Greece

David Willett
Rosemary Hall
Paul Hellander
Corinne Simcock

Greece

3rd edition

Published by
Lonely Planet Publications
Head Office: PO Box 617, Hawthorn, Vic 3122, Australia
Branches: 155 Filbert St, Suite 251, Oakland, CA 94607, USA
10a Spring Place, London NW5 3BH, UK
71 bis rue du Cardinal Lemoine, 75005 Paris, France

Printed by
SNP Printing Pte Ltd, Singapore

Photographs by

Greg Alford	Michelle Coxall	Mark Daffey	Dimitri Gatzouras	David Hall
Rosemary Hall	Paul Hellander	Mark Honan	Ann Jousiffe	Helen Rowley
Corinne Simcock	Linda Welters	Tamsin Wilson		

Front cover: Cat & Blue Wall (Reimund Zunde)

First Published
February 1994

This Edition
February 1998

Although the authors and publisher have tried to make the information as accurate as possible, they accept no responsibility for any loss, injury or inconvenience sustained by any person using this book.

National Library of Australia Cataloguing in Publication Data

Willett, David
Greece

3rd ed.
Includes index.
ISBN 0 86442 527 9

1. Greece – Guidebooks. I. Willett, David.

914.950476

text & maps © Lonely Planet 1998
photos © photographers as indicated 1998
climate charts for Corfu, Iraklio, Lesvos, Rhodes and Thessaloniki compiled from information supplied by
Patrick J Tyson, © Patrick J Tyson, 1998

David Willett

David is a freelance journalist based near Bellingen on the mid-north coast of New South Wales, Australia. He grew up in Hampshire, England, and wound up in Australia in 1980 after stints working on newspapers in Iran (1975-78) and Bahrain. He spent two years working as a sub-editor on the Melbourne *Sun* before trading a steady job for a warmer climate. Between jobs, David has travelled extensively in Europe, the Middle East and Asia.

Paul Hellander

Like a number of authors who ended up working for Lonely Planet, Paul came to Australia from England, having temporarily satiated his wanderlust along the way in over 30 countries. After leaving England, Paul spent five years seeking fame and fortune in Greece, but ended up being exported to Australia to teach Greek instead. Paul is a former lecturer in Modern Greek from Adelaide University and now runs an Internet-based translation agency in Adelaide in between writing and travelling. Paul worked on the 1st edition of *Greece* as language consultant and also wrote Lonely Planet's *Greek phrasebook*. He has also contributed to the *Mediterranean Europe* and *Eastern Europe* shoestring guides. When not writing, translating or travelling, Paul lives in Cyberspace at paul@planetmail.net and welcomes comments and discussion about Greece.

Corinne Simcock

Corinne, based in London, spent the first 10 years of her career as a sound engineer in the music industry. In 1988, sick of spending 18 hours a day in a basement listening to people who couldn't play make mistakes, she chucked it all in to become a journalist, writing for national newspapers and magazines about everything from travel and crime to business and personal finance. She has travelled through more than 30 countries and her passion in life is deserts.

Rosemary Hall

Rosemary was born in Sunderland, England. She graduated in fine art, but fame and fortune as an artist eluded her, so she spent a few months bumming around Europe and India. After teaching in northern England, she decided to find somewhere more exotic, finally landing a job in Iraq. When, after two years, the Iraqi government refused to renew her work permit, she settled in London, tried to make it again as a painter, did supply teaching, and then travelled in India, South-East Asia and Africa. Rosemary researched Iraq for Lonely Planet's *West Asia on a shoestring* and wrote the 1st edition of *Greece*. She is the co-author of four walking guides to London.

From the Authors

David Willett My thanks go first to my partner, Rowan, and our son, Tom, for holding the fort at home during my extended stay in Greece. Thanks also to my friends Tolis and Lisa in Athens for their continued hospitality during my frequent visits; to Maria Economou from the Greek National Tourism Office for continually finding the unfindable; to Kev for his flow of useful (and not so useful) e-mails; and to Sacha Pearson from LP's Oakland office and Isabelle from LP Paris for help with travel information. Last but not least, I'd like to thank Rosemary Hall for doing such a good job on the 1st edition.

Paul Hellander Special thanks must be given to the following organisations who made my research in Greece a breeze: Olympic Airways and the Greek National Tourism

Office (EOT) for valuable transport assistance; the Greek Railways Organisation (OSE) for on-ground transport assistance on mainland Greece; Strintzis Lines for ferry assistance to/from Italy and Greece; the Maritime Company of Lesvos (NEL) for welcome transport assistance and Miniotis Lines for the lift from Chios to Ikaria. In Greece, the following persons offered me practical assistance, moral support and a place to unwind during a busy schedule: Christos & Litsa Kotronis (Thessaly); Areti Billini & Nikos Konstantinidis (Athens); Maria Haristou, Antonis Konstantinidis (Halkidiki); Alekos & Valentini Papadopoulos (Thessaloniki); Maria Aïvazidis & Apostolos Kyriakidis (Thrace); Stavros & Katerina Parissos (Limnos); Julia Galanaki (Agios Efstratios); Georgos & Barbara Ballis (Lesvos); Vassilis Dionissos (Ikaria). Special thanks yet again to Dimitra Kaplanelli at the Office of Tourism for the NE Aegean (Mytilini) for hospitality and assistance beyond the call of duty. A big thank you to Stella for holding the fort and for being patient while I wandered off once more around Greece. Byron and Marcus, thanks for helping with the road-testing around the Sporades. This one's for you too!

Corinne Simcock A huge thank you to Despina from the Naxos Tourist Information Centre, Mike from Rooms Mike on Paros, Alexis from Pension Alexis (Kos), Francesco, Maria and Henry from Francesco's (Ios), Manolis from Pension Vasso (Samos), Anna from Dakoutros Travel (Santorini), Pete Plumbley from Laskarina Holidays (Tilos) and Anna Pilatou from Themis Minimarket (Kalymnos) – who took it upon herself to be a one-woman tourist board – for spectacular assistance way beyond the call of duty.

Among other friends who helped, thanks go to Tansy and Manolis at Pallas Travel (Rhodes), the staff at Karpathos Travel, Angelidi from Astypalea Tours, Nikos from Symi Tours, AquaNet on Kalymnos, Luna from Laskarina Travel (Leros), Bianca and Patricia from Astoria Travel (Patmos), Rena from Paradise Travel and Anna from Lipsos Travel (Lipsi), Sabine and George on Agathonisi, Marianna from Greek Sun Holidays (Andros), Sharon from Windmills Travel & Tourism (Tinos), all at Rhapsody bar (Mykonos), Panayiotis Boudouris from TeamWork (Syros), all at Café Picasso (Naxos), Irene from Aegialis Tours (Amorgos), Flavio from Sottovento (Folegandros), Theresa from Terry's Travel Services (Milos) and Anni from Krinas Travel (Serifos).

Rosemary Hall In London, I am grateful to Anastasia Caramanis at the GNTO and Andrew Stoddart at the Hellenic Book Service for their assistance. Thanks also to my cousin, David Hall, for encouragement and support, especially when I was struggling with a new computer. In Greece, I would like to thank the staff of the EOT and municipal tourist offices on Crete and the Ionian islands. Also, warm thanks for assistance, and hospitality to Lena and Jenny (Hania), Heracles Papadakis (Spili), Apostolis Kimalis (Sitia), Ruth & Peter Thompson and Naomi (Lassithi plateau), Regina Schroder, Denis Lahr, Bridget Hoffman and Ingrid Rausdouck (Plakias), Chris (Plakias), Dee & Noel Simpson (Mirtos), Simon & Vassiliki Hill and Nikos Tranacs (Kalamata), Angelo Megalokonomos (Kythira), Vivian & Nik (Kefallonia), Angeliki Digaletou (Ithaki), James & Carol Woodward and Richard & Linda Barnes (Meganisi) and Helen Morgan (Lefkada). Finally, thanks to David Willett for his good humour and patience and thanks to all the LP staff involved with the production of the book.

This Book

This is the 3rd edition of LP's *Greece* guide. Rosemary Hall wrote the 1st edition. David Willett was the coordinating author of this edition, and he also updated the introductory chapters as well as the chapters on Athens, the Peloponnese and the Saronic Gulf islands. Paul Hellander updated the chapters on Northern Greece, Central Greece, the North-Eastern Aegean Islands and Evia & the Sporades. Corinne Simcock looked after the Dodecanese and Cyclades chapters, and Rosemary Hall was responsible for the Crete and Ionian chapters. Anne Moffat wrote the text for the art section.

From the Publisher

This book was edited at Lonely Planet in Melbourne by Bethune Carmichael with assistance from Ṣarah Mathers and Quentin Frayne. Anthony Phelan drew the maps, designed and laid out the book with assistance from Lyndell Taylor and Marcel Gaston. Margaret Jung, Trudi Canavan and Ann Jeffree helped with the illustrations and Simon Bracken designed the cover. Thanks to Anne Mulvaney, Paul Harding and Sue Harvey for proofing. Thanks also to Dan Levin for the soft fonts and Rowan McKinnon for the philosophy aside.

Thanks

Many thanks to the travellers who used the last edition and wrote to us with helpful hints, useful advice and interesting anecdotes:

Helen Alice, Allan Allsopp, Marcus Angwin, Nancy Austen, Al & Joan Bailey, S Barkley, Matt Barrett, Lloyd Barrett, James Bartlett, E A Bayley, Joakim Bejbom, Joke Bekkering, A J Bond, Iain Booth, A Bostock, Tony Bostock, Brady Bowles, Lawrence Bradley, Rachel Brandt, Nancy Breynaert, Mary Briggs, Neil Briscoe, Rebecca Burton, Riccardo Cadoni, Roderick Campbell, Bonnie Cediel, Ken Chandler, Wong Yik Chin, Sandy Clendenen, Joan Cooper, Nicholas Couis, Anthony Crawford, Michael Cummins, C Davies, Willy de Jong, Tony Del Prete, Myrosia Dragon, John Dutton, Dave & Carol Eales, J Edwards, David Edwards, R Fairchild, Lynda Fanning, S & S Fellows, C & A Fernando, Carl Ferris, Simona Fino, D Fletcher, G & E Fokion, Bill Freeman, J M Fyne, Andrew Ganner, P Gardiner, Lloyd Garrett, Karl Gebert, Juston Gellatly, Timothy George, Bernice Gerrand, Dr Michael Gibson, Sofia Granstrom, Janice Hamer, Julie Hardiman, E & C Harris, Helen Hatzimaggio, David Hawley, Emma Hill, Katrin Hohmann, Kathy Hood, Michelle House, Gareth Hovey, Stephen Hopkins, L G Hunt, Colin J Jordan, Anne Jack, Bernard Jacks, Kristin Jacobson, Romanna Jakymec, Michelle Jones, Penny Jones, Nils Olof Jonsson, Vibeke Jorgensen, Francesca Joyce, V Junge, Merilee Karr, R Kaufman, Ruth Keene Jones, Debbie Keffer, Geoff Kent, Ales Kermauner, Anthony Kleanthous, Doris Krysanski, Hilary Lang, Katherine Langton, J Laverock, Sara Lodge, Richard Loren, Campbell Lyle, Angus MacDonald, John MacDougall, Angela McGregor, James McLennan, Marianthe McLiesh, Emanuele Magrone, Jayne Marek, Donald Mathews, Michael Melvin, Pamela Mertens, Steffen Metzner, Marilyn Milota, Ken Mirkin, Kate Moore, Rebecca Mowling, Lai Wai Mun, Denise Murphy, Doug Myers, Irene Nakamura, Monique Nazzari, Fr Tony Noble, Clive Noffke, Janet Nowottny, Michael O'Flaherty, Lisa Olszewski, Jane Organ, A Panagiotopoulos, Tanya Papadopoulos, John Peake, Torbjorn Petterson, C & P Pilsworth, Tally Rabinovitch, Paul Rawcliffe, Itamar Raz, Vincent Reidy, Sylvia Rose, Gert Ruiter, Peter Savic, Lisa Schildt, Amy Schuler, Winfried Schwarz, Bruce Scott, Joy Sealey, H Seymoure, Sam Sharpe, Mike Sharrocks, Jessica Siegel, Sandra Sljivic, Phil Smith, Richard Smith, S Sonnino, Anne Stanley, Barbara Stephenson, Rae Stewart, Jordan Stolper, G & R Strand, Anne Strydom, J & R Stucker, Jan Tepper, E & R Thomas, J & J Thorne, Alan Tonks, Cheryl Tummons, Marit Undeborn, Colin Unsworth, Steven Vallen, K & J van Dam, Koen Vande Wiell, Shiayax Vazifdar, Christian Vincent, Tadej Vodopivec, Joan Weaver, Morten Wendt, E & U WernerReiss, Ken West, James Wilde, P & P Wilson, William Wilson, Alexander Winter, Barbra Wolf, Stan Woods, Brian Worthen, Peggy Wright, Kris Wyld, Humphrey Yin, Liz Zavazal, Nicolas Zervos.

Warning & Request

Things change – prices go up, schedules change, good places go bad and bad places go bankrupt – nothing stays the same. So, if you find things better or worse, recently opened or long since closed, please tell us and help make the next edition even more accurate and useful.

We value all of the feedback we receive from travellers. Julie Young coordinates a small team who read and acknowledge every letter, postcard and e-mail, and ensure that every morsel of information finds its way to the appropriate authors, editors and publishers.

Everyone who writes to us will find their name in the next edition of the appropriate guide and will also receive a free subscription to our quarterly newsletter, *Planet Talk*. The very best contributions will be rewarded with a free Lonely Planet guide.

Excerpts from your correspondence may appear in new editions of this guide; in our newsletter, *Planet Talk*; or in updates on our Web site – so please let us know if you don't want your letter published or your name acknowledged.

Contents

Transliteration & Variant Spellings: an Explanation

The issue of correctly transliterating Greek is a vexed one. While the alphabet itself is not difficult to learn, and despite the fact that there are only 24 letters in the alphabet, giving a Latin alphabet rendition of Greek is fraught with inconsistencies and pitfalls.

The Greeks themselves are not very consistent when it comes to providing transliterated names on their signs, though things are gradually improving. The word 'Piraeus', for example, has been variously represented by the following transliterations: Pireas, Piraievs and Pireefs; and when appearing as a street name (eg Piraeus Street) you will also find Pireos!

The legacy of various military dictatorships in Greece, the most recent foray being from 1967 to 1974, has left another linguistic minefield in its wake: that of diglossy, or two forms of the Greek language. There is a purist form called Katharevousa and a popular form called Dimotiki. The Katharevousa form was never more than an artificiality and Dimotiki has always been spoken as the mainstream language, but this linguistic schizophrenia means there are often two Greek words for each English word. Thus, the word for 'baker' in everyday language is *fournos*, but the shop sign will more often than not say *artopoieion*. The product of the baker's shop will be known in the street as *psomi*, but in church as *artos*.

As if all that was not enough, there is also the issue of anglicised vs hellenised forms of place names: for example, Athina vs Athens, Patra vs Patras, Thiva vs Thebes, Evia vs Euboia – the list goes on and on! Toponymic diglossy (the existence of both an official and everyday name for a place) is responsible for Kerkyra – Corfu, Zante – Zakynthos, and Santorini – Thira. In this guide we have tended to provide modern Greek equivalents for town names, with one or two well-known exceptions, eg Athens and Patras. Where mention is made of ancient sites, settlements or people closely related to antiquity, we have attempted to stick to the more familiar classical names. Thus we have Thucydides instead of Thoukididis; Mycenae instead of Mykines.

Problems in transliteration have particular implications for vowels, especially given that Greek has six ways of rendering the vowel sound *ee*, two ways of rendering the *o* sound and two ways of rendering the *e* sound. In most instances in this book, *y* has been used for the *ee* sound when a Greek *upsilon* (υ, Υ) has been used, and *i* for Greek *ita* (η, H) and *iota* (ι, I). In the case of the Greek vowel combinations that make the *ee* sound, that is οι, ει and υι, an *i* has been used. For the two Greek *e* sounds, αι and ε, an *e* has been employed.

As far as consonants are concerned, the Greek letter *gamma* (γ, Γ) appears as *g* rather than *y* throughout this book. This means that *agios* (Greek for male saint) is used rather than *ayios*, and *agia* (Greek for female saint) rather than *ayia*. The letter *delta* (δ, Δ) appears as *d*, rather than *dh*, throughout this book, so *domatia* (Greek for rooms), rather than *dhomatia*, is used. The letter *fi* (φ, Φ) can be transliterated as either *f* or *ph*. Here, a general rule of thumb is that classical names are spelt with a *ph* and modern names with an *f*. So Phaistos is used rather than Festos, and Folegandros is used rather than Pholegandros. The Greek letter *chi* (ξ, Ξ) has been more or less uniformly represented as *h* in order to give as close as possible an approximation of the pronunciation of the Greek. Thus, we have 'Haralambos' instead of 'Charalambos' and 'Polytehniou' instead of 'Polytechniou'. Bear in mind that the *h* is to be pronounced as an aspirated *h*, much like the *ch* in loch. The letter *kapa* (κ, K) has been used to represent that sound, except where well-known names from antiquity have adopted by convention the letter *c*, eg Polycrates, Acropolis.

Wherever reference to a street name is made, we have omitted the Greek word 'odos'. Words for avenue *(leoforos)* and square *(plateia)* have, however, been included to assist in differentiating types of locations.

For a list of useful words and phrases, see the language guide at the back of this book. For a more detailed guide to the Greek language, check out Lonely Planet's *Greek phrasebook*.

Greece Map Index

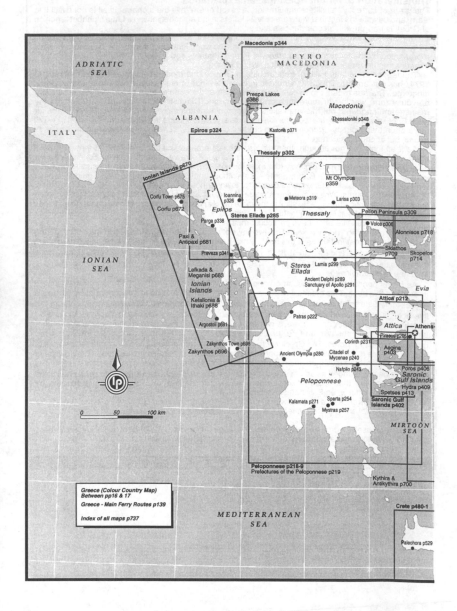

ADRIATIC SEA

ITALY

ALBANIA

IONIAN SEA

Macedonia p344

FYRO MACEDONIA

Prespa Lakes p366

Macedonia

Thessaloniki p348

Epiros p324

Kastoria p371

Thessaly p302

Ionian Islands p570

Mt Olympus p359

Corfu Town p675

Ioannina p326

Meteora p319

Larisa p303

Corfu p672

Epiros

Sterea Ellada p285

Thessaly

Pelion Peninsula p309

Parga p338

Volos p306

Alonnisos p718

Paxi & Antipaxi p681

Preveza p341

Sterea Eliada

Lamia p299

Skiathos p709

Skopelos p714

Lefkada & Meganisi p683

Ancient Delphi p289
Sanctuary of Apollo p291

Evia

Ionian Islands

Kefallonia & Ithaki p688

Attica p212

Attica

Athens

Argostoli p691

Patras p222

Piraeus p205

Zakynthos Town p696

Corinth p231

Aegina p403

Zakynthos p696

Ancient Olympia p280

Citadel of Mycenae p240

Poros p406
Saronic Gulf Islands

Nafplio p243

Hydra p409

Peloponnese

Spetses p413

Kalamata p271

Sparta p254

Saronic Gulf Islands p402

Mystras p257

MIRTOÖN SEA

0   50   100 km

Peloponnese p218-9
Prefectures of the Peloponnese p219

Kythira & Antikythira p700

Greece (Colour Country Map) Between pp16 & 17

Greece - Main Ferry Routes p139

Index of all maps p737

MEDITERRANEAN SEA

Crete p480-1

Paleohora p529

which destroyed the palaces at Knossos, Phaestos, Malia and Zakros. The Minoans rebuilt them to a more complex, almost labyrinthine design with multiple storeys, sumptuous royal apartments, reception halls, storerooms, workshops, living quarters for staff and an advanced drainage system. The interiors were decorated with the celebrated Minoan frescoes, now on display in the archaeological museum at Iraklio.

The Minoans were also literate. Their first script resembled Egyptian hieroglyphics, the most famous example of which is the inscription on the Phaestos disc (1700 BC). They progressed to a syllable-based script which 20th-century archaeologists have dubbed Linear A, because it consists of linear symbols. Like the earlier hieroglyphics, it has not yet been deciphered, but archaeologists believe that it was used to document trade transactions and the contents of royal storerooms, rather than to express abstract concepts.

Some historians have suggested that the civilisation's decline after 1500 BC was accelerated by the effects of the massive volcanic explosion on the Cycladic island of Santorini (Thira), an eruption vulcanologists believe was more cataclysmic than any on record. They theorise that the fall-out of volcanic ash from the blast may have caused a succession of crop failures – with resulting social unrest.

Mycenaean Civilisation The decline of the Minoan civilisation in the Late Minoan period coincided with the rise of the first great civilisation on the Greek mainland, the Mycenaean (1900-1100 BC), which reached its peak between 1500 and 1200 BC. Named after the ancient city of Mycenae, where the German archaeologist Heinrich Schliemann made his celebrated finds in 1876, it is also known as the Achaean civilisation after the Indo-European branch of migrants who had settled on mainland Greece and absorbed many aspects of Minoan culture.

Unlike Minoan society, where the lack of city walls seems to indicate relative peace under some form of central authority, Mycenaean civilisation was characterised by independent city-states such as Corinth, Pylos, Tiryns and, the most powerful of them all, Mycenae. These were ruled by kings who inhabited palaces enclosed within massive walls on easily defensible hilltops.

The Mycenaeans' most impressive legacy is magnificent gold jewellery and ornaments, the best of which can be seen in the National Archaeological Museum in Athens. The Mycenaeans wrote in what is called Linear B (an early form of Greek unrelated to the Linear A of Crete), which has been deciphered. They also worshipped gods who were precursors of the later Greek gods.

Examples of Linear B have also been found on Crete, suggesting that Mycenaean invaders may have conquered the island, perhaps around 1500 BC, when many Minoan palaces were destroyed. Mycenaean influence stretched further than Crete: the Mycenaean city-states banded together to defeat Troy (Ilium) and thus to protect their trade routes to the Black Sea, and archaeological research has unearthed Mycenaean artefacts as far away as Egypt, Mesopotamia and Italy.

The Mycenaean civilisation came to an end during the 12th century BC when it was overrun by the Dorians.

Geometric Age
The origins of the Dorians remain uncertain. They are generally thought to have come from Epiros or northern Macedonia, but some historians argue that they only arrived from there because they had been driven out of Doris, in central Greece, by the Mycenaeans.

The warrior-like Dorians settled first in the Peloponnese, but soon fanned out over much of the mainland, razing the city-states and enslaving the inhabitants. They later conquered Crete and the south-west coast of Asia Minor. Other Indo-European tribes known as the Thessalians settled in what is now Thessaly. Of the original Greek tribal groups, the Aeolians fled to the north-west coast of Asia Minor; the Ionians sought refuge on the central coast and the islands of

Geometric detail from an urn, 750 BC

Lesvos, Samos and Chios, although they also held out in mainland Greece – in Attica and the well-fortified city of Athens.

The Dorians brought a traumatic break with the past, and the next 400 years are often referred to as Greece's 'dark age'. But it would be unfair to dismiss the Dorians completely; they brought iron with them and developed a new style of pottery, decorated with striking geometrical designs – although art historians are still out to lunch as to whether the Dorians merely copied the designs perfected by Ionians in Attica. The Dorians worshipped male gods instead of fertility goddesses and adopted the Mycenaean gods of Poseidon, Zeus and Apollo, paving the way for the later Greek religious pantheon.

Perhaps most importantly, the Dorian warriors developed into a class of land-holding aristocrats. This worsened the lot of the average farmer but also brought about the demise of the monarchy as a system of government, along with a resurgence of the Mycenaean pattern of independent city-states, this time led by wealthy aristocrats instead of absolute monarchs – the beginnings of 'democratic' government.

Archaic Age

By about 800 BC, local agriculture and animal husbandry had become productive enough to trigger a resumption of maritime trading. New Greek colonies were established in north Africa, Italy, Sicily, southern France and southern Spain to fill the vacuum

left by the decline of those other great Mediterranean traders, the Phoenicians.

The people of the various city-states were unified by the development of a Greek alphabet (of Phoenician origin, though the Greeks introduced vowels), the verses of Homer (which created a sense of a shared Mycenaean past), the establishment of the Olympic Games (which brought all the city-states together), and the setting up of central sanctuaries such as Delphi (a neutral meeting ground for lively negotiations), giving Greeks, for the first time, a sense of national identity. This period is known as the Archaic, or Middle, Age.

Most city-states were built to a similar plan, with a fortified acropolis (high city) at the highest point. The acropolis contained the cities' temples and treasury and also served as a refuge during invasions. Outside the acropolis was the agora (market), a bustling commercial quarter, and beyond it the residential areas.

The city-states were autonomous, free to pursue their own interests as they saw fit. Most city-states abolished monarchic rule in favour of an aristocratic form of government, usually headed by an *archon* (chief magistrate). Aristocrats were often disliked by the population because of their inherited privileges, and some city-states fell to the rule of tyrants after Kypselos started the practice in Corinth around 650 BC. Tyrants seized their position rather than inheriting it. These days they've got an image problem, but in ancient times they were often seen as being on the side of ordinary citizens.

Athens & Solon The seafaring city-state of Athens, meanwhile, was still in the hands of aristocrats, and a failed coup attempt by a would-be tyrant led the legislator Draco to draw up his infamous laws in 620 BC (hence the word 'draconian'). These were so harsh that even the theft of a cabbage was punishable by death.

Solon was appointed archon in 594 BC with a far-reaching mandate to defuse the mounting tensions between the haves and the have-nots. He cancelled all debts and freed

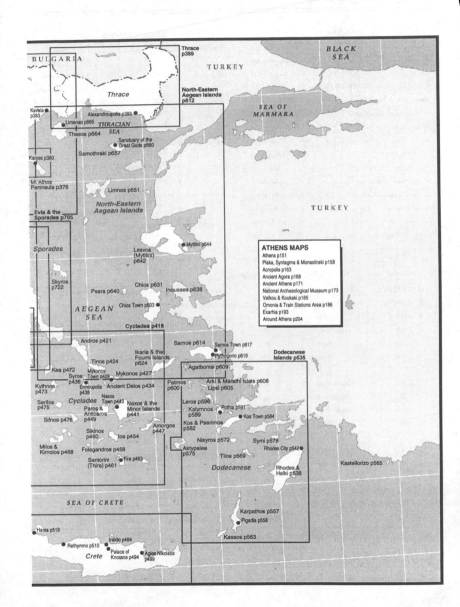

BULGARIA

Thrace
p389

TURKEY

BLACK
SEA

Thrace

North-Eastern
Aegean Islands
p612

SEA OF
MARMARA

Kavala
p383

Alexandroupolis p393

Limenas p665   *THRACIAN*
Thasos p664   *SEA*

Sanctuary of the
Great Gods p660

Karyes p380

Samothraki p657

Mt Athos
Peninsula p376

Limnos p651

TURKEY

Evia & the
Sporades p705

*North-Eastern
Aegean Islands*

Sporades

Mytilini p644

Lesvos
(Mytilini)
p642

ATHENS MAPS
Athens p151
Plaka, Syntagma & Monastiraki p158
Acropolis p163
Ancient Agora p168
Ancient Athens p171
National Archaeological Museum p173
Velkou & Koukaki p185
Omonia & Train Stations Area p186
Exarhia p193
Around Athens p204

Skyros
p722

Psara p640   Chios p631

Inousses p638

Chios Town p633

*AEGEAN
SEA*

Cyclades p418

Andros p421

Samos p614   Samos Town p617

Pythagorio p619

*Dodecanese
Islands p535*

Tinos p424

Ikaria & the
Fourni Islands
p624

Kea p472

Mykonos
Syros   p429
p436   Mykonos p427

Agathonisi p609

Kythnos
p473

Ermoupolis   Ancient Delos p434

Naxos
Town p443

Patmos
p600

Arki & Marathi Islets p608

Lipsi p605

Serifos
p475

Paros &
Antiparos
p449

Naxos & the
Minor Islands
p441

Leros p596

Kalymnos
p589

Pothia p591

Cyclades

Sifnos p476

Kos & Pserimos
p582

Kos Town p584

Amorgos
p447

Sikinos
p460   Ios p454

Nisyros p572

Symi p578

Milos &
Kimolos p468

Folegandros p458

Astypalea
p575

Tilos p569

Rhodes City p542

Santorini
(Thira) p461   Fira p463

Dodecanese

Rhodes &
Halki p538

Kastellorizo p565

SEA OF CRETE

Hania p519

Karpathos p557

Pigadia p558

Iraklio p484

Rethymno p510   Palace of
Knossos p494   Agios Nikolaos
p499

Kassos p563

Crete

Map Legend

BOUNDARIES

.... International Boundary
.... Provincial Boundary

ROUTES

E25 ..... Freeway, with Route Number
.... Major Road
.... Minor Road
.... Minor Road - Unsealed
.... City Road
.... City Street
.... City Lane
.... Train Route, with Station
.... Metro Route, with Station
.... Cable Car or Chairlift
.... Ferry Route
.... Walking Track

AREA FEATURES

.... Building
.... Beach
.... Cemetery
.... Market
✿ .... Park, Gardens
.... Pedestrian Mall
.... Forest
.... Urban Area

HYDROGRAPHIC FEATURES

.... Canal
.... Coastline
.... Creek, River
.... Lake, Intermittent Lake
.... Rapids, Waterfalls
.... Swamp

SYMBOLS

○ CAPITAL .... National Capital	✈ .... Airport	⛫ .. Museum, Art Gallery
◉ CAPITAL .... Provincial Capital	... Ancient or City Wall	← .... One Way Street
● CITY .... City	∴ .... Archaeological Site	Ⓟ .... Parking
● Town .... Large Town	☺ .... Bank	)(....................... Pass
● Town .... Town	✕ .... Battle Site	⛽ .... Petrol Station
● Village .... Village	🏃 .... Beach	★ .... Police Station
	↘ .... Bird Sanctuary	✉ .... Post Office
■ .... Place to Stay	∿ .... Border Crossing	❖ .... Shopping Centre
Å .... Camping Ground	⚓ .... Canoeing	⚑ .... Ski Field
⊞ .... Caravan Park	🏯 .... Castle	◎ .... Spring
🏠 .... Hut or Chalet	⌒ .... Cave	🏛 .... Stately Home
	⬚ 🛈 .... Church	⬛ .... Swimming Pool
▼ .... Place to Eat	⌒ .... Cliff or Escarpment	☎ .... Telephone
ⓤ .... Pub or Bar	☯ .... Embassy	❶ .... Tourist Information
	✚ .... Hospital	▣ .... Tomb
	☀ .... Lookout	⚐ .... Trailhead
	⚱ .... Monument	⊝ .... Transport
	☪ .... Mosque	⚘ .... Vineyard
	▲ .... Mountain or Hill	🐘 .... Zoo

Note: not all symbols displayed above appear in this book

Introduction

Greece has always attracted travellers, drawn by the fascination of some of Europe's earliest civilisations. Philosophers muse that to journey to Greece is to return home, for the legacy of ancient Greece pervades the consciousness of all western nations. Greek Doric, Ionic and Corinthian columns adorn many of our buildings, and much of our greatest early literature drew on the Greek myths for inspiration. Some of our most evocative words are Greek – chaos, drama, tragedy and democracy, to name a few. Perhaps the greatest legacy is democracy itself.

While it was this underlying awareness of Greek culture that drew the wealthy young aristocrats of the 19th century to the country, the majority of today's visitors are drawn by Greece's beaches and sunshine. Island-hopping has become something of an initiation rite for the international singles set. Their numbers are dwarfed, however, by the millions of package holiday-makers who come to Greece every year in search of two weeks of sunshine by the sea.

Package tourism took off with the advent of cheaper airfares in the 1960s and gathered pace through the 70s and 80s. By the early 1990s, almost nine million visitors a year were pouring through the turnstiles, making tourism easily the most important industry in the country.

The ancient sites are an enduring attraction. The Acropolis needs no introduction as the most remarkable legacy of the classical period. At Knossos on Crete, you can wander around the ancient capital of one of Europe's oldest civilisations: the Minoan. The many Minoan, Mycenaean and classical Greek sites, and elaborate Byzantine churches, stand alongside the legacies left by foreign occupiers: towering Venetian, Frankish and Turkish castles, and crumbling, forgotten mosques.

Reminders of the past are everywhere. The Greek landscape is littered with broken columns and crumbling fragments of ancient

walls. Moreover, there is hardly a meadow, river or mountaintop which is not sacred because of its association with some deity, and the spectres of the past linger still.

Greece has clung to its traditions more tenaciously than most European countries. Through hundreds of years of foreign occupation by Franks, Venetians, Turks and others, tradition and religion were the factors that kept the notion of Greek nationhood alive. Greeks today remain only too well aware of the hardships their forebears endured. Even hip, young Greeks defend these traditions and enthusiastically participate in many of them.

The traditions manifest themselves in a variety of ways, including regional costumes, such as the baggy pantaloons and high boots worn by elderly Cretan men, and in the embroidered dresses and floral headscarves worn by the women of Olymbos, on Karpathos. Many traditions take the form of festivals, where Greeks express their *joie de vivre* through dancing, singing and feasting.

Festival time or not, the Greek capacity for enjoyment of life is immediately evident. If you arrive in a Greek town in the early evening in summer, you could be forgiven for thinking you've arrived mid-festival. This is the time of the *volta*, when everyone takes to the streets, refreshed from their siesta, dressed up and raring to go. All this adds up to Greece being one of Europe's most relaxed and friendliest countries. But Greece is no European backwater locked in a time warp. In towns and cities you will find discos as lively as any in Italy, France or Britain, and boutiques as trendy.

If you're a beach-lover, Greece, with its 1400 islands, has more coastline than any other country in Europe. You can choose between rocky outcrops, pebbled coves or long swathes of golden sand.

Greece's scenery is as varied as its beaches. There is the semitropical lushness of the Ionian and North-Eastern Aegean islands and southern Crete; the bare sunbaked rocks of the Cyclades; and the forested mountains, icy lakes and tumbling rivers of northern Greece. Much of this breathtaking landscape is mantled with vibrant wildflowers.

There is yet another phenomenon which even people cynical about anything hinting of the esoteric comment upon. It takes the form of inexplicable happenings, coincidences, or fortuitous occurrences. It could be meeting up with a long-lost friend, or bumping into the same person again and again on your travels; or missing the ferry and being offered a lift on a private yacht; or being hot, hungry, thirsty and miles from anywhere, then stumbling upon a house whose occupants offer hospitality.

Perhaps these serendipitous occurrences can be explained as the work of the gods of ancient Greece, who, some claim, have not entirely relinquished their power, and to prove it, occasionally come down to earth to intervene in the lives of mortals.

MARK HONAN

MARK HONAN

MARK HONAN

Top Left: Ceremonial guards patrol the tomb of the Unknown Warrior, Athens
Top Right & Bottom: Olympian Zeus Temple, Athens: the largest temple in Greece, it was
completed by Hadrian in 131 AD

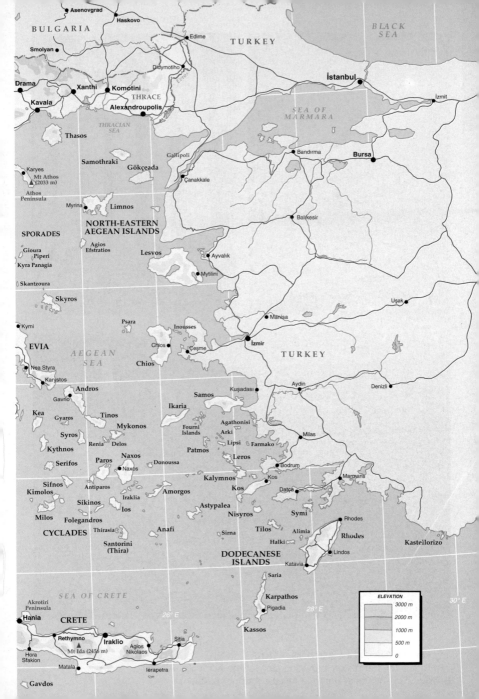

ROSEMARY HALL

MARK DAFFEY

DAVID HALL

Top Left: Entrance to the Acropolis, Athens
Top Right: The Parthenon, crowning glory of the Acropolis, Athens
Bottom: The Theatre of Herodes Atticus, Acropolis, Athens

Facts about the Country

HISTORY

From ancient Minoan palaces and classical Greek temples to spectacular Byzantine churches and remote Frankish castles, the legacy of Greece's long and colourful history is everywhere.

Stone Age

The discovery of a Neanderthal skull in a cave on the Halkidiki peninsula of Macedonia has confirmed the presence of humans in Greece 700,000 years ago. Bones and tools from Palaeolithic times have been found in the Pindos mountains.

The move to a pastoral existence came during Neolithic times (7000-3000 BC). The fertile area that is now Thessaly was the first area to be settled. The people grew barley and wheat, and bred sheep and goats. They used clay to produce pots, vases and simple statuettes of the Great Mother (the earth goddess), whom they worshipped.

By 3000 BC, people were living in settlements complete with streets, squares and mud-brick houses. The villages were centred around a large palace-like structure which belonged to the tribal leader. The most complete Neolithic settlements in Greece are Dimini (inhabited from 4000 to 1200 BC) and Sesklo, both near the city of Volos.

Bronze Age

Around 3000 BC, Indo-European migrants introduced the processing of bronze (an alloy of copper and tin) into Greece – so began three remarkable civilisations: the Cycladic, Minoan and Mycenaean.

Cycladic Civilisation The Cycladic civilisation, centred on the Cyclades islands, is divided into three periods: Early (3000-2000 BC), Middle (2000-1500 BC) and Late (1500-1100 BC). The most impressive legacy of this civilisation is the statuettes carved from Parian marble – the famous Cycladic figurines. Like statuettes from

Neolithic times, they depicted images of the Great Mother. Other remains include bronze and obsidian tools and weapons, gold jewellery, and stone and clay vases and pots.

The peoples of the Cycladic civilisation were accomplished sailors who developed prosperous maritime trade links. They exported their wares to Asia Minor (the west of present-day Turkey), Europe and north Africa, as well as to Crete and continental Greece. The Cyclades islands were influenced by both the Minoan and Mycenaean civilisations.

Minoan Civilisation The Minoan civilisation of Crete was the first advanced civilisation to emerge in Europe, drawing its inspiration from two great Middle Eastern civilisations: the Mesopotamian and Egyptian. Archaeologists divide the Minoan civilisation, like the Cycladic, into three phases: Early (3000-2100 BC), Middle (2100-1500 BC) and Late (1500-1100 BC).

Many aspects of Neolithic life endured during the Early period, but by 2500 BC most people on the island had been assimilated into a new and distinct culture which we now call the Minoan, after the mythical King Minos. The Minoan civilisation reached its peak during the Middle period, producing pottery and metalwork of remarkable beauty and a high degree of imagination and skill. The Late period saw the civilisation decline both commercially and militarily against Mycenaean competition from the mainland, until its abrupt end around 1100 BC, when Dorian invaders and natural disasters ravaged the island.

Like the Cycladic civilisation, the Minoan was a great maritime power which exported goods throughout the Mediterranean. The polychrome Kamares pottery, which flourished during the Middle period, was highly prized by the Egyptians.

The first calamity to strike the Minoans was a violent earthquake in about 1700 BC,

CHRONOLOGY OF MAJOR EVENTS

Period/Age		Events
Cycladic & Minoan civilisations 3000-1100 BC	2800 BC	– Marble figurines carved in Cyclades
	2000 BC	– First palaces built on Crete
	1700 BC	– Minoan palaces (Knossos, Phaestos, Malia & Zakros) rebuilt after earthquake
Mycenaean Age 1900-1100 BC	c 1450 BC	– Massive volcanic eruption on Thira; Minoan palaces destroyed
Dark Age 1200-800 BC	1200 BC	– Dorians conquer Greece, introducing Iron Age technology
	1000 BC	– First appearance of pottery with geometric patterns (the Geometric Age)
Archaic (Middle) Age 800-480 BC	800 BC	– Emergence of the independent city-states
	776 BC	– First Olympic Games held
	c 750 BC	– Homer thought to have composed the *Iliad* and the *Odyssey*
	490 BC	– Persians defeated at the Battle of Marathon
Classical Age 480-338 BC	461-429 BC	– Pericles presides over golden age of Athens; plays by Sophocles and Euripides written
	438 BC	– Parthenon completed
	431-421 BC	– First Peloponnesian War
	399 BC	– Socrates sentenced to death
	338 BC	– Philip of Macedon conquers Greece
	324 BC	– Death of Alexander the Great
	168 BC	– Romans defeat Macedon at the Battle of Pydnaa
Roman Rule 146 BC to 324 AD	67 AD	– Nero starts work on the Corinth Canal
	132	– Temple of Olympian Zeus completed in Athens
Byzantine Age 324-1453	384	– Christianity becomes the official religion of Greece
	529	– Emperor Justinian closes schools of philosophy in Athens
	1204	– Crusaders sack Constantinople
	1210	– Venetians occupy Crete
Ottoman Rule 1453-1829	1453	– Ottoman Turks capture Constantinople
	1669	– Iraklio, Crete, surrenders to Turks after a 21-year siege
	1821	– Bishop Germanos raises the Greek flag at Patras, starting the War of Independence
Modern Greece 1829-present	1829	– Turks accept Greek independence by the Treaty of Adrianople
	1893	– French company completes Corinth Canal
	1896	– First modern Olympics in Athens
	1923	– Compulsory population exchange with Turkey agreed at the Treaty of Lausanne
	1946-49	– Greek civil war
	1981	– Andreas Papandreou becomes Greece's first socialist leader when PASOK wins elections; Greece joins EC
	1990	– Konstantinos Mitsotakis' conservative ND party wins the general election
	1993	– Papandreou's socialist PASOK party back in power

those who had become enslaved because of their debts. Declaring all free Athenians equal by law, he abolished inherited privileges and restructured political power along four classes based on wealth. Although only the first two classes were eligible for office, all four were allowed to elect magistrates and vote on legislation in the general assembly, known as the ecclesia. His reforms have led him to be regarded as the harbinger of democracy.

Sparta Sparta, in the Peloponnese, was a very different kind of city-state. The Spartans were descended from the Dorian invaders and used the Helots, the original inhabitants of Lakonia, as their slaves. They ran their society along strict military rules laid down by the 9th-century BC legislator Lycurgus.

Newborn babies were inspected and, if found wanting, were left to die on a mountain top. At the age of seven, boys were taken from their homes to start rigorous training that would turn them into crack soldiers. Girls were spared military training but were forced to keep very fit in order to produce healthy sons. Spartan indoctrination was so effective that dissent was unknown and a

Sixth-century Spartan pottery design depicting a trading scene

degree of stability was achieved that other city-states could only dream of.

While Athens became powerful through trade, Sparta became the ultimate military machine. They towered above the other city-states.

The Persian Wars The Persian drive to destroy Athens was sparked by the city's support for a rebellion in the Persian colonies on the coast of Asia Minor. Emperor Darius spent five years suppressing the revolt, and emerged hellbent on revenge. He appealed to Sparta to attack Athens from behind, but the Spartans threw his envoy in a well and Darius was left to do the job alone.

A 25,000-strong Persian army reached Attica in 490 BC, but suffered a humiliating defeat when outmanoeuvred by an Athenian force of 10,000 at the Battle of Marathon.

Darius died in 485 BC before he could mount another assault, so it was left to his son Xerxes to fulfil his father's ambition of conquering Greece. In 480 BC Xerxes gathered men from every nation of his far-flung empire and launched a coordinated invasion by army and navy, the size of which the world had never seen. The historian Herodotus estimated that there were five million Persian soldiers. No doubt this was a gross exaggeration, but it was obvious Xerxes intended to give the Greeks more than a bloody nose.

The Persians dug a canal near present-day Ierissos so that their navy could bypass the rough seas around the base of the Mt Athos peninsula (where they had been caught out before), and spanned the Hellespont with pontoon bridges.

Some 30 city-states of central and southern Greece met in Corinth to devise a common defence (others, including Delphi, sided with the Persians). They agreed on a combined army and navy under Spartan command, with the Athenian leader Themistocles providing the strategy. The Spartan King Leonidas led the army to the pass at Thermopylae, near present-day Lamia, the main passage into central Greece from the north. This bottleneck was easy to defend, and although the Greeks were greatly outnumbered they held the pass until a traitor showed the Persians a way over the mountains. The Greeks were forced to retreat, but Leonidas, along with 300 of his elite Spartan troops, fought to the death. The fleet which held off the Persian navy north of Euboea (Evia) had no choice but to retreat as well.

The Spartans and their Peloponnesian allies fell back on their second line of defence (an earthen wall across the Isthmus of Corinth), while the Persians advanced upon Athens. Themistocles ordered his people to flee the city: the women and children to Salamis, and the men to sea with the Athenian fleet. The Persians razed Attica and burned Athens to the ground.

Things did not go so well for the Persian navy. By skilful manoeuvring, the Greek navy trapped the larger Persian ships in the narrow waters off Salamis, where they became easy pickings for the more mobile Greek vessels. Xerxes, who watched the defeat of his mighty fleet from the shore, returned to Persia in disgust, leaving his general Mardonius and the army to subdue Greece. The result was quite the reverse. A year later the Greeks, under the Spartan general Pausanias, obliterated the Persian army at the Battle of Plataea. The Athenian navy then sailed to Asia Minor and destroyed what was left of the Persian fleet at Mykale, freeing the Ionian city-states there from Persian rule.

Classical Age

After the defeat of the Persians, the disciplined Spartans once again retreated to their Peloponnesian 'fortress', while Athens basked in its role as liberator and embarked on a policy of blatant imperialism. In 477 BC it founded the Delian League, so called because the treasury was kept on the sacred island of Delos. The league consisted of almost every state with a navy, no matter how small, including many of the Aegean islands and some of the Ionian city-states in Asia Minor.

Ostensibly its purpose was twofold: to create a naval force to liberate the city-states that were still occupied by Persia, and to protect against another Persian attack. The swearing of allegiance to Athens and an annual contribution of ships (later just money) were mandatory. The league, in effect, became an Athenian empire.

Indeed, when Pericles became leader of Athens in 461 BC, he moved the treasury from Delos to the Acropolis and used its contents to begin a building programme in which no expense was spared. His first objectives were to rebuild the temple complex of the Acropolis which had been destroyed by the Persians, and to link Athens to its lifeline, the port of Piraeus, with fortified walls designed to withstand any future siege.

Under Pericles' leadership (461-429 BC), Athens experienced a golden age of unprecedented cultural, artistic and scientific achievement. With the Aegean Sea safely under its wing, Athens began to look westward for further expansion, bringing it into conflict with the city-states of the mainland. It also encroached on the trade area of Corinth, which belonged to the Sparta-dominated Peloponnesian League. A series of skirmishes and provocations led to the Peloponnesian Wars.

First Peloponnesian War One of the major triggers of the first Peloponnesian War (431-421 BC) was the Corcyra incident, in which Athens supported Corcyra (present-day Kerkyra or Corfu) in a row with its mother city, Corinth. Corinth, now under serious threat, called on Sparta to help. Sparta's power depended to a large extent on Corinth's wealth, so it rallied to the cause.

Athens knew it couldn't defeat Sparta on land, so it abandoned Attica to the Spartans and withdrew behind its mighty walls, opting to rely on its navy to put pressure on Sparta by blockading the Peloponnese. Athens suffered badly during the siege. Plague broke out in the overcrowded city, killing a third of the population – including Pericles – but the defences held firm. The blockade of the Peloponnese eventually began to hurt, and the two reached an uneasy truce.

The Sicilian Adventure Throughout the war Athens had maintained an interest in Sicily and its grain, which the soil in Attica was too poor to produce. The Greek colonies there mirrored the city-states in Greece, the most powerful being Syracuse, which had remained neutral during the war.

In 416 BC, the Sicilian city of Segesta asked Athens to intervene in a squabble it was having with Selinus, an ally of Syracuse. A hot-headed second cousin of Pericles, Alcibiades, convinced the Athenian assembly to send a flotilla to Sicily; it would go on the pretext of helping Segesta, and then attack Syracuse.

The flotilla, under the joint leadership of Alcibiades, Nicias and Lamachos, was ill-fated from the outset. Nicias' health suffered and Lamachos, the most adept of the three, was killed. After laying siege to Syracuse for over three years, Alcibiades was called back to Athens on blasphemy charges arising from a drinking binge in which he knocked the heads off a few sacred statues. Enraged, he travelled not to Athens but to Sparta and persuaded the surprised Spartans to go to the aid of Syracuse. Sparta followed Alcibiades' advice and broke the siege in 413 BC, destroying the Athenian fleet and army.

Second Peloponnesian War Athens was depleted of troops, money and ships; its subject states were ripe for revolt, and Sparta was there to lend them a hand. In 413 BC the Spartans occupied Decelea in northern Attica and used it as a base to harass the region's farmers. Athens, deprived of its Sicilian grain supplies, soon began to feel the pinch. Its prospects grew even bleaker when Darius II of Persia, who had been keeping a close eye on events in Sicily and Greece, offered Sparta money to build a navy in return for a promise to return the Ionian cities of Asia Minor to Persia.

Athens went on the attack and even gained the upper hand for a while under the leadership of the reinstated Alcibiades, but its days were numbered once Persia entered the fray in Asia Minor, and Sparta regained its composure under the outstanding general,

Greek warriors were known to fight barefoot

Lysander. Athens surrendered to Sparta in 404 BC.

Corinth urged the total destruction of Athens but Lysander felt honour-bound to spare the city that had saved Greece from the Persians. Instead he crippled it by confiscating its fleet, abolishing the Delian League and tearing down the walls between the city and Piraeus.

Spartan Rule The Peloponnesian Wars had exhausted the city-states, leaving only Sparta in a position of any strength. During the wars, Sparta had promised to restore liberty to the city-states who had turned against Athens, but Lysander now changed his mind and installed oligarchies (governments run by the super-rich) supervised by Spartan garrisons. Soon there was widespread dissatisfaction.

Sparta found it had bitten off more than it could chew when it began a campaign to reclaim the cities of Asia Minor from Persian rule. This brought the Persians back into Greek affairs, where they found willing clients in Athens and increasingly powerful Thebes. Thebes, which had freed itself from Spartan control and had revived the Boeotian League, soon became the main threat to Sparta. Meanwhile, Athens regained some of its former power at the head of a new league of Aegean states known as the Second Confederacy – this time aimed against Sparta rather than Persia.

The rivalry culminated in the decisive Battle of Leuctra in 371 BC, where Thebes, under the leadership of the remarkable statesman and general Epaminondas, inflicted Sparta's first defeat in a pitched battle. Spartan influence collapsed, and Thebes filled the vacuum.

In a surprise about-turn Athens now allied itself with Sparta, and their combined forces met the Theban army at Mantinea in the Peloponnese in 362 BC. The battle was won by Thebes, but Epaminondas was killed. Without him, Theban power soon crumbled. Athens was unable to take advantage of the situation. The Second Confederacy became embroiled in infighting fomented by the Persians and when it eventually collapsed, Athens lost its final chance of regaining its former glory.

The city-states were now spent forces and a new power was rising in the north: Macedon. This had not gone unnoticed by the inspirational orator Demosthenes in Athens, who urged the city-states to prepare to defend themselves. Only Thebes took heed of his warnings and the two cities formed an alliance.

The Rise of Macedon

While the Greeks engineered their own decline through the Peloponnesian Wars, Macedon (geographically the modern nome, or province, of Macedonia) was gathering strength in the north. Macedon had long been regarded as a bit of a backwater, a loose assembly of primitive hill tribes nominally ruled by a king. The Greeks considered the people to be barbarians (those whose speech sounded like 'bar-bar', which meant anyone who didn't speak Greek).

The man who turned them into a force to be reckoned with was Philip II, who came to the throne in 382 BC.

As a boy, Philip had been held hostage in Thebes where Epaminondas had taught him about military strategy. After organising his rebellious hill tribes into an efficient army of cavalry and long-lanced infantry, Philip made several forays south and manipulated his way into membership of the Amphyctionic Council (a group of states whose job it was to protect the oracle at Delphi).

In 339 BC, on the pretext of helping the Amphyctionic Council sort out a sacred war with Amfissa, he marched into Greece. The result was the Battle of Khaironeia in Boeotia (338 BC), in which the Macedonians defeated a combined army of Athenians and Thebans. The following year, Philip called together all the city-states (except Sparta, which remained aloof) at Corinth and persuaded them to form the League of Corinth and swear allegiance to Macedonia by promising to lead a campaign against Persia. The barbarian upstart had become leader of the Greeks.

Philip's ambition to tackle Persia never materialised, for in 336 BC he was assassinated by a Macedonian noble. His son, the 20-year-old Alexander, who had led the decisive cavalry charge at Khaironeia, became king.

Alexander the Great Alexander, highly educated (he had been tutored by Aristotle), fearless and ambitious, was an astute politician and intent upon finishing what his father had begun. Philip II's death had been the signal for rebellions throughout the budding empire, but Alexander wasted no time in crushing them, making an example of Thebes by razing it to the ground. After restoring order, he turned his attention to the Persian Empire and marched his army of 40,000 men into Asia Minor in 334 BC.

After a few bloody battles with the Persians, most notably at Issus (333 BC), Alexander succeeded in conquering Syria, Palestine and Egypt – where he was proclaimed pharaoh and founded the city of Alexandria. Intent on sitting on the Persian throne, he then began hunting down the Persian king, Darius III, defeating his army in Mesopotamia in 331 BC. Darius III fled east while Alexander mopped up his empire behind him, destroying the Persian palace at Persepolis in revenge for the sacking of the

Alexander the Great (356-323 BC) hoped to conquer the world

Seleucid dynasty which ruled over Persia and Syria (capital: Antiochia); and Antigonus, who ruled over Asia Minor and whose Antigonid successors would win control over Macedonia proper.

Macedonia lost control of the Greek city-states to the south, which banded together into the Aetolian League centred on Delphi and the Achaean League based in the Peloponnese; Athens and Sparta joined neither. One of Alexander's officers established the mini-kingdom of Pergamum in Asia Minor, which reached its height under Attalos I (ruled 241-196 BC) when it rivalled Alexandria as a centre of culture and learning. The island of Rhodes developed into a powerful mini-state by taxing passing ships.

Still, Alexander's formidable achievements during his 13 years on the world stage earned him the epithet 'the Great'. He spread Greek culture throughout a large part of the 'civilised' world, encouraged intermarriage and dismissed the anti-barbarian snobbery of the classical Greeks. In doing so, he ushered in the Hellenistic period of world history, in which Hellenic ('Greek') culture broke out of the narrow confines of the ancient Greek world and merged with the other proud cultures of antiquity to create a new, cosmopolitan tradition.

Acropolis 150 years earlier, and confiscating the royal treasury. Darius' body was found a year later: he had been stabbed to death by a Bactrian (Afghan) dissident.

Alexander continued east into what is now known as Uzbekistan, Bactria (where he married a local princess, Roxane) and northern India. His ambition was now to conquer the world, which he believed ended at the sea beyond India. But his soldiers grew weary and in 324 BC forced him to return to Mesopotamia, where he settled in Babylon and drew up plans for an expedition south into Arabia. The following year, however, he fell ill suddenly and died, heirless, at the age of 33. His generals swooped like vultures on the empire.

When the dust settled, Alexander's empire had fallen apart into three large kingdoms and several smaller states. The three generals with the richest pickings were Ptolemy, founder of the Ptolemaic dynasty in Egypt (capital: Alexandria), which died out when the last of the dynasty, Cleopatra, committed suicide in 30 BC; Seleucus, founder of the

Roman Rule

While Alexander the Great was forging his vast empire in the East, the Romans had been expanding to their west and now also began making inroads into Greece. They found willing allies in Pergamum and Rhodes, who feared Syrian and Macedonian expansionism. The Romans defeated the Seleucid king, Antiochus III, in a three-year campaign and in 189 BC gave all of Asia Minor to Pergamum. Several wars were needed to subjugate Macedon, but in 168 BC Macedon lost the decisive Battle of Pydnaa.

The Achaean League was defeated in 146 BC; the Roman consul Mummius made an example of the rebellious Corinthians by completely destroying their beautiful city, massacring the men and selling the women and children into slavery. Attalos III, king of

Pergamum, died without an heir in 133 BC, donating Asia Minor to Rome in his will.

In 86 BC, Athens joined in a rebellion against the Romans in Asia Minor staged by the king of the Black Sea region, Mithridates VI. In return, the Roman statesman Sulla invaded Athens, destroyed its walls and took off with its most valuable sculptures.

Greece then became a battleground as Roman generals fought for supremacy. In a decisive naval battle off Cape Actium (31 BC) Octavian was victorious over Mark Antony and Cleopatra and consequently became Rome's first emperor, assuming the title Augustus, the Grand One.

For the next 300 years Greece, as the Roman province of Achaea, experienced an unprecedented period of peace, the Pax Romana. The Romans had always venerated Greek art, literature and philosophy, and aristocratic Romans sent their offspring to the many schools in Athens. Indeed, the Romans adopted most aspects of Hellenistic culture, spreading its unifying traditions throughout their empire.

Christianity & the Byzantine Empire

The Pax Romana began to crumble in 250 AD when the Goths invaded Greece, the first of a succession of invaders spurred on by the 'great migrations', which included the Visigoths in 395, the Vandals in 465, the Ostrogoths in 480, the Bulgars in 500, the Huns in 540 and the Slavs after 600.

Christianity, meantime, had emerged as the country's new religion. St Paul had made several visits to Greece in the 1st century AD and made converts in many places. The definitive boost to the spread of Christianity in this part of the world came with the conversion of the Roman emperors and the rise of the Byzantine Empire, which blended Hellenistic culture with Christianity.

In 324 Emperor Constantine I (also known as Constantine the Great), a Christian convert, transferred the capital of the empire from Rome to Byzantium, a city on the western shore of the Bosphorus, which was renamed Constantinople (present-day İstanbul). This was as much due to insecurity in

Italy itself as to the growing importance of the wealthy eastern regions of the empire. By the end of the 4th century, the Roman Empire was formally divided into a western and eastern half. While Rome went into terminal decline, the eastern capital grew in wealth and strength, long outliving its western counterpart (the Byzantine Empire lasted until the capture of Constantinople by the Turks in 1453).

Emperor Theodosius I made Christianity the official religion in Greece in 394 and outlawed the worship of Greek and Roman gods, now branded as paganism. Athens remained an important cultural centre until 529, when Emperor Justinian forbade the teaching of classical philosophy in favour of Christian theology, then seen as the supreme form of intellectual endeavour. The Hagia Sophia (Church of the Divine Wisdom) was built in Constantinople and many magnificent churches were also built in Greece, especially in Thessaloniki, a Christian stronghold much favoured by the Byzantine emperors.

The Crusades

It is one of the ironies of history that the demise of the Byzantine Empire was accelerated not by invasions of infidels from the east, nor barbarians from the north, but by fellow Christians from the West – the Frankish crusaders.

The stated mission of the crusades was to liberate the Holy Land from the Muslims, but in reality they were driven as much by greed as by religious fervour. By the time the First Crusade was launched in 1095, the Franks had already made substantial gains in Italy at the empire's expense and the rulers of Constantinople were understandably nervous about giving the crusaders safe passage on their way to Jerusalem. The first three crusades passed by without incident, but the fourth proved that the fear was justified. The crusaders struck a deal with Venice, which had a score to settle with the Byzantines, and was able to persuade the crusaders that Constantinople presented richer pickings than Jerusalem.

Constantinople was sacked in 1204 and the crusaders installed Baldwin of Flanders as head of the short-lived Latin Empire of Constantinople. Much of the Byzantine Empire was partitioned into feudal states ruled by self-styled 'Latin' (mostly Frankish) princes. Greece now entered one of the most tumultuous periods of its history. The Byzantines fought to regain their lost capital and to keep the areas they had managed to hold on to (the so-called Empire of Nicaea, south of Constantinople in Asia Minor), while the Latin princes fought among themselves to expand their territories.

The Venetians, meanwhile, had secured a foothold in Greece. Over the next few centuries they acquired all the key Greek ports, including the island of Crete, and became the wealthiest and most powerful traders in the Mediterranean.

Despite this disorderly state of affairs, Byzantium was not yet dead. In 1259, the Byzantine emperor Michael VIII Palaeologos recaptured the Peloponnese from the Frankish de Villehardouin family, and made the city of Mystras his headquarters. Many eminent Byzantine artists, architects, intellectuals and philosophers converged on the city for a final burst of Byzantine creativity. Michael VIII managed to reclaim Constantinople in 1261, but by this time Byzantium was a shadow of its former self.

The Ottoman Empire

Constantinople was soon facing a much greater threat from the East. The Seljuk Turks, a tribe from central Asia, had first appeared on the eastern fringes of the empire in the middle of the 11th century. They established themselves on the Anatolian plain by defeating a Byzantine army at Manzikert in 1071. The threat looked to have been contained, especially when the Seljuks were themselves overrun by the Mongols. By the time Mongol power began to wane, the Seljuks had been supplanted as the dominant Turkish tribe by the Ottomans – the followers of Osman, who ruled from 1289 to 1326. The Muslim Ottomans rapidly expanded the areas under their control and by

the mid-15th century were harassing the Byzantine Empire on all sides. Western Europe was too embroiled in the Hundred Years' War to come to the rescue, and in 1453 Constantinople fell to the Turks under Mohammed II (the Conqueror). Once more Greece became a battleground, this time fought over by the Turks and Venetians. Eventually, with the exception of the Ionian islands, Greece became part of the Ottoman Empire.

Much has been made of the horrors of the Turkish occupation in Greece. However, in the early years at any rate, Greeks probably marginally preferred Ottoman to Venetian or Frankish rule. The Venetians in particular treated their subjects little better than slaves. But life was not easy under the Turks, not least because of the high taxation they imposed. One of their most hated practices was the taking of one out of every five male children to become janissaries, personal bodyguards of the sultan. Many janissaries became infantrymen in the Ottoman army, but the cleverest could rise to high office – including grand vizier (chief minister).

Ottoman power reached its zenith under Sultan Süleyman the Magnificent (ruled 1520-66), who expanded the empire through the Balkans and Hungary to the gates of Vienna. His successor, Selim the Sot, added Cyprus to their dominions in 1570, but his death in 1574 marked the end of serious territorial expansion.

Although they captured Crete in 1670 after a 25-year campaign and briefly threatened Vienna once more in 1683, the ineffectual sultans that followed in the late 16th and 17th centuries saw the empire go into steady decline. They suffered a series of reversals on the battlefield, and Venice succeeded in holding onto the Peloponnese after a campaign in 1687 that saw them advance as far as Athens. The Parthenon was destroyed during the fighting when a shell struck a store of Turkish gunpowder.

Chaos and rebellion spread across Greece. Corsairs terrorised coastal dwellers, gangs of klephts (anti-Ottoman fugitives and brigands) roamed the mountains, and there was an upsurge of opposition to Turkish rule by freedom fighters – who fought each other when they weren't fighting the Turks.

Russian Involvement

Russia's link with Greece went back to Byzantine times, when the Russians had been converted to Christianity by Byzantine missionaries. The Church hierarchies in Constantinople and Kiev (later in Moscow) soon went separate ways, but when Constantinople fell to the Turks, the metropolitan (head) of the Russian Church declared Moscow the 'third Rome', the true heir of Christianity, and campaigned for the liberation of its fellow Christians in the south. This fitted in nicely with Russia's efforts to expand southwards and south-westwards into Ottoman territory – perhaps even to turn the Ottoman Empire back into a Byzantine Empire dependent on Russia.

When Catherine the Great became Empress of Russia in 1762, both the Republic of Venice and the Ottoman Empire were weak. She sent Russian agents to foment rebellion, first in the Peloponnese in 1770 and then in Epiros in 1786. Both rebellions were crushed ruthlessly – the latter by Ali Pasha, the governor of Ioannina, who proceeded to set up his own power base in Greece in defiance of the sultan.

Independence Parties In the 1770s and 1780s Catherine booted the Turks from the Black Sea coast and created a number of towns in the region, which she gave Ancient Greek or Byzantine names. She offered Greeks financial incentives and free land to settle the region, and many took up her offer.

One of the new towns was Odessa, and it was there in 1814 that businessmen Athanasios Tsakalof, Emmanuel Xanthos and Nikolaos Skoufas founded the first Greek independence party, the Filiki Eteria (Friendly Society). The message of the society spread quickly and branches opened throughout Greece. The leaders in Odessa believed that armed force was the only effective means of liberation, and made generous monetary contributions to the freedom fighters.

There were also stirrings of dissent among Greeks living in Constantinople. The Ottomans regarded it as beneath them to participate in commerce, and this had left the door open for Greeks to become a powerful economic force in the city. These wealthy Greek families were called Phanariots. Unlike the Filiki Eteria, who strove for liberation through rebellion, the Phanariots believed that they could effect a takeover from within.

The War of Independence

Ali Pasha's private rebellion against the sultan in 1820 gave the Greeks the opportunity they had been waiting for. On 25 March 1821, Bishop Germanos of Patras signalled the beginning of the War of Independence when he hoisted the Greek flag at the monastery of Agia Lavra in the Peloponnese. Fighting broke out almost simultaneously across most of Greece and the occupied islands, with the Greeks making big early gains. The fighting was savage, with atrocities committed on both sides. In the Peloponnese, 12,000 Turkish inhabitants were massacred after the capture of the city of Tripolitsa (present-day Tripolis) and Maniot freedom fighters razed the homes of thousands of Turks. The Turks retaliated with massacres in Asia Minor, most notoriously on the island of Chios, where 25,000 civilians were killed.

The fighting escalated and within a year the Greeks had captured Monemvasia, Navarino (modern Pylos), Nafplio and Tripolitsa in the Peloponnese, and Messolongi, Athens and Thiva (Thebes). Greek independence was proclaimed at Epidaurus on 13 January 1822.

The western powers were reluctant to intervene, fearing the consequences of creating a power vacuum in south-eastern Europe, where the Turks still controlled much territory. Help came from the philhellenes – aristocratic young men, recipients of a classical education, who saw themselves as the inheritors of a glorious civilisation and were willing to fight to liberate its oppressed descendants. These philhellenes included Shelley, Goethe, Schiller, Victor Hugo, Alfred de Musset and Lord Byron. Byron arrived in Messolongi – an important centre of resistance – in January 1824 and died three months later of pneumonia.

The prime movers in the revolution were the klephts Theodoros Kolokotronis (who led the siege on Nafplio) and Markos Botsaris; Georgos Koundouriotis (a ship owner) and Admiral Andreas Miaoulis, both from Hydra; and the Phanariots Alexandros Mavrokordatos and Dimitrios Ypsilantis. Streets all over Greece are named after these heroes.

The cause was not lacking in leaders; what was lacking was unity of objectives and strategy. Internal disagreements twice escalated into civil war, the worst in the Peloponnese in 1824. The sultan took advantage of this and called in Egyptian reinforcements. By 1827 the Turks had captured Modon (Methoni) and Corinth, and recaptured Navarino, Messolongi and Athens.

At last the western powers intervened, and a combined Russian, French and British fleet destroyed the Turkish-Egyptian fleet in the Bay of Navarino in October 1827. Sultan Mahmud II defied the odds and proclaimed a holy war. Russia sent troops into the Balkans and engaged the Ottoman army in yet another Russo-Turkish war. Fighting continued until 1829 when, with Russian troops at the gates of Constantinople, the sultan accepted Greek independence by the Treaty of Adrianople.

Birth of the Greek Nation

The Greeks, meanwhile, had been busy organising the independent state they proclaimed several years earlier. In April 1827 they elected as their first president a Corfiot who had been the foreign minister of Tsar Alexander I, Ioannis Kapodistrias. Nafplio, in the Peloponnese, was selected as the capital.

With his Russian past, Kapodistrias believed in a strong, centralised government. Although he was good at enlisting foreign support, his autocratic manner at home was unacceptable to many of the leaders of the War of Independence, particularly the Maniot chieftains who had always been a law unto themselves, and he was assassinated in 1831.

Amid the ensuing anarchy, Britain, France and Russia once again intervened and declared that Greece should become a monarchy and that the throne should be given to a non-Greek so that they would not be seen to be favouring one Greek faction. A fledgling kingdom was now up for grabs among the offspring of the crowned heads of Europe, but no-one exactly ran to fill the empty throne. Eventually the 17-year-old Prince Otto of Bavaria was chosen, arriving in Nafplio in January 1833. The new kingdom (established by the London Convention of 1832) consisted of the Peloponnese, Sterea Ellada, the Cyclades and the Sporades.

King Otho (as his name became) got up the nose of the Greek people from the moment he set foot on their land. He arrived with a bunch of upper-class Bavarian cronies, to whom he gave the most prestigious official posts, and he was just as autocratic as Kapodistrias. Otho moved the capital to Athens in 1834.

Patience with his rule ran out in 1843 when demonstrations in the capital, led by the War of Independence leaders, called for a constitution. Otho mustered a National Assembly which drafted a constitution calling for parliamentary government consisting of a lower house and a senate. Otho's cronies were whisked out of power and replaced by War of Independence freedom fighters, who bullied and bribed the populace into voting for them.

The Great Idea

By the middle of the 19th century the people of the new Greek nation were no better off materially than they had been under the Ottomans, and it was in this climate of despondency that the Megali Idea (Great Idea) of a new Greek Empire was born. This empire was to include all the lands that had once been under Greek influence and have Constantinople as its capital. Otho enthusiastically embraced the idea, which increased his popularity no end. The Greek politicians, however, did not; they sought ways to increase their own power in the face of Otho's autocratic rule.

By the end of the 1850s, most of the stalwarts from the War of Independence had been replaced by a new breed of university graduates (Athens University had been founded in 1837). In 1862 they staged a bloodless revolution and deposed the king. But they weren't quite able to set their own agenda, because in the same year Britain returned the Ionian islands (a British protectorate since 1815) to Greece, and in the general euphoria the British were able to push forward young Prince William of Denmark, who became King George I (the Greek monarchy retained its Danish links from that time).

His 50-year reign brought stability to the troubled country, beginning with a new constitution in 1864, which established the power of democratically elected representatives and pushed the king further towards a ceremonial role. An uprising in Crete against Turkish rule was suppressed by the sultan in 1866-68, but in 1881 Greece acquired Thessaly and part of Epiros as the result of another Russo-Turkish war.

When Harilaos Trikoupis became prime minister in 1882, he prudently concentrated his efforts on domestic issues rather than pursuing the Great Idea. The 1880s brought the first signs of economic growth: the country's first railway lines and paved roads were constructed; the Corinth Canal (begun in 62 AD!) was completed – enabling Piraeus to become a major Mediterranean port; and the merchant navy grew rapidly.

However, the Great Idea had not been buried, and reared its head again after Trikoupis' death in 1896. In 1897 there was another uprising in Crete, and the hot-headed prime minister Theodoros Deligiannis responded by declaring war on Turkey and sending help to Crete. A Greek attempt to invade Turkey in the north proved disastrous

– it was only through the intervention of the great powers that the Turkish army was prevented from taking Athens.

Crete was placed under international administration. The day-to-day government of the island was gradually handed over to Greeks, and in 1905 the president of the Cretan assembly, Eleftherios Venizelos, announced Crete's union *(enosis)* with Greece, although this was not recognised by international law until 1913. Venizelos went on to become prime minister of Greece in 1910 and was the country's leading politician until his republican sympathies brought about his downfall in 1935.

The Balkan Wars

Although the Ottoman Empire was in its death throes at the beginning of the 20th century, it was still clinging onto Macedonia. It was a prize sought by the newly formed Balkan countries of Serbia and Bulgaria, as well as by Greece, leading to the Balkan wars. The first, in 1912, pitted all three against the Turks; the second, in 1913, pitted Serbia and Greece against Bulgaria. The outcome was the Treaty of Bucharest (August 1913), which greatly expanded Greek territory by adding the southern part of Macedonia, part of Thrace, another chunk of Epiros, and the North-East Aegean islands, as well as recognising the union with Crete.

In March 1913, King George was assassinated by a lunatic and his son Constantine became king.

WWI & Smyrna

King Constantine, who was married to the sister of the German emperor, insisted that Greece remain neutral when WWI broke out in August 1914. As the war dragged on, the Allies (Britain, France and Russia) put increasing pressure on Greece to join forces with them against Germany and Turkey. They made promises which they couldn't hope to fulfil, including land in Asia Minor. Venizelos favoured the Allied cause, placing him at loggerheads with the king. Tensions between the two came to a head in 1916, and Venizelos set up a rebel government, first in

Crete and then in Thessaloniki, while the pressure from the Allies eventually persuaded Constantine to leave Greece in June 1917. He was replaced by his more amenable second son, Alexander.

Greek troops served with distinction on the Allied side, but when the war ended in 1918 the promised land in Asia Minor was not forthcoming. Venizelos took matters into his own hands and, with Allied acquiescence, landed troops in Smyrna (present-day İzmir) in May 1919 under the guise of protecting the half a million Greeks living in that city (just under half its population). With a firm foothold in Asia Minor, Venizelos now planned to push home his advantage against a war-depleted Ottoman Empire. He ordered his troops to attack in October 1920 (just weeks before he was voted out of office). By September 1921, the Greeks had advanced as far as Ankara.

The Turkish forces were commanded by Mustafa Kemal (later to become Atatürk), a young general who also belonged to the Young Turks, a group of army officers pressing for western-style political reforms. Kemal first halted the Greek advance outside Ankara in September 1921 and then routed them with a massive offensive the following spring. The Greeks were driven out of Smyrna and many of the Greek inhabitants were massacred. Mustafa Kemal was now a national hero, the sultanate was abolished and Turkey became a republic. The outcome of the failed Greek invasion and the revolution in Turkey was the Treaty of Lausanne of July 1923. This gave eastern Thrace and the islands of Imvros and Tenedos to Turkey, while the Italians kept the Dodecanese (which they had temporarily acquired in 1912 and would hold until 1947).

The treaty also called for a population exchange between Greece and Turkey to prevent any future disputes. The Great Idea, which had been such an enormous drain on the country's finances over the decades, was at last laid to rest. Almost 1.5 million Greeks left Turkey and almost 400,000 Turks left Greece. The exchange put a tremendous strain on the Greek economy and caused great hardship for the individuals concerned. Many Greeks abandoned a privileged life in Asia Minor for one of extreme poverty in shantytowns in Greece.

The Republic of 1924-35
The arrival of the refugees coincided with, and compounded, a period of political instability unprecedented even by Greek standards. In October 1920, King Alexander had died from a monkey bite, resulting in the restoration of his father, King Constantine. Constantine identified himself too closely with the war against Turkey, and abdicated after the fall of Smyrna. He was replaced by his first son, George II, but he was no match for the group of army officers who seized power after the war. A republic was proclaimed in March 1924 amid a series of coups and counter-coups.

A measure of stability was attained with Venizelos' return to power in 1928. He pursued a policy of economic and educational reforms, but progress was inhibited by the Great Depression. His anti-royalist Liberal Party began to face a growing challenge from the monarchist Popular Party, culminating in defeat at the polls in March 1933. The new government was preparing for the restoration of the monarchy when Venizelos and his supporters staged an unsuccessful coup in March 1935. Venizelos was exiled to Paris, where he died a year later. In November 1935 King George II was restored to the throne by a rigged plebiscite, and he installed the right-wing General Ioannis Metaxas as prime minister. Nine months later, Metaxas assumed dictatorial powers with the king's consent under the pretext of preventing a communist-inspired republican coup.

WWII
Metaxas' grandiose vision was to create a Third Greek Civilisation based on its glorious ancient and Byzantine past, but what he actually created was more like a Greek version of the Third Reich. He exiled or imprisoned opponents, banned trade unions and the KKE (Kommunistiko Komma Ellados, the Greek Communist

Party), imposed press censorship, and created a secret police force and a fascist-style youth movement. Metaxas is best known, however, for his reply of *ohi* (no) to Mussolini's request to allow Italians to traverse Greece at the beginning of WWII, thus maintaining Greece's policy of strict neutrality. The Italians invaded Greece, but were driven back into Albania.

A prerequisite of Hitler's plan to invade the Soviet Union was a secure southern flank in the Balkans. The British, realising this, asked Metaxas if they could land troops in Greece. He gave the same reply as he had given the Italians, but died suddenly in January 1941. The king replaced him with the timorous Alexandros Koryzis, who agreed to British forces landing in Greece and then committed suicide when German troops marched through Yugoslavia and invaded Greece on 6 April 1941. The defending Greek, British, Australian and New Zealand troops were seriously outnumbered, and the whole country was under Nazi occupation within a month. King George II and his government went into exile in Egypt. The civilian population suffered appallingly during the occupation, many dying of starvation. The Nazis rounded up more than half the Jewish population and transported them to death camps.

Numerous resistance movements sprang up. The three dominant ones were ELAS (Ellinikos Laïkos Apeleftherotikos Stratos), EAM (Ethnikon Apeleftherotikon Metopon) and EDES (Ethnikos Dimokratikos Ellinikos Syndesmos). Although ELAS was founded by communists, not all of its members were left wing, whereas EAM consisted of Stalinist KKE members who had lived in Moscow in the 1930s and harboured ambitions of establishing a postwar communist Greece. EDES (Ethnikos Dimokratikos Ellinikos Syndesmos) consisted of right-wing and monarchist resistance fighters. These groups fought one another with as much venom as they fought the Germans.

By 1943 Britain had begun speculating on the political complexion of postwar Greece. Winston Churchill wanted the king back and was afraid of a communist takeover, especially after ELAS and EAM formed a coalition and declared a provisional government in the summer of 1944. The Germans were pushed out of Greece in October 1944, but the communist and monarchist resistance groups continued to fight one another.

Civil War

On 3 December 1944, the police fired on a communist demonstration in Syntagma Square. The ensuing six weeks of fighting between the left and the right were known as the Dekemvriana (events of December), the first round of the civil war, and only the intervention of British troops prevented an ELAS-EAM victory. An election held in March 1946 and boycotted by the communists was won by the royalists, and a rigged plebiscite put George II back on the throne.

In October the left-wing Democratic Army (DA) was formed to resume the fight against the monarchy and its British supporters. Under the leadership of Markos Vafiadis, the DA swiftly occupied a large swathe of land along Greece's northern border with Albania and Yugoslavia.

By 1947, the US had replaced Britain as Greece's 'minder' and the civil war had developed into a setting for the new Cold War as the Americans fought to contain the spread of Soviet influence in Europe. Inspired by the Truman Doctrine, the US poured in cash and military hardware to shore up the anti-communist coalition government. Communism was declared illegal and the government introduced its notorious Certificate of Political Reliability (proof that the carrier was not left wing), which remained valid until 1962 and without which Greeks couldn't vote and found it almost impossible to get work.

US aid did little to improve the situation on the ground. The DA continued to be supplied through the communist states to the north, and by the end of 1948 large chunks of the mainland and most of the Peloponnese were under its control. It was unable, though, to capture the major town it needed as a base for a rival government declared by Vafiades. The tide began to turn the government's way early in 1949 when the DA was forced out of the Peloponnese, but the fighting dragged on until October 1949, when Yugoslavia fell out with the Soviet Union and cut off the DA's supply lines. Vafiades was assassinated by a group of his Stalinist underlings and the DA capitulated.

If this was a victory, there was nothing to celebrate. The country was in an almighty mess, both politically and economically. More Greeks had been killed in the three years of bitter civil war than in WWII; a quarter of a million people were homeless, many thousands more had been taken prisoner or exiled, and the DA had taken some 30,000 Greek children from northern Greece to Eastern-bloc countries, ostensibly for protection.

The sense of despair left by the civil war became the trigger for a mass exodus. Almost a million Greeks headed off in search of a better life elsewhere, primarily to Australia, Canada and the USA. Villages – whole islands even – were abandoned as people gambled on a new start in the suburbs of cities like Melbourne, New York and Chicago. While some have drifted back (including half the restaurant owners in the Peloponnese!), most have stayed away.

Reconstruction & the Cyprus Issue

A general election was held in 1950. The system of proportional representation resulted in a series of unworkable coalitions, and the electoral system was changed to majority voting in 1952 – which excluded the communists from future governments. The next election was a victory for the newly formed right-wing Ellinikos Synagermos (Greek Rally) party led by General Papagos, who had been a field marshal during the civil war. General Papagos remained in power until his death in 1955, when he was replaced by Konstantinos Karamanlis, the minister of public works.

Greece joined NATO in 1951, and in 1953 the US was granted the right to operate sovereign bases. Intent on maintaining a right-wing government, the US gave generous aid and even more generous military support. Living standards improved during the 1950s, but Greece remained a poor country.

Cyprus occupied centre stage in Greece's foreign affairs, and has remained close to it to this day. Since the 1930s, Greek Cypriots (four-fifths of the island's population) had demanded union with Greece, while Turkey had maintained its claim to the island ever since the British occupied it in 1914 (it became a British crown colony in 1925). After an outbreak of communal violence between Greek and Turkish Cypriots in 1954, Britain stated its intention to make Cyprus an independent state.

The right-wing Greek Cypriot EOKA (National Organisation of Cypriot Freedom Fighters) took up arms against the British, but Greece and Turkey finally accepted independence in 1959. Cyprus duly became a republic the following August with Archbishop Makarios as president and a Turk, Fasal Kükük, as vice president. The changes did little to appease either side. EOKA resolved to keep fighting, while Turkish Cypriots continue to clamour for partition of the island.

Back in Greece, Georgos Papandreou, a former Venizelos supporter, founded the broadly based EK (Centre Union) in 1958, but an election in 1961 returned the ERE (National Radical Union), Karamanlis' new name for Papagos' Greek Rally party, to power for the third time in succession. Papandreou accused the ERE of ballot-rigging – probably true, but the culprits were almost certainly right-wing, military-backed groups (rather than Karamanlis) who feared communist infiltration if the EK came to power. Political turmoil followed, culminating in the murder, in May 1963, of Grigorios Lambrakis, the deputy of the communist EDA (Union of the Democratic Left). All this proved too much for Karamanlis, who resigned and left the country.

Despite the ERE's sometimes rather desperate measures to stay in power, an election in February 1964 was won by the EK.

Papandreou wasted no time in implementing a series of radical changes. He freed political prisoners and allowed exiles to come back to Greece, reduced income tax and the defence budget, and increased spending on social services and education. Papandreou's victory coincided with King Constantine II's accession to the Greek throne, and with a renewed outbreak of violence in Cyprus, which erupted into a full-scale civil war before the UN intervened and installed a peace-keeping force.

The Colonels' Coup

The right in Greece was rattled by Papandreou's tolerance of the left, fearing that this would increase the EDA's influence. The climate was one of mutual suspicion between the left and the right, each claiming that the other was plotting a takeover. Finally, Papandreou decided the armed forces needed a thorough overhaul, which seemed fair enough, as army officers were more often than not the perpetrators of conspiracies. King Constantine refused to cooperate with this, and Papandreou resigned. Two years of ineffectual interim governments followed before a new election was scheduled for May 1967.

The election was never to be. A group of army colonels led by Georgos Papadopoulos and Stylianos Patakos staged a coup d'état on 21 April 1967. King Constantine tried an unsuccessful counter-coup in December, after which he fled the country. A military junta was established with Papadopoulos as prime minister.

The colonels imposed martial law, abolished all political parties, banned trade unions, imposed censorship, and imprisoned, tortured and exiled thousands of Greeks who opposed them. Suspicions that the coup had been aided by the CIA remain conjecture, but criticism of the coup, and the ensuing regime, was certainly not forthcoming from the CIA or the US government. In June 1972 Papadopoulos declared Greece a republic (confirmed by rigged referendum in July) and appointed himself president.

In November 1973 students began a sit-in at Athens' Polytechnic college in protest against the junta. On the night of 16 November, tanks stormed the building, injuring many and killing at least 20. On 25 November, Papadopoulos was deposed by the thuggish Brigadier Ioannidis, head of the military security police.

The following July, desperate for a foreign policy success to bolster the regime's standing, Ioannidis decided it was time to play the Cyprus card. He hatched a wild scheme to assassinate President Makarios and unite Cyprus with Greece. The scheme went disastrously wrong after Makarios got wind of the plan and escaped. The junta installed Nikos Sampson, a former EOKA leader, as president, and Turkey reacted by invading the island.

The junta quickly removed Sampson and threw in the towel, but the Turks continued to advance until they occupied the northern third of the island, forcing almost 200,000 Greek Cypriots to flee their homes for the safety of the south.

After the Colonels

The army now called Karamanlis from Paris to clear up the mess in Greece. An election was arranged for November 1974 (won handsomely by Karamanlis' New Democracy party), and the ban on communist parties was lifted. Andreas Papandreou (son of Georgos) formed PASOK (the Panhellenic Socialist Union), and a plebiscite voted 69% against restoration of the monarchy. (Former king Constantine, who now lives in London, didn't revisit Greece until the summer of 1993. The New Democracy government sent missile boats and a transport plane to follow his yacht. Nonetheless the ex-king said he and his family enjoyed the holiday, and he had no wish to overthrow the Greek constitution.)

Karamanlis' New Democracy (ND) party won the election in 1977, but his personal popularity began to decline. One of his biggest achievements before accepting the largely ceremonial post of president was to engineer Greece's entry into the European Community (now the European Union), which involved jumping the queue ahead of other countries who had waited patiently to be accepted. On 1 January 1981 Greece became the 10th member of the EC.

The Socialist 1980s

Andreas Papandreou's PASOK party won the election of October 1981 with 48% of the vote, giving Greece its first socialist government. PASOK promised removal of US air bases and withdrawal from NATO.

Seven years into government, these promises remained unfulfilled (although the US military presence was reduced), unemployment was high and reforms in education and welfare had been limited. Women's issues had fared better, though: the dowry system was abolished, abortion legalised, and civil marriage and divorce were implemented. The crunch came in 1988 when Papandreou's love affair with air hostess Dimitra Liani (whom he subsequently married) hit the headlines, and PASOK became embroiled in a financial scandal involving the Bank of Crete.

In July 1989 an unlikely coalition of conservatives and communists took over to implement a *katharsis* (campaign of purification) to investigate the scandal. In September it ruled that Papandreou and four former ministers be tried for embezzlement, telephone tapping and illegal grain sales. The trial of Papandreou ended in January 1992 with his acquittal on all counts.

The 1990s

An election in 1990 brought the ND back to power with a majority of only two seats, and with Konstantinos Mitsotakis as prime minister. Intent on redressing the country's economic problems – high inflation and high government spending – the government imposed austerity measures, including a wage freeze for civil servants and steep increases in public-utility costs and basic services. It also announced a privatisation programme aimed at 780 state-controlled enterprises; OTE (the telecommunications company), electricity and Olympic Airways were first on the list. The government also cracked down on tax evasion, which is still so rife it's described as the nation's favourite pastime.

The austerity measures sparked off a series of strikes in the public sector in mid-1990 and again in 1991 and 1992. The government's problems were compounded by an influx of Albanian refugees (see the People section later in this chapter), and the dispute over the use of the name Macedonia for the southern republic of former Yugoslavia (see the aside 'What's in a Name?' in the Northern Greece chapter).

By late 1992 corruption allegations were being made against the government and it was claimed that Cretan-born Mitsotakis had a large, secret collection of Minoan art, and in mid-1993 there were allegations of government telephone tapping. Former Mitsotakis supporters began to cut their losses: in June 1993 Antonis Samaras, the ND's former foreign minister, founded the Political Spring party and called upon ND members to join him. So many of them joined that the ND lost its parliamentary majority and hence its capacity to govern.

An early election was held in October, which Andreas Papandreou's PASOK party won with 47% of the vote against 39% for ND and 5% for Political Spring. Through the majority voting system, this translated into a handsome parliamentary majority for PASOK.

Given the 74-year-old Papandreou's heart condition and generally poor health, the focus of political interest now shifted to speculation on the succession. Papandreou was rarely sighted outside his villa, where he lived surrounded by his ministerial coterie of family and friends. He was finally forced to step down as PASOK leader in early 1996 after another bout of ill-health, and his death on June 26 marked the end of an era in Greek politics.

Papandreou's departure produced a dramatic change of direction for PASOK, with the party abandoning his left-leaning politics and electing economic reformer Costas Simitis as prime minister. The new leader had been an outspoken critic of Papandreou and had been sacked as industry minister four months previously. He surprised many by calling a snap poll in September 1996, and campaigned hard in support of his Mr Clean image. He was rewarded with almost 42% of the vote, which translated into a comfortable parliamentary majority.

Simitis belongs to much the same school of politics as Britain's Tony Blair. Since he took power, PASOK policy has shifted right to the extent that it now agrees with the opposition New Democracy on all major policy issues. Simitis can be expected to push for further integration with Europe,

including monetary union. This will mean very little change to domestic policy, with more tax reform and more talk of austerity.

MYTHOLOGY

Mythology was an integral part of the lives of all ancient peoples. The myths of ancient Greece are the most familiar to us, for they are deeply entrenched in the consciousness of western civilisation. They are accounts of the lives of the deities whom the Greeks worshipped and of the heroes they idolised.

The myths are all things to all people – a rollicking good yarn, expressions of deep

Olympian Creation Myth

According to mythology, the world was formed from a great shapeless mass called Chaos. From Chaos came forth Gaea, the earth goddess. She bore a son, Uranus, the Firmament, and their subsequent union produced three 100-handed giants and three one-eyed Cyclopes. Gaea dearly loved her hideous offspring, but not so Uranus, who hurled them into Tartarus (the underworld).

The couple then produced the seven Titans, but Gaea still grieved for her other children. She asked the Titans to take vengeance upon their father, and free the 100-handed giants and Cyclopes. The Titans did as they were requested, castrating the hapless Uranus, but Cronos (the head Titan), after setting eyes on Gaea's hideous offspring, hurled them back into Tartarus, whereupon Gaea foretold that he (Cronos) would be usurped by one of his own offspring.

Cronos married his sister Rhea, but wary of his mother's warning, he swallowed every child Rhea bore him. When Rhea bore her sixth child, Zeus, she smuggled him to Crete, and gave Cronos a stone in place of the child, which he duly swallowed. Rhea hid the baby Zeus in the Dikteon cave in the care of three nymphs.

On reaching manhood, Zeus, determined to avenge his swallowed siblings, became Cronos' cupbearer and filled his cup with poison. Cronos drank from the cup, then disgorged first the stone and then his children Hestia, Demeter, Hera, Poseidon and Hades, all of whom were none the worse for their ordeal. Zeus, aided by his regurgitated brothers and sisters, deposed Cronos, and went to war against the Titans who wouldn't acknowledge him as chief god. Gaea, who still hadn't forgotten her imprisoned, beloved offspring, told Zeus he would only be victorious with the help of the Cyclopes and the 100-handed giants, so he released them from Tartarus.

The Cyclopes gave Zeus a thunderbolt, and the three 100-handed giants threw rocks at the Titans, who eventually retreated. Zeus banished Cronos, as well as all of the Titans except Atlas (Cronos' deputy), to a far-off land. Atlas was ordered to hold up the sky.

Mt Olympus became home-sweet-home for Zeus and his unruly and incestuous family. Zeus, taking a fancy to Hera, turned himself into a dishevelled cuckoo whom the unsuspecting Hera held to her bosom, whereupon Zeus violated her, and Hera reluctantly agreed to marry him. They had three children: Ares, Hephaestus and Hebe. ∎

Hermes, Zeus & Aphrodite

psychological insights, words of spine-tingling poetic beauty and food for the imagination. They have inspired great literature, art and music, by providing archetypes through which we can learn much about the deeper motives of human behaviour.

The myths we know are thought to be a blend of Dorian and Mycenaean mythology. Most accounts derive from the works of the poets Hesiod and Homer, produced in about 900 BC. The original myths have been chopped and changed countless times – dramatised, moralised and even adapted for ancient political propaganda, so numerous versions exist.

The Greek Myths, by Robert Graves, is regarded as being the ultimate book on the subject. It can be heavy going, though. *An Iconoclast's Guide to the Greek Gods* by Maureen O'Sullivan makes more entertaining reading.

The Twelve Deities

The main characters of the myths are the 12 deities, who lived on Mt Olympus – which the Greeks thought to be at the exact centre of the world.

The supreme deity was **Zeus**, who was also god of the heavens. His job was to make laws and keep his unruly family in order by brandishing his thunderbolt. He was also the possessor of an astonishing libido and vented his lust on just about everyone he came across, including his own mother. Mythology is littered with his offspring.

Zeus was married to his sister, **Hera** (see the Olympian Creation Myth aside earlier in this section), who was the protector of women and the family. Hera was able to renew her virginity each year by bathing in a spring. She was the mother of Ares and Hephaestus.

Ares, god of war, was a nasty piece of work. He was fiery-tempered and violent, liking nothing better than a good massacre. Athenians, who fought only for such noble ideals as liberty, thought that Ares must be a Thracian – whom they regarded as bloodthirsty barbarians.

Hephaestus was worshipped for his matchless skills as a craftsman. When Zeus decided to punish man, he asked Hephaestus to make a woman. So Hephaestus created Pandora from clay and water, and, as everyone knows, she had a box, from which sprang all the evils afflicting humankind.

The next time you have a bowl of corn flakes, give thanks to **Demeter**, the goddess of earth and fertility. The English word 'cereal', for products of corn or edible grain, derives from the goddess' Roman name, Ceres. The Greek word for such products is *demetriaka*.

The goddess of love (and lust) was the beautiful **Aphrodite**. Her *tour de force* was her magic girdle which made everyone fall in love with its wearer. The girdle meant she was constantly pursued by both gods and goddesses – the gods because they wanted to make love to her, the goddesses because they wanted to borrow the girdle. Zeus became so fed up with her promiscuity that he married her off to Hephaestus, the ugliest of the gods.

In contrast **Hestia**, the goddess of the hearth, symbol of security, happiness and hospitality, was as pure as driven snow. She spurned disputes and wars and swore to be a virgin forever.

Athena, the powerful goddess of wisdom and guardian of Athens, is said to have been born (complete with helmet, armour and spear) from Zeus' head, with Hephaestus acting as midwife. Unlike Ares, she derived no pleasure from fighting, but preferred to use her wisdom to settle disputes peacefully. If need be, however, she went valiantly into battle.

Poseidon, the brother of Zeus, was god of the sea and preferred his sumptuous palace in the depths of the Aegean to Mt Olympus. When he was angry (which was often) he would use his trident to create massive waves and floods. His moods could also trigger earthquakes and volcanic eruptions. He was always on the lookout for some real estate on dry land and challenged Dionysos for Naxos, Hera for Argos and Athena for Athens.

Apollo, god of the sun, and **Artemis**, goddess of the moon, were the twins of Leto and Zeus. Many qualities were attributed to Apollo, for the ancient Greeks believed that

The Twelve Deities

Zeus
Domain: supreme deity
Aegis: thunderbolt

Hera
Domain: marriage, childbirth
Aegis: cuckoo, peacock

Ares
Domain: war
Aegis: armour

Hephaestus
Domain: fire, industry
Aegis: hammer, anvil

Demeter
Domain: fertility
Aegis: sheaf of wheat

Aphrodite
Domain: love, beauty
Aegis: dove, girdle

Hestia
Domain: domesticity
Aegis: hearth

Athena
Domain: wisdom
Aegis: owl, armour

Poseidon
Domain: sea, earthquakes
Aegis: trident

Apollo
Domain: sun, music, poetry
Aegis: bow, lyre

Artemis
Domain: moon, hunting, chastity
Aegis: she-bear, stag

Hermes
Domain: commerce
Aegis: winged sandals

the sun not only gave physical light, but that its light was symbolic of mental illumination. Apollo was also worshipped as the god of music and song, which the ancients believed were heard only where there was light and security. Artemis was worshipped as the goddess of childbirth, yet she asked Zeus if he would grant her eternal virginity. She was also the protector of suckling animals, but loved to hunt stags!

Hermes was born of Maia, daughter of Atlas and one of Zeus' paramours. He had an upwardly mobile career. His first job was as protector of the animal kingdom. As the chief source of wealth was cattle, he therefore became the god of wealth. However, as civilisation advanced, trade replaced cattle as the main source of wealth, so Hermes became god of trade. However, a prerequisite for good trade was good commerce, so he became the god of commerce. To progress in commerce a merchant needed to be shrewd, so this attribute was assigned to Hermes. Later it was realised that to excel in commerce one needed to use the art of persuasion, so oratory was added to his portfolio.

Lesser Gods

After his brothers Zeus and Poseidon had taken the heavens and seas, **Hades** was left with the underworld (the earth was common ground). This vast and mysterious region was thought by the Greeks to be as far beneath the earth as the sky was above it. The underworld was divided into three regions: the Elysian Fields for the virtuous, Tartarus for sinners and the Asphodel Meadows for those who fitted neither category. Hades was also the god of wealth, in the form of the precious stones and metals found deep in the earth.

Some versions of mythology include **Dionysos**, the god of wine and revelry, in the first rank of the Olympians in place of Hestia. Dionysos was a son of Zeus by another of the supreme deity's dalliances. He had the job of touring the world with an entourage of fellow revellers spreading the word about the vine and wine.

Pan, the son of Hermes, was the god of the shepherds. Born with horns, beard, tail and goat legs, his ugliness so amused the other gods that eventually he fled to Arcadia where he danced, played his famous pipes and watched over the pastures, shepherds and herds.

Other gods included **Asclepius**, the god of healing; **Eros**, the god of love; and **Hypnos**, the god of sleep.

Mythical Heroes

Heroes such as **Heracles** and **Theseus** were elevated almost to the ranks of the gods. Heracles, yet another of Zeus' offspring, was performing astonishing feats of strength before he had left the cradle. His 12 labours were performed to atone for the murder of his wife and children in a bout of madness. The deeds of Theseus included the slaying of the Minotaur at Knossos.

Other heroes include **Odysseus**, whose wanderings after the fall of Troy are recorded in Homer's Odyssey, and **Jason**, who led his Argonauts to recover the golden fleece from Colchis (in modern Georgia).

GEOGRAPHY

Greece, at the southern extremity of the Balkan peninsula, is the only member of the EU without a land frontier with another member. To the north, Greece has land borders with Albania, the Former Yugoslav Republic of Macedonia, and Bulgaria; and to the east with Turkey.

Greece consists of a peninsula and about 1400 islands, of which 169 are inhabited. The land mass is 131,900 sq km and Greek territorial waters occupy 400,000 sq km. The islands are divided into six groups: the Cyclades, the Dodecanese, the islands of the North-Eastern Aegean, the Sporades and the Saronic Gulf islands. The two largest islands, Crete and Evia, do not belong to any group. In Greece, no area is much more than 100 km from the sea. The much indented coastline has a total length of 15,020 km.

Roughly four-fifths of Greece is mountainous, with most of the land over 1500m above sea level. The Pindos mountains, which are an offshoot of the Dinaric Alps, run north to south through the peninsula, and are known as the backbone of Greece. The mountains of the Peloponnese and Crete are part of the same formation. The highest mountain is Mt Olympus (2917m). Greece does not have many rivers, and none which are navigable. The largest are the Aheloös, Aliakmonas, Aoös and Arahthos, all of which have their source in the Pindos range in Epiros. The long plains of the river valleys, and those between the mountains and the coast, are the only lowlands. The mountainous terrain, dry climate and poor soil restricts agriculture to less than a quarter of the land. Greece is, however, rich in minerals, with reserves of oil, manganese, bauxite and lignite.

CLIMATE

Greece can be divided into a number of main climatic regions. Northern Macedonia and northern Epiros have a climate similar to the Balkans, with freezing winters and very hot, humid summers; while the Attic peninsula, the Cyclades, the Dodecanese, Crete, and the central and eastern Peloponnese have a more typically Mediterranean climate with hot, dry summers and milder winters.

Snow is very rare in the Cyclades (it snowed on Paros for the first time in 15 years in 1992), but the high mountains of the Peloponnese and Crete are covered in snow during the winter, and it does occasionally snow in Athens. In July and August, the mercury can soar to 40°C in the shade just about anywhere in the country. July and

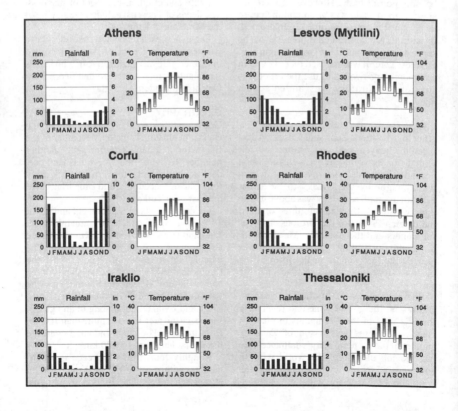

August are also the months of the meltemi, a strong northerly wind that sweeps the eastern coast of mainland Greece (including Athens) and the Aegean islands, especially the Cyclades. The wind is caused by air pressure differences between North Africa and the Balkans. The wind is a mixed blessing: it reduces humidity, but plays havoc with ferry schedules and sends everything flying – from beach umbrellas to washing hanging out to dry.

The western Peloponnese, western Sterea Ellada, south-western Epiros and the Ionian islands escape the meltemi and have less severe winters than northern Greece, but are the areas with the highest rainfall. The North-Eastern Aegean islands, Halkidiki and the Pelion peninsula fall somewhere between the Balkan-type climate of northern Greece and the Mediterranean climates. Crete stays warm the longest – you can swim off its southern coast from mid-April to November.

Mid-October is when the rains start in most areas, and the weather stays cold and wet until February – although there are also occasional winter days with clear blue skies and sunshine.

ECOLOGY & ENVIRONMENT

Greece is belatedly becoming environmentally conscious; regrettably, it is often a case of closing the gate after the horse has bolted. Deforestation and soil erosion are problems that go back thousands of years. Olive cultivation (see the accompanying Evil Olive aside) and goats have been the main culprits, but firewood gathering, shipbuilding, housing and industry have all taken their toll. Forest fires are also a major problem, with an estimated 25,000 hectares destroyed by fire every year.

The result is that the forests of ancient Greece have all but disappeared. Epiros and Macedonia in northern Greece are now the only places where extensive forests remain. The loss of forest cover elsewhere has been accompanied by serious soil erosion problems. The problem is finally being addressed with the start of a long overdue reafforestation programme.

General environmental awareness remains at a very low level, especially where litter is concerned. The problem is particularly bad in rural areas, where roadsides are strewn with soft-drink cans and plastic packaging hurled from passing cars. Environmental education is just beginning in schools, so it will be some time before community attitudes change.

One area where Greece is aiming to be a leader rather than a follower is in the exploitation of solar energy. Crete looks set to become the site of Europe's first major solar

The Evil Olive

It is a sad irony that the tree most revered by the Greeks is responsible for the country's worst ecological disaster. The tree is the olive. It was the money tree of the early Mediterranean civilisations, providing an abundance of oil that not only tasted great but could also be used for everything from lighting to lubrication. The ancient Greeks thought it was too good to be true and they concluded it must be a gift from the gods.

In their eagerness to make the most of this gift, native forest was cleared on a massive scale to make way for the olive. Landowners were urged on by decrees such as those issued in the 6th century BC by the archon of Athens, Solon, who banned the export of all agricultural produce other than olive oil and made cutting down an olive tree punishable by death.

Much of the land planted with olives was unsuitable hill country. Without the surface roots of the native forest to bind it, the topsoil of the hills was rapidly washed away. The olive tree could do nothing to help. It has no surface root system, depending entirely on its impressive tap root.

Thus, the lush countryside so cherished by the ancient Greeks was transformed into the harsh, rocky landscape that greets the modern visitor. ■

power station, and Athens has announced an ambitious long-term plan to become the first city in the world to operate solar-powered buses.

FLORA & FAUNA
Flora

Greece is endowed with a variety of flora unrivalled in Europe. The wildflowers are spectacular. There are over 6000 species, some of which occur nowhere else, and more than 100 varieties of orchid. They continue to thrive because most of the land is too poor for intensive agriculture and has escaped the ravages of chemical fertilisers.

The regions with the most wildflowers are the mountains of Crete and the Mani area of the Peloponnese. Trees begin to blossom as early as the end of February in warmer areas, and the wild flowers start to appear in March. During spring the hillsides are carpeted with flowers, which seem to sprout even from the rocks. Spring flowers include anemones, white cyclamens, irises, lilies, poppies, gladioli, tulips, countless varieties of daisy and many more. By summer, the flowers have disappeared from all but the northern mountainous regions. Autumn brings flowers too, especially crocuses.

Fauna

Greece also has a large range of fauna, but

Wildflowers

The Greek countryside is the showcase for a spectacular display of wildflowers. Autumn is often described as Greece's 'second spring'.

Of Europe's 200 wild orchids, around half grow in Greece. They flower from late February to early June. Another spring flower is the iris. The word 'iris' is Greek for rainbow – an appropriate name for these multicoloured flowers. Greece's wild irises include the white and yellow *Iris ochroleuca* and the blue and orange *Iris cretica*. The latter is one of 120 wildflowers unique to Crete. Others include the pink Cretan ebony, the white-flowered symphyandra and the white-flowered *Cyclamen cretic*. Other unique species include the *Rhododendron luteum*, a yellow azalea, which grows only on Mytilini, and a peony, which is unique to Rhodes.

Spectacular plants include the coastal giant reed. You may get lost among its high, dense groves on your way to a beach. The giant fennel, which grows to 3m, and the tall yellow-horned poppy also grow by the sea. Another showy coastal plant is the magenta-flowered Hottentot fig, which was introduced from Africa. The white-flowered sea squill grows on hills above the coast.

Conspicuous thistles include the milk thistle which has green and white variegated leaves and grows in meadows and by road sides. In rocky terrain you will see the stemless carline thistle, whose silvery-white petalled flowers are used in dried flower displays.

The beautifully perfumed sea daffodil grows along southern coasts, particularly on Crete and Corfu. The conspicuous snake's-head fritillary *(Fritillaria graeca)* has pink flowers shaped like snakes' heads, and the markings on the petals resemble a chequer board – the Latin word *fritillu* means dice box.

Interesting trees include the evergreen carob which grows up to 10m. John the Baptist is said to have eaten its pods when he lived in the desert. Mineral-rich carob is sold in some countries as a healthy substitute for chocolate. The flowers of the Judas tree, unusually, appear before the leaves. According to legend they were originally white, but when Judas hanged himself from the tree they turned pink in shame. ■

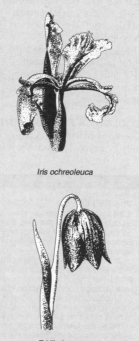

Iris ochreoleuca

Fritillaria graeca

you won't encounter much of interest unless you venture out into the prime habitat areas.

Bird-watchers have more chance of coming across something unusual than animal spotters. Greece has all the usual Mediterranean small birds – wagtails, tits, warblers, bee-eaters, larks, swallows, flycatchers, thrushes and chats – as well as some more distinctive species such as the hoopoe.

They include a large number of migratory birds, most of which are merely passing by on their way from winter feeding sites in north Africa to summer nesting grounds in eastern Europe. Out of a total of 408 species of migratory birds in Europe, 240 have been sighted in Greece. One very visible visitor is the stork. Storks arrive in early spring from Africa, and return to the same nest year after year. The nests are built on electricity poles, chimney tops and church towers, and can weigh up to 50kg; look out for them in northern Greece, especially in Thrace.

Lake Mikri Prespa, in Macedonia, has the richest colony of fish-eating birds in Europe, including egrets, herons, cormorants and ibises, as well as the Dalmatian pelican – Turkey and Greece are now the only countries in Europe where this bird is found.

The hoopoe, a member of the kingfisher family, has a prominent black-tipped crest

The wetlands at the mouth of the Evros River, close to the border with Turkey, are home to two easily identifiable wading birds – the avocet, which has a long upcurved beak, and the black-winged stilt, which has extremely long pink legs.

Upstream on the Evros River in Thrace, the dense forests and rocky outcrops of the 7200-hectare Dadia Forest Reserve play host to the largest range of birds of prey in Europe. Thirty-six of the 38 European species can be seen here, and it is a breeding ground for 23 of them. Permanent residents include both the giant black vulture, whose wingspan reaches three metres, the griffon vulture and golden eagles. Europe's last 15 pairs of royal eagles nest on the river delta. The reserve is managed by the Worldwide Fund for Nature (☎ 01-363 4661). About 350 pairs (60% of the world's population) of the rare Eleonora falcon nest on the remote island of Piperi in the Sporades.

The mountains of northern Greece also support a much greater range of wildlife than anywhere else in the country, although you're extremely unlikely to spot animals such as the brown bear or the grey wolf (see Endangered Species later in this section). Wild boar are still found in reasonable numbers in the north and are a favourite target for hunters. Squirrels, rabbits, hares, foxes and weasels are all fairly common on the mainland; less common is the cute European suslik – a small ground squirrel. Reptiles are well represented. The snakes include several viper species, which are poisonous. For more information on snakes in Greece, see the Health section in the Facts for the Visitor chapter. You're more likely to see lizards, all of which are harmless.

One of the pleasures of island hopping in Greece is watching the dolphins as they follow the boats. Although there are many dolphins in the Aegean, the striped dolphin has recently been the victim of murbilivirus – a sickness that affects the immune system. Research into the virus is being carried out in the Netherlands.

Cruelty to Animals
The Greek attitude to animals depends on

whether the animal is a cat or not. It's definitely cool to be a cat. Even the mangiest-looking stray can be assured of a warm welcome and a choice tidbit on approaching the restaurant table of a Greek. Most other domestic animals are greeted with a certain indifference. You don't see many pet dogs, or pets of any sort for that matter. The various societies for animal protection in Greece are listed in *Atlantis* magazine.

The main threat to animal welfare is hunting. Greek hunters are notorious for blasting anything that moves, and millions of animals are killed during the long 'open' season, from 20 August to 10 March, which encompasses the bird migratory period. The Hellenic Wildlife Hospital (☎ 0297-22 882), on the island of Aegina, reports that 80% of the animals it treats have been shot.

Endangered Species

The brown bear, Europe's largest land mammal, still survives in very small numbers in the Pindos mountains, the Peristeri range that rises above the Prespa Lakes and in the mountains which lie along the Bulgarian border. Other countries where the brown bear survives are France, Italy, Spain and Turkey.

The wolf is also an endangered species, but is not protected in Greece as it is in other countries. It survives in small numbers in the forests of the Pindos in Epiros as well as in the Dadia Reserve area.

Europe's rarest mammal, the monk seal, was once very common in the Mediterranean, but it's now on the brink of extinction in Europe – it survives in slightly larger numbers in the Hawaiian islands. There are only about 350 left in Europe, all of which live in Greece. There are about 30 in the Ionian Sea and the rest are found in the Aegean. Until recently the seals were killed by fishers because they damaged nets. The monk seal requires a gently sloping sandy beach on which to give birth; but unfortunately tourists 'require' these beaches for sunbathing, so fewer and fewer are available for the seals. The Hellenic Society for the Study & Protection of the Monk Seal (☎ 01-

The grey wolf still survives in small numbers in the mountains of northern Greece

364 4146), Solomnou 35, Athens 10682, has a seal-rescue centre on Alonnisos, and the WWF funds seal-watch projects on Kefallonia, Ithaki and Lefkada.

The waters around Zakynthos and Kefallonia are home to the last large sea turtle colony in Europe, that of the loggerhead turtle *(careta careta)*. The Sea Turtle Protection Society of Greece (☎ 01-364 4146), Solomnou 35, Athens 10682, runs monitoring programs and is always looking for volunteers.

National Parks

Greece's national parks are Vikos-Aoös and Prespa national parks in Epiros, Olympus National Park on the border of Thessaly and Macedonia, Parnassos and Iti national parks in Central Greece, Parnitha National Park in Attica and Samaria National Park in Crete. All of these have refuges and some have marked hiking trails. Greece also has a National Marine Park off the coast of Alonnisos in the Sporades.

GOVERNMENT & POLITICS

Since 1975, democratic Greece has been a parliamentary republic with a president as head of state. The president and parliament, which has 300 deputies, have joint legislative power. The PASOK party of Prime Minister Simitis holds 163 seats in the current parliament. Greek governments traditionally name very large cabinets – Simitis fronts a team of 41, with 19 ministries. Papandreou had 52 in his last cabinet!

Greece is divided into regions and island groups. The regions of the mainland are the Peloponnese, Central Greece (officially called Sterea Ellada), Epiros, Thessaly, Macedonia and Thrace. The island groups are the Cyclades, Dodecanese, North-Eastern Aegean, Sporades and Saronic Gulf, all in the Aegean Sea, and the Ionian, which is in the Ionian Sea. The large islands of Evia and Crete do not belong to any group. For administrative purposes these regions and groups are divided into prefectures or nomes (*nomoi* in Greek).

ECONOMY

Greece is an agricultural country, but the importance of agriculture to the economy has declined rapidly since WWII. Some 50% of the workforce is now employed in services (contributing 59% of GDP), 22% in agriculture (contributing 15%), and 27% in industry and construction (contributing 26%). Tourism is by far the biggest industry; shipping comes next. The eight million tourists who visit Greece each year contribute around US$3 billion to the economy.

Although Greece has the second-lowest income per capita of all the EU countries (after Portugal), its economic future looks brighter now than for some time. The economy suffered badly from the fighting in the Balkans in the early 90s, which cut Greece's major overland trade route to the rest of Europe. Peace in the Balkans has done much to restore business confidence. The austerity measures imposed by successive governments also appear to have had the desired effect, with inflation cut to single figures (8.5%) for the first time in 22 years, and unemployment officially running at 10%. Its economy is unlikely to be in good enough health to meet the criteria for the first phase of European monetary union in 1999, but the government is confident that it will be ready for the second phase.

POPULATION

A census is taken every 10 years in Greece. The 1991 census recorded a population of 10,264,156 – an increase of 5.4% on the 1981 figure. Women outnumber men by more than 200,000. Greece is now a largely urban society, with 68% of the population living in cities. By far the largest is Athens, with more than 3.1 million people living in the greater Athens area. The population figures of other major cities are: Thessaloniki (750,000), Piraeus (171,000), Patras (153,000), Iraklio (127,600), Larisa (113,400) and Volos (110,000). Less than 15% of people live on the islands, the most populous of which are Crete (537,000), Evia (209,100) and Corfu (105,000).

PEOPLE

It is doubtful that any Greek alive today is directly descended from an ancient Greek. Contemporary Greeks are a mixture of all of the invaders who have occupied the country since ancient times. Today, there are a number of distinct ethnic minorities living in the country.

The country's small Roman Catholic population is of Genoese or Frankish origin. They live mostly in the Cyclades, especially on the island of Syros, where they make up 40% of the population. The Franks dominated the island from 1207 AD to Ottoman times.

About 300,000 ethnic Turks who were exempt from the population exchange of 1923 live in western Thrace. There are also small numbers of Turks on Kos and Rhodes which, along with the rest of the Dodecanese, did not become part of Greece until 1947.

There are small Jewish communities in several large towns. In Ioannina, Larisa, Halkidi and Rhodes, they date back to the Roman era, while in Thessaloniki, Kavala and Didymotiho, most are descendants of 15th-century exiles from Spain and Portugal. In 1429, 20,000 exiled Jews arrived in Thessaloniki and by the 16th century they constituted the major part of the population. In 1941, the Germans entered Thessaloniki and herded 46,000 Jews off to Auschwitz, most never to return. They comprised 90% of Thessaloniki's Jews and more than half the total number in Greece. The small number of Jews in Athens are mostly German Jews who came over with King Otho in the 1830s. Today there are only about 5000 Jews living in Greece.

Very small numbers of Vlach and Sarakatsani shepherds live a semi-nomadic existence in Epiros. They take their flocks to the high ground in summer and return to the valleys in winter. The Vlachs originate from the region that is now Romania; the origins of the Sarakatsani are uncertain.

You will come across Gypsies everywhere in Greece, but especially in Macedonia, Thrace and Thessaly. There are large communities of Gypsies in the Thracian towns of Alexandroupolis and Didymotiho.

The shedding of years of hardline Stalinism and isolation in Albania has left that country in turmoil and the people in a state of abject poverty. Consequently, thousands of Albanians have been illegally crossing the poorly guarded border into Greece. Estimates of their number vary wildly, but 250,000 is probably closer to the mark than the 500,000 that café statisticians claim. The Greek government claims that the Albanian authorities are encouraging this exodus, and the government in Tiranë accuses Greece of violating human rights in its treatment of the refugees.

EDUCATION

Education in Greece is free at all levels of the state system from kindergarten to tertiary. Primary schooling begins at the age of six, but most children attend a state-run kindergarten from the age of five. Private kindergartens are popular with those who can afford them. Primary school classes tend to be larger than those in most European countries – usually 30 to 35 children. Primary school hours are short (8 am to 1pm), but children get a lot of homework.

At 12, children enter the *gymnasio*, and at 15 they may leave school, or enter the *lykeio*, from where they take university-entrance examinations. Although there is a high percentage of literacy, many parents and pupils are dissatisfied with the education system, especially beyond primary level. The private sector therefore flourishes, and even relatively poor parents struggle to send their children to one of the country's 5000 *frontistiria* (intensive coaching colleges) to prepare them for the very competitive university-entrance exams. Parents complain that the education system is badly underfunded. The main complaint is about the lack of modern teaching aids in both gymnasio and lykeio.

Grievances reached a peak in 1991, when lykeio students staged a series of sit-ins in schools throughout the country, and organised protest marches. In 1992, gymnasio pupils followed suit, and the government responded by making proposals that called for stricter discipline and a more demanding curriculum. More sit-ins followed, and in the end the government changed its plans and is still reassessing the situation.

ARTS

See the colour art section for a detailed look at the history of art and architecture in Greece.

Music & Dance

The folk dances of today derive from the ritual dances performed in ancient Greek temples. One of these dances, the *syrtos*, is depicted on ancient Greek vases, and there are references to dances in Homer's works. Many Greek folk dances, including the syrtos, are performed in a circular formation; in ancient times, dancers formed a circle in order to seal themselves off from evil influences.

Each region of Greece has its own dances, but one dance you'll see performed everywhere is the *kalamatianos*, originally from Kalamata in the Peloponnese. It's the dance in which dancers stand in a row with their hands on one another's shoulders.

Singing and the playing of musical instruments have also been an integral part of life in Greece since ancient times. Cycladic figurines holding musical instruments

Georgos Dalaras

Georgos Dalaras is a musical phenomenon in Greece. With a successful career spanning over 29 years, more than 40 albums of his own and participation in over 50 other albums, he is Greece's undisputed ambassador of song. Essentially unknown to the wider public outside his homeland, Georgos Dalaras nonetheless performs regularly to captive audiences in the USA, Australia, Israel and in many countries in Europe. His songs are hummed as much by youth in Greece as by the youth of Belgrade or Helsinki. Two of his albums have achieved the status of the first gold and platinum records in Greece.

Who is Georgos Dalaras and why is he so popular? His success is due to his remarkable voice and his commitment to the preservation of the popular Greek song in a musical world dominated by disco and techno. Georgos Dalaras is a political singer too, and managed to tread that fine line between acceptability and political pariah status during the dark years of the military Junta (1967-74). In recent times his musical output has embraced the tragedy of the Turkish occupation of Cyprus with two major concerts at Wembley Arena, London, in 1992 and the Palais des Congrès in Paris in 1993. He has participated in cultural and political festivals in Cuba, sung with Mikis Theodorakis in 1981 and alongside Peter Gabriel and Sting for Amnesty International in 1988 at the Olympic Stadium in Athens.

More than anyone else, Georgos Dalaras was responsible for the re-awakened respect for and interest in the *rembetika* genre of music – the Greek blues of the 20s. His double album *50 Chronia Rembetiko* sold over 100,000 copies. His concerts still pack stadiums and sports halls and his popularity is stronger than ever. If you are in Greece, try and catch one of his concerts. It will be a rare treat. It is hard to suggest a representative work from his vast discography, but for a retrospective, have a listen to the aforementioned *50 Chronia Rembetiko*. For a live song collection, listen to *Dalaras – Papakonstantinou – Live at the Attikon*, a recent work featuring Vasilis Papakonstantinou, another Greek musical genius. The 1972 album *Mikra Asia*, a nostalgic tribute to the 1921 Asia Minor disaster, is one of the masterpieces of contemporary Greek music ■

---

resembling harps and flutes date back to 2000 BC. Musical instruments of ancient Greece included the lyre, lute, *piktis* (pipes), *kroupeza* (a percussion instrument), *kithara* (a stringed instrument), *aulos* (a wind instrument), *barbitos* (similar to a violin cello) and the *magadio* (similar to a harp).

If ancient Greeks did not have a musical instrument to accompany their songs, they imitated the sound of one. It is believed that unaccompanied Byzantine choral singing derived from this custom.

The bouzouki, which you will hear everywhere in Greece, is a mandolin-like instrument similar to the Turkish *saz* and *baglama*. It is one of the main instruments of rembetika music – the Greek equivalent of the American Blues. The name rembetika may come from the Turkish word *rembet* which means outlaw. Opinions differ as to

the origins of rembetika, but it is probably a hybrid of several different types of music. One source was the music that emerged in the 1870s in the 'low life' cafés, called *tekedes* (hashish dens), in urban areas and especially around ports. Another source was the Arabo-Persian music played in sophisticated Middle Eastern music cafés *(amanedes)* in the 19th century. Rembetika was popularised in Greece by the refugees from Asia Minor.

The songs which emerged from the tekedes had themes concerning hashish, prison life, gambling, knife fights etc, whereas café aman music had themes which centred around erotic love. These all came together in the music of the refugees, from which a subculture of rebels, called *manges*, emerged. The manges wore showy clothes even though they lived in extreme poverty.

They worked long hours in menial jobs, and spent their evenings in the tekedes, smoking hashish and singing and dancing. Although hashish was illegal, the law was rarely enforced until Metaxas did his clean-up job in 1936. It was in a tekes in Piraeus that Markos Vamvakaris, now acknowledged as the greatest *rembetis*, was discovered by a recording company in the 1930s.

Metaxas' censorship meant that themes of hashish, prison, gambling and the like disappeared from recordings of rembetika in the late 1930s, but continued clandestinely in some tekedes. This polarised the music, and the recordings, stripped of their 'meaty' themes and language, became insipid and bourgeois; recorded rembetika even adopted another name – *laiko tragoudi* – to disassociate it from its illegal roots. Although WWII brought a halt to recording, a number of composers emerged at this time. They included Apostolos Kaldaras, Yiannis Papaïoanou, Georgos Mitsakis and Manolis Hiotis, and one of the greatest female rembetika singers, Sotiria Bellou, appeared at this time.

During the 1950s and 1960s rembetika became increasingly popular, but less and less authentic. Much of the music was glitzy and commercialised, although the period also produced two outstanding composers of popular music (including rembetika) in Mikis Theodorakis and Manos Hatzidakis. The best of Theodorakis' work is the music which he set to the poetry of Seferis, Elytis and Ritsos.

During the junta years, many rembetika clubs were closed down, but interest in genuine rembetika revived in the 1980s – particularly among students and intellectuals. There are now a number of rembetika clubs in Athens.

Since independence, Greece has followed mainstream developments in classical music. The Athens Concert Hall has performances by both national and international musicians.

Literature

The first, and greatest, ancient Greek writer was Homer, author of the *Iliad* and *Odyssey*. Nothing is known of Homer's life or where or when he lived, or whether, as it is alleged, he was blind. The historian Herodotus thought Homer lived in the 9th century BC, and no scholar since has proved nor disproved this.

Herodotus was the author of the first historical work about western civilisation. His highly subjective account of the Persian Wars has, however, led him to be regarded as the 'father of lies' as well as the 'father of history'. The historian Thucydides was more objective in his approach, but took a high moral stance. He wrote an account of the Peloponnesian Wars, and also the famous *Melian Dialogue*, which chronicles the talks between the Athenians and Melians prior to the Athenian siege of Melos. Pindar (518-438 BC) is regarded as the pre-eminent lyric poet of ancient Greece. He was commissioned to recite his odes at the Olympic Games. The greatest writers of love poetry were Sappho and Alcaeus, both of whom lived on Lesvos in the 5th century. Sappho's poetic descriptions of her affections for other women gave rise to the term 'lesbian'.

In Byzantine times, poetry, like all of the arts, was of a religious nature. During Ottoman rule, poetry was inextricably linked with folk songs, which were not written down but passed on by word of mouth. Many of these songs were composed by the klephts, and told of the harshness of life in the mountains and of their uprisings against the Turks.

Dionysios Solomos (1798-1857) and Andreas Kalvos (1796-1869), who were both born on Zakynthos, are regarded as the first modern Greek poets. Solomos' work was heavily nationalistic and his *Hymn to Freedom* became the Greek national anthem. At this time there were heated debates among writers, politicians and educators about whether the official language should be Demotiki or Katharevousa. Demotic was the spoken language of the people and Katharevousa was an artificial language loosely based on Ancient Greek. Almost all writers favoured demotic, and from the time of

THREE PILLARS OF WESTERN PHILOSOPHY

Socrates – 'Know thyself'

Very little is certain about Socrates because he committed none of his thoughts to paper. Historians and philosophers have constructed a picture of the man and his ideas mostly through the writings of Xenophon, in his *Memorabilia*, and more importantly through the work of Plato, a one-time pupil of Socrates, in his 'dialogues'. Socrates is represented in Plato's dialogues both as a historical figure and as a character called 'Socrates' who articulated many of Plato's own ideas. As a result, the distinction between the ideas of the Platonic Socrates and Socrates himself is hard to make. Of all Plato's writings about Socrates, the only one that is considered reasonably historical is the *Apology* – an account of Socrates' speech at his own trial where he was sentenced to death as an enemy of the state. Plato was present at the trial, but it was some years later that he wrote the *Apology* based on his recollections. Socrates was already an old man when Plato came to him as a pupil, so there is much about the man that remains unknown.

Socrates was born around 470 BC in Athens and fought in the First Peloponnesian War as an infantry soldier. When serving in the trenches it is said that he would become transfixed in torpid states for up to 24 hours at a time, utterly lost in thought. The chaos of the war affected him greatly and thereafter he gave his life over to teaching in the streets, the marketplace and, particularly, the gymnasia – a mission that he believed was bestowed on him by his god, the *daimon*. He was a man of very meagre means and most tales of Socrates have him dressed in rags and walking barefoot.

He was deeply religious and regarded mythology with disdain, claiming that tales of gods were merely the contrivance of poets. However, the *daimon's* existence was demonstrated by the perfect order of nature, by the universality of people's belief in the divine, and by the revelations that come in dreams and omens. Socrates not only believed that the soul was immortal, but that it was the very essence of an individual: his or her character and intellect – the *self*.

Socrates' method was dialectic, that is, he sought to illuminate truth by a process of question and answer. He would teach his pupils by responding to a question with another question, and then another, until the pupil came to answer his or her own inquiry. He believed that knowledge is inside everybody but that it needs to be revealed to them.

He was most concerned with moral questions and, for him, goodness was a fixed and knowable thing. It was the nature of people's actions and their character, rather than the nature of the world as revealed to the senses, that he spoke most about. He sought a 'way to live'. He believed that people are corrupted by putting the desires of the body and of the material world before the need to care for the soul, and that the condition of a person's soul is directly responsible for his or her happiness and well-being. The soul itself was seen as neither good nor bad, but well or poorly realised, and people's unhappiness was thought to result from their not knowing what happiness really is. Accordingly, actions that are unethical are in some sense involuntary – people are responsible for their wrong-doings, but they commit them because they have poor conceptions of themselves. However, those who know the true good will always act in accordance with it, for to do otherwise would be to knowingly choose sadness over happiness.

Socrates believed that the duty of government was to look after the souls of the citizens of the state, and that a profound understanding of goodness should be an essential prerequisite for members of a government. He held that democracy was a flawed system because it left the state in the hands of the unenlightened and it valued all opinion as equal.

It's likely that Socrates did some work on what was to become Plato's theory of Ideas. The problem of how to define class-names, or 'universals' (nouns like 'tree' that cover whole classes of objects) had been touched on by previous thinkers, but Socrates' work was significant. (For a further discussion about the nature of class-names see the following sections on Plato and Aristotle.)

In 399 BC, at the age of 70, Socrates was indicted for 'impiety'. He was charged with 'corruption of the young' and 'neglect of the gods whom the city worships and the practice of religious novelties'. He was contemptuous of the charges but was convicted and the prosecutors sought the death penalty.

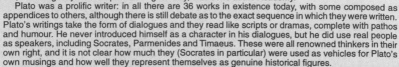

Under Athenian law, the accused was entitled to suggest a lesser penalty than that proposed by the prosecutors, and the judges would choose between the two – it seems unlikely that the death penalty would have been insisted upon. But Socrates incensed the court by suggesting a mere fine of 30 minae, and a larger majority than that which had found him guilty condemned him to death by the drinking of hemlock. He preferred to face death than to give credence to the charges by proposing a more substantial penalty. Socrates' friends had plans for his escape both before trial and during the 30 days that he was interned awaiting execution, but he would have none of it. He argued that the court was a legitimate one, and although the verdict was wrong, he was compelled to obey its rulings. The story of Socrates' day of execution, when he explains that the soul must be immortal for 'universals' to exist, is told in Plato's *Phaedo*.

Socrates lived a life of deep conviction and died as a martyr. It is remarkable that a man born nearly 2500 years ago, who wrote nothing and of whom so little is known, should be revered as such a giant in the development of western thought.

Plato – 'Until philosophers are kings ... cities will never cease from ill, nor the human race'

Plato was born around 428 BC in Athens, or perhaps Aegina, in the early years of the First Peloponnesian War into an aristocratic and very well-connected family. He was a student of Socrates, who had a great influence upon him. In his early years, Plato had political ambitions but these waned in later life. He lived through turbulent times as a young man, through the Second Peloponnesian War and the fall of Athens. Plato was still a young man when Socrates was executed in 399 BC by the Athenian democrats. This, and the fact that his family was well connected in Periclean politics, caused Plato to despise democracy, and this theme ran through all of his work.

Around 387 BC, Plato founded the Academy in Athens as an institute of philosophical and scientific studies. Although he is remembered as a great thinker, during his life he regarded the founding and administration of the Academy as his most important work. Aristotle came to the Academy at the age of 17 and remained there for nearly 20 years. Most of the important mathematical work of the 4th century BC, including major developments in geometry, was done at the Academy.

Plato was a prolific writer: in all there are 36 works in existence today, with some composed as appendices to others, although there is still debate as to the exact sequence in which they were written. Plato's writings take the form of dialogues and they read like scripts or dramas, complete with pathos and humour. He never introduced himself as a character in his dialogues, but he did use real people as speakers, including Socrates, Parmenides and Timaeus. These were all renowned thinkers in their own right, and it is not clear how much they (Socrates in particular) were used as vehicles for Plato's own musings and how well they represent themselves as genuine historical figures.

There are three main themes to Plato's work: metaphysics; ethics and politics; and aesthetics and mysticism. His greatest dialogue, the *Republic*, weaves these disparate elements into a more or less coherent whole.

Politically, Plato was an authoritarian. He, like all ancient Greeks, believed in a static universe where goodness and reality are fixed, unchanging qualities. The *Republic* is, in part, given over to Plato's view of the ideal state. He begins by dividing all people into three classes: the commoners, the soldiers and the rulers. He believed the state should seek to emulate the static perfection of heaven, and the rulers of this state should be those who best understand the nature of goodness and who are exponents of a certain moral and intellectual rigour. Furthermore, Plato thought that leisure was essential to wisdom and that only those who were free of the need to earn a livelihood were capable of enlightenment and thereby suitable as leaders of the perfect state. However, Plato also believed that the ego is the flaw in human nature and that both wealth and poverty are harmful. So, in the ideal state, rulers and citizens alike would act for the good of the whole rather than the benefit of one class. To this end, Plato declared that all people should live in modest houses and eat simple food – all extravagances would be forbidden; that women and men should be equal, should be given the same

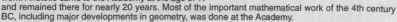

education and have the same prospects; that marriages should be arranged by the State and children should be removed from their parents at birth, never knowing their natural parents. He believed these initiatives, among others, would minimise personal, possessive emotions so that public spirit would be the overwhelming thing that an individual felt. Plato made the distinction between 'ideal' and ordinary desires: an ideal desire is one that the desirer feels on behalf of all people and bears no relation to his or her own ego.

Plato was a pious man and his philosophical ideas reflected his conviction that there was a heaven, or rather a dwelling place of the gods that the soul could enter if the person had led a good life in accordance with the highest principles of philosophy. The notion of divine perfection was a central tenet in his thinking. The problem of class-ideas or 'universals' had been a conundrum for thinkers until Socrates – for example, 'woman' is greater, more real and more enduring than any individual woman. The problem was in determining the meaning of nouns like 'woman' or 'house' that can be applied to whole classes of individual instances, ie the meaning of 'woman' in its broadest sense is not this woman or that woman, or even these two women together.

For Plato, the answer to this riddle was that objects in the world are merely appearances of perfect 'Ideas' or 'Forms'. These things were seen as singular, determinate and unchanging objects which could be apprehended by the intellect only. So, every tree that is perceivable is of the material world – it's born and it dies – and is merely a copy of the perfect tree created by God, and God's tree bears no relation to time or space. It is this idealised tree that determines the properties of 'treeness'. When a person describes something as beautiful, what they mean is that the Form 'beauty' has become present in that thing.

Knowledge, for most contemporary thinkers, is founded on perception. Plato, however, held that knowledge cannot be derived from the senses, and that true knowledge belongs to the realm of concepts. He argued that we perceive *through* our senses, not *with* them. It is the intellect that makes good of the information gathered through the senses. We know that smells and shapes are different, and yet there is no sense-organ that can perceive both. Furthermore, we have knowledge of concepts that are not derived from experience: perfect symmetry has no manifestation in the world we apprehend with our senses. Plato claimed that all knowledge is recollection – that it comes as revelation to the intellect. For him, each person has knowledge within, but they need to get at it, and this is achieved by philosophical instruction and through introspection.

Plato's ideas embraced a dualism that exists between reality and appearance, pure forms and sensible objects, intellect and sensory apprehension and, ultimately, soul and body. For him, the body and earthly desires impede wisdom, and wisdom is the soul transcending.

Aristotle – 'He who exercises his reason and cultivates it seems to be both in the best state of mind and most dear to the gods'

At the end of an extraordinary period of Greek thought came Aristotle, and his legacy cannot be overstated. It took 2000 years after his death until another great thinker came along who might be regarded as his equal: Descartes. Almost every significant philosophical advance since has been initiated by some reaction to an Aristotelian idea. In the case of logic (Aristotle's famous syllogisms), his work remained unsurpassed until the writings of German philosopher Gottlob Frege began to attract attention at the beginning of this century.

Aristotle was born in 384 BC in Stagira on the Halkidiki peninsula of Macedonia. His father was physician to the Macedonian King Amyntas III (father of Philip II and grandfather of Alexander the Great). Aristotle learned much about medicine from his father and studied the case histories in Hippocrates' *Epidemiai*. He would later become a great authority on biology. In 367 BC, Aristotle went to Athens to become a pupil of Plato at the Academy. He remained there for nearly 20 years, until Plato's death.

After Plato's death a rift appeared between Aristotle and the Academy. This was perhaps because Aristotle was overlooked as Plato's successor to head the Academy, a position that was filled by

Speusippus, or possibly because of the strong anti-Macedonian sentiment that came over Athens after Philip had plundered the Greek city-state of Olynthus in 348 BC. Aristotle left the Academy and travelled widely with another graduate, Xenocrates. Over the next few years he immersed himself in biological studies – a departure from the theoretical work he had done at the Academy. He wrote in his treatise *On Generation of the Animals*: 'credit must be given to observation rather than theories, and to theories only in so far as they are confirmed by the observed facts'. This kind of methodology was at odds with that employed by Plato – who held that no knowledge could be gleaned from observations – and was the kind of approach that would be taken on by the empiricist philosophers of the 17th and 18th centuries.

In 343 BC, he was commissioned to tutor Alexander, then aged 13, and he maintained the position for three years, until Alexander was pronounced regent.

At nearly 50, Aristotle returned to Athens and, after the death of Speusippus, was once again denied the presidency of the Academy, this time in favour of Xenocrates, his old travelling companion. Shortly thereafter, under the protection of Alexander (who had just become king of the Greeks), he founded a rival institution, the Lyceum. He stayed in Athens for another 12 years, working and lecturing in philosophy and the sciences. He often strolled with his pupils as he taught them, and the Lyceum became known as the Peripatetic ('walking around') school.

Alexander the Great died in 323 BC, and Athens was again gripped by strong anti-Macedonian sentiments. Aristotle, with his Macedonian background, was swept up in this. Like Socrates, Aristotle was indicted for 'impiety', ostensibly over some of his writings, but the real motives were political, due to his connections with the Macedonian nobility. He fled Athens with some of his followers. One year later, aged 62 or 63, he died of a stomach condition.

Aristotle wrote voluminously on metaphysics, ethics, politics, logic and physics. Much of his writing has been lost. Of more than 170 manuscripts, only 47 remain.

He attacked Plato's theory that Ideas were separate from the material world. He regarded class-names as descriptive words, more like adjectives. Proper names, like 'Syntagma Square', signify a 'this', while class-names, or universals, like 'square', signify a 'such', indicating a kind of thing rather than a specific thing. For Plato, class-names referred to a single specific thing, the Idea or Form, but Aristotle held that this was simply wrong. For him, a universal derives its meaning from the fact that there are many individual instances of it. If there were no red things in the world, then the notion of 'redness' would be nonsensical.

However, Aristotle had his own metaphysic that is hard enough to grapple with. Central to this was his distinction between 'form' and 'matter'. In the case of a statue, the sculptor confers shape (the form) onto marble (the matter). The Aristotelian idea is that, more than merely determining shape, a thing's form is that which is unified about it – its *essence*. Matter without form is just potentiality, but by acquiring form its actuality increases; and change consists of giving form to matter. God has no matter, but is pure form and absolute actuality, and therefore unchanging (this conforms to the classical Greek idea of a static universe). Thus humans, by increasing the amount of form in the world, by building houses and bridges, are making it more divine.

Aristotle's main argument for God's existence was that there had to be something that initiated motion. He viewed the soul as 'the form of a material body having life potentially within it...soul is the actuality of the body'. And yet, Aristotle's view of the soul was quite different from Plato's and from the view that was to be espoused by Christianity. For Aristotle, the soul was inseparable from the body. However, he made a distinction between the irrational soul and the rational soul, or the *mind*. The irrational soul, it seemed, determined such things as the vagaries of taste and was inexorably connected to the body. Mind, however, was seen as divine and impersonal – provided they thought clearly, all people should agree on issues of pure reason like mathematics. Thus, the immortality of the mind was not a personal immortality. Rather, when exercising pure reason, people partook in the divine – in God's immortality.

Aristotle's considerable influence on the development of western philosophy has been most keenly felt in the area of logic. He was the first thinker to look at structures of deductive arguments, or syllogisms. A syllogism is an argument in three parts: a major premise, a minor premise and a conclusion. He found that many deductive arguments could be expressed this way and also that they existed in recurring forms. For example, all people are mortal (major premise), Socrates is a person (minor premise), therefore Socrates is mortal (conclusion) – this form is called 'Barbara'. Or, all people are rational, some animals are people, therefore some animals are rational – this form is called 'Darii', and there are others. Notice that by replacing 'person' with 'A', 'mortal' with 'B' and 'Socrates' with 'C', then 'Barbara' can be expressed thus: all As are B, C is an A, therefore C is a B. This is symbolic logic, and this is loosely where Frege and Bertrand Russell picked up Aristotle's thread more than 2000 years after his death. ■

Solomos, most wrote only in that language. The highly acclaimed poet Constantine Cavafy (1863-1933) was less concerned with nationalism, being a resident of Alexandria in Egypt; he wrote many love poems.

The best known 20th-century Greek poets are George Seferis (1900-71), who won the Nobel prize for literature in 1963, and Odysseus Elytis (1911-96), who won the same prize in 1979. Seferis drew his inspiration from the Greek myths, whereas Elytis' work is surreal. Angelos Sikelianos (1884-1951) was another poet who drew inspiration from ancient Greece, particularly Delphi, where he lived. His poetry is highly evocative, and includes incantatory verses emulating the Delphic oracle. Yiannis Ritsos is another highly acclaimed Greek poet; his work draws on many aspects of Greece – its landscape, mythology and social issues. The most celebrated 20th-century Greek novelist is Nikos Kazantzakis. See the Books section in the Facts for the Visitor chapter for a commentary on his works.

Drama

Drama in Greece can be dated back to the contests staged at the Ancient Theatre of Dionysos in Athens during the 6th century BC for the annual Dionysia festival. During one of these competitions, Thespis left the ensemble and took centre stage for a solo performance regarded as the first true dramatic performance. The term Thespian for actor derives from this event.

Aeschylus (525-456 BC) is the so-called 'father of tragedy'; his best known work is the *Oresteia* trilogy. Sophocles (496-406 BC) is regarded as the greatest tragedian. He is thought to have written over 100 plays, of which only seven major works survive. These include *Ajax*, *Antigone*, *Electra*, *Trachiniae* and his most famous play, *Oedipus Rex*. His plays dealt mainly with tales from mythology and had complex plots. Sophocles won first prize 18 times at the Dionysia festival, beating Aeschylus in 468BC, whereupon Aeschylus went off to Sicily in a huff.

Euripides (485-406 BC), another famous tragedian, was more popular than either Aeschylus or Sophocles because his plots were considered more exciting. He wrote 80 plays of which 19 are extant (although one, *Rhesus*, is disputed). His most famous works are *Medea*, *Andromache*, *Orestias* and *Bacchae*. Aristophanes (427-387BC) wrote comedies – often ribald – which dealt with topical issues. His play *The Wasp* ridicules Athenians who resorted to litigation over trivialities; *The Birds* pokes fun at Athenian gullibility, and *Plutus* deals with the unfair distribution of wealth. You can see plays by the ancient Greek playwrights at the Athens and Epidaurus festivals (see the Athens and Peloponnese chapters), and at various other festivals around the country.

Film

Greeks are avid cinema goers, although most of the films shown are North American or British. The Greek film industry is in the doldrums. This is largely due to inadequate government funding, which is compounded by the type of films which the Greeks produce. Greek films have a reputation for being slow moving, with symbolism and ambiguity often used to convey complex themes. Although they are well made and the cinematography is often outstanding, they are too avant-garde to have mass appeal.

Greece's most acclaimed film director is Theodoros Angelopoulos, whose films include *The Beekeeper*, *Alexander the Great*, *Travelling Players*, *Landscapes in the Mist* and *The Hesitant Step of the Stork*. All have received awards at both national and international festivals.

SOCIETY & CONDUCT
Traditional Culture

Greece is steeped in traditional customs. Name days (see the accompanying aside), weddings and funerals all have great significance. On someone's name day an open-house policy is adopted and refreshments are served to wellwishers who stop by to give gifts. Weddings are highly festive occasions, with dancing, feasting and drinking sometimes continuing for days.

Greeks tend to be more superstitious than other Europeans. Tuesday is considered an unlucky day because on that day the Byzantine Empire fell to the Ottomans. Many Greeks will not sign an important transaction, get married or begin a trip on a Tuesday. Greeks also believe in the 'evil eye', a superstition prevalent in many Middle Eastern countries. If someone is the victim of the evil eye, then bad luck will befall them. The bad luck is the result of someone's envy, so one should avoid being too complimentary about things of beauty, especially newborn babies. To ward off the evil eye, Greeks often wear a piece of blue glass, resembling an eye, on a chain around their necks.

Dos & Don'ts

The Greeks' reputation for hospitality is not a myth. Greece is probably the only country in Europe where you may be invited into a stranger's home for coffee, a meal or even to spend the night. This can often lead to a feeling of uneasiness in the recipient if the host is poor, but to offer money is considered offensive. The most acceptable way of saying thank you is through a gift, perhaps to a child in the family. A similar situation arises if you go out for a meal with Greeks; the bill is not shared as in northern European countries, but paid by the host.

When drinking wine it is the custom to only half fill the glass. It is bad manners to empty the glass, so it must be constantly replenished. When visiting someone you will be offered coffee and it is bad manners to refuse. You will also be given a glass of water and perhaps a small serve of preserves. It is the custom to drink the water, then eat the preserves and then drink the coffee.

Personal questions are not considered rude in Greece, and if you react as if they are you will be the one causing offence. You will be inundated with queries about your age, salary, marital status etc – expect commiserations if you are over 25 and not married!

If you go into a *kafeneio*, taverna, or shop, it is the custom to greet the waiters or assistant with *kalimera* (good day) or *kalispera* (good evening) – likewise if you meet someone in the street.

You may have come to Greece for sun, sand and sea, but if you want to bare all, other than on a designated nude beach, remember that Greece is a traditional country, so take care not to offend the locals.

Namedays

Namedays, not birthdays, are celebrated in Greece. Great significance is attached to the name given a child, and the process of choosing a name follows fairly rigid conventions. The idea of a child being given a name just because the parents like the sound of it is unknown in Greece. Even naming a child after someone as a mark of respect or admiration is unusual. That so many children were named Vyronis (the Greek form of Byron) was a measure of the tremendous gratitude the Greeks felt for the philhellene, Lord Byron.

Children are never named after parents, but the eldest son in a family is often called after his paternal grandfather, and the eldest daughter after her paternal grandmother. Names are usually of religious origin. Each island or area in Greece has a patron saint, and people living in that area often name a child after its patron saint. The patron saint of Corfu is Agios Spyridon and it seems as if about half of the men who were born there are called Spyridon. Exceptions to this custom occur if a family is not religious – quite a rarity in Greece. A non-religious family will often give their offspring a name derived from ancient Greece or mythology. Socrates, Aristotle, Athena and Aphrodite are popular.

Each saint has a special feast day. A person's nameday is the feast day of the saint after which they were named. On someone's nameday, open house is held and a feast is laid on for the friends and neighbours who call. They will give a small gift to the person whose nameday it is, but there is less emphasis on the giving of presents than there is in birthday celebrations.

If you meet someone in Greece on his or her nameday, the customary greeting is *chronia polla!*, which means 'many years'. ■

Sport

Greek men are football (soccer) and basketball mad, both as spectators and participants. If you happen to be eating in a taverna on a night when a big match is being televised, expect indifferent service.

RELIGION

About 98% of Greeks belong to the Greek Orthodox Church. Most of the remainder are either Roman Catholic, Jewish or Muslim.

Philippi, in Macedonia, is reputedly the first place in Europe where St Paul preached the gospel. This was in 49 AD, and during the next five years he preached also in Athens, Thessaloniki and Corinth.

The Greek Orthodox Church is closely related to the Russian Orthodox Church and together with it forms the third-largest branch of Christianity. Orthodox, meaning 'right belief', was founded in the 4th century by Constantine the Great, who was converted to Christianity by a vision of the Cross.

By the 8th century, there were a number of differences of opinion between the pope in Rome and the patriarch of Constantinople, as well as increasing rivalry between the two. One dispute was over the wording of the Creed. The original Creed stated that the Holy Spirit proceeds 'from the Father', which the Orthodox Church adhered to, whereas Rome added 'and the Son'. Another bone of contention concerned the celibacy of the clergy. Rome decreed priests had to be celibate; in the Orthodox Church, a priest could marry before he became ordained. There were also differences in fasting: in the Orthodox Church, not only was meat forbidden during Lent, but wine and oil were also.

By the 11th century these differences had become irreconcilable, and in 1054 the pope and the patriarch excommunicated one another. Ever since, the two have gone their own ways as the (Greek/Russian) Orthodox Church and the Roman Catholic Church.

During Ottoman times membership of the Orthodox Church was one of the most important criteria in defining a Greek, regardless of where he or she lived. The church was the principal upholder of Greek culture and traditions.

Religion is still integral to life in Greece, and the Greek year is centred on the festivals of the church calendar. Most Greeks, when they have a problem, will go into a church and light a candle to the saint they feel is most likely to help them. On the islands you will see hundreds of tiny churches dotted around the countryside. Most have been built by individual families in the name of their selected patron saint as thanksgiving for God's protection.

If you wish to look around a church, you should dress appropriately. Women should wear skirts that reach below the knees, and men should wear long trousers and have their arms covered. Regrettably, many churches are kept locked nowadays, but it's usually easy enough to locate caretakers, who will be happy to open them up for you.

Greek Art
through the Ages

Greece has preserved its art and architecture over a period of some 4000 years. This heritage remains remarkably accessible and is part of modern Greek life today. It also draws people back to Greece again and again. Visitors come to search for ancient frescoes, marble temples, crusader castles, and Byzantine churches, icons and mosaics. There are also relics of Greece's more recent history: the monuments and art which recall the War of Independence, traditional village life and folk arts, and contemporary art.

There is a variety of museums, too, through which each region reveals its own story.

Wherever the search leads, the journey can be as rewarding as the goal.

Previous page: Fisherman; fresco from Akrotiri, Santorini (Thira), c. 1600 BC (National Archaeological Museum, Athens)

Right: Children boxing; fresco from Akrotiri, Santorini (Thira), c. 1600 BC

NATIONAL ARCHAEOLOGICAL MUSEUM, ATHENS

CYCLADES & MINOAN CRETE

The prehistoric art of Greece has been discovered only recently, notably in the Cyclades and on Crete. Smooth, flattish figurines, carved from the high-quality marble of Paros and Naxos in the middle of the 3rd millennium BC, caught the imagination of 20th-century artists and collectors because of their pared-down style.

Even more recently, in the 1960s and 1970s, excavations on Santorini (Thira) have revealed houses with frescoes preserved by the eruption of the island's volcano in the late 17th century BC. They were painted in fresco technique using yellow, blue, red and black pigments, with some details added after the plaster had dried. Plants and animals are depicted as well as men and women. Figures are usually shown in profile or in a combination of profile and frontal views. Stylistically, the frescoes are similar to the paintings of Minoan Crete, which are less well preserved. Some of these frescoes are now in the National Archaeological Museum in Athens, while others, such as the narrative frieze showing ships and harbour towns, will be displayed in a new museum on Santorini.

Minoan culture, dating from the third millennium until around 1400 BC, is named after the legendary King Minos, whose wife gave birth to the Minotaur.

In 1899 Sir Arthur Evans began excavations of the huge palace and residential complex at Knossos and over the next 30 years substantially reconstructed it, restoring many of its very fragmentary frescoes *in situ*. Similar palaces on Crete, usually of two storeys and built around a large courtyard, have since been excavated at Phaestos, Agia Triada, Malia, Gournia and Zakros.

Left: Marble figurine of a woman; Early Cycladic, c. 2800-2300 BC

Right: Marble figurine of a seated figure proposing a toast; Early Cycladic, c. 2800-2300 BC

Ceramics are ubiquitous on Greek sites, especially after the introduction of wheel-made pottery in about 2000 BC. Minoan pottery is often characterised by a high centre of gravity and beak-like spouts. Painted decoration was applied as a white clay slip (a thin paste of clay and water) or one which fired to a greyish black or dull red. Flowing designs with spiral or marine and plant motifs were used. The Archaeological Museum in Iraklio has a wealth of Minoan material, including frescoes and intricately carved seals.

MYCENAEAN GREECE

In the 1870s Heinrich Schliemann, after excavating at Troy near the entrance to the Dardanelles, had turned to the mainland Greek sites of Mycenae and Tiryns. This mainland Greek-speaking Mycenaean culture superseded the Minoan culture on Crete and flourished from around 1600 to 1200 BC. Characteristic of these sites are walls of massive, 'Cyclopean' stonework, such as at Tiryns, and palaces with a megaron (reception room) which had a central hearth and a roof supported by four internal columns.

Prestigious beehive-shaped stone tombs covered by a mound of earth have been found not only at Mycenae, where two large ones are romantically known as the tombs of Agamemnon and Clytaemnestra, but also at Pylos and elsewhere.

Mycenaean pottery shapes include a long-stemmed goblet and a globular vase with handles resembling a pair of stirrups. Decorative motifs are similar to those on Minoan pottery but rather stiffer. Small terracottas of women with a circular body or with arms upraised are known to modern scholars as phi (ϕ) and psi (ψ) figurines from their resemblance to these letters of the Greek alphabet. Such artefacts have been found over a wide area around the Mediterranean, indicating extensive trade. Spectacular Mycenaean gold masks, diadems, cups and dress ornaments; dagger blades with battle scenes inlaid in gold and silver; carved ivory and seal-stones; and pottery occupy the central hall of the Archaeological Museum in Athens.

The Mycenaean palaces were burnt and the culture was largely destroyed for reasons unknown around 1200 BC. This is also the traditional date given for the Greek sacking of Troy, but Homer's epics, given written form first in the 8th century BC, reflect an earlier stage of Mycenaean culture.

PROTOGEOMETRIC & GEOMETRIC POTTERY

The archaeological record picks up again around 1000 BC with substantial pots decorated with blackish-brown horizontal lines around the circumference, hatched triangles, and compass-drawn concentric circles. This Protogeometric style was followed by the more crowded decoration of geometric patterning, often in bands or panels, and with stylised animal friezes. Some geometric pots from around 750 BC, used as grave markers in the Dipylon cemetery in Athens, have panels depicting the corpse on a bier surrounded by stick-like figures tearing at their hair in mourning. Terracotta figurines of horses suggest an equestrian aristocracy. By the 7th century BC, Corinth was producing pottery with added white and purple-red clay slip and friezes of lions, goats and swans, with details incised and a background fill of rosettes.

Facing page: The palace at Knossos, Crete

ARCHAIC PERIOD

In the 6th century BC the first large stone temples were built, like that at Corinth with its unusual monolithic columns. The first life-size marble statues, the stiff nude male kouros and draped female kore, were carved with an obvious debt to Egyptian sculpture. Athens took over from Corinth in pottery production using red clay with a high iron content. A thick colloidal slip made from this clay produced a glossy black surface which contrasted with the red and was enlivened with added white and purple-red. Details were incised through the slip before firing. Scenes from Greek mythology, especially showing Heracles and his labours or Dionysos, the god of wine, replaced animal motifs. The ability to draw three-quarter views of the human figure on vases, and presumably also on lost wooden panels, coincided with the steady development of naturalism in sculpture, as seen in the reliefs from the 6th-century BC temple-like treasuries at Delphi. By 480 BC, after the sacking of Athens' Acropolis by the Persians, naturalism was being achieved for the first time in European art. This period, through to the death of Alexander the Great in 323 AD, is known as 'classical'.

Left: Theseus fights the Minotaur; Attic black-figure belly amphora, c. 540 BC

Right: Triptolemos on his wheeled and winged throne; Attic red-figure column krater, by the Nausikaa Painter, 450-445 BC

Bottom: Detail from Eastern Greek Caeretan hydria; 520-51 BC

NICHOLAS P GOULANDRIS FOUNDATION & MUSEUM OF CYCLADIC ART

NICHOLAS P GOULANDRIS FOUNDATION & MUSEUM OF CYCLADIC ART

NICHOLAS P GOULANDRIS FOUNDATION & MUSEUM OF CYCLADIC ART

CLASSICAL PERIOD

The art of classical Greece shows an obsession with the human figure and with drapery. At first the classical style was rather severe, as with the bronze charioteer at Delphi, the Zeus from Artemision in the Athens Archaeological Museum, and the sculpture from the temple at Olympia. Sculptors sought ideal proportions for the human figure. New poses were explored and the figures became increasingly sinuous, with smaller heads in relation to the body. The nude female figure first appeared in the 4th century BC as Aphrodite.

Apart from the 5th-century marble relief sculpture on the temples and some very moving Attic tombstones, little original work of the classical period survives. Most free-standing classical sculpture described by ancient writers was made of bronze and survives only as marble copies made by the Romans. In the last century, however, some classical

NATIONAL ARCHAEOLOGICAL MUSEUM, ATHENS

Grave stele of a woman with her maid; Attic, early 4th century BC

bronzes, lost when they were being shipped abroad in antiquity, have been recovered from the sea.

Europeans first drew on Roman works for their knowledge of Greek architecture. The three major Greek styles were known from the tiers of columns on the Colosseum in Rome. Whereas the rather plain Doric and the Ionic voluted capitals were more commonly used in Greece, for example on the colonnades surrounding temples, Romans preferred the Corinthian capitals based on the acanthus leaf. Thus, when the Romans finally completed the large temple of Olympian Zeus in Athens, it was in the Corinthian order.

It was only after the publication in the 18th century of engravings made from measured architectural drawings of monuments like the Parthenon and Erechtheion on the Acropolis that a genuine Greek Revival style was possible in Europe. It is the 5th-century temples such as the Parthenon, Erechtheion and Temple of Athena Nike on the Acropolis of Athens, and the temples at Olympia and on Aegina, that epitomise classical Greek art.

The classical period was also the time when the Greek tragedies of Aeschylus, Sophocles and Euripides and the comedies of Aristophanes were written and first performed in the theatre built into the slope of Athens' Acropolis. The ancient theatres at Dodoni, Megalopolis, Epidaurus and Argos are larger, the latter seating about 20,000; most are still used for summer festivals and have excellent acoustics.

The Parthenon, Athens;
5th century BC

ANN JOUSIFFE

HELLENISTIC PERIOD

During the Hellenistic period (323-31 BC) sculpture often showed greater realism than the classical. It was able to express suffering and old age, and delighted in the grotesque. In this period, too, when the empire won by Alexander was centred on Macedon in Northern Greece, Antioch in Syria, and Alexandria in Egypt, portraiture first came into its own in sculpture and on coins. There are also traces of paintings on tombstones at Volos and on the walls of some of the temple-like tombs of Macedonia. Gold was again available at this time in some quantity, as can be seen from the furnishings of Philip of Macedon's tomb, now in the Archaeological Museum in Thessaloniki, and from the exquisite jewellery of the period.

Cities of the eastern Mediterranean became increasingly wealthy and Delos, which had been a sacred island, developed as a cosmopolitan commercial centre in the 2nd century BC judging from the remains of lavish houses with floor mosaics, a theatre and sanctuaries for Eastern cults as well as for Apollo.

NATIONAL ARCHAEOLOGICAL MUSEUM, ATHENS

Statuette of a boy playing with a goose; marble, 3rd century BC

ROMAN PERIOD

In the Hellenistic and Roman period Athens, with its marble from Mt
Pendeli, continued to produce sculpture, largely for export. It received
prestigious buildings such as the theatre donated by Herodes Atticus
(now lacking a roof but again used for concerts and drama) and large
colonnaded stoas were added to frame the Agora.

From the middle of the 2nd century BC, when Rome gained control
of Greece, Corinth became an important Roman city with fountains,
baths and gymnasia which have been excavated in recent years. Athens
obtained a new commercial agora (now known as the Roman Agora) in
the time of Augustus, at the end of the 1st century BC, and a century and
a half later the emperor Hadrian endowed the city with a library and built
an elegant arch which still stands between the old and new parts of the
city.

In the northern town of Philippi there are substantial architectural
remains of large early Christian churches, and early mosaics have
survived in the Church of St Dimitrios in Thessaloniki.

BYZANTINE PERIOD

During the Byzantine period, through to 1453, Constantinople was the
most important Greek-speaking city. The Parthenon in Athens was
converted into a church and smaller churches were built throughout
Greece, especially from the 10th century on. Usually they had a central
dome supported by four arches on piers and flanked by vaults, with
smaller domes at the four corners and three apses to the east. The
external brickwork, which alternates with stone, is sometimes set in
patterns. The churches were usually decorated with frescoes on a
dark-blue ground with a bust of Christ in the dome; the four Gospel-
writers in the pendentives supporting the dome; the Virgin and Child in
the apse; then scenes from the life of Christ (Annunciation, Nativity,
Baptism, Entry into Jerusalem, Crucifixion and Transfiguration); and,
below that, at the lowest level, figures of the saints. In the later centuries
the scenes involve more detailed narratives, including cycles of the life
of the Virgin and the miracles of Christ.

Judas' Betrayal of Christ;
mosaic from the monas-
tery church at Dafni, 11th
century

DAFNI MONASTERY & THE GREEK MINISTRY OF CULTURE

Three 11th-century churches – at Dafni, at Moni Osiou Louka near Delphi, and at Nea Moni on Chios – retain their mosaic wall decoration with tesserae of coloured glass for the figures, and glass with gold leaf for the background. At Kastoria, in Epiros, and in the Mani there are small chapels of simple design; some at Kastoria have scenes painted on the exterior walls. At Mt Athos and on Patmos, where the first monasteries were built in the 10th century, the monastic buildings as well as the churches survive, though much has changed through centuries of continuous use and a number of fires. At Meteora, in Central Greece, the monasteries are built high on precipitous rocks and for centuries were almost inaccessible. In addition to their frescoes, all these monasteries retain some of their ecclesiastical treasures, including manuscripts, vestments, icons and silver. Marble reliefs from the earliest churches and early icons are a special feature of the Byzantine Museum in Athens.

After the temporary fall of Constantinople to a crusading army in 1204, much of Greece became the fiefdoms of Western aristocrats. The most notable of these was the Villehardouin family, who built castles in the Peloponnese at Hlemoutsi, Nafplio, Kalamata and Mystras. At Mystras

The Virgin Enthroned, with a border of scenes from the life of Christ and portraits of saints; icon of the Cretan school, 16th century

BENAKI MUSEUM, ATHENS

BYZANTINE MUSEUM, ATHENS

BYZANTINE MUSEUM, ATHENS

BYZANTINE MUSEUM, ATHENS

BENAKI MUSEUM, ATHENS

they also built a palace which became, for two centuries prior to the Turkish conquest, a court of the Byzantine imperial family, second only to Constantinople. The now empty frescoed churches and two-storey houses on the steep hillside of Mystras convey the spirit of this late Byzantine administrative and intellectual centre which also had strong links with Renaissance Italy. The Byzantines also held onto Monemvassia with its castle and churches on the south-eastern tip of the Peloponnese, while the Venetians built castles on the south-western tip at Koroni and at Methoni. Byzantines, Franks and Venetians all contributed in turn to building the fortress above Corinth.

The Venetian settlements on Crete and other islands were long-lasting as they profited from supplying the ships which ferried crusaders to the Holy Land and from trading with Constantinople and the Ottomans.

The Byzantine fortress at Lindos on Rhodes, like the town of Rhodes itself, was taken over by the Knights of St John of Jerusalem. These medieval towns and most of the great enceintes have been carefully restored.

BENAKI MUSEUM, ATHENS

Facing page:
Top left: The Archangel Michael; icon, 14th century

Top right: St John the Theologian on Patmos dictating the Book of Revelations to Prochoros; icon, 17th to 18th century

Bottom left: St Constantine the Great and St Helena; icon, 18th century

Bottom right: The Presentation of Christ in the Temple and the Baptism of Christ in the River Jordan by John the Baptist; icon of the Cretan school, 16th century

This page:
Left: Gold pendant with enamels and pearls, from Patmos; 18th century

TURKISH OCCUPATION

Few of the wooden houses of the Ottoman period survive and there are now only a few mosques, mostly in the north, but also in Athens. Kavala, Xanthi and Didymotiho near the Turkish border retain some of this architecture.

In Ioannina the local ruler Ali Pasha maintained an idiosyncratic court in the late 18th and early 19th centuries in what had been the Byzantine fortress. One of the mosques by the lake is now a museum housing Epirote costumes of this period.

The numerous folk museums of Greece, such as those at Kastoria and Thessaloniki, illustrate the culture of Greeks under Turkish rule which, in northern Greece, lasted into the 20th century.

MODERN GREECE

After the War of Independence, Greece continued the neoclassical style, dominant in Western European architecture and sculpture at the turn of the century, thus providing a sense of continuity with its ancient past. This neoclassical style is apparent in Nafplio, initially the capital, and in Athens, notably in the Doric and Ionic ensemble of the National Library and the university. Notable, too, are the old royal palace, the Polytehnio, and the mansions which are now the Byzantine, Benaki and Kanellopoulos museums. Architects working in this style were mainly Germans or Greeks: C and T von Hansen, E Ziller, L Kaftanzoglu, Leo von Klenze and S Kleanthes. In many towns the archaeological museums, town halls, law courts and mansions exhibit the same

Blind Eros and Two Sirens; *painting on wood by Agapios Manganaris of Sifnos;1825*

BYZANTINE MUSEUM, ATHENS

PAUL HELLANDER

BENAKI MUSEUM, ATHENS

BENAKI MUSEUM, ATHENS

Top: Painted ceiling, Kastoria Folk Museum

Middle: Embroidery from Ioannina; 18th century

Bottom: Cushion embroidered with a forked-tailed Gorgon in the centre; from Crete, 18th to 19th century

restrained form of neoclassicism. The cemetery of Ermoupolis, on Syros, and the First Cemetery of Athens are virtual museums of 19th-century Greek sculpture, again in the classical tradition.

With the German Otho on the Greek throne, the Munich school of art, working in the traditions of classicism and romanticism, was the main influence on Greek painters after independence. During the 19th century, however, Greek artists trained in various centres of Europe, including Rome and Paris. Andreas Kriezis specialised in portraits and nautical themes, and Dionysios Tsokos and Theodoros Vryzakis often focused on the War of Independence. Nikiphoros Lytras, Konstantinos Volanakis and Nicholas Gyzis, in the second half of the century, chose genre scenes and their paintings became more pictorial than descriptive. Gyzis' historical paintings were more visionary, coinciding with the fascination with the Great Idea of a new Greek empire. The settings, costumes and historical subjects of many of these 19th-century paintings express Greek conditions of the time.

From the first decades of the 20th century, artists like Konstantinos Parthenis and Konstantinos Kaleas and, later, George Bouzianis were able to use the heritage of the past and at the same time assimilated various developments in modern art. These paintings are best studied in the National Art Gallery in Athens where there is also some sculpture and works of the naive painters and water colourists, notably Panayiotis Zographos.

Naive painters are also represented in folk-art museums. Theses artists often paint directly onto wood panels, as with icons, and choose subjects like ships, wedding festivities, portraits and village life. Painted shop signs and painted wooden ceiling and wall panels and frescoes in houses are special genres.

Weaving and embroidery display regional characteristics. They survive in some quantity from the 17th century on. Geometric and stylised animal and bird motifs on a natural linen ground are most common in needlework, the designs laid out by counting threads. On the mainland, embroidery was applied particularly to dress, and on the islands to household articles like bed curtains, cushion covers and towels. Rich reds, greens, browns, deep blues and pale yellows predominate.

Floral designs, pastel colours and freehand patterns usually reflect Turkish influence, as in Epiros or the islands near Turkey. Italian influence occurs in Crete and in white embroideries and drawn-thread work. Ecclesiastical vestments and altar cloths are also often richly embroidered. The conservatism of designs may be linked to the desire to preserve local traditions in the face of Turkish rule.

Ceramics, woodcarving and metal work have achieved rather less prominence. Wooden chests and icon screens and sanctuary doors in churches were often elaborately carved and there was a folk tradition of carved figures on ships' prows. Silversmiths produced liturgical vessels and crosses, ornate Gospel covers, icon frames, and sword sheaths. The Benaki Museum in Athens has the finest collection of decorative arts from medieval and modern Greece as well as some from earlier centuries.

Ann Moffatt, Australian National University, Canberra

Further reading:

Greek Art and Archaeology by J G Pedley, Cassell, London, 1992
The Greek Museums by M Andronicos et al, Athens, 1975

Facts for the Visitor

PLANNING

When to Go

Spring and autumn are the best times to visit Greece. Winter is pretty much a dead loss outside the major cities. Most of Greece's tourist infrastructure goes into hibernation from the end of November until the beginning of April – hotels and restaurants are closed and bus and ferry services are either drastically reduced or plain cancelled.

The cobwebs are dusted off in time for Easter, when the first tourists start to arrive. Conditions are perfect between Easter and mid-June, when the weather is pleasantly warm in most places, but not too hot; beaches and ancient sites are relatively uncrowded; public transport operates on close to full schedules; and accommodation is cheaper and easier to find.

Mid-June until the end of August is the high season. It's party time on the islands and everything is in full swing. It's also very hot – in July and August the mercury can soar to 40°C in the shade just about anywhere in the country; the beaches are crowded, the ancient sites are swarming with tour groups and in many places accommodation is booked solid.

The season starts to wind down after August and conditions are ideal once more until the shutdown at the end of November. Before ruling out a winter holiday entirely, it's worth considering going skiing (see the Activities section later in this chapter for details).

What Kind of Trip?

Travelling Companions Travelling alone is not a problem in Greece. If you decide to travel with others, bear in mind that travel can put relationships to the test in a way that few other experiences can. Many a long-term friendship has collapsed under the strain of constant negotiations on where to stay and eat, what to do and where to go next. Other friendships become much closer than before

– there's no way of knowing until you try it. It's a good idea to agree on a rough itinerary before you go, and to be operating with similar budgets. Above all, you will need to be flexible.

One of the great advantages of travelling with others is that you can share the cost of big-budget items like car hire, which might be beyond the means of lone travellers.

Move or Stay? Greece is a place where travellers tend to keep on the move. If you're heading for the islands, island-hopping on the ferries is the name of the game – just keep hopping until you find an island that catches your mood. The advantage of staying somewhere for a while is that you can settle in and get to know a place. You will also be able to save a bit of money by negotiating a cheaper deal on accommodation.

Maps

Unless you are going to trek or drive, the free maps given out by the EOT will probably suffice, although they are not 100% accurate. On islands where there is no EOT there are usually tourist maps for sale for around 400 dr, but again, these are not very accurate.

The best motoring maps are produced by Road Editions, newcomers on the mapping

scene who advertise boldly that their maps are produced with the cooperation of the Hellenic Army Geographic Service. Whatever the source of their information, the maps are excellent. They are all produced to a scale of 1:250,000, and even the smallest roads and villages are clearly marked. The distance indicators on the Peloponnese and Central Greece maps proved spot on – important when negotiating your way around the back blocks. Useful features include symbols to indicate the location of petrol stations and tyre shops.

The company is working on a six-part, purple-cover series covering the mainland and Crete, and a six-part, blue-cover series for the major islands. Central Greece, the Peloponnese and Crete were the only maps in the mainland series at the time of research; the others were due out later in 1997. The only island map available was Corfu.

If you're looking for one map to cover the mainland, try the Bartholomew/RV Euromap (1:800,000). Freytag & Berndt's 15-map Greece series has good coverage of the islands and the Peloponnese.

If you are going to trek, then the best available topographical survey maps of Greece are the *Karta Nomos* (1:200,000), published by the Ethniki Statistiki Ypiresia (National Statistical Office). There are 52 sheets; each covers a single administrative area. Relief is shown by colour tints with contours at 200m intervals. All names are given in Greek script only. The maps may be bought at the Athens Statistical Service Office, Lykourgou 14, 3rd floor, near Omonia (show your passport). The maps are available at Stanfords, 12-14 Long Acre, London, WC2E 9LP (☎ 0171-836 1321; fax 0171-836 0189). Lonely Planet's *Trekking in Greece* has over 40 contoured sketch maps, which should suffice for most of the standard treks.

Under present Greek government regulations, larger-scale topographic surveys published by the military authorities are not available to the general public. All is not lost, however. The bimonthly EOS magazine *Korfes* publishes a series of walking maps

(1:50,000) based on the military topographical maps. Copies of these maps may be purchased in Greece at the EOS office (☎ 01-246 1528), Plateia Kentriki 16, Aharnes (a satellite suburb north of Athens). Before trekking out to Aharnes, it's probably worth checking if the maps are also available from the head office of the EOS (☎ 01-321 2429/2355) at Plateia Kapnikareas 2, Athens – on Ermou, 500m west of Syntagma. The maps cover the most popular trekking and climbing areas in Greece. Recent editions have names in both Greek and Latin script; earlier ones have names in Greek only. These maps are also available at Stanfords.

What to Bring

Sturdy shoes are essential for clambering around ancient sites and wandering around historic towns and villages, which tend to have lots of steps and cobbled streets. Footwear with ankle support is preferable for trekking, although many visitors get by with trainers.

A day pack is useful for the beach, and for sightseeing or trekking. A compass is essential if you are going to trek in remote areas, as is a whistle, which you can use should you become lost or disoriented. A torch (flashlight) is not only needed if you intend to explore caves, but comes in handy during occasional power cuts. If you like to fill a washbasin or bathtub (a rarity in Greece), bring a universal plug as Greek bathrooms rarely have plugs.

Many camp sites have covered areas where tourists without tents can sleep in summer, so you can get by with a lightweight sleeping bag and foam bedroll. Whether or not you are going to self-cater, a plastic food container, plate, cup, cutlery, bottle opener, water container and an all-purpose knife are useful, not only for picnics, but for food you take with you on long boat trips.

You will need only light clothing – preferably cotton – during the summer months. But if you're going to climb Mt Olympus (or any other high mountain) you will need a sweater and waterproof jacket, even in July and August. During spring and autumn you'll need a light sweater or jacket in the evening. In winter take a heavy jacket or coat, warm sweaters, winter shoes or boots, and an umbrella.

In summer a sun hat and sunglasses are essential (see the Health section later in this chapter). Sunscreen creams and suntan oil are expensive, as are moisturising and cleansing creams. Film is not wildly expensive, especially in larger towns and tourist areas, but the stock tends to hang around for a while in remoter areas.

If you read a lot, it's a good idea to bring along a few disposable paperbacks to read and swap.

SUGGESTED ITINERARIES

One of the most difficult aspects of travel is organising an itinerary. The following list of suggested itineraries provides a choice of one-week and two-week itineraries for each of the major regions and island groups. The one-week itineraries are for people who want no more than a quick tour of the highlights of each region, while the two-week itineraries are for people with a bit more time to spare.

The list can be used to create the individual itinerary of your choice. A month in Greece, for example, could be divided up into a week in the Peloponnese, followed by a couple of weeks in the Cyclades and a week on Crete.

Athens
One Week

Combine a walking tour of Plaka with a visit to the Acropolis (one day); National Archaeological Museum (one day); day trip to Cape Sounion (one day); an early morning climb up Lykavittos Hill followed by visits to the Goulandris Museum of Cycladic & Ancient Greek Art and the Byzantine Museum (one day); day trip to Elefsina, stopping at Moni Dafniou on the way (one day); visit the Ancient Agora and the Keramikos (one day); day trip to Moni Kaissarianis (one day). Evening activities to schedule in include the Dora Stratou folk dancers on Filopappos Hill; summer performances of ancient Greek drama at the Theatre of Herodes Atticus; and a visit to a *rembetika* club.

Peloponnese
One Week

Head from Athens to Nafplio (two days) and use it as a base for side trips to Epidaurus and Mycenae; go south to Sparta (two days) and visit Mystras; travel across the Taygetos mountains to Kalamata and then up the west coast to Ancient Olympia (one day); visit the site early and continue north around the coast through Patras to Diokofto and ride the rack-and-pinion railway up to Kalavryta (one day); travel back to Diokofto via Zahlorou and take the train back to Athens.

Two Weeks

People with more time can follow the above itinerary as far as Sparta/Mystras, and then head south-east to Monemvasia (one day). From Monemvasia, travel west through Gythio to Aeropoli and use it a base for exploring the Lakonian Mani (two days) before moving up the coast to Kardamyli (two days). From Kardamyli, head west via Kalamata to the old Venetian town of Methoni (one day) and then go north to Olympia (one day). Visit the site early and then catch the bus to Tripolis (one day), and then take the bus that runs north through the mountains to Kalavryta (one day). From Kalavryta, ride the rack-and-pinion railway to Diokofto via Zahlorou and catch a train to Athens.

Central Greece
One Week

Start at Volos and work your way towards Meteora. Head southwards across the mountains via Karditsa, Lamia and Amfissa and visit the Oracle of Delphi. Allow two days for this magical place. If time and patience allow, head along the north coast of the Gulf of Corinth from Delphi and visit Messolongi in Etolo-Akarnania. Take along some of Byron's poetry, to get in the mood. Central Greece offers two main sightseeing areas for the short-term visitor – the Meteora and the Pelion peninsula.

Two Weeks

Start at Volos but allow an extra two to three days to visit the villages of the Pelion peninsula, overnighting in perhaps Tsangarada and Vyzitsa. Frofn Volos traverse Thessaly – perhaps including a short visit to workaday Larisa – before halting at Meteora. A stay of at least two to three days should be allowed for Meteora, especially if you wish to visit all the monasteries at walking pace. With more time on your hands you might detour slightly to the Monastery of Osios Loukas in Central Greece before resuming the one-week itinerary at Delphi. From Messolongi you might care to loop back to Central Greece via the little-visited mountains of the Agrafa and the capital of Greece's 'little Switzerland', Karpenisi.

Northern Greece

One Week

Start in Epirus and use Ioannina as your base to visit Ioannina and the Zagoria villages. Head eastwards to Macedonia via Konitsa and make for Kastoria. Visit the Prespa Lakes basin and move on to Thessaloniki via Edessa. Then head further east to Alexandroupolis. Look out for the Turkish-speaking villages of central Thrace and the 'Turkish' town of Komotini. From Alexandroupolis, you can head east to Turkey or catch a weekly ferry down as far as the Dodecanese.

Two Weeks

Allow at least four to five days to visit the Zagoria villages and if walking is your cup of tea then base yourself at Papingo or Konitsa. Include the Vlach village of Metsovo as a side trip from Ioannina then head east via Konitsa to western Macedonia. Other than the sights listed in the one-week itinerary you should also visit Vergina and Pella and spend some more time soaking up the culture in Europe's 1997 cultural capital, Thessaloniki.

Saronic Gulf Islands

One Week

Starting from Athens, head to Aegina (two days), visiting the Temple of Aphaia and exploring the ruins of Paleohora; Poros warrants no more than a brief stopover on the way to tranquil Hydra (three days); continue to Spetses (two days). From Spetses, you can either return to Athens or continue by hydrofoil to one of the ports of the eastern Peloponnese.

Cyclades

One Week

Visit Santorini (one day), party on Ios (three days) and continue on Mykonos (two days).

Two Weeks

Visit Santorini (two days), party on Ios (three days), recover on Naxos and take a day trip to the Minor islands (three days), lose yourself in the nightlife of Mykonos and take an excursion to ancient Delos (three days), relax on Tinos (two days).

Dodecanese

One Week

Explore the medieval city of Rhodes (two days), then base yourself in Kos and take day trips to Nisyros and Bodrum (four days).

Two Weeks

Explore the medieval city of Rhodes and take a bus to Lindos (two days), visit Tilos (two days), then base yourself on Kos for day trips to Nisyros and Bodrum and nightlife in Kos town (five

days). Relax on Leros (two days) and spend a day on Patmos en route to Piraeus.

North-Eastern Aegean Islands

One Week

With only seven days, you will be a bit pushed so plan your ferry trips carefully. Fly out to Lesvos (Mytilini) or take the overnight boat. Make sure you visit Mythimna (Molyvos) and maybe Skala Eresou for some beach life. Take a boat to Chios and visit the Mastihohoria (Mastic villages) and maybe sit on Homer's stone (Daskalopetra) for some poetic inspiration. Head for Samos if you want some organised tourism, or Ikaria if you want a very laid-back and idiosyncratic visit. Fly or sail back to the mainland.

Two Weeks

Start your itinerary on the under-rated but worthwhile island of Limnos, reached by ferry from either Kavala or Thessaloniki. From here, try to make a two-day visit the remote community on Agios Efstratios, one of Greece's most remote islands. Fly to Lesvos (Mytilini) and follow the one-week itinerary to Samos. Definitely include Ikaria for three to four days with perhaps a side trip to the Fourni islands while en route from Samos. Take the overnight boat to Piraeus to finish your trip.

Evia & the Sporades

One Week

Starting in Athens, take the bus to Kymi in Evia and then the ferry to Linaria in Skyros. Give delectable Skyros at least two days of your time. Take a hydrofoil to Alonnisos and work your way to Volos on the mainland, visiting the islands of Skopelos and Skiathos en route.

Two Weeks

Try this adventurous route if you have time at your disposal. From Athens head to Rafina in Attica and take the ferry to Karystos in Evia. Work your way up to Kymi in Evia at your own pace, perhaps taking in Eretria on Evia's west side and some walking up Mt Dirfys from the inland village of Steni. From Kymi in Evia follow the one-week itinerary, allowing two to three days on each island of the Sporades. Finally exit from Skiathos to Thessaloniki (ferry or hydrofoil) and return to Athens by train.

Northern Ionian Islands

One Week

Spend two days in Corfu town; explore the narrow streets of the old town and visit the museums. Spend one night in Paleokastritsa or Lakones; walk the path between the two, visit Moni Theotokou and Angelokastro, and have a meal at one of the restaurants on the Lakones-Makrades road. If you have your own transport visit old Perithia. Spend two days at a west-coast resort and catch a sunset at Pelekas. If you have your own transport visit Lake Korission and surrounds. Spend one or two nights on Paxi.

Southern Ionian Islands

One Week

Spend one day and night on Lefkada. Look around the capital and relax on one of the west coast beaches. Overnight on Meganisi. Spend two days on Ithaki. Visit Vathi's museums and the villages of Anogi, Frikes and Kioni. Have two days in Fiskardo on Kefallonia (in the high season stay elsewhere and visit on a day trip), to see the village of Assos and Myrtos beach. Spend one day in Sami to visit the nearby caves.

Two Weeks

Spend three days in Corfu town; explore the narrow streets of the old town and visit the museums, Ahillion palace and the villages of Kastellani, Kamara and Agios Prokopias. Spend one night in Paleokastritsa or Lakones; walk the path between the two, visit Moni Theotokou and Angelokastro, and have a meal at a restaurant on the Lakones-Makrades road. If you have your own transport visit old Perithia. Spend two days at a west coast resort and catch a sunset at Pelekas. If you have your own transport visit Lake Korission and surrounds. Spend two nights on Paxi. Spend two nights on Lefkada to see Lefkada town and relax on one of the west-coast beaches. Spend one night on Meganisi. Spend two days on Ithaki. Visit Vathi's museums and the villages of Anogi, Frikes and Kioni. Have one day in Fiskardo on Kefallonia (in the high season stay elsewhere and visit on a day trip), to see Assos and Myrtos beach.

Crete

One Week

Spend two days in Iraklio; visit the archaeological museum, historical museum of Crete and the Minoan site of Knossos. Overnight in Sitia, Zakros or Kato Zakros and walk the gorge, visit ancient Zakros and have a swim. Have two days in Rethymno to visit the fortress and museums and explore the old quarter. If you have time take a day trip to the mountain town of Spili, or the resort of Plakias, if you prefer a beach. Spend two days in Hania to visit the museums and explore the old quarter. Round off your trip with an evening of music and drinking at Café Crete.

Two Weeks

Spend two days in Iraklio; visit the archaeological museum, historical museum of Crete and the Minoan site of Knossos. Overnight at one of the Lassithi plateau villages and visit the Dikteon

cave and walk on the plateau. Spend two nights in Sitia; visit the archaeological museum, walk the gorge to Kato Zakros, visit ancient Zakros and have a swim. If you have time, visit ancient Lato. Have two days in Rethymno to visit the fortress and museums and explore the old quarter. Overnight in Agia Galini to visit Phaestos and Agia Triada. Spend two nights in the mountain town of Spili, or the resort of Plakias, if you prefer beaches, and visit Moni Preveli. Spend two nights in Hania to explore the old town, visit the archaeological and folk museums and trek the Samaria gorge. Take the boat from Agia Roumeli to Loutro, or to Sougia or Paleohora, for one or two days of relaxation and swimming.

THE BEST & THE WORST

It's tough trying to pick just 10 of the best things about Greece. These are our personal favourites, the places, things and activities the authors of this book would most like to dedicate a lot more of their time to:

1 Cycladic architecture
2 Dining out beneath the floodlit Acropolis
3 The Peloponnese in spring
4 *Rembetika* music clubs
5 Ice-cold retsina
6 Ancient Olympia
7 Easter festivities
8 Nafplio's old Venetian quarter
9 Meteora
10 The Zaghoria villages in Epiros

We'd be quite content not to experience the following again:

1 Athens airport
2 Bar scams
3 Package tourism in northern Crete
4 Ouzo-induced hangovers
5 Sleazy Plateia Omonias in Athens
6 Corinth
7 Xenia hotels
8 Macho motorcyclists
9 Olympic Airways
10 The attitude to rubbish

TOURIST OFFICES

Tourist information is handled by the Greek National Tourist Organisation, known by the initials GNTO abroad and EOT (Ellinikos Organismos Tourismou) in Greece.

Local Tourist Offices

The address of the EOT's head office is Amerikis 2, Athens 105 64 (☎ 01-322 3111). There are about 25 EOT offices throughout Greece. Most EOT staff speak English, but they vary in their enthusiasm and helpfulness. All of the offices have maps, glossy brochures and information on transport and accommodation. In addition to EOT offices, there are municipal tourist offices, which serve the same function.

Tourist Police

The tourist police work in cooperation with the regular Greek police and EOT. Each tourist police office has at least one member of staff who speaks English. Hotels, restaurants, travel agencies, tourist shops, tourist guides, waiters, taxi drivers and bus drivers all come under the jurisdiction of the tourist police. If you think that you have been ripped off by any of these, report it to the tourist police and they will investigate. If you need to report a theft or loss of passport, then go to the tourist police first, and they will act as interpreters between you and the regular police. The tourist police also fulfil the same functions as the EOT and municipal tourist offices, dispensing maps and brochures, and giving information on transport. They can often help you to find accommodation.

Tourist Offices Abroad

GNTO offices abroad include:

Australia
    51 Pitt St, Sydney NSW 2000 (☎ 02-9241 1663)
Austria
    Opernring 8, Vienna 10105 (☎ 1-512 5317)
Belgium
    173 Ave Louise Louizalaan, 1050 Bruxelles (☎ 2-647 5770)
Canada
    1300 Bay St, Toronto, Ontario MSR 3K8 (☎ 416-968 2220); 1233 Rue de la Montagne, Suite 101, Montreal, Quebec H3G 1Z2 (☎ 514-871 1535)
Denmark
    Vester Farimagsgade 1, 1606 Kobenhavn (☎ 3-325 332)

France
    3 Ave de l'Opéra, Paris 75001 (☎ 01 42 60 65 75)
Germany
    Neue Mainzerstrasse 22, 6000 Frankfurt (☎ 69-237 735); Pacellistrasse 2, W 8000 Munich 2 (☎ 89-222 035); Abteistrasse 33, 2000 Hamburg 13 (☎ 40-454 498); Wittenbergplatz 3A, 10789 Berlin 30 (☎ 30-217 6262)
Italy
    Via L Bissolati 78-80, Rome 00187 (☎ 06-474 4249); Piazza Diaz 1, 20123 Milan (☎ 02-860 470)
Japan
    Fukuda Building West, 5F 2-11-3 Akasaka, Minato-Ku, Tokyo 107 (☎ 03-350 55 911)
Netherlands
    Leidsestraat 13, Amsterdam NS 1017 (☎ 020-625 4212)
Norway
    Ovre Slottsgate 15B, 0157 Oslo 1 (☎ 2-426 501)
Sweden
    Birger Jarlsgatan 8, Box 5298 S, 10246 Stockholm (☎ 8-679 6480)
Switzerland
    Loewenstrasse 25, CH 8001 Zürich (☎ 01-221 0105)
UK
    4 Conduit St, London W1R ODJ (☎ 0171-499 9758)
USA
    Olympic Tower, 645 5th Ave, New York, NY 10022 (☎ 212-421 5777); Suite 600, 168 North Michigan Ave, Chicago, Illinois 60601 (☎ 312-782 1084); Suite 2198, 611 West 6th St, Los Angeles, California 92668 (☎ 213-626 6696)

VISAS & DOCUMENTS
Passport

To enter Greece you need a valid passport or, for EU nationals, travel documents (ID cards). You must produce your passport or EU travel documents when you register in a hotel or pension in Greece. You will find that many accommodation proprietors will want to keep your passport during your stay. This is not a compulsory requirement; they need it only long enough to take down the details.

See Useful Organisations later in this chapter for contact details. For information on student cards see the aside later in this chapter.

Visas

Nationals of Australia, Canada, all EU

countries, Iceland, Israel, Japan, New Zealand, Norway, South Africa, Switzerland and the USA can stay in Greece for up to three months without a visa. Greek embassies have a list of other nationalities allowed in without a visa. The list changes, but includes nationals of the European principalities of Monaco and San Marino and most South American countries. Those not on the list can expect to pay about US$20 for a three-month visa.

Turkish-Occupied North Cyprus Greece will refuse entry to people whose passport indicates that they have visited Turkish-occupied North Cyprus since November 1983. This can be overcome if, upon entering North Cyprus, you ask the immigration officials to stamp a piece of paper (loose-leaf visa) rather than your passport. If you enter North Cyprus from the Greek Republic of Cyprus (only possible for a day visit), an exit stamp is not put into your passport.

Visa Extensions If you wish to stay in Greece for longer than three months, apply at a consulate abroad or at least 20 days in advance to the Aliens' Bureau (☎ 01-770 5711), Leoforos Alexandras 173, Athens. Take your passport and four passport photographs along. You may be asked for proof that you can support yourself financially, so keep all your bank exchange slips (or the equivalent from a post office). These slips are not always automatically given – you may have to ask for them. The Aliens Bureau is open from 8 am to 1 pm on weekdays. Elsewhere in Greece apply to the local police authority. You will be given a permit which will authorise you to stay in the country for a period of up to six months. Most travellers get around this by visiting Turkey briefly and then re-entering Greece.

Photocopies

The hassles created by losing your passport, travellers cheques and other important documents can be reduced considerably if you take the precaution of taking photocopies. It is a good idea to have photocopies of the passport pages that cover personal details, issue and expiry date and the current entry stamp or visa. Other documents worth photocopying are airline tickets, credit cards, driving licence and insurance details. You should also keep a record of the serial numbers of your travellers cheques, and cross them off as you cash them.

This emergency material should be kept separate from the originals, so that hopefully they won't both get lost (or stolen) at the same time. Leave an extra copy with someone you can rely on at home just in case.

Travel Permits

You need a special permit to visit the monasteries of the Mt Athos peninsula in Macedonia. The permits can be issued in either Athens or Thessaloniki. See the Mt Athos section of the Northern Greece chapter for details of the application process.

Travel Insurance

A travel insurance policy to cover theft, loss and medical problems is a good idea. The policies handled by STA Travel and other student travel organisations are usually good value. Some policies offer lower and higher medical-expense options; the higher ones are chiefly for countries such as the USA, which have extremely high medical costs. There is a wide variety of policies available; check the small print.

Some policies specifically exclude 'dangerous activities' which can include scuba diving, motorcycling, even trekking. A locally acquired motorcycle licence is not valid under some policies.

You may prefer a policy that pays doctors or hospitals direct rather than you having to pay on the spot and claim later. If you have to claim later make sure you keep all documentation. Some policies ask you to call back (reverse charges) to a centre in your home country where an immediate assessment of your problem is made.

Check that the policy covers ambulances or an emergency flight home.

Student Cards

An ISIC (International Student Identity Card) is a plastic ID-style card displaying your photograph. These cards are widely available from budget travel agencies (take along proof that you are a student). In Athens you can get one from the International Student & Youth Travel Service (ISYTS; ☎ 01-323 3767), 2nd floor, Nikis 11.

Some travel agencies in Greece offer discounts on organised tours to students. However, there are no student discounts for travel within Greece (although Olympic Airways gives a 25% discount on domestic flights which are part of an international flight). Turkish Airlines (THY) gives 55% student discounts on its international flights. THY has flights from Athens to İstanbul and İzmir. Most ferries to Cyprus, Israel and Egypt from Piraeus give a 20% student discount and a few of the services between Greek and Italian ports do so also. If you are under 26 years but not a student, the Federation of International Youth Travel Organisation (FIYTO) card gives similar discounts. Many budget travel agencies issue FIYTO cards including London Explorers Club, 33 Princes Square, Bayswater, London W2 (☎ 0171-792 3770); and SRS Studenten Reise Service, Marienstrasse 23, Berlin (☎ 030-2 83 30 93). ■

Driving Licence & Permits

EU nationals can use their normal licence to drive in Greece. Others will have to get an International Driving Permit. They are best obtained before you leave home, but ELPA (Greek Automobile Touring Club) offices will issue them on production of a national driving licence, passport and photograph.

Hostel Card

A Hostelling International (HI) card is of limited use in Greece. The only place you will be able to use it is at the Athens International Youth Hostel (for more information, see the Hostels section of the Athens chapter).

Student & Youth Cards

The most widely recognised (and thus the most useful) form of student ID is the International Student Identity Card (ISIC). Holders qualify for half-price admission to museums and ancient sites and for discounts at some budget hotels and hostels. The International Student & Youth Travel Service (☎ 01-323 3767), 1st floor, Nikis 11, Athens, issues ISIC cards. You will need to show documents proving you are a student, provide a passport photo and cough up 2500 dr.

There are no student discounts on domestic flights (unless linked to an international flight), and none to be had on buses, ferries or trains either. Students will, however, find some good deals on international airfares.

Seniors' Cards

See the Senior Travellers section later in this chapter.

EMBASSIES

Greek Embassies Abroad

The following is a selection of Greek diplomatic missions abroad:

Albania
    Rruga Frederik Shiroka, Tiranë (☎ 342 90)
Australia
    9 Turrana St, Yarralumla, Canberra ACT 2600 (☎ 062-73 3011)
Bulgaria
    Klement Gottwald 68, Sofia (☎ 02-44 3770)
Canada
    76-80 Maclaren St, Ottawa, Ontario K2P OK6 (☎ 613-238 6271)
Cyprus
    Byron Boulevard 8-10, Nicosia (☎ 02-44 18802)
Denmark
    Borgergade 16, 1300 Copenhagen K (☎ 33 11 4533)
Egypt
    18 Aisha el Taymouria, Garden City, Cairo (☎ 02-355 1074)
France
    17 Rue Auguste Vacquerie, 75116 Paris (☎ 01 47 23 72 28)
Germany
    Koblenzer Str 103, 5300 Bonn 2 (☎ 228-83010)

Ireland
    1 Upper Pembroke St, Dublin 2
    (☎ 01-767 254/255)
Israel
    35 Shaul Hameleck St, PO Box 33631
    (☎ 03-695 9704)
Italy
    Via S Mercadante 36, Rome 00198
    (☎ 06-854 9630)
Japan
    16-30 Nishi Azabu, 3-chome, Minato-ku, Tokyo
    106 (☎ 03-340 0871/0872)
Netherlands
    Dr Kuiper 10, The Hague
    (☎ 070-363 87 00)
New Zealand
    5-7 Willeston St, Wellington
    (☎ 04-473 7775)
Norway
    Nobels Gate 45, 0244 Oslo 2
    (☎ 22 44 2728)
South Africa
    Reserve Bank Building, St George's Rd,
    Capetown (☎ 21-24 8161)
Spain
    Avenida Doctor Arce 24, Madrid 28002
    (☎ 01-564 4653)
Sweden
    Riddargatan 60, 11457 Stockholm
    (☎ 08-663 7577)
Switzerland
    Jungfraustrasse 3, 3005 Bern
    (☎ 31-352 1637)
Turkey
    Ziya-ul-Rahman Caddesi 9-11, Gaziosmanpaşa
    06700, Ankara (☎ 312-446 5496)
UK
    1A Holland Park, London W11 3TP
    (☎ 0171-229 3850)
USA
    2221 Massachusetts Ave NW, Washington DC
    20008 (☎ 202-667 3169)

Foreign Embassies in Greece

All foreign embassies in Greece are in
Athens and its suburbs. There are consulates
of various countries in Thessaloniki, Patras,
Corfu, Rhodes and Iraklio. See the relevant
chapters for details. Foreign embassies in
Athens (telephone code 01) include:

Albania
    Karahristou 1, Athens 115 21
    (☎ 723 4412)
Australia
    Dimitrou Soutsou 37, Athens 115 21
    (☎ 644 7303)

Bulgaria
    Stratigou Kallari 33A, Psyhiko, Athens 154 52
    (☎ 647 8105)
Canada
    Genadiou 4, Athens 115 21 (☎ 725 4011)
Cyprus
    Herodotou 16, Athens 106 75
    (☎ 723 7883)
Egypt
    Leoforos Vasilissis Sofias 3, Athens 106 71
    (☎ 361 8612)
France
    Leoforos Vasilissis Sofias 7, Athens 106 71
    (☎ 339 1000)
Germany
    Dimitriou 3 & Karaoli, Kolonaki, Athens 106 75
    (☎ 728 5111)
Ireland
    Leoforos Vasileos Konstantinou 7, Athens 106
    74 (☎ 723 2771)
Israel
    Marathonodromou 1, Psyhiko, Athens 154 52
    (☎ 671 9530)
Italy
    Sekeri 2, Athens 106 74 (☎ 361 7260)
Japan
    Athens Tower, Leoforos Messogion 2-4, Athens
    115 27 (☎ 775 8101)
Netherlands
    Vasileos Konstantinou 5-7, Athens 106 74
    (☎ 723 9701)
New Zealand (Consulate)
    Semitelou 9, Athens 115 28
    (☎ 771 0112)
South Africa
    Kifissias 60, Maroussi, Athens 151 25
    (☎ 680 6645)
Turkey
    Vasilissis Georgiou B 8, Athens 106 74
    (☎ 724 5915)
UK
    Ploutarhou 1, Athens 106 75
    (☎ 723 6211)
USA
    Leoforos Vasilissis Sofias 91, Athens 115 21
    (☎ 721 2951)

CUSTOMS

There are no longer duty-free restrictions
within the EU. This does not mean, however,
that customs checks have been dispensed
with: random searches are still made for
drugs.

Arrival & Departure

Upon entering the country from outside the
EU, customs inspection is usually cursory

for foreign tourists. There may be spot-checks, but you probably won't have to open your bags. A verbal declaration is usually all that is required.

You may bring the following into Greece duty free: 200 cigarettes or 50 cigars; 1L of spirits or 2L of wine; 50g of perfume; 250mL of eau de cologne; one camera (still or video) and film; a pair of binoculars; a portable musical instrument; a portable radio or tape recorder; a typewriter; sports equipment; and dogs and cats (with a veterinary certificate).

Importation of works of art and antiquities is free, but they must be declared on entry, so that they can be re-exported. Import regulations for medicines are strict; if you are taking medication, make sure you get a statement from your doctor before you leave home. It is illegal, for instance, to take codeine into Greece without an accompanying doctor's certificate.

An unlimited amount of foreign currency and travellers cheques may be brought into Greece. If, however, you intend to leave the country with foreign banknotes in excess of US$1000, you must declare the sum upon entry.

Restrictions apply to the importation of sailboards into Greece. See the Activities section later in this chapter for more details.

It is strictly forbidden to export antiquities (anything over 100 years old) without an export permit. This crime is second only to drug smuggling in the penalties imposed. It is an offence to remove even the smallest article from an archaeological site.

The place to apply for an export permit is Antique Dealers & Private Collections Section, The Archaeological Service, Polignotou 13, Athens.

Vehicles

Cars can be brought into Greece for four months without a carnet; only a green card (international third-party insurance) is required. Your vehicle will be registered in your passport when you enter Greece in order to prevent you leaving the country without it.

MONEY
Costs

Greece is still a cheap country by northern European standards, but it is no longer dirt cheap. A rock-bottom daily budget would be 6000 dr. This would mean hitching, staying in youth hostels or camping, staying away from bars, and only occasionally eating in restaurants or taking ferries. Allow at least 10,000 dr per day if you want your own room and plan to eat out regularly as well as travelling about and seeing the sights. You will still need to do a fair bit of self-catering. If you really want a holiday – comfortable rooms and restaurants all the way – you will need closer to 15,000 dr per day. These budgets are for individuals. Couples sharing a double room can get by on less.

Prices vary quite a lot between islands, particularly for accommodation. Hydra and Mykonos are the most expensive; the cheapest tend to be the less well-known ones.

Museum Fees Cultural excursions can quickly cut into your budget. Most small museums charge 500 dr, and major sites and museums cost between 1200 and 2000 dr. Museums and sites are free on Sunday from October to the end of April, but normal charges apply in summer.

Card-carrying students, teachers and pensioners from the EU pay half-price, and an International Student Identification Card (ISIC) enables students from outside the EU to claim the discount.

Carrying Money

The safest way of carrying cash and valuables (passport, travellers cheques, credit cards etc) is a favourite topic of travel conversation. The simple answer is that there is no foolproof method. The general principle is to keep things out of sight. The front pouch belt, for example, presents an obvious target for a would-be thief – only marginally less inviting than a fat wallet bulging from your back pocket.

The best place is under your clothes in contact with your skin where, hopefully, you will be aware of an alien hand before it's too late. Most people opt for a money belt, while others prefer a leather pouch hung around the neck. Another possibility is to sew a secret stash pocket into the inside of your clothes. Whichever method you choose, put your valuables in a plastic bag first – otherwise they will get soaked in sweat as you wander around in the heat. After a few soakings, they will end up looking like they've been through the washing machine.

Cash

Nothing beats cash for convenience – or for risk. If you lose it, it's gone for good and very few travel insurers will come to your rescue. Those that will, normally limit the amount to about US$300. It's best to carry no more cash than you need for the next few days, which means working out your likely needs when you change travellers cheques or withdraw cash from an ATM.

It's also a good idea to set aside a small amount of cash, say US$50, for your emergency stash.

Travellers Cheques

The main reason to carry travellers cheques rather than cash is the protection they offer against theft. They are, however, losing popularity as more and more travellers opt to put their money in a bank at home and withdraw it at ATMs as they go along.

American Express, Visa and Thomas Cook cheques are all widely accepted and have efficient replacement policies. Maintaining a record of the cheque numbers and recording when you use them is vital when it comes to replacing lost cheques. Keep this record separate from the cheques themselves. US dollars are a good currency to use.

ATMs

ATMs are to be found in almost every town large enough to support a bank – and certainly in all the tourist areas. If you've got MasterCard or Visa, there are plenty of places to withdraw money.

Cirrus and Maestro users can make withdrawals in all major towns and tourist areas.

AFEMs (Automatic Foreign Exchange Machines) are starting to make an appearance. They take all the major European currencies, Australian and US dollars and Japanese yen.

Credit Cards

The great advantage of credit cards is that they allow you to pay for major items without carrying around great wads of cash. Credit cards are now an accepted part of the commercial scene in Greece, especially in major towns and tourist areas. They can be used to pay for a wide range of goods and services such as up-market meals and accommodation, car hire and souvenir shopping.

If you are not familiar with the card options, ask your bank to explain the workings and relative merits of the various schemes: cash cards, charge cards and credit cards. You should explain what you want to do with the card and push for a credit limit that meets your needs. Ask whether the card can be replaced in Greece if it is lost or stolen.

The main credit cards are MasterCard, Visa (Access in the UK) and Eurocard, all of which are widely accepted in Greece. They can also be used as cash cards to draw drachma from the ATMs of affiliated Greek banks in the same way as at home. Daily withdrawal limits are set by the issuing bank. Cash advances are given in local currency only. Credit cards can be used to pay for accommodation in all the smarter hotels. Some C-class hotels will accept credit cards, but D and E-class hotels rarely do. Most up-market shops and restaurants accept credit cards.

The main charge cards are American Express and Diner's Card, which are widely accepted in tourist areas but unheard of elsewhere.

International Transfers

If you run out of money or need more for whatever reason, you can instruct your bank back home to send you a draft. Specify the city and the bank as well as the branch that you want the money sent to. If you have the choice, select a large bank and ask for the international division.

Money sent by telegraphic transfer (which usually involves a charge of US$20 or more, but ask) should reach you within a week; by mail, allow at least two weeks. When it arrives, it will most likely be converted into drachmas – you can take it as it is or buy travellers cheques. US citizens can also use Western Union, which has offices in Athens, Piraeus and Thessaloniki.

Currency

The unit of currency is the drachma. Coins come in denominations of five, 10, 20, 50 and 100 dr. Banknotes come in 50 (fast disappearing), 100, 200, 500, 1000, 5000 and 10,000 dr. The larger notes can be difficult to change in remote areas.

Currency Exchange

Following are approximate cash exchange rates in effect at the time of going to press.

Australia	A$1	=	208.39 dr
Canada	C$1	=	199.14 dr
France	1FF	=	46.22 dr
Germany	DM1	=	159.57 dr
Italy	L1000	=	163 dr
Japan	¥100	=	235.87 dr
New Zealand	NZ$1	=	195.45 dr
United Kingdom	UK£1	=	449.58 dr
United States	US$1	=	274.53 dr

What to Carry & Where to Exchange It

Banks will exchange all major currencies in either cash, travellers cheques or Eurocheques. To obtain Eurocheques you need a European bank account, and you will usually have to wait at least two weeks to receive the cheques. The best known travellers cheques in Greece are Thomas Cook and American Express. A passport is required to change travellers cheques, but not cash.

Commission charged on the exchange of banknotes and travellers cheques varies not only from bank to bank but from branch to branch. It's less for cash than for travellers cheques. The lowest charges levied are 200 dr for cash (banknotes only; no coins) with

a value of up to 20,000 dr, and 400 dr for cash with a value above 20,000 dr.

For travellers cheques the commission levied is 350 dr up to 20,000 dr; 450 dr for amounts between 20,000 and 30,000 dr; and a flat rate of 1.5% on amounts over 30,000 dr. No commission is charged on Eurocheques.

All post offices have exchange facilities for banknotes, travellers cheques and Eurocheques, and charge less commission than banks. It is often quicker to change money at a post office than in a bank. Many travel agencies and hotels will also change money, travellers cheques and Eurocheques at bank rates, but their commission charges are higher.

Tipping

In restaurants the service charge is included in the bill but it is the custom to leave a small amount. The practice is often just to round off the bill. Likewise for taxis – a small amount is appreciated.

Bargaining

Bargaining is not as widespread in Greece as it is further east. Prices in most shops are clearly marked and non-negotiable. The same applies to restaurants and public transport. It is always worth bargaining over the price of hotel rooms or *domatia* (the Greek equivalent of the British bed & breakfast, minus the breakfast), especially if you are intending to stay a few days. You may get short shrift in peak season, but prices can drop dramatically in the off season. Souvenir shops and market stalls are other places where your negotiating skills will come in handy. If you feel uncomfortable about haggling, walking away can be just as effective – you can always go back.

POST & COMMUNICATIONS

Post offices *(tahydromio)* are easily identifiable by means of the yellow signs outside. Regular post boxes are also yellow. The red boxes are for express mail only.

Postal Rates

The postal rate for postcards and air-mail letters to destinations within the EU is 120 dr for up to 20g and 200 dr for up to 50g. To other destinations the rate is 150 dr up to 20g and 240 dr for up to 150g. Post within Europe takes five to eight days and to the USA, Australia and New Zealand, nine to 11 days. *Periptera* (kiosks) also sell stamps, but with a 10% surcharge.

Express mail costs an extra 400 dr and should ensure delivery in three days within the EU – use the special red post boxes. Valuables should be sent registered post, which costs an extra 350 dr.

Sending Mail

Do not wrap a parcel until it has been inspected at a post office. In Athens, take your parcel to the Parcel Post Office (☎ 01-322 8940) in the arcade at Stadiou 4, and elsewhere to the parcel counter of a regular post office.

Receiving Mail

Mail can be sent poste restante (general delivery) to any main post office. The service is free of charge, but you are required to show your passport. Ask your friends and relatives to write your family name in capital letters and underline it, and to mark the envelope 'poste restante'. It is a good idea to ask the post-office clerk to check under your first name as well if letters you are expecting cannot be located. After one month, uncollected mail is returned to the sender. If you are about to leave a town and expected mail hasn't arrived, ask at the post office to have it forwarded to your next destination, c/- poste restante. See the Post & Communications section in the Athens chapter for addresses of post offices that hold poste-restante mail.

Parcels are not delivered in Greece; they must be collected from the parcel counter of a post office – or, in Athens, from the Parcel Post Office.

Telephone

The Greek telephone service is maintained by the public corporation known as Organis-mos Tilepikoinonion Ellados, which is always referred to by the acronym OTE (pronounced O-tay). The system is modern and efficient. Public telephones all use phonecards. They cost 1500 dr for 100 units, 6500 dr for 500 units, and 11,500 dr for 1000 units. The 100-unit cards are widely available from outlets such as periptera, corner shops and tourist shops. The 500 and 1000-unit cards can be bought at OTE offices. A local call costs one unit.

The phones are easy to use. The 'i' at the top left of the push-button dialling panel brings up the operating instructions in English. Don't remove your card before you are told to do so or you will wipe out the remaining credit.

Direct-dial long-distance and international calls can be made from public phones. It is also possible to use various national card schemes, such as Telecom Australia's Telecard, to make international calls. You will still need a phonecard to dial the scheme's access number, which will cost you one unit. International calls can also be made from OTE offices. They contain cubicles equipped with meters. A counter clerk tells you which cubicle to use, and payment is made afterwards. Villages and remote islands without OTE offices almost always have at least one metered phone for international and long-distance calls – usually in a shop, *kafeneio* (café) or taverna.

Another option is to use a periptero telephone. Almost every periptero has a metered telephone which can be used for local, long-distance and direct-dial international calls. There is a small surcharge, but it is less than that charged by hotels.

Reverse-charge (collect) calls can be made from an OTE office. The time you have to wait for a connection can vary considerably, from a few minutes to two hours. If you are using a private phone to make a reverse-charge call, dial the operator (domestic ☎ 151; international ☎ 161).

To call overseas direct, dial the Greek overseas-access code (00), followed by the country code for the country you are calling, then the local area code (dropping the leading zero if there is one) and then the number. The table below lists often used country codes and per-minute charges:

Country	Code	Cost per minute
Australia	61	236 dr
France	33	183 dr
Germany	49	183 dr
Ireland	353	183 dr
Italy	39	183 dr
Japan	81	319 dr
Netherlands	31	183 dr
New Zealand	64	319 dr
Turkey	90	183 dr
UK	44	183 dr
USA & Canada	1	236 dr

Off-peak rates are 25% cheaper. They are available to Africa, Europe, the Middle East and India from 10 pm to 6 am; to the Americas from 11 pm to 8 am; and to Asia and Oceania between 8 pm and 5 am.

Calls to Greece The international access code for Greece is ☎ 30.

Fax, Telex & Telegraph
Telegrams can be sent from any OTE office; larger offices have telex facilities. Main city post offices have fax machines.

E-mail
Greece has been slow off the mark in embracing the wonders of the Internet, but it's now striving to make up for lost time. Internet cafés are springing up everywhere, except it seems in Athens, and more and more hotels and businesses are adding e-mail to their addresses. The main problem at the time of writing was the limited number of lines operated by the main service providers.

BOOKS
Most books are published in different editions by different publishers in different countries. As a result, a book might be a hardcover rarity in one country while it's readily available in paperback in another. Fortunately, bookshops and libraries search by title or author, so your local bookshop or library is best placed to advise you on the availability of the following recommendations.

Lonely Planet
The Lonely Planet shoestring guides to *Mediterranean Europe* and *Western Europe* also include coverage of Greece. Lonely Planet's *Trekking in Greece* by Marc S Dubin is an in-depth guide to Greece's mountain paths, complemented with excellent maps.

These titles are available at major English-language bookshops in Athens, Thessaloniki, Rhodes and Iraklio. See the Bookshop entries in these sections for more details.

Guidebooks
The ancient Greek traveller Pausanias is acclaimed as the world's first travel writer. *The Guide to Greece* was written in the 2nd century BC. Umpteen editions later, it is now available in English in paperback. For archaeology buffs, the *Blue Guides* are hard to beat. They go into tremendous detail about all the major sites, and many of the lesser known ones. They have separate guides for Greece and Crete. In contrast, *Ebdon's Odyssey* by John Ebdon is a highly entertaining and irreverent account of travels in Greece.

Travel
During the 19th century many books about Greece were written by philhellenes who went to the country to help in the struggle for self-determination. *Travels in Northern Greece* by William Leake is an account of Greece in the last years of Ottoman rule. Leake was the British consul in Ioannina during Ali Pasha's rule. The English painter and writer Edward Lear, of *The Owl and the Pussy Cat* fame, spent some time in Greece in the mid-19th century and wrote *Journeys of a Landscape Painter* and *A Cretan Diary*.

Lawrence Durrell, who spent an idyllic childhood on Corfu, is the best known of the 20th-century philhellenes. His evocative books *Prospero's Cell* and *Reflections on a Marine Venus* are about Corfu and Rhodes respectively. His coffee-table book *The Greek Islands* is one of the most popular books of its kind. Even if you disagree with Durrell's opinions, you will probably concede that the photographs are superb. *My Family and Other Animals* by Gerald Durrell is a hilarious account of the Durrell family's chaotic and wonderful life on Corfu – Gerald and Lawrence were brothers.

Patrick Leigh Fermor, another ardent philhellene, is well-known for his exploits in rallying the Cretan resistance in WWII. He now lives in Kardamyli in the Peloponnese. His highly acclaimed book *The Mani* is an account of his adventures in the Mani peninsula during the 1950s, when many traditional customs were still in evidence. By the same author, *Roumeli* relates travels in northern Greece. *Deep into Mani* by Peter Greenhalgh & Edward Eliopoulis is a journey through the Mani some 25 years after Fermor's book about the area was written. If you are going to explore the Mani, this book (as well as those by Fermor) will greatly aid your appreciation of the region, which is one of the most strikingly beautiful in Greece.

Travels in the Morea by Nikos Kazantzakis is a highly readable account of the great writer's travels through the Peloponnese in the 1930s.

Under Mount Ida: A Journey into Crete by Oliver Burch is a compelling portrayal of this diverse and beautiful island – full of insights into its landscape, history and people.

If you are planning a trip to Mt Athos, and wish to get the most out of the experience, some preliminary reading is essential. The most informative and interesting accounts are *The Station* by Robert Byron and *Athos: the Holy Mountain* by Sidney Loch.

Katherine Kizilos vividly evokes Greece's landscapes, people and politics in her book *The Olive Grove: Travels in Greece*. She explores the islands and borderlands of her father's homeland, and experiences life in her family's village deep in the mountains of the Peloponnese. This is one of the many exciting titles in Journeys, Lonely Planet's new travel literature series.

People & Society

Of the numerous festivals held in Greece,

one of the most bizarre and overtly pagan is the carnival held on the island of Skyros. The definitive book on the subject is *The Goat Dancers of Skyros* by Joy Coulentianou.

The Cyclades, or Life Amongst the Insular Greeks by James Theodore Bent (first published 1885) has stood the test of time and is still the greatest English-language book about the Greek islands. It relates the experiences of the author and his wife during a year of travelling around the Cyclades in the late 19th century. Sadly, the book is out of print. (The Hellenic Book Service may have a second-hand copy; see the Bookshops section later in this chapter.)

Time, Religion & Social Experience in Rural Greece by Laurie Kain Hart is a fascinating account of village traditions – many of which are alive and well beneath the tourist veneer.

Portrait of a Greek Mountain Village, by Juliet du Boulay, is in a similar vein, based on the author's experiences in an isolated village.

A Traveller's Journey is Done and *An Affair of the Heart* , by Dilys Powell, wife of archaeologist Humfry Payne, are very readable, affectionate insights into village life in the Peloponnese during the 1920s and 1930s when Payne was excavating there.

Road to Rembetica: Music of a Greek Subculture – Songs of Love, Sorrow and Hashish by Gail Holst is an exploration of the intriguing subculture which emerged from the poverty and suffering of the refugees from Asia Minor.

The Colossus of Maroussi by Henry Miller is now regarded as a classic. With senses heightened, Miller relates his travels in Greece at the outbreak of WWII with feverish enthusiasm. Another book which will whet your appetite if you are contemplating a holiday in Greece is *Hellas: A Portrait of Greece* by Nicholas Gage.

Vanishing Greece by Clay Perry, with an introduction by Patrick Leigh Fermor, is a large and expensive book with magnificent photographs of the landscapes and people of rural Greece. But the message of the book is a sad one: that the rural culture of Greece, little changed since Homer's time, is fast vanishing.

History & Mythology

A Traveller's History of Greece by Timothy Boatswain & Colin Nicholson is probably the best choice for the layperson who wants a good general reference on the historical background of Greece. It gives clear and comprehensive coverage from Neolithic times to the present day. *Modern Greece: A Short History* by CM Woodhouse is in a similar vein, although it has a right-wing bent; Woodhouse makes no attempt to hide his glee at the fall of PASOK in 1990. The book covers the period from Constantine the Great to 1990.

Mythology was an intrinsic part of life in ancient Greece, and some knowledge of it will enhance your visit to the country. One of the best publications on the subject is *The Greek Myths* by Robert Graves (two volumes) which relates and interprets the adventures of the main gods and heroes worshipped by the ancient Greeks. Maureen O'Sullivan's *An Iconoclast's Guide to the Greek Gods* presents entertaining and accessible versions of the myths. The two volumes of Homer's *Odyssey* and *Iliad* translated by EV Rien are possibly the best translations of these epics – Homer's account of the Trojan War and Odysseus' (known as Ulysses in Latin) subsequent adventures. *Ovid's Metamorphoses* translated by AD Melville is a beautiful poetic interpretation of the Greek myths. Ovid (Publius Ovidius Naso) was a Roman who lived in the 1st century BC.

Women in Athenian Law and Life by Roger Just is the first in-depth study of the role of women in ancient Greece.

The Argonautica Expedition by Theodor Troev encompasses Greek mythology, archaeology, travel and adventure. It relates the voyage undertaken by the author and his crew in the 1980s following in the footsteps of Jason and the Argonauts. The aim of the expedition was to investigate the possibility that maritime and cultural links had existed between what is now the Georgian coast and other points in the ancient world.

Mary Renault's novels provide an excellent feel for ancient Greece. *The King Must Die* and *The Bull from the Sea* are vivid tales of Minoan times.

Mistras and Byzantine Style and Civilisation by Sir Steven Runciman and *Fourteen Byzantine Rulers* by Michael Psellus are both good introductions to the Byzantine Age – a period in the country's history which is often overlooked by visitors to Greece.

Farewell Anatolia and *The Dead are Waiting* by Dido Soteriou are two powerful novels focusing on the population exchange of 1923. Soteriou was born in Asia Minor in 1909 and was herself a refugee.

The Villa Ariadne by Dilys Powell is centred around the dwelling of the title, which was built by Sir Arthur Evans and still stands near Knossos. Many people who were prominent in the shaping of modern Crete were either residents or guests at this house at one time or another, so the book is a very readable account of recent Cretan history. Crete played a pivotal role during WWII and many books have been written about this period of the island's history. *The Cretan Runner* by Georgios Psychoundaki (translated by Patrick Leigh Fermor) is a graphic account of this traumatic time – the author was active in the island's resistance movement.

In a similar vein, *The Jaguar* by Alexander Kotzias is a moving story about the leftist resistance to the Nazi occupation of Greece. Although a novel, it is packed with historical facts. *Greek Women in Resistance* by Eleni Fountouri is a compilation of journals, poems and personal accounts of women in the resistance movement from the 1940s to the 1950s. The book also contains poignant photographs and drawings.

Eleni by Nicholas Gage is an account by the author of his family's struggle to survive the horrors of the civil war, and his mother's death at the hands of the communists. It was made into a film in 1985.

The third volume of Olivia Manning's Balkan trilogy, *Friends & Heroes* has Greece as its setting. It is based on the author's own experiences as the wife of a British Council lecturer, and is a riveting account of the chaos and confusion among the émigré community fleeing the Nazi invasion of Europe. *The Flight of Ikaros* by Kevin Andrews is another classic. The author relates his travels in Greece during the 1940s civil war. *Greece in the Dark* by the same author is an account of his life in Greece during the junta years.

Poetry

Sappho: A New Translation by Mary Bernard is the best translation of this great ancient poet's works.

Collected Poems by George Seferis, *Selected Poems* by Odysseus Elytis and *Collected Poems* by Constantine Cavafy are all excellent translations of Greece's greatest modern poets.

Novels

The most well-known and widely read Greek author is the Cretan writer Nikos Kazantzakis, whose novels are full of drama and larger-than-life characters. His most famous works are *The Last Temptation*, *Zorba the Greek*, *Christ Recrucified* and *Freedom or Death*. The first two have been made into films.

The Mermaid Madonna and *The Schoolmistress with the Golden Eyes* are two passionate novels by Stratis Myrivilis. Their settings are two villages on the island of Lesvos, the writer's birthplace. *When the Tree Sings* by Stratis Haviaras is a beautifully lyrical and impressionistic novel inspired by the author's experiences as a young boy in Greece during the traumatic 1940s.

The Australian journalists George Johnston and Charmian Clift wrote several books with Greek themes during their 19 years as expatriates, including Johnston's novel *The Sponge Divers*, set on Kalymnos, and Clift's autobiographical *A Mermaid Singing*, which is about their experiences on Hydra. Most evocative is Johnston's award-winning *Clean Straw For Nothing*, second in a trilogy, which was followed by the tragic *A Cartload of Clay*. The last two are clas-

sified as fiction but many close to Johnston and Clift believed the books mirrored their lives in Greece, England and Australia.

The experiences of Australian writer Gillian Bouras are recounted in her books about living in Greece – *A Foreign Wife* and *Aphrodite and the Others*. Fellow-Australian Beverley Farmer has two collections of beautifully written short stories, *Home Time* and *Milk*, many of which are about the experiences of foreigners who endeavour to make their home in Greece.

Museum Guides

Museums and Galleries of Greece and Cyprus by Maria Kontou, of the Ministry of Culture, lists 165 museums in Greek and English with about 1000 photographs to illustrate exhibits that relate to visual arts, natural history, navigation, science, technology and the theatre.

Botanical Field Guides

The Flowers of Greece & the Aegean by William Taylor & Anthony Huxley is the most comprehensive field guide to Greece. The Greek writer, naturalist and mountaineer George Sfikas has written many books on wildlife in Greece, some of which have been translated into English. Among them are *Wildflowers of Greece*, *Trees & Shrubs of Greece*, *Medicinal Plants of Greece* and *Wildflowers of Mt Olympos*.

Children's Books

Greek publishers Malliaris-Paedia put out a good series of books on the myths, retold in English for young readers by Aristides Kesopoulos. The titles are *The Gods of Olympus and the Lesser Gods*, *The Labours of Hercules*, *Theseus and the Voyage of the Argonauts*, *The Trojan War and the Wanderings of Odysseus* and *Heroes and Mythical Creatures*.

Robin Lister's retelling of *The Odyssey* is aimed at slightly older readers (ages eight to 10), but makes compelling listening for younger children when read aloud.

Bookshops

The bookshops in Greece which have the most comprehensive selections of foreign-language books (including English) are in Athens and Thessaloniki (see those sections). All other major towns and tourist resorts have bookshops that sell some foreign-language books. Imported books are expensive – normally two to three times the recommended retail price in the UK and the USA. Larger shops, such as Compendium in Athens, have some good deals, including the Penguin classics for 800 dr each. The Greek publisher Efstathiadis specialises in English translations of books by Greek authors as well as books about Greece by foreign authors. Many hotels have small collections of second-hand books to read or swap.

Abroad, the best bookshop for new and second-hand books about Greece, written in both English and Greek, is the Hellenic Book Service (☎ 0171-267 9499), 91 Fortress Rd, Kentish Town, London NW5 1AG. It stocks almost all of the books recommended here, and will take mail or telephone orders.

NEWSPAPERS & MAGAZINES

Greeks are great newspaper readers. There are 15 daily newspapers, of which the most widely read are *Ta Nea*, *Kathimerini* and *Eleftheros Typos*.

English-language newspapers are the daily (except Monday) *Athens News* (200 dr) which carries world news and Greek news, and the *Weekly Greek News* (250 dr), which carries predominantly Greek news. Both are widely available in Athens and at major resorts.

Atlantis (750 dr) is a monthly magazine with articles on politics, travel and the arts. It was previously known as *The Athenian*. *Scope* (400 dr) is a weekly listings magazine for the Athens entertainment scene.

Foreign newspapers are also widely available, although only between April and October in smaller resort areas. They include almost every British newspaper, the *Herald Tribune*, the *European* and international magazines such as *Time*, *Newsweek* and the *Economist*. The papers reach Athens (Syntagma) at 1 pm on the day of publication on weekdays, and at 7 pm on weekends. They are not available until the following day in other areas.

RADIO & TV

Greece has two state-owned radio channels, ET 1 and ET 2. ET 1 runs three programmes; two are devoted to popular music and news, while the third plays mostly classical music. It has a news update in English at 7.30 am from Monday to Saturday, and at 9 pm from Monday to Friday. It can be heard on 91.6 MHz and 105.8 MHz on the FM band, and 729 KHz on the AM band. ET 2 broadcasts mainly popular music. Local radio stations are proliferating at such a rate that the mountains around Athens have begun to look like pincushions. Western music fans can check out Radio Gold (105 FM), which plays mainly music from the 60s, or Kiss FM (90.9 FM), which plays a mixture of rock and techno. Athens International Radio (107.1 FM) broadcasts the BBC World Service live from 6.30 am to 11 pm. It has British and American news every hour on the hour. The broadcast area covers Aegina and much of Attica as well as Athens and Piraeus. Elsewhere, the best short-wave frequencies for picking up the World Service are:

GMT	Frequency
3 to 7.30 am	9.41 MHz (31m band)
	6.18 MHz (49m band)
	15.07 MHz (19m band)
7.30 am to 6 pm	12.09 MHz (25m band)
	15.07 MHz (19m band)
6.30 to 11.15 pm	12.09 MHz (25m band)
	9.41 MHz (31m band)
	6.18 MHz (49m band)

As far as Greek TV is concerned, quantity rather than quality is the operative word. There are nine TV channels and various pay-TV channels. All the channels show English and US films and soapies with Greek subtitles. A bit of channel-swapping will normally turn up something in English.

VIDEO SYSTEMS

If you want to record or buy video tapes to

play back home, you won't get a picture unless the image registration systems are the same. Greece uses PAL, which is incompatible with the North American and Japanese NTSC system. Australia uses PAL.

PHOTOGRAPHY & VIDEO
Film & Equipment
Major brands of film are widely available, although they can be expensive in smaller towns. In Athens, expect to pay about 1500 dr for a 36-exposure roll of Kodak Gold ASA 100; less for other brands. You'll find all the gear you need in the photography shops of Athens and major cities.

Photography
Because of the brilliant sunlight in summer, you'll get better results using a polarising lens filter.

Developing Film
As elsewhere in the world, developing film is a competitive business. Most places charge around 80 dr per print, plus a 400 dr service charge.

Video
Properly used, a video camera can give a fascinating record of your holiday. As well as videoing the obvious things – sunsets, spectacular views – remember to record some of the ordinary everyday details of life in the country. Often the most interesting things occur when you're actually intent on filming something else. Remember too that, unlike still photography, video 'flows' – so, for example, you can shoot scenes of countryside rolling past the train window, to give an overall impression that isn't possible with ordinary photos.

Video cameras these days have amazingly sensitive microphones, and you might be surprised how much sound will be picked up. This can also be a problem if there is a lot of ambient noise – filming by the side of a busy road might seem OK when you do it, but viewing it back home might simply give you a deafening cacophony of traffic noise. One good rule to follow for beginners is to try to film in long takes, and don't move the camera around too much. Otherwise, your video could well make your viewers seasick! If your camera has a stabiliser, you can use it to obtain good footage while travelling on various means of transport, even on bumpy roads. And remember, you're on holiday – don't let the video take over your life, and turn your trip into a Cecil B de Mille production.

Make sure you keep the batteries charged, and have the necessary charger, plugs and transformer for the country you are visiting. In most countries, it is possible to obtain video cartridges easily in large towns and cities, but make sure you buy the correct format. It is usually worth buying at least a few cartridges duty free to start off your trip.

Restrictions
Never photograph a military installation or anything else that has a sign forbidding photography.

Photographing People
Greeks usually love having their photos taken but always ask permission first. The same goes for video cameras, probably even more annoying and offensive for locals than a still camera.

TIME
Greece is two hours ahead of GMT/UTC and three hours ahead on daylight-saving time, which begins at 12.01 am on the last Sunday in March, when clocks are put forward one hour. Clocks are put back an hour at 12.01 am on the last Sunday in September.

So, when it is noon in Greece it is also noon in İstanbul, 10 am in London, 11 am in Rome, 2 am in San Francisco, 5 am in New York and Toronto, 8 pm in Sydney and 10 pm in Auckland.

ELECTRICITY
Electricity is 220v, 50 cycles. Plugs are the standard continental type with two round

pins. All hotel rooms have power points and most camping grounds have supply points.

WEIGHTS & MEASURES

Greece uses the metric system. Liquids – especially barrel wine – are often sold by weight rather than volume: 959g of wine, for example, is equivalent to 1000mL.

Remember that, like other continental Europeans, Greeks indicate decimals with commas and thousands with points.

LAUNDRY

Large towns and some islands have laundrettes, which charge from 2000 to 2500 dr to wash and dry a load whether you do it yourself or have it service-washed. Hotel and room owners will usually provide you with a washtub if requested.

HEALTH

Travel health depends on your predeparture preparations, your day-to-day health care while travelling and how you handle any medical problem or emergency that does develop. While the list of potential dangers can seem quite frightening, few travellers experience more than upset stomachs.

Predeparture Planning

Health Insurance Refer to Travel Insurance under Visas & Documents earlier in this chapter for information on health insurance.

Medical Kit It's wise to carry a small, straightforward medical kit. The kit should include:

- Aspirin or paracetamol (acetaminophen in the US) – for pain or fever.
- Antihistamine (such as Benadryl) – useful as a decongestant for colds and allergies, to ease the itch from insect bites or stings, and to help prevent motion sickness. There are several antihistamines on the market, all with different pros and cons (eg a tendency to cause drowsiness), so it's worth discussing your requirements with a pharmacist or doctor. Antihistamines may cause sedation and interact with alcohol so care should be taken when using them.
- Loperamide (eg Imodium) or Lomotil for diarrhoea; prochlorperazine (eg Stemetil) or

metaclopramide (eg Maxalon) for nausea and vomiting. Antidiarrhoea medication should not be given to children under the age of 12.
- Rehydration mixture – for treatment of severe diarrhoea. This is particularly important if travelling with children, but is recommended for everyone.
- Antiseptic such as povidone-iodine (eg Betadine), which comes as a solution, ointment, powder and impregnated swabs – for cuts and grazes.
- Bandages and plasters (Band-aids) – for minor injuries.
- Scissors, tweezers and a thermometer (note that mercury thermometers are prohibited by airlines).
- Insect repellent, sunscreen, chap stick and water purification tablets.

Warning Codeine, which is commonly found in headache preparations, is banned in Greece; check labels carefully, or risk prosecution. There are strict regulations applying to the importation of medicines into Greece, so obtain a certificate from your doctor which outlines any medication you may have to carry into the country with you.

Health Preparations Make sure you're healthy before you start travelling. If you are embarking on a long trip make sure your teeth are OK.

If you wear glasses take a spare pair and your prescription.

If you require a particular medication take an adequate supply, as it may not be available locally. Take the prescription or, better still, part of the packaging showing the generic rather than the brand name (which may not be locally available), as it will make getting replacements easier.

Immunisations

No jabs are required for travel to Greece but a yellow fever vaccination certificate is required if you are coming from an infected area. There are, however, a few routine vaccinations that are recommended. These should be recorded on an international health certificate, available from your doctor or government health department. Don't leave your vaccinations until the last minute as some require more than one injection. Recommended vaccinations include:

Tetanus & Diphtheria Boosters are necessary every 10 years and protection is highly recommended.

Polio A booster of either the oral or injected vaccine is required every 10 years to maintain our immunity from childhood vaccination. Polio is a very serious, easily transmitted disease which is still prevalent in many developing countries.

Hepatitis A The most common travel-acquired illness that can be prevented by vaccination. Protection can be provided in two ways – either with the antibody gamma globulin or with the vaccine Havrix 1440. Havrix 1440 provides long-term immunity (possibly more than 10 years) after an initial injection and a booster at six to 12 months. Gamma globulin is not a vaccination but a ready-made antibody which has proven very successful in reducing the chances of hepatitis infection. It should be given as close as possible to departure because it is at its most effective in the first few weeks after administration and the effectiveness tapers off gradually between three and six months.

Rabies Pretravel rabies vaccination involves having three injections over 21 to 28 days and should be considered by those who will spend a month or longer in a country where rabies is common, especially if they are cycling, handling animals, caving, travelling to remote areas, or children (who may not report a bite). If someone who has been vaccinated is bitten or scratched by an animal they will require two booster injections of vaccine; those not vaccinated will require more.

Basic Rules

Care in what you eat and drink is the most important health rule; stomach upsets are the most likely travel health problem (between 30% and 50% of travellers in a two-week stay experience this) but the majority of these upsets will be relatively minor. Don't become paranoid; trying the local food is part of the experience of travel, after all.

Food & Water Tap water is safe to drink in Greece, but mineral water is widely available if you prefer it. You might experience mild intestinal problems if you're not used to copious amounts of olive oil; however, you'll get used to it and current research says it's good for you.

If you don't vary your diet, are travelling hard and fast and missing meals, or simply lose your appetite, you can soon start to lose weight and place your health at risk. Fruit and vegetables are good sources of vitamins and Greece produces a greater variety of these than almost any other European country. Try to eat plenty of grains (including rice) and bread. If your diet isn't well balanced or if your food intake is insufficient, it's a good idea to take vitamin and iron pills.

In hot weather make sure you drink enough – don't rely on feeling thirsty to indicate when you should drink. Not needing to urinate or very dark yellow urine is a danger sign. Always carry a water bottle with you on long trips. Excessive sweating can lead to loss of salt and therefore muscle cramping. Salt tablets are not a good idea as a preventative, but in places where salt is not used much adding salt to food can help.

Everyday Health Normal body temperature is 37°C or 98.6°F; more than 2°C (4°F) higher indicates a high fever. The normal adult pulse rate is 60 to 100 per minute (children 80 to100, babies 100 to140). You should know how to take a temperature and a pulse rate. As a general rule the pulse increases about 20 beats per minute for each °C (2°F) rise in fever.

Respiration (breathing) rate is also an indicator of illness. Count the number of breaths per minute: between 12 and 20 is normal for adults and older children (up to 30 for younger children, 40 for babies). People with a high fever or serious respiratory illness (such as pneumonia) breathe more quickly than normal. More than 40 shallow breaths a minute may indicate pneumonia.

Avoid climatic extremes: keep out of the sun when it's hot, dress warmly when it's cold. Avoid potential diseases by dressing sensibly. You can avoid insect bites by covering bare skin when insects are around, by screening windows or beds and by using insect repellents.

Seek local advice: if you're told the water is unsafe due to jellyfish, crocodiles or bilharzia, don't go in. In situations where there is no information, discretion is the better part of valour.

Environmental Hazards

Sunburn By far the biggest health risk in Greece comes from the intensity of the sun. You can get sunburnt surprisingly quickly, even through cloud. Use a sunscreen and take extra care to cover areas which don't normally see sun – eg your feet. A hat provides added protection, and you should also use zinc cream or some other barrier cream for your nose and lips. Calamine lotion is good for mild sunburn. Greeks claim that yoghurt applied to sunburn is soothing. Protect your eyes with good-quality sunglasses.

Prickly Heat Prickly heat is an itchy rash caused by excessive perspiration trapped under the skin. Keeping cool but bathing often, using a mild talcum powder or even resorting to air-conditioning may help until you acclimatise.

Heat Exhaustion Dehydration or salt deficiency can cause heat exhaustion. Take time to acclimatise to high temperatures and make sure you drink sufficient liquids. Wear loose clothing and a broad-brimmed hat. Do not do anything too physically demanding.

Salt deficiency is characterised by fatigue, lethargy, headaches, giddiness and muscle cramps and in this case salt tablets may help. Vomiting or diarrhoea can deplete your liquid and salt levels.

Heat Stroke This serious, sometimes fatal, condition can occur if the body's heat-regulating mechanism breaks down and the body temperature rises to dangerous levels. Long, continuous periods of exposure to high temperatures can leave you vulnerable to heat stroke. You should avoid excessive alcohol consumption or strenuous activity when you first arrive in a hot climate.

The symptoms are feeling unwell, not sweating very much or at all and a high body temperature (39°C to 41°C or 102°F to 106°F). Where sweating has ceased the skin becomes flushed and red. Severe, throbbing headaches and lack of coordination will also occur, and the sufferer may be confused or aggressive. Eventually the victim will become delirious or convulse. Hospitalisation is essential, but in the interim get victims out of the sun, remove their clothing, cover them with a wet sheet or towel and then fan continually.

Fungal Infections Fungal infections, which occur with greater frequency in hot weather, are most likely to occur on the scalp, between the toes or fingers, in the groin and on the body. You get ringworm (which is a fungal infection, not a worm) from infected animals or by walking on damp areas, like shower floors.

To prevent fungal infections wear loose, comfortable clothes, avoid artificial fibres, wash frequently and dry carefully. If you do get an infection, wash the infected area daily with a disinfectant or medicated soap and water, and rinse and dry well. Apply an antifungal cream or powder like the widely available Tinaderm. Try to expose the infected area to air or sunlight as much as possible and wash all towels and underwear in hot water as well as changing them often.

Hypothermia Too much cold is just as dangerous as too much heat, particularly if it leads to hypothermia. Although everyone associates Greece with heat and sunshine, the high mountainous regions can be cool, even in summer. There is snow on the mountains from November to April. On the highest mountains in the north, snow patches can still be seen in June. Keeping warm while trekking in these regions in spring and autumn can be as much of a problem as keeping cool in the lower regions in summer.

Hypothermia occurs when the body loses heat faster than it can produce it and the core temperature of the body falls. It is surprisingly easy to progress from very cold to dangerously cold due to a combination of wind, wet clothing, fatigue and hunger, even if the air temperature is above freezing. It is best to dress in layers; silk, wool and some of the new artificial fibres are all good insulating materials. A hat is important, as a lot of heat is lost through the head. A strong, waterproof outer layer is essential, as keeping dry is vital. Carry basic supplies, including food containing simple sugars to generate heat quickly and lots of fluid to drink. A space blanket is something all travellers in cold environments should carry.

Symptoms of hypothermia are exhaustion, numb skin (particularly toes and fingers), shivering, slurred speech, irrational or violent behaviour, lethargy, stumbling, dizzy spells, muscle cramps and violent bursts of energy. Irrationality may take the form of sufferers claiming they are warm and trying to take off their clothes.

To treat mild hypothermia, first get the person out of the wind and/or rain, remove their clothing if it's wet and replace it with dry, warm clothing. Give them hot liquids – not alcohol – and some high-kilojoule, easily digestible food. Do not rub victims, instead allow them to slowly warm themselves. This should be enough to treat the early stages of hypothermia. The early recognition and treatment of mild hypothermia is the only way to prevent severe hypothermia, which is a critical condition.

Motion Sickness Sea sickness can be a problem. The Aegean is very unpredictable and gets very rough when the meltemi wind blows. Eating lightly before and during a trip will reduce the chances of motion sickness. If you are prone to motion sickness try to find a place that minimises disturbance – near the wing on aircraft, close to midships on boats, near the centre on buses. Fresh air usually helps; reading and cigarette smoke don't. Commercial motion-sickness preparations, which can cause drowsiness, have to be taken before the trip commences; when you're feeling sick it's too late. Ginger (available in capsule form) and peppermint (including mint-flavoured sweets) are natural preventatives.

Infectious Diseases
Diarrhoea Simple things like a change of water, food or climate can all cause a mild bout of diarrhoea, but a few rushed toilet trips with no other symptoms is not indicative of a major problem.

Dehydration is the main danger with any diarrhoea, particularly in children or the elderly as dehydration can occur quite quickly. Under all circumstances *fluid replacement* (at least equal to the volume being lost) is the most important thing to remember. Weak black tea with a little sugar, soda water, or soft drinks allowed to go flat and diluted 50% with clean water are all good.

Hepatitis Hepatitis is a general term for inflammation of the liver. It is a common disease worldwide. The symptoms are fever, chills, headache, fatigue, feelings of weakness and aches and pains, followed by loss of appetite, nausea, vomiting, abdominal pain, dark urine, light-coloured faeces, jaundiced (yellow) skin and the whites of the eyes may turn yellow. **Hepatitis A** is transmitted by contaminated food and drinking water. The disease poses a real threat to the western traveller. You should seek medical advice, but there is not much you can do apart from resting, drinking lots of fluids, eating lightly and avoiding fatty foods. People who have had hepatitis should avoid alcohol for some time after the illness, as the liver needs time to recover.

Hepatitis E is transmitted in the same way, and can be very serious in pregnant women.

There are almost 300 million chronic carriers of **Hepatitis B** in the world. It is spread through contact with infected blood, blood products or body fluids, for example through sexual contact, unsterilised needles and blood transfusions, or contact with blood via small breaks in the skin. Other risk situations include having a shave, tattoo, or having your body pierced with contaminated equipment. The symptoms of type B may be more severe and may lead to long-term problems. **Hepatitis D** is spread in the same way, but the risk is mainly in shared needles.

Hepatitis C can lead to chronic liver disease. The virus is spread by contact with blood – usually via contaminated transfusions or shared needles. Avoiding these is the only means of prevention.

Tetanus This potentially fatal disease is found worldwide. It is difficult to treat but is preventable with immunisation.

Rabies Rabies is a fatal viral infection found in many countries and is caused by a bite or scratch by an infected animal. It's rare, but it's found in Greece. Dogs are noted carriers as are monkeys and cats. Any bite, scratch or even lick from a warm-blooded, furry animal should be cleaned immediately and thoroughly. Scrub with soap and running water, and then clean with an alcohol or iodine solution. If there is any possibility that the animal is infected medical help should be sought immediately to prevent the onset of symptoms and death. Even if the animal is not rabid, all bites should be treated seriously as they can become infected or can result in tetanus. A rabies vaccination is now available and should be considered if you are in a high-risk category – eg if you intend to explore caves (bat bites can be dangerous), work with animals, or travel so far off the beaten track that medical help is more than two days away.

Sexually Transmitted Diseases Sexual contact with an infected sexual partner spreads these diseases. While abstinence is the only 100% preventative, using condoms is also effective. Gonorrhoea, herpes and syphilis are among these diseases; sores, blisters or rashes around the genitals, discharges or pain when urinating are common symptoms. In some STDs, such as wart virus or chlamydia, symptoms may be less marked or not observed at all in women. Syphilis symptoms eventually disappear completely but the disease continues and can cause severe problems in later years. The treatment of gonorrhoea and syphilis is with antibiotics.

There are numerous other sexually transmitted diseases, for most of which effective treatment is available. However, there is no cure for herpes and there is also currently no cure for AIDS.

HIV/AIDS HIV, the Human Immunodeficiency Virus, may develop into AIDS, Acquired Immune Deficiency Syndrome. HIV is a major problem in many countries. Any exposure to blood, blood products or bodily fluids may put the individual at risk. In many developing countries transmission is predominantly through heterosexual sexual activity. This is quite different from industrialised countries where transmission is mostly through contact between homosexual or bisexual males, or via contaminated needles shared by IV drug users. Apart from abstinence, the most effective preventative is always to practise safe sex using condoms. It is impossible to detect the HIV-positive status of an otherwise healthy-looking person without a blood test.

HIV/AIDS can also be spread through infected blood transfusions; some developing countries cannot afford to screen blood for transfusions. It can also be spread by dirty needles – vaccinations, acupuncture, tattooing and ear or nose piercing can be potentially as dangerous as intravenous drug use if the equipment is not clean. If you do need an injection, ask to see the syringe unwrapped in front of you, or better still, take a needle and syringe pack with you overseas – it is a cheap insurance package against infection with HIV.

Fear of HIV infection should never preclude treatment for serious medical conditions. Although there may be a risk of infection, it is very small indeed.

Insect-Borne Diseases
Typhus Tick typhus is a problem from April to September in rural areas, particularly areas where animals congregate. Typhus begins with a fever, chills, headache and muscle pains, followed a few days later by a body rash. There is often a large painful sore at the site of the bite and nearby lymph nodes are swollen and painful. There is no vaccine available. The best protection is to check your skin carefully after walking in danger

areas such as long grass and scrub. A strong insect repellent can help, and serious walkers in tick areas should consider having their boots and trousers impregnated with benzyl benzoate and dibutylphthalate. (See the Cuts, Bites & Stings section below for information about ticks.)

Lyme Disease Lyme disease is a tick-transmitted infection which may be acquired throughout Europe. The illness usually begins with a spreading rash at the site of the tick bite and is accompanied by fever, headache, extreme fatigue, aching joints and muscles and mild neck stiffness. If untreated, these symptoms usually resolve over several weeks but over subsequent weeks or months disorders of the nervous system, heart and joints may develop. The response to treatment is best early in the illness. The longer the delay, the longer the recovery period.

Cuts, Bites & Stings

Skin punctures can easily become infected in hot climates and may be difficult to heal. Treat any cut with an antiseptic such as povidone-iodine. Where possible avoid bandages and Band-aids, which can keep wounds wet.

Although there are a lot of bees and wasps in Greece, their stings are usually painful rather than dangerous. Calamine lotion or Stingose spray will give relief and ice packs will reduce the pain and swelling.

Snakes To minimise your chances of being bitten always wear boots, socks and long trousers when walking through undergrowth where snakes may be present. Don't put your hands into holes and crevices, and be careful when collecting firewood.

Snake bites do not cause instantaneous death and antivenenes are usually available. Keep the victim calm and still, wrap the bitten limb tightly, as you would for a sprained ankle, and then attach a splint to immobilise it. Then seek medical help, if possible with the dead snake for identification. Don't attempt to catch the snake if there is even a remote possibility of being bitten

again. Tourniquets and sucking out the poison are now comprehensively discredited.

Jelly Fish, Sea Urchins & Weever Fish Watch out for sea urchins around rocky beaches; if you get some of their needles embedded in your skin, olive oil will help to loosen them. If they are not removed they will become infected. Be wary also of jelly fish, particularly during the months of September and October. Although they are not lethal in Greece, their stings can be painful. Dousing in vinegar will deactivate any stingers which have not 'fired'. Calamine lotion, antihistamines and analgesics may reduce the reaction and relieve the pain. Much more painful than either of these, but thankfully much rarer, is an encounter with the weever fish. It buries itself in the sand of the tidal zone with only its spines protruding, and injects a painful and powerful toxin if trodden on. Soaking your foot in very hot water (which breaks down the poison) should solve the problem. It can cause permanent local paralysis in the worst instance.

Bedbugs & Lice Bedbugs live in various places, but particularly in dirty mattresses and bedding. Spots of blood on bedclothes or on the wall around the bed can be read as a suggestion to find another hotel. Bedbugs leave itchy bites in neat rows. Calamine lotion or Stingose spray may help.

All lice cause itching and discomfort. They make themselves at home in your hair, your clothing or in your pubic hair. You catch lice through direct contact with infected people or by sharing combs, clothing and the like. Powder or shampoo treatment will kill the lice and infected clothing should then be washed in very hot water.

Leeches & Ticks Leeches may be present in damp rainforest conditions; they attach themselves to your skin to suck your blood. Trekkers often get them on their legs or in their boots. Salt or a lighted cigarette end will make them fall off. Do not pull them off, as the bite is then more likely to become infected. An insect repellent may keep them away. You should always check your body if you have been walking through a potentially tick-infested area as ticks can cause skin infections and other more serious diseases.

Sheepdogs In Greece these dogs are trained to guard penned sheep from bears, wolves and thieves. They are often underfed and sometimes ill-treated by their owners. They are almost always all bark and no bite, but if you are going to trek into remote areas, you should consider having rabies injections (see Rabies). You are most likely to encounter these dogs in the mountainous regions of Epiros and Crete. Wandering through a flock of sheep over which one of these dogs is vigilantly (and possibly discreetly) watching is simply asking for trouble.

Women's Health
Gynaecological Problems Poor diet, lowered resistance due to the use of antibiotics for stomach upsets and even contraceptive pills can lead to vaginal infections when travelling in hot climates. Maintaining good personal hygiene, and wearing skirts or loose-fitting trousers and cotton underwear will help to prevent infections.

Yeast infections, characterised by a rash, itch and discharge, can be treated with a vinegar or lemon-juice douche, or with yoghurt. Nystatin, miconazole or clotrimazole suppositories are the usual medical prescription. Trichomoniasis and gardnerella are more serious infections; symptoms are a smelly discharge and sometimes a burning sensation when urinating. Male sexual partners must also be treated, and if a vinegar-water douche is not effective medical attention should be sought. Metronidazole (Flagyl) is the prescribed drug.

Pregnancy Most miscarriages occur during the first three months of pregnancy, so this is the most risky time to travel as far as your own health is concerned. Miscarriage is not uncommon, and can occasionally lead to

severe bleeding. The last three months should also be spent within reasonable distance of good medical care. A baby born as early as 24 weeks stands a chance of survival, but only in a good modern hospital. Pregnant women should avoid all unnecessary medication, but vaccinations and malarial prophylactics should still be taken where possible. Additional care should be taken to prevent illness and particular attention should be paid to diet and nutrition. Alcohol and nicotine, for example, should be avoided.

Hospital Treatment
Citizens of EU countries are covered for free treatment in public hospitals within Greece on presentation of an E111 form. Enquire at your national health service or travel agent in advance. Emergency treatment is free to all nationalities in public hospitals. In an emergency, dial ☎ 166. There is at least one doctor on every island in Greece and larger islands have hospitals. Pharmacies can dispense medicines which are available only on prescription in most European countries, so you can consult a pharmacist for minor ailments.

All this sounds fine, but although medical training is of a high standard in Greece, the health service is underfunded and one of the worst in Europe. Hospitals are overcrowded, hygiene is not always what it should be and relatives are expected to bring in food for the patient – which could be a problem for a tourist. Conditions and treatment are better in private hospitals, which are expensive. All this means that a good health-insurance policy is essential.

TOILETS
Other than at airports, and bus and train stations, public toilets are few and far between. If you're caught short, a visit to the nearest café is the best solution, although you will be expected to buy something while you are there.

WOMEN TRAVELLERS
Many women travel alone in Greece and, as

the crime rate is low, they are probably safer than they would be in most European countries. This does not mean that you should be lulled into complacency; bag snatching and rapes do occur, although violent offences are rare.

The biggest nuisance to foreign women travelling alone are the guys the Greeks have nicknamed *kamaki*. The word means 'fishing tridents' and refers to the kamaki's favourite pastime, which is 'fishing' for foreign women in order to have a sexual encounter which they can boast to their friends about.

A kamaki will approach and ask something like 'Where do you come from?' or 'Do you like Greece?'. A woman looking at a map gives him a good reason to approach and offer help. Ignoring him at this stage does not always work because a kamaki enjoys a challenge. He'll follow you for a while, but give up eventually. Unfortunately, in your efforts to shake him off, you've probably walked in the opposite direction to the way you wanted to go, and are hopelessly lost, so out will come the map again...

Dressing conservatively helps to a certain extent to keep kamakia at bay, as does looking as if you know where you are going, even if you haven't got a clue. However, these men are very much in the minority, and are a hassle rather than a threat. The majority of Greek men treat foreign women with respect, and are genuinely helpful.

GAY & LESBIAN TRAVELLERS

In a country where the church still plays a prominent role in shaping society's views on issues such as sexuality, it should come as no surprise that homosexuality is generally frowned upon – especially outside the major cities. While there is no legislation against homosexual activity, it pays to be discreet and to avoid open displays of togetherness.

This has not prevented Greece from becoming a popular destination for gay travellers. Athens has a busy gay scene, but most gay travellers head for the islands. Mykonos has long been famous for its bars, beaches and general hedonism, while Paros,

Rhodes, Santorini and Skiathos all have their share of gay hang outs.

The island of Lesvos (Mytilini), birthplace of the lesbian poet Sappho, has become something of a place of pilgrimage for lesbians.

Information The *Spartacus International Gay Guide*, published by Bruno Gmünder (Berlin), has 10 pages of information on Greece in its 1996/97 guide, listing gay venues everywhere from Alexandroupolis to Xanthi. For lesbians, the comprehensive international guide *Women Going Places* (Women Going Places Productions) is recommended. *Anfi* magazine is Greece's oldest gay and lesbian magazine. The monthly magazine *To Kraximo* has information about the local gay scene, but is published in Greek. There is also a *To Kraximo* bilingual pocket guide to gay Greece and Cyprus. On the Internet, a site called *Roz Mov* can be found at www.geocities.com/westhollywood/2225/index.html. It's in English and Greek, and contains travel info, gay press, organisations, events and legal issues.

Organisations The address of the Greek Gay Liberation Organisation is PO Box 2777, Athens GR 100 22.

DISABLED TRAVELLERS

If mobility is a problem and you wish to visit Greece, the hard fact is that most hotels, museums and ancient sites in Greece are not wheelchair accessible. This is partly due to the uneven terrain of much of the country, which, with its abundance of stones, rocks and marble, presents a challenge even for able-bodied people.

If you are determined, then take heart in the knowledge that disabled people do come to Greece for holidays. But the trip needs careful planning, so get as much information as you can before you go. The British-based Royal Association for Disability and Rehabilitation (RADAR) publishes a useful guide called *Holidays & Travel Abroad: A Guide for Disabled People*, which gives a good overview of facilities available to disabled travellers in Europe. Contact RADAR (☎ 0171-637 5400) at 25 Mortimer St, London W1N 8AB.

Lavinia Tours (☎ 031-23 2828; fax 031-21 9714), Egnatia 101 (PO Box 111 06), Thessaloniki 541 10, specialises in arranging tours for disabled travellers. The managing director, Eugenia Stravropoulou, has travelled widely both in Greece and abroad in her wheelchair.

SENIOR TRAVELLERS
Card-carrying EU pensioners can claim a range of benefits such as reduced admission charges at museums and ancient sites and discounts on trains.

TRAVEL WITH CHILDREN
Greece is a safe and relatively easy place to travel with children. Hotels and restaurants are both very accommodating when it comes to meeting their needs. The service in restaurants is normally very quick, which is great when you've got hungry children on your hands.

Children under four travel for free on ferries, while children between four and 10 pay half fare. Full fares apply for children over 10. Children under four also travel free on Greek buses, and pay half fare up to the age of 12. On domestic flights, you'll pay 10% of the fare to have a child under two sitting on your knee. Kids aged two to 12 pay half fare.

The main problem is a shortage of playgrounds and other recreational facilities for children – not a problem if you're at the beach. Many parents are surprised by how much their children enjoy the ancient sites. Young imaginations go into overdrive when let loose at somewhere like the 'labyrinth' at Knossos.

USEFUL ORGANISATIONS
Mountaineering Clubs
Ellinikos Orivatikos Syndesmos (EOS – Greek Alpine Club; ☎ 01-321 2429/2355) is the largest and oldest Greek mountaineering and trekking organisation. Its headquarters are at Plateia Kapnikareas 2, Athens – on

Ermou, 500m west of Syntagma. The headquarters of the Hellenic Federation of Mountaineering Clubs (☎ 01-323 4555; fax 01-323 7666) is at Karageorgi Servias 7, Athens – on the edge of Syntagma. Both of these organisations are underfunded and staffed by volunteers, but if you call or visit between 7 and 9 pm on a weekday, there should be someone there.

Automobile Associations
ELPA (☎ 01-779 1615), the Greek automobile club, has its headquarters on the ground floor of Athens Tower, Messogion 2-4, Athens 115 27. The ELPA offers reciprocal services to members of national automobile associations on production of a valid membership card. If your vehicle breaks down, dial ☎ 104.

DANGERS & ANNOYANCES
Theft
Crime, especially theft, is low in Greece, but unfortunately it is on the increase. The worst area is Omonia in Athens – keep track of your valuables here, on the metro and at the Sunday flea market. The vast majority of thefts from tourists are still committed by other tourists. Bearing this in mind, the biggest danger of theft is probably in dormitory rooms in hostels and at camp sites. So make sure you do not leave valuables unattended in such places. If you are staying in a hotel room, and the windows and door do not lock securely, ask for your valuables to be locked in the hotel safe – hotel proprietors are happy to do this.

Bar Scams
A warning needs to be given to solo male travellers about an unpleasant practice which is currently largely confined to Athens, although there have been cases in other cities. The practice follows this pattern: a male traveller enters a bar and buys a drink; the owner then offers him another drink. Women appear, more drinks are provided and the visitor relaxes as he realises that the women are not prostitutes, just friendly Greeks. The crunch comes at the end of the evening when

the traveller is presented with an exorbitant bill.

LEGAL MATTERS
Consumer Advice
The Tourist Assistance Programme operates in conjunction with various Greek consumer associations to help people who are having trouble with any tourism-related service. Legal advice is available in English, French and German. The main office (☎ 01-330 0673) is at Valtetsiou 43-45 in Athens. In Iraklio, Crete, contact the Consumers Association of Crete (☎ 081-240 666), Milatou 1 and Agiou Titou, and in Volos contact the Consumers Association of Volos (☎ 0421-39 266), Haziagari 51.

Drugs
Greek drug laws are the strictest in Europe. Greek courts make no distinction between possession and pushing. Possession of even a small amount of marijuana is likely to land you in jail.

BUSINESS HOURS
Banks are open Monday to Thursday from 8 am to 2 pm, and Friday from 8 am to 1.30 pm. Some banks in large towns and cities open from 3.30 to 6.30 pm in the afternoon and on Saturday morning.

All post offices are open Monday to Friday from 7.30 am to 2 pm. In the major cities they stay open until 8 pm, and open on Saturday from 7.30 am to 2 pm.

The opening hours of OTE offices (for long-distance and overseas telephone calls) vary according to the size of the town. In smaller towns they are usually open every day from 7.30 am to 3 pm; from 6 am until 11 pm in larger towns; and 24 hours in major cities like Athens and Thessaloniki.

In summer, shops are open from 8 am to 1.30 pm and from 5.30 to 8.30 pm on Tuesday, Thursday and Friday, and from 8 am to 2.30 pm on Monday, Wednesday and Saturday. They open 30 minutes later in winter. These times are not always strictly adhered to. Many shops in tourist resorts are open seven days a week. Periptera are open from early morning until late at night. They sell everything from bus tickets and cigarettes to hard-core pornography. Opening times of museums and archaeological sites vary, but most are closed on Monday.

PUBLIC HOLIDAYS
All banks and shops and most museums and ancient sites close during public holidays. National public holidays in Greece are:

New Year's Day	–	1 January
Epiphany	–	6 January
First Sunday in Lent	–	February
Greek Independence Day	–	25 March
Good Friday	–	March/April
(Orthodox) Easter Sunday	–	March/April
Spring Festival/Labour Day	–	1 May
Feast of the Assumption	–	15 August
Ohi Day	–	28 October
Christmas Day	–	25 December
St Stephen's Day	–	26 December

SPECIAL EVENTS
The Greek year is a succession of festivals and events, some of which are religious, some cultural, others an excuse for a good knees-up, and some a combination of all three. The following is by no means an exhaustive list, but it covers the most important events, both national and regional. If you're in the right place at the right time, you'll certainly be invited to join the revelry.

January
Feast of Agios Vasilios (Feast of St Basil)
The year kicks off with this festival on 1 January. A church ceremony is followed by the exchanging of gifts, singing, dancing and feasting; the New Year pie *(vasilopitta)* is sliced and the person who gets the slice containing a coin will supposedly have a lucky year.

Epiphany (the Blessing of the Waters)
On 6 January, Christ's baptism by St John is celebrated throughout Greece. Seas, lakes and rivers are blessed and crosses immersed in them. The largest ceremony takes place at Piraeus.

Gynaikratia
On 8 January a day of role reversal occurs in villages in the prefectures of Rodopi, Kilkis and Seres in northern Greece. Women spend the day in kafeneia (cafés) and other social centres where men usually congregate, while the men stay at home to do the housework.

February-March

Carnival

The Greek carnival season is the three weeks before the beginning of Lent (the 40-day period before Easter, which is traditionally a period of fasting). The carnivals are ostensibly Christian pre-Lenten celebrations, but many derive from pagan festivals. There are many regional variations, but fancy dress, feasting, traditional dancing and general merrymaking prevail. The Patras carnival is the largest and most exuberant, with elaborately decorated chariots parading through the streets. The most bizarre carnival takes place on the island of Skyros where the men transform themselves into grotesque 'half-man, half-beast' creatures by donning goat-skin masks and hairy jackets. Other carnivals worth catching are those at Athens, Veria, Zakynthos, Kefallonia, and at Naoussa in Macedonia.

Shrove Monday (Clean Monday)

On the Monday before Ash Wednesday (the first day of Lent), people take to the hills throughout Greece to have picnics and fly kites.

March

Independence Day

The anniversary of the hoisting of the Greek flag by Bishop Germanos at Moni Agias Lavras is celebrated on 25 March with parades and dancing. Germanos' act of revolt marked the start of the War of Independence. Independence Day coincides with the *Feast of the Annunciation*, so is also a religious festival.

March-April

Easter

In the Greek Orthodox religion, Easter is the most important festival. Emphasis is placed on the Resurrection rather than on the Crucifixion, so it is a joyous occasion. The festival commences on Good Friday with the procession of a shrouded bier (representing Christ's funeral bier) through the town or village. On Saturday evening the Resurrection mass takes place. At midnight, packed churches are plunged into darkness to symbolise Christ's passing through the underworld.

The ceremony of the lighting of candles which follows is the most significant moment in the Orthodox year, for it symbolises the Resurrection. Its poignancy and beauty are spellbinding. If you are in Greece at Easter you should endeavour to attend this ceremony, which ends with the setting off of fireworks and candle-lit processions through the streets. The Lenten fast ends on Easter Sunday with the cracking of red-dyed Easter eggs and an outdoor feast of roast lamb followed by Greek dancing. The day's greeting is *Hristos anesti* ('Christ is risen'), to which the reply is *Alithos anesti* ('Truly He is risen'). On both Palm Sunday (the Sunday before Easter) and Easter Sunday, St Spiridon (the mummified patron saint of Corfu) is taken out for an airing and joyously paraded through the town. He is paraded again in Corfu town on 11 August.

Feast of Agios Georgos

The feast day of St George, Greece's patron saint, and patron saint of shepherds, takes place on 23 April or the Tuesday following Easter (whichever comes first). It is celebrated at several places, but with particular exuberance in Arahova, near Delphi.

May

May Day

On the first day of May there is a mass exodus from towns to the country. During picnics, wildflowers are gathered and made into wreaths to decorate houses.

Anastenaria

This fire-walking ritual takes place on 21 May in Langadas near Thessaloniki. Villagers clutching icons dance barefoot on burning charcoal. See the Northern Greece chapter for more details about this ritual.

June

Navy Week

This naval festival is celebrated in June in fishing villages and ports throughout the country. Volos and Hydra have unique versions of these celebrations: in Volos there is a re-enactment of the departure of the *Argo*, for legend has it that Iolkos (from where Jason and the Argonauts set off in quest of the Golden Fleece) was near the city. Hydra commemorates Admiral Andreas Miaoulis, who was born on the island and was a hero of the War of Independence. There is a re-enactment of one of his naval victories, accompanied by feasting and fireworks.

Feast of St John the Baptist

This feast day on 24 June is widely celebrated. Wreaths made on May Day are kept until this day, when they are burned on bonfires.

July

Feast of Agia Marina (Feast of St Marina)

This feast day is celebrated on 17 July in many parts of Greece, and is a particularly important event on the Dodecanese island of Kassos.

Feast of Profitis Ilias

This feast day on 20 July is celebrated at hill-top churches and monasteries dedicated to the prophet, especially in the Cyclades.

August
Assumption

Greeks celebrate Assumption Day (15 August) with family reunions. The whole population seems to be on the move either side of the big day, so it's a good time to avoid public transport. The island of Tinos gets particularly busy because of its miracle-working icon of Panagia Evangelistria. It becomes a place of pilgrimage for thousands, who come to be blessed, healed or baptised, or just for the excitement of being there. Many are unable to find hotels and sleep out on the streets.

September
Genesis tis Panagias (the Virgin's Birthday)

This day is celebrated on 8 September throughout Greece with religious services and feasting.

Exaltation of the Cross

This is celebrated on 14 September throughout Greece with processions and hymns.

October
Feast of Agios Dimitrios

This feast day is celebrated in Thessaloniki on 26 October with wine drinking and revelry.

Ohi (No) Day

Metaxas' refusal to allow Mussolini's troops to traverse Greece in WWII is commemorated on 28 October with remembrance services, military parades, folk dancing and feasting.

December
Christmas Day

Although not as important as Easter, Christmas is still celebrated with religious services and feasting. Nowadays much 'western' influence is apparent, including Christmas trees, decorations and presents.

Summer Festivals & Performances
There are cultural festivals throughout Greece in summer. The most important are the Athens Festival (June-September), with drama and music performances in the Theatre of Herodes Atticus, and the Epidaurus Festival (July-September), with drama performances in the ancient theatre at Epidaurus. Others include the Philippi and Thasos Festival (July and August); the Renaissance Festival in Rethymno (July and August); the Dodoni Festival in Epiros (August); the Olympus Festival at Katerini and Litohoro (August); the Hippocratia Festival on Kos (August); and the Patras Arts Festival (August and September).

Summer is also the time for wine festivals where, for a nominal admission charge, you can drink as much as you like. The biggest are held at Rethymno and Alexandroupolis.

Thessaloniki hosts a string of festivals and events during September and October, including the International Trade Fair and the Feast of Agios Dimitrios (details on the latter in the list above).

The nightly son et lumière (sound and light) shows in Athens and Rhodes run from April to October. The Corfu show runs from May to September.

Greek folk dances are performed in Athens from mid-May to September and in Rhodes from May to October.

ACTIVITIES
Windsurfing
Windsurfing is the most popular water sport in Greece. Hsrysi Akti on Paros, and Vasiliki on Lefkada vie for the best windsurfing

Greece has plenty of beaches
ideally suited to windsurfing

beaches. According to an Australian magazine, Vasiliki is one of the best places in the world to learn the sport, but you'll see sailboards for hire on almost every beach, except the least developed ones. Hire charges range from 2000 to 2500 dr an hour. If you are a novice, most places that rent equipment also give instruction.

Sailboards may only be brought into Greece if a Greek national residing in Greece guarantees that it will be taken out again. To find out the procedure for arranging this, contact the Hellenic Windsurfing Association (☎ 01-323 0330), Filellinon 7, Athens.

Water-Skiing

Islands with water-ski centres are Chios, Corfu, Crete, Kythira, Lesvos, Paros, Skiathos and Rhodes.

Snorkelling & Diving

Snorkelling is enjoyable just about anywhere along the coast off Greece. Especially good places are Monastiri on Paros, Velanio on Skopelos, Paleokastritsa on Corfu, Telendos islet (near Kalymnos) and anywhere off the coast of Kastellorizo.

Diving is a another matter. Any kind of underwater activity using breathing apparatus is strictly forbidden other than under the supervision of a diving school. This is to protect the many antiquities in the depths of the Aegean. There are diving schools on the islands of Corfu, Crete (at Rethymno), Evia, Mykonos and Rhodes, and Halkidiki and Glyfada (near Athens) on the mainland. At Glyfada, contact the Aegean Dive Shop (☎ 01-894 5409), Pandoras 31.

Trekking

More than half of Greece is mountainous. It could be a trekkers' paradise, but there is one drawback. Like all organisations in Greece, the EOS (Ellinikos Orivatikos Syndesmos), the Greek Alpine Club, is grossly underfunded. Most EOS staff are volunteers who have full-time day jobs. Consequently, many of the paths in Greece are overgrown and inadequately marked. Don't be put off by this, however, as the most popular routes are

well walked and maintained. For trekking in more remote places, see Lonely Planet's *Trekking in Greece*.

On small islands it's fun to discover pathways for yourself. You are unlikely to get into danger as settlements or roads are never far away. You will encounter a variety of paths: *kalderimi* are cobbled or flagstone paths which link settlements and date back to Byzantine times. Sadly, many have been bulldozed to make way for roads. Donkey and mule paths are identifiable by droppings and brown dust on the paths. They are used by farmers, are easy to walk along, and usually lead to a settlement, field or farm. Goat tracks are also useful, as goats follow contours and zigzag up slopes – they never charge straight uphill. They can be very narrow and tricky to negotiate, but widen as they approach 'home' – a compound or enclosure.

There are also a number of companies running organised treks. One of the biggest is Trekking Hellas (☎ 01-323 4548; fax 01-325 1474), Filellinon 7, Athens 105 57.

Skiing

Greece provides some of the cheapest skiing in Europe. There are 16 resorts dotted around the mountains of mainland Greece, mainly in the north. The main skiing areas are Mt Parnassos, 195km north-west of Athens, and Mt Vermio, 110km west of Thessaloniki. There are no foreign package holidays to these resorts; they are used mainly by Greeks. Most have all the basic facilities and are a pleasant alternative to the glitzy resorts of northern Europe.

The season depends on snow conditions but runs approximately from January to the end of April. For further information pick up a copy of *Greece: Mountain Refuges & Ski Centres* from an EOT office. Information may also be obtained from the Hellenic Skiing Federation (☎ 01-524 0057; fax 01-524 8821), PO Box 8037, Omonia, Athens 100 10.

COURSES
Language

If you are serious about learning the language, an intensive course at the start of your stay is a good way to go about it. Most of the courses are in Athens, but there are also courses on the islands in summer.

The Athens Centre (☎ 01-701 2268; fax 01-701 8603), Arhimidous 48, has a very good reputation. Its courses cover five levels of proficiency from beginner to advanced. It holds eight immersion courses a year for beginners, packing 60 hours of class time into three weeks for 100,000 dr. The centre occupies a fine neoclassical building in the quiet residential suburb of Mets. In June and July, it runs additional courses at the Anargyrios and Korgialenios College on the island of Spetses.

XEN (the YWCA) (☎ 01-362 4291; fax 01-362 2400), at Amerikis 11, runs six-week beginners' courses starting in February, May and October. Courses involve 40 hours of class time and cost 50,000 dr.

Other places in Athens offering courses are the Hellenic American Union (☎ 01-362 9886), Massalias 22, and the Hellenic Language School, Zalongou 4 (☎ 01-362 8161; fax 01-363 9951). The Hellenic Language School also offers courses in Hania, Crete, during June, July and August.

The Hellenic Culture Centre (☎ & fax 01-647 7465, or 0275-61 482) runs courses on the island of Ikaria from June to October. Three-week beginners' courses are 125,000 dr, and there are also two-week courses for 95,000 dr. The centre can also arrange accommodation.

Courses in Modern Greek and Greek Civilisation are conducted at Corfu's Ionian University in July and August. Details are available at Deligiorgi 55-59 (☎ 01-522 9770) in Athens, or from the Secretariat of the Ionian University (☎ 0661-22 993/994) at Megaron Kapodistria 49, Corfu town.

Information about language courses is also available from EOT offices and Greek embassies.

Other Courses

XEN (see earlier in this section) also has courses in cookery, painting, photography, jewellery-making and Greek dancing – but

you will need to have done the Greek language course first because the instruction is in Greek.

The Dora Stratou Dance Company (☎ 01-324 4395) holds a series of folk-dancing workshops for amateurs during July and August. The *Weekly Greek News* carries information about this and other workshops.

WORK
Permits

EU nationals don't need a work permit, but they need a residency permit if they intend to stay longer than three months. Nationals of other countries are supposed to have a work permit.

English Tutoring

If you're looking for a permanent job, the most widely available option is to teach English. A TEFL (Teaching English as a Foreign Language) certificate or a university degree is an advantage but not essential. In the UK, look through the *Times Educational Supplement* or Tuesday's edition of the *Guardian* newspaper – in other countries, contact the Greek embassy.

Another possibility is to find a job teaching English once you are in Greece. You will see language schools everywhere. Strictly speaking, you need a licence to teach in these schools, but many will employ teachers without one. The best time to look around for such a job is late summer.

The notice board at the Compendium bookshop in Athens sometimes has advertisements looking for private English lessons.

Bar Work

The bars of the Greek islands could not survive without foreign workers and there are thousands of summer jobs up for grabs every year. The pay is not fantastic, but you get to spend a summer in the islands. May is the time to go looking. Hostels and travellers' hotels are other places that regularly employ foreign workers.

Summer Harvest

Seasonal harvest work seems to be monopolised by migrant workers from Albania, and is no longer a viable option for travellers.

Volunteer Work

The Hellenic Society for the Study & Protection of the Monk Seal and the Sea Turtle Protection Society of Greece both use volunteers for their monitoring programmes on the Ionian islands and the Peloponnese. The two organisations share a telephone number (☎ 01-364 4146) and address – Solomnou 35, Athens 106 82.

Street Performers

The richest pickings are to be found on the islands, particularly Mykonos, Paros and Santorini. Plaka is the place to go in Athens. The area outside the church on Kydathineon is the most popular spot.

Other Work

There are often jobs advertised in the classifieds of the English-language newspapers, or you can put an advertisement in one yourself. EU nationals can also make use of the OAED (Organismos Apasholiseos Ergatikou Dynamikou), the Greek National Employment Service, in their search for a job. The OAED has offices throughout Greece.

ACCOMMODATION

There is a range of accommodation available in Greece to suit every taste and pocket. All places to stay are subject to strict price controls set by the tourist police. By law, a notice must be displayed in every room, which states the category of the room and the price charged in each season. The price includes a 4.5% community tax and 8% VAT.

Accommodation owners may add a 10% surcharge for a stay of less than three nights, but this is not mandatory. A mandatory charge of 20% is levied if an extra bed is put into a room. During July and August, accommodation owners will charge the maximum price, but in spring and autumn, prices will drop by up to 20%, and perhaps by even more in winter. These are the times to bring your bargaining skills into action.

Rip-offs rarely occur, but if you suspect you have been exploited by an accommodation owner, report it to either the tourist police or regular police and they will act swiftly.

Mountain Refuges

There are 55 mountain refuges dotted around the Greek mainland, Crete and Evia. They range from small huts with outdoor toilets and no cooking facilities to comfortable modern lodges. They are run by the country's various mountaineering and skiing clubs. The EOT publication *Greece: Mountain Refuges & Ski Centres* has details about each refuge. Prices range from 1500 to 2000 dr per person, depending on the facilities.

Camping

There are almost 350 camping grounds in Greece. A few are operated by the EOT, but most are privately run. Very few are open outside the high season (April-October). The Greek Camping Association (☎ 01-346 5262) publishes an annual booklet listing all of the country's camp sites and their facilities. The association's address is Solonos 102, GR-196 80 Athens.

Camping fees are highest from 15 June to the end of August. Most camping grounds charge from 920 to 1000 dr per adult and 550 to 600 dr for children aged four to 12. There's no charge for children aged under four. Tent sites cost from 900 dr per night for small tents, and from 1200 dr per night for large tents. Caravan-site rates start at around 1400 dr.

Between May and mid-September it is warm enough to sleep out under the stars, although you will still need a lightweight sleeping bag to counter the pre-dawn chill. It's a good idea to have a foam pad to lie on and a waterproof cover for your sleeping bag.

Camping at nonofficial sites is illegal, but the law is not always strictly enforced. If you do decide to take a chance on this, make sure you are not camping on private land, and clear up all rubbish when you leave. If you are told to move by the police, do so without protest, as the law is occasionally enforced. Freelance camping is more likely to be tolerated on islands that don't have camp sites. It's wise to ask around before freelance camping anywhere in Greece.

Apartments

Self-contained family apartments are available in some hotels and domatia. There are also a number of purpose-built apartments, particularly on the islands, which are available for either long or short-term rental. Prices vary considerably according to the amenities offered. In Athens, the classified sections of the *Athens News* and *Weekly Greek News* both advertise apartments. The notice board at the Compendium bookshop in Athens is also worth a look. The tourist police may be able to help in other major towns. In rural areas and islands, ask in a kafeneio.

Domatia

Domatia are the Greek equivalent of the British bed & breakfast, minus the breakfast. Once upon a time domatia comprised little more than spare rooms in the family home which could be rented out to travellers in summer; nowadays, many are purpose-built appendages to the family house. Some come complete with fully equipped kitchens. Standards of cleanliness are generally high. The décor runs the gamut from cool grey marble floors, coordinated pine furniture, pretty lace curtains and tasteful pictures on the walls, to places so full of kitsch, you are almost afraid to move in case you break an ornament.

They remain a popular option for budget travellers. Domatia are classified A, B and C. Expect to pay 4000 to 6000 dr for a single, and 6000 to 9000 dr for a double, depending on the class, whether bathrooms are shared or private, and the season. In some domatia, you may be charged between 300 and 400 dr for hot water. Domatia are found throughout the mainland (except in large cities) and on almost every island which has a permanent population. Most domatia are available only between April and October.

From June to September domatia owners are out in force, touting for customers. They meet buses and boats, shouting 'Room, room!', and often carry photographs of their rooms. In peak season, it can prove a mistake not to take up an offer – but be wary of owners who are vague about the location of their accommodation. 'Close to town' can turn out to be way out in the sticks. If you are at all dubious, insist they show you the location on a map.

Hostels

There is only one youth hostel in Greece affiliated to the International Youth Hostel Federation (IYHF), the excellent Athens International Youth Hostel (☎ 01-523 4170). You don't need a membership card to stay there; temporary membership costs 500 dr per day.

Most youth hostels in Greece are run by the Greek Youth Hostel Organisation (☎ 01-751 9530), Damareos 75, 116 33 Athens. There are affiliated hostels in Athens, Mycenae, Olympia, Patras and Thessaloniki on the mainland, and on the islands of Corfu, Crete, Ios, Naxos, Santorini and Tinos. There are six on Crete – at Iraklio, Malia, Myrthios, Plakias, Rethymno and Sitia.

Other hostels belong to the Greek Youth Hostels Association (☎ 01-323 4107), Dragatsaniou 4, 105 59 Athens. It has hostels on the islands of Corfu, Crete (at Hersonisos and Iraklio) and Santorini.

Both organisations appear to be equally underfunded and facilities are often fairly primitive, but they are mostly very casual places. Their rates vary from 1500 to 2000 dr and you don't have to be a member to stay in any of them. Few have curfews.

There are XEN (YWCA) hostels for women only in Athens and Thessaloniki.

Traditional Settlements

Traditional settlements are old buildings of architectural merit that have been renovated and converted into tourist accommodation. These are terrific places to stay, but they are expensive – most are equivalent in price to an A or B-class hotel. The EOT publishes a leaflet with details of these places and you can reserve a room through them. Most of them are in the Peloponnese – tower houses at Aeropolis and Vathi on the Mani peninsula, a stone mansion in the central Aracadian mountain village of Dimitsana and converted monks' cells in Monemvasia. There are other traditional settlements on the islands of Santorini, Psara and Chios, and on the Pelion peninsula.

Pensions

Pensions in Greece are virtually indistinguishable from hotels. They are classed A, B or C. An A-class pension is equivalent in amenities and price to a B-class hotel, a B-class pension is equivalent to a C-class hotel and a C-class pension is equivalent to a D or E-class hotel.

Hotels

Hotels in Greece are divided into six categories: deluxe, A, B, C, D and E. Hotels are categorised according to the size of the room, whether or not they have a bar, and the ratio of bathrooms to beds, rather than standards of cleanliness, comfort of the beds and friendliness of staff – all elements which may be of greater relevance to guests. As one would expect, deluxe, A and B-class hotels have many amenities, private bathrooms and constant hot water. C-class hotels have a snack bar, rooms have private bathrooms, but hot water may only be available at certain times of the day. D-class hotels may or may not have snack bars, most rooms will share bathrooms, but there may be some with private bathrooms, and they may have solar-heated water, which means hot water is not guaranteed. E classes do not have a snack bar, bathrooms are shared and you may have to pay extra for hot water – if it exists at all.

Prices are controlled by the tourist police and the maximum rate that can be charged for a room should be displayed on a board behind the door. The classification is not often much of guide to price. Rates in D and E-class hotels are generally comparable with

domatia. You can pay anywhere from 9000 to 19,000 dr for a single in high season in C class and 12,000 to 25,000 dr for a double. Prices in B class range from 15,000 to 23,000 dr for singles, and from 23,000 to 30,000 dr for doubles; A-class prices are not much higher.

FOOD

Greek food does not enjoy a reputation as one of the world's great cuisines. Maybe that's because many travellers have experienced Greek cooking only in tourist resorts. The old joke about the Greek woman who, on summer days, shouted to her husband 'Come and eat your lunch before it gets hot', is based on truth. Until recently, food was invariably served lukewarm – which is how Greeks prefer it. Most restaurants that cater to tourists have now cottoned on that foreigners expect cooked dishes to be served hot, and improved methods of warming meals (including the dreaded microwave) have made this easier. If it is not hot, ask that it be served *zesto* or order grills, which have to be cooked to order. Greeks are fussy about fresh ingredients, and frozen food is rare.

Greeks eat out regularly, regardless of socioeconomic status. Enjoying life is paramount and a large part of this enjoyment comes from eating and drinking with friends.

By law, every eating establishment must display a written menu including prices. Bread will automatically be put on your table and usually costs between 100 and 200 dr, depending on the restaurant's category.

Where to Eat

Tavernas The taverna is usually a traditional place with a rough-and-ready ambience, although some are more up-market, particularly in Athens, resorts and big towns. In simple tavernas, a menu is usually displayed in the window or on the door, but not all have menus and you may be invited into the kitchen to peer into the pots and point to what you want. This is not merely a privilege for tourists; Greeks also do it because they want to see the taverna's version of the dishes on offer. Some tavernas don't open until 8 pm, and then stay open until the early hours. Some are closed on Sunday.

Restaurants A restaurant *(estiatorio)* is more sophisticated than a taverna, with damask tablecloths, smartly attired waiters and printed menus at each table – often with an English translation. Ready-made food is usually displayed in a *bain-marie* and there may be a charcoal grill. Some restaurants offer breakfast and remain open all day while others serve lunch between 1 and 3 pm and dinner from 8 pm to 1 am. Some close on Sunday. Restaurants specialising in spit roasts and charcoal-grilled food – usually lamb, pork or chicken – are called *psistaria*.

Ouzeria An *ouzeri* serves ouzo. Greeks believe it is essential to eat when drinking alcohol so, in traditional establishments, your drink will come with a small plate of titbits or *mezedes* (appetisers) – perhaps olives, a slice of feta and some pickled octopus. Ouzeria are becoming trendy and are increasingly offering menus with larger choices of appetisers and main courses.

Galaktopoleia A *galaktopoleio* (literally 'milk shop') sells dairy produce including milk, butter, yoghurt, rice pudding, cornflour pudding, custard, eggs, honey and bread. It may also sell home-made ice cream in several flavours. Look for the sign *pagoto politiko* displayed outside. Most have seating and serve coffee and tea. They are inexpensive for breakfast and usually open from very early in the morning until evening.

Zaharoplasteia A *zaharoplasteio* (pâtisserie) sells cakes (both traditional and western), chocolates, biscuits, sweets, coffee, soft drinks and, possibly, bottled alcoholic drinks. They usually have some seating.

Kafeneia Kafeneia are often regarded by foreigners as the last bastion of male chauvinism in Europe. With bare light bulbs, nicotine-stained walls, smoke-laden air, rickety wooden tables and raffia chairs, they are frequented by middle-aged and elderly

Greek men in cloth caps who while away their time fiddling with worry beads, playing cards or backgammon or engaged in heated political discussion. It was once unheard of for women to enter kafeneia but, in large cities, this situation is changing.

In rural areas, Greek women are rarely seen inside kafeneia. When a female traveller enters one, she is inevitably treated courteously and with friendship if she manages a few Greek words of greeting. If you feel inhibited about going into a kafeneio, opt for outside seating. You'll feel less intrusive. Kafeneia originally only served Greek coffee but, now, most also serve soft drinks, Nescafé and beer. They are generally fairly cheap, with Greek coffee for about 150 dr and Nescafé with milk for 250 dr or less. Most kafeneia are open all day every day, but some close during siesta time (roughly from 3 to 5 pm).

Other Eateries Infiltrations from other countries include pizzerias, crêperies and *gelaterias* (which sell Italian-style ice cream in various flavours). You'll also find the occasional Chinese, Japanese or Indian restaurant in Athens and Thessaloniki but authenticity of cuisine cannot be guaranteed and prices tend to be high.

Meals

Breakfast Most Greeks have Greek coffee and perhaps a cake or pastry for breakfast. Budget hotels and pensions offering breakfast provide it continental style (rolls or bread with jam, and tea or coffee) and up-market hotels serve breakfast buffets (western and continental styles). Otherwise, restaurants and galaktopoleia serve bread with butter, jam or honey; eggs; and the budget travellers' favourite, yoghurt *(yiaourti)* with honey. In tourist areas, many menus offer an 'English' breakfast – which means bacon and eggs.

Lunch This is eaten late – between 1 and 3 pm – and may be either a snack or a complete meal. The main meal can be lunch or dinner

– or both. Greeks enjoy eating and often have two large meals a day.

Dinner Greeks also eat dinner late. Many people don't start to think about food until about 9 pm, which is why some restaurants don't bother to open their doors until after 8 pm. In tourist areas dinner is often served earlier.

A full dinner in Greece begins with appetisers and/or soup, followed by a main course of either ready-made food, grilled meat, or fish. Only very posh restaurants or those pandering to tourists include western-style desserts on the menu. Greeks usually eat cakes separately in a galaktopoleio or zaharoplasteio.

Greek Specialities
Snacks Favourite Greek snacks include pretzel rings sold by street vendors, *tost* (toasted sandwiches), *tyropitta* (cheese pie), *bougatsa* (custard-filled pastry), *spanakopitta* (spinach pie) and *sandouits* (sandwiches). Street vendors sell various nuts and dried seeds such as pumpkin for 200 to 400 dr a bag. Chestnuts are roasted on the roadsides in the autumn.

Mezedes In a simple taverna, possibly only three or four mezedes (appetisers) will be offered – perhaps taramasalata (fish-roe dip), tzatziki (yoghurt, cucumber and garlic dip), olives and feta (sheep's or goat's milk cheese). Ouzeria and restaurants usually offer wider selections.

Mezedes include *ohtapodi* (octopus), *garides* (shrimps), *kalamaria* (squid), dolmades (stuffed vine leaves), *melitzanosalata* (aubergine or eggplant dip) and *mavromatika* (black-eyed beans). Hot mezedes include *keftedes* (meatballs), *fasolia* (broad white beans), *loukanika* (little sausages), *tyropitta* (cheese pie), spanakopitta (spinach pie), *bourekaki* (tiny meat pie), *kolokythakia* (deep-fried zucchini), *melitzana* (deep-fried aubergine) and *saganaki* (fried cheese). It is quite acceptable to make a full meal of these instead of a main course. Three plates of mezedes are about equivalent in price and quantity to one main course. You can also order a *pikilia* (mixed plate).

Soups Soup is a satisfying starter or, indeed, an economical meal in itself with bread and a salad. Psarosoupa is a filling fish soup with vegetables, while kakavia (Greek bouillabaisse) is laden with seafood and more expensive – but heavenly. Economical fasolada (bean soup) is also a meal in itself. Avgolemano soupa (egg and lemon soup) is usually prepared from a chicken stock. And, if you're into offal, don't miss the traditional Easter soup mayiritsa at this festive time.

Salads The ubiquitous (and no longer inexpensive) Greek or village salad *horiatiki salata* is a side dish for Greeks, but many drachma-conscious tourists make it a main dish. It consists of peppers, onions, olives, tomatoes and feta cheese, sprinkled with oregano and dressed with olive oil and lemon juice. A tomato salad often comes with onions, cucumber and olives, and, with bread, makes a satisfying lunch. In winter, try the cheaper *radikia salata* (dandelion salad).

Main Dishes The most common main courses are *moussaka* (layers of eggplant or zucchini, minced meat and potatoes topped with cheese sauce and baked), *pastitsio* (baked cheese-topped macaroni and béchamel, with or without minced meat), dolmades (stuffed vine leaves) and *yemista* (stuffed tomatoes or green peppers). Other main courses include *giouvetsi* (casserole of lamb or veal and pasta), *stifado* (meat stewed with onions), *soutzoukakia* (spicy meatballs in tomato sauce, also known as Smyrna sausages) and *salingaria* (snails in oil with herbs). *Melizanes papoutsakia* is baked eggplant stuffed with meat and tomatoes, and topped with cheese, which looks, as its Greek name suggests, like a little shoe. Spicy loukanika (sausage) is a good budget choice and comes with potatoes or rice. Lamb fricassee, cooked with lettuce *arni fricassée me maroulia* is usually filling enough for two to share.

A Greek Feast

Greek dishes are easy to prepare at home. Here's a simple lunch or dinner to share with friends. Recipes serve four people.

Tzatziki (Cucumber & Yoghurt Dip) Peel and grate a medium cucumber. Add a cup of yoghurt, a tablespoon of olive oil, a pinch of salt, a teaspoon of vinegar, 1 teaspoons of freshly chopped dill and a minced garlic clove and refrigerate for two hours. Garnish with an olive and serve with fresh crusty bread or as a companion to vegetables or fried fish.

Soupa Avgolemono (Egg & Lemon Soup) Add 6 tablespoons of uncooked rice to six cups of boiling chicken, fish or beef stock, then cover and simmer until the rice is tender. Beat two eggs, adding a pinch of salt and the juice of a large lemon. Add the stock to this mixture slowly, so that it doesn't curdle, then pour the mixture into a pot for reheating. Stir and ensure it does not boil.

Soutzoukakia (Sausages from Smyrna) This hearty dish originated in Smyrna (İzmir) in the days of Greek occupation and has subsequently been adopted by the cooks of Thessaloniki. Soak two slices of white bread in a half cup of water, mash and add three garlic cloves finely chopped, half a teaspoon of pepper and a dessertspoon of cumin.

Add 500g (1lb) of minced lamb or beef and a beaten egg, mix well and form into small sausages. Place in an oiled roasting pan and bake in a medium to hot oven until the sausages brown on the base side. Turn the sausages and add 500g (1lb) of tomatoes, a dollop of butter and teaspoon of sugar and return to the oven for about 15 minutes – or until the tomatoes are soft and the *soutzoukakia* are brown on the other side. Serve with fried potatoes or rice, and salad.

Halvas tou Fournou (Baked Halva) Here's a delightful dessert that is simple to make. Sift half a cup of flour with two teaspoons of baking powder and a pinch of salt. Add two cups of semolina and a cup of finely chopped nuts. Cream ¾ of a cup of butter or margarine with a cup of sugar and add three beaten eggs and grated lemon peel. Combine the mixtures well, then pour into a greased, square, 25cm (10-inch) pan. Bake in a medium oven until golden. Boil three cups of water with three cups of sugar, add four cloves and a half stick of cinnamon, then pour over the rest of the dessert. Leave it to stand until the cinnamon and clove mixture has been absorbed, then serve with or without cream, warm or cold. It's filling and keeps for days. ■

Fish is usually sold by weight in restaurants but is not as cheap nor as widely available as it used to be. The Mediterranean has been overfished – sometimes legally, to satisfy a growing demand from restaurateurs in big cities, and sometimes illegally by dynamiting. Calamari (squid), deep-fried in batter, remains a tasty option for the budget traveller at 900 to 1300 dr for a generous serve. Other reasonably priced fish (about 1000 dr a portion) are *marides* (whitebait), sometimes cloaked in onion, pepper and tomato sauce, and *gopes*, which are similar to sardines. More expensive are *ohtapodi* (octopus), *bakaliaros* (cod), *xifias* (swordfish) and *glossa* (sole). Ascending the price scale further are *synagrida* (snapper) and *barbounia* (red mullet). *Astakos* (lobster) and *karabida* (crayfish) are top of the range at about 10,000 dr per kg.

Fish is mostly grilled or fried. More imaginative fish dishes include shrimp casserole and mussel or octopus saganaki (fried with tomato and cheese) and psarosoupa (fish soup). As Greece has few rivers and lakes, freshwater fish are not widely available, although reasonably priced *pestrofa* (trout) is found in Epiros, from Lake Pamvotis in Ioannina, the Aoös river in Zagoria, and also from the Prespa Lakes in Macedonia.

Desserts Greek cakes and puddings include *baklava* (layers of filo pastry filled with honey and nuts), *loukoumades* (puffs or fritters with honey or syrup), *kataïfi* (chopped nuts inside shredded wheat pastry or filo soaked in honey), *rizogalo* (rice pudding), *loukoumi* (Turkish delight), *halva* (made from semolina or sesame seeds) and *pagoto* (ice cream). Tavernas and restaurants usually only have a few of these on the menu. The best places to go for these delights are galaktopoleia or zaharoplasteia.

Regional Dishes

Greek food is not all moussaka and souvlaki. Every region has its own specialities and it need not be an expensive culinary adventure to discover some of these. Corfu, for example, which was never occupied by the Turks, retains traditional recipes of Italian, Spanish and ancient Greek derivations. Corfiot food is served in several restaurants and includes *sofrito* (lamb or veal with garlic, vinegar and parsley), *pastitsada*, (beef with macaroni, cloves, garlic, tomatoes and cheese) and *burdeto* (fish with paprika and cayenne). Look for poultry and venison in the Peloponnese, citrus-flavoured dishes in Argolis (along with succulent fresh oranges and lemons), and eggplant dishes in Argos and try the famed olives when in Kalamata. Only in Epiros will you find freshwater crustaceans, trout, carp and eel, cooked to special recipes. Game is inevitably on the menu in Thessaly and Macedonia.

Santorini's baby tomatoes flavour distinctive dishes, not least a rich soup as thick and dark as blood. The *myzithra* (soft ewe's milk cheese) of Ios is unique, and the lamb pies of Kefallonia and Crete are worth searching for. Andros' speciality, *froutalia* (spearmint-flavoured potato and sausage omelette), is good value. Rhodes' special, baked omelette is loaded with meat and zucchini. Spetses' baked fish is renowned. Soutzoukakia, while available nationally, are best in Thessaloniki where most cooks dare to add the cumin needed to give them oomph.

If you're out in the countryside and the loud bangs disturbing you are not caused by children setting off fire crackers in celebration of Easter or Independence Day, it will be shooting season. Be prepared to be offered pigeon, partridge, duck and hare (sometimes written on the menu as rabbit).

Vegetarian Food

Greece has few vegetarian restaurants. Unfortunately, many vegetable soups and stews are based on meat stocks. Fried vegetables are safe bets as olive oil is always used – never lard. The Greeks do wonderful things with artichokes *(aginares)*, which thrive in Greece. Stuffed, served as a salad, as a meze, (particularly with raki in Crete) and as the basis of a vegetarian stew, the artichoke warrants greater discovery by visitors. Vegetarians who eat eggs can be assured that an economical omelette can be whipped up anywhere. Salads are cheap, fresh, substantial and nourishing. Other options are yoghurt, rice pudding, cheese and spinach pies, and nuts. Crêperies also offer tasty vegetarian selections.

Lent, incidentally, is a good time for vegetarians because the meat is missing from many dishes.

Fast Food

Western-style fast food has arrived in Greece in a big way. Fans of McDonald's will find their favourite burger in a number of locations in Athens and major towns. There are also a host of similar franchises like Wendy's and Goody's, as well as chicken and pizza chains.

It's hard, though, to beat eat-on-the-street Greek offerings. Foremost among them are the *gyros* and the souvlaki. The gyros is a giant skewer laden with slabs of seasoned meat which grills slowly as it rotates and the meat is trimmed steadily from the outside; souvlaki are small individual kebab sticks. Both are served wrapped in pitta bread, with salad and lashings of tzatziki.

Fruit

Greece grows many varieties of fruit. Most visitors will be familiar with *syka* (figs), *rodakina* (peaches), *stafylia* (grapes), *karpouzi* (watermelon), *milo* (apples), *portokalia* (oranges) and *kerasia* (cherries).

Many will not, however, have encountered the *frangosyko* (prickly pear). Also known as the Barbary fig, it is the fruit of the opuntia cactus, recognisable by the thick green spiny pads that form its trunk. The fruit are borne around the edge of the pads in late summer and autumn and vary in colour from pale orange to deep red. They are delicious but need to be approached with extreme caution because of the thousands of tiny prickles (invisible to the naked eye) that cover their skin. Never pick one up with your bare hands. They must be peeled before you can eat them. The simplest way to do this is to trim the ends off with a knife and then slit the skin from end to end.

Another fruit that will be new to many people is the *mousmoula* (loquat). These small, orange fruit are among the first of summer, reaching the market in mid-May. The flesh is juicy and pleasantly acidic.

Self-Catering

Eating out in Greece is as much an entertainment as a gastronomic experience, so to self-cater is to sacrifice a lot. If, however, you are on a low budget you will need to make the sacrifice – for breakfast and lunch at any rate. All towns and villages of any size have well-stocked supermarkets, fruit and vegetable stalls, bakeries, and a weekly *laïki agora* market.

Many towns also have huge indoor food markets which feature fruit and vegetable stalls, butchers, dairies and delicatessens, all under one roof.

Only in isolated villages and on remote islands is food choice limited. There may only be one all-purpose shop – a *pantopoleio* which will stock meat, vegetables, fruit, bread and tinned foods.

DRINKS
Nonalcoholic Drinks

Coffee & Tea Greek coffee is the national drink. It is a legacy of Ottoman rule and, until the Turkish invasion of Cyprus in 1974, the Greeks called it Turkish coffee. It is served with the grounds, without milk, in a small cup. Connoisseurs claim there are at least 30 variations of Greek coffee, but most people know only three – *glyko* (sweet), *metrio* (medium) and *sketo* (without sugar).

The next most popular coffee is instant, called Nescafé (which it usually is). Ask for Nescafé *me ghala* (pronounced 'me GA-la') if you want it with milk. In summer, Greeks drink Nescafé chilled, with or without milk and sugar – this version is called *frappé*.

Espresso and filtered coffee are served only in trendy cafés. Cappuccino is often seen on menus but tends to be the Viennese rather than the Italian version. Or at least, the Greek version of a Viennese cappuccino, which is a strange concoction of black instant coffee with synthetic cream floating on top. You'll pay through the nose for it – more than 500 dr. If you want an Italian cappuccino, ensure it's what the café serves before you order. Tea is inevitably made with a tea bag.

Fruit Juice Packaged fruit juices are available everywhere. The Life range is especially good. It includes peach, *sanguini* (blood orange), Ruby grapefruit and Valencia orange. Fresh orange juice is not hard to find, but doesn't come cheap.

Milk Fresh milk can be hard to find on the islands and in remote areas. Elsewhere, you'll have no problem. A litre costs about 330 dr. UHT milk is available almost everywhere, as is condensed milk.

Soft Drinks Coca-Cola, Pepsi, Seven-Up,

Sprite and Fanta are available everywhere in cans and bottles.

Water Tap water is safe to drink in Greece but, if you prefer it, bottled spring water is sold widely in 500mL and 1.5L plastic bottles. If you're happy with tap water, fill a container with it before embarking on ferries or you'll wind up paying through the nose for bottled water. Sparkling mineral water is seldom seen.

Alcohol

Beer All the beers produced in Greece are brewed under licence by off-shoots of major northern European breweries. The most popular beers are Amstel and Heineken. Amstel is cheaper than Heineken, and bottles are cheaper than cans. Supermarkets are the cheapest place to buy beer. A 500mL bottle of Amstel costs about 190 dr (including 25 dr deposit on the bottle), while a 500mL can costs about 240 dr. Amstel also produces a low-alcohol beer and a bock, which is dark, sweet and strong.

Other beers brewed locally are Henniger, Kaiser, Kronenbourg and Tuborg. Imported lagers, stouts and beers are found in tourist spots such as music bars and discos. You might even spot Newcastle Brown, Carlsberg, Castlemaine XXXX and Guinness.

Wine According to mythology, the Greeks invented or discovered wine and it has been produced in Greece on a large scale for more than three thousand years.

The modern wine industry, though, is still very much in its infancy. Until the 1950s, most Greek wines were sold in bulk and were seldom distributed any further afield than the nearest town. It wasn't until industrialisation (and the resulting rapid urban growth) that there was much call for bottled wine. Quality control was unheard of until 1969, when appellation laws were introduced as a precursor to applying for membership of the European Community, and wines have improved significantly since then. The big private wineries have introduced new tech-nology, and cooperative wineries and some smaller growers are following suit.

Don't expect Greek wines to taste like French wines. The varieties grown in Greece are quite different. Some of the most popular and reasonably priced labels include Rotonda, Kambas, Boutari, Calliga and Lac des Roches. Boutari's Naoussa is worth looking out for. It's a dry red wine from the Naoussa area of north-west Macedonia.

More expensive, but of good quality, are the Achaïa-Clauss wines from Patras. The most expensive wines are the Kefallonian Robola de Cephalonie, a superb dry white, and those produced by the Porto Carras estate in Halkidiki. Good wines are produced on Rhodes (famous in Greece for its champagne) and Crete. Other island wines worth sampling are those from Samos (immortalised by Lord Byron), Santorini, Kefallonia and Paros. *Aspro* is white, *mavro* is red and *kokkinelli* is rosé.

Strong Liquor Ouzo is the most popular aperitif in Greece. Distilled from grape stems and flavoured with anise, it is similar to the Middle Eastern *arak*, Turkish *raki* and French Pernod. Clear and colourless, it turns white when water is added. A 700mL bottle of a popular brand like Ouzo 12, Olympic or Sans Rival costs about 1000 dr. In an ouzeri, a glass costs from 250 to 400 dr. It will be served neat, with a separate glass of water to be used for dilution.

The second-most popular spirit is Greek brandy, which is dominated by the Metaxa label. Metaxa comes in a wide choice of grades, starting with three star – a high-octane product without much finesse. You can pick up a bottle in a supermarket for about 1500 dr. The quality improves as you go through the grades: five star, seven star, VSOP, Golden Age and finally the top-shelf Grand Olympian Reserve (4400 dr). Other reputable brands include Cambas and Votrys. The Cretan speciality is raki, a fiery clear spirit that is served as a greeting (regardless of the time of day).

If you're travelling off the beaten track, you may come across *chipura*. Like ouzo, it's made from grape stems but without the

Retsina

A holiday in Greece would not be the same without a jar or three of retsina, the famous – some might say notorious – resinated wine that is the speciality of Attica and neighbouring areas of Central Greece.

Your first taste of retsina may well leave you wondering whether the waiter has mixed up the wine and the paint stripper, but stick with it – it's a taste that's worth acquiring. Soon you will be savouring the delicate pine aroma, and the initial astringency mellows to become very moreish. Retsina is very refreshing consumed chilled at the end of a hot day, when it goes particularly well with tzatziki.

Contrary to popular belief, the resinous flavour of retsina does not come from its storage barrels

Greeks have been resinating wine, both white and rosé, for millennia. The ancient Greeks dedicated the pine tree to Dionysos, also the god of wine, and held that land that grew good pine would also grow good wine.

No-one seems quite sure how wine and pine first got together. The consensus is that it was an inevitable accident in a country with so much wine and so much pine. The theory that resin entered the wine-making process because the wine was stored in pine barrels does not hold water, since the ancients used clay amphora rather than barrels. It's more likely that it was through pine implements and vessels used elsewhere in the process. Producers discovered that wine treated with resin kept for longer, and consumers discovered that they liked it.

Resination was once a fairly haphazard process, achieved by various methods such as adding crushed pine cones to the brew and coating the insides of storage vessels. The amount of resin also varied enormously. One 19th-century traveller wrote that he had tasted a wine 'so impregnated with resin that it almost took the skin from my lips'. His reaction was hardly surprising; he was probably drinking a wine with a resin content as high as 7.5%, common at the time. A more sophisticated product awaits the modern traveller, with a resin content no higher than 1% – as specified by good old EU regulations. That's still enough to give the wine its trademark astringency and pine aroma.

The bulk of retsina is made from two grape varieties, the white *savatiano* and the red *roditis*. These two constitute the vast majority of vine plantings in Attica, Central Greece and Evia. Not just any old resin will do; the main source is the Aleppo pine *(Pinus halepensis)*, which produces a resin known for its delicate fragrance.

Retsina is generally cheap and it's available everywhere. Supermarkets stock retsina in a variety of containers ranging from 500mL bottles to 5L casks and flagons. Kourtaki and Cambas are both very good, but the best (and worst) still flows from the barrel in traditional tavernas. Ask for *heema*, which means 'loose'. ■

anise. It's an acquired taste, much like Irish poteen and packing a similar punch. You'll most likely encounter chipura in village kafeneia or private homes.

There have been reports, mainly from Ios and Paros, about hooch (flavoured to taste like well-known spirits) being sold in place of the genuine article. Beware of citrus-flavoured shots, often given or sold cheaply, to give one a thirst for more strong, straight stuff.

ENTERTAINMENT
Cinemas

Greeks are keen movie-goers and almost every town of consequence has a cinema. English-language films are shown in English with Greek subtitles. Admission ranges from 1000 dr in small-town movie houses to 1800 dr at plush big-city cinemas.

Discos & Music Bars

Discos can be found in big cities and resort areas, though not in the numbers of a decade ago.

Most young Greeks prefer to head for the music bars that have proliferated to fill the void. These bars normally specialise in a particular style of music – Greek, modern rock, 60s rock, techno and, very occasionally, jazz.

Ballet, Classical Music & Opera

Unless you're going to be spending a bit of time in Athens or Thessaloniki, you're best off forgetting about ballet, classical music and opera while in Greece. See the Entertainment section of the Athens chapter for information on venues.

Theatre

The highlight of the Greek dramatic year is the staging of ancient Greek dramas at the Theatre of Herodes Atticus in Athens during the Athens Festival from late June to early September. Performances are also staged at the amazing Theatre of Epidaurus. See the Special Events section of the Athens chapter and the Epidaurus section of the Peloponnese chapter for more information.

Rock

Western rock music continues to grow in popularity, but live music remains a rarity outside Athens and Thessaloniki.

Traditional Music

Most of the live music you hear around the resorts is tame stuff laid on for the tourists. If you want to hear music played with a bit

---

Traditional Greek Music & Dancing

Music and dancing have played an important role in Greek social life since the dawn of Hellenism. You may even think at times that Greeks live solely for the chance to sing and to participate in dancing. You wouldn't be that wrong. Whether it be at a traditional wedding, a night club, an Athenian *boîte* or a simple village *kafeneion*, a song and a dance are not far from people's minds.

The style of dancing often reflects the climate or disposition of the participants. In Epirus, the stately *tsamiko* is slow and highly emotive, reflecting the often cold and insular nature of mountain life. The Pontian Greeks, on the contrary, have a highly visual, vigorous and warlike form of dancing reflecting years of altercations with their Turkish neighbours. The *kotsari* is one of the best examples of this unique dance form. The islands with their bright and cheery atmosphere give rise to lilting music and matching dances such as the *ballos* or the *syrtos*, while the graceful *kalamatianos* circle dance, most commonly seen at Greek festive occasions, reflects years of proud Peloponnese tradition. The so-called 'Zorba's dance' or *syrtaki* is a stylised dance for two or three men or women with linked arms on shoulders, while the often spectacular solo male *zeïmbekikos* with its whirling improvisations has its roots in the Greek blues of the hashish dens and prisons of prewar times. The women counterpoint this self-indulgent and showy male display with their own sensuous *tsifteteli*, a svelte, sinewy show of femininity evolved from the Middle-Eastern belly dance.

Music is as widely divergent as dancing. The ubiquitous stringed *bouzouki* closely associated with contemporary music is a relative newcomer to the game, while the plucked strings of the bulbous *outi* (oud), the strident sound of the Cretan *lyra* (lyre) and the staccato rap of the *toumberleki* lap drum bear witness to a rich range of musical instruments that share many common characteristics with instruments all over the Middle East. Musical forms range from the *rembetika* – the Greek blues, to *dimotika* – humble folk poetry sung and more often than not accompanied by the *klarino* (clarinet) and *defi* (tambourine) and to the widely popular middle-of-the-road *elafrolaïka*, best exemplified by the songs of Giannis Parios. The unaccompanied, polyphonic *pogonisia* songs of northern Epirus and southern Albania are spine-chilling examples of a musical genre that owes its origins to Byzantium. At the lesser end of the scale, the curiously popular *skyladika* or 'dog-songs' – presumably because they resemble a whining dog – are hugely popular in night clubs known as *bouzouxidika* where the bouzouki reigns supreme, but where musical taste sometimes takes a back seat. ■

The distinctly Greek bouzouki

of passion, the rembetika clubs in Athens are strongly recommended.

Folk Dancing

The pre-eminent folk dancers in Greece are the ones who perform at the Dora Stratou Theatre on Filopappos hill in Athens, where performances take place nightly in summer. Another highly commendable place is the Old City Theatre, Rhodes City, where the Nelly Dimoglou Dance Company performs during the summer months. Folk dancing is an integral part of all festival celebrations and there is often impromptu folk dancing in tavernas.

SPECTATOR SPORT

Soccer (football) remains the most popular spectator sport, although basketball is catching up fast following the successes of Greek sides in European club competition in recent years. Greek soccer teams, in contrast, have seldom had much impact on European club competition, and the national team is the source of constant hair-wrenching. The side's only appearance in the World Cup finals, in the USA in 1994, brought a string of heavy defeats.

The two glamour clubs of Greek soccer are Olympiakos of Piraeus and Panathinaikos of Athens. The capital supplies almost a third of the clubs in the first division (see under Spectator Sports in the Athens chapter for more information). The season lasts from September to the middle of May; cup matches are played on Wednesday night and first division games on Sunday afternoon. Games are often televised. Entry to a match costs around 1500 dr for the cheapest terrace tickets, or 3000 dr for a decent seat. Fixtures and results are given in the *Athens News*.

Olympiakos and Panathinaikos are the glamour clubs of Greek basketball. Panathinaikos was European champion in 1996, and Olympiakos followed suit in 1997.

THINGS TO BUY

Greece produces a vast array of handicrafts. The Centre of Hellenic Tradition, at Pandrossou 36, Plaka, Athens, has a good range.

Antiques

It is illegal to buy, sell, possess or export any antiquity in Greece (see the Customs section earlier in this chapter). However, there are antiques and 'antiques'; a lot of items only a century or two old are regarded as junk, rather than part of the national heritage. These items include handmade furniture and odds and ends from rural areas in Greece, ecclesiastical ornaments from churches and items brought back from far-flung lands. Good hunting grounds for this 'junk' are Monastiraki and the flea market in Athens and the Piraeus market held on Sunday morning (see the Piraeus section in the Athens chapter).

Ceramics

You will see ceramic objects of every shape and size – functional and ornamental – for sale throughout Greece. The best places for high-quality handmade ceramics are Athens, Rhodes and the islands of Sifnos and Skyros.

There are a lot of places selling plaster copies of statues, busts, grave steles etc.

Leather Work

There are leather goods for sale throughout Greece; most are made from leather imported from Spain. The best place for buying leather goods is Hania on Crete. Bear in mind that the goods are not as high quality or as good value as those available in Turkey.

Jewellery

You could join the wealthy North Americans who spill off the cruise ships onto Mykonos to indulge themselves in the high-class gold jewellery shops there. But although gold is good value in Greece, and designs are of a high quality, it is priced beyond the capacity of most tourists' pockets. If you prefer something more reasonably priced, go for filigree-silver jewellery. Ioannina is the filigree-jewellery centre of Greece.

Bags

Tagari bags are woven wool bags – often brightly coloured – which hang from the shoulder by a rope. Minus the rope, they make attractive cushion covers.

Getting There & Away

Most travellers arrive in Greece by air, the cheapest and quickest way to get there. Whichever way you're travelling, make sure you take out travel insurance. This covers you not only for medical expenses and luggage theft or loss, but also for cancellations or delays in your travel arrangements under certain circumstances (you might fall seriously ill two days before departure, for example). The kind of cover you get depends on your insurance and type of ticket, so ask both your insurer and your ticket-issuing agency to explain where you stand. Ticket loss is also (usually) covered by travel insurance. Make sure you have a separate record of all your ticket details – or better still, a photocopy. Buy travel insurance as early as possible. If you buy it just before you fly, you may find that you're not covered for such problems as delays caused by industrial action.

Paying for your ticket with a credit card sometimes provides limited travel insurance, and you may be able to reclaim the payment if the operator doesn't deliver. In the UK, for instance, credit-card providers are required by law to reimburse consumers if a company goes into liquidation and the amount in contention is more than UK£100. Ask your credit-card company what it's prepared to cover.

AIR
Airports & Airlines
Greece has 16 international airports, but only those at Athens, Thessaloniki, Iraklio (Crete), Rhodes and Corfu take scheduled flights. Athens handles the vast majority of flights, including all intercontinental traffic.

Thessaloniki has direct connections to Brussels, Copenhagen, Dusseldorf, Frankfurt, İstanbul, Cyprus, London, Milan, Munich, Nuremberg, Paris, Stockholm, Tiranë, Vienna and Zürich. Most of these flights are with Greece's national airline, Olympic Airways, or the flag carrier of the country concerned. Iraklio has Olympic Airways flights to Rome and Vienna, while Transavia flies to Amsterdam, and Lufthansa to Frankfurt. From the middle of June, Olympic Airways has direct links from Corfu to Milan and Rome.

Greece's other international airports are at Mykonos, Santorini (Thira), Hania (Crete), Kos, Karpathos, Samos, Skiathos, Hrysoupolis (for Kavala), Preveza (for Lefkada), Kefallonia and Zakynthos. These airports are used exclusively for charter flights, mostly from the UK, Germany and the Scandinavian countries. Charter flights also fly to all of Greece's other international airports.

In Greece, as with everywhere else, always remember to reconfirm your onward or return bookings by the specified time – usually 72 hours before departure on international flights. If you don't, there's a risk that you'll turn up at the airport only to find that you've missed your flight because it was rescheduled, or that the airline has given the seat to someone else.

There is an airport tax of 6100 dr on all international departures. This is paid when you buy your ticket, not at the airport.

If you are buying a ticket out of Greece, Athens is one of the major centres in Europe for budget airfares.

Buying Tickets
If you are flying to Greece from outside Europe, the plane ticket will probably be the most expensive item in your budget, and buying it can be an intimidating business. There will be a multitude of airlines and travel agents hoping to separate you from your money, and it's well worth taking time to research the options. Start early: some of the cheapest tickets have to be bought months in advance, and popular flights tend to sell out early.

Discounted tickets fall into two distinct categories: official and unofficial. Official discount schemes include advance-purchase

Air Travel Glossary

Apex Apex, or 'advance purchase excursion' is a discounted ticket which must be paid for in advance. There are penalties if you wish to change it.

Baggage Allowance This will be written on your ticket: usually 20kg to go in the hold, plus one item of hand luggage.

Bucket Shop An unbonded travel agency specialising in discounted airline tickets.

Bumped Just because you have a confirmed seat doesn't mean you're going to get on the plane – see Overbooking.

Cancellation Penalties If you have to cancel or change an Apex ticket there are often heavy penalties involved; insurance can sometimes be taken out against these penalties. Some airlines impose penalties on regular tickets as well, particularly against 'no show' passengers. See the Getting Around chapter for details on cancellation penalties levied on domestic Olympic Airways flights.

Check In Airlines ask you to check in a certain time ahead of the flight departure (usually 1 hours before international flights). If you fail to check in on time and the flight is overbooked the airline can cancel your booking and give your seat to somebody else.

Lost Tickets If you lose your airline ticket, an airline will usually treat it like a travellers' cheque and, after enquiries, issue you with another one. Legally, however, an airline is entitled to treat it like cash and if you lose it then it's gone forever. Take good care of your tickets.

No Shows No shows are passengers who fail to show up for their flight, sometimes due to unexpected delays or disasters, sometimes due to simply forgetting, sometimes because they made more than one booking and didn't bother to cancel the one they didn't want. Full-fare passengers who fail to turn up are sometimes entitled to travel on a later flight. The rest of us are penalised (see Cancellation Penalties).

Overbooking Airlines hate to fly empty seats and since every flight has some passengers who fail to show up (see No Shows) airlines often book more passengers than they have seats. Usually the excess passengers balance those who fail to show up but occasionally somebody gets bumped. If this happens, guess who it is most likely to be? The passengers who check in late.

Reconfirmation At least 72 hours prior to the departure time of an onward or return flight you must contact the airline and 'reconfirm' that you intend to be on the flight. If you don't do this the airline can delete your name from the passenger list and you could lose your seat. You don't have to reconfirm for the first flight on your itinerary or if you're on a stopover of less than 72 hours. It doesn't hurt to reconfirm more than once.

Restrictions Discounted tickets often have various restrictions on them – advance purchase is the most usual one (see Apex). Others are restrictions on the minimum and maximum period you must be away, such as a minimum of 14 days or a maximum of one year. See Cancellation Penalties.

Tickets Out An entry requirement for many countries is that you have an onward or return ticket, in other words, a ticket out of the country. If you're not sure what you intend to do next, the easiest solution is to buy the cheapest onward ticket to a neighbouring country or a ticket from a reliable airline which can later be refunded if you do not use it.

Transferred Tickets Airline tickets cannot be transferred from one person to another. Travellers sometimes try to sell the return half of their ticket, but officials can ask you to prove that you are the person named on the ticket. This is unlikely to happen on domestic flights, but on an international flight tickets may be compared with passports.

Travel Periods Some officially discounted fares, Apex fares in particular, vary with the time of year. There is often a low (off-peak) season and a high (peak) season. Sometimes there's an intermediate or shoulder season as well. At peak times, when everyone wants to fly, not only will the officially discounted fares be higher but so will unofficially discounted fares or there may simply be no discounted tickets available. Usually the fare depends on your outward flight – if you depart in the high season and return in the low season, you pay the high-season fare. ■

---

tickets, budget fares, Apex, Super-Apex and a few other variations on the theme. These tickets can be bought both from travel agents and direct from the airline. They often have restrictions on them – advance purchase is the usual one. Others are restrictions on the

minimum and maximum period you must be away, such as a minimum of 14 days and a maximum of one year.

Unofficial tickets are simply discounted tickets that the airlines release through selected travel agents. Don't go looking for discounted tickets straight from the airlines because they are available only through travel agents.

Return tickets always work out much cheaper than two one-way tickets; in some cases, *cheaper* than a one-way ticket. Generally, you can find discounted tickets at prices as low, or even lower, than Apex or budget tickets. Phone around the travel agents for bargains.

Charter Flights

Charter-flight tickets are usually the cheapest of all – and the most restrictive. These tickets are for seats left vacant on flights which have been block booked by package-tour companies. However, conditions apply on charter flights to Greece. A ticket must be accompanied by an accommodation booking. This is normally circumvented by issuing accommodation vouchers which are not meant to be used – even if the hotel named on the voucher actually exists. The law requiring accommodation bookings was introduced in the 1980s to prevent budget travellers flying to Greece on cheap charter flights and sleeping rough on beaches and in parks. It hasn't worked.

The main catch for travellers using charter flights involves visits to Turkey. If you fly to Greece with a return ticket on a charter flight, you will forfeit the return portion if you visit Turkey. Greece is one of several popular charter destination countries which have banded together to discourage tourists from leaving the destination country during the duration of the ticket. The countries involved want to ensure that people don't flit off somewhere else to spend their tourist dollars. The result is that if you front up at the airport for your return charter flight with a Turkish stamp in your passport, you will be forced to buy another ticket.

This does not apply if you take a day excursion into Turkey, because the Turkish immigration officials do not stamp your passport. Neither does it apply to regular or excursion-fare flights.

Charter-flight tickets are valid for up to four weeks, and usually have a minimum-stay requirement of at least three days. Sometimes it's worth buying a charter return even if you want to stay for longer than four weeks. The tickets can be so cheap that you can afford to throw away the return portion.

The place to look for cheap charter deals is the travel sections of major newspapers. More information on charter flights is given later in this chapter under specific point-of-origin headings.

Courier Flights

Another option (sometimes even cheaper than a charter flight) is a courier flight. This deal entails accompanying freight or a parcel that will be collected at the destination. The drawbacks are that your time away may be limited to one or two weeks, your luggage is usually restricted to hand luggage (the parcel or freight you carry comes out of your luggage allowance), and you may have to be a resident of the country that operates the courier service and apply for an interview before they'll take you on.

Travel Agents

Many of the larger travel agents use the travel pages of national newspapers and magazines (like *Time Out)* to promote their special deals. Before you make a decision, there are a number of questions you need to ask about the ticket. Find out the airline, the route, the duration of the journey, the stopovers allowed, any restrictions on the ticket and – above all – check the price. Ask whether the fare quoted includes all taxes and other possible inclusions.

You may discover when you start ringing around that those impossibly cheap flights, charter or otherwise, are not available – but the agency just happens to know of another one that 'costs a bit more'. Or the agent may claim to have the last two seats available for Greece for the whole of July, which they will hold for a maximum of two hours. Don't panic – keep ringing around.

If you are flying to Greece from the USA, South-East Asia or the UK, you will probably find that the cheapest flights are being advertised by obscure agencies whose names haven't yet reached the telephone directory – the proverbial bucket shops. Many such firms are honest and solvent, but there are a few rogues who will take your money and disappear, only to reopen elsewhere a month or two later under a new name. If you feel suspicious about a firm, don't give them all the money at once – leave a small deposit and pay the balance when you get the ticket. If they insist on cash in advance, go somewhere else or be prepared to take a big risk. Once you have booked the flight with the agency, ring the airline to check that you have a confirmed booking.

It can be easier on the nerves to pay a bit more for the security of a better known travel agent. Firms such as STA Travel, which has offices worldwide, Council Travel in the USA or Travel CUTS in Canada offer good prices to Europe (including Greece), and are unlikely to disappear overnight.

The fares quoted in this book are intended as a guide only. They are approximate and are based on the rates advertised by travel agents at the time of going to press.

Travellers with Special Needs

If you've broken a leg, you're a vegetarian or require a special diet, you're travelling in a wheelchair, taking a baby or whatever, let the airline staff know as soon as possible – preferably when booking your ticket. Check that your request has been registered when you reconfirm your booking (at least 72 hours before departure) and again when you check in at the airport.

Children under two years of age travel for 10% of the standard fare (or free, on some airlines) as long as they don't occupy a seat. But they do not get a baggage allowance. 'Skycots' should be provided by the airline if requested in advance; these will take a child weighing up to about 10kg. Olympic Airways charges half-fare for accompanied children aged between two and 12 years, while most other airlines charge two-thirds.

UK

British Airways, Olympic Airways and Virgin Atlantic operate daily, direct flights between London and Athens. The pricing is very competitive, with all three offering return tickets for around UK£200 in high season, plus UK£21 tax. These prices are for midweek departures; you will pay about UK£40 more for weekend departures. At these prices, there are no longer savings to be made by taking a connecting flight via Timbuktu with some obscure airline. There are connecting flights to Athens from Edinburgh, Glasgow and Manchester.

British Airways also has daily flights from London to Thessaloniki, stopping in Turin for an hour en route, while Olympic Airways has four direct flights a week. Most scheduled flights from London leave from Heathrow airport, but a few leave from Gatwick.

London is Europe's major centre for discounted fares. The following are the addresses of some of the most reputable agencies selling discount tickets:

Campus Travel
    52 Grosvenor Gardens, SW1
    (☎ 0171-730 3402; www.campustravel.co.uk/);
    tube stn: Victoria
STA Travel
    86 Old Brompton Rd, SW7
    (☎ 0171-361 6161; www.statravel.co.uk); tube
    stn: South Kensington
Trailfinders
    215 Kensington High St, W8
    (☎ 0171-937 5400); tube stn: High St Kensington.

The listings magazines such as *Time Out*, the Sunday papers, the *Evening Standard* and *Exchange & Mart* carry ads for cheap fares. Also look through the *Yellow Pages* for travel agents' ads and look out for the free magazines and newspapers widely available in London, especially *TNT*, *Footloose*, *Supertravel Magazine* and *Trailfinder* – you can pick them up outside the main train and tube stations.

Some travel agents specialise in flights for students aged under 30 and travellers aged under 26 (you need an ISIC card or an official youth card). Whatever your age, you should be able to find something to suit your pocket. You can also contact the Air Travel Advisory Bureau (☎ 0171-636 5000; www.tcol.co.uk/orgs/atab/atab.html) for information about current charter-flight bargains.

Most British travel agents are registered with ABTA (Association of British Travel Agents). If you have paid for your flight to an ABTA-registered agent who then goes out of business, ABTA will guarantee a refund or an alternative. If an agency is registered with ABTA, its ads will usually say so.

In areas of London with large numbers of ethnic Greeks, there are travel agencies which specialise in package holidays and charter flights to Greece. Their prices may well be as competitive as those offered by the more centrally located agencies, and their staff are usually very helpful. Two agencies worth trying are:

Anemone
    109 Myddleton Rd, N22
    (☎ & fax 0181-889 9207)
Hermes Travel
    8 Wordsworth Parade, Green Lanes, N8
    (☎ 0181-881 0268)

Typical charter fares to Athens from London are UK£79/129 one way/return in the low season and UK£99/189 in the high season. These prices are for advance bookings. Even in high season it's possible to pick up last-minute deals for as little as UK£59/99. Many travel agencies also offer charter flights to the islands as well as to Athens. Most island destinations cost about UK£109/209 in high season.

Charter flights to Greece also fly from Birmingham, Luton, Manchester and Newcastle. Look in the *Yellow Pages* and local press for ads.

In Athens, budget fares to London start from as low as 25,000 dr, plus the airport tax.

Continental Europe

Athens is linked to every major city in Europe by either Olympic Airways or the flag carriers of each country.

Though London is the discount capital of Europe, Amsterdam, Frankfurt, Berlin and Paris are also major centres for cheap airfares.

Albania Olympic Airways has at least one flight a day from Tiranë to Athens (US$204/369 one way/return), going via Thessaloniki (US$160/291) twice a week. Student discounts of 25% are available.

France Olympic Airways and Air France have at least three flights a day from Paris to Athens between them. Advance purchase fares starts at around 3300FF. Olympic also has three flights a week to Athens from Marseille.

Charter flights are much cheaper. You'll pay around 2000FF in high season for a return flight from Paris to Athens, and 2050FF to Rhodes or Santorini. The fare to Athens drops to 1500FF in low season. Reliable travel agents include:

Héliades
    23-25 rue Basfroi, 75011 Paris
    (☎ 01 53 27 28 29)
Air Sud
    18 rue du Pont-Neuf, 75001 Paris
    (☎ 01 40 41 66 66)
La Grèce Autrement, 72 boulevard Saint Michel,
    75006 Paris (☎ 01 44 41 69 95)
Atsaro
    9 rue de l'Echelle, 75001 Paris
    (☎ 01 42 60 98 98)
Bleu Blanc, 53 avenue de la République, 75011 Paris
    (01 40 21 31 31)
Nouvelles Frontières
    87 boulevard de Grenelle, 75015 Paris
    (☎ 01 41 41 58 58)
Planète Havas, 26 Avenue de l'Opéra, 75001 Paris
    (☎ 01 53 29 40 00)

Germany For cheap air tickets in Frankfurt, try SRID Reisen (☎ 069-43 01 91), Berger Strasse 118. In Berlin, Alternativ Tours (☎ 030-8 81 20 89), Wilmersdorfer Strasse 94 (U-Bahn: Adenauerplatz), specialises in discounted fares to just about anywhere in the world. SRS Studenten Reise Service (☎ 030-2 83 30 94), at Marienstrasse 23 near Friedrichstrasse station, offers flights with discounted student (aged 34 or less) or youth (aged 25 or less) fares. Travel agents offering unpublished cheap flights advertise in *Zitty*, Berlin's fortnightly entertainment magazine.

The Netherlands Reliable travel agents in Amsterdam include:

Budget Air
    Rokin 34 (☎ 020-627 12 51)
ILC Reizen
    NZ Voorburgwal 256 (☎ 020-620 51 21)
Malibu Travel
    Damrak 30 (☎ 020-626 66 11)
NBBS Reizen
    Rokin 38 (☎ 020-624 09 89) or Leidsestraat 53
    (☎ 020-638 17 36)

From Athens to Europe Budget fares from Athens to a host of European cities are widely advertised by the travel agents around Syntagma. Typical one-way fares include:

Destination	One-Way Fare
Amsterdam	46,000 dr
Copenhagen	44,000 dr
Frankfurt	from 35,000 dr
Geneva	52,000 dr
Hamburg	52,000 dr
Madrid	52,000 dr
Milan	42,000 dr
Munich	49,000 dr
Paris	52,000 dr
Rome	39,000 dr
Zürich	52,000 dr

These fares do not include airport tax.

Turkey

Olympic Airways and Turkish Airlines share the İstanbul-Athens route, with at least one flight a day each. The full fare is US$243 one way. Olympic also flies three times a week between İstanbul and Thessaloniki (US$186). Students qualify for a 50% discount on both routes.

There are no direct flights from Ankara to Athens; all flights go via İstanbul.

Cyprus

Olympic Airways and Cyprus Airways share the Cyprus-Greece routes. Both airlines have two flights a day from Larnaca to Athens (CY£234/424 one way/return), and there are five flights a week to Thessaloniki (CY£235/449).

In summer, Cyprus Airways flies twice a week to Iraklio and Rhodes. All of these flights have a 55% student discount.

Cyprus Airways also flies from Paphos to Athens once a week in winter, and twice a week in summer (CY£163/294).

USA

The North Atlantic is the world's busiest long-haul air corridor, and the flight options to Europe – including Greece – are bewildering. Microsoft's popular Expedia website (www.msn.com) gives a good idea of the possibilities. Other sites worth checking out are ITN (www.itn.net) and Travelocity (www.travelocity.com).

The *New York Times*, *LA Times*, *Chicago Tribune* and *San Francisco Chronicle Examiner* all publish weekly travel sections in which you'll find any number of travel agents' ads. Council Travel (www.ciee.org/travel/) and STA Travel (www.sta-travel.com) have offices in major cities nationwide.

New York has the most direct scheduled flights to Athens. Both Delta Airlines and Olympic have daily flights. The fare on Olympic Airways is US$1070 one way. Apex fares range from US$960 to US$1550, depending on the season and how long you want to stay away.

Boston is the only other east-coast city with direct flights to Athens. Olympic has flights on Wednesday and Saturday. Fares are the same as from New York.

There are no direct flights to Athens from the west coast. Delta has daily flights via New York for US$1750.

There are connecting flights to Athens from many other US cities, stopping at New York's John F Kennedy airport. Most European national airlines fly from New York (and some from other cities) to their home countries, and then on to Athens. These connections usually mean a stopover of three or four hours.

One-way fares can work out very cheap on a stand-by basis. Airhitch (☎ 212-864 2000; e-mail airhitch@netcom.com) specialises in this sort of thing, and can get you to Europe one way for US$175 from the east coast and US$269 from the west coast.

Courier flights are another possibility. Discount Travel International in New York (☎ 212-362 3636; fax 212-362 3236) offers New York-Athens for US$499 in summer and Los Angeles-London for US$399 – but nothing from LA to Athens. Call two or three months in advance, at the beginning of the calendar month.

The *Travel Unlimited* newsletter, PO Box 1058, Allston, MA 02134, publishes details of the cheapest airfares and courier possibilities for destinations all over the world from the USA and other countries, including the UK. It's a treasure-trove of information. A single monthly issue costs US$5, and a year's subscription costs US$25 (US$35 outside the USA).

From Athens to the USA The travel agents around Syntagma offer the following one-way fares to the USA (prices do not include airport tax): Atlanta 110,000 dr; Chicago 110,000 dr; Los Angeles 125,000 dr; and New York 85,000 dr.

Canada
Olympic Airways has two flights a week from Toronto to Athens via Montreal. There are no direct flights from Vancouver, but there are connecting flights via Toronto, Amsterdam, Frankfurt and London on Canadian Airlines, KLM, Lufthansa and British Airways.

Budget flights are also available from Canada. Travel CUTS has offices in all major cities including Toronto (☎ 416-798 2887), Vancouver (☎ 604-681 9136) and Edmonton (☎ 403-488 8487). It can get you to Athens from Toronto and Montreal for C$1140 or from Vancouver for C$1480. The *Toronto Globe & Mail*, the *Toronto Star* and the *Vancouver Province* all carry ads for cheap tickets.

For courier flights originating in Canada, contact FB On Board Courier Services in Montreal (☎ 514-631 2677) and Vancouver (☎ 604-278 1266). Prices to London return are C$525 from Montreal or Toronto and C$570 from Vancouver.

At the time of writing, budget travel agencies in Athens were advertising flights to Toronto for 107,000 dr and to Montreal for 100,000 dr, plus airport tax.

Australia
There are two Olympic Airways flights a week from Sydney and Melbourne to Athens. Return excursion fares range from A$2249 in the low season to A$2899 in high season, but there are normally special deals available which bring the price down to about A$1799 in low season and A$2199 in high season. Olympic Airways has offices in Melbourne (☎ 03-9629 2411, toll free 008-331 448) and Sydney (☎ 02-9251 2044, toll free 1800-221 663).

It's worth checking out special deals offered by other airlines. Some include free side trips within Europe. KLM and Alitalia are two likely candidates.

STA Travel and Flight Centres International are two of Australia's major dealers in cheap fares. The Sunday tabloid newspapers are the best place to look for cheap flights, as well as the Saturday travel sections of the *Sydney Morning Herald* and the Saturday edition of the Melbourne *Age*.

From Athens to Australia A one-way ticket from Athens to Sydney or Melbourne costs 180,000 dr, plus airport tax.

New Zealand
There are no direct flights from New Zealand to Athens, though there are connecting flights via Sydney, Melbourne, Bangkok and Singapore on Olympic Airways, United Airlines, Qantas Airways, Thai Airways and Singapore Airlines.

LAND
Turkey
Bus There is one bus a day between Athens and İstanbul (22 hours) every day except

Wednesday. They travel via Thessaloniki and Alexandroupolis. The buses are run by the Hellenic Railways Organisation (OSE) and leave the Peloponnese train station in Athens at 7 pm. In İstanbul, they use the Anadolu Terminal (Anatolia Terminal) at the Topkapı *otogar* (bus station), leaving at 6.30 pm. One-way fares from Greece are 17,000 dr from Athens, 10,900 dr from Thessaloniki and 4000 dr from Alexandroupolis. Students qualify for a 15% discount and children under 12 travel for half-fare. See the Getting There & Away sections for each city for information on where to buy tickets. (See the Alexandroupolis Getting There & Away section for alternative ways of getting to Turkey by public transport.)

Citizens of most western countries, including Australia, Canada, New Zealand and the USA, don't need a visa for stays of up to three months. British passport-holders will have to hand over US$20 for a Turkish visa at the border. It cannot be obtained in advance.

You may not be allowed into Turkey if your passport is due to expire within three months.

Train There are daily trains between Athens and İstanbul (14,750 dr), via Thessaloniki (10,100 dr), Alexandroupolis (5350 dr) and many more places en route. The service is incredibly slow and the train gets uncomfortably crowded. There are often delays at the border and the journey can take up to 35 hours. You'd be well advised to take a bus. Inter-Rail passes are valid in Turkey, but Eurail passes are not.

Car & Motorcycle The crossing points are at Kipi, 43km north-east of Alexandroupolis, and at Kastanies, 139km north-east of Alexandroupolis. Kipi is much more convenient if you're heading for İstanbul, but the route through Kastanies goes via the fascinating towns of Soufli and Didymotiho, in Greece, and Edirne (ancient Adrianople) in Turkey.

Hitching If you want to hitchhike to Turkey, try to get a lift from Alexandroupolis right through to Turkey as you cannot hitchhike across the border.

Bulgaria

Bus There are two OSE buses a day from Athens to Sofia (15 hours, 10,000 dr) every day except Monday, leaving at 7 am and 4.30 pm. The OSE also operates three buses a day between Thessaloniki and Sofia (7½ hours, 4100 dr). There is a private bus service to Plovdiv (7000 dr) and Sofia (8000 dr) from Alexandroupolis on Wednesday and Sunday at 8.30 am.

Train There is a daily train running between Sofia and Athens (18 hours, 10,100 dr) via Thessaloniki (nine hours, 5500 dr).

Car & Motorcycle The Bulgarian crossing is at Promahonas, 145km north-east of Thessaloniki and 50km from Serres.

Hitching If you want to hitchhike to Bulgaria, try to get a lift from Thessaloniki or Serres straight through to Sofia. Lifts can be hard to come by beyond Serres.

Albania

Bus There is a daily OSE bus from Athens to Tiranë (9800 dr) and vice versa, via Ioannina and Gjirokastër. The bus departs Athens (Larisis train station) at 9 pm and arrives in Tiranë the following day at 5 pm. It leaves Ioannina at 7.30 am and passes through Gjirokastër at 10.30 am. It departs from Tiranë at 7 am. There are buses from Thessaloniki to Korçë (Korytsa in Greek) every day except Sunday. The fare is 5100 dr.

Car & Motorcycle There are two crossing points between Greece and Albania. The main one is 60km north-west of Ioannina. Take the main Ioannina-Konitsa road and turn left at Kalpaki. This road leads to the border town of Kakavia. The other border crossing is at Krystallopigi, 14km west of Kotas on the Florina-Kastoria road. Kapshtica is the closest town on the Albanian side. It is possible to take a private vehicle into Albania, although it's not a great idea. Always carry your passport in areas near the Albanian border.

Former Yugoslav Republic of Macedonia

Train There are local trains from Skopje, capital of the Former Yugoslav Republic of Macedonia (FYROM), to the town of Gevgelija, near the Greek border. From Gevgelija, there are three trains a day to Thessaloniki. Two of them are international services originating in Belgrade, capital of Serbia.

There are no trains between Florina and FYROM, although there may be trains to Skopje from the FYROM side of the border.

Car & Motorcycle There are two border crossings with FYROM. One is at Evzoni, 68km north of Thessaloniki. This is the main highway to Skopje which continues to Belgrade. The other border crossing is at Niki, 16km north of Florina. This road leads to Bitola, and continues to Ohrid, once a popular tourist resort on the shores of Lake Ohrid.

Western Europe

Overland travel between western Europe and Greece is almost a thing of the past. Airfares are so cheap that land transport cannot compete. Travelling from the UK to Greece through Europe means crossing various borders, so check whether any visas are required before setting out. Australians, for example, will need a visa to travel through France.

Bus Fear of flying is about the only reason anyone would opt to go to Greece by bus instead of by plane. If you like the idea of spending days on a bus instead of hours on a plane, there are a couple of companies willing to oblige.

Olympic Bus used to operate the only year-round service from London, but at the time of writing it was travelling only from Brussels. The bus leaves Brussels on Saturday at 7 am and travels via Frankfurt, Munich, Innsbruck, Venice and Brindisi,

reaching Athens at 5 pm on Monday. Olympic's London office (☎ 0171-837 9141) is at 70 Brunswick Centre, WC1 1AE. One-way/return fares from Brussels are UK£100/150. Athens bookings are handled by Iason Tours (☎ 01-324 4633), Eolou 100, near Omonia.

The only service still operating out of the UK is run by Eurolines. It does the trip in just 51 hours, taking the short route across France and northern Italy to Ancona, and then taking the ferry to Igoumenitsa via Corfu. The buses run only from 1 August to 15 September, when they leave London's Victoria Coach Terminus on Friday at 10.30 am. Fares are UK£126/218 one way/return. Eurolines (☎ 0171-730 8235) is at 52 Grosvenor Gardens, Victoria, London SW1.

Train Unless you have a Eurail pass or are aged under 26 and eligible for a discounted fare, travelling to Greece by train is prohibitively expensive. The full fare one way/return from London is UK£204/371, or UK£148/264 if you're under 26.

Greece is part of the Eurail network, and Eurail passes are valid on ferries operated by Adriatica di Navigazione and Hellenic Mediterranean Lines that ply between the Italian port of Brindisi and Corfu, and between Igoumenitsa and Patras. The passes can only be bought by residents of non-European countries and are supposed to be purchased before arriving in Europe. They can, however, be bought in Europe as long as your passport proves that you've been there for less than six months. In London, head for the French National Railways office (☎ 0990 300 003) at 179 Piccadilly, W1. If you are starting your European travels in Greece, you can buy your Eurail pass from the Hellenic Railways Organisation offices at Karolou 1 and Filellinon 17 in Athens, and at Patras and Thessaloniki stations.

Greece is also part of the Inter-Rail pass system, but the pass for those aged over 26 is not valid in France, Italy and Switzerland – rendering it useless if you want to use the pass to get to Greece. Inter-Rail youth passes for those under 26 are divided into zones. A

Global pass (all zones) costs UK£276 and is valid for a month. You need to be under 26 on the first day of travel and to have lived in Europe for at least six months.

Car & Motorcycle Before the troubles in former Yugoslavia began, most motorists driving from the UK to Greece opted for the direct route: Ostend, Brussels, Salzburg and then down the Yugoslav highway through Zagreb, Belgrade and Skopje and crossing the border to Evzoni.

These days most people drive to an Italian port and get a ferry to Greece. Coming from the UK, this means driving through France, where petrol costs and road tolls are exorbitant.

SEA
Turkey
There are five regular ferry services between Turkey's Aegean coast and the Greek islands. Tickets for all ferries to Turkey must be bought a day in advance. You will almost certainly be asked to turn in your passport the night before the trip. You'll get it back the next day before you board the boat. Port tax for departures to Turkey is 5000 dr. (See the relevant sections under individual island entries for more information about the following trips.)

Rhodes to Marmaris There are three ferries a day from Rhodes to Marmaris between April and October and less frequent services in winter. Prices vary, so shop around. There are also hydrofoils to Marmaris daily (weather permitting) from April to October for 12,000/19,000 dr one way/return.

Chios to Çeşme There are daily boats between Chios and Çeşme from July to September, dropping steadily back to one boat a week in winter. Tickets cost 14,000/18,000 dr one way/return, including port taxes.

Kos to Bodrum There are daily ferries in summer from Kos town to Bodrum (ancient Halicarnassus) in Turkey. Boats leave at 8 am and return at 4 pm. The journey takes one hour and costs 13,000 dr return (including the port taxes).

Lesvos to Ayvalık See the Lesvos section of the North-Eastern Aegean Islands chapter for information on the political problems bedevilling this service. There are normally daily ferries on this route from late May to September, and one or two boats a week at other times. Tickets cost 17,000 dr one way or return.

Samos to Kuşadası There are two boats a day to Kuşadası (for Ephesus) from Samos town in summer, dropping to one or two boats a week in winter. Tickets cost 5000/9000 dr one way/return (plus 5000 dr Greek port tax and US$10 Turkish port tax).

Italy
There are ferries to Greece from the Italian ports of Ancona, Bari, Brindisi, Otranto, Ortona, Trieste and Venice. For more information about these services, see the Patras, Igoumenitsa, Corfu and Kefallonia sections.

The ferries can get very crowded in summer. If you want to take a vehicle across it's a good idea to make a reservation. In the UK, reservations can be made on almost all of these ferries at Viamare Travel Ltd (☎ 0171-431 4560; fax 0171-431 5456), Graphic House, 2 Sumatra Rd, London NW6IPU.

You can find the latest information on services operated by ANEK and Minoan Lines on the Internet. For ANEK, contact www.conceptum.com.gr/anek, and for Minoan Lines dial up www.minoan.gr.

ANEK bookings can be made by e-mail on bookings@anek.cha.forthnet.gr, and Minoan bookings can be made on booking-eta@minoan.gr.

The prices listed below are for one-way deck class in the high season (July and August). Deck class on these services means exactly that. If you want a reclining, aircraft-type seat, you'll be up for another 10% to 15% on top of the listed fares. Most companies offer discounts for return travel.

Ancona to Patras The ferry operators in Ancona all have booths at the *stazione marittima* (ferry terminal), off Piazza Candy, where you can pick up timetables and price lists and make bookings.

Superfast Ferries (☎ 71-20 28 05) is the fastest and most convenient, but also the most expensive. They have boats from Ancona every day except Wednesday and from Patras every day except Tuesday. They do the trip in just 20 hours for L138,000. Minoan Lines (☎ 71-5 67 89) operates three ferries a week direct to Patras (22 hours, L126,000) and one a week via Igoumenitsa and Corfu (31 hours). ANEK (☎ 71-20 59 99) runs two direct boats a week (25 hours, L106,000) and three via Igoumenitsa (33 hours, L112,000). Marlines (☎ 71-20 25 66) has three boats a week (33 hours, L100,000), stopping at Igoumenitsa.

Bari to Corfu, Igoumenitsa & Patras Ventouris Ferries (☎ 80-52 17 699) operates daily on this route, charging L65,000 to Corfu and Igoumenitsa and L85,000 to Patras. It also offers student discounts. Marlines (☎ 80-52 31 824) has daily boats from Bari to Igoumenitsa (25 hours, L65,000).

Bari to Kefallonia Ventouris Ferries has boats to Kefallonia every second day from mid-July to mid-August for L85,000.

Brindisi to Corfu, Igoumenitsa & Patras The route from Brindisi to Patras (18 hours) via Corfu (nine hours) and Igoumenitsa (10 hours) is the cheapest and most popular of the various Adriatic crossings.

The major companies operating ferries from Brindisi are: Adriatica di Navigazione (☎ 831-52 38 25), Corso Garibaldi 85-87 (open from 9 am to 1 pm, 4 to 7 pm), and on the 1st floor of the stazione marittima, where you must go to check in; Hellenic Mediterranean (☎ 831-52 85 31), Corso Garibaldi 8; Med Link Lines (☎ 831-52 76 67), represented by Discovery Shipping, Corso Garibaldi 49; and Vergina Ferries (☎ 831-52 48 69), represented by Angela Gioia Agenzia Marittima, Via F Consiglio 55.

Adriatica and Hellenic are the most expensive at L90,000 for deck-class passage to Corfu, Igoumenitsa or Patras, but they are the best. They are also the only lines which officially accept Eurail passes. You will still have to pay port tax and a high-season loading in summer – usually about L15,000. If you want to use your Eurail pass, it is important to reserve some weeks in advance, particularly in summer. Even with a booking, you must still go to the Adriatica or Hellenic embarkation office in the stazione marittima to have your ticket checked. Med Link and Vergina charge L70,000 to Igoumenitsa or Patras.

Prices are about 30% less in the low season. The cheapest cabin accommodation costs around L30,000 more than deck class in low season, and L45,000 more in high season. Fares for cars range from L57,500 to L90,000 in the high season.

Other companies sail only between Brindisi, Corfu and Igoumenitsa. They include Fragline (☎ 831-56 03 50), Corso Garibaldi 88; and Minoan Lines (☎ 831-59 03 05), Corso Garibaldi 96-8. The fares are L79,000 with Fragline and L96,000 with Minoan. Ventouris Ferries (☎ 831-52 16 14), represented by Venmare at Corso Garibaldi 79, charges L60,000 to Igoumenitsa. Its boats don't stop in Corfu.

Brindisi to Kefallonia Hellenic Mediterranean has daily services to the port of Sami on Kefallonia from the beginning of July through to mid-September. The trip takes 13½ hours and costs L90,000 for deck class.

Trieste to Patras ANEK Lines (☎ 40-302 888), whose tickets can be bought from Stazione Marittima di Trieste, has three boats a week travelling via Igoumenitsa. The trip takes 39 hours and costs L106,000 for deck class.

Venice to Patras Minoan Lines (☎ 41-27 12 345), Magazzino 17, Santa Marta, has boats from Venice (40 hours, L132,000). All services stop at Corfu and Igoumenitsa on the way, and from mid-May until late September two boats a week call at Kefallonia.

Cyprus & Israel

Salamis Lines operates a weekly year-round service connecting Piraeus and Rhodes with Limassol on Cyprus and the Israeli port of Haifa. The service leaves Haifa at 8 pm on Sunday and Limassol at 2 pm on Monday, reaching Rhodes at 10 am on Tuesday and Piraeus at 7 am on Wednesday. Approximate deck-class fares from Haifa are US$105 to Rhodes and US$110 to Piraeus. The fares from Limassol are US$70 to Rhodes and US$75 to Piraeus. Bookings in Haifa are handled by Allalouf Shipping (☎ 04-867 1743), 40 Hanamal St, and in Limassol by Salamis Tours (☎ 05-355 555) at Salamis House, 28 October Ave.

Poseidon Lines operates an additional weekly service from early July until mid-September. Boats leave Haifa at 8 pm on Thursday and Limassol at 1 pm on Friday, calling at Rhodes as well as Crete on the way to Piraeus.

For more information about these services, see the Piraeus, Iraklio and Rhodes sections.

DEPARTURE TAXES

There is no departure tax as such, but there is an airport tax of 6100 dr for all international departures. The money goes, in theory, to a good cause – the funding of the new international airport at Athens. The tax is paid when you buy your ticket, not on departure. Port taxes vary from 1500 to 5000 dr, depending on the port.

ORGANISED TOURS

If a package holiday of sun, sand and sea doesn't appeal to you, but you would like to holiday with a group, there are several companies that organise special-interest holidays.

The UK-based Explore Worldwide (☎ 0125-234 4161; www.explore.co.uk) organises reasonably priced, small-group holidays which include visits to many of the country's ancient sites. Island Holidays (0176-477 0107) specialises in cultural holidays on Crete.

If you wouldn't mind a holiday of sun, sand and sea, but don't like crowded, tacky resorts, UK companies specialising in package holidays to unspoilt areas of Greece include: Laskarina (☎ 0162-982 4881; fax 0162-982 2205), Greek Islands Club (☎ 0193-222 0477; fax 0193-222 9346), Simply Ionian (☎ 0181-995 1121) and Simply Crete (☎ 0181-994 4462).

WARNING

The information in this chapter is particularly vulnerable to change: prices for international travel are volatile, routes are introduced and cancelled, schedules change, special deals come and go, and rules and visa requirements are amended. Airlines and governments seem to take a perverse pleasure in making price structures and regulations as complicated as possible. You should check directly with the airline or a travel agent to make sure you understand how a fare (and ticket you may buy) works. In addition, the travel industry is highly competitive and there are many lurks and perks.

The upshot of this is that you should get opinions, quotes and advice from as many airlines and travel agents as possible before you part with your hard-earned cash. The details given in this chapter should be regarded as pointers and are not a substitute for your own careful, up-to-date research.

Getting Around

AIR

Greece has an extensive domestic air network. Olympic Airways handles virtually all flights together with its offshoot, Olympic Aviation. Olympic lost its monopoly on domestic routes in 1993, but no serious competition has emerged. The only newcomer to show any sign of permanence is the Crete-based Air Greece, which offers a cheaper alternative to Olympic on some of the major routes, such as Athens-Thessaloniki, Athens-Rhodes and Athens-Iraklio.

Olympic Airways has offices wherever there are flights, as well as in other major towns. The head office in Athens (☎ 01-966 6666) is at Leoforos Syngrou 96. The airline accepts American Express, Visa, Master-Card, Diners Club and Eurocard.

Olympic Airways domestic tickets are nontransferable. If a passenger cancels a reservation between eight and 24 hours prior to departure, a cancellation charge of 30% of the fare is imposed. If the cancellation occurs within eight hours of departure or the passenger does not show up for the flight, the cancellation charge is 50% of the fare. Different conditions may apply for special fares – check when you buy your ticket. Travel insurance will generally cover you if you have to cancel due to ill health or an emergency, but check your policy.

The free-baggage allowance on domestic flights is 15kg. However, this does not apply when the domestic flight is part of an international journey. The international free-baggage allowance is then extended to the domestic sector. A free-baggage allowance of 20kg applies if tickets for domestic travel are sold and issued outside Greece. Olympic offers a 25% student discount on domestic Olympic Airways flights, but only if the flight is part of an international journey.

Domestic passengers are also funding the building of Athens' new international airport. The airport tax for domestic flights is 3100 dr, which is paid as part of the ticket. All prices quoted in this book include this tax.

Mainland Flights

Athens is far and away the busiest of the nine airports on the Greek mainland. The only mainland route that doesn't involve Athens is the Thessaloniki-Ioannina service (six per week, 50 minutes, 10,800 dr). See the table in this section for details of flights to mainland cities from Athens.

Mainland to Island Flights

Olympic Airways operates a busy schedule to the islands in summer. Athens has flights to a total of 22 islands, with services to all

---

Air Greece Flights
One-way fares (including airport taxes), frequency and duration of flights operated by Air Greece:

Route	Flights/Week	Duration	Fare
Athens – Hania	7	60 mins	16,100 dr
Athens – Iraklio	28	60 mins	17,600 dr
Athens – Rhodes	14	75 mins	19,100 dr
Athens – Thessaloniki	14	60 mins	17,100 dr
Iraklio – Thessaloniki	14	105 mins	23,000 dr
Iraklio – Rhodes	3	60 mins	17,100 dr
Thessaloniki – Rhodes	4	120 mins	25,000 dr

Mainland Flights from Athens
One-way fares (including airport taxes), frequency and duration of flights from Athens are:

City	Flights/Week	Duration	Fare
Alexandroupolis	15	55 mins	17,100 dr
Ioannina	13	70 mins	17,100 dr
Kalamata	7	50 mins	12,700 dr
Kastoria	4	75 mins	17,900 dr
Kavala	12	60 mins	16,800 dr
Kozani	4	70 mins	16,100 dr
Preveza	5	60 mins	12,800 dr
Thessaloniki	55	50 mins	20,700 dr

Summer Flights from Athens to the Greek Islands
This table lists one-way fares (including airport taxes) from **Athens**, the frequency of flights and their duration.

Island	Flights/Week	Duration	Fares
Astypalea	6	65 mins	19,100 dr
Chios	31	50 mins	14,600 dr
Corfu	24	50 mins	19,200 dr
Crete (Hania)	25	45 mins	18,600 dr
Crete (Iraklio)	41	45 mins	20,500 dr
Crete (Sitia)	3	85 mins	22,800 dr
Ikaria	5	50 mins	16,100 dr
Karpathos	4	80 mins	24,700 dr
Kassos	1	130 mins	24,700 dr
Kefallonia	13	60 mins	16,900 dr
Kos	14	50 mins	19,800 dr
Kythira	12	50 mins	13,400 dr
Leros	7	65 mins	20,100 dr
Lesvos (Mytilini)	28	45 mins	15,800 dr
Limnos	17	60 mins	13,900 dr
Milos	14	45 mins	12,700 dr
Mykonos	37	45 mins	17,300 dr
Naxos	14	45 mins	18,600 dr
Paros	52	45 mins	17,100 dr
Rhodes	45	55 mins	23,100 dr
Samos	28	60 mins	16,100 dr
Santorini (Thira)	43	50 mins	20,200 dr
Skiathos	8	40 mins	15,300 dr
Skyros	2	45 mins	13,900 dr
Syros	17	35 mins	13,800 dr
Zakynthos	7	55 mins	16,400 dr

This information is for flights between 14 June and 26 September. Outside these months, the number of flights to the islands drops dramatically – especially to Mykonos, Paros, Skiathos and Santorini (Thira).

the island groups as well as to three destinations on Crete – Hania, Iraklio and Sitia.

There are flights from Thessaloniki to Hania and Iraklio on Crete; to Chios, Lesvos (Mytilini) and Limnos in the North-Eastern Aegean group; to Mykonos and Santorini in the Cyclades; to Rhodes in the Dodecanese; and to Corfu. See the tables on summer flights from Athens & Thessaloniki to the Greek islands below and on the previous page. In spite of the number of flights, it can be hard to find a seat during July and August. Early bookings are recommended.

Flight schedules are greatly reduced in winter, with only a few services to smaller islands.

Interisland Flights

There are year-round, interisland flights between Rhodes and Iraklio, Karpathos, Kassos, Kastellorizo, Kos and Santorini; between Karpathos and Kassos; between Limnos and Lesvos (Mytilini); and between Sitia (Crete) and Karpathos via Kassos.

BUS

All long-distance buses on both the mainland and the islands are operated by KTEL (Koino

Summer Flights from Thessaloniki to the Greek Islands
One-way fares (excluding airport taxes), frequency and duration of flights from **Thessaloniki** are:

Island	Flights/Week	Duration	Fares
Chios	2	50 mins	21,100 dr
Corfu	3	50 mins	19,600 dr
Crete (Hania)	2	105 mins	27,700 dr
Crete (Iraklio)	17	110 mins	27,700 dr
Lesvos (Mytilini)	9	60 mins	19,600 dr
Limnos	7	50 mins	14,100 dr
Mykonos	3	75 mins	25,100 dr
Rhodes	2	70 mins	29,900 dr
Samos	2	105 mins	23,700 dr
Santorini (Thira)	3	90 mins	27,300 dr

Interisland Flights

Islands	Flights/Week	Duration	Fares
Chios – Lesvos (Mytilini)	2	25 mins	10,200 dr
Iraklio – Mykonos	2	60 mins	20,400 dr
Iraklio – Rhodes	4	45 mins	20,300 dr
Iraklio – Santorini (Thira)	3	40 mins	13,900 dr
Karpathos – Kassos	4	15 mins	6000 dr
Karpathos – Rhodes	14	40 mins	12,200 dr
Karpathos – Sitia	1	25 mins	11,500 dr
Kassos – Rhodes	7	40 mins	12,200 dr
Kassos – Sitia	1	55 mins	10,700 dr
Kastellorizo – Rhodes	3	45 mins	10,600 dr
Kos – Rhodes	2	30 mins	13,200 dr
Lesvos (Mytilini) – Limnos	7	35 mins	12,700 dr
Mykonos – Rhodes	3	60 mins	20,400 dr
Mykonos – Santorini (Thira)	6	30 mins	13,900 dr
Rhodes – Santorini (Thira)	4	60 mins	20,400 dr

Tamio Eispraxeon Leoforion), a collective of private bus companies. Drivers take great pride in their buses, staking out a little territory where they sit and adorning it with icons, pin-ups, psychedelic love hearts and plastic mobiles. Bus fares are fixed by the government.

The bus network is comprehensive and major routes have frequent services. With the exception of towns in Thrace, which are reached by buses from Thessaloniki, all the major towns on the mainland, including those in the Peloponnese, are served by frequent buses from Athens. The islands of Corfu, Kefallonia and Zakynthos can also be reached directly from Athens by bus – the fare includes the price of the ferry ticket.

Villages in remote areas are often served by only one or two buses a day. These operate for the benefit of school children and people going into the nearest town to shop, rather than for tourists. These buses leave the villages very early in the morning and return early in the afternoon. On islands where the capital is inland rather than a port, buses normally meet the boats. Some of the very remote islands have not yet acquired a bus, but most have some sort of motorised transport – even if it is only a bone-shaking, three-wheeled truck.

In large and medium-size towns there is usually a central, covered bus station with seating, waiting rooms, toilets, and a snack bar selling pies, cakes and coffee. In some larger towns and cities, there may be more than one bus station, each serving different destinations. In small towns and villages the 'bus station' may be no more than a bus stop outside a *kafeneio* or taverna which doubles as a booking office – here a timetable will be displayed and tickets will be sold. In remote areas, the timetable may be in Greek only, but in most booking offices timetables are in both Greek and Roman script. The timetables give both the departure and return times – useful if you are making a day trip. Times are listed using the 24-hour-clock system.

When you buy a ticket you will be allotted a seat, and the seat number will be noted on the ticket. The seat number is indicated on the back of each seat of the bus, not on the back of the seat in front; this causes confusion among Greeks and tourists alike. You can board a bus without a ticket and pay on board, but on a popular route, or during the high season, this may mean that you have to stand. Keep your ticket for the duration of the journey as it will be checked several times en route.

It's best to turn up at least 20 minutes before departure to make sure you get a seat. Buses often leave a few minutes before their scheduled time of departure – another reason to give yourself plenty of time. Check the destination with the driver before you board the bus, and check that your luggage has been placed in the appropriate hold.

The buses are comfortable. Not all are air-conditioned, but they all have either curtains or blinds which you can pull down for shade. Buses do not have toilets on board and they don't have refreshments available, so make sure you are prepared on both counts. Buses stop about every three hours on long journeys. Smoking is prohibited on all buses in Greece; only the chain-smoking drivers dare to ignore the no-smoking signs.

Bus fares are reasonably priced, with a journey costing approximately 1000 dr per 100km. Fares and journey times on some of the major routes are: Athens-Thessaloniki, 7½ hours, 7700 dr; Athens-Patras, three hours, 3350 dr; Athens-Volos, five hours, 4900 dr; and Athens-Corfu, 11 hours, 8600 dr (including ferry).

TRAIN

The Greek Railways Organisation, OSE (Organismos Sidirodromon Ellados), is gradually getting its act together and modernising its creaky rolling stock; but train travel in Greece is still viewed by most people as a poor alternative to road travel.

For starters, the rail system is not huge. There are essentially two main, standard-gauge lines: Athens to Thessaloniki and Thessaloniki to Alexandroupolis. The Peloponnese system uses a narrow-gauge track, as does the Volos to Kalambaka line.

There are also two distinct levels of service: the slow, stopping-all-stations services that crawl around the countryside, and the faster, modern intercity trains that link most major cities.

Travel by the former is cheaper than by bus, but it is painfully slow and certainly not more comfortable. There seems to be no effort to upgrade the dilapidated rolling stock on these services. Unless you are travelling on a very tight budget, they are best left alone – except on shorter runs such as Athens-Halkida and Volos-Kalambaka. Sample journey times and fares include Athens-Thessaloniki, 7½ hours, 5580/3720 dr (1st/2nd class); Athens-Patras, five hours, 2370/1580 dr; and Athens-Volos, seven hours, 4250/2830 dr.

The intercity network, which links Athens with Thessaloniki, Volos and Alexandroupolis, and Athens with the Peloponnese, is a much better way to travel. The services are not necessarily express – the Greek terrain is too mountainous – but the trains are modern and comfortable. There are 1st and 2nd-class smoking/nonsmoking seats and there is a café-bar on board. On some services, meals can be ordered and delivered to your seat. There is a comfortable night service between Athens and Thessaloniki – especially if you travel in a 1st-class sleeper – on which you can also transport your vehicle.

Ticket prices for intercity services are subject to a distance loading on top of the normal fares. This ranges from a 400 dr supplement for up to 100km to 4000 dr for over 751km. Seat reservations should be made as far in advance as possible, especially in summer. Sample journey times and 1st-class intercity fares include Athens-Thessaloniki, six hours, 9560 dr; Athens-Patras, 3½ hours, 3580 dr; and Athens-Volos, five hours, 6830 dr.

Eurail and Inter-Rail cards are valid in Greece, but it's not worth buying one if Greece is the only place you plan to use it. The passes are valid only for 2nd-class travel, but can be used on intercity services without paying the loading. If you want to travel 1st class, you will have to pay the difference.

Another option if you're planning on using the trains a lot is to buy a tourist rail pass, which are available for individual passengers, as well as for families and groups of up to five people. They are valid for 10, 20 or 30 days and entitle the holder to make an unlimited number of journeys on all the rail routes. An individual pass costs 14,150 dr for 10 days, 21,250 dr for 20 days and 28,320 dr for 30 days. Whatever pass you have, you must have a reservation. You cannot board a train without one.

Senior cards are available to passengers over 60 years of age on presentation of their IDs or passports. They cost 15,550 dr for 1st-class travel and 10,400 dr for 2nd class, and are valid for one year from the date of issue. The cards entitle passengers to a 50% reduction on train travel plus five free journeys per year. Free journeys may not be taken 10 days before or after Christmas or Easter, or between 1 July and 30 September.

Tickets can be bought from OSE booking offices in a few major towns, otherwise from train stations. There is a 20% discount on return tickets, and a 30% discount for groups of 10 or more.

CAR & MOTORCYCLE

No-one who has travelled on Greece's roads will be surprised to hear that the country's road-fatality rate is the highest in Europe. More than 2000 people die on the roads every year, with overtaking listed as the greatest cause of accidents. Stricter traffic laws were introduced in 1992 (see the following subsection) but they have had little impact on the toll. Greek roads remain a good place to practise your defensive-driving techniques.

Heart-stopping moments aside, your own car is a great way to explore off the beaten track. Bear in mind that roads in remote areas are often either dirt or poorly maintained asphalt. Get a good road map (see the Maps section in the Facts for the Visitor chapter) before you set off.

There are seven stretches of highway in Greece where tolls are levied. They are Athens-Corinth, Corinth-Patras, Corinth-

Tripolis, Athens-Lamia, Lamia-Larisa, Larisa-Thessaloniki and Thessaloniki-Ev-zoni. The rates depend on how far you're going. It costs, for example, 500 dr from Athens to Corinth and 600 dr from Corinth to Patras for a car.

Almost all islands are served by car ferries, but they are expensive. Sample prices for small vehicles include: Piraeus to Mykonos, 17,560 dr; Piraeus to Crete (Hania and Iraklio), 21,250 dr; Piraeus to Rhodes, 22,675 dr; and Piraeus to Lesvos, 21,030. The charge for a large motorbike is about the same as the price of a 3rd-class passenger ticket.

Petrol in Greece is expensive, and the further you get from a major city the more it costs. Prices vary from petrol station to petrol station. Super can be found as cheaply as 210 dr per litre at big city discount places, but 225 to 235 dr is the normal range. You may pay closer to 245 dr per litre in remote areas. The price range for unleaded – available everywhere – is from 200 to 225 dr per litre. Diesel costs about 160 dr per litre. See the Documents section in the Facts for the Visitor chapter for information on licence requirements for EU nationals and travellers from other countries.

Road Rules

In Greece, as throughout Continental Europe, you drive on the right and overtake on the left. Outside built-up areas, traffic on a main road has right of way at intersections. In towns, vehicles coming from the right have right of way. Seat belts must be worn in front seats, and in back seats if the car is fitted with them. Children under 12 years are not allowed in the front seat. It is compulsory to carry a first-aid kit, fire extinguisher and warning triangle, and it is forbidden to carry cans of petrol. Helmets are compulsory for motorcyclists if the motorbike is 50cc or more.

Outside residential areas the speed limit is 120km/h on highways, 90km/h on other roads and 50km/h in built-up areas. The speed limit for motorbikes up to 100cc is 70km/h and for larger motorbikes, 90km/h.

Drivers exceeding the speed limit by 20% are liable for a fine of 10,000 dr; and by 40%, 30,000 dr. Other offences and fines include:

- driving on the wrong side of the road – 20,000 dr
- going through a red light – 50,000 dr
- violating right of way at a crossroads – 20,000 dr
- overcrowding a vehicle – 10,000 dr
- use of undipped headlights in towns – 10,000 dr
- illegal reversing – 5000 dr

Drink-driving laws are strict – a blood-alcohol content of 0.05% is liable to incur a penalty, and over 0.08% is a criminal offence.

The police can issue traffic fines, and payment cannot be made on the spot – you will be told where to pay.

If you are involved in an accident and no-one is hurt, the police will not be required to write a report, but it is advisable to go to a nearby police station and explain what happened. A police report may be required for insurance purposes. If an accident involves injury, a driver who does not stop and does not inform the police may face a prison sentence.

See the Useful Organisations section in the Facts for the Visitor chapter for information about the Greek automobile club (ELPA).

Rental

Car If the deadly driving has not put you off getting behind a wheel in Greece, then perhaps the price of hiring a car will. Rental cars are widely available, but they are more expensive than in most other European countries. Most of the big multinational car-hire companies are represented in Athens and large towns, on large islands and at international airports. The smaller islands often have only one car-hire outlet.

The multinationals are, however, the most expensive places to hire a car. High-season weekly rates with unlimited mileage start at about 110,000 dr for the smallest models, such as a 900cc Fiat Panda. The rate drops to about 90,000 dr per week in winter. To these prices must be added VAT of 18%, or 13% on the islands of the Dodecanese, the North-

Eastern Aegean and the Sporades. Then there are the optional extras, such as a collision-damage waiver of 3300 dr per day (more for larger models), without which you will be liable for the first 1,500,000 dr of the repair bill (much more for larger models). Other costs include a theft waiver of at least 1000 dr per day and personal-accident insurance. It all adds up to an expensive exercise. The major companies offer much cheaper prebooked and prepaid rates.

Local companies offer some good deals for those prepared to shop around. They are normally more open to negotiation, especially if business is slow. Their advertised rates are about 25% cheaper than those offered by the multinationals.

If you want to take a hire car to another country or onto a ferry, you will need advance written authorisation from the hire company. Unless you pay with a credit card, most hire companies will require a minimum deposit of 20,000 dr per day. See the Getting Around sections of cities and islands for details of places to rent cars.

The minimum driving age in Greece is 18 years, but most car-hire firms require you to be at least 23 years old, although a few will rent vehicles to 21-year-olds.

Motorcycle Mopeds and motorcycles are available for hire wherever there are tourists to rent them. In many cases their maintenance has been minimal, so check the machine thoroughly before you hire it – especially the brakes: you'll need them!

Greece is not the best place to initiate yourself into motorcycling. Apart from the reckless drivers with whom you will be sharing the road, the roads are hilly and they are badly maintained in remote areas. Every year many tourists have motorcycle accidents in Greece. Take care!

Rates range from 3000 to 3500 dr per day for a moped or 50cc motorbike to 6000 dr per day for a 250cc motorbike. Out of season these prices drop considerably, so use your bargaining skills. By October it is sometimes possible to hire a moped for as little as 1500 dr per day. Most motorcycle hirers include

third-party insurance in the price, but it is wise to check this. This insurance will not include medical expenses; see the following warning.

Warning If you are planning to hire a motorcycle or moped, check that your travel insurance covers you for injury resulting from a motorbike accident. Many insurance companies don't offer this cover. Check the fine print!

Purchase
Greece has no automotive industry and imported cars are heavily taxed. Several firms in Athens are authorised to buy and sell tax-free cars in transit. One is Auto Imports at Liossion 220. Other possibilities are Transco (☎ 01-959 4827), Syngrou 336, and Kyriakos (☎ 01-922 2746), Syngrou 144. You will pay at least 600,000 dr for a decent, second-hand, small car.

BICYCLE
Cycling has not caught on in Greece, which isn't surprising considering the hilly terrain. Tourists are beginning to cycle in Greece, but if you decide to do so you'll need strong leg muscles. You can hire bicycles in most tourist places, but they are not as widely available as cars and motorbikes. Prices range from 1000 to 3000 dr per day, depending on the type and age of the bike. Bicycles are carried free on ferries.

HITCHING
Hitching is never entirely safe in any country in the world, and we don't recommend it. Travellers who decide to hitch should understand that they are taking a small but potentially serious risk. People who do choose to hitch will be safer if they travel in pairs and should let someone know where they are planning to go.

Some parts of Greece are much better for hitching than others. Getting out of major cities tends to be hard work, and Athens is notoriously difficult. Hitching is much easier in remote areas and on islands with poor public transport. On country roads, it is not unknown for someone to stop and ask if you want a lift even if you haven't stuck a thumb out. You can't afford to be fussy about the mode of transport – it may be a tractor or a spluttering old truck.

Greece has a reputation for being a relatively safe place for women to hitch, but it is still unwise to do it alone. It's better to hitch with a companion, preferably a male one.

WALKING

Unless you have come to Greece just to lie on a beach, the chances are you will do quite a bit of walking. You don't have to be a trekker to start clocking up the kilometres. The narrow, stepped streets of many towns and villages can only be explored on foot, and visiting the archaeological sites involves a fair amount of legwork. See the What to Bring, Health and Trekking sections in the Facts for the Visitor chapter for more information about walking.

BOAT
Ferry

For most people, travel in Greece means island-hopping. Every island has a ferry service of some sort, although in winter services to some of the smaller islands are fairly skeletal. Services start to pick up again from April onwards, and by July and August there are countless services criss-crossing the Aegean. Ferries come in all shapes and sizes, from the giant 'superferries' that work the major routes to the small ageing open ferries that chug around the backwaters.

Prices are fixed by the government, and are determined by the distance travelled rather than by the facilities of a particular boat. There can be big differences in the size, comfort and facilities of boats offering rival services on a given route, but the fares will be the same. The small differences in price you may find at ticket agencies are the results of some agents sacrificing part of their designated commission to qualify as a 'discount service'. The discount is seldom more than 50 dr.

The hub of Greece's ferry network is

Piraeus, the port of Athens. Ferries leave here for the Cyclades, Dodecanese, the North-Eastern Aegean, Saronic Gulf islands and Crete. Athens' second port is Rafina, 70km away from the city and connected by an hourly bus service. There are ferries from Rafina to several of the Cyclades, and to Evia. The port of Lavrio, in southern Attica, offers the only ferry link from the mainland to the Cycladic island of Kea. There are regular buses from Athens to Lavrio.

Ferries for the Ionian islands leave from the Peloponnese ports of Patras (for Kefallonia, Ithaki, Paxoi and Corfu) and Kyllini (for Kefallonia and Zakynthos); from Astakos (for Ithaki and Kefallonia) and Mytikas (for Lefkada and Meganisi), both in Sterea Ellada; and from Igoumenitsa in Epiros (for Corfu).

Ferries for the Sporades islands leave from Volos, Thessaloniki, Agios Konstantinos, and Kymi on Evia. The latter two ports are easily reached by bus from Athens. Some of the North-Eastern Aegean islands have connections with Thessaloniki as well as Piraeus. The odd ones out are Thasos, which is reached from Kavala, and Samothraki, which can be reached from Alexandroupolis year-round and also from Kavala in summer. See the table in this section, as well as the relevant port and island sections throughout the book.

Ferry timetables change from year to year and season to season, and ferries are subject to delays and cancellations at short notice due to bad weather, strikes or boats simply conking out. No timetable is infallible, but the comprehensive weekly list of departures from Piraeus put out by the EOT in Athens is as accurate as humanly possible. The people to go to for the most up-to-date ferry information are the local port police (limenarheio), whose offices are usually on or near the quay side.

If you're going to do a lot of island-hopping and you enjoy poring over timetables, you may want a copy of the Greek Travel Pages. This weighty tome is published monthly, primarily for the tourist industry, and has timetables for the major routes as well as lots

Major Ferry Routes from Ports in Mainland Greece

This table shows the high-season deck-class prices at the time of writing. It should be considered a guide only; fares can change at short notice and sailing times can also vary, according to how many islands are visited en route and prevailing weather conditions. For more up-to-date information, contact the EOT or local port police.

Cyclades

	Piraeus	Rafina
Andros	-	2 hours (2310 dr)
Tinos	5 hours (4170 dr)	3½ hours (3335 dr)
Mykonos	5½ hours (4430 dr)	4½ hours (3780 dr)
Syros	4 hours (3875 dr)	5½ hours (3230 dr)
Naxos	6 hours (4320 dr)	8 hours (3865 dr)
Paros	5 hours (4295 dr)	7 hours (3740 dr)
Ios	7½ hours (4700 dr)	-
Folegandros	8-10 hours (4610 dr)	-
Santorini	9 hours (5405 dr)	-
Serifos	4½ hours (3435 dr)	-
Sifnos	5½ hours (3900 dr)	-

Crete

	Piraeus
Iraklio	12 hours (6095 dr)
Hania	11 hours (5200 dr)
Rethymno	12 hours (6050 dr)

Dodecanese Islands

	Piraeus
Rhodes	14-18 hours (7940 dr)
Astypalea	16 hours (6130 dr)

North-Eastern Aegean Islands

	Piraeus
Samos	13 hours (5950 dr)
Chios	8 hours (5130 dr)
Lesvos	12 hours (6240 dr)

Ionian Islands

	Igoumenitsa	Patras	Killini
Corfu	1½ hours (1400 dr)	10 hours (5100 dr)	-
Kefallonia	-	4 hours (2900 dr)	2½ hours (2700 dr)
Ithaki	-	6 hours (3015 dr)	-
Zakynthos	-	-	1½ hours (1470 dr)

Sporades

	Volos	Agios Konstantinos
Skiathos	3-4 hours (2300 dr)	3½ hours (3000 dr)
Skopelos Town	4½ hours (2800 dr)	4½ hours (3500 dr)
Alonnisos	6 hours (3200 dr)	6 hours (3900 dr)

Saronic Gulf Islands

	Piraeus
Aegina	1½ hours (1190 dr)
Poros	3 hours (1650 dr)
Hydra	3½ hours (1950 dr)
Spetses	4½ hours (2600 dr)

Evia

	Glyfa	Arkitsa	Oropou	Agia Marina	Rafina
Agiokambos	30 minutes (330 dr)	-	-		
Loutra Edipsou	-	1 hour (650 dr)	-	-	-
Eretria	-	-	30 minutes (240 dr)	-	-
Nea Styra	-	-	-	40 minutes (540 dr)	-
Marmari	-	-	-	-	1½ hrs (1230 dr)
Karystos	-	-	-	-	1 hour (1630 dr)

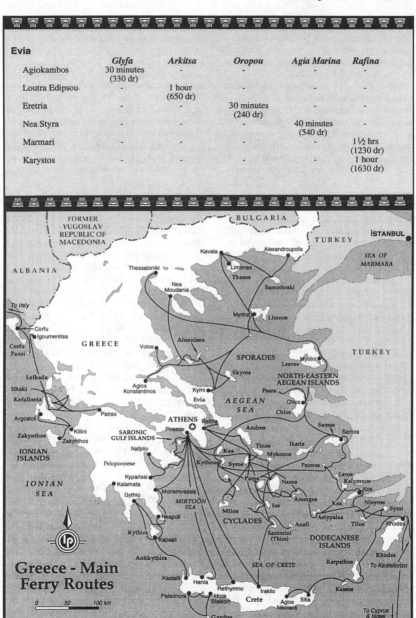

Greece - Main Ferry Routes

0   50   100 km

of other travel facts. You can pick up a copy from Eleftheroudakis bookshop, Nikis 4, Athens, for 5000 dr. If you don't want to spend this much money, a travel agency may let you browse through their copy.

Throughout the year there is at least one ferry a day from a mainland port to the major island in each group, and during the high season (from June to mid-September) there are considerably more. Ferries sailing from one island group to another are not so frequent, and if you're going to travel in this way you'll need to plan carefully, otherwise you may end up having to backtrack to Piraeus.

The large ferries usually have four classes: 1st class has air-con cabins and a posh lounge and restaurant; 2nd class has smaller cabins and sometimes a separate lounge; tourist class gives you a berth in a shared four-berth cabin; and 3rd (deck) class gives you access to a room with 'airline' seats, a restaurant, a lounge/bar and, of course, the deck.

Deck class remains an economical way to travel (see the accompanying table of fares), while a 1st-class ticket can cost almost as much as flying on some routes. Children under four travel for free, while children between four and 10 pay half fare. Full fares apply for children over 10. Unless you state otherwise, when purchasing a ticket, you will automatically be given deck class. As deck class is what most tourists opt for, it is those prices which will be quoted in this book. The ticket prices include embarkation tax, a contribution to NAT (the seaman's union) and 8% VAT.

Given that ferries are prone to delays and cancellations, do not purchase a ticket until it has been confirmed that the ferry is leaving, as getting a refund usually proves to be either impossible or a lot of hassle. If you need to reserve car space, however, you may need to pay prior to the day of departure.

Travelling time can vary considerably from one ferry to another, depending on how many islands are called in at on the way to your destination. For example, the Piraeus-Rhodes trip can take between 14 and 18 hours depending on the route. Before buying

your ticket, check how many stops the boat is going to make, and its estimated arrival time.

Agencies selling tickets line the waterfront of most ports, but rarely is there one that sells tickets for every boat, and often an agency is reluctant to give you information about a boat they do not sell tickets for. This means you have to check the timetables displayed outside each agency to find out which ferry is next to depart – or ask the port police. In high season, a number of boats may be due at a port at around the same time, so it is not beyond the realms of possibility that you might get on the wrong boat. The crucial thing to look out for is the name of the boat; this will be printed on your ticket, and in large English letters on the side of the vessel.

If for some reason you haven't purchased a ticket from an agency, makeshift ticket tables are put up beside a ferry about an hour before departure. Tickets can also be purchased on board the ship after it has sailed. If you are waiting at the quay side for a delayed ferry, don't lose patience and wander off. Ferry boats, once they turn up, can demonstrate amazing alacrity – blink and you may miss the boat.

Once on board the fun really begins – in high season, chaos reigns. No matter how many passengers are already on the ferry, more will be crammed on. Bewildered black-shrouded grannies are steered through the crowd by teenage grandchildren, children get separated from parents, people almost get knocked over by backpackers, dogs get excited and bark, and everyone rushes to grab a seat. As well as birds in cages and cats in baskets there is almost always at least one truck of livestock on board – usually sheep, goats or cattle – who will vociferously make their presence known.

Greeks travelling third class usually make a beeline for the lounge/snack bar, whereas tourists often make for the deck where they can sunbathe. In high season, you need strong nerves and lungs to withstand the lounge/snack bar, which usually has at least two TVs turned on full blast, tuned to different channels and crackling furiously from interference. A couple of other people will have ghetto blasters pumping out heavy metal, and everyone will be engaged in loud conversation. Smoke-laden air adds the final touch to this delightful ambience. Unlike other public transport in Greece, smoking is not prohibited on ferries.

On overnight trips, backpackers usually sleep on deck in their sleeping bags – you can also roll out your bag between the 'airline' seats. If you don't have a sleeping bag, claim an 'airline' seat as soon as you board. Leave your luggage on it – as long as you don't leave any valuables in it. The noise on board usually dies down around midnight so you should be able to snatch a few hours sleep. Outside the high season, ferries can be very subdued places, and sometimes it may seem as if you are the only passenger on board.

The food sold in the snack bars ranges from mediocre to inedible, and the choice is limited to packets of biscuits, sandwiches, very greasy pizzas and cheese pies. Most large ferries also have a self-service restaurant where the food is OK and reasonably priced, with main courses starting at around 1200 dr. If you are budgeting, have special dietary requirements, or are at all fussy about what you eat, then take some food along with you.

Interisland Boat

In addition to the large ferries which ply between the large mainland ports and island groups, there are smaller boats which link two, three or four islands in a group, and occasionally, an island in one group with an island in another. In the past these boats were always caïques – sturdy old fishing boats – but gradually these are being replaced by new purpose-built boats, which are usually called express or excursion boats. Tickets tend to cost more than those for the large ferries, but the boats are very useful if you're island-hopping.

Taxi Boat

Taxi boats are small boats which transport people to places inaccessible or difficult to get to by land. Most islands have at least one of these boats; some owners charge a set price for each person, others charge a flat rate for the boat, and this cost is divided by the number of passengers. Either way, prices are usually quite reasonable.

Hydrofoil

Hydrofoils are an alternative to ferries for reaching some of the islands. They take half the time and cost twice the price, and do not take cars or motorbikes. Some routes operate only during high season, and according to demand, and all are prone to cancellations if the sea is at all rough. A well-established service links Piraeus and the Saronic Gulf islands. Some hydrofoils continue from the Saronic Gulf islands to Porto Heli, Tolo and Nafplio in the Peloponnese and some to Leonidio, Kyparissi, Monemvasia, Neapoli (all in the Peloponnese) and then on to the island of Kythira.

Another well-established service (summer only) links Thessaloniki and the Sporades; some call in at Moudania on the Halkidiki peninsula. From Moudania there are hydrofoils to Alonnisos, which continue on to either Volos or Agios Konstantinos. The Sporades are also served by hydrofoils from Volos and Agios Konstantinos.

The Dodecanese has a well-established service between Rhodes and Kos and a high-season service between Rhodes, Leros and Samos. Other high-season hydrofoils link Rhodes with Halki, Tilos, Nisyros, Karpathos and Kastellorizo; and Rafina with the Cycladic islands of Andros, Tinos, Mykonos and Naxos. Some examples of hydrofoil prices are: Agios Konstantinos to Skopelos (7920 dr) and Alonnisos (8475 dr); and from Piraeus to Hydra (3900 dr) and Spetses (5300 dr). Tickets cannot be bought on board hydrofoils – you must buy them in advance from an agent. You will be allocated a seat number.

Catamaran

Catamarans are the new guys on the interisland travel scene. They operate alongside hydrofoils on some of the hydrofoil routes. The Flying Cats (as the company calls them) operated by Ceres offer VIP class as well as economy travel. Economy fares are the same as for hydrofoils, while an extra 7500 dr gets you a plush, red-leather seat and free drinks in the VIP lounge.

Yacht

Despite the disparaging remarks about yachting among backpackers, yacht is *the* way to see the Greek islands. Nothing beats the peace and serenity of sailing the open sea, and the freedom of being able to visit remote and uninhabited islands.

The free EOT booklet *Sailing the Greek Seas*, although long overdue for an update, contains lots of information about weather conditions, weather bulletins, entry and exit regulations, entry and exit ports and guidebooks for yachties. You can pick up the booklet at any GNTO/EOT office either abroad or in Greece.

If you are not rich enough to buy a yacht there are several other options open to you. You can hire a bare boat (a yacht without a crew) if two crew members have a sailing certificate. Prices start at US$1300 per week for a 28-footer that will sleep six. It will cost an extra US$700 per week for a skipper. Yacht-charter companies operating in and around Athens and Piraeus include:

Aegean Cruises
    Poseidonos 15, Glyfada, Attica (☎ 01-984 9984)
Alpha Yachting
    Vasilissis Georgio Sofias 12, Athens
    (☎ 01-721 9360)
Fine Yachting & Travel
    Koundouriotou 131, Piraeus (☎ 01-412 0414)
Ghiolman Yachts
    Filellinon 7, Athens (☎ 01-323 3696)
GM Yachting
    Makariou 2, Alimos, Attica (☎ 01-984 6812)
Hellas Yachting
    Akademias 43, Athens (☎ 01-362 5698)
Koutsoukelis Yachting
    Stadiou 5, Athens (☎ 01-322 7011)
Seahorse
    Alkyonidon 83, Voula, Attica
    (☎ 01-895 2212/6733)

There are many more yacht-charter companies in Greece; the EOT can give you some addresses. Also check the Dodecanese chapter in this book.

Ghiolman Yachts (see the preceding list) also offers a range of yachting holidays for those who just want to go sailing without the hassle of chartering a yacht. The possibilities include a week sailing the Sporades for US$700, or US$900 in July and August, and two weeks in the Aegean for US$1100/1300.

A number of UK-based holiday companies also offer holidays sailing around the Greek islands. You can book holidays with them either excluding or including the airfare to Greece. Some of these include:

Greek Islands Touring Club
    66 High St, Walton-on-Thames,
    Surrey KT12 1BU (☎ 01932-220416)
Tenrag Yacht Charters
    Bramling House, Bramling, Canterbury,
    Kent CT3 1NB (☎ 01227-721874)
World Expeditions
    7 North St, Maidenhead,
    Berkshire SL6 6BP (☎ 01628-74174)

LOCAL TRANSPORT
Airports

Olympic Airways operates buses to a few domestic airports (see individual entries in the appropriate chapters). Where the service exists, buses leave the airline office about 1½ hours before departure. In many places, the only way to get to the airport is by taxi. This means that in at least one case (Karpathos-Kassos) you will fork out more for the taxi than the flight. Check-in is an hour before departure for domestic flights.

Transport to and from international airports in Greece is covered in the Getting Around section of the relevant city.

Bus

Most Greek towns are small enough to get around on foot. The only places where you may need to use local buses are Athens, Piraeus and Thessaloniki. The procedure for buying tickets for local buses is covered in the Getting Around section for each city.

Metro
Athens is the only city in Greece with an underground system. At the moment, the service is restricted to a single line running from the port of Piraeus to the northern suburb of Kifissia, with 21 stations in between. A new line, due to be completed in 2000, will greatly expand the network. There will be stops at Syntagma and at the Larisis train station.

Taxi
Taxis are widely available in Greece except on very small or remote islands. They are reasonably priced by European standards, especially if three or four people share costs.

Yellow city cabs are metered. Flagfall is 200 dr, followed by 62 dr per km (120 dr per km outside town). These rates double between midnight and 5 am. Additional costs (on top of the per-km rate) are 300 dr from an airport, 150 dr from a bus, port or train station and 55 dr for each piece of luggage. Grey rural taxis do not have meters, so you should always settle on a price before you get in.

The taxi drivers of Athens are legendary for their ability to part locals and tourists alike from their drachma – see the Dangers & Annoyances section in the Athens chapter. If you have a complaint about a taxi driver, take the cab number and report your complaint to the tourist police. Taxi drivers in other towns in Greece are, on the whole, friendly, helpful and honest.

ORGANISED TOURS
Tours are worth considering only if your time is very limited, in which case there are countless companies vying for your money. The major players are CHAT, GO Tours and Key Tours, all based in Athens and offering almost identical tours. They include day trips to Delphi (16,300 dr) and Mycenae and Epidaurus (16,300 dr). They also offer longer trips such as a four-day tour calling at Mycenae, Nafplio, Epidaurus, Olympia and Delphi (from 89,000 dr). These prices include twin-share accommodation and half-board. For details of these companies, see Organised Tours in the Activities section of the Athens chapter.

Organised Treks
Trekking Hellas, at Filellinon 7, Athens 105 57 (☎ 01-325 0853; fax 323 4548; e-mail trekking@compulink.gr), is a well-established company which specialises in treks and other adventure activities for small groups. It offers a wide range of treks lasting from four to nine days and graded from introductory to challenging. They have fairly easy introductory walks in the foothills of the Taygetos mountains in the Peloponnese, on the Ionian island of Ithaki and on the Cycladic islands of Andros and Tinos. The treks around Meteora and the Pelion peninsula are a bit more demanding, while only fit, experienced walkers should attempt the challenging treks in the Pindos ranges and to the summits of Mt Olympus. Other activities include canoeing, river-rafting (January-April), canyoning and cycling. Prices for all these activities work out at about 25,000 dr per day, including full board.

Other tours are recommended throughout the book.

The Mainland

Athens Αθήνα

• pop 3.7 million • postcode 102 00 (Omonia), 103 00 (Syntagma) • area code ☎ 01

The perpetual 'high' which the novelist Henry Miller experienced during his travels in Greece did not flag when he came to the capital (in Greek Ath**ee**na). In the *Colossus of Maroussi*, Miller waxed lyrical about the extraordinary quality of the city's light and rhythm. Few visitors today, however, share his bubbling enthusiasm. Most beat a hasty retreat after the obligatory visit to the Acropolis and the National Archaeological Museum. Despite its glorious past and its influence on western civilisation, it is a city which few fall in love with. Modern Athens is a vast concrete urban sprawl that suffers badly from the curse of the modern age, pollution.

To appreciate Athens, it's important to be aware of the city's traumatic history. Unlike most capital cities, Athens does not have a history of continuous expansion; it is one characterised by glory, followed by decline and near annihilation, and then resurgence in the 19th century – when it became the capital of independent Greece.

The historical event which, more than any other, shaped the Athens of today was the compulsory population exchange between Greece and Turkey that followed the signing of the Treaty of Lausanne in July 1923. The population of Athens virtually doubled overnight, necessitating the hasty erection of concrete apartment blocks to house the newcomers.

The expansion of Athens in all directions began at this time, and accelerated during the 1950s and 1960s when the country began the transition from an agricultural to an industrial nation. Young people began to flock to the city from the islands and rural areas, and this trend has continued ever since.

Athens has many redeeming qualities. The city is bounded on three sides by Mt Parnitha (1413m), Mt Pendeli (1109m) and Mt Hymettos (1026m). The latter was once famed for its violet sunsets – these days

HIGHLIGHTS

- The Acropolis (and dining beneath it)
- The National Archaeological Museum
- The view from Lykavittos hill
- *Rembetika* clubs
- Sunset at Cape Sounion

normally obliterated by the city's appalling pollution. At least one of these mountains can be glimpsed from almost every street in Athens. Within the city there are no less than eight hills, of which the most prominent are Lykavittos (277m) and the Acropolis (156m). These hills are a pleasant place to escape from the traffic-congested streets. Athens improves considerably when viewed from a height, and there are stunning views over the city to the glistening waters of the Saronic Gulf – its boundary on the fourth side.

Travelling east, Athens is the last European city in the Mediterranean. King Otho and the middle class that evolved after Independence might have been intent upon making Athens European in every sense of

147

the word, but the influence of Asia Minor is still immediately evident – the coffee, the raucous street vendors on every square and the bustling outdoor markets.

Some of the older parts of the city have a ramshackle Third World feel about them, in contrast with the elegant neoclassical mansions of the smarter suburbs. One of the most endearing aspects of the city is the congeniality of the local people, in contrast to the anonymity one feels in many western capitals. Within a week of staying in Athens the chances are you'll be passing the time of day, or stopping for a chat, with new acquaintances.

Perhaps most significant of all is the fact that wherever you are in the centre of the city the Acropolis, with its transcendent and compelling aura, stands proudly on the skyline. It serves as a constant reminder that whatever trials and tribulations might have befallen the city, its status as the birthplace of western civilisation is beyond doubt.

History

Early History The early history of Athens is inextricably interwoven with mythology, making it impossible to disentangle fact from fiction. What is known is that the hilltop site of the Acropolis, endowed with two bounteous springs, drew some of Greece's earliest Neolithic settlers. When a peaceful agricultural existence gave way to the war-orientated city-states, the Acropolis provided an ideal defensive position: its steep slopes formed natural defences on three sides and it was an excellent vantage point from which to spot potential danger approaching from land or sea.

By 1400 BC, the Acropolis had become a powerful Mycenaean city. Unlike the cities of Mycenae, Pylos and Tiryns, it survived the Dorian assault on Greece in 1200 BC. It couldn't, however, escape the dark age that enveloped Greece for the next 400 years, and very little is known of this period.

After its emergence from the dark age in the 8th century BC, a period of peace followed, both for Athens and the surrounding united towns. During this time the city be-

came the artistic centre of Greece, excelling in ceramics. The geometric designs of vases from the dark ages evolved into a narrative style, depicting scenes from everyday life and mythology. This pottery subsequently became known as the Proto-Attic style.

By the 6th century BC, Athens was ruled by aristocrats, generals and the archon (chief magistrate). A person's position in the hierarchy depended on their wealth, which was gained either from commerce or agriculture. Labourers and peasants had no say at all in the functioning of the city – until the reform-oriented Solon became archon in 594 BC.

Solon did much to improve the lot of the poor and is regarded as the harbinger of Athenian democracy. His most significant reforms were the annulment of all debts and the implementation of trial by jury. Continuing unrest over the reforms created the pretext for the tyrant Peisistratos, formerly head of the military, to seize power in 560 BC.

Peisistratos built up a formidable navy, much to the consternation of other city-states, and extended the boundaries of Athenian influence on land. He was a patron of the arts as well as a general, inaugurating the Festival of the Great Dionysia, which was the precursor of Attic drama, and commissioning many splendid sacred and secular buildings – most of which were destroyed by the Persians on the eve of the Battle of Salamis in 480 BC.

Peisistratos was succeeded by his son Hippias, who was very much a tyrant. Athens managed to rid itself of this oppressor in 510 BC only by swallowing its pride and accepting the help of Sparta. Hippias wasn't finished, however, heading off to Persia to stir up trouble and returning with Darius 20 years later to be defeated at the Battle of Marathon.

Athens' Golden Age After Athens had finally repulsed the challenge of the Persian Empire at the battles of Salamis and Plataea (again, with the help of Sparta), its power knew no bounds.

In 477 BC Athens established a confed-

Athena & the Olive Tree

According to mythology, Cecrops, a Phoenician, came to Attica, where he founded a city on a huge rock near the sea. The gods of Olympus proclaimed that the city should be named after the deity who could produce the most valuable legacy for mortals. Athena (goddess of wisdom) and Poseidon (god of the sea) contended. Athena produced an olive tree, symbol of peace and prosperity. Poseidon struck a rock with his trident and a horse sprang forth, which symbolised all the qualities of strength and fortitude for which he was renowned. Athena was the victor, for the gods proclaimed that her gift would better serve the citizens of Athens than the arts of war personified by Poseidon's gift. ∎

Poseidon and Athena

eracy on the sacred island of Delos and demanded tributes from the surrounding islands to protect them from the Persians. It was little more than a standover racket because the Persians were no longer much of a threat. The treasury was moved to Athens in 461 BC and Pericles (ruled from 461 to 429 BC) used the money to transform the city. The period has become known as Athens' golden age, the pinnacle of the classical era.

Most of the monuments on the Acropolis today date from this time. Drama and literature flourished in the form of the tragedies written by Aeschylus, Sophocles and Euripides. The sculptors Pheidias and Myron and the historians Herodotus, Thucydides and Xenophon also lived at this time.

Rivalry with Sparta Arch rival Sparta wasn't prepared to sit back and allow Athens to revel in its new-found glory. The increasing jockeying for power between the two led to the outbreak of the Peloponnesian Wars in 431 BC. The warring dragged on until 404 BC, when Sparta gained the upper hand. Athens was never to return to its former glory. The 4th century BC did, however, produce three of the West's greatest orators and philosophers: Socrates, Plato and Aristotle. The degeneracy into which Athens had fallen was perhaps epitomised by the ig-

nominious death sentence passed on Socrates for the crime of corrupting the young with his speeches.

Athens' days of glory were now numbered. In 338 BC, along with the other city-states of Greece, Athens was conquered by Philip II of Macedon. After Philip's assassination, his son Alexander the Great, a cultured young man, favoured Athens over other city-states. After his untimely death, Athens passed in quick succession through the hands of several of his generals.

Roman & Byzantine Rule After the Romans conquered Greece in 31 BC, Athens continued to be a major seat of learning, and many wealthy young Romans attended Athens' schools. Anybody who was anybody in Rome at the time spoke Greek. The Roman emperors, particularly Hadrian, graced Athens with many grand buildings.

After the subdivision of the Roman Empire into east and west, Athens remained an important cultural and intellectual centre until Emperor Justinian closed its schools of philosophy in 529 AD. The city then declined into nothing more than an outpost of the Byzantine Empire.

Between 1200 and 1450, Athens was continually invaded – by Franks, Catalans, Florentines and Venetians, all opportunists preoccupied only with grabbing for themselves principalities from the crumbling Byzantine Empire.

Ottoman Rule & Independence Athens was captured by the Turks in 1456, and nearly 400 years of Ottoman rule followed. The Acropolis became the home of the Turkish governor, the Parthenon was converted into a mosque and the Erechtheion was used as a harem.

In the early stages of the War of Independence (1821-27), fierce fighting broke out in the streets of Athens, with the city changing hands several times between Turks and Greek liberators. In 1834 Athens superseded Nafplio as the capital of independent Greece and King Otho set about transforming the sparsely populated, war-scarred town into something worthy of a capital. Bavarian architects created a city of imposing neoclassical buildings, tree-lined boulevards, flower gardens and squares. Sadly, many of these buildings have been demolished. The best surviving examples are on Vasilissis Sofias.

The 20th Century Athens grew steadily throughout the latter half of the 19th and early 20th centuries, and enjoyed a brief heyday as the 'Paris of the eastern Mediterranean'. This came to an abrupt end in 1923 with the Treaty of Lausanne. The treaty resulted in nearly a million refugees from Turkey descending on Athens – an event which marked the beginning of its much-maligned concrete sprawl.

Athens, along with the rest of Greece, suffered appallingly during the German occupation of WWII. During this time more Athenians were killed by starvation than by the enemy. This suffering was perpetuated in the civil war that followed.

The industrialisation programme that was launched during the 1950s, with the help of US aid, brought another population boom as people from the islands and mainland villages headed to Athens in search of work.

The colonels' junta (1967-74), with characteristic insensitivity, tore down many of the crumbling old Turkish houses of Plaka and the imposing neoclassical buildings of

King Otho's time. Subsequent governments have become steadily more conservation-conscious, and these days many old buildings of architectural merit are being restored. The sleazy bars, nightclubs and strip joints of Plaka have been closed down and many of its streets have become pedestrian ways.

Orientation

City Centre Although Athens is a huge, sprawling city, nearly everything of interest to travellers is located within a small area bounded by Plateia Omonias to the north, Plateia Monastirakiou to the west, Plateia Syntagmatos to the east and the Plaka district to the south. The city's two major landmarks, the Acropolis and Lykavittos hill, can be seen from just about everywhere and are useful for getting one's bearings. The streets are clearly signposted in Greek and English. If you do get lost, it's very easy to find help – a glance at a map is often enough to draw an offer of assistance. Anyone you ask will be able to direct you to Syntagma.

Plateia Syntagmatos (Πλατεία Συντάγ-ματος) Syntagma is the heart of the modern city of Athens. It is flanked by luxury hotels, banks, airline offices and expensive coffee shops and is dominated by the old royal palace. It was from the palace balcony that the constitution *(syntagma)* was declared on 3 September 1843. The building has housed the Greek parliament since 1935.

Syntagma is a pleasant introduction to the city, despite the manic speed at which the traffic zooms around it. At its centre is a large, paved square, planted with orange, oleander and cypress trees. If you're arriving on the airport bus and want to stay in Plaka, Syntagma is the place to get off. The stop is opposite the National Gardens, just before the square. Syntagma will have its own metro stop when the new line is finished.

Plaka (Πλάκα) Plaka is the old Turkish quarter of Athens and virtually all that existed when Athens was declared the capital of independent Greece. Its narrow, labyrinthine streets nestle

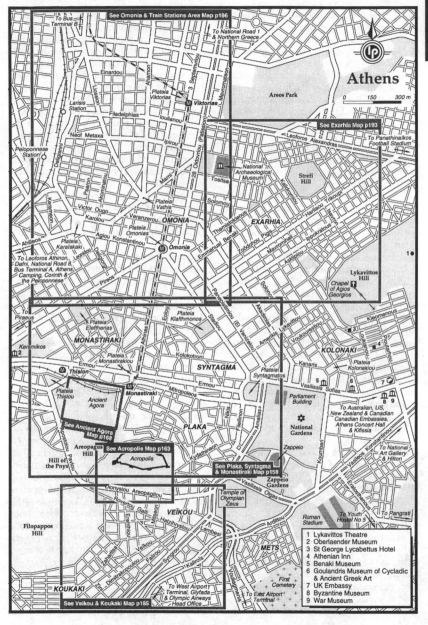

Athens

0   150   300 m

To Bus
Terminal B
See Omonia & Train Stations Area Map p186
To National Road 1
& Northern Greece

Einardou

Areos Park

Plateia
Viktorias
Viktorias

Larisis
Station

Filadelphias

See Exarhia Map p193

Neof Metaxa

Leoforos Alexandras
To Panathinaikos
Football Stadium

Peloponnese
Station

National
Archaeological
Museum

Strefi
Hill

Tositsa

Plateia
Vathis

Solomou

EXARHIA

Victor Ougo

Plateia
Omonias

Karolou

Veranzerou

OMONIA

Agiou Konstantinou

Plateia
Karaiskaki

To Leoforos Athinon,
Dafni, National Road 8,
Bus Terminal A, Athens
Camping, Corinth &
the Peloponnese

Omonia

Pireos

Lykavittos
Hill

1

Chapel
of Agios
Georgios

To
Piraeus

Plateia
Eleftherias

Plateia
Klafthmonos

Kleomenous

3

Keramikos

2

MONASTIRAKI

Plateia
Monastirakiou

Kolokotroni

KOLONAKI

4

Thision

Ermou

Monastiraki

SYNTAGMA

Plateia
Syntagmatos

Kanaris

Plateia
Kolonakiou

7

Ermou

Mitropoleos

Vasilissis Sofias

5

6

Plateia
Thisiou

Ancient
Agora

See Ancient Agora
Map p168

Niki

Filellinon

Parliament
Building

To Australian, US,
New Zealand & US
Canadian Embassies,
Athens Concert Hall
& Kifissia

8   9

PLAKA

National
Gardens

Areopagus
Hill

See Acropolis Map p163

Acropolis

Zappeio

To National
Art Gallery
& Hilton

Hill of
the Pnyx

See Plaka, Syntagma
& Monastiraki Map p158

Dionysiou Areopagitou

Zappeio
Gardens

Filopappos
Hill

VEÏKOU

Temple of
Olympian
Zeus

Roman
Stadium

To Youth
Hostel No 5

To Pangrati

METS

First
Cemetery

KOUKAKI

To West Airport
Terminal, Glyfada
& Olympic Airways
Head Office

To East Airport
Terminal

See Veikou & Koukaki Map p185

1 Lykavittos Theatre
2 Oberlaender Museum
3 St George Lycabettus Hotel
4 Athenian Inn
5 Benaki Museum
6 Goulandris Museum of Cycladic
   & Ancient Greek Art
7 UK Embassy
8 Byzantine Museum
9 War Museum

into the north-eastern slope of the Acropolis, and most of the city's ancient sites are close by. Plaka is touristy in the extreme. Its main streets, Kydathineon and Adrianou, are packed solid with restaurants and souvenir shops. It is the most attractive and interesting part of Athens and the majority of visitors make it their base. The most convenient trolleybus stop is on Filellinon, near the junction with Kydathineon.

Plateia Monastirakiou (Πλατεία Μονα–στηρακίου) Monastiraki is in the heart of the city's market district. The central meat and fish market is on Athinas, opposite the fruit and vegetable market, halfway between Monastiraki and Omonia. Shops along the streets bordering the markets sell cheeses, nuts, herbs, honey, dried fruits and cold meats. On Eolou most shops sell cut-price clothing and street vendors offer items such as sheets, towels, tablecloths and underwear.

The famous flea market is to the south-west on Ifestou, while Areos, to the south, is the favourite hang-out of a colourful bunch of freaks and travellers selling Indian paraphernalia. Ermou and Mitropoleos, which run almost parallel between Monastiraki and Syntagma, offer somewhat more up-market shopping. Ermou is lined with fashion and textile shops, and Mitropoleos is the best place in Athens to buy carpets and flokati rugs. Athens Cathedral dominates the large square halfway along Mitropoleos.

Monastiraki is the metro stop for Plaka.

Plateia Omonias (Πλατεία Ομόνιας) Omonia is more of a transport hub than a square. The major streets of central Athens all meet here: the two most important are El Venizelou and Stadiou, which run parallel south-east to Syntagma, 1km away. Athens University is halfway along El Venizelou, which is more commonly known as Panepistimiou (university). Athinas heads south from Omonia to Plateia Monistirakiou; Pireos runs south-west to Piraeus; Agiou Konstantinou goes west towards the train stations; and 3 Septemvriou heads north – although the major

street heading north is 28 Oktovriou-Patission, which starts 50m along Panepistimiou from the square. South of Panepistimiou, the street becomes Eolou and runs almost to the foot of the Acropolis. Omonia is a stop on the metro system, as well as being on almost every trolleybus route.

The square is not a pleasant place to hang out (see Dangers & Annoyances, below). A lot of homeless people sleep rough in the underground hall and passages connected to the metro station. Their numbers have been boosted by refugees from the troubles in the Balkans. Junkies seem to prefer Plateia Vathis, 300m to the north-west.

Beyond the City Centre To get a glimpse of how today's Athenians live, it's well worth exploring the streets beyond the city centre.

Around Syntagma Amalias is the main street heading south from the eastern side of Syntagma. Next to it are the National Gardens – a park of subtropical trees and ornamental ponds – and the more formal Zappeio gardens. Amalias skirts the Arch of Hadrian and the Temple of Olympian Zeus and leads into Syngrou, which runs all the way to the coast at Faliro. Buses from the airport and Piraeus approach Syntagma along Amalias.

Vasilissis Sofias runs east from Syntagma, skirting the northern edge of the National Gardens. One of Athens' most imposing streets, it was laid out by the Bavarian architects brought in by King Otho. Its neoclassical buildings now house a collection of museums, embassies and government offices. To the north of Vasilissis Sofias, at the foot of Lykavittos hill, is the opulent residential district of Kolonaki with its ultra-trendy boutiques, expensive coffee shops and private art galleries. Kolonaki has long been the favoured address of Athenian socialites. More recently it has become a popular area with gays, who frequent its sophisticated bars.

Around Plaka South of the Acropolis is Filopappos hill, and flanking it are the pleasant residential districts of Veïkou and Koukaki. To the east, on the other side of Syngrou, is the district of Mets, which still has some delightful old Turkish houses. North-east of Mets is Pangrati. Both are pleasant residential neighbourhoods.

West of Plateia Monastirakiou The stretch of Ermou west of Monastiraki is the site of the famous Sunday markets. North of Ermou is the district of Psiri, which stretches north to the central markets. This is Athens at its most clapped out, with a ramshackle Third World feel. There are lots of second-hand shops with a bizarre array of bric-a-brac overflowing onto the pavements.

South of Ermou (and the metro line) is Thisio, once as run-down as Psiri but now booming like never before. Young people began buying the cheap property a few years ago and Thisio has rapidly been transformed into one of the city's trendiest addresses. Iraklidon and Nileos are both packed with bars and restaurants.

North of Omonia Venturing north from Omonia the seediness gradually recedes and, beyond Plateia Vathis, gives way to a respectable, if characterless, neighbourhood. Athens' two train stations are at the western edge of this area, on Deligianni. The National Archaeological Museum is on the eastern side, on 28 Oktovriou-Patission. The area's main square is Plateia Viktorias, near which is the red-light district on Filis.

Just south of the National Archaeological Museum is the Athens Polytehnio. This establishment has university status, with faculties of fine arts and engineering, whereas most students at Athens University read law or medicine. The Polytehnio has a long tradition of radical thinking and alternative culture, and led the student sit-in of 1973 in opposition to the junta.

Squashed between the Polytehnio and Strefi hill is the student residential area of Exarhia. It's a lively area with graffiti-covered walls and lots of cheap restaurants catering for Bohemian-looking professors and crowds of rebellious-looking students.

Information

Tourist Offices EOT's head office (☎ 322 3111; fax 323 1048; e-mail gnto@eexi.gr) at Amerikis 2 does not deal with enquiries from the general public. The organisation's public face is a small information window (☎ 322 2545) in the National Bank of Greece building on Syntagma Square, Syntagma. It is a very unsatisfactory and impersonal arrangement which requires you to talk into a microphone to someone on the other side of a heavy plate-glass window, who responds in kind. They can slide photocopied information sheets out to you, provided you know what to ask for. It's worth asking for their free map of Athens, which has most of the places of interest clearly marked and also shows the trolleybus routes. Unfortunately, the map is designed to last the length of the average tourist's stay – about a day – before it falls to bits.

There's also a notice board with transport information, including a very useful timetable of the week's ferry departures from Piraeus. The window is open Monday to Friday from 8 am to 6 pm and on Saturday from 9 am to 2 pm.

If your question concerns Athens, you can call at the much friendlier municipal information kiosk on Syntagma at the top of Ermou.

The EOT office (☎ 979 9500) at the East Air Terminal is open Monday to Friday from 9 am to 7 pm and Saturday from 10 am to 5 pm.

Tourist Police The head office (☎ 902 5992) of the tourist police is at Dimitrakopoulou 77, Veïkou. It is open 24 hours a day, but it's quite a trek from the city centre – take trolleybus No 1, 5 or 9 from Syntagma. The tourist police also have a 24-hour information service (☎ 171). You can call them for general tourist information or in an emergency – someone who speaks English is always available.

They will also act as interpreters for any dealings you might have with the crime police (☎ 770 5711/5717), Leoforos Alexandras

173, or the traffic police (☎ 523 0111), Agiou Konstantinou 28, near Omonia.

Foreign Embassies See Visas & Embassies in the Facts for the Visitor chapter for a list of foreign embassies in Athens.

Money Most of the major banks have branches around Plateia Syntagmatos, open Monday to Thursday from 8 am to 2 pm and Friday from 8 am to 1.30 pm. The National Bank of Greece at Syntagma is open extended hours for foreign exchange dealings only: from 3.30 to 6.30 pm Monday to Thursday; from 3 to 6.30 pm on Friday; from 9 am to 3 pm on Saturday; and from 9 am to 1 pm on Sunday. Both the National Bank and the Credit Bank, on opposite sides of Stadiou, have 24-hour automatic exchange machines.

American Express (☎ 324 4975/4979), Ermou 2, Syntagma, is open Monday to Friday from 8.30 am to 4 pm and on Saturday from 8.30 am to 1.30 pm. It also has a free poste-restante service for card-holders. Non-members can use the service, but there's a collection fee of 600 dr per item. Thomas Cook (☎ 322 0155) has an office at Karageorgi Servias 4, open Monday to Friday from 8.30 am to 8 pm, Saturday from 9 am to 6.30 pm and Sunday from 10 am to 2.30 pm.

In Plaka, Acropole Foreign Exchange, Kydathineon 23, is open from 9 am to midnight every day. It does, however, charge a hefty 2.5% commission. Ergobank, at the junction of Adrianou and Kydathineon, has a 24-hour automatic exchange machine.

The banks at both the East and West airport terminals are open 24 hours a day, although you may have trouble tracking down the staff late at night.

Post & Communications Athens' central post office (☎ 321 6023) is at Eolou 100, Omonia, just east of Plateia Omonias. Unless specified otherwise, poste restante will be sent here.

If you're staying in Plaka, it's far more convenient to get your mail sent to the poste restante at the large post office on Plateia Syntagmatos, on the corner of Mitropoleos. Both are open Monday to Friday from 7.30 am to 8 pm and Saturday from 7.30 am to 2 pm.

Parcels for abroad that weigh over 2kg must be taken to the parcel post office (☎ 322 8940), Stadiou 4, Syntagma. The office is in the arcade that runs between Amerikis and Voukourestiou. Parcels should be taken along unwrapped for inspection.

The OTE office, 28 Oktovriou-Patission 85, Omonia, is open 24 hours a day. There are also offices at Stadiou 15, Syntagma, and on the southern corner of Plateia Omonias, Omonia; both of these offices are open from 7 am to 11.30 pm daily. There is also an office at Athinas 50. Some useful telephone numbers include:

general telephone information	☎ 134
numbers in Athens & Attica	☎ 131
numbers elsewhere in Greece	☎ 132
international telephone information	☎ 161 or 162
international telegrams	☎ 165
domestic operator	☎ 151 or 152
domestic telegrams	☎ 155
wake-up service	☎ 182

If you simply cannot live without a mobile phone, they can be rented from Trimtel Mobile Communications (☎ 729 1964), Menandrou 9.

Travel Agencies The bulk of the city's travel agencies are around Omonia and Syntagma squares, but only the agencies at Syntagma deal in discounted air tickets. There are lots of them just south of the square on Filellinon, Nikis and Voulis. The International Student & Youth Travel Service (ISYTS) (☎ 323 3767), Nikis 11 (2nd floor), is the city's official student and youth travel service and also issues International Student Identity Cards (ISIC). Magic Bus (☎ 323 7471), Filellinon 20, specialises in discount airfares, and has some very good last-minute deals on charter flights. It no longer operates its own buses to Europe (see the Getting There & Away chapter). Consolas Travel

(☎ 323 2812), right next door to Magic Bus, is also worth checking out.

Cultural Centres Following is a list of international cultural centres in Athens:

British Council
    Plateia Eterias (also known as Plateia Kolonakiou) 17 (☎ 363 3215)
French Institute of Athens
    Sina 31 (☎ 362 4301)
Goethe Institute
    Omirou 14-16 (☎ 360 8114)
Hellenic-American Union
    Massalias 22 (☎ 362 9886)

These cultural centres hold concerts, film shows and exhibitions from time to time. Major events are listed in various English-language newspapers and magazines.

Warning Lonely Planet has received several letters of complaint from travellers who have bought cheap accommodation packages for the Greek islands from travel agencies in the Plaka/Syntagma area. Some are relatively mild cases involving substandard hotels, others involve slick salespeople pressuring people into buying outrageously overpriced packages, and others involve travellers who have turned up at hotels to be told that their vouchers are worthless because the travel agency hasn't paid the hotel for months.

There is no need to buy a package; you will always be able to negotiate a better deal yourself when you get to the island of your choice. If you are worried that everywhere will be full, select a place from the pages of Lonely Planet and make a booking.

Bookshops Athens has three good English-language bookshops. The pick of them is Compendium (☎ 322 1248), upstairs at Nikis 28, Plaka. It has a second-hand section as well as a good selection overall. The place is also child-friendly, and holds a children's story hour on the second and fourth Saturday of every month at 11 am. The English-language notice board outside has information about jobs, accommodation and courses in Athens. You'll find the largest selection of books at

Eleftheroudakis (☎ 331 4180), Panepistimiou 17. Eleftheroudakis has a chain of stores around Athens, including a Syntagma branch at Nikis 4 and an Omonia branch in the Minion department store. Pantelides Books (☎ 362 3673), Amerikis 11, stocks a range of feminist books as well as paperbacks, travel guides, maps etc. All these shops stock Lonely Planet guides, but Eleftheroudakis has the largest range.

Ippokratous, in the student suburb of Exarhia, is packed solid with bookshops. The foreign-language bookshop *(xenoglosso vivliopoleio)* at No 10-12 stocks books in French, Italian and German as well as English.

The second-hand bookshop in the flea market at Ifestiou 24, Monastiraki, is an amazing place: a dusty cavern with piles of books everywhere – stacked to the ceiling in places. One of these stacks is devoted to books in English, dumped totally at random. You'll find everything from bundles of Marvel comics to books on neurology.

French, German, English, Italian and Spanish books are available at Kauffmann (☎ 322 2160), Stadiou 28, Syntagma, and The Booknest (☎ 323 1703), Panepistimiou 25-29.

International newspapers reach the *periptera* (kiosks) on Syntagma on the same day as they are published at 1 pm on weekdays and 7 pm on weekends.

Laundries Plaka has a very convenient laundrette at Angelou Geronta 10, just off Kydathineon near the outdoor restaurants. It is also the cheapest, charging 2000 dr to wash and dry 5kg. Others are at Psaron 9 near Plateia Karaïskaki (2500 dr), at Kolokinthous 41 on the corner of Leonidou (both in Omonia) and at Erehthiou 9 in Koukaki (2500 dr).

Luggage Storage Many of Athens' hotels will store luggage free for guests, although a lot of them do no more than pile the bags in a hallway. The Student & Travellers' Inn (see Places to Stay – Plaka) charges nonresidents 400 dr per day (per piece), 1600 per week or 2600 dr per month. Pacific Travel (☎ 324 1007),

Nikis 26, Plaka, charges 500 dr per day, 1500 dr per week and 3000 dr per month. Opening hours are Monday to Saturday from 8 am to 8 pm, Sunday and holidays from 8 am to 2 pm.

Supermarkets Supermarkets are a bit thin on the ground in central Athens. The Marinopoulos chain has a branch near Omonia on Athinas; the food section is downstairs. Basilopolou at Stadiou 18, Syntagma, is a large, well-stocked delicatessen that almost qualifies as a supermarket.

Emergency For the fire brigade ring ☎ 199. For emergency medical treatment ring the tourist police (☎ 171) and they will tell you the location of the nearest hospital. Hospitals give free emergency treatment to tourists. For hospitals with out-patient departments on duty, call ☎ 106; for the telephone number of an on-call doctor, ring ☎ 105 (from 2 pm to 7 am); for a pharmacy open 24 hours call ☎ 107; and for first-aid advice phone ☎ 166. US citizens can ring ☎ 721 2951 for emergency medical aid.

Dangers & Annoyances Be alert to the following traps:

Pickpockets Pickpockets have become a major problem in Athens. Their favourite hunting grounds are the metro system and the crowded streets around Omonia, particularly Athinas. The Sunday market on Ermou is another place where it pays to take extra care of your valuables. There have been numerous reports of thefts from day packs and bags.

Slippery Surfaces Many of Athens' pavements and other surfaces underfoot are made of marble and become incredibly slippery when wet, so if you are caught in the rain, be very careful how you tread.

Taxi Drivers Athens residents will tell you that their taxi drivers are the biggest bunch of bastards in the world. It seems that they have as much trouble getting a fair deal as

tourists do. Most of the rip-off stories involve cabs picked up from the airport or from Bus Terminal A at Kifissou. A favourite trick is to set the meter on night rate (tariff 2) during the day. They should be charging the day rate (tariff 1) between 6 am and midnight. Every now and again, the police conduct well-publicised clamp-downs. At the time of research, one cabby was caught at the airport with a handy remote-controlled device that could make the meter spin round at 2000 dr per minute!

If you are catching a cab to Athens from the airport, agree on the price before you get in. If the driver still attempts to charge you more, ask to see the official tariff list (which every driver must keep in the cab) and point out the error. If there is still a dispute over the fare, take the driver's number and report it to the tourist police.

Taxi Touts Taxi drivers working in league with some of the overpriced C-class hotels around Omonia are a problem that many have to contend with. The scam involves taxi drivers picking up late-night arrivals, particularly at the airport and Bus Terminal A, and persuading them that the hotel they want to go to is full – even if they have a booking. The taxi driver will pretend to phone the hotel of choice, announce that it's full and suggest an alternative. You can ask to speak to your chosen hotel yourself, or simply insist on going where you want.

Taxi drivers frequently attempt to claim commissions from hotel owners even if they have just gone where they were told. If the taxi driver comes into the hotel, make it clear to hotel staff that there is no reason to pay a commission.

Bar Scams Lonely Planet continues to receive a steady flow of letters from readers who have been taken in by one of the various bar scams that operate around central Athens, particularly around Syntagma. The basic scam runs something like this: friendly Greek approaches solo male traveller and discovers that the traveller knows little about Athens; friendly Greek then reveals that he, too, is from out of town. Why don't they go to this great little bar that he's just discovered and have a beer? They order a drink, and the equally friendly owner then offers another drink. Women appear, more drinks are provided and the visitor relaxes as he realises that the women are not prostitutes, just friendly Greeks. The crunch comes at the end of the evening when the traveller is presented with an exorbitant bill and the smiles disappear. The con men who cruise the streets playing the role of the friendly Greek can be very convincing: some people have been taken in more than once.

Other bars (see under Bars in the Entertainment section) don't bother with the acting. They target intoxicated males with talk of sex and present them with outrageous bills.

Walking Tour

This walk takes in most of Plaka's main sites. It takes about 45 minutes without detours. Plaka is a fascinating place to explore, full of surprises tucked away in the labyrinthine streets that weave over the undulating terrain.

The walk begins at the former royal palace, now the **parliament building**, which flanks the eastern side of Syntagma. The palace was designed by the Bavarian architect Von Gartner and was built in 1836-42. The building remained the royal palace until 1935, when it became the seat of the Greek parliament. (The royal family moved to a new palace on the corner of Vasileos Konstantinou and Herod Atticus, which became the presidential palace upon the abolition of the monarchy in 1974.)

Plateia Syntagmatos has been a favourite place for protests and rallies ever since the rally that led to the granting of a constitution on 3 September 1843, declared by King Otho from the balcony of the royal palace. In 1944 the first round of the civil war began here after police opened fire on a rally organised by the communists. Known as the Dekembriana (events of December), it was followed by a month of fierce fighting between the communist resistance and the British forces. In 1954 the first demonstration demanding the *enosis* (union) of Cyprus with Greece took place here. At election time, political parties stage their rallies in the square and most protest marches end up here.

The parliament building is guarded by the much photographed *evzones* (guards traditionally from the village of Evzoni in Macedonia). Their somewhat incongruous uniform of short kilts and pom-pom shoes is the butt of much mickey-taking by sightseers. Their uniform is based on the attire worn by the klephts, the mountain fighters who battled so ferociously in the War of Independence. Every Sunday at 11 am the evzones perform a full changing-of-the-guard ceremony.

Standing with your back to the parliament building you will see ahead of you, to the right, the **Hotel Grande Bretagne**. This, the grandest of Athens' hotels, was built in 1862 as a 60-room mansion to accommodate visiting dignitaries. In 1872 it was converted into a hotel and became the place where the crowned heads of Europe and eminent politicians stayed. The Nazis made it their headquarters during WWII. The hotel was the scene of an attempt to blow up the British prime minister Winston Churchill on Christmas Eve 1944 while he was in Athens to discuss the Dekembriana fighting. A bomb was discovered in the hotel sewer.

At the time of writing, it was not possible to cross over Amalias and walk through the middle of the square because of the metro works. Instead, cross Amalias and follow Othonos, on the southern flank of the square, down to Mitropoleos, which starts at the post office. Take the first turn left into Nikis, and walk up to the crossroads with Kydathineon, a pedestrian walkway and one of Plaka's main thoroughfares.

Turn right and a little way along you will come to the **Church of Metamorphosis** on Plateia Satiros; opposite is the **Museum of Greek Folk Art**. Continue along here, and after Plateia Filomousou Eterias (more commonly known as Plateia Plakas), the square with the outdoor tavernas, take the first turn left into Adrianou, another of Plaka's main

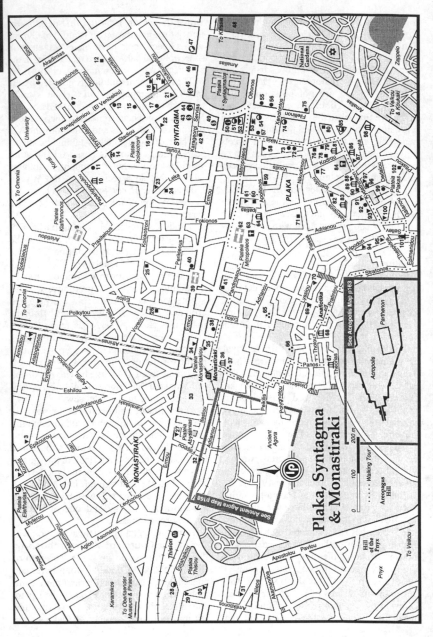

Plaka, Syntagma & Monastiraki

PLACES TO STAY
12 XEN
24 Hotel Achilleas
25 Hotel Carolina
26 Hotel Tempi
41 Hotel Plaka
46 Hotel Grande
   Bretagne; GB
   Corner Restaurant
59 Hotel Omiros
60 John's Place
71 Electra Palace
76 Hotel Myrto
77 Acropolis House
   Pension
78 Hotel Kouros
79 George's
   Guesthouse
80 Festos Youth &
   Student
   Guesthouse
82 Hotel Nefeli
90 Student &
   Travellers' Inn
102 Hotel Dioskouros
   House

PLACES TO EAT
2 Olympic Restaurant
3 O Telis Psistaria
4 Fruit & Vegetable
   Market
5 Meat & Fish Market
   Tavernas
19 Zonar's
20 Brazil Coffee Shop
21 Wendy's
22 Far East Restaurant
23 Orient Restaurant
27 Taverna Abyssinia
29 Taverna Steki tou
   Elia Restaurant
30 Pit Poule
31 Stavlos Restaurant
   & Music Bar
32 Ipiros Taverna
34 Savas & Grigoris
35 Thanasis
53 Neon Café
58 Souvlaki tou Hasepi
61 Peristeria Taverna
69 Traditional Music
   Tavernas

70 Eden Vegetarian
   Restaurant
87 Taverna Saita
88 The Cellar &
   Galaktopoleio
91 Vizantino Restaurant
93 Plaka Psistaria
94 Ouzeri Kouklis
95 Taverna O Thespis
96 Café Ionou
97 Michiko Japanese
   Restaurant
100 Taverna Damigos

THINGS TO SEE
9 Church of Agii
   Theodori
10 City of Athens
   Museum
16 National Historical
   Museum
36 Museum of
   Traditional Greek
   Ceramics
37 Library of Hadrian
38 Centre of Hellenic
   Tradition
39 Church of
   Kapnikarea
48 Parliament
62 Athens Cathedral
63 Church of Agios
   Eleftherios
64 National Welfare
   Organisation's Folk
   Art Gallery
65 Tower of the Winds
66 Roman Agora
67 Paul & Alexandra
   Kanellopoulos
   Museum
68 Museum of the
   University
81 Museum of
   Children's Art
83 Centre of Folk Arts
   & Traditions
84 Church of
   Metamorphosis
86 Museum of Greek
   Folk Art
89 Children's Museum
98 Jewish Museum

101 Monument of
   Lysicrates

OTHER
1 Buses to Dafni &
   Elefsina
6 Buses to Moni
   Kaissariannis
7 OSE (Railways
   Office)
8 Kauffmann Books
11 Basilopoulou
   Delicatessen
13 Eleftheroudakis
   Books
14 OTE
15 Pantilides Books
17 Festival Box Office
18 Parcel Post Office
28 Buses to Peania &
   Koropi
33 Flea Market
40 EOS (Greek Alpine
   Association)
42 Eleftheroudakis
   Books
43 Thomas Cook
44 EOT; National Bank
   of Greece
45 Credit Bank
47 Egyptian Consulate
49 American Express
50 Municipal Tourist
   Information Kiosk
51 Buses to Airport
52 Post Office
54 Bus 040 to Piraeus
55 Flying Dolphin
   (Ceres) Office
56 Olympic Airways
57 International
   Student & Youth
   Travel Service
72 Compendium Books
73 Pacific Travel
74 Buses to Cape
   Sounion
75 OSE (Railways
   Office)
85 Trolley Stop for
   Plaka
92 Cine Paris
99 Laundrette

thoroughfares. At the end, turn right, and this will bring you to the square with the **Choregic Monument of Lysicrates**. (The name *choregos* was given to the wealthy citizens who financed choral and dramatic performances.) This monument was built in 334 BC to com-memorate a win in a choral festival. An inscription on the architrave states:

Lysicrates of Kykyna, son of Lysitheides, was Choregos; the tribe of Akamantis won the victory with a chorus of boys; Theon played the flute; Lysiades of Athens trained the chorus; Euainetos was archon.

Choregic Monument of Lysicrates

The reliefs on the monument depict the battle between Dionysos and the Tyrrhenian pirates, whom the god had transformed into dolphins. It is the earliest known monument using Corinthian capitals externally. It stands in a cordoned-off archaeological site which is part of the **Street of Tripods**. It was here that winners of ancient dramatic and choral contests dedicated their tripod trophies to Dionysos.

In the 19th century, the monument was incorporated into the library of a French Capuchin convent, in which Byron stayed in 1810-11 and wrote *Childe Harold*. The convent was destroyed by fire in 1890. Recent excavations around the monument have revealed the foundations of other choragic monuments.

Facing the monument, turn left and then right into Epimenidou. At the top of the steps, turn right into Stratonos, which skirts the Acropolis. A left fork after 150m leads to the highest part of Plaka, an area called Anafiotika. The little whitewashed cube houses are the legacy of the people from the small Cycladic island of Anafi who were used as cheap labour in the building of Athens after Independence. It's a beautiful spot, with brightly painted olive-oil cans brimming with flowers bedecking the walls of the tiny gardens.

The path winds between the houses and comes to some steps on the right, at the bottom of which is a curving pathway leading downhill to Pratiniou. Turn left at Pratiniou and veer right after 50m into Tholou. The yellow-ochre building with brown shutters at No 5 is the old university, built by the Venetians. The Turks used it as public offices and it was Athens University from 1837 to 1841. It is now the **Museum of the University**, and its displays include some wonderful, old anatomical drawings and gruesome-looking surgical instruments. It is open Monday and Wednesday from 2.30 to 7 pm, and Tuesday, Thursday and Friday from 9.30 am to 2.30 pm. Admission is free.

At the end of Tholou, turn left into Panos. At the top of the steps on the left is a restored 19th-century mansion which is now the **Paul & Alexandra Kanellopoulos Museum**. Retracing your steps, go down Panos to the ruins of the **Roman Agora**, then turn left into Polygnotou and walk to the crossroads. Opposite, Polygnotou continues to the **Ancient Agora**. At the crossroads, turn right and then left into Peikilis, then immediately right into Areos. On the right are the remains of the **Library of Hadrian** and next to it is the **Museum of Traditional Greek Ceramics**, open Wednesday to Monday from 10 am to 2 pm. Admission is 500 dr. The museum is housed in the Mosque of Tzistarakis, built in 1759. After Independence it lost its minaret and was used as a prison.

Ahead is **Plateia Monastirakiou**, named after the small church. To the left is the metro station and the **flea market**. Plateia Monastirakiou is Athens at its noisiest, most colourful and chaotic. It teems with street vendors selling nuts, coconut sticks and fruit.

Turn right just beyond the mosque into Pandrossou. This street is a relic of the old Turkish bazaar. Today it is full of souvenir shops, selling everything from cheap kitsch to high-class jewellery and clothes. The street is named after King Cecrops' daughter, Pandrosos, who was the first priestess of Athens. At No 89 is Stavros Melissinos, the 'poet sandalmaker' of Athens who names the Beatles, Rudolph Nureyev and Jackie Onassis among his customers. Fame and fortune have not gone to his head, however – he still makes the best-value sandals in Athens, costing between 2400 and 3700 dr per pair.

Pandrossou leads to **Plateia Mitropoleos** and the **Athens Cathedral**. The cathedral has little architectural merit, which isn't surprising considering that it was constructed from the masonry of over 50 razed churches and from the designs of several architects. Next to it stands the much smaller, and far more appealing, **Church of Agios Eleftherios**, which was once the cathedral.

Turn left after the cathedral, and then right into Mitropoleos and follow it back to Syntagma.

The Acropolis

Athens exists because of the Acropolis, the most important ancient monument in the western world (see the Acropolis map). Crowned by the Parthenon, it stands sentinel over Athens, visible from almost everywhere within the city. Its monuments of Pentelic marble gleam white in the midday sun and gradually take on a honey hue as the sun sinks. At night they are floodlit and seem to hover above the city. No matter how harassed you may become in Athens, a sudden unexpected glimpse of this magnificent sight cannot fail to lift your spirits. Inspiring as these monuments are, they are but faded remnants of Pericles' city, and it takes a great leap of the imagination to begin to comprehend the splendour of his creations. Pericles spared no expense – only the best materials, architects, sculptors and artists were good enough for a city dedicated to the cult of Athena, tutelary goddess of Athens.

The Acropolis in classical times (c 400 BC)

The city was a showcase of colossal buildings, lavishly coloured and gilded, and of gargantuan statues, some of bronze, others of marble plated with gold and encrusted with precious stones.

The crowds that swarm over the Acropolis need to be seen to be believed. It's best to get there as early as possible. You need to wear shoes with good soles because the paths around the site are uneven and very slippery.

Between April and October, the Acropolis archaeological site (☎ 321 0219) is open Monday to Friday from 8 am to 6.30 pm, and on Saturday, Sunday and holidays from 8.30 am to 2.30 pm. The Acropolis **museum** is open Tuesday to Friday from 8 am to 6.30 pm; Saturday, Sunday and holidays from 8.30 am to 2.30 pm; and on Monday from 11 am to 6.30 pm. In winter, both site and museum close at 5 pm instead of 6.30 pm. The combined admission fee is 2000 dr.

There is only one entrance to the Acropolis, but there are several approaches to this entrance. The main approach from the north is along the path that is a continuation of Dioskouron in the south-west corner of Plaka. From the south, you can either walk or take bus No 230 along Dionysiou Areopagitou to just beyond the Theatre of Herodes Atticus, where a path leads to the entrance.

History The Acropolis (high city) was first inhabited in Neolithic times. The first temples were built during the Mycenaean era in homage to the goddess Athena. All the buildings on the Acropolis were reduced to ashes by the Persians on the eve of the Battle of Salamis (480 BC).

People lived on the Acropolis until the late 6th century BC, but in 510 BC the Delphic oracle declared that it should be the province of the gods. When Pericles set about his ambitious rebuilding programme, he transformed the Acropolis into a city of temples which has come to be regarded as the zenith of classical Greek achievement.

All four of the surviving monuments of the Acropolis have received their fair share of battering through the ages. Ravages inflicted upon them during the years of foreign occupation, pilfering by foreign archaeologists, inept renovation following Independence, visitors' footsteps and earthquakes have all taken their toll. The year 1687 was a particularly bad one. The Venetians attacked the Turks and opened fire on the Acropolis, causing an explosion in the Parthenon, where the Turks were storing gunpowder. The resulting fire blazed for two days, damaging all of the buildings.

However, the most recent menace, acid rain, caused by industrial pollution and traffic fumes, is proving to be the most irreversibly destructive. It is dissolving the very marble of which the monuments are built. Major renovation work is taking place in an effort to save the monuments for future generations.

Beulé Gate & Monument of Agrippa Once you've bought your ticket for the Acropolis and have walked a little way along the path, you will see on your left the Beulé Gate, named after the French archaeologist Ernest Beulé, who uncovered it in 1852. The 8m pedestal on the left, halfway up the zigzag ramp leading to the Propylaia, was once topped by the Monument of Agrippa, a bronze statue of the Roman general riding a chariot. It was erected in 27 BC to commemorate victory in a chariot race at the Panathenaic games.

Propylaia The Propylaia formed the towering entrance to the Acropolis in ancient times. Built by Mnesicles in 437-432 BC, its architectural brilliance ranks with that of the Parthenon. It consists of a central hall, with two wings on either side. Each section had a gate, and in ancient times these five gates were the only entrances to the 'upper city'. The middle gate (which was the largest) opened onto the Panathenaic Way. The western portico of the Propylaia must indeed have been imposing, consisting of six double columns, Doric on the outside and Ionic on the inside. The fourth column along has been restored. The ceiling of the central hall was painted with gold stars on a dark blue back-

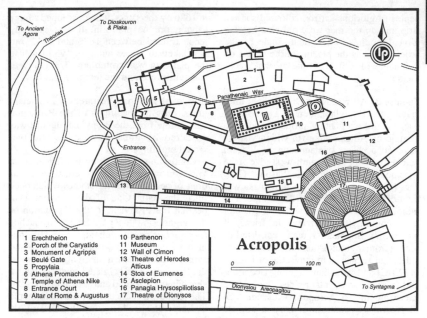

1 Erechtheion
2 Porch of the Caryatids
3 Monument of Agrippa
4 Beulé Gate
5 Propylaia
6 Athena Promachos
7 Temple of Athena Nike
8 Entrance Court
9 Altar of Rome & Augustus
10 Parthenon
11 Museum
12 Wall of Cimon
13 Theatre of Herodes
   Atticus
14 Stoa of Eumenes
15 Asclepion
16 Panagia Hrysospiliotissa
17 Theatre of Dionysos

Acropolis

0   50   100 m

ground. The northern wing was used as a picture gallery *(pinakotheke)* and the south wing was the antechamber to the Temple of Athena Nike.

The Propylaia is aligned with the Parthenon – the earliest example of a building designed in relation to another. It remained intact until the 13th century when various occupiers started adding to it. It was badly damaged in the 17th century when a lightning strike set off an explosion in a Turkish gunpowder store. Heinrich Schliemann paid for the removal of one of its appendages – a Frankish tower – in the 19th century. Reconstruction took place between 1909 and 1917 and there was further restoration after WWII. Once you're through the Propylaia, there is a stunning view of the Parthenon ahead.

Panathenaic Way The Panathenaic Way, which cuts across the middle of the Acropolis, was the route taken by the Panathenaic procession. The procession was the climax of the Panathenaia, the festival held to venerate the goddess Athena. The origins of the Panathenaia are uncertain. According to some accounts it was initiated by Erichthonius; according to others, by Theseus. There were two festivals: the Lesser Panathenaic Festival took place annually on Athena's birthday, and the Great Panathenaic Festival was held every fourth anniversary of the goddess' birth.

The Great Panathenaic Festival began with dancing and was followed by athletic, dramatic and musical contests. The Panathenaic procession, which took place on the final day of the festival, began at the Keramikos and ended at the Erechtheion. Men carrying animals sacrificed to Athena headed the procession, followed by maidens carrying rhytons (horn-shaped drinking vessels). Behind them were musicians playing a fanfare for the girls of noble birth who followed, proudly holding aloft the sacred peplos (a glorious saffron-coloured shawl). Bringing up the rear were old men bearing olive branches. The grand finale of the procession was the placing of the peplos on the statue of Athena Polias in the Erechtheion.

Temple of Athena Nike On the right after leaving the Propylaia, there is a good view back to the exquisitely proportioned little Temple of Athena Nike (to which visitors have no access). It stands on a platform perched atop the steep south-west edge of the Acropolis, overlooking the Saronic Gulf. The temple, designed by Callicrates, was built of Pentelic marble in 427-424 BC. The building is almost square, with four graceful Ionic columns at either end. Its frieze, of which only fragments remain, consisted of scenes from mythology on the east and south sides, and scenes from the Battle of Plataea (479 BC) and Athenians fighting Boeotians and Persians on the other sides. Parts of the frieze are in the Acropolis Museum. The platform was surrounded by a marble parapet of relief sculptures; some of these are also in the museum, including the beautiful sculpture of Athena Nike fastening her sandal.

The temple housed a statue of the goddess Athena. In her right hand was a pomegranate (symbol of fertility) and in her left a helmet (symbol of war). The temple was dismantled in 1686 by the Turks, who positioned a huge cannon on the platform. It was carefully reconstructed between 1836 and 1842, but was taken to pieces again in 1936 because the platform was crumbling. The platform was reinforced and the temple rebuilt.

Statue of Athena Promachos In ancient times, only the pediment of the Parthenon was visible from the Propylaia; the rest was obscured by numerous statues and two sacred buildings.

Continuing ahead along the Panathenaic Way you will see, to your left, the foundations of pedestals for the statues which once lined the path. One of them, about 15m beyond the Propylaia, is the foundation of the gigantic statue of Athena Promachos (*promachos* means 'champion'). The 9m-high statue was the work of Pheidias, and symbolised Athenian invincibility against the Persians. The helmeted goddess held a shield in her left hand and a spear in her right. The statue was carted off to Constantinople by Emperor Theodosius in 426 AD. By 1204 it had lost its spear, so the hand appeared to be gesturing. This led the inhabitants to believe that the statue had beckoned the crusaders to the city, so they smashed it to pieces.

Parthenon You have now reached the Parthenon, the monument which more than any

---

Greek Marble

So you thought Italy produced the world's best marble? Wrong, say the Greeks. The Italians import enormous amounts of raw marble from Greece.

In fact, Greece has been renowned for its fine marble since ancient times. For example, the most impressive legacy of the Cycladic civilisation is the figurines sculpted from the islands' magnificent white marble. The Temple of Athena Nike, in the Acropolis, was built entirely of Pentelic marble – from Attica – between 427 and 424 BC. Paros is famous for its pure, white marble which was once considered the world's finest – the Venus de Milo was carved from it and Napoleon's tomb is a Parian marble creation.

In addition to yielding excellent white marble, Greece is also renowned for its pink marble (found around Ioannina and Volos) and green marble (from the island of Timos).

Today, Greek marble is sliced and used for floors, staircases, gravestones, fireplaces, tables and bar tops. Unsliced pieces are made into pots, lamp bases, candlesticks and whole sinks for bathrooms or kitchens. Highly polished leftovers are made into figurines and marble eggs or set in jewellery. ∎

other epitomises the glory of ancient Greece. The name Parthenon means 'virgin's apartment'. It is the largest Doric temple ever completed in Greece, and the only one to be built completely (apart from its wooden roof) of Pentelic marble. It is built on the highest part of the Acropolis, halfway between the eastern and western boundaries.

The Parthenon had a dual purpose – to house the great statue of Athena which had been commissioned by Pericles, and to serve as a treasury for the tribute money which had been moved from Delos. It was built on the site of at least four earlier temples, all dedicated to the worship of Athena. It was designed by Ictinus and Callicrates, under the surveillance of Pheidias, to be the pre-eminent monument of the Acropolis. Building began in 447 BC and was completed in time for the Great Panathenaic Festival of 438 BC.

The temple consisted of eight fluted Doric columns at either end and 17 on each side. To achieve perfect form, its lines were ingeniously curved in order to counteract inharmonious optical illusions. As a result the foundations are slightly concave and the columns slightly convex, to make both look straight. Supervised by Pheidias, the sculptors Agoracritos and Alcamenes worked on the pediments and the sculpted sections of the frieze (metopes). All of the sculptures they created were brightly coloured and gilded. There were 92 metopes, 44 statues and a frieze which went all the way around.

The metopes on the eastern side depicted Athenians fighting giants (*gigantions*), and on the western side Theseus leading the Athenians into battle against the Amazons. Those on the southern side represented the contest of the Lapiths and Centaurs at the marriage feast of Pierithoös. An Ionic frieze 159.5m long ran all around the Parthenon. Much of it was damaged in the explosion of 1687, but the greatest existing part (just over 75m) consists of the much publicised Elgin Marbles, now in the British Museum in London. The British Government continues to scorn Greek requests for their return.

The ceiling of the Parthenon, like that of the Propylaia, was painted blue and gilded with stars. At the eastern end was the cella (inner room of a temple), the holy of holies, into which only a few privileged initiates could enter.

Here stood the statue for which the temple was built – the **Athena Polias** (Athena of the City), which was considered one of the wonders of the ancient world. The statue was designed by Pheidias and completed in 432 BC. It was made of gold plate over an inner wooden frame, and stood almost 12m high on its pedestal. The face, hands and feet were made of ivory, and the eyes were fashioned from jewels. The goddess was clad in a long dress of gold with the head of Medusa carved in ivory on the breast. In her right hand, she held a statuette of Nike – the goddess of victory – and in her left a spear; at the base of the spear was a serpent. On her head she wore a helmet, on top of which was a sphinx with griffins in relief at either side. In 426 BC the statue was taken to Constantinople, where it disappeared. There is a Roman copy (the Athena Varvakeion) in the National Archaeological Museum.

Erechtheion Although the Parthenon was the most impressive monument of the Acropolis, it was more of a showpiece than a sanctuary. That role fell to the Erechtheion, built on the part of the Acropolis that was held most sacred. It was here that Poseidon struck the ground with his trident and that Athena produced the olive tree. The temple is named after Erichthonius, a mythical king of Athens. It housed the cults of Athena, Poseidon and Erichthonius.

If you follow the Panathenaic Way around the northern portico of the Parthenon, you will see the Erechtheion to your left. It is immediately recognisable by the six larger-than-life maidens who take the place of columns to support its southern portico, its much-photographed **Caryatids**. They are so called because the models for them were women from Karyai (modern-day Karyes) in Lakonia.

The Erechtheion was part of Pericles' plan

The Caryatids, which support the southern
portico of the Erectheion

for the Acropolis, but the project was
postponed after the outbreak of the Peloponnesian Wars, and work did not start until 421
BC, eight years after his death. It is thought
to have been completed in 406 BC.

The Erechtheion is architecturally the
most unusual monument of the Acropolis.
Whereas the Parthenon is considered the
supreme example of Doric architecture, the
Erechtheion is considered the supreme example of Ionic. It was ingeniously built on
several levels to counteract the unevenness
of the ground. It consists of three basic parts
– the main temple, the northern porch and the
southern porch – all with different dimensions.

The main temple is of the Ionic order and
is divided into two cellae: one is dedicated to
Athena, the other to Poseidon; thus the
temple represents a reconciliation of the two
deities after their contest. In Athena's cella

stood an olive-wood statue of Athena Polias
holding a shield on which was a gorgon's
head. It was this statue on which the sacred
peplos was placed at the culmination of the
Panathenaic Festival. The statue was illuminated by a golden lantern placed at its
feet.

The northern porch consists of six graceful Ionic columns; on the floor are the
fissures supposedly cleft by Poseidon's trident. This porch leads into the **Temenos of
Pandrossos**, where, according to mythology, the sacred olive brought forth by
Athena grew. To the south of here was the
Cecropion – King Cecrops' burial place.

The southern porch is that of the Caryatids, which prop up a heavy roof of Pentelic
marble. The ones you see are plaster casts –
the originals (except for one removed by
Lord Elgin) are in the site's museum.

Acropolis Museum The museum at the
south-east corner of the Acropolis houses a
collection of sculptures and reliefs from the
site. The rooms are organised in chronological order, starting with finds from the
temples that predated the Parthenon and
were destroyed by the Persians. They include
the pedimental sculptures of Heracles slaying the Lernaian Hydra and of a lioness
devouring a bull, both in Room I. The Kora
(maiden) statues in Room IV are regarded as
the museum's prize exhibits. Most date from
the 6th century BC and were uncovered from
a pit on the Acropolis, where they were
buried by the Athenians after the Battle of
Salamis. The statues were votives dedicated
to Athena, each once holding an offering to
the goddess. The earliest of these Kora
statues are quite stiff and formal in comparison with the later ones, which have
flowing robes and elaborate headdresses.

Room VIII contains the few pieces of the
Parthenon's frieze that escaped the clutches
of Lord Elgin. They depict the Olympians at
the Panathenaic procession. It also holds the
relief of Athena Nike adjusting her sandal.
Room IX is home to four of the five surviving Caryatids, safe behind a perspex screen.
The fifth is in the British Museum.

Southern Slope of the Acropolis

The entrance to the southern slope of the Acropolis is on Dionysiou Areopagitou. The site (☎ 322 4625) is open every day from 8.30 am to 2.30 pm. Admission is 500 dr.

Theatre of Dionysos The importance of theatre in the life of the Athenian city-state can be gauged from the dimensions of the enormous Theatre of Dionysos on the south-eastern slope of the Acropolis.

The first theatre on this site was a timber structure erected sometime during the 6th century BC, after the tyrant Peisistratos had introduced the Festival of the Great Dionysia to Athens. This festival, which took place in March or April, consisted of contests where men clad in goatskins sang and performed dances. Everyone attended, and the watching of performances was punctuated by feasting, revelry and generally letting rip.

During the golden age in the 5th century BC, the annual festival had become one of the major events on the calendar. Politicians would sponsor the production of dramas by writers such as Aeschylus, Sophocles and Euripides, with some light relief provided by the bawdy comedies of Aristophanes. People came from all over Attica, their expenses met by the state – if only present-day governments were as generous to the arts!

The theatre was reconstructed in stone and marble by Lycurgus between 342 and 326 BC. The auditorium had a seating capacity of 17,000 spread over 64 tiers of seats, of which about 20 survive. Apart from the front row, the seats were built of Piraeus limestone and were occupied by ordinary citizens, although women were confined to the back rows. The front row consisted of 67 thrones built of Pentelic marble, which were reserved for festival officials and important priests. The grandest was in the centre and reserved for the Priest of Dionysos, who sat shaded from the sun under a canopy. The seat can be identified by well-preserved lion-claw feet at either side. In Roman times, the theatre was also used for state events and ceremonies as well as for performances.

The reliefs at the rear of the stage, mostly of headless figures, depict the exploits of Dionysos and date from the 2nd century BC. The two hefty, hunched-up guys who have managed to keep their heads are *selini*. Selini were worshippers of the mythical Selinos, the debauched father of the satyrs whose chief attribute seems to have been an out-sized phallus. His favourite pastime was charging up mountains in lecherous pursuit of nymphs. He also happened to be Dionysos' mentor.

Asclepion & Stoa of Eumenes Directly above the Theatre of Dionysos, wooden steps lead up to a pathway. On the left at the top of the steps is the Asclepion, which was built around a sacred spring. The worship of Asclepius, the physician son of Apollo, began in Epidaurus and was introduced to Athens in 429 BC at a time when plague was sweeping the city.

Beneath the Asclepion is the Stoa of Eumenes, a long colonnade built by Eumenes II, King of Pergamum (197-159 BC), as a shelter and promenade for theatre audiences.

Theatre of Herodes Atticus The path continues west from the Asclepion to the Theatre of Herodes Atticus, built in 161 AD. Herodes Atticus was a wealthy Roman who built the theatre in memory of his wife Regilla. It was excavated in 1857-58 and completely restored in 1950-61. There are performances of drama, music and dance here during the Athens Festival. The theatre is open to the public only during performances.

Panagia Hrysospiliotissa If you retrace your steps back to the Theatre of Dionysos, you will see an indistinct rock-strewn path leading to a grotto in the cliff face. In 320 BC, Thrasyllos turned the grotto into a temple dedicated to Dionysos. Today it is the tiny Panagia Hrysospiliotissa (Chapel of our Lady of the Cavern). It is a poignant little place with old pictures and icons on the walls. Above the chapel are two Ionic columns which are the remains of Thrasyllos' temple.

Ancient Agora

The Agora (market) was Athens' meeting place in ancient times (see the Ancient Agora map). It was the focal point of administrative, commercial and political life, not to mention social activity. All roads led to the Agora, and it was a lively, crowded place. Socrates spent a lot of time here expounding his philosophy, and in 49 AD St Paul disputed daily in the Agora, intent upon winning converts to Christianity.

The site was first developed in the 6th century BC. It was devastated by the Persians in 480 BC, but a new agora was built in its place almost immediately. It was flourishing by Pericles' time and continued to do so until 267 AD, when it was destroyed by the Herulians, a Gothic tribe from Scandinavia. The Turks built a residential quarter on the site, but this was demolished by archaeologists after Independence. If they'd had their way the archaeologists would have also knocked down the whole of Plaka, which was also Turkish. The area has been excavated to classical and, in parts, Neolithic levels.

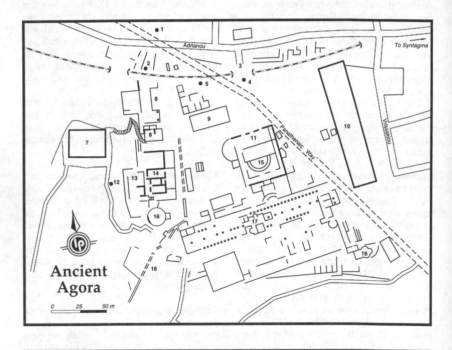

Ancient Agora

0   25   50 m

1	Stoa Poikile	6	Stoa of Zeus Eleutherios	13	New Bouleuterion
2	Stoa of Basileios			14	Metroön
3	Entrance	7	Temple of Hephaestus	15	Odeon of Agrippa
4	Mosaic showing reconstruction of Agora	8	Temple of Apollo	16	Tholos
		9	Temple of Ares	17	Middle Stoa
		10	Stoa of Attalos	18	Sewer
5	Altar of the Twelve Gods	11	Stoa of the Giants	19	Church of the Holy Apostles
		12	Plan of Site		

The main monuments are the Temple of Hephaestus, the Stoa of Attalos and the Church of the Holy Apostles.

The site is bounded by Areopagus hill in the south, the Athens-Piraeus metro line to the north, Plaka to the east and Leoforos Apostolou Pavlou to the west. There are several entrances, but the most convenient is the southern entrance at the western end of Polygnotou (see the Walking Tour section earlier). The Ancient Agora (☎ 321 0185) is open from Tuesday to Sunday from 8.30 am to 3 pm, and admission costs 1200 dr.

Stoa of Attalos The Agora Museum in the reconstructed Stoa of Attalos is a good place to start if you want to make any sense of the site. The museum has a model of the Agora upstairs as well as a collection of finds from the site.

The original stoa was built by King Attalos II of Pergamum (159-138 BC). It was two storeys high with two aisles, and housed expensive shops. A popular stamping ground for wealthy Athenians, people also gathered here to watch the Panathenaic procession, which crossed in front of the stoa. It was authentically reconstructed in 1953-56 by the American School of Archaeology. The reconstruction deviates from the original in only one detail: the façade has been left in natural Pentelic marble, but it was originally painted red and blue. The stoa has a series of 45 columns which are Doric on the ground floor and Ionic on the upper gallery.

Temple of Hephaestus This temple on the western edge of the Agora was surrounded by foundries and metalwork shops, and was dedicated to Hephaestus, god of the forge. It was one of the first buildings of Pericles' rebuilding programme and is the best preserved Doric temple in Greece. Built in 449 BC by Ictinus, one of the architects of the Parthenon, it has 34 columns and a frieze on the eastern side depicting nine of the Twelve Labours of Heracles. In 1300 AD it was converted into the **Church of Agios Georgios**. The last service held here was on

13 December 1834 in honour of King Otho's arrival in Athens.

Unlike the Parthenon, the monument does not evoke a sense of wonder, but it's nevertheless a pleasant place to wander around. The garden that surrounds the temple has been reconstructed to resemble the Roman garden that existed there in antiquity.

To the north-east of the temple are the foundations of the **Stoa of Zeus Eleutherios**, one of the places where Socrates expounded his philosophy. Further north are the foundations of the **Stoa of Basileios** and the **Stoa Poikile** (Painted Stoa), both currently inaccessible to the public. The Stoa Poikile was so called because of its murals, which were painted by the leading artists of the day and depicted mythological and historical battles. At the end of the 4th century BC, Zeno taught his Stoic philosophy here. To the south-east of the Temple of Hephaestus was the **New Bouleuterion**, or council house, where the Senate (originally created by Solon) met. To the south of here was the circular **Tholos** where the heads of government met.

Church of the Holy Apostles This charming little church, which stands near the southern entrance, was built in the early 11th century to commemorate St Paul's teaching in the Agora. In 1954-57 it was stripped of its 19th-century additions and restored to its original form. It contains some fine Byzantine frescoes.

The Keramikos

The Keramikos was the city's cemetery from the 12th century BC to Roman times. It was discovered in 1861 during the construction of Pireos, the street which leads to Piraeus. Despite its location on the seedier part of Ermou, beyond Monastiraki, it is one of the most green and tranquil of Athens' ancient sites.

The entrance to the site (☎ 346 3552) is at Ermou 148. It is open Tuesday to Sunday from 8 am to 3 pm, and admission is 500 dr.

Sacred & Dipylon Gates The first place to check out once you have entered the site is the small knoll ahead and to the right from the entrance: here you will find a plan of the site. A path leads down to the right from the knoll to the remains of the city wall, which was built by Themistocles in 479 BC, and rebuilt by Konon in 394 BC. The wall is broken by the foundations of two gates (see the Ancient Athens map).

The first, the Sacred Gate, spanned the Sacred Way and was the one by which pilgrims from Eleusis entered the city during the annual Eleusian procession. The Dipylon Gate, to the north-east of the Sacred Gate, was the city's main entrance and was where the Panathenaic procession began. It was also the stamping ground of the city's prostitutes, who gathered there to offer their services to jaded travellers.

From a platform outside the Dipylon Gate, Pericles gave his famous speech extolling the virtues of Athens and honouring those who died in the first year of the Peloponnesian Wars. The speech stirred many more to battle – and to their deaths.

Between the Sacred and the Dipylon gates are the foundations of the **Pompeion**. This building was used as a dressing room for participants in the Panathenaic procession.

Street of Tombs The Street of Tombs leads off the Sacred Way to the left as you head away from the city. This avenue was reserved for the tombs of Athens' most prominent citizens. The surviving stele are now in the National Archaeological Museum, and what you see are replicas. They consist of an astonishing array of funerary monuments, and their bas-reliefs warrant more than a cursory examination.

Ordinary citizens were buried in the areas bordering the Street of Tombs. One very well preserved stele shows a little girl with her pet dog. You will find it by going up the stone steps on the northern side of the Street of Tombs. The site's largest stele, that of sisters Demetria and Pamphile, is on the path running from the south-east corner of the street of tombs. Pamphile is seated beside a standing Demetria.

Oberlaender Museum The site's Oberlaender Museum is named after its benefactor, Gustav Oberlaender, a German-American stocking manufacturer. It contains steles and sculpture from the site, as well as an impressive collection of vases and terracotta figurines. The museum is to the left of the site entrance.

Roman Athens
Tower of the Winds & Roman Agora These are next to one another to the east of the Ancient Agora and north of the Acropolis (see the Ancient Athens map).

The well-preserved Tower of the Winds was built in the 1st century BC by a Syrian astronomer named Andronicus. The octagonal monument of Pentelic marble is an ingenious construction which functioned as a sundial, weather vane, water clock and compass. Each side represents a point of the compass, and has a relief of a figure floating through the air, which depicts the wind associated with that particular point. Beneath each of the reliefs are the faint markings of sundials. The weather vane, which disappeared long ago, was a bronze Triton that revolved on top of the tower. The Turks, not ones to let a good building go to waste, allowed dervishes to use the tower.

The entrance to the Roman Agora is through the well-preserved **Gate of Athena Archegetis**, which is flanked by four Doric columns. It was erected sometime in the 1st century AD and financed by Julius Caesar.

The rest of the Roman Agora appears to the layperson as little more than a heap of rubble. To the right of the entrance are the foundations of a 1st-century public latrine. In the south-east area are the foundations of a propylon and a row of shops.

The site (☎ 321 0185) is open Tuesday to Sunday from 8.30 am to 3 pm. Admission is 500 dr.

City of Hadrian The Roman emperor Hadrian had a great affection for Athens. Although, like all Roman emperors, he did his fair share of spiriting its classical artwork

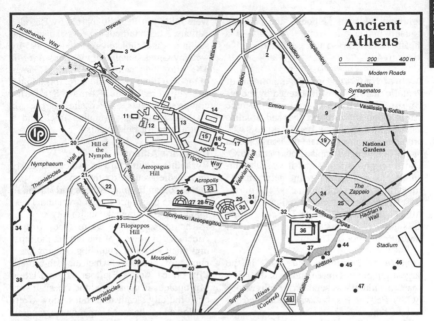

Ancient Athens

0   200   400 m

Modern Roads

to Rome, he also embellished the city with many monuments influenced by classical architecture. Grandiose as these monuments are, they lack the refinement and artistic flair of their classical predecessors.

Library of Hadrian This library is to the north of the Roman Agora. The building, which was of vast dimensions, was erected in the 2nd century AD and included a cloistered courtyard bordered by 100 columns. As well as books, the building housed music and lecture rooms and a theatre. The library is at present inaccessible to visitors.

Arch of Hadrian This lofty monument of Pentelic marble – now blackened by the effluent of exhausts – stands where traffic-clogged Vasilissis Olgas and Amalias meet. It was erected by Hadrian in 132 AD, probably to commemorate the consecration of the Temple of Olympian Zeus (see below). The inscriptions show that it was also intended as a dividing point between the ancient city and the Roman city. The northwest frieze bears the inscription, 'This is Athens, the Ancient city of Theseus'; while the south-east frieze states 'This is the city of Hadrian, and not of Theseus'.

Temple of Olympian Zeus This is the largest temple in Greece and took over 700 years to build. It was begun in the 6th century BC by Peisistratos, but was abandoned for lack of funds.

Various other leaders had stabs at completing the temple, but it was left to Hadrian to complete the work in 131 AD. The temple is impressive for the sheer size of its 104 Corinthian columns (17m high with a base diameter of 1.7m), of which 15 remain – the fallen column was blown down in a gale in 1852. Hadrian put a colossal statue of Zeus in the cella and, in typically immodest fashion, placed an equally large one of himself next to it. The site (☎ 922 6330) is open Tuesday to Sunday from 8.30 am to 3 pm. Admission is 500 dr.

Roman Stadium The last Athenian monument with Roman connections is the Roman Stadium, which lies in a fold between two pine-covered hills between the neighbourhoods of Mets and Pangrati (see the Athens map). The stadium was originally built in the 4th century BC as a venue for the Panathenaic athletic contests. A thousand wild animals are said to have been slaughtered in the arena at Hadrian's inauguration in 120 AD. Shortly after this, the seats

were rebuilt in Pentelic marble by Herodes Atticus. After hundreds of years of disuse the stadium was completely restored in 1895 by wealthy Greek benefactor Georgios Averof. The following year the first Olympic Games of modern times were held here. It is a faithful replica of the Roman Stadium, comprising seats of Pentelic marble for 70,000 spectators, a running track and a central area for field events.

Byzantine Athens
Byzantine architecture in Athens is fairly thin on the ground. By the time of the split in the Roman Empire, Athens had shrunk to little more than a provincial town and Thessaloniki had become the major city.

The monastery at Dafni (see Around Athens), 10km west of the city, is the most important Byzantine building. Athens has a number of churches, of which the 11th-century **Church of Agios Eleftherios** on Plateia Mitropoleos is considered the finest. It was once the city's cathedral, but is now overshadowed by the much larger new cathedral. It is built partly of Pentelic marble and decorated with an external frieze of symbolic beasts in bas-relief.

The **Church of Kapnikarea**, halfway down Ermou, is another small 11th-century church. Its dome is supported by four large Roman columns. The **Church of Agii Theodori**, just off Plateia Klafthmonos on Stadiou, has a tiled dome and the walls are decorated with a terracotta frieze of animals and plants. Other churches worth peering into are the **Church of the Holy Apostles** (see Ancient Agora, earlier) and the **Church of Agios Dimitrios** (see West of the Acropolis in the Hills of Athens section, later).

Museums
Athens has 25 museums to choose from, covering everything from Mycenaean treasures to old theatre props.

National Archaeological Museum This museum (☎ 821 7717), opened in 1874, stands supreme among the nation's finest.

Despite all the pilfering by foreign archaeologists in the 19th century, it still has the world's finest collection of Greek antiquities. It is so crammed with treasures that to do the place justice you need to visit several times. If time is very short, at least ensure you visit the magnificent Hall of Mycenaean Antiquities and the Thira Exhibition, which contains the celebrated collection of Minoan frescoes unearthed at Akrotiri on the island of Santorini (Thira).

Several guidebooks to the museum are on sale in the foyer. There are comprehensive explanations in English in each room.

The museum is at 28 Oktovriou-Patission 44 (see the Exarhia map) and is open Tuesday to Friday from 8 am to 7 pm; Saturday, Sunday and holidays from 8.30 am to 3 pm; and on Monday from 12.30 to 7 pm. It closes at 5 pm instead of 7 pm between November and March. Admission is 2000 dr (free on Sunday and public holidays). To reach the museum take trolleybus No 2, 4, 5, 9, 11, 12, 15 or 18 from Amalias.

Hall of Mycenaean Antiquities The museum's *tour de force* is the Hall of Mycenaean Antiquities, where gold gleams

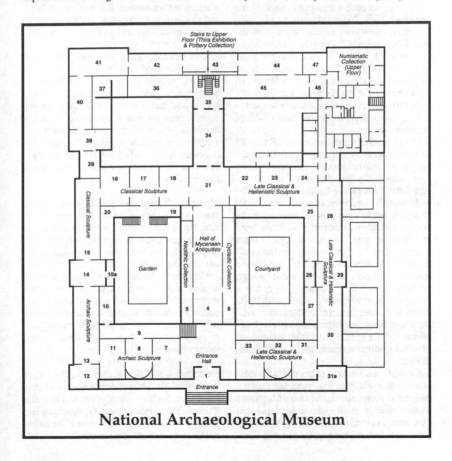

National Archaeological Museum

at you from everywhere. The chief exhibits are from the six shaft graves of Grave Circle A at Mycenae. Shaft graves were rectangular pits about 6m deep. The pit bottom was covered with pebbles, and stone walls measuring about 1.5m high were built around the sides. After the body and treasures were placed in the pit, it was covered with tree trunks, which rested upon the top of the stone wall. The pit was then filled with soil. Graves one to five were excavated by Heinrich Schliemann in 1874-76 and the sixth by Panagiotes Stamatakis in 1886-1902. Just beyond case 25 are four grave steles, two on each side. On the back of the one nearest case 25 are two pictures of Grave Circle A; one shows a reconstruction of the site. The five cases beyond the steles – numbers 3, 4, 23, 24 and 27 – contain the most valuable finds from these shaft graves. Most famous of all is the golden **Mask of Agamemnon** in case 3. It has subsequently been proven that the death mask belonged to a king who died three centuries before Agamemnon.

In the centre of the hall, cases 28 and 29 contain objects from the third grave, including gold sheets that covered the bodies of two royal babies. On the left, cases 5 and 6 contain finds from Grave Circle B (from 1650 to 1550 BC), which was outside the citadel at Mycenae. In case 5 is an unusual rock-crystal vase in the shape of a duck: its head and neck are gracefully turned back to form a handle. On the right, against the blue partition, is the head of a woman, possibly a sphinx or goddess, carved in limestone with brightly painted lips, eyes and fringe. It is a rare example of a Mycenaean sculpture in the round and dates from the 13th century BC. On the other side of the partition are fragments of frescoes from the palace at Mycenae, which reveal a strong Minoan influence.

Case 30, also in the centre, contains miscellaneous finds from Mycenae, including a delightful ivory carving of two voluptuous women and a child, who may represent Demeter, Persephone and Iacchus. On the right, just beyond here, is the famous **War-** **rior Vase** which, along with the Mask of Agamemnon, Schliemann rated as one of his greatest finds. It depicts men leaving for war and a woman waving them goodbye.

The rest of the hall is devoted to other Mycenaean sites. On the left, case 9 contains tablets with inscriptions in Cretan Linear B script. In case 15, on the right, are objects from Tiryns, including the famous **Tiryns Treasure**. The treasure is believed to have been looted by a tomb robber, who then reburied it and failed to retrieve it. Back in the centre, case 32 contains the famous gold cups from the beehive-shaped tomb at Vaphio, which depict the taming of wild bulls. These magnificent cups are regarded as among the finest examples of Mycenaean art.

Towards room 21, at the far end of the hall, on the right-hand wall, is an explanation in English of the three different types of Mycenaean graves: shaft graves, chamber tombs and tholos tombs. The latter are the most elaborate and impressive, and the entrance to one of them, the **Treasury of Atreus**, has been reconstructed around the doorway at this end of the hall. To the right are some slabs which decorated the façade of this treasury.

Cycladic Collection Room 6, to the right of the Hall of Mycenaean Antiquities, is devoted to Cycladic art. At the western end is the largest Cycladic figurine ever found. It is almost life-size and was discovered on the island of Amorgos.

Cases 56, 57 and 58 contain ceramic 'frying pans' from early Cycladic cemeteries on Syros. They are black with intricate inlaid patterns in white. In case you're wondering why on earth these people took frying pans to the grave with them, they are so called merely because of their shape.

Neolithic Collection Room 5, to the left of the Hall of Mycenaean Antiquities, contains Neolithic finds – mainly from Thessaly. There is also a case of pottery, figurines and jewellery from Troy, including a beautiful necklace of delicate gold beads. These finds were presented to the museum by Sophie Schliemann, wife of Heinrich.

Archaic Sculpture Rooms 7 to 14, entered from the left side of the vestibule, contain archaic sculpture. The main feature of room 7 is the huge sepulchral amphora (a jar with two handles and a narrow neck) dating from 760 BC and found in the Keramikos. It is considered the most masterful example of the geometric style of pottery.

The chief exhibit in room 8 is the huge *kouros* dating from 600 BC. This was a votive offering found in the Temple of Poseidon at Cape Sounion. To the right of the entrance to room 9 is the torso of a kore figure with elaborately folded drapery.

Room 10 contains gravestones from the 6th century and two well-preserved sphinxes, one from Piraeus (540 BC) and the other from Sparta (570 BC). In Room 11 is the torso of another colossal kouros (540 BC), found at Megara in Attica.

Room 13 is dominated by the sepulchral kouros named Croesus. To the left of this sculpture is the base of a kouros found in the Keramikos. It has reliefs on three sides: one shows four clothed youths provoking a fight between a cat and dog; another shows naked youths wrestling; and the third shows youths playing a ball game.

Room 14 is given over to provincial stele monuments. The gravestone by Alxenor is one of the finest in the room and bears an endearing, if egocentric, inscription by the artist: 'Alxenor the Naxian made me. Admire me'.

Classical Sculpture The bronze statue of **Poseidon of Artemision** (450 BC) in room 15 is one of the highlights of the museum. The statue was hauled out of the sea off Cape Artemision in 1928, and shows Poseidon poised to hurl his trident (now missing). More than any other statue of Poseidon, it conveys the god's strength and unlimited power.

Just within the door of this room is a beautiful and well-preserved relief from Eleusis (440 BC). It depicts Demeter, ac-companied by her daughter Persephone, giving Triptolemos an ear of wheat to sprout.

Room 16 contains classical grave monuments, most of which were found in Attica. Rooms 17 and 19 contain classical votive sculpture. Room 20 consists mostly of Roman copies of classical Greek statues. At the far end is the statue of Athena Varvakeion, which was made in about 200 BC. It is the most famous copy – much reduced in size – of the statue of Athena Polias by Pheidias that once stood in the Parthenon. Room 18 contains late 5th and early 4th-century sepulchral monuments.

Late Classical & Hellenistic Sculpture In room 21, the central hall, your eye will be drawn to another outstanding piece – the 2nd-century bronze statue of the **Horse and Jockey of Artemision**, which was found with the statue of Poseidon. It is a remarkably animated sculpture; especially impressive is the jockey's anxious expression.

There is an unusual grave monument (540 BC) in the centre of room 24 consisting of a floral column which supports a cauldron decorated with griffins.

Room 25 is mostly devoted to charming diminutive reliefs of nymphs. They are not individually labelled, but there is an explanation in English of their role. On the left, just before room 26, is a highly unusual votive relief of a snake and a huge sandal on which is carved a worshipping figure. It dates from 360 BC and is believed to depict the Hero of the Slipper, who was worshipped near the Theatre of Dionysos. Rooms 26 and 27 contain more votive reliefs.

Room 28 contains some extremely realistic funerary monuments, particularly the Grave Monument of Aristonautes (330 BC), found in the Keramikos. The large sepulchral relief of a boy attempting to restrain a frisky horse is a powerful and unprecedented piece of realist sculpture, especially the leg muscles of both the horse and boy, and the magnificent drapery. It was found near Larisis Station in 1948, and dates from the second half of the 3rd century. The famous **Ephebos of Antikythira** (340 BC) stands in the centre of the room. The amazingly lifelike eyes are almost hypnotic. Behind this statue, to the right, is the head of a bronze statue – probably of the Elean boxer Satyros. He certainly looks a nasty piece of work in contrast to the calm 'other world' expressions on the faces surrounding him.

Room 29 is dominated by the statue of Themis (the goddess of justice). Behind her is a head of Alexander the Great which has graffitied cheeks (added later). Next to him is a head of the orator Demosthenes, looking very perplexed.

The comic masks on the right in room 30 provide some light relief, although some of their expressions are as menacing as they are funny. A little way down, in the middle of the room, is a delightful and sensitive sculpture of a naked boy with his hand on a goose – note his gentle smile and the apparent softness of his skin. Dominating the room is yet another statue of the sea god, Poseidon (140 BC), which was found on Milos in 1877. Behind this statue is the bronze head of a melancholic-looking guy; it was found on Delos. To the right is an amusing sculpture of Pan making amorous advances towards Aphrodite, who is about to clobber him with her sandal.

Room 34 is built to simulate an open-air sanctuary and displays objects from the **Sanctuary of Aphrodite** which existed near Dafni. Room 36 houses the **Karapanos Collection**, which includes a chariot from the Roman period. Room 37 was the first bronze room to be opened. A case on the left shows casting techniques; another shows burial offerings. In the middle is a bronze statue of a youth (337 BC), which was found in the Bay of Marathon.

Thira Exhibition The hall at the top of the stairs houses the celebrated frescoes unearthed by Spyridon Marinatos at the Minoan settlement of Akrotiri on Santorini (Thira) in the late 1960s.

The frescoes are more varied and better preserved than the Minoan frescoes found on Crete. Extremely beautiful and harmonious in both colour and form, they give a comprehensive insight into the everyday life of the Minoans. Scenes depicted in the frescoes include two boxing youths, a youth holding two strings of fish, and women performing religious rites. The most unusual is the one which shows a flotilla of ships sailing from one coastal town to another. The frescoes will remain here until a suitable museum has been built on Santorini.

Pottery Collection On leaving the Thira exhibition, turn left to reach the first of the pottery rooms. These house the world's most comprehensive collection of ancient Greek pottery. The collection traces the development from the Bronze Age, through the Protogeometric and Geometric periods to the beginning of simple decorative motifs.

Flora, fauna and human figures first featured on pottery in the 8th century BC, and mythical scenes appeared a century later. The 6th century BC saw the emergence of the famous Attic black-figured pottery. By the middle of the 5th century, the pots with black figures had been superseded by red-figured pottery, which reached the peak of perfection during Pericles' rule.

Numismatic Collection The numismatic exhibit, to the left at the top of the stairs and through room 56, is a vast collection comprising 400,000 coins from ancient Greek, Hellenic, Roman and Byzantine times.

Benaki Museum This museum contains the sumptuous and eclectic collection of Antoine Benaki, accumulated during Antoine's 35 years of avid collecting in Europe and Asia. In 1931 he turned the family house into a museum and presented it to the Greek nation. The collection includes Bronze Age finds from Mycenae and Thessaly; two early works by El Greco; ecclesiastical furniture brought from Asia Minor by refugees; pottery, copper, silver and woodwork from Egypt, Asia Minor and Mesopotamia; and a stunning collection of Greek regional costumes.

The museum is on the corner of Vasilissis Sofias and Koumbari Kolonaki (see the

Athens map). At the time of writing, it was closed for a complete refit and was not scheduled to reopen until mid-1998. The museum shop (☎ 362 7367) remains open Monday to Friday from 8.30 am to 3 pm, selling books, cards and replicas.

Goulandris Museum of Cycladic & Ancient Greek Art This private museum (☎ 801 5870) houses a collection of Cycladic art which is second in importance only to that displayed at the National Archaeological Museum. The museum was custom-built for the collection and the finds are beautifully displayed, lit and labelled. Although the exhibits cover all periods from Cycladic to Roman times, the emphasis is on the Cycladic from 3000 to 2000 BC. The 230 exhibits include the marble figurines with folded arms which inspired many 20th-century artists with their simplicity and purity of form.

The museum has now taken over the 19th-century mansion next door, which it uses for temporary exhibitions. The entrance to the museum is at Neofytou Douka 4, Kolonaki, just around the corner from Vasilissis Sofias (see the Athens map). It is open on Monday, Wednesday, Thursday and Friday from 10 am to 4 pm, and on Saturday from 10 am to 3 pm. Admission is 400 dr.

Byzantine Museum This museum (☎ 723 1570) has a large collection of Christian art from the 4th to the 19th century, housed in the Villa Ilissia, an attractive, mock-Florentine mansion at Vasilissis Sofias 22, Kolonaki (see the Athens map).

Unfortunately, the museum will be operating at half-capacity until at least 1998, as the wing to the right of the courtyard is being completely rebuilt. This wing housed many of the finest frescoes and icons; some are in storage, others have been moved temporarily to Thessaloniki.

The downstairs rooms in the surviving wing are given over to re-creations of churches, starting with a very solemn basilica from the 5th to the 7th century. The reconstruction of an 11th-century Byzantine

church is beautiful in its simplicity, in contrast to the elaborate decorations of the post-Byzantine church next door. The bishop's throne in this room was brought to Athens by refugees from Asia Minor. The upstairs rooms contain icons and frescoes.

The museum is open Tuesday to Sunday from 8.30 am to 3 pm. Admission is 500 dr.

Museum of Greek Folk Art This museum (☎ 322 9031) houses a superb collection of secular and religious folk art, mainly from the 18th and 19th centuries. On the 1st floor is embroidery, pottery, weaving and puppets. On the 2nd floor is a reconstructed traditional village house with paintings by the primitive artist Theophilos of Lesvos (Mytilini). Greek traditional costumes are displayed on the 3rd and 4th floors.

The museum is at Kydathineon 17, Plaka, and is open Tuesday to Sunday from 10 am to 2 pm. Admission is 500 dr.

National Art Gallery The emphasis in this gallery (☎ 721 1010) is on Greek painting and sculpture from the 19th and 20th centuries. There are also 16th-century works and a few works by European masters, including paintings by Picasso, Marquet and Utrillo and Magritte's sculpture *The Therapist*.

Paintings by the primitive painter Theophilos are displayed on the mezzanine floor and 20th-century works are on the 1st floor. The 2nd floor has mostly 19th-century paintings, with one room of earlier works. It has four El Greco paintings, including *The Crucifixion* and *Symphony of the Angels*.

Greek sculpture of the 19th and 20th centuries is effectively displayed in the sculpture garden and sculpture hall, which are reached from the lower floor. There are several works by Giannolis Halepas (1851-1937), one of Greece's foremost sculptors.

The gallery is at Vasileos Konstantinou 50 (opposite the Hilton Hotel) and is open Wednesday to Saturday and Monday from 9 am to 3 pm and Sunday from 10 am to 2 pm. Admission is 500 dr.

War Museum This museum (☎ 729 0543) is

a relic of the colonels' junta. Greece seems to have been at war since time immemorial, and a look around helps to get the country's history in perspective. All periods from the Mycenaean to the present day are covered, and displays include weapons, maps, armour and models of battles.

The museum is at Vasilissis Sofias 24, just beyond the Byzantine Museum (see the Athens map), and it's open Tuesday to Saturday from 9 am to 2 pm. Entry is free.

Centre of Folk Arts & Traditions

There's no entry charge for this small museum (☎ 324 3987) either. It has a good display of costumes, embroideries, pottery and musical instruments.

It's at Angelika Hatzimihali 6, Plaka, and is open Tuesday and Thursday from 9 am to 9 pm and on Wednesday, Friday and Saturday from 9 am to 1 pm and 5 to 9 pm.

Paul & Alexandra Kanellopoulos Museum

This museum (☎ 321 2313), on the corner of Panos and Theorias, houses the small but fascinating private collection of the Kanellopoulos family. Exhibits include pieces from Cycladic, Minoan and classical times, Attic vases, Byzantine jewellery and embroideries, Persian jewellery from the 5th century BC, icons and coins. It was closed for restoration at the time of writing.

National Historical Museum

This museum (☎ 323 7617) specialises in memorabilia from the War of Independence, including Byron's helmet and sword. There is also a series of paintings depicting events leading up to the war, Byzantine and medieval exhibits and a collection of photographs and royal portraits.

The museum is housed in the old parliament building at Plateia Kolokotroni, Stadiou, in Syntagma. Theodoros Deligiannis, who succeeded Trikoupis as prime minister of Greece, was assassinated on the steps of the building in 1905. It's open Tuesday to Sunday from 9 am to 1.30 pm, and admission is 500 dr.

City of Athens Museum

This museum (☎ 324 6164) occupies the palace where King Otho and his consort Amalia lived for a few years during the 1830s. It contains some of the royal couple's furniture, costumes and personal mementoes, as well as paintings, prints and models of Athens in the 19th century.

The museum is at Paparigopoulou 7 in Plaka and is open on Monday, Wednesday, Friday and Saturday from 9 am to 1.30 pm. Admission is 400 dr.

Jewish Museum

This museum (☎ 323 1577) traces the history of the Jewish community in Greece back to the 3rd century BC through an impressive collection of religious and folk art and documents. It includes a reconstruction of a synagogue.

The museum is housed on the 3rd floor of a 19th-century building at Amalias 36, Plaka. It's open Sunday to Friday from 9 am to 1 pm and entry is free.

Theatre Museum

Aspiring Thespians may be interested in visiting this museum (☎ 362 9430), which contains theatre memorabilia from the 19th and 20th centuries. Exhibits include photographs, costumes, props and reconstructions of the dressing rooms of Greece's most celebrated 20th-century actors.

The museum is at Akadimias 50 (see the Exarhia map). Opening times are Monday to Friday from 9 am to 3 pm. Admission is 300 dr. It, too, was temporarily closed at the time of writing.

Hills of Athens

Lykavittos Hill The name Lykavittos means 'hill of wolves' and derives from ancient times when the hill was in remote countryside and wolves menaced the sheep that grazed there. Today, it is no longer remote or inhabited by wolves, but rises out of a sea of concrete to offer the finest views in Athens. Pollution permitting, there are panoramic views of the city, the Attic basin, the surrounding mountains and the islands of Salamis and Aegina. A path leads to the summit from the top of Loukianou. Alternatively, you can take the funicular railway from the top of Ploutarhou (400/800 dr, one way/return).

There is an expensive café halfway up the path and another at the top, as well as a restaurant looking down towards the Acropolis. Also on the summit is the little **Chapel of Agios Giorgios**. The chapel is floodlit at night and from the streets below looks like a vision from a fairy tale. The open-air **Lykavittos Theatre**, to the northeast of the summit, is used for performances of jazz and rock during the Athens Festival.

West of the Acropolis The low **Areopagus hill** lies between the Acropolis and the Ancient Agora. According to mythology, it was here that Ares was tried by the council of the gods for the murder of Halirrhothios, son of Poseidon. The council accepted his defence of justifiable deicide on the grounds that he was protecting his daughter, Alcippe, from unwanted advances.

The hill became the place where murder trials were heard before the Council of the Areopagus, whose jurisdiction by the 4th century had been extended to cover treason and corruption. In 51 AD, St Paul delivered his famous 'Sermon to an Unknown God' from Areopagus hill and gained his first Athenian convert, Dionysos, who became patron saint of the city.

The hill is linked to the Acropolis by a saddle and can be climbed by steps cut into the rock. There are good views of the Ancient Agora from the summit. The rock is very slippery, so wear suitable shoes.

Filopappos hill, also called the Hill of the Muses, is clearly identifiable to the west of the Acropolis by virtue of the **Monument of Filopappos** at its summit (see the Veïkou & Koukaki map). The monument was built in 114-116 AD in honour of Julius Antiochus Filopappos, who was a prominent Roman consul and administrator. There are small paths all over the hill, but the paved path to the top starts next to the Dionysos Taverna on Dionysiou Areopagitou. The pine-clad slopes are a pleasant place for a stroll and

offer good views of the plain and mountains of Attica and of the Saronic Gulf.

After 250m, the path passes the **Church of Agios Dimitrios**, which contains some fine frescoes. It was sensitively restored in 1951-57. Above here is the rocky **Hill of the Pnyx**. This was the meeting place of the Democratic Assembly in the 5th century BC. Among the great orators who addressed assemblies here were Aristides, Demosthenes, Pericles and Themistocles.

To the north-west of the Hill of the Pnyx is the **Hill of the Nymphs**, on which stands an observatory built in 1842. It is open to visitors on the last Friday of each month.

Parks
Athens is sadly lacking in parks. Only three are large enough to be worthy of a mention and a visit.

National Gardens These gardens are a delightful shady refuge during the summer months and are the favourite haunt of Athens' many stray cats. They were formerly the royal gardens and were designed by Queen Amalia.

The garden contains subtropical trees, ornamental ponds with waterfowl, and a **botanical museum**, which houses interesting drawings, paintings and photographs. There are entrances to the gardens from Vasilissis Sofias and Amalias.

Zappeio Gardens These gardens are laid out in a network of wide walkways around the Zappeio, which was built in the 1870s with money donated by the wealthy Greek-Romanian benefactor Konstantinos Zappas. Until the 1970s, the Zappeio was used mainly as an exhibition hall. It was used for Council of Europe meetings during Greece's presidency of the EC.

Areos Park This pleasant park is north of the National Archaeological Museum on Leoforos Alexandras. It is a large park with wide, tree-lined avenues, one of which has a long line of statues of War of Independence heroes.

Athens' First Cemetery Athens' First Cemetery (Proto Nekrotafeion Athinon) is not strictly a park, but it bears more than a passing resemblance to one. In the absence of real parks, any patch of greenery is welcome. Athenian families who come to attend the graves of loved ones certainly seem to take this attitude, turning duty into an outing by bringing along a picnic. It's a peaceful place to stroll around and is the resting place of many famous Greeks and philhellenes.

The cemetery is 600m south-east of the Temple of Zeus at the end of Anapafseos. You'll know you're getting close when you see all the stone masons and flower shops. Other shops sell cemetery paraphernalia, ranging from life-size figures of Christ to miniature picture frames – used to put photographs of the deceased on the gravestones.

The cemetery is well kept and most of the tombstones and mausoleums are lavish in the extreme. Some are kitsch and sentimental, others are works of art created by the foremost Greek sculptors of the 19th century, such as the *Sleeping Maiden* by Halepas, which is the tomb of a young girl. Someone places a red rose in her hand every day.

Among the cemetery's famous residents are the writers Rangavis (1810-92) and Soutsos (1800-68); the politician Harilaos Trikoupis (1832-96); the archaeologists Heinrich Schliemann (1822-90) and Adolph Furtwängler (1853-1907); the benefactors Antoine Benaki, Georgios Averof and Theodoros Syngros; and War of Independence heroes Sir Richard Church (1784-1873), Kolokotronis (1770-1843), Makrygiannis and Androutsos. Schliemann's mausoleum is decorated with scenes from the Trojan War. Located near the entrance is a memorial – poignant in its simplicity – to the 40,000 citizens who died of starvation during WWII.

Activities

Skiing The nearest ski fields to Athens are on Mt Parnassos, where the season lasts from mid-December to March or April. The ski department (☎ 324 1915) at Klaoudatos, the big department store on Athinas, organises

excursions to the resort of Kalaria. Their buses leave from the stadium in Athens every morning at 5.40 am and get to Kalaria at 8.30 am. They return at 4 pm. Tickets are 7000 dr, including a lift pass. An extra 3000 dr gets you all the gear – skis, bindings, boots and poles.

Tennis Visitors are welcome to use the courts at the Glyfada Golf Club (☎ 894 6820), near the airport, for 3000 dr per hour. Otherwise, getting a game involves wangling your way into one of the exclusive clubs, such as the Athens Tennis Club (☎ 923 2872), next to the Temple of Olympian Zeus at Vasilissis Olgas 2.

Golf The Glyfada Golf Club (☎ 894 6820), near the airport, is Athens' only course. Green fees are 12,000 dr on weekdays, 16,000 dr on weekends and public holidays. You'll be up for another 3000 dr for a bag of clubs, and 800 dr for a buggy.

Other Sports Clubs Addresses of other sports clubs include:

Gliding
  Gliding Club of Athens, Pafsaniou 8
  (☎ 723 5158)
Horse Riding
  Horse Riding Club of Athens, Gerakas
  (☎ 661 1088)
  Horse Riding Club of Greece, Paradissos
  (☎ 682 6128)
Jogging
  Hash House Harriers Jogging Club, Kifissia
  (☎ 621 9821)

Bird-Watching Keen bird-watchers might like to contact the Hellenic Ornithological Society (☎ 361 1271), Benaki 53.

Bridge Players of the world's most popular card game can contact the Greek Federation of Bridge Clubs (☎ 321 0490), Evripidou 6.

Language Courses If you are serious about learning Greek, an intensive course at the start of your stay is a good way to go about it. Most of the courses are in Athens, but there are also courses on the islands in summer.

The Athens Centre (☎ 701 2268; fax 701 8603), Arhimidous 48, in the quiet residential suburb of Mets, has a very good reputation. Its courses cover five levels of proficiency from beginners to advanced. There are eight immersion courses a year for beginners, packing 60 hours of class time into three weeks for 100,000 dr. The centre occupies a fine neoclassical building.

XEN (the YWCA) (☎ 362 4291; fax 362 2400), at Amerikis 11, Syntagma, runs six-week beginners' courses starting in February, May and October. Courses involve 40 hours of class time and cost 50,000 dr.

Other places in Athens offering courses are the Hellenic American Union (☎ 362 9886), Massalias 22, Mets, and the Hellenic Language School (☎ 362 8161; fax 363 9951), Zalongou 4, Mets.

Private lessons are sometimes advertised on the notice board outside the Compendium Bookshop, Nikis 28, Plaka.

Children's Activities The Children's Museum, Kydathineon 14, in Plaka, is more of a play group than a museum. It has a games room and a number of 'exhibits', such as a mock-up of a metro tunnel, for children to explore.

It's open on Monday and Wednesday from 9.30 am to 1.30 pm, Friday from 9.30 am to 1.30 pm and from 5 to 8 pm, and on weekends from 10 am to 1 pm. Entry is free. Parents have to stay and supervise their children.

The Museum of Children's Art, nearby at Kodrou 9, Plaka, has a room set aside where children can let loose their creative energy. Admission is free and crayons and paper are supplied. It's open Tuesday to Saturday from 10 am to 2 pm and on Sunday from 11 am to 2 pm. The 500-dr fee applies only to children attending special programmes.

Organised Tours
The three main companies running organised tours around Athens are CHAT (☎ 322 3137), Stadiou 4; GO Tours (☎ 322

5951/5955), Voulis 31-33; and Key Tours (☎ 923 3166/3266), Kaliroïs 4. You will find their brochures everywhere, all offering similar tours and prices. They include a half-day sightseeing tour of Athens (8800 dr), which does nothing more than point out all the major sights, and Athens by Night (11,700 dr), which takes in the son et lumière (sound-and-light show) before a taverna dinner with folk dancing.

The companies also have one-day tours to Cape Sounion (6700 dr); Delphi (16,300 dr, 18,800 dr with lunch); the Corinth Canal, Mycenae, Nafplio and Epidaurus (same prices); and one-day cruises to Aegina, Poros and Hydra (17,000 dr including lunch).

Future Travel & Tourism (☎ 323 3131; fax 323 1894), at level four, Kolokotroni 9, Syntagma, specialises in tailor-made tours for either individuals or groups.

Special Events
Athens Festival The state-sponsored Athens Festival is the city's most important cultural event, running from mid-June to the end of September. It includes classical-music concerts and dance performances by national and international orchestras and dance companies.

The main attraction is the performance of ancient Greek drama at the Theatre of Herodes Atticus. The plays are performed in modern Greek, but somehow it doesn't seem to matter if you don't understand. The setting is superb, backed by the floodlit Acropolis, and the atmosphere is electric. There are also performances at the Lykavittos Theatre, the open-air amphitheatre in Piraeus and the Theatre of Epidaurus – special buses run here from Athens. (See also the Nafplio and Epidaurus sections in the Peloponnese chapter).

Tickets sell out quickly, so try to buy yours as soon as possible. They can be bought at the festival box office (☎ 322 1459), in the arcade at Stadiou 4, Syntagma.

Opening times are Monday to Friday from 8.30 am to 1.30 pm and from 6 to 8.30 pm. Tickets may also be bought on the day of the performance at the theatre box offices, but queues can be very long. There are student discounts for most performances on production of an ISIC.

Alternative Athens Festival A privately sponsored alternative festival runs concurrently with the established festival. It features jazz and rock artists at venues including the Lykavittos Theatre, the Panathinaïkos Football Stadium on Leoforos Alexandras and the clubs listed under Live Music in the Entertainment section later in this chapter. Tickets for these performances can be purchased at the box offices of the respective venues and at major music shops. The EOT does not give out a programme for the alternative festival, but events are listed in English-language newspapers as well as being widely advertised on posters.

Places to Stay
Athens is a noisy city and Athenians keep late hours, so an effort has been made to select hotels in quiet areas, pedestrian precincts or side streets. Except where specified, the prices quoted here are for the 1997 high season. Most places offer considerable discounts in the off season.

The enormous influx of refugees from the troubles in neighbouring Albania (in particular) and other Balkan nations has had a major impact on the budget accommodation scene. Many cheap hotels and hostels that once were popular with travellers have now become little more than refugee camps. The budget places recommended in this section all attempt to ensure a secure environment for their guests.

Plaka is the most popular place to stay. Most of the sights are close by and it's convenient for every transport connection other than the train station. It has a choice of accommodation right across the price spectrum, from travellers' hostels to smart mid-range hotels and pensions. Not surprisingly, rooms fill up quickly in July and August, so it's wise to make a reservation. If you haven't booked, a telephone call can save a fruitless walk.

The other main hotel area is around Plateia Omonias, but the options are not very attractive. They all seem to be either cheap bordellos, where you won't get a wink of sleep, or characterless modern C-class places. An added drawback to the Omonia region is the general seediness after dark. There are, however, a couple of good budget places in the streets north of Omonia.

Koukaki, south of the Acropolis, is a quiet residential suburb with some good pensions and mid-range hotels.

If you arrive in the city late and cannot find anywhere to stay, don't be tempted to sleep out. It is illegal and could be dangerous. You would be better off going to one of the many all-night cafés, some of which are recommended in Places to Eat later.

Hotel Touts Many of the budget hotels and hostels in Athens employ touts to meet tourists who arrive by train, particularly the late train from Patras. Some of the hostels recommended in the Places to Stay section in this chapter do this, and it often saves a lot of hassle to take up an offer. Before doing so, however, ask to see the hostel leaflet. This will have a picture of the hostel, information about the facilities offered and (very importantly) a map showing its location. Be very suspicious of a tout who cannot show you a leaflet. It's a good idea to agree upon a price in writing before taking up an offer.

Places to Stay – bottom end
Camping There are no camp sites in central Athens. The EOT's *Camping in Greece* brochure lists all 17 sites in Attica. The nearest to the city centre is *Athens Camping* (☎ 581 4114), Leoforos Athinon 198, 7km from the centre. It has hot water, a mini-market and snack bar and is open year-round. To get there, take bus No A16 to Elefsina from Plateia Eleftherias on Panepistimiou. From Piraeus, take bus No 802 or 845. These buses can also drop you at *Dafni Camping* (☎ 581 1562/1563), a good shady site next to the famous monastery in Dafni 3km further on.

If you prefer to be by the sea, there are several camp sites on the coast road to Cape

Sounion (see the Coast Rd to Sounion and Cape Sounion sections later).

Hostels There are a few places around Athens making a pitch for the hostelling market by tagging 'youth hostel' onto their names. There are some truly dreadful dumps among them.

There are only a couple of youth hostels worth knowing about. They include the excellent HI-affiliated *Athens International Youth Hostel* (☎ 523 4170), Victor Hugo 16, in Omonia. The location isn't overly salubrious, but otherwise the place is almost too good to be true. It occupies the former C-class Hotel Victor Ougo, which has been completely renovated – it even has double-glazed windows. The spotless rooms, all with private bathroom, sleep two to four people and come complete with sheets and pillow cases. Rates are 1500 dr per person for those with an HI card. If you don't have a card, you can either pay 3000 dr to join or 500 dr for a daily stamp. There is no curfew. The manager is a friendly guy called Akis, who speaks good English.

Another possibility is the *Youth Hostel No 5* (☎ 751 9530), at Damareos 75 in the suburb of Pangrati. Location again is a problem – 1.5km from Syntagma (east of the old Athens stadium) and a long way from anything else of interest. It is, however, a cheery place that looks all the better for a long overdue paint job. It charges 1500 dr per night for dorm beds, plus 100 dr per sheet and 100 dr for a pillow case. There are coin-operated hot showers. Facilities include a communal kitchen and a TV room. To get there, take trolleybus No 2 or 11 from Syntagma to the Filolaou stop on Frinis, just past Damareos.

The only other hostel that warrants a mention is *Youth Hostel No 2* (☎ 644 2421) at Drossi 1, Gizi. It's a squalid dump that should be avoided like the plague. The hostel is a long way from the centre of town – 1.5km east of Oktovriou-Patission, along Alexandras. It's above the Restaurant Babis, a *rembetika* club, and is open only from May to September. Facilities are extremely primitive. It charges 1500 dr for dorm beds.

Hotels – Plaka & Syntagma The *Student & Travellers' Inn* (☎ 324 4808; fax 321 0065; e-mail students-inn@ath.forthnet.gr), right in the heart of Plaka at Kydathineon 16, is hard to look past. It's a friendly, well-run place with polished timber floors and spotless rooms. It has beds in four-person dorms for 2500 dr (2800 dr in July/August), or 3000 dr (3300 dr) in three-person dorms. Singles/doubles are 5500/7000 dr with shared bathroom, rising to 6000/7500 dr. Student card-holders qualify for a 10% discount on singles and doubles, but not on dorm beds. In summer, a choice of breakfasts is served in the vine-covered courtyard at the back – which becomes a bar from 2 to 10 pm. Breakfast is served indoors in winter. All rooms have central heating.

The *Festos Youth & Student Guesthouse* (☎ 323 2455), Filellinon 18, has been a popular place with travellers for a long time despite its noisy location on one of the busiest streets in Athens. It has beds in eight-person dorms for 2500 dr, rising to 3000 dr between June and August. Beds in smaller four-person dorms are 3500 dr all year, and there are a few doubles for 6000 dr, rising to 7500 dr. In July and August, you can sleep on the roof for 2500 dr. A popular feature of the place is the bar on the 1st floor, which also serves meals and has at least one vegetarian item on the menu.

The *Hotel Kouros* (☎ 322 7431), Kodrou 11, looks extremely promising, but guests appear to be regarded as a bloody nuisance. It's a shame, because it's an old house with beautiful moulded ceilings and loads of character. It charges 5000/10,000 dr for rooms with shared bathroom. Kodrou is on the northern edge of Plaka, five minutes walk from Syntagma, and is the southern (pedestrian) extension of Voulis, which leads into Kydathineon.

The huge timber spiral staircase at *George's Guest House* (☎ 322 6474) at Nikis 46 speaks of grander times. It has fairly grubby singles/doubles for 4000/6000 dr with shared bathroom – if you can persuade the staff to stop watching TV for long enough to give you a key.

The *XEN* (YWCA) (☎ 362 4291), Amerikis 11, is an option for women only. It has singles/doubles with shared bathroom for 5000/8000 dr, and for 6000/9000 dr with private bathroom. There are laundry facilities and a snack bar which charges 800 dr for continental breakfast. Annual membership costs 600 dr.

The rooms at *John's Place* (☎ 322 9719), Patröou 5, are very basic but clean. Singles/doubles/triples with shared bathroom are 4000/6000/9000 dr. Patröou is on the left heading down Mitropoleos from Syntagma.

The D-class *Hotel Dioskouros* (☎ 324 8165), Pittakou 6, looks all the better for a change of management and a coat of paint. It's at the top end of the budget bracket with doubles for 9000 dr with outside bathroom, but the rooms are large. There's a shady courtyard at the back with a snack bar that serves breakfast and light meals.

Hotels – Monastiraki There are a couple of good budget hotels around Plateia Monastirakiou. The D-class *Hotel Tempi* (☎ 321 3175; fax 321 4179), Eolou 29, is a friendly family-run place on the pedestrian precinct part of Eolou. Yiannis and Katerina keep the place spotless and the rooms at the front have balconies overlooking a little square with a church and a flower market. Rates are 5200/7800/9000 dr with shared bathroom, or 8800 dr for doubles with private bathroom. Credit cards are accepted – unusually for a budget hotel. A washing machine is an added attraction.

The *Hotel Carolina* (☎ 331 1784) is close by at Kolokotroni 55 with singles/doubles with shared bathroom for 6000/9000 dr, or 7000/10,000 dr with private bathroom. Ask for a room overlooking the pedestrian precinct on Kalamiotou. The rooms at the other end are above a bar that belts out rock music until 3 am.

Hotels – Veïkou & Koukaki This isn't exactly backpacker territory, but the *Marble*

House Pension (☎ 923 4058 or 922 6461), Zini 35A, Koukaki, is one of Athens' best budget hotels. Monica, the French manager, is friendly and helpful, and rates for the immaculate rooms are 5800/8900 dr for singles/doubles with shared bathroom and 6800/9900 dr with private bathroom. The pension is on a quiet cul-de-sac off Zini. To get there, catch trolleybus No 1, 5, 9 or 18 from Syntagma to the Zini stop on Veïkou, turn left into Zini and the cul-de-sac is the first turn-off on the left.

Hotels – Omonia & Surrounds This section includes the area around the train stations as well as Omonia.

The *Hostel Aphrodite* (☎ 881 0589; fax 881 6574; e-mail hostel-aphrodite@ath.forthnet.gr), Einardou 12, is one of the best budget places in Athens. It is very clean, with dazzling white walls and good-sized rooms, many with balconies. It has beds in six-bed dorms for 1500 dr (1800 dr in July/August), or 2200 dr in four-bed dorms. There are also singles/doubles with shared bathroom for 4500/5500, or 5000/6000 dr with private bathroom. These rates rise by 500 dr in July/August.

The Aphrodite's lively basement bar is a good place to compare notes with fellow travellers until the wee small hours. In the morning, it becomes the breakfast room, turning out a range of breakfasts until midday. The English-speaking staff are helpful and knowledgeable about Athens, and the hostel's travel service sells ferry tickets as cheaply as you'll find anywhere. Einardou is a small street off Mihail Voda, about 1.5km north of Plateia Omonias. Trolleybus No 1 goes up Mihail Voda, although the route is not shown on the EOT map. Get off at the Proussis stop, just south of Einardou. The hostel is only 10 minutes walk from Larisis train station. The nearest metro station is Viktorias, five minutes walk south-east at Plateia Viktorias.

Zorbas Hotel (☎ 823 4239; fax 823 4239), 100m west of Plateia Viktorias at Gilfordiou 10, is open again after closing its doors for a year or so. It occupies a quaint old building

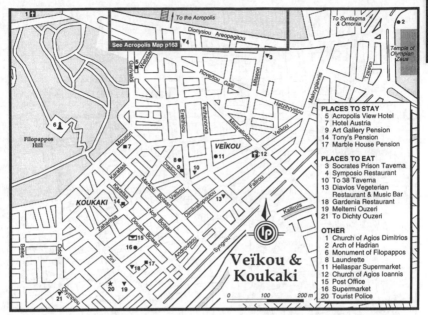

PLACES TO STAY
5 Acropolis View Hotel
7 Hotel Austria
9 Art Gallery Pension
14 Tony's Pension
17 Marble House Pension

PLACES TO EAT
3 Socrates Prison Taverna
4 Symposio Restaurant
10 To 38 Taverna
13 Diavlos Vegeterian
Restaurant & Music Bar
18 Gardenia Restaurant
19 Meltemi Ouzeri
21 To Dichty Ouzeri

OTHER
1 Church of Agios Dimitrios
2 Arch of Hadrian
6 Monument of Filopappos
8 Laundrette
11 Hellaspar Supermarket
12 Church of Agios Ioannis
15 Post Office
16 Supermarket
20 Tourist Police

Veïkou &
Koukaki

and the new manager, Nikos, has put a lot of effort into giving the place a facelift. There are dorms for 2000 dr and singles/doubles for 3500/5000 dr. Breakfast is available in the 1st-floor bar.

The *Hostel Argo* (☎ 522 5939), Victor Hugo 25, is just along the street from the International Youth Hostel. It has beds in four-person dorms for 2000 dr, and singles/ doubles are 4000/5000 dr with shared bathroom – 4500/5500 dr with private bathroom. There is a bar and breakfast room, and also a washing machine.

Hotels – Exarhia Exarhia is off the beaten track as far as hotels go, but there are a couple of good places tucked away at the base of Strefi hill.

The *Hotel Orian* (☎ 382 7362/7116/ 0191) and *Hotel Dryades* (with the same owner and telephone numbers) are 50m apart on Anehartisias, which skirts the western side of the hill. They are managed by a friendly

guy who speaks English. The Orion is clean and well kept with singles/doubles for 6000/7500 dr with shared bathroom, while the Dryades charges 8000/10,500 dr for rooms with private bathroom. The hotels are to the left at the top of the steps leading off Emmanual Benaki at the junction with Kalidromiou. You can save yourself a long uphill trek by catching bus No 230 from Amalias to the Kalidromiou stop on Harilaou Trikoupi, which runs parallel to Benaki.

The *Museum Hotel* (☎ 380 5611/5613), Bouboulinas 16, is a long-established hotel behind the National Archaeological Museum. The rooms are plain but comfortable, and reasonably priced at 6000/9000 dr with private bathroom.

The *Hotel Exarhion* (☎ 360 3296/1256/ 8684) is right in the heart of student territory on Plateia Exarhion. It's a modern hotel and the light, airy rooms have large French windows which open out onto balconies.

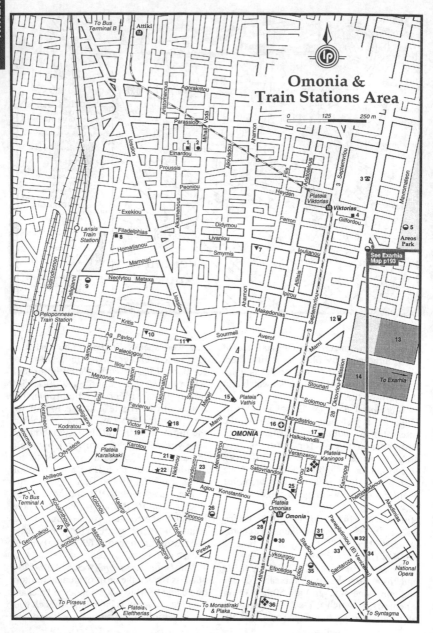

Omonia &
Train Stations Area

0   125   250 m

PLACES TO STAY	34	Ideal Restaurant	16	First-Aid Centre
1 Hostel Aphrodite			20	Laundrette
4 Zorba's Hotel		**OTHER**	21	OSE (Railways Office)
8 Oscar Hotel	2	Atlantik Supermarket	22	Traffic Police
18 Athens International	3	OTE	23	National Theatre
Youth Hostel	5	Buses to Marathon &	24	Minion Department
19 Hostel Argo		Rafina		Store
32 Titania Hotel	6	Buses to Lavrion and	26	Buses to Bus
		Cape Sounion		Terminal A
PLACES TO EAT	9	Trolley Stop for Train	27	Laundrette
7 Dafni Taverna		Stations	29	Bus 049 to Piraeus
10 O Makis Psistaria	12	Rodon Club	30	Marinopoulos
11 O Vaggelis Taverna	13	National		Supermarket
17 Grigoris Coffee Shop		Archaeological	31	Central Post Office
25 Neon Cafeteria		Museum	35	Buses to Airport
28 Pitta Pan	14	Polytehnio	36	Klaoudatos
33 Vegetarian Fast Food	15	Public Toilets		Department Store

Singles/doubles are 5500/7700 dr with private bathroom. The square is surrounded by bars, clubs and restaurants and can be noisy at night, so ask for a room at the back.

Places to Stay – middle
Plaka & Syntagma The *Acropolis House Pension* (☎ 322 2344/6241), Kodrou 6-8, is a beautifully preserved 19th-century house which retains many original features. The rooms are attractively furnished and have 24-hour hot water. The hotel is centrally heated and some rooms also have air-conditioning. The price structure is incredibly complicated. Among the options are singles/doubles with outside bathroom for 11,700/14,000 dr, singles/doubles with private bathroom for 13,600/16,400 dr and air-con doubles with bathroom for 20,600 dr. Breakfast costs 1500 dr per person.

The *Hotel Myrto* (☎ 322 7237 or 323 4560) is nearby at Nikis 40. It has immaculate singles for 12,000 dr and doubles from 20,000 dr with *en suite* bathroom, as well as doubles with shared bathroom for 15,000 dr. All rooms come with central heating, air-con and TV, and breakfast is included. The modern *Hotel Nefeli* (☎ 322 8044/8045), Iperidou 16, is a popular place. It has singles/doubles for 11,000/12,000 dr, including breakfast. To get there from Syntagma, head south down Voulis and turn right into Iperidou.

The *Hotel Plaka* (☎ 322 2096) is the best of a cluster of B and C-class hotels on busy Mitropoleos. The hotel is at the junction with Kapnikareas and has singles/doubles with breakfast for 17,800/22,900.

The *Hotel Omiros* (☎ 323 5486/5487), Apollonos 15, is a B-class hotel with large air-con singles/doubles for 10,850/14,200 dr. Apollonos runs roughly parallel to Mitropoleos, one street closer to Plaka.

In Syntagma, the *Hotel Achilleas* (☎ 323 3197), Leka 21, is a comfortable, modern hotel with large, airy rooms. Rooms on the top floor open onto garden terraces. It charges 14,000/17,800 dr for singles/doubles with breakfast. To get there from Syntagma, head west along Ermou, turn right into Voulis and you'll see Leka leading off diagonally to the left.

Veïkou & Koukaki The *Art Gallery Pension* (☎ 923 8376; fax 923 3025), Erehthiou 5, Veïkou, is a small, friendly place run by the brother-and-sister team of Ada and Yannis Assimakopoulos. It has comfortable singles/doubles/triples for 11,000/13,000/15,000 dr with balcony and private bathroom. To get there, take trolleybus No 1, 5, 9 or 18 from Syntagma to the Drakou stop on Veïkou. Erehthiou runs north from Veïkou towards the Acropolis.

Tony's Pension (☎ 923 6370/0561), Zaharitsa 26, Koukaki, is another clean, well-maintained pension. It offers singles/doubles for 9000/11,000 dr with private bathroom. There is a small communal kitchen downstairs for making tea/coffee and breakfast. Tony also has well-equipped two-person studio apartments nearby for long or short-term rental. Short-term prices are the same as for rooms at the pension. Take the trolleybus to the Drakou stop on Veïkou, head north-west along Drakou, and Zaharitsa is the second on the left.

The *Hotel Austria* (☎ 923 5151; fax 924 7350), Mouson 7, is in a quiet spot on the slopes of Filopappos hill, with good views over the city from its roof garden. The place is spotless, but the rooms are on the spartan side. Singles/doubles are 13,500/17,400 dr, including breakfast. Mouson is on the left at the top of Drakou.

There are indeed views of the Acropolis from many of the rooms at the *Acropolis View Hotel* (☎ 921 7303/3035; fax 923 0705), just south of the Theatre of Herodes Atticus at Webster 10. The best views are from the roof terrace. Some of the rooms look out over Filopappos hill. Rates are 17,500/24,000 dr for air-con singles/doubles with buffet breakfast. Bus No 230 from Syntagma stops at the Theatre of Herodes Atticus, two minutes walk away.

Around Omonia Omonia is not really the place to be looking for up-market accommodation – you can do much better for your money elsewhere.

There are a couple of exceptions. The *Oscar Hotel* (☎ 883 4215), on the corner of Samou and Filadelphias opposite Larisis train station, is a smart B-class hotel that has a roof garden with small swimming pool. Singles/doubles here cost 17,000/23,500 dr, including breakfast.

The *Titania Hotel* (☎ 330 0111; fax 330 0700), with an imposing façade at Panepistimiou 52, is a comfortable modern hotel with large singles/doubles for 21,900/26,800 dr, including breakfast. All the rooms have satellite TV. There are great views over the city from the rooftop bar at night.

Kolonaki This posh area has the B-class *Athenian Inn* (☎ 723 8097/9552; fax 721 5614), Haritos 22. It's a small but distinguished place on a quiet street in the heart of Kolonaki that was reputably a favourite of Lawrence Durrell. It has a cosy intimacy which is often lacking in hotels of this category. The rooms are unpretentious but comfortable with air-con and pretty pictures of island scenes on the walls. It has singles/doubles for 18,000/24,800 dr, including breakfast. Haritos is five blocks north of Vasilissis Sofias, and just north-east of Plateia Kolonakiou.

Places to Stay – top end
If you are wealthy, *the* place to stay in Athens is – and always has been – the deluxe *Hotel Grande Bretagne* (☎ 331 4444; fax 322 8034), on Plateia Syntagmatos. Built in 1862 to accommodate visiting heads of state, it ranks among the grand hotels of the world. No other hotel in Athens can boast such a rich history (see the Walking Tour section earlier). It has undergone much expansion since it first became a hotel in 1872, but still has an old-world grandeur. The elegantly furnished rooms have air-con, minibar, satellite TV and video. Singles/doubles are priced from US\$315/345, and suites start at US\$630.

St George Lycabettus Hotel (☎ 729 0711; fax 729 0439), Kleomenous 2, Kolonaki, has a prime location at the foot of Lykavittos hill. It looks a bit tatty on the outside, but it's deluxe inside. The big attraction here is that you can lie in bed at night and gaze at the floodlit Acropolis – or satellite TV, if you prefer. The roof garden surrounds a good-sized swimming pool. Prices depend on the view from the window. It charges 58,800/66,900 dr for singles/doubles with a view of the Acropolis – much less if you don't care about the view. The price includes a buffet breakfast. The hotel is at the western end of Kleomenous, on the edge of Plateia Dehamenis.

Hilton-hoppers will find their favourite (☎ 725 0201; fax 725 3110) at Vasilissis Sofias 46 Ilissia, opposite the National Art

Gallery. The Athens version is a vast concrete edifice. From the outside, it looks more like a 1950s housing project than a luxury hotel. Inside, no expense has been spared. It has lashings of marble and bronze, public areas with enormous chandeliers and carpets which were especially designed by eminent Greek artists. Singles/doubles are US$254/275, plus tax, while suites start from US$400.

Plaka's smartest hotel is the A-class *Electra Palace* (☎ 324 1401; fax 324 1875) at Nikodimou 18. Facilities include a rooftop pool with views over to the Acropolis. The official rates are 27,800/31,800 dr for singles/doubles, but there are often special deals.

The posh leafy suburb of Kifissia also has a number of luxury hotels. The A-class *Theoxenia Palace* (☎ 801 2751/2765), on the corner of Filadelpheos and Kolokotroni, charges from 22,000/29,000 dr for singles/doubles. Facilities include a swimming pool. Likewise the A-class *Semiramis Hotel* (☎ 808 8101), Harilaou Trikoupi 48, where the rates are 25,000/34,700 dr. The deluxe *Pentelikon Hotel* (☎ 808 0311; fax 801 0314), Deligianni 66, is an exquisite place built in traditional style with a swimming pool and a lovely garden. All of the beautifully furnished rooms have minibar and satellite TV. The rates are 68,000/80,000 dr for singles/doubles and suites start at 98,000 dr for suites.

Places to Eat

Plaka is the part of town where most visitors wind up eating. The streets are lined with countless restaurants, tavernas, cafés, pâtisseries and gyros stalls.

There's more to Athens eating than Plaka though. There are a lot of good places in the Exarhia area, where prices are more in line with the average student's pocket. The waiters may not speak any English, but you'll find tasty food and reasonable prices. Every neighbourhood of Athens has its good eating places. These are often small, friendly, unpretentious tavernas tucked away on side streets.

Places to Eat – inexpensive

Plaka For most people, Plaka is the place to be. It's hard to beat the atmosphere of dining out beneath the floodlit Acropolis.

You do, however, pay for the privilege – particularly at the outdoor restaurants around the square on Kydathineou. It's the setting you're paying for, not the food, which is hard to get excited about. The best of the bunch is the *Taverna Vizantino*, which prices its menu more realistically and is popular with locals year-round. Their daily specials are good value, with dishes like stuffed tomatoes (1050 dr), pastitsio (990 dr) and baked fish (1550 dr).

One of the best deals in the Plaka is the *Plaka Psistaria*, Kydathineon 28, with a range of gyros and souvlaki to eat there or take away.

Another place that is worth seeking out is the *Ouzeri Kouklis*, Tripodon 14, an old-style ouzeri with an oak-beamed ceiling, marble tables and wicker chairs. It serves only mezedes, which are brought round on a large tray so you can take your pick. They include flaming sausages (ignited at your table) and cuttlefish for 1100 dr, as well as the usual dips for 500 dr. The whole selection, enough for four hungry people, costs 8500 dr. Draught red wine is 900 dr and ouzo is 1200 dr. The ouzeri is open for lunch and dinner and it gets very busy later in the evening. Looking west, Tripodon is the first street on the right off Thespidos (the continuation of Kydathineon) as you climb up the hill from Adrianou.

Vegetarian restaurants are thin on the ground in Athens. The *Eden Vegetarian Restaurant*, Lyssiou 12, is one of only three. (The others are in Koukaki and Omonia and are discussed later.) The Eden has been around for years, substituting soya products for meat in tasty vegetarian versions of moussaka (1500 dr) and other Greek favourites. Lyssiou leads off to the left at the north-western end of Tripodon.

With such an emphasis on outdoor eating in summer, it's no great surprise that the three cellar restaurants on Kydathineon are closed from mid-May until October. They are also three of Plaka's cheapest places, where you can expect to pay about 1800 dr per person for a main dish washed down with half a litre of draught retsina. They include the *Taverna Damigos*, at No 41, which claims to be the oldest taverna in Plaka and was opened in 1865 by the Damigos family. Unfortunately, the family photographs that bedeck the walls are much more interesting than the food. The *galaktopoleio* (shop selling dairy products) next door, at No 43, has takeaway crêpes, both savoury and sweet. Prices start at 450 dr. The taverna known as *The Cellar* is downstairs at No 10. It looks promising, with its colourful murals of carousing Athenians, but the food is a bit pale. The *galaktopoleio* at No 10 serves breakfast. In the evening, the tables outside are a popular spot for a beer.

The third of the cellar places is the *Taverna Saita*, at No 21, near the Museum of Greek Folk Art. It is more rough and ready but turns out tastier food.

Peristeria Taverna, next to John's Place at Patröou 5, is the best of the Plaka cheapies and is open all year. Chicken, moussaka and meatballs are all 1000 dr and draught retsina is 600 dr. Patröou is the fourth street on the left down Mitropoleos from Syntagma.

Most hotels serve breakfast, but if you're not happy with what's on offer you'll find breakfast advertised at many of the Plaka restaurants. Prices start at around 650 dr for continental breakfast.

Monastiraki There are some excellent cheap eats around Plateia Monastirakiou, particularly for gyros and souvlaki fans. *Thanasis*, at the bottom end of Mitropoleos, is famous among Athenians for its special souvlaki. It uses a traditional house recipe that combines minced lamb, minced beef and seasonings. You'll pay 270 dr for the takeaway version wrapped in a small pitta, or 1300 dr to sit down to a plate of four souvlaki and a large pitta. The place is always packed out and the service is pure theatre – the waiters have to run to keep up with the demand.

Opposite Thanasis at Mitropoleos 86 is *Savas*, which specialises in gyros. It has a takeaway stall with a choice of chicken (340 dr), pork or minced beef (both 310 dr), and a restaurant (there's a shop in between) with seating in the square opposite. The restaurant charges an extra 60 dr per gyros, but also has salads and side dishes such as baked peppers. *Grigoris*, at Mitropoleos 88, serves good coffee a lot cheaper than anywhere else around. Greek coffee is 180 dr, filter coffee 260 dr and cappuccino 350 dr.

The best taverna food in this part of town is at the *meat market*, 400m along Athinas from Plateia Monastirakiou, on the right. The place must resemble a vegetarian's vision of hell, but the food is great and the tavernas are open 24 hours a day, except Sunday. They serve traditional meat dishes such as patsas (tripe soup) and podarakia (pig-trotter soup), as well as less exotic dishes such as stifado (meat stewed with onions) and meatballs. Soups start at 800 dr, and main dishes at 1000 dr.

Opposite the meat market is the main *fruit & vegetable market*, where you'll find the widest range of whatever's in season and the best prices. The stretch of Athinas between the meat market and Plateia Monistirakiou is the place to shop for nuts and nibblies.

O Telis psistaria, at the junction of Evripidou and Epikourou near Plateia Eleftherias, is famous for its only dish – pork chops and chips. A huge pile of chips topped by three or four chops costs 1400 dr. The *Olympic Restaurant*, nearby on Plateia Eleftherias, is a very good cheap taverna. It has spaghetti with tomato sauce for 600 dr and soups for 700 dr as well as delicious macaroni with octopus for 1100 dr. To get to these restaurants, head north along Athinas from Plateia Monastirakiou and turn left onto Evripidou before the meat market.

There are a couple of good places to eat in the flea market. *Ipiros Taverna*, Filippou 16, has cheap, tasty food. The outdoor tables are great in summer for watching the market's hustle and bustle. The *Taverna Abyssinia*, on the western side of nearby Plateia Abyssinias, does a roaring trade on Sunday market days when it has live folk music.

Just south of Monastiraki in Thision, the

Taverna Steki tou Elia, Thessalonikis 3, has quickly become one of the trendiest eating spots in town. You'll find everyone from pop stars to politicians lining up alongside the masses to enjoy the speciality of the house: pork or lamb chops and chips, washed down with a few glasses of draught retsina. A good meal costs about 2500 dr per person. Thessalonikis runs alongside the metro line west of Thision station, starting beyond the bus stops on Eptahalkou. The family runs a second restaurant of the same name further west on Thessalonikis at the junction of Erissihithonos.

Syntagma Fast food is the order of the day at busy Syntagma. The self-serve salad bar at *Wendy's*, at the junction of Stadiou and Voukourestiou, is one of the best deals around, with a choice of about 20 salads. Vegetarians beware – many of the salads have meat in them. You can pile enough salad on a small plate (920 dr) to constitute a meal. A large serve is 1150 dr.

Meat is the only item on the menu at the tiny *Souvlaki tou Hasepi* (The Butcher's Souvlaki) at Apollonos 3. Pork souvlakis are 150 dr each and come with a slice of bread. A large cold beer costs 270 dr.

The *Neon Café*, on the south-western corner of Plateia Syntagmatos, is a stylish self-service cafeteria. It has spaghetti or fettucine napolitana for 950 dr, or bolognese/carbonara for 1280 dr. Main dishes range from moussaka (1450 dr) to whole baked trout (2500 dr). It is probably the only eating place in Athens with a nonsmoking area.

It's very hard to ignore the delicious aromas emanating from the *Brazil Coffee Shop* on Voukourestiou (between Panepistimiou and Stadiou). It has Greek coffee for 400 dr and filter coffee for 550 dr, plus cakes and croissants priced from 300 dr.

Veïkou & Koukaki The *Gardenia Restaurant*, Zini 31, at the junction with Dimitrakopoulou, claims to be the cheapest taverna in Athens. I wouldn't doubt it. A plate of gigantes beans is 550 dr, chicken and potatoes 650 dr, and moussaka is 700 dr. A large Amstel beer costs 350 dr, and a litre of draught retsina is 450 dr. What's more, the food is good and the service is friendly. The owner is an effervescent woman called Gogo who speaks English.

On the opposite side of the road at Zini 26 is *Meltemi Ouzeri*, Zini 26, a pleasant spot with white stucco walls, marble-topped tables and blue-painted wooden chairs – all of which give the place a Cycladic-island feel. In summer, an outside eating area is shielded from the traffic by large pot plants. There is a wide choice of delicious mezedes priced from 600 dr, or you can try a mixed plate for 1300 dr.

To 38 Taverna, Veïkou 38, is another good-value establishment. The restaurant is lively, rough and ready, and very popular. A generous serving of crisp fried cod costs 1400 dr, and a plate of cuttlefish cooked with spinach is 1150 dr. There is no name on the door, only the number. There's a barber's shop next door. It is open in the evening from 8 pm, but is closed from 1 June to 15 September.

Socrates Prison, Mitseon 20, is a delightful taverna with an Art Nouveau interior and 19th-century Parisian posters on the walls. It also has garden seating in summer. The restaurant is not named after the philosopher, but after the owner (also called Socrates), who reckons the restaurant is his prison. It has an imaginative range of mezedes from 600 dr and main dishes from 1500 dr.

The *Diavlos Vegetarian Restaurant & Music Bar*, Drakou 9, has the most extensive vegetarian menu in town, with more than 50 dishes to choose from. These include homemade pies with chips and salad (from 1250 dr), croquettes and fritters (1250 dr), soya moussaka (1600 dr) and tofu curry with rice (1750 dr). Diavlos is open every day from 10 am to 3 am. The place tends to be deserted until the rembetika music starts at about 11 pm.

Omonia The *Vegetarian Fast Food* restaurant, Panepistimiou 55, offers a choice of three dishes from its buffet for 700 dr, as well as portions of wholemeal pizza and pies for

400 dr. You can wash your meal down with a fresh carrot juice for 300 dr. There is also a well-stocked health-food shop, which carries a small range of biodynamic produce.

The choice of fast-food outlets at Plateia Omonias includes *Pitta Pan*, which brings McDonald's-style marketing slickness to the humble gyros and souvlaki. Their basic-model pork gyros sell for 425 dr and a plain souvlaki goes for 360 dr. Pitta Pan is on the corner of the square between Athinas and Pireos.

The *Neon Cafeteria* occupies a beautiful neoclassical building on the corner of Dorou, on the opposite side of the square. It is a stable mate of the Neon at Syntagma and serves the same fare.

The *Grigoris* coffee shop, at the junction of Oktovriou-Patission and Halkokondili, is a good spot to stop for coffee after visiting the National Archaeological Museum.

Around the Train Stations Wherever you choose to eat in this area you will find the lack of tourist hype refreshing – it's a million miles from the strategically placed menus and restaurant touts of Plaka.

O Makis Psistaria, at Psaron 48 opposite the church, is a lively place serving hunks of freshly grilled pork or beef, plus chips, for 1500 dr. It also does delicious grilled chicken with lemon sauce for 1200 dr. Just north of Plateia Vathis, *O Vaggelis Taverna*, Liossion 21 (the entrance is around the corner on Sahini), is an unpretentious traditional taverna with garden seating in summer. Main dishes are priced from 1000 to 1600 dr, and a litre of retsina is 800 dr.

The *Dafni Taverna*, further north at Ioulianou 65, offers equally good value with very tasty gigantes beans for 750 dr or baked fish with potatoes for 1400 dr. In summer, there's outdoor seating in the small courtyard.

Exarhia Exarhia has lots of ouzeria and tavernas to choose from, and prices are tailored to suit the pockets of the district's student clientele. It's quite a long hike to the area from Syntagma. The alternative is to catch a No 230 bus from Amalias or Panepistimiou to Harilaou Trikoupi and walk across. It is, however, only a short walk from the National Archaeological Museum to lively Plateia Exarhion. The square (triangle actually) is lined with cafés and snack bars, many with seating under shade.

The *café* behind the National Archaeological Museum, at Bouboulinas 34, has a mixed plate of mezedes for two people for 1400 dr and toasted sandwiches with a large choice of fillings priced from 350 dr. It's closed on Sunday.

Most of the better eating places are south of Plateia Exarhion. You'll find a string of small ouzeris along the upper reaches of Emmanual Benaki, including the excellent *Ouzeri I Gonia* on the corner of Emmanual Benaki and Arahovis. It has a good range of tasty mezedes priced between 600 and 1400 dr, and has draught wine as well as ouzo.

The *Taverna Barbargiannis*, Emmanual Benaki 94 on the corner of Dervenion, is an excellent place with a blackboard list of daily specials. Your best bet is to line up at the counter and ask to have a look. They make a delicious thick chicken soup for 1150 dr that comes with a generous portion of chicken on the side, as well as a tasty bean soup for 800 dr. Most meat dishes are priced around 1500 dr, and draught retsina is 700 dr for a litre.

Another good place is the *Taverna Rozalia*, Valtetsiou 58. In summer, it has outdoor seating in the garden opposite under a tangle of trees and vines. It has a large range of mezedes priced from 600 dr, but casseroles are the speciality. The pork in lemon sauce and the beef in wine both cost 1700 dr and come in individual clay pots.

Gargadovas Taverna, Isavron 29B, serves mezedes to serious night owls. There is no menu; the night's offerings are brought round on a tray for you to take your pick. All are priced from 500 to 900 dr. It's open from 9.30 pm to 6 am, and is closed on Sunday.

Places to Eat – mid-range

Plaka The *Taverna O Thespis*, at the top end of Thespidos, has a great setting on the lower

See Omonia &
Train Stations
Area Map p196

Areos Park

National
Archaeological
Museum

Polytehnio

EXARHIA

Strefi
Hill

NEAPOLI

Exarhia

0   100   200 m

To
Omonia

To Syntagma
& Veikou

Lykavittos
Hill

Funicular
Railway

1 Café
2 Museum Hotel
3 Ach Marie Club
4 Boemissa Rembetika Club
5 AN Club
6 Hotel Exarchion
7 Taverna Rozalia
8 Ouzeri I Gonia
9 Taverna Barbargiannis
10 Hotel Dryades
11 Hotel Orian
12 Green Door Club
13 Sklavenitis Supermarket
14 Gargadovas Taverna
15 Xenoglosso Bibliopoleio
16 National Opera
17 Theatre Museum
18 Chapel of Agios Georgios
19 Restaurant Dionysos

slopes of the Acropolis with seating under the trees in the small square outside. The speciality here is bekri meze (beef in a spicy tomato sauce) for 2400 dr. Thespidos is the south-western extension of Kydathineon, beyond Adrianou, that leads uphill towards the Acropolis.

The *Michiko Japanese Restaurant* (☎ 322 0980), Kydathineon 27, is housed in Plaka's largest surviving mansion. It has a shady front garden with seating around an ornamental pool. The menu includes a range of three-course meals priced from 5500 dr.

Ionou is a stylishly renovated café right in

the middle of Plaka on Plateia Filomousson. In summer, there's outdoor seating where you can drink good filter coffee (750 dr) or a range of imported draught beers (1000 dr). In winter, you can retreat indoors and keep warm around the open fire.

Syntagma There are a couple of good Asian restaurants around Syntagma that will appeal to those looking for something a bit different. The *Orient Restaurant*, Leka 26, has an extensive menu of Szechwan, Cantonese and Korean dishes, including a range of set menus for 6000 dr per person. The *Far East*

Restaurant, in the arcade at Stadiou 7, has a spacious, elegant Oriental interior and serves Korean, Japanese and Chinese food at similar prices.

Zonar's, on the corner of Panepistimiou and Voukourestiou, is the establishment coffee shop. It charges a hefty 1000 dr for a Greek coffee and 800 dr for filter coffee. It specialises in ice creams and sundaes, which are priced from 1700 dr.

Veïkou *To Dichty*, near the corner of Veïkou and Olympiou, is an up-market ouzeri with a nautical bent. Its walls are decked out with fishing nets, plastic lobsters and lifebuoys. The range of mezedes includes peppers with regato cheese (950 dr), fried savoury octopus (1800 dr), mussels with fried cheese (1600 dr) and cuttlefish cooked in red wine (1850 dr). It's open Monday to Saturday from 6 pm to 2 am.

Places to Eat – expensive
The following is a selection of Athens' top-end, blow-the-budget restaurants. The resort of Glyfada also has a range of top-end restaurants (see the Coast Road to Sounion section later in this chapter).

Plaka, Syntagma & Monastiraki The Hotel Grande Bretagne's *GB Corner* restaurant has a range of set menus priced from 7500 to 10,000 dr for both lunch and dinner. It serves international dishes as well as local specialities such as Athenian tripe soup.

Pit Poule (☎ 342 3665), Apostolou Pavlou 51, on the corner of Poulopoulou, serves French Mediterranean food. Count on paying upwards of 12,000 dr per person, excluding wine. It's open from 8 pm every day except Sunday.

Omonia The *Ideal Restaurant* (☎ 461 4604), Panepistimiou 46 (next to the Ideal Cinema), is a long-established favourite with Athenians. The interior is Art Deco and the menu has a mixture of Greek, Turkish and European dishes with daily specials. Expect to pay upwards of 8000 dr per person, excluding wine.

Veïkou *Symposio* (☎ 922 5321), south of the Acropolis at Erehthiou 46, is one of Athens' most elegant restaurants. It occupies a beautifully restored 1920s house, and offers a menu loaded with regional specialities from all over Greece. They include a plate of Lake Ioannina frogs' legs for 3500 dr. Symposio's signature dish is fish baked in a salt crust (16,000 dr per kg). The wine list is similarly top of the range. You can reckon on paying at least 12,000 dr per person, excluding wine. It's open from 8 pm until late, closed Sunday. Reservations are recommended.

Kolonaki There's no finer view in Athens than that offered by the *Restaurant Dionysos*, at the top of Lykavittos hill – accessible by the funicular railway (see the Exarhia map). It has set menus for 4800 and 6500 dr as well as à la carte. It's open from 9 am until midnight.

Ilissia The Athens Hilton, in the district of Ilissia, just east of Kolonaki, has several restaurants. *Ta Nissia Restaurant* does a four-course menu for 11,000 dr, while the *Kellari* specialises in mezedes. A selection of 10 costs 4800 dr.

Entertainment
Cinema Athenians are avid cinema-goers. Most cinemas show recent releases from Britain and the USA in English. The two areas with the highest concentration of cinemas are the main streets running between Syntagma and Omonia and the Patission and Plateia Amerikis area.

The major cinemas in central Athens are the *Apollon* (☎ 323 6811), Stadiou 19; *Astor* (☎ 323 1297), Stadiou 28; *Asty* (☎ 322 1925), Koraï 4; *Cine Paris* (☎ 322 0721), Kydathineon; *Elly* (☎ 363 2789), Akadimias 64; *Ideal* (☎ 382 6720), Panepistimiou 46; and *Titania* (☎ 381 1147), on the corner of Panepistimiou and Themistokleous. The Asty shows mostly avant-garde films; the others show mostly first-run films (usually from Britain or the USA with Greek subtitles).

All the major cinemas have listings in the *Athens News*, *Scope* and the *Hellenic Times*. Admission costs between 1200 and 1500 dr.

Theatre Athens has a dynamic theatre scene, but, as you'd expect, most performances are in Greek. If you're a theatre buff you may enjoy a performance of an old favourite, provided you know the play well enough. The *Hellenic Times* has a cursory listing, but the listings in *Scope* are more comprehensive. They both state when a performance is in English – which happens occasionally.

Greek Folk Dancing In summer, performances of Greek folk dances are given by the *Dora Stratou Dance Company* at their own theatre (☎ 324 4395) on Filopappos hill. The company was formed many years ago and has gained an international reputation for authenticity and professionalism. Performances are held nightly at 10.15 pm from May to October, with additional performances at 8.15 pm on Wednesday and Sunday. Tickets can be bought at the door and cost from 2500 to 3000 dr. The theatre is signposted from the western end of Dionysiou Areopagitou. The troupe occasionally holds dance workshops, which are advertised in the *Hellenic Times*.

Concerts, Opera, Ballet & Contemporary Dance There are frequent classical-music concerts, by both international and Greek performers, at the *Athens Concert Hall* (Megaron Mousikis) (☎ 728 2333), Vasilissis Sofias, Illissa (next to the US Embassy). Dance performances and jazz concerts are also held here. The *Pallas Theatre* (☎ 322 4434), Voukourestiou 1, Syntagma, also has performances of classical music. The *Olympia Theatre* (☎ 361 2461) has performances of both ballet and opera by the National Opera (Ethniki Lyriki Skini) (☎ 361 2461), Akadimias 59. Dance performances are also given at the *Politechno Theatres* (☎ 651 4746), opposite the Alphaville cinema on Mavromihali, Exarhia, and at *Athens College Theatre* (☎ 647 4676), Stefanou Delta, Psyhiko.

If anything big is happening, posters will be displayed, and tickets will be for sale at the box office in the arcade at Stadiou 4, Syntagma. The English-language newspapers, *Scope* and the *Athenian* publish listings.

Son et Lumière This spectacle is not one of the world's best, but it is an enduring and integral part of the Athens tourist scene. There are shows in English every night at 9 pm from the beginning of April until the end of October at the theatre on the Hill of the Pnyx (%y322 1459). There are shows in French at 10 pm every night except Tuesday and Friday, when the show is in German. During the performance, the monuments of the Acropolis are lit up in synchronisation with the accompanying music, sound effects and historical narration. The lights are the most exciting part of the performance. Tickets cost 1200 dr. The Hill of the Pnyx is west of the Acropolis off Dionysiou Areopagitou. Bus No 230 from Syntagma will get you there.

Music Bars Athens has a huge number of music bars, each with its own atmosphere and style of music. You'll find most of them listed in the pages of *Scope* magazine. Lots of them are in Exarhia, where the *Green Door Club*, Kalidromiou 52, at the junction with Emmanual Benaki, is one of the most popular. There's no name, just a green door.

Thision is another good area to look. *Stavlos*, Iraklidon 10, occupies an amazing old rabbit warren of a building. It has a rock bar playing mainly alternative British music, and more mellow sounds in the café/brasserie outside.

You are best off staying away from the bars around Syntagma. *Club 11*, Nikis 11, and *Athens Club*, Nikis 1, both employ touts to roam Syntagma and Plaka, targeting single male tourists with talk of beautiful girls. The girls then persuade suckers to buy them ludicrously overpriced drinks.

Gay Bars The popular *Alexander Club*, Anagnostopoulou 44, Kolonaki, is a relaxed,

Nes Frappé

You can hardly miss the forest of straws sprouting from glasses of frothy-topped black liquid at countless street cafés throughout Greece. Nes(café) frappé has almost universally overtaken the traditional Greek (or Turkish) coffee as the nation's favourite beverage. But what could possibly be the attraction of a glass of cold water, flavoured with a spoonful of instant coffee and sugar, processed to resemble a glass of Guinness stout and then chilled with ice cubes?

Nes frappé is not a beverage to be taken in a hurry; it is certainly not a beverage to be drunk for the caffeine hit that you might expect from traditional coffee. Its primary role is that of a 'ticket' to sit at a street café in order to idly chat and smoke. Its arrival at the table, however, is treated with almost reverential ceremony. Firstly the imbiber will dutifully stir the ice cubes to ensure that every molecule of Nes frappé is equally chilled, and then the first minuscule sip is taken. It is considered extremely bad form to drink the mixture quickly, so never order one if you intend to quench your thirst in Greek company. The next sip may follow between five and ten minutes later; in fact the whole drinking procedure may take up to an hour.

The drink's universal popularity throughout the country and at all times of the year may be a puzzle to observers, for its appeal as a beverage is surely limited. The café owners, however, are not complaining: at 500 dr a shot, it is a sure-fire money spinner. ∎

---

friendly place that draws a mixed crowd of younger gays and lesbians. There's a cruising bar upstairs and a disco downstairs. It's open every night from 9 pm to 2 am throughout the year. *Alekos Island*, Tsalakof 42, Kolonaki, comes highly recommended by no less an authority than *Spartacus*. The crowd here is mainly gay. Another popular gay place is *Granazi Bar*, Lembesi 20, which is south of Hadrian's Arch and east of Syngrou. You'll find more gay bars listed in the pages of *Scope* magazine.

Discos Discos operate in Athens only between October and April. In summer, the action moves to the coastal suburbs of Ellinikon and Glyfada. There are more discos around the Mikrolimano in Piraeus. *Aerodhromio*, opposite the airport (East Terminal) at Ellinikon, has an open-air dance floor.

Admission at most places ranges from 1000 dr on weekdays to 3000 dr on Friday and Saturday nights. The price often includes one free drink. Subsequently, expect to pay about 800 dr for soft drinks, 1000 dr for a beer and 1500 dr for spirits. Discos don't start to get busy until around midnight.

You'll find a full list of discos in *Scope* magazine.

Live Music The best place to hear rock music is the *Rodon Club* (☎ 524 7427), north of Plateia Omonias at Marni 24, which has bands most Fridays and Saturdays. It often has international bands. Gigs are listed in *Scope*. Venues in Exarhia include the *Ach Maria Club* (☎ 363 9217), Solomou 20, and the *AN Club*, Solomou 13-15. If anything exciting is going on at any of these places you'll see posters all over Exarhia.

Traditional Music Tavernas There is a cluster of tavernas on the upper reaches of Mnissikleos in Plaka that feature live Greek music, occasionally accompanied by folk dancing. The main places are the *Taverna Geros tou Moria*, at No 27, and its neighbour the *Taverna Alexandros*. Both get packed out with tour groups and the performances are fairly uninspiring. You don't have to eat to watch the shows, but drinks are expensive. If you want to see real Greek music, you're better off going to a rembetika club (see below).

Rembetika Clubs Athens has a good number of rembetika clubs, but many close down from May to September. Performances in these clubs start at around 11.30 pm; most places do not have a cover charge but drinks are expensive – sometimes as much as 3000 dr for spirits. Clubs open up and close down with great rapidity – telephone to check if a club is still open. The biggest concentration of clubs is in and around Exarhia.

A good place to check out is *Boemissa* (☎ 384 3836), Solomou 19, in Exarhia. It's open from 11 pm to 4 pm, and it pays to get in early – particularly on Friday and Saturday when it's packed out. It's closed on Monday. The *Diavlos Vegetarian Restaurant & Music Bar* (☎ 923 9588) has music every night between 11 am and 3 pm. The *Rembetiki Stoa Athanaton* (☎ 321 4362), next to the central meat market at Sofokleous 19, is open in the afternoon from 3 to 6 pm and reopens from midnight until 6 am. It's closed on Sunday.

Soccer Six of the 18 teams in the Greek Soccer League's first division are from Athens. They are AEK, Apollon, Athinikos, Olympiakos, Panathinaïkos and Panionios. Two other Athenian clubs, Ethnikos and Ionikis, fluctuate between the first and second divisions. AEK plays at the Nea Philadelphia Stadium; Apollon at Rizoupolis; Athinikos at Vyronas; Panionios at Nea Smyrni; and Panathinaïkos at the Panathinaïkos Stadium, Leoforos Alexandras 160, just north of Lykavittos hill.

Olympiakos and Ethnikos play at the Karaïskaki Stadium in Piraeus on alternate weeks. Olympiakos is the most popular team, the Greek equivalent of Manchester United. The club's runaway success in the 1996/97 Greek championship was its 26th in 72 years. Its main rival is wealthy Panathinaïkos, which reached the semifinals of the European championship in 1996 – the best result achieved by a Greek team. First division matches are played on Sunday and cup matches on Wednesday. They are often televised. Admission charges start at 1500 dr.

The soccer season lasts from September to the middle of May. Fixtures and results are given in the *Athens News*.

Horse Racing Horse races are held three times a week at the Faliro Ippodromo (☎ 941 7761), at the southern end of Syngrou in Faliro. Bus No 126 from Syntagma will take you there. Meetings are normally held on Monday, Wednesday and Friday, starting at about 2 pm.

Things to Buy

Flea Market This market is the first place which springs to most people's minds when they think of buying things in Athens. The flea market is the commercial area which stretches both east and west of Plateia Monastirakiou and consists of shops selling goods running the whole gamut from high quality to trash. However, when most people speak of the Athens flea market, they are referring to the outdoor flea market that takes place on Sunday morning. This market spills over into Plateia Monastirakiou and all the way down Ermou to the entrance to the Keramikos.

A visit to Athens isn't complete without a visit to this market. All manner of things are on sale – new, second-hand, third-hand and fourth-hand. There's everything from clocks to condoms, binoculars to bouzoukis, tyres to telephones, giant evil eyes to jelly babies, and wigs to welding kits. Wandering around the market, you'll soon realise that Greece is top of the league of European countries when it comes to mass-produced kitsch. If you're looking for a plastic jewellery box with a psychedelic picture of the Virgin Mary on the lid, which plays 'Never on a Sunday' when you open it, you might just be in luck at the flea market.

Flokati Rugs Karamihos Mazarakis Flokati, at Voulis 31-33, Plaka, has the largest selection of rugs.

Traditional Handicrafts The National Welfare Organisation's Hellenic Folk Art Gallery, on the corner of Apollonos and Ipatias, Plaka, is a good place to go shopping for handicrafts. It has top-quality merchandise and the money goes to a good cause – the preservation and promotion of traditional Greek handicrafts. It has a wide range of knotted carpets, kilims, flokatis, needlepoint rugs and embroidered cushion covers as well as a small selection of pottery, copper and woodwork. The shop is open Tuesday to Friday from 9 am to 8 pm, Monday and Saturday from 9 am to 3 pm, and is closed on Sunday.

The Centre of Hellenic Tradition, Pandrossou 36, Plaka, has a display of traditional and modern handicrafts from each region of Greece. Most of the items are for sale.

Mado, next to the Lysicrates monument on Sellev, Plaka, is a workshop that turns out beautiful, hand-woven wall-hangings. Many depict island scenes.

Good-quality leather sandals may be bought from Stavros Melissinos, Pandrossou 89 (see the Plaka Walking Tour section earlier).

Getting There & Away

Air Athens is served by Ellinikon airport, on the coast 9km south-east of the city. There are two main terminals with separate entrances 1.5km apart: the West Terminal for all Olympic Airways flights (domestic and international) and the East Terminal for all other flights. From 1 April until the end of October, charter flights use the old military terminal 500m south of the East Terminal.

The facilities are dreadful at all the terminals, and are the subject of constant complaint by hotel and tour operators as well as travellers. Nothing is likely to change, however, until the new international airport at Spata (21km east of Athens) is completed. Ellinikon will then handle only domestic flights.

For Olympic Airways flight information ring ☎ 936 3363, and for all other airlines ring ☎ 969 9466/7. The head office of Olympic Airways (☎ 926 7251/4) is at Leoforos Syngrou 96. The most central Olympic Airways branch office (☎ 926 7444; international: ☎ 926 7489) is at Filellinon 13, just off Plateia Syntagmatos. For information about domestic flights from Athens see the Getting Around chapter. There is luggage storage (open 24 hours; 1600 dr per piece) at the East Terminal, opposite the domestic arrivals.

Athens is one of Europe's major centres for buying discounted air tickets. There are dozens of travel agents on Filellinon, Nikis and Voulis that sell low-priced air tickets to Europe and the USA. See the Travel Agencies section under Information at the beginning of this chapter for some recommendations. Airline offices in Athens include:

Aeroflot	☎ 322 0986
Air Canada	☎ 322 3206
Air France	☎ 960 1100
Air India	☎ 360 3584
Alitalia	☎ 995 9200/3
American Airlines	☎ 325 5061
British Airways	☎ 325 0601
Continental Airlines	☎ 323 7853
CSA-Czech Airlines	☎ 323 2303
Cyprus Airways	☎ 322 6413/4/5
Delta Airlines	☎ 331 1660/1/2/3/4/5
Egypt Air	☎ 323 8907/8
El Al	☎ 363 8642
Garuda Indonesia	☎ 360 6198
Gulf Air	☎ 322 5157
Iberia	☎ 323 4523/6
Japan Airlines	☎ 325 2075
KLM	☎ 988 0177
Lufthansa	☎ 771 6002
Malaysian Airlines	☎ 323 0344/5/6/7
Qantas Airways	☎ 323 9063/4/5/6
SAS	☎ 960 1003/8
Singapore Airlines	☎ 323 9111
South African Airways	☎ 361 6305
Thai Airways	☎ 364 7610
Turkish Airlines	☎ 324 6024
TWA	☎ 322 6451
United Airlines	☎ 924 2645
Virgin Atlantic	☎ 924 9100

Bus Athens has two main intercity bus stations. Terminal A is about 7km north-west of Omonia at Kifissou 100 and has departures to the Peloponnese, the Ionian islands and western Greece. Terminal B is about 5km north of Omonia off Liossion and has departures to central and northern Greece as well as to Evia. The EOT gives out an intercity bus schedule.

Terminal A Like the infamous airport, Terminal A is not a good introduction to Athens – particularly if you arrive between midnight and 5 am when there is no public transport. The taxi fare from Terminal A to Syntagma should be no more than 1500 dr at any time of day. See the following Getting Around section for details of fares, and the Dangers and Annoyances section earlier in this chapter for information on avoiding rip-offs. The only public transport to the city centre is bus No 051, which runs between the terminal and the junction of Zinonos and Menandrou, near Omonia. Buses run every 15 minutes from 5 am to midnight. Don't bother visiting the Tourist Information office at the terminal. It's a booking agency.

The table below shows the destination, journey time, fare and frequency of buses departing from this terminal:

Destination	Duration	Fare	Frequency
Argos	2 hours	2150 dr	hourly
Astakos	5 hours	4750 dr	3 daily
Corfu	11 hours	8600 dr	3 daily
	(including 1000 dr ferry ticket)		
Corinth	1½ hours	1450 dr	half-hourly
Epidaurus	2½ hours	2250 dr	2 daily
Gythio	4½ hours	4150 dr	4 daily
Igoumenitsa	8½ hours	7750 dr	4 daily
Ioannina	7½ hours	6750 dr	8 daily
Kalamata	4½ hours	3950 dr	9 daily
Kalavryta	3½ hours	3000 dr	1 daily
Kavala	10 hours	10,350 dr	3 daily
Kefallonia	8 hours	7000 dr	3 daily
Lefkada	5½ hours	5700 dr	4 daily
Loutraki	1½ hours	1450 dr	9 daily
Monemvasia	6 hours	5150 dr	2 daily
Nafplio	2½ hours	2350 dr	hourly
(via Mycenae)		1950 dr	
Olympia	5½ hours	5000 dr	4 daily
Patras	3 hours	3350 dr	half-hourly
Pyrgos	5 hours	4650 dr	10 daily
Sparta	4½ hours	3450 dr	10 daily
Thessaloniki	7½ hours	7700 dr	10 daily
Tripoli	2¼ hours	2800 dr	12 daily
Zakynthos	7 hours	5850 dr	3 daily
	(with boat ticket)		

Terminal B Terminal B is much easier to handle than Terminal A, although again there is no public transport from midnight to 5 am. The EOT information sheet misleadingly lists the address of the terminal as being Liossion 260, which turns out to be a small car repair workshop. Liossion 260 is where you should get off the No 024 bus that runs from outside the main gate of the National Gardens on Amalias. From Liossion 260,

turn right onto Gousiou and you'll see the terminal at the end of the road on Agiou Dimitriou Oplon. A taxi from the terminal to Syntagma should cost no more than 1500 dr at any time. The table following shows the destination, journey time, fare and frequency of buses departing from this terminal:

Destination	Duration	Fare	Frequency
Agios Konstantinos	2½ hours	2650 dr	hourly
Delphi	3 hours	2700 dr	5 daily
Edipsos	3¼ hours	2450 dr	7 daily
Halkida	1½ hours	1250 dr	half-hourly
Karpenisi	6 hours	4450 dr	2 daily
Kymi	3½ hours	2750 dr	7 daily
Lamia	3¼ hours	3300 dr	hourly
Livadia	2 hours	1570 dr	hourly
Trikala	5½ hours	5000 dr	8 daily
Volos	6¼ hours	4900 dr	9 daily

Buses for nearly all destinations in Attica leave from the Mavromateon terminal at the junction of Alexandras and 28 Oktovriou-Patission, 250m north of the National Archaeological Museum. Buses for southern Attica leave from this terminal, while buses to Rafina and Marathon leave from the bus stops 150m north on Mavromateon.

Train Trains for northern Greece, Evia and Europe leave from Larisis train station, Deligianni, about 1km north-east of Plateia Omonias. Selected destinations, journey times, fares and frequency are:

Destination	Duration	Fare	Frequency
Alexan-droupolis	14 hours	6710 dr** 10,070 dr*	3 daily
Halkida	1½ hours	600 dr**	16 daily
Larisa	5 hours	2660 dr** 3990 dr*	14 daily
Thessaloniki	8 hours	3720 dr** 5580 dr*	10 daily
Volos	7 hours	2830 dr** 4250 dr*	5 daily
Xanthi	12 hours	5880 dr** 8880 dr*	3 daily
*1st class **2nd class			

Four of the trains to Thessaloniki are express intercity services which take six hours and cost more than twice the standard fare – 7700 dr in 2nd class, 9560 dr in 1st class. The 7 am service from Athens is express right through to Alexandroupolis, arriving at 7 pm. It will get you to Larisa in four hours and to Xanthi in 10½ hours. There are also two express trains a day to Volos, taking 4¾ hours. These express services cost about double the standard fare.

Couchettes are available on overnight services to Thessaloniki, priced from 1400 dr in 2nd class and 5400 dr in 1st class.

All trains for the Peloponnese leave from the Peloponnese train station, which is on Sidirodromon. Selected destinations, journey times, fares and frequency are:

Destination	Duration	Fare	Frequency
Corinth	1¾ hours	780 dr** 1170 dr*	14 daily
Kalamata	6½ hours	2160 dr** 3240 dr*	4 daily
Kyparissia	6-8 hours	2560 dr** 3840 dr*	5 daily
Mycenae	2½ hours	900 dr** 1350 dr*	5 daily
Nafplio	3½ hours	1400 dr**	2 daily
Patras	3½-4½ hours	1580 dr** 2370 dr*	8 daily
Pyrgos	5-7 hours	2160 dr** 3240 dr*	6 daily
Tripolis	4 hours	1500 dr** 2250 dr*	3 daily

*1st class **2nd class

The two stations are very close to one another. To reach them take trolleybus No 1 from Plateia Syntagmatos. The stop is the same for both stations, but to get to the Peloponnese train station, cross over the metal bridge at the southern end of Larisis train station.

There is baggage storage at Larisis train station, open from 6.30 am to 9.30 pm, and the cost is 400 dr per piece. More information on services is available from the following OSE offices: Filellinon 17 (☎ 323 6747); Sina 6 (☎ 362 4402); and Karolou 1 (☎ 524 0647). These offices also handle advance bookings.

Car & Motorcycle National Road 1 is the main route north from Athens. It starts at Nea Kifissia. To get there from central Athens, take Vasilissis Sofias from Syntagma. National Road 8, which begins beyond Dafni, is the road to the Peloponnese. Take Agiou Konstantinou from Omonia.

The northern reaches of Syngrou, just south of the Temple of Olympian Zeus, are packed solid with car-rental firms. Local companies offer much better deals than their international rivals. Just Rent a Car (☎ 923 9104), Syngrou, is one of the best. Other outlets include:

Avis
    Amalias 48 (☎ 322 4951)
Budget
    Syngrou 8 (☎ 921 4771)
Eurodollar Rent a Car
    Syngrou 36-38 (☎ 923 0548)
Hertz
    Syngrou 12 (☎ 922 0102)

Hitching Athens is the most difficult place in Greece to hitchhike from. Your best bet is to ask the truck drivers at the Piraeus cargo wharves for a ride. Otherwise, for the Peloponnese, take bus No 860 or 880 from Panepistimiou to Dafni, where National Road 8 begins. For northern Greece, take the metro to Kifissia, then a bus to Nea Kifissia and walk to National Road 1.

Getting Around

The Airport Express-line bus No 91 operates 24 hours a day between central Athens and the East and West terminals, stopping also at the charter terminal when it's in use. The buses are blue and have their destination marked on the front in English.

Going to the airport, the main stops are just south of Plateia Omonias on Stadiou (opposite Emmanual Benaki) and Plateia Syntagmatos, Syntagma (outside the post office). The buses run every 20 minutes between 7 am and 10.45 pm, and then (roughly) hourly until 5.40 am. The night buses leave

Stadiou at 11.50 pm and at 0.50, 1.50, 2.50, 3.50, 4.50, 5.40, 6.20 and 7 am, and from Plateia Syntagmatos five minutes later. The fare is 160 dr, or 200 dr from 11.50 pm to 5.40 am. Tickets can be bought from booths adjacent to the stops or on the bus. During rush hour the journey can take up to an hour. At other times, it should take about 30 minutes.

Coming from the airport, the service starts at the West Terminal and calls at the East and charter terminals before heading for the city. It stops at Stiles, just south of the Temple of Olympian Zeus (for Veïkou and Koukaki); at Amalias, opposite the National Gardens (for Syntagma); and at the northern end of Stadiou (for Omonia). Night services leave the airport hourly from 11.12 pm to 5.12 am, then half-hourly until 8.42 am and then every 20 minutes.

Olympic Airways passengers also have the option of taking the special buses that leave from the Olympic Airways terminal at Syngrou 96 (every 30 minutes, 6.30 am to 8.20 pm, 160 dr). Bus No 133 from Plateia Syntagmatos, Syntagma, to Agios Kosmas (every 15 minutes, 5.40 am to midnight, 100 dr) and bus No A2 from Stadiou or Plateia Syntagmatos to Voula (every 15 minutes, 5.30 am to 11.30 pm, 100 dr) can drop you outside the West Terminal on Leoforos Poseidonos.

There are also express buses from all the airport terminals to Plateia Karaïskaki in Piraeus. Buses leave the East Terminal at 1.45, 3.55, 5.05, 7.05, 8.05, 9.05, 10.05, 10.55 and 11.45 am, and at 12.25, 1.15, 2.05, 2.25, 3.35, 4.35, 5.35, 6.35, 7.45, 8.55, 10.05 and 11.15 pm. They leave Plateia Karaïskaki at 0.20, 2.40, 5, 6, 8, 9.10, 10.10 and 11.10 am, at midday and at 12.50, 1.30, 2.40, 3.10, 3.50, 4.40, 5.40, 6.40, 7.40, 8.50, 10 and 11.10 pm.

Airport Taxis Welcome to Athens! It seems to be virtually impossible to catch a cab from the airport without getting involved in an argument about the fare. One way of avoiding a dispute is to agree a set rate with the driver before you get in. Many drivers will insist on using the meter, in which case you should check that it is set to the correct tariff (see following Taxi section for details). You will also have to pay a 300 dr airport surcharge. Fares vary according to the time of day and level of traffic, but you should expect to pay between 1500 and 2000 dr to get from the airport to the city centre or to Piraeus during the day, and between 2000 and 2500 dr at night. If you have any problems, do not hesitate to threaten to involve the tourist police. See the Dangers & Annoyances section earlier in this chapter for more information on how to handle the city's notorious taxi drivers.

Bus & Trolleybus Since most of Athens' ancient sites are within easy walking distance of Syntagma, and many of the museums are close by on Vasilissis Sofias near Syntagma, the chances are that you won't have much need for public transport.

The blue-and-white buses that serve Athens and the suburbs operate every 15 minutes from 5 am until midnight. There are also green buses operating 24 hours a day between the city centre and Piraeus, every 20 minutes from 6 am until midnight and then hourly. Bus No 040 runs from Filellinon to Akti Xaveriou in Piraeus, and No 049 runs from the northern end of Athinas to Plateia Themistokleous.

Trolleybuses also operate from 5 am until midnight. The free map handed out by EOT shows most of the routes.

There is a flat fare of 100 dr throughout the city on both buses and trolleybuses. Tickets must be purchased before you board, either at a transport kiosk or a *periptero*. Most, but not all, periptera sell tickets. The same tickets can be used on either buses or trolleybuses. Tickets can be bought in blocks of 10, but there is no discount for bulk buying. Tickets must be validated using the red ticket machine as soon as you board a bus or trolleybus. Plain-clothed inspectors make spot checks, and the penalty for travelling without a validated ticket is 1500 dr. Monthly travel cards also are available for buses and trolleybuses. They are valid from the first day of each month to the last and cost 5000 dr.

Metro Athens' metro is simple to understand and you cannot get lost as there is only one line, which is divided into three sections: Piraeus to Omonia, Omonia to Perissos and Perissos to Kifissia. The stations are: Piraeus, Faliro, Moshato, Kalithea, El Venizelou/Tavros, Petralona, Thision, Monastiraki, Omonia, Plateia Viktorias, Attiki, Agios Nikolaos, Kato Patissia, Perissos, Pefkakia, Nea Ionia, Iraklio, Irini, Maroussi, Kat and Kifissia. The line runs underground between Monastiraki and Attiki. The price of a ticket for travel within one or two sections is 100 dr and 150 dr for three sections. There are ticket machines and ticket booths at all stations. The machines for validating tickets are at the platform entrances. As with bus tickets, the penalty for travelling without a validated ticket is 1500 dr. The trains run every five minutes between 5 am and midnight.

A new metro system is under construction. It was originally scheduled to open in 1998, but a series of archaeological discoveries made during construction means that it won't be completed until the year 2000 at the earliest.

Taxi Athens' taxis are yellow. If you see an Athenian standing in the road bellowing and waving their arms frantically, the chances are they will be trying to get a taxi at rush hour. Despite the large number of taxis careering around the streets of Athens, it can be incredibly difficult to get one.

To hail a taxi, stand on a pavement and shout your destination as they pass. If a taxi is going your way the driver may stop even if there are already passengers inside. This does not mean the fare will be shared: each person will be charged the fare shown on the meter. If you get in one that does not have other passengers, make sure the meter is switched on.

The flag fall is 200 dr, with a 160 dr surcharge from ports and railway and bus stations, and a 300 dr surcharge from the airport. After that, the day rate (tariff 1 on the meter) is 62 dr per km. The rate doubles between midnight and 5 am (tariff 2 on the meter). Baggage is charged at the rate of 55 dr per item over 10kg. The fare should be less than 500 dr for most journeys in central Athens. It sometimes helps if you can point out your destination on a map – many taxi drivers in Athens are extremely ignorant of their city.

If it is absolutely imperative that you get somewhere on time (eg to the airport), and you want to go by taxi, it is advisable to book a radio taxi – you will be charged 300 dr extra, but it's worth it. The radio taxis operating out of central Athens include:

Athina 1	☎ 921 7942
Enotita	☎ 645 9000
Ermis	☎ 411 5200
Ikaros	☎ 513 2240
Kosmos	☎ 420 0042
Parthenon	☎ 582 1292
Proödos	☎ 643 3400
Sata	☎ 862 5407

For more information about Athens' taxi drivers see Dangers & Annoyances earlier in this chapter.

Car & Motorcycle Appalling traffic, confusing signposting and the one-way system that operates on most streets in the city centre combine to make Athens a nightmarish place to drive in. The traffic jams do at least offer an opportunity to work out where you're going!

Athenian drivers have a cavalier attitude towards driving laws. Contrary to what you will see, parking *is* illegal alongside kerbs marked with yellow lines, where street signs prohibit parking and on pavements and in pedestrian malls.

Athens has numerous small car parks, but these are totally insufficient for the large number of cars used in the city. There is an underground car park opposite the meat market on Athinas, with entry from Sokratous.

For details of car and motorcycle-rental

Traffic Chaos

If your first introduction to Greece is Athens, the chances are you will soon be cursing cars like you've never done before. Despite the fact that Greeks have the second-lowest GDP per capita of all EU countries, there are more cars per head of population in Athens than in any other Mediterranean city.

The problems of traffic congestion and pollution have been testing the ingenuity of politicians and town planners for years. Ironically, the measures adopted to date have succeeded only in increasing the number of vehicles on the road.

The first measures came in 1980, when the famous odds and evens number-plate legislation was introduced. It bans odd and even plates from the city centre on alternate days. This, it was calculated, would halve the number of cars in the city centre. Instead, it has resulted in many families purchasing a second car with the requisite odd or even number plate.

The next attempt, at the beginning of 1993, was more sophisticated – but equally ill fated. It was decreed that all cars in use in central Athens must be fitted with catalytic converters. This was promoted by a 1991 regulation reducing import taxes on cars with catalytic converters, as long as the owner scrapped a vehicle at least 15 years old. Many low-income families then became car owners for the first time by buying an old banger and trading in for a new 'clean' car.

With these measures only increasing the congestion, the municipal authorities have now persuaded offices in central Athens to stagger the starting times of employees to lessen the impact of peak hour.

The situation is unlikely to improve much, however, until the completion of the new metro system, hopefully by the year 2000. In the meantime, the construction works merely worsen the situation. ∎

agencies in Athens, see the previous Getting There & Away section.

Around Athens

PIRAEUS Πειραιάς
• *pop 171,000* • *postcode 185 01* • *area code* ☎ *01*

Piraeus (in Greek Pireás) is the port of Athens, the main port of Greece and one of the major ports of the Mediterranean. It's the hub of the Aegean ferry network, the centre for Greece's maritime export-import and transit trade and the base for its large merchant navy. Nowadays, Athens has expanded sufficiently to meld imperceptibly into Piraeus. The road linking the two passes through a grey, urban sprawl of factories, warehouses and concrete apartment blocks. Piraeus is as bustling and traffic-congested as Athens. It's not a place in which many visitors want to linger; most come merely to catch a ferry.

History

The histories of Athens and Piraeus are inextricably linked. Piraeus has been the port of Athens since classical times, when Themis-tocles transferred his Athenian fleet from the exposed port of Phaleron (modern Faliro) to the security of Piraeus. After his victory over the Persians at the Battle of Salamis in 480 BC, Themistocles fortified Piraeus' three natural harbours. In 445 BC Pericles extended these fortifying walls to Athens and Phaleron. The Long Walls, as they were known, were destroyed as one of the peace conditions imposed by the Spartans at the end of the Peloponnesian Wars, but were rebuilt in 394 BC.

Piraeus was a flourishing commercial centre during the classical age, but by Roman times it had been overtaken by Rhodes, Delos and Alexandria. During medieval and Turkish times it diminished to a tiny fishing village, and by the time of Independence it was home to less than 20 people. Its resurgence began in 1834 when Athens became the capital of independent Greece. By the beginning of this century it had superseded the island of Syros as Greece's principal port. In 1923 its population was swollen by the arrival of 100,000 refugees from Turkey. The Piraeus which then evolved from this influx had a seedy but somewhat romantic appeal with its bordellos, hashish dens and rembetika

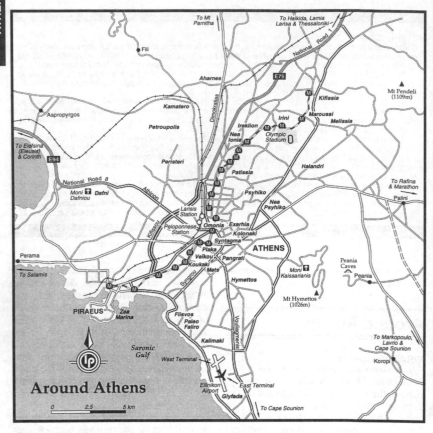

Around Athens

0   2.5   5 km

music – all vividly portrayed in the film
Never on a Sunday.

These places have long since gone and
beyond its façade of smart, new shipping
offices and banks, much of Piraeus is now
just plain seedy. The exception is the eastern
quarter around Zea Marina and Mikrolimano, where the seafront is lined with
seafood restaurants, bars and discos.

Orientation

Piraeus is 10km south-west of central
Athens. The largest of the three harbours is
the Great Harbour (Megas Limin), on the

western side of the Piraeus peninsula. All
ferries leave from here. Zea Marina (Limin
Zeas), on the other side of the peninsula, is
the port for hydrofoils to the Saronic Gulf
islands (except Aegina) as well as being the
place where millionaires moor their yachts.
North-east of here is the picturesque Mikrolimano (small harbour), which is
brimming with private yachts.

The quickest and easiest way of getting to
Piraeus from central Athens is by metro,
which terminates at the north-eastern corner
of the Great Harbour on Akti Kalimassioti.
Most ferry departure points are a short walk

PLACES TO STAY
8 Hotel Delfini
10 Hotel Acropole
23 Hotel Castella
24 Hotel Mistral
27 Hotel Cavo d'Oro

PLACES TO EAT
9 Restaurant I Folia
26 Restaurant Moruragio

FERRIES & HYDROFOILS
2 Ferries for Crete
3 Ferries for Eastern
  Cyclades
4 Ferries for Western
  & Central Cyclades
16 Ferries for Saronic Gulf
17 Hydrofoils for Aegina
19 Ferries for Crete
20 Ferries for the Dodecanese
22 International Ferries
31 Hydrofoil Ticket Office

34 Hydrofoils for Saronic
   Gulf

OTHER
1 Train Station for
  Northern Greece
5 Train Station for
  Peloponnese
6 Metro Station
7 Buses to Zea Marina
11 Bus Station
12 Buses to Airport
13 National Bank of Greece
14 OTE
15 Post Office
18 Bus 049 to Omonia
21 Olympic Airways
25 Amphitheatre
28 Archaeolgical Museum
29 Bus 040 to Syntagma
30 EOT
32 Buses to Great Harbour
33 Maritime Museum

Piraeus

Saronic
Gulf

0   200   400 m

from here. A left turn out of the metro station leads after 250m to Plateia Karaïskaki, which is the terminus for buses to the airport. Jutting out into the harbour behind the square is Akti Tzelepi with its mass of ticket agencies.

The departure points for the various ferry destinations are shown on the map of Piraeus. Note that there are two departure points for Crete. Ferries for Iraklio leave from the western end of Akti Kondyli, but ferries for other Cretan ports occasionally dock there as well. It's a long way to the other departure point for Crete on Akti Miaouli, so

check where to find your boat when you buy your ticket. All ferries display a clock face showing their departure time, and have their ports of call written in English above their bows.

Piraeus also has train stations for both northern Greece and the Peloponnese. The station for the Peloponnese is one block north of the metro, and the station for northern Greece is at the western end of Akti Kondyli.

There are buses (No 904 or 905) to Zea Marina from the bus stop next to the metro. If you want to walk, it takes about 30

Unfinished Buildings

Unfinished buildings are a constant blot on the landscape wherever you go in Greece. Most people don't actually have the money to build a house when they buy the land, so they do it in stages. Planning permission costs one million drachma per 100 sq m and usually takes around a year to obtain, after which the concrete frame is erected and left until there is money available to pay for the next step.

After three years the licence expires, and if the house doesn't look finished they have to re-apply for planning permission and pay all over again. In practice this often means that frenetic building activity takes place as the deadline approaches, and by the time the three years is up the house looks finished. At least, it does from the outside; inside is a different story – work may not have started on the interior at all.

A receipt has to be obtained for every single bit of building work, and electricity will not be connected until the owner has shown where he got the money to build the house in the first place.

Steel rods are usually left sticking up through the roof so that another floor can be added later on if required. As Greece is a matriarchal society, the extension is often built to provide a home for a daughter upon her marriage. ∎

---

minutes. Head up Vasileos Georgiou Androutsou from Plateia Themistokleous and turn right onto Vasileos Konstantinou at Plateia Kora. Continue along Vasileos Konstantinou (also known as Iroön Polytehniou) for almost 1km, and then turn left down Afendouli after the Hotel Savoy. Turn right at the end of Afendouli, and then take the second street on the left (Freatidas) and you will emerge at the Maritime Museum, overlooking the hydrofoil departure point. If you are coming to Zea Marina on bus No 040 from Syntagma, get off at the stop opposite the Hotel Savoy.

Information

Thanks to some kind of bureaucratic bad joke, the Piraeus EOT (☎ 413 5716) is at Zea Marina. Why it should be here and not at the Great Harbour defies imagination. Doubtless the office is kept busy telling millionaire yacht owners where to stock up on caviar and champagne, but it's useless for the thousands of travellers who pour through the Great Harbour every day. The office is open Monday to Friday from 8 am to 3 pm. The telephone number of Piraeus' port police is ☎ 417 2657.

Money The National Bank of Greece is just north of Plateia Themistokleous on the corner of Antistaseos and Tsamadou. The Emporiki Bank, closer to the square on the corner of Antistaseos and Makras Stoas, has a 24-hour automatic exchange machine. Thomas Cook (☎ 422 5000) has a branch at Akti Poseidonos 26. It's open Monday to Friday from 8.30 am to 8 pm, Saturday from 9 am to 6.30 pm and Sunday from 10 am to 2.30 pm.

Post & Communications The main post office is on the corner of Tsamadou and Filonos, just north of Plateia Themistokleous. It's open Monday to Friday from 7.30 am to 8 pm and Saturday from 7.30 am to 2 pm. The OTE is just north of here at Karaoli 19 and is open 24 hours.

Archaeological Museum

If you have time to spare in Piraeus, the archaeological museum is a good place to spend it. It's well laid out and contains some important finds from classical and Roman times. These include some very fine tomb reliefs dating from the 4th to the 2nd century BC. The star piece of the museum, however, is the magnificent statue of Apollo, the Piraeus Kouros. It is the oldest larger-than-life, hollow bronze statue yet found. It dates from about 520 BC and was discovered, buried in rubble, in 1959. The museum (☎ 452 1598) is at Trikoupi 31 and is open Tuesday to Sunday from 8.30 am to 3 pm. Admission is 500 dr.

Maritime Museum

The maritime museum's collection spans the history of the Greek navy from ancient times to the present day, with drawings and plans of battles, models of ships, battle scenes, uniforms and war memorabilia. There are various nautical oddments in the small park outside the museum, including a submarine conning tower which children love to climb. The museum (☎ 451 6822) is on Akti Themistokleous at Zea Marina, very close to the hydrofoil quay. It's open Tuesday to Saturday from 8.30 am to 1.30 pm. Admission is 200 dr.

Places to Stay – bottom end

There's no reason why anyone should stay in Piraeus when Athens is so close. If you do get stuck, don't attempt to sleep out – Piraeus is the most dangerous place in Greece to do so.

Most of the cheap hotels are geared more towards accommodating sailors than tourists. The *Hotel Acropole* (☎ 417 3313), Gounari 7, has dorm beds for 3000 dr, and tidy but plain singles/doubles with shared bathroom for 6000/8000 dr. Gounari is the main thoroughfare running inland from Plateia Karaïskaki.

The C-class *Hotel Delfini* (☎ 412 9779), nearby at Leoharous 7, is a bit smarter with singles/doubles for 7000/10,000 dr with private bathroom. Make sure you don't get taken there by one of the touts who hang around the port or you will wind up paying the official prices of 14,000/16,000 dr.

Places to Stay – middle

The best hotels are to be found around the Mikrolimano. There are three good B-class options on Vasilissis Pavlou, which runs around the hillside above the harbour. The pick of them is the plush *Hotel Mistral* (☎ 411 7675) at No 105. It charges 17,000/22,000 dr for very comfortable air-con rooms with great views over the harbour below. The rates include buffet breakfast,

and facilities include a roof garden with restaurant, bar and swimming pool. The *Hotel Castella* (☎ 411 4735/4737), at No 75, has singles/doubles with air-con for 16,000/25,000 dr, including breakfast. It also has views of the harbour, as does the *Hotel Cavo d'Oro* (☎ 412 2210), at No 19, where air-con singles/doubles are 14,000/20,000 dr.

Places to Eat

If all you want is a quick bite before catching a ferry, then there are several reasonably priced places on Akti Poseidonos and along Gounari. The tiny *Restaurant I Folia*, opposite Plateia Karaïskaki on Akti Poseidonos, does a bowl of gigantes beans for 500 dr, calamari for 600 dr and moussaka for 780 dr.

The setting around the Mikrolimano is rather more relaxed, with a string of seafood restaurants right on the waterfront. The *Restaurant Mouragio*, Akti Koumoundourou 60, has a good range and reasonable prices. Expect to pay about 5000 dr per person, plus drinks.

Entertainment

The Piraeus *open-air amphitheatre* features drama and dance performances as part of the Athens Festival (see Special Events in the Athens section earlier). The theatre is on the Hill of Kastella behind the Mikrolimano.

Things to Buy

Many locals will tell you that the Piraeus flea market is infinitely better than its famous counterpart in Athens. As well as stalls selling junk, there are small shops selling high-quality jewellery, ceramics and antiques. The market is held on Sunday mornings on Alipedou and Skilitsi, near Plateia Ippodamias, which is behind the metro station.

Getting There & Away

Air Olympic Airways (☎ 452 0968) has an office at Akti Miaouli 27.

Bus There are no intercity buses to or from Piraeus. There are buses to central Athens, to the airport and to the coastal suburbs of Glyfada and Voula, south of the airport.

Green bus Nos 040 and 049 operate 24 hours a day to Athens – every 20 minutes from 6 am until midnight and then hourly. No 040 runs between Akti Xaveriou and Filellinon and is the service that goes closest to Zea Marina. The most convenient stop is outside the Hotel Savoy. No 049 runs between Plateia Karaïskaki and Plateia Omonias. The fare is 100 dr for both services.

Buses to the airport leave from the southwestern corner of Plateia Karaïskaki. Departure times are listed under To/From the Airport in the Getting Around section earlier in this chapter. The fare is 160 dr, or 200 dr from 11.30 pm to 6 am. Blue bus No 110 runs from Plateia Karaïskaki to Glyfada and Voula every 15 minutes (100 dr). It stops outside the airport's West Terminal.

Metro The metro is the fastest and easiest way of getting from the Great Harbour to central Athens (see the Getting Around section earlier in this chapter). The station is at the northern end of Akti Kalimassioti.

Train Piraeus train station is one block north of the metro. All the railway services to the Peloponnese (see Getting There & Away in the Athens chapter) actually start and terminate at Piraeus, although most schedules don't mention it. There are about 15 trains a day to Athens – enough to make them a reasonable option if you want to stay close to the stations.

The single service from the northern line train station (via Larisis train station) is of purely academic interest, leaving at 1.30 pm and taking more than seven hours to crawl to Volos, stopping all stations.

Ferry – domestic The following islands and island groups are linked to Piraeus by ferries: Crete, the Cyclades (except Kea), the Dodecanese (Kastellorizo, Agathonisi, Lipsi, Nisyros and Tilos cannot be reached directly – ferries change in Rhodes), the Saronic Gulf and the North-Eastern Aegean (except Thasos and Samothraki; for Psara and Inousses ferries change on Chios). The EOT in Athens gives out a ferry schedule which is updated weekly.

The following information applies only to the high season from June to mid-September. There are daily ferries to the Cycladic islands of Kythnos, Serifos, Sifnos, Milos, Kimolos, Syros, Mykonos, Paros, Naxos, Ios and Tinos; and two or three ferries a week to Iraklia, Shinoussa, Koufonisi, Donoussa, Amorgos, Folegandros, Sikinos and Anafi. In the shoulder season (April, May and October) ferry schedules are reduced to some extent and in winter they are reduced drastically.

There are daily ferries to the Dodecanese islands of Rhodes, Kos, Kalymnos, Leros and Patmos; and two or three a week to Astypalea, Karpathos and Kassos. Daily ferries also operate to the North-Eastern Aegean islands of Chios, Lesvos (Mytilini), Ikaria and Samos. Limnos has two or three connections a week. The Saronic Gulf islands are linked by daily ferries all year. Crete has a host of ferry connections. There are two a day to Iraklio year-round and at least one a day to Hania, as well as three or four a week to Rethymno, two or three a week to Kastelli-Kissamos (via Monemvasia, Neapoli, Gythio, Kythira and Antikythira) and one a week to Agios Nikolaos.

Ferry ticket prices are fixed by the government. All ferries charge the same for any given route, although the facilities on board differ – quite radically at times. The small differences in prices charged by agents are the result of agents sacrificing part of their allotted commission to increase sales. These discounts seldom amount to more than 50 dr. Agents cannot charge more than the fixed price. If you want to book a cabin or take a car on board a ferry, it is advisable to buy a ticket in advance in Athens. Otherwise, wait until you get to Piraeus; agents selling ferry tickets are thick on the ground around Plateia Karaïskaki. If you're running short of time, you can buy your ticket at the quay from the tables set up next to each ferry. It costs no more to buy your ticket at the boat, contrary to what some agents might tell you.

See Boat in the Getting Around chapter and the Getting There & Away sections for each island for more information.

Ferry – international There are three ferries a week in summer to Limassol in Cyprus and Haifa in Israel, one a week in winter. Salamis Lines operates the F/B *Nissos Kypros* all year-round via Rhodes. It leaves Piraeus on Thursday at 8 pm and Rhodes on Friday at 5 pm, arriving at Limassol at 11 am on Saturday and Haifa at 7 am on Sunday. In summer, Vergina Ferries runs the F/B *Vergina* to Cyprus and Haifa via Iraklio on Crete, leaving Piraeus on Thursday at 7 am, while Poseidon Lines operates the F/B *Sea Harmony* via Rhodes and Crete. The high season runs from 15 June until 13 September. Deckclass fares from Piraeus to Limassol are 13,000/15,000 dr in low/high season, and 21,000/23,000 dr to Haifa. The fares from Crete and Rhodes are virtually the same, although Rhodes is halfway to Cyprus. All three lines offer 20% student (up to 28 years), youth (up to 24 years) and returnticket discounts.

Hydrofoil There are year-round, daily hydrofoils from Zea Marina to the Saronic Gulf islands of Aegina, Hydra, Poros and Spetses. Some of these also call at Ermioni, Porto Heli, Leonidio, Tolo, Nafplio, Monemvasia and Neapoli in the Peloponnese and the island of Kythira. In addition, there are hourly hydrofoils (on the hour) from Great Harbour to Aegina. You can buy tickets at the kiosks adjacent to the departure points. For more information, see Hydrofoils in the Getting Around chapter and the Getting There & Away sections of the island chapters.

Getting Around
Green bus No 040 goes from Vasileos Konstantinou to Syntagma every 20 minutes during the day and hourly during the night.

This bus can take up to 45 minutes to get from Athens to Piraeus; the metro is quicker.

DAFNI Δαφνί
Moni Dafniou
This monastery, 10km north-west of Athens along the busy road to Corinth, is Attica's most important Byzantine monument. It is built on the route of the Sacred Way and on the site of an ancient Sanctuary of Apollo. Its name derives from the daphne laurels which were sacred to Apollo.

The monastery's 11th-century church contains some of Greece's finest **mosaics**. These were created at a time when the artistic and intellectual achievements of Byzantium had reached unprecedented heights. The monastery was sacked in 1205 by the renegades of the Fourth Crusade who had earlier captured Constantinople. It was rebuilt and occupied by monks until the time of the War of Independence, after which it was used as army barracks and as a hospital for the mentally ill. Much restoration has taken place since.

The mosaics on the church walls depict saints and monks, while the ones on the dome depict apostles, prophets and guardian archangels. Exquisite though these mosaics are, they fade into insignificance once the visitor has gazed upon the Christos Pantokrator (Christ in Majesty) which occupies the centre of the dome. Even a confirmed atheist cannot help but be impressed by this masterpiece of Byzantine art. The monastery (☎ 581 1558) is open daily from 8.30 am to 3 pm, and entry is 800 dr.

Getting There & Away
Bus No A16 from Plateia Eleftherias, north of Monastiraki, can drop you at the Venzini stop right outside the monastery. The buses run every 20 minutes and take about 30 minutes in reasonable traffic. Don't catch the buses to Dafni from Syntagma, which go to a suburb of the same name to the south-east.

ELEFSINA (ELEUSIS) Ελευσίνα
The ruins of ancient Eleusis are in the modern industrial town of Elefsina, 12km

further along the road from Moni Dafniou and on the same bus route.

The ancient city of Eleusis was built around the **Sanctuary of Demeter**. The site dates back to Mycenaean times, when the cult of Demeter began.

The cult became one of the most important in ancient Greece. By classical times it was celebrated with a huge annual festival, which attracted thousands of pilgrims wanting to be initiated into the Eleusian mysteries. They walked in procession from the Acropolis to Eleusis along the Sacred Way, which was lined with statues and votive monuments. Initiates were sworn to secrecy on punishment of death, and during the 1400 years that the sanctuary functioned its secrets were never divulged. The sanctuary was closed by the Roman emperor Theodosius in the 4th century AD.

Although the sanctuary was the most important in ancient Greece after Delphi, the modern site is not particularly inspiring. Most of it is overgrown, and an industrial complex occupies the western edge. A visit to the site's **museum** first will help you to make some sense of the ruins. Both the site and museum are open Tuesday to Sunday from 8.30 am to 3 pm. Admission is 500 dr.

MONI KAISSARIANIS
Μονή Καισσαριανής

This 11th-century monastery, 5km east of Athens, is set amid pines, plane and cypress trees on the slopes of Mt Hymettos. The air is permeated with the aroma of herbs which grow on the mountain.

The source of the river Ilissos is on the hill above the monastery. Its waters were once believed to cure infertility and were sacred

The Abduction of Persephone

The story of the abduction of Persephone to the underworld and her subsequent return is the mythological explanation for the changing of the seasons and the cycle of life, death and rebirth.

According to one version of the myth, Hades, the god of the underworld, fell in love with Persephone, daughter of Demeter, the goddess of wheat and fertility. Zeus was placed in a tricky spot when he was asked to give his consent to their marriage. He didn't want to upset his big brother by saying no, but he knew that Demeter doted on Persephone and would not want to lose her to the underworld. He ended up saying nothing, so Hades just went ahead and grabbed Persephone, swooping down on her while she was picking flowers in a field near Eleusis. A distraught Demeter searched everywhere for her daughter, but to no avail. Eventually she came in disguise to the city of Eleusis and was taken in by King Celeus. His son, Triptolemus, recognised her and told her that Hades had been spotted dragging Persephone off.

Hades and Persephone

Demeter was furious, sensing that her fellow gods and goddesses had been holding out on her. In revenge, she cursed the soil so that nothing would grow while her daughter was kept from her. Zeus was forced into a diplomatic shuffle to negotiate Persephone's release, which was obtained on the condition that she had not eaten anything while in the underworld, for no-one can return to the world of the living after tasting the food of the dead. The diplomatic shuffle became ever more desperate after it was discovered that Persephone had eaten a seed of the pomegranate that Hades had given her as a token of his love. It was finally agreed that Persephone could spend nine months of the year with her mother on earth, and the other three months in the underworld. Demeter lifted her curse, apart from the three-month period when Persephone had to return to the underworld. During this time the earth's soil became infertile again. In thanks to King Celeus and Triptolemus, Demeter gave permission for her principal temple in Greece to be built at Eleusis. ■

to Aphrodite; a temple dedicated to her stood nearby. The spring feeds a fountain on the eastern wall of the monastery, where the water gushes from a marble ram's head (this is a copy – the 6th-century original is in the National Archaeological Museum).

Surrounding the courtyard of the monastery are a mill, bakery, bathhouse and refectory. The church is dedicated to the Presentation of the Virgin and is built to the Greek-cross plan. Four columns taken from a Roman temple support its dome. The 17th-century frescoes in the narthex are the work of Ioannis Ipatos. Those in the rest of the church date from the 16th century, and were painted by a monk from Mt Athos.

The monastery is best visited during the week – it's swarming with picnickers at weekends. The grounds are open until sunset and the monastery buildings are open Tuesday to Sunday from 8.30 am to 3 pm; admission is 800 dr. To get to the monastery take bus No 224 from Plateia Kaningos (at the north end of Akadimias), or from the junction of Akadimias and Sina, to the terminus. From here it's a walk of about 30 minutes to the monastery.

Attica Αττική

Attica, a *nomos* of Sterea Ellada, contains more than just the capital and its port of Piraeus. There are several places of interest, most of which can be reached by the orange buses which depart from the Mavromateon bus terminal.

COAST ROAD TO CAPE SOUNION
This road skirts Attica's Apollo coast. It's a beautiful coastline of splendid beaches and stunning sea vistas which has been spoilt by overdevelopment. Many of the beaches are either EOT pay beaches or belong to hotels. The beaches have boats and water-sports equipment for hire, tennis and volleyball courts and children's playgrounds.

The first resort you'll encounter travelling south is **Glyfada**, Attica's largest resort. The

place is overrun with package tourists in summer, and they are joined by half the population of Athens at weekends. In addition, Glyfada has a permanent population of wealthy expatriates. Loads of bars and discos and noisy air traffic complete the picture – you'd be better off staying on the bus.

If you want to stay in Glyfada, the *Hotel Ilion* (☎ 894 6011) has clean singles/doubles with private bathroom for 4900/5900 dr. The hotel is at Kondyli 4, on the corner of Plateia Bizaniou, which is where the No 120 bus from Syntagma terminates. Konstantinoupoleos, which runs parallel to Kondyli one block south, is packed with bars and tavernas.

Foodwise, *Tzavelas Taverna*, away from the main pack at the junction of Konstantinoupoleos and Lazaridi Sabba, has the best prices. *Tiller's Pub*, at No 9, is the favourite haunt of the expatriate community. It turns out a traditional English Sunday lunch of roast beef and veg for a traditional 1009 dr. The *Joker Club*, opposite, has live bands on Thursday night.

The beach-resort belt continues south through Voula, Vouliagmeni and Varkiza. There are camp sites by the beach at both Voula (☎ 01-895 2712) and Varkiza (☎ 01-897 4329). The coast south of Varkiza to Cape Sounion is dotted with the weekenders of well-to-do Athenians, but it's still possible to find stretches of beach with hardly a soul in sight. Cape Sounion, 70km from Athens, is at the south-eastern tip of Attica.

Getting There & Away
Blue city buses can take you as far south as Varkiza for 100 dr. There are buses from Syntagma to Glyfada (A3) and Voula/Vouliagmeni (A2). The A2 buses are much faster and also stop at Glyfada. If your destination is Sounion, take one of the *paraliako* (coastal) buses which leave hourly, on the half-hour (two hours, 1150 dr), from the Mavromateon bus terminal (see Athens, Getting Around for details). The buses also stop on Filellinon, on the corner of Xenofondos just south of Plateia Syntagmatos, 10

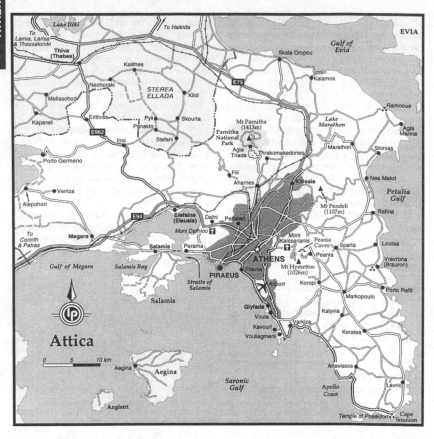

Attica

minutes later, but by this time they're usually very crowded.

INLAND ROAD TO CAPE SOUNION

The inland road to Cape Sounion passes through the Mesogeia (middle land) region, renowned for the fine olives and grapes grown on its red soil. **Peania**, a village 18km east of Athens in the eastern foothills of Mt Hymettos, was the birthplace of the orator Demosthenes (384-322 BC). Little remains of the ancient town. Visitors come today not for the ruins, but to look around the **Vorres Museum** (☎ 01-664 2520/4771), which houses folkloric items, prints and pictures, and an impressive collection of contemporary Greek paintings. Modern sculptures stand in the courtyard. The museum is a fair hike from the bus stop on Peania's main square, Plateia Vasileos Konstantinou. Walk down Demosthenous (which has the New Democracy building on the corner and the post office next to it) and turn right onto Dimihounta at the bottom. Walk to the top of Dimihounta, and turn left onto Diadohou Konstantinou – where you'll soon find a reassuring sign pointing straight ahead to the museum. The museum is open on weekends only, from 10 am to 2 pm. Admission is 500 dr.

The **Peania Caves** (☎ 01-664 2108), 4km west of Peania on the slopes of Mt Hymettos, have an impressive array of stalactites and stalagmites that are very effectively lit. The cave is signposted from Peania, but there is no public transport. It is open daily from 9 am to 4.30 pm. Admission is 1500 dr.

The largest of the villages of Mesogeia is **Koropi**, a lively market town 7km south of Peania. Its Church of the Transfiguration, on the road to Markopoulo, is one of the oldest churches in Attica and contains the remains of 10th-century frescoes. The road continues to **Markopoulo** – home of the Kourtaki company, producer of Greece's most popular bottled retsina. The road south continues to Lavrio and Cape Sounion.

Getting There & Away
There are Athens suburban blue buses to Peania and Koropi from Eptahalkou, just south of the metro line at Thision. Bus Nos 125, 307 and 308 all terminate at Koropi. Markopoulo is on the route of the *mesogiaki* (inland) buses bound for Sounion from the Mavromateon terminal in Athens. They leave hourly, on the hour, and take 2¼ hours to get to Sounion (1050 dr).

CAPE SOUNION Ακρωτήριο Σούνιο
Temple of Poseidon
The ancient Greeks chose their temple sites carefully, with the prime considerations being a site's natural beauty and its appropriateness to the god in question. Nowhere is this more evident than at Cape Sounion, where the Temple of Poseidon stands on a craggy spur that plunges 65m to the sea. The temple was built in 444 BC at the same time as the Parthenon. It is constructed of local marble from Agrilesa and its slender columns – of which 16 remain – are Doric. It is thought that the temple was built by Ictinus, the architect of the Temple of Hephaestus in Athens' Ancient Agora.

The temple looks gleaming white when viewed from the sea and is discernible from a long distance away. It gave great comfort

to sailors in ancient times: they knew that once they'd spotted it, they were nearly home. The views from the temple are equally impressive. On a clear day, you can see Kea, Kythnos and Serifos to the south-east, and Aegina and the Peloponnese to the west. The site also contains scanty remains of a propylon, a fortified tower and, to the north-east, a 6th-century temple to Athena.

You'll have to visit early in the morning before the tourist buses arrive if you wish to indulge the sentiments of Byron's lines from *Don Juan*:

> Place me on Sunium's marbled steep,
> Where nothing save the waves and I,
> May hear our mutual murmurs sweep...

Byron was so taken by Sounion that he carved his name on one of the columns – many others have followed suit.

The site is open Monday to Saturday from 9 am to sunset and on Sunday from 10 am to sunset. Admission is 800 dr.

Places to Stay & Eat
There are two camp sites at Cape Sounion, *Camping Vakchos* (☎ 0292-39 571/262) and *Sounio Beach Camping* (☎ 0292-39 358/718). Both are on the road to Lavrio.

The café at the cape is expensive, so it's a good idea to bring along something to eat and drink. The nearest tavernas are at Sounio beach on the way to Lavrio.

Getting There & Away
You can take either the inland or coastal bus to Cape Sounion. See the Coast Road to Sounion and the Inland Road to Sounion sections for more information.

LAVRIO Λαύριο
• pop 2500 • postcode 195 00 • area code ☎ 0292
Lavrio is an unattractive industrial town on the east coast of Attica, 10km north of Sounion. It is only worth a mention because it is the departure point for ferries to the islands of Kea and Kythnos. The town has definitely seen better days. In ancient times its silver mines, worked by slaves, helped to

finance Pericles' building programme. The island of Makronisos, opposite the port, was used as a place of exile during the civil war. If you have time to spare you could visit the **mineralogical museum** (☎ 26 270), Plateia Iroön Polytehniou. It's open on Wednesday, Saturday and Sunday from 10 am to noon. Admission is 100 dr.

Getting There & Away

Bus There are buses every 30 minutes to Lavrio from the Mavromateon terminal in Athens (1½ hours, 900 dr).

Ferry Goutos Lines runs the F/B *Myrina Express* from Lavrio to Kea (1680 dr) and Kythnos (2260 dr). From mid-June, there are ferries to Kea every morning and evening from Monday to Friday, and up to six a day at weekends. Three ferries a week continue to Kythnos. In winter there are ferries to Kea every day except Monday, returning every day except Wednesday. One service a week continues to Kythnos. The EOT in Athens gives out a timetable for this route.

The ticket office at Lavrio is opposite the quay.

RAFINA Ραφήνα
• *pop* • *postcode 190 09* • *area code* ☎ *0294*

Rafina, on Attica's east coast, is Athens' main fishing port and second-most important port for passenger ferries. The port is much smaller than Piraeus and less confusing – and fares are about 20% cheaper, but you have to spend an hour on the bus and 440 dr to get there.

The port police (☎ 22 888) occupy a kiosk near the quay, which is lined with fish restaurants and ticket agents. The main square, Plateia Plastira, is at the top of the ramp leading to the port.

There's no reason to hang about in Rafina and there are frequent bus connections with Athens. If, however, you want to stay the night and catch an early ferry or hydrofoil, there are a couple of reasonable hotels. The D-class *Hotel Koralli* (☎ 22 477), on Plateia Plastira, has singles/doubles/triples for 5000/7300/10,200 dr. The C-class *Hotel*

Avra (☎ 22 780) overlooks the port just south of the square. It has large singles/doubles with sea views for 10,000/14,000 dr, including breakfast.

Getting There & Away

Bus There are frequent buses from the Mavromateon terminal in Athens to Rafina (one hour, 380 dr) between 5.45 am and 10.30 pm. The first bus leaves Rafina at 5.50 am and the last at 10.15 pm.

Ferry Agoudimos Lines, Ventouris Ferries and Strintzis Lines all operate ferries to the Cycladic islands of Andros (two hours, 2310 dr), Tinos (3½ hours, 3335 dr) and Mykonos (4½ hours, 3780 dr). There are ferries every morning at 8 am and every afternoon between 5 and 6.30 pm. From 15 June until the end of August, there is an additional service leaving at 2.15 pm.

The Agoudimos Lines ferry leaving at 5 pm on Thursday continues from Mykonos to Syros (5½ hours, 3230 dr), Paros (seven hours, 3740 dr), Naxos (eight hours, 3865 dr), Amorgos (11 hours, 4360 dr), Koufonisi (11½ hours, 4405 dr), Shinoussa (12 hours, 4405 dr) and Iraklia (12½ hours, 4405 dr).

The Maritime Company of Lesvos has four boats a week to Limnos (10-13 hours, 5315 dr), two of them stopping at Lesvos (8½ hours, 4150 dr). There are also ferries to the ports of Karystos and Marmari on the island of Evia. There are three services a day to Marmari (1230 dr) and two to Karystos (1630 dr). Both take about an hour.

Catamaran Goutos Lines has services to Andros, Tinos and Mykonos every day except Thursday, leaving at 7.30 am. Fares are the same as for the ferries, but journey times are slightly shorter. Strintzis Lines operates on the same route every day at 7.45 am. The Tuesday service also calls at Syros and continues to Paros and Naxos.

Hydrofoil Ilio Lines operate services to the Cyclades. There are morning departures at 7.35 am every day to Andros (70 minutes, 4490 dr), Tinos (two hours, 6850 dr) and

Mykonos (2½ hours, 7750 dr). The Thursday service continues to Paros (3¾ hours, 7650 dr), Sifnos (five hours, 7225 dr) and Serifos (5¾ hours, 6585 dr). There are also afternoon departures at 4 pm every day to Andros, Tinos, Mykonos and Paros, continuing to Naxos (four hours, 7898 dr), Ios (five hours, 7893 dr) and Santorini (5¾ hours, 9135 dr).

MARATHON REGION
Marathon Μαραθώνας
The plain surrounding the unremarkable small town of Marathon, 42km north-east of Athens, is the site of one of the most celebrated battles in world history. In 490 BC, an army of 9000 Greeks and 1000 Plataeans defeated the 25,000-strong Persian army, proving that the Persians were not invincible. The Greeks were indebted to the ingenious tactics of Miltiades, who altered the conventional battle formation so that there were fewer soldiers in the centre, but more in the wings. This lulled the Persians into thinking that the Greeks were going to be a pushover. They broke through in the centre, but were then ambushed by the soldiers in the wings. At the end of the day, 6000 Persians and only 192 Greeks lay dead. The story goes that after the battle a runner was sent to Athens to announce the victory. After shouting *Enikesame!* ('We won!') he collapsed in a heap and never revived. It is the origin of today's marathon foot race.

Marathon Tomb
This burial mound stands 350m from the Athens-Marathon road, 4km before the town of Marathon. In ancient Greece, the bodies of those who died in battle were returned to their families for private burial, but as a sign of honour the 192 men who fell at Marathon were cremated and buried in this collective tomb. The mound is 10m high and 180m in circumference. The tomb site is signposted from the main road and is open Tuesday to Sunday from 8.30 am to 3 pm. The **museum**, nearer to the town, has the same opening hours. The admission fee of 500 dr covers both sites.

Lake Marathon
This huge dam, 8km west of Marathon, was Athens' sole source of water until 1956. The massive dam wall, completed in 1926, is faced with the famous Pentelic marble that was used to build the Parthenon. It's an awesome sight, standing over 50m high and stretching for more than 300m.

Ramnous Ραμνούς
The ruins of the ancient port of Ramnous are 15km north-east of Marathon. It's an evocative, overgrown and secluded little site, standing on a plateau overlooking the sea. Among the ruins are the remains of a Doric **Temple of Nemesis** (435 BC), which once contained a huge statue of the goddess. Nemesis was the goddess of retribution and mother of Helen of Troy. There are also ruins of a smaller 6th-century temple dedicated to Themis, goddess of justice. The site is open Tuesday to Sunday from 8.30 am to 3 pm, and admission is 500 dr.

Shinias Σχοινιάς
The long, sandy, pine-fringed beach at Shinias, south-east of Marathon, is the best in this part of Attica. It's also very popular, particularly at weekends. *Camping Ramnous* (☎ 0294-55 855) is on the way to the beach.

Getting There & Away
There are hourly buses from the Mavromateon terminal to Marathon (1¼ hours, 700 dr). The tomb, the museum and Shinias beach are all within short walking distance of bus stops (tell the driver where you want to get out). There are no buses to Lake Marathon or Ramnous; you need your own transport.

VRAVRONA (BRAURON) Βραυρώνα
The ruins of the ancient city of Brauron lie just outside the small village of Vravrona (pronounced Vravro**na**), 40km east of Athens. Brauron belonged to King Cecrops' league of 12 cities (King Cecrops was the mythical founder of Athens). Remains dating back to 1700 BC have been found at the site, but it is best known for the

Sanctuary of Artemis. According to mythology, it was to Brauron that Iphigenia and Orestes brought the *xoanon* (sacred image) of Artemis that they removed from Tauris. The site became a sanctuary to Artemis during the time of the tyrant Peisistratos, who made the worship of Artemis the official religion of Athens.

The cult centred around a festival, held every five years, at which girls aged between five and 10 performed a ritual dance that imitated the movements of a bear. The ruins of the dormitories where the girls stayed can be seen at the site. The sanctuary's Doric temple, of which only a small section still stands, was built in the 5th century BC on the site of an earlier temple that was destroyed by the Persians. The site's **museum** (☎ 0299-27 020) houses finds from the sanctuary and the surrounding area. Both site and museum are open Tuesday to Sunday from 8.30 am to 3 pm. Admission is 500 dr.

Getting There & Away
Extremely early risers can follow the tourist office's advice and catch the 5.50 am bus from Mavromateon to Cape Sounion as far as Markopoulo, where you can then catch the 6.50 am bus to Vravrona. A less painful option is to catch a regular A5 bus from the junction of Sina and Akadimias to the ERT (radio and TV) office at Agia Paraskevi on the outskirts of Athens. There are buses to Vravrona (100 dr) from here every 20 minutes.

Peloponnese Πελοπόννησος

The Peloponnese (Pelo**po**nisos in Greek) is the southernmost section of the Balkan peninsula. The construction of the Corinth Canal through the Isthmus of Corinth in the late 19th century effectively severed it from the mainland, and now the only links are the bridges that span the canal. Indeed, the Peloponnese has every attraction of an island – and better public transport.

It's a region of outstanding natural beauty, with lofty, snow-crested mountains, valleys of citrus groves and cypress trees, cool springs and many fine beaches. The landscape is diverse and dotted with the legacies of the many civilisations which took root in the region: ancient Greek sites, crumbling Byzantine cities and Frankish and Venetian fortresses. The best-known attraction is the ancient site at Olympia. Less well known is that the beaches of the Messinian Mani, south of Kalamata, are some of the finest in Greece. The rugged Mani peninsula has additional attractions – the remnants of the many fortified tower houses that were built as refuges from clan wars from the 17th century onwards.

With your own transport, two weeks is sufficient to visit the major attractions. On public transport, allow at least three weeks, or be selective about your destinations. Ideally, the Peloponnese warrants a month's wandering, such is the variety of its magnificent natural and ancient splendours. Accommodation prices quoted in this section are for high season (July and August). Expect to pay less at other times, and certainly try bargaining.

History & Mythology

The name Peloponisos derives from the mythological hero, Pelops, and from the word for island, nisos. Literally translated, it means 'island of Pelops'. The region's medieval name was the Morea *(mouria* is

HIGHLIGHTS

- Ancient Olympia in springtime
- Trekking in the hills above Kardamyli
- Accommodation in the traditional tower settlements of the Mani
- The train ride up the Vouräkos gorge from Diakofto to Kalavryta
- Kalavryta's Cave of the Lakes
- The old Venetian town of Nafplio

Greek for mulberry tree), perhaps because mulberry trees grow so well in the area.

The deities may have resided on Mt Olympus, but they made frequent jaunts to the Peloponnese. It is a region rich in myths, and Pelops features in many of them.

Since ancient times, the Peloponnese has played a major role in Greek history. When the Minoan civilisation declined after 1450 BC, the focus of power in the ancient Aegean world moved from Crete to the hill-fortress palaces of Mycenae and Tiryns in the Peloponnese. As elsewhere in Greece, the 400 years following the Dorian conquests in

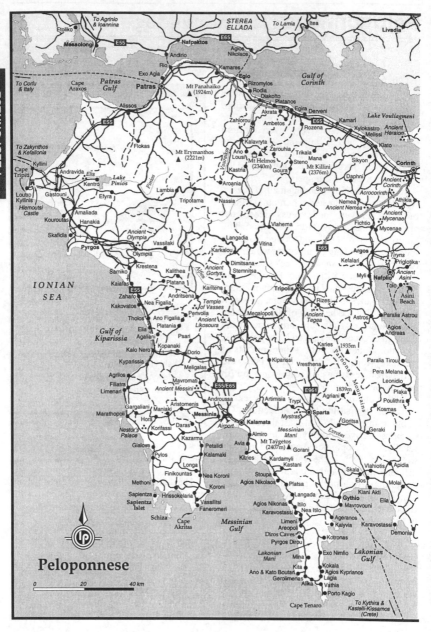

Peloponnese

0   20   40 km

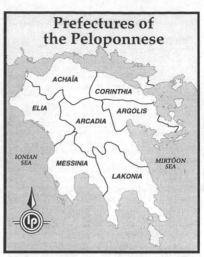

Prefectures of the Peloponnese

the 12th century BC are known as the dark age. When the region emerged from it in the 7th century BC, Sparta, Athens' arch rival, had surpassed Mycenae as the most powerful city in the Peloponnese. The period of peace and prosperity under Roman rule (146 BC to around 250 AD) was shattered by a series of invasions by Goths, Avars and Slavs.

The Byzantines were slow to make inroads into the Peloponnese, and did not become firmly established until the 9th century. In 1204, after the fall of Constantinople to the crusaders, the crusader chiefs William de Champlitte and Geoffrey de Villehardouin divided the region into 12 fiefs, which they parcelled out to various barons of France, Flanders and Burgundy. These fiefs were overseen by de Villehardouin, the self-appointed Prince of Morea (as the region was then called).

The Byzantines gradually won back the Morea. Although the empire as a whole was now in terminal decline, a glorious renaissance took place in the Morea, centred on Mystras, which Byzantine Emperor Michael VIII Paleologus made the region's seat of government.

The Morea fell to the Turks in 1460 and

Pelops

Pelops was the son of the conniving Tantalos, who invited the gods to a feast and served up the flesh of his son to test their power of all-knowing. Of course, the omniscient gods knew what he had done and refrained from eating the flesh. However, Demeter, who was in a tizz over the abduction of her daughter, Persephone, by Hades, accidentally ate a piece of Pelops' shoulder. Fortunately, the gods reassembled Pelops, and fashioned another shoulder of ivory. Tantalos was suspended from a fruit tree overhanging a lake, and was punished with eternal tantalising thirst.

Pelops took a fancy to the beautiful Hippodameia, daughter of Oinomaos, king of Elia. Oinomaos, who was a champion chariot racer, was told by an oracle that his future son-in-law would bring about his death. Oinomaos announced that he would give his daughter in marriage to any suitor who defeated him in a chariot race, but that he would kill those who failed – a fate which befell many suitors. Pelops took up the challenge and bribed the king's charioteer, Myrtilos, to take a spoke out of a

Ancient coin depicting a chariot race

wheel of the king's chariot. The chariot crashed during the race and Oinomaos was killed, so Pelops married Hippodameia and became king of Elia. The couple had two children, Atreus and Thyestes. Atreus became king of Mycenae and was the father of that kingdom's greatest king, Agamemnon. Pelops' devious action is blamed for the curse on the Royal House of Atreus, which ultimately brought about its downfall. ■

hundreds of years of power struggles between the Turks and Venetians followed. The Venetians had long coveted the Morea and had succeeded in establishing profitable trading ports at Methoni, Pylos, Koroni and Monemvasia.

The War of Independence began in the Peloponnese. Bishop Germanos of Patras raised the flag of revolt near Kalavryta on 25 March 1821. The Egyptian army, under the leadership of Ibrahim Pasha, brutally restored Turkish rule in 1825.

In 1827, the Triple Alliance of Great Britain, France and Russia, moved by Greek suffering and the activities of philhellenes (Byron's death in 1824 was particularly influential), came to the rescue of the Greeks by destroying the Egyptian-Turkish fleet at the Battle of Navarino, ending Turkish domination of the area.

The Peloponnese became part of the inde-pendent state of Greece, and Nafplio in Argolis became the first national capital. Kapodistrias, Greece's first president, was assassinated on the steps of Nafplio's Church of St Spyridon in October 1831. The new king Otho moved the capital to Athens in 1834.

Like the rest of Greece, the Peloponnese suffered badly during WWII. The town clock of Kalavryta, in the central north, is forever stopped at 2.34, the time at which, on 13 December 1943, the Germans began a massacre of all the males aged over 15 in reprisal for resistance activity.

The civil war (1944-49) brought widespread destruction and, in the 1950s, many villagers migrated to Athens, Australia, Canada, South Africa and the USA. More recently, the towns of Corinth and Kalamata have suffered devastating earthquakes. Both are still recovering.

Getting There & Away

Air Kalamata, in the south-west, has the only (domestic) airport in the Peloponnese.

Bus There are buses from Athens to most towns in the Peloponnese. For details, see Getting There & Away in the Athens chapter. There are also connections to Patras from Ioannina in northern Greece and from the Ionian island of Lefkada. Both run via the ferry that operates between Andirio, in Sterea Ellada, and Rio, 9km east of Patras. If you don't have your own transport, travelling by bus is a pleasant way to explore the Peloponnese. Services are adequate to all but the most remote areas.

Train The Peloponnese rail network is run on narrow-gauge lines. The network starts in Athens and splits into two main lines at Corinth, both of which then terminate in Kalamata. One line runs around the north and west coasts via Diakofto, Patras, Pyrgos and Kyparissia, while the other cuts diagonally across the centre via Argos and Tripolis. Intercity trains run only on the coast line, and only as far as Kyparissia. Nafplio has its own rail link to Athens via Argos and Corinth.

There are also branch lines from Diakofto to Kalavryta (rack-and-pinion) and from Pyrgos to Olympia.

Car & Motorcycle If you are travelling from Athens to the Peloponnese with your own vehicle, you have the choice of the New National Road (a toll highway) or the slower Old National Road, which hugs the coast and has fine sea views. Coming from Central Greece, you can get to the Peloponnese on the ferries that cross the Gulf of Corinth from Andirio to Rio and from Agios Nikolaos to Egio.

Ferry Patras is one of Greece's major ports with ferries to the Italian ports of Ancona, Bari, Brindisi, Trieste and Venice. It also has numerous services to Corfu and daily links to the islands of Ithaki, Kefallonia and Zakynthos. Kyllini, south-west of Patras, has

ferry connections to Kefallonia and Zakynthos. Ferries for Crete (Kastelli-Kissamos) leave from Gythio and stop at Kythira and Antikythira.

Hydrofoil Hydrofoil services from Piraeus to the Saronic gulf islands also call at a range of ports on the east coast of the Peloponnese, including Leonidio, Porto Heli, Tolo, Nafplio, Monemvasia and Neapoli. See the Saronic Gulf Islands chapter for more details.

Achaïa Αχαΐα

Achaïa owes its name to the Achaeans, an Indo-European branch of migrants who settled on mainland Greece and established what is more commonly known as the Mycenaean civilisation. When the Dorians arrived, the Achaeans were pushed into this north-western corner of the Peloponnese, displacing the original Ionians. Legend has it that the Achaeans founded 12 cities, which later developed into the powerful Achaean Federation that survived until Roman times. Principle among these cities were the ports of Patras and Egio.

The coast of modern Achaïa consists of a string of resorts which are more popular with Greeks than with tourists. Inland are the high peaks of Mt Panahaïko, Mt Erymanthos (where Heracles captured the Erymanthian boar) and Mt Helmos.

The village of Diakofto, 55km east of Patras, is the starting point for a ride on the fantastic rack-and-pinion railway to Zahlorou and Kalavryta. Overnight stops at Zahlorou and Kalavryta are highly recommended.

PATRAS Πάτρα

• *pop 153,300* • *postcode 260 01* • *area code ☎ 061*
Achaïa's capital, Patras (in Greek, **Pa**tra), is Greece's third-largest city and the principal port for boats to and from Italy and the Ionian islands. It is named after King Patreas, who ruled Achaïa in about 1100 BC. Despite a

PELOPONNESE

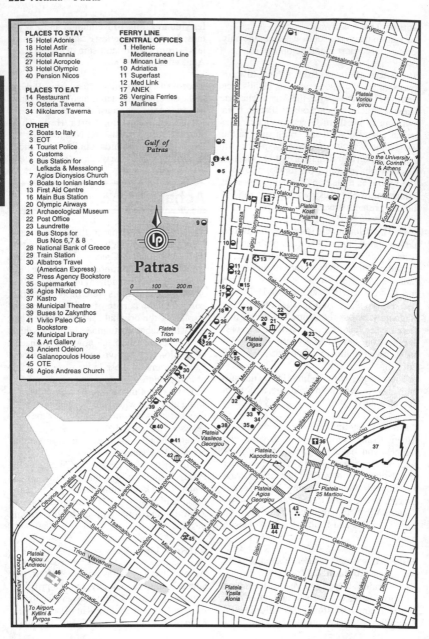

PLACES TO STAY
15 Hotel Adonis
18 Hotel Astir
25 Hotel Rannia
27 Hotel Acropole
33 Hotel Olympic
40 Pension Nicos

PLACES TO EAT
14 Restaurant
19 Osteria Taverna
34 Nikolaros Taverna

OTHER
2 Boats to Italy
3 EOT
4 Tourist Police
5 Customs
6 Bus Station for
  Lefkada & Messalongi
7 Agios Dionysios Church
9 Boats to Ionian Islands
13 First Aid Centre
16 Main Bus Station
20 Olympic Airways
21 Archaeological Museum
22 Post Office
23 Laundrette
24 Bus Stops for
  Bus Nos 6,7 & 8
28 National Bank of Greece
29 Train Station
30 Albatros Travel
  (American Express)
32 Press Agency Bookstore
35 Supermarket
36 Agios Nikolaos Church
37 Kastro
38 Municipal Theatre
39 Buses to Zakynthos
41 Vivlio Paleo Clio
  Bookstore
42 Municipal Library
  & Art Gallery
43 Ancient Odeion
44 Galanopoulos House
45 OTE
46 Agios Andreas Church

**FERRY LINE
CENTRAL OFFICES**
1 Hellenic
  Mediterranean Line
8 Minoan Line
10 Adriatica
11 Superfast
12 Med Link
17 ANEK
26 Vergina Ferries
31 Marlines

Gulf of Patras

Patras

0   100   200 m

history stretching back 3000 years, Patras is not wildly exciting. Few travellers stay around any longer than it takes to catch the next boat, bus or train.

The city was destroyed by the Turks during the War of Independence, and rebuilt on a modern grid plan of wide, arcaded streets, large squares and ornate neoclassical buildings. Some look in dire need of a facelift, but many are now being restored. The higher you climb up the steep hill behind the teeming, somewhat seedy waterfront, the better Patras gets.

Orientation

Patras' grid system means easy walking. The waterfront is known as Iroön Polytehniou at the north-eastern end, Othonos Amalias in the middle and Akti Dimeon to the south. Customs is at the Iroön Polytehniou end, and the main bus and train stations are on Othonos Amalias. Most of the agencies selling ferry tickets are on Iroön Polytehniou and Othonos Amalias. The main thoroughfares of Agiou Dionysiou, Riga Fereou, Mezonos, Korinthou and Kanakari run parallel to the waterfront. A small square, Plateia Trion Symahon, faces the train station. The main square is Plateia Vasileos Georgiou, up from the waterfront along Gerakostopolou. South along Mezonos, almost to the intersection with Pantanassis, is the municipal library which houses an art gallery. On the square is a small replica of Milan's La Scala, the municipal theatre. The prettiest and largest square is Plateia Ypsila Alonia in the upper city at the end of Kanari. Bordered by pines and cafés, it is where locals relax. Sisini runs north from the square to triangular Plateia Agiou Georgiou, surrounded by dilapidated neoclassical residences.

Information

Tourist Offices The EOT (☎ 361 653) is outside customs. The English-speaking staff have information on transport schedules and a map. It is open daily from 7 am to 9.30 pm. The tourist police (☎ 220 902), opposite, are open 24 hours.

Money The National Bank of Greece is on Plateia Trion Symahon. In summer, the opening times are Monday to Thursday from 8 am to 2 pm and 6 to 8.30 pm, Friday from 8 am to 1.30 pm and 6 to 8.30 pm, and weekends from 11 am to 1 pm and 6 to 8.30 pm. In winter, it is closed on weekends. American Express is represented by Albatros Travel (☎ 220 993), Othonos Amalias 48.

Post & Communications The main post office is on the corner of Zaïmi and Mezonos. It is open Monday to Friday from 7.30 am to 8 pm; Saturday from 7.30 am to 2 pm; and Sunday from 9 am to 1.30 pm. A mobile post office outside the customs office is open Monday to Saturday from 8 am to 8 pm and Sunday from 9 am to 6 pm.

The main OTE office is on the corner of Dimitriou Gounari and Kanakari in the western part of the city.

Bookshops The Press Agency Bookstore (☎ 277 396), Agiou Nikolaou 32, sells English-language books, newspapers and magazines. For books only, try Vivlio Paleo Clio (☎ 225 659) on Patreos 27.

Laundry The laundrette on Zaïmi, just uphill from Korinthou, charges 2500 dr to wash and dry a load and is open from 9 am to 9 pm every day except Sunday.

Emergency There is a first-aid centre (☎ 277 386) at the corner of Karolou and Agiou Dionysiou.

Kastro

The medieval Venetian kastro, built on the ruins of an ancient acropolis, dominates the city. Set in an attractive pencil-pined park, it is reached by climbing steps at the end of Agiou Nikolaou. Great views over to the Ionian islands of Zakynthos and Kefallonia are the reward.

Archaeological Museum

The small museum (☎ 275 070) is well laid out, and the collection of finds from the Mycenaean, Hellenic and Roman periods is labelled in English. Exhibits include funerary objects; sculptures; figurines; a mosaic; and an ivory-framed, blue-glass disc found in a Roman house in Patras.

Facing shady Plateia Olgas, a favourite spot for families and tame, hungry pigeons, the museum is at Mezonos 42. Opening times are Tuesday to Sunday from 8.30 am to 3 pm. Admission is free.

Achaïa Clauss Winery
This picturesque hillside winery, 9km south-east of Patras, was founded in 1854 by the Bavarian Baron Gustav von Clauss. It produces some of Greece's best-known wines, including the very popular Demestica label reds and whites. The winery's speciality is Mavrodaphne (black daphne), a fortified dessert wine first produced in 1861. It was named after the object of the baron's unrequited love – she died of tuberculosis.

The winery is open for a free tour and tastings from 9 am to 7 pm (10 am to 4.30 pm in the off season). Take bus No 7 from the corner of Kolokotroni and Kanakari to get there.

About 1km from the winery is the Church of Agios Konstantinos, which overlooks the pretty village of Saravali.

Other Attractions
There are a couple of places worth checking around Plateia Agiou Georgiou. **Galano-poulos House**, built in 1930 for a wealthy merchant, exemplifies eclectic, 19th-century European architecture, combining Art Nouveau and neoclassicism.

Behind Plateia Agiou Georgiou there is an **ancient odeum** (theatre) which predates the odeum of Herodus Atticus in Athens. The odeum was restored after WWII.

Special Events
It is claimed that the Patras Carnival is the world's biggest noncommercial (unlike Rio's) celebration. Euphoria and high spirits are shared as floats and about 50,000 people in fancy dress parade the streets for many of the 40 days from 17 January (St Anthony's Day). The International Patras Festival of the

Arts is held from July until September on an annual theme featuring music (from classical to jazz), art exhibitions, theatre and other events. EOT can supply details. Patras celebrates Independence Day on 25 March with colourful parades and much music.

Places to Stay – bottom end
The absence of decent budget accommodation is one of the reasons few travellers stick around.

Kavouri Camping (☎ 42 8066/2145), 2km north of Patras in the village of Exo Agia, is the closest camping ground. Take bus No 1 from Agios Dionysios church. There are two more camping grounds at Rio, 9km north-east of Patras. *Rio Camping* (☎ 99 1585/1450/3388) and *Rio Mare* (☎ 992 263) can both be reached on bus No 6 from Kanakari.

It's hard to recommend the *YHA hostel* (☎ 427 278) following a string of complaints from travellers. It's a fair haul from the city centre at Iroön Polytehniou 68, 1.5km east of the customs building. Dorm beds are 1500 dr.

It's hard to get much more enthusiastic about *Pension Nicos* (☎ 623 757), up from the waterfront on the corner of Patreos and Agiou Andreou 121, which is where most people head. It has singles/doubles with shared facilities for 4000/5500 dr, and doubles with bathroom for 7000 dr.

The cheap hotels tend to double as bordellos. They are normally clean enough, but you will have to put up with comings and goings. You're better off hunting around for deals at some of the smarter hotels (see below).

Places to Stay – middle
The C-class *Hotel Rannia* (☎ 220 114/435), facing Plateia Olgas at Riga Fereou 53, is a good place to check out. It has been known to offer substantial discounts on the official rates of 12,000/16,500 dr for good, clean rooms with bathroom. The *Hotel Olympic* (☎ 224 103) is a bit on the gloomy side, but is centrally located at Agiou Nikolaou 45. Singles/doubles with bath are 10,000/15,000 dr. Another reasonable option is the *Hotel*

Acropole (☎ 279 809), opposite the train station at Othonos Amalias 39. The *Hotel Adonis* (☎ 22 4213/4235), Zaïmi 9, opposite the bus station, has well-furnished single/ double air-con rooms for 17,000/ 20,600 dr, including breakfast.

Places to Stay – top end

The best place in town – which isn't saying much – is the *Hotel Astir* (☎ 277 502; fax 271 644), near the bus station on Agiou Andreou 16. It looks too run-down to be charging 29,800/32,300 dr for singles/doubles, despite an impressive list of facilities that includes a private garage. If you've got a car, there are better options along the coast north of town. The *Achaïa Beach* (☎ 991 801) at Bozaitika, 4km north of Patras, comes complete with a bar, restaurant, pool and nightclub. Singles/doubles are 12,300/ 15,400 dr, including breakfast. On the same stretch of coast, *To Tzaki Hotel* (☎ 42 8303/8325; fax 42 6750) has a bar, restaurant and TV lounge. Doubles are 23,000 dr, including breakfast.

Places to Eat

The waterfront eateries seem to specialise in overpriced souvlaki, moussaka and English breakfasts. Takeaway and budget sit-down meals improve from Agiou Andreou upwards. *Nikolaros Taverna*, Agiou Nikolaou 50, and the nameless *restaurant* at Michalakopoulou 3, both serve good traditional food.

For a treat that won't blow the budget, try the green-shuttered *Osteria Taverna*, Aratou 5, near the Hotel Astir. The imaginative selection of mezes includes special fare such as burekia – a filling starter of minced meat, eggplant and cheeses (900 dr). The seafood platter (4000 dr) is enough for two generous servings. A liqueur (made to a secret recipe) comes free with the bill, not necessarily to soften the blow.

Self-caterers can stock up with supplies at the large Cronos supermarket on Kanakari.

Entertainment

Performances from comedy to ancient Greek

tragedy are staged at the *municipal theatre*. Patras also has a lively nightclub and disco scene centred on the streets below the kastro.

Getting There & Away

Many first-time visitors to Greece assume that the best way to get from Patras to Athens is by bus. The bus is faster, but is more expensive and drops you off a long way from the city centre at Terminal A on Kifissou. It will cost at least 1000 dr for a taxi to the inner city if the connecting bus is full, and there is no public transport after midnight. The train takes you close to the city centre, within easy walking distance of good accommodation.

Bus The main bus station on Othonos Amalias has buses every half-hour to Athens (three hours, 3350 dr); 10 a day to Pyrgos (two hours, 1700 dr); four a day to both Ioannina (four hours, 4050 dr) and Kalavryta (1450 dr); three a day to Thessaloniki (9½ hours, 7700 dr); two a day to Kalamata (four hours, 3800 dr) and Tripolis (four hours, 2550 dr).

There are four buses a day to the Ionian island of Lefkada (3050 dr), leaving from a small bus station on the corner of Faverou and Konstantinopoleos. Buses to Zakynthos (3½ hours, 2600 dr) leave from the special Zakynthos bus station at the corner of Othonos Amalias and Gerokostopolou. There are up to five buses a day, travelling via the port of Kyllini.

Take bus No 6 from Kanakari for the Rio-Andirio ferry (30 minutes, 240 dr).

Train There are at least eight trains a day to Athens. Half of them are slow trains, which take five hours and cost 1580 dr. They travel via Diakofto (one hour, 510 dr) and Corinth (2½ hours, 1000 dr). The intercity trains to Athens take 3½ hours and cost 2600 dr in 2nd class. The last intercity train leaves Patras at 6.30 pm. Holders of Eurail passes can travel free, but may have to pay for their baggage.

There are also seven trains a day to Pyrgos

(two hours, 820 dr); and two a day to Kalamata (six hours, 1500 dr).

Ferry – domestic There are daily ferries from Patras to the Ionian islands of Kefallonia (four hours, 2900 dr), Ithaki (six hours, 3015 dr) and Corfu (10 hours, 5100 dr). See also the following section on International Ferries. Patras' port police are on ☎ 341 002.

Ferries between Rio, 9km north-east of Patras, and Andirio (for Lefkada), operate every 15 minutes between 7 am and 11 pm and every 30 minutes through the night (15 minutes, 110 dr; car 1300 dr).

Ferry – international Patras is Greece's main port for ferry services to Italy. The most popular crossing is the 18-hour trip to Brindisi. In summer, there are up to five boats a day on this route. One-way, deck-class fares range from 11,000 dr with Med Link and Vergina Ferries to 14,000 dr with the more comfortable Adriatica di Navigazione and Hellenic Mediterranean. Adriatica and Hellenic are the only lines that officially accept Eurail passes, although you will still have to pay the port tax of 1500 dr. In July and August, you will also have to pay a high-season loading of about 3000 dr.

There is also a choice of boats to Ancona. Superfast provides the fastest service, doing the trip in 20 hours for 15,800 dr. Other lines operating on this route are Minoan (22 hours, 13,600 dr), ANEK (25 hours, 12,200 dr) and Marlines (33 hours, 12,000 dr).

Ventouris Ferries has a daily service to Bari (17½ hours, 12,600 dr), and Minoan has daily boats to Venice (40 hours, 18,600 dr). ANEK has three boats a week to Trieste (39 hours, 17,300 dr).

With the exception of the express services to Ancona, most of these ferries stop at Igoumenitsa and Corfu. Some allow a free stopover on Corfu; ask when you buy your ticket. See the Getting There & Away chapter for more details of services. Ferries to Italy leave from two points on the waterfront (see the Patras map).

The addresses and routes of the central offices or representatives of the ferry lines operating out of Patras are:

Adriatica di Navigazione
    Othonos Amalias 8 (☎ 422 138): Brindisi via Igoumenitsa and Corfu
ANEK
    Othonos Amalias 25 (☎ 226 053): Ancona and Trieste via Corfu and Igoumenista
Hellenic Mediterranean
    Corner of Pente Pigadion & Iroön Polytehniou (☎ 652 521): Brindisi via Kefallonia and Corfu
Marlines
    Othonos Amalias 56 (☎ 223 444): Ancona via Igoumenitsa
Med Link Lines
    Giannatos Travel, Othonos Amalias 15 (☎ 623 011): Brindisi direct or via Kefallonia and Igoumenitsa
Minoan
    On the corner of Norman 1 & Athinon (☎ 421 500): Ancona direct; Venice via Igoumenitsa and Corfu
Superfast Ferries
    Othonos Amalias 12 (☎ 622 500): Ancona direct
Ventouris Ferries
    Othonos Amalias 81 (☎ 279 997): Bari via Kefallonia, Igoumenitsa and Corfu
Vergina Ferries
    Othonos Amalias 32 (☎ 277 204): Brindisi via Igoumenitsa

Getting Around

Bus Local bus Nos 6, 7 and 8 leave from bus stops on either side of Aratou (see map).

Car Car-hire outlets include Europcar (☎ 621 360), Agiou Andreou 6; Hertz (☎ 220 990), Karolou 2; and Reliable Rent A Car (☎ 272 764), Othonos Amalias 44.

DIAKOFTO Διακοφτό
• *pop 2250* • *postcode 251 00* • *area code* ☎ *0691*
Diakofto (Deeakof**to**), 55km east of Patras and 80km north-west of Corinth, is a serene village, tucked between steep mountains and the sea amid lemon and olive groves.

Orientation & Information
Diakofto's layout is easy to figure out. The train station is in the middle of the village. To reach the waterfront, cross the railway track and walk down the road ahead. You will come to pebbly Egali beach after 1km.

The post office, OTE and the National Bank of Greece are all on the main street that leads inland from the station. There is no EOT in Diakofto and no tourist police.

Diakofto-Kalavryta Railway

This rack-and-pinion railway runs through the spectacular Vouraïkos gorge, ascending 700m in 22.5km. It was built by an Italian company between 1885 and 1895 and it is a remarkable feat of engineering. The original steam engines were replaced in the early 1960s by diesel cars, but the old steam engines can still be seen outside Diakofto and Kalavryta stations. The line crosses narrow bridges and goes through tunnels and along precariously overhanging ledges. Down below, the Vouraïkos river tumbles over massive boulders, and the surrounding countryside is a riot of wild flowers in spring. The journey from Diakofto to Kalavryta, stopping en route at Zahlorou, takes just over an hour. See the following Getting There & Away section for departure times.

Places to Stay

The *Hotel Lemonies* (☎ 41 229/ 41 821), on the right, halfway down the road to the sea, has pleasant doubles/triples with bathroom for 7000/8500 dr. The *Hotel Helmos* (☎ 41 236), 50m from the station on the main street, has basic rooms with shared bathroom for 5000/8000 dr.

Diakofto's best accommodation is at the C-class *Chris Paul Hotel* (☎ 41 715/855; fax 42 128). The air-con singles/doubles are 8200/13,700 dr including breakfast. The hotel has its own swimming pool, bar and restaurant. It's conveniently situated near the train station, and well signposted.

Places to Eat

There are several places along the main street heading inland from the station. *Costas* is a very popular psistaria opposite the National Bank. It's run by a friendly Greek-Australian family and has a choice of taverna-style dishes alongside the usual grilled meats. A hearty meal for two with wine costs about 4000 dr. Further up is *Soulekas*, another psis-

taria offering similar fare. The more up-market *Kohili Taverna* is on the seafront at the end of the road leading from the station.

People heading up to Kalavryta on the train can stock up for the trip at the shops opposite the station.

Getting There & Away

Bus There's not much point in catching a bus to/from Diakofto – the trains are much more convenient. Most Patras-Athens buses bypass the village on the New National Road.

Train Diakofto is on the main Athens-Patras line and there are frequent trains in both directions. There are also six trains a day on the rack-and-pinion line to Kalavryta. Departure times from Diakofto are 7.35, 10.05 and 11.30 am and 1.35, 3.30 and 5.24 pm. The journey takes just over an hour, and the fare is 630 dr in 2nd class. You'll enjoy the journey more if you pay an extra 210 dr to travel 1st class. The seats are the same, but the 1st-class compartments at the front and rear of the train have the best views.

ZAHLOROU Ζαχλωρού

The picturesque and unspoilt settlement of Zahlorou, the halfway stop on the Diakofto to Kalavryta train line, straddles both sides of the river and railway line. Many people take the train to this point and walk back to Diakofto.

Moni Mega Spileou

Μονή Μεγάλου Σπήλαιου

A steep path (signposted) leads up from Zahlorou to the Moni Mega Spileou (Monastery of the Great Cavern). The original monastery was destroyed in 1934 when gunpowder stored during the War of Independence exploded. The new monastery houses illuminated gospels, relics, silver crosses, jewellery and the miraculous icon of the Virgin Mary which, like numerous icons in Greece, is said to have been painted by St Luke. It was supposedly discovered in the nearby cavern by St Theodore and St Simeon in 362 AD. A monk will show visitors around. Modest dress is required of both sexes – no bare arms or legs. The 3km walk up to the monastery takes about an hour.

Places to Stay & Eat

The quaint D-class *Hotel Romantzo* (☎ 0692-22 758) is one of Greece's more eccentric little hotels. It stands right next to the railway line at the end of the platform and has singles/doubles with shared bathroom for 4000/8000 dr. You can almost reach out and touch the trains from the windows of its seven rooms. It's advisable to book at weekends. During the week, the manager uses one room as a dorm where hikers can roll out their sleeping bags for 2000 dr. The hotel has a restaurant with outdoor seating on the opposite side of the railway.

Getting There & Away

All Diakofto-Kalavryta trains stop at Zahlorou. The fare is 550 dr to Diakofto and 260 dr to Kalavryta. You can drive to Zahlorou on a dirt road leading off the Diakofto-Kalavryta road. The turn-off is 7.5km north of Kalavryta.

KALAVRYTA Καλάβρυτα

• *pop 2200* • *postcode 250 01* • *area code* ☎ *0692*

At an elevation of 756m, Kalavryta (Kalav-rita) is a cool mountain resort with copious springs and shady plane trees. Two relatively recent historical events have assured the town a special place in the hearts of all Greeks. The revolt against the Turks began here on 25 March 1821 when Bishop Germanos of Patras raised the banner of revolt at the monastery of Agia Lavra, 6km from Kalavryta. And, on 13 December 1943, in one of the worst atrocities of WWII, the Nazis set fire to the town and massacred all its male inhabitants over 15 years old in a reprisal against resistance activity. The total number killed in the region was 1436. The hands of the old cathedral clock stand eternally at 2.34, the time the massacre began.

Orientation & Information

Most people arrive at the train station, which is on the northern edge of town. Facing the train station is a large building that was being converted into the Municipal Museum of the Kalavryta Holocaust at the time of writing. Kalavryta is the founding member of the Union of Martyred Towns. To the right of the museum-to-be is Syngrou, which is a pedestrian precinct. After one block, it becomes 25 Martiou. To the left of the museum is Konstantinou. The central square, Plateia Eleftherias, is between these two streets, two blocks up from the train station.

The bus station is on Kapota. From the train station, walk up Syngrou and turn right at the Hotel Maria onto Kapota, cross Ethnikis Antistassis and you'll see the buses parked outside at the bottom of the hill on the left. The post office is on the main square and the OTE is on Konstantinou. The National Bank of Greece is on 25 Martiou, just before the central square. Kalavryta has no EOT or tourist police.

Martyrs' Monument

A huge white cross on a cypress-covered hillside just east of town marks the site of the 1943 massacre. Beneath this imposing monument is a poignant little shrine to the victims. The site is signposted off Konstantinou.

Places to Stay

Kalavryta does not have a lot of accommodation, and it's wise to book in advance if you want to visit during the ski season, particularly at weekends. Most Kalavryta hotels do not offer single rooms at this time. They are open to negotiation at other times.

The cheapest hotel in Kalavryta is the D-class *Hotel Paradissos* (☎ 22 303) at the junction of Kapota and Ethnikis Antistassis. The attractive doubles/triples with bathroom are listed at 9000/12,000 dr, but outside the ski season you'll find doubles for 6000 dr and singles can be accommodated for 3000 dr. It's the same story at the C-class *Hotel Maria* (☎ 22 296), Syngrou 10, where you'll normally pay 6000/10,000 dr for very comfortable singles/doubles with bathroom that cost 10,000/16,000 dr in peak season. All rooms are equipped with colour TV. Breakfast (1300 dr) is served in the café down-stairs.

The B-class *Hotel Filoxenia* (☎ 22 422), opposite the Paradissos, has singles/doubles with bathroom, minibar and TV for 9800/15,000 dr.

Places to Eat

Most of the places to eat are on 25 Martiou. *To Tzaki Taverna*, opposite the church, is large and cheerful. Main meals are reasonably priced. *Taverna Stani*, opposite the National Bank, has excellent staples. You can wash down house specialities like roast goat in white sauce (1800 dr) or roast lamb in vine leaves (2000 dr) with a litre of house wine (1200 dr).

Getting There & Away

Bus There are five buses a day to Patras (1400 dr), two to Athens (3000 dr) and one to Tripolis (1500 dr).

Train The narrow-gauge train to Diakofto (via Zahlorou) leaves at 8.48 and 11.25 am, and at 1.30, 3.27, 5.19 and 7.10 pm.

Taxi Kalavryta's taxi rank (☎ 22 127) is on the central square.

AROUND KALAVRYTA

Moni Agias Lavras

The original 10th-century monastery was burnt by the Nazis. The new monastery has a small museum where the banner standard is displayed along with other monastic memorabilia. Buses heading south from Kalavryta to Klitoria or Tripolis can drop you a short walk from the monastery, or take a taxi.

Cave of the Lakes

The remarkable Cave of the Lakes lies 16.5km south of Kalavryta near the village of Kastria. The cave features in Greek mythology and is mentioned in the writings of the ancient traveller Pausanias, but its whereabouts remained unknown in modern times until 1964. Locals had noticed water pouring from the roof of a smaller, lower cave after heavy rain and decided to investigate. They found themselves in a large bat-filled cavern at the start of a winding 2km-long cave carved out by a subterranean river.

The cavern is now reached by an artificial entrance that is the starting point for a 350m raised walkway that snakes up the riverbed. It passes some wonderfully ornate stalactites, but they are mere sideshows alongside the lakes themselves. These lakes are actually a series of 13 stone basins formed by mineral deposits over the millennia. In summer, the waters dry up to reveal a curious lace work of walls, some up to 3m high.

The cave (0692-31 633) is open daily from 9.30 am to 4.30 pm, and admission is 800 dr. Getting there is difficult without your own transport. The daily bus from Kalavryta to Kastria isn't much help. A taxi to the cave from Kalavryta will cost about 6000 dr return.

Ski Centre

The ski centre (elevation 1650m to 2100m), with nine pistes and one chair lift, is 14km east of Kalavryta on Mt Helmos. It has a cafeteria and first-aid centre but no overnight accommodation. The ski centre has an office in Kalavryta (☎ 0692-22 661; fax 22 415), at the top of 25 Martiou. Opening times are Monday to Friday from 7 am to 3 pm. Several outlets on Konstantinou rent skis for approximately 3000 dr per weekday, 3500 dr on weekends. There is no transport to the centre from Kalavryta, so you will need to organise your own.

Mt Helmos Refuge

The EOS-owned B Leondopoulos Mountain Refuge is situated at 2100m on Mt Helmos. A marked footpath leads to the refuge from the ski centre (one hour). Another leads from the village of Ano Loussi (1½ hours), on the way to Kastria. If you would like to stay in the refuge, or want more details on walks or climbs on Mt Helmos, talk to the ski-centre staff in Kalavryta.

Mavroneri Waterfall

This waterfall, which plunges into a ravine on the northern side of Mt Helmos, is one of several places in Greece claiming to be the source of the River Styx, across which the dead must journey before they can enter Hades.

It is possible to trek to the waterfall from the EOS refuge of B Leondopoulos on Mt Helmos (two hours) or from the village of Peristera (five hours). Peristera is one of a cluster of remote mountain villages lying west of a road that runs south from Akrata, about 10km east of Diakofto.

With your own transport (you may need chains in winter), you can explore this remote region. Buses are infrequent. For more information about trekking to the waterfall, contact the Egio branch of the EOS (☎ 0691-25 285), on the corner of Sotiriou Pontou and Aratou. Egio is on the coast, 13km west of Diakofto.

Corinthia Κορινθία

Corinthia occupies a strategic position adjoining the Isthmus of Corinth. The region was once dominated by the mighty, ancient city of Corinth, now one of the main attractions. Few travellers opt to linger long, although there are several minor sites in the pretty hinterland west of Corinth that are worth a detour if you have your own transport.

CORINTH Κόρινθος
• pop 27,400 • postcode 201 00 • area code ☎ 0741

Modern Corinth (in Greek **Co**rinthos), 6km west of the Corinth Canal, is the dull administrative capital of Corinthia prefecture. The town was rebuilt here after the old town was destroyed by an earthquake in 1858. The new town was wrecked by another, equally violent earthquake in 1928 and badly damaged again in 1981.

The modern town is dominated by concrete buildings built to withstand future earthquakes, but it has a pleasant harbour,

friendly people, tasty food and warrants an overnight stay because of its proximity to ancient Corinth and Nemea. Old Corinth is a mere village near the ancient site.

Orientation & Information

It is not difficult to negotiate Corinth, which is laid out on a grid of wide streets stretching back from the waterfront. Social activity centres around the large square by the harbour, Plateia El Venizelou, while transport and administrative activity is based around the small park 200m inland on Ethnikis Antistaseos. The National Bank of Greece is one of several banks on Ethnikis Antistaseos; the post office is on the edge of the park at Adimantou 33; and the OTE is nearby on the corner of Kolokotroni and Adimantou.

Corinth has no EOT. The helpful tourist police (☎ 23 282) are located next to the park at Ermou 51, open daily from 8 am to 2 pm and 5 to 8 pm. The regular police (☎ 22 143) are in the same building.

Folk Museum

This museum, to the south of the wharf, focuses on bridal and festive costumes from the past three centuries. There are costumes from the islands and the mainland, as well as metalwork, embroidery, gold and silver objects, and carvings, both secular and ecclesiastical. The museum is open daily, except Monday, from 8.30 am to 1 pm. Admission is 400 dr.

Places to Stay – bottom end

Corinth Beach Campground (☎ 27 967/968) is about 3km west of the town centre. Buses to ancient Corinth can drop you there. The *Blue Dolphin Campground* (☎ 25 766/767) is 3km from ancient Corinth, on the beach. Take the bus to Lecheon from the stop on Koliatsou, just off Ethnikis Antistaseos.

Corinth's budget hotels are as grim a bunch as you'll find anywhere. The cheapest rooms in town are at the *Hotel Akti* (☎ 23 337), Ethnikis Antistaseos 1. It has singles/doubles with shared bathroom for 3000/6000 dr, but you'll need to be suffering from a heavy cold to put up with the pong of decom-

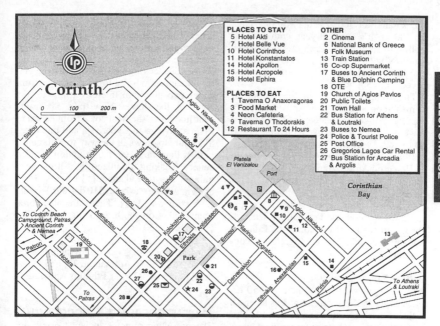

PLACES TO STAY
5 Hotel Akti
7 Hotel Belle Vue
10 Hotel Corinthos
11 Hotel Konstantatos
14 Hotel Apollon
15 Hotel Acropole
28 Hotel Ephira

PLACES TO EAT
1 Taverna O Anaxoragoras
3 Food Market
4 Neon Cafeteria
9 Taverna O Thodorakis
12 Restaurant To 24 Hours

OTHER
2 Cinema
6 National Bank of Greece
8 Folk Museum
13 Train Station
16 Co-op Supermarket
17 Buses to Ancient Corinth
    & Blue Dolphin Camping
18 OTE
19 Church of Agios Pavlos
20 Public Toilets
21 Town Hall
22 Bus Station for Athens
    & Loutraki
23 Buses to Nemea
24 Police & Tourist Police
25 Post Office
26 Gregorios Lagos Car Rental
27 Bus Station for Arcadia
    & Argolis

posing carpet. The decrepit-looking *Hotel Belle Vue*, Damaskinou 41, was closed in search of a new owner at the time of writing – which leaves the *Hotel Apollon* (☎ 22 587), near the train station at Pirinis 18. This place looks to be on the verge of collapse from the outside, and that impression continues right up to the bedroom doors. The rooms, however, have recently been redecorated and 4000/6000 dr is a good price for clean singles/doubles with bathroom. The drawback is that the hotel doubles as a bordello, so you'll have to put up with late-night comings and goings.

Places to Stay – middle
The best deal in town is at the friendly family-run *Hotel Ephira* (☎ 24 021; fax 24 514), Ethnikis Antistaseos 52. It offers excellent value for a C-class hotel with comfortable air-con singles/doubles with bathroom and TV for 7500/10,000 dr. Breakfast is available for 1200 dr.

The other C-class places in town all look overpriced in comparison. The *Hotel Acropole* (☎ 26 568), at the corner of Damaskinou and Ethnikis Anexartisias, certainly does – even when doubles are discounted from the official 14,500 dr to 10,000 dr. The *Hotel Corinthos* (☎ 26 701; fax 23 693), Damaskinou 26, has pleasant singles/doubles for 12,000/15,000 dr with bathroom and balcony. The well-furnished (complete with stuffed fox in the lounge) *Hotel Konstantatos* (☎ 22 120; fax 85 634), also on Damaskinou, has singles without bath for 11,000 dr and rooms with private facilities for 14,000/16,500 dr. Air-con doubles are 20,000 dr.

Places to Eat
The *Taverna O Thodorakis*, just back from the waterfront near the folkloric museum, is a lively place specialising in fresh grilled fish, priced from 7000 dr per kg. You can have a plate of sardines for 1000 dr, a large

Greek salad for 900 dr and a litre of retsina for 700 dr. It's open all year, with outdoor seating in summer. *Taverna O Anaxagoras*, Agiou Nikolaou 31, at the opposite end of the waterfront, specialises in mezedes, priced from 500 to 1200 dr.

The *Neon Cafeteria*, at the corner of Damaskinou and Ethnikis Antistaseos, is a popular self-service cafeteria with a good range of daily specials like moussaka (1400 dr) or roast veal with potatoes (1800 dr) as well as a salad bar (900 dr). *Restaurant To 24 Hours* on Agiou Nikolaou is more expensive but, as the name suggests, it never closes.

Corinth's lively *food market* is on the corner of Kyprou and Periandrou. The *Co-Op supermarket*, at the corner of Ethnikis Anexartisias and Pilarinou Zografon, is convenient.

Getting There & Away

Bus Buses to Athens (1½ hours, 1450 dr) leave every half-hour from the bus terminal at the corner of Ermou and Koliatsou. This is also the departure point for frequent buses to Loutraki (20 minutes, 260 dr). There are seven buses a day to Nemea (one hour, 750 dr) from the bus stop 50m south-east of here along Koliatsou.

Buses to most other parts of the Peloponnese leave from the terminal at the corner of Aratou and Ethnikis Antistaseos. Buses leave here every hour for Nafplio (1¼ hours, 1050 dr) via Mycenae (45 minutes, 650 dr) and Argos (one hour, 950 dr). Nine buses go to Tripolis (1½ hours, 1450 dr); eight a day to Sparta (three hours, 2250 dr); and seven to Kalamata (four hours, 2800 dr). Tickets are bought on the bus.

Buses to ancient Corinth (20 minutes, 210 dr) leave from the bus stop north-west of the central park on Koliatsou. This is also the place to catch a bus to Lecheon (for Blue Dolphin Campground).

Buses to Patras leave from out of town. You're better off catching the train.

Train There are 15 trains a day to Athens (1¾ hours, 780 dr). Four of them are inter-city services, but they are only 15 minutes faster. The Peloponnese rail network divides at Corinth, with eight trains a day heading along the north coast to Diakofto and Patras. It's worth checking the timetable before you set out: journey times to Patras range from under two hours on intercity trains to 3½ hours on the slowest slow train. Six trains continue down the west coast from Patras to Pyrgos; five go to Kyparissia and one takes 8½ hours to crawl all the way to Kalamata.

If Kalamata is your destination, you're better off taking the inland line. It has four trains a day to Kalamata (5½ hours, 1650 dr), via Argos (one hour, 510 dr) and Tripolis (2½ hours, 980 dr). There are also three trains a day on the branch line to Nafplio (1¼ hours, 650 dr).

Car Car-hire outlets in Corinth include Rent a Car (☎ 25 573), Adimantou 39, and Gregorios Lagos (☎ 22 617), Ethnikis Antistaseos 42.

ANCIENT CORINTH & ACROCORINTH

The sprawling ruins of ancient Corinth are 7km south-west of modern Corinth. Towering 575m above them is the massive, fortified bulk of Acrocorinth.

Allow a day to see both ancient Corinth and Acrocorinth. Most people come on day trips from modern Corinth, but there are tavernas and a few *domatia* in the village near the ancient site. Look for the signs. Acrocorinth has a restaurant.

The site (☎ 0741-31 207) and its museum are open daily, except Monday, from 8 am to 6 pm (7 pm in summer). Admission to the site (including the museum) is 1200 dr.

History

During the 6th century BC, Corinth was one of ancient Greece's richest cities. It owed its wealth to its strategic position on the Isthmus of Corinth, which meant it was able to build twin ports, one on the Aegean sea (Kenchreai) and one on the Ionian sea (Lecheon). From these ports it traded throughout the Mediterranean. It survived the Peloponnesian Wars and flourished under Macedonian rule, but it was sacked by the Roman consul Mummius in 146 BC for rebelling against Roman rule. In 44 BC, Julius Caesar began rebuilding the city and it again became a prosperous port.

During Roman times, when Corinthians weren't clinching business deals, they were paying homage to the goddess of love, Aphrodite, in a temple dedicated to her (which meant they were having a rollicking time with the temple's sacred prostitutes, both male and female). St Paul, perturbed by the Corinthians' wicked ways, spent 18 fruitless months preaching here.

Ancient Corinth

Exploring the Site Earthquakes and sackings by a series of invaders have left little standing in ancient Corinth. The remains are mostly from Roman times. An exception is the 5th-century BC Doric **Temple of Apollo**, the most prominent ruin on the site. To the south of this temple is a huge **agora**, or forum, bounded at its southern side by the foundations of a **stoa**. This was built to accommodate the bigwigs who were summoned here in 337 BC by Philip II, to sign oaths of allegiance to Macedon. In the middle of the central row of shops is the **bema**, a marble podium from which Roman officials addressed the people.

At the eastern end of the forum are the remains of the **Julian Basilica**. To the left (north) is the **Lower Peirene fountain** – the Upper Peirene fountain is on Acrocorinth. According to mythology, Peirene wept so much when her son Kenchrias was killed by Artemis that the gods, rather than let all the precious water go to waste, turned her into a fountain. In reality, it's a natural spring which has been used since ancient times and still supplies old Corinth with water. The water tanks are concealed in a fountain house with a six-arched façade. Through the arches can be seen the remains of frescoes.

West of the fountain, steps lead to the **Lecheon road**, which used to be the main thoroughfare to the port of Lecheon. On the right (east) side of the road is the **Peribolos of Apollo**, a courtyard flanked by Ionic col-

umns. Some have been restored. Nearby is a **public latrine**. Some seats remain. The site's **museum** houses statues, mosaics, figurines, reliefs and friezes.

Acrocorinth Ακροκόρινθος

Earthquakes and invasions compelled the Corinthians to retreat to Acrocorinth, a sheer bulk of limestone which was one of the finest natural fortifications in Greece. The original fortress was built in ancient times and was coveted and strengthened by streams of invaders. The ruins are a medley of imposing Roman, Byzantine, Frankish, Venetian and Turkish ramparts, harbouring remains of Byzantine chapels, Turkish houses and mosques.

On the higher of Acrocorinth's two summits is the **Temple of Aphrodite** where the sacred courtesans, who so raised the ire of St Paul, catered to the desires of the insatiable Corinthians. Little remains of the temple, but the views are tremendous. The site is open Tuesday to Sunday from 8.30 am to 7 pm. Admission is free.

Getting There & Away

Buses to ancient Corinth leave Corinth hourly on the hour, returning on the half-hour. There is no public transport between ancient Corinth and Acrocorinth. You can drive or take a taxi, otherwise it's a strenuous 1½-hour walk.

CORINTH CANAL

The concept of cutting a canal through the Isthmus of Corinth to link the Ionian and Aegean seas was first proposed by the tyrant Periander, founder of ancient Corinth. The enormity of the task defeated him, so he opted instead to build a paved slipway across which sailors dragged small ships on rollers – a method used until the 13th century.

In the intervening years, many leaders, including Alexander the Great and Caligula, toyed with the canal idea, but it was Nero who actually began digging in 67 AD. In true megalomaniac fashion, he struck the first blow himself using a golden pickaxe. He then left it to 6000 Jewish prisoners to do the

PELOPONNESE

hard work. The project was soon halted by invasions by the Gauls. Finally, in the 19th century (1883-93), a French engineering company completed the canal.

The Corinth Canal, cut through solid rock, is over 6km long and 23m wide. The vertical sides rise 90m above the water. The canal did much to elevate Piraeus' status as a major Mediterranean port. It's an impressive sight, particularly when a ship is passing through it.

Getting There & Away

The canal can be reached on a Loutraki bus from modern Corinth to the canal bridge. Any bus or train between Corinth and Athens will also pass over the canal. Heraion Tours (☎ 0744-21 062) in Loutraki offers cruises through the canal to the Saronic gulf on the ketch *Anna* for 5500 dr. Departure times are fairly erratic, so phone first.

ISTHMIA Ισθμία

At the south-eastern end of the canal is the site of ancient Isthmia. The remains of the **Sanctuary of Poseidon**, a defensive wall, and **Roman theatre** are of interest only to archaeology buffs. As with Nemea, Delphi and Olympia, ancient Isthmia was one of the sites of the Panhellenic Games, and the site's excellent **museum** (open daily except Tuesday) contains various ancient athletic exhibits. The modern village of Isthmia lies a short distance to the east of the ancient site.

The Old National Road to Athens crosses the canal at Isthmia by a submersible bridge, which is lowered to allow ships to pass over it.

LOUTRAKI Λουτράκι

Loutraki (population 7000), 6km north of the Corinth Canal, lounges between a pebbled beach and the tall cliffs of the Gerania mountains. Once a traditional spa town patronised by elderly and frail Greeks, it remains a major producer of bottled mineral water. The town was devastated by the 1981 earthquake; subsequent reconstruction has resulted in its reincarnation as a tacky resort

with dozens of modern, characterless hotels along the seafront. Loutraki hardly warrants an overnight stay.

Getting There & Away

Half-hourly buses run from Corinth to Loutraki (20 minutes, 260 dr) and there are eight buses a day form Athens (1½ hours, 1250 dr).

LAKE VOULIAGMENI Λιμνι Βουλιαμενισ

Tranquil Lake Vouliagmeni, 23km northwest of Loutraki, is a lovely little lagoon linked to the sea by a narrow channel. It's a popular spot at weekends and there are half a dozen small fish tavernas dotted around the shore.

The road continues beyond the lake to the ruins of **ancient Heraion**, surrounding a tiny natural harbour below Cape Melanhavi. The site was excavated by Humfry Payne from 1930 to 1933. Payne was accompanied by his wife, Dilys Powell, who describes her stay in the area in her book *An Affair of the Heart*. At the site are the ruins of an agora, a stoa and an 8th-century BC temple in a **Sanctuary to Hera**. The site is not enclosed and entry is free.

Getting There & Away

There is no public transport to Lake Vouliagmeni, so you will have to find your own way there. There are several places in Loutraki which rent motorcycles.

WEST OF CORINTH

The coastline stretching west from Corinth towards Patras is dotted with a series of fishing villages and small resorts. Places such as **Derveni** (which has a sandy beach), **Kamari, Xylokastro** and **Kiato** are popular mainly with Greek holiday-makers and groups from northern Europe. Beach buffs will be unimpressed. There are several interesting minor sites inland that are worth a detour if you have the time.

Stymfalia Στυμφαλία

If you've got your own transport, the 36km drive from Kiato to Stymfalia is worth the effort for the scenery as much as anything else. Little remains of the ancient site apart from the ruins of three temples. The site is next to a marshy lake of the same name, which was the home of the mythical, man-eating Stymfalian birds that Heracles was ordered to shoo away as the sixth of his 12 labours. The birds were depicted in sculptures on the Temple of Artemis Stymfalia.

Nemea Νεμύα

Ancient Nemea lies 4km north-east of the modern village of the same name. According to mythology, it was here that Heracles carried out the first of his labours – the slaying of the lion that had been sent by Hera to destroy Nemea. The lion became the constellation Leo – each of the 12 labours is related to a sign of the zodiac.

Like Olympia, Nemea was not a city but a sanctuary and venue for the biennial Nemean Games, held in honour of Zeus. These games became one of the great Panhellenic festivals. Remarkably, three columns of the 4th-century BC Doric **Temple of Zeus** remain. Other ruins include a bathhouse and hostelry. The site's **museum** is excellent and includes models of the site and English explanations.

At the **stadium**, 500m back on the road, you can see the athletes' starting line and distance markers. The site and museum (☎ 0746-22 739) are open Tuesday to Sunday from 8.30 am to 3 pm. Admission is 500 dr for each.

Getting There & Away Nemea is 35km south-west of Corinth, which has seven buses a day to Nemea (one hour, 750 dr). Ask the driver to drop you at the site, 4km before the village. There are also buses from Argos (550 dr).

Argolis Αργολίδα

The Argolis peninsula, which separates the Saronic and Argolic gulfs in the north-east,

is a veritable treasure trove for archaeology buffs. The town of Argos, from which the region takes its name, is thought to be the longest continually inhabited town in Greece. Argolis was the seat of power of the Mycenaean Empire that ruled Greece from 1600 to 1200 BC. The ancient cities of Mycenae, Tiryns, Argos and Epidaurus are the region's major attractions.

ARGOS Αργος
• *pop 22,300 • postcode 212 00 • area code ☎ 0751*
Argos (**Arghos**) is the oldest continuously inhabited town in Greece, but vestiges of its past glory lie mostly beneath the uninspiring modern town. The ruins that have been excavated are perhaps only of interest to aficionados, but Argos is a convenient base from which to explore the sites of Argolis and has a refreshing lack of tourist hype. It is also a major transport hub for buses.

Orientation & Information
Argos' showpiece and focal point is the magnificent central square, Plateia Agiou Petrou, with its Art Nouveau street lights, citrus and palm trees and the impressive Agios Petros church. Beyond, Argos deteriorates into an unremarkable working town.

Argos has two bus stations. The Argolis bus station, which also handles Athens services, is just south of the central square on Kapodistriou. The Arcadia-Lakonia bus station is nearby on Pheidonos. To get there from the Athens bus station, turn left from the ticket office, cross Kallergi and then turn left onto Pheidonos. The bus station is on the right. The train station is 500m south-east of the central square along Vasileos Georgiou and Filellinon.

The post office and OTE are both close to Plateia Agiou Petrou. The post office is clearly signposted on Kapodistriou, and the OTE office is on Nikitara, which leads off the square next to the National Bank of Greece. Argos' hospital (☎ 24 455/456; emergency ☎ 166) is on Corinth, off the north side of the central square. There is no tourist office and no tourist police. The regular police can be contacted on ☎ 100.

Archaeological Museum

Even if you're only passing through Argos, try to pause long enough to visit the archaeological museum, on the edge of the central square. The collection includes some outstanding Roman mosaics and sculptures; Neolithic, Mycenaean and Geometric pottery; and bronze objects from the Mycenaean tombs. The museum (☎ 68 819) is open Tuesday to Sunday from 8.30 am to 3 pm. Admission is 500 dr.

Roman Ruins

There are Roman ruins on both sides of Tripolis, the main Argos-Tripolis road. To get there from the central square, head south along Danaou for about 500m and then turn right onto Theatron. Theatron joins Tripolis opposite the star attraction, the enormous **theatre**, which could seat up to 20,000 people (more than at Epidaurus). It dates from classical times but was greatly altered by the Romans. Nearby are the remains of a 1st-century AD **odeum** (indoor theatre) and **Roman baths**. The site is open every day from 8.30 am to 3 pm. Admission is free.

It's 45 minutes of hard slog by footpath from the theatre up to the **Fortress of Larissa**, a conglomeration of Byzantine, Frankish, Venetian and Turkish architecture, standing on the foundations of the city's principal ancient citadel.

The **Sanctuary of Apollo & Athena** and the nearby remains of a **Mycenaean necropolis**, where some chamber tombs and shaft graves have been excavated, lie to the north of the Roman ruins. The hill to the northeast of these ruins is the site of a small, ancient citadel and an early Bronze Age settlement, now crowned by the chapel of Agios Elias. To reach these ruins from the Roman ruins, walk north along Tripolis and turn left at the intersection with Tsokri. From the central square, walk up Vasileos Konstantinou, which becomes Tsokri.

Places to Stay

All five hotels in town are close to the central square. The best budget choice is the *Hotel* *Apollon* (☎ 68 065), behind the National Bank of Greece at Papaflessa 13. It has singles/doubles with bathroom for 4700/6500 dr, and singles with shared bathroom for 4000 dr. The *Hotel Theoxenia* (☎ 67 808), Tsokri 31, is similarly priced – 4200/6500 dr for rooms with shared bathroom. From the central square walk up Vasileos Konstantinou, which becomes Tsokri.

The *Hotel Palladion* (☎ 67 807), on the northern side of the square on Vasilissas Sophias, has reasonable singles/doubles for 5000/7000 dr with private bathroom. The C-class *Hotel Mycenae* (☎ 68 754), on the central square, has large, comfortable rooms for 8000/14,000 dr, and a four-bed 'apartment' is 22,000 dr. Breakfast costs 2000 dr per person.

Places to Eat

The restaurants on the central square are either relatively expensive or serve fast food. Head for the backstreets for traditional, cheap fare. You'll find a few simple *ouzeria* between the main square and the train station. Argos' *food market* is in the neoclassical agora on Tsokri.

Getting There & Away

Bus The Argolis bus station has buses every half-hour to Nafplio (30 minutes, 240 dr); hourly buses to Athens (two hours, 1900 dr); six buses a day to Mycenae (25 minutes, 240 dr); and two buses a day to Nemea (one hour, 550 dr). The fare to Corinth is 950 dr.

The Arcadia-Lakonia bus station has nine buses a day to Tripolis (1¼ hours, 1000 dr) and eight via Tripolis to Sparta (2½ hours, 1350 dr). The solitary service to Leonidio takes three hours and costs 1350 dr.

Train There are seven trains a day to Athens (three hours, 1040 dr), also stopping at Nemea (45 minutes, 310 dr) and Corinth (one hour, 510 dr). There are also four trains a day to Kalamata (3½ hours, 1280 dr) via Tripolis (one hour, 590 dr).

AROUND ARGOS

About 7km from Argos off the main road to Tripolis is the pretty village of **Kefalari**. It is surrounded by vineyards, which sprawl out either side of the 2km dirt road that climbs up to the **Pyramid of Helenekion** (or Pyramid of Kenchreai). It was built in 4 BC to commemorate a victory over Sparta and evolved into a fort. It stands – fenced, crude and crumbling – on a hilltop by a church. It's hardly worth the walk, but the deviation to Kefalari is. The village centrepiece is the substantial and beautiful **Church of the Virgin & Child Life-Giving Spring**. Framed by trees and bougainvillea, beneath grottos sacred to Dionysos and Pan on the slope of Mt Haon, it spans a gushing mountain stream. Visitors can soak up the tranquillity at open-air summer tavernas. Buses headed for Kefalari leave from Argos' Arcadia-Lakonia bus station. (See the South-East section for details of the scenic coastal route from Myli to Leonidio).

MYCENAE Μυκήνες

• *pop 450* • *postcode 212 00* • *area code* ☎ *0751*
The modern village of Mycenae (in Greek Mi**ki**nes) is 12km north of Argos, just east of the main Argos-Corinth road. It has little to commend it other than its proximity to the ancient site, 2km to the north. The village is geared towards the hordes of package tourists visiting ancient Mycenae. There is accommodation along its single street. There's no bank, but there is a post office with a currency-exchange service at the ancient site.

Places to Stay – bottom end

The two camping grounds at Mycenae are *Camping Mycenae* (☎ 76 247), near the bus stop in Mycenae village, and *Camping Atreus* (☎ 76 221), near the Corinth-Argos road.

Don't bother with the disgusting *youth hostel* (☎ 76 255), located above the Restaurant Iphigenia on the main road. It charges 1500 dr per person, which would have to be more than has been spent on maintenance in the last 10 years.

Places to Stay – middle

You'll find some good deals at the hotels along the main road. The C-class *Belle Helene Hotel* (☎ 76 255) has singles/doubles for 5000/7000 dr. The renowned amateur archaeologist Heinrich Schliemann (see under Ancient Mycenae) stayed here while excavating. Other famous guests have included Claude Debussy and Virginia Woolf. Further up, the friendly *Hotel Klitemnistra* (☎ 76 451) has an airy restaurant and singles/doubles for 4000/6000 dr. The B-class *La Petit Planete* (☎ 76 240), between the village and ancient site, has smart singles/doubles for 11,000/15,000 dr. It also has a swimming pool, a restaurant and bar.

Places to Eat

Restaurants cater for day-trippers. The best value is to be found at the *Hotel Klitemnistra Restaurant*, which serves good three-course meals for between 2000 and 2500 dr.

Getting There & Away

Bus There are three buses a day from Nafplio (one hour, 550 dr) and six from Argos (30 minutes, 240 dr). Most buses stop at the village and the ancient site. Otherwise, take an hourly Corinth-Argos bus, which will leave you on the main road at Fichtio with a 3km uphill walk to the site.

ANCIENT MYCENAE

In the barren foothills of Mt Agios Ilias (750m) and Mt Zara (600m) stand the sombre and mighty ruins of ancient Mycenae, vestiges of a kingdom which, for 400 years (1600-1200 BC), was the most powerful in Greece, holding sway over the Argolid (the modern-day prefecture of Argolis) and influencing the other Mycenaean kingdoms.

The site (☎ 76 585) is open daily from 8 am to 7 pm. Admission to the citadel and the Treasury of Atreus is 1500 dr. After exploring, revive yourself with Argolis orange juice, sold from a van opposite the mobile post office.

PELOPONNESE

PELOPONNESE

The Life of Heinrich Schliemann

Heinrich Schliemann is often dismissed as being too eccentric and monomaniacal to be taken seriously in the dry, academic world of archaeology – someone who was driven more by impulse than carefully correlated facts. Despite his inaccurate dating of his finds, Schliemann must be acknowledged as the archaeologist who proved that the kingdom of Mycenae had existed and was not merely a product of Homer's imagination.

The life of Heinrich Schliemann was as dramatic, fantastic and eventful as any of Homer's tales. He was born in the Baltic German state of Mecklenburg in 1822. His father was a feckless womaniser and drunkard whose long-suffering wife died when Schliemann was only nine years old. Forced to leave school at 14, Schliemann got a job stacking crates in a local grocery shop. Five years later he'd had enough, and set off to seek his fortune. He walked to Hamburg and got a job as a ship's boy on a vessel bound for Venezuela. The ship was wrecked off the Dutch Frisian island of Texel, but against all odds Schliemann survived and wandered into Amsterdam half-naked, half-dead and destitute.

Heinrich Schliemann

With a thirst for both knowledge and money, he worked for various trading companies in Holland and studied obsessively in his spare time. Languages were one of his passions; he learnt modern European languages in six weeks, but Ancient Greek took him a while longer. By the age of 24 he was working for an international Dutch trading company, and in 1846 he was appointed their representative in St Petersburg. Already fluent in English, Portuguese, French, Dutch, Spanish and Italian, he was now able to add Russian to his repertoire.

Over the next 20 years Schliemann made a considerable amount of money in various business ventures. One particularly lucrative enterprise was as a private banker in California during the gold rush. By the time he was 40, he had so much money in the bank he decided it was time to indulge a

History & Mythology

Mycenae is synonymous with Homer and Schliemann. In the 9th century BC, Homer told in his epic poems, the *Iliad* and the *Odyssey*, of 'well-built Mycenae, rich in gold'. These poems were, until the 19th century, regarded as gripping and beautiful legends. In the 1870s, the amateur archaeologist Heinrich Schliemann (1822-90), despite derision from professional archaeologists, struck gold, first at Troy then at Mycenae.

In Mycenae, myth and history are inextricably linked. According to Homer and Aeschylus' *Oresteia*, the city of Mycenae was founded by Perseus, the son of Danaë and Zeus. Perseus' greatest heroic deed was the killing of the hideous snake-haired Medusa, whose looks literally petrified the

beholder. Eventually, the dynasty of Perseus was overthrown by Pelops, a son of Tantalus. The Mycenaean Royal House of Atreus was probably descended from Pelops, although myth and history are so intertwined, and the genealogical line so complex, that no-one really knows. Whatever the bloodlines, by Agamemnon's time the House of Atreus was the most powerful of the Achaeans (Homer's name for the Greeks). It eventually came to a sticky end, fulfilling the curse which had been cast because of Pelops' misdeeds.

The historical facts are that Mycenae was first settled by Neolithic people in the 6th millennium BC. Between 2100-1900 BC, during the Old Bronze Age, Greece was invaded by people of Indo-European stock who had crossed Anatolia via Troy to Greece. The invaders brought an advanced

The death mask Schliemann mistakenly thought to be that of Agamemnon

fantasy that had obsessed him for many years. Since his time in Amsterdam, he had steeped himself in Greek mythology and was convinced that Homer's epics were based, albeit loosely, on fact.

In 1868 he decided to prove this, but wanted a sympathetic partner to help him. He wrote to a friend, a bishop in Athens, asking him to find him a suitable wife. The bishop came up with a number of likely candidates, including 17-year-old Sophia Engastromenos (later the family name was changed to Kastomenos). When they met, Schliemann asked her a number of questions. The two crucial ones were: Could she recite some of Homer by heart? And, would she like to travel? The highly intelligent Sophia passed the test, they were married and she was whisked off to Hissartik (ancient Ilium, alias Troy) in Asia Minor to assist Schliemann in his excavations.

In his overenthusiasm Schliemann dug too deep and uncovered treasures which belonged to a pre-Homeric period, not that of King Priam as he believed. The same happened in Mycenae, where he excavated next. The gold mask which he unearthed and excitedly proclaimed as the death mask of Agamemnon actually belonged to a king who lived three centuries earlier.

His marriage to Sophia was a happy one: she accompanied him in all his expeditions, ever-supportive, hard-working and enthusiastic. Marriage did not, however, diminish Schliemann's eccentricities and obsessions – the Schliemanns' house, on El Venizelou in Athens (built by the esteemed German architect, Ernst Ziller) was named Iliou Melathron (Palace of Troy) and their son and daughter were called Agamemnon and Andromache.

Appropriately, his mausoleum in Athens' First Cemetery, designed by Ziller, is adorned with scenes from the Trojan War. ■

culture to the then-primitive Mycenae and other mainland settlements. This new civilisation is now referred to as the Mycenaean, named after Mycenae, its most powerful kingdom. The other kingdoms included Pylos, Tiryns, Corinth and Argos in the Peloponnese. Evidence of Mycenaean civilisation has also been found at Thiva (Thebes) and Athens.

The city of Mycenae consisted of a fortified citadel and surrounding settlement. Due to the sheer size of the walls of the citadel (13m high and 7m thick), the ancient Greeks believed they must have been lifted by a Cyclops, one of the giants described by Homer in the *Odyssey*.

Archaeological evidence indicates that the palaces of the Mycenaean kingdoms were destroyed around 1200 BC. It was long thought that the destruction was the work of the Dorians, but later evidence indicates that the decline of the Mycenaean civilisation was symptomatic of the general turmoil around the Mediterranean at the time. The great Hittite Empire in Anatolia, which had reached its height between 1450 and 1200 BC, was now in decline, as was the Egyptian civilisation.

The Mycenaeans, Hittites and Egyptians had all prospered through their trade with each other, but this had ceased by the end of the 1200s. Many of the great palaces of the Mycenaean kingdoms were destroyed 150 years before the Dorians arrived.

Whether the destruction was the work of outsiders or due to internal division between the various Mycenaean kingdoms remains unresolved.

Exploring the Site

The **Citadel of Mycenae** is entered through the **Lion Gate,** so called because of the relief above the lintel of two lionesses supporting a pillar. This motif is believed to have been the insignia of the Royal House of Atreus.

Inside the citadel, you will find **Grave Circle A** on the right as you enter. This was the royal cemetery and contained six grave shafts. Five were excavated by Schliemann in 1874-76 and the magnificent gold treasures he uncovered are in Athens' National Archaeological Museum. In the last grave shaft, Schliemann found a well-preserved gold death mask with flesh still clinging to it. Fervently, he sent a telegram to the Greek king stating, 'I have gazed upon the face of Agamemnon'. The mask turned out to be that of an unknown king who had died some 300 years before Agamemnon.

To the south of Grave Circle A are the remains of a group of houses. In one was found the famous **Warrior Vase** which Schliemann regarded as one of his greatest discoveries.

The main path leads up to Agamemnon's palace, centred around the **Great Court**. The rooms to the north were the private royal apartments. One of these rooms is believed to be the chamber in which Agamemnon was murdered. Access to the **throne room**, west of the Great Court, would originally have been via a large staircase. On the south-eastern side of the palace is the **megaron** (reception hall).

On the northern boundary of the citadel is the **Postern Gate** through which, it is said, Orestes escaped after murdering his mother. In the far north-eastern corner of the citadel is the **secret cistern**. It can be explored by torchlight, but take care – the steps are slippery.

Until the late 15th century BC, the Mycenaeans put their royal dead into shaft graves. They then devised a new form of burial – the tholos tomb, shaped like a beehive. The

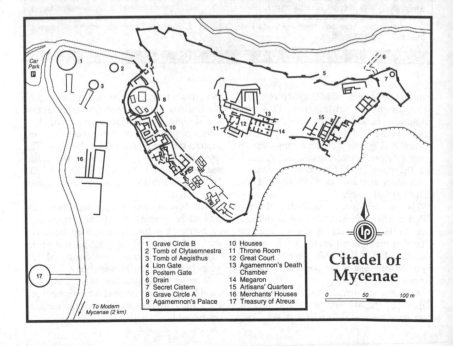

1 Grave Circle B	10 Houses
2 Tomb of Clytaemnestra	11 Throne Room
3 Tomb of Aegisthus	12 Great Court
4 Lion Gate	13 Agamemnon's Death
5 Postern Gate	Chamber
6 Drain	14 Megaron
7 Secret Cistern	15 Artisans' Quarters
8 Grave Circle A	16 Merchants' Houses
9 Agamemnon's Palace	17 Treasury of Atreus

Car Park

To Modern Mycenae (2 km)

Citadel of Mycenae

0   50   100 m

The Trojan War & the Fall of the House of Atreus

In his epic poems, the *Iliad* and the *Odyssey*, Homer related the events of a crucial period in Mycenaean history – the Trojan War and its aftermath. Homer called Troy 'Ilium' (hence the epic's title, the *Iliad*). The 10-year war took place around 1250 BC between the Achaeans and the Trojans, during the reign of Mycenae's King Agamemnon and Troy's King Priam.

Agamemnon's brother, Menelaus, king of Sparta, had suffered great humiliation when his beautiful wife, Helen, was abducted by Paris, the son of King Priam. Menelaus sought the advice of Nestor, king of Pylos, the oldest and wisest of the Mycenaean kings, who told him that nothing less than a combined force of all the armies of Greece would be sufficient to get Helen back. So, accompanied by Agamemnon, Menelaus visited all the princes and heroes in the land to ask for their assistance. Amongst them were Odysseus, king of Ithaca (Ithaki), Patroclus, Achilles and Nestor. Agamemnon, as the most powerful and richest king in Greece, headed the Greek expedition to Troy. Fighting on the Trojan side were Paris, his brother Hector and Priam. The war dragged on for 10 years, during which time Hector killed Patroclus, Achilles killed Hector and Paris killed Achilles, and still there was no end in sight. Odysseus then came up with the idea of the wooden horse filled with soldiers.

While all this was going on in Troy, back in Mycenae, Agamemnon's wife, Clytaemnestra, had taken a lover, Aegisthus. On his return to Mycenae, Agamemnon was greeted lovingly by his wife (despite his being accompanied by his Trojan concubine, Cassandra). However, later while he was taking a bath, Clytaemnestra, assisted by her lover, stabbed him to death. Orestes, her son, then avenged the murder of his father by murdering her, and so the Mycenaen Royal House of Atreus came to its dramatic end. ■

The Trojan horse: the trick that brought Troy's downfall

---

approach road to Mycenae passes to the right of the best preserved of these, the **Treasury of Atreus** or tomb of Agamemnon. A 40m-long passage leads to this immense beehive-shaped chamber. It is built with stone blocks that get steadily smaller as the structure tapers to its central point. Further along the road on the right is **Grave Circle B**, and nearby are the tholos tombs of Aegisthus and Clytaemnestra.

Getting There & Away

Buses depart several times daily for both ancient and modern Mycenae from Nafplio and Argos. See the Getting There & Away section under (modern) Mycenae for details.

NAFPLIO Ναύπλιο

• *pop 11,900* • *postcode 211 00* • *area code* ☎ *0752*

Nafplio (**Naf**plio), 12km south-east of Argos on the Argolic gulf, is one of Greece's prettiest towns. The narrow streets of the old town are filled with elegant Venetian houses and gracious neoclassical mansions. The setting is dominated by the towering Palamidi Fortress.

Nafplio was the first capital of Greece after independence and has been a major port since the Bronze Age. So strategic was its position that it had three fortresses – the massive principal fortress of Palamidi, the smaller Akronafplia and the diminutive Bourtzi on an islet east of the old town.

Removed from the spotlight as capital of Greece after Kapodistrias' assassination by the Maniot chieftains Konstantinos and Georgos Mavromihalis, Nafplio has settled into a more comfortable role as a peaceful seaside resort. With good bus connections, the city is an absorbing base from which to explore many ancient sites.

Orientation

The old town occupies a narrow promontory

with the Akronafplia fortress on the southern side and the promenades of Bouboulinas and Akti Miaouli on the north side. The principal streets of the old town are Amalias, Vasileos Konstantinou, Staïkopoulou and Kapodistriou. The old town's central square is Plateia Syntagmatos (Syntagma Square), at the western end of Vasileos Konstantinou. The bus station is on Syngrou, the street separating the old town from the new. The main street of the new town is 25 Martiou, an easterly continuation of Staïkopoulou.

Information

Nafplio's post office is on Syngrou, and the OTE is on the northern side of 25 Martiou. The National Bank of Greece is on Plateia Syntagmatos. The municipal tourist office (☎ 24 444) is on 25 Martiou, opposite the OTE. The tourist police (☎ 27776) can be found at the western end of 25 Martiou, sharing an office with the traffic police (☎ 22 972).

There is a laundry at 22 Papanikolaou. It's open from Monday to Saturday from 9 am to 2 pm and 6 to 8.30 pm. It charges 2000 dr to wash and dry a load.

Palamidi Fortress

This vast citadel stands on a 216m-high outcrop of rock. Within its walls stand three separate Venetian fortresses, built between 1711 and 1714, but seized by the Turks only a year after completion. Above each of the gates of the citadel is the Venetian emblem of the Lion of St Mark. During the War of Independence, the Greeks, under the leadership of the venerable klepht chief, Theodoros Kolokotronis, besieged the citadel for 15 months before the Turks surrendered. In the new town, north of the OTE, stands a splendid equestrian statue of Kolokotronis, who was known as the Grand Old Man of the Morea.

The fortress affords marvellous views. The energetic can tackle the seemingly endless steps (999) that begin south-east of the bus station. Climb early and take water. There's also a road to the fortress. A taxi costs about 800 dr one way. The fortress (☎ 28

036) is open every day from 8.30 am to 2.45 pm. Admission is 800 dr.

Akronafplia Fortress

The Akronafplia fortress, which rises above the old part of town, is the oldest of Nafplio's three castles. The lower sections of the walls date back to the Bronze Age. Up until the arrival of the Venetians, the town was restricted to within its walls. The Turks called it İç Kale (meaning 'inner castle'). It was used as a political prison from 1936-1956. It has now been converted into tourist hotels by the government-run Xenia group.

Bourtzi

This small island fortress lies about 600m east of the port. Most of the existing structure was built by the Venetians. There are frequent boats out to the island in the summer (400 dr return), leaving from the north-eastern end of Akti Miaouli. The Bourtzi is used as a venue for the Nafplio folk music festival in May/June.

Museums

Nafplio's **Popular Art Museum** (☎ 28 379) won the European Museum of the Year award in 1981 for its displays of traditional textile-producing techniques (with in-depth explanations in English) and folk costumes. The museum is in the old town at Ypsilandou 1 and is open Tuesday to Sunday from 9 am to 2.30 pm. Admission is 500 dr. The museum was closed for repairs at the time of writing and was not scheduled to reopen until 1999. The museum shop has been temporarily relocated to the corner of Vasilissis Olgas and Ferraou, opposite the Hotel Tiryns.

The **archaeological museum** (☎ 27 502) on Plateia Syntagmatos is in an 18th-century Venetian building. The collection includes pottery from Neolithic to classical times, and finds from Mycenae and Tiryns. The prize piece is a suit of bronze Mycenaean armour from Tiryns that is virtually intact. The museum is open Tuesday to Sunday from 8.30 am to 3 pm. Admission is 500 dr.

The **military museum** on Amalias traces

PELOPONNESE

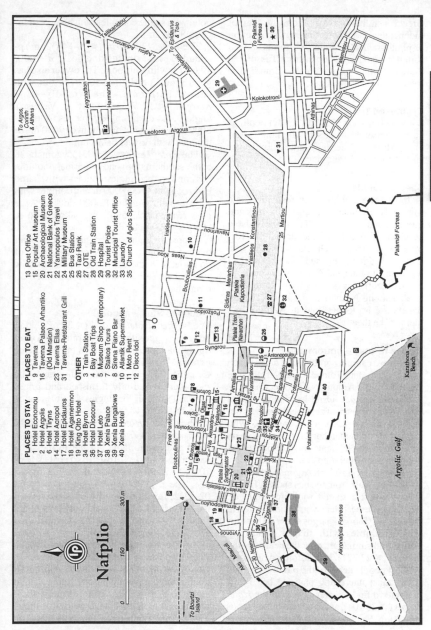

Nafplio

0   150   300 m

PLACES TO STAY
1 Hotel Economou
2 Hotel Argolis
6 Hotel Tiryns
14 Hotel Acropol
17 Hotel Epidauros
18 Hotel Agamemnon
19 King Otto Hotel
34 Hotel Byron
36 Hotel Dioscouri
37 Hotel Leto
38 Xenia Palace
39 Xenia Bungalows
40 Xenia Hotel

PLACES TO EAT
9 Taverna
16 Taverna Palaeo Arhantiko (Old Mansion)
23 Taverna Ellas
31 Taverna-Restaurant Grill

OTHER
3 Train Station
4 Bay Boat Trips
5 Museum Shop (Temporary)
7 Staikos Tours
8 Sirena Piano Bar
10 Atlantik Supermarket
11 Moto Rent
12 Disco Idol

13 Post Office
15 Popular Art Museum
20 Archaeological Museum
21 National Bank of Greece
22 Yannopoulos Travel
24 Military Museum
25 Bus Station
26 Taxi Rank
27 OTE
28 Old Train Station
29 Hospital
30 Tourist Police
32 Municipal Tourist Office
33 Laundry
35 Church of Agios Spiridon

Greece's military history from the War of Independence onwards through a collection of photographs, paintings, uniforms and assorted weaponry. It's open from Tuesday to Sunday from 9 am to 2 pm. Admission is free.

Organised Tours
Staikos Tours (☎ 27 950), at Bouboulinas 50, organises bus tours to Olympia (Monday), Mystras (Tuesday) and to Epidaurus and Mycenae (Wednesday).

Special Events
Nafplio hosts a folk music festival in late May and early June featuring both Greek and international performers. The town is also a good base for visits to Epidaurus for performances of ancient Greek dramas at the famous theatre during the Epidaurus festival between late June and August. The local bus syndicate operates special buses to the festival, leaving Nafplio at 7.30 pm. Theatre tickets are no longer sold in Nafplio; buy them at the theatre.

Places to Stay – bottom end
The closest camping grounds are at the beach resorts, including Tolo, east of Nafplio (see Beaches in the Around Nafplio section).

Nafplio's *youth hostel* has finally closed its doors after years of zero maintenance, but all is not lost. George Economou, who opened the original hostel some 25 years ago, offers special deals for backpackers at the D-class *Hotel Economou* (☎ 23 955), opposite the ex-hostel on Argonafton – about 20 minutes walk from the bus station. He can offer beds in a shared room for 2000 dr, which is the best deal you'll find in town. Otherwise, George charges 4000/7000 dr for singles/doubles with shared bathroom. You'll find similar prices at the nearby *Hotel Argolis* (☎ 27 721), on Leoforos Argous.

Most people head for the old town, which is the most interesting place to be. You'll struggle to find a better deal than the *Hotel Tiryns* (☎ 28 104), at the junction of Othonos and Riga Fereou. It's a clean, family-run

hotel with singles/doubles with bathroom for 6000/8000 dr.

The *Hotel Epidaurus* (☎ 27 541), on Ypsilandou, has singles/doubles for 9000/12,000 dr with bathroom. The owner also has good rooms nearby for 5000/7000 dr with shared bathroom. The friendly *Hotel Acropol* (☎ 17 796), nearby at Vasilissis Olgas 9, has clean singles/doubles for 6500/8000 dr with shared bathroom or 9000 dr for doubles with private bathroom.

The *Hotel Leto* (☎ 28 093) Zygomala 28 at the southern (top) end of Farmakopoulou, has comfortable singles/doubles with shared bathroom for 6600/8000 dr and doubles with private bathroom for 12,000 dr. The *King Otto Hotel* (☎ 27 585), Farmakopoulou 3, charges 6500/8000 dr.

There are signs advertising domatia all over town, but the highest concentration of domatia is in the old town on the narrow streets between Staïkopoulou and the Akronafplia.

Places to Stay – middle
The stylish *Hotel Byron* (☎ 22 351; fax 26338), opposite the church of Agiou Spiridona on Kapodistriou, is the best place in town – in spite of earning no more than a C rating from the tourist authorities. The rooms are beautifully furnished and prices start at 11,000 dr for singles. Doubles range from 14,000 to 18,000 dr.

The C-class *Hotel Dioscouri* (☎ 28 550), on the corner of Zygomala 6 and Vyronos, is clean and comfortable but not in the same league. Singles/doubles/triples are 10,000/13,700/17,000 dr, including breakfast. The B-class *Hotel Agamemnon* (☎ 28 021/022; fax 28 022), at Akti Miaouli 3 on the waterfront, offers mandatory half-board (breakfast and lunch or dinner) for 13,500/21,400 dr.

Places to Stay – top end
Going on price alone, Nafplio's top hotels are the three government-run Xenia that sit atop the Akronafplia. Unfortunately, location is about all they have going for them. The A-class *Xenia Hotel* (☎ 28 991/2) is an

A-grade crumbling concrete eyesore with flaking paint and a general air of dereliction. The alleged luxury-class *Xenia Palace* (☎ 28 981/3) welcomes customers with a carpet that any self-respecting household would take straight to the tip. It would be unwise to expect any better from the nearby *Xenia Bungalows*, also rated deluxe.

Places to Eat
The streets of the old town are filled with literally dozens of restaurants. Staïkopoulou appears to be one long chain of restaurants. It would take months to eat at all of them. Most of these places close down in winter, when the choice shrinks to a few long-standing favourites.

Top of the list is the excellent *Taverna Palaeo Arhontiko* (Old Mansion), on the corner of Ypsilandou and Sofroni. It's a tiny place that is open for dinner only. It's very popular with locals and there's nothing on the menu priced over 1400 dr. The owner is a friendly guy who speaks good English. He can usually be found partying along with guests until the small hours.

Taverna Ellas, on the corner of Plateia Syntagmatos and Vasileos Konstantinou, is fun for people-watching as you tuck into staples such as meatballs or chicken in tomato sauce (1000 dr).

The simple *Taverna-Restaurant Grill*, at 25 Martiou 11 in the new town, serves wine from the barrel and has long had a reputation for hearty home-cooked lunches and grills at night. Prices are reasonable.

For seafood, check out the restaurants along the promenade on Bouboulinas.

Entertainment
Nafplio seems to have almost as many nightclubs and bars as it has restaurants. Most of them are on Bouboulinas – just cruise along until you find a sound that you like at a volume you can handle.

You'll find live Greek music at the *Sirena Piano Bar*, set back behind the severe-looking bust of War of Independence heroine Lascarina Bouboulinas at the junction of Bouboulinas and Sofroni.

Disco-lovers can head for *Disco Idol*, on the corner of Syngrou and Flessa.

Getting There & Away
Bus There are hourly buses from Nafplio to Athens (2½ hours, 2100 dr); half-hourly buses to Argos (30 minutes, 240 dr); hourly buses to Tolo (30 minutes, 240 dr); three a day to Porto Heli (two hours, 1400 dr); and three a day to Mycenae (one hour, 550 dr), Epidaurus (40 minutes, 550 dr) and Galatas (two hours, 1450 dr). Other destinations include Ligourio (40 minutes, 550 dr), Tripolis (1¼ hours, 1000 dr) and Corinth (1¼ hours, 1050 dr).

Hydrofoil There are hydrofoils from Nafplio to Zea Marina (four hours, 7615 dr) every day except Monday from mid-May until the end of September. They travel via Spetses (one hour, 2840 dr), Hydra (two hours, 3625 dr), Poros (2½ hours, 5125 dr) and Aegina (three hours, 6600 dr). You can buy tickets from Yannopoulos Travel (☎ 27 456 or 28 054) on Plateia Syntagmatos.

Train Train services from Nafplio are of little more than academic interest. There are three trains a day to Athens (900 dr), leaving at 5.36 am, and 6 and 8.18 pm. They take three hours. The station is by the port at the western end of Bouboulinas. An old train has been converted into the ticket office and *kafeneion*.

Getting Around
Moto Rent (☎ 25 642), Polizoidou 8, has a wide range of motorcycles, starting with 50cc models for 3500 dr per day. It also hires cars.

AROUND NAFPLIO
Beaches
The nearest sandy beach to Nafplio is **Karathona beach**, at the far side of the Palamidi Fortress. There is no access from the fortress. To get there, walk (one hour) or take a bus from 25 Martiou, which doubles back to the coast. It's also possible to walk around the base of the headland.

Further around the coast, a line of beaches begins with **Asini**, 9km from Nafplio, followed by **Tolo**, **Drepano**, **Plaka**, **Kadia** and **Iria**. Tolo, 11km from Nafplio, is the most developed.

Places to Stay Most hotels along this coast are block-booked by package-holiday companies, but there's a plethora of prominently signposted camping grounds. There's *Kastraki Camping* (☎ 59 386/387) near Asini beach; *Lido II* (☎ 59 369), *Sunset Camping* (☎ 59 566) and *Xeni* (☎ 59 338) at Tolo; *Plaka Beach* (☎ 92 194/195) at Plaka; and *Argolic Strand* (☎ 92 376) and *Triton* (☎ 92 228) at Drepano. The telephone code for all these sites is ☎ 0752.

Getting There & Away There are hourly buses from Nafplio to Tolo (30 minutes, 240 dr) via Asini.

Ancient Asini Ασίνη

The ruins of ancient Asini, on a rocky headland 1km inland from Asini beach, offer a diversion from sun-seeking. There are the remains of an acropolis, Mycenaean tombs, Roman baths and Venetian fortifications.

Tiryns Τίρυνθα

The ruins of Homer's 'wall-girt Tiryns' are 4km north-west of Nafplio. The walls of Tiryns are the apogee of Mycenaean architectural achievement (or paranoia), being even more substantial than those at Mycenae. In parts, they are 20m thick. The largest stones are estimated to weigh 14 tons. Within the walls there are vaulted galleries, secret stairways, and storage chambers. Frescoes from the palace are in Athens' National Archaeological Museum. Tiryns' setting is less awe-inspiring than Mycenae's and much less visited. The site (☎ 0752-22 657) is open daily from 8 am to 7 pm, and admission is 500 dr. The ruins stand to the right of the Nafplio-Argos road. Any Nafplio-Argos bus can drop you outside the site.

EPIDAURUS Επίδαυρος

Epidaurus (Ep**ee**davros), 30km east of Nafplio, is one of the most renowned of Greece's ancient sites. Epidaurus was a sanctuary of Asclepius, the god of medicine. The difference in the atmosphere here, compared with that of the war-orientated Mycenaean cities, is immediately obvious. Henry Miller wrote in *The Colossus of Maroussi* that Mycenae 'folds in on itself', but Epidaurus is 'open, exposed ... devoted to the spirit'. Epidaurus seems to emanate joy, optimism and celebration.

History & Mythology

Legend has it that Asclepius was the son of Apollo and Coronis. While giving birth to Asclepius, Coronis was struck by a thunder bolt and killed. Apollo took his son to Mt Pelion where the physician Chiron instructed the boy in the healing arts.

Apollo was worshipped at Epidaurus in Mycenaean and Archaic times but, by the 4th century BC, he had been superseded by his son. Epidaurus became acknowledged as the birthplace of Asclepius. Although there were sanctuaries to Asclepius throughout Greece, the two most important were at Epidaurus and on the island of Kos. The fame of the sanctuary spread, and when a plague was raging in Rome, Livy and Ovid came to Epidaurus to seek help.

It is believed that licks from snakes were one of the curative practices at the sanctuary. Asclepius is normally shown with a serpent, which – by renewing its skin – symbolises rejuvenation. Other treatments provided at the sanctuary involved diet instruction, herbal medicines and occasionally even surgery. The sanctuary also served as an entertainment venue. Every four years the Festival of Asclepieia took place at Epidaurus. Dramas were staged and athletic competitions were held.

Theatre

Today, the 3rd-century theatre, not the sanctuary, pulls the crowds to Epidaurus. It is one of the best preserved classical Greek buildings, renowned for its amazing acoustics. A coin dropped in the centre can be heard from the highest seat. Built of limestone, the theatre seats up to 14,000 people. Its entrance is flanked by restored Corinthian pilasters. The Festival of Epidaurus takes place each year in July and August. See the Entertainment section for details.

Museum

The museum, between the sanctuary and the theatre, houses statues, stone inscriptions recording miraculous cures, surgical instruments, votives and partial reconstructions of the sanctuary's once-elaborate tholos. After the theatre, the tholos is considered to have been the site's most impressive building and fragments of beautiful, intricately carved reliefs from its ceiling are also displayed.

Sanctuary

The vast ruins of the sanctuary are less crowded than the theatre. In the south is the huge **katagogeion**, which was a hostelry for pilgrims and patients. To the west is the large **banquet hall** in which the Romans built an **odeum**. It was in this building that the Festival of Asclepieia took place. Opposite is the **stadium**, venue for the festival's athletic competitions.

To the north are the foundations of the **Temple of Asclepius** and next to them is the **abaton**. The therapies practised here seemed to have depended on the influence of the mind upon the body. It is believed that patients were given a pep talk by a priest on the powers of Asclepius then put to sleep in the abaton to dream of a visitation by the god. The dream would hold the key to the healing process.

East is the **Sanctuary of Egyptian Gods**, which is an indication that the cult of Asclepius was an adaptation of the cult of Imhotep. Imhotep was worshipped in Egypt for his healing powers. To the west of the Temple of Asclepius are the remains of the **tholos**, built in 360-320 BC. The function of the tholos is unknown.

Set among the green foothills of Mt Arahneo, the air redolent with herbs and pine trees, it's easy to see how the sanctuary

would have had a beneficial effect upon the ailing. Considering the state of Greece's current health system, perhaps the centre should be resurrected.

Places to Stay & Eat

The only accommodation at the site is the B-class *Xenia Hotel* (☎ 0753-22 003). Several readers have written to complain that the place is an absolute dump, which will come as no surprise to anyone familiar with this government-run chain.

The village of Ligourio, 4km north of Epidaurus on the main road to Nafplio, offers cheaper options. The *Hotel Asklepios* (☎ 0753-22 251), in the middle of town on the Nafplio-Epidaurus road, charges 3500/5000 dr for singles/doubles with shared facilities. The *Hotel Koronis* (☎ 0753-22 267), on the opposite side of the road, was in the middle of a complete refit at the time of research.

There are several restaurants on the main road through Ligourio.

Entertainment

The theatre at Epidaurus is used to stage performances of ancient Greek dramas during the Festival of Epidaurus, from 26 July to 30 August each year. Performances are held on Friday and Saturday nights, starting at 9 pm. Tickets can be bought in Epidaurus (☎ 0753-22 006) at the site office on Thursday, Friday and Saturday from 9.30 am to 1 pm and 6 to 9 pm. They can also be bought from the Athens Festival box office (see the Entertainment section in the Athens chapter). Prices vary according to seating. Student discounts are available. There are special buses from Athens and Nafplio.

Getting There & Away

There are four buses a day from Nafplio to Epidaurus (40 minutes, 550 dr) via Ligourio (also 550 dr).

ANCIENT TROIZEN Τροιζήν

Troizen (also known as Trizin), 49km southeast of Ligourio, was an Ionian colony, the birthplace of Theseus and a refuge for

Athenian women and children during the Persian invasion beginning in 480 BC. It shared many traditions and cults with Athens. The site is a few minutes walk from the picturesque, hillside village of **Trizin**.

The **Sanctuary of Hippolytos** is the first ruin you come across, followed by the remains of the city wall with an Hellenic tower. Small stones in the upper construction indicate Frankish rebuilding. A further 10 minutes climbing brings you to the **Devil's Bridge**, a natural extension across the deep Gefyron gorge.

Buses from Nafplio to the seaside village of **Galatas** (two hours, 1450 dr) can drop you at the turn-off to Trizin, from where it's a steep climb to the site. The alternative is to continue to Galatas and take a bus (210 dr) or taxi back to Trizin. Galatas and Trizin can also be visited from the island of Poros (see the Saronic Gulf Islands chapter).

Arcadia Αρκαδία

The picturesque rural prefecture of Arcadia occupies much of the central Peloponnese. Its name evokes images of grassy meadows, forested mountains, gurgling streams and shady grottoes. It was a favourite haunt of Pan, who played his pipes, guarded herds and frolicked with nymphs in this sunny, bucolic idyll.

Almost encircled by high mountains, Arcadia was remote enough in ancient times to remain largely untouched by the battles and intrigues of the rest of Greece. It was the only region of the Peloponnese not conquered by the Dorians. It remains a backwater, dotted with crumbling medieval villages, remote monasteries and Frankish castles, visited only by determined tourists. It also has 100-odd km of unspoilt coastline on the Argolic gulf, running south from the pretty town of Myli to Leonidio.

TRIPOLIS Τρίπολη
• *pop 22,500* • *postcode 221 00* • *area code ☎ 071*
The violent recent history of Arcadia's capi-

tal, Tripolis (**Tripolee**), is in stark contrast with the surrounding rural idyll. In 1821, during the War of Independence, the town was captured by Kolokotronis and its 10,000 Turkish inhabitants massacred. The Turks retook the town three years later, and burnt it to the ground before withdrawing in 1928.

Tripolis itself is not a place to linger long, but it's a major transport hub for the Peloponnese. It also has some impressive neoclassical buildings and Byzantine churches, a large park and wonderful window-shopping for consumer goods.

Orientation
Tripolis can be a bit confusing at first. The streets radiate out from the central square, Plateia Vasileos Georgiou, like an erratic spider's web. The main streets are Washington, which runs south from Plateia Georgiou to Kalamata; Ethnikis Antistaseos, which runs north from the square and becomes the road to Kalavryta; and Vasileos Georgiou, which runs east from the square to Plateia Kolokotroni. El Venizelou runs east from Plateia Kolokotroni, leading to the road to Corinth.

The main Arkadias bus station is conveniently central on Plateia Kolokotroni. The city's other bus station is opposite the train station, about 10 minutes walk away, at the south-eastern end of Lagopati – which is the street that runs behind the Arkadias terminal.

Information
There's a tourist information office (☎ 239 392) in the town hall, about 250m north of Plateia Vasileos Georgiou at Ethnikis Antistaseos 43. It's on the ground floor to the right, open Monday to Friday from 7 am to 2 pm. The tourist police (☎ 222 265) cohabit with the regular police at Plateia Petrinou, which is the square between Plateia Georgiou and the town hall. The police station is next to the ornate Malliaropoulio Theatre.

The post office is just off Plateia Vasileos Georgiou, behind the Hotel Galaxy at the junction of Athanasiadou and Nikitara. The OTE is nearby on 28 Oktovriou. Tripolis has branches of all the major banks. The National Bank of Greece is on the corner of 28 Oktovriou and Ethnikis Antistaseos. The bookshop on the northern side of Plateia Vasileos Georgiou sells English-language newspapers.

Archaeological Museum

The city's archaeological museum occupies a neoclassical mansion on Evagistrias, and is clearly signposted off Vasileos Georgiou next to the Hotel Alex. The museum houses finds from the surrounding ancient sites of Megalopoli, Gortys, Lykosoura and Mantinea. The museum is open from Tuesday to Sunday from 8.30 am to 3 pm. Admission is 500 dr.

Places to Stay

The *Hotel Alex* (☎ 223 465), Vasileos Georgiou 26, has the cheapest rooms in town. It charges 5000/7000 dr for basic singles/doubles, and 6000/8000 dr with private bathroom.

The best deal is to be found at the friendly *Hotel Anactoricon* (☎ 222 545; fax 223 845), beyond the town hall at Ethnikis Antistaseos 48. It has large, comfortable singles/doubles with TV and bathroom for 9000/11,000 dr, as well as smaller singles/doubles with shared bathroom for 5500/8000 dr. The *Galaxy Hotel* (☎ 225 195), on the main square, is a reasonable option if the other places are full. It has singles/doubles with bathroom for 5000/6700 dr.

The smartest place is supposedly the B-class *Hotel Arkadia* (☎ 225 551) on Plateia Kolokotroni. The interior is better maintained than the exterior (which wouldn't be difficult), but it's not worth the 8500/14,000 dr it asks for singles/doubles.

Places to Eat

There are lots of cafés and restaurants on and around Plateia Kolokotroni and Plateia Vasileos Georgiou. The *Taverna Atia*, near the train station at the junction of Lampraki and Iroon, is a popular spot with a good range of reasonably priced traditional fare.

Getting There & Away

Bus The Arkadias bus station on Plateia Kolokotroni is the city's main terminal. There are 12 buses a day to Athens (2¼ hours, 2800 dr) and frequent buses to Corinth (1½ hours, 1450 dr). There are also regular services to Patras (four hours, 2850 dr), Monemvasia (3½ hours, 2600 dr), Olympia (2½ hours, 2200 dr) and Pyrgos (three hours, 2500 dr).

Regional services include hourly buses to Tegea (20 minutes, 230 dr); eight a day to Megalopoli (40 minutes, 600 dr); two to Dimitsana (one hour, 1150 dr) via Stemnitsa (one hour, 950 dr), and two to Andritsena (1½ hours, 1400 dr) via Karitena (850 dr).

The bus station on Lagopati handles departures to Achaïa, Argolis, Lakonia and Messinia. They include nine buses a day to Argos (1¼ hours, 1000 dr) and Sparta (1½ hours, 950 dr); six to Kalamata (two hours, 1450 dr); three to Nafplio (1¼ hours, 1000 dr); and one to Kalavryta (2½ hours, 1500 dr).

Train Tripolis is on the main Athens-Kalamata line. There are four trains a day to Athens (four hours, 1500 dr), travelling via Argos (1½ hours, 950 dr) and Corinth (2½ hours, 1000 dr). There are also four trains a day to Kalamata (three hours, 840 dr).

AROUND TRIPOLIS

Ancient Tegea Αρχαία Τεγέα

Ancient Tegea, 8km south-east of Tripolis, was the most important city in Arcadia in classical and Roman times. Tegea was constantly bickering with its arch rival, Mantinea, and fought a long war with Sparta, to which it finally capitulated and became allied in the Peloponnesian Wars. It was laid waste in the 5th century AD but rebuilt by the Byzantines, who called it Nikli. The ruins of the city lie scattered around the modern village of Tegea (also called Alea).

The bus from Tripolis stops outside Tegea's **museum**, which houses thrones, statues and reliefs from the site, including fragments of the pediment from the 4th-century BC Doric **Temple of Athena Alea**. The temple's pediment was regarded as one of the greatest artworks of its time. The museum has erratic opening times: Tuesday to Sunday, supposedly from 8.30 am to 3 pm. Try calling first (☎ 55 6153). Admission is 300 dr.

Standing on the site of an ancient theatre, the **Church of Episkopi** in Tegea, once a forum for matchmaking, has a festival on Assumption Day, 15 August.

MEGALOPOLI Μεγαλόπολη
• *pop 4700* • *postcode 222 00* • *area code* ☎ *0791*

Despite its name, Megalopoli (Meghalopolee, which means 'great city'), there's little left that reflects its former grandeur. It was founded in 371 BC as the capital of a united Arcadia nestled in a leafy valley on the banks of the Elisson river. The modern town is dominated by a large hydroelectric plant, but it is surrounded by rolling orchard country with mountain backdrops. Megalopoli is an important transport hub astride the main route from Tripolis to Kalamata and Pyrgos.

Places to Stay & Eat
There are six modest hotels to choose from, all located on the streets leading off the large central square, Plateia Polyviou. The *Hotel Paris* (☎ 22 410), close to the bus station at Agiou Nikolaou 9, has tidy singles/doubles with bathroom for 4400/7500 dr, while the *Hotel Leto* (☎ 22 302), P Kefala 9, is a bit cheaper at 4000/6000 dr.

There are several restaurants around Plateia Polyviou, but the best place is the very popular *Psistaria O Meraklis*, just off the square on Papanastasiou – the road to Tripolis. It has a range of grilled food, starting with souvlaki sticks for 90 dr, as well as salads and vegetable dishes. It's run by an extended Greek-Canadian family.

Getting There & Away
Bus departures include eight a day to Athens (4½ hours, 3300 dr), via Tripolis (40 minutes, 600 dr); eight to Kalamata (one hour, 950 dr); and two a day to Andritsena (1¼ hours, 800 dr).

AROUND MEGALOPOLI
Poetically described as the first city which saw the sun, **Ancient Likosoura**, the holy city of the Arcadians, is regarded as Greece's oldest ruin. A small **museum** has copies of statues from the nearby **Sanctuary of Despina and Demeter**. The originals are housed in the National Archaeological Museum in Athens. The site is 10km west of Megalopoli, just past the village of **Lykeo** where the museum caretaker lives. The route passes through oak woods, and there are beautiful mountain views.

CENTRAL ARCADIA
The area to the west of Tripolis is a tangle of medieval villages, precipitous ravines and narrow winding roads, woven into valleys of dense vegetation beneath the slopes of the Menalon mountains. This is the heart of the Arcadia prefecture, an area with some of the most breathtaking scenery in the Peloponnese. The region is high above sea level and nights are chilly, even in summer. Snow is common in winter.

You need your own transport to do the area justice, but the three most important villages – Karitena, Stemnitsa and Dimitsana – are within reach of Tripolis by public transport. Stemnitsa and Dimitsana are on the 37km stretch of road that cuts through the mountains from the Pyrgos-Tripolis road in the north to the Megalopoli-Andritsena road in the south.

Karitena Καρίταινα
High above the Megalopoli-Andritsena road is the splendid medieval village of Karitena (Karitena, population 320), aptly called the 'Toledo of Greece'. A stepped path leads from the central square to the village's 13th-century **Frankish castle** atop a massive rock.

Karitena's 13th-century **Church of Agios Nikolaos** has well-preserved frescoes. The church is locked. Ask around and someone will direct you to the caretaker. From the church, a path leads down to the **Frankish bridge** which spans the River Lousios (a tributary of the Alfios). The bridge features on the 5000 dr note. Karitena has domatia. North of Karitena, the road runs to the east of the Lousios gorge. After 10km, south of the small village of Elliniko, a dirt track to the left leads in 1½ hours of walking to the site of **ancient Gortys**, which can also be reached by hardy vehicle. It's on the west side of the gorge, approached via a bridge. Gortys was an important city from the 4th century BC. Most ruins date from Hellenistic times, but to the north are the remains of a **Sanctuary to Asclepius**.

Getting There & Away Most buses from Megalopoli and Tripolis to Andritsena call at Karitena. A few will leave you on the main road, from where it's an arduous uphill walk to the village. The staff at the bus station you leave from will be able to tell you where the bus will stop.

Stemnitsa Στεμνίτσα
• *pop 550* • *postcode 220 24* • *area code* ☎ *0795*
Stemnitsa (Stem**nit**sa), 15km north of Karitena, is a spectacular village of stone houses and Byzantine churches. North of the village, a path to the left leads to **Moni Agiou Ioannitou Prodromou**. The walk takes about an hour. A monk will show visitors the chapel's splendid 14th and 15th-century frescoes. From here, paths lead to the deserted monasteries of **Paleou** and **Neou Philosophou** and also south along the riverbank to the site of ancient Gortys. The monks at Prodromou can direct you.

Stemnitsa has one hotel, the C-class *Hotel Triokolonion* (☎ 81 297). It has singles/doubles with bathroom for 7000/9500 dr and a restaurant. It also serves good food.

Getting There & Away On weekdays, there's a daily bus from Tripolis (one hour, 950 dr).

Dimitsana Διμιτσάνα
• *pop 650* • *postcode 220 07* • *area code* ☎ *0795*
Built amphitheatrically on two hills at the beginning of the Lousios gorge, Dimitsana (Dimit**san**a, population 650), 11km north of Stemnitsa, is a lovely medieval vil-

lage. Despite its remoteness, Dimitsana played a significant role in the country's struggle for self-determination. Its Greek school, founded in 1764, was one spawning ground for the ideas leading to the uprisings against the Turks. Its students included Bishop Germanos of Patras and Patriarch Gregory V, who was hanged by the Turks in retaliation for the massacre in Tripolis. The village also had a number of gunpowder factories and a branch of the secret Filiki Eteria ('friendly society') where Greeks met to discuss the revolution (see the History section in the Facts about the Country chapter for more details on the Filiki Eteria).

From the heady days before independence, Dimitsana has become a sleepy village where the most exciting event is the arrival of the daily Tripolis bus. Apart from the beauty of the village and its surroundings, tourists will appreciate the **folk museum** and **library**, on Nikolaou Makri (open daily from 8 am to 2 pm, free admission) and the **Moni Aimialon**, 3km south on the road to Stemnitsa (open daily from 9 am to 2 pm).

Places to Stay You'll see signs for a couple of domatia in the middle of town (Plateia Agia Kyriaki), as well as a sign pointing the way to the *Xenonas Kazakou* (☎ 31 660), another EOT-run traditional settlement. It was closed at the time of research, but has doubles with breakfast for 12,600 dr when open.

Dimitsana's one hotel, the C-class *Hotel Dimitsana* (☎ 31 518), is south of the village on the road to Stemnitsa. It has doubles with bathroom for 13,500 dr, including breakfast.

Getting There & Away There are two buses a day from Tripolis to Dimitsana (one hour, 1150 dr).

ANDRITSENA Ανδρίτσαινα
• *pop 900* • *postcode 270 61* • *area code* ☎ *0626*
The village of Andritsena, 81km west of Tripolis, is perched on a hillside overlooking the valley of the River Alfios. Crumbling

stone houses with rickety wooden balconies flank its narrow cobbled streets and a stream gushes through its central square.

The post office, OTE and bank are near the central square. The village's only concession to tourism is its small **folk museum**, which is usually open daily from 11 am to 1 pm and 5 to 6 pm. Admission is free. Most people come to Andritsena to visit the Temple of Vasses, 14km away.

Temple of Vasses

The Temple of Vasses, 14km south of Andritsena, stands at an altitude of 1200m on a hill overlooked by Mt Paliavlakitsa. The road from Andritsena climbs steadily along a mountain ridge, through increasingly dramatic scenery, to Greece's most isolated temple.

Well preserved, it was built in 420 BC by the people of nearby Figalia, who dedicated it to Apollo Epicurus (the Helper) for delivering them from pestilence. Designed by Ictinus, the architect of the Parthenon, it combines Doric and Ionic columns and a single Corinthian column – the earliest example of this order.

At the time of research, the temple was enclosed by a giant tent and was in the middle of a much-needed restoration programme. The site is open Tuesday to Sunday from 8 am to 5 pm. Admission is 500 dr.

There are no buses to Vasses. In summer, it's usually possible to find people in the square to share a taxi for about 4000 dr return.

From Vasses, a dirt road continues for 11km to the village of **Perivolia**, from where a 2km track leads to the village of **Ano Figalia**, which is built on the site of ancient Figalia (see the Elia section for more details). This Fagalia is not to be confused with the village of Nea Fagalia, 19km west of Perivolia on the road to Tholos.

Places to Stay & Eat

Andritsena's only hotel is the uninspiring *Theoxenia* (☎ 22 219). Singles/doubles are 9000/13,000 dr, including breakfast.

Andritsena's few eateries are on the central square. Meals are also served at the Theoxenia Hotel.

Getting There & Away

There are two buses a day to Andritsena from Athens Bus Terminal A (four hours, 3900 dr). There are also services from Megalopoli (1¼ hours, 800 dr), Pyrgos (1½ hours) and Tripolis (two hours, 1400 dr).

MYLI TO LEONIDIO

There are lots of opportunities to explore on the scenic coast road that runs south from the pretty town of Myli, 46km east of Tripolis, to Leonidio.

The opening 34km leg from Myli to **Astros** is a delight. Astros, notable for its dahlias and roses, is perched above Paralia Astrou, which has a kastro and camping by the beach. From Astros, a good road hugs the coast, curving above tiny pebble-beached villages. Along the way there are some shady camping grounds, domatia, studios and tavernas. The first settlement of any consequence is the isolated seaside village of **Paralia Tyrou**, also known as **Tyrosapounakia**, which has several hotels and tavernas.

LEONIDIO

• *pop 3800* • *postcode 223 00* • *area code* ☎ *0757*

The small town of Leonidio, 20km south of Paralia Tyrou, has a dramatic setting at the mouth of the Badron river gorge. Its tiny Plateia 25 Martiou is an archetypal, unspoiled, whitewashed Greek village square, surrounded by shady trees. The OTE is visible from the square, and the friendly police (☎ 22 222) are close at hand on Kiloso. Many of the older people around here still speak *chakonika*, the language of ancient Sparta, in preference to Greek.

There are excellent unspoiled beaches at the nearby seaside villages of **Lakos**, **Plaka** and **Poulithra**. The fertile alluvial river flats between Leonidio and the coast are intensively farmed.

Places to Stay

There are apartments for rent in town, but most people head for the beach at Plaka.

There are several domatia as well as the D-class *Katavros Hotel* (☎ 51 214) on the small square by the port. It has doubles for 12,000 dr. You'll find cold beer and excellent seafood at the nearby *Restaurant Akroyali*.

There are more domatia and the *Hotel Kentauros* (☎ 51 214) at Poulithra, 7km south of Plaka.

Getting There & Away

Bus Getting there by bus takes a bit of effort. There is one bus a day that runs down the coast from Argos departing at 9 am (three hours, 1350 dr).

Hydrofoil It's much easier to use the hydrofoil – Leonidio's port of Plaka is part of the Flying Dolphin circuit around the Saronic gulf and the eastern Peloponnese. In summer there are at least two hydrofoils a day to Zea Marina at Piraeus (2½ hours, 6300 dr), travelling via Spetses (45 minutes, 2200 dr), and Hydra (80 minutes, 2970 dr). There are also five services a week to Monemvasia (80 minutes, 3475 dr).

SOUTH OF LEONIDIO

The road south from Leonidio over the rugged Parnon mountains to the town of Geraki in Lakonia, 48km away, is one of the most scenic in the Peloponnese. For the first 12km, the road snakes west up the Badron gorge, climbing slowly away from the river until at times it is no more than a speck of silver far below. The road then leaves the Badron and climbs rapidly through a series of dramatic hairpin bends towards Kosmas.

Just before the top of the climb, there's a dirt road to the left leading to **Moni Profitas Ilonas**, an amazing little monastery perched precariously on the mountainside. Visitors are welcome providing they are suitably dressed. Almost as amazing as the monastery is the cardphone outside.

It's another 14km from the monastery to the beautiful red-tiled mountain village of **Kosmas**, where you can stay at *To Balkoni tis Kynourias* (☎ 0757-22 821), a renovated

traditional house just off the central square. It's open from April to November.

The final 15km is no more than a gentle coast down to Geraki. From here you can head 40km west to Sparta, or continue south through **Vlahiotis**, **Molai** and **Sikia** to Monemvasia.

Lakonia Λακωνία

The modern region of Lakonia occupies almost identical boundaries to the powerful kingdom ruled by King Menelaus in Mycenaean times. Menelaus ruled from his capital at Sparta, which was later to achieve much greater fame as the arch rival of Athens in classical times. The Spartans who fought Athens were the descendants of the Dorians, who had arrived in about 1100 BC after the decline of the Mycenaean empire.

Little remains of ancient Sparta, but the disappointment is more than compensated for by the glorious Byzantine churches and monasteries at Mystras, just to the west. Another place not to be missed is the evocative, medieval town of Monemvasia, in the south-east.

English-speakers can thank the Lakonians for the word laconic – brief of speech, which many Lakonians still are.

SPARTA Σπάρτη

• *pop 14,100* • *postcode 231 00* • *area code* ☎ *0731*

Modern Sparta (in Greek **Spar**ti) is an easy-going town of wide, tree-lined streets that is very much in contrast with the ancient image of discipline and deprivation. The town lies at the heart of the Evrotas valley, an important citrus and olive-growing region. The Taÿgetos mountains, snow-capped until early June, provide a stunning backdrop to the west.

Orientation

You won't get lost in Sparta. It was constructed in 1834 on a grid system, and has two main thoroughfares. Palaeologou runs

PELOPONNESE

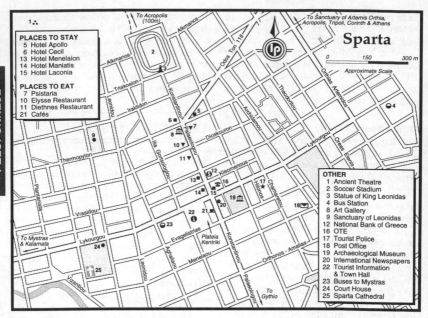

PLACES TO STAY
5 Hotel Apollo
6 Hotel Cecil
13 Hotel Menelaion
14 Hotel Maniatis
15 Hotel Laconia

PLACES TO EAT
7 Psistaria
10 Elysse Restaurant
11 Diethnes Restaurant
21 Cafés

OTHER
1 Ancient Theatre
2 Soccer Stadium
3 Statue of King Leonidas
4 Bus Station
8 Art Gallery
9 Sanctuary of Leonidas
12 National Bank of Greece
16 OTE
17 Tourist Police
18 Post Office
19 Archaeological Museum
20 International Newspapers
22 Tourist Information
   & Town Hall
23 Buses to Mystras
24 Court House
25 Sparta Cathedral

north to south through the town, and Lykourgou runs east to west. They intersect in the middle of town. The central square, Plateia Kentriki, is one block west of the intersection. The bus station is at the eastern end of Lykourgou.

Information

Sparta's enthusiastic tourist information office (☎ 24 852) is on the 1st floor of the town hall on the main square. It's open Monday to Friday from 8 am to 2.30 pm. The tourist police (☎ 26 229) are at Hilonos 8, one block east of the museum.

The post office is clearly signposted off Lykourgou on Archidamou, and the OTE is between Lykourgou and Kleomvrotou, one block east of Palaeologou. The National Bank of Greece is one of many banks on Palaeologou.

Exploring Ancient Sparta

If the city of the Lacedaemonians were destroyed, and only its temples and the foundations of its buildings left, remote posterity would greatly doubt whether their power were ever equal to their renown.

Thucydides

To witness the accuracy of Thucydides' prophecy, wander around ancient Sparta's meagre ruins. Walk north along Palaeologou. At the top is a large statue of a belligerent King Leonidas, standing in front of a soccer stadium. West of the stadium, a path leads to the southern gate of the **acropolis**. Pathways from here lead to forlorn ruins amid olive groves. Away to the left (west) is the 2nd or 3rd-century BC **ancient theatre**, the site's most discernible ruin. Along the road to Tripolis, a path leads to the **Sanctuary of Artemis Orthia**. Like most of the deities in Greek mythology, the goddess Artemis had many aspects, one of which was Artemis Orthia. In earliest times, this aspect of the goddess was honoured through human sacrifice. The Spartans gave this activity

PELOPONNESE

away for the slightly less gruesome business of flogging young boys in honour of the goddess.

Museum & Gallery
Sparta's **archaeological museum** (☎ 28 575) is just east of the town centre on Lykourgou and includes votive sickles which Spartan boys dedicated to Artemis Orthia, heads and torsos of various deities, a statue of Leonidas, masks and a stele. The museum is open Tuesday to Saturday from 8.30 am to 3 pm and Sunday from 8.30 am to 2.30 pm. Admission is 500 dr.

The **John Coumantarios Art Gallery**, Palaeologou 123, has a collection of 19th and 20th-century French and Dutch paintings and also holds changing exhibitions of works by contemporary Greek painters. It's open Tuesday to Saturday from 9 am to 3 pm and Sunday from 10 am to 2 pm. Admission is free.

Places to Stay – bottom end
Camping Mystras (☎ 22 724) and *Camping Castleview* (☎ 93 384), both about 4km west of town on the Sparta-Mystras road, have good facilities and charge similar rates. Buses to Mystras can drop you off at either place.

There's a good choice of hotels back in town. Most travellers head to the friendly family-run *Hotel Cecil* (☎ 24 980), Palaeologou 125. The owners had just finished a major upgrade when we visited, and the rooms are top value at 6000/8000 dr for singles/doubles with private bathroom. If it's full, try the *Hotel Laconia* (☎ 28 951), down the street at Palaeologou 61. It has singles/doubles/triples for 6000/9000/10,500 dr.

The *Hotel Apollo* (☎ 22 491), Thermopylon 84, is not as expensive as its marble-filled foyer might suggest. It charges 7000/10,000 dr for large singles/doubles with bathroom and balcony.

Places to Stay – middle
There's very little to choose between the C-class *Hotel Maniatis* (☎ 22 665; fax 29 994), Palaeologou 72, and the B-class *Hotel Menelaion* (☎ 22 161; fax 26 332), nearby at No 91. Both have immaculate singles/doubles with bathroom and TV for 11,000/14,000 dr. The swimming pool just tips the scales in the Menelaion's favour.

Places to Eat
There are lots of restaurants along Palaeologou. The *Diethnes Restaurant*, Palaeologou 105, is long-established and serves tasty, traditional food, while the nearby *Restaurant Elysse* makes a play for the tourist trade with its 'We Speak English' sign.

Locals seem to prefer the rough and ready *psistaria* opposite the art gallery. It turns out a large plate of delicious grilled pork for 1200 dr, Greek salad for 800 dr and half a litre of wine for 350 dr – and the owner speaks English. Prices at the elegant *Dias Restaurant*, next to the Hotel Maniatis, are much more reasonable than the décor suggests. There are *supermarkets* and *fast-food outlets* on Palaeologou.

Getting There & Away
Sparta's well-organised new bus station is at the east end of Lykourgou. Departures are clearly displayed in English on a large information board. They include 10 buses a day to Athens (4½ hours, 3450 dr) via Corinth (three hours, 2250 dr); five to Gythio (one hour, 750 dr); four to Neapoli (four hours, 2350 dr) and Tripolis (1¼ hours, 950 dr); and two a day to Kalamata (2½ hours, 950 dr) via Artemissia (600 dr). There are also buses to Geraki (45 minutes, 700 dr) and to Monemvasia (2½ hours, 1700 dr). Departures to the Mani peninsula include two buses a day to Gerolimenas (three hours, 1700 dr) via Areopoli (two hours, 1150 dr) and a 9 am service to the caves at Pyrgos Dirou.

There are also 12 buses a day to Mystras (30 minutes, 210 dr). You can also catch these services on their way out to Mystras at the bus stop on Aghsilaou, around the corner from Lykourgou.

MYSTRAS Μυστράς
The captivating ruins of the once awesome town of Mystras (Mis**tras**), crowned by an imposing fortress, spill from a spur of Mt Taÿgetos.

History
The fortress of Mystras was built by Guillaume de Villehardouin in 1249. When the Byzantines won back the Morea from the Franks, Emperor Michael VIII Paleologus made Mystras its capital and seat of government. It soon became populated by people from the surrounding plains seeking refuge from the invading Slavs. From this time, until the last despot, Dimitrios, surrendered to the Turks in 1460, a despot of Morea (usually a son or brother of the ruling Byzantine emperor) lived and reigned at Mystras.

While the empire plunged into decline elsewhere, Mystras enjoyed a renaissance under the despots. A school of humanistic philosophy was founded by Gemistos Plethon (1355-1452). His enlightened ideas attracted intellectuals from all corners of Byzantium. After Mystras was ceded to the Turks, Plethon's pupils moved to Rome and Florence where they made a significant contribution to the Italian Renaissance. Art and architecture also flourished, evidenced in the splendid buildings and vibrant frescoes of Mystras.

Mystras declined under Turkish rule. It was captured by the Venetians in 1687 and thrived again with a flourishing silk industry and a population of 40,000. It was recaptured by the Turks in 1715, and from then on it was downhill all the way. It was burned by the Russians in 1770, by the Albanians in 1780 and by Ibrahim Pasha in 1825. By the time of Independence, it was in a very sorry state; virtually abandoned and in ruins. Since the 1950s, much restoration has taken place.

Exploring the Site
A day is needed to do Mystras justice. Wear sensible shoes, bring plenty of water and begin at the upper entrance to the site to walk down, rather than uphill. The site is divided into three sections – the **kastro** (the fortress on the summit), the **upper town** (hora) and the **lower town** (kato hora).

Kastro & Upper Town From opposite the upper-entrance ticket office, a path (signposted 'kastro') leads up to the fortress. It was built by the Franks and extended by the Turks. The path descending from the ticket office leads to **Agia Sofia**, which served as the palace church – some frescoes survive. Steps descend from here to a T-junction. A left turn leads to the **Nafplio Gate**, which was the main entrance to the town. Near the gate is the huge **Palace of the Despots**, a complex of several buildings constructed at different times. The vaulted audience room, the largest of its buildings, was added in the 14th century. Its façade was painted, and its

HELEN ROWLEY

MARK HONAN

DAVID HALL

MARK HONAN

Top: The ruins of Mystras, Peloponnese, contain fine frescoes and stone carvings
Middle Left: An ancient dream, the Corinth Canal, Peloponnese, finally realised in 1893
Middle Right: Entrance to the stadium, Ancient Olympia, Peloponnese
Bottom: The Fortress of Bourtzi on an islet east of the old town of Nafplio, Peloponnese

MARK DAFFEY

ROSEMARY HALL

GREG ALFORD

Top: The tranquil fishing village of Gerolimenas on the Lakonian peninsula, Peloponnese
Bottom Left: The main street of Monemvasia, Lakonian peninsula, Peloponnese
Bottom Right: Ancient Delphi, Central Greece

Mystras

0   50   100 m

Kastro
(621m)

Upper
Entrance

Agia Sofia

UPPER TOWN

Nafplio
Gate

Agios
Nikolaos

Small
Palace

Convent
of Pantanassa

Monemvassia
Gate

Taxiarhes

Palace of the
Despots

House of
Frangopoulos

Aphentiko

Vrontokhion
Monastery

Monastery of
Perivleptos

Laskaris
Mansion

Agios
Hristoforos

LOWER
TOWN

Agios
Georgios

Agios
Theodoros

Vaulted
Passage

Evangelistria

Marmara
Fountain

To Neos Mystras
& Sparta

Episcopal
Palace

Museum

Mitropolis
(Cathedral
of Agios
Dimitrios)

window frames were very ornate, but
hundreds of years of neglect have robbed it
of its former opulence.

From the palace, a winding, cobbled path
leads down to the **Monemvasia Gate**, the
entrance to the lower town.

Lower Town Through the Monemvasia gate,
turn right for the well-preserved, 14th-century
Convent of Pantanassa. The nuns who live
here are Mystras' only inhabitants. The
building has beautiful stone-carved or-
namentation on its façade and the capitals of

its columns. It's an elaborate, perfectly
proportioned building – never overstated.
Exquisite, richly coloured 15th-century frescoes are among the finest examples of late
Byzantine art. There is a wonderful view of
the pancake-flat and densely cultivated plain
of Lakonia from the columned terrace on the
northern façade.

The path continues down to the
Monastery of Perivleptos, which is built
into a rock. Its 14th-century frescoes are
equal to those of Pantanassa and have been
preserved virtually intact. Each scene is an
entity – enclosed in a simple symmetrical

Icons

The word icon derives from the Greek word *ekenai* which means 'to be like'. Icons are religious paintings, on polished wooden boards, usually depicting a saint, Christ, or the Virgin Mary. The background of an icon is often of gold leaf, the colour gold being symbolic of heaven.

All churches in Greece have a collection of icons, and even the smallest chapels have at least one. Icons are often painted on panels in an iconostasis – the screen which separates the nave from the altar and the name of which derives from the word, icon. Almost every home in Greece has at least one icon, usually standing on a shelf and illuminated by a candle.

Icons are highly stylised works of art. The painter of icons sublimates his individuality to an ideal. Icons are meant to invoke an exalted state in the viewer. It is said they are meant to be 'looked through', not at. Because of the insignificance of the painter, many icons are believed to have appeared miraculously. Many are said to have been washed up by the sea: the Mediterranean must have contained as many icons as fish in the Middle Ages.

In the 8th century a movement known as Iconoclasm (the breaking of images) began to take hold. Iconoclasts, influenced by Judaism and Islam, declared the use of icons to be idolatry. This led to the Emperor Leo III issuing a decree that all icons be destroyed. Opponents of the movement, the Iconodules, eventually overruled the decree, but not before many icons had been destroyed. After this, schools of icon painters developed, most notably at Mystras and on Crete. Most icons are unsigned, but a few icon painters, such as Mikhail Damaskinos, a contemporary of El Greco, did sign their work. Some of Damaskinos' icons can be seen in the museum at the former Church of Agia Ekaterini in Iraklio. Other impressive icon collections are housed at the Byzantine museums in Athens and Corfu, the neo-Byzantine museum in Zakynthos town and the Monastery of St John the Theologian on Patmos. Greece's most celebrated icon is the miracle-working icon of the Madonna in the Church of Panagia Evangelistria on Tinos. Quite often, the greatest pleasure comes from accidentally encountering an icon in a remote chapel, for in these circumstances the sense of personal discovery often heightens the appreciation of the work. Sadly many of Greece's churches and chapels are now kept locked. It seems too many light-fingered tourists regard icons as prized souvenirs. However, it is usually easy enough to find someone to open a church for you.

Icon painting continues today. Many towns and cities have an area, or a street, of icon painters' workshops. Ask a local to direct you to such a street or area. ∎

---

shape. The overall effect is of numerous icons, placed next to one another, relating a visual narrative. The church has a very high dome. In the centre is the Pantokrator, surrounded by the apostles, and the Virgin flanked by two angels.

As you continue down towards the Mitropolis, you will pass **Agios Georgios**, one of Mystras' many private chapels. Further down and above the path on the left is the **Laskaris Mansion**, a typical Byzantine house where the ground floor was used as stables and the upper floor was the residence.

The **Mitropolis** (Cathedral of Agios Dimitrios) consists of a complex of buildings enclosed by a high wall. The original church was built in the 13th century but was greatly altered in the 15th century. The church stands in an attractive courtyard surrounded by stoas and balconies. Its impressive ecclesiastical ornaments and furniture include a carved marble iconostasis, an intricately carved wooden throne and a marble slab in the floor on which is carved a two-headed eagle (symbol of Byzantium). This is located exactly on the site where Emperor Constantine XI was crowned. The church also has some fine frescoes. The adjoining **museum** houses fragments of sculpture and pottery from Mystras' churches.

Beyond the Mitropolis is the **Vrontokhion Monastery**. This was once the wealthiest monastery of Mystras, the focus of cultural activities and the burial place of the despots. Of its two churches, **Agios Theodoros** and **Aphentiko**, the latter is the most impressive, with striking frescoes.

In summer, Mystras is open every day from 8 am to 6 pm and in winter from 8 am to 3.30 pm. Admission is 1200 dr. Students from EU countries are admitted free on production of an ISIC card. Outside the lower entrance to Mystras is a *kantina* (mobile café), which sells snacks and fresh orange juice.

Places to Stay
Most people visit Mystras on a day trip from Sparta. There is limited accommodation in the village of Nea Mystras, near the site. The *Hotel Byzantion* (☎ 0731-93 309), near the central square, has singles/doubles for 6000/10,000 dr. There are domatia on the road opposite the hotel.

Getting There & Away
Frequent buses go to Mystras from Sparta (see the Getting There & Away section for Sparta). A taxi from Sparta to Mystras' lower entrance costs 1000 dr, 1500 dr to the upper entrance.

GERAKI Γεράκι
Geraki (Ye**ra**kee), 40km east of Sparta, is an unsung Mystras. While the latter is on almost everyone's list of 'must sees' in the Peloponnese, the medieval city of Geraki crumbles in obscurity on a remote hillside. The modern village of Geraki was built over the site of ancient Geronthrai, which dates back to Mycenaean times. Fragments of the walls remain to the north and east of the village in an open site. The ruins of the medieval city lie 4km to the east, about 50 minutes walk along a road from the modern village.

The city was one of the 12 Frankish fiefs of the Peloponnese. The fortress was built by Jean de Nivelet in 1245 but was ceded to the Byzantines in 1262. It is reached by a steep path and has breathtaking views of the surrounding plain and mountains. The site is open and unattended but its 15 small chapels are locked. Ask in the village taverna for the caretaker who will give you the keys to the most important churches. People in the village square can suggest domatia.

Getting There & Away
If you are driving, the road to Geraki is signposted to the right a little way out of Sparta along the Tripolis road. Several buses

a day come from Sparta to the modern village (45 minutes, 700 dr).

GEFYRA & MONEMVASIA
Γέφυρα & Μονεμβασία
• *pop 900* • *postcode 230 70* • *area code* ☎ *0732*
Monemvasia (Monemvas**ee**a), 99km southeast of Sparta, is the Gilbratar of Greece – a massive rock rising dramatically from the sea just off the east coast. It is reached by a causeway from the mainland village of Gefyra (also called Nea Monemvasia). In summer, Gefyra and Monemvasia brim with tourists, but the extraordinary impact of the first encounter with the medieval town of Monemvasia – and the delights of exploring it – override the effects of mass tourism. The poet Yiannis Ritsos, who was born and lived for many years in Monemvasia, wrote of it: 'This scenery is as harsh as silence'.

From Gefyra, Monemvasia is a huge rock topped by a fortress with a few scattered buildings at sea level. But cross the causeway and follow the road that curves around the side of the rock and you will come to a narrow tunnel in a massive fortifying wall. The tunnel is L-shaped so you cannot see the other side. You emerge into the magical town of Monemvasia, concealed until that moment. Unlike Mystras, Monemvasia's houses are inhabited, mostly by weekenders from Athens.

History
The island was part of the mainland until it was separated by a devastating earthquake in 375 AD. Its name means 'single entry' *(moni* – single, *emvasia* – entry), as there is only one way to the medieval town. During the 6th century, barbarian incursions forced the inhabitants of the surrounding area to retreat to this natural rock fortress. By the 13th century, it had become the principal commercial centre of Byzantine Morea – complementary to Mystras, the spiritual centre. It was famous throughout Europe for its highly praised Malvasia (also called Malmsey) wine.

Later came a succession of invasions from Franks, Venetians and Turks. During the War of Independence, its Turkish inhabitants were massacred on their surrender following a three-month siege.

Orientation & Information

All the practicalities are located in Gefyra. The main street is 23 Iouliou, which runs south around the coast from the causeway, while Spartis runs north up the coast and becomes the road to Molai. Malvasia Travel, just up from the causeway on Spartis, acts as the bus stop. The post office and the National Bank of Greece are opposite. The OTE is at the top of 28 Oktovriou, which runs inland off 23 Iouliou.

There is no tourist office and no tourist police. Malvasia Travel (☎ 61 752; fax 61 432) can arrange accommodation and rents out cars and motorcycles.

Medieval Town

The narrow, cobbled main street is lined with souvenir shops and tavernas, flanked by winding stairways which weave between a complex network of stone houses with walled gardens and courtyards. The main street leads to the central square and the **Cathedral of Christ in Chains**, dating from the 13th century. Opposite is the **Church of Agios Pavlos**, built in 956 and now a small **museum**. Above it is the **Church of Mirtidiotissa**, virtually in ruins, but still with a small altar and a defiantly flickering candle. Overlooking the sea is the recently restored, whitewashed 16th-century **Church of Panagia Hrysaphitissa**.

The **fortress** and the upper town are reached up the signposted steps to the left, shortly after entering the old town. The upper town is now a vast and fascinating jumbled ruin, except for the **Church of Agia Sophia**, which perches on the edge of a sheer cliff.

Places to Stay – bottom end

Camping Paradise (☎ 61 680), on the coast 3.5km south of Gefyra, is a pleasant, well-shaded camping ground. It's right next to a beach and has its own minimarket, bar and disco.

There is no budget accommodation in Monemvasia, so if your budget is tight you'll have to stay in Gefyra. The basic E-class *Hotel Akrogiali* (☎ 61 360), facing the National Bank of Greece on Spartis, has the cheapest rooms – singles/doubles with shower for 5500/8000 dr. The C-class *Hotel Minoa* (☎ 61 224/398/209), up from the causeway, has large well-furnished singles/doubles for 8000/10,000 dr.

The *Hotel Glyfada* (☎ 61 719), by the sea on the northern edge of town, has spacious doubles/triples with bathroom, refrigerator, cutlery and crockery for 9000/11,000 dr.

Places to Stay – middle & top end

If you've got money to spend, Monemvasia is the place to spend it. There's a range of impeccably restored traditional settlements to choose from. They include the excellent *Malvasia Hotel* (☎ 61 113/323; fax 61 722), which has rooms spread around several locations in the old town. Beautifully furnished singles/doubles/triples are 9000/13,500/17,500 dr, which includes a generous breakfast. *Byzantino* (☎ 61 254; fax 61 331) has doubles/triples for 12,500/15,500 dr and a suite for 19,300 dr.

The EOT-run traditional settlement *Kellia*, (☎ 61 520), is above the sea next to the Panagia Hrysaphitissa. Former monastery cells have been converted into delightful doubles/triples, but 17,000/26,600 dr is a bit steep – even with breakfast.

Staying in Monemvasia is a memorable experience, and the mystery of the town increases under night stars.

Places to Eat

The *Taverna Nikolas* and the *T' Agnantio Taverna* are a couple of places on 23 Iouliou in Gefyra that serve tasty, reasonably priced dishes.

As with the accommodation, the restaurants in Monemvasia are markedly more up-market.

To Kanoni, on the right of the main street, has an imaginative and extensive menu, while the *Matoula* has a great setting with a terrace overlooking the sea.

Getting There & Away
Bus Buses leave from Malvasia Travel, which also sells tickets. Some services from Monemvasia involve a change of bus in the small town of Molai, 24km to the north, but it is possible to buy a ticket to your final destination. There are four buses a day to Athens (6½ hours, 5150 dr) via Sparta (two hours, 1700 dr) and Tripolis (3½ hours, 2600 dr). There's also a daily express bus to Athens at 4.10 am (5½ hours, 3500 dr). In summer, there's one bus a day to Gythio (1½ hours, 1300 dr).

Hydrofoil In summer, there is at least one Flying Dolphin service a day to Zea Marina at Piraeus (four hours, 7920 dr), travelling via Spetses (2½ hours, 3775 dr). There are also five services a week to Leonidio (80 minutes, 3475 dr) and Hydra (three hours, 4680 dr). Buy tickets from Angelakos Travel (☎ 61 219), by the petrol station on the Monemvasia side of the causeway.

Getting Around
Car & Motorcycle These can be rented from Malvasia Travel (☎ 61 752/432) up from the bus station. The medieval town of Monemvasia is inaccessible to cars and motorcycles but parking is available outside.

NEAPOLI Νεάπολη
Neapoli (Neapolee, population 2500), 42km south of Monemvasia, lies close to the southern tip of the eastern prong of the Peloponnese. It's a fairly uninspiring town, in spite of its location on a huge horseshoe bay. The western flank of the bay is formed by the small island of Elafonisi (see below). Few travellers make it down this far, but the town is popular enough with local holiday-makers to have three hotels and domatia.

Getting There & Away
Bus There are four buses a day to Neapoli from Sparta (four hours, 2100 dr).

Ferry The F/B *Maria* leaves Neapoli for Agia Pelagia on Kythira (1¾ hours, 1600 dr) on Tuesday, Thursday and Sunday.

Hydrofoil In July and August, there are four hydrofoils a week to Kythira (20 minutes, 2845 dr). They continue to Zea Marina (five hours, 8860 dr) via Monemvasia and Spetses.

ELAFONISI Ελαφονήσι
Like Neapoli, Elafonisi sees few foreign tourists, but it's popular with Greeks who pop over from the mainland for fish lunches in summer, particularly on Sunday. Locals insist that the *barbounia* (red mullet) from the waters around here are the best you'll find. The island's main attractions, apart from the seafood, are its superb beaches – which the Greeks liken to the those of the South Seas. They're not exaggerating.

As well as fish tavernas, there are two pensions and a few domatia. There is no official camping ground.

Getting There & Away
From July to September, there are frequent caïques to Elafonisi (10 minutes, 160 dr) from the village of Viglafia, about 14km west of Neapoli. They shuttle backwards and forwards constantly from 9.30 am to 10 pm. At other times, there are infrequent boats from both Neapoli and Viglafia.

GYTHIO Γύθειο
• *pop 4600* • *postcode 232 00* • *area code* ☎ *0733*
Once the port of ancient Sparta, Gythio (**Yitheeo**) is the gateway to the Lakonian Mani. It's an attractive fishing town with a bustling waterfront of 19th-century, pastel-coloured buildings, behind which crumbling old Turkish houses clamber up a steep, wooded hill.

Orientation
Gythio is not too hard to figure out. Most things of importance to travellers are along the seafront on Akti Vasileos Pavlou. The bus station is at the northern end of the seafront, next to a small triangular park. The town's central square, Plateia Mavromihali, is halfway along the waterfront. The quay is opposite this square. Beyond it, the waterfront continues south and becomes the road to

Areopoli. A causeway leads out to Marathonisi islet at the southern edge of town.

At the time of research, a tourist office was about to open at Vasileos Georgiou 20. Vasileos Georgiou runs inland from the northern end of the seafront and becomes the road to Sparta. The tourist police (☎ 22 271) share lodgings with the regular police (☎ 22 100) on the waterfront between the bus station and Plateia Mavromihali. The post office is on Ermou, in the newer part of the town two blocks north of the bus station, and the OTE office is between the two at the corner of Herakles and Kapsali.

Marathonisi Islet

According to mythology, tranquil pine-shaded Marathonisi is ancient Cranae where Paris (prince of Troy) and Helen (wife of Menelaus) consummated the affair that sparked the Trojan Wars. The islet's 18th-century tower once belonged to the famous Mavromihalis family, the Maniot rebels involved in the assassination of Kapodistrias, Greece's first president, in Nafplio. The tower now houses a small **museum**, open 9 am to 1 pm and 3 to 9 pm, focusing on Mani history. The islet is perfect for a picnic.

Ancient Theatre

Gythio's small but well-preserved ancient theatre is next to an army camp on the northern edge of town. To get there, follow Ermou inland from the post office and turn right on to Arheou Theatrou. Most of ancient Gythio lies beneath the nearby Lakonian gulf.

Beaches

There's safe swimming off the 6km of sandy beaches which extend from the village of **Mavrovouni**, 2km south of Gythio.

Places to Stay – bottom end

There are four camping grounds near Gythio, all on the coast south of Mavrovouni on the road to Areopoli. They are *Meltemi* (☎ 22 833), *Gythion Beach* (☎ 23 441), *Mani Beach* (☎ 23 450) and *Kronos* (☎ 93 093). There are bus stops at all camping

grounds except Kronos, which is 3km from the nearest stop.

You'll find plenty of domatia on the streets running inland from Plateia Mavromihali. They include *Koutsouris Rooms to Rent* (☎ 22 321), which has singles/doubles with small kitchen and bathroom for 4000/5000 dr and a triple for 6000 dr. Guests can relax in a garden filled with citrus trees and tortoises. Walk up Tzannibi Gregoraki, turn right at the church with the clock tower, and the rooms are on the left.

The *Saga Pension* (☎ 23 220), on the seafront south of Plateia Mavromihali, has immaculate singles/doubles with bathroom for 6000/9000 dr, while the *Hotel Kranai* (☎ 24 394), just north of Plateia Mavromihali at Akti Vasileos Pavlou 17, charges 7000/11,000/14,000 dr for large singles/doubles/triples with bathroom.

Places to Stay – middle

The smart *Hotel Pantheon* (☎ 22 166; fax 22 284), Akti Vasileos Pavlou 33, has singles/doubles with air-con, colour TV and sea views for 15,000/26,500 dr.

Places to Eat

The waterfront is lined with countless fish tavernas with very similar menus. You'll find the best value at the nameless *farotaverna* next to the Hotel Kranai, which is where the locals go to eat. A big plate of calamari costs 1200 dr, and there's fresh fish by the kg. Fresh fish also features prominently on the menu at the excellent *Saga Pension Restaurant* (see Places to Stay) together with traditional taverna food.

Self-caterers can stock up at the *Kourtakis supermarket*, around the corner from the bus station on Heracles, or at the *laïki agora* on Ermou on Tuesday and Friday mornings.

Getting There & Away

Bus There are five buses a day south to Areopoli (30 minutes, 450 dr); five to Athens (5½ hours, 4150 dr) via Sparta (one hour, 750 dr); four to Kalamata, two via Sparta and two via Itilo and Limeni (40 minutes, 650 dr); two to Gerolimenas (two hours, 1000 dr); and one to the Diros caves (one hour, 650 dr). There's a daily bus to Monemvasia (1½ hours, 1250 dr) from June to September.

Ferry In summer, the F/B *Maria* operates to Kythira (2½ hours, 1535 dr) every day except Monday. On Thursday and Sunday it continues to Kastelli-Kissamos on Crete (eight hours, 4525 dr) via Antikythira (3230 dr). Rozakis Travel (☎ 22 207), on the waterfront before Plateia Mavromihali, handles tickets. The port police (☎ 22 262) are on the waterfront before the causeway.

Getting Around

Car & Motorcycle Gythio has no car-hire outlets. Motorcycles can be rented from Super Cycle Moto (☎ 24 407/001), a little way up Tzannibi Gregoraki from Plateia Mavromihali.

The Mani Η Μάνη

The region referred to as the Mani covers the central peninsula in the south of the Peloponnese. For centuries, the Maniots were a law unto themselves, renowned for their fierce independence and resentment of any attempt to govern them.

Today, the Maniots are regarded by other Greeks as independent, royalist and right-wing. But don't be deterred from visiting the region by descriptions of the Maniots as hostile, wild and hard people. Contact with the outside world and lack of feuding have mellowed them. The Maniots are as friendly and hospitable as Greeks elsewhere, despite the fierce appearance of some older people who dress like the Cretans and offer fiery raki as a gesture of hospitality. But the music and dance of the two differ.

The Mani is generally divided into the Messinian Mani (also called the outer Mani) and the Lakonian (or inner) Mani. The Messinian Mani starts south-east of Kalamata and runs south between the coast and the Taÿgetos mountains, while the Lakonian Mani covers the rest of the peninsula south

of Itilo. Such was the formidable reputation of the inhabitants of the remote inner Mani that foreign occupiers thought they were best left alone.

The Mani has no significant ancient sites, but it well compensates with medieval and later remains, bizarre tower settlements – particularly in the inner Mani – and some magnificent churches, all enhanced by the distant presence of the towering peaks of the Taÿgetos mountains. The Diros caves in the south are another major attraction.

History

The people of the Mani regard themselves as direct descendants of the Spartans. After the decline of Sparta, citizens loyal to the principles of Lycurgus, founder of Sparta's constitution, chose to withdraw to the mountains rather than serve under foreign masters. Later, refugees from occupying powers joined these people who became known as Maniots, from the Greek word *mania*.

The Maniots claim they are the only Greeks not to have succumbed to foreign invasions. This may be somewhat exaggerated but the Maniots have always enjoyed a certain autonomy and a distinctive lifestyle. Until independence, the Maniots lived in clans led by chieftains. Fertile land was so scarce that it was fiercely fought over. Blood feuds were a way of life and families constructed towers as hide-outs.

The Turks failed to subdue the Maniots, who eagerly participated in the War of Independence. But, after 1834, although reluctant to relinquish their independence, they became part of the new kingdom.

For background reading, try *Mani* by Patrick Leigh Fermor, *Deep into Mani* by Eliopoulis & Greenhold and *The Architecture of Mani* by Ioannis Saïtis.

LAKONIAN MANI

Grey rock, mottled with defiant clumps of green scrub and the occasional stunted olive or cypress tree characterises the bleak mountains of inner Mani. The lower slopes are terraced wherever this unyielding soil has been cultivated. A curious anomaly is the profusion of wildflowers which mantle the valleys in spring, exhibiting nature's resilience by sprouting from the rocks.

The indented coast's sheer cliffs plunge into the sea and rocky outcrops shelter pebbled beaches. This wild and barren landscape is broken only by austere and imposing stone towers, mostly abandoned, but still standing sentinel over the region. Restoration of Maniot buildings is increasing and many refugee Albanians, who are fine stonemasons, have been engaged on these projects.

To explore the Lakonian Mani, head from Gythio to Areopoli and then south to Gerolimenas, loop round and return to Areopoli via Kotronas. You can then continue north from Areopoli to Itilo and continue to the Messinian Mani.

Areopoli Αρεόπολη
• *pop 980* • *postcode 230 62* • *area code* ☎ *0733*
Areopoli (Areopolee), capital of the Mani, is aptly named after Ares, the god of war. Dominating the central square is a statue of Petrobey Mavromihalis, who proclaimed the Maniot insurrection against the Turks. Konstantinos and Georgos Mavromihalis, who assassinated Kapodistrias, belonged to the same family. The town retains many other reminders of its rumbustious past.

In the narrow, cobbled streets of the old town, grim tower houses stand proudly vigilant. Stroll around during siesta time when the heat and silence make it especially evocative.

Also have a look at the unusual reliefs above the doors of the Church of Taxiarhes, on Kapetan Matapan, which depict feuding archangels and signs of the zodiac.

Orientation & Information The bus stop is in front of Nicola's Corner Taverna on Plateia Athanaton, the central square. The post office and OTE are on the corner of the square and Kapetan Matapan, the main thoroughfare through the old town that leads downhill of the square. The National Bank of Greece is on P Mavromihali – turn right at the first church on Kapetan Matapan and the bank is on the left after 150m. It's open normal banking hours in July and August, and on Tuesday and Thursday from 9 am to noon for the rest of the year. There is no tourist office and no tourist police.

Places to Stay – bottom end The cheapest rooms belong to *Petros Bathrellos* (☎ 51 205), who rents out three rooms above his taverna, Barbar Petros, 70m down Kapetan Matapan from the square. He charges 4000/6000/8000 dr for basic singles/doubles/triples with shared facilities.

Keep going down Kapetan Matapan and you'll see a sign at the Church of Taxiarhes pointing to *Tsimova Rooms* (☎ 51 301), housed in a beautiful old renovated tower behind the church. Owner George Versakos has cosy rooms, filled with ornaments, family photos and icons, for 6000/10,000 dr, and a two-room apartment with kitchen for 15,000 dr. George will show you around his minimuseum of daggers, pistols, a stele and ancient coins.

The *Hotel Kouris* (☎ 51 340), on the main square, has spotless singles/doubles with bathroom for 7500/9500 dr.

Places to Stay – middle The *Pyrgos Kapetanakas* (☎ 51 233), signposted to the right at the bottom end of Kapetan Matapan, is another EOT-run traditional tower settlement. It is austerely authentic, in keeping with the spirit of the Mani. Singles/doubles/triples with shared bathroom are 9400/13,300/16,700 dr, which includes breakfast.

Places to Stay – top end The most stylish rooms are at *Londas Pension* (☎ 51 360; fax 51 012), a 200-year-old tower signposted to the right off Kapetan Matapan at the Church of Taxiarhes. The rooms have white-washed stone walls and beamed ceilings. Doubles/triples are 17,000/23,000 dr, including breakfast.

Places to Eat The most popular place is *Nicola's Corner Taverna*, open all day on the central square. It has a good choice of tasty Greek staples with nothing over 1500 dr. *Barbar Petros* on Kapetan Matapan (see Places to Stay) is primarily a psistaria serving grilled steak and chops, but it also has daily specials like eggplant and potato pie – 1000 dr for an enormous serving.

There's a small *supermarket* near the square on Kapetan Matapan.

Getting There & Away

The bus office (☎ 51 229) is inside Nicola's Corner Taverna. There are five buses a day to Gythio (30 minutes, 450 dr); three to Itilo (20 minutes, 310 dr) via Limeni; two to Gerolimenas (30 minutes, 400 dr); two to the Diros caves (15 minutes, 210 dr); one to Lagia (40 minutes, 650 dr) via Kotronas; and three a week (on Monday, Wednesday and Friday) to Vathia (40 minutes, 700 dr).

Diros Caves Σπήλαιο Διρού

These extraordinary caves are 11km south of Areopoli, near the village of Pyrgos Dirou – notable for its towers.

The natural entrance to the caves is on the beach and some experts believe they may extend as far north as Sparta. The caves were inhabited in Neolithic times, but were abandoned after an earthquake. They were rediscovered in 1895, and systematic exploration began in 1949.

The caves are famous for their stalactites and stalagmites, which have fittingly poetic names such as the Palm Forest, Crystal Lily and the Three Wise Men.

Unfortunately, the guided tour through the caves is a huge disappointment. It covers only the lake section, and bypasses the dry section that features the most spectacular formations. Tourists are punted through the caves at breakneck speed without a word of commentary. Our guide managed the course in a shade under 20 minutes. It's not good enough to justify an admission charge of 3500 dr.

The caves are open daily from 8 am to 5.30 pm from June to September, and from 8 am to 2.30 pm from October to May.

Places to Stay & Eat

Most people visit the caves on day trips from Areopoli or Gythio, but there is accommodation closer to the caves. The nearest hotel is the D-class *To Panorama* (☎ 0733-52 280), 1km from the caves on the right coming from Pyrgos Dirou. Comfortable singles/doubles with private bathroom are 5000/7000 dr. *Kambinara Domatia & Restaurant* (☎ 0733-52 256), 2km from the caves on the right, has tidy singles/doubles with shared bathroom for 4000/6000 dr. The restaurant has good grilled food.

Pyrgos Dirou to Gerolimenas

Πύργος Διρού **to** Γερολιμένας

Journeying south down Mani's west coast from Pyrgos Dirou to Gerolimenas, the barren mountain landscape is broken only by deserted settlements with mighty towers. From one of these settlements, Stavri, reached by turning right (west) from the main road, you can trek in 40 to 50 minutes over rough terrain to the **Castle of Mina**, on the Tigani promontory. This Frankish castle was built by William II de Villehardouin in 1248. Back on the main road, **Kita**, with a plethora of towers, is worth a stroll. Although 17km separates Pyrgos Dirou and Gerolimenas, there is only one place to stay in between: the *Tsitsiris Castle Guest House* (☎ 0733-56 297) at Stavri. The 'castle' is a wonderfully restored tower house on the edge of the village. It has air-con singles/doubles with bathroom for 12,700/17,000 dr, which includes a generous buffet breakfast. At night, you'll find delicious home-cooked meals in the restaurant at standard taverna prices. The guesthouse is signposted off the main road 4km north of Gerolimenas.

Gerolimenas Γερολιμένας

• *pop 100* • *postcode 230 71* • *area code* ☎ *0733*

Gerolimenas (Yerolimenas) is a tranquil fishing village built around a small, sheltered bay at the south-western tip of the peninsula. The village has a post office with a currency-exchange service (open Monday to Friday from 8 am to 2 pm), but no bank.

Walk to Ano Boulari & Kato Boulari From the village, walk back along the road towards Pyrgos Dirou. About 100m beyond the Hotel Akrogiali, a road off to the right (Mantoivaloi) leads 2km to the almost deserted village of Ano (upper) Boulari. The **Church of Agios Stratigos** has some well-preserved frescoes mostly dating from the 12th century. Further on at the village of Kato (lower) Boulari, the **Anemodoura Tower**, built around 1600, is thought to be one of the earliest Maniot towers.

Places to Stay & Eat The best rooms in town are at the *Hotel Akrogiali* (☎ 54 204), overlooking the beach on the way into town. It charges 5000/7500 dr for singles/doubles with bathroom, or 6000/8500 dr with aircon. The owners also rent out four-person apartments nearby for 15,000 dr.

The *Hotel Akrotenaritis* (☎ 54 205), by the bus stop, looks very shoddy by comparison. It does, however, have reasonable singles/doubles in another building right next door for 4000/8000 dr.

Both hotels have restaurants. There is a so-called *supermarket* on the road behind the Hotel Akrogiali.

Getting There & Away There are buses to Sparta (three hours, 1700 dr); to Gythio (two hours, 1000 dr); and to Areopoli (30 minutes, 400 dr).

Gerolimenas to Porto Kagio
Γερολιμένας **to** Πόρτο Κάγιο
South of Gerolimenas, the road continues 4km to the small village of Alika, where it divides. One road leads east to Lagia and the other goes south to Vathia and Porto Kagio. The southern road follows the coast, passing pebbly beaches. It then climbs steeply inland to **Vathia** (**Va**theea), the most dramatic of all the traditional Mani villages, comprising a cluster of closely packed tower houses perched on a rocky spur.

Nine km south of Alika, a turn-off to the right leads to two sandy beaches at Marmari, while the main road cuts across the peninsula

to the tiny east-coast fishing village of **Porto Kagio** on the shore of an almost circular bay.

Places to Stay & Eat The only accommodation at Vathia is at the traditional settlement of *Vathia Towers* (☎ 0733-55 244). Accommodation is spread around six of the towers. Singles/doubles are 14,000/17,900 dr, including breakfast. In spite of these prices, the place is often full and bookings are recommended.

Porto Kagio has one place to stay, the *Akroteri Domatia* (☎ 0733-21 103). It has large doubles with balcony and bathroom from 10,000 to 13,000 dr a double, depending on size and position. The three *tavernas* all specialise in fish dishes.

Lagia to Kotronas Λάγια **to** Κότρωνας
Approached from Alika, Lagia, at 400m above sea level, is formidable. It was once the chief town of the south-eastern Mani. Now, the village is permeated with a strange aura of insularity and brooding, as if the ghosts of old Mani still linger in its deserted towers.

From Lagia, the road winds down with spectacular views of the little fishing harbour of **Agios Kyprianos** – a short diversion from the main road. The next village is **Kokala**, busy, friendly and with two pebbled beaches. The bus stop is in front of Synantisi Taverna.

After Kokala, the road climbs again. After 4km, there are more beaches at the sprawling village of **Nyfi**. A turn-off to the right leads to the sheltered beach of **Alipa**. Continuing north, a turn-off beyond Flomochori descends to **Kotronas**.

Places to Stay & Eat Lagia has no accommodation but there are several possibilities in Kokala. The *Pension Kokala* (☎ 0733-21 107), on the main street, has comfortable doubles with bathroom for 6000 dr.

You'll see signs promoting *To Kastro Pension* (☎ 0733-21 090), formerly *Papa's Rooms*, all the way down the east coast. The place is perched high above the village, reached by a steep concrete road leading up the hill next to the *Hotel Soleteri*. The rooms are owned by jovial Papageorgis, the local priest. He has doubles priced from 10,000 dr, but Papa, like most Greek owners, is not averse to bargaining. The *Marathos Taverna*, on the beach, has good food and a great setting.

At Nyfi, *Pension Nifi* (☎ 21 242) has pleasant doubles with shared bathroom for 4500 dr. The pension doesn't have a sign, but it's a distinctive cream and brown building, above a taverna on the right at the beginning of the village.

Kotronas Κοτρώνας
* *pop 600* • *area code* ☎ *0733*

Around Kotronas (Kotronas) the barrenness of the Mani gradually gives way to relative lushness, with olive groves and cypress trees. Kotronas bustles compared to the Mani's half-deserted tower villages. Its main thoroughfare leads to the waterfront where the bus turns around. To the left is a bay with a small, sandy beach.

The post office is on the right of the main thoroughfare as you go towards the sea. The islet off the coast is linked by a causeway. Walk inland along the main thoroughfare and turn left at the fork. Take the first left and walk to a narrow road, which soon degenerates into a path, leading to the causeway. On the island are ruins surrounding a small well-kept church.

Places to Stay & Eat Accommodation is a problem – unless the *Adelfia Pension* (☎ 21 209), on the right of the main road as you head down towards the sea, is open. It wasn't at the time of research. The other budget option is at grotty *Kotroni Domatia* (☎ 21 269), above a taverna overlooking the beach. Singles/doubles with shared bathroom are 3000/5000 dr.

The *Kotronas Bay Bungalows* (☎ 21 340; fax 21 402) are 500m east of the village on the road that skirts the bay. They can accommodate up to four people and cost 25,000 dr a day. They come with fully-equipped kitchens, but there is also the co-owned *To Timoniera* restaurant.

There are two *minimarkets* and a *bakery* on the main street.

Limeni Λιμένι
The tiny village of Limeni is 3km north of Areopoli on the southern flank of beautiful Limeni bay. There are spectacular views over the bay to Itilo from *Limeni Village Bungalows* (☎ 0733-51 111), a complex of replica Maniot towers on the cliff top overlooking the village. Singles/doubles are 11,000/13,000 dr and the facilities include a pool, bar and restaurant. The village proper has domatia and a taverna.

Itilo & Nea Itilo Οίτυλο & Νέο Οίτυλο
* *pop 550* • *postcode 230 62* • *area code* ☎ *0733*

Itilo (**Iteelo**), 11km north of Areopoli, was the medieval capital of the Mani. To travel between Lakonian and Messinian Mani, you must change buses at Itilo.

The village is now a crumbling and tranquil backwater, severed by a ravine which was traditionally regarded as the border between outer and inner Mani. Above the ravine is the massive 17th-century **Castle of Kelefa** from which the Turks attempted to constrain the Maniots. You can't miss it on a hill above the road from Neo Itilo. Nearby, the **Monastery of Dekoulou** has colourful frescoes in its church. Neo Itilo, 4km before, lies at the back of secluded Limeni bay.

Places to Stay & Eat Apart from a few domatia down by Limeni bay in Neo Itilo, there is no budget accommodation. You'd have to be desperate to take up the offer of free camping extended by the owners of the *O Faros Fish Restaurant*, signposted off the Neo Itilo-Itilo road at the small village of Karavostassi. The restaurant is fine, but the camping area is just a patch of wasteland by the road.

The plush C-class *Hotel Itilo* (☎ 59 222), right on the beach in Neo Itilo, has singles/doubles for 11,500/17,000 dr including breakfast. *Xenonas Studios* (☎ 59 388), on the main road just south of Itilo, has superb views from its well-equipped studio

PELOPONNESE

rooms. Doubles/triples with bathroom and breakfast facilities are 15,000/17,000 dr.

Getting There & Away There are three buses a day to Areopoli (30 minutes, 310 dr) and three to Kalamata (two hours, 1250 dr). Areopoli-Itilo buses go via Neo Itilo and Limeni.

MESSINIAN MANI

The Messinian Mani, or outer Mani, lies to the north of its Lakonian counterpart, sandwiched between the Taÿgetos mountains and the west coast of the Mani peninsula. Kalamata lies at the northern end of the peninsula. The indented coast is scattered with superb beaches at the feet of guardian mountains. There are glorious views between the villages of Kambos and Almyro and on the ascent to Kardamyli and the village of Stavropigi. There are many camp sites along this stretch of coast, unlike the inner Mani.

Stoupa Στούπα
• *pop 730* • *postcode 240 54* • *area code* ☎ *0721*
Stoupa, 10km south of Kardamyli, has undergone a rapid transformation from fishing village to up-market resort. Tourist development remains fairly low-key; it's billed as a resort for discriminating package tourists intent on discovering the unspoilt Greece. Although not as picturesque as Kardamyli, it does have two lovely beaches. It was the founding place of the ancient kingdom of Lefktron. Like Kardamyli, Stoupa also has literary connections. Nikos Kazantzakis lived here for a time and based the protagonist of his novel *Zorba the Greek* on Alexis Zorbas, who worked as a coal-mine supervisor in Pastrova, near Stoupa.

Orientation & Information Stoupa is 1km west of the main Areopoli-Kalamata road, connected by link roads both north and south of town. Both roads lead to the larger of Stoupa's two main beaches – a glorious crescent of golden sand.

Stoupa's development has been so rapid that its amenities have yet to catch up.

Katerina's supermarket, to the south of the main beach, doubles as both the post office and the OTE. It sells stamps, accepts mail for delivery, changes money and sells phone cards.

There is no tourist office, but most tourists treat Thomeas Travel (☎ 77 689; fax 77 571) as if it were one. Manager Bob Barrow is a keen student of Mani history and a mine of information about local attractions. He can also change money, organise hire cars and advise on accommodation.

Places to Stay & Eat *Camping Delfinia* (☎ 77 318) is a nicely maintained camping ground near Kaminia beach, 2km away on the Kardamyli side of Stoupa. It has a restaurant, minimarket, playground and also apartments. *Camping Kalogria* (☎ 54 319), above Stoupa's small beach, is well kept, with shady sites, a children's playground, minimarket and bar.

Stoupa's growing band of pensions and custom-built domatia all seem to be block-booked by package-tour operators. Thomeas Travel may know of vacancies. Alternatively, you can seek out Thanasis, who you will find in a small office (more like a hole in the wall without a telephone) at the beginning of the large beach. The wacky Thanasis is the champion of independent and out-of-season travellers, renting a variety of houses in Stoupa. None are purpose-built and he doesn't let to tour groups. Reckon on paying about 8000 dr for two.

The C-class *Stoupa Hotel* (☎ 54 308/485) has doubles with bathroom and balcony for 10,500 dr. The hotel is on the southern approach road to Stoupa.

Stoupa has lots of restaurants and tavernas, none particularly cheap. The *Taverna Akrogiali* has a top location at the southern end of the beach, and good food if their fish soup (950 dr) is any guide.

Getting There & Away Stoupa is on the main Itilo-Kalamata bus route. Some buses come as far as Plateia Agias Fotineas on the southern approach to town, but most go further than the bakery at the junction of the approach road and the main road – making the bakery the best place to wait for a bus.

Kardamyli Καρδαμύλη
• *pop 350* • *postcode 240 22* • *area code ☎ 0721*

The tiny village of Kardamyli (Kardameelee) has one of the prettiest settings in the Peloponnese, nestled between the calm waters of the Messinian gulf and the highest peaks of the Taÿgetos mountains. The deep Vyros gorge, which emerges just north of town, runs straight up to the foot of Mt Taÿgetos (2404m). The gorge and surrounding areas are very popular with trekkers.

Kardamyli was one of the seven cities offered to Achilles by Agamemnon.

Orientation & Information Kardamyli is on the main Areopoli-Kalamata road. The bus stops at the central square, Plateia 25 Martiou 1821, at the northern end of the main thoroughfare. The post office is back towards Stoupa on the main street.

Kardamyli's main pebble-and-stone beach is off the road to Kalamata; turn left beyond the bridge on the northern edge of town. The road up to Old (or Upper) Kardamyli is on the right before the bridge.

Trekking Trekking has become Kardamyli's biggest drawcard. The hills behind the village are crisscrossed with an amazing network of colour-coded trails. All the accommodation places in the village will be able to supply you with a map that explains the routes. Most of the treks are strenuous. Strong footwear is essential to support your ankles on the rough ground, particularly if you venture into the boulder-strewn gorge itself. You will also need to carry plenty of drinking water. Many treks pass through the mountain village of Exohorio, perched on the edge of the Vyros gorge at an altitude of 450m. The village is also accessible by road, and it's a good place for nontrekkers to do a spot of more gentle exploration. The turn-off to Exohorio is 3km south of Kardamyli.

Places to Stay & Eat *Melitsina Camping* (☎ 73 461), by the beach on the northern side

of town, has good shady sites among the olive trees. There are plenty of domatia signs along the main road. The street down to the sea opposite the post office is the place to look. Olivia Koumounakou (☎ 73 326/623), on the left after 150m, has immaculate double *rooms* with private bathroom for 7500 dr and a communal kitchen. Opposite are the equally agreeable *apartments* of Statis Bravacos (same telephone number as Olivia's rooms), where doubles are also 7500 dr.

If you keep going down this street and turn right, you'll come to *Lela's Taverna & Rooms* (☎ 73 541). It has good doubles with bathroom for 10,000 dr, but the real attraction is the excellent restaurant with terrace seating overlooking the sea. Lela, who runs the kitchen, is the former housekeeper of author Patrick Leigh Fermor, who still lives in the village.

Anniska Apartments (☎ 73 600; fax 73 000), by the sea 200m north of Lela's, has a range of spacious, well-appointed studios and apartments, all with kitchen facilities. The studios cost 12,000 dr for two people, while the larger apartments cost 15,500 dr for three people and 21,000 dr for four.

Self-caterers will find all they need at *Kardimilis market* at the Kalamata end of town.

Getting There & Away Kardamyli is on the main bus route from Itilo to Kalamata (one hour, 650 dr).

Getting Around The Pandora souvenir shop (☎ 73 415) hires mopeds. Early birds can catch the sole bus to Exohoria at 6.15 am; most prefer to take a cab (1200 dr).

Messinia Μεσσηνία

Messinia occupies the south-western corner of the Peloponnese. Its boundaries were established in 371 BC following the defeat of Sparta by the Thebans at the Battle of Leuctra. The defeat ended more than 300 years of Spartan domination of the Peloponnese – during which Messinian exiles founded the city of Messinia in Sicily – and the Messinians were left free to develop their kingdom in the region stretching west from the Taÿgetos mountains. Their capital was Ancient Messini, about 25km north-west of Kalamata on the slopes of Mt Ithomi.

Few travellers make it to Messinia, which is a shame. Finikounda has one of the best beaches in the country, and the old Venetian towns of Koroni and Methoni are delightful little hideaways that have yet to feel the weight of package tourism.

KALAMATA Καλαμάτα
• *pop 44,000* • *postcode 241 00* • *area code* ☎ *0721*
Kalamata is Messinia's capital and the second-largest city in the Peloponnese. 'Calamitous Kalamata' aptly sums up this hapless city. The old town was almost totally destroyed by the Turks during the War of Independence and rebuilt unimaginatively by French engineers in the 1830s. On 14 September 1986, Kalamata was devastated by an earthquake which registered 6.2 on the Richter scale. Twenty people died, hundreds were injured and more than 10,000 homes were destroyed.

Orientation
The old town around the kastro is picturesque, and the waterfront along Navarinou is lively – but it's a long (3km), hot walk between the two. The main streets linking the old town with the waterfront are Faron and Aristomenous. The city centre is around Plateia Georgiou on Aristomenous.

The main bus station is on the northwestern edge of town on Artemidos, while local buses leave from Plateia 25 Martiou – the No 1 goes to the waterfront. The train station is on Frantzi, near Plateia Georgiou.

Information
EOT has a small tourist office (☎ 86 868) by the yachting marina, but it's not worth heading out there. The many 'tourist information' signs around town direct people to the tourist police (☎ 22 622), close to the port on Miaouli

opposite the Lambos supermarket. They are open Monday to Friday from 8 am to 2 pm. The regular police (☎ 23 187) are in the city centre at Aristomenous 46.

The post office is near the train station at Iatropoulou 4, and the OTE is on the northwestern side of Plateia Georgiou.

There are branches of all the major banks, including the National Bank of Greece, opposite the OTE on Aristomenous. There's another branch on the waterfront on the corner of Ariti and Navarinou. The bookshop at Faron 210 sells English-language newspapers and books. There is a laundrette near the waterfront on Mezonos.

Kastro
Looming over the town is the 13th-century kastro. Remarkably, it survived the 1986 earthquake. There are excellent views from the battlements. The kastro is the setting for an annual summer festival, which includes cultural events such as contemporary musical performances and plays.

Archaeological Museum
The Archaeological Museum of Kalamata is just north of Plateia 25 Martiou on Papazoglou. It's signposted off Ypapantis. The museum is slowly being reopened after being badly damaged in the 1986 earthquake. It's open from Tuesday to Saturday from 8 am to 2.30 pm and on Sunday from 8.30 am to 3 pm. Admission is 500 dr.

Places to Stay – bottom end
Camping Fare (☎ 29 250) is on the waterfront east of town, and can be reached by bus No 1 from Plateia 25 Martiou. *Maria's Sea and Sun Camping* (☎ 41 314) is a much better site, but it's 4km east of town. It has a minimarket, bar, restaurant and two-person bungalows. Buses to Avias (from the main bus station) can drop you close by.

The best budget place in the northern part of town is the spotless D-class *Hotel George* (☎ 27 225), close to the train station at the corner of Frantzi and Dagre. Singles/doubles with private bathroom are 5000/6000 dr. Ask for a room away from the street.

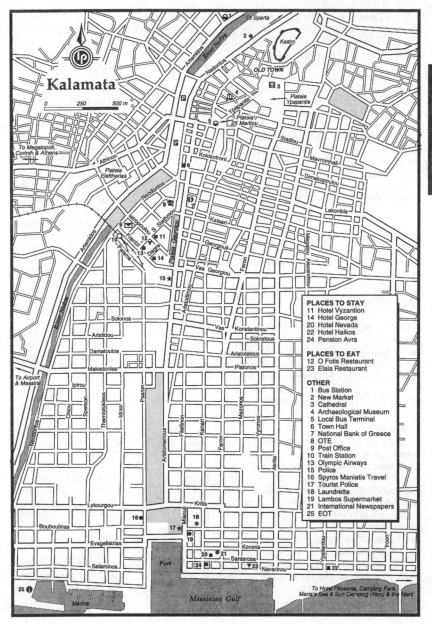

PLACES TO STAY
11 Hotel Vyzantion
14 Hotel George
20 Hotel Nevada
22 Hotel Haikos
24 Pension Avra

PLACES TO EAT
12 O Fotis Restaurant
23 Elaia Restaurant

OTHER
 1 Bus Station
 2 New Market
 3 Cathedral
 4 Archaeological Museum
 5 Local Bus Terminal
 6 Town Hall
 7 National Bank of Greece
 8 OTE
 9 Post Office
10 Train Station
13 Olympic Airways
15 Police
16 Spyros Maniatis Travel
17 Tourist Police
18 Laundrette
19 Lambos Supermarket
21 International Newspapers
25 EOT

If the George is full, try the nearby *Hotel Vyzantion* (☎ 86 824/5), nearby at the corner of Sidirodromikou Stathmou and Iatropoulou. It has singles/doubles with private bathroom for 6000/7000 dr.

There are a couple of good places down by the seafront on Santarosa, which runs parallel to Navarinou one block back from the sea. The D-class *Hotel Nevada* (☎ 82 429), Santa Rosa 9, has clean singles/doubles with shared bathroom for 4000/5500 dr. All rooms have balconies. Opposite is the homely *Pension Avra* (☎ 82 759), charging 4000/6000 dr with shared bathroom. There is a communal kitchen upstairs. Both these places are on the section of Santarosa between Faron and Kanari.

Places to Stay – middle
The waterfront east of Faron is lined with numerous C-class hotels. The *Hotel Haikos* (☎ 88 902/924), Navarinou 115, charges a typical 11,000/13,000 dr for singles/doubles with bathroom.

Places to Stay – top end
The B-class *Filoxenia Hotel* (☎ 23 166/167/168) overlooks the beach at the eastern end of Navarinou. It has a restaurant, bar, pool and disco. Mandatory half-board (breakfast and lunch or dinner) rates are 16,000/24,700 dr for singles/doubles.

Places to Eat
O Fotis Taverna, close to the train station on Sidirodromikou Stathmou, is a good traditional taverna where you can eat and drink well for 2500 dr. Navarinou is lined with countless cafés, fast-food restaurants and seafood tavernas. Among them is Kalamata's best restaurant, the *Elaia* (☎ 93 956), which occupies a beautifully restored neoclassical building at No 41. Allow around 6500 dr per person, plus drinks.

Self-caterers should visit Kalamata's large *food market* across the bridge from the bus station. Kalamata is noted for its olives, olive oil, figs, raki and mastica (a surprisingly smooth mastic-based liqueur).

Things to Buy
Kalamata silk mantillas or kerchiefs, still woven Byzantine-style by nuns at the Convent of Agios Konstantinos and Agia Eleni, are on sale at the base of the kastro.

Getting There & Away
Air There are daily flights to Athens (12,700 dr). The Olympic Airways office (☎ 22 724) is at Sidirodromikou Stathmou 17.

Bus Heading north, there are nine buses a day to Athens (4½ hours, 3950 dr) via Tripolis (two hours, 1450 dr) and Corinth (four hours, 2800 dr); and two to Patras (four hours, 3600 dr) via Pyrgos (two hours, 2100 dr). Heading west, there are nine buses a day to Koroni (1½ hours, 850 dr) and nine to Pylos (1½ hours, 850 dr). Five of the buses to Pylos continue past Methoni (two hours, 1050 dr) and three keep going to Finikoundas (2½ hours, 1200 dr). Heading east, there are two buses a day to Sparta (2½ hours, 950 dr) via Artimisia (450 dr), and two to Gythio via Kardamyli, Stoupa and Itilo.

Train Kalamata is the end of the line for both branches of the Peloponnese railway. There are four trains a day to Athens (seven hours, 2160 dr) on the inland line via Tripolis (2½ hours, 840 dr), Argos (four hours, 1260 dr) and Corinth (5¼ hours, 1650 dr). There are also two trains a day to Patras (six hours, 1500 dr) on the west-coast line via Kyparissia (two hours, 590 dr) and Pyrgos (3¼ hours, 860 dr). One train keeps going to Athens (11 hours, 2860 dr).

Ferry Ferry services from Kalamata to Crete had been suspended at the time of research. Spyros Maniatis Travel (☎ 20 704), by the port on Psaron, will know the latest developments.

Getting Around
The Airport Kalamata's airport is 10.5km west of the city. There is no airport shuttle bus. A taxi costs about 1500 dr.

Bus Local buses leave from Plateia 25 Martiou. The most useful service is bus No 1, which goes south along Aristomenous to the seafront, and then east along Navarinou to the Filoxenia Hotel. The flat fare is 110 dr.

Car & Motorcycle There are lots of places to hire cars and motorcycles from on the waterfront and on Faron. It pays to compare prices.

LANGADA PASS

The 59km road from Kalamata to Sparta is one of the most stunning routes in Greece, twisting and turning through the Taÿgetos mountains by way of the Langada pass. It's a lonely road, but in the middle of nowhere, on a hairpin bend, it can yield a surprise – an old man, his donkey tethered, patiently waiting for motorists to stop and buy honey from his stall. The highest point of the pass is 1524m, after which it begins descending through the **Langada gorge** to the village of **Trypi**. To the north of this gorge is where the ancient Spartans threw babies too weak or deformed to become good soldiers. The *Hotel Keadas* (☎ 0731-98 222) in Trypi has singles/doubles for 4500/7500 dr.

You can travel this route by bus, but most services along this route involve a change of bus in Artimisia. Drivers and hikers will find some great picnic areas on the Kalamata side of the pass.

KORONI Κορώνη
• *pop 1420* • *postcode 240 04* • *area code* ☎ *0725*

Koroni (Koronee) is a delightful old Venetian town on the coast 43km south-west of Kalamata. Its narrow streets lead up to the old castle, most of which is taken up by the **Timios Prodromos Convent**. The small promontory beyond the castle is a tranquil place for a stroll with lovely views over the Messinian gulf to the Taÿgetos mountains. Koroni's main attraction is **Zaga beach**, a long sweep of golden sand just south of the town.

Orientation & Information

Buses will drop you in the main square outside the Church of Agios Dimitrios, one block back from the harbour. There is no tourist office, but you'll find all the information you need on the large map of town on the church wall. It shows the location of the post office, OTE and both banks, all of which are nearby. There are no tourist police. The main street runs east from the square, one block back from the sea.

It takes about 20 minutes to walk to Zaga beach. To get there, take the road that leads up to the castle from above the square; turn right at the top of the hill and follow the road that curves uphill around the castle. You'll see a sign to the beach on the left after 500m.

Places to Stay

Camping Koroni (☎ 22 119) is a good camping ground with a restaurant, bar, shop, pool, kitchen and wash room. It's just north of town on the road from Kalamata. Buses stop outside.

Koroni does not have a lot of accommodation. Most of the rooms are spread around a cluster of domatia by the sea at the eastern end of the main street. Expect to pay around 5000/7000 dr for singles/doubles. George, the amiable Greek-American owner of the popular Symposium restaurant on the main street, has rooms above the restaurant at the *Koroni Pension* (☎ 22 385/448). It has clean rooms with bathroom for 7000/8000 dr and there's a communal kitchen. At the time of research, George was about to open a new hotel on the coast road that runs south-west from town overlooking Zaga beach. Also out this way, about 3km south-west of town, is the *Hotel de la Plage* (☎ 22 401) with singles/doubles for 10,000/13,000 dr. It's normally booked out by tour groups. There are more domatia at the beginning of Zaga beach.

Places to Eat

The *Symposium* (see Places to Stay above), on the main street, is about as traveller-friendly as you could ever want a restaurant to be. Years of New York living have taught George all about keeping the customer satisfied. He has seafood and grills as well as a daily selection of taverna staples for around

1200 dr. Vegetarians will find at least six dishes to choose from.

Locals prefer to sip their coffee at the cafés along the seafront, where you'll find a couple of more expensive seafood restaurants.

Getting There & Away

There are nine buses a day to Kalamata (1½ hours, 750 dr) and two to Finikounda.

FINIKOUNDA Φοινικούντα

• *pop 650* • *postcode 240 06* • *area code ☎ 0723*

The fishing village of Finikounda, midway between Koroni and Methoni, is a popular place for backpackers to hang out. The attraction is the string of fine beaches that stretch either side of the village. The area has a reputation for good windsurfing. There are plenty of places hiring out windsurfers and offering lessons.

Finikounda has spread steadily along the beach over the years. All the shops and facilities are in the old village around the port. The bus stop is outside the Hotel Finikountas, 100m from the port on the way to Methoni.

Places to Stay

Most people head to one of the two camp sites. *Camping Ammos* (☎ 71 262) is 3km west of Finikounda off the road to Methoni, and *Camping Loutsa Beach* (☎ 71 169) is 2km east of town off the road to Koroni. Both are by the beach and have windsurfers and water-sports equipment as well as the usual facilities.

There are a few domatia in the village and a growing band of mid-range hotels. The *Hotel Finikountas* (☎ 71 308) has singles/doubles for 11,000/13,000 dr with breakfast. You'll find similar prices at the *Hotel Korakakis Beach* at the eastern end of the beach. The best rooms are at the *Hotel Porto Finissia* (☎ 71 457; fax 71 458), which charges 15,000/17,000 dr with breakfast.

Getting There & Away

Three buses a day go to Kalamata (two hours, 1000 dr) via Methoni (30 minutes, 280 dr) and Pylos; and two a day go to

Koroni. If the lousy bus service tempts you to take a taxi, reckon on about 2000 dr to Methoni and 2500 dr to Koroni.

METHONI Μεθώνη

• *pop 1200* • *postcode 240 06* • *area code ☎ 0723*

Methoni (Methonee), 12km south of Pylos, was another of the seven cities offered to Achilles by Agamemnon. Homer described it as 'rich in vines'. Today, it's a pretty seaside town, with a sandy beach that's crowded in summer, and a magnificent 13th-century fortress. This vast fortification is built on a promontory south of the modern town, surrounded on three sides by the sea and separated from the mainland by a moat. The medieval port town, which stood within the fortress walls, was the Venetians' first and longest-held possession in the Peloponnese, and a stopover point for pilgrims en route to the Holy Land. In medieval times, the twin fortresses of Methoni and Koroni were known as 'the Eyes of the Serene Republic'.

Orientation & Information

The road from Pylos forks on the edge of town to create Methoni's two main streets, which then run parallel through town 100m apart to the fortress. Coming from Pylos, the fork to the right is the main shopping street. It has shops, a supermarket and a branch of the National Bank of Greece. The left fork leads directly to the fortress car park, passing the post office on the way. Turn left at the fortress end of either street to get to Methoni beach. The small square by the beach is surrounded by fairly characterless C-class hotels and several seafood restaurants.

There is no tourist office and no tourist police. The regular police (☎ 22 316) are signposted near the post office.

Fortress

This splendid fortress, a supreme example of military architecture, is vast and romantic. It's easy to spend half a day wandering around. Within the walls are a Turkish bath, a cathedral, houses, a cistern, parapets and underground passages. See how many Lion of St Mark insignias you can spot. A short causeway leads from the fortress to the diminutive octagonal Turkish castle on an adjacent islet. Bring a torch to explore the interior. The site is open Monday to Saturday from 8 am to 7 pm and on Sunday from 8 am to 6 pm. Admission is free.

Boat Trips
From June to September, the managers of the Hotel Albatros (see below) operate daily trips around the islands south of Methoni on the cruiser *Clea*. The trips last from 9 am to 5 pm and cost 3000 dr.

Places to Stay – bottom end
Camping Methoni (☎ 31 228) has a good location right behind the beach, but could use a few shade trees. You'll see several signs for domatia in the streets near the fortress, including those of *Dimitrios Tsonis* (☎ 31 640/588), above Cafeteria George at the fortress end of the main shopping street. He has spotless doubles/triples for 6000/7000 dr, with use of a communal kitchen. Family apartments are also available for 15,000 dr. The *Hotel Dionysos* (☎ 31 317), on the same street, has singles/doubles for 5000/7000 dr.

Places to Stay – middle
The best place is the friendly *Hotel Albatros* (☎ 31 160; fax 31 114), next to the post office. It has comfortable air-con doubles with bathroom, refrigerator and balcony for 9000/13,000 dr. Breakfast costs an extra 1000 dr a head. The C-class *Hotel Castello* (☎ 31 300/280), facing the fortress, has beautifully furnished singles/doubles with breakfast for 13,000/15,000 dr. The hotel is closed in August.

Places to Eat
You'll find better value away from the restaurants on the beachside square. The *Restaurant Oinouses*, 150m along the beach, serves tasty food at more reasonable prices. In town, the *Restaurant Kali Karthia*, on the shopping street, has an interesting menu with main courses from 1200 to 2000 dr. The

Restaurant Klimitaria, behind the post office, is recommended by other travellers.

Getting There & Away
Buses leave from the fork at the Pylos end of town where the two main streets meet. You'll find a timetable pinned to the door of the newsagent on the left 100m towards Pylos. There are seven buses a day to Kalamata (1½ hours, 850 dr), seven to Pylos (15 minutes, 210 dr) and three to Finikounda (30 minutes, 360 dr). There are no direct buses to Koroni – change at Finikounda and keep your fingers crossed.

PYLOS Πύλος
• *pop 2500* • *postcode 240 01* • *area code* ☎ *0723*
Pylos (**Pilos**), on the coast 51km south-west of Kalamata, presides over the southern end of an immense bay. On this bay on 20 October 1827, the British, French and Russian fleets, under the command of Admiral Codrington, fired at point-blank range on Ibrahim Pasha's combined Turkish, Egyptian and Tunisian fleet, sinking 53 ships and killing 6000 men, with negligible losses on the Allies' side.

It was known as the Battle of Navarino (the town's former name) and was decisive in the War of Independence, but it was not meant to have been a battle at all. The Allied fleet wanted to achieve no more than to persuade Ibrahim Pasha and his fleet to leave, but things got out of hand. George IV, on hearing the news, described it as a 'deplorable misunderstanding'.

With its huge natural harbour almost enclosed by the Sfaktiria islet, a delightful tree-shaded central square, two castles and surrounding pine-covered hills, Pylos is one of the most picturesque towns in the Peloponnese.

Orientation & Information
Everything of importance is within a few minutes' walk of the central square, Plateia Trion Navarhon, down by the seafront. The bus station is on the inland side of the square. The post office is on Nileos, which runs uphill from the bus station towards the

PELOPONNESE

Arviniti Hotel. The National Bank of Greece and the police station (☎ 22 316) are also on the square. There is no tourist office. The main Kalamata-Methoni road runs around the square.

Castles

Pylos has castles at each side of the bay. **Paleokastro** is 6km north of Pylos at the other side of the bay, but it's in such a bad state that it's hardly worth visiting. **Neo Kastro** is right on the southern edge of town and in good nick. It was used as a prison until this century. Within its walls are a citadel, a mosque converted into a church and a courtyard surrounded by dungeons. The castle is open daily, except Monday, from 8.30 am to 3 pm. Admission is 800 dr. The road to Methoni from the central square goes past the castle.

Boat Tours

You can ask around the waterfront for fishers to take you around the Bay of Navarino and the island of Sfaktiria. The price will depend on the number of passengers, but reckon on about 3000 dr each. On the trip around the island, stops can be made at memorials to admirals of the Allied ships. Boats may pause so you can see wrecks of sunken Turkish ships, discernible in the clear waters.

Places to Stay

The nearest camping ground is *Navarino Beach Camping* (☎ 22 761), 8km north of Pylos on Gialova beach. Take a Kyparissia bus from Pylos.

There are several domatia on the approach road from Kalamata. Look for signs. The D-class *Hotel Navarino* (☎ 22 564), on the waterfront south of Plateia Trion Navarhon, has singles/doubles with shared bathroom for 4000/5500 dr. The hotel is open only from May to October.

The C-class *Hotel Galaxy* (☎ 22 780), right on the square, charges 8750/12,500 dr for rather run-down singles/doubles with bathroom. The C-class *Arvaniti Hotel* (☎ 23 050/341), on Nileos beyond the post office,

is a better choice with spacious rooms for 8800/11,600 dr with breakfast.

Places to Eat

Ta Adelfia, below the Hotel Navarino, is a good little taverna with outdoor seating overlooking the bay. It turns out a tasty plate of stuffed tomatoes for 800 dr or moussaka for 1000 dr. *Johnny's Fast Food*, on the main square by the bus station, has cheap eats and cheap cold beer.

There are *supermarkets*, *fruit and vegetable stalls*, a *baker* and *psistaria* on lively Ipiskoupou, which is up the steps leading off the northern side of the square.

Getting There & Away

There are nine buses a day to Kalamata (1½ hours, 850 dr); five to Kyparissia (two hours, 1000 dr), via Nestor's Palace (30 minutes, 340 dr) and Hora (35 minutes); five to Methoni (20 minutes, 210 dr); three to Finikounda (45 minutes) and two to Athens (seven hours, 4800 dr) via Tripolis (three hours, 2250 dr).

AROUND PYLOS
Nestor's Palace

This is supposedly Homer's 'sandy Pylos' where Telemachos (with Athena disguised as Mentor) was warmly welcomed when he came to ask of the wise old King Nestor the whereabouts of his long-lost father, Odysseus, King of Ithaca.

The palace, originally a two-storey building, is the best preserved of all Mycenaean palaces. Its walls stand 1m high, giving a good idea of the layout of a Mycenaean palace complex. The main palace, in the middle, was a vast building of many rooms. The largest, the **throne room**, was where the king dealt with state business. In the centre was a large, circular hearth surrounded by four ornate columns which supported a 1st-floor balcony. Some of the fine frescoes discovered here are in the museum in the nearby village of Hora (see the following section). Rooms surrounding the throne room include the sentry box, pantry, waiting room, a vestibule and, most fascinating, a bathroom with a terracotta tub still in place.

The most important finds were about 1200 Linear B script tablets, the first discovered on the mainland. Some are in Hora's museum. The site was excavated later than the other Mycenaean sites, between 1952 and 1965. An excellent guidebook by Carl Blegen, who led the excavations, is sold at the site for 500 dr.

Nestor's Palace is 17km north of modern Pylos. It is open daily from 8.30 am to 3 pm, Sunday from 9.30 am to 2.30 pm. Admission is 500 dr.

Hora Χώρα

Hora's fascinating little **archaeological museum**, 3km north-east of Nestor's Palace, houses finds from the site and other Mycenaean artefacts from Messinia. The prize pieces are the frescoes from the throne rooms at Nestor's Palace. The museum is open Monday, Wednesday and Saturday from 8.45 am to 3 pm and Sunday from 8.30 am to 3 pm. Admission is 500 dr.

Getting There & Away

Buses from Pylos to Kyparissia stop at Nestor's Palace and Hora.

Elia Ηλία

The western prefecture of Elia is home to some of the best farming country in Greece. The main agricultural areas are along the broad valley of the River Alfios, the 'Sacred Alph' of Samuel Taylor Coleridge's *Kubla Khan*, and in the north-west around Gastouni and Andravida. The rich alluvial flats around here are watered by the River Pinios, which has been dammed upstream to create Lake Pinios, the largest water storage facility in the Peloponnese.

Ancient Elia took its name from the mythical King Helios. Its capital was the city of Elis, now a forgotten ruin on the road from Gastouni to Lake Pinios. When the Franks arrived, they made Andravida the capital of

their principate of Morea. Pyrgos is the dull modern capital. Most people come to Elia for just one reason: to visit ancient Olympia.

THOLOS TO PYRGOS

Heading north into Elia from Messinia, the mountains to the east give way to interrupted plains fringed by golden-sand beaches. Interspersed by pebbled shores and rocky outcrops, these beaches stretch right around Elia's coastline. The best beaches in the south are at **Tholos**, where there's a camping ground, and at **Kakovatos** and **Kouroutas**. There's seaside accommodation in each village, but most of it is in uninspiring, concrete buildings.

A sign outside Tholos points to the mountain village of **Nea Figalia**, 14km inland. From here, it's a further 21km to the tranquil site of **Ancient Figalia**, set high above the River Nedron almost at its source. Laurels, cypresses and citrus trees are clustered around the ruins of this ancient Arcadian marketplace, with towers, a small acropolis, an agora, and a temple to Dionysos, the wine pourer. A rough road leads east from Nea Figalia to Andritsena (see the Arcadia section).

PYRGOS Πύργος

• *pop 28,700* • *postcode 271 00* • *area code* ☎ *0621*

Pyrgos, 98km south-west of Patras and 24km from Olympia, is an unattractive agricultural service town with little of interest except its municipal theatre and market. It is, however, the capital of Elia prefecture and all forms of public transport pass through here, including buses and trains to Olympia. The bus and train stations are about 100m apart, the former on Manolopoulou and the latter a short walk away. If you must stay overnight, try the C-class *Hotel Olympos* (☎ 23 650), on the corner of Vasileos Pavlou and Karkavitsa; or the *Hotel Pantheon* (☎ 29 746), Themistokleous 7. Both are near the train station and charge around 8000 dr a double.

Getting There & Away

Bus There are 16 buses a day to Olympia

(30 minutes, 360 dr) on weekdays, 14 on Saturday, and nine on Sunday. There are 10 buses a day to both Athens (five hours, 4650 dr) and Patras (two hours, 1700 dr); seven a day to Lehena (one hour, 950 dr); three each to Kyllini (50 minutes, 950 dr), Tripolis (four hours, 2500 dr), Kalamata (two hours, 2100 dr) and Andritsena (1½ hours, 1450 dr).

Train There are eight trains a day north to Patras (two hours, 820 dr) and six to Athens (seven hours, 2160 dr). Three of these trains are intercity, which take five hours to Athens and Kyparissia (1¼ hours); five go to Olympia (36 minutes, 210 dr); and four go to Kalamata (3¼ hours, 860 dr). To Corinth, it's 5½ hours (2100 dr).

OLYMPIA Ολυμπία
• pop 1000 • postcode 270 65 • area code ☎ 0624
The modern village of Olympia (Olim**bee**a) panders unashamedly to the hundreds of thousands of tourists who pour through here each year on their way to ancient Olympia, half a km to the south on the road to Tripolis. The main street is lined with countless overpriced souvenir shops, coffee shops and restaurants.

Orientation
The modern village lies along the main Pyrgos-Tripolis road, known as Praxitelous Kondyli. The bus stops for Pyrgos and Tripolis are opposite one another towards the southern end of Praxitelous Kondyli, and the train station is close to the centre on Douma.

Information
Olympia's outstanding municipal tourist office (☎ 23 100/173) is by the bus stops on Praxitelous Kondyli. The staff offer a good map of the village, have comprehensive information on bus, train and ferry schedules (from Kyllini and Patras) and can change currency. It's open daily from 9 am to 9 pm from June to September. The rest of the year it opens from 11 am to 2 pm and 5 to 8 pm. The tourist police (☎ 22 550) are behind the tourist office on Spiliopoulou, which runs

parallel to Praxitelous Kondyli one block up the hill.

The post office is up the first street to the right as you walk along Praxitelous Kondyli towards ancient Olympia from the tourist office. The OTE is on Praxitelous Kondyli, beyond the turn-off for the post office. The National Bank of Greece is on the corner of Praxitelous Kondyli and Stefanopoulou.

Things to See
The **Historical Museum of the Olympic Games** is two blocks west of Praxitelous Kondyli, open Tuesday to Sunday from 8.30 am to 3 pm. Although most of the labelling is in French, the collection of commemorative stamps and literature needs little explanation. Admission is 500 dr.

Places to Stay – bottom end
Olympia has three good sites to choose from. The most central is *Camping Diana* (☎ 22 314), 250m west of the village. A sign by the National Bank of Greece points the way. *Camping Olympia* (☎ 22 745) is opposite the BP service station 1km north of town on the road to Pyrgos, and *Camping Alphios* (☎ 22 950) shares a million-dollar view with the neighbouring Hotel Europa in the hills 1km south-west of town. There are signs pointing the way at the southern end of town. All three sites have swimming pools.

The cheery *youth hostel* (☎ 22 580), Praxitelous Kondyli 18, has dorm beds for 1500 dr, including hot shower. There is no curfew.

The *Pension Achilleys* (☎ 22 562), Stefanopoulou 4, has cosy singles/doubles/ triples with shared facilities for 3000/6000/ 9000 dr. The pension is just uphill from the National Bank of Greece. Further up the hill at Stefanopoulou 9 is the *Pension Posidon* (☎ 22 567), offering spotless singles/ doubles with shared bathroom for 6800/ 9000 dr.

The D-class *Hotel Hermes* (☎ 22 577) is a friendly little family-run hotel on the right as you come into town from Pyrgos. It has singles/doubles with shared bathroom for 5000/5500 dr, or 6000/7000 dr with private bathroom. The rooms at the back look out over fields. Another option is the *Hotel Praxiteles* (☎ 22 592), next to the police station at Spiliopoulou 9, where singles/doubles with shared bathroom are 4800/6000 dr.

Place to Stay – top end
Olympia's unattractive collection of mid-range hotels are invariably block-booked by tour groups. If you want a bit of style, the place to go is the excellent A-class *Best Western Hotel Europa International* (☎ 22 650/700/306; fax 23 166), which has sensational views from its hilltop location south-west of the village. Singles/doubles with buffet breakfast are 15,000/25,500 dr, and facilities include a bar, restaurant, swimming pool and tennis court.

Places to Eat
With so many one-off customers passing through, Olympia's restaurants have little incentive to strive for excellence – and they don't. One exception is the *Taverna Praxitelous*, next door to the police station and well patronised by the boys in blue. Locals recommend a walk out to the *Restaurant Klimitaria*, signposted to the right by the BP station on the edge of town as you go out towards Pyrgos.

If you've got your own transport, you can head out to the friendly *Restaurant Bacchus* in the village of Miraka, 3km south-east of Olympia off the road to Tripolis. A hearty meal of grilled fish, salad and wine costs under 5000 dr for two people.

Self-caterers will find *supermarkets* along Praxitelous Kondyli.

Entertainment
The *Touris Club* puts on displays of folk dancing for tour groups every evening at 9 pm between 1 February and 30 October. Admission is 4000 dr. Individuals don't fit in very well with the policy of providing one free bottle of cheap plonk and a bowl of peanuts for every four people.

Getting There & Away
Bus There are four buses a day to Athens

(5½ hours, 5000 dr), travelling via Pyrgos and the coast, as well as numerous services to Pyrgos (30 minutes, 360 dr). Three buses a day go east to Tripolis (3½ hours, 2200 dr).

Train There are five trains a day to Pyrgos (36 minutes, 210 dr).

ANCIENT OLYMPIA
Ancient Olympia was a complex of temples, priests' dwellings and public buildings. It was also the venue of the Olympic Games, which took place every four years. During these games the city-states were bound by *ekeheiria* (a sacred truce) to stop beating the hell out of one another, and compete in races and sports instead.

The site is open Monday to Friday from 8 am to 7 pm and Saturday and Sunday from 8.30 am to 3 pm. Admission is 1200 dr (free on Sunday and public holidays).

History & Mythology
The origins of Olympia date back to Mycenaean times. The Great Goddess, identified with Rea, was worshipped here in the 1st millennium BC. By the classical era, Rea had been superseded by her son Zeus. A small regional festival, which probably included athletic events, was introduced in the 11th century BC.

The first official quadrennial Olympic Games were declared in 776 BC by King Iphitos of Elis. By 676 BC, they were open to all male Greeks, reaching their height of prestige in 576 BC. The games were held in honour of Zeus, popularly acclaimed as their founder. They took place at the time of the first full moon in August.

The athletic festival lasted five days and included wrestling, chariot and horse racing, the pentathlon (wrestling, discus and javelin throwing, long jump and running), and the pancratium (a vicious form of fisticuffs).

Originally only Greek-born males were allowed to participate, but later Romans were permitted. Slaves and women were not allowed to enter the sanctuary as participants or spectators. Women trying to sneak in were thrown from a nearby rock.

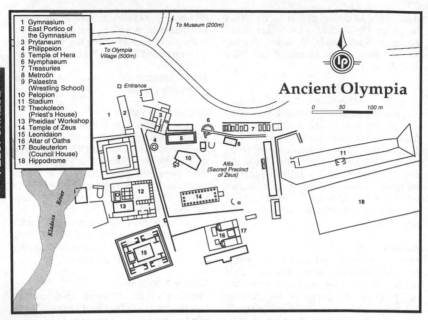

1 Gymnasium
2 East Portico of the Gymnasium
3 Prytaneum
4 Philippeion
5 Temple of Hera
6 Nymphaeum
7 Treasuries
8 Metroön
9 Palaestra (Wrestling School)
10 Pelopion
11 Stadium
12 Theokoleon (Priest's House)
13 Pheidias' Workshop
14 Temple of Zeus
15 Leonidaion
16 Altar of Oaths
17 Bouleuterion (Council House)
18 Hippodrome

To Museum (200m)

To Olympia Village (500m)

Entrance

Ancient Olympia

0   50   100 m

Altis (Sacred Precinct of Zeus)

Kladeos River

The event served purposes besides athletic competition. Writers, poets and historians read their works to a large audience, and the citizens of various city-states got together. Traders clinched business deals and city-state leaders talked in an atmosphere of festivity that was conducive to resolving differences through discussion, rather than battle.

The games continued during the first years of Roman rule. By this time, however, their importance had declined and, thanks to Nero, had become less edifying. In 67 AD, Nero entered the chariot race with 10 horses, ordering that other competitors could have no more than four. Despite this advantage, he fell and abandoned the race. He was still declared the winner by the judges.

The games were held for the last time in 394, before they were banned by Emperor Theodosius I as part of a purge of pagan festivals. In 426, Theodosius II decreed that the temples of Olympia be destroyed.

The modern Olympic Games were instituted in 1896 and, other than during WWI and WWII, have been held every four years in different cities around the world ever since. The Olympic flame is lit at the ancient site and carried by runners to the city where the games are held.

Exploring the Site
Ancient Olympia is signposted from the modern village. The entrance is beyond the bridge over the Kladeos river (a tributary of the Alfios). Thanks to Theodosius II and various earthquakes, little remains of the magnificent buildings of ancient Olympia, but enough remains to sustain an absorbing visit in an idyllic, leafy setting. The first ruin encountered is the **gymnasium**, which dates from the 2nd century BC. South of here is the partly restored **palaestra**, or wrestling school, where contestants practised and trained. The next building was the **theokoleon** (the priests' house). Behind it was

least 30,000 spectators. Slaves and women spectators had to be content to watch from the Hill of Cronos. South of the stadium was the **hippodrome**, where the chariot contests thrilled the crowds.

To the north of the Temple of Zeus was the **pelopion**, a small, wooded hillock with an altar to Pelops. It was surrounded by a wall and the remains of its Doric portico can be seen. Many artefacts, now displayed in the museum, were found buried on the hillock.

North is the 6th-century Doric **Temple of Hera**, the site's most intact structure. Hera was worshipped along with Rea until the two were superseded by Zeus.

To the east of this temple is the **nymphaeum**. This monument was erected by the wealthy Roman banker Herodes Atticus from 156-160 AD. Typical of buildings financed by Roman benefactors, it was grandiose, consisting of a semicircular building with Doric columns flanked at each side by a circular temple. The building contained statues of Herodes Atticus and his family. Despite its elaborate appearance, the nymphaeum had a practical purpose: it was a fountain house supplying Olympia with fresh spring water.

From the nymphaeum, a row of 12 **treasuries** stretched to the stadium. These looked like miniature temples. Each was erected by a city-state for use as a storehouse. These buildings marked the northern boundaries of the altis. The remains are reached by ascending a flight of stone steps.

At the bottom of these steps are the scant remains of the 5th-century BC **metroön**, a temple dedicated to Rea, the mother of the gods. Apparently the ancients worshipped Rea in this temple with orgies.

To the west of the Temple of Hera are the foundations of the **philippeion**, a circular construction with Ionic columns built by Philip of Macedon to commemorate the Battle of Khaironeia (338 BC), where he defeated a combined army of Athenians and Thebans. The building contained statues of Philip and his family.

North of the philippeion was the **prytaneum**, the magistrate's residence. Here,

The ancient Greeks used circular stones or plates for discus throwing

the **workshop** where Pheidias sculpted the gargantuan chryselephantine Statue of Zeus, one of the Seven Wonders of the Ancient World. The workshop was identified by archaeologists after the discovery of tools and moulds. Beyond the theokoleon is the **leonidaion**, an elaborate structure which accommodated dignitaries.

The **altis**, or **Sacred Precinct of Zeus**, lies to the left of the path. Its most important building was the immense 5th-century Doric **Temple of Zeus** in which stood Pheidias' statue. The 12m-high statue was later removed to Constantinople by Theodosius II, where it was destroyed by a fire in 475 BC. The temple consisted of 13 lateral columns and six at either end. None are still standing.

The **stadium** lies to the east of the altis and is entered through an archway. The start and finish lines of the 120m sprint track and the judges' seats still survive. There are normally plenty of athletic types weaving through the tourists as they time themselves over the distance. The stadium could seat at

winning athletes were entertained and feasted.

South of the Temple of Zeus is the **bouleuterion** (council house), where competitors swore to obey the rules decreed by the Olympic Senate.

Museum

The museum is 200m north of the site, on the opposite side of the road. The star piece is the 4th-century Parian marble statue of **Hermes of Praxiteles**, a masterpiece of classical sculpture from the Temple of Hera. Hermes was charged with taking the infant Dionysos to Mt Nysa. The statue portrays the god in repose.

Other important exhibits are a sculptured **Head of Hera** and the pediments and metopes from the Temple of Zeus. The eastern pediment depicts the chariot race between Pelops and Oinomaos. The western pediment shows the fight between the Centaurs and Lapiths and the metopes depict the Twelve Labours of Heracles.

The museum is open Tuesday to Friday from 8 am to 7 pm, Saturday and Sunday from 8.30 am to 3 pm, and Monday from 11 am to 7 pm. Admission is 1200 dr.

KYLLINI Κυλλήνη

The tiny port of Kyllini (**Kilee**ni), 78km south-west of Patras, warrants a mention only as the jumping-off point for ferries to Kefallonia and Zakynthos. Most people pass through Kyllini on buses from Patras that board the ferries. If you get stuck in Kyllini, the tourist/port police (☎ 0623-92 211) at the quay can suggest accommodation.

Kyllini is near the first of a succession of excellent beaches stretching south.

Getting There & Away

Bus There are between three and seven buses a day to Kyllini (1¼ hours, 1300 dr) from the Zakynthos bus station, as well as at least three buses a day from Pyrgos (50 minutes, 950 dr).

Boat Depending on the season, there are between three and seven boats a day to

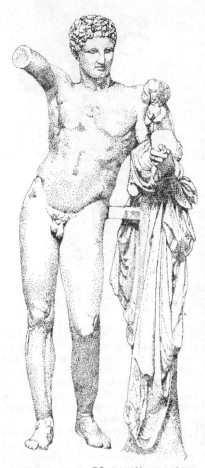

The 4th-century BC statue Hermes of Praxiteles resides in the museum at Olympia

Zakynthos (1½ hours, 1470 dr), and two boats a day to Poros (1½ hours, 1940 dr) and Argostoli (2¾ hours, 2700 dr) on Kefallonia.

HLEMOUTSI CASTLE

The castle is 6km south of Kyllini near the appropriately named village of Kastro. It stands on the only hill for miles, and dominates the surrounding agricultural plain.

Hlemoutsi was built by the Franks in 1223 AD. Destroyed in 1430, it was later rebuilt by the Turks to withstand artillery fire.

The castle's battlement walls, hexagonal keep, vaulted galleries and rock location make it one of Morea's most impressive medieval constructions, with a round tower by the entry gate and a western bastion dating from its Turkish period.

The castle can be reached in a roundabout way from **Gastouni**, but it's easier to visit direct from Kyllini.

PELOPONNESE

Central Greece Κεντρική Ελλάδα

Steeped in history, central Greece is a land of mountains and plains whose attractions, with some exceptions, are subtle rather than obvious. From the rugged mountains of the South Pindos to densely populated Attica, from the sleepy wetlands of the south-west to the verdant Pelion, central Greece covers a wide range of varied landscapes and two major regions: Thessaly and Sterea Ellada.

Three major attractions draw travellers to this ancient land – the oracle of Delphi, the amazing rock forest of Meteora and its monasteries, and the lush Pelion peninsula with its traditional stone houses.

Sterea Ellada
Στερεά Ελλάδα

Sterea Ellada is bordered by Thessaly and Epiros to the north and the narrow gulfs of Corinth and Patras in the south. The region acquired the name Sterea Ellada (mainland Greece) in 1827, because it was the only continental portion of the newly formed Greek state – the Peloponnese was classed as an island. To the west is the prefecture of Etolo-Akarnania where England's most famous philhellene bard, Lord Byron, died at Messolongi while assisting in the Greek War of Independence.

To the east is the large island of Evia, which is separated from the mainland by a narrow gulf, and is a jumping-off point for the Sporades islands. Evia is covered in the Sporades chapter.

ATHENS TO THIVA

If you have your own transport and intend travelling from Athens to Delphi you have a choice of two routes: the main highway or the old mountain road to Thiva; the latter is a turn inland just west of Elefsina (Eleusis). Along the way you can take a turn-off left to

HIGHLIGHTS

- The rock-pillar monasteries of Meteora
- The Oracle of Delphi and Sanctuary of Apollo
- The lush, green mountain villages of the Pelion peninsula
- The Byzantine monastery of Osios Louka

the 4th-century BC **Fortress of Aigosthena**, and have a swim at nearby **Porto Germeno**, on the north coast of the Gulf of Corinth. The fortress is well preserved, with its towers still standing. Within the walls are two Byzantine churches.

Porto Germeno is a pleasant low-key resort with a pebble beach, inexpensive fish tavernas and one hotel, the C-class *Hotel Egosthenion* (☎ 0263-41 226), though it's set back somewhat from the beach. Singles/doubles go for 8500/10,500 dr.

Back on the Thiva road, 2km beyond the turn-off for the Fortress of Aigosthena and Porto Germeno, you will see the **Fortress of Eleutherai** to the right. This fortress also dates from the 4th century BC, but is less

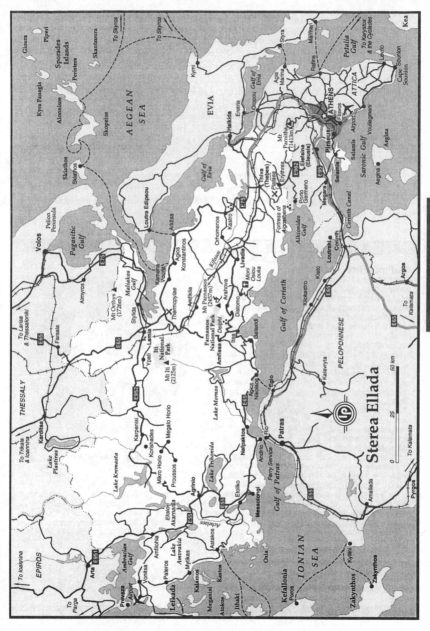

impressive than Aigosthena. The fortress stands at the entrance to the pass over Mt Kythairon. According to mythology, baby Oedipus was left to perish on this mountain.

If you are a battle buff you may like to make the 5km detour to the remains of **Plataea**, which once overlooked the plain where the famous Battle of Plataea (479 BC) took place. The ruins are reached by turning left at Erythres.

THIVA (THEBES) Θήβα
• *pop 19,000 • postcode 322 00 • area code ☎ 0262*
Thiva (Thíva), 87km north-west of Athens, figures prominently in history and mythology, and the two are inextricably linked. The tragic fate of its royal dynasty, centred

around the myth of Oedipus, rivalled that of Mycenae.

Present-day Thiva is a lively enough town in the central area, but has few vestiges of its past glory as a city-state.

History
After the Trojan War, Thebes became the dominant city of the region of Boeotia. In 371 BC the city was victorious in a battle against Sparta, which had hitherto been invincible.

In 336 BC, Thebes was sacked by Alexander the Great for rebelling against Macedonian control. The bloody battle saw 6000 Thebans killed and 30,000 taken prisoner.

Oedipus Rex
Laius, ruler of Thebes, had been warned by the Delphic oracle that any child born to his wife, Jocasta, would murder him. When, despite this, Jocasta gave birth to Oedipus, Laius took him away, drove a nail through his feet (hence the name 'Oedipus', which means 'swollen foot') and left him on Mt Cithaeron. However, Oedipus did not perish – a shepherd found him and took him to Corinth, where Oedipus was adopted by King Polybus and his wife, Periboea.

As a young man, Oedipus consulted the oracle about his future and heard to his dismay that he would kill his father and marry his mother. Unaware that Polybus and Periboea were not his real parents, Oedipus fled, determined not to let the oracle's prophecy come true. While heading towards Thebes, Oedipus entered into an argument with a stranger and became so enraged that he killed him, not realising that the man was Laius, his real father. At the entrance to the city of Thebes, Oedipus came upon the Sphinx, a monster who posed a riddle to all passers-by and devoured those who could not answer it. Having been outwitted by Oedipus, who guessed correctly, the Sphinx killed herself.

Oedipus meets the Sphinx

As a reward for having destroyed this vexatious creature, the Thebans proclaimed Oedipus their king and gave him the hand in marriage of the recently widowed Queen Jocasta, thereby fulfilling the oracle's prophecy. Following their union, Thebes was besieged by a plague so Oedipus consulted the oracle once more, which said he should banish the murderer of Laius. The renowned prophet Tiresias appeared at Oedipus' court at this time and revealed the gods' wishes: the plague would end only at the death of the man who had killed his father and married his mother. Only now did Oedipus and Jocasta discover the truth. Jocasta hanged herself; Oedipus blinded himself and went into exile and eventually died in Colonus in Attica.

The riddle, in case you're wondering, was 'What creatures have four legs in the morning, two at midday, and three in the evening, and are at their weakest when they have the most?' The answer is people – they crawl on all fours as babies, walk upright when mature and use a cane in old age. ■

Archaeological Museum

Thiva has an impressive archaeological museum (☎ 27 913). The collection includes pottery from prehistoric and Mycenaean times, Linear B tablets found in the Mycenaean palaces and some Mycenaean clay coffins, which are unique to mainland Greece.

The museum is open Tuesday to Sunday from 8.30 am to 3 pm. Admission is 500 dr. It's at the northern end of Pindarou, which runs parallel to Epaminondou.

Places to Stay

If you get stuck in Thiva there are really only two hotels to choose from. The C-class *Neobe Hotel* (☎ 27 949), Epaminondou 63, has singles/doubles with shared bathroom for 5000/7000 dr and rooms with private bathroom for 5500/7500 dr.

A better choice is the C-class *Meletiou Hotel* (☎ 27 333; fax 23 334), at Epaminondou 58, which has singles/doubles for 9000/15,000 dr. These hotels are opposite each other.

Getting There & Away

Bus Hourly buses operate to both Athens (1½ hours, 1450 dr) and Livadia (45 minutes, 850 dr) from Thiva's small but modern bus station.

Train There are 10 services to and from Athens daily (1½ hours, 880 dr), as well as nine services northwards.

LIVADIA Λειβαδιά
• *pop 18,000 • postcode 321 00 • area code* ☎ *0261*
Livadia is on the Athens-Delphi road, 45km north-west of Thiva. The town flanks both sides of a gorge through which the River Erkinas flows. A 14th-century Frankish castle overlooks Livadia from Profitis Elias hill.

The town's main claim to fame is as the site of the oracle of Trophonios. According to legend, the ordeal one had to go through in order to consult this oracle resulted in a permanent look of fright. First, the pilgrim drank from the fountain of Lethe (Waters of

Forgetfulness) and then of the Mnemosyne (Waters of Remembrance). They were then lowered into a hole in a cave and left there for days on end to commune with the oracle.

Springs, which are supposedly the original Lethe and Mnemosyne, can be seen in a very attractive park. The pleasant *Xenia Restaurant* in the park is signposted from the Athens-Delphi road, just south of the town.

Places to Stay

The C-class *Hotel Philippos* (☎ 24 931; fax 24 934), on Athinon, has singles/doubles for 9900/13,800 dr. The hotel is on the outskirts of town on the Thiva side.

The B-class *Levadia Hotel* (☎ 23 611; fax 28 266), at Plateia L Katsoni 4, has singles/doubles for 13,600/19,500 dr.

Getting There & Away

Bus Frequent buses run from Livadia to Athens, Thiva, Delphi and Distomo (for Moni Osiou Louka).

Train There are 13 services to and from Athens daily (1½ hours, 1550 dr), as well as to most destinations north.

DELPHI Δελφοί
• *pop 2400 • postcode 330 54 • area code* ☎ *0265*
If the ancient Greeks hadn't chosen Delphi (Delphí) as their navel of the earth and built the Sanctuary of Apollo here, someone else would have thought of a good reason to make this eagle's eyrie village a tourist attraction. Its location on a precipitous cliff edge is spectacular and despite its overt commercialism and the constant passage of tour buses through the narrow streets of the modern village, it still has a special feel. Modern Delphi is 178km north-west of Athens and is the base for exploring one of Greece's major tourist sites.

Orientation & Information

Almost everything you'll need in Delphi is on Vasileon Pavlou & Friderikis. The bus stop is here next to the Taverna Castri at the Itea side of town. The post office, OTE and two banks are also on this street. Ancient

Delphi is 1.5km along the main road to Arahova.

Delphi's municipal tourist office (☎ 82 900) is at the Arahova end of Vasileon Pavlou & Friderikis. Opening times are Monday to Friday from 7.30 am to 2.30 pm. Both the National Bank and the Commercial Bank close by have automatic exchange machines.

Places to Stay – bottom end
Delphi's nearest and best camp site is *Apollon Camping* (☎ 82 750), 1.5km west of modern Delphi. *Delphi Camping* (☎ 28 944) is 4km down the Delphi-Itea road.

Finding a room in Delphi generally does not present any problems, as hotels are plentiful. Ring ahead in peak season and during public holidays to be on the safe side.

The *Pension Delphi* (☎ 82 268), Apollonos 31, was formerly Delphi's youth hostel. It is run by a helpful and courteous woman from New Zealand, and has double rooms for 9000 dr. The hostel is open from March to November and on Friday and Saturday in winter. Apollonos runs north of and parallel to Vasileon Pavlou & Friderikis.

Places to Stay – middle
Most of Delphi's hotels are on Vasileon Pavlou & Friderikis. The D-class *Hotel Athina* (☎ 82 239), at No 55, has nicely furnished singles/doubles for 5000/7000 dr with shared bathroom and 6500/8000 dr with private bathroom.

The C-class *Hotel Pan* (☎ 82 294; fax 82 320), at No 53, has pleasant single/double rooms for 7000/10,000 dr with private bathroom. The very pleasant C-class *Hotel Parnassos* (☎ 82 321; fax 82 621) at No 32 has singles/doubles for 7000/9000 dr and is run by Greek-Australians who make visitors from down under very welcome.

The B-class *Hotel Hermes* (☎ 82 318; fax 82 639), at No 29, has spacious, tastefully furnished singles/doubles for 10,000/12,000 dr with private bathroom and breakfast. This hotel has spectacular views down to the Gulf of Corinth.

Places to Stay – top end
Delphi's most luxurious hotel is the A-class *Hotel Amalia* (☎ 82 101-3; fax 82 290), at Apollonos 1. The hotel has a bar, café, restaurant and swimming pool. Rates are 23,000/30,000 dr for singles/doubles.

Another plush place is the A-class *Hotel Vouzas* (☎ 82 232; fax 82 033 or 01-984 6861), Vasileon Pavlou & Friderikis 1. Singles/doubles here are a budget-shattering 25,100/35,500 dr. The hotel has a bar, restaurant and roof garden.

Places to Eat
The *Taverna Vakhos*, Apollonos 31, next door to the Pension Delphi, serves tasty Greek staples at a reasonable price and offers an unparalleled view over the deep valley and olive groves below.

Down on the main street is a string of establishments catering mainly to the tourist traffic and offering set-menu choices for around 2600 dr. Look out for *Lefas* and the *Iniohos* for piano music while you dine. Most also offer good views along with the food. The *Arahova* is a smaller, more economical place that you may want to look out for. It doesn't have the views, but the food is as good.

Getting There & Away
Bus There are seven buses a day from Delphi to Amfissa (30 minutes, 320 dr); six to Itea (30 minutes, 300 dr) and five to Arahova (20 minutes, 200 dr); five or six to Athens (three hours, 2700 dr); one direct bus to Patras (2200 dr); three to Lamia (two hours, 1600 dr) and two to Nafpaktos (three hours, 1900 dr). For Kalambaka and Meteora (4½ hours, 3850 dr) there is a daily bus at 10.15 am (3.15 pm on Friday and Sunday) to Larisa, where you must change buses. For Thiva, take a bus to Livadia, from where there are frequent buses. The bus to/from Athens gets very crowded in the summer, so turn up early to buy a ticket. Ask for Mike at the ticket office for current details.

Train The nearest train station to Delphi is in Livadia (47km away), which is on the

Agia Triada perched on one of the massive pinnacles of Meteora, Central Greece

PAUL HELLANDER

LINDA WELTERS

DAVID HALL

Top: The little-visited Prespa lakes, Northern Greece, a haven for birdlife
Bottom Left: Man in foustanella, Metsovo, Northern Greece
Bottom Right: Monastery of Dionysiou on the Mt Athos peninsula, Northern Greece

Athens-Thessaloniki line. Taking the train is only worth considering if you have a rail pass.

ANCIENT DELPHI Αρχαιοι Δελφοι

To the majority of people, Delphi, of all the ancient sites in Greece, is the one with the most potent 'spirit of place'. Built on the slopes of Mt Parnassos, overlooking the Gulf of Corinth and extending into a valley of cypress and olive trees, Delphi's allure lies both in its stunning setting and its awe-inspiring ruins. The ancients regarded Delphi as the centre of the world, for according to mythology Zeus released two eagles at opposite ends of the world and they met here.

The site is open Monday to Friday from 7.30 am to 7.15 pm and weekends from 8.30 am to 2.45 pm. Admission is 1200 dr. Admission is free on Sunday and public holidays from 1 November to 31 March. Students from EU countries are admitted free; students from non-EU countries pay 600 dr. Student cards are required in both cases.

History

Delphi reached its height in the 4th century BC as a sanctuary dedicated to Apollo, when multitudes of pilgrims bearing expensive votive gifts came to ask advice of its oracle. The Delphic oracle was believed to be Apollo's mouthpiece, and was the most powerful in Greece. Battles were fought, marriages took place, journeys were embarked upon and business deals clinched on the strength of its utterances.

Following battles between the city-states, the oracle was showered with treasures by the victors and accused of partiality by the vanquished. Not surprisingly, the sanctuary became a hotbed of chicanery, coveted for its priceless treasures. It eventually brought about Greece's demise at the hands of the Macedonians.

Delphi was protected by a federation of Greek states called the Amphyctionic Council. However, the surrounding territory belonged to the city of Krisa, which took advantage of this by charging visitors an exorbitant fee for the privilege of disembarking at its port of Kirrha. This angered the city-states, especially Athens, who called upon the Amphyctionic Council to do something about it. The result was the First Sacred War (595-586 BC), which resulted in the council destroying Krisa and its port.

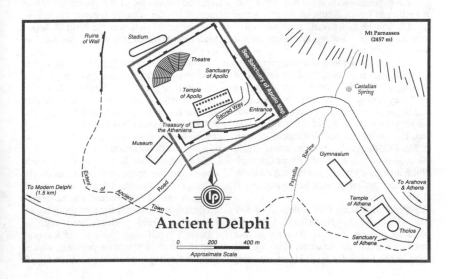

Ancient Delphi

The Delphic Oracle

During early Mycenaean times, the earth goddess, Gaea, was worshipped at Delphi, and it is believed the oracle originated at that time. Later Delphi became a sanctuary to Themis, then Demeter and later Poseidon, but by the end of the Mycenaean period, Apollo had replaced the other deities. The oracle was a priestess over 50 years of age, who sat on a tripod at the entrance to a chasm which emitted vaporous fumes. When the priestess inhaled these fumes, they induced a frenzy. Her seemingly unintelligible utterances in answer to a pilgrim's question were translated into verse by a priest.

In summer Apollo was worshipped at Delphi, but in winter, he and the oracle took a rest and Dionysos stepped into his place. As everywhere, the god of wine was honoured with merrymaking and feasting, which must have come as a welcome relief from the serious business of trying to comprehend the oracle's cryptic and grave messages. ∎

The council now took control of the sanctuary, and Delphi became an autonomous state. The sanctuary enjoyed great prosperity, receiving tributes from numerous benefactors, including the kings of Lydia and Egypt. Struggles for its control ensued, and Delphi passed from one city-state to another, resulting in further sacred wars.

The Third Sacred War was precipitated by a dispute between Thebes and the district of Phocis, in 356 BC, over control of the sanctuary. Philip II, the king of Macedon, seized the opportunity to exert power over the city-states by acting as arbitrator in this war. He brought an end to the conflict and, in 346 BC, the sanctuary again came under the protection of the Amphyctionic Council. Philip now took Phocis' place in the council, which had probably been his intention all along.

The Fourth Sacred War broke out in 339 BC when the Amphyctionic Council declared war on Amfissa because it had staked a claim to the sanctuary. The council appealed to Philip for help. Philip saw this as an opportunity to bring his formidable army into Greece and, in so doing, not only destroyed Amfissa, but fought, and defeated, a combined army of Athenians, Thebans and their allies in the Battle of Khaironeia, in Boeotia (north-west of Athens). Philip had now achieved his ambition – control of Greece.

In 191 BC, Delphi was taken by the Romans and the oracle's power dwindled. It was consulted on personal, rather than political issues. Along with the country's other pagan sanctuaries, it was abolished by Theodosius in the late 4th-century AD.

Exploring the Site

The **Sanctuary of Apollo** is on the left of the main road as you walk towards Athens. From the entrance, at the site of the old **Roman agora**, steps lead to the **Sacred Way**, which winds up to the foundations of the Doric **Temple of Apollo**.

Once you have entered the site, you will pass on your right the pedestal which held the statue of a bull dedicated by the city of Kerkyra (Corfu). Further along are the remains of monuments erected by the Athenians and Lacedaemonians. The semicircular structures on either side of the Sacred Way were erected by the Argives (people of Argos). The one to the right was the **King of Argos Monument**, which was built in the 4th century BC.

In ancient times the Sacred Way was lined with treasuries and statues given by grateful city-states, including Thebes, Siphnos, Sikyon, Athens and Knidos, in thanks to Apollo for helping them win battles. The **Athenian treasury** has been reconstructed. To the north of this treasury are the foundations of the **bouleuterion** (council house).

The 4th-century BC Temple of Apollo dominated the entire sanctuary. Inside the cella was a gold statue of Apollo and a hearth where an eternal flame burned. On the temple architrave were inscriptions of the wise utterings of Greek philosophers, such as 'Know Thyself' and 'Nothing in Excess'. The chasm from which the priestess inhaled the intoxicating vapours has not been found;

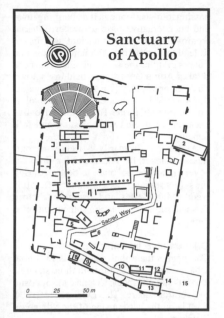

Sanctuary of Apollo

0   25   50 m

1   Theatre
2   Stoa of Attalos
3   Temple of Apollo
4   Bouleuterion (Council House)
5   Athenian Treasury
6   Knidos Treasury
7   Thebes Treasury
8   Siphnos Treasury
9   Sikyon Treasury
10   King of Argos Monument
11   Votive Offering of Athens
12   Site of Bull of Kerkyra
13   Votive Offering of Athens
14   Main Entrance
15   Roman Agora (Market Place)

all that is known is that it was somewhere within the temple.

Above the temple is the well-preserved 4th-century BC **theatre**, which was restored by the Romans. From the top row of seats there are magnificent views. Plays were performed here during the Pythian Festival, which, like the Olympic Games, was held every four years. From the theatre another path leads up to the **stadium**, the best preserved in all of Greece.

From the Sanctuary of Apollo, walk towards Arahova and you will come to the **Castalian spring** on the left, where pilgrims had to cleanse themselves before consulting the oracle. Opposite is the **Sanctuary of Athena** (free admission), where Athena Pronaia was worshipped. This is the site of the 4th-century BC **tholos**, the most striking of Delphi's monuments. It was a graceful circular structure comprising 20 columns on a three-stepped podium – three of its columns have been re-erected. The purpose of the tholos is unknown.

Museum

Ancient Delphi managed to amass a considerable treasure-trove, and this is reflected in its magnificent museum collection. Most labels are in Greek and French only, with the exception of some of the major exhibits.

On the landing is the **omphalos**, a sculpted cone, which once stood at what was considered the centre of the world – the spot where the eagles released by Zeus met. In the second room along from here are two 6th-century BC **kore figures**. To the right of this room are displayed parts of the frieze from the **Siphnian treasury**, which depicts the battle between the gods and the giants, and the gods watching the fight over the corpse of Patroclus during the Trojan War.

In the rooms to the left are fragments of metopes from the **Athenian treasury** depicting the Labours of Hercules, the Exploits of Theseus and the Battle of the Amazons. Further on you can't miss the large **Acanthus Column**, with three women dancing around it. In the end room is the celebrated life-size **Bronze Charioteer**, which commemorates a victory in the Pythian Games of 478 or 474 BC.

The museum (☎ 82 313) is open Tuesday to Friday from 7.30 am to 7.15 pm; weekends and public holidays from 8.30 am to 2.45 pm; and Monday from noon to 6.15 pm. Admission is 1200 dr. Admission is free

CENTRAL GREECE

on Sunday and public holidays from 1
November to 31 March. Students from EU
countries are admitted free; students from
non-EU countries pay 600 dr. Student cards
are required in both cases.

Getting There & Away
Buses between Arahova and modern Delphi
will drop you off at the site. See Getting
There & Away under modern Delphi for
details.

MT PARNASSOS Παρνασσός Ορος
There are two ski centres on Mt Parnassos,
both with overnight accommodation. The
largest is the EOT centre at Fterolakkas
(1750m), which also has facilities higher up
at Kelaria (1950m). For more information
contact the municipal tourist office in Delphi
or the EOT in Athens, or the ski centre
(☎ 0267-22 689). The centre is 24km from
Arahova and 17km from Amfiklia. The
Athens department store Klaoudatos organises trips to this ski centre. For more
information, see Skiing in the Activities section of the Athens chapter.

The second centre is at Gerondovrahos.
For more information contact Athens Ski-
Lovers Club (☎ 01-643 3368), Sarantapihou
51, Athens, or Nikos Georgakos (☎ 0267-31
391) in Arahova. The centre is 25km from
Arahova and 34km from Delphi.

Getting There & Away
There is no public transport to either centre
– you'll need to take a taxi or hitch from
Delphi or Arahova.

ARAHOVA Αράχωβα
• *pop 2800* • *postcode 320 04* • *area code ☎ 0267*
Arahova (Arahova) is built on a rocky spur
of Mt Parnassos at an altitude of 960m. It's
12km from Delphi on the main Athens-
Delphi road. The main street is flanked by
shops selling embroideries, hand-woven
goods, flokati rugs and various other
souvenirs. The town is also noted for its
cheese, honey, hilopittes (dried pasta) and
a pleasant, unresinated red wine.

Despite this overt flaunting of its assets to

passing tourists, Arahova is a charming town
and an alternative base to modern Delphi
from which to visit the ancient site. In the
little alleys bordering the main street, stone
houses cling to the steep hillside. The **Festival of Agios Georgios** is held in the town
on St George's Day (23 April). However, if
this date falls during Lent, the festival is
postponed until Easter Tuesday. It's a joyous
occasion celebrated with feasting and folk
dancing.

Arahova is primarily a trendy accommodation resort for skiers, and for Greeks it
is very much the 'in' place to be seen during
the skiing season. Prices in winter reflect this
trend. Many cafés and restaurants close
down in summer, including some mentioned
here.

Orientation & Information
The town's main thoroughfare is Delphon,
which snakes its way through three squares.
The bus station is at the Celena Café opposite
the central square. The EOT office (☎ 31
630) is on the eastern side of the village on
Delphon.

Opening hours are 8 am to 3.30 pm Monday to Thursday and 8 am to 10 pm on Friday
and Saturday. The post office and OTE are
on Plateia Xenias, one block west of the
central square.

Places to Stay & Eat
The town has some rooms to rent in private
houses where you pay around 6000 dr a
double, depending on the season. Prices are
higher in winter. For information about these
enquire at the Celena Café.

The D-class *Apollon Hotel* (☎ 31 427),
Delphon 20, has pleasant, spotless
singles/doubles for 4000/5000 dr, with
shared bathroom. Under the same management, the *Apollon Inn* (☎ 31 057) at Delphon
106 has neat single/double domatia for
5000/7000 dr with private bathroom. *Pension Nostos* (☎ 31 385; fax 31 765) is a
homely little place with double/triple
domatia for 10,000/12,000 dr. It is just off
Plateia Xenias.

The very trendy C-class *Arahova Inn*

(☎ 31 353; fax 31 134) on the east side of the village is one of the town's more popular hotels. Rooms cost 9000/14,000 dr in low (summer) season, but rocket to 18,000/22,000 dr in high (winter) season. The hotel also has a bar, restaurant and central heating.

The older B-class *Hotel Xenia* (☎ 31 230; fax 32 175), Plateia Xenias, also has a bar, restaurant and central heating. The rates are 9500/15,000 dr with breakfast.

There are many restaurants and cafés lining Delphon and many only open during the skiing season. *To Agnantio* and *Taverna O Sakis* are easy to locate and have good views from the restaurant. The *I Liakoura* near the Xenia hotel specialises in soups and other local dishes.

Getting There & Away
The five buses a day which run between Athens and Delphi stop at Arahova. In addition there are some local buses to Delphi (20 minutes, 200 dr). A taxi from Arahova to Delphi will cost 1700 dr.

AROUND ARAHOVA
Moni Osiou Louka Μονή Οσίου Λουκά
The Moni Osiou Louka (Monastery of St Luke Stiris) is 8km east of the village of Distomo, which lies just south of the Athens-Delphi road. Its principal church contains some of Greece's finest Byzantine frescoes.

The monastery is dedicated to a local hermit who was canonised for his healing and prophetic powers. The monastic complex includes two churches. The interior of the main one of **Agios Loukas** is a glorious symphony of marble and mosaics. There are also icons by Michael Damaskinos, the 16th-century Cretan icon painter.

In the main body of the church the light is partially blocked by the ornate marble window decorations. This creates striking contrasts of light and shade, which greatly enhance the atmosphere. The crypt where St Luke is buried also contains fine frescoes. Bring a torch, since there is little lighting. The other church, **Theotokos** (Church of St Mary), built in the 10th century, has a less impressive interior.

The monastery is in an idyllic setting, with breathtaking vistas from its leafy terrace. There is a small café in the monastery grounds. The monastery is open from 8 am to 7 pm daily but closes from 2 to 4 pm from May to September. Admission is 800 dr, and modest dress is required (no shorts).

Distomo Δίστομο
• *pop 2156* • *postcode 320 05* • *area code* ☎ *0267*
The only thing worth seeking out in Distomo is the **war memorial** built on the hill on the east side of the village. Look for the 'mausoleum' sign. The memorial is in commemoration of the slaying of over 200 villagers from Distomo by the Nazis in 1944 in reprisal for a guerrilla attack. The large, white marble slab on the memorial wall with an inscription in both Greek and German is an official German government apology for the atrocity, offered by the German president Roman Herzog in June 1996.

Places to Stay Moni Osiou Louka is a hassle to get to by public transport, so if you get really stuck, there are a couple of budget hotels in Distomo, including the D-class *Hotel America* (☎ 22 079), I Kastriti 1, where singles/doubles are 4300/7500 dr with private bathroom. Nearby, the D-class *Hotel Koutriaris* (☎ 22 268), on the central square of Plateia Ethnikis Antistasis, has singles/doubles for 4300/7500 dr with shared bathroom.

Getting There & Away There is one direct bus a day from Athens, which leaves Bus Terminal B at 11 am (3½ hours, 1690 dr) – change at Livadia. Otherwise you can take the Delphi bus from Athens and ask the driver to stop at the turn-off for Distomo, from where you should be able to flag down a taxi for the 9km to the monastery. That will set you back about 1000 dr. Otherwise it's a 2km walk from Distomo to the taxi stand at Distomo. From Livadia there are 11 buses a day to Distomo (45 minutes, 650 dr) and one to the monastery at 1.30 pm (one hour, 800 dr). There are hourly buses to Athens from Livadia (two hours, 1570 dr).

CENTRAL GREECE

DELPHI TO NAFPAKTOS

The 80km route from Delphi westwards along the Gulf of Corinth is via the much less travelled, but no less attractive drive as far as Nafpaktos, where there is an imposing Venetian fortress. This route skirts the north shore of the Gulf of Corinth, passing a number of seaside towns and villages before meeting the important ferry-boat link at Andirio. Boats here run every half-hour or so. The coast is more popular as a holiday destination with Greeks than with foreign tourists.

The market town of **Itea**, 10km down the road to the coast, is less attractive and more commercial. From Itea an alternative road branches left for 2km to **Kira**. This was ancient Kirrha, the port of Delphi, which was destroyed by the Amphyctionic Council in the First Sacred War (595-586 BC). Kira has a good beach and two camp sites, *Kaparelis Camping* (☎ 0265-32 330) and *Ayannis Camping* (☎ 0265-32 555).

Galaxidi, a bit further along the road, is perhaps the prettiest town along this coast. It was a prosperous caïque-building centre in the 19th century, and some fine stone mansions survive from this time. Its naval museum houses models of ships, marine paintings and paraphernalia from the War of Independence (1821-26).

Galaxidi has a number of hotels, and *Galaxidi Camping* (☎ 0265-41 530) is just west of town.

Nafpaktos (Ναύπακτοϖ), just inside the region of Etolo-Akarnania and 9km east of Andirio, is a little resort with an attractive harbour, a good beach and a well-preserved Venetian castle. It sits in a lush region with a backdrop of pine-covered mountains. Nafpaktos was known as Lepanto in medieval times and it was here in 1571 that the famous naval battle of Lepanto took place.

Nafpaktos has several hotels as well as two camp sites between it and Andirio: *Platanitis Beach* (☎ 0634-31 555) and *Dounis Beach* (☎ 0634-31 565). There is another camp site, *Doric Camping* (☎ 0266-31 722), further east along the coast at **Agios Nikolaos**. If you are looking for a hotel here,

try the nifty C-class *Akti* (☎ 0634-28 464; fax 24 171) near the eastern promenade. Singles/doubles are 8500/11,500 dr. There are also a couple of more expensive hotels nearby.

Getting There & Away

The Delphi-Patras bus goes along this stretch of coast. There are five buses a day from Itea to Nafpaktos and vice versa, stopping at the coastal towns along the way, and six buses a day from Delphi to Itea and vice versa.

MESSOLONGI Μεσολόγγι

• *pop 10,916* • *postcode 302 00* • *area code* ☎ *0631*

Most people come to Messolongi for historical or sentimental reasons, rather than to seek a lively holiday spot. Its location is rather melancholy, as it lies between the outlets of the rivers Aheloös and Evinos, on the shores of a bleak and seemingly endless lagoon. It is Messolongi's connection with the War of Independence and the role played by Britain's philhellene bard Lord Byron that gives the town its historic reputation. The siege by the Turks and ultimate self-sacrificial exodus of the men, women and children of Messolongi in 1826 is recognised as one of the most heroic deeds of the war and was immortalised in Dionysios Solomos' epic poem *I Eleftheri Poliorkimeni* (The Free Besieged).

History

Lord Byron arrived in Messolongi in 1824, already a famous international philhellene, with the intention of lending his weight, reputation and money to the independence cause. After months of vainly attempting to organise the motley Greek forces, who spent much time squabbling among themselves, Byron's efforts came to nought. He contracted a fever, no doubt hastened on by the unsanitary and damp conditions of what was, at the time, a miserable outpost, and died, his immediate aims unfulfilled, on 19 April 1824.

Ironically, his death spurred on internationalist forces to precipitate the end of the War of Independence and Byron became a Greek national hero. One hundred years after Byron's death, many male children, now men in their seventies, were christened with the name Byron, or Vyronas in Greek, and most Greek towns have a street with the same name.

Orientation & Information
Messolongi is the capital of the prefecture of Etolo-Akarnania, though it is only a small town. The town is laid out in a roughly rectangular grid and the two main streets, running more or less parallel along its length, are Eleftheron Poliorkimenon and Spyrou Moustakli. Both bring you to the main square, Plateia Markou Botsari. The OTE and post office are both within shouting distance of the square.

Things to See
All arrivals to Messolongi enter via the **exodus gate** through which the besieged residents of Messolongi attempted to escape on the night of 22-23 April 1826, only to be caught and slaughtered by a mercenary force nearby. The gate is narrow and dangerous for traffic, so beware if you are entering by car.

Just beyond the gate, to the right, is the **Garden of the Heroes** translated incorrectly as Heroes' Tombs on the road sign. This memorial garden was established on the orders of the then governor of Greece, Yiannis Kapodistrias who, in 1829, issued the following decree:

...within these walls of the city of Messolongi lie the bones of those brave men, who fell bravely while defending the city...it is our duty to gather together, with reverence, the holy remains of these men and to lay them to rest in a memorial where our country may, each year, repay its debt of gratitude.
Aegina, 14 May 1829

You will find the Greek text of this decree on the marble slab to the right as you enter the garden. Within the leafy grounds of the garden you will find memorials to many other philhellenes as well. Beneath the statue of **Lord Byron**, which features prominently in

the garden, is buried the heart of the poet. A much larger and more modern bronze statue of Byron outside the garden now over-shadows the smaller sculpted one inside. The garden is open from 9 am to 8 pm (it closes earlier in winter).

On the main square and housed in the town hall is a **museum** dedicated to the revolution. There is also a collection of Byron memorabilia, although its credibility is a bit stretched at times. Bone up on your War of Independence history beforehand in order to get a full feel for the importance of these historic events. Museum opening times are 9 am to 1.30 pm and 4 to 8 pm in summer. Entry is free.

Places to Stay
There isn't a huge choice here. The D-class *Avra* (☎ 22 284) is as central as you can get and is quite homy, with singles/doubles for 7000/9000 dr. The B-class *Theoxenia* (☎ 22 493) is out of town somewhat on the lagoon side and has single/double rooms in the 9000/11,000 dr price bracket. The B-class *Liberty* (☎ 24 831; fax 24 832), close to the Garden of the Heroes, is rather large and impersonal and has single/double rooms for 8500/10,450 dr.

Places to Eat
There is a brace of eating places in the street running off the main square, Harilaou Trikoupi. *To Elliniko* is one option and the *Pikantiko* further along on the same side is another. There are fast-food joints scattered along here as well, and in the side streets you will find one or two reasonable cafeterias. Look out for the stylish *Taverna tou Karveli* on Ioanni Rangou, near the Pikantiko. Both major hotels have restaurants attached.

Getting There & Away
The bus station is on Mavrokordatou 5. This street forms one side of the main square. From here buses go to Athens, Patras and most destinations north, though you may need to change at Agrinio.

SOUTH-WEST COASTAL RESORTS

Amfilohia Αμφιλοχία

This attractive little place at the south-eastern corner of the Gulf of Ambracia attracts a small holiday crowd. Most visitors are merely passing through, since it is on the main highway between Epiros and the south. It is a lively town of 5000 inhabitants and although it would probably not warrant a long-term stay, it is an amenable enough stopover point. Swimming is touch and go despite the town touting an official beach. You might want to try a bit further north up the gulf towards Menidi. There is a long, curving promenade with many restaurants and cafés to relax in. If you are here in August or September, look out for the strange luminescence of the water at night.

There are five recognised hotels to choose from, of which the *Oscar* (0642-22 155; fax 22 867) is probably your best choice; singles/doubles here are 6500/9000 dr. There is also a small camp site, *Stratis Beach Park*, at Katafourko beach, north of Amfilohia, with a bar, restaurant, supermarket and shaded sites.

Vonitsa Βόνιτσα

The town of Vonitsa is popular enough with local holiday-makers, but doesn't have any real beach scene to speak of, since it is on the still waters of the Gulf of Ambracia. It is quiet and pleasant and conveniently located for the town of Preveza and the Aktio airport. Its waterfront is being developed and there are a number of modern cafés and restaurants. The route through Vonitsa from Preveza is a quicker way through to the main north-south highway to the Peloponnese. There is one D-class and four C-class hotels to choose from.

Mytikas Μύτικας

The small village of Mytikas is built on the gulf of the same name. This place has yet to feel the effect of mass tourism since it is mainly confined to Greeks and the few foreign visitors who find their way here. It's an oddly pleasant kind of place, though, with its palm trees and houses built right up to the water's edge. The beach is pebbly and un-commercialised, but is being gradually developed. There are only a couple of hotels, a few domatia and a scattering of tavernas. You can take a local caïque to the island of Kalamos that looms over Mytikas, or Kastos tucked away on the other side, if the isolation of Mytikas is not enough for you.

Astakos Αστακός

Slightly more up-market and bigger than Mytikas, Astakos is another place for a quiet, hassle-free holiday, though it lacks Mytikas' cosiness. It can also be used as a more convenient stepping stone for access to the Ionian islands, via the daily ferry to/from Ithaki in summer. There is one C-class establishment, the *Hotel Stratos* (☎ 0646-41 096) and some domatia in summer. Restaurants and tavernas cater mainly to domestic tourists and locals.

Getting There & Away

Public transport to these locations is by bus from either Agrinio or Vonitsa.

KARPENISI Καρπενήσι

• *pop 10,000* • *postcode 361 00* • *area code* ☎ *0237*

Karpenisi (altitude 960m) is in the foothills of Mt Tymfristos (2315m), 82km west of Lamia. The town itself is not especially attractive but lies in a beautiful, well-wooded region the EOT brochures tout as the 'Switzerland of Greece'. There are many opportunities for trekking and, if you have your own transport, you can explore some delightful mountain villages. Karpenisi receives tourists all year round and the skiing centre, 17km from the town, is particularly popular with Greeks in winter.

Information

Karpenisi has a tourist office (☎ 21 016; fax 21 016) on the main square, which is open from Monday to Thursday from 10 am to 2 pm and 5 to 9 pm, Friday and Saturday from 9 am to 11 pm and on Sunday from 9 am to 8 pm.

The Commercial Bank has an ATM and

there is the usual OTE and post office both centrally located.

Activities
If you are keen to participate in some kind of organised adventure sport activity, get in contact with Trekking Hellas (☎ & fax 25 940) at Zinopoulou 7, on the main square. They organise group activities in trekking, kayaking, canyoning and rafting.

Places to Stay
The most convenient option if you arrive by bus are the *domatia* of Konstantinos Koutsikos (☎ 21 400). His domatia are high up (51 steps) overlooking the main square, close to the bus station. Beautiful singles/doubles with a view go for 6000/7000 dr with private bathroom.

The C-class *Hotel Galini* (☎ 22 914; fax 25 623), Riga Fereou 3, has single/double rooms with private bathroom for 6000/12,000 dr. In the same class but decidedly better, and somewhat more expensive, the *Hotel Helvetia* (☎ 22 465), Zinopoulou 33, has very comfortable rooms for 13,000/14,000 dr.

The supposedly B-class and rather grungy *Mont Blanc* (☎ 21 341), known in Greek as Lefko Oros, Ethnikis Antistasis 2, has drab rooms for 7700/12,100 dr.

The beautifully renovated B-class but expensive *Anesis Hotel* (☎ 22 840; fax 22 305), Zinopoulou 50, has single/double rooms for 14,000/22,000 dr with private bathroom. Breakfast is included.

The Mt Tymfristos refuge of *Takis Flengas* (☎ 22 002), at 1840m, can be reached along a 12km road from Karpenisi, or is a 2½-hour walk along a path. If you wish to stay at the refuge, contact the Karpenisi EOS (☎ 23 051), Georgiou Tsitsara 2, Karpenisi.

Places to Eat
For a no-nonsense meal the *Restaurant Triandafylli*, opposite the OTE, is as good and economical a place as any. About 2000 dr should get you a decent feed. At Kosma Etolou 25 the English/Italian-speaking *Klimataria* restaurant with occasional live music, includes boiled goat, hare in oregano and rooster in red-wine sauce among its specialities. Plan on 2000 to 2500 dr for a meal.

Greeks prefer the family ambience of the *Panorama* taverna with its outdoor eating area, though the whole ambience is somewhat marred by a ghastly unfinished hotel complex overlooking the garden. It is 100m past the Galini hotel on the right. Otherwise the homely *Esy Oti Pis* with its folksy wooden sign in Greek is open, like the Panorama, both at lunchtime and in the evening. Turn left after the police station and it is 50m along on your left. Prices at both establishments are slightly higher than the previous two places mentioned.

Entertainment
If you have not come here for the skiing and its ensuing après-ski social life, you might want to try and catch some late-night, authentic live Greek music at the *Mousikes Epafes* club at Kosma Etolou 17. It is open only on Friday and Saturday and on public holidays and things don't get going until after midnight. To find it, go down Athanasiou Karpenisioti – the street leading steeply down from the main square – turn right onto Kosma Etolou after 50m and the tiny club is on your left.

Getting There & Away
There are three buses a day from Athens to Karpenisi (six hours, 4450 dr) and another four to Lamia (1¾ hours, 1300 dr). There are also two buses a day to and from Agrinio in Etolo-Akarnania (3½ hours, 1900 dr). For Mikro and Megalo Horio there are three buses a day (20 minutes, 250 dr) and for Proussos, two a week on Monday and Friday (45 minutes, 600 dr).

AROUND KARPENISI
From Karpenisi a scenic mountain road leads south for 37km to the village of **Proussos**. Along the way you'll pass several picturesque villages. The charming village of **Koryshades** has well-preserved mansions and is 5km south-west of Karpenisi, reached

by a turn-off right along the Proussos road. **Mikro Horio** and **Megalo Horio** are 12km further along the road.

The **Monastery of the Virgin of Proussiotissa**, just before the village of Proussos, has a miracle-working icon. There are more icons, wood-carvings and ecclesiastical ornaments in the monastery's 18th-century church. A small number of monks live at the monastery and pilgrims flock there in August for the Feast of the Assumption.

Places to Stay

The D-class *Hotel Antigone* (☎ 0237-41 395), at Megalo Horio, has single/double rooms with private bathroom for 5500/8000 dr. The *Agathidis Pension* (☎ 0237-91 248), at Proussos, has rooms with private bathroom for 6000/8500 dr. The A-class pension *Dryas* (☎ 0237-41 131) at Megalo Horio is your most comfortable option. A double room with breakfast will cost you 16,000 dr.

KARPENISI TO AGRINIO

Two buses a day run along this tortuous (but sealed) road across the mountains and villages of the Agrafa to Agrinio (Αγρίνιο) in Etolo-Akarnania. During the Tourkokratia (the period of Turkish occupation of Greece), the villages of this region were considered too remote to be recorded for taxation purposes, so they were classified as *agrafa* (unrecorded). The bus covers the distance in a slow 3½ hours and it is quite a spectacular drive.

The beauty of this trip is the emptiness of the countryside, through which the road climbs and twists downwards as far as the first main centre of habitation, the twin villages of **Anatoliki** and **Dytiki Frangista**, just before which is the modern taverna *Sotira* with a children's play park and, surprisingly, a swimming pool. The road then crosses the long bridge over the artificial Lake Kremasta into Etolo-Akarnania, climbs high over the last ridge and eventually winds down through small farm holdings into Agrinio. If you suffer from motion sickness, think twice before making this trip.

LAMIA Λαμία
•pop 44,000 • postcode 351 00 • area code ☎ 0231

Lamia is the capital of the prefecture of Fthiotida and is an attractive town at the western end of the Maliakos gulf, built in the form of an amphitheatre along the foothills of Mt Orthys. Lamia rarely figures on people's itineraries, but it deserves a look-in. Like most towns that are not dependent on tourism for their livelihood, Lamia is a vibrant and lively place all year round. It is famous for its lamb on the spit, its *kourabiedes* (almond shortcake) and its *xynogala* (sour milk).

To the east of Lamia is the narrow pass of Thermopylae, where, in 480 BC, Leonidas and 300 Spartans managed to temporarily halt the Persian advance of Xerxes and his 30,000-strong army.

Orientation

The main cluster of activity in Lamia is centred around Plateia Eleftherias, Plateia Laou and Plateia Parkou, where most public services can also be found. The main bus stations are towards the end of Satovriandou. This is the street that leads south from Plateia Parkou and then dips down a hill by the primary school building. The local train station is south of the centre on Konstantinoupoleos, close to the bus terminals.

Information

The EOT office is at Plateia Laou 3 (☎ 30 065; fax 30 066) and is open Monday to Friday from 7 am to 2.30 pm. The OTE is on Plateia Eleftherias and the post office is on Athanasiou Diakou, south from Plateia Eleftherias. You will find most banks on, or near, Plateia Parkou.

Things to See & Do

Lamia's **frourio**, or fort, is worth a hike up just for the views. The **Gorgopotamos railway bridge** is a fairly famous landmark in recent Greek history. It is 7km south-east of Lamia. It was blown up by the united national forces on 25 November 1944 to delay the German advance and was considered one of the greatest acts of sabotage of the time. If

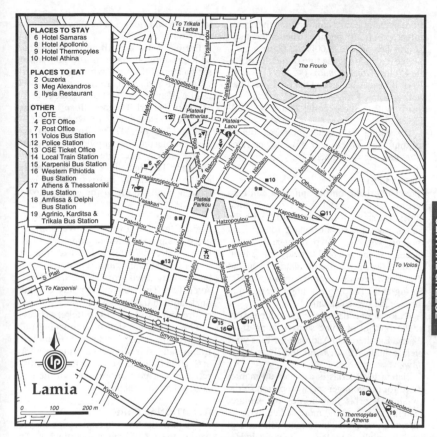

PLACES TO STAY
6 Hotel Samaras
8 Hotel Apollonio
9 Hotel Thermopyles
10 Hotel Athina

PLACES TO EAT
2 Ouzeria
3 Meg Alexandros
5 Ilysia Restaurant

OTHER
1 OTE
4 EOT Office
7 Post Office
11 Volos Bus Station
12 Police Station
13 OSE Ticket Office
14 Local Train Station
15 Karpenisi Bus Station
16 Western Fthiotida
    Bus Station
17 Athens & Thessaloniki
    Bus Station
18 Amfissa & Delphi
    Bus Station
19 Agrinio, Karditsa &
    Trikala Bus Station

Lamia

0   100   200 m

The Frourio

To Trikala & Larisa

To Volos

To Karpenisi

To Volos

To Thermopylae & Athens

CENTRAL GREECE

you are heading south by train to Athens, you will cross the reconstructed bridge over a deep ravine, shortly after leaving Lianokladi station.

Thermopylae (Thermopyles in modern Greek) is 18km from Lamia on the main Athens highway. A large statue of Leonidas marks the spot where the Persian army was delayed on its way to Thessaly, but where Leonidas and his brave Spartans ultimately perished.

Today the pass is much wider than it was in antiquity because of a gradual silting up of the land on the sea side.

Places to Stay

The hotel scene in Lamia does not allow for much choice or great quality. Since Lamia is not a tourist town, its hotel owners don't seem to make much effort to make their establishments attractive. The D-class *Thermopyles* (☎ 21 366) at Rozaki Angeli 36 has unassuming but OK singles/doubles for 9000/12,000 dr. Directly opposite at Rozaki Angeli 47 is the more presentable D-class *Athina* (☎ 27 700) with air-con single/double rooms and TV for 7500/ 10,000 dr.

The C-class *Apollonio* (☎ 22 668; fax 23 032) on Plateia Parkou doesn't offer much more in facilities and comfort than the above hotels apart from a phone and better location. Rooms here go for 11,000/14,000 dr.

One exception to the rule of mediocrity is the C-class *Hotel Samaras* (☎ 28 971; fax 42 704). It is at Athanasiou Diakou 14 and has well-appointed rooms with TV and air-con (both with remote control) for 12,000/15,000 dr.

Try asking for a better room rate out of season: most hotels will have lower rates than the prices listed here.

Places to Eat
If you like lamb on the spit, you can't go wrong here. Karaïskaki, a tree-shaded pedestrian street, is full of psistarias with the rather grotesque sight of whole roast lambs in their windows. Two point-and-choose places offering reasonable ready-made food are the *Meg Alexandros* on Plateia Laou and the *Ilysia* round the corner on Kalyva Bakogianni. The English-language menu at this second place is a killer!

A cluster of little ouzeria are hidden away at the bottom of some steps leading from Plateia Eleftherias to Androutsou. Take your pick from the *Allo Schedio*, the *Trata* and *O Spyros*.

Plateia Eleftherias is a rather up-market place for the younger set, who patronise the swish cafeterias that border the square. Plateia Laou is a little more sedate, with its kafeneia, and overall has a more relaxed feel to it, especially since the square is shaded by large plane trees. Similarly, Plateia Parkou has outdoor cafés, but they are a bit more impersonal.

Getting There & Away
Bus The scene here is a tad confusing. There are a few terminals, all within walking distance of each other, but all serving different destinations.

The main terminal for Athens and Thessaloniki buses is on Papakyriazi, which runs off Satovriandou. There are almost hourly buses for Athens (three hours, 3300 dr) and two a day (three on weekends) for Thessaloniki (four hours, 4500 dr). There is a bus

for Patras on Friday and Sunday (3½ hours, 4500 dr).

Further down the hill and on the corner of Konstantinoupoleos is the bus station for western Fthiotida, which includes the village of Ypati in its route.

The Karpenisi ticket agency is on Markou Botsari 3, again close by. There are four buses a day to Karpenisi (1¾ hours, 1300 dr). There are another two sub-stations on Thermopylon, 100m south of the railway line: one for Agrinio, Karditsa and Trikala and the other for Amfissa and Delphi. Finally, buses for Volos leave from a small station at the end of Rozaki Angeli.

Train Lamia has a very inconveniently located main train station 7km west of the town centre at Lianokladi. Most intercity trains stop at Lianokladi. Train tickets can be pre-purchased from the OSE office at Averof 28. The No 6 bus (to Stavros) links the Lianokladi station with the Lamia town centre and passes the OSE ticket office.

The small train station in town has only two trains a day linking Lamia with Lianokladi from the branch line terminus at Stylida (14km east of Lamia) – hardly a reliable transport option, though the train does go on to Athens.

ITI NATIONAL PARK
If you have the time, an exploration the area west of the city of Lamia is worthwhile. The attractive village of **Ypati**, 25km past Lamia and 8km south of the Karpenisi-Lamia road, has the remains of a fortress and is the starting point for treks on Mt Iti (2152m).

This mountain is the focus of the Iti National Park, established in 1966. It's a verdant region with forests of fir and black pine. According to mythology, Mt Iti was the place where the dying Hercules built his own funeral pyre and was burned to death. While the mortal elements in Hercules perished, the immortal Hercules joined his divine peers on Mt Olympus.

From Ypati it's a four-hour walk along a marked path to the mountain's *Trapeza*

Refuge (1850m). For information about this refuge contact the Lamia EOS (☎ 0231-26 786), Ipsilandou 20, Lamia.

Ypati has two hotels. The D-class *Hotel Panellinion* (☎ 0231-59 640) is open in July and August only and has singles/doubles with shared bathroom for 4500/6500 dr. The D-class *Hotel Panorama* (☎ 0231-59 222) has rooms with shared bathroom for 5000/7000 dr and doubles with private bathroom for 7500 dr. This hotel operates from April to October only. Ypati is served by frequent buses from Lamia.

From the Ypati turn-off the road is fast and relatively flat and runs along the valley of the River Sperhios. After Makri, the road begins to climb through forested hills and really climbs at the village of Tymfristos, winding slowly upwards to a pass at the summit of which you enter the prefecture of Evrytania. This road gets quite a bit of snow in winter.

A new road then winds down fairly quickly to Karpenisi, bypassing the village of Agios Nikolaos.

AGIOS KONSTANTINOS
Αγιος Κωνσταντίνος
• *pop 2360* • *postcode 350 06* • *area code* ☎ *0235*
Agios Konstantinos, on the main Athens-Thessaloniki route, is one of the three mainland ports that serve the Sporades islands (the other two are Thessaloniki and Volos).

There are a number of hotels in the town. However, with judicious use of buses from Athens to the port, you will probably not need to stay overnight before catching a Sporades-bound ferry or hydrofoil. If you get stuck, try the *Hotel Poulia* (☎ 31 663). Rates are 4500/6500 dr for singles/doubles. A more comfortable option is the A-class *Motel Levendi* (☎ 32 251; fax 32 255), where singles/doubles are 13,800/15,200 dr.

Getting There & Away
Bus Buses depart hourly for Agios Konstantinos from Athens Terminal B bus station (2½ hours, 2650 dr).

Ferry There are one or two daily ferries from

Agios Konstantinos to Skiathos (3½ hours, 3000 dr) and one or two to Skopelos town (4½ hours, 3500 dr) and Alonnisos (six hours, 3850 dr).

Hydrofoil Hydrofoils depart up to four times daily for Skiathos (1½ hours, 6000 dr), and four times daily for Skopelos town (2½ hours, 7900 dr) and Alonnisos (three hours, 7400 dr).

Thessaly Θεσσαλία

Thessaly is the proud possessor of two of Greece's most extraordinary natural phenomena: the giant rock pinnacles of Meteora and the riotously fertile Pelion peninsula. On a more modest scale it also has the beautiful Vale of Tembi. Travelling north from Thessaly to Macedonia, whether by road or train, you will pass through this 12km-long valley, which is a narrow passageway between Mt Olympus and Mt Ossa. The road and railway line share the valley with a river, whose richly verdant banks contrast dramatically with the sheer cliffs on either side. If you have your own transport there are viewpoints at the most scenic spots.

The valley has also been a favoured place for invaders of Greece. The Persian king Xerxes gained access to central Greece via Tembi in 480 BC, as did the Germans in 1941.

LARISA Λάρισα
• *pop 112,777* • *postcode 410 00* • *area code* ☎ *041*
Larisa is the kind of place you would normally bypass on your travels through Greece, but it is worth more than a fleeting glance. Larisa occupies a position as an important transport hub and since it is pretty well central to the Thessaly region, it is likely that you are going to find yourself at least passing through here, if only fleetingly, on the train heading either north or south. Despite its initial lack of promise, Larisa is nonetheless a lively and sophisticated Greek town, almost bereft of tourists, and is a very

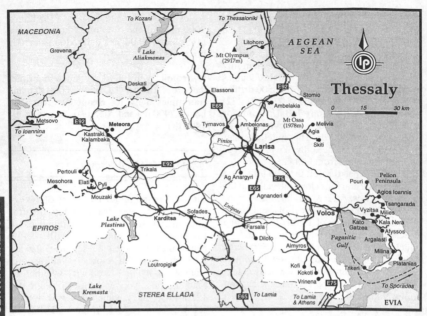

important service centre for the whole of the vast agricultural plain of Thessaly. It is a vibrant student town, as the bustling cafeterias around the central area testify, and has a military and air-force base.

Larisa has been inhabited for over 8000 years and its multifarious and fascinating past is only gradually being uncovered, since in recent years fast-growing residential development has tended to disguise what historical remains lie beneath the modern city.

Orientation

Larisa is built on the east bank of the River Pinios, which eventually flows through the Vale of Tembi to the sea. Its main square is called Plateia Laou. The train station is on the southern side of town and the main bus station on the northern side. To get to the town centre from the train station, bear left onto the road outside the station towards a busy intersection and then turn to the right

from the intersection, along Alex Panagouli. This street leads directly north to Plateia Laou.

Kyprou and Nikitara run across the south end of this square and Eleftheriou Venizelou and 31 Avgoustou across the north end. Plateia Ethnarhou Makariou (more commonly known as Plateia Tahydromiou) and Plateia Mihail Sapka are the other two squares around which most of the social life revolves. The streets around these squares are mainly a pedestrian zone.

To get to Plateia Laou from the main bus station, walk directly south along Olympou for about 100m.

Information

The Larisa EOT office is at Koumoundourou 18 (☎ 250 919) near the prefecture office (*nomarhia*) building. Opening hours are from 8 am to 2.30 pm Monday to Saturday. The post office is on the corner of A Papanastasiou and Athanasiou Diakou, which runs to

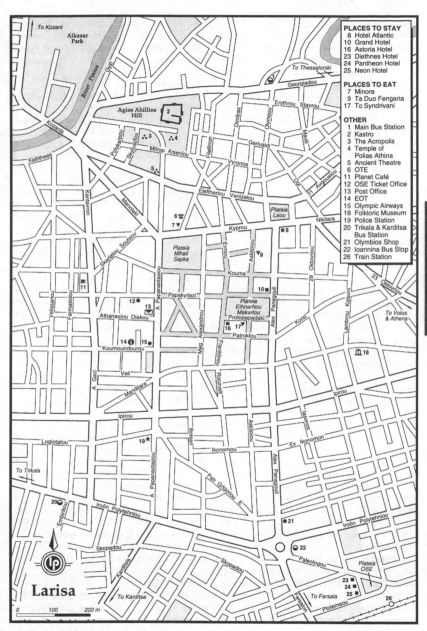

PLACES TO STAY
8 Hotel Atlantic
10 Grand Hotel
16 Astoria Hotel
23 Diethnes Hotel
24 Pantheon Hotel
25 Neon Hotel

PLACES TO EAT
7 Minore
9 Ta Duo Fengaria
17 To Syndrivani

OTHER
1 Main Bus Station
2 Kastro
3 The Acropolis
4 Temple of
  Polias Athina
5 Ancient Theatre
6 OTE
11 Planet Café
12 OSE Ticket Office
13 Post Office
14 EOT
15 Olympic Airways
18 Folkloric Museum
19 Police Station
20 Trikala & Karditsa
   Bus Station
21 Olymbios Shop
22 Ioannina Bus Stop
26 Train Station

CENTRAL GREECE

Larisa

the left off Kyprou, and the OTE office is on Filellinon, which is 100m to the west of Plateia Laou. There is an ATM at the train station. The police station is at the southern end of A Papanastasiou, just past the church of Agios Nikolaos.

Greece's first Internet café opened in Larisa in late 1996. It is called Planet Café and is at Skarlatou Soutsou 20. Check their web page www.planet-cafe.com for details, or send e-mail to cafe@planet-cafe.com. They charge 1200 dr per hour of access time. Big screens and all major Internet programmes are available.

Things to See

The **Acropolis** on Agios Ahillios hill has archaeological evidence that indicates this area had been settled since the Neolithic Age (6000 BC), but was used as the ancient settlement's Acropolis during classical times, when the temple of **Polias Athina** once existed. The Acropolis is now the site of the **kastro**. Nearby are the excavations of a newly discovered **ancient theatre** which, when fully excavated, could rival that of the theatre at Epidaurus. The excavation site is on the corner of A Papanastasiou and Eleftheriou Venizelou. It is not particularly impressive at the moment and to fully uncover it will mean demolishing a good section of the neighbouring streets.

The **folkloric museum** at Mandilara 74 (☎ 239 446) has an interesting collection of tools and utensils from the pre-industrial age, beginning with exhibits showing how crops were sown and grown. There are Greek traditional costumes, displays about nomads and semi-nomads and, in the reception area, some samples of weaving and bronze ware from Tyrnavos, a town not far from Larisa. Opening hours are from 10 am to 2 pm Monday to Saturday. Admission is free.

Alkazar Park, just across the river on the right at the end of Eleftheriou Venizelou is a nice place to relax and cool down after the heat of the day. Larisa, along with Agrinio in Etolo-Akarnania, shares the unenviable record of being the hottest place in Greece. The grandly titled **sculpted river** is an Art Nouveau set of marble sculptures in the middle of Plateia Laou, with gushing, running water. If nothing else, it is a refreshing sight on a hot day.

Activities

For adventure sports fans, the Olymbios Shop, at Alex Panagouli 99, is very good and able to supply your hiking, climbing, windsurfing and skiing needs. There is also a good mountain bike shop next door and another sports shop next to that.

Places to Stay – bottom end

There are three D-class hotels right outside the train station on Plateia OSE that are convenient, if not inspiring, for travellers in transit. The *Neon* doesn't make much of an effort to operate as a hotel, but you might get a room if you're desperate. The *Pantheon* (☎ 236 726) has singles/doubles with shared bathroom for 4500/6000 dr and with private bathroom for 6000/7100 dr. The *Diethnes* (☎ 234 210), next door, is an old-fashioned place with functional rooms with shared bathroom for 4500/5600 dr.

Places to Stay – middle

The C-class *Hotel Atlantic* (☎ 287 711; fax 230 022) is reasonable enough and has rooms for 7000/10,000 dr. It is at Panagouli 1, off the south side of Plateia Laou.

Places to Stay – top end

Larisa has a couple of overpriced B-class hotels where you will probably get up to 30% discount most times. The *Astoria* (☎ 252 941; fax 229 097) at Protopapadaki 4 is as central as you can get and there's a lively nightlife in the immediate area. Single/double rooms here go for 18,500/25,420 dr. The *Grand Hotel* (☎ 257 111; fax 557 888) at Papakyriazi 16, on the opposite corner of the square from the Astoria, has single/double rooms for 16,000/25,000 dr.

Places to Eat

On Plateia Makariou is the *To Syndrivani*, which spills out onto the square when the going gets busy. Food here runs from ready-made to *tis oras* (to order) but is a bit pricey. Another traditional food place is *Ta Duo Fengaria* at Asklipiou 7, on the north side of Plateia Makariou. Expect to pay 2000 dr for a reasonable meal with wine here.

For live rembetika music and dancing with your food, try *Minore* (☎ 536 779) at Filellinon 3, hidden away in a little arcade near the post office. It won't be cheap, but you will hear some authentic Greek blues music. Live music is only played at weekends during the winter season.

Getting There & Away

Bus Buses leave from Larisa for many destinations including the following: six a day to Athens (4½ hours, 5500 dr), 13 to Thessaloniki (two hours, 2700 dr) and 12 to Volos (one hour, 1000 dr). Buses run regularly to and from Karditsa and Trikala from a separate bus station south of the city centre on Iroön Polytehniou, near the junction with Embirikou. Buses for Ioannina originating in Thessaloniki stop at the busy road junction near the train station.

A considerable number of intercity buses make a stop in front of the Neon Hotel outside the train station. The bus destinations include towns in western Macedonia, Evia, central Greece, the Peloponnese and even Crete. For this last destination you will buy your ferry ticket when you arrive in Piraeus. Tickets and further information are available from the shop below the Neon Hotel.

Train Larisa is on the main train line to and from Thessaloniki (two hours, 1300 dr) and Athens (five hours, 2660 dr), so there are a number of trains a day between both cities passing through Larisa. In addition to the five intercity services between both cities, there are also two extra intercity services to Athens that originate in Volos and another intercity service to/from Kozani. These better-appointed trains attract a supplementary charge. There are also 15 local trains to Volos (one hour, 560 dr) and you can get to Kalambaka (for Meteora), via Paleofarsalos (Stavros), should you prefer to make the journey by train. You can buy train tickets

and make reservations at the OSE office in town at Papakyriazi 41, near the post office. Luggage storage is available at the train station.

VOLOS Βόλος

• *pop 110,000* • *postcode 380 01* • *area code* ☎ *0421*

Volos is a large and bustling city attractively positioned on the northern shores of the Pagasitic gulf. According to mythology, Volos was the ancient Iolkos from where Jason and the Argonauts set sail on their quest for the Golden Fleece. The city's name was recorded as Golos by a 14th-century historian, but the current name is generally believed to be a corruption of the original Iolkos.

Volos is not a holiday destination in its own right: the lure of the Pelion peninsula or the Sporades islands draws people to the city while they are in transit. It is nonetheless a very pleasant place to spend a night or two, or even as a base for touring the Pelion villages. Travellers arriving by bus or train will immediately feel its spaciousness – the legacy of a rebuilding plan after the disastrous 1955 earthquake. Its broad waterfront is conducive to relaxing strolls.

Since the early 1980s, Volos has been a thriving university town, as it is home to the University of Thessaly. Its growing number of students and accompanying student life add a youthful feel to the city.

Orientation

The waterfront street of Argonafton is, for half its length, a pedestrian area; running parallel to it are the city's main thoroughfares of Iasonos, Dimitriados and Ermou. The central section of Ermou and its side streets are, in fact, a very lively pedestrian precinct. Heading north-east out of the town centre towards the hills and at right angles to the main thoroughfares are K Kartali and Eleftheriou Venizelou: this latter street is known to the locals as Iolkou. The central square of Plateia Riga Fereou is at the north-western end of the main waterfront. To the west of this square is the train station. The modern

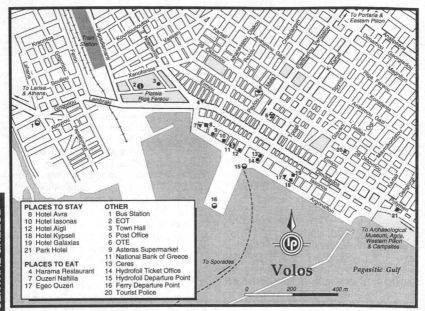

PLACES TO STAY
8   Hotel Avra
10 Hotel Iasonas
12 Hotel Aigli
18 Hotel Kypseli
19 Hotel Galaxias
21 Park Hotel

PLACES TO EAT
4   Harama Restaurant
7   Ouzeri Naftilia
17 Egeo Ouzeri

OTHER
1   Bus Station
2   EOT
3   Town Hall
5   Post Office
6   OTE
9   Asteras Supermarket
11 National Bank of Greece
13 Ceres
14 Hydrofoil Ticket Office
15 Hydrofoil Departure Point
16 Ferry Departure Point
20 Tourist Police

bus station is 500m further along Grigoriou Lambraki.

Information
The EOT (☎ 23 500; fax 24 750) is on the northern side of Plateia Riga Fereou. The helpful and multilingual staff give out town maps, information on bus, ferry and hydrofoil schedules, and have a list of hotels in all categories for the whole of Thessaly. Opening times are Monday to Friday from 7.30 am to 2.30 pm and 6 to 8.30 pm, and weekends and holidays from 9.30 am to 1.30 pm. In the low season (September to June), opening hours are 7.30 am to 2.30 pm Monday to Friday. The tourist police (☎ 72 421) are in the same building as the regular police at 28 Oktovriou 179.

The post office is at Pavlou Mela 45. The OTE is at Eleftheriou Venizelou 22 and is open from 6 am to midnight every day.

The National Bank of Greece, in the middle of the waterfront, has an ATM. Volos'

General Hospital (☎ 24 531) is in the eastern part of town near the archaeological museum.

Archaeological Museum
This excellent museum, in the south-east of town, has a comprehensive collection of finds from the area. Especially impressive is the large collection of painted grave steles from the nearby Hellenistic site of Dimitrias. The museum is open Tuesday to Saturday from 8.30 am to 3 pm and Sunday and public holidays from 9.30 am to 2.30 pm. Admission is 400 dr.

Places to Stay – bottom end
Camping The nearest camp sites to Volos are at Kato Gatzea, 20km away, on the west coast of the Pelion peninsula. They are *Camping Marina* (☎ 0423-22 167), an OK sort of camping place, but there is no beach to speak of. Further along, and the best of the bunch, is *Camping Hellas* (☎ 0423-22 267;

fax 22 492) with restaurant, minimarket and beachside bar. Book if you plan to come in July or August. Not far behind is *Sikia Fig Tree Camping* (☎ 0423-22 279), with restaurant and bar and all the usual good camping facilities. This place is right next to Camping Hellas and shares the same beach. There are also some domatia at Sikia Camping. The buses to Milies and Platanias pass all three sites.

Hotels There are 18 hotels to choose from in Volos, so you will not miss out on a bed too easily. Listed below are some of the more central hotels, clustered close to the waterfront. You can get a full list from the EOT office when you arrive.

An agreeable, cheap hotel is the D-class *Hotel Avra* (☎ 25 370), Solonos 5, on the corner of Iasonos. Rates are 4000/5600 dr for singles/doubles with shared bathroom, and 5000/7000 dr with private bathroom. Despite its prime location on the waterfront at Agiou Nikolaou 1, the C-class *Hotel Kypseli* (☎ 24 420) has a rather dingy interior, but clean and functional rooms with air-con for 8000/12,000 dr.

Places to Stay – middle
The C-class *Hotel Galaxias* (☎ 20 750; fax 31 444) at Agiou Nikolaou 3 is a modern-looking and very clean hotel with rooms for 10,000/14,000 dr. The C-class *Iasonas* (☎ 26 075; fax 26 975) at Pavlou Mela 1, more or less on the waterfront, has light and breezy single/double rooms with double-glazed windows for 6500/10,000 dr.

Places to Stay – top end
Volos' fanciest hotel is the rather snooty B-class *Park Hotel* (☎ 36 511; fax 28 645), Deligiorgi 2. The stylish rooms have all expected amenities. Single/double rates are 12,000/18,000 dr including breakfast. On the waterfront at Argonafton 24 is one of Volos' longest-established hostelries, the B-class *Aigli* (☎ 24 471; fax 33 006); it has an impressive neoclassical façade and a warm interior. Single/double rooms here are an equally impressive 13,000/20,000 dr including breakfast.

Places to Eat
Since Volos is considered the ouzeri capital of Greece, it would be a shame not to eat and drink as the locals do. Some typical mezedes are spetsofaï (chopped sausages and peppers in a rich sauce); ohtapodi (octopus); htypiti (a mixed feta cheese and hot pepper dip); and fried calamari.

There is a cluster of ouzeria along the Argonafton waterfront of which the most popular seem to be *Naftilia*, at the western end, and the *Egeo* towards the middle. There are, of course, many other ouzeria along the waterfront and throughout the city itself, so half the fun may well be in seeking out your own favourite place. Bear one thing in mind: an ouzeri can get a bit expensive if you don't keep track of what you are eating and drinking.

For more traditional restaurant fare, try the *Harama Restaurant*, Dimitriados 49, which serves very tasty, cheap dishes.

If this is all too hard, the well-stocked *Asteras Supermarket* right in the middle of the waterfront will supply you with all you need for a picnic lunch.

Getting There & Away
Bus From the bus station there are nine buses a day to Athens (five hours, 4900 dr); 12 a day to Larisa (one hour, 1000 dr); five a day to Thessaloniki (three hours, 3300 dr); and four to Kalambaka (three hours, 2800 dr).

Buses to the major villages of the Pelion peninsula are as follows: 11 a day to Kala Nera and five a day to Afyssos; 10 a day to Makrynitsa (via Portaria); seven to Vyzitsa (via Milies); six to Milina (via Argalasti and Horto); three a day to Platanias; and three a day to both Zagora (via Hania) and Agios Ioannis (via Tsangarada). Buses also run to many of the smaller villages, but often only two or three times a day. Check the board at the bus station and bear in mind possible seasonal changes.

Train There are 15 trains a day to Larisa

The Ouzeri

An *ouzeri* (strictly speaking, a *tsipouradiko*), if you have not already come across one, is like a little restaurant where you eat from various plates of *mezedes* (tasty titbits) and drink little bottles of *tsipouro*. When you have finished one round of mezedes or tsipouro, you order some more and so on, until you are full, or can't stand up. Tsipouro is a distilled spirit like ouzo, but stronger. You can dilute it with water, if you want it to last a little longer. It costs around 450 dr a pop.

The ouzeri is not purely a Volos institution, but Volos is famous throughout Greece for the quality and quantity of its ouzeria. The institution came about as a result of refugees from Asia Minor who established themselves in Volos after the exchange of populations in 1922, when Greeks and Turks were forced to swap homelands. Most of the refugees who came to Volos were seafarers who would gather on the harbour at lunchtime and drink tsipouro accompanied by various mezedes. As the eating and drinking progressed, the demand for all the more exotic and different mezedes grew and so too did the repertoire of the establishment serving them. Seafood mezedes were the mainstay of this eating and drinking routine. ■

(560 dr). Two direct intercity trains a day go to Athens (the *Trikoupis* at 6.25 am and the *Thessalia* at 5.25 pm, 5410 dr) and three local trains go to Thessaloniki, with a connection at Larisa. However, there are many connections a day to both Thessaloniki and Athens from Larisa. You can make reservations for these connections and the Athens or Thessaloniki intercity trains from the on-line booking office at the station. Four trains a day go to Kalambaka (four hours, 1140 dr) via Paleofarsalos, for travellers wishing to get to Meteora.

Ferry There are one to two ferries daily from Volos to Skiathos (three hours, 2300 dr); Glossa (Skopelos; 3½ hours, 2630 dr); Skopelos town (4½ hours, 2814 dr); and Alonnisos (five hours, 3100 dr).

Hydrofoil In summer, there are five or six daily hydrofoils to Skiathos (1½ hours, 5100 dr); Glossa (1¾ hours, 6150 dr); Skopelos town (two hours, 6580 dr); and Alonnisos (three hours, 7250 dr). Additional services

operate to Evia and some of the Sporades services stop at Trikeri island, Agia Paraskevi and Platanias. Tickets are available from Ceres (☎ 39 786; fax 24 388), Antonopoulou 14A.

Getting Around

Cars can be rented from European Car Rental (☎ 24 381; fax 24 192), at Iasonos 83, and from Avis (☎ 20 849; fax 32 360), at Argonafton 41.

PELION PENINSULA Πήλιον Ορος

The well-watered Pelion peninsula lies to the east and south of Volos. It consists of a mountain range, of which the highest peak is Mt Pliassidi (1651m). The inaccessible eastern flank consists of high cliffs which plunge dramatically into the sea. The gentler western flank coils around the calm sea of the Pagasitic gulf. The interior is a green wonderland where trees heavy with fruit vie with wild olive groves, forests of horse chestnut, oak, walnut, eucalyptus and beech trees to reach the light of day.

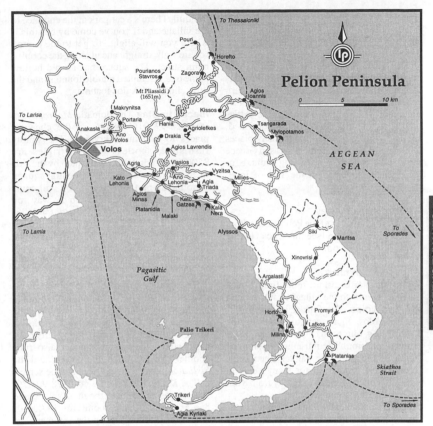

The villages tucked away in this profuse foliage are characterised by whitewashed, half-timbered houses with overhanging balconies and grey slate roofs, and cobbled mule paths winding around their vibrant gardens. Flagstone squares harbouring little Byzantine churches and sculpted fountains shaded by enormous gnarled plane trees are another feature of these settlements.

If you have your own transport you can see a great deal of the peninsula in one day, but bear in mind that driving here is a tortuous affair with so many bends and turns. If you're travelling by bus, allow for two or three days: no single bus route goes around the whole peninsula, so it isn't possible to tour the coast and inland villages in a single day.

Many of the places to stay in the Pelion are traditional mansions tastefully converted into pensions. They are wonderful places to spend a night or two, but they don't necessarily come cheap.

The Pelion has an enduring tradition of regional cooking. Be sure to try some of the local specialities, such as *fasolada* (bean soup), *kouneli stifado* (rabbit stew), *spetsofaï* and *tyropsomo* (cheese bread).

History & Mythology

In mythology the Pelion was inhabited by centaurs – reprobate creatures who took delight in deflowering virgins.

The Turkish occupation did not extend into the inaccessible central and eastern parts of the Pelion, and as a result the western coastal towns were abandoned in favour of mountain villages. In these remote settlements, culture and the economy flourished; silk and wool were exported to many places in Europe. Like other remote areas in Greece the Pelion became a spawning ground for ideas that culminated in the War of Independence.

Getting There & Away

Buses to the villages of the Pelion leave from the Volos bus station (see the Volos Getting There & Away section).

Volos to Makrynitsa

Taking the north-eastern route from Volos, the road climbs to the villages of **Anakasia** and **Ano Volos**. The former is 4km north-east of Volos. In its central square is the **Theophilos Museum**, housed in an 18th-century mansion. The museum features the works of the primitive painter Theophilos (1866-1934), who lived for many years in Volos. It's open Monday to Friday from 8 am to 2 pm. Admission is free.

Portaria, the next village, is 13km north-east of Volos. True to form, its plateia has a splendid old plane tree, and the little 13th-century **Church of Panagia of Portaria** has fine frescoes. A fork to the left in the village leads to Makrynitsa, 17km north-east of Volos.

Makrynitsa Μακρυνίτσα

Makrynitsa (Makrynitsa), clinging to a mountainside at an elevation of 750m, is aptly called the Balcony of Pelion. The traditional houses were built with three storeys at the front and only one at the back, giving the impression they are stacked on top of one another. It is one of the loveliest of the Pelion villages, but is also the most touristy. However, as it is closed to traffic, it remains tranquil. There's a car park at the entrance to the village and if you've come by bus this is where you will alight. To get to the central square walk straight ahead along the cobbled main street. The square has an old hollow plane tree, a sculpted marble fountain and the little church of Agios Ioannis.

Places to Stay The domatia *Makropoulou* (☎ 0428-99 016) is one of the cheapest places to stay in Makrynitsa. The simply furnished, spotless doubles/triples are 8500/10,000 dr. Walk up the path by the side of Restaurant Galini, on the central square, continue along the path and you will come to the domatia on the right. On the way you will pass the *Archontiko Diomidi* (☎ 0428-99 430; fax 0428-99 114), a traditional mansion featuring lots of wall-hangings, brass and ceramic ornaments and carved-wood furniture. Rates are 10,500 dr for a double.

The *Pension Xiradaki* (☎ 0428-99 250) is a beautiful old stone mansion, with minimal but tasteful traditional décor. Double/triple rates are 17,000/21,000 dr, with breakfast. Look for the pension sign pointing left on the main street. This establishment also runs another two arhontika, the *Mousli* and the *Sislianou*, where room prices are the same.

The *Kentavros Xenonas* (☎ 0428-99 075) is a spotless place near the main square and has exquisite double rooms for 14,000 dr which drop to 8000 dr in the summer. The *Hotel Achilles* (☎ 0428-99 177; fax 0428-99 140), which is on the main square, has single/double rooms for 9000/11,500 dr.

Places to Eat Try the reasonably priced *Restaurant Galini* on the central square for excellent spetsofaï, fasolada and kouneli stifado. The *Pantheon* nearby on the square offers much the same fare, but has a much better view. Meals at both establishments should cost around 2600 dr with wine.

Makrynitsa to Tsangarada

Back on the main Volos-Zagora route the road continues to the modern village of **Hania**. Some 16km uphill from here is the ski resort of **Agriolefkes**, where there is a ski centre (☎ 0428-39 136) with three downhill runs and one cross-country run. Information can be obtained either from the EOT in Volos or the Volos EOS (Greek Alpine Club) (☎ 0421-25 696) at Dimitriados 92.

From Hania the road zigzags down through chestnut trees to a road junction. The left turn leads to **Zagora** (population 3000), the largest of the Pelion villages and a major fruit-growing centre. Zagora is a long, strung-out village, as the approach along the main road will testify, and is not as dependent on tourism as other villages in the area. The very successful Zagora agricultural cooperative was founded in 1916 and has been instrumental in promoting the growing and export of fruit (mainly apples) as a means of sustaining growth in the village region. The cooperative has its own restaurant, cafeteria and minimarket complex in town called *Milon tis Eridos* (Apple of Discord). Just down past the turn-off to Horefto, you will pass, on the left, the **Ellinomousio**, a museum dedicated to Rigas Fereos, one of the intellectual instigators of the War of Independence. The museum is open daily from 9.30 am to 1.30 pm and 5.30 to 8.30 pm.

Horefto, 8km downhill from Zagora, is a popular resort with a long sandy beach. The main beach is OK, but there are a couple of better beaches, within walking distance, north and south of the main village. There is a reasonable camp site here. At the moment, Horefto takes some getting to by road because of the terrain, but you can always jump off a hydrofoil from the Sporades or Thessaloniki if the mood takes you.

North of Zagora, **Pouri**, another charming village, spills down a steep mountainside. This is the last of the central Pelion villages and is worth the detour from Zagora to have a look.

Back at the road junction, the right turn-off takes you through a series of villages to Tsangarada. This route is one of the most scenically spectacular in the Pelion.

The most delightful of the villages is **Kissos**, which is built on steep terraces. Its 18th-century Church of Agia Marina has fine

frescoes. From Kissos, a 6km road leads down to the coastal resort of **Agios Ioannis**, which is popular enough, though it wouldn't rank among the best. It is connected to Thessaloniki and the Sporades by a summer hydrofoil service.

Tsangarada Τσαγκαράδα

Tsangarada (Tsangarada), nestling in oak and plane forests, is an extremely spread-out village comprising the four separate communities of Agii Taxiarhes, Agia Paraskevi, Agios Stefanos and Agia Kyriaki. The largest is Agia Paraskevi, which is just north of the main Volos-Milies-Tsangarada road. The bus stops near the central square of Plateia Paraskevis. The plane tree on this square is reputedly the largest and oldest in Greece – locals claim it is 1500 years old. No doubt this is an exaggeration, but whatever its age it's a magnificent specimen with a girth of 14m.

The small seaside resort of **Mylopotamos**, with a sheltered beach, is 8km down the road from Tsangarada. The beach here has earned an EU Blue Flag for cleanliness, so enjoy and respect it.

Places to Stay There are several domatia on the main road near Plateia Paraskevis. Walking south along the main road, you will first find the *Paradisos Pension* (☎ 0426-49 209; fax 0426-49 551) on your right – a lovely place run by the friendly and enthusiastic Rigakis brothers. The pension's immaculate and cosy single/double rooms are 8700/13,000 dr.

The *Konaki Pension* (☎ 0426-49 481), further along the road on the left (before the turn-off for Mylopotamos), is a traditional mansion with singles/doubles for 8000/12,000 dr, including breakfast. If you'd rather be on the coast, then Mylopotamos has a few domatia.

Places to Eat The *Paradisos Restaurant* (at the pension of the same name) is excellent. Their roast kid and local retsina is top notch. Their home-made apple and cherry preserve is ambrosia to anyone with a sweet tooth.

CENTRAL GREECE

There are plenty of other psistarias and tavernas to choose from as well.

Volos to Milies & Vyzitsa

After leaving Volos, the west-coast road passes through the touristy villages of **Agria**, **Kato Lehonia** and **Ano Lehonia**. Several roads off to the left lead to one of the most beautiful areas of Pelion; the road from Ano Lehonia to **Vlasios** is particularly lovely. A right turn leads to the seaside resorts of **Platanidia**, **Malaki** and **Kato Gatzea**. After the tortuous and narrow roads of the eastern Pelion villages, this stretch of road is a blessing.

Further along the coast road just past **Kala Nera**, 22km from Volos, there is a turn-off to the left for Tsangarada. A little way along here, another turn-off to the left leads through apple orchards to the photogenic villages of Milies and Vyzitsa.

Milies Μηλιές

• *pop 952* • *postcode 370 10* • *area code* ☎ *0423*

Built in the late 16th century, Milies (Mili**es**) was a rich agricultural centre, prospering on olive oil, fruit and silk production. Like most of the Pelion it enjoyed semi-autonomy and, largely due to its excellent school, it played a major role in the intellectual and cultural awakening that led to Greek independence.

Milies was the birthplace of Anthinos Gazis (1761-1828), the man who raised the Thessalian revolt in 1821. Shortly after independence a railway line was built between Volos and Milies and the town became a prosperous centre of commerce. *To Trenaki*, the steam train which used to chug along this route, retired formally long ago, but has recently been revived as a weekend tourist attraction (600 dr). It currently runs a limited route from Milies to Ano Lehonia, though whether its route would ever be extended to Volos is debatable, since it would mean some serious realignment of the old track which is clearly visible under the surface of the main Volos-Gatzea road. The train stations at Milies and Ano Lehonia have been renovated and you can take a delightful walk along the track between the two stations.

To reach the station from Milies' central square, turn left at the clock tower as you face towards Vyzitsa (the next village along), then walk across the car park and take the cobbled path by the side of Aigli Taverna. If you are approaching under your own steam from Kala Nera, look for the left turn-off to the station just before you reach the main village turn-off. While you are at the station, look out for the memorial to the 29 residents of Milies who were executed by the Germans in 1942.

The **Milies folk museum**, which houses a display of local crafts, is on the right beyond the central square.

Places to Stay The A-class *Palios Stathmos* (☎ 86 425), by the station in Milies, is an old stone house with traditional furnishings. Doubles go for 12,000 dr, including breakfast.

Places to Eat The setting of the *Palios Stathmos Restaurant* is idyllic and the food is tasty and reasonably priced. Just up the road from the station is the *Hryso Milo* restaurant, while up in the main village, the striking-looking *Panorama* psistaria offers a range of local foods. However, the gastronomic highlight of Milies is the scrumptious tyropsomo (cheese pie). You can buy it at the Korbas bakery on the main Volos-Tsangarada road, just before the Milies turn-off.

Vyzitsa Βυζίτσα

• *pop 295* • *postcode 370 10* • *area code* ☎ *0423*

Just 2km beyond Milies is the peaceful little village of Vyzitsa (altitude 555m). Vyzitsa is a photographer's delight. Proclaimed a state heritage village by EOT, here you will find a model Pelion community. It is less touristy than Makrynitsa and in many ways is more attractive. Cobbled pathways wind between its traditional slate-roof houses. To reach Vyzitsa's shady central square walk 50m up a cobbled path to your right from the main parking area.

Places to Stay Vyzitsa has several domatia where doubles average 9000 dr – have a look for the signs. The *Karagiannopoulos Mansion* (☎ 86 373) is a beautiful place – the lounge has a carved-wood ceiling and stained-glass windows. Rates are 12,000 dr for a double and 16,000 dr for a suite, both with breakfast. The mansion is on the road coming from Milies.

The *Kontos Mansion* (☎ 86 793) is equally appealing, and is the village's largest mansion. Rates here are 12,000/17,000 dr for singles/doubles. The pension is signposted to the right from the bus terminal, which is in the main parking area. The *Thetis Xenonas* (☎ 86 111), just off the main car park and with its accompanying café, has doubles for 11,800 dr including breakfast.

Places to Eat The *Thetis Café*, just beyond the bus terminal, is a serene place, with tables and chairs on a patio shaded by walnut trees. On the main square, nestled in between two enormous plane trees, you have a choice of two establishments, the *Drosia* and the *Balkonaki*. The newer *Georgaras* restaurant on the right of the road leading back to Milies has the views, but not the village intimacy.

South to Platanias Πλατανιάς
Continuing south from Kala Nera the bus goes as far as Platanias. Although not as fertile as the northern part of the peninsula, the southern part of the Pelion is still attractive, with pine-forested hills and olive groves. Before heading inland once more, the road skirts the little coastal village of Afyssos, winds upwards through to the large unexceptional inland farming community of Argalasti, and then forks – the left fork continues inland, the right goes to the coastal resorts of Horto and Milina. From Milina the road heads inland and then south to Platanias. If you are really keen, you can take a twice-daily bus from Volos, all the way to the end of the desolate-looking peninsula to Trikeri and finally to Agia Kyriaki.

CENTRAL GREECE

The Evil Eye

When travelling through Greece – particularly in the rural areas – you may notice that some bus drivers keep a chain bearing one or two blue stones dangling over the dashboard. Or you may spot a small, plastic blue eye attached to the cross hanging around someone's neck. Or maybe you'll wonder why there is a string of blue beads hanging from the front fender of a tractor.

Puzzle no longer. The Greeks are not sporting blue colours in support of their favourite soccer team or to show a particular political leaning. No – they are wearing blue to ward off the evil eye.

The evil eye is associated with envy, and can be cast – apparently unintentionally – upon someone or something which is praised or admired (even secretly). So those most vulnerable to the evil eye include people, creatures or objects of beauty, rarity and value. Babies are particularly vulnerable, and those who admire them will often spit gently on them to repel any ill effects. Adults and older children who are worried about being afflicted by the evil eye will wear blue.

Who then is responsible for casting the evil eye? Well, most culprits are those who are already considered quarrelsome or peculiar in some way by the local community. And folk with blue eyes are regarded with extreme suspicion – no doubt more than partly because being blue-eyed is a trait Greeks associate with Turks. All these quarrelsome, peculiar or blue-eyed folk have to do is be present when someone or something enviable appears on the scene – and then the trouble starts.

If, during your travels, someone casts the evil eye on you, you'll soon know about it. Symptoms include dizziness, headaches, a feeling of 'weight' on the head or of tightening in the chest. The locals will be able to point you in the direction of someone, usually an old woman, who can cure you.

What happens next is usually along these lines: the curer will make the sign of the cross over a glass of water; then she will pray silently, at the same time dropping oil into the glass. If the oil disappears from the surface, it proves that you have the evil eye – and it also cures it, for the 'blessed' water will be dabbed on your forehead, stomach and at two points on your chest (at the points of the crucifix).

Apparently, the cure works. But you know the old adage about prevention being better than cure. If you're worried about the evil eye, don't take any chances: wear blue. ∎

Afyssos Αφψσσος
This up-market resort features a long and attractive promenade, but it tends to get pretty busy in the summer. There is one A-class hotel, the *Maïstrali* (☎ 0423-33 472), with doubles in the 13,000 dr range, and several domatia/pension places, if you do really prefer the hustle and bustle of the place.

Horto & Milina Χόρτο & Μηλίνα
These are the next two villages down that you will meet, if you take the right fork after Argalasti at Metohi. Horto is very low-key and small, while Milina is larger and probably offers a better balance of amenities. Both are on a quiet part of the peninsula with clean water but no spectacular beaches. There are two camp sites at Milina, the *Olizon* (☎ 0423-65 236) and the *Kentauros*, a little further on. Of the two, Olizon is probably a better choice.

Just beyond Milina at **Mavri Petra** is an appealing roadside taverna called *Flavios*. Set on a wide bay with fishing boats at anchor, it is a pleasant culinary oasis. Sardines, chips and salad with draught retsina should cost you about 2000 dr.

Trikeri Τρικέρι
The road from Milina to Trikeri now becomes more and more desolate and the vegetation more stunted as rock takes over. Apart from one or two small sections, the road is sealed all the way and is wide and fast, with little to distract your attention other than the odd house-cum-taverna or goat pen. There is an end-of-the-world feel about this part of the Pelion and Trikeri may come as a surprise when you discover this lively and historically important little community perched on the hill top, keeping guard over the straits that separate the mainland from Evia.

Donkeys outnumber cars here and the residents pride themselves on their tradition as seafarers, fighters against the Turks in the War of Independence and as upholders of traditional customs and dress. The week following Easter is one of continual revelry as dancing takes place every day and women try to outdo each other in their local costume finery.

Agia Kyriaki Αγία Κψριακή
• *pop 285• area code ☎ 0423*
This is the last stop on the Pelion peninsula, a winding 5km drive down the hill, or a fast 15-minute walk down a stone path. This is a fishing village without the tourist trappings and most people only see it during a five-minute stopover on the Flying Dolphin from, or to, the Sporades. Here you will find bright, orange-coloured fishing boats put to good use by a lively, hard-working community.

Rooms are available at *Lambis domatia* (☎ 91 587), just out of Agia Kyriaki at **Mylos**. Follow a dirt road for about 500m and look for the Greek sign. Walk down the path and then look for the EOT sign on the wall, on your left. Haralambos Karapetis, an expat Australian-Greek, should be able to accommodate you as well. Ask around Mylos to be directed to Haralambos.

There are a couple of reasonable-looking places to eat on the waterfront, but the *Mouragio* has that more authentic fish taverna look, with tables right next to the water.

Palio Trikeri Παλιό Τρικέρι
• *pop 91 • postcode 370 09 • area code ☎ 0423*
If you really must go that one step further to get away from it all, then head for this little island just off the coast and inside the Pagasitic gulf. The hydrofoil is supposed to make a stop here four times a week, but you may have to ask to make sure. Alternatively, you can twist someone's arm at Agia Kyriaki to take you down a farm track to the end of the headland, where they will whistle or shout to get someone to come from the island to take you over on a caïque.

The *Palio Trikeri* domatia-cum-restaurant (☎ 91 432) can probably offer you accommodation and food, as can *Hariklia Brouzou-Roumbakia* (☎ 91 031), which, similarly, has domatia with an attached restaurant.

Platanias Πλατανιάς
• *pop 171 • postcode 370 06 • are code ☎ 0423*
Platanias (Platanias) is a popular resort with

a good sand and pebble beach. It's a fun place to spend a day or two, even though it's quite developed. Les Hirondelles Travel Agency (☎ 71 231) rents a variety of water-sports equipment, such as canoes, *pedalos* (paddleboats), water skis, scooters and motorboats. Turn left at the sea to reach the agency.

Places to Stay *Kastri Beach Camping* (☎ 71 209) is at Kastri beach, 5km east of Platanias. Look for the left turn-off to Kastri on the approach road to Platanias. *Louisa Camping* (☎ 71 260) is just 500m before Platanias on the left.

A cheap hotel in Platanias is the D-class *Hotel Platanias* (☎ 65 565), where pleasant singles/doubles are 6200/7500 dr with private bathroom. Turn left at the waterfront to reach the hotel. Another agreeable option is the D-class *Hotel des Roses* (☎ 65 568), by the bus stop. Rates are 5500/6500 dr with shared bathroom; doubles with private bathroom are 7500 dr.

The C-class *Hotel Drosero Akrogiali* (☎ 71 210) has doubles/triples for 8500/10,000 dr with private bathroom. Turn right at the waterfront to reach this hotel.

Places to Eat There are no less than six eating places in Platanias among which *To Steki Restaurant* has a large choice of well-prepared dishes. A decent meal here will cost you about 2200 dr with wine or beer. Turn left at the waterfront to reach this place.

Getting There & Away See the Getting There & Away section under Volos for bus services to Platanias.

There is a daily caïque running to Skiathos in the Sporades and whispered rumour of a future car ferry link as well. Don't bank on it yet; though it would be a great service, given the distance and high cost of shipping a vehicle from Volos to the Sporades.

At least two hydrofoils call by Platanias from 1 June onwards on their way to Skiathos (2900 dr), Glossa (3400 dr), Skopelos town (3900 dr) and Alonnisos (4100 dr), and there are five a week to Volos.

Tickets can be purchased from Les Hirondelles Travel Agency.

Getting Around Les Hirondelles Travel Agency rents motorbikes of varying sizes. There are ad hoc excursion boats to Skiathos in addition to the regular caïque service. Other caïques run daily to local, but less-accessible, beaches.

TRIKALA Τρίκαλα
• *pop 48,000* • *postcode 421 00* • *area code* ☎ *0431*
Trikala (Trikala) is ancient Trikki, the reputed birthplace of Asclepius, the god of healing. It's a bustling agricultural town, through which flows the River Litheos, and is a major hub for buses. While Trikala's attractions hardly warrant a special trip, the chances are if you're exploring central Greece you'll eventually pass through here en route to somewhere else.

Orientation
Trikala's main thoroughfare is Asklipiou, the northern end of which is a pedestrian precinct. Facing the river, turn left from the bus station to reach Plateia Riga Fereou at the northern end of Asklipiou. The train station is at the opposite end of Asklipiou, 600m from Plateia Riga Fereou.

To reach the central square of Plateia Iroön Polytehniou turn right at Plateia Riga Fereou and cross the bridge over the river.

Information
Trikala does not have an EOT or tourist police; the regular police (☎ 32 777) are on the corner of Kapodistriou and Asklipiou. The National Bank of Greece is on the central square. The post office is at Saraphi 13; turn left at the central square and it's a little way along on the left. To reach the OTE walk along the left side of the central square and turn left onto 25 Martiou. The OTE is a little way along here on the right at the far side of a small square.

Things to See
The **River Litheos** which bisects the town is crossed by 10 bridges, half of which are for

pedestrians only. The central iron bridge was built in France in 1886. The **Fortress of Trikala** is currently closed for restoration. In any case it's worth a wander up to the gardens which surround it for the views. Walk 400m up Saraphi from the central square and look for the sign pointing right. To get to the old **Turkish quarter** of Varousi, take a sharp right at the sign for the fortress. It's a fascinating area of peaceful narrow streets and fine old houses with overhanging balconies. If you keep on walking through Varousi and up the hill, you will come to the chapel of **Profitis Ilias**. It is a pleasant tree-lined walk after the town centre and you will eventually reach a **zoo** of sorts, if you keep on walking. The zoo is open from 8 am to 8 pm. If you don't mind looking at a collection of sad-looking animals – including an incongruous pair of lions – it's a pleasant enough place to spend an hour or so. Entrance is free.

At the other side of town is the **Koursoun Tzami**, a Turkish mosque built in the 16th century by Sinan Pasha, the same architect who built the Blue Mosque in İstanbul. This mosque has been the subject of a EU-funded restoration project and has now been restored to its former glory – minus the top of the minaret. It is now used as a community concert hall and exhibition centre. From the bus station, turn right, follow the river and you'll reach the mosque after 300m.

Places to Stay – bottom end

Trikala isn't a tourist centre so finding accommodation is easy. The cheapest place is the gloomy – despite a rejuvenating facelift of the façade – D-class *Hotel Panellinio* (☎ 27 644) on Plateia Riga Fereou. Rates are 3500/5000 dr for singles/doubles with shared bathroom.

The C-class *Hotel Palladion* (☎ 28 091), Vyronos 4, is an agreeable budget option, with well-maintained rooms for 7000/10,000 dr with shared bathroom. The hotel is behind the Hotel Achillion (see below). Practically on top of the bus station is the brightly painted C-class *Litheon* (☎ 20 690; fax 37 390), which has been tastefully

renovated and has single/double rooms for 8000/10,000 dr.

Places to Stay – middle

The C-class *Hotel Dina* (☎ 74 777; fax 29 490), at Karanasiou 1, has immaculate rooms with air-con, telephone and balconies for 10,000/14,000 dr. The hotel is 100m along the main pedestrian mall down from Plateia Riga Fereou, on the right.

Places to Stay – top end

The palatial, renovated B-class *Hotel Achillion* (☎ 28 291; fax 74 858), at Asklipiou 2 on Plateia Riga Fereou, has singles/doubles for 15,000/22,000 dr. The B-class *Hotel Divani* (☎ 27 286; fax 20 519), Dionysiou 13 on Plateia Kitrilaki, overlooking the river, is Trikala's best hotel. Single/double room rates are 18,600/24,000 dr. Rates at both these hotels are usually negotiable.

Places to Eat

Quality fast-food joints have sprung up all over Trikala, so if you really want your hamburger and fried chicken fix, you can't go wrong. For ready-made food at a reasonable kind of place, try *O Kostaras* on Plateia Kitrilaki, where you can get a feed for about 2000 dr. There are other eateries on this square in the warm months, too.

Taverna o Babis, four doors down from the Hotel Dina on Karanasiou, is a very pleasant restaurant for lunch as well as for dinner, with ready-made dishes as well as made-to-order grills. Budget for about 2500 dr for a meal.

The *Pliatsikas* restaurant on Ioulietas Adam and diagonally opposite, the *Yali Kafene*, a hip kind of ouzeri joint, are both slightly upper-market establishments, but are popular with the locals for a night out. Ioulietas Adam runs at right angles to Karanasiou.

Getting There & Away

Bus From Trikala's bus station there are 20 buses a day to Kalambaka (30 minutes, 380 dr); almost half-hourly buses to Larisa (one hour, 1100 dr); eight to Athens (5½ hours,

5000 dr); six to Thessaloniki (5½ hours, 3350 dr); four to Volos (2½ hours, 2400 dr); and two to Ioannina (3½ hours, 2550 dr).

Train Trikala is on the narrow-gauge Volos-Kalambaka line. There are 10 departures a day, though only four trains go through to Volos. Five trains connect for Athens and six for Thessaloniki. The connection is at Paleofarsalos (Stavros). Check the timetable (in Greek) at the station. Sample ticket prices are Volos (three hours, 1010 dr); Athens (six to seven hours, 2660 dr); and Thessaloniki (4½ hours, 2220 dr). Travel on intercity trains attracts an extra supplement on top of these prices.

Upgrading of this narrow-gauge line to standard-gauge commenced in 1997. Delays or cancellations may be experienced.

AROUND TRIKALA

About 18km from Trikala is the little village of **Pyli**, which means 'gate' – and rightly so, for just beyond Pyli is a spectacular narrow gorge leading into one of Greece's more attractive wilderness areas and one that is currently embroiled in a vigorous ecological debate. Industrial progressives, despite the protests of the ecological lobby and the local inhabitants, have been building a large, 135m-high dam near Mesohora village on the upper Aheloös River. Once completed, the area behind the dam, which includes two villages and three settlements, will be flooded, thereby bringing about the destruction of the area's native flora and fauna. If that isn't bad enough, the dam builders also want to divert part of the flow of the Aheloös River to the plain of Thessaly, thus radically reducing the natural water flow of the river to the wetlands of Messolongi in Etolo-Akarnania. This, it is claimed, would result in the destruction of the natural habitat of the bird life in the region. The issue has even reached the hallowed halls of the European Parliament and is still under heated discussion.

The area beyond Pyli is gradually being opened up to tourism. If you have your own transport, you can drive comfortably and on a very scenic, almost completely sealed road from Pyli to Arta (three hours), via Stournareïka and Mesohora and the disputed upper Aheloös dam. This provides a much-needed alternative route across the south Pindos ranges to and from Epiros. Buses do not currently cover this route.

There is a small, but locally popular skiing centre near **Pertouli**, 30km beyond Pyli. Here you will find forested, alpine scenery, reminiscent of Switzerland. Skis can be hired here and the centre has a cosy, family atmosphere. Buses for Pertouli leave from the main bus station in Trikala.

For some time now, kayaking enthusiasts have been coming to the **Tria Potamia** area, which is 15km north of Mesohora, to ride the waters of the Aheloös River. The sport is not as organised as it is in Konitsa in northern Epiros, but nonetheless attracts a growing number of white-water jockeys. How long this activity will last, once the dam is built, is anyone's guess.

KALAMBAKA Καλαμπάκα
• *pop 12,000* • *postcode 422 00* • *area code ☎ 0432*
Kalambaka (Kalambaka) is almost entirely modern, having been devastated by the Nazis in WWII. Its chief claim to fame is its proximity to Meteora. It takes a whole day to see all of the monasteries of Meteora, so you'll need to spend the night either in Kalambaka or the village of Kastraki, which is closer to the rocks. First-time visitors to Kalambaka will be amazed at the vertical rocks that guard the northern flank of the town. It is an unusual sight and gives Kalambaka a special feel. The rocks are illuminated at night to great effect.

Orientation
The central square is the hub of the town and the main thoroughfares of Rodou, Trikalon, Ioanninon, Kastrakiou and Vlahavas radiate from it. Kalambaka's other large square is Plateia Riga Fereou – Trikalon connects the two.

The bus station is on the right side of Rodou if you're walking from the central square. Most incoming buses stop on the central square to let passengers alight. To get to the train station from the central square walk along Trikalon, take the right fork after Plateia Riga Fereou, turn right at Kondili and the station is opposite the end of this road.

Information
There is no EOT in Kalambaka but the Tourist Services Office (☎ 75 306; fax 25 343) at Kondyli & Hatzipetrou 38 has a wide range of information on all aspects of local tourism. In the summer months it has a mobile office on the main square near the taxi rank. The tourist police (☎ 22 109) are at Hatzipetrou 10, near the bus station.

The National Bank of Greece is on Plateia Riga Fereou and sports both an ATM and automatic exchange machine. The post office and OTE are both on Ioanninon.

Places to Stay – bottom end
There are several camp sites in the area. *Theopetra Camping* (☎ 81 405) is the first site you come across if you're coming from Trikala. *Camping Philoxenia* (☎ 24 446) with good shade and a children's play area – including a water slide – is next on the right and *Rizos International* (☎ 22 239) is last. *Camping Kalambaka* (☎ 22 309) is on a road off to the right just before you enter Kalambaka.

There is no shortage of rooms in Kalambaka and you may well be approached as you arrive by train or bus. Choose with care. Look for the EOT-approved sign, wherever possible and avoid rooms offered by a Mr Tottis, if at all possible. *Koka Roka Rooms* (☎ 24 554), at the beginning of the path to Agia Triada Monastery, is a bit of an institution among travellers and has an impressive visitors' book. The few rooms are clean and nicely furnished and cost 8000 dr for doubles with private bathroom. The host Sakis is an affable Greek-Australian who will most probably proudly show you his guest books. From the central square, walk 700m to the top of Vlahavas, and you'll come to the rooms on the left.

Kalambaka's cheapest hotel is the D-class *Hotel Astoria* (☎ 22 213), G Kondili 93. The

clean pine-furnished single/double rooms with shared bathroom cost 5000/6000 dr. The hotel is on the road opposite the train station. The C-class *Hotel Meteora* (☎ 22 367; fax 75 550), Ploutarhou 14, is a charming and cosy place, with single/double/triple rooms for 5000/7000/9000 dr with private bathroom. The price includes breakfast. From the central square, walk along Patriarhou Dimitriou, and Ploutarhou is the second turn right.

The C-class *Aeolic Star* (☎ 22 325; fax 22 444) at Athanasiou Diakou 4 has clean, compact rooms for 6000/8500 dr. It is just north of the main square. The C-class *Hotel Odysseon* (☎ 22 320; fax 75 307), at Patriarhou Dimitriou 54, heading out to Kastraki, has light, spacious rooms; rates are 8500/10,000 dr for singles/doubles including breakfast. The *Hotel Helvetia* (☎ 23 041; fax 25 241), which is nearby at Patriarhou Dimitriou 45, has very pleasant rooms for 9100/11,000 dr.

Places to Stay – middle
The B-class *Hotel Famisi* (☎ 24 117; fax 24 615), Trikalon 103, has singles/doubles for 13,500/20,600 dr. All the rooms have balconies, a radio and direct-dial telephone. The hotel has a restaurant and bar.

Places to Stay – top end
A top-end choice in town is the A-class *Hotel Divani* (☎ 22 584; fax 23 638), the first hotel you come to on the left as you enter Kalambaka from Trikala. Single/double rooms here are 18,000/22,000 dr and naturally include breakfast.

Places to Eat
For a good range of look-and-point fare, the *Diethnes* restaurant is your best bet. It is on the corner of Trikalon on Plateia Riga Fereou. You can eat here for under 2000 dr and at the same time avoid the tourist groups that sometimes plague other establishments.

The *Koka Roka Taverna*, below Koka Roka Rooms (see Places to Stay), serves tasty low-priced food in a warm and homy environment. Grills prepared on the open hearth are their speciality. Their splendid rosé wine is, however, wicked when over-indulged in. The *Taverna Stathmos*, at Kondili 56, which is the street directly opposite the train station, is open all day and operates as an ouzeri at lunchtime. At night it is a very good psistaria with many spit-roast dishes. Prices are in the 2500 dr range for a decent meal.

Getting There & Away
Bus From Kalambaka there are frequent buses to Trikala (30 minutes, 380 dr) and to the surrounding villages and two through buses to Ioannina (three hours, 2100 dr). There are two buses a day to Grevena (1¼ hours, 1200 dr) and four buses a day to Volos (three hours, 2800 dr). Four buses a day run to Megalo Meteoro (via Kastraki, 210 dr); they leave from Kalambaka's central square. Buses to other major destinations depart from Trikala.

Train Kalambaka is the western terminus of the narrow-gauge line to Volos. There are 10 departures a day, though only four trains go through to Volos. Five trains connect for Athens and six for Thessaloniki. The connection is at Paleofarsalos (Stavros). Check the timetable (in Greek) at the station. Sample ticket prices are Volos (three hours, 1140 dr); Athens (six to seven hours, 2700 dr); and Thessaloniki (five hours, 2220 dr). Travel on intercity trains attracts an extra supplement on top of these prices.

Upgrading of this narrow-gauge line to standard gauge commenced in 1997. Delays or cancellations may be experienced.

Getting Around
Motorbikes can be hired from the Hobby Shop (☎ 25 262; fax 25 262) at Patriarhou Dimitriou 28. This is the main Kastraki road and the shop is on the right as you head out of Kalambaka. A 50cc motorbike rental will cost you 3500 dr. They also offer a full motorbike service, and rent bicycles for 1500 dr a day. The owner also speaks English. There is another rental shop called Moto Service (☎ 23 526), on Meteoron. From the central square, walk along Ioanninon, turn

right at the post office and the outlet is on the right.

METEORA Μετέωρα
Meteora (Meteora) is an extraordinary place. The massive pinnacles of smooth rocks with holes in them like Emmenthal cheese are ancient and yet, paradoxically, could be a setting for a science fiction story. The monasteries are the icing on the cake in this already strange and beautiful landscape.

Each monastery is built around a central courtyard surrounded by monks' cells, chapels and a refectory. In the centre of each courtyard stands the *katholikon* (main church).

History
The name Meteora derives from the adjective *meteoros*, which means suspended in the air. The word 'meteor' is from the same root. Many theories have been put forward as to the origins of this 'rock forest', but it remains a geological enigma.

From the 11th century, solitary hermit monks lived in the caverns of Meteora. By the 14th century, Byzantine power was on the wane and incursions into Greece were on the in-

crease, so monks began to seek peaceful havens away from the bloodshed. The inaccessibility of the rocks of Meteora made them an ideal retreat, and the less safe the monks became, the higher they climbed, until eventually they were living on top of the rocks.

The earliest monasteries were reached by climbing articulated, removable ladders. Later, windlasses were used so monks could be hauled up in nets, and this method was used until the 1920s. A story goes that when apprehensive visitors enquired how frequently the ropes were replaced, the monks' stock reply was 'When the Lord lets them break'. These days access to the monasteries is by steps hewn into the rocks. Some windlasses can still be seen (you can have a good look at one at Agia Triada), but they are now used for hauling up provisions.

Monasteries

The monasteries are linked by asphalt roads, but the area is best explored on foot on the old paths, where they still exist. You could walk around all the monasteries in one day, but you would need an early start and plan at least a two-hour break from 1 to 3 pm when most monasteries close. In any case, they are all only open at the same time on weekends. Opening times and closure days do vary from season to season. Walking and climbing around the rocks can be thirsty work, but there are mobile canteens selling drinks and snacks at most monastery car parks.

Entry to all monasteries is currently 400 dr unless you are Greek, or can convince the ticket seller that you are, in which case entry is free. Strict dress codes are enforced. Women must wear skirts below their knees, men must wear long trousers and arms must be covered. Skirts, which you can wear over your trousers, are often provided for women upon entering the monastery.

A dirt track leads in 15 minutes from Kastraki (see later in this section) to the **Moni Agiou Nikolaou Anapafsa**. To reach it walk to the end of the main road in Kastraki, which peters out to a dirt track. After about 10 minutes the path crosses a stream bed. Im-

mediately after the stream, scramble up a steep grassy slope towards the monastery which you will see perched on a rock high up on your left. You will come out on the main road just to the right of the path leading to the monastery. A slightly longer but more straightforward route is to follow the main road from Kastraki.

The Monastery of Agiou Nikolaou Anapafsa was built in the 15th century. The superlative frescoes in its katholikon were painted by the monk Theophanes Strelizas from Crete. Especially beautiful is the one of Adam naming the animals. The monastery is open every day from 9 am to 6 pm.

On leaving the monastery, turn left onto the road and five minutes along, just before the road begins to wind, take a path off to the left. The start of the path is not marked, so look out for a white chevron road sign on the bend. The path starts here. In five minutes you will come to a fork. Take the left fork and soon you will come to a T-junction at the base of the rocks. Turn left here and after about 20 minutes of steep, zigzag climbing you will reach the **Moni Megalou Meteorou** (Metamorphosis), the best known of the monasteries.

The majestic and imposing Megalo Meteoro monastery is built on the highest rock at 613m above sea level. Founded by St Athanasios in the 14th century, it became the richest and most powerful of the monasteries, thanks to the Serbian emperor Symeon Uros, who turned all his wealth over to the monastery and became a monk. Its katholikon has a magnificent 12-sided central dome. Its striking, although gory, series of frescoes entitled *Martyrdom of Saints* depicts the persecution of Christians by the Romans. The monastery is open from 9 am to 1 pm and 3 to 6 pm, but is closed on Tuesday and Wednesday.

From Megalo Meteoro turn sharp right on the road to reach the nearby **Moni Varlaam**. It has fine late Byzantine frescoes by Frangos Kastellanos. Varlaam is open from 9 am to 1 pm and 3.30 to 6 pm (closed on Friday).

On leaving Varlaam walk back to the main road and veer right. In about 15 minutes you will come to a fork: the right fork has a signpost to Rousanou and the left to the Agiou Stefanous Nannery (sic). The best approach is to take the left fork and in about 10 minutes you will come to a signpost pointing right to the Rousanou monastery. A 10-minute walk along a path will lead to **Moni Agias Varvaras Rousanou**; access is across a vertiginous bridge. The katholikon features more gory frescoes. Rousanou is open from 9 am to 1 pm and from 3.30 to 5 pm. It is closed on Wednesday.

After Rousanou you have the choice of either a short walk down the steps to the Agios Nikolaos-Metamorphosis road or going back along the path and continuing along the road to Moni Agias Triados. If you decide to do this you will reach the Agia Triada monastery in about 45 minutes (you may be able to hitch a lift on this stretch). A path leads down to Kalambaka from this monastery. If you want to take this path then it is better to visit the Agiou Stefanou monastery first and then backtrack to Agia Triada.

Of all the monasteries, **Moni Agias Triados** has the most primitive and remote feel about it. It gained meteoric, though temporal fame, when it featured in the James Bond film *For Your Eyes Only*. The monastery is open from 9 am to 1 pm every day.

Moni Agiou Stefanou is another 10 minutes walking further along the road. After Agia Triados it feels like returning to civilisation, with business-like nuns selling souvenirs and even videotapes of Meteora. Among the exhibits in the monastery's **museum** is an exquisite embroidered Epitaphios (a picture on cloth of Christ on his bier), executed with gold threads and sequins. Agiou Stefanou is open from 9 am to 1 pm and 3 to 5 pm.

To find the path to Kalambaka from Agias Triados, walk straight ahead when you leave the monastery; the path is off to the left. It's well marked with red arrows, dots and slashes. The monks will tell you this walk takes 10 minutes, but unless you're James Bond or have the agility of a mountain goat, it'll take you around 30 minutes. On the walk

there are tremendous views of the rocks at close quarters, where you see not only their dramatic contours but the details of their strata, too. The path ends near the Koka Roka Taverna in Kalambaka.

For your lunchtime break try to picnic on the *Psaropetra* lookout, with some great photo opportunities. It is along the road to the Agios Triados and Agiou Stefanou monasteries close to the point where the track down to the Rousanou monastery begins.

Activities
Trekking Hellas (☎ 75 214; fax 23 134; mobile 094-313 898) runs a rock-climbing school for beginners, and rock-climbing packages in the Meteora region for both beginner and advanced climbers. For further information contact Hristos Lambris, Trekking Hellas, Rodou 11, 422 00 Kalambaka. Meteora is a mecca for rock climbers and if you are one of those people whose feet are firmly and permanently planted on terra firma, you will not cease to be amazed at the daily spectacle of fly-like climbers inching their way up those almost vertical pillars of rock that dot Meteora.

If that wasn't enough for you, Trekking Hellas also organises ultralite flights over Meteora (8000 to 10,000 dr) as well as paragliding and parachuting. Trekking Hellas can also be contacted via Vrachos Camping (see under Kastraki).

KASTRAKI Καστράκι
• *pop 1500* • *postcode 422 00* • *area code* ☎ *0432*
The small village of Kastraki nestles at the foot of the rocks, 2km from Kalambaka. Its location right under the rocks is most impressive and the view all around the village has an other-world feel about it, since there is really no other place in Greece quite like it. Despite its small size, more than a million people pass through here each year, so it can feel a bit crowded at times. As an alternative base for exploring the Meteora monasteries, or climbing the rocks themselves, Kastraki is a much better choice than Kalambaka.

There is a nice walk from Kastraki to

CENTRAL GREECE

Kalambaka along the base of the rocks. From the main square take the steps down and follow the road opposite up the hill. Turn right at the top and follow the road until you reach the junction with the main road after about 10 minutes walking. There are a couple of scenically located benches along the way, if you feel like taking in the views for a few minutes. Kalambaka is a brisk 15-minute walk away.

Places to Stay

Camping If you decide to stay here, *Vrachos Camping* (☎ 22 293; fax 23 134), on the left as you enter the village, has excellent facilities and a swimming pool. The sites are reasonably level and many are powered. The toilet blocks are new and there is a covered, communal eating area. Kastraki also has a couple of other camping sites should this one be full: the *Meteora Garden* and *Boufidis Camping*.

Hotels *Zozas Pallas* (☎ 24 408; fax 25 344) has very comfortable singles/doubles for 4000/8000 dr with private bathroom. The domatia are on the left (west) side of the Kalambaka-Kastraki road. One hundred metres further up towards the village are the domatia of *Spanias Rooms* (☎ 75 966), with ample car parking and a relaxed and spacious environment. Single/double rooms at Spanias go for 5500/7000 dr. Both Zozas and Spanias have a bar and cafeteria and both are more like hotels than your average domatia. There are more domatia, too numerous to mention, scattered throughout the village.

Between Zozas and Spanias is the newer C-class *Sydney Hotel* (☎ & fax 23 079) run by a welcoming Greek-Australian. Pleasant single/double rooms go for 7000/8000 dr. Some of them have a TV. The C-class *Hotel France* (☎ 24 186; fax 24 186), opposite Vrachos Camping, is run by a French-speaking Greek man and his wife who can fill you in on some 'hidden' walks around the rocks. Good singles/doubles here go for 6000/8000 dr. The hotel also has a restaurant and bar.

Places to Eat

There is no shortage of eating places here, but prices reflect Kastraki's popularity as a tourist destination. Opposite Vrachos Camping is the unmarked *Dellas Psistaria*, which serves standard grilled fare at a reasonable price. Further up the main road to the monasteries is the *Philoxenia Restaurant*, which is open year-round. Their speciality is moussaka. It's on the main road, so you'll have to put up with the passing tourist coaches. There are a number of places around the main village square area, away from the traffic. Look out for the *Gardenia* or the *Platania* where you can eat for around 2000 dr.

Northern Greece Βόρεια Ελλάδα

Northern Greece comprises the regions of Epiros, Macedonia and Thrace. With thickly forested mountains and tumbling rivers, these areas resemble the Balkans more than they do other parts of Greece. Northern Greece offers great opportunities for trekking, but it is an area where you don't have to go into the wilds to get off well-worn tourist tracks, for its towns are little visited by foreign holiday-makers. Unlike the unglamorous and noisy towns of the Peloponnese and central Greece, many of which serve as transport hubs to get out of quickly, most towns in northern Greece have considerable appeal, with atmospheric old quarters of narrow streets and wood-framed houses.

Epiros Ηπειρος

Epiros occupies the north-west corner of the Greek mainland. To the north is Albania, to the west is the Ionian sea and Corfu. Its port of Igoumenitsa is a jumping-off point for ferries to Corfu and Italy. The high Pindos mountains form the region's eastern boundary, separating it from Macedonia and Thessaly.

The road from Ioannina to Kalambaka cuts through the Pindos mountains and is one of the most scenically spectacular in Greece, particularly the section between Metsovo and Kalambaka, which is called the Katara pass. In northern Epiros the Vikos-Aoös National Park is a wilderness of lofty mountains, cascading waterfalls, precipitous gorges, fast-flowing rivers and dense forests harbouring villages of slate-stone houses. These settlements are known as the Zagorohoria villages (Zagoria).

The beaches fronting the Ionian sea are very popular with Greeks, and also with visiting Italians and Germans. The oracle at

- The slate and stone villages of the Zagorohoria
- The awe-inspiring Vikos gorge
- The independent monastic community of Mt Athos
- Thessaloniki – dynamic, bustling capital of Northern Greece
- The Vergina tombs of Phillip II and their splendid gold treasures
- The lonely beauty of the Prespa lakes
- Mt Olympus – home of the ancient gods

Dodoni predates the more illustrious oracle of Delphi.

History

In early times Epiros' remote mountainous terrain was inhabited by tribes unaffected by, and oblivious to, what was happening in the rest of the country. Eventually one tribe, the Molossi, became so powerful that it dominated the whole region, and its leader became king of Epiros. The most renowned of these was King Pyrrhus (319-272 BC),

NORTHERN GREECE

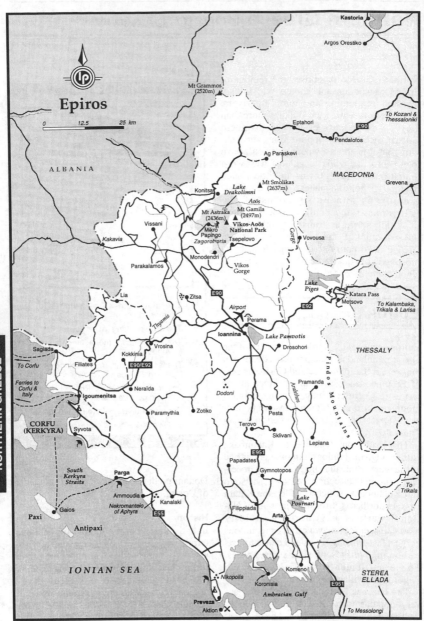

whose foolhardy fracas in Italy against the Romans gave rise to the phrase 'Pyrrhic victory' – a victory achieved at too great a cost.

King Pyrrhus came to an undignified end. After unsuccessful attempts to gain control of Macedonia and parts of Rome he decided to have a go at Argos in the Peloponnese. As he entered the city, an old woman threw a tile from her rooftop which hit him on the head and killed him.

Epiros fell to the Turks in 1431, although its isolation ensured it a great degree of autonomy. It became part of independent Greece in 1913 when the Greek army seized it from the Turks during the second Balkan War. During WWII many Greeks took to the mountains of Epiros, forming a strong resistance movement. When the resistance split into the factions which culminated in the civil war (1944-45), Epiros was the scene of heavy fighting.

During this time, as in Macedonia, many children from Epiros were forcibly evacuated to Eastern-bloc countries by the communists.

IOANNINA Ιωάννινα
• *pop 90,000* • *postcode 450 00* • *area code* ☎ *0651*

Ioannina (Ioannina) is the capital and largest town of Epiros, and the gateway to the Vikos-Aoös National Park. It stands on the western shore of Lake Pamvotis, which is the site of a tranquil island. During Ottoman rule Ioannina became a major commercial and intellectual centre and one of the largest and most important towns in Greece. The city reached its height during the reign of the ignominious, swashbuckling tyrant Ali Pasha. The old town within the city walls has picturesque narrow lanes flanked by traditional Turkish buildings, which include two mosques.

These days, Ioannina is an important commercial hub on the new de facto Via Egnatia since travel through the former Yugoslavia is still fraught with some difficulty.

Orientation
Ioannina's main bus station is on the corner

of Sina and Zosimadon (the northern extension of Markou Botsari). To get to the town centre from here, find the pharmacy outside the bus station, walk left along Markou Botsari opposite, turn right at the Hotel Egnatia and then left into 28 Oktovriou which is the first main road you come to. Continue along 28 Oktovriou to the major road junction; this is Ioannina's main street – to the left it is called Averof and to the right Dodonis.

To reach the old town, turn left into Averof, continue along here and you will come to Plateia Georgiou; on the right is the gateway into the old town. To reach the quay from where boats leave for the island, walk across Plateia Georgiou and follow the *kastro* walls along Karamanli, which leads towards the lakefront. The ferry quay is on the right. Ioannina's other bus station is at Vizaniou 28, the southerly continuation of 28 Oktovriou.

Information
The EOT (☎ 25 086) is on Napoleonda Zerva 2. Turn right at the bottom of 28 Oktovriou into Dodonis and you will come to it on the right, set back on a square. Most people come to Epiros to trek in the mountains, and Ioannina is a good place to get information or arrange an organised trek. For example, the EOT has information on the Vikos gorge trek. The office is open all year round from 7.30 am to 2.30 pm and 5.30 to 8.30 pm Monday to Friday, and 9 am to 1 pm on Saturday.

The tourist police (☎ 25 673) are opposite the post office on 28 Oktovriou.

If you wish to trek in more remote areas than the Vikos gorge then talk to someone at the EOS (Greek Alpine Club; ☎ 22 138), Despotatou Ipirou 2. The office is open Monday to Friday evenings from 7 to 9 pm.

The OTE and post office are on 28 Oktovriou, though there is a new post office on Georgiou Papandreou, about a 10-minute walk from Limnopoula Camping in the direction of the kastro and just past the Big Atlantik supermarket.

For your e-mail, or Web fix, visit the *Internet Café* (☎ 77 925) at Napoleonda Zerva

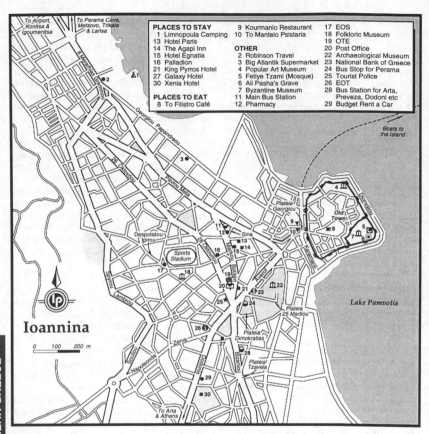

PLACES TO STAY
1 Limnopoula Camping
13 Hotel Paris
14 The Agapi Inn
15 Hotel Egnatia
16 Palladion
21 King Pyrros Hotel
27 Galaxy Hotel
30 Xenia Hotel

PLACES TO EAT
8 To Filistro Café

9 Kourmanio Restaurant
10 To Manteio Psistaria

OTHER
2 Robinson Travel
3 Big Atlantik Supermarket
4 Popular Art Museum
5 Fetiye Tzami (Mosque)
6 Ali Pasha's Grave
7 Byzantine Museum
11 Main Bus Station
12 Pharmacy

17 EOS
18 Folkloric Museum
19 OTE
20 Post Office
22 Archaeological Museum
23 National Bank of Greece
24 Bus Stop for Perama
25 Tourist Police
26 EOT
28 Bus Station for Arta,
      Preveza, Dodoni etc
29 Budget Rent a Car

Ioannina

0   100   200 m

4-6 (downstairs), or point your browser before you go at www.icafe.gr. Access is 1000 dr per hour.

Museums

Archaeological Museum This is an excellent museum which is spacious and well laid out. In the first room on the right there is a collection of Palaeolithic tools, including a 200,000 BC hand axe from Kokkinopolis, near Preveza. Also in this room are finds from Dodoni, including two charming bronze statuettes of children; one is throwing a ball and the other is holding a dove.

Another delightful piece is a terracotta rattle in the shape of a tortoise.

The far room on the left houses a permanent exhibition of 19th and 20th-century paintings, sculptures and prints, including some mildly risqué nudes in among the stuffy portraits of local dignitaries. Don't miss the beautiful little terracotta sculpture entitled *Two Friends* by Theodoros Hrisohoïdou.

The museum (☎ 25 490) is in a small park set back from the east side of Averof. It is open Tuesday to Friday from 8 am to 6 pm and Saturday and Sunday from 8.30 am to 3 pm all year round. Admission is 500 dr, or free with student card.

Byzantine Museum This museum (☎ 25 989) is a new addition to the Ioannina cultural scene and is worth visiting for its collection of Byzantine art. It is in the kastro and is open from Tuesday to Sunday from 8.30 am to 3 pm. Entry is 500 dr.

Popular Art Museum Known also as the Municipal Museum (☎ 26 356), it is housed in the Aslan Pasha mosque, in the old town. Its eclectic collection includes some local costumes and photographs of old Ioannina. It's open Monday to Friday from 8 am to 3 pm and weekends from 9 am to 3 pm. Admission is 700 dr, or 400 dr with student card.

Folkloric Museum This museum (☎ 20 515) is located at Mihail Angelou 42 and is open only on Monday from 5.30 to 8 pm and Wednesday from 10 am to 1 pm. Admission is 100 dr. It contains a small display of local costumes, embroidery and cooking utensils.

Vrellis Wax Museum This (☎ 92 128) is a mini Madame Tussaud's, but with an emphasis on modern Greek history. The museum is at Bizani, 14km out of Ioannina on the road to Athens. Admission is 1000 dr, or 500 dr for students. It is open from 10 am to 5 pm every day.

Organised Treks
Robinson Travel (☎ 29 402; fax 27 071), 8 Merarhias Grammou 10, specialises in treks to remote areas of Epiros. Treks are usually block-booked by groups. Call or fax to see if you can join a group as a 'blow-in'.

Every Sunday between October and June the Ioannina EOS (see Information) organises a one-day trek in the Pindos mountains. Anyone is welcome and the cost is approximately 2000 dr per person.

Special Events
During July and August the Festival of An-

cient Drama takes place at the restored theatre at the nearby site of Dodoni. Information may be obtained from the EOT in Ioannina.

Places to Stay – bottom end
Limnopoula Camping (☎ 25 265; fax 38 060) is on the edge of the lake, 2km north-west of town. The cost is 1200 dr per person and 770 dr per tent. The site has a restaurant and bar and is supposed to be open all year. To reach the site take a Perama-bound bus from Plateia Eleftherias. Alight at the round-about with the two petrol stations.

The rather dingy but functional D-class *Hotel Paris* (☎ 20 541), Tsirigoti 6, has clean single/double rooms for 5000/8000 dr with shared bathroom. The hotel is near the main bus station. In the same alleyway as the entrance to the Hotel Paris is the cheap E-class pension *Agapi Inn* (☎ 20 541) which offers doubles/triples for 5000/7000 dr, and shares the same management as the Hotel Paris.

Places to Stay – middle
Back in Ioannina proper, the C-class *Hotel Egnatia* (☎ 25 667; fax 75 060), near the main bus station on the corner of Dangli and Aravantinou, has comfortable single/double rooms for 10,000/14,000 dr. The C-class *King Pyrros Hotel* (☎ 27 652; fax 29 980), Gounari 3, charges 10,000/15,000 dr. Gounari is opposite the clock tower on Averof.

At Tsirigoti 10, near the Agapi Inn, is the comfortable and family-oriented C-class *Dioni* (☎ 27 864; fax 27 032) which has rooms for 9000/12,000 dr. On King Pyrros square, nestled away in the far right corner as you face the square from Dodonis, is the decidedly pleasant and modern C-class *Galaxy Hotel* (☎ 25 432; fax 30 724) with rooms for 12,000/17,000 dr. The Galaxy has fine views over the lake. All hotels in this category have TVs and private bathroom.

Places to Stay – top end
The most luxurious hotel in Ioannina is

NORTHERN GREECE

the B-class *Xenia* (☎ 47 301; fax 47 189), Dodonis 33. Room rates are 15,250/22,100 dr with breakfast. The hotel has a bar and restaurant. The *Palladion* (☎ 25 856; fax 74 034), at Noti Botsari 1, is 100m up the pedestrian street from the Hotel Egnatia. This modern B-class hotel offers very well-appointed rooms for 12,000/15,500 dr.

Places to Eat

There are several eating places on Plateia Georgiou. One of the nicest is *To Manteio Psistaria*, opposite the entrance to the old city. A meal here will cost about 2000 dr. To the right of the Manteio is the more intimate and slightly cheaper *Kourmanio* with excellent home cooking as well as the usual grills. For a wide choice of teas, coffee and liqueurs, visit the small but very atmospheric *Filistro* café inside the kastro at Andreou Paleologou 20. This is also a good place for breakfast.

Things to Buy

Ioannina has for a long time been a centre for the manufacture of filigree silver. Shops selling this type of jewellery line Averof and Karamanli. Prices start at around 3000 dr for rings and earrings.

You can also buy various wood carvings and other tourist-oriented items from the same area. Epiros is also famous for its flokati rugs, also known as *velenzes*.

Getting There & Away

Air There are usually two flights a day to Athens (17,100 dr) and a daily flight to Thessaloniki (10,800 dr). The Olympic Airways office (☎ 26 518) is on the right side of Dodonis as you walk towards the EOT.

Bus From the main bus station there are nine buses a day to Igoumenitsa (2½ hours, 1700 dr); nine to Athens (7½ hours, 6750 dr) and 11 to Konitsa (two hours, 1050 dr); five to Thessaloniki (seven hours, 5650 dr – once a week via Kozani); four to Metsovo (1½ hours, 1000 dr); two to Trikala (3½ hours, 2550 dr); two a day to Kozani (4½ hours, 3300 dr) and one summer service to Parga (three hours, 1800 dr). Buses to the Zagorohoria also leave from this bus station. The schedule is as follows: Papingo villages (Monday, Wednesday and Friday at 5.30 am and 2.30 pm; two hours, 1000 dr); the Wednesday buses also call in at Vikos; Tsepelovo (Monday, Wednesday and Friday at 6 am and 3.05 pm; 1½ hours, 850 dr); Monodendri (every day at 6 am and 4.15 pm; 1½ hours, 650 dr).

From Ioannina's other bus station, at Vizaniou 28, there are 10 buses a day to Arta

---

Flokati

There are few better souvenirs of a visit to Greece than the luxuriant woollen flokati rugs produced in the mountain areas of central and northern Greece. They make beautiful, cosy floor coverings.

The process by which these rugs are produced has changed little over the centuries. The first step is to weave a loose woollen base. Short lengths of twisted wool are then looped through it, leaving the two ends on top to form the pile – the more loops, the denser the pile.

At this point, the rug looks like a scalp after stage one of a hair transplant – a series of unconvincing little tufts. The twisted threads can easily be pulled through.

A transformation takes place during the next stage, the 'waterfall treatment'. The rugs are immersed in fast-running water for between 24 and 36 hours, unravelling the twisted wool and shrinking the base so that the pile is held fast. They can then be dyed.

The main production areas are the villages of Epiros, around the town of Tripolis in the Peloponnese and around the towns of Trikala and Karditsa in Thessaly. All these villages have plenty of the running water required for the waterfall treatment.

The rugs are sold by weight. A rug measuring 150 x 60cm will cost from 10,000 to 40,000 dr, depending on the length and density of the pile. ∎

Ali Pasha

Ali Pasha, one of the most flamboyant characters of recent Greek history, was born in 1741 in the village of Tepeleni in Albania. In 1787 the Turks made him Pasha of Trikala and by 1788 he ruled Ioannina. His life was a catalogue of brigandage, murder, warfare and debauchery.

Tales abound about Ali. He supposedly had a harem of 400 women, but as if that were not enough he was also enamoured of Kyra Frosyni, his eldest son's mistress. When she rejected his amorous overtures, she and 15 other women were put into sacks and tipped into the lake.

Ali's sons seem to have taken after their father: one was a sex maniac who was in the habit of raping women; the other had the more innocuous hobby of collecting erotic literature.

Ali's lifelong ambition was to break away from the Ottoman Empire and create an independent state. In 1797 he collaborated with Napoleon, but in 1798 he wrested Preveza from the French. In 1817 he courted the British, who rewarded him with Parga.

In 1822 Sultan Mahmud II decided he had had enough of Ali's opportunistic and fickle alliances and sent his troops to execute him. The 82-year-old Ali took refuge on the 1st floor of the guesthouse of Agios Panteleimon monastery on the island, but was killed when the troops fired bullets at him through the ceiling from below. Ali was then beheaded, and his head paraded around Epiros before being buried in Constantinople (İstanbul) – the rest of his body was buried in Ioannina. ■

(2½ hours, 1700 dr); and two buses a day to Patras (4½ hours, 3900 dr). Buses also leave here for Preveza, Parga and Dodoni (see the Dodoni Getting There & Away section for details).

Car Budget Rent a Car (☎ 43 901; fax 43 901) is at Dodonis 109, though it has a booth at Ioannina airport to meet all incoming flights.

Albania See the Getting There & Away chapter for information on going to/from Albania from Ioannina.

Getting Around

The Airport Ioannina's airport is 5km northwest of town on the road to Perama. Take bus No 7, which runs every 20 minutes from the bus stop just south of Averof near the clock tower. Bus Nos 1 and 2 run less frequently, but they also go past the airport.

Bus & Taxi The local bus service covers most parts of Ioannina. Buses from the lakefront usually take you up to the main square. Buy your ticket before you board the bus. There is a ticket kiosk near the Olympic Airways office. Within the central area a single-trip ticket costs 150 dr.

AROUND IOANNINA

The Island Το Νησί

This traffic-free island is a serene place to wander around. It has four monasteries and a whitewashed village which was built in the 17th century by refugees from the Mani in the Peloponnese. It is now a permanent home to about 90 families. If you wish to stay here, there are also some *domatia*.

The **Moni Panteleïmonos**, where Ali Pasha was killed, houses a small museum. The museum was damaged when a tree fell on it during a storm, but it has been rebuilt using the original stones. Entry is 100 dr and it is usually open as long as the ferry is running.

The monastery is signposted, as are all the other monasteries on the island.

Places to Stay & Eat Sotirios Dellas (☎ 81 894) rents pleasant single/double *domatia* for 5000/6500 dr. From the quay walk straight ahead along Monahon Nektariou for about 100m till you come to a square where the primary school is located. You will see a sign on your right leading you to the Saraï, a small square where Sotirios has his rooms. Look for the EOT sign. Another possibility are the nearby *domatia* of Varvara Varvaka (☎ 81 596). Rates are about the same price as at Sotirios', but are always negotiable.

NORTHERN GREECE

For a memorable meal in a lakeside setting, head for the *Gripos* restaurant. It is to the right as you disembark from the ferry, is very good and serves exquisite grilled trout. The *Pamvotis* restaurant, to the left of the quay, is owned by the same proprietor and is equally good and more likely to be open in the low season. A trout meal here will cost about 3000 dr.

Getting There & Away There are regular boats to the island (10 minutes, 180 dr). They usually run every hour in winter and every half-hour in summer, leaving from near the gate to the fortress, 50m west of Plateia Mavili.

Perama Cave Σπήλαιο Περάματος
This cave (☎ 81 521), 4km north of Ioannina, is one of the largest in Greece. It was discovered in 1940 by locals searching for a hiding place from the Nazis, and explored by the speleologists Ioannis and Anna Petrohilos, who also explored the Diros caves in the Peloponnese. The Perama cave is second in Greece only to the Diros caves in its astonishing array of stalactites and stalagmites. It consists of many chambers and passageways and is 1100m long. It's open from 8 am to 8 pm. Admission is 1000 dr; 500 dr for students.

Getting There & Away Take bus No 8 from near the clock tower to the village of Perama. The buses run every 20 minutes.

Dodoni Δωδώνη
Dodoni, 21km south-west of Ioannina and lying in a fertile valley at the foot of Mt Tomaros, is Epiros' most important ancient site.

The site is open from 8 am to 7 pm Monday to Friday and from 8.30 am to 3 pm Saturday and Sunday. Admission is 500 dr or 400 dr for students.

History An earth goddess was worshipped here as long ago as 2000 BC. She spoke through an oracle which was reputedly the oldest in Greece. By the 13th century BC

Zeus had taken over and it was believed he spoke through the rustling of leaves from a sacred oak tree. Around 500 BC a temple to Zeus was built, but only the foundations and a few columns of this and other smaller temples remain. The oracle was the most important in Greece until it was superseded by the Delphic oracle.

Exploring the Site The site's colossal 3rd-century BC **theatre**, an ambitious project overseen by King Pyrrhus, has been restored, and is now the site of the Festival of Ancient Drama (see under Special Events in the Ioannina section for details). To the north of the theatre a gate leads to the **acropolis**; part of its once substantial walls are still standing. To the east of the theatre are the foundations of the **bouleuterion** (council house) and a small temple dedicated to Aphrodite. Close by are the scant remains of the **Sanctuary of Zeus**. This sacred precinct was the site of the oracle of Zeus and the sacred oak.

Christianity also left its mark on Dodoni, as evidenced by the remains of a 6th-century Byzantine basilica, which was built over the remains of a sanctuary dedicated to Hercules.

Places to Stay The *Pension Andromahi* (☎ 0651-82 296) is in the village of Dodoni, near the site.

Getting There & Away The bus service to Dodoni is pretty abysmal considering it's Epiros' major ancient site. There are buses from Ioannina on Monday, Tuesday, Wednesday, Friday and Saturday at 6.30 am and 4.30 pm. There are no buses on a Thursday and only one bus on a Sunday at 6 pm, which returns at 6.45 pm.

Buses leave from Ioannina's Vizaniou bus station for the village of Dodoni, and return at 7.30 am and 5.30 pm. An alternative is to get a Zotiko bus, which stops 1.5km from the site. This bus leaves the Bizaniou bus station on Monday, Wednesday and Friday at 5.30 am and 2 pm and returns at 7.15 am and 4.30 pm. If your interest in archaeology is not enough to get you out of bed at dawn, then a taxi will cost around 4500 dr return plus 600 dr per hour of waiting time.

THE ZAGOROHORIA Ζαγοροχώρια

The 44 Zagoria villages lie north of Ioannina in the region of Zagoria. The villages are collectively known as the Zagorohoria. This area offers some breathtaking vistas and is drawing more and more visitors. As with many inaccessible mountainous areas in Greece, the Zagorohoria maintained a high degree of autonomy in Turkish times, so their economy and culture flourished.

An outstanding feature of the villages is their architecture. The houses are built entirely of slate from the surrounding mountains – a perfect blending of nature and architecture. With their winding, cobbled and stepped streets the villages could have leapt straight out of a Grimm's fairy tale. Some of the villages are sadly depopulated, with only a few elderly inhabitants, while others, like Papingo, Monodendri and Tsepelovo, are beginning to thrive on the new-found tourism in the area.

Good roads connect most of the villages, and with a car you can see many of them in one day.

The Vikos-Aoös National Park encompasses much of the area. Within the park is the Tymfi massif which is part of the north Pindos range and comprises Mt Astraka, Mt Gamila and Mt Tsouka Rossa, the Vikos gorge and the Aoös river gorge. It's an area of outstanding natural beauty and is becoming popular with trekkers. So far it is untouched by mass tourism, but several companies organise treks in the region, including the British-based Exodus Expeditions and Robinson Travel Agency in Ioannina.

The area is thickly forested; hornbeam, maple, willow and oak predominate, but there are also fir, pine and cedar trees. Bears, wolves, wild boars, wild cats, wild goats and the rare Rissos quadruped roam the mountains. Vlach and Sarakatsani shepherds still live a seminomadic existence taking their flocks up to high grazing ground in the summer and returning to the valleys in the autumn.

The telephone code (excluding Konitsa) for the Zagorohoria is ☎ 0653. For information about buses to these villages, see Ioannina's Getting There & Away section.

Vikos Gorge Χαράδρα του Βίκου

The focal point of the region is the 10km-long Vikos gorge, which begins at the village of **Monodendri** (elevation 1090m), at the southern end of the gorge. Monodendri is 38km north of Ioannina, and is reached by taking a right-hand turn from the main Ioannina-Konitsa road at the village of Karyes.

The Vikos gorge is the most trekked gorge in Greece, after the Samaria gorge on Crete. It doesn't require any special expertise but it is a strenuous walk of around 7½ hours ending at the twin villages of either **Megalo Papingo** or **Mikro Papingo**. Stout walking boots are recommended. You can tackle the gorge from either end, but if you have come by car, you will have to arrange a lift back to your vehicle via the long road route.

Before you come to Monodendri visit the EOT or the EOS in Ioannina. They will give you a map of the gorge, and answer any questions you may have. Whatever you do, come prepared for some serious walking; this is not a Sunday afternoon stroll in the park.

At the far end of Monodendri there is a spectacular view down into the gorge from the 15th-century **Moni Agias Paraskevis**. The descent into the gorge is down a steep marked path between the village and the monastery. Once in the gorge, it's a four-hour walk to the end, from where a trail up to the right leads to the settlement of Mikro Papingo (2½ hours). The larger settlement of Megalo Papingo is 2km west of here, but the track splits into two at the base of the climb. You can also terminate your trek at the village of Vikos if you wish.

Klima spring, about halfway along the gorge, is the only source of water, so take plenty along with you. Probably the most breathtaking view of the gorge for the less-energetic is from the **Oxya lookout**, 5km beyond Monodendri. You will have to hitch or walk since there is no public transport here.

If you come by road to Papingo, the view is awe-inspiring as you approach the village from the bed of the **Voïdomatis river**, after you have passed through **Aristi**, the last village before Papingo. There are no less than 15 hairpin bends that switchback in rapid succession up to the ledge where the Papingo villages nestle under the looming hulk of Mt Gamila. As you wind your way up, there are spectacular views into the Vikos gorge on your right.

The village of Vikos, 5km beyond Aristi is a good starting point for the gorge trek and it is a shorter hike to Monodendri or vice-versa than from the Papingo villages. The view from the panoramic platform in Vikos is stunning.

Papingo is popular with wealthy Greeks, so be prepared to pay for services accordingly. Trekkers with less lavish means can buy some food items, though it might be a good idea to stock up on provisions from Ioannina before you come, since there are limited supplies in the Papingo villages.

After a strenuous hike along the gorge to Papingo you might want to cool off in the natural **rock pools**, which are exquisitely refreshing on a hot day. The 300m path to the pools starts at a bend in the road between Megalo and Mikro Papingo. Look out for the EU stars with the word 'Life' in the middle of the telltale stone gateway.

Places to Stay & Eat Monodendri's choicest accommodation is the lovely traditional *Monodendri Pension & Restaurant* (☎ 71 300), where doubles are 8000 dr. The restaurant serves reasonably priced, well-prepared food, specialising in pittes, which are oven-baked pies made from filo pastry and various delicious fillings. The pension is on the upper square on the main road. Another pleasant place is the *Vikos Hotel* (☎ 71 232), with doubles for 8750 dr. There are also rooms available in private houses – look for signs.

Megalo Papingo has domatia and a couple of hostelries. The *Xenonas tou Kouli* (☎ 41 138) has six rooms in various combinations from 10,000 to 12,000 dr for doubles/quadruples. There is a minimarket and café-bar as well. It is best to book in advance. The owners of this place also serve as official EOS tour guides. The *Xenonas Kalliopi* (☎ 41 081) on the south side of the village has eight rooms, again in various combinations ranging in price from 10,000/15,000 dr for singles/triples. There is also a small restaurant-bar here serving home cooking and the regional specialities, pittes.

Mikro Papingo has one pleasant place to stay – the *Xenonas Dias* (☎ 41 257) with 12 rooms for 10,00/12,000 dr for doubles/triples. There is also a little restaurant for breakfast and meals and the place is open all year round.

For a special treat, try *Nikos Tsoumanis Restaurant*. He offers local pittes, among other regular fare, and has a good wine selection. Expect to pay between 3000 and 4000 dr.

If you are planning to start your trek from Vikos itself, the *domatia* of Sotiris Karpouzas (☎ 41 176) should serve you well. Modern doubles/triples with private bathroom cost 12,000/15,000 dr. Food is also available.

Mt Gamila to Tsepelovo
From Mikro Papingo there is a good marked path to the *Gamila Refuge* (1950m) (also called Rodovoli Refuge), owned by the EOS in Megalo Papingo (☎ 41 138), which you must contact for bookings (2500 dr per person per night). Cooked meals, soft drinks, beer and wine are all available from the refuge at somewhat inflated prices. If it is fully booked you should be able to camp by the *xiroloutsa* dry lake on the next valley floor.

From this refuge there are marked trails to Drakolimni (dragon) lake (one hour) and to the village of Tsepelovo (six to seven hours). For rock climbers there are over 20 routes up Mt Astraka. The EOS in Ioannina gives out a leaflet detailing these.

Tsepelovo Τσεπέλοβο
Tsepelovo is a delightful Zagoria village, 51km north of Ioannina. There are many opportunities for scenic day walks from the village. There is a post office and public phone.

Places to Stay & Eat The *Gouris Pension* (☎ 81 214) is an immaculate place where doubles cost 8000 dr. The enterprising owner, Alekos Gouris, also runs a grocery shop and restaurant in the village's main square. He speaks excellent English and is very knowledgeable about treks in the area. There are a few domatia to let in the village. Try Erasmia Deligianni (☎ 81 232) who has *domatia* to let for 8000/10,000 dr for doubles/triples. Her domatia are on the main (upper) square. The *Hagiati Hotel* (☎ 81 301) is just back from the same square and charges 12,000 dr for studios for two persons with a 20% loading for each extra person. Buffet breakfast is included. Winter prices are higher.

There is a taverna on the main square and another one on the right of the main road as you approach from Ioannina.

KONITSA Κόνιτσα
• pop 4000 • postcode 441 00 • area code ☎ 0655
Konitsa (**Konitsa**), 64km north of Ioannina, is the largest settlement in the area. It's a lively market town and is a good base from which to explore the northern Zagorohoria. In recent times it has become a centre of sorts for kayaking and trekking in the Vikos-Aoös National Park. Konitsa is built amphitheatrically on a hillside, and the view over the Voïdomatis valley, as the sun sets over the mountains in Albania, is quite a sight. A serpentine road leads up to Konitsa's centre from the main Ioannina-Kozani road.

Information
The bus station is on the central square, where you will also find the post office and the National Bank of Greece. There is no EOT or tourist police.

Things to See & Do
Museums There is a small **folkloric museum** just above To Dentro guesthouse. The opening hours are erratic, so check with the staff at the guesthouse. Opposite the town hall near the main square there is a **natural history museum**, organised by the Konitsa Hunting Club!

Walk to Stomio Monastery (Μονή Στομίου)
This scenic walk along the Aoös river gorge takes about 1½ hours. Cross the stone bridge at the beginning of the town (coming from Ioannina), turn left and follow the Aoös river to the waterfall. Cross the bridge and follow the path up to the monastery. Occasionally there is a lone monk in residence here who shows visitors around the monastery, but even if you find it locked, the walk is worthwhile for the tremendous views.

Adventure Sports Paddler (☎ 23 102; fax 23 101), at Averof 16, organises kayaking, rafting, canyoning, paragliding and trekking expeditions. Ask for Nikos Kyritsis, or call ☎ S22 385 and ask for Mihalis Oikonomou.

Places to Stay & Eat
To Dentro Guesthouse (☎ & fax 22 055), 500m before the town centre on the Ioannina road, is Konitsa's best deal. Look out for the bright orange-coloured exterior on the last bend of the road up to the main square. It has beautifully furnished, spotless doubles/triples for 8000/12,000 dr with private bath. English-speaking Ioannis, the owner, can advise on local walks. To Dentro also has the best restaurant in town. Pot-roast goat or lamb is a good bet and trout is an equally satisfying choice, but make sure you ask for their speciality: grilled fetta with chilli and tomato.

There is a proliferation of domatia all along the road leading up to Konitsa from Ioannina. Down near the old bridge is the *Potamolithos* (☎ 23 790), a stone-clad hostel offering domatia. This place is very conveniently placed for the Aoös river gorge walks. Look for the wooden sign 100m along

NORTHERN GREECE

the Konitsa turn-off road. Rooms are 12,000 dr for a double.

There is a fast-food joint and the *Zourloukas Psistaria* on the main square. There is also a small *supermarket* on the main market street behind the post office.

Getting There & Away

From Monday to Friday there are seven buses to Ioannina (two hours, 1000 dr) from Konitsa; and on weekends there are four buses. Two buses a day from Ioannina to Kozani (2460 dr) pass through here. If you want to go further, go to Kozani first, then take another bus onwards from there. There are also buses from Ioannina to Thessaloniki that pass through Konitsa once a week in winter (Monday, 4450 dr), and twice a week (Monday and Friday) in summer.

METSOVO Μέτσοβο

• *pop 2900* • *postcode 442 00* • *area code ☎ 0656*

The village of Metsovo (Metsovo) sprawls down a mountainside at an elevation of 1160m, just south of the Katara pass, at the junction of Epiros, Thessaly and Macedonia, 58km from Ioannina and 90km from Trikala. The inhabitants are descendants of Vlach shepherds, most of whom have hung up their crooks to make a living in the tourist trade.

Metsovo has many tourist trappings: locals dressed in traditional costumes, local handcrafts, regional cuisine, stone-built mansions, invigorating air, a superb mountain setting and good conditions for skiing. Some visitors find the village twee and artificial, while others are enamoured of its considerable charm.

Despite its peasant origins, Metsovo attracts an urban set and there is a wide choice of high quality hotels and restaurants. If you are on your way by road across the Pindos range, make a stop at Metsovo for a day or two and sample its ambience.

History

Originally a small settlement of shepherds, the inhabitants of Metsovo were granted many privileges in Ottoman times as reward for guarding the mountain pass upon which Metsovo stands. This pass was the only route across the Pindos range, and the Metsovite guards' vigilance facilitated the passage of Ottoman troops. These privileges led to Metsovo becoming an important centre of finance, commerce, handcraft production and sheep farming. A school was established in the town in 1659 at a time when Greek-language schools were not allowed in other parts of the country.

Metsovo's privileges were abolished in 1795 by that spoilsport, Ali Pasha. In March 1854 it suffered considerable damage from Ottoman troops. But Metsovo was very lucky in that it had many prosperous benefactors: locals who had gone on to achieve national and international recognition. The most famous of them were Georgios Averof (1815-99) and Mihail Tositsas (1885-1950). Both bequeathed large amounts of money to Metsovo. This was used to restore the town to its former glory and to finance several small industries.

Orientation & Information

Orientation in Metsovo is easy as there is only one main thoroughfare. Coming from Kalambaka, turn-off to the left after the Katara pass to reach Metsovo. The main thoroughfare loops down to the central square, passing many restaurants, hotels and souvenir shops. A maze of stone pathways winds between the fine, traditionally built houses.

The bus stop is on the central square in front of Café Diethnes. The post office is on the right side of the main thoroughfare, when you're walking from the central square. To reach the OTE, walk along the road opposite the bus station, keep veering right and you will come to the OTE on the right. The building is a bit inconspicuous, so keep your eyes open. The National Bank of Greece is on the far side of the central square and there are another two banks as well.

The new Pindos vehicle tunnel from Metsovo to Malakasi in Thessaly has been completed, but bureaucracy has so far prevented the completion of the new Via Egnatia, which will traverse the tunnel, so the Katara pass is still the only option to cross the Pindos range. The tunnel and Via Egnatia are expected to be completed by 2000.

There is no EOT or tourist police. The regular police (☎ 41 233) are on the right, a little way along the road opposite the bus stop.

Things to See

The restored **Tositsas mansion** has been turned into a folk museum, and is a faithful reconstruction of a wealthy 19th-century Metsovite household, with exquisitely hand-crafted furniture, artefacts and utensils. The museum is about halfway up the main street. Look out for the wooden sign. Opening times are every day except Thursday from 8.30 am to 1 pm and 4 to 6 pm. Wait at the door until the guide opens it and lets you in (every half-hour). Admission is 500 dr.

The 14th-century **Moni Agiou Nikolaou** stands in a gorge below Metsovo. Its chapel has post-Byzantine frescoes and a beautiful carved-wood iconostasis. The monastery is a 30-minute walk from Metsovo and is signposted to the left, just before the Hotel Athens.

The **Averof Gallery** was financed by Georgios Averof's three children. It houses a permanent collection of 19th and 20th-century works by Greek painters and sculptors. To reach the gallery turn left at the far side of the central square and the gallery is on the right. It's open every day except Tuesday from 9 am to 1.30 pm and 5 to 7.30 pm. Admission is 500 dr, or 300 dr for students.

Activities

Coming from Kalambaka, Metsovo's ski centre (☎ 41 211) is on the right-hand side of the main Kalambaka-Ioannina highway, just before the turn-off for the town. There is a taverna at the centre and an 82-seat ski lift, two downhill runs and a 5km cross-country run. Ski hire is available in Metsovo.

Places to Stay – bottom end

There is no shortage of accommodation in Metsovo, with no less than 14 hotels and abundant domatia. Metsovo's hotels, pre-dictably, have a folksy ambience, right down to the town's one E-class establishment. The E-class *Hotel Athens* (☎ 41 332; fax 42 009), just off the central square, is old but clean, and the woven rugs on the floors add a homely touch. Double/triple rooms cost 8000/10,000 dr with private bathroom. Allied to the Athens are the *Filoxenia* domatia (☎ 41 021; fax 42 009) just behind the central park area and close to the art gallery. Singles/doubles cost 8000/10,000 dr, while 15,000 dr will get you a suite for four persons with one of the most spectacular views in town.

The D-class *Hotel Acropolis* (☎ 41 672) has traditional furniture, wooden floors and ceilings, and very colourful wall-hangings. Rates here are 10,000/14,000 dr for doubles/triples with private bathroom. Look out for it on the right at the beginning of the road down to Metsovo.

Places to Stay – middle

The *Hotel Galaxias* (☎ 41 202; fax 41 124) is the closest hotel to the bus stop. Very comfortable singles/doubles cost 12,000/16,000 dr. The C-class *Hotel Egnatia* (☎ 41 263; fax 41 485) has cosy rooms with balcony and wood-panelled walls. Room rates here are 11,000/13,200 dr for singles/doubles. The hotel is on the right side of the main road as you approach the central square.

On the opposite side, further up the hill, the C-class *Hotel Bitouni* (☎ 41 217; fax 41 545) has immaculate rooms and a charming lounge with a flagstone floor, brass plates, embroidered cushions and carved wooden coffee tables. Rates here are 10,830/13,000/18,000 dr for singles/doubles/suites.

Places to Stay – top end

The *Hotel Apollon* (☎ 41 844; fax 42 110) is Metsovo's best hotel. The gorgeous carpeted rooms cost 14,500/18,000/28,500 dr for singles/doubles/suites. To reach the hotel, walk along the road opposite the bus station and look for the sign pointing right.

Places to Eat

The *Athens Restaurant* (in the hotel of the same name; see Places to Stay) has tasty, reasonably priced food with many local specialities. Expect to pay under 2000 dr for an average meal. The *Restaurant Galaxias* next to its associated hotel is a very good choice. Try the local pittes and hilopittes (pasta) with veal, accompanied by fine rosé for around 2250 dr.

The 1st-floor *Taverna Metsovitiko Saloni* is a largish establishment with a beautiful interior of traditional carved-wood furniture and colourful wall-hangings. A meal here will go for about 2600 dr. The restaurant is just up from the post office.

Things to Buy

Craft shops selling both high-quality stuff and kitsch are ubiquitous in Metsovo. The old-fashioned food shop opposite the bus stop sells local cheeses, for which the town is famous.

Getting There & Away

From Metsovo there are six direct buses to Ioannina (1000 dr) and two or three to Trikala (1500 dr). In summer there is also a direct bus to Athens (7000 dr). To catch a Thessaloniki bus you will have to walk up to the main road and wave the bus down. These buses normally come from Ioannina.

IGOUMENITSA Ηγουμενίτσα
• *pop 6800* • *postcode 461 00* • *area code* ☎ *0665*

Once a sleepy little outpost, the west-coast port of Igoumenitsa (Igoumenitsa), 100km from Ioannina, is where you get ferries to Corfu and Italy. It is growing at a fast rate thanks to its strategic position as an important port to western Europe from the southern Balkans and Middle East. There is little of interest to keep you here, but if you are travelling to or from Greece by ferry and using Igoumenitsa as your entry or exit point, then you are likely to be spending some time here, if only to have a meal or wait out a few hours for a boat or bus. There is actually a very pleasant beach and taverna at Dre-

panos, about 6km north of town, if you feel like a relaxing swim and a meal.

Orientation

Ferries for Italy and domestic ferries for Corfu leave from three separate quays quite close to one another on the waterfront of Ethnikis Antistasis. Ferries to/from Ancona and Venice depart from the new port on the south side of town; ferries for Kerkyra/Paxi from just north of the new port and ferries for Brindisi/Bari from the old port in front of the main shipping offices.

To get to the bus station turn left from the ferry quays, walk along Ethnikis Antistasis, turn right into 23 Fevrouariou – look out for the sign – and two blocks inland turn left into Kyprou. The bus station is a little way along on the left.

Information

The main EOT office (☎ 22 227), on the waterfront and inside the old port area, is open every day from 7 am to 2.30 pm. There is also an EOT booth just outside the arrivals area of the new port. The post office and OTE are next to each other on Evangelistrias. Automatic currency exchange machines are available at the Commercial and National Bank.

Places to Stay & Eat

Ferries leave Igoumenitsa in the morning and evening these days so you may not have to stay overnight here before your departure. However, budget hotels are in short supply in Igoumenitsa. Campers might head for *Il Sole Mare* on the south side of town, or if you have independent transport, there is a quiet camping site at *Drepanos Beach* 6km north of town. There are also domatia in the area of the new port. Look for signs.

The D-class *Egnatia* (☎ 23 648) has comfortable rooms for 7000/10,000 dr with private bathroom. Cross over Kyprou from El Venizelou and the hotel is on the right. The C-class *Oscar Hotel* (☎ 23 338; fax 23 557) right opposite the new port arrivals area has reasonable singles/doubles for 8870/11,830 dr. The C-class *Hotel Aktaion* (☎ 22 330; fax

22 330), on the waterfront between the Kerkyra ferry quay and the old port, has singles/doubles for 11,000/15,000 dr.

To Astron Restaurant, El Venizelou 9, and the *Restaurant Martinis-Bakalis*, on the corner of 23 Fevrouariou and Grigoriou Lambraki, serve reasonably priced, tasty food. The locals eat here so you can be assured of good value. Plan on about 2500 dr for a meal.

Getting There & Away

Bus From Igoumenitsa's bus station there are nine buses to Ioannina (two hours, 1700 dr); five to Parga (one hour, 1050 dr); three to Athens (eight hours, 7750 dr); two to Preveza (2½ hours, 1950 dr); and one to Thessaloniki (eight hours, 7250 dr).

Ferry – Corfu There are ferries every hour to Corfu town between 5 am and 10 pm (1½ hours, 1050 dr). Ferries also go to Lefkimmi in southern Corfu five times a day (one hour, 1400 dr) and to Paxi three times a week (1½ hours, 1250 dr). Agency booths opposite the quay sell tickets. Match the name of the boat that you are planning to leave on with the name on the appropriate ticket booth.

Most of the ferries to/from Italy also stop at Corfu. There are also weekly passenger and car ferries to Kerkyra from Sagiada (one hour, 600 dr) 20km north of Igoumenitsa (see Sagiada).

Ferry & Catamaran – Italy There is a veritable plethora of options for leaving Igoumenitsa in the direction of Italy and most of the harbour-front street Ethnikis Antistasis is full of shipping agencies, or travel agencies selling their tickets. There are different prices for low, middle and high seasons and return tickets are 30% cheaper than two outward tickets.

There are six to eight ferries a day from Igoumenitsa to Brindisi (11 hours) and between two and four ferries a day to Bari (13 hours); two to three ferries a day to Ancona (24 hours); two ferries a week to Otranto (nine hours); nine ferries a week to Venice (27½ hours) and six ferries a week to Trieste (28 hours). Some of the ferries to Italy go direct, but go via Corfu

(two hours) where some lines allow you to stop over free of charge. Boats leave in the morning between 6 and 8 am and in the evening between 6 and 9 pm. You should turn up at the port at least two hours before departure. Check in at the shipping agent's office. Timetables are subject to change and demand is high in summer. Book ahead if you can.

The following table will give you some idea of rates with various lines. Fares are based on high season deck rates.

Destination	Company	Single	Return
Ancona	ANEK	16,600 dr	28,200 dr
Ancona	Minoan	18,600 dr	32,200 dr
Ancona	Strintzis	18,400 dr	31,200 dr
Bari	Marlines	13,000 dr	22,100 dr
Bari	Ventouris	9000 dr	18,000 dr*
Brindisi	Fragline	12,800	21,900 dr
Brindisi	Hellenic Mediterranean	14,000 dr	23,500 dr
Brindisi	Minoan	13,800 dr	24,400 dr
Brindisi	Ventouris	8000 dr	15,200 dr
Trieste	ANEK	17,300 dr	29,400 dr
Venice	Minoan	18,600 dr	32,200 dr
* student rate			

All of the main shipping offices are on Ethnikis Antistasis. For a comprehensive brochure of most ferry options, go to Chris Travel at No 60 (☎ 25 351; fax 25 350).

Hellenic Mediterranean is at No 32 (☎ 25 682; fax 24 960; Minoan is at No 58a (☎ 22 952; fax 22 101); ANEK is at No 34 (☎ 22 104; fax 25 421); Marlines is at No 42 (☎ 23 301; fax 25 428) and Strintzis (☎ 24 252; fax 25 492) is at No 62.

A catamaran service operates, in the summer months, between Igoumenitsa and Brindisi (every day, 3½ hours, 9000 to 14,000 dr low/high season). Tickets are available from Alpha Travel (☎ 22 797; fax 26 330) at Agion Apostolon 167, opposite the new port entrance.

Sagiada Σαγιάδα

Sagiada is a sleepy fishing village 20km north of Igoumenitsa and is favoured by the

NORTHERN GREECE

day-tripping yachty set from Corfu as well as the passengers on the weekly ferry service to/from Corfu. Aside from the five tavernas and five bars that crowd its waterfront, there is not much activity other than just lazing around. If all goes to plan, this will become Greece's last waterside settlement before a border crossing to Konispol in Albania. The crossing is due to open soon. There are a few rooms to be had, and the village is linked by two daily buses to both Igoumenitsa and Filiates further inland.

PARGA Πάργα

• *pop 1700* • *postcode 480 60* • *area code* ☎ *0684*

Parga, 77km north of Preveza and 48km south of Igoumenitsa, spills down to a rocky bay, flanked by coves and islets. Add to this a Venetian kastro and the long pebble and sand Valtos beach and you have somewhere truly alluring. So it will come as no surprise to be told that it's overrun with tourists in midsummer and that hotels, domatia and travel agents have swamped this once serene fishing village.

Despite this, it is still a very attractive place for a day or two and is Epiros' number-one tourist resort. Try and visit Parga in early or late summer. If you are travelling along this coast, it would be a shame to miss this gem.

Orientation & Information

The bus station is at Alexandrou Baga 18 and the post office is in the same building. Turn left at the bus station and walk straight ahead past the crossroads into Vasila and you will come to the National Bank of Greece and the OTE; continue along this street to reach the waterfront.

There is no EOT, but there is now a tourist-police department in the same building as the regular police (☎ 31 222), which is shared with the post office and the bus station. There is an ATM at the National Bank and at the

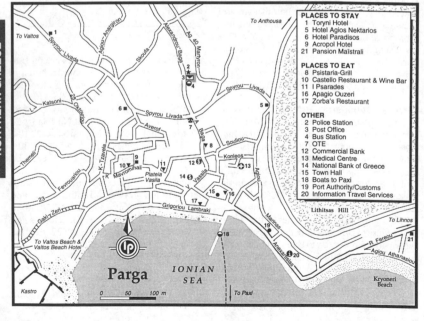

PLACES TO STAY
1 Toryni Hotel
5 Hotel Agios Nektarios
6 Hotel Paradisos
9 Acropol Hotel
21 Pension Maïstrali

PLACES TO EAT
8 Psistaria-Grill
10 Castello Restaurant & Wine Bar
11 I Psarades
16 Apagio Ouzeri
17 Zorba's Restaurant

OTHER
2 Police Station
3 Post Office
4 Bus Station
7 OTE
12 Commercial Bank
13 Medical Centre
14 National Bank of Greece
15 Town Hall
18 Boats to Paxi
19 Port Authority/Customs
20 Information Travel Services

Commercial Bank for card-equipped travellers.

Nekromanteio of Aphyra

Just about every travel agent in Parga advertises trips to the Nekromanteio of Aphyra. This involves taking a boat ride down the coast to the Aheron river (believed to be the ancient River Styx) and then up the navigable river as far as the Nekromanteio itself, which you approach on foot. The day trip costs about 1500 dr. If you have your own transport, take the Preveza road as far as the village of Mesopotamos and look out for the sign to the Nekromanteio, 1km off the main road. Entrance is 500 dr or 300 dr for students.

The Nekromanteio is a truly fascinating place if you have time to ponder over the mysteries of the ancient rituals of the dead and the underworld. There is a good colour guidebook written in English by Professor Sotiris Dakaris of the University of Ioannina. It's available at the sanctuary entrance and costs 1500 dr. The site is open daily from 8.30 am to 4.30 pm and on weekends from 8.30 am to 3 pm.

According to mythology the Aheron river was the River Styx across which the ferryman of the dead, Charon, rowed the departed souls to the underworld. Until the departed had taken this journey they could not enter Hades (the world of the dead) and so were in a state of limbo.

The Nekromanteio was the ancients' venue for the equivalent of a modern-day seance. They believed this to be the gate of Hades, god of the underworld, and so it became an oracle of the dead and a sanctuary to Hades and Persephone. Pilgrims came here with offerings of milk, honey and the blood of sacrificed animals in the hope that the souls of the departed would communicate with them through the oracle.

The labyrinth of buildings was only discovered in 1958 and revealed not only the Nekromanteio itself, but the monastery of Agios Ioannis Prodromos and a graveyard. The eerie underground vault, the purpose of which is still not known, could easily have been the meeting place for the dead and the living.

Other Attractions

The **kastro** dominates the town of Parga and separates **Valtos beach** from Parga proper. The kastro, a reminder of the 400 years of Venetian presence in Epiros, is a bit overgrown with vegetation, but its ramparts provide some lovely rambling as well as superb views of the coastline.

If you like scuba diving, contact Information Travel Services (☎ 31 833; fax 31 834) and they will put you in touch with the diving school. A one-day beginner's course costs around 12,000 dr. ITS also organises Aheron river cruises for about 2500 dr. Cruises with a beach barbecue and unlimited drinks cost 7000 dr.

Places to Stay – bottom end

There is a veritable plethora of accommodation available in Parga during the tourist season, from top hotels to camping grounds, from domatia to studios. Avoid mid-July to the end of August if you are not planning to stay more than a week here. Rates are expensive and places are hard to find. Take your pick during the low season.

For help with accommodation, try Information Travel Services, Anexartisias 37, on the main waterfront, or at their other office on Kryoneri beach.

There are three camp sites serving Parga: *Lihnos Beach Camping* (☎ 31 161); *Elia Camping* (☎ 31 130); and probably the best choice, *Valtos Camping* (☎ 31 287) at Valtos beach.

One of Parga's nicest hotels is the D-class *Hotel Agios Nektarios* (☎ 31 150) on the corner of the turn-off to the north end of Parga. To reach the hotel from the bus station turn left and left again at Spyrou Livada and the hotel is on the right.

Places to Stay – middle

Hotels in this range cost about 14,000 dr for a double room in high season. Worth mentioning is the C-class *Acropol* (☎ 31 239; fax 31 834) at Agion Apostolon 6, which is a small but cosy hotel. The C-class *Hotel Paradisos* (☎ 31 229; fax 31 266) is at Spyrou Livada 23. Rooms go for 11,200/ 14,000 dr for singles/doubles. The C-class *Toryni* (☎ 31 219; fax 32 376) is north-west along Spyrou Livada and is a another good choice. Rooms at both these places go for about 13,000/15,600 dr for doubles/triples.

The *Pansion Maïstrali* at Riga Fereou 4 (☎ 31 275) is a very clean and convenient option. It is on the south side of town, up from Kryoneri beach. Double/triple rooms in this category cost 12,000/14,500 dr.

Places to Stay – top end
The B-class *Valtos Beach Hotel* (☎ 31 610; fax 31 904), on the beach at Valtos, has singles/doubles for 13,000/16,500 dr, with breakfast. The hotel has a café and restaurant. The *Lihnos Beach Hotel* (☎ 31 257; fax 31 157) has rates of 13,500/17,000 dr. These two hotels both have a bar, restaurant and tennis court. Valtos beach is just north of Parga and Lihnos beach is just to the south.

Places to Eat
Not surprisingly, there are plenty of places to eat, many of them touting tourist menus and English breakfasts. In high season, tourist prices are all the rage.

Zorba's Restaurant is open all year round and caters for locals as well as visitors. It is on the waterfront, 50m to the right as you face the pier, by the statue of Ioannis Dimoulitsas. It offers good food, draught wine and has the most picturesque location.

For a couple of cheap and tasty options, try the *I Psarades*, just back from the seafront on Plateia Vasila, or the nameless *Psistaria-Grill* at Alexandrou Baga 4, 100m down from the bus station.

Try the homely *Apagio Ouzeri* in a little alley just off the promenade. It is one of the few places that deals mainly with a Greek clientele. Spetsofaï with salad and draught wine will cost about 2300 dr.

The *Castello Restaurant & Wine Bar* is an up-market joint with professionally prepared food served in an enticing outdoor garden. It is part of the Hotel Acropol. It's worth a look-in for that special night out.

Getting There & Away
Bus From Parga's bus station there are four buses a day to Igoumenitsa (one hour, 1050 dr), five to Preveza (two hours, 1250 dr), one to Ioannina in summer (three hours, 2100 dr) and three to Athens (seven hours, 7150 dr).

Excursion Boat The small Ionian islands of Paxi and Antipaxi lie just 20km off the coast. In summer there are daily excursion boats to Paxi (4000 dr) from Parga. The excursions are widely advertised by Parga's travel agents.

PREVEZA Πρέβεζα
• *pop 13,340* • *postcode 481 00* • *area code* ☎ *0682*
Preveza (Preveza), built on a peninsula between the Ionian sea and the gulf of Ambracia, is primarily a port from which ferries cross the narrow strait to Aktion, but it is also a popular holiday destination for Greek tourists and German and Austrian tour groups. Most people coming to Preveza are either heading out to the resorts at Parga, or to the beach resorts north of the town. Preveza is a pleasant town in its own right and a leisurely stroll through its narrow pedestrian-only central streets is a great pleasure.

Orientation & Information
If you arrive by bus, you will alight at the bus station on Irinis, which is the main commercial thoroughfare. Turn left from the bus station along Irinis and walk about 500m, bearing left until you reach the harbour. The EOT, post office and National Bank of Greece are in a row on the waterfront – turn left as you reach the quay. There are a couple of ATMs around town.

If you arrive by plane, there is an Olympic Airways bus that will take you to the Aktion ferry and across to Preveza proper. The ferry ticket costs extra.

Special Events
In July each year there is an International

Choral Festival with up to 20 or more international choirs taking part. Preveza's own choir has won considerable international acclaim. For detailed information, check with Preveza's municipal tourist office (☎ 28 120; fax 27 553) in the town hall.

At the beginning of August you may come across a mildly whimsical sardine festival. The Nikopolia Festival is an umbrella event for various musical and theatrical presentations held in August on Nikopolis to the west of town. Again, check with the municipal tourist office for details.

Places to Stay

If you wish to camp, you have a choice of four camping grounds, the best of which is *Camping Kalamitsi* (☎ 22 192; fax 28 660) which has 116 sites. This site boasts a large pool, restaurant, laundry facilities, communal fridges and a minimarket, and grassed tent sites with ample shade. It's 4km along the main Preveza-Igoumenitsa road.

Nearest the bus station is the C-class *Preveza City* (☎ 27 370; fax 23 872) at Irinis 81-83, 200m from the bus station on the left in the direction of the waterfront. It has clean singles/doubles for 11,300/14,500 dr. The spartan C-class *Minos Hotel* (☎ 28 424) at 21 Oktovriou 11 has singles/doubles for 10,400/13,600 dr. Within the town precinct, the C-class *Hotel Dioni* (☎ 27 381; fax 27 3) is a good, but somewhat pricey choice. The hotel is on a quiet square, Plateia Theodorou Papageorgiou, and has singles/doubles for 10,500/14,800 dr. The bar has a pool table.

Places to Eat

The main road along the waterfront has a large number of drinks and snacks places, but there is a clutch of fish tavernas along the street leading to the clock tower of the St Haralambos church from the waterfront. For a no-nonsense, unadorned meal in a low-ceilinged room lined with wine barrels that are actually used, head for the *Amvrosios*. Sardines, salad and draught wine will cost you less than 2000 dr. Next door the *Gafa* offers similar fare, but you can sit outside.

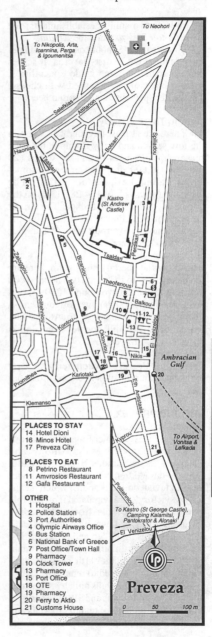

PLACES TO STAY
14 Hotel Dioni
16 Minos Hotel
17 Preveza City

PLACES TO EAT
8 Petrino Restaurant
11 Amvrosios Restaurant
12 Gafa Restaurant

OTHER
1 Hospital
2 Police Station
3 Port Authorities
4 Olympic Airways Office
5 Bus Station
6 National Bank of Greece
7 Post Office/Town Hall
9 Pharmacy
10 Clock Tower
13 Pharmacy
15 Port Office
18 OTE
19 Pharmacy
20 Ferry to Aktio
21 Customs House

Kastro
(St Andrew
Castle)

Ambracian
Gulf

To Neohori

To Nikopolis, Arta,
Ioannina, Parga
& Igoumenitsa

To Airport,
Vonitsa &
Lefkada

To Kastro (St George Castle),
Camping Kalamitsi,
Pantokrator & Alonaki

Preveza

0   50   100 m

NORTHERN GREECE

Nearby are two similar establishments: the *Taverna tou Stavraka* and the *I Trata*.

The *Petrino* at Sapountzaki 4, is a tastefully modern but touristy taverna. It serves some excellent home-made specialities, such as baked peppers stuffed with cheese. The owner specialises in imported beers.

Getting There & Away
Air There are at least five flights a week in the low season and daily flights in the high season from Preveza airport to Athens (20 minutes, 12,800 dr). The airport is sometimes called Lefkada or Aktion. The Olympic Airways office (☎ 28 343) is on the corner of Spiliadou and Balkou. The airport is 7km south of Preveza and the Olympic Airways bus to the airport costs 450 dr, plus the Aktion ferry fare.

Bus From the intercity bus station there are ten buses a day to Ioannina (two hours, 1800 dr); five to Parga (two hours, 1250 dr) and Arta (one hour, 900 dr); two to Igoumenitsa (2½ hours, 1950 dr); four to Athens (six hours, 6100 dr) and one to Thessaloniki (eight hours, 7150 dr).

Ferry The Preveza-Aktion ferry departs every half-hour (80 dr per person; 750 dr per car).

AROUND PREVEZA
Nikopolis Νικόπολη
In 31 BC, Octavian (later Emperor Augustus of Rome) defeated Mark Antony and Cleopatra in the famous Battle of Actium (present-day Aktion). To celebrate this victory, Octavian built Nikopolis, which means 'city of victory', and populated it by forcible resettlement of people from surrounding towns and villages. It was plundered by Vandals and Goths in the 5th and 6th centuries, but rebuilt by Justinian. It was sacked again by the Bulgars in the 11th century, after which nobody bothered to rebuild it.

Little is left of the walls built by Augustus, but the Byzantine walls and a theatre survive, and there are remains of temples to Mars and Poseidon (an appropriate choice of gods for the war-mongering Octavian), an aqueduct, Roman baths and a restored Roman odeum. The immense site sprawls over both sides of the Preveza-Arta road.

There is an **archaeological museum** at the Nikopolis site (☎ 41 336) open every day except Monday from 8.30 am to 3 pm. It has exhibits from the ancient citadel. Admission is 500 dr or 300 dr for students. Other exhibits may be viewed at the Ioannina Archaeological Museum.

Getting There & Away Preveza-Arta buses stop at the site.

Beaches
From just north of the Preveza there are beaches strung out for some 30km all along the **Bay of Nikopolis**. The beaches at **Monolithi**, 10km out of Preveza, and **Kastrosykia**, 15km from Preveza, are particularly popular. They are accessible on Parga-bound buses.

ARTA Αρτα
• *pop 18,000* • *postcode 471 00* • *area code* ☎ *0681*
Arta (**A**rta), the second-largest town of Epiros, is 76km south of Ioannina and 50km north-east of Preveza. Arta is easy to miss if you're speeding on your way to Athens or locations further south, which is a pity, because Arta is worth a visit. After the barren agricultural scene of Ioannina and further north, it is a refreshing break to come across grove upon grove of citrus plantations as you leave the Louros valley and reach the open plains and wetlands of the north Ambracian gulf.

The town is built over the ancient city of Ambracia which King Pyrrhus of Epiros made his capital in the 4th century BC. In the 14th century the Frankish despot of Epiros made it his seat of government. The town has a wealth of Byzantine monuments of which the locals are justifiably proud.

Today it is a bustling supply centre for the north Ambracia region and is a pleasant place to stroll around.

Orientation & Information

The main bus station is on the Ioannina-Athens road on the east side of town and just outside the town walls. From the bus station, walk about 200m to your right and look for Krystalli, which will lead you to Arta's main street Nikiforou Skoufa. Half of this street is for pedestrians only.

The OTE is on the main square, Plateia Ethnikis Antistasis, which is halfway along Skoufa. The post office is on Amvrakias, about a five-minute walk from the OTE in the general direction of the fortress walls.

Things to See

The town's most distinguished feature is its fine 18th-century **Bridge of Arta**, which crosses the River Arahthos. This bridge, made famous by Greek demotic poetry, is probably Arta's most photographed monument. Legend has it that the master builder, who was having difficulty in preventing the bridge from being washed away every time he tried to complete it, was advised to entomb his wife in the stonework of the central arch. The bridge is still standing, although it has had a facelift or two in recent times and is now used by local pedestrians.

Arta also has several churches of note: the 13th-century **Church of Panagia Parigoritisa**, overlooking Plateia Skoufa, just south of the central square of Plateia Kilkis, is a well-preserved and striking building. The churches of **Agios Vasilios** and **Agia Theodora** have attractive ceramic decorations on their exterior walls. Both of these churches are just west of the main thoroughfare of Pyrrou which runs south from the fortress to Plateia Kilkis.

Places to Stay & Eat

The town has just two C-class hotels. The *Hotel Cronos* (☎ 22 211; fax 73 795), Plateia Kilkis, has singles/doubles for 10,000/13,000 dr with private bathroom. The *Hotel Amvrakia* (☎ 28 311; fax 78 544) has single/double rooms for 8500/10,000 dr with private bathroom. The Amvrakia is at Priovolou 13, one block east of Pyrrou.

There are several restaurants on Plateia Kilkis and you can always get a snack at the cafeterias on Plateia Ethnikis Antistasis. The Amvrakia Hotel has an associated restaurant next to it called the *Skaraveos*. Here you can get some genuine and tasty home cooking for around 2000 dr.

On either side of the bridge are two pricier establishments, the *Mylos* on the Ioannina side and the *Protomastoras* on the Arta side.

Getting There & Away

There are 10 buses a day to Ioannina (2½ hours, 1300 dr) and five buses a day between Preveza and Arta (one hour, 900 dr). You can also get four direct buses to Athens (five hours, 5600 dr) and one daily to Thessaloniki (7½ hours, 6550 dr).

Macedonia Μακεδονία

Macedonia is the largest prefecture in Greece, and its capital, Thessaloniki, is Greece's second city. With abundant and varied attractions it's surprising that more travellers don't find their way here. Tucked up in the left-hand corner are the beautiful Prespa lakes, home to one of Europe's most important bird sanctuaries. To the south, Mt Olympus, at 2917m Greece's highest peak, rises from a plain just 6km from the sea. The unsung towns of Veria, Edessa and Florina unfold their charms to only the occasional visitor. For archaeological buffs there is Alexander the Great's birthplace of Pella; the sanctuary of Dion, where Alexander made sacrifices to the gods; Vergina, where the Macedonian kings (apart from Alexander) were buried; and Philippi, where the battle which set the seal on the future of the western world was fought. Macedonia is also the site of the Monastic Republic of Athos.

THESSALONIKI Θεσσαλονίκη
• pop 750,000 • postcode 541 00 • area code ☎ 031

Thessaloniki (Thessaloníki) was the second city of Byzantium and is the second city of modern Greece. However, being second does not mean that Thessaloniki lies in the

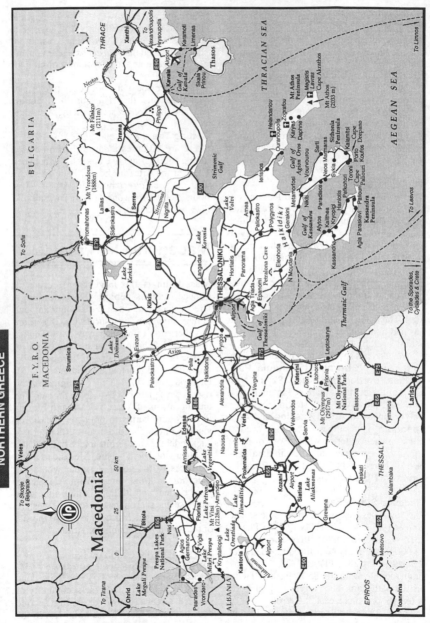

shadow of, or tries to emulate, the capital. It is a sophisticated city with a distinct character of its own. It has a lively nightlife, good restaurants and, although it doesn't have the impressive ancient monuments of the capital, it has several good museums, a scattering of Roman ruins and superlative Byzantine churches.

Thessaloniki sits at the top of the wide Thermaic gulf. The oldest part of the city is the kastro, the old Turkish quarter, whose narrow streets huddle around a Byzantine fortress on the slopes of Mt Hortiatis.

Thessaloniki is best avoided during festival time (September-October), as accommodation is almost impossible to find and rates are at a premium. Finding a room at other times should not be a problem.

History

Like almost everywhere in Greece, Thessaloniki has had not only its triumphs but more than its fair share of disasters. As with Athens, an awareness of these helps greatly in one's appraisal of the city.

The city was named Thessaloniki in 316 BC by the Macedonian general, Kassandros, after his wife, daughter of Philip II and half-sister of Alexander the Great. While Philip was successfully expanding his territory in Thessaly, his wife gave birth to their daughter. When he arrived home Philip announced that the child would be called Thessaloniki, which means 'Victory in Thessaly'.

After the Roman conquest in 168 BC, Thessaloniki became capital of the province of Macedonia. Thessaloniki's geographical location on the Thermaic gulf and its position on the Via Egnatia helped to promote its development. It was also an important staging post on the trade route to the Balkan region.

The Roman Emperor Galerius made it the imperial capital of the eastern half of the Roman Empire, and after the empire split it became the second city of Byzantium, flourishing as both a spiritual and economic centre. Inevitably, its strategic position brought attacks and plundering by Goths, Slavs, Muslims, Franks and Epirots. In 1185

it was sacked by the Normans, and in 1204 was made a feudal kingdom under Marquis Boniface of Montferrat. In 1246 it was reunited with the Byzantine Empire. After several sieges it finally capitulated to Ottoman rule when Murad II staged a successful invasion in 1430.

Along with the rest of Macedonia, Thessaloniki became part of Greece in 1913. In August 1917 a fire broke out in the city and, as there was no fire brigade, the flames spread quickly, destroying 9500 houses and rendering 70,000 inhabitants homeless. The problem of homelessness was exacerbated by the influx of refugees from Asia Minor after the 1923 population exchange. During the late 1920s the city was carefully replanned and built on a grid system with wide streets and large squares.

In 1978 Thessaloniki experienced a severe earthquake. Most of the modern buildings were not seriously damaged, but the Byzantine churches suffered greatly and most are still in the process of being restored. Thessaloniki was chosen as Europe's 'Cultural Capital' in 1997.

Orientation

Thessaloniki's waterfront of Leoforos Nikis stretches from the port in the west to the White Tower (Lefkos Pyrgos) in the east. North of the White Tower are the exhibition grounds where Thessaloniki's annual International Trade Fair is held. The university campus is north of here. The city's other principal streets of Mitropoleos, Tsimiski and Ermou run parallel to Nikis. Egnatia, the next street up, is the city's main thoroughfare and most of Thessaloniki's Roman remains are between here and Agiou Dimitriou. The city's two main squares are Plateia Eleftherias, and Plateia Aristotelous, both of which abut the waterfront.

The central food market is between Egnatia, Irakliou, Aristotelous and Dragoumi. Plateia Eleftherias is one of the city's local bus terminals, although the main terminal is at Plateia Dikastirion. The train station is on Monastiriou, a westerly continuation of Egnatia. The city does not have one general intercity bus station; there are several terminals for different destinations. The airport is 16km south-east of the city. Kastra, the old Turkish quarter, is north of Athinas and just within the ramparts.

Information

Tourist Office The EOT (☎ 271 888), Plateia Aristotelous 8, is open Monday to Friday from 8 am to 8 pm and Saturday from 8 am to 2 pm.

Tourist Police The tourist police (☎ 554 871) are at Dodekanisou 4, 5th floor. The office is open from 7.30 am to 11 pm all year round.

Money The National Bank of Greece, Plateia Dimokratias, is open Monday to Friday from 8 am to 2 pm and 6 to 8 pm, on Saturday from 8 am to 1.30 pm and on Sunday from 9.30 am to 12.30 pm. Another branch, at Tsimiski 11, opens on weekends for the benefit of people wishing to change currency. There is an automatic exchange machine at the train station. American Express (☎ 269 521) is at Tsimiski 19 and is open from Monday to Thursday from 8.30 am to 2 pm and on Friday from 8 am to 1.30 pm.

Post & Communications The main post office is at Tsimiski 45. It's open Monday to Friday from 7.30 am to 8 pm, Saturday from 7.30 am to 2.15 pm and Sunday from 9 am to 1.30 pm. The OTE is at Karolou Dil 27 and is open 24 hours a day.

Online Services There is an Internet café, Netcafé (☎ 943 939) at Agiou Spyridona, Triandria. It is open from 11 am to 1 am and charges 1000 dr per hour, if you want to infosurf or just read your e-mail. Check their URL for further details: www.netcafe.gr. Triandria is the suburb immediately to the east of the Kaftanzoglio stadium on the east side of the university campus. Take the No 32 bus to get there. Alight at the Church of Agios Spyridon.

What's in a Name?

An awful lot if you are Greek and the name is Macedonia. In January 1992, the Yugoslav Republic of Macedonia declared its full independence. After this pronouncement the Greek government protested vociferously, insisting that the new country change its name before the European Community granted it recognition. In May 1992, Greece stated it would recognise the republic's independence and cooperate with it to ensure stability in the region, so long as its name did not include the word Macedonia. In response, the EC recognised Macedonia in June 1992, provided it adopted another name. Among the Greek people, the issue has resulted in a surge of unprecedented nationalism with slogans throughout the country declaring 'Macedonia is Greek, always was, and always will be'.

The Greeks' objections to the name Macedonia are twofold. They believe that it is an infringement of their cultural heritage, and they read into it undercurrents of territorial claims. The 'Greekness' of Alexander the Great, the greatest of Macedonian kings, is indisputable. After all, it was he who spread Greek culture to India and the Middle East, and in so doing established Greek as the international language of the ancient world. Whether Alexander the Great's ancestors were Greek is a different matter. The ethnic origins of the ancient Macedonians has, since the beginning of recorded history, been a conundrum, for it seems that Macedonia has always been a mélange of languages and nationalities.

After Alexander's death, Macedonia continued to be part of Greece until, with the rest of the country, it came under Roman domination. When the Roman Empire split in the 4th century, Macedonia, traversed by the Via Egnatia (the long straight road which linked Rome to Byzantium), became a powerful region with a relatively stable population. This stability came to an end in the 7th century when the region was invaded by Serbs, who were followed by Bulgars and Muslims. During Byzantine times, Samuel, a Slav Macedonian king, fought against the Byzantines, and his army made inroads into Macedonia. In the 14th century the Serb Stefan Dusan (who ruled from 1331 to 1355) occupied all of Macedonia, except Thessaloniki. This occupation was short-lived as it was quickly superseded by the Ottoman conquest.

The Greeks' concern about claims on the territory of Macedonia stem from the late 19th century, when the Ottoman Empire was on the point of collapse. At this time, countries welling over with

There is also the more centrally located Globus Internet Café (☎ 232 901) at Amynta 12. However, it is closed for one month during summer.

Foreign Consulates Foreign consulates in Thessaloniki include:

Bulgaria
    N Manou 12 (☎ 829 210)
Canada
    Tsimiski 17 (☎ 256 350; fax 256 351)
Czech Republic
    Ploutarhou 8 (☎ 267 041)
France
    McKenzie King 8 (☎ 244 030; fax 244 032)
Germany
    Karolou Dil 4a (☎ 236 349)
Hungary
    Danaïdou 4 (☎ 547 397; fax 530 988)
Italy
    Vasilissis Olgas 63 (☎ 830 055)
Netherlands
    Komninon 26 (☎ 227 477; fax 283 794)
Norway
    McKenzie King 12 (☎ 234 110)
Romania
    Leoforos Nikis 13 (☎ 225 481; fax 225 428)
South Africa
    Tsimiski 51 (☎ 722 519; fax 274 393)
Sweden
    Komninon 26 (☎ 236 410)
Turkey
    Ag Dimitriou 151 (☎ 248 452; fax 204 438)
UK
    El Venizelou 8 (☎ 278 006; fax 283 868) open 8 am to 1 pm
USA
    Leoforos Nikis 59 (☎ 242 905; fax 242 915) open Tue & Thu, 9 am to 12 pm
Yugoslavia
    Komninon 4, (☎ 244 266)

Australia and New Zealand are represented by the UK Consulate.

Mt Athos Permits Permits for the monastic region of Mt Athos may be obtained from the Ministry of Macedonia & Thrace (☎ 257 012), on Plateia Diikitiriou. For information about applying for one, see under Mt Athos in the Halkidiki section later in this chapter.

nationalistic fervour were poised to pick up the spoils. The Serbs made no secret of the fact that they coveted Macedonia, but a much greater threat came from King Ferdinand of Bulgaria.

This volatile situation culminated in the two Balkan wars (1912-13). In the first Balkan war, the Serbs, Bulgarians and Greeks fought the Turks, and in the second round the Serbs and Greeks fought the Bulgarians. The second Balkan war was ended by the Treaty of Bucharest, which ceded more than half of Macedonia to Greece and divided the rest between Serbia and Bulgaria. In both world wars Bulgaria fought against Greece and in WWII parts of Macedonia were occupied by Bulgaria, which implemented a policy of enforced 'Bulgarianisation'. After the victory of the Allies in WWII, the threat from Bulgaria was replaced by one from Yugoslavia.

In April 1945, Tito proclaimed the Socialist Republic of Macedonia. Greece is convinced that Tito did this to strengthen the southern flank of his territory and that his ultimate ambition was to create an independent Macedonian state which would include the Greek province of Macedonia, and the Bulgarian region of Macedonia known as Pirin. Greece says it was too busy fighting the civil war to protest at the time, a situation that Tito was only too aware of. In 1952 a Macedonian grammar was published in Tito's republic and in 1968 the republic acquired the autocephalous Macedonian church. To Greece, these factors added credence to its suspicions.

Greece continued to protest against the name Macedonia throughout 1992 and into 1993. Then in April 1993, Macedonia was admitted to the UN under the temporary name of the Former Yugoslav Republic of Macedonia (FYROM), which doesn't exactly trip off the tongue. By mid-1997 the issue of the 'name' was no closer to being resolved, though tensions between the two neighbours have eased and visitors from both sides of the border are now seen in greater numbers in each other's country.

To this day there are people in Greek villages on the borders of Bulgaria and the new republic who speak Macedonian. This is one of the south Slavonic group of languages, which is a dialect of Bulgarian, with some Turkish, Greek, Albanian and Vlach words. An offshoot of the present nationalistic fervour is that a minority of these people are demanding greater autonomy for Macedonian-speaking Greeks within Greece. The country is not without other ethnic minorities. Could it be that Greece, in its much ado about Macedonia, has inadvertently opened a Pandora's box? ■

NORTHERN GREECE

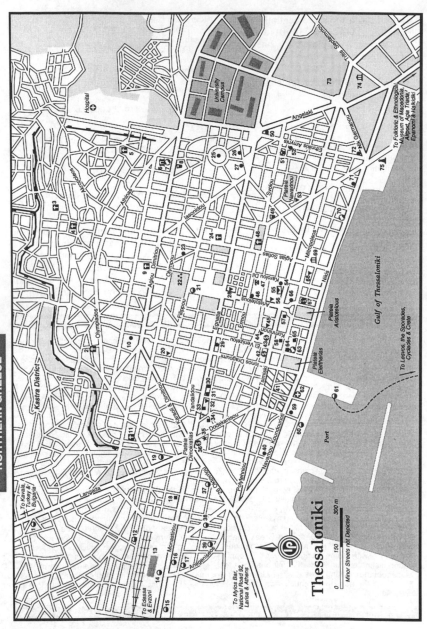

Thessaloniki

0   150   300 m

Minor Streets not Depicted

PLACES TO STAY
18 Capsis Hotel
30 Hotel Atlas
31 Hotel Averof
33 Hotel Atlantis
34 Hotel Acropol
50 ABC Hotel
51 GYHA Hostel
57 Electra Palace Hotel
58 Tourist Hotel
65 Continental Hotel

PLACES TO EAT
20 Life Restaurant
28 Ta Spata Psistaria
32 Ta Nea Ilysia
41 Ta Ladadika
44 O Loutros Fish
    Taverna
45 Babel Snack Bar
53 Taverna ta Aderfia tis
    Pyxarias
56 Ouzeri Aristotelous
68 Ta Nisia Taverna

THINGS TO SEE
2 Church of Agia
   Ekaterini
3 Monastery of
   Vlatadon
4 Church of Osios David
5 Church of Nikolaos
   Orfanos
6 Atatürk's House
9 Church of Agios
   Dimitrios

11 Church of the Dodeka
    Apostoli
22 Roman Agora
24 Church of Panagia
    Ahiropiitos
25 The Rotonda
27 Arch of Galerius
48 Church of Agia Sofia
69 Museum of the
    Macedonian
    Struggle
73 International
    Exhibition
    Fairground
74 Archaeological
    Museum
75 White Tower
    (Monument)

OTHER
1 Kavala Bus Station
7 Turkish Consulate
8 Show Avantaz
10 Ministry of Macedonia
    & Thrace
12 Alexandroupolis Bus
    Station
13 Train Station
14 Airport Bus Terminal
15 Ioannina Bus Station
16 Athens & Trikala Bus
    Station
17 Florina Bus Station
19 Langadas Bus Station
21 Local Bus Station
23 Globus Internet Cafe

26 Bianca Laundrette
29 Molho Bookshop
35 Tourist Police
36 National Bank of
    Greece
37 Veria Bus Station
38 Katerini Bus Station
39 Pella, Kastoria, Volos
    & Edessa Bus
    Station
40 Olympic Airways
    Office
42 National Bank of
    Greece
43 American Express
46 Train Tickets Office
    (OSE)
47 OTE
49 Rivoli Club
52 En Chordais Music
    Store
54 EOS (Climbing Club)
55 Main Post Office
59 Nomikos Lines
60 Hydrofoil Departure
    Point
61 Ferry Departure
    Point
62 First-Aid Centre
63 UK Consulate
64 Doucas Tours
66 Olympian Cinema
67 EOT
70 US Consulate
71 Cinema Pallas
72 Aristotelion Cinema

NORTHERN GREECE

Bookshops Molho, Tsimiski 10, has a comprehensive stock of English-language books, magazines and newspapers. Malliaris Kaisia, at Aristotelous 9, also has many English-language publications.

Laundry Wash & Go, just north-east of the university campus at Nestoros Telloglou 15, is a trendy, airy-looking place. Follow Agiou Dimitriou from the city until just past the university and it's set back on your left, off a small grassy square, opposite the dental school. It's open Monday to Saturday from 9 am to 8.30 pm; closed on Sunday. A wash and dry will cost you 1800 dr.

Bianca Laundrette, on Antoniadou, has a more utilitarian ambience. Walk up D Gournari from the Arch of Galerius and Antoniadou is off to the right. It's open Monday to Friday from 8 am to 8.30 pm. This place charges 1400 dr a load for a wash and dry.

Emergency There is a first-aid centre (☎ 530 530) at Navarhou Koundourioti 6, near the port. The largest public hospital is the Ippokration (☎ 830 024), Konstantinoupoleos 49.

Business Hours Commercial shops are open during the following hours: Monday, Wednesday and Saturday from 8.30 am to 2.30 pm; Tuesday, Thursday and Friday from 8.30 am to 2.30 pm and 5 to 8.30 pm. They're not open on Sunday.

Department stores and supermarkets are open during the following hours: Monday to Friday from 8 am to 8 pm and Saturday from

8 am to 3 pm, though supermarkets are open until 6 pm. They are, however, closed on Sunday.

Things to See

Archaeological Museum In 1977 one of Greece's most eminent archaeologists, Professor Andronikos, was excavating at Vergina near Thessaloniki when he found an unlooted tomb which turned out to be that of King Philip II of Macedon. The spectacular contents of this tomb, now on display in this museum, are comparable to the grave treasures of Mycenae.

Among the exhibits are exquisite gold jewellery, bronze and terracotta vases, tiny ivory reliefs of intricate detail and a solid gold casket with lion's feet, embossed with the symbol of the royal house of Macedonia, which contained the bones of Philip II. The most mind-boggling exhibit is the bones themselves, which are carefully laid out to reconstruct an almost complete skeleton. There is something very strange about looking at someone who until that moment was just a name in a history book.

The opening hours of the museum (☎ 830 538) are Monday from 12.30 to 7 pm; Tuesday to Friday from 8 am to 7 pm; and weekends and holidays from 8.30 am to 3 pm. In winter, it opens from 10.30 am to 5 pm on Monday; on the other days, it opens at the same time as in summer but closes at 5 pm. Admission costs 1500 dr. The museum is opposite the entrance to the exhibition grounds. To get there either walk east along Tsimiski or take bus No 3.

Folkloric & Ethnological Museum of Macedonia

This museum (☎ 830 591), housed in a beautiful 19th-century mansion, is one of the best of its kind in Greece. As well as elaborate costumes and intricate embroidery, the collection also includes traditional agricultural and craft tools.

The upstairs exhibition is titled 'Thessaloniki 1913 to 1919'. Life in the city at that time is presented through photographs taken by Fred Boissonas, a pioneer photographer and philhellene. The exhibition also includes eyewitness accounts (translated into English) of the fire of 1917.

The museum is at Vasilissis Olgas 68, but in 1997 it was closed for renovations. It should be open by early 1998. It is 15 minutes walk from the archaeological museum, or you can take eastbound bus No 5, 7 or 33 and get off at the Fleming stop.

White Tower This 15th-century tower is both the city's symbol and most prominent landmark. During the 18th century it was used as a prison for insubordinate janissaries, the elite troops of forcibly converted Christian boys, who became servants of the sultan. In 1826, at the order of Mahmud II, many of the janissaries were massacred in this tower and thereafter it became known as the bloody tower. After independence it was whitewashed as a symbolic gesture to expunge its function during Turkish rule. The whitewash has now been removed and it has been turned into a very fine **Byzantine Museum** (☎ 267 832), with splendid frescoes and icons.

In the pleasant museum café a 30-minute audiovisual is shown every hour between 10 am and 4 pm (except at 2 pm).

The opening hours of the museum are Monday from 12.30 to 7 pm, Tuesday to Friday from 8 am to 7 pm, weekends and holidays from 8.30 am to 3 pm. Admission is 800 dr.

Other Museums The **Museum of the Macedonian Struggle** (☎ 229 778) outlines the story of the liberation of Macedonia from the Ottomans and the threat of Bulgarian nationalism. The museum is at Proxenou Koromila 23, in what was the Greek consular building when Macedonia was still part of the Ottoman Empire. Proxenou Koromila runs parallel to, and between, Mitropoleos and Nikis. Opening times are Tuesday to Friday from 9 am to 2 pm; and also Wednesday from 6 to 8 pm. On weekends it opens from 11 am to 2.30 pm. It is closed on Monday. Admission is free.

Kemal Atatürk, the founder of the Republic of Turkey, was born in Thessaloniki in 1881. The Turkish timber-framed house where he was born and spent his childhood has been faithfully restored and is now a museum called **Atatürk's House**. It is at Apostolou Pavlou 17. A visit is a bit of a cloak-and-dagger affair, but is worth the effort. You must ring the bell of the Turkish Consulate building (around the corner on Agiou Dimitriou); you will be asked to produce your passport, and then someone will show you around. The museum is open every day from 2 to 6 pm. Admission is free.

Roman & Byzantine Thessaloniki Thessaloniki has few remaining Roman ruins, but its churches represent every period of Byzantine art and architecture, and were once the city's foremost glory. Not withstanding the extensive damage they have received due to fire and earthquakes, and their conversion to mosques; a visit to the most renowned ones is still worthwhile. You can see the Roman remains and the major churches in a circular walk.

The **Roman agora**, in the upper part of Plateia Dikastirion, is reached by crossing Egnatia from Aristotelous. Excavations began in the 1970s and are still in progress, so the site is cordoned off from the public. So far the odeum and two stoas have come to light.

From the north-east corner of this site, walk up Agnostou Stratioti, cross over Olympou, walk straight ahead, and you will see the 5th-century **Church of Agios Dimitrios** on the opposite side of the road.

Dimitrios was born in the city in the 3rd century and became an eminent scholar, and an early convert to Christianity. He was martyred on the orders of Galerius, who was not a Christian and who was ruthless in his persecution of those who were. Several claims of appearances of Dimitrios' ghost in warrior-like guise at apposite moments during sieges caused the enemy to flee in terror. This, coupled with claims of miraculous cures at the site of his martyrdom, gained him a sainthood. The church is Greece's largest and was built on the site where he was martyred.

The church was converted into a mosque by the Turks who plastered over the interior walls. When it was restored to the Christians again, it was discovered to have the finest mosaics of all the city's churches.

The frescoes and the buildings were extensively damaged in the fire of 1917. However, five 8th-century mosaics have survived and can be seen on either side of the altar. The church is open to the public daily from 7.30 am to 12 pm and from 5 to 8.30 pm. Entry is free.

On leaving the church turn left and walk along Agiou Dimitriou till you come to Dragoumi, which leads off to the right. Walk down here until you reach Filippou and you will see ahead the 3rd-century BC **Rotonda**, the oldest of Thessaloniki's churches. It is a Roman brickwork rotunda, which was originally intended as a mausoleum for Galerius, but never fulfilled this function. Constantine the Great transformed it into a church. The minaret, erected during its days as a mosque, remains. The church is closed for eventual restoration, opening only for occasional services.

Walk a little way around the church and turn right into D Gounari, and you will see ahead the imposing **Arch of Galerius**, which was erected in 303 AD to celebrate the emperor's victories over the Persians in 297 AD. Its eroded bas-reliefs depict battle scenes with the Persians. Turn right into Egnatia, and then left to reach the 8th-century **Church of Agia Sofia**, on Agias Sofias, which emulates its renowned namesake in İstanbul. The dome has a striking mosaic of the Ascension.

On leaving the Church of Agia Sofia, retrace your steps back to Egnatia, cross the road, and continue a little way up Agias Sofias to the **Church of the Panagia Ahiropiitos**, on the right. This church, built in the 5th century, is an early example of basilica form; some mosaics and frescoes remain. The name means 'made without hands' and derives from the 12th century, when an icon supposedly miraculously appeared in the church.

Several of the smaller churches are also

worth a look. They include the 13th-century **Church of Agia Ekaterini**, the **Church of the Dodeka Apostoloi** (Church of the Twelve Apostles) and the 4th-century **Church of Nikolaos Orfanos**, which has exquisite frescoes. The little 5th-century **Church of Osios David**, in Kastra, was allegedly built to commemorate Galerius' daughter, Theodora, whose clandestine baptism took place while her father was on one of his campaigns.

Kastra & the Ramparts The Turkish quarter of Kastra is all that is left of 19th-century Thessaloniki. The original ramparts of Kastra were built by Theodosius (379-475), but were rebuilt in the 14th century.

Kastra's streets are narrow and steep, with lots of steps, flanked by timber-framed houses, with overhanging upper storeys and tiny whitewashed dwellings with shutters. From Kastra there are stunning views of modern Thessaloniki and the Thermaic gulf. To get there, either take bus No 22 or 23 from Plateia Eleftherias; or walk north along Agias Sophias, which becomes Dimadou Vlatadou after Athinas. At the top turn right into Eptapyrgiou.

Organised Tours
Doucas Tours (☎ 269 984; fax 286 610), El Venizelou 8, organises a wide range of half-day and full-day tours around northern Greece for prices ranging from 6000 to 12,000 dr.

Special Events
Thessaloniki hosts a string of festivals during September and October, which are held in the exhibition grounds. The first is the International Trade Fair, followed by a cultural festival, which includes film shows and Greek song performances and culminates in the celebration of St Dimitrios' Day on 26 October. This is followed by military parades on Ohi Day on 28 October.

Places to Stay – bottom end
There are no camp sites close to Thessaloniki; the nearest ones are the EOT-run camp on the crowded beach at *Agia Triada* (☎ 0392-51 360), which opens on June 1 and is 27km from Thessaloniki, and at *Epanomi* (☎ 0392-41 358) which is open from April 1 and is 33km from Thessaloniki. Both charge about 1200 dr per person and 650 dr per tent. Take bus No 69 for Epanomi, and for Agia Triada, either bus No 67 or 72 from Plateia Dikastirion.

Thessaloniki's *GYHA hostel* (☎ 225 946; fax 262 208), Alex Svolou 44, has dorm beds for 2000 dr. It is not part of the HI organisation. The dormitory doors are locked between 11 am and 6 pm, but you can use the lounge area. With a HI or ISIC student card you get a 10% discount.

The E-class *Hotel Atlantis* (☎ 540 131), Egnatia 14, has pokey but clean double/triple rooms for 5400/8640 dr with shared bathroom. The D-class *Hotel Acropol* (☎ 536 670), Tandalidou 4, is Thessaloniki's best budget hotel. It's clean, quiet and owned by a friendly English-speaking family. The single/double rooms cost 6000/9000 dr with shared bathroom. The hotel is just beyond the central police station.

Another quiet option is the D-class *Hotel Averof* (☎ 538 498), Leontos Sofou 24, around the corner from Egnatia. The attractive pine-furnished rooms cost 4500/8000 dr with shared bathroom for singles/doubles. The D-class *Hotel Atlas* (☎ 537 046; fax 537 046), Egnatia 40, has clean, carpeted singles/doubles for 5500/9000 dr with shared bathroom (shower 1000 dr); doubles with private bathroom are 12,000 dr. This is a reasonable hotel, but the rooms at the front get a lot of traffic noise.

The D-class *Tourist Hotel* (☎ 270 501; fax 226 865), Mitropoleos 21, has pleasant rooms and a spacious lounge with comfortable armchairs and a TV. The cost is a hefty (for its category) 11,880/18,360 dr for a single/double room.

The C-class *Continental Hotel* (☎ 277 553), at Komninon 5, has better priced singles/doubles for 5400/7600 dr with shared bathroom, or 11,000/14,000 dr with private bathroom. All of the rooms have a refrigerator and the ones with private bathroom have colour TV and air-con. The hotel has an idiosyncratic lift which should be donated to an industrial archaeological museum.

Places to Stay – middle

The B-class *ABC Hotel* (☎ 265 421; fax 276 542), Angelaki 41, has 102 rooms all with private bathroom, telephone and balcony. Singles/doubles here cost 20,900/28,900 dr including breakfast. The hotel is at the eastern end of Egnatia. Further east, the modern B-class *Hotel Queen Olga* (☎ 824 621; fax 868 581), Vasilissis Olgas 44, has cosy rooms with a warm, mellow décor and private bathroom, radio, colour TV, minibar and air-con. The rates are 24,000/30,300 dr. This hotel has a car park. Travelling east, the hotel is on the right. A little further along, on the opposite side of the road, is the B-class *Hotel Metropolitan* (☎ 824 221; fax 849 762), at Vasilissis Olgas 65. It has attractively furnished rooms with bathroom, telephone and radio. Singles/doubles cost 23,500/ 32,500 dr including breakfast. All of the middle-range hotels recommended have bars and restaurants.

Places to Stay – top end

Thessaloniki's A-class *Electra Palace Hotel* (☎ 232 221; fax 235 947), Plateia Aristotelous 5a, has an impressive façade in the style of a Byzantine palace. The cost for singles/doubles is 28,800/35,000 dr including breakfast. The hotel has two restaurants and a bar.

Places to Eat

There are lots of fast-food places and snack bars in Thessaloniki where you can get gyros, pizza or cheese pie for around 350 dr. *Babel Snack Bar*, Komninon 18, is a good place for a snack or breakfast with reasonably priced crêpes, pies, toasted sandwiches and filter coffee.

The bright and busy *Life Restaurant*, Filippou 1, on the corner of Syngrou and Filippou, offers a rarity in Greece – instant service. The menu is large and the food well prepared: moussaka, pastitsio and spaghetti are all around the 1300 dr mark. The restaurant is open every day for lunch and dinner. Another popular place with similarly priced Greek staples is *Ta Nea Ilysia* on Leontos Sofou, opposite the Hotel Averof.

For a lively evening out you could try the long-established *O Loutros Fish Taverna*, in an old Turkish hammam (bathhouse) on Komninon, near the flower market. Don't be misled by the rough-and-ready ambience – this taverna has a cult following. If you go there you'll be rubbing shoulders with politicians, professors and actors. Excellent fish dishes cost around 2000 to 3000 dr. The taverna is always crowded and there are often spontaneous renderings of *rembetika* music, usually on Tuesday and Thursday evenings.

At the popular *Ta Spata Psistaria*, Aristotelous 28, a tasty meal of gyros, chips, aubergine salad, fried zucchini and retsina will cost about 2400 dr. Choose your meal from the dishes on display and order. Service is smart and business-like. The *Taverna Ta Aderfia tis Pyxarias*, at Plateia Navarinou 9, is another popular place worth checking out. It has a pleasing ambience, with enlarged pictures of old Thessaloniki on the walls; its very tasty kebabs cost around 1250 dr.

The *Ouzeri Aristotelous* has first-rate mezedes, which include cuttlefish stuffed with cheese, grilled eggplant with garlic and prawns in red sauce. The restaurant, which has a Parisian ambience with marble-top tables, is in an arcade off the left side of Aristotelous as you walk towards the waterfront. It's open Monday to Saturday all day until late, but closes on Sunday at 6 pm.

Ta Nisia Taverna, Koromila 13, is another wonderful place. It has white stucco walls, a wood-beamed ceiling, lots of plants, and pretty plates on the walls. The unusual, imaginative mezedes include cuttlefish with spinach in wine and little triangles of pastry filled with eggplant.

Ta Ladadika This is a small area consisting of a few blocks of formerly derelict commercial warehouses and small shops close to the ferry terminal. Over the last few years the area has been gradually restored and is now the focus for a number of tavernas, music bars and pubs. The *Psarotaverna Istira* on Egyptou got the thumbs up from the 1997 Thessaloniki Cultural Capital committee as a 'traditional dining place'. Meat dishes start from 1200 dr; fish, however, is fairly expensive.

Further up along the same street is the *Kokoretsina* offering kokoretsi (spit-grilled offal) for around 1600 dr – and naturally retsina – and around the corner on Katouni the small *Iatros tis Pinas* doubles as a fastfoudadiko and ouzeri.

On Fasianou, leading to the seafront, two unassuming Greek fish & chip joints *Ta Bakaliarakia sto Limani* and *Ta Bakaliarakia tou Aristou* do a reasonable job with this staple Anglo dish and are as popular with locals as they are with visitors from northern Europe.

The *Zithos* pub on Plateia Katouni does an admirable pint of Murphy's stout for 1200 dr and offers an imaginative lunch and dinner menu. Over on Plateia Morihovou the *Sirines* doubles as a restaurant and funky music bar. If all that isn't enough, the *Kali Orexi* on the Plateia Eleftherias side of the Ladadika is a Chinese restaurant, should you be hankering after an oriental banquet.

Entertainment

Discos & Music Bars *Mylos* (☎ 525 968), Andreou Georgiou 56, is a huge old mill which has been converted into an entertainment complex with an art gallery, restaurant, bar and live-music club (classical and rock). Andreou Georgiou is off the map in a grim part of town. Either take a westbound bus No 31, or walk down 26 Oktovriou from Plateia Vardari to Andreou Georgiou, which is off to the right next to the petrol station at 26 Oktovriou 36. Mylos is a spruce cream and terracotta building, 250m along on the right. Music bars abound in the Ladadika area (see the preceding Places to Eat section), where the main entertainment emphasis is on music and pubs with all kinds of draught and bottled beer.

Live bouzouki and Greek folk are played at *Show Avantaz*, Agiou Dimitriou 156. There is no cover charge but spirits cost 1500 dr. The club is open from 11 pm to 4 am nightly, but closes from June to September.

One of Thessaloniki's biggest winter discos is *Traffic* on Tritis Septemvriou, two blocks down from Egnatia on the right. *L'Apogée* at Ethnikis Andistasis 16 and *Troll*, almost next door, are lively winter discos in the eastern part of town – any taxi driver will be able to take you there.

Thessaloniki's summer discos are out towards the airport – the hippest are *Club Privé* and *Amnesia*. Back in the centre the *Rivoli*, formerly known as Loft, Pavlou Mela 40, is a popular *bouzouksidiko* – a nightclub for die-hard bouzouki fans.

Cinema

Thessaloniki's cinemas showing first-run English-language films include the revamped *Olympian* on Plateia Aristotelous, *Aristotelion*, opposite the White Tower, and *Cinema Pallas*, at Nikis 69. *Natali* is an open-air summer cinema on Megalou Alexandrou.

Things to Buy

Thessaloniki's women have a reputation for being the most chic in Greece so, to supply a demand, Thessaloniki has many clothes and shoe shops selling ultra-fashionable gear. Bargains can be found along Egnatia and the shops around the indoor food market, and you can pick up high-quality and expensive stuff on Tsimiski. Also look out for vendors on Tsimiski, some of whom sell trendy handmade jewellery at reasonable prices.

If you are seriously interested in Greek or Middle-Eastern music, you can buy some genuine traditional musical instruments at En Chordais (☎ 282 248) which is hidden away somewhat at L Margariti. The store is at the back end of the same block as the GYHA Hostel. Kyriakos Kalaïtzidis, the owner of En Chordais, is also an accomplished musician and runs a music school, should you have a burning desire to learn the oud, the *toumberleki* (lap drum), or Byzantine choral music.

Getting There & Away

Air The Olympic Airways office (☎ 230 240) is at Navarhou Koundourioti 3. The airport phone number is ☎ 425 011.

Domestic Olympic has at least seven flights a day to Athens (20,700 dr), daily flights to Limnos (14,100 dr), daily flights to Ioannina (10,800 dr) and three a week to Iraklio (27,700 dr). There are two flights per week to Corfu (19,600 dr), Mytilini (19,600 dr), Samos (23,700 dr) and Chios (21,100 dr).

International There are international flights between Thessaloniki and the following destinations:

Belgrade	four a week
Budapest	four a week
Cyprus	five a week
Frankfurt	two a day
London	11 a week
Munich	two a day
Paris	one a week
Vienna	nine a week
Zürich	seven a week

Bus – domestic Most of Thessaloniki's bus terminals are close to the train station. Frequent buses for Athens and Trikala leave from Monastiriou 65 and 67, opposite the train station. Buses for Alexandroupolis leave from Koloniari 17 behind the train station. Buses for Pella, Edessa, Volos and Kastoria leave from Anageniseos 22 and for Florina from Anageniseos 42. Ioannina buses leave from Hristou Pipsou 19 (off Giannitson). Buses for Veria leave from 26 Oktovriou 10.

The Katerini bus station is at Promitheos 10, on a corner with Sapphous, a turn-off right (heading west) just beyond the Veria station. Kavala buses leave from Langada 59. This is the main road north out of Thessaloniki starting at Plateia Vardari.

All buses for the Halkidiki peninsula leave from Karakasi 68 which is in the eastern part of the city and off this book's map. To reach the Halkidiki terminal take bus No 10 to the Botsari stop (near Markou Botsari) from either the train station or anywhere along Egnatia.

Bus – international Greek Railways (OSE) runs buses to the following destinations: Sofia, at 7 am, 4 and 10 pm daily (4100 dr); İstanbul, at 2.30 am daily except Thursday (10,900 dr); and Korça (Korytsa) in Albania, every day except Sunday at 8 am (5100 dr). Buses leave from the station forecourt and tickets can be bought in the station. These services, however, are subject to frequent changes.

Train – domestic All domestic trains leave from the station on Monastiriou (☎ 517 517). There are four regular trains a day to Athens (7½ hours, 3720 dr), four to Kozani (four hours, 1580 dr) with connections to Florina (3¼ hours, 1370 dr). There are three trains a day to Alexandroupolis (2990 dr) and a further three local trains to Larisa with connections to Volos (4½ hours, 1730 dr).

There are five additional express intercity services to Athens (six hours, 7770 dr) – one of which is a nonstop service with a meal included in the ticket price; two services to Alexandroupolis (5½ hours, 4870 dr) and one service to Kozani (3¼ hours, 2080 dr). Note that tickets to all destinations and intermediate stations using the intercity services attract a supplement which is worked out on a sliding scale, depending on the distance travelled. There are also a couple of night-sleeper trains to Athens.

Tickets may be bought at the train station or the OSE office (☎ 276 382), Aristotelous 18. The station has a National Bank of Greece, a post office, an OTE and a restaurant which is open from 6 am to 10 pm. Luggage storage is 270 dr per piece, per day.

Train – international There are currently four international services operating out of Thessaloniki. There are two trains a day to Belgrade (9500 dr); one departs at 6 am and the other at 7.30 pm, which continues on to

NORTHERN GREECE

Budapest (26,400 dr) and to other destinations in Eastern and western Europe. There is one train for İstanbul (10,100 dr) leaving at 10.20 pm. Finally, there is one train a day to Sofia (5500 dr), with a connection for Bucharest, leaving at 8.30 am. These times are subject to seasonal changes, so do check before making plans.

Car The ELPA (Greek Automobile Club; ☎ 426 319) is at Vasilissis Olgas 228. Cars may be hired from Budget Rent a Car (☎ 274 272), Angelaki 15; and InterRent-Europcar (☎ 826 333), G Papandreou 5, among others.

Ferry A ferry sails on Sunday throughout the year to Chios (18 hours, 7750 dr) via Limnos (eight hours, 5050 dr) and Lesvos (13 hours, 7700 dr). In summer there are three to six boats a week to Iraklio, on Crete (10,650 dr). Boats go via Paros and Santorini and one of them also stops at Tinos and Mykonos.

There are also boats to the Sporades islands (Skiathos, Skopelos and Alonnisos) three times a week (5½-7 hours, 3500 dr) in July and August, and one a week to Rhodes (21 hours, 12,000 dr) throughout the year via Samos and Kos.

The telephone number of Thessaloniki's port police is ☎ 531 504. Ferry tickets may be purchased from Nomikos Lines (☎ 524 544; fax 532 289), Koundourioti 8.

Hydrofoil In summer there are more or less daily hydrofoils to the Sporades islands of Skiathos (3¼ hours, 9500 dr), Skopelos (four hours, 9500 dr) and Alonnisos (4½ hours, 11,100 dr). These also stop at Nea Moudania, Horefto and Agios Ioannis on the Pelion peninsula. Hydrofoil tickets can be purchased from Egnatias Tours (☎ 223 811), Kambouniou 9.

Getting Around
The Airport Thessaloniki's airport is 16km south-east of town. There is no Olympic Airways transfer service. Public bus No 78 plies to and from the airport; it leaves from in front of the train station and stops in front

of the ferry terminal. It costs 130 dr. A taxi to or from the airport costs around 2000 dr.

Bus Orange articulated buses operate within the city, and blue and orange buses operate both within the city and out to the suburbs. The local bus station is on Filippou and there is a flat fare of 100 dr within the city.

On the articulated orange buses you buy a ticket from the conductor sitting next to the door. On the driver-only buses you buy tickets from a machine on the bus. Make sure you have change before you board. There are three different tickets for the three zones: 100 dr within the city, 135 dr for the suburbs and 150 dr for outlying villages.

Taxi Thessaloniki's taxis are blue and white and the procedure for hailing one is the same as in Athens – stand on the edge of the pavement, and bellow your destination as they pass. For a radio taxi telephone ☎ 217 218.

AROUND THESSALONIKI
Langadas Λαγκαδάς
The village of Langadas, 12km north-east of Thessaloniki, is famous for the fire-walking ritual *anastenaria* which takes place on 21 May, the feast day of St Constantine and his mother, St Helena. The fire walkers, or *anastenarides* (groaners) believe the ritual originated in the village of Kosti (an abbreviation of Konstantinos) in eastern Thrace. The story is that in 1250 AD the Church of St Constantine caught fire and the villagers, hearing groans from the icons, entered the church, retrieved them, and escaped unscathed. The icons were kept by the families concerned, and descendants and devotees honoured the saint each year by performing the ritual. In 1913, when the village was occupied by Bulgarians, the families fled to the villages of Serres, Drama and Langadas, taking the icons with them.

The anastenarides step barefoot onto burning charcoal. Holding the icons and waving coloured handkerchiefs, they dance while emitting strange cries, accompanied by drums and lyres. They believe they will not be burned because God's spirit enters into them. Each year new fire walkers are initiated.

The church condemns the ritual as pagan, and indeed the celebration seems to have in it elements of the pre-Christian worship of Dionysos. If you would like to see this overtly commercial but intriguing spectacle, it begins at 7 pm – turn up early to get a ringside seat. Frequent buses leave for Langadas from the terminal at Irinis 17, near Langada in Thessaloniki.

PELLA Πέλλα

Pella (Pella), most famous as the birthplace of Alexander the Great, lies on the plain of Macedonia astride the Thessaloniki-Edessa road. Its star attraction is its marvellous mosaics. King Archelaos (who ruled 413-399 BC) moved the Macedonian capital from Aigai to Pella, although Aigai remained the royal cemetery.

The mosaics, most of which depict mythological scenes, are made from naturally coloured stones and the effect is one of subtle and harmonious blends and contrasts. They were discovered in the remains of houses and public buildings, on the north (right, coming from Thessaloniki) side of the road. Some are *in situ* and others are housed in the museum. Also on the north side of the road there is a courtyard laid out with a black and white geometric mosaic and six re-erected columns.

The **museum**, which is at the southern side of the site, is one of Greece's best on-site museums. In Room 1, there's a reconstruction of a wall from a house at Pella, and a splendid circular table inlaid with intricate floral and abstract designs, which is thought to have belonged to Philip II. In Room 2 are the mosaics which have been lifted from the site.

The site (☎ 0382-31 160) is open every day from 8 am to 7 pm. Admission (including museum entry) is 500 dr. There is a drinking fountain outside the museum, and a *kafeneio* next to the north side of the site. The museum is open from 8 am to 7 pm from Tuesday to Friday, 8.30 am to 3 pm on Saturday and Sunday, and from 12.30 to 7 pm on Monday.

Getting There & Away

There are frequent buses to Pella from Thessaloniki (40 minutes, 650 dr). If you use the bus and wish to visit Pella and Vergina in one day, after visiting Pella, take a Thessaloniki bus back along the main road and get off at Halkidona, from where you can pick up a bus to Vergina.

MT OLYMPUS Ολυμπος Ορος

Mt Olympus, chosen by the ancients as the abode of their gods, is Greece's highest and most awe-inspiring mountain. It has around 1700 plant species, some of which are rare and endemic. The lower slopes are covered with forests of holm oak, arbutus, cedar and conifers; the higher ones with oak, beech and black and Balkan pine. The mountain also maintains a varied bird life. In 1937 it became Greece's first national park.

In August 1913, Christos Kakalos, a native of Litohoro and the Swiss climbers Frederic Boissonas and Daniel Baud-Bovy were the first mortals to reach the summit of Mytikas (2917m), Mt Olympus' highest peak.

Litohoro Λιτόχωρο

• *pop 6600* • *postcode 602 00* • *area code* ☎ *0352*
The village of Litohoro (Litohoro, altitude 305m) is the place to go if you wish to climb Olympus. The village was developed in the 1920s as a health resort for the tubercular; later it settled comfortably into its role as 'base camp' for climbing Olympus. The approach to Litohoro along the main road is picture-postcard stuff on a fine day. Directly in front of you as you make the final approach to the village, the gorge of the Enipeas river parts to reveal the towering peaks of Olympus. The ancients sure knew how to choose an abode for their gods.

In recent years Litohoro has once again begun to promote its health-resort image. This has resulted in difficulties in finding a hotel room in July and August, particularly at weekends.

NORTHERN GREECE

Orientation Litohoro's main road is Agiou Nikolaou, which, if you are coming from Thessaloniki or Katerini, is the road by which you will enter the village; it leads up to the central square of Plateia Kentriki. On the right side of this road is a large army camp. The road to Prionia, where the main trail up Olympus begins, is a turn-off to the right, just before the central square. Leading off to the left from the main square up the hill is 28 Oktovriou where you will find most of the provision stores.

The bus terminal is on Plateia Kentriki, to the right as you face the sea.

Information The post office is on Plateia Kentriki. The OTE is on Agiou Nikolaou, almost opposite the turn-off for Prionia.

The National Bank of Greece is on Plateia Kentriki. Both this bank and the Commercial Bank nearby sport ATMs. The police station (☎ 81 100) is on the corner of the road to Prionia. There is a health centre (☎ 22 222) 5km away, at the turn-off for the village from the main coastal highway.

There is an EOT office in a little white building with wooden eves on Agiou Nikolaou, just before the turn-off for Prionia.

The EOS (☎ 81 944) in Litohoro has helpful English-speaking staff who give information about Olympus and a free pamphlet giving details of some of the treks. To get to this office, when you are facing inland on Agiou Nikolaou, turn left opposite the Mirto Hotel and follow the signs. The office is open Monday to Friday from 9 am to 1 pm and 6 to 8.30 pm, and on Saturday from 9 am to 1 pm. It's closed on Sunday. The EOS has three refuges on Olympus.

The SEO (Association of Greek Climbers; ☎ 82 300) also gives information, but you are more likely to find someone who speaks English at the EOS. To get to the SEO, walk along the road to Prionia and take the first turn left and first left again. The SEO office is open from 6 to 10 pm every day, and has one refuge on Olympus.

Places to Stay There's a plethora of camp sites along the coast around the turn-off for Litohoro. They include *Olympios Zeus* (☎ 22 115), *Olympos Beach* (☎ 22 112) and *Minerva* (☎ 22 177). All of these sites have good facilities and a taverna, snack bar and minimarket.

Litohoro's once-popular youth hostel is now closed and the slack has been taken up by one or two domatia around the village, though the supply is not great.

Litohoro's cheapest hotel is the clean, well-kept D-class *Hotel Markesia* (☎ 81 831), which costs 5500/6500 dr for singles/doubles with private bathroom. However, this place only opens from June onwards. From Plateia Kentriki, facing inland, turn left into 28 Oktovriou and the hotel is along here on the left.

The rather gloomy-looking C-class *Hotel Aphrodite* (☎ 81 415), on Plateia Kentriki, has OK rooms for 6000/8500 dr with private bathroom. However, directly opposite the main entrance of the Aphrodite is the newer and much brighter and breezier *Hotel Enipeas* (☎ 81 328), with doubles/triples for 8500/10,000 dr and probably the best views in town of Olympus from the balconies.

Litohoro's poshest hotel is the C-class *Mirto Hotel* (☎ 81 398; fax 82 298), where all the rooms have a telephone, private bathroom and balcony. Singles/doubles cost 9000/9900 dr. The hotel is near the central square.

Places to Eat There is a selection of places to eat both on the main square and on the approach road coming up from the army barracks. The choice ranges from fast to traditional. *Olympos Taverna*, on Agiou Nikolaou opposite the Park Hotel, is reasonably good value. *Deas Psistaria*, next to the OTE, has generous portions of charcoal grill chicken for a reasonable price.

To Pazari, just down from the Hotel Markesia on 28 Oktovriou, specialises in fish dishes. On the main square itself, the *Olympus Café* serves tasty mezedes and ready-made food. Don't forget to try their unusual red retsina.

Getting There & Away There are 18 buses

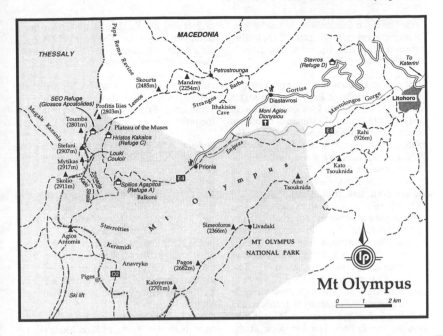

Mt Olympus

a day between Litohoro and Katerini (25 minutes, 400 dr). There are ten a day between Thessaloniki and Litohoro (1½ hours, 1550 dr). There are three buses a day from Litohoro to Athens (via Katerini, 5½ hours, 6750 dr). Thessaloniki-Athens and Thessaloniki-Volos buses will drop you off on the main highway, from where you can catch the Katerini-Litohoro bus.

Litohoro train station is on the Athens-Volos-Thessaloniki line (10 trains a day) but the station is 9km from Litohoro.

Mt Olympus Trails

The following trails by no means exhaust the possibilities on Olympus, but they are the ones which (between June and September) can be tackled by anyone who is fit – no mountaineering experience or special equipment is required. It takes two days to climb Olympus, spending one night at a refuge. However, if you are a keen trekker you'll want to spend longer exploring the mountain

– it really deserves more than a couple of days.

You will need to take warm clothing as it can become very cold and wet, even in August. Sunblock cream is also essential as much of the climbing is above the tree line. Climbing boots are the most suitable footwear, but sturdy shoes or trainers will suffice. A good topographical map of the region is essential. The relevant Korfes map of the Olympus region is probably the best available. Maps can be obtained from EOS (☎ 01-246 1528) – Aharnes, Kentriki Plateia, 136 71 Aharnes. The Olympus map sells for around 2000 dr but the legend and place names are only in Greek.

Do your homework before you begin the trek by talking with someone at the EOS or SEO (see Information in the previous section on Litohoro). Let them know how long you plan to trek and when you will return. Bear in mind that Olympus is a high and challenging mountain – it has claimed its share of lives. For more comprehensive trekking information on Mt Olympus, including detailed trail descriptions, see Lonely Planet's *Trekking in Greece*.

Litohoro to Prionia The most popular trail up Olympus begins at Prionia (Πριόνια), a tiny village 18km from Litohoro. It has a car park, basic taverna and a source of water, but no telephone and there is no bus service. The EOS-owned *Dimitris Boundolas Refuge* (Refuge D) is halfway along the Litohoro-Prionia road at Stavros (930m). It is open from April to November. If you plan to do the six-hour trek from Diastavrosi to the SEO refuge you may wish to stay here.

Most people either opt to drive, hitch or take a taxi (5500 dr) to Prionia, but if you have sufficient stamina, you can trek there along an 18km marked trail, which follows the course of the Enipeas river. The strenuous four-hour trek is over sharply undulating terrain but offers glorious views. It begins beyond the cemetery in Litohoro and ends just before the taverna at Prionia. Just 1km before Prionia you can look at the ruined **Moni Agiou Dionysiou** which was built at the beginning of the 16th century and blown up by the Turks in 1828. It was rebuilt only to be blown up again in 1943 by the Nazis who believed resistance fighters were using it as a hide-out.

Prionia to Spilios Agapitos The trail begins just beyond the taverna in Prionia. You'll have to fill up with water here as it is the last source before Refuge A at Spilios Agapitos (Σπήλαιος Αγαπητός). The trail is well maintained and well used – there is no chance of getting lost and you will meet other trekkers along the way. The steep trail passes first through thick forests of deciduous trees and then through conifers. It takes around 2½ hours to reach the refuge.

Refuge A (☎ 0352-81 800) can accommodate up to 90 people. It has cold showers and serves very good meals from 6 am to 9 pm, both to guests and to people just popping in. The warden, Kostas Zolotas, speaks fluent English, is an experienced moun-

taineer and will be able to answer any questions you may have. The cost of staying at the refuge, which is open from May to October, is 2500 dr a night (2000 dr for Alpine Club members). If you wish to stay during July and August it is advisable to make a reservation either through the EOS in Litohoro or Thessaloniki, or by telephoning the refuge.

Refuge A to Mytikas (via Kaki Skala) The path to Mytikas (Μύτικας) begins just behind Refuge A. Fill up your water bottles because there is no source of water beyond here. The last of the trees thin out rapidly; the path is still marked by red slashes and once again it is easy to follow. After one to 1½ hours you will come to a sign pointing right to the SEO refuge. To reach Mytikas continue straight ahead. The path now zigzags over the scree for another hour before reaching the summit ridge. From the ridge there is a 500m drop into the chasm of Kazania (the cauldron).

Just before the drop, in an opening to the right, is the beginning of Kaki Skala (Κακή Σκάλα; bad stairway), which leads, after 40 minutes of rock scrambling, to the summit of Mytikas. The route is marked by red slashes on the rocks. It is perhaps surprising that no-one has yet coined the nickname 'the original Stairway to (Olympian) Heaven', given the divine destination of the Kaki Skala. The route keeps just below the drop into Kazania, although at a couple of places you can look down into the cauldron – a dramatic sight. If you have never done rock scrambling before, take a look at Kaki Skala and decide then and there if you want to tackle it. Many turn back at this stage, but just as many novices tackle Kaki Skala. If you decide against it, all is not lost, for if you turn left at the summit ridge, an easy path leads in 15 to 20 minutes to Skolio (Σκολιό) peak (2911m), Mt Olympus' second highest peak.

Mytikas to Giossos Apostolides (SEO Refuge) After you've admired the breathtaking views from Mytikas, signed the summit book and said a prayer of thanks to the gods for helping you up (and another, asking them to help you down), you are faced with the choice of returning to Refuge A via Kaki Skala, or continuing on to the *SEO Refuge* of Giossos Apostolides (Γιόσος Αποστολίδης). At 2720m this is the highest refuge in the whole of the Balkans and has a stunning panorama of the major peaks of Olympus. The refuge has beds for 90 people and meals are served. It has no showers or natural drinking water, but bottled water is sold; it is much less visited than Refuge A. The EOS *Refuge C*, called Hristos Kakalos (Χρήστος Κάκαλος), is nearby, and has beds for 18 people. It is open only during July and August.

Neither of these refuges has a telephone. To get to them you can return via Kaki Skala to the path signposted to the SEO Refuge; this path is called Zonaria (Ζωνάρια) and leads to the refuge in one hour. Alternatively, you can descend Mytikas via Louki couloir, which begins just north of the summit and is another 45-minute rock scramble. A few experienced climbers claim Louki couloir is easier than Kaki Skala, but the general consensus is that it's more difficult. It is certainly more sheer and prone to rock falls – more of a danger to those climbing up, than to those descending. At the bottom of Louki couloir you meet up with the Zonaria path. Turn left onto the path and you will reach the SEO lodge in 20 minutes.

SEO Refuge to Diastavrosi The refuge is on the edge of the Plateau of the Muses and from here a well-maintained path leads, in 4½ hours, to Diastavrosi (Διασταύρωση), on the Prionia-Litohoro road. From the plateau the path goes along a ridge called Lemos (Λαιμός; neck) with the Enipeas ravine on the right and the Papa Rema ravine on the left. After one hour you arrive at Skourta summit (2485m) and from here it is 1½ hours to **Petrostrounga** (the stony sheepfold). The next stretch of path leads through woodland to a small meadow known as **Barba** and from here it is 40 minutes to Diastavrosi, which is 14km from Litohoro.

Ancient Dion Δίον
Recently discovered ancient Dion is an extensive, well-watered site at the foot of Mt Olympus, just north of Litohoro and 16km south of Katerini. It was the sacred city of the Macedons, who gathered here to worship the Olympian gods. Alexander the Great made sacrifices to the Olympian gods here, before setting off to conquer the world.

Dion's origins are unknown but there is evidence that an earth goddess of fertility was first worshipped here. Later other gods were worshipped, including Asclepius, the god of medicine. The most interesting discovery so far is the evocative **Sanctuary to Isis**, the Egyptian goddess, in a lush low-lying part of the site.

Its votive statues were found virtually intact with traces of colour remaining. Copies of these statues have been placed in the positions of the originals, which are now in the site's museum. Also worth seeking out is the magnificent well-preserved mosaic floor, dating from 200 AD, which depicts the **Dionysos Triumphal Epiphany**. During the Olympus Festival, which takes place during August, plays are performed at the reconstructed theatre at the site.

The site's **museum** (☎ 0351-53 206) is well laid out with a large collection of statues and offerings from ancient Dion; labelling is in English and Greek. It is open from Tuesday to Friday from 8 am to 7 pm, and Monday from 12.30 to 7 pm. Admission is 800 dr; 400 dr for students.

The **Dion Archaeological Park** (the actual site) is open daily from 8 am to 7 pm, but closes in winter at 6 pm. Admission is 800 dr; 400 dr for students.

Places to Stay As it is a bit of a hassle to get to Dion, you may wish to stay overnight in the modern village. The pleasant C-class *Dion Hotel* (☎ 0351-53 222; fax 0351-31 202) is on the main road in (modern) Dion, near the bus stop. Singles/doubles with private bathroom are 6500/7000 dr.

Getting There & Away There are no buses from Litohoro to Dion; you must first go to

Katerini from where there are 12 buses a day (220 dr). The Dion bus terminal is 400m from Katerini's intercity bus station. To reach it, walk out of the intercity bus station, cross the road, and walk along Karaïskaki towards the town centre. Continue along here for 150m and you will come to a crossroad; turn left into Pangari Tsaldari.

Walk a little way along here to a T-junction and turn right into Tsaldari. Walk 100m along Tsaldari and you will come to a five-road intersection. Cross the road to the Restaurant Olympos, make a right turn and take the second turn left into Kosma Ioannou. Continue up here for 40m and you will come to the Dion bus station on the left, opposite the Orfeas cinema.

Once you're in the village of modern Dion, both the site and museum are clearly signposted.

VERIA Βέροια
• *pop 37,000 • postcode 591 00 • area code ☎ 0331*
Most people merely pass through Veria (Veria), 75km west of Thessaloniki, en route to the ancient site of Vergina. But Veria, capital of the prefecture of Imathia, is a fascinating town with over 70 churches – it is called 'Little Jerusalem' by some people. There are many rather dilapidated houses from the Turkish era, but a government preservation order is in force and most of them are now undergoing gradual restoration. Mineral springs are located all over the town and the local tap water is said to be very good. Veria is also the centre of a vast peach-growing industry and wines made from grapes grown on the escarpment from Veria to Edessa are among Greece's most well-known exports.

Orientation & Information
The town's two main squares, Plateia Antoniou and Plateia Raktivan – more commonly known as Plateia Orologiou – are 1km apart. Connecting them are the town's two main thoroughfares: the modern Venizelou which halfway along becomes Mitropoleos, and the traditional Vasileos Konstantinou (also called Kentrikis). To reach Plateia Antoniou from the intercity bus station, walk out of the rear end of the station onto Iras, turn right and immediately left into Malakousi, and the square is a little way along here with Venizelou and Vasileos Konstantinou both running off to the left. The train station is 3km from the town centre on the old road to Thessaloniki.

The National Bank of Greece is on the corner of Mitropoleos and Ippokratous. There is no tourist office or tourist police. The regular police (☎ 22 391) are next door to the post office on Mitropoleos. The post office is at Mitropoleos 33 and the OTE at No 45.

Things to See
The most interesting part of Veria is the old Turkish quarter. For a short walk around this area, begin by walking down Vasileos Konstantinou from Plateia Antoniou. The narrow and winding Vasileos Konstantinou is the commercial street of old Veria, flanked by old-fashioned tailor shops, bookbinders, kafeneia and antique shops. Halfway along on the right is a huge ancient-looking plane tree where in 1430 the Turks, after taking Veria, hanged the archbishop Arsenios. Directly opposite the plane tree is the dilapidated **old cathedral** which dates from the 12th century. A rather incongruous and now decapitated minaret bears testament to the cathedral's conversion to a mosque during the Turkish era. To reach the residential part of the old Turkish quarter, turn right at the plane tree into Goudi and just wander among the old streets with their many abandoned houses.

The **archaeological museum** is in this part of town on Leoforos Anixeos, which snakes its way to the left across the escarpment from the end of Elias. It contains some finds from the tombs of Vergina and Levkadia. The museum is open from 8.30 am to 3 pm from Tuesday to Sunday. Admission is 400 dr. To reach it, take any of the roads running east from Venizelou, which will bring you to Leoforos Anixeos.

St Paul the Apostle visited Veria twice on his second and third voyages (49-52 and

53-58 AD). Veria was known as Beroea in the New Testament and there is now a shrine at Mavromihali 1 where Paul is believed to have held his sermons. Mavromihali runs off Plateia Orologiou and leads to the Papakia district (see Places to Eat).

Places to Stay – bottom end

The best value among Veria's few hotels is *Hotel Veroi* (☎ 22 866; fax 20 014) on Plateia Orologiou. The hotel is very clean with large, comfortably furnished single/double rooms with balcony, costing 8300/11,600 dr with private bathroom.

At the *Hotel Villa Elia* (☎ 26 800; fax 21 880), Elias 16, single/double room rates are 12,000/15,000 dr with private bathroom. Both Elias and Megalou Alexandrou are left turns off Venizelou, coming from Plateia Antoniou.

Places to Stay – middle

The best of Veria's hotels is the B-class *Hotel Macedonia* (☎ 66 902; fax 66 902), Kontogiorgaki 50. The spacious, tastefully furnished rooms are 12,000/15,000 dr with private bathroom. To reach the hotel walk along Venizelou, turn left into Elias and then right at the Top Café into Paster. Kontogiorgaki is the continuation of Paster. The hotel is at the end of this street on the right.

Places to Eat

Veria is famous for its revani, a sweet syrupy cake found throughout most of the town. It's also known for the infamous bean concoction, fasolada, usually cooked in an oven.

The long-established *Estiatorion-Kosmas Sarafopoulos* is on Kentrikis (Vasileos Konstantinou) 100m around the corner and down the hill from the Hotel Veroi. This place is popular with locals. There is a similar but slightly more modern place next to the Kozani bus terminal on Plateia Orologiou called the *Menou*.

For more relaxed eating in a pleasant location, head for the Papakia district. Follow Mavromihali, near the Kozani bus station, up the hill for about 200m. Here is a pleasant square with waterfalls, little streams and a

couple of pleasant places to eat. The *Saroglou* is a slightly pretentious place, but very popular. Next to it is the traditional *Kostalar*, in business since 1939.

For that special treat, go to the *Gri Gri* at Kapetan Agra 4. This is an ouzeri, but is refreshingly modern, well-presented and has some exquisite specialities. Try their htypiti (feta cheese and chilli dip), or the mydia saganaki (pan-fried mussels in chilli sauce).

Getting There & Away

Bus Frequent buses leave from Veria's intercity bus station for Thessaloniki (1250 dr), Athens (7900 dr), Edessa (950 dr) and the ancient site of Vergina (280 dr). Buses for Kozani (1050 dr) depart from a separate bus station on Plateia Orologiou and through buses to/from Ioannina also stop on this square.

Train There are eight trains a day, in both directions, along the Thessaloniki-Kozani/Florina line. Two additional intercity services to and from Kozani pass through Veria twice a day. One goes to Athens and the other to Thessaloniki.

VERGINA Βεργίνα

• *pop 1255* • *postcode 590 31* • *area code* ☎ *0331*

The ancient site of Vergina (Vergína), 11km south-east of Veria, is ancient Aigai, the first capital of Macedon. The capital was later transferred to Pella, but Aigai continued to be the royal burial place. Philip II was assassinated here in 336 BC at the wedding reception of his daughter, Cleopatra.

To fully appreciate the significance of the discoveries, you need to visit Thessaloniki's archaeological museum, where the magnificent finds of Philip II's tomb are displayed, along with Philip II himself! Unfortunately, Philip's tomb is off limits to visitors as it is still being excavated.

The ruins of ancient Vergina are spread out, but well signposted from the modern village of the same name. The **Macedonian tomb**, 500m uphill from the village, has a façade of four Ionic half-columns. Inside is a marble throne. Continue 400m further up the road to reach the ruins of an extensive palatial complex, built as a summer residence for King Antigonos Gonatas (278-240 BC). The focal point of the site is a large Doric peristyle which was surrounded by pebble mosaic floors. One of the mosaics, with a beautiful floral design, is well preserved and *in situ*. A large oak tree on the highest point of the site affords some welcome shade.

Both this site (☎ 92 347) and the Macedonian tomb are open Tuesday to Sunday from 8.30 am to 3 pm, and to 7 pm in summer. Entrance to the museum is 500 dr and to the site 1200 dr.

There is a café opposite the Macedonian tomb and for those who wish to stay overnight, there is a choice of the *Pansion Vergina*, or *Ikos* domatia, both on the same road as the tombs.

EDESSA Εδεσσα
• *pop 16,000* • *postcode 582 00* • *area code* ☎ *0381*
Edessa (Edessa) is the capital of the prefecture of Pella. Extolled by Greeks for its many waterfalls, it is little visited by foreign tourists. Edessa is a truly delightful town which has water and greenery, unlike the majority of towns in Greece. Little streams and bridges and cool and shady parks dot the whole of Edessa which, being a small town, is very easy and pleasant to discover on foot. The town is perched precariously on a ledge overlooking the seemingly endless agricultural plain below and is the most northern of the Mt Vermion escarpment centres.

Until the discovery of the royal tombs at Vergina, Edessa was believed to be the site of the ancient Macedonian city of Aigai.

Orientation
Edessa's intercity bus station is on the corner of Filippou and Pavlou Mela. To reach the town centre, cross over Filippou and walk straight ahead along Pavlou Mela to the T-junction, and turn right into Egnatia. Almost immediately the road forks: the left fork continues as Egnatia; the right fork is Dimokratias. These two streets, along with Filippou, are the town's main thoroughfares.

The train station is opposite the end of 18 Oktovriou. To reach the town centre from here, walk straight ahead up 18 Oktovriou for 400m to a major road junction. From here the biggest waterfall is signposted sharp left; veer right for Dimokratias.

Information
There is no EOT or tourist police; the regular police are on Iroön Polytehniou, which runs between Filippou and Dimokratias.

The National Bank of Greece is at Dimokratias 1 and has an ATM. The post office is at Dimokratias 26. The OTE is on Agiou Dimitriou. To reach it turn right from Pavlou Mela (by the Hotel Pella) and you will find it off to the left.

Things to See
Edessa's main attraction is its **waterfalls**. There are a number of little ones (usually artificial) dotted around the town, but the biggest waterfall, called *katarraktes* (waterfalls), plunges dramatically down a cliff to the agricultural plain below. There are actually two falls: one that drops more or less vertically and another, a little way to the left, that tumbles and twirls, zigzag fashion, down the cliff face.

The whole set-up is actually very becoming, if you discount the tacky tourist stalls on the street. The cliff is mantled with abundant vegetation and there are wonderful views of the vast plain, which extends all the way to Thessaloniki.

Places to Stay – bottom end
The D-class *Hotel Elena* (☎ 23 218; fax 23 951), Plateia Timenidon, has light and airy single/double rooms for 7500/12,000 dr with private bathroom and TV. From the bus station turn right at Filippou, walk three blocks to the road junction with signposts to the waterfalls and Florina, turn right into Arch Panteleimonos and you will see the hotel a little way along there on the left.

The D-class *Hotel Pella* (☎ 23 541), which is right next door to the Hotel Alfa (see next section) at Egnatia 26, has single/double rooms for 7500/9900 dr with private bathroom.

Places to Stay – middle
The C-class *Hotel Alfa* (☎ 22 221; fax 24 777) in Egnatia has double-glazed and soundproofed rooms with air-con for 8000/12,000 dr. It is much nicer than its immediate neighbour, the aforementioned Hotel Pella. Edessa's best hotel is the B-class *Hotel Katarraktes* (☎ 22 300; fax 27 237) at Karanou 18, where single rates are 11,200/16,200 dr. The hotel has comfortable, traditionally furnished rooms with private bathroom and balcony. Follow the signposts for the cataracts, and look for the hotel on the left, just before the waterfalls.

Places to Eat
Close to the bus station and on the same street as the Hotel Pella and Hotel Alfa, at Egnatia 20 is the *Estiatorion Omonia* (the sign is in Greek only). The food is cheap and good and this is a long-established eating place with ready-made dishes for you to point at and choose from. A meal with draught wine will cost about 2000 dr.

Closest to the bus station is a nameless *taverna/psistaria* at Filippou 26, diagonally opposite the bus station. This place is convenient, though a little uninspiring. Another traditional place is *Taverna Roloï* (clock tavern), at Agiou Dimitriou 5, near the OTE and on the street leading to the clock tower. Behind the clock tower is *Pavlos Taverna*, worth trying even though it looks a bit old and decrepit.

The younger set's bar and café life is centred on the little brick-paved street Angeli Gatsou, which starts just opposite the post office and by the little bridge.

Getting There & Away
Bus From the main bus station there are hourly buses to Thessaloniki (one hour and 40 minutes, 1500 dr), six a day to Veria (one hour, 850 dr) and three a day to Athens (eight hours, 8250 dr). Four buses a day go to Florina and Kastoria from a second bus station, marked by a bus sign on the corner of Egnatia and Pavlou Mela.

Train There are eight trains a day both ways on the Thessaloniki-Kozani/Florina line, plus an additional two intercity services. The stretch between Edessa and Amyndeo is particularly beautiful as it skirts the western shore of Lake Vegoritida.

FLORINA Φλώρινα
• *12,500 pop* • *postcode 531 00* • *area code ☎ 0385*
The mountain town of Florina (Fl**o**rina) is the capital of the prefecture of Florina. Tourists used to come to Florina only because it was the last town in Greece before the former Yugoslav border. Now its economy is seriously compromised by the continuing political troubles with its neighbour to the north. Despite the recent changes, it's a lively town, and a pleasant place for an overnight stopover if you are touring the area.

Despite local protestations, a consortium has converted the old Tottis Hotel up on the hill into a hotel and casino. Whether this will bolster Florina's flagging fortunes is a moot point. At the time of writing an operating licence had not been granted because of alleged building irregularities and the whole project may eventually turn into a fiscal white elephant.

If you enjoy your stay in Florina you're in good company. Greece's most famous film director, Theodoros Angelopoulos, loves Florina (although it is not his birthplace). Two of his films, *Alexander the Great* and *The Hesitant Step of the Stork* were made on location here.

Florina is the only place from which you can take a bus to the Prespa lakes and there is also a low-key skiing resort at Vigla, just west of Florina on the Prespa lakes road.

Orientation & Information
Florina is laid out in a long curving shape, much like a boomerang, and is divided by the river that flows along the length of the town. The main street is Pavlou Mela, which leads to the central square of Plateia Georgiou

NORTHERN GREECE

Modi. Half of Pavlou Mela is a pedestrian mall. To reach this street from the train station, walk straight ahead keeping the archaeological museum to your left. Bear left and you are on Pavlou Mela. From Plateia Georgiou Modi, turn right into Stefanou Dragoumi to reach the intercity bus station, which is 250m up the street. Bear right at the end of the street, cross the road and look for the KTEL office, opposite the national stadium. If you turn left from Plateia Georgiou Modi, into 25 Martiou, you will reach the river. Megalou Alexandrou is the continuation of Pavlou Mela on the other side of the square.

The post office is at Kalergi 22; walk along Stefanou Dragoumi towards the bus station and Kalergi is off to the left. The OTE is at Tyrnovou 5. As you walk along Pavlou Mela from the train station, Tyrnovou is a turn-off to the left. The gaudily coloured National Bank of Greece is about 50m up Megalou Alexandrou on the right and the Commercial Bank is just behind it. Both banks provide ATM facilities.

There is no EOT or tourist police; the telephone number of the regular police is ☎ 22 100.

Things to See & Do

The **archaeological museum** is housed in a modern building near the train station. It is well laid out, even though the downstairs section feels a little bare. Only the labels downstairs are in English. The curator will show you around but his English is limited. Downstairs there is pottery from the Neolithic, early Iron Age and Bronze Age and grave steles and statues from the Roman period. Upstairs there are some Byzantine reliefs and fragments of frescoes, and finds from an as yet unidentified town built by Philip II, discovered on the nearby hill of Agios Panteleimonas. The museum is open every day except Monday from 8.30 am to 3 pm. Admission is free.

Close to the archaeological museum and easily mistaken for a railway building, is the **Florina Artists' Gallery**. It is open Wednesday to Saturday from 5 to 8 pm and on Sunday and holidays from 10 am to 1 pm, and houses a collection of local artists' works.

Old Florina occupied both river banks, and many Turkish houses and neoclassical mansions survive. The town has a thriving artistic community, and the Society for the Friends of Art of Florina has restored one of the neoclassical mansions on the river bank, which is now the **Museum of Modern Art** at Leoforos Eleftherias 103. The museum houses a permanent collection of works by contemporary Greek artists and hosts frequent exhibitions. It is open from 5 to 8 pm every day and from 10 am to 1 pm on Sunday. Admission is free.

To reach the museum walk down 25 Martiou, cross the bridge over the river and turn right. Walk for about 200m. Even if you are not interested in art, this is a pleasant walk along the river bank.

If you feel energetic, there is a pleasant walk up to the new (would-be) casino from where you can enjoy an unparalleled view of Florina. From the little **Church of Koimisis Theotokou** there is an established path that snakes up the hill. The blue and white church is on the south side of the river, just above Plateia Sholion. Walk down 25 Martiou, cross the river and turn left. Walk about 200m and you will come across the square, and the church above it.

Places to Stay

The nearest hotel to the train station is the C-class *Hotel Ellenis* (☎ 22 671; fax 22 815), Pavlou Mela 39. It's pleasantly clean, if somewhat basic. The single/double room rates are 8000/11,000 dr with private bathroom. Coming from the train station the hotel is on the left.

Up a notch, the C-class *Hotel Antigone* (☎ 23 180; fax 45 620), Arianou 1, has slightly jaded but pleasant rooms for 11,000/14,700 dr. Turn right into Stefanou Dragoumi from Plateia Georgiou Modi, and the hotel is 200m along on the left, close to the bus station.

The B-class *Hotel Lingos* (☎ 28 322; fax 29 643), Tagmatarhou Naoum 1, just north of Plateia Georgiou Modi, has comfortable, but essentially functional rooms for 11,000/18,000 dr.

The B-class *King Alexander* (☎ 23 501; fax 29 643), a little out of town at Leoforos Nikis 68 (the road leading to Prespa), has comfortable single/double rooms for 11,000/16,500 dr.

Places to Eat

Florina has an array of eating places, from fast food to traditional, centred on the Pavlou Mela/Plateia Modi area, so you can't go far wrong. Florina is famous for its large red peppers – piperies Florinis – some hot and some sweet. Make sure you try them out.

The *Taverna Takis*, 25 Martiou 18, serves tasty, reasonably priced grilled food. It's a favourite port of call of this author. A meat dish with salad and wine will cost about 2300 dr. *Restaurant Olympos*, Megalou Alexandrou 22 (on the right as you walk from Plateia Modi) has a good choice of well-prepared, low-priced, ready-made food. This restaurant is only open at lunchtime, but is a very good choice. Lunch with wine here will cost about 1800 dr.

If you are waiting for a bus, or have just arrived by bus, the *Tria Adherfia*, 70m to the left as you exit the bus station ticket office, is unpretentious, clean and convenient. If you arrive on a late train and fancy a pizza, try *Ramona Pizza* on the corner of Pavlou Mela and Sidirodromikou Stathmou. It's the first eating place you come to after leaving the station.

Of all the fast-food joints, *Perfetto*, on the corner of Pavlou Mela and Arhimandritou Papathanasiou is the best of the bunch.

Getting There & Away

Bus – domestic From the main bus station there is one bus a day to Athens (leaving at 8.30 am, nine hours, 9000 dr), six buses a day to Thessaloniki (three hours, 2800 dr), seven to Kozani (1¾ hours, 1500 dr), and two to Agios Germanos (for the Prespa lakes, 1½ hours, 800 dr), at 6.45 am and 2.30 pm. For Kastoria, you have to take a bus to Amyndeo and another one from there.

If you are planning to enter the Former Yugoslav Republic of Macedonia (FYROM) from Florina, there are three buses a day to the border town of Niki (30 minutes, 320 dr). For Albania, there are two buses daily to the border post near Krystallopigi (1½ hours, 1000 dr).

Bus – international There is a bus to Korça (Korytsa in Greek) in Albania run by the Greek Railways Organisation (OSE), that operates on Monday, Tuesday, Wednesday, Friday and Saturday. The bus leaves Florina train station sometime between 11.30 am and 12.30 pm and the one-way ticket costs 2500 dr. This bus originates in Thessaloniki. (See also the introductory Getting There & Away chapter for details on transport to Albania).

Train – domestic Florina is at the end of the Thessaloniki-Edessa-Amyndeo line. There are five to seven trains a day (depending on the season) in both directions. The approximate journey time from Thessaloniki is 3½ hours and the ticket costs 1370 dr. You can also take the train to Kozani (1¾ hours, 810 dr), via Amyndeo. If you plan to pick up the Athens or Thessaloniki-bound Intercity service at Amyndeo, there is a surcharge.

Train – international There is currently no through service to Bitola, or beyond, in the Former Yugoslav Republic of Macedonia (FYROM). See also the introductory Getting There & Away chapter for details on getting to FYROM from Florina.

PRESPA LAKES Λίμνες Πρεσπ

In the mountainous north-west corner of Greece, at an altitude of 850m, are the two lakes of Megali Prespa and Mikri Prespa, separated by a narrow strip of land. The area is one of outstanding natural beauty and is little visited by foreign tourists. The road from Florina crosses the Pisoderi pass and winds its way through thick forests and lush meadows with grazing cattle; if you have your own transport, there are lots of picnic tables.

Mikri Prespa has an area of 43 sq km and

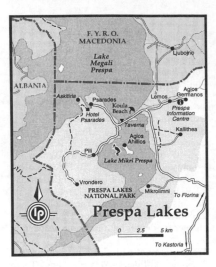

is located almost entirely in Greece, except for the south-western tip, which is in Albania. Megali Prespa is the largest lake in the Balkans; the biggest part is in FYROM (1000 sq km); 38 sq km is in Greece and a small part in the south-west is in Albania. Much of the shore of Megali Prespa is of precipitous rock, which rises dramatically from the chilly blue water. The Prespa area became a national park in 1977. There is an excellent information centre in Agios Germanos.

Mikri (little) Prespa is a wildlife refuge of considerable interest to ornithologists. It is surrounded by thick reed beds where numerous species of birds, including cormorants, pelicans, egrets, herons and ibis, nest.

The lake's islet of **Agios Ahillios** has ancient Byzantine remains. The boat operator will take you across and back for about 2000 dr for a boatload of four people. Phone ☎ 0385-46 112 to call the ferryman.

Incidentally, one of the best viewing places for the lake's wildlife is from the top of the sizeable hillock harbouring the little jetty for Agios Ahillios. It is often swarming with school groups on fieldwork.

Getting There & Away

Bus The only town with a direct bus link to the lakes is Florina. There are two buses on weekdays to Agios Germanos village, 16km east of Psarades. The buses leave Florina at 7.45 am and 2.30 pm. These buses stop at the road junction between the two lakes: the left fork leads to Koula beach and Psarades, and the right fork leads to the villages of Lemos and Agios Germanos. Another bus bound for Pyli meets the second bus twice a week on Tuesday and Thursday. If you get this bus, ask to be let off at Koula beach, which is 5km from Psarades.

From here you have the choice of either hitching a lift to Psarades, a long uphill walk, or asking someone at the taverna at Koula beach to telephone for a taxi (☎ 0385-51 247) – they will willingly do this. The bus for Florina leaves Agios Germanos at 6.45 am and 3.45 pm on weekdays. On a Saturday there is only one bus at 7.45 am and there are none on Sunday.

Taxi If you decide to use a taxi for part or all of the journey, prices from Psarades are approximately 2000 dr to Lemos (to pick up the bus to Florina), 6500 dr to Florina and 7500 dr to Kastoria.

Agios Germanos Αγιος Γερμανός
• *pop 267 • postcode 530 77 • area code* ☎ *0385*
This little village serves as the main transport hub to the Prespa region and, although it is a little way back from the lakes themselves, it is an attractive village and a convenient base. There are some good walks to be made from the village and there is always a taxi (☎ 51 207) handy, should you need to move further afield. The village is primarily an agricultural settlement and is renowned for its bean crops. The mounds of cut cane you will see in springtime as you enter the village are used entirely for supporting the bean plants.

Orientation & Information Agios Germanos contains a bus terminus and the only post office in the Prespa basin. There are no banking facilities, but you can change money at the post office. The phone number of the local police is ☎ 51 203.

Things to See There are two churches that may be of interest to fans of Byzantium: **Agios Athanasios** and **Agios Germanos**, named after the patron saint of the village.

For friends of nature, the Prespa Information Centre (☎ 51 452; fax 51 452), which is on the right just before you enter the village proper, is a very well-presented display and resource centre for information on the Prespa National Park. There is some excellent material in Greek, but not too much in English. Nonetheless, the photos, maps and diagrams are pretty self-explanatory. It is open from 10 am to 2.30 pm.

Places to Stay & Eat The well-run and comfortable *Agios Germanos Hostel* (☎ 51 320) is run by the local women's cooperative and is at the top end of the village. Follow the signs. Doubles/triples here cost 7000/8000 dr. *Les Pelicans* (☎ 51 442) is an EOT-approved domatia place and is just below the main square.

Lefteris Taverna, opposite the hostel, is the best place in the village for a meal. Bank on about 3000 dr for a good feed. There is another restaurant of sorts on the main square and there is also one ouzeri and one kafeneio.

Psarades Ψαράδες
• *pop 143* • *postcode 530 77* • *area code* ☎ *0385*
The village of Psarades, on Megali Prespa, 70km from Florina, is a revelation. It's positioned within a small inlet of Megali Prespa and is Greece's last village before the three-nation border point out on Megali Prespa lake. Psarades is a delectable little village with traditional stone houses, which are subject to a National Trust preservation order; old fishing boats made of cedar and oak; and some of the most unusual miniature cows you will see in Greece.

From a pre-war population of 770, only 143 permanent residents remain, according to the 1991 census. Many live overseas in the USA and Australia. Six hundred people from Psarades live in Perth, Western Australia. A large marble memorial on the lakefront from the Macedonian Association of Chicago attests to the strong bonds between Psarades and its former residents overseas.

Orientation & Information You will need your own transport to get to Psarades, or you can take a taxi from either Lemos or Agios Germanos. The village consists of an attractive, landscaped lakefront lined with numerous modern restaurants and fish tavernas.

There is no bank or post office, but Philippos Papadopoulos, the owner of the grocery shop on the village square, will exchange cash. So too will Lazaros Hristianopoulos at the Syntrofia taverna. There is no OTE, but the Syntrofia taverna has metered telephones, as does the grocery store and the Psarades Hotel on the other side of the bay.

Things to See & Do It will be hard to resist taking a **boat trip** out onto Megali Prespa, since Psarades is Greece's only village with anchorage on this lake. More specifically, you should strive to be taken to the three *askitiria* (places of solitary worship) that can only be visited by boat. All three are out past the Roti headland to the left. The first one, Metamorphosi, dates from the 13th century. There are only a few remnants of the rich painting that once decorated this site and two sections from the wood-carved *temblon* (votive screen), the rest of which is in the Florina museum. The second is called Mikri Analipsi and is from the 14th or 15th century. Access to this one is a little difficult. The third and probably the best one is called Panagia Eleousa. A typical trip will cost you about 750 dr for the short tour and 1250 dr for the full tour, assuming there are at least four people per boatload.

More or less opposite the village, there are rock paintings of the **Panagia Vlahernitisa** (1455-56) and of **Panagia Dexiokratousa** (1373) along with some inscriptions. These are included in the boat tour mentioned above.

The church of **Kimisis Theotokou** in the village itself dates from 1893 and is decorated on the outside with the double-headed eagle of the Byzantine Empire. There is also an inscription that refers to the old name of the village, Nivitsa.

Places to Stay If you plan on coming to the area in July or August without a reservation, think twice, as the region is getting very popular and accommodation is limited.

There is no official camp site but you can camp freelance at Koula beach on the southern shore of Megali Prespa, 5km east of Psarades.

Psarades' only official, EOT-approved *domatia* are the clean, comfortable rooms of Lazaros & Eleni Hristianopoulos (☎ 46 107), which cost 7500 dr for a double room with private bathroom. The domatia are above the family taverna (Syntrofia) at the far end of the village. Several other families rent rooms unofficially.

The *Hotel Psarades* (☎ 46 015) is right opposite the village of Psarades. It has excellent single/double rooms for 6400/8000 dr, all with views over the village. There is also a bar and restaurant here.

Places to Eat Five tavernas line the waterfront at Psarades. They all dish up excellent fresh fish, straight from the lake. Lazaros Hristianopoulos from the *Syntrofia* taverna is a very amenable host and his trout and house wine are recommended. The *Paradosi* is another good choice and is probably the only eating place open out of season.

KASTORIA Καστοριά
• *pop 17,000* • *postcode 521 00* • *area code* ☎ *0467*
Kastoria (Kastoriá) lies between Mt Grammos and Mt Vitsi in western Macedonia, 200km west of Thessaloniki. It is regarded by many Greeks as their most beautiful town. Indeed its setting is exemplary, occupying the isthmus of a promontory which projects into the tree-fringed Lake Orestiada, surrounded by mountains.

Its architecture is also outstanding, featuring many Byzantine and post-Byzantine churches and many 17th and 18th-century mansions, known as *arhontika*, because they were the homes of the *arhons* – the town's leading citizens. In Kastoria the arhontika were the dwellings of rich fur merchants.

The town has a long tradition of fur production. Jewish furriers (refugees from Europe) came to Kastoria because of the large numbers of beavers living by the lake. They carried out their trade with such zeal that by the 19th century the beaver was extinct in the area. The furriers then began to import scraps of fur. Whatever your feelings are about the fur trade, you are not going to escape them in Kastoria; every street has some kind of office or business associated with the fur trade.

Orientation
Kastoria's main bus station is one block inland from the south lakeside, on 3 Septemvriou. To reach the town centre from here, with your back to the station office turn left and keep walking, bearing right just past the soccer stadium, to Plateia Davaki, which is one of the city's main squares. Mitropoleos, the town's main commercial thoroughfare, runs south-east from here to the other main square of Plateia Omonias.

Information
Kastoria's EOT (☎ 24 484) is in the town hall on Ioustinianou, which runs north-east from Plateia Davaki. The staff are helpful and give out lots of brochures, maps and information.

The National Bank of Greece is on 11 Noemvriou, just north of Plateia Davaki and has an ATM. The post office is at the northern end of Leoforos Megalou Alexandrou, which skirts the lakeside. The OTE is on Agiou Athanasiou, which runs off Plateia Davaki just north of Mitropoleos. The phone number for the regular police is ☎ 83 333.

Byzantine Churches
Many of the numerous churches in Kastoria were originally private chapels attached to the arhontika houses. Almost all of the churches are locked, and gaining access to them is something of a Byzantine experience in

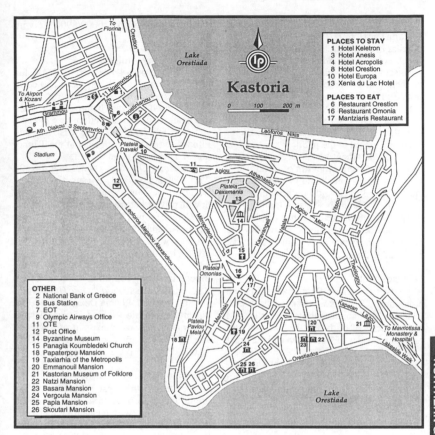

Kastoria

PLACES TO STAY
1 Hotel Keletron
3 Hotel Anesis
4 Hotel Acropolis
8 Hotel Orestion
10 Hotel Europa
13 Xenia du Lac Hotel

PLACES TO EAT
6 Restaurant Orestion
16 Restaurant Omonia
17 Mantziaris Restaurant

OTHER
2 National Bank of Greece
5 Bus Station
7 EOT
9 Olympic Airways Office
11 OTE
12 Post Office
14 Byzantine Museum
15 Panagia Koumbledeki Church
18 Papaterpou Mansion
19 Taxiarhia of the Metropolis
20 Emmanouil Mansion
21 Kastorian Museum of Folklore
22 Natzi Mansion
23 Basara Mansion
24 Vergoula Mansion
25 Papia Mansion
26 Skoutari Mansion

itself. The key man (literally) for the ones around Plateia Omonias is Hristos Philikas. If you can track him down he will be happy to open them up for you – ask around the kafeneia on the square. Another possibility is the Byzantine Museum's curator who may be able to contact someone who can show you some of the churches.

Even if you don't manage to get a look inside any churches, all is not lost, for some of them have external frescoes. One such church is the **Taxiarhia of the Metropolis**, on Plateia Pavlou Mela, south of Plateia Omonias, which has a 13th-century fresco of

the Madonna and Child above the entrance. Inside the church is the tomb of Pavlos Melas, a Macedonian hero who was killed by Bulgar terrorists during the struggles that culminated in the Balkan Wars. Melas' life is documented in Thessaloniki's Museum of the Macedonian Struggle. Many Macedonian streets are named Pavlou Mela in memory of this hero.

Museums
The **Byzantine Museum** houses outstanding icons from many of the town's churches. It will help you to appreciate the churches if

you visit this museum first. It is adjacent to the Xenia du Lac Hotel on Plateia Dexamenis. The museum is open from 8.30 am to 5 pm every day except Monday. Admission is free.

Most of the surviving **arhontika** are in the southern part of the town in the area called Doltso. The most important ones are the Emmanouil, Basara, Natzi, Skoutari, Papia, Vergoula and Papaterpou mansions – named after the families who once lived in them. These are closed to the public.

One of the arhontika has been converted into the **Kastorian Museum of Folklore**. A visit to the museum should be considered a must. The 530-year-old house belonged to the wealthy Neranzis Alvazis family. It is sumptuously furnished and has displays of ornaments, kitchen utensils and tools. The museum is open every day from 10 am to 12 pm and 3 to 5 pm. Admission is 300 dr.

Lakeside Walk
A pretty tree-shaded 9km road skirts the promontory. The lake is fringed by reeds, which are the habitat of frogs and turtles and many species of birds. On the lake you will see many species of water fowl and the great crested grebe.

Just under halfway is the **Moni Mavriotissas**. The resident monk will give you a guided tour. Next to the monastery is the 11th-century **Agia Maria** and the 16th-century **Church of St John the Theologian**. Both churches are liberally festooned with frescoes and icons, and are usually open. Beside the monastery there is a reasonably priced restaurant, which is the only source of refreshment on the walk. To begin the walk, take the road to the hospital (see the Kastoria map).

Places to Stay – bottom end
There is a free *camp site* in the grounds of the Moni Mavriotissas.

The vaguely seedy C-class *Hotel Keletron* (☎ 22 676), 11 Noemvriou 52, has reasonable single/double rooms for 5300/6800 dr with private bathroom. The C-class *Hotel Acropolis* (☎ 83 737), Grammou 14, has tidy rooms for 5500/6060 dr for singles/doubles

without bathroom, or 6000/8900 dr with bathroom.

Places to Stay – middle
The neat C-class *Hotel Anesis* (☎ 83 908; fax 83 768), Grammou 10, has clean and comfortable single/double rooms for 8500/11,000 dr with private bathroom. To reach this hotel from the bus station, face the lake and turn left, then take the first left into Filikis Eterias, then turn right at the T-junction and the hotel is on the left.

The *Hotel Orestion* (☎ 22 257; fax 22 258), Plateia Davaki 1, is a superior C-class with very pleasant rooms for 10,500/12,800 dr with private bathroom. In a similar vein is the *Hotel Europa* (☎ 23 826; fax 25 154) at Agiou Athanasiou 12, just up from Plateia Davaki with single/double rooms for 10,000/12,500 dr.

Places to Stay – top end
Kastoria's A-class *Xenia du Lac Hotel* (☎ 22 565; fax 26 391), Plateia Dexamenis 11, is a quaintly old-fashioned kind of place despite its A rating. It's in a quiet part of town and singles/doubles are good value at 10,000/18,000 dr with private bathroom.

Places to Eat
One of the town's best restaurants is the bright and modern *Restaurant Omonia* on Plateia Omonias, with meals for under 2000 dr. Nearby the *Mantziaris Restaurant*, Valala 8, is also good and reasonably cheap, with meals for about 1800 dr.

The *Restaurant Orestion*, Ermou 37, is an unpretentious little place, which dishes up tasty low-priced ready-made food. It is closed on Saturday evening and on Sunday. A meal here will cost around 1800 dr.

Getting There & Away
Air The airport is 10km south of Kastoria. Between May and October, there are four flights a week from Kastoria to Athens (17,900 dr) on Sunday, Tuesday, Wednesday and Friday. The Olympic Airways office (☎ 22 275) is at Leoforos Megalou Alexandrou 15.

Bus From Kastoria's main bus station there are six buses a day to Thessaloniki (four hours, 3450 dr), five a day to Kozani (two hours, 1600 dr) and two to Athens (nine hours, 9000 dr). The 6.30 am and 3.30 pm Thessaloniki buses go via Kozani and Veria. There are more buses in summer.

HALKIDIKI Χαλκιδική

The Halkidiki peninsula is a large blob to the south-east of Thessaloniki, from which three long 'fingers' extend from the peninsula into the Aegean. The two large lakes of Koronia and Volvi separate the peninsula from the rest of Macedonia.

Halkidiki boasts 500km of coastline, with superb sandy beaches surrounded by calm, aquamarine sea. Unfortunately, these assets have been ruthlessly exploited and the two fingers of Kassandra and Sithonia consist of either luxurious holiday complexes for the rich and famous, or package-tourist ghettos. The easternmost promontory of Halkidiki is the Monastic Republic of Mt Athos (Agion Oros).

Halkidiki is not a place for budget or independent travellers as virtually all accommodation is booked solid throughout the summer. If you are camping, however, a visit is more practicable: Halkidiki has many camp sites which, even if they are bursting at the seams, are unlikely to turn you away.

Northern Halkidiki

The **Petralona cave**, 56km south-east of Thessaloniki in northern Halkidiki, has stalactites and stalagmites and is where a 700,000-year-old Neanderthal skull (evidence of one of Europe's earliest inhabitants) was found. The cave is open daily from 9 am to 7 pm (5 pm in winter). Admission is 1500 dr; students 800 dr. There is a booklet about the cave in English on sale for 700 dr. Doucas Tours (see Organised Tours in the Thessaloniki section) sometimes has tours to the caves.

The **archaeological museum** at Polygyros, the capital of Halkidiki, houses finds from the peninsula's ancient sites including the Sanctuary of Zeus at Aphytis and the ancient city of Acanthos. The museum is open Tuesday to Sunday from 8.30 am to 3 pm. Admission is 500 dr.

Getting There & Away A bus goes to Petralona cave (one hour, 1000 dr) at 1.15 pm every day, except Sunday and public holidays, and continues on to the village of Krini where it turns round and heads back for Thessaloniki straight away. This hardly leaves you time to see the cave, so to get back to Thessaloniki you must walk or hitch to the village of Eleohoria, 5km south, from where you can pick up a regular Nea Moudania bus to Thessaloniki. A number of buses to the Sithonia 'finger' stop at Polygyros.

Kassandra Peninsula

The Kassandra peninsula is less beautiful than the Sithonian peninsula. Its commercialism is horrendous and, even if you're not averse to package tourists, roaring motorbikes, fast-food joints and discos, you're unlikely to easily find independent accommodation. However, if you have a tent, there are lots of well-advertised camp sites. Free camping is not allowed and there are large signs alerting you to the fact.

For what it is worth, the western side of the finger is somewhat quieter, with a couple of almost get-away-from-it camp sites at Posidi and Nea Skioni. The little resort of Siviri, also on the west side, has a sandy beach, but has been taken over by the luxurious private apartments of Thessaloniki's élite.

Getting There & Away There are 13 buses to Kallithea (1½ hours, 1600 dr) on the east coast; 11 buses to Pefkohori (two hours, 2100 dr), also on the east coast, via Kryopigi and Haniotis; seven buses to Paliouri (two hours, 2300 dr) and three buses to Agia Paraskevi (2½ hours, 2350 dr), both on the southern tip. All the buses leave from the bus terminal at Karakasi 68 in Thessaloniki.

Sithonian Peninsula

Sithonia is an improvement on Kassandra.

The landscape en route is quite spectacular with sweeping vistas of thickly forested hills.

An undulating road makes a loop around Sithonia, skirting wide bays, climbing into the pine-forested hills and dipping down to the resorts. Travelling down the west coast there are good stretches of sandy beach between **Nikiti** and **Paradisos**. Beyond here, **Neos Marmaras** is Sithonia's biggest resort, with a very crowded beach but lots of domatia available. Look out for the big information boards on both waterfronts. The gigantic monstrosity of Porto Carras sits at one side of the bay. This is a luxury holiday complex for 3000 guests built by the wine-producing magnate John G Carras and modelled on Spanish Marbella – ugh.

Beyond Neos Marmaras the road climbs into the hills from where dirt roads lead down to several beaches and camp sites. **Toroni** and **Porto Koufos** are small resorts at the south-western tip. The latter is a picturesque little place with a good beach. The southern tip of Sithonia is still relatively isolated and is scenically the most spectacular region of Halkidiki (excluding the Athos peninsula) – rocky, rugged and dramatic. As the road rounds the south-eastern tip, Mt Athos comes into view across the gulf, further adding to the spectacular vistas.

Kalamitsi The resort of Kalamitsi is the most delightful corner of the Sithonian peninsula. This little enclave has a gorgeous sandy beach, a couple of tavernas, some domatia, two camp sites – *Porto Camping* on the main beach and *Camping Kalamitsi* around the headland – and boat-hire facilities. Not yet commercialised, it's one of the Sithonian peninsula's hidden delights. *O Giorgakis* (☎ 0375-41 338; fax 0375-41 013), just above the restaurant of the same name, is a stone's throw from the beach. Fully equipped studios here will cost from 9000 for two persons to 13,000 dr for four persons.

Continuing up the east coast, the bus does a little 2km detour inland to the pleasant village of **Sykia**, which has less tourist hype than the coastal resorts. Back on the coast, the resort of Sarti is next along the route.

Sarti Sarti has not succumbed entirely to the package-tourist industry and has a good laid-back atmosphere. From its excellent, long sandy beach there are splendid views of the startling pyramid-like hulk of Mt Athos. The town is compact and pleasant enough and tends to cater for local tourism, though it is popular with Germans and Austrians.

Sarti consists of two streets: one is on the waterfront and the other is parallel and one block inland. The bus terminal is on the latter – a timetable is pinned to a nearby tree. There is no tourist office but the staff of Koutras Travel (☎ 0375-94 017; fax 94 387), near the bus terminal, are helpful and speak English. The agency organises half-day mule treks in the mountains for 5000 dr, and Mt Athos cruises for 5000 dr.

Places to Stay If you decide to stay, *Sarti Beach Camping* (☎ 0375-94 450; fax 94 211) is not only a camp site, but a holiday complex with a variety of accommodation. The camp site itself is well shaded, but offers little greenery. Travelling north it's on the right side of the main approach road – buses stop outside.

In Sarti itself, *Hotel Three Stars* (☎ 0375-94 370) has smallish but modern apartments for 12,000 dr for three persons and 15,000 dr for four persons. Ask at the cigarette kiosk next to the bus stop for directions. There are many other domatia in Sarti too. Ask Koutras Travel for advice if you are stuck.

Places to Eat The *Pergola Café Restaurant* in Sarti is a great place to have a drink, a snack or a full meal; it's open all day till late evening. Their pergola plate has a bit of everything – meatballs, calamari, souvlaki – and is generally good value. From the bus stop turn left opposite Koutras Travel and you'll see the restaurant on the right – painted purple, grey and orange.

Getting There & Away Buses to Halkidiki leave from the bus terminal at Karakasi 68 in Thessaloniki. There are four buses a day to Neos Marmaras (2½ hours, 2300 dr); and three buses to Sarti (3½ hours, 3250 dr).

Most of the Sarti buses do a loop around the Sithonian peninsula, enabling you to see its magnificent southern tip.

Athos Peninsula (Secular Athos)

Most of the easternmost portion of the three prongs of the Halkidiki peninsula is occupied by the Athonite monasteries. You will probably only want to pass through secular Athos on your way to see the monasteries. The beaches are admittedly very fine in parts, but they have long been developed for the package-tour industry. Soulless resorts based on large hotels with no interest in, or of interest to, independent travellers are dotted along the coast. **Ierissos** is one of the few real towns, notable mainly for being the terminus for the irregular boat serving the east-coast monasteries, but you can't enter Athos this way. The **canal**, dug across the peninsula by the Persian king Xerxes in the 5th century BC for his invading fleet, is featured proudly on most maps, but it was filled in centuries ago and there's precious little for the untrained eye to see.

Ouranoupolis (Ουρανούπολη) The village of Ouranoupolis is at the northern end of secular Athos. The most obvious feature of the village is the 14th-century tower built to guard what was then a dependency of Vatopediou monastery. A building in a side street, one block back from the waterfront, is, despite appearances, actually early 20th century. It once housed a monastic copper works (now a pharmacy). Most of the rest of the village was founded in 1922 by refugees from Asia Minor.

As well as the ferry for pilgrims to Athos, boats from here run tourist trips along the coast of Mt Athos for those unwilling or unable (because of their gender) to set foot there. Ouranoupolis' postcode is 630 75 and the telephone code is ☎ 0377.

Places to Stay & Eat There are domatia and a few hotels, including the D-class *Hotel Galini* (☎ 71 217), one block back from the coast road. It has singles/doubles for 7000/9000 dr with shared facilities – you take breakfast in the family's dining room behind the small grocer's shop they run beneath the hotel rooms. The D-class *Hotel Akrogiali* (☎ 71 201; fax 71 395), on the waterfront, has singles/doubles for 6000/ 9000 dr.

If you want to splurge before plunging into the rigours of Athonite monastic life, the waterfront A-class *Xenia* (☎ 71 202; fax 71 362) has pricey singles/doubles for 24,300/ 36,000 dr but this includes most meals each day.

There are a number of restaurants facing the sea on the beach; between these and the road, not far away from the tower, *O Kokkinos* is reasonably priced and has good fish dishes.

Mt Athos (Agion Oros)

This semiautonomous monastic area, known in Greek as the 'Holy Mountain', occupies most of the Athos peninsula. To set foot here is to step back in time – literally by 13 days, because the Athonite community still uses the Julian calendar – and metaphorically by 500 years, as this is a remnant of the Byzantine Empire, which otherwise ended with the fall of Constantinople in 1453.

Setting foot here, however, is not straightforward. Foreign men are allowed to stay in the monasteries for four nights (extendible up to six) after completing some formalities (see Obtaining a Permit later in this section). Visitors walk from monastery to monastery, enjoying the landscape (Athos is also called the Garden of the Virgin Mary) on the way, experiencing a little of the ascetic life of the monks. Despite some of the rigours associated with a visit to the Holy Mountain, this unique experience can be a very enriching one.

Women cannot enter the area at all. The closest approach they can make to the monasteries is to view them from one of the round-trip cruises. Boats carrying women must stay at least 500m offshore.

History Hermits gravitated to Mt Athos from the very early years of the Byzantine Empire. The first monastery on Athos, Megistis

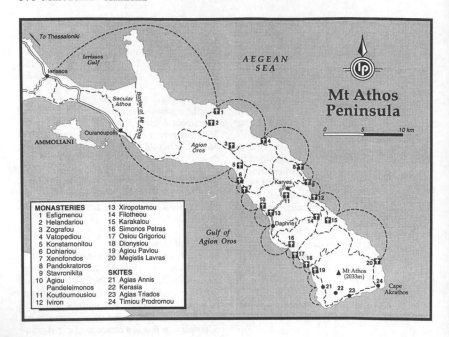

Mt Athos
Peninsula

MONASTERIES
1 Esfigmenou
2 Helandariou
3 Zografou
4 Vatopediou
5 Konstamonitou
6 Dohiariou
7 Xenofondos
8 Pandokratoros
9 Stavronikita
10 Agiou
   Pandeleimonos
11 Koutloumousiou
12 Iviron

13 Xiropotamou
14 Filotheou
15 Karakalou
16 Simonos Petras
17 Osiou Grigoriou
18 Dionysiou
19 Agiou Pavlou
20 Megistis Lavras

SKITES
21 Agias Annis
22 Kerasia
23 Agias Triados
24 Timiou Prodromou

Lavras, was founded between 961 and 963 AD by St Athanasios with support from the emperor, Nikephoros II Phokas. The next emperor, Ioannis Tsimiskis, gave Athos its first charter. The Athonite community flourished under the continuing support of the Byzantine emperors, who issued decrees reinforcing its status. The most notorious decree was that made under Constantine IX Monomahos barring access to women, beardless persons and female domestic animals. This is still in force, except that it is no longer a requirement to be bearded. Hens (for eggs) are tolerated; birds are apparently too lowly to be included in the ban.

Monasteries continued to be founded, particularly when Christians from outside the area came in during the first crusades. By 1400 there were said to be 40 monasteries, including foundations by Bulgarians, Russians and Serbian princes. The Athos community submitted to Turkish rule after the fall of Constantinople, but managed to retain its semi-independent status. The last monastery to be founded was Stavronikita, in 1542. The community declined over the centuries and today there are 20 ruling monasteries.

In the Greek War of Independence (1821-29) many monasteries were plundered and entire libraries burned by Turkish troops. The present constitution of Athos dates from 1924. It was guaranteed by the 1975 Greek constitution, and recognises Athos as a part of Greece (all the monks, regardless of their origin, must become Greek nationals), with the Iera Synaxis (holy council; composed of one representative from each of the 20 monasteries) responsible for all of the internal administration.

Obtaining a Permit Only 10 foreign adult males may enter Mt Athos per day, but unrestricted numbers of Greek men may enter. Start the procedure early, particularly for summer visits, when you may have to wait weeks for a place – make a reservation. Athos can get quite crowded at weekends.

You can start the process in Athens or Thessaloniki, but you are supposed to complete the paperwork in the city in which you started it. As you have to be in Northern Greece anyway, it is simplest to start in Thessaloniki.

Ordained clergymen should have an introduction from their bishop, and need permission to visit Athos from the Ecumenical Patriarchate of Constantinople – apply at the Metropolis of Thessaloniki, Vogatsikou 5 (☎ 031-227 677).

Applying in Thessaloniki You must first book a date for your visit. This is done through the Ministry for Macedonia & Thrace (open from 11 am to 1.45 pm, Monday to Friday) and can be done by phone. Call 031-257 010 and ask for Ms Plessa. Otherwise call in person at the Ministry which is on Plateia Diikitiriou (see Thessaloniki map).

You then need a letter of recommendation from your consulate. There are a number of foreign consulates listed under the Thessaloniki section. The British Consulate also acts for Australians and New Zealanders. The consulate will confirm your reservation with the Ministry.

The British consular hours are Monday to Friday from 8 am to 1 pm. The US consular hours are Tuesday and Thursday from 9 am to noon. Try telephoning the US Consulate (☎ 031-242 915) if you need your letter of recommendation urgently.

The British charge the highest consular fees in Greece for letters of recommendation – UK£20 payable in drachma. Australians and New Zealanders should technically use their embassies in Athens, but the UK consulate will issue a letter if the need is very urgent. The US Consulate doesn't levy a charge.

Take your letter of recommendation to the Ministry of Macedonia & Thrace. In Room 218 (1st floor, east wing), Directorate of Political Affairs, the staff exchange your letter of recommendation for a permit to enter

Athos on a particular date. This completes the initial paperwork.

In busy seasons, the ministry may give you a date for your visit several weeks or even months away. You can reserve a place from countries outside Greece either via your consulate or by directly contacting the Ministry of Macedonia & Thrace (☎ 031-270 092), Directorate of Political Affairs, Room 218, Plateia Diikitiriou, Thessaloniki, 541 23.

Applying in Athens First obtain your letter of recommendation (ask for a *note verbale*) from the consular section of your embassy. Consular fees for this (payable in drachma) are: British UK£20; US gratis; Canadian C$10; Australian A$25.

Take your letter of recommendation to the Ministry of Foreign Affairs, Zalakosta 2, to obtain the permit to enter Athos on a specific date. No further paperwork is required.

It is also possible to make an advance reservation for a particular date through your embassy.

Orientation & Information There is no land access from secular Greece; all visitors enter the Athonite community by boat from Ouranoupolis to Daphne, the small port of Athos. This has a port-authority building, police and customs, post office, a couple of general stores selling food and religious artefacts made on Athos, and a café. There is no OTE office, but one of the shops has a telephone with a meter. The only other town is Karyes, the administrative capital, which includes the headquarters building of the Holy Epistasia (holy council), an inn, post office, OTE office, doctor and a couple of shops. There are no tourist police, but there is a regular police station in Karyes.

The remaining settlements are the 20 monasteries plus 12 scattered *skites*, and the isolated dwellings of hermits – the total population of monks and resident laymen is about 1600. In addition to Karyes and Daphne, police are based at Agiou Pandeleimonos, Megistis Lavras, Agias Annis, Zografou and Helandariou.

Visitors & the Monastic Life

Don't imagine that all the monks are simple, otherworldly men. Although some of the hermits in the south of the peninsula are, to put it politely, weird, many of the monks in the monasteries are highly educated men very familiar with the outside world – you will come across monks who spend much of their life outside the monasteries, as university professors or missionary doctors.

The monks have not chosen their way of life primarily for the benefit of visitors. Your reception will vary from correct but distant to warm and hospitable, and this partly depends on you. Every aspect of your behaviour in a monastery will be under close scrutiny (even if you think everyone is ignoring you) and will be eagerly discussed by the monks (who are apparently great gossips).

Certain behaviour is expected of you. Wear long trousers, not shorts, everywhere on Athos; it's polite to wear long-sleeved shirts. Inside the monasteries, do not wear a hat, do not smoke or behave inconsiderately (for example by singing or whistling). When you meet a monk along the way, greet him by saying 'evloite' (evloyite, literally 'bless me'); the usual response is the blessing 'o kyrios' (the Lord). Photography is often forbidden within monasteries, and you should never photograph a monk without his permission.

Remain dressed on the way to and from the washrooms, and even in them. Exposing skin is a big no-no, so attempt to wash with your shirt on, unless the guest quarters have enclosed showers. Do not swim within sight of a monastery, however hot and sweaty you feel after walking; not only is this forbidden, but raw sewage is discharged into the sea.

The monasteries have a common ground plan; from the outside, each resembles a fortified castle having one gateway for access. In the central courtyard is the katholikon (monastery church), frequently blood-red in colour, and behind this is the trapeza (refectory). Most monasteries now accommodate only a fraction of the monks they once did, and have abandoned derelict sections; some of these are being renovated with the aid of EU funds for heritage protection.

The monastic day begins at sunset, which is midnight in the Byzantine time kept in the monasteries (distrust the clocks, which must be adjusted every day). This is when the outer gate is shut, and it is not reopened until daybreak. When you reach a monastery, head for the guest quarters, arhontariki (usually signposted), and find the guest master. The monks traditionally welcome visitors by offering them home-distilled tsipouro and loukoumi, or coffee. The guest master will show you to a two to 10-bed guest room.

Visitors are not expected to participate completely in the monastic religious life, and some monasteries do not permit the non-Orthodox within the church; however, you should, if permitted, attend the morning and evening services which usually precede the meal times (it's bad form to sneak straight into the refectory for the food).

Services are indicated by a monk walking round the monastery striking a simandro, a large wooden plank, with a mallet in a distinctive rhythm. The only music permitted is that of the human voice (heavenly in some monasteries, diabolical in others), and the liturgical language used is an archaic form of Greek. The apparently endless repetition of some sections has a hypnotic effect.

Religious practice on Athos derives from the 14th-century Hesychast movement, according to which the divine light radiated at the Transfiguration can be perceived by certain practices of meditation and repetitive chanting.

The landscape is dominated in the south by the white peak of Mt Athos itself; the northerly part is densely wooded. Wildlife abounds; the small population of monks and absence of any industry (apart from some logging) have virtually turned the area into a reserve.

Leave video cameras behind – they're prohibited on Athos.

Exploring Athos Once you have obtained your diamonitirion (permit to stay in the monasteries), you are free to roam. There are few proper roads, and not many vehicles – you get around on foot, following the old paths, or by boat.

A caïque leaves Agias Annis every day at 9.45 am for Daphne, serving intermediate west-coast monasteries or their arsanas (landing stage for monasteries not immediately by the sea) and returning from Daphne every afternoon. A more irregular caïque serves points on the east coast (theoretically three times a week, weather permitting on this exposed coast) between Ierissos and Mandraki, the harbour for Megistis Lavras.

If the non-Orthodox are permitted in the church, they will usually be confined to the *exonarthex*, the outer porch (the double narthex is a peculiarity of the Athos churches). When there is no service in progress some monasteries make a point of showing non-Orthodox visitors the church interior – most of them are stuffed with more relics and icons than you can shake a censer at.

The monks dine twice a day, or only once on the frequent fasting days. The simple vegetarian meals rely heavily on produce from the monastery gardens, but are occasionally supplemented by fish. Common accompaniments to the cooked vegetables include home-baked bread, olives, eggs and cheese. Some monasteries serve very palatable wine with the meals, an uncharacteristic epicurean touch.

In some monasteries, non-Orthodox visitors eat separately from the monks, at others they eat with them, in which case you must stop eating as soon as the monks rise and leave, no matter how much food remains. On fasting days the monks normally provide some light refreshment for their guests.

Older books classify the monasteries into coenobite or idiorhythmic type, depending on whether communal life is centrally or more loosely organised. This distinction is now obsolete: the last idiorhythmic monastery, Pandokratoros, became coenobite on 8 June 1992 (Byzantine calendar), along with much feasting and celebration.

The lives of monks who live in *skites* – clusters of houses around a church – are not as strict as those of the monks who reside in the monasteries. Monks in the skites have more free time, and produce most of the Athos artefacts sold in Daphne and Karyes. One of the houses acts as the guest quarters, and visitors are received hospitably. Some *kelloi* – literally cells, but more like small farmhouses, and usually accommodating two to four monks – also receive guests.

The accommodation offered by the monasteries can be spartan, the food frugal and you won't meet any women, but you will have been in exalted company. The Byzantine emperor John VI Cantacuzenus, on his enforced abdication in 1354, became a monk on Athos for the rest of his life. Rasputin, the Mad Monk (an unfair name, as technically speaking he wasn't a monk) walked here in 1891 from Siberia, a journey of 2000 miles. ∎

David Hall

NORTHERN GREECE

Another service around the south connects Mandraki and Agias Annis. The caïques are inexpensive; for example, at the time of writing the trip from Daphne to Dionysiou cost 250 dr.

Unless you travel exclusively by boat, you need to be reasonably fit and prepared to walk for several hours a day in the heat. Carry water with you and, as food often becomes an obsession among visitors, take extra supplies, such as biscuits and dried fruit. You will need a map; the best one of Athos is the 1:50,000 contour map published by Reinhold & Klaus Zwerger available through Stanfords of London (☎ 0171-836 1321) or from the cartographers themselves at Wohlmutstrasse 8, A-1020 Vienna, Austria.

Other useful things to take include a torch (flashlight), compass, a whistle (in case you get lost), a small shaving mirror (not all monastic washrooms have mirrors) and mosquito coils.

You can only spend one night in each monastery. Some of the heavily visited ones near Karyes request that you telephone them

Karyes

0   0.5   1 km

1   Skiti Agiou Andreou
2   Athonia School
3   Administrator
4   Hospital
5   Iosafeon
6   Bus stop
7   Guest house
8   WC
9   Government House (Kyvernio)
10 OTE
11 Protaton
12 Post Office
13 Dionysios Fournas
14 Police
15 Guesthouse
16 Bakery

in advance to be sure of a place (the numbers are displayed in the Holy Epistasia, where you wait for the diamonitirion), but this can be a frustrating experience, as the telephone is not answered for many hours of the day during periods of rest and meditation. You must reach the monastery before sunset, as the gate is then shut, and not opened for anyone.

In **Karyes** you should see the 10th-century **Protaton**, the basilican church opposite the Holy Epistasia, which contains a number of treasures including paintings by Panselinos, the master of the Macedonian School. Karyes itself is a strange place – like a ghost town, with many derelict buildings testifying to a former, grander era. If you've had a long day, you may decide to stay at the monastery of **Koutloumousiou** in Karyes. Otherwise, you should now decide on your itinerary.

A popular route is to head for one of the monasteries on the east coast, and then to continue to Megistis Lavras, returning to Daphne on the west coast. This can involve some lengthy walks unless you use the caïques, but these can be unreliable on the east coast.

From Karyes, you can walk to either **Stavronikita** or **Iviron** on the coast, to continue by caïque, or coastal paths (easier to follow than the inland paths). Alternatively, from Karyes you can walk to **Filotheou** along a pleasant shady path (spring water available) in about 3½ hours. About 30 minutes further on is **Karakalou**. Beyond here the old Byzantine path has been converted into a road, and you face a 5½-hour walk along it (unless a monastic vehicle gives you a lift) to **Megistis Lavras**.

Not only is this the oldest monastery on Athos, it is also the only one to remain undamaged by fire during its history. Its 10th-century structure protects a number of treasures, including frescoes by Theophanes of Crete and the tomb of St Athanasios, the founder.

A caïque leaves Megistis Lavras at about 3 pm for the *skiti* (hermit's dwellings) of Agias Annis. Alternatively, you can follow the path around the wilderness of the south end of the peninsula. You come first to the skiti of **Timiou Prodromou**, then **Agias Triados** on the coast (off the main track), then **Kerasia**, and subsequently to **Agias Annis**, either of which (although Agias Annis has a better reputation for hospitality) can be used as a base for climbing Mt Athos (2030m).

This climb should not be undertaken lightly, and it is wise not to attempt it alone. It also wouldn't hurt to inform someone of your plans before setting off. Remember that it will be cold at the top, and you will need to take food and water. Water is available from a well at the chapel of Panagia (Virgin Mary), a short distance below the summit. You can return to Daphne by caïque from Agias Annis.

An alternative route is to head from Karyes to see the architecturally interesting monasteries on the west coast, including the spectacular Simonos Petras, clinging to a cliff like a Tibetan lamasery. From Karyes you climb over the central spine of the hills and head down again. You'll come first to **Xiropotamou**, which has newly renovated guest rooms (still lit by oil lamps) and serves good food and wine to guests separately from the monks. A path leads from here to Daphne; you can follow the coastal path from here or take the daily caïque leaving at 12.30 pm for Agias Annis calling at Simonos Petras, Grigoriou, Dionysiou and Pavlou. Alternatively, from Karyes you could head for Filotheou and then take a path to Simonos Petras from there.

Simonos Petras, also called Simopetra, is an awesome sight from its sea-level arsanas. From here it's a stiff climb to the monastery. The monastery's outside walls are surrounded by wooden balconies – as you walk along these from the guest rooms to the washroom, you can see the sheer drop beneath your feet. Swallows nest in the eaves and delight in taking vertiginous swoops to the sea. You can't normally get outside the monasteries to experience Athos at night – standing on these balconies in the dark, listening to the swallows and staring down towards the light of a solitary fishing boat is a magical experience.

From Simonos Petras you can descend to a coastal path which branches off the path to the arsanas at a small shrine. The path brings you to **Osiou Grigoriou**, which has a very pleasant position by the sea, and a comfortable guesthouse by the harbour outside the main monastery building. This has electric light and the rare luxury of showers.

The coastal path from here onwards is quite strenuous as it climbs and descends three times before coming to **Dionysiou**,

another cliff-hanger of a monastery resembling Simonos Petras in some ways. One of the treasures of its *katholikon* (main church), in a separate chapel, is an age-blackened icon claimed as the oldest in Athos. It is said to have been carried round the walls of Constantinople to inspire its successful defence against a combined siege by the Persians and Avars in 626. The coastal path from here continues to **Agiou Pavlou** and Agias Annis.

A road less travelled takes in the monasteries north of Karyes. First stop could be the slightly out of the way **Pandokratoros** monastery with its own pretty harbour, or you can keep on going to **Vatopediou**, also on the coast. This picturesque monastery is an oddity in that it keeps to the European calendar. When Athos was at its height, Vatopediou had a celebrated school (now in ruins). A coastal path leads on to **Esfigmenou**, and further on, little visited because of its isolation, is **Helandariou**, a Serbian foundation still inhabited by Serbs and noted for its hospitality.

The somewhat hard to get to and humble **Konstamonitou** monastery might be worth a visit if you are really keen, but further north and between the east and west coasts is the Bulgarian monastery, **Zografou** (which means 'painter', named for a miraculous icon not painted by human hands). On the west coast, the most northerly monastery is **Dohiariou**, which is considered to have some of the best architecture on Athos.

Coming south on the coastal path you reach **Xenofondos** and then **Agiou Pandeleimonos**, the Russian monastery – which welcomes visitors with tea. This enormous building used to accommodate over 1000 monks, who came in swarms from Russia in the 19th century. Most of the distinctive Russian-style buildings date from that period and many are now derelict. The monastery was once renowned for the quality of its singing, which has been through a low point in the recent past, but is happily picking up again. Be aware that accommodation may not be available here. These west-coast monasteries are served by the Ouranoupolis-Daphne ferry.

NORTHERN GREECE

Many alternative routes are possible using the network of old Byzantine paths – most of which have been recently marked by the Thessaloniki Mountaineering Club, but unmarked logging tracks make it amazingly easy to get lost in the woods. Monks' paths, which cross vehicle tracks and lead directly to (or away from) monasteries, are marked at the roadside by small crosses.

Getting There & Away Entry is by boat from Ouranoupolis, which is accessible by bus from Thessaloniki's Halkidiki terminal at Karakasi 68. There are seven buses a day (2½ hours, 2080 dr). The first bus (6 am) from Thessaloniki arrives just in time for the boat, but leaves you little time to organise your diamonitirion (see the next section; Entering Athos); otherwise you need to stay overnight in Ouranoupolis. This gives you a chance to buy easily carried food, and find somewhere to store unwanted gear (probably for a fee). Take only the bare minimum to Athos, as you'll have to lug it round all the time.

You may prefer to store unneeded baggage in Thessaloniki – when you return from Athos to Ouranoupolis, the bus to Thessaloniki is waiting for the boat, and you may miss it while recovering luggage. Also, you might want to leave Athos via the west-coast boat to Ierissos – no big advantage if all your worldly goods are in Ouranoupolis.

Entering Athos When you arrive in Ouranoupolis, you must first call in at the Pilgrims' Office which is on a street to the right, just before a petrol station, as you enter the village. Look for the Byzantine flag. Officials will check your passport and entry permit and issue you a document called a diamonitirion for 3000 dr to actually enter Athos. Both diamonitirion and passport will be checked as you board the ferry for Athos. Make sure you get to Ouranoupolis early as there may be queues, especially on weekends.

The boat, usually the small car ferry *Axion Esti*, leaves Ouranoupolis at 9.45 am for the small port of Daphne (850 dr). The journey

takes about two hours; some intermediate stops are made for monks and other residents and if you are not heading directly to Karyes you may alight at these intermediate stops. Once you arrive in Daphne, a clapped-out bus waits to take you to Karyes for 500 dr.

Once in the main square of Karyes you are free to start your walk to the monastery of your choice for the first night. The monasteries will not expect any further donations for accommodating you, but technically you're supposed to spend only one night in each monastery. You might get two nights if you ask politely. The diamonitirion can be extended (for a further two days) in Karyes at the end of the four days.

Leaving Athos The daily boat to Ouranoupolis leaves Daphne at noon – there is a fairly rigorous customs check to ensure that you're not walking off with any antiquities (even visiting clerics have been known to snaffle valuable relics).

The morning caïque from Agias Annis arrives in Daphne in ample time for the Ouranoupolis boat. The irregular east-coast caïque provides an alternative exit to Ierissos.

KAVALA Καβάλα
• *pop 57,000* • *postcode 655 00* • *area code ☎ 051*
Kavala (Kavala), 163km east of Thessaloniki, is one of the most attractive of Greece's large cities. It spills gently down the foothills of Mt Symvolon to a commodious harbour. The old quarter of Panagia nestles under a massive Byzantine fortress.

Modern Kavala is built over ancient Neopolis, which was the port of Philippi. Mehmet Ali (1769-1849), who became Pasha of Egypt and founder of the last Egyptian royal dynasty, was born in Kavala. Like Athens and Thessaloniki, its population was almost doubled by the population exchange with Asia Minor.

Orientation
Kavala's focal point is Plateia Eleftherias. The town's two main thoroughfares, Elef-

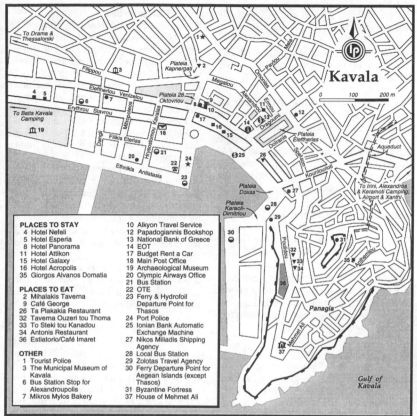

Kavala

0   100   200 m

PLACES TO STAY
4 Hotel Nefeli
5 Hotel Esperia
8 Hotel Panorama
11 Hotel Attikon
15 Hotel Galaxy
16 Hotel Acropolis
35 Giorgos Alvanos Domatia

PLACES TO EAT
2 Mihalakis Taverna
9 Café George
26 Ta Plakakia Restaurant
32 Taverna Ouzeri tou Thoma
33 To Steki tou Kanadou
34 Antonis Restaurant
36 Estiatorio/Café Imaret

OTHER
1 Tourist Police
3 The Municipal Museum of Kavala
6 Bus Station Stop for Alexandroupolis
7 Mikros Mylos Bakery
10 Alkyon Travel Service
12 Papadogiannis Bookshop
13 National Bank of Greece
14 EOT
17 Budget Rent a Car
18 Main Post Office
19 Archaeological Museum
20 Olympic Airways Office
21 Bus Station
22 OTE
23 Ferry & Hydrofoil Departure Point for Thasos
24 Port Police
25 Ionian Bank Automatic Exchange Machine
27 Nikos Miliadis Shipping Agency
28 Local Bus Station
29 Zolotas Travel Agency
30 Ferry Departure Point for Aegean Islands (except Thasos)
31 Byzantine Fortress
37 House of Mehmet Ali

NORTHERN GREECE

theriou Venizelou and Erythrou Stavrou run west from here parallel with the waterfront Ethnikis Antistasis. The old quarter of Panagia occupies a promontory to the southeast of Plateia Eleftherias. To get to the old quarter, walk east along Eleftheriou Venizelou from Plateia Eleftherias, turn left at the T-junction and take the first right (signposted Panagia and the Castle).

The intercity bus station is on the corner of Hrysostomou Kavalas and Filikis Eterias, near the Thasos ferry quay.

One of the town's most prominent landmarks is an imposing aqueduct, which

was built during the reign of Süleyman the Magnificent (1520-66).

Information

Tourist Office The EOT (☎ 222 425) is on the west side of Plateia Eleftherias. The helpful staff give out a map of the town, provide information on transport and have a list of the town's hotels with prices. They also have information on the summer drama festivals at Philippi and Thasos.

Opening times of the office are Monday to Friday from 7 am to 2.30 pm. If staffing allows, the office is also open from 5 to 8 pm and on Saturday from 8 am to 1 pm. It's closed on Sunday.

Tourist Police The tourist police (☎ 222 905) are in the same building as the regular police at Omonias 119.

Money The National Bank of Greece is on the corner of Megalou Alexandrou and Dragoumi and has an automatic exchange machine and ATM. There is a 24-hour Ionian Bank automatic exchange machine and ATM on the harbour front, and the Midas Exchange office next to the EOT operates over fairly extended hours.

Post & Communications The main post office is on the corner of Hrysostomou Kavalas and Erythrou Stavrou. The OTE is on the corner of Antistasis and Averof.

Bookshops The Papadogiannis Bookshop, at Omonias 46 on the corner of Amynta, stocks a wide range of international newspapers and magazines. It also has a few English-language paperbacks.

Panagia Παναγία
The pastel-coloured houses in the narrow tangled streets of the Panagia quarter are less dilapidated than those of Thessaloniki's Kastra and the area is less commercialised than Athens' Plaka.

Its most conspicuous building is the **Imaret**, a huge structure with 18 domes, which overlooks the harbour from Poulidou. In Turkish times the Imaret was a hostel for theology students. It has recently been restored and is now a pleasant café and restaurant (see Places to Eat). Within the café are some cabinets displaying memorabilia from Mehmet Ali's time. The carefully restored Turkish house where Mehmet Ali was born is now open to the public. If you ring the bell the caretaker will show you around; along with other rooms, you will see Ali's harem. The house is at the southern end of Poulidou. Nearby is an equestrian statue of Ali.

Other Things to See
Kavala's **archaeological museum** (☎ 222 335) houses well-displayed finds from ancient Amphipolis, between Thessaloniki and Kavala. Amphipolis was a colony of Athens, and a gold-rush town with mines on Mt Pangaeum. The finds include sculpture, jewellery, grave steles, terracotta figurines and vases. The museum entrance is at the western end of Ethnikis Antistasis. It's open Tuesday to Sunday from 8.30 am to 6 pm. Admission is 500 dr, but is free on Sunday and public holidays.

The **Municipal Museum of Kavala** is also worth a visit. On the ground floor are pictures and sculptures by contemporary Greek artists including a large collection of works by Polygnotos Vagis (1894-1965), who was born in Potamia on Thasos, and emigrated to the USA where he gained an international reputation.

On the upper floor is a superb folk-art collection with costumes, jewellery, handcrafts, household items and tools. The museum is at Filippou 4.

Places to Stay – bottom end
Irini Camping (☎ 229 785) is the military-looking EOT camp site and is 2km east of Kavala on the coast road. *Alexandros Camping* (☎ 316 347) is another 8km out of town by the beach at Nea Karvali. *Batis Kavala Camping* (☎ 243 051) is 3km west of Kavala at Batis beach. Finally out at Keramoti, 37km from Kavala there is *Keramoti Camping* (☎ 0591-51 279). They all charge in the region of 1100 dr per person and 700 dr per tent per night.

The best deal for budget travellers and perhaps the nicest environment in Kavala to spend the night are the cosy *domatia* in the beautiful 300-year-old house rented by Giorgos Alvanos (☎ 228 412), Anthemiou 35, in Panagia. Single/double rates are 4000/6000 dr with shared bathroom.

The E-class *Hotel Attikon* (☎ 222 257), Megalou Alexandrou 8, is pretty dire and sleazy and is only included here because there is a dearth of budget accommodation in Kavala. Singles/doubles are 4000/5000 dr

PAUL HELLANDER

PAUL HELLANDER

Top: Vikos gorge, Northern Greece, one of Greece's most popular trekking routes
Bottom: Mt Olympus, Northern Greece: home of the ancient gods and today a national park

Top: A boat under construction in Ierissos on the Mt Athos peninsula, Northern Greece
Bottom: View of Poros town, Poros, Saronic Gulf Islands

with shared bathroom. D-class *Hotel Acropolis* (☎ 223 543; fax 830 752), Eleftheriou Venizelou 29, is marginally better and has singles with shared bathroom for 7500 dr and doubles with private bathroom for 14,000 dr. Take the lift to reception as you enter the building.

Places to Stay – middle
The C-class *Hotel Panorama* (☎ 224 205; fax 224 685), Eleftheriou Venizelou 26 C, has reasonable singles/doubles for 9000/12,500 dr with shared bathroom and 12,000/16,000 dr with private bathroom. Nearer the waterfront the C-class *Hotel Nefeli* (☎ 227 441; fax 227 440), Leoforos Erythrou Stavrou 50, has pleasant singles/doubles for 12,000/15,000 dr with private bathroom. The C-class *Hotel Esperia* (☎ 229 621; fax 220 621), Erythrou Stavrou 44, has similar singles/doubles for 13,700/17,000 dr.

Places to Stay – top end
The B-class *Hotel Galaxy* (☎ 224 812; fax 226 754), Eleftheriou Venizelou 27, is Kavala's best hotel, with spacious, attractively furnished single/double rooms for 14,200/19,250 dr. All rooms have air-con, refrigerator, telephone, radio and private bathroom.

Always bear in mind that the list prices given here may be heavily discounted out of season, sometimes by as much as 55%.

Places to Eat
Kavala's restaurant scene is a vast improvement on its accommodation. *Ta Plakakia Restaurant*, Doïranis 4, near Plateia Eleftherias, is a conveniently located eating place with a huge choice of low-priced dishes. The *Mihalakis Taverna*, Kassandrou 3, on Plateia Kapnergati, is more up-market. Don't be put off by the tacky murals and folksy wall-hangings – the food is good. Prices at these two places range from 1800 to 2500 dr for a generous meal.

There are at least three popular restaurants on Poulidou, opposite the Imaret. The first is *Taverna Ouzeri tou Thoma*; their fried mussels are delectable. Another one, *To Steki tou*

Kanadou, has a wide-ranging fish menu and other seafood specialities. Try their mussels in tomato sauce. *Antonia Restaurant*, next door, is also recommended by locals and is equally well patronised. Prices at these three are similar. Expect to part with at least 2500 dr for a delectable meal. For a unique eating environment, try the *Estiatorio Imaret* in the Imaret itself, further up Poulidou on the right. This is probably Kavala's most atmospheric eating location. The price of a meal here is also in the 2500 dr bracket.

The *Café George*, on a side street off Eleftheriou Venizelou, has good cheese pies and custard pies and filter coffee, and you can get great bread and cakes at the modern *Mikros Mylos* bakery a block south of the Municipal Museum. If you don't want a meal, then the *café* in the Imaret is in a lovely serene setting around a courtyard of fruit trees. Here you can play backgammon or other board games to while away an hour or so.

Getting There & Away
Air Kavala shares Hrysoupolis airport with Xanthi. There is one flight a day to Athens (16,800 dr) at 6.50 pm (7.20 pm on Sunday) and four additional flights a week in summer at 6.30 am. The airport is 29km east of Kavala.

Bus From the intercity bus station there are half-hourly buses to Xanthi (one hour, 1000 dr); hourly buses to Keramoti (one hour, 800 dr) and hourly services to Thessaloniki (two hours, 2650 dr). For Philippi, take one of the frequent Drama buses and ask to be let off at the ancient site of Philippi (20 minutes, 320 dr).

Buses for Alexandroupolis (2½ hours, 2750 dr), which originate in Thessaloniki, do not leave from the intercity bus station, but from outside the Dore Café (☎ 227 601), Erythrou Stavrou 34, from where you can get departure times and buy a ticket.

To/From Turkey There are daily OSE buses that originate in Thessaloniki and depart daily from Kavala at 4.30 am, except Thursday.

Tickets cost 9450/16,100 dr for a single/return. Student and youth discounts apply to student card-holders. You can buy tickets from Alkyon Travel Service (☎ 231 096; fax 836 251) at Eleftheriou Venizelou 26d, next door to the Hotel Panorama.

Train The nearest train station to Kavala is at Drama, 30km away. Drama is on the Thessaloniki-Alexandroupolis line and there are eight trains a day in either direction. There is a frequent bus service between Kavala and Drama. Train tickets can be bought in advance from Alkyon Travel Service on Eleftheriou Venizelou, which also acts as an OSE agency.

Car Budget Rent a Car (☎ 228 785) is on the 1st floor of Eleftheriou Venizelou 35, opposite the Hotel Panorama. You can also rent a car from the Europcar agency at Alkyon Travel Service.

Ferry There are ferries every hour from Kavala to Skala Prinou on Thasos (1¼ hours, 650 dr). There is also a service every hour or so in summer (35 minutes, 330 dr, plus 2700 dr if you are taking a car across) from the small port of Keramoti, 46km east of Kavala, to Limenas.

In summer there are ferries from Kavala to Samothraki (four hours, 3000 dr). Times and frequency vary month by month. Buy tickets and check the latest schedule at Zolotas Travel Agency (☎ 835 671) near the entrance to the Aegean islands ferry departure point.

There are ferries to Limnos (4½ hours, 3100 dr), Agios Efstratios (six hours, 3400 dr) and Lesvos (11½ hours, 5200 dr). Some services also go through to Rafina (in Attica) and Piraeus via Chios and Samos.

You can buy tickets and get the latest schedules from Nikos Miliadis Shipping Agency (☎ 226 147; fax 838 767), Karaoli-Dimitriou 36.

Hydrofoil There are about nine hydrofoils a day to Limenas (30 minutes, 1500 dr), and a further two per day to Potos (2500 dr), via Kallirahi, Maries and Limenaria. Purchase tickets at the departure point at the port. There used to be hydrofoil connections to Lesvos, Plomari (Lesvos) and Chios but these have been discontinued in recent years. Check with the port police in case they have been re-instated.

Both hydrofoil and ferry schedules are posted in the window of the port police near the hydrofoil departure point.

Greek Weddings

Greek weddings are lavish affairs and if you have ever been lucky enough to attend one and its ensuing lively wedding feast, you have indeed been privileged. While civil weddings in Greece have been legal for over fifteen years, most Greek couples still prefer the ritualistic ceremony of an orthodox church service followed by an afternoon and evening, or even weekend of eating, drinking and dancing.

The church ceremony is redolent of incense and ceremony. The participation of the bride and bridegroom is mainly passive since the main action is conducted by the priest and the *koumbaros* (best man) or *koumbara* (best woman) who literally 'crowns' the couple with a pair of interlinked garlands. The real excitement starts with the 'dance' during which the newly-wed couple are led around in a circle by the priest while church participants shower them with rice.

After the ceremony it is customary for everyone in the church to line up and congratulate the couple, their family, the best man or woman and the bridesmaids with wishes such as *na zisete* (may you enjoy long life) to the couple and *na sas zisoun* (may they live for many years) to the parents. If the bridesmaids are single they are greeted with *kai sta dika sou* (your turn next).

Those invited to the wedding feast, which in rural areas often means the whole village, will retire to an evening of revelry and entertainment, part of which sees the bride and groom take the first dance and then literally get covered with money that is pinned to their clothes by guests. The party will often carry on all night and into the next day. ■

Getting Around

The Airport There is no Olympic Airways bus to the airport but KTEL buses leave from the intercity bus station at 6.30 am and 6.30 pm (700 dr, 30 minutes), timed to connect with departing and incoming flights.

PHILIPPI Φίλιπποι

The ancient site of Philippi (Filippi) lies 15km inland from Kavala astride the Kavala-Drama road. The original city was called Krenides. Philip II seized it from the Thasians in 356 BC because it was in the foothills of Mt Pangaion, and there was 'gold in them thar hills', which he needed to finance his battles to gain control of Greece.

During July and August the Philippi Festival is held at the site's theatre. Information about this can be obtained from the EOT in Kavala. The site (☎ 051-516 470) and museum (☎ 051-516 251) are open Tuesday to Sunday from 8.30 am to 6 pm. Admission to each is 800 dr; 400 dr for students.

History

A visit to Philippi is worthwhile more for the significance of the events that happened there than for what can actually be seen, so some knowledge of its history is essential. Philippi is famous for two reasons: it was the scene of one of the most decisive battles in history, and it was the first European city to accept Christianity.

By the 1st century AD, Greece had become the battleground for factions of the Roman republic, and Philippi was coveted for its strategic position on the Via Egnatia. Julius Caesar's death at the hands of the republicans Cassius and Brutus had created a power vacuum. Eager to fill this gap, the two most powerful armies of Rome (with 80,000 men per side) met in battle on the plain of Philippi. One side was led by the imperial Mark Antony (great nephew of Julius Caesar) and Octavian, and the other by Julius Caesar's assassins. Octavian was the victor, causing Cassius and Brutus to commit suicide.

The battle set the seal on the future of a new Rome, which was to be imperialist (and as things turned out, Christian as well).

Octavian, after this victory, waged another famous battle (the Battle of Actium) in 31 AD, where he fought his former ally Mark Antony and Antony's consort, Cleopatra. Again, Octavian was the victor (and again the defeated committed suicide) and so now in control, he established an autocracy, and became Augustus, first emperor of Rome.

Neopolis (present-day Kavala), the port of Philippi, was the landing stage in Europe for travellers from the Orient. And so it was here that St Paul came in 49 AD to embark on his conversion of the pagan Europeans. His overzealous preaching landed him in prison – a misadventure which would be repeated many times in the future.

Exploring the Site

Despite Philippi being the first Christian city in Europe, its people didn't have much luck in their church-building endeavours. The 5th-century **Basilica A** was the first church built in the city, but it was wrecked by an earthquake shortly after completion. The remains of this church can be seen on the north side of the site (on the right coming from Kavala), near the road and to the west of the theatre.

Their next attempt was the 6th-century **Basilica B**, on the southern side of the site, next to the large and conspicuous forum. This church was an ambitious attempt to build a church with a dome, but the structure was top heavy and collapsed before it was dedicated. In the 10th century its sole remaining part, the narthex, was made into a church – several of its Corinthian columns can be seen.

Philippi's best preserved building is the **theatre**, which isn't Roman but was built by Philip II. Also in good nick are 50 marble latrines at the southern end of the forum. The site's **museum**, on the north side, houses both Roman and Christian finds from Philippi, and also Neolithic finds from the nearby site of Dikili Tach. It was closed for renovation in 1997, but should be up and running again by 1998.

Getting There & Away

Buses between Kavala and Drama will let passengers off at the ancient site (20 minutes, 320 dr).

Thrace Θράκη

Thrace is the north-eastern region of Greece and the backwater of the mainland. If you ask Greeks from elsewhere what it has to offer, chances are most will reply 'nothing', and some will add in words weighted with meaning 'and Turks live there'. The Turkish population of Thrace, along with the Greek population of Constantinople and the former Greek islands of Imvros (Gökçeada) and Tenedos (Bozcaada) were exempt from the 1923 population exchange. This phenomenon alone sets the area apart from the rest of Greece.

The landscape is dotted with the slender minarets of mosques and villages of Turkish-style red-roofed houses. There is also a more pronounced Turkish influence in the food, and a greater proliferation of Eastern-style bazaars and street vendors.

Besides being of ethnographical interest, the region has some picturesque towns and a varied landscape. It has a long coastline interspersed with wetlands and a hinterland of mountains (the Rodopi range) covered in thick forest and undergrowth. The mountains are punctuated by valleys through which flow several rivers. The most important is the River Evros, which marks the boundary with Turkey.

Between the coast and the mountains is a fertile plain where sunflowers, grown for their oil, create a pretty foreground to the mountainous backdrop. Tobacco is also grown, to supply a thriving industry – although the rest of Europe is giving up the noxious weed, smoking among Greeks is increasing at an alarming rate. Another feature of the area is its large number of storks. Look out for their huge, untidy nests on high extremities of buildings.

History

The earliest Thracian tribes were of Indo-European extraction, and the ethnic and cultural origins of the region have more of an affinity with Bulgaria and Turkey than Greece. During the 7th century BC, the Thracian coast was conquered by the most powerful Greek city-states, but during the 6th and 5th centuries BC it was subjugated by the Persians.

After the Persian defeat at the Battle of Plataea, Thrace was governed by Athens. In 346 BC, Philip II of Macedon gained control. During Roman times it was an insignificant backwater, but after the split of the empire, the region developed culturally and economically, because of its strategic position on the Via Egnatia. Later, its fate was similar to that of pretty much everywhere else in Greece, with invasions by Goths, Huns, Vandals and Bulgars and finally the Turks in 1361.

In 1920 the Treaty of Sèvres decreed that all of Thrace become part of the modern Greek state, but after the 1923 population exchange, Greece lost eastern Thrace to Turkey.

XANTHI Ξάνθη

• *pop 31,000* • *postcode 671 00* • *area code ☎ 0541*

Travelling east from Thessaloniki or Kavala, Xanthi (Xanthi) is the first town you will come to in Thrace. The old town of Xanthi has many beautiful, well-maintained Turkish dwellings from the 19th century. Xanthi is a lively and flourishing town where Turks make up 10% of the population, and live amicably with Greeks. The town is the centre of Thrace's tobacco-growing industry. The areas to the north of Xanthi, though you can technically visit them, are subject to military control and a pass is required to travel there.

Orientation & Information

The main thoroughfare is 28 Oktovriou, which runs north-south through the town. Halfway along here is Plateia Eleftherias, and just west of here on Iroön is a huge, fascinating indoor food market. The main bus station is at the northern end of this food

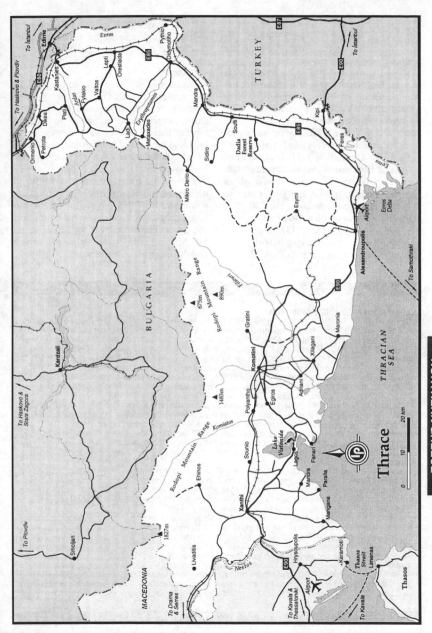

market and the bus station for Kavala is opposite the southern end on Eklission. The train station is 2km from town – just off the main Kavala-Xanthi road.

If you continue up 28 Oktovriou from Plateia Eleftherias, you will come to the central square of Plateia Kentriki, with a prominent clock tower on its western side. To reach the old town from here, continue north along Vasileos Konstantinou, a picturesque cobbled street. The post office is at A Giorgiou 16, and the OTE is at Michael Vogdou 2; both streets lead west from Plateia Kentriki. Walk one block up Vasileos Konstantinou, turn right and you'll see the National Bank of Greece on the left. The Olympic Airways office (☎ 22 944) is at Michael Vogdou 4, near the OTE.

There is no tourist office or tourist police in Xanthi, but the regular police (☎ 22 100), at 28 Oktovriou 223, will do what they can to help, bringing in an English speaker off the street if necessary.

Old Xanthi

Old Xanthi is built on a hillside overlooking the modern town. The narrow winding streets have some lovely neoclassical mansions, which once belonged to wealthy tobacco merchants. The more modest dwellings also have considerable charm; most are pastel coloured and have overhanging timber-framed floors.

Two of the old town's mansions, which adjoin one another, have been converted into a **museum**. They were built for the Koumtzogli brothers, who were tobacco magnates. The museum is well laid out and exhibits include traditional agricultural and household implements, carpets,

---

The Turkish Minority Question

The issue of the Turkish minority in Greece is a touchy and sensitive matter. The Treaty of Lausanne (1923) settled the boundaries of modern Turkey and resolved the territorial disputes raised in Anatolia by WWI. At the end of the war the Allies imposed the Treaty of Sévres (1920) on the defeated Ottoman Empire; it effectively dismembered the empire, leaving only Anatolia (minus a Greek enclave at Smyrna, or İzmir) under Turkish rule. This settlement was rejected by the Turkish nationalists led by Mustafa Kemal (later Kemal Atatürk). Although they accepted the loss of Iraq, Syria, Arabia, and other non-Turkish areas, they objected to the loss of Smyrna to Greece. After driving the Greek troops out of Smyrna and ousting the sultan, Kemal's government was able to force the negotiation of a new treaty, which was finally concluded at Lausanne, Switzerland, on July 24, 1923.

According to the Treaty of Lausanne, Turkey regained not only Smyrna but also eastern Thrace and some of the Aegean islands. It also resumed control of the Dardanelles (internationalised under the previous treaty) on the condition that they were kept demilitarised and open to all nations in peacetime. A separate agreement between Turkey and Greece provided for the exchange of minority populations. In the exchange, whole communities of Greeks and Turks were forcibly relocated to new homelands, with the exception of the Turks of central Thrace and the Greeks of İstanbul (Constantinople).

It is the result of this incomplete exchange of populations that is today causing Greece a considerable headache. Officially, there are no Turkish minorities in Greece, but 'Muslim Greeks'. However any visitor to Komotini and the villages around this town in central Thrace could easily be mistaken in believing that they are in Turkey. The Turkish language is spoken everywhere and it is hard to miss the women dressed in Muslim attire.

Paradoxically, and in a country where individual television satellite dishes cost a small fortune, there is not a Turkish-speaking village that does not sprout a forest of these expensive antennae, ostensibly for the purpose of receiving Turkish television and apparently paid for indirectly by the Turkish government, via its consulate in Thessaloniki. This 'Turkish Trojan Horse' positioned deep within Greece's vulnerable eastern flank causes jitters whenever the term 'Turkish minority' is raised. An unofficial visit in May 1995 by the Turkish minister for information, Yıldırım Aktouna, caused a storm when the said minister boldly called for greater self-determination for Greece's Turkish-speaking population. How Greece will handle this delicate issue in a region already beset by ethnic conflicts will be a subject of close scrutiny by all Balkan watchers. ■

embroidery and jewellery. While you're in the museum cast your eyes upwards to the ceilings, which are amazing. Some are made of carved wood, others are painted with intricate designs. Also, don't miss the antique toilet upstairs (no longer useable). The toilet's bowl is decorated both inside and out with elaborate floral designs.

Labelling of exhibits is in Greek, but the curator will do his best to explain things, although his English is limited. The museum is at Antika 7 and is open every day from 11 am to 1 pm. Admission is 300 dr.

Places to Stay – bottom end

The rather sleazy D-class *Lux Hotel* (☎ 22 341), Georgiou Stavriou 18, near Plateia Kentriki, has singles/doubles for 4000/5000 dr with shared bathroom. If you're coming from Vasileos Konstantinou, turn right at the National Bank of Greece to reach the hotel. The town's two clean and comfortable C-class hotels are much better options. The C-class *Hotel Dimokritos* (☎ 25 111; fax 25 537), 28 Oktovriou 41, near Plateia Kentriki, has single/double rates of 8000/10,450 dr with private bathroom. The C-class *Hotel Xanthippion* (☎ 77 061; fax 77 076), 28 Oktovriou 212, has singles/doubles for 11,000/14,000 dr with private bathroom. This hotel has a car park, and is at the southern end of town. Prices at both these places are negotiable most of the time.

Places to Stay – middle

Xanthi's best hotel is the modern B-class *Hotel Nestos* (☎ 27 531; fax 27 535). The rooms go for 14,000/17,500 dr with private bathroom. The hotel is 1km south of the town centre. Coming from Kavala by road, it's on the right as you enter the town. This hotel also has a car park.

Places to Eat

Locals rate the *Klimataria Restaurant* on Plateia Kentriki as the town's best eating place. It has a large selection of ready-made food: this author had fasolia, Greek salad and retsina and paid a comparatively pricey 2400 dr for the privilege.

Students hang out at *Haradra Taverna* which has outdoor eating in a walled garden. This restaurant only opens in the summer. Walk to the top of Vasileos Konstantinou and you will see a sign on a wall pointing left to the taverna. Turn left and you will find the restaurant immediately, though not obviously, to your left. A decent meal will cost about 2500 dr.

Close by, just where Paleologou begins to climb to old Xanthi, are two ouzeria, the *Kivotos* and the *Arhontissa*. Give them a try, if you can manage to order one or two mezedes in Greek. Keep track of what you are eating and drinking or the bill might be higher than you'd anticipated. Expect to pay over 2500 dr if you eat and drink at an ouzeri.

On Vasileos Konstantinou there are many *zaharoplasteia* (pastry shops) selling Turkish cakes and confectionery. One of the best of these is *Anesti*, at the northern end of the street, on the right.

Getting There & Away

Air Xanthi shares Hrysoupolis airport with Kavala in Macedonia (see the Kavala section for flight details). The airport is 47km away.

Bus From the main bus terminal there are eight buses a day to Komotini (45 minutes, 950 dr) and seven to Thessaloniki (four hours, 3300dr). There are no direct buses to Alexandroupolis; you must change buses at Komotini. Thessaloniki-bound buses go via Kavala (one hour, 1000 dr). Finally there are two daily buses to Athens (10 hours, 11,150 dr).

Train There are six trains a day to both Alexandroupolis (1½ hours, 860 dr) and Thessaloniki (four hours, 2160 dr). The Thessaloniki-bound intercity trains leave Xanthi in the morning and early evening. The equivalent services to Alexandroupolis depart mid-morning and early evening respectively. These trains attract a ticket supplement. The İstanbul-bound train calls by at the ungodly hour of 3.30 am – presumably to discourage travellers.

Train tickets may be purchased either at

the station; or from the OSE agent, Tarpidis Tours (☎ 22 277 or 27 840), at Tsaldari 5, which is in the Agora Nousa (an indoor shopping precinct) just east of Plateia Kentriki. A taxi to the train station will cost you about 600 dr.

Getting Around

The Airport There are no Olympic Airways buses to Hrysoupolis. A taxi costs 6000 dr. Alternatively you can take a Kavala-bound bus to the town of Hrysoupolis, and take a taxi to the airport 12km away.

KOMOTINI Κομοτηνή
• *pop 37,000* • *postcode 691 00* • *area code* ☎ *0531*
Komotini (Komotiní), 57km east of Xanthi, is the capital of the prefecture of Rodopi. Its population is half Greek and half Turkish. It lacks the character of Xanthi and is unremarkable except for its outstanding **archaeological museum** (☎ 22 411), Simeonidi 4, which houses well-displayed finds from little-known ancient sites in Thrace, most notably Abdera and Maronia.

The latter was Homer's Ismaros, where Odysseus obtained the wine which he used to intoxicate the Cyclops Polyphemus. While in this drunken state, Polyphemus had a stake driven into his one remaining eye by villagers who sought revenge for his misdeeds. (The scant remains of the ancient site of Maronia are near the modern village of Maronia, 31km south-east of Komotini.) The museum is well signposted and opening times are Tuesday to Sunday from 9 am to 5 pm. Admission is 500 dr.

The blinding of the Cyclops Polyphemus

Have a look at the **Museum of Folk Life & History** (☎ 25 975; fax 37 145), at Agiou Georgiou 13. It's worth a visit if you are in between buses. Housed in the Peïdi Mansion, the display has samples of home wares, manuscripts and costumes. The more important displays are labelled in English also. A useful book on the history of Komotini and the Rodopi prefecture is available for 1000 dr. Entrance to the museum is free. It is open from 10 am to 1 pm only; closed on Sunday. To get there, walk 100m right from the bus station, turn left onto Georgiou Mameli, walk another 100m and you will find it on your right.

Places to Stay

The nearest camp site to Komotini is *Fanari Komotinis Camping* (☎ 0535-31 217). The site is by the sea near the village of Fanari, about 26km south-east of Komotini.

If you get stuck in Komotini, finding a place to stay shouldn't be too much of a problem. Among the possibilities are the E-class *Hotel Hellas* (☎ 22 055), Dimokritou 31, where singles/doubles with shared bathroom are 4500/6500 dr. The *Pension Olympos* (☎ 37 690; fax 37 693), Orfeos 37, has singles/doubles with private bathroom for 8500/10,000 dr. The *Democritos Hotel* (☎ 22 579; fax 23 396), Plateia Vizynou 8, has singles/doubles for 10,500/15,500 dr with private bathroom.

The snazzy-looking *Hotel Astoria* (☎ 35 054; fax 22 707) right on Plateia Irinis has neat, modern single/double rooms with air-con for 14,000/19,000 dr. Most hotel prices are negotiable.

Getting There & Away

Bus There are frequent buses from Komotini to Xanthi (45 minutes, 850 dr) and Alexandroupolis (70 minutes, 1100 dr). There are also eight buses a day to Thessaloniki (4½ hours, 4200 dr) which all stop at Kavala (1½ hours, 1750 dr).

Train There are six trains a day to both Alexandroupolis (one hour, 590 dr) and Thessaloniki (4½ hours, 2500 dr). The Thessaloniki-bound intercity trains leave from Komotini in the morning and early evening. The equivalent services to Alexandroupolis depart at about midday and mid-evening. These trains attract a ticket supplement. The 4.08 am eastbound train goes to İstanbul.

ALEXANDROUPOLIS Αλεξανδρούπολη
• pop 37,000 • postcode 681 00 • area code ☎ 0551

Alexandroupolis (Alexandr**ou**polis), the capital of the prefecture of Evros, is a modern, dusty and prosaic town with a heavy military presence. Most travellers come here simply to transit east to Turkey, or to catch the ferry to Samothraki. Still, Alexandroupolis' maritime ambience and its liveliness all year round make it a pleasant stopover.

Alexandroupolis' hotels get surprisingly full, since Greek holiday-makers from northern Evros flock here in July and August. Their numbers are swelled by overlanders who descend upon the town en route to Turkey. During these months try to continue your journey to Samothraki or Turkey; otherwise, reserve accommodation in advance.

Orientation
The town is laid out roughly on a grid sys-

NORTHERN GREECE

PLACES TO STAY
2 Hotel Okeanis
3 Hotel Lido
5 Apartment Hotel Athina
10 Hera Hotel
18 Hotel Erika

PLACES TO EAT
13 Klimataria Restaurant
14 Neraïda Restaurant
16 Psarotaverna Anestis

OTHER
1 St Nicholas Cathedral & Ecclesiastical Art Museum of Alexandroupolis

4 Bus Station
6 Kikon Travel Agency
7 OTE
8 Municipal Tourist Office
9 National Bank of Greece
11 Folkloric & Historical Museum
12 Police
15 Vatitsis Shipping Agency
17 Train Station
19 Arsinoi ticket office
20 Lighthouse
21 Main Post Office
22 Olympic Airways Office
23 Ferries to Samothraki

THRACIAN SEA

To Samothraki

Alexandroupolis

0   125   250 m

tem, with the main streets running east-west, parallel with the waterfront, where the lively evening *volta* (promenade) takes place. Karaoli Dimitriou is at the eastern end of the waterfront, with Megalou Alexandrou at the western end. The town's most prominent landmark is the large 19th-century lighthouse on the middle of the waterfront. The two main squares are Plateia Eleftherias and Plateia Polytehniou. Both are just one block north of Karaoli Dimitriou.

The train station is on the waterfront just south of Plateia Eleftherias and east of the port where boats leave for Samothraki. The intercity bus station is at Eleftheriou Venizelou 36, five blocks inland. The local bus terminal is on Plateia Eleftherias.

Information

The municipal tourist office (☎ 24 998) is in the town hall on Dimokratias. The helpful staff dispense maps and have information on accommodation and transport.

The main post office is on the waterfront on the corner of Nikiforou Foka and Megalou Alexandrou. The OTE is on the corner of Mitropolitou Kaviri and Eleftheriou Venizelou.

The National Bank of Greece is at Dimokratias 246. The police (☎ 26 418) are at Karaïskaki 6. The port police telephone number is ☎ 26 468.

Things to See

The outstanding **Ecclesiastical Art Museum of Alexandroupolis** is one of the best of its kind in the country. It contains a priceless collection of icons and ecclesiastical ornaments brought to Greek Thrace by refugees from Asia Minor. Unfortunately, due to a cutback in government funding, the museum is unable to keep regular opening hours, but if you ring the bell of the offices next door, someone will show you around. Entrance is free. The museum is in the grounds of the St Nicholas Cathedral.

The **Folkloric and Historical Museum** (☎ 28 926) on the corner of Dimokratias and Kanari in a brand-new, swish building is organised by the Society of the Friends of

Antiquities of the Evros Prefecture. The displays offer an insight into the life and culture of Eastern Thrace. Opening hours are Tuesday to Saturday, 10.30 am to 1.30 pm and 6.30 to 9.30 pm. Visits on Sunday and holidays are by appointment only. Entry is free.

Places to Stay

The EOT-run *Camping Alexandroupolis* (☎ 28 735) is on the beach 2km west of the town. It's a clean, well-run site with good facilities. Take a local bus from Plateia Eleftherias to reach the site.

The *Hotel Lido* (☎ 28 808), Paleologou 15, is an outstanding D-class hotel with comfortable single/double rooms for 3500/4500 dr with shared bathroom, and 6000/6500 dr for doubles/triples with private bathroom. The hotel is one block north of the bus station. The *Hotel Erika* (☎ 34 115; fax 34 117), is a very superior D-class place where room rates are a rather high 10,000/12,000 dr for its singles/doubles. All rooms have private bathroom, telephone, TV and balcony. The hotel is on the corner of Karaoli Dimitriou and Kountourioti.

The C-class *Hotel Okeanis* (☎ 28 830; fax 34 118) on Paleologou 20, almost opposite the Lido, has excellent, spacious single/double rooms for 10,000/14,950 dr. C-class *Hera Hotel* (☎ 23 941; fax 34 222) on Leoforos Dimokratias 179, closer to the railway station, has pricey, but smaller rooms for 12,650/15,400 dr.

One other excellent option for groups of two or more is the *Apartment Hotel Athina* (☎ 34 492; fax 37 301) at Paleologou 53. Here you can be self-contained with air-con and modern kitchen facilities. Doubles here go for 22,000 dr and suites for three to five people are 27,500 dr. Prices are negotiable and are usually considerably lower than these published rates.

Places to Eat

The *Neraïda Restaurant*, on Kyprou where it widens to form a small square, is a good choice and has a range of standard fare and some local specialities for 1600 to 2200 dr.

In a similar vein and with similar prices, but with an English language menu that takes some beating, is the *Klimataria* which is diagonally opposite the Neraïda.

For a special treat at night, try a restaurant not on the usual tourist beat. The *Psarotaverna Anestis*, on Athanasiou Diakou 5, one street east of Kyprou, looks very unassuming, but has a fine choice of mezedes, especially those with fish. Mydia saganaki (chilli mussels) are highly recommended. Prices are reasonable for a fish taverna.

Getting There & Away

Air The Olympic Airlines office (☎ 26 361) is at Ellis 6. Alexandroupolis' domestic Dimokritos airport, which is 7km east of town and near the village of Loutra, does receive occasional international charter flights. The airport has a morning and evening flight to Athens and possibly extra flights in summer. The cost is 17,100 dr.

Bus From Alexandroupolis' bus station there are frequent buses to Soufli, Didymotiho, Orestiada (two hours, 1800 dr) and Komotini (70 minutes, 1100 dr). There are six buses a day to Thessaloniki (six hours, 5200 dr) via Xanthi and Kavala.

For what it's worth, there is one daily bus to Athens (12 hours, 12,700 dr).

Turkey There is a daily OSE bus to İstanbul, leaving at 8.30 am. The journey takes between five and seven hours and costs 4000 dr. There are currently no private buses running to Turkey, but Kikon Travel Agency (☎ 25 455; fax 34 755), Eleftheriou Venizelou 68, can organise for you to join a bus group departing from Thessaloniki.

Otherwise, you can take a bus from the intercity bus station to the border town of Kipi (three departures a day, 700 dr), 43km from Alexandroupolis. You cannot walk across the border but it is easy enough to hitch across – you may be lucky and get a lift all the way to İstanbul. Otherwise take a bus to İpsala (5km beyond the border) or Keşan (30km beyond the border) from where there are many buses to İstanbul.

Bulgaria There is a private bus service to Plovdiv (7000 dr) and Sofia (8000 dr) which departs from Alexandroupolis on Wednesday and Sunday at 8.30 am. Return dates and times from Bulgaria are the same. Contact Kikon Travel Agency (☎ 25 455; fax 34 755), Eleftheriou Venizelou 68, for details.

Train There are five trains a day to Thessaloniki (seven hours, 3000 dr), including one which continues on to Athens and intermediate stations (14 hours, 6700 dr). Two of these are intercity services; the *Alexandros* terminates in Thessaloniki and the *Vergina* terminates in Athens – both attract a ticket supplement. There are also seven trains a day to Dikea via Pythio, Didymotiho, Orestiada and Kastanies for the Turkish border crossing. However, only the 5.15, 5.45 and 9.45 am services will get you to Kastanies in time to cross the border before it closes at 1 pm.

Turkey There is one train a day to İstanbul, which currently leaves Alexandroupolis in the early morning. This time is subject to frequent changes, so check with OSE. Tickets cost 5350 dr and the journey can take 10 hours. The train is hot and crowded in summer – the OSE bus is a marginally better choice.

Bulgaria There is one service a day to Svilengrad with an ongoing connection to Plovdiv and Sofia. The ticket costs 2800 dr as far as Svilengrad and the trip takes four hours. The train currently leaves Alexandroupolis at 5.20 am. Double-check with OSE in case of any timetable change.

Ferry In July and August there are two to three sailings a day to Samothraki. In spring and autumn there are two and in winter, one. Tickets for the *Saos* ferry and the latest departure details may be obtained from Vatitsis Shipping Agency (☎ 26 721; fax 32 007), Kyprou 5 (opposite the port), or for the *Arsinoi* ferry from the Arsinoi ticket office (☎ 22 215; fax 24 256) diagonally opposite.

Tickets cost 2200 dr and the trip takes two hours.

There is a weekly summer ferry to Rhodes, via five other islands en route. Sample base prices are: Limnos (2440 dr), Lesvos (4100 dr) and Rhodes (9500 dr). Contact Kikon Travel Agency (see details previously) for tickets and reservations.

Hydrofoil Hydrofoil (Flying Dolphin) services occasionally operate during the summer months, linking Alexandroupolis with Limnos and sometimes destinations further afield. Tickets to Limnos cost 5000 dr. Contact the Arsinoi ticket office for full details.

Getting Around
The Airport There is no airport shuttle bus. Take a Loutra-bound bus from Plateia Eleftherias. A taxi to the airport will cost about 1200 dr.

EVROS DELTA Δέλτα Εβρου
The Evros delta, 20km south-east of Alexandroupolis, is ecologically one of Europe's most important wetlands. Three hundred species of birds have been recorded, including the last 15 surviving pairs of royal eagles; and more than 200,000 migrating waterfowl spend part of their winter here. Unfortunately, the wetlands are in a highly sensitive area due to their proximity to Turkey, and permission from the security police in Alexandroupolis is technically required in order to visit. Contact the regular police or the Feres municipal tourist office (☎ 0555-22 211) for further information on organised tours.

ALEXANDROUPOLIS TO DIDYMOTIHO
North-east of Alexandroupolis the road, railway line and River Evros run close together, skirting the Turkish border. This is a highly sensitive area with many signs prohibiting photography. It's also a lush and attractive region with fields of wheat and sunflowers, and forests of pine trees.

Feres, 29km north-east of Alexandroupolis, has the interesting 12th-century Byzantine Church of Panagia Kosmosotira. It is signposted from the main road.

Continuing north, the little town of **Soufli**, 67km north-east of Alexandroupolis and 31km south of Didymotiho, has lots of character. It has retained a number of its Turkish wattle-and-daub houses and is renowned in Greece for its production of silk. This is because the mulberry tree, upon which the silkworms feed, used to thrive in the region.

Unfortunately, most of the mulberry trees have been chopped down to make way for crops, but the town still has one silk factory.

Soufli has an interesting **silk museum** with a display of silk-producing equipment. The museum is signposted from the town's main through road, but opening times are subject to change.

If you decide to spend the night in Soufli, the D-class *Egnatia Hotel* (☎ 0554-22 124), Vasileos Georgiou 225, has singles/doubles for 4000/6000 dr with shared bathroom. The most up-market place to stay is the C-class *Hotel Orpheas* (☎ 0554-22 922; fax 22 305), on the corner of Vasileos Georgiou and Tsimiski. Rates are 8700/13,000 dr with private bathroom.

Soufli is on the Alexandroupolis to Didymotiho bus and train routes.

DIDYMOTIHO Διδυμότειχο
• *pop 8500* • *postcode 683 00* • *area code* ☎ *0553*
Didymotiho (Didimotiho) is the most interesting of the towns north of Alexandroupolis, although few tourists venture here. The town's name derives from the double walls that once enclosed it (*didymo* – 'twin', *tihos* – 'wall').

In Byzantine times it was an important town. When it fell to the Turks in 1361, Murad I made it the capital. In 1365 he transferred the capital to Adrianople (present-day Edirne). The town's most prominent landmark is a large mosque, with a pyramidal-shaped roof, on Plateia Kentriki.

Fifteen per cent of the town's population is Turkish and there are also Gypsies here.

Orientation & Information

Orientation is easy in this small town, as almost everything you need is on or near Plateia Kentriki, the central square, which you can't miss because of the mosque. The OTE and the National Bank of Greece are on Plateia Kentriki and the post office is just north of here. Walk along Vasileos Alexandrou, and take the first left into Kolokotroni, and it's on the right.

To get to Plateia Kentriki from the bus station, walk along the road straight ahead, and turn right into Venizelou, which is the town's main thoroughfare – the square is at the end of here. From the train station turn left, keep walking to 25 Maïou, and continue along here to Venizelou. There is no tourist office or tourist police.

Things to See

Didymotiho is yet another place to wander in. With the mosque on your left, walk straight ahead from Plateia Kentriki to the picturesque, tree-shaded Plateia Vatrahou ('Frog Square' in English), so named because of its frog-shaped fountain. Continue straight ahead up Metaxa. In this area there are many Turkish timber-framed houses. Continue uphill to the **Cathedral of Agios Athanasios**. Next to the cathedral are some well-preserved sections of the town's Byzantine walls.

If you walk back down Metaxa, and turn left into Vatatzi, you will come to the **folk museum** on the right. This outstanding museum has displays of Thracian costumes; 19th and early 20th-century agricultural equipment and household implements; and a reconstructed kitchen from a 1920s house. The museum is open Wednesday and Thursday from 5 to 8 pm and on weekends from 10 am to 2 pm. Call ☎ 0554-22 154 if you wish to visit out of hours.

Construction of the **mosque** on Plateia Kentriki was started by Murad I and finished by his son, Bayazıt, in 1368. It is the oldest and largest mosque in Europe. Its minaret, which has two intricate ornate balconies, has lost its top, all the windows are smashed and the walls are crumbling. It is still obvious,

however, that it must once have been a fine building.

Places to Stay

Didymotiho has two hotels. The tidy D-class *Hotel Anesis* (☎ 24 850) has single/double rooms for 7800/9400 dr with private bathroom. The hotel is on the left side of Vasileos Alexandrou, coming from Plateia Kentriki. The other option is the posh B-class *Hotel Plotini* (☎ 23 400; fax 22 251), Agias Paraskevis 1, 1km south of town on the road to Alexandroupolis – approaching the town, it's on the left. Rooms here go for 9000/16,000 dr.

Places to Eat

Fast-food and cheap souvlaki places are on Venizelou. *Zythestiatorio Kipsilaki*, opposite the OTE, is about the only place resembling a traditional eatery within the central area. At lunchtime a meal will cost you about 1800 dr with wine.

Didymotiho has some fine old *kafeneia*. The one at the top of Kolokotroni looks as if it's jumped straight out of the museum opposite. The one on Plateia Vatrahou has tables and chairs set under shady plane trees.

Getting There & Away

There are many buses a day from Alexandroupolis to Didymotiho (two hours, 1000 dr). There are also seven trains a day from Alexandroupolis (three hours, 750 dr).

NORTH OF DIDYMOTIHO

From Didymotiho the road continues for another 20km to **Orestiada** (population 13,000). This town was built in the 1920s to house refugees who came from Turkey during the population exchange. It's a modern town with little character. If you get stuck it has a couple of budget hotels. The cheapest one is the D-class *Hotel Acropolis* (☎ 0552-22 277), Vasileos Konstantinou 48, where singles/doubles are 4000/7000 dr with private bathroom. The C-class *Hotel Vienna* (☎ 0552-22 578; fax 22 258), Orestou 64, has rates of 10,000/13,500 dr with private bathroom.

NORTHERN GREECE

The best hotel in this area is the gaudily-coloured *Hotel Electra* (☎ 0552-23 540; fax 23 133), at A Pantazinou 50. The rooms here cost 8500/12,000 dr.

On the same street as the Electra, some 300m north on the right, is the *Koutoukaki* grill and restaurant. Their chicken and draught retsina are recommended and are very good value.

It's another 19km to **Kastanies**, Greece's northern road-border point into Turkey. Unless you're planning to continue to Turkey there's little point coming here.

If you cross the border into Turkey the first town you'll arrive at is the eastern Thracian town of **Edirne**, 9km from Kastanies. The town (formerly called Adrianoupolis) is overlooked by most tourists and retains much of its traditional character. If you want to cross the border here by bus, the municipal tourist offices in Alexandroupolis will provide you with information. Bear in mind that the border crossing is only open from 9 am to 1 pm, so time your arrival at the border accordingly. Three morning trains will get you to the border in time for the crossing (see the Alexandroupolis section earlier in this chapter).

The Islands

Saronic Gulf Islands
Νησιά του Σαρωνικού

The five islands of the Saronic Gulf are the closest group to Athens. The closest, Salamis, is little more than a suburb of the sprawling capital. Aegina is also close enough to Athens for people to commute to work. Along with Poros, the next island south, it is a popular package-holiday destination. Hydra, once famous as the rendezvous of artists, writers and beautiful people, manages to retain an air of superiority and grandeur. Spetses, the most southerly island in the group, receives an inordinate number of British package tourists.

Spetses has the best beaches, but these islands are not the place to be if long stretches of golden sand are what you want. With the exception of the Temple of Aphaia, on Aegina, the islands have no significant archaeological remains.

The islands are a very popular escape for Athenians. Accommodation can be nigh on impossible to find between mid-June and mid-September, and weekends are busy all year round. If you plan to go at these times, it's a good idea to reserve a room in advance.

The islands have a reputation for high prices, which is a bit misleading. What is true is that there are very few places for budget travellers to stay – no camp sites and only a couple of cheap hotels. There is good accommodation available if you are happy to pay 10,000 dr or more for a double. Midweek visitors can get some good deals. Food is no more expensive than anywhere else.

The Saronic Gulf is named after the mythical King Saron of Argos, a keen hunter who drowned while pursuing a deer that had swum into the gulf to escape.

Getting There & Away
Ferry At least 10 ferries a day sail from Piraeus' Great Harbour to Aegina town

HIGHLIGHTS

- Rambling through the ruins of the old town of Paleohora on Aegina
- Views over the Saronic Gulf from the Temple of Aphaia on Aegina
- Accommodation in Hydra's gracious old stone mansions
- Exploring the back roads of Spetses by motorcycle

(1½ hours, 1190 dr). Many continue to Methana in the Peloponnese (two hours, 1350 dr), and Poros (3½ hours, 1650 dr); two or three continue from Poros to Hydra (4½ hours, 1950 dr), Ermioni in the Peloponnese (five hours, 2600 dr), and Spetses (5½ hours, 2600 dr).

Hydrofoil The Ceres Group operates a busy schedule to the islands and nearby Peloponnesian ports with its fleet of Flying Dolphin hydrofoils. Services to Hydra, Poros and Spetses leave from Zea Marina in Piraeus; services to Aegina leave from the Great

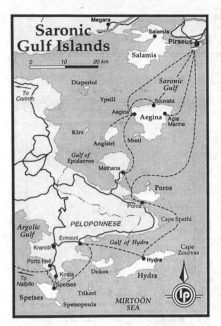

Athens for 17,000 dr, which includes a buffet lunch. The cruises operate all year.

Trekking Hellas (☎ 01-325 0853), Filellinon 7, Athens, organises seven-day caïque tours through the Saronic Gulf. The tours include short treks on all the major islands as well as visits to some of the smaller islets.

Aegina Αίγινα

• *pop 11,000* • *postcode 180 10* • *area code* ☎ *0297*
Unassuming Aegina (**Eyee**na) was once a major player in the Hellenic world, thanks largely to its strategic position at the mouth of the Saronic Gulf. It began to emerge as a commercial centre in about 1000 BC. By the 7th century BC, it was the premier maritime power in the region and amassed great wealth through its trade with Egypt and Phoenicia. The silver 'turtle' coins minted on the island at this time are thought to be the first coins produced in Europe. The Aeginian fleet made a major contribution on the Greek side at the Battle of Salamis.

Athens, uneasy about Aegina's maritime prowess, attacked the island in 459 BC; defeated, Aegina was forced to pull down its city walls and surrender its fleet. It did not recover.

The island's other brief moment in the spotlight came in 1827-29, when it was declared the temporary capital of partly liberated Greece. The first coins of the modern Greek nation were minted here.

Aegina has since slipped into a humbler role as Greece's premier producer of pistachio nuts. The writer Nikos Kazantzakis was fond of the island and wrote *Zorba the Greek* while living in a house in Livadi, just north of Aegina town.

According to mythology, Aegina – named after the daughter of the river god, Asopus – was abducted by Zeus and taken to the island. Aegina's son by Zeus, Aeacus, was the grandfather of Achilles of Trojan War fame.

Getting There & Away
Ferry In summer there are at least 10 ferries

Harbour. See individual island entries for details. Ceres also operates high-speed catamarans on some routes. These Flying Cats, as the company calls them, have both economy and VIP classes. Economy fares are the same as for hydrofoils. VIP class costs an extra 7500 dr, and gets you a plush red-leather seat, free drinks and headphone music.

Getting Around
There is a comprehensive network of ferries and hydrofoils linking the Saronic Gulf islands. See individual island entries for details.

Organised Tours The *Aegean Glory* does a daily cruise from Piraeus to the islands of Aegina, Poros and Hydra. Passengers get to spend about an hour on shore at each island – long enough to buy a souvenir and take the obligatory 'been-there, done-that photo'. You'll see the cruise advertised all over

a day from Aegina town to Piraeus (1½ hours, 1190 dr) as well as services from Agia Marina (1000 dr) and Souvala (950 dr). There are at least three boats a day to Poros (1½ hours, 1050 dr) via Methana (40 minutes, 800 dr), and a daily boat to Hydra (two hours, 1450 dr) and Spetses (three hours, 2000 dr). The ferry companies have ticket offices at the quay, where you'll find a full list of the day's sailings.

Hydrofoil The easiest way of getting to Aegina is on the hydrofoils that operate almost hourly from 7 am to 8 pm between Aegina town and the Great Harbour at Piraeus (35 minutes, 2182 dr). Two others go to Zea Marina (2136 dr). Four hydrofoils a day go to Methana (20 minutes, 1804 dr) and Poros (40 minutes, 2206 dr). Two continue to Hydra (1¼ hours, 2836 dr), Ermioni (1½ hours, 3595 dr) and Spetses (two hours, 4237 dr); and one keeps going to Porto Heli (2½ hours, 4469 dr) in the Peloponnese. There is only one service on Sunday from Aegina to the other islands. It goes right through to Porto Heli.

From mid-May until the end of September, there's a service from Aegina to Nafplio

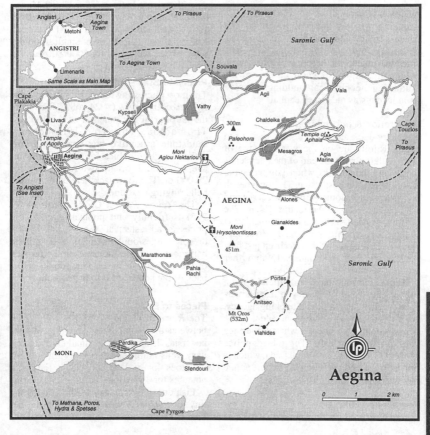

(3¼ hours, 6594 dr) daily except Sunday, travelling via Tolo.

Hydrofoil tickets are sold at the quay in Aegina town.

Getting Around
Frequent buses go from Aegina town to Agia Marina (30 minutes, 350 dr), via Paleohora and the Temple of Aphaia. Other buses go to Perdika (15 minutes, 210 dr) and Souvala (20 minutes, 250 dr). Departure times are displayed outside the ticket office in Plateia Ethnegersias.

There are numerous places to hire motorcycles.

AEGINA TOWN
Aegina town, on the west coast, is the island's capital and main port. The town is a charming and bustling, if slightly ramshackle, place; its harbour is lined with colourful caïques. Several of the town's crumbling neoclassical buildings survive from its days as the Greek capital.

Orientation & Information
The ferry dock and nearby small quay used by hydrofoils are on the western edge of town. A left turn at the end of the quay leads to Plateia Ethnegersias, where you'll find the bus terminal and post office. The town beach is 200m further along. A right turn at the end of the quay leads to the main harbour. The OTE is off Aiakou, which heads inland next to the port authority building. The National Bank of Greece is on the waterfront just past Aiakou, and the Credit Bank is 150m further around the harbour.

Aegina doesn't have an official tourist office. The 'Tourist Office' you'll see advertised on the waterfront is a booking agency, which will do no more than add a 25% commission to the price of whatever service you care to nominate. The tourist police (☎ 23 333) are on Leonardou Lada, which is opposite the hydrofoil quay. The port police have a kiosk at the hydrofoil quay.

Temple of Apollo
'Temple' is a bit of a misnomer for the one Doric column which stands at this site. This column is all that's left of the 5th-century Temple of Apollo which once stood on the Hill of Koloni. The hill was the site of the ancient acropolis, and there are remains of a Helladic settlement. The site, on the far side of the town beach, also has a small **museum**. Both are open Tuesday to Sunday from 8.30 am to 3 pm. Admission is 500 dr.

Places to Stay – bottom end
The best place to head for is the *Hotel Plaza* (☎ 25 600), on the waterfront 100m past Plateia Ethnegersias. It has good singles/ doubles overlooking the sea for 4000/7000 dr with private bathroom. *Antonios Marmarinos Rooms to Rent* (☎ 22 954), next to the Hotel Marmarinos at the top of Leonardou Lada, has very clean, quiet singles/doubles with private bathroom for 5000/8000 dr.

Places to Stay – middle
The most interesting rooms in town are at the *Eginitiko Arhontiko* (☎ 24 968), 100m from the harbour at the junction of Aiakou and Thomaïdou. This fine 19th-century sandstone arhontiko has beautifully furnished singles/doubles for 9200/12,700 dr, and a splendid, ornate two-room suite for 28,000 dr. The drawback here is the church bells ringing next door.

The *Xenon Pavlou Guest House* (☎ 22 795) is friendly and popular, even if the prices are a bit steep at 9000/11,000/ 13,000 dr for singles/doubles/triples with private bathroom. The guesthouse is on the far side of the harbour from the ferry dock, at the back of the square next to the church.

Places to Eat
The *Restaurant Lekka*, on the waterfront between the Hotel Plaza and Plateia Ethnegersias, is an excellent small taverna. It is very reasonably priced, serving stuffed tomatoes for 800 dr and baked fish with potatoes for 1200 dr.

Fish doesn't come any fresher than at the tiny *Restaurant Agora*, at Pan Irioti 47, behind the fish market.

Local pistachio nuts are on sale everywhere at about 900 dr for 500 grams.

AROUND AEGINA
Temple of Aphaia
The splendid, well-preserved Doric Temple of Aphaia, a local deity of pre-Hellenic times, is the major ancient site of the Saronic Gulf islands. It was built in 480 BC when Aegina was at its most powerful.

The temple's pediments were decorated with outstanding Trojan War sculptures, most of which were spirited away in the 19th century and eventually fell into the hands of Ludwig I (father of King Otho). They now have pride of place in Munich's Glyptothek. The temple is impressive even without these sculptures. It stands on a pine-covered hill and commands imposing vistas of the Saronic Gulf and Cape Sounion.

The site (☎ 32 398) is open Monday to Friday from 8.15 am to 7 pm and Saturday and Sunday from 8.30 am to 3 pm. Admission is 800 dr. Aphaia is 10km east of Aegina. Buses to Agia Marina stop at the site.

Paleohora Παλαιοχώρα
The ruins of Paleohora, on a hillside 6.5km east of Aegina town, are fascinating to explore. The town was the island's capital from the 9th century to 1826, after pirate attacks had forced the islanders to flee the coast and settle inland. (It didn't do them much good when the notorious pirate Barbarossa arrived in 1537, laid waste to the town and took the inhabitants off into slavery.)

The ruins are far more extensive than at first appearance. The only buildings left intact are the churches. There are more than two dozen of them, in various states of disrepair, dotted around the hillside. Beautiful frescoes can be seen in some of them.

In the valley below Paleohora is **Moni Agiou Nektariou**, an important place of pilgrimage. The monastery contains the relics of a hermit monk, Anastasios Kefalas, who died in 1920. When his body was exhumed in 1940 it was found to have mummified – a sure sign of sainthood in Greek Orthodoxy, especially after a lifetime of performing miracle cures. Kefalas was canonised in 1961 – the first Orthodox saint of the 20th century. The enormous new church that has been built to honour him is a spectacular sight beside the road to Agia Marina. A track leads south from here to the 16th-century **Moni Hysoleontissas**, in a lovely mountain setting.

The bus from Aegina town to Agia Marina stops at the turn-off to Paleohora.

Beaches
Beaches are not Aegina's strong point. The east coast town of **Agia Marina** is the island's premier tourist resort, but the beach is no great shakes – if you can see it for package tourists. There are a couple of sandy patches that almost qualify as beaches between Aegina and Perdika, at the southern tip of the west coast.

MONI & ANGISTRI ISLETS
Νήσος Μονή & Νήσος Αγκίστρι
The Moni and Angistri islets lie off the west coast of Aegina, opposite Perdika. Moni, the smaller of the two, is a 10-minute boat ride from Perdika – frequent boats do the trip in summer.

Angistri is much bigger with around 500 inhabitants. There's a sandy beach at the port and other smaller beaches around the coast. Both package-holiday tourists and independent travellers find their way to Angistri, which has tavernas, hotels and domatia. In summer, five caïques a day do the 25-minute trip from Aegina town to Angistri (400 dr).

Poros Πόρος

• *pop 4000* • *postcode 180 20* • *area code* ☎ *0298*
The island of Poros is little more than a stone's throw from the mainland. The slender passage of water that separates it from the Peloponnesian town of Galatas is only 360m wide at its narrowest point.

Poros was once two islands, Kalavria and Sferia. These days they are connected by a

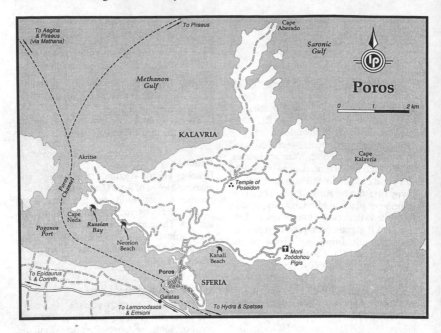

narrow isthmus, cut by a canal for small boats and rejoined by a road bridge. The vast majority of the population lives on the small volcanic island of Sferia, which is more than half-covered by the town of Poros. Sferia hangs like an appendix from the southern coast of Kalavria, a large, well-forested island that has all the package hotels. The town of Poros is not wildly exciting, but it can be used as a base for exploring the ancient sites of the adjacent Peloponnese.

Getting There & Away

Ferry There are eight ferries a day to Piraeus (three hours, 1650 dr), via Methana and Aegina; three a day to Hydra (one hour, 850 dr); and at least one to Spetses (two hours, 1410 dr). The ticket agencies are opposite the ferry dock.

Small boats shuttle constantly between Poros and Galatas (85 dr) on the mainland. They leave from the quay opposite Plateia Iroön in Poros town.

Hydrofoil There are up to 10 hydrofoils a day from Poros to Zea Marina (3500 dr), as well as two a day to the Great Harbour in Piraeus (3550 dr). Direct services take an hour; those via Methana and Aegina take 1½ hours.

There are four hydrofoils a day to Aegina (40 minutes, 2226 dr), up to nine to Hydra (30 minutes, 1527 dr) and eight to Spetses (one hour, 2442 dr). Less frequent services operate to Ermioni, Leonidio, Nafplio, Neapoli, Tolo and Tyros.

The Flying Dolphin agency is on Plateia Iroön, and has a timetable of departures outside.

Getting Around

The Poros bus operates almost constantly along a route that starts near the hydrofoil dock on Plateia Iroön in Poros town. It crosses to Kalavria and goes east along the south coast as far as Moni Zoödohou Pigis (210 dr), then turns around and heads west as far as Neorion beach. Numerous places along the waterfront offer bikes for hire, both motorised and pedal-powered. Motor Stelios, next to Family Tours, rents out 50cc mopeds for 3000 dr per day, good mountain bikes for 1500 dr and regular bikes for around 1000 dr.

Some of the boats operating between Poros and Galatas switch to ferrying tourists to beaches in summer. Operators stand on the waterfront and call out their destinations.

POROS TOWN

Poros town is the island's only settlement. It's a pretty place of white houses with terracotta-tiled roofs, and there are wonderful views over to the mountains of Argolis. It is a very popular weekend destination for Athenians as well as for package tourists and cruise ships.

Orientation & Information

The main ferry dock is at the western tip of Poros town, overlooked by the striking blue-domed clock tower. A left turn from the dock puts you on the waterfront road leading to Kalavria. The OTE building is on the right after 100m. A right turn at the ferry dock leads along the waterfront facing Galatas. The first square (triangle actually) is Plateia Iroön, which is where the hydrofoils dock. The bus leaves from next to the kiosk at the eastern end of the square.

The next square along is Plateia Karamanou, home of the post office. The National Bank of Greece is 500m further along the waterfront. The Credit Bank, on Plateia Iroön, is more convenient.

Poros does not have a tourist office. The tourist police (☎ 22 462/254) are 300m past the National Bank on the waterfront, above the Meskes music bar.

Suzi's Laundrette Service, next to the OTE, charges 2000 dr to wash and dry a 5kg load.

Places to Stay – bottom end

The nearest camp site to town is *Camping Kyragelo* (☎ 24 520), 600m north-west of Galatas on the mainland. It's open from May to October and charges 800 dr per person and 400 dr per tent. It also has a few basic double rooms for 3000 dr.

Poros itself has very little cheap accommodation. The cheapest rooms are at the *Hotel Aktaion* (☎ 22 281) on Plateia Iroön, which charges 6000/7300 dr for basic singles/doubles with shared bathroom.

The *Hotel Latsi* (☎ 22 392), 600m from the ferry dock on the road to Kalavria, has doubles with shared bathroom for 5000 dr as well as singles/doubles/triples for 6000/8000/11,000 dr with private bathroom.

If things are not too hectic, you may be offered a room by one of the domatia owners when you get off the ferry. Otherwise, head left along the waterfront and turn right at the sign to the Litrivi bar. There are lots of *domatia* on the streets around here.

Places to Stay – middle

The place to be for a room with a view is the charming *Villa Tryfon* (☎ 22 215 or 25 854), on top of the hill overlooking the port. The double rooms are 9000 dr, and all have private bathroom and kitchen facilities as well as great views over to Kalavria. To get there, turn left from the ferry dock and take the first right up the steps 20m past the Agricultural Bank of Greece. Turn left at the top of the steps on Aikaterinis Hatzopoulou Karra, and you will see the place signposted up the steps to the right after 150m.

The Seven Brothers Hotel (☎ 23 412), Plateia Iroön, is a smart C-class hotel with large, comfortable singles/doubles for 12,000/15,000 dr.

The travel agents opposite the ferry dock also handle accommodation. They include Hellenic Sun Travel (☎ 22 636; fax 25 653) and Family Tours (☎ 23 743; fax 24 480).

Places to Eat

O Pantelis Taverna is a lively, unpretentious place next to the markets on the backstreet running between Plateia Iroön and Plateia Karamanou.

The seafront facing Galatas is lined with restaurants offering virtually identical menus. Seafood dominates, and most main courses are priced around 1500 dr.

If you're prepared to spend a bit more, the upmarket *Taverna Sotiri*, 100m before the police station, on the waterfront facing Galatas, is the place. The food is excellent, but you will need to get in early. The place gets packed after 9 pm.

The *Taverna Platanos*, uphill from the Litrivi bar on Dimosthenous, has excellent spit-roast meat (chicken, lamb or pork) and a great setting beneath a huge old plane tree.

Entertainment

The *Litrivi Bar*, on Dimosthenous, specialises in revelry of the Greek-dancing, plate-smashing kind. It's open from 11 pm until late between April and November.

AROUND POROS

Poros has few places of interest and its beaches are no great shakes. **Kanali beach**, on Kalavria 1km east of the bridge, is a mediocre pebble beach. **Neorion beach**, 3km west of the bridge, is marginally better.

The best beach is reputedly at **Russian bay**, 1.5km past Neorion.

The 18th-century **Moni Zoödohou Pigis** has a beautiful gilded iconostasis which came from Asia Minor and is decorated with paintings from the gospels. The monastery, on Kalavria, is well-signposted and is 4km east of Poros town.

From the road below the monastery you can strike inland to the 6th-century **Temple of Poseidon**. The god of the sea and earthquakes was the principal deity worshipped on Poros. There's very little left of this temple, but the walk is worthwhile for the scenery on the way. From the site there are superb views of the Saronic Gulf and the Peloponnese. The orator Demosthenes, after failing to shake off the Macedonians who were after him for inciting the city-states to rebel, committed suicide here in 322 BC.

From the ruins you can continue along the road, which eventually winds back to the bridge. The road is drivable, but it's also a fine 6km walk that will take around 1½ hours.

PELOPONNESIAN MAINLAND

The Peloponnesian mainland opposite Poros can easily be explored from the island.

A couple of kilometres south-east of **Galatas** are the vast citrus groves of **Lemonodasos**.

About 9km north-west of Galatas is the ancient site of **Troizen**, legendary birthplace of Theseus. Take a bus to Dhamala, 6km from Galatas, and walk to the site from there. Alternatively, a Methana-bound bus will let you off at Agios Georgios, from where it is a 3km walk inland to the site.

Camping Kyragelo is about 1km northwest of Galatas (see the preceding Places to Stay section). There are also a couple of hotels and domatia in town.

Getting There & Around

Small boats do the five-minute run between Galatas and Poros (85 dr) every 10 minutes. A couple of buses a day depart for Nafplio (two hours, 1300 dr) and can drop you off at the ancient site of Epidaurus (see the Peloponnese chapter for details on this site).

The district around Galatas is ideal for exploring by bicycle. These can be hired on the seafront in Galatas.

Hydra Υδρα

• *pop 3000* • *postcode 180 10* • *area code* ☎ *0298*

Hydra (**Ee**dra) is the Saronic Gulf island with the most style. The gracious stone, white and pastel mansions of Hydra town are stacked up the rocky hillsides that surround the fine natural harbour. The first foreigners to be seduced by the beauty of Hydra were the film-makers who began arriving in the 1950s; the island was used as a location for the film *Boy on a Dolphin*, among others. The artists and writers moved in next, followed by the celebrities, and nowadays it seems the whole world is welcomed ashore.

If you've been in Greece for some time you may fall in love with Hydra for one reason alone: the absence of kamikaze motorcyclists. Hydra has no motorised

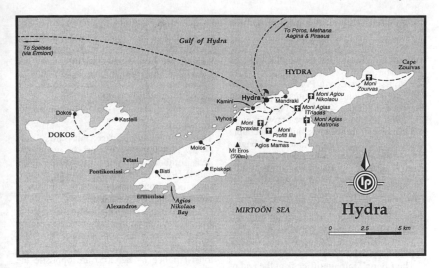

transport except for sanitation and construction vehicles. Donkeys (hundreds of them) are the only means of transport.

The name Hydra suggests that the island once had plenty of water. Legend has it that the island was once covered with forests, which were destroyed by fire. Whatever the story, these days the island is almost totally barren and imports its water from the Peloponnese.

History

Like many of the Greek islands, Hydra was ignored by the Turks, so many Greeks from the Peloponnese settled on the island to escape Ottoman suppression and taxes. The population was further boosted by an influx of Albanians. Agriculture was impossible, so these new settlers began building boats. By the 19th century, the island had become a great maritime power. The canny Hydriots made a fortune by running the British blockade of French ports during the Napoleonic Wars. The wealthy shipping merchants built most of the town's grand old *arhontika* from the considerable profits. It became a fashionable resort for Greek socialites, and lavish balls were a regular feature.

Hydra made a major contribution to the War of Independence. Without the 130 ships supplied by the island, the Greeks wouldn't have had much of a fleet with which to blockade the Turks. It also supplied leadership in the form of Georgios Koundouriotis, who was president of the emerging Greek nation's national assembly from 1822 to 1827, and Admiral Andreas Miaoulis, who commanded the Greek fleet. Streets and squares all over Greece are named after these two.

A mock battle is staged in Hydra harbour during the Miaoulia Festival held in honour of Admiral Miaoulis in late June.

Getting There & Away

Ferry Ventouris Lines has ferries to Piraeus (3½ hours, 1950 dr) from Monday to Saturday at 3.55 and 6.30 pm and on Sunday at noon, 1.45 and 5.30 pm. They sail via Poros (850 dr), Methana (1300 dr) and Aegina (1350 dr). There is a daily boat to Spetses (one hour, 950 dr), leaving between 10.30 and 11.30 am. Ferry departures are listed on a board at the ferry dock.

You can buy your tickets from Idreoniki Travel (☎ 54 007), just off the waterfront on the street leading to the post office and market.

Hydrofoil At least eight hydrofoils a day go to Zea Marina (4088 dr). Direct services take 1¼ hours; services via Poros (30 minutes, 1527 dr), Methana (45 minutes, 2689 dr) and Aegina (1¼ hours, 2836 dr) take between eight and 10 hours. There are between eight and 10 hydrofoils to Poros, but only a couple via Methana and Aegina – and at the beginning of the season just one a week. There are also frequent services to Spetses (30 minutes, 2017 dr), half of which call at Ermioni (20 minutes, 1700 dr) – adding 20 minutes to the trip. Many of the services to Spetses continue to Porto Heli (50 minutes, 2235 dr). There are also occasional services to Geraki, Leonidio, Monemvasia, Nafplio, Tolo and Tyros.

The Flying Dolphin office is at the end of the cul de sac leading off the waterfront between Saitis Tours and the Commercial Bank of Greece. Departure times are displayed on a board outside.

Getting Around
In summer, there are caïques from Hydra town to the island's beaches. There are also water taxis which will take you anywhere you like. A water taxi to Kamini costs 1600 dr, and 2200 dr to Mandraki and Vlyhos.

The donkey owners clustered around the port charge around 2500 dr to transport your bags to the hotel of your choice.

HYDRA TOWN
Most of the action in Hydra town is concentrated around the waterfront cafés and shops, leaving the upper reaches of the narrow, stepped streets virtually deserted – and a joy to explore.

Orientation
Ferries and hydrofoils both dock on the eastern side of the harbour. The town's three main streets all head inland from the waterfront at the back of the harbour. Walking around from the ferry dock, the first street you come to is Tombazi, at the eastern

corner. The next is Miaouli, on the left before the clock tower, which is the town's main thoroughfare. The third is Lignou, at the western extreme, which leads up over the hill to Kamini. Lignou is best reached by heading up Votsi, on the left after the clock tower, and taking the first turn right.

Information
There is no tourist office, but Saitis Tours (☎ 52 184; fax 53 469), on the waterfront near Tombazi, puts out a useful free guide called *Holidays in Hydra*. You can find information about the island on the Internet at www.forthnet.gr/hydranet.

Most things of importance are close to the waterfront. The post office is on a small side street between the Commercial (Emporiki) Bank and the National Bank of Greece. The tourist police (☎ 52 205) are opposite the OTE on Votsi.

There's a laundry service in the small market square just past the post office. It's open from 9 am to 9 pm (4 to 9 pm on Sunday) and charges 2200 dr to wash and dry a load.

Things to See
The new **Historical Archives Museum of Hydra** is close to the ferry dock on the eastern side of the harbour. It houses a collection of portraits and naval oddments, with an emphasis on the island's role in the War of Independence. The museum is open Tuesday to Sunday from 10 am to 5 pm and admission is 500 dr.

Several of the town's arhontika are worth seeking out, even if you can only look at them from the outside. They include the **Georgios Koundouriotis mansion** to the west of the harbour. Koundouriotis was a wealthy shipowner as well as a War of Independence leader, and the mansion houses a large portrait collection. The mansion is owned by the Ministry of Defence, which appears to be renovating it, but there is no indication of when it will be opened to the public.

Moni Panagias, behind the waterfront clock tower, is now used as offices but it has a peaceful courtyard and quite lavish ecclesiastical decorations inside its church.

Places to Stay – bottom end

The accommodation in Hydra is generally of a very high standard, and you pay accordingly for it. The cheapest rooms are at the *Pension Theresia* (☎ 53 983), which has quaint little singles/doubles around a leafy courtyard for 5000/7000 dr. All the rooms have private bathrooms, although they are very cramped. There is also a refrigerator and facilities for making tea or coffee. To get there, head up Tombazi from the port, fork right at the Amalour Café and follow the signs to the Restaurant Doukas, which lead to a small square. Pension Theresia is on the left of the square – the entry is around the corner on a side street.

The only other budget option is the *Hotel Sofia* (☎ 52 313) on the corner of the waterfront and Miaouli. The rather tatty singles/doubles/triples with shared bathroom are not particularly good value at 6000/7700/9900 dr – unless you can get a room overlooking the harbour.

Places to Stay – middle

The *Hotel Hydra* (☎ 52 102) has a great setting overlooking the town from the west. It has large, comfortable singles/doubles for 11,000/15,500 dr with en suite bathroom. It's a fair haul to get there – up more than 100 steps from Lignou, but the views over the town and harbour are worth it.

Finding the *Hotel Leto* (☎ 53 385) involves no more than a gentle stroll up Miaouli. It's a stylish place with beautiful polished timber floors. Singles are 15,000 dr and doubles start from 17,500 dr. Prices include a buffet breakfast. The Leto is about 250m from the port. Follow Miaouli to the far side of the small park and then turn left up some steps into a narrow alleyway. You'll see the hotel on the right after 50m.

A little bit further up Miaouli is the *Hotel Miranda* (☎ 52 230), originally the mansion of a wealthy Hydriot sea captain. It has been beautifully renovated and converted into a

Sailing out of Hydra Town

very smart hotel. Singles/doubles are 13,500/15,500 dr with breakfast, and a two-room suite is 22,000 dr.

Places to Stay – top end

The two hotels at the top of the comfort scale both offer something special. The *Hotel Orloff* (☎ 52 564; fax 53 532) is a beautiful old mansion with a cool, vine-covered courtyard at the back. The furnishings are elegant without being overstated, and each of the 10 rooms has a character of its own. Singles/doubles are 21,000/28,000 dr, which includes a buffet breakfast – served in the courtyard in summer.

The *Hotel Bratsera* (☎ 53 971; fax 53 626) is a converted sponge factory. The architects have left the rich stonework and solid timbers and have added some nice touches like doors made up from old packing cases. Doubles are priced from 29,000 to 36,000 dr, and four-bed suites start at 48,000 dr. The Bratsera has the town's only swimming pool. It's for guests only, but you'll qualify if you eat at their restaurant.

Places to Eat – inexpensive

Hydra has one of the best budget tavernas around. The owners of *The Terrace*, opposite Pension Antonios, are people who really care about their food. Try their beetroot salad – a bowl of baby beets and boiled greens with a dollop of cold, very garlicky, mashed potato on top. The flavours complement each other perfectly. You can eat well for 2000 dr per person, including a jug of retsina, but get in early or you'll have a long wait.

The *Garden Restaurant*, on Sahtouri, is a good psistaria with a large range of grilled food at reasonable prices. As the name suggests, the setting is a pleasant walled garden. To get there, turn left at the Amalour Café and you'll see it on the right after about 300m.

Lulu's, 50m from the port on Miaouli, is a popular taverna but the food is no better than average.

Places to Eat – middle

The *Veranda Restaurant*, halfway up the steps to the Hotel Hydra, occupies a terrace with great views over the town and harbour. The food is Mediterranean, and a meal for two will cost about 7000 dr, plus wine.

Strofilia is an excellent ouzeri just up from the waterfront on Miaouli. It specialises in mezes, including spetsofai (sausages in spicy sauce) for 1300 dr, mussels saganaki for 1400 dr and vegetable croquettes for 700 dr.

Entertainment

Kavos, with its sign made up of nautical oddments, is a popular disco just west of town on the coastal path to Kamini, but there is no point heading out there before 11 pm. The *Amalour*, 100m up Tombazi, is a more sophisticated café-bar that sells a wide range of fresh juices as well as alcohol. For rock music, head to the *Pirate* at the western end of the waterfront.

AROUND HYDRA

It's a strenuous but worthwhile one-hour walk up to **Moni Profiti Ilia**, starting from Miaouli. Monks still live in the monastery, which has fantastic views down to the town. It's a short walk from here to the convent of **Moni Efpraxias**.

The beaches on Hydra are a dead loss, but the walks to them are enjoyable. **Kamini**, about 20 minutes walk along the coastal path from town, has rocks and a very small pebble beach. **Vlyhos**, 20 minutes further on, is an attractive village with a slightly larger pebble beach, two tavernas and a ruined 19th century stone bridge. There are *domatia* at Vlyhos as well as *Antigoni's Apartments* (☎ 53 228), which has self-catering apartments to sleep four/six for 15,000/22,000 dr.

From here, walkaholics can continue to the small bay at **Molos**, or take a left fork before the bay to the inland village of **Episkopi**. There are no facilities at Episkopi. A seasonal café may be open at Molos but don't bank on it – take sustenance with you.

An even more ambitious walk is the three-hour stint from Hydra town to **Moni Zourvas**, in the north-east of the island. Along the way you will pass **Moni Agias Triadas** and **Moni Agiou Nikolaou**.

A path leads east from Hydra town to the pebble beach at **Mandraki**. The beach is the exclusive reserve of the *Hotel Miramare* (☎ 52 300; fax 52 301), which has doubles with breakfast for 19,000 dr. There's a range of water-sport equipment for hire, including sailboards (3000 dr per hour) and canoes (1200 dr).

Spetses Σπέτσες

• *pop 3700* • *postcode* • *180 50* • *area code* ☎ *0298*
Pine-covered Spetses (**Spet**ses), the most distant of the group from Piraeus, is a favourite of British package-tour operators.

Spetses' history is similar to Hydra's. It became wealthy through shipbuilding, ran the British blockade during the Napoleonic Wars and refitted its ships to join the Greek fleet during the War of Independence. Spetsiot fighters achieved a certain notoriety through their pet tactic of attaching small boats laden with explosives to the enemy's ships, setting them alight and beating a hasty retreat.

The island was known in antiquity as Pityoussa (meaning 'pine-covered'), but the original forest cover disappeared long ago. The pine-covered hills that greet the visitor today are a legacy of the far-sighted and wealthy philanthropist Sotirios Anargyrios.

Anargyrios was born on Spetses in 1848 and emigrated to the US, returning in 1914 an exceedingly rich man. He bought two-thirds of the then largely barren island and planted the Aleppo pines that stand today. He also financed the island's road system and commissioned many of the town's grand buildings, including the Hotel Possidonion. He was a big fan of the British public (ie private) school system, and established Anargyrios & Korgialenios College, a boarding school for boys from all over Greece.

British author John Fowles taught English at the college from 1950-51, and used the island as a setting for his novel *The Magus*.

Getting There & Away

Ferry There is at least one ferry a day to Piraeus (4½ hours, 2597 dr), via Hydra (950 dr), Poros (1410 dr), Methana (1620 dr) and Aegina (1990 dr). Two companies operate the service on alternate days. Ventouris Lines tickets are sold by Meledon Travel on the seafront in Spetses town, and Lefakis Lines tickets from Alasia Travel next door.

Between July and September, there are ferries from Spetses to Kosta, 25 minutes away on the Peloponnese. The ferries depart at 7.15 and 10 am, and at 1 and 4.30 pm; they return half an hour later.

Get your ticket (130 dr) on the boat. Water taxis do the trip in 10 minutes for 3000 dr. The port police (☎ 72 245) are opposite the quay.

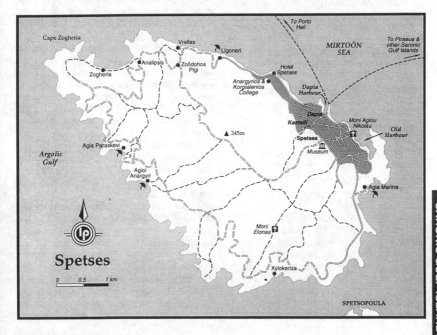

Hydrofoil There are at least five Flying Dolphins a day to Zea Marina (5560 dr). Direct services take 1¾ hours, but most go via Hydra (30 minutes, 2017 dr) and/or Poros (70 minutes, 2442 dr) and take about 2½ hours. In high season, one or two services a day go to Aegina (two hours, 4237 dr). There are also daily connections to Leonidio (one hour, 2196 dr) and Monemvasia (1½ hours, 3775 dr).

Getting Around
Spetses has two bus routes. There are three or four buses a day from Plateia Agias Mamas in Spetses town to Agioi Anargyri (750 dr return), via Agia Marina and Xylokeriza. Departure times are displayed on a board by the bus stop. There are hourly buses to Ligoneri (140 dr) from in front of the Hotel Possidonion.

No cars are permitted on the island. Unfortunately this ban has not been extended to motorbikes, resulting in there being more of the critters here than just about anywhere else.

The colourful horse-drawn carriages are a pleasant but expensive way of getting about. Prices are displayed on a board where the carriages gather by the port.

Boat Water taxis (☎ 74 885) go anywhere you care to nominate from opposite the Flying Dolphin office at Dapia harbour. Fares are displayed on a board. Samples include 4000 dr to Agia Marina and 6000 dr to Agioi Anargyri. In summer, there are caïques from the harbour to Anargyri (1500 dr return) and Zogheria (1000 dr return).

SPETSES TOWN
Spetses town sprawls along almost half the north-east coast of the island, reflecting the way in which the focal point of settlement has changed over the years.

There's evidence of an early Helladic settlement near the old harbour, about 1.5km east of the modern commercial centre and port of Dapia. Roman and Byzantine remains have been unearthed in the area

behind Moni Agiou Nikolaou, halfway between the two.

The island is thought to have been uninhabited for almost 600 years before the arrival of Albanian refugees fleeing fighting between the Turks and the Venetians in the 16th century. They settled on the hillside just inland from Dapia, the area now known as Kastelli.

The Dapia district has a few impressive arhontika, but the prettiest part of town is around the old harbour.

Orientation & Information
The quay at Dapia harbour serves both ferries and hydrofoils. A left turn at the end of the quay leads east along the waterfront on Sotirios Anargyris, passing through the square where the horse-drawn carriages wait. The road is flanked by a string of uninspiring, concrete C-class hotels, and emerges after 200m on Plateia Agias Mamas, next to the town beach. The bus stop for Anargyri is next to the beach. The post office is on the street running behind the hotels; coming from the quay, turn right at the Hotel Soleil and then left.

The waterfront to the right of the quay is also called Sotirios Anargyris. It skirts the small Dapia harbour, passes the decaying shell of the once-grand Hotel Possidonion and continues west around the bay to the Hotel Spetses. The OTE is behind Dapia harbour, next to the National Bank of Greece.

There is no tourist office on Spetses. The tourist police (☎ 73 100) are based in the police station – on the left as you walk up N Spetson from the quay – from June to September. N Spetson leads inland from the south-western corner of the square which has the horse-drawn carriages. The road at the south-eastern corner leads to the main square, known as Plateia Orologiou.

Things to See
The **old harbour** is a delightful place to explore. It is ringed by old Venetian buildings, and filled with boats of every shape and size – from colourful little fishing boats to

sleek luxury cruising yachts. The ship-builders of Spetses still do things the traditional way and the shore is dotted with the hulls of emerging caïques. The walk from Dapia harbour takes about 20 minutes. **Moni Agiou Nikolaou** straddles a headland at the halfway mark.

The **museum** is housed in the arhontiko of Hadzigiannis Mexis, a shipowner who became the island's first governor. While most of the collection is devoted to folkloric items and portraits of the island's founding fathers, there is also a display of ships' figureheads. It's open Tuesday to Sunday from 8.30 am to 3 pm. Admission is 500 dr. The museum is clearly signposted from Plateia Orologiou.

Organised Tours
Meledon Travel (☎ 74 497) organises trips around the island by caïque for 2500 dr, including wine and commentary. Meledon Travel is on the waterfront east of the quay.

Places to Stay
Spetses town has very little budget accommodation, as is the case throughout the Saronic islands.

The best option is the *Villa Marina* (☎ 72 646), just off Plateia Agias Mamas beyond the row of restaurants. It has good singles/doubles with bathroom for 9000/13,000 dr – available most of the year for 5000/8000 dr. All rooms have refrigerators and there is a well-equipped communal kitchen downstairs.

Another good place is the pretty, whitewashed *Villa Kristina* (☎ 72 218), on Ikoniou, a left turn off Spetson about 300m beyond the police station. It has singles/doubles with private bathroom for 7500/10,000 dr, as well as four-person studios for 15,000 dr.

If these two are full, try the *Hotel Kamelia* (☎ 72 415), signposted to the right at the supermarket, 100m past Plateia Agias Mamas on the road that leads inland to Agioi Anargyri. The place is almost hidden beneath a sprawling burgundy bougainvillea.

Lascarina Bouboulina
Spetses contributed one of the most colourful figures of the War of Independence, the dashing heroine Lascarina Bouboulina. Her exploits on and off the battlefield were the stuff of legend. She was widowed twice by the time the war began – both her ship-owning husbands had been killed by pirates, leaving her a very wealthy woman – and she used her money to commission her own fighting ship, the *Agamemnon*, which she led into battle during the blockade of Nafplio. Bouboulina was known for her fiery temperament and her countless love affairs, and her death was in keeping with her flamboyant lifestyle – she was shot during a family dispute in her Spetses home. Bouboulina was featured on the old 50 dr note in a dramatic portrayal showing her directing cannon fire.

The Bouboulina mansion is on the western side of the square behind the OTE building. It houses a small museum, which is open from Tuesday to Sunday from 9 am to 5 pm; admission is 700 dr. ■

Spotless singles/doubles with private bathroom are 8500/10,500 dr.

Otherwise you will be forced to fall back on one of the uninspiring C and D-class places that line the waterfront between the ferry dock and Plateia Agias Mamas, or seek help from one of the travel agents.

Places to Eat
The *Restaurant Stelios*, between Plateia Agias Mamas and the post office, is a popular taverna that pitches for the tourist trade with a series of set menus. Prices start at under 2100 dr for three courses.

The *Taverna O Roussos*, on Plateia Mamas, also has solid taverna fare at prices that won't break the bank.

Getting away from the tourist hype involves a bit of walking. The *Restaurant Exedra*, halfway around the bay on the road to the Hotel Spetses, is a good little place with seating on a small platform built out over the beach. Surprisingly, given its location, fish hardly features on the menu.

Fish fans should keep walking around the

bay to the *Restaurant Patralis*. It has a great setting, a good menu and fish supplied by the restaurant's own boat. The fish à la Spetses (1800 dr), a large tuna or swordfish steak baked with vegetables and lots of garlic, goes down perfectly with a cold beer.

If character is what you are after, you won't find a better place than *Byzantino*, halfway to the old harbour on the other side of town. The early 19th-century port-authority building has been converted into a stylish restaurant specialising in mezedes. Reckon on about 8000 dr for two, with drinks.

Self-caterers can head to the *Kritikos Supermarket*, next to the Hotel Soleil on the waterfront near Plateia Agias Mamas. There is a very well stocked bottle shop across the alleyway behind it.

AROUND SPETSES

Spetses' coastline is speckled with numerous coves with small, pine-shaded beaches. A 24km road (part sealed, part dirt) skirts the entire coastline, so a motorcycle is the ideal way to explore the island.

The beach at **Ligoneri**, west of town, has the attraction of being easily accessible by bus. **Agia Marina**, to the south of the old harbour, is a small resort with a crowded beach. **Agia Paraskevi** and **Anargyri**, on the south-west coast, have good, albeit crowded, beaches; both have water sports of every description. A large mansion between the two beaches was the inspiration for the Villa Bourani in John Fowles' *The Magus*.

The small island of **Spetsopoula** to the south of Spetses is owned by the family of the late shipping magnate, Stavros Niarchos.

Top: The cliffs of Santorini in the Cyclades are ideal for viewing spectacular sunsets
Bottom Left: The striking silhouette of a windmill at sunset in Oia, Santorini, Cyclades
Bottom Right: An evening ferry glides through golden waters to Fira, Cyclades

MARK DAFFEY

DAVID HALL

DAVID HALL

MARK DAFFEY

DAVID HALL

Top Left: Sun worship on scorching black sand at Kamari, Santorini, Cyclades
Top right: Passing the time in Naxos town, Naxos, Cyclades
Middle: Waves lap the shore of Mykonos town, Mykonos, Cyclades
Bottom Left: Church bells overlooking Perissa, Santorini, Cyclades
Bottom Right: Moni Hozoviotissas clings to a cliff above the coast of Amorgos, Cyclades

Cyclades Κυκλάδες

The Cyclades (Cyclades) are the archetypal Greek islands – rugged outcrops of rock dotted with brilliant white buildings offset by vividly painted balconies and bright blue church domes, all bathed in dazzling light and fringed with golden beaches lapped by aquamarine seas.

Goats and sheep are raised on the mountainous, barren islands, as well as some pigs and cattle. Naxos alone is sufficiently fertile to produce crops for export. Many islanders still fish, but tourism is becoming the dominant source of income.

Some of the Cyclades, like Mykonos, Santorini (Thira) and Ios, have been eager to embrace tourism, and their shores are spread with sun lounges, umbrellas and watersports equipment. Others, such as Andros, Syros, Kea, Kythnos, Serifos and Sifnos, are less visited by foreigners, but are popular weekend and summer retreats for Athenians, thanks to their proximity to the mainland.

Tinos is not a holiday island but the country's premier place of pilgrimage – a Greek Lourdes. Other islands, such as Anafi and the tiny islands east of Naxos, are little more than clumps of rock with tiny depopulated villages and few tourists.

The islands of the Cyclades are small and closely grouped, making them ideal for an island-hopping holiday.

It's best to avoid these islands in July and August, when accommodation can be hard to find. Most places are open only from April to October. Accommodation prices quoted in this section are for the July/August high season; expect to pay less at other times.

The Cyclades are more prone to the northwesterly *meltemi* wind than other island groups, but this provides a welcome respite from the heat.

History

The Cyclades have been populated since at least 5000 BC. Around 3000 BC, Phoenician colonists settled on the islands and their ad-

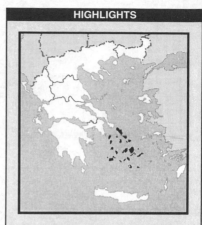

HIGHLIGHTS

- Spectacular sunsets over Santorini's submerged volcano
- Wild partying on Ios
- Trekking on Naxos
- Clubbing on Mykonos
- The archaeological site of ancient Delos

vanced culture heralded the Cycladic civilisation. During the Early Cycladic period (3000-2000 BC), people on Milos lived in houses, built boats and mined obsidian which was exported throughout the Mediterranean. It was during this time that the famous Cycladic marble statues were sculpted.

In the Middle Cycladic period (2000-1500 BC), the islands were occupied by the Minoans. Around the 15th century BC, at the beginning of the Late Cycladic period (1500-1100 BC), the Cyclades passed to the Mycenaeans. The Dorians followed, but by the 8th century BC Archaic culture was burgeoning.

After the Greek victory over Persia, the

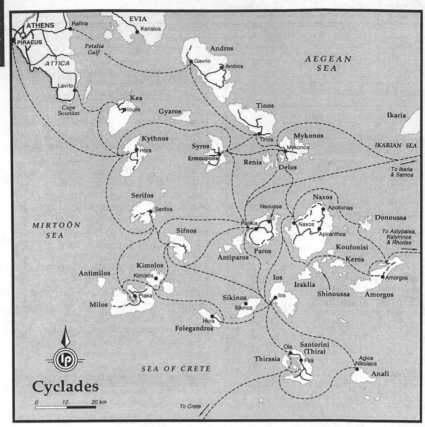

Cyclades

0   10   20 km

Cyclades became part of the Delian League and were incorporated into the Athenian empire, thus suffering the onerous annual tax imposed by Athens.

In 190 BC, the islands were conquered by the Romans and trade links were established with many parts of the Mediterranean, bringing prosperity.

In 1204, the Franks gave the Cyclades to Venice, which parcelled the islands out to opportunistic aristocrats. Most powerful was Marco Sanudo (self-styled Duke of Naxos), who acquired Naxos, Paros, Amorgos and Folegandros.

The islands came under Turkish rule in 1453. Neglected by the Ottomans, they became backwaters, prone to pirate raids – hence the labyrinthine character of their towns. The mazes of narrow lanes were designed to disorientate attackers. On some islands, people moved inland to escape pirates.

The Cyclades' participation in the War of Independence was minimal but they became havens for people fleeing from islands where insurrections against the Turks had led to massacres.

The fortunes of the islands have been

revived by the tourism boom that began in the 1970s. Until then, many islanders lived in abject poverty and many more gave up the battle and headed for the mainland in search of work.

Getting There & Away

For specific details, see sections under individual islands.

Air In summer there is at least one flight a day between Naxos and Athens (15,500 dr), and at least two a day to/from Syros (10,500 dr). There are three flights a day to/from Milos (9600 dr), four a day to/from Mykonos (14,200 dr), seven to/from Paros (14,000 dr) and at least four to/from Santorini (17,100 dr). In addition there are direct flights between Santorini and Mykonos, Thessaloniki and Crete, and between Mykonos and Thessaloniki and Crete. Both Santorini and Mykonos have direct connections with Rhodes.

Ferry Most ferries serving the Cyclades connect a particular group of islands with Piraeus or Rafina on the mainland. However, Paros is the ferry hub of the Cyclades, and connections between different groups of islands are usually possible via Paros, if not direct.

Agapitos Express Ferries operates three boats, *Express Olympia*, *Express Apollon* and *Express Santorini*, connecting Piraeus variously with Syros, Paros, Naxos, Amorgos, Ios, Santorini, Anafi, Folegandros and Sikinos.

Agapitos Lines – a totally different company – operates F/B *Naias 11*, which sails between Piraeus, Syros, Tinos and Mykonos. Its *Naias Express* and *Super Naias* connect Piraeus via Paros and Naxos and the Minor Islands (Donoussa, Amorgos, Iraklia and Shinoussa) with the southern islands of Ios, Santorini, Folegandros and Sikinos, as well as Anafi, and Astypalea in the Dodecanese. The F/B *Golden Vergina* sails from Piraeus to Paros and Naxos, and on to Ikaria and Samos in the North-Eastern Aegean.

Ventouris Ferries' *Pegasus* and Lindos

Shipping's *Milos Express* serve the Western Cyclades, with services from Piraeus to Kythnos, Serifos, Sifnos, Milos, Folegandros and Sikinos, and on to Ios and Santorini. The only ferry to Kea is the *Myrina Express*, which leaves from Lavrio, on the mainland.

Minoan Lines has the F/B *El Greco*, which sails three times a week from Thessaloniki to Santorini and on to Crete, either via Tinos and Paros or via Syros and Naxos.

The F/B *Paros Express* sails from Syros and Mykonos to Santorini via Paros, Naxos and Ios, and on to the Western Cyclades. It does not connect with the mainland.

GA Ferries operates the *Milena*, which connects Piraeus with Paros and Naxos in the Cyclades and Ikaria and Samos in the North-Eastern Aegean. The F/Bs *Romilda*, *Marina* and *Daliana* all connect Piraeus, Paros and Naxos with Rhodes in the Dodecanese. The *Daliana* also calls at Santorini and Iraklio (Crete).

The LANE F/B *Vitsentsos Kornaros* links Piraeus with Milos, Sitia and Agios Nikolaos (Crete), and Karpathos and Kassos in the Dodecanese.

Lesvos, in the North-Eastern Aegean, has a weekly ferry connection with Syros and Piraeus on the F/B *Agios Rafail*.

Ferry prices from Piraeus to the Cyclades are listed below:

Tinos	4120 dr
Mykonos	4380 dr
Syros	3840 dr
Kythnos	2820 dr
Serifos	3390 dr
Sifnos	3860 dr
Paros	4260 dr
Naxos	4280 dr
Milos	4330 dr
Folegandros	4560 dr
Sikinos	5500 dr
Ios	4720 dr
Amorgos	4450 dr
Santorini	5350 dr
Anafi	6080 dr

From early June to mid-October you can buy a 20-day island pass which offers unlimited travel from Piraeus to the islands of Paros, Naxos, Ios and Santorini for 11,500 dr. The passes are issued by Agapitos Lines and are available from most travel agents in Athens.

Hydrofoil Ilio Lines is the major operator for the Cyclades. Regular hydrofoils connect Rafina with Andros, Tinos, Mykonos, Syros, Naxos, Amorgos, Paros, Ios and Santorini, as well as the Minor Islands (Koufonisi, Iraklia, Shinoussa and Donoussa) and most of the Western Cyclades. Ceres Hydrofoils, operating out of Piraeus, serves Kea and Kythnos. At the time of writing, a new consortium was about to start operating out of Santorini. Strintzis Lines and Goutos Lines operate catamaran services from Rafina.

Getting Around
Air The only inter-island flights are between Mykonos and Santorini.

Bus The standard of bus services varies according to the size of the island and its popularity as a tourist destination. The most popular islands have good bus services, the less visited islands have less frequent services, and the tiny islands of Anafi, Donoussa, Koufonisi, Shinoussa and Iraklia have no public transport at all.

Car, Motorcycle & Bicycle There are cars for hire on Andros, Tinos, Milos, Syros, Mykonos, Naxos, Paros, Ios, Santorini and Sifnos. Motorcycle and moped hire is possible on most other islands, and bicycle hire is available on a few. For details, see the sections on individual islands.

Andros Ανδρος

• *pop 8781* • *postcode 845 00* • *area code ☎ 0282*
Andros (**And**ros) is the most northerly of the Cyclades and the second largest after Naxos. It is also one of the most fertile islands, producing citrus fruit and olives. The island is unusual in that it has retained its pine forests and mulberry woods. More distinc-

tive features are its dovecotes (although Tinos has more) and elaborate stone walls.

Getting There & Away
Ferry At least two ferries a day leave Rafina for Andros' main port of Gavrio (two hours, 2310 dr), continuing to Tinos (1800 dr) and Mykonos (2550 dr) and returning via the same route. One ferry a week from Rafina links Andros with Paros and Naxos, which both offer better connections with the other islands. See Getting There & Away at the start of the Cyclades chapter for further details. The telephone number of the port police in Gavrio is ☎ 71 213.

Hydrofoil There are daily hydrofoils from Rafina to Andros (70 minutes, 4100 dr), continuing to Tinos (3440 dr) and Mykonos (5270 dr), and returning by the same route. Every afternoon, a hydrofoil from Rafina calls at Andros, Tinos, Mykonos, and continues to Paros, Naxos and Ios. All services dock at the main port of Gavrio. Strintzis Lines' *Sea Jet 1* provides a daily catamaran service to and from Rafina, Tinos and Mykonos.

Getting Around
Theoretically, six buses a day link Gavrio and Andros town via Batsi, but they tend to run only when ferries arrive.

GAVRIO Γαώριο
Gavrio, on the west coast, is the main port of Andros. The capital, Andros town, is on the east coast. Nothing much happens in Gavrio, but in high season it may be easier to find accommodation here than at the resort of Batsi or in Andros town, and there are lovely beaches nearby.

Orientation & Information
The ferry quay is in the middle of the waterfront and the bus stop is next to it. Turn right from the quay and walk along the waterfront for the OTE, turn left for the post office. Andros doesn't have a tourist office or tourist police.

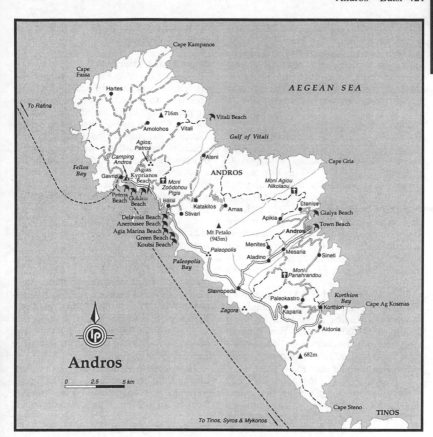

Andros

CAPE Kampanos

Cape Fassa

Hartes

▲716m

Amolohos Vitali

▲Vitali Beach

AEGEAN SEA

Agios. Petros

Gulf of Vitali

To Rafina

Camping Andros

▲Ateni

Cape Gria

Fellos Bay

Agias Kyprianos Beach

Gavrio

ANDROS

Moni Agiou Nikolaou

Petros Beach

Golden Beach

Moni Zoödohou Pigis

Batsi

Delavoia Beach

Katakilos

Amas

Ctenies

Gialya Beach

Stivari

Apikia

Andros

Town Beach

Anerousee Beach

Agia Marina Beach

Green Beach

Koutsi Beach

Mt Petalo
(945m)

Menites

Mesaria

Sineti

Aladino

Paleopolis

Paleopolis Bay

Moni Panahrandou

Stavropeda

Paleokastro

Korthion Bay

Cape Ag Kosmas

Zagora

Kaparia

Korthion

Aidonia

0 2.5 5 km

▲682m

Cape Steno

TINOS

To Tinos, Syros & Mykonos

Places to Stay – bottom end

The island's only camp site, *Camping Andros* (☎ 71 444), is 300m from the harbour along the Batsi road. It has a restaurant, minimarket, bar and pool. If you decide to stay in town, look for domatia signs along the waterfront or try the *Hotel Galaxy* (☎ 71 005/228) to the left of the quay. It has clean doubles/triples with private bathroom for 7000/10,000 dr.

Places to Stay – middle

The B-class *Andros Holiday Hotel* (☎ 71 384), overlooking the beach, is regarded as

Gavrio's best. It has a restaurant, bar, tennis court, sauna, jacuzzi and gym. Singles/doubles/triples cost 13,000/18,000/22,000 dr.

Places to Eat

The reasonably priced *Restaurant O Valmas* is one of Gavrio's best. Turn right from the quay, then left one block before the Batsi road.

BATSI Μπατσί

Batsi, 8km south of Gavrio, is Andros' major resort. The attractive town encircles a bay with a fishing harbour at one end and a nice sandy beach at the other. There is no EOT, but Greek Sun Holidays (☎ 41 198; fax 41 239) is particularly helpful and can take care of everything from accommodation to sightseeing. Car hire is available at Auto Europe (☎ 41 995; fax 41 239).

Places to Stay & Eat

Scan the waterfront for domatia signs. The *Karanassos Hotel* (☎ 41 480), 50m from the beach, has singles/doubles with private bathroom for 8500/10,700 dr. The *Scouna Hotel* (☎ 41 165/240), overlooking the beach, has pleasant rooms for 8500/12,000 dr. *Hotel Chryssi Akti* (☎ 41 237), right on the beach, is one of the best, with rooms for 9000/12,000/13,000 dr. The improbably named *Villa Erotica* (☎ 41 198), overlooking Stivari Bay, has double/triple studios with balconies and great sea views for 12,000/13,000 dr.

Likio Studios (☎ 41 050/811) is set back from the beach amid masses of geraniums. Its spotless studios cost 14,000 dr for a double, or 22,000 dr for a two-bedroom apartment which sleeps four. All studios have cooking facilities. The owner meets ferries year-round if phoned.

Cavo d'Oro (☎ 41 776) at the beach end of the waterfront is a pizzeria with *domatia* (9000 dr for doubles with private bathroom). It specialises in Andros' famed fourtalia, an omelette made with potatoes and home-made sausages. On the waterfront, *Esthesis Restaurant* has good food at reasonable prices as well as live music, including rembetika. Dishes include country sausage with capsicum, beefburger stuffed with cheese, and divine shrimp saganaki.

Sweet-toothed travellers should seek out the island's speciality, karydhaki – Andros walnuts cooked with honey, sugar, cinnamon and cloves.

ANDROS TOWN

Andros town is on the east coast, 35km east of Gavrio. The town's setting, along a narrow peninsula, is more striking than the town itself, although there are some fine old neoclassical mansions and a tiny central square shaded by trees.

Orientation & Information

The bus station is on Plateia Goulandri. To the left, as you face the sea, is the main pedestrian thoroughfare where you'll find the post office, OTE and National Bank of Greece. Walk along here towards the sea for Plateia Kaïri, the central square, beyond which is the headland. Steps descend to beaches from both sides of the square. The street traversing the promontory ends at Plateia Riva where there is a bronze statue of an unknown sailor. The ruins of a Venetian fortress stand at the tip of the headland.

Museums

Andros town has two outstanding museums; both were endowed by Vasilis Goulandris, a wealthy ship owner and Andriot. The town's **archaeological museum** is north of Plateia Kaïri. Its contents include the 1st-century BC Hermes of Andros made of Parian marble and finds from Andros' two ancient cities of Zagora and Paleopolis. The museum is open Tuesday to Sunday from 8.30 am to 3 pm. Admission is 500 dr.

The **museum of modern art** has a collection of 20th-century Greek and European paintings. It's open Saturday to Monday from 10 am to 2 pm. Admission is 700 dr.

Places to Stay & Eat

The best value is at the *Hotel Egli* (☎ 22 303), off the right side of the main road as you head towards the sea, between the two squares. Doubles/quads with private bathroom are 7500/13,500 dr including breakfast.

Restaurant Stathmos, on Plateia Goulandri by the bus station, has tasty, low-priced fare. The *Parea Taverna* on the central square has a commanding beach view and daily specials for 800 to 1400 dr.

AROUND ANDROS

About 2.5km from Gavrio, the **Agios Petros tower** is an imposing circular watchtower, dating at least from Hellenistic times – possibly earlier. It's a 30-minute walk to the tower from Camping Andros. Look for the signpost for Agios Petros, also the name of a village.

Along the coast road from Gavrio to Batsi is a turn-off left leading 5km to the 12th-century **Moni Zoödohou Pigis**. A few nuns still live here. Between Gavrio and Paleopolis bay are several nice beaches – **Agios Kyprianos**, (where a former church is now a beachfront taverna), **Delavoia** (nudist), **Green beach** and **Anerousa**. The *Anerousa Beach Hotel* (☎ 41 044/045), open from May to October, offers singles/doubles/triples for 14,500/18,000/22,000 dr.

Paleopolis, 9km south of Batsi on the coast road, is the site of ancient Andros, where the Hermes of Andros was found. There is little to see, but the mountain setting is lovely. At Stavropedan, the main road strikes inland for Andros town. From the village of Mesaria, it's a strenuous two hour walk to the 12th-century **Moni Panahrandou**, the island's largest and most important monastery.

The pretty blue-green bay at **Korthion**, in the south-east, remains almost untouched by tourism. Its *Hotel Korthion* (☎ 61 218), on the shore, has inexpensive singles/doubles with bath and breakfast for 3600/7200 dr. The hotel can arrange windsurfing and jet-skiing.

Tinos Τήνος

• *pop 7747* • *postcode 842 00* • *area code ☎ 0283*
Tinos (**Tee**nos) is green and mountainous, like nearby Andros. The island is a place of pilgrimage for the Greek Orthodox, so it's hardly surprising that churches feature prominently among the attractions. The celebrated **Church of Panagia Evangelistria** dominates its capital, while more modest churches, unspoilt hill villages and ornate whitewashed dovecotes are rural attractions. Tinos also has a large Roman Catholic population – the result of its long occupation by the Venetians. The Turks didn't succeed in wresting the island from

the Venetians until 1715, long after the rest of the country had surrendered to Ottoman Turkey.

Getting There & Away

Ferry Tinos shares the same ferry services to Rafina (3½ hours, 3335 dr) as Andros, but Agapitos Lines' F/Bs *Naias II* and *Naias Express* provide an additional daily service to Mykonos and Piraeus (4½ hours, 4120 dr) via Syros. Twice a week these boats continue past Mykonos to the Minor Islands (Donoussa, Iraklia and Shinoussa) and Amorgos. Nomicos Lines and Minoan Lines each run two ferries a week from Tinos to Crete (5750 dr) via Mykonos, Paros (1735 dr) and Santorini (3710 dr), starting out from Thessaloniki. Tinos' port police (☎ 22 348) are on the waterfront near the quay.

Hydrofoil There are daily hydrofoils from Rafina to Tinos (two hours, 6200 dr), continuing to Mykonos and returning via the same route. Every afternoon a hydrofoil from Rafina calls at Tinos, Mykonos, Paros, Naxos and Ios. Strintzis Lines' *Sea Jet 1* provides a daily catamaran service to and from Rafina, Tinos and Mykonos. On Thursday there is a hydrofoil from Rafina to Tinos, Mykonos, Paros, Sifnos and Serifos, returning via the same route.

Getting Around

There are frequent buses from Tinos town to Kionia and several a day to Panormos via Pyrgos and Kambos, and to Porto. However, the best way to explore the island is by motorcycle (prices start at 2500 dr a day) and overall the roads are pretty good. Motorcycles and cars can be hired along Tinos town's waterfront.

TINOS TOWN

Tinos town, the island's picturesque capital and port, has a lively waterfront and little streets with shops and stalls catering for pilgrims and tourists. The Church of Panagia Evangelistria presides over the action from its elevated position in the centre of town.

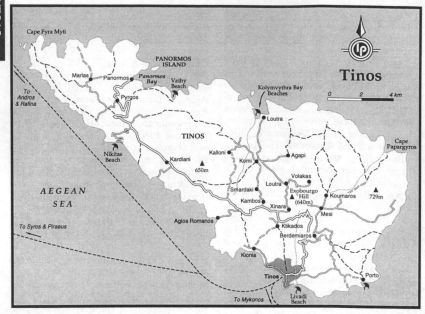

Orientation & Information

The main ferry quay is in the middle of the waterfront, but there is one either side, so check which one your boat departs from. Leoforos Megaloharis, straight ahead from the main ferry quay, is the route pilgrims take to the church. The narrow Evangelistria, to the right facing inland, also leads to the church.

The post office is at the south-eastern end of the waterfront, past the bus station and the National Bank of Greece. To reach it turn right from the quay. The town beach of Agios Fokas is a 20-minute walk south from the waterfront.

Tinos has no tourist office, but there are many travel agencies supplying information as well as providing accommodation and car hire services. Sharon Turner from Windmills Travel (☎ 23 398), at Kionion 2, has been living on Tinos for more than 11 years and is a mine of information. Ask her about excursions, or anything else you need to know.

Turn left from the quay and you will find the office near the children's park.

The tourist police (☎ 22 255) and regular police (☎ 22 100) are two blocks past the Asteria Hotel on the main road to Kionia.

Church of Panagia Evangelistria

This church is a neoclassical marble confection of white and cream, with a high bell tower. The ornate façade has graceful white upper and lower colonnades. The final approach is up carpeted steps, doubtless a relief to pious souls choosing to crawl up. Enter for an ecclesiastical extravaganza: the miracle-working icon draped with gold, silver, jewels and pearls, surrounded by gifts from those hopeful of its powers.

A lucrative trade in candles, icon copies, incense and evil-eye deterrents is carried out on Evangelistria. The largest candles cost around 5000 dr, and after an ephemeral existence burning in the church, the wax remains are gathered, melted down and resold.

Not only the frail, elderly and dying make the pilgrimage here. On the feasts of the Annunciation and Assumption and during Advent, Tinos also swarms with children. It is considered auspicious to be baptised at the church, a privilege costing nothing but a donation, though many of these are very large.

Hotels are crammed during pilgrimages, but most people sleep out because they can neither find nor afford a room.

Within the church complex, several **museums** house religious artefacts, icons, and secular artworks. Below the church, a crypt marks the spot where the icon was found. Next to it is a mausoleum to the sailors killed on the *Elle*, a Greek cruise ship blown up in Tinos port on 15 August 1940, allegedly by an Italian submarine. The church and museums are open daily from 8 am to 8 pm.

Archaeological Museum

The archaeological museum (☎ 22 670), below the church on Leoforos Megaloharis, contains a mosaic, Roman sculptures, a 1st-century sundial designed by Andronicus of Kyrrhos and impressive clay *pithoi* (large jars). Opening times are Tuesday to Sunday from 8 am to 3 pm. Admission is 500 dr.

Places to Stay

Avoid Tinos at pilgrimage times, unless you want to join the huddled masses who sleep anywhere.

Camping Tinos (☎ 22 344) is a nice site with good facilities south of the town. Follow the sign on the waterfront.

Look for domatia signs along Evangelistria and other streets leading inland

---

As Long as It's Black

A bent old lady clad from head to foot in black, silhouetted against sparkling, sugar cube buildings, makes a striking, evocative image – so much so that you will see it reproduced on 'arty postcards' throughout Greece. But it is not only elderly women who dress in black, the colour of mourning; many younger people do, too. Traditionally, Greek women marry men much older than themselves, so are often widowed in middle age. Until recently a widow was expected to wear black for the rest of her life, or until she remarried, something she could not do during the first five years after her husband's death. She was also expected to wear a black kerchief that completely covered her hair, forehead and neck. You will still see elderly women wearing this headdress.

In the Greek Orthodox faith, the five years following death is known as the liminal period. It is believed that during this time the soul of the deceased journeys to heaven. Throughout the liminal period a widow makes daily visits to her husband's grave, lighting candles and leaving food there.

At the end of the liminal period the body is exhumed and the bones are cleaned and placed in a casket. This symbolises the final purification of the soul and its readiness to enter heaven. Nowadays widows are expected to wear black only during the liminal period following their husband's death. After this the care of the grave is carried out collectively. Five times a year, on All Souls Days, neighbouring widows exchange plates of food, which are then blessed by a priest and placed on the graves.

Likewise, if a child dies, the mother wears black for at least five years, and tends the grave daily. Upon the death of a parent or sibling the mourning time is one to five years, for an in-law it is one year, and for a more distant relation it is 40 days. If the deceased is a child, a relation she was close to, or someone who died in tragic circumstances, a woman is expected to wear black for longer. After the period of mourning, a woman is expected to dress in a subdued manner, replacing black with dark blue, then with brown and then gradually adding brighter colours. During the time of mourning a woman is not expected to socialise or entertain.

In comparison men get off lightly. The only requirement expected of a man is that he wears a black armband and refrains from socialising for the 40 days following a death.

In keeping with the rest of the western world's hip, young Greek women have come to hold the maxim 'any colour as long as it's black' with regard to clothes. However it is not difficult to spot the difference between a woman wearing black to make a fashion statement and one wearing black because she is in mourning. ■

from the waterfront. *Manthos' Rooms* (☎ 22 675), at Ioannou Voulgari 7, has rooms surrounding a vine-covered patio. To get there, turn right from the ferry quay and left at the supermarket into Zanaki Alavanou. Ioannou Voulgari is six streets up. Doubles are 6500 dr, or 7500 dr with bathroom. New studios with balconies are also available. Ask about the home-made lemonade.

Hotel Eleana (☎ 22 561) has well-kept doubles/triples with private bathroom for 10,000/13,200 dr. From the quay, turn right and then left at the Hotel Possidonion. The hotel is opposite the Church of Agios Ioannis.

The C-class *Hotel Meltemi* (☎ 22 881/ 882/883), on Megaloharis, has airy singles/doubles for 8500/12,700 dr with private bathroom and breakfast. The C-class *Hotel Delfinia* (☎ 22 289), on the waterfront, has pleasant singles/doubles for 8000/ 11,000 dr with private bathroom. The C-class *Oasis Hotel* (☎ 23 055 or 22 455), on Evangelistria, offers doubles for 11,000 dr.

The B-class *Hotel Tinion* (☎ 22 261) has spacious doubles for 13,200 dr with private bathroom. The hotel is en route to the camp site which is signposted from the waterfront. The *Hotel Aigli* (☎ 22 240), opposite the quay, has doubles with private bathroom starting at 16,500 dr.

Other options include *Aeolos Bay* (☎ 23 339), a five-minute walk from the town centre, with great views and a swimming pool; *Hotel Theoxenia* (☎ 22 274), near the Church of Panagia Evangelistria; and *Hotel Leandros* (☎ 23 545), near the children's park. Singles/doubles with private bathroom and breakfast cost 11,100/16,200 dr. Discounts are available through Windmills Travel (see Orientation & Information), which also has studios and apartments at the beach and several houses in villages such as Berdemiaros and Pyrgos.

Places to Eat

The following restaurants are all reasonably priced. *Xinari Restaurant*, at the waterfront end of Evangelistria, serves exceptional Greek food, homemade bread and great pizzas. *Old Pallada Taverna*, just off the waterfront, serves basic Greek fare and you can eat outside under the grape vines. Turn left from the quay (facing inland) and you'll find it on the way to Windmills Travel. It's opposite the only **bakery** on Tinos which still uses wood ovens.

Mixhalis Taverna, in the first lane to the right off Evangelistria, is noted for its high quality meat. *Galera Restaurant*, on the waterfront just past Hotel Oceanis, has decent food and a pretty view. To get to *Kypos Taverna* turn right from the quay, and then left at the Hotel Possidonion. Then take the third turn left. A full meal with retsina will cost about 2600 dr.

AROUND TINOS

At **Kionia**, 3km north-west of Tinos town, there are several small beaches, the nearest overlooked by the Tinos Beach Hotel. The site of the **Sanctuary of Poseidon and Amphitrite**, before the hotel, dates from the 4th century BC. The Tiniots worshipped Poseidon because they believed he banished the snakes which once inundated the island.

At **Porto**, 6km east of Tinos town, is a sandy, uncrowded beach. Out of Loutra, **Kolymvythra bay**, on the north coast, has two lovely sandy beaches. Further along the coast is a small beach at **Panormos bay** from where distinctive green marble quarried in nearby **Marlas** and **Panormos** was once exported. **Pyrgos** is a picturesque village where sculptors still carve the marble. Figurines and other marble artefacts are on sale. Take the bus to Pyrgos village from where it's a pleasant 4km walk to the bay of Panormos.

The ruins of the **Venetian Fortress of Exobourgo**, on a 640m hill, stand sentinel over a cluster of unspoilt hill villages. At the fortress, built on an ancient acropolis, the Venetians made their last stand against the Turks. The ascent can be made from several villages. The shortest is from Xinara. It's a steep climb, but the views are worth it.

The tiny, traditional Cycladic village of **Volakas**, nestled on a rocky plain in the centre of the island, is where the famous basket-weavers of Tinos are based. You can usually buy baskets direct from the workshops, but if they're shut, there's a café which sells them. There is a small folkloric museum (entry free), an attractive Catholic chapel and one of the best tavernas on the island, serving home-produced meat and vegetables. It's difficult to get to, but worth the effort. You need to take the Skalados bus from Tinos Town: unfortunately it departs at 2 pm and returns at 2.30 pm on Monday and Friday only, so you'll need to get a taxi either there or back (2000 dr), or hire a motorcycle.

Mykonos Μύκονος

• *pop 6170* • *postcode 846 00* • *area code* ☎ *0289*

Mykonos (**Mee**konos) is the most visited and expensive of all Greek islands and has the most sophisticated nightlife. Despite its reputation as 'the gay capital of Greece', this shouldn't – and doesn't – deter others. The days when Mykonos was the favourite rendezvous for the world's rich and famous may be over, but the island probably still has more poseurs per square metre than any other Mediterranean resort. Depending on your temperament, you'll either be captivated or take one look and stay on the ferry. Barren, low-lying Mykonos would never win a Greek-island beauty competition, but it has good beaches and is the jumping-off point for the sacred island of Delos.

Getting There & Away

Air There are six flights a day to Athens (17,300 dr), six weekly to Santorini (13,900 dr), three a week to Rhodes (20,400 dr), two a week to Iraklio (20,400 dr) and three a week to Thessaloniki (25,100 dr).

Ferry Mykonos has daily services to Rafina (4¼ hours, 3800 dr) via Tinos and Andros; to Piraeus (5½ hours, 4400 dr) via Tinos and

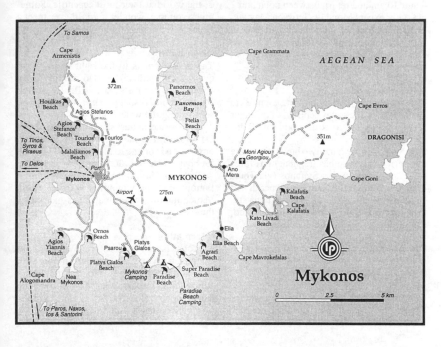

Syros; and to Naxos (1720 dr), Paros (1700 dr), Ios (2980 dr) and Santorini (3200 dr). There are two ferries a week to Amorgos (3000 dr) and one a week to Samos in the North-Eastern Aegean via Ikaria. On Sunday the F/B *Leros* sets out from Kos in the Dodecanese to Kalymnos, Astypalea, Amorgos, Mykonos, Syros and Piraeus. For Thessaloniki/Crete connections see Getting There & Away in the Tinos section.

The port police (☎ 22 218) are on the waterfront, above the National Bank of Greece.

Hydrofoil There are daily hydrofoils connecting Mykonos with Paros, Naxos, Ios and Santorini, as well as with Rafina via Andros and Tinos. There is a weekly service linking Mykonos with Sifnos (6000 dr) and Serifos (6200 dr) in the Western Cyclades.

Excursion Boats These boats leave for Delos (30 minutes, 1600 dr return) between 8 and 10 am and return between noon and 2 pm daily except Monday. Between May and September, guided tours are conducted in English, French and German for 7500 dr. Tickets are available from several waterfront outlets.

Getting Around
The Airport Mykonos' airport, about 3km south-east of the town centre, is no longer served by bus. A taxi costs around 1000 dr.

Bus Mykonos town has two bus stations: the northern bus station has frequent departures to Ornos beach, Agios Stefanos (via Tourlos), Ano Mera, Elia, Kato Livadi beach and Kalafatis beach, while the southern bus station has buses to Agios Yiannis beach, Psarou, Platys Gialos and Paradise beach.

Car & Motorcycle Most car and motorcycle rental firms are around the southern bus station.

Caïque Caïques leave Mykonos town for Super Paradise, Agrari and Elia beaches (June to September only) and from Platys Gialos to Paradise, Super Paradise, Agrari and Elia beaches.

MYKONOS TOWN
Mykonos town, the island's port and capital, is the epitome of warren-like Cycladic villages. Some visitors are enamoured, others find it claustrophobic. It can be very hard to find your bearings, and just when you think you've got it worked out, you'll find yourself back at square one. Throngs of pushy people add to the frustration. However, familiarise yourself with the three main streets that form a horseshoe behind the waterfront and you will have a fighting chance of finding your way around. Even the most disenchanted could not deny that Mykonos town is beautiful – a conglomeration of chic boutiques, houses with brightly painted balconies and geraniums, clematis and bougainvillea growing against whiter than white walls. Mykonos is also a great place to people-watch – not Greeks but the holiday-makers of the world at their most eccentric. Sometimes you may wonder if you'll ever meet a Greek.

Orientation
The waterfront is to the right of the ferry quay (facing inland) beyond the tiny town beach. The central square is Plateia Manto Mavrogenous (usually called Taxi Square), south along the waterfront.

The northern bus station is behind the OTE (see Information), while the southern bus station is on the road to Ornos. The quay for boats to Delos is at the western end of the waterfront. South of here is Mykonos' famous row of windmills and the Little Venice quarter, where balconies hang over the sea.

Information
Mykonos has no tourist office. When you get off the ferry, you will see a low building with four numbered offices. No 1 is the Hotel Reservation Department (☎ 24 540), open from 8 am to midnight; No 2 is the Association of Rooms & Apartments (☎ 26 860), open from 10 am to 6 pm; No 3 has camping

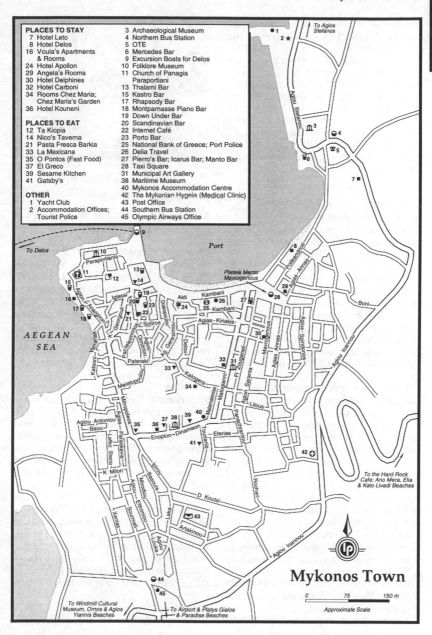

PLACES TO STAY
7 Hotel Leto
8 Hotel Delos
16 Voula's Apartments
    & Rooms
24 Hotel Apollon
29 Angela's Rooms
30 Hotel Delphines
32 Hotel Carboni
34 Rooms Chez Maria;
    Chez Maria's Garden
36 Hotel Kouneni

PLACES TO EAT
12 Ta Kiopia
14 Nico's Taverna
21 Pasta Fresca Barkia
33 La Mexicana
35 O Pontos (Fast Food)
37 El Greco
39 Sesame Kitchen
41 Gatsby's

OTHER
1 Yacht Club
2 Accommodation Offices;
   Tourist Police

3 Archaeological Museum
4 Northern Bus Station
5 OTE
6 Mercedes Bar
9 Excursion Boats for Delos
10 Folklore Museum
11 Church of Panagia
    Paraportiani
13 Thalami Bar
15 Kastro Bar
17 Rhapsody Bar
18 Montparnasse Piano Bar
19 Down Under Bar
20 Scandinavian Bar
22 Internet Café
23 Porto Bar
25 National Bank of Greece; Port Police
26 Delia Travel
27 Pierro's Bar; Icarus Bar; Manto Bar
28 Taxi Square
31 Municipal Art Gallery
38 Maritime Museum
40 Mykonos Accommodation Centre
42 The Mykonian Hygeia (Medical Clinic)
43 Post Office
44 Southern Bus Station
45 Olympic Airways Office

Mykonos Town

0   75   150 m

Approximate Scale

information (☎ 22 852); and No 4 houses the tourist police (☎ 22 482), who have variable opening times.

The National Bank of Greece is on the waterfront and has an ATM. Two doors away, Delia Travel (☎ 22 322) represents American Express. The Mykonian Hygeia (☎ 27 464, or 094-33 8292/35 1253 in an emergency) is a medical clinic on Agiou Ioannou, the ring road behind the town.

The post office is south of the town and the OTE is beside the northern bus terminal. There's an **internet café** on Kouzi Georgouli.

The famous windmills of Mykonos

Museums & Galleries

Mykonos town has four museums. The **archaeological museum**, near the quay, houses pottery from Delos and some grave steles and jewellery from the island of Renia (the necropolis of Delos). Chief exhibits are a pithos featuring a Trojan War scene in relief and a statue of Heracles. It's open Tuesday to Sunday from 8.30 am to 3 pm. Admission is 500 dr, free on Sunday.

The **maritime museum** has well-displayed nautical paraphernalia. It's open 10.30 am to 1 pm and 6.30 to 9 pm daily. Admission is 350 dr.

The excellent **folklore museum**, which is housed in an 18th-century sea captain's mansion, features a large collection of memorabilia, a reconstructed 19th-century kitchen and a bedroom with a four-poster bed. There's also a rather macabre stuffed pelican, the erstwhile Petros, who was run over by a car in 1985. He was hastily replaced by Petros II, whom you'll probably meet while wandering. Petros I crash-landed on Mykonos during a mid-1950s storm. The islanders regarded him as a lucky omen because his arrival heralded Mykonos' status as the premier Cycladic resort. The museum, near the Delos quay, is open daily from 5.30 to 8.30 pm. Entrance is free.

On the road to Ornos is the **Windmill Cultural Museum**. Entrance is free but opening times are erratic.

The **municipal art gallery** (☎ 27 190) on Matogianni is open daily from 10 am to 6 pm, but don't rely on these times.

Church of Panagia Paraportiani

Of Mykonos' many churches, the Panagia Paraportiani is the most famous. It is actually four little churches amalgamated into one – a white, lumpy asymmetrical building which seems to have been cobbled together without rhyme or reason, and yet the result is one of great beauty. The interplay of light and shade on the multifaceted structure creates subtle nuances. It's a photographer's delight.

Activities

Watersports There's a massive new watersports complex built on 40 acres of land close to Elia beach. **Watermania** (☎ 71 477) has a range of giant water slides and a **scuba diving** school. There are restaurants, bars and nightclubs where party-goers can play till dawn. Continuous shuttle buses run to and from the northern bus station in Mykonos town.

Dive Adventures (☎ 26 539), on Paradise beach, offers the full range of scuba-diving courses right up to instructor level. The new **Aphrodite Diving School**, is owned by Hotel Aphrodite (☎ 71 367) on Kalafatis beach. Other facilities include tennis, horse-riding, a gymnasium and aerobics.

Organised Tours

Excursion boats run day trips to the sacred

island of Delos. See the Mykonos Getting There & Away section for details.

Places to Stay – bottom end

Mykonos has two camping grounds: *Paradise Beach Camping* (☎ 22 852) on Paradise beach and *Mykonos Camping* (☎ 24 578), on Paraga beach (10 minutes walk from Platys Gialos beach). Both sites have good facilities. Minibuses from the camping grounds meet the ferries.

Mykonos' hotel prices will make your jaw drop. They're about double most places in Greece, although the standard of service doesn't always match the price. If you arrive without a reservation between June and September and manage to barter for suitably priced accommodation, take it. Otherwise seek the assistance of organisations mentioned in the Information section or head for John at the Mykonos Accommodation Centre (☎ 23 408). If you choose domatia from owners meeting ferries, ask if they charge for transport. Some do.

The D-class *Hotel Carboni* (☎ 22 217), on Andronikou Matogianni, has doubles/triples with private bathroom for 10,000/13,000 dr. *Angela's Rooms* (☎ 22 967), on Taxi Square, has doubles with private bathroom for 12,000 dr. The old-world D-class *Hotel Apollon* (☎ 22 223), on the waterfront, has singles/doubles/triples with shared bathroom for 10,000/12,500/13,000 dr. *Rooms Chez Maria* (☎ 22 480) has attractive doubles/triples for 12,000/15,000 dr with private bathroom.

Places to Stay – middle

The C-class *Hotel Delos* (☎ 22 517), on the town beach, has doubles/triples with private bathroom for 14,800/17,000 dr. *Hotel Delphines* (☎ 24 505), on Matogianni, is nicely furnished and has singles/doubles/ triples for 13,000/16,500/20,000 dr. Little Venice's only seafront accommodation is *Voula's Apartments & Rooms* (☎ 22 951/157). Its balconied rooms are above a club and taverna so bring earplugs if you're not prepared to party. Doubles/triples with private bathroom and basic cooking facilities are

18,000/20,000 dr. Voula meets boats and does not charge for transport.

The *Hotel Kouneni* (☎ 22 301) on Tria Pigadia, a square set just back from the road, has a charming garden and singles/doubles with private bathroom and breakfast for 16,000/21,000 dr.

Places to Stay – top end

The newly refurbished *Hotel Leto* (☎ 22 207), facing the town beach, has been host to guests including Greece's king and international celebrities. Doubles/triples cost 58,000/70,000 dr including breakfast. For more top-end hotel listings, see the Beaches and Ano Mera sections.

Places to Eat

The high prices charged in many of Mykonos' eating establishments are not always indicative of quality or quantity. *Gatsby's* is one of the best, with gourmet burgers from 2200 dr and salmon fillet for 2700 dr. *Pasta Fresca Barkia* serves fresh pasta made on the premises; spaghetti bolognese is 2200 dr. *La Mexicana* does great fajitas for 2600 dr.

Nico's Taverna, up from the Delos quay, and *Ta Kiopia*, opposite, are both popular. *Sesame Kitchen*, next to the marine museum, serves mostly vegetarian dishes at reasonable prices.

Chez Maria's Garden is renowned for its 'seafood treasure' – a mere 40,000 dr for two! – and veal T-bone (6200 dr). *El Greco* serves interesting dishes such as rooster (2150 dr) and leg of lamb (2850 dr).

There's a cluster of cheap fast-food outlets in the centre of town: *O Pontos* serves gyros for 300 dr. There are several supermarkets and fruit stalls, particularly around the southern bus station.

Entertainment

The nightlife on Mykonos leaves all other Greek islands in the shade. New places come and go but the following are perennials. The *Down Under* bar, run by Australian Theo, is the cheapest, with beers at 500 dr, and the nearby *Scandinavian Bar* is also popular.

Mercedes, near the archaeological museum, is an expensive, sophisticated disco with an older clientele. The atmospheric waterfront *Thalami Bar* features Greek music.

For classy ambience try *Montparnasse Piano Bar* in Little Venice; it plays classical music at sunset. Next door, *Rhapsody* is a great new bar playing jazz and blues. If you're roomless or an insomniac, head for the *Yacht Club*, by the quay, which is open 24 hours.

The *Hard Rock Café*, about 4km along the Ano Mera road, is an astonishing complex serving Greek and US food. It has a nightclub and offers free use of a pool between noon and 4 am. A pink courtesy bus shuttles ravers to the café complex from the Yacht Club every half-hour between noon and 4 am.

The new *Club Paradiso*, 300m above Paradise beach, has all-night raves starting at 3 am with international DJs. Entry is 5000 dr.

Gay & Lesbian Venues *Porto* has a reputation for being the best pick-up bar in town. *Kastro Bar* in Little Venice plays classical music at sunset, while *Pierro's* is the place for late-night dancing. Adjoining it, *Icarus* and *Manto* are popular haunts.

Super Paradise is the nudist gay beach.

Things to Buy

Nothing is cheap on Mykonos but it offers beautiful cotton and lace curtains, and museum copies of early Mykonian and Cycladic designs. Look in Little Venice for feather-soft hand knits of angora wool which is spun outside a few shops by old women.

Greek jewellery is much in evidence, as are handwoven rugs with Mykonian motifs. You can also find Byzantine-style items, and icon replicas fashioned from old wood collected from all over Greece.

AROUND MYKONOS
Beaches

The nearest beaches to Mykonos town are **Malaliamos** and the tiny, crowded **Tourlos**, 2km to the north. **Agios Stefanos**, 2km

beyond here, is larger but just as crowded. To the south, beyond **Ornos**, is **Agios Yiannis**, the attractive beach where the movie *Shirley Valentine* was filmed. Unless you're pushed for time, jump on a bus to **Platys Gialos**, on the south-west coast. The beach is long and sandy but inevitably crowded. From here, caïques call at the island's best beaches further around the south coast. They are **Paradise**, **Super Paradise**, **Agrari** and **Elia** beaches. Nudism is accepted on all these beaches. Elia is the last caïque stop, so is the least crowded. The next beach along, **Kato Livadi**, is also relatively uncrowded.

Beaches on the north coast are prone to the meltemi wind. The best is **Panormos beach**, reached along a road or a path just before Ano Mera.

Places to Stay There are many places for a splurge around the coast. The newly refurbished *Ornos Beach Hotel* (☎ 23 216) has great sea views and a swimming pool. Doubles cost 30,000 dr. *Villa Katerina* (☎ 23 414), a quiet, romantic place, 300m up the hill above Agios Ioannis beach, has a garden and pool. Double studios cost 24,000 dr. Close by, the A-class *Appollonia Bay* (☎ 27 890) has doubles for 42,200 dr.

On Kalafatis beach, the A-class *Aphrodite Beach Hotel* (☎ 71 367) has masses of facilities including water sports and scuba diving. Doubles/triples cost 40,000/52,000 dr. At Platys Gialos, the A-class *Petinos Beach* (☎ 24 310) has a bar, pool and watersports equipment. Doubles are 38,500 dr. Nearby, under the same management, *Hotel Petinos* (☎ 23 680) has doubles for 24,000 dr. At Agios Stefanos, The A-class *Princess of Mykonos* (☎ 23 806 or 24 713) was once a Jane Fonda hang-out. Singles/doubles are 40,000/45,000 dr.

Ano Mera Ανω Μέρα

The stark village of Ano Mera, 7km east of Mykonos town, is the island's only inland settlement. On its pretty central square is the 6th-century **Moni Panagias Tourlianis**, which has a fine stone carved bell tower, an ornate wood iconostasis carved in Florence in the late 1700s and 16th-century icons of the Cretan School. There's a small **museum** here.

The A-class *Ano Mera Hotel* (☎ 71 215) has a pool, restaurant and disco. Singles/doubles/triples with breakfast are 23,600/28,000/33,800 dr.

Delos Δήλος

Despite its diminutive size, Delos is one of the most important archaeological sites in Greece, and certainly the most important in the Cyclades. The Cyclades are so named because they form a circle *(kyklos)* around Delos. Lying a few kilometres off the west coast of Mykonos, the sacred island of Delos is the mythical birthplace of Apollo and Artemis. Like many archaeological sites it is closed on Monday.

History
Delos was first inhabited in the 3rd millennium BC. In the 8th century BC, the annual Delia festival was established on the island to celebrate the birth of Apollo. For a long time, the Athenians coveted Delos, seeing its strategic position as one from where they could control the Aegean. By the 5th century BC, it had come under their jurisdiction.

After Athens defeated the Persians, it established the Delian League in 477 BC, and its treasury was kept on Delos. It carried out a number of 'purifications', decreeing that no-one could be born or could die on Delos, thus strengthening its control over the island by removing the native population.

Delos reached the height of its power in Hellenistic times, becoming one of the three most important religious centres in Greece and a flourishing centre of commerce. It traded throughout the Mediterranean and was populated with wealthy merchants, mariners and bankers from as far away as Egypt and Syria. These inhabitants built temples to the various gods worshiped in their countries of origin, although Apollo remained the principal deity.

The Romans made Delos a free port in 167 BC, which brought even greater prosperity. But, by then, it had become debased and was the most lucrative slave market in the Mediterranean. In 88 BC, it was sacked by Mithridates and 10,000 of the island's inhabitants were massacred. From then on, Delos was prey to pirates and, later, to looters of antiquities.

Getting There & Away
See Excursion Boats under Mykonos for schedules and prices.

ANCIENT DELOS
Orientation & Information
The small modern quay is south of the *Sacred Harbour*. Many of the most significant finds from Delos are in the National Archaeological Museum in Athens. The on-site **museum** has a modest collection.

Overnight stays on Delos are forbidden, and the boat schedule allows only three hours there. Bring water and food as the island's cafeteria is poor value. Wear a hat and sensible shoes. Entrance to the site costs 1200 dr (including entrance to the museum).

Exploring the Site
Following is an outline of some significant archaeological remains on Delos. For further site details, buy a guidebook at the ticket office.

If you have the energy, climb Mt Kythnos (113m), to the south-east of the harbour to see the layout of Delos. There are terrific views of surrounding islands on clear days.

The path is reached by walking through the **theatre quarter**. Delos' wealthiest inhabitants built their houses here in the precincts of the **Theatre of Delos**. The houses surrounded peristyled courtyards. Mosaics, apparently a status symbol, were the most striking feature of each house.

These colourful mosaics were exquisite art works, mostly representational and offset by intricate geometric borders. The most lavish dwellings were the **House of Dionysos**, named after its mosaic depicting the wine god riding a panther; and the **House**

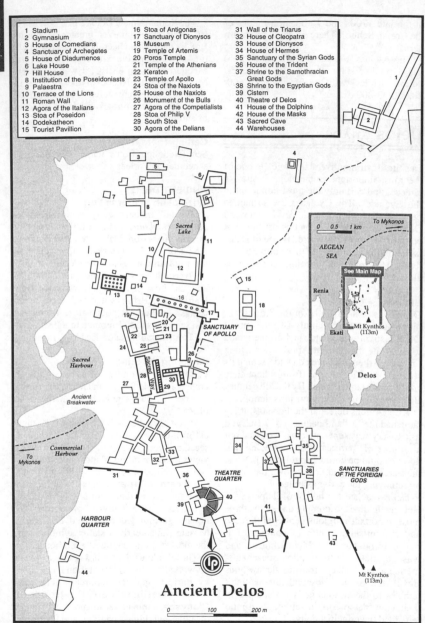

1	Stadium
2	Gymnasium
3	House of Comedians
4	Sanctuary of Archegetes
5	House of Diadumenos
6	Lake House
7	Hill House
8	Institution of the Poseidoniasts
9	Palaestra
10	Terrace of the Lions
11	Roman Wall
12	Agora of the Italians
13	Stoa of Poseidon
14	Dodekatheon
15	Tourist Pavillion
16	Stoa of Antigonas
17	Sanctuary of Dionysos
18	Museum
19	Temple of Artemis
20	Poros Temple
21	Temple of the Athenians
22	Keraton
23	Temple of Apollo
24	Stoa of the Naxiots
25	House of the Naxiots
26	Monument of the Bulls
27	Agora of the Competialists
28	Stoa of Philip V
29	South Stoa
30	Agora of the Delians
31	Wall of the Triarus
32	House of Cleopatra
33	House of Dionysos
34	House of Hermes
35	Sanctuary of the Syrian Gods
36	House of the Trident
37	Shrine to the Samothracian Great Gods
38	Shrine to the Egyptian Gods
39	Cistern
40	Theatre of Delos
41	House of the Dolphins
42	House of the Masks
43	Sacred Cave
44	Warehouses

Ancient Delos

of **Cleopatra**, where headless statues of the house's owners were found. These are now in the museum. The **House of the Trident** was one of the grandest houses. The **House of the Masks**, probably a hostelry for actors, has another mosaic of Dionysos resplendent astride a panther. The **House of the Dolphins** has another exceptional mosaic.

The theatre dates from 300 BC and had a large cistern, the remains of which can be seen. It supplied much of the town with water. The houses of the wealthy had their own cisterns – essential appendages as Delos was almost as parched and barren then as it is today.

On the descent from Mt Kythnos, explore the **Sanctuaries of the Foreign Gods**. Here, at the **Shrine to the Samothracian Great Gods**, the Kabeiroi (the twins Dardanos and Aeton) were worshipped. At the **Sanctuary of the Syrian Gods** there are remains of a theatre. Here, an audience watched orgies held in honour of the Syrian deities. There is also an area where Egyptian deities, including Serapis and Isis, were worshipped.

Leto with the twins Apollo and Artemis

The **Sanctuary of Apollo**, to the north of the harbour, contains temples dedicated to him. It is also the site of the much photographed **Terrace of the Lions**. These proud beasts, carved from marble, were offerings from the people of Naxos that were presented to Delos in the 7th century BC. Their function was to guard the sacred area. To the east of them is the **Sacred Lake** (dry since 1925) where, according to legend, Leto gave birth to Apollo and Artemis.

Syros Σύρος

• *pop 19,870* • *postcode 841 00* • *area code* ☎ *0281*
Many tourists come to Syros (**See**ros) merely to change ferries. This is a pity because its capital, Ermoupolis, named after Hermes, god of trade, is a beautiful city whose inhabitants have not become tourist-weary. Syros' economy depends little on tourism, and though its ship-building industry has declined, it has textile factories, dairy farms and a horticultural industry supplying the rest of the Cyclades with plants and flowers. It's also the summer home of several celebrities such as French actress Catherine Deneuve.

History
In the Middle Ages, Syros was the only Greek island with an entirely Roman Catholic population, the result of conversions by the Franks who took over the island in 1207. This gave it the support and protection of the west (particularly the French) during Ottoman times.

Syros remained neutral during the War of Independence and thousands of refugees from islands ravaged by the Turks fled here. They brought their Orthodox religion and built a new settlement on a hill (now called Vrodado) and the port town of Ermoupolis. After Independence, Ermoupolis became the commercial, naval and cultural centre of Greece. Today, Syros' Catholic population is 40% and Orthodox makes up the other 60%. The city's ornate churches and neoclassical

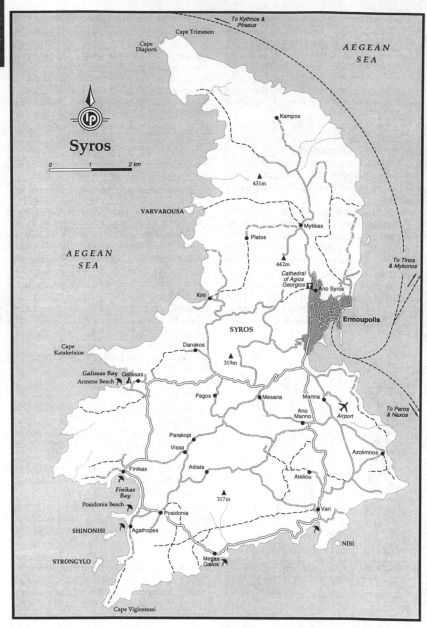

Syros

0   1   2 km

*AEGEAN
SEA*

To Kythnos &
Piraeus

Cape Trimeson

Cape
Diaporti

Kampos

▲
431m

VARVAROUSA

*AEGEAN
SEA*

Mytikas

Platos

▲
442m

*Cathedral
of Agios
Georgios*

Ano Syros

Kini

Ermoupolis

To Tinos
& Mykonos

SYROS

Danakos

▲
319m

Cape
Katakefalos

Galissas Bay Galissas
Armeos Beach △

Pagos

Mesaria

Manna

Ano
Manno

Airport

To Paros
& Naxos

Parakopi

Vissa

Azolimnos

Finikas

Adiata

Ateliou

*Finikas
Bay*

Posidonia Beach

▲
317m

Vari

SHINONISI

Agathopes

Posidonia

NISI

STRONGYLO

Megas
Gialos

Cape Viglostassi

mansions (many now being restored) are testimonies to its former grandeur.

Getting There & Away

Air Syros has at least two flights a day to/from Athens (13,800 dr). The Olympic Airways office (☎ 88 018) is on the waterfront, around the corner from Naxou. Tickets can also be bought from TeamWork Holidays (☎ 83 400; fax 83 508), on the waterfront just before Plateia Kanari.

Ferry Syros has at least two ferries a day to Piraeus (four hours, 4000 dr), Tinos and Mykonos; at least one to Paros (1600 dr) and Naxos; at least four a week to Amorgos; and one a week to Rafina (four hours, 3250 dr). On Saturday the F/B *Leros* leaves Syros for Paros, Amorgos, and the Dodecanese islands of Astypalea, Kalymnos and Kos, returning via Mykonos early Monday morning. On Tuesday GA Ferries' *Daliana* leaves Syros for Crete (5120 dr), Halki (5920 dr) and Rhodes (6610 dr). On Sunday morning the F/B *Agios Rafail* arrives from Lesvos, in the North-Eastern Aegean, and heads back for Lesvos at 9 pm.

Syros' port police (☎ 82 690 or 88 888) are on the eastern side of the waterfront.

Hydrofoil There are daily hydrofoils to Tinos (2220 dr), Mykonos (2920 dr), Paros (3000 dr), Naxos (3930 dr), Ios (7000 dr) and Santorini (7750 dr); as well as one or two services a week to the smaller islands. There are daily hydrofoils and catamarans to Rafina on the mainland (6640 dr).

Getting Around

Frequent buses do a southern loop around the island from Ermoupolis, calling at all beaches mentioned in the text. Cars can be hired from TeamWork Holidays (see Getting There & Away) from 9000 dr a day.

ERMOUPOLIS Ερμούπολη

During the 19th century, a combination of fortuitous circumstances resulted in Ermou-

polis becoming Greece's major port. It was superseded by Piraeus long ago but is still the Cyclades' largest city and its capital, with a population of 12,000. As the boat sails into Syros' port of Ermoupolis you will see the Catholic settlement of Ano Syros to the left, and the Orthodox settlement of Vrodado to the right, both set on hills. Spilling down from them both and skirting the harbour is Ermoupolis. It's an impressive sight.

Orientation & Information

Most boats dock at the west of the bay. In summer there is an information booth to the right of the quay after the wharf. The bus station is also by the quay. There are public toilets and showers (700 dr) around the bay to the east, near the port police.

To reach the central square of Plateia Miaouli from the quay, turn right and then left into El Venizelou. The National Bank of Greece and the OTE are to the right of the square. The police station (☎ 82 610) is one block west of the Ionian Bank (which has an ATM) on Eleftheriou Venizelou, the post office is on Protopapadaki and the EOT (☎ 82 375) is on Dodekanisou.

Things to See

Vrodado and Ermoupolis merge but **Ano Syros** (Ανω Σώρος) is quite different – a typical Cycladic settlement of narrow alleyways and whitewashed houses. It's a fascinating place to wander around and has views of neighbouring islands. On the way up, check the **Agios Georgios Cemetery** which has ostentatious mausoleums reminiscent of Athens' First Cemetery. The finest of Ano Syros' Catholic churches is the baroque **Cathedral of St George**. Close by is the **Capuchin Monastery of St Jean**, founded in 1535 to minister to the poor. Ano Syros was the birthplace of Markos Vamvakaris, the celebrated rembetika singer. To reach Ano Syros, walk up Omirou.

Plateia Miaouli is the hub of bustling Ermoupolis. It's flanked by palm trees and cafés and dominated by the town hall, a magnificent neoclassical building designed by the German architect Ernst Ziller. The

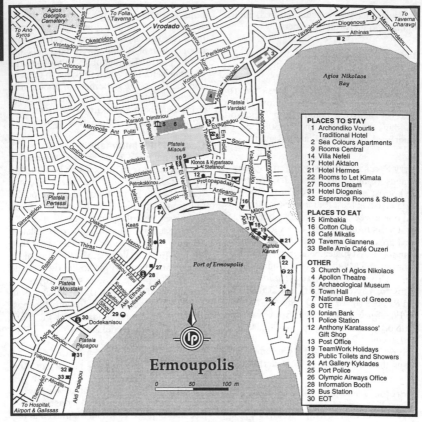

PLACES TO STAY
1 Archondiko Vourlis
   Traditional Hotel
2 Sea Colours Apartments
9 Rooms Central
14 Villa Nefeli
17 Hotel Aktaion
21 Hotel Hermes
22 Rooms to Let Kimata
27 Rooms Dream
31 Hotel Diogenis
32 Esperance Rooms & Studios

PLACES TO EAT
15 Kimbakia
16 Cotton Club
18 Café Mikalis
20 Taverna Giannena
33 Belle Amie Café Ouzeri

OTHER
3 Church of Agios Nikolaos
4 Apollon Theatre
5 Archaeological Museum
6 Town Hall
7 National Bank of Greece
8 OTE
10 Ionian Bank
11 Police Station
12 Anthony Karatassos'
    Gift Shop
13 Post Office
19 TeamWork Holidays
23 Public Toilets and Showers
24 Art Gallery Kyklades
25 Port Police
26 Olympic Airways Office
28 Information Booth
29 Bus Station
30 EOT

small **archaeological museum** in the town hall houses a mediocre collection of vases, grave steles, heads and torsos – hardly worthy of the capital of the Cyclades. It's open Tuesday to Sunday from 8.30 am to 3 pm. Entry is free.

The **Apollon Theatre**, on Plateia Vardaki, was designed by the French architect Chabeau and is a replica of La Scala in Milan. There are terrific views from the **Church of Anastasis**, on top of Vrodado hill – reached by walking up Louka Ralli.

The **Art Gallery Kyklades**, behind the port police, is open Tuesday to Friday from

10.30 am to 1.30 pm and from 7 to 9 pm; Saturday from 7 to 9 pm and Sunday from 10.30 am to 1.30 pm.

Organised Tours
TeamWork Holidays (see Getting There & Away) offers excursions around the island by bus or boat.

Places to Stay
Domatia owners are discouraged from meeting ferries, but there are plenty of rooms in the centre of town. Anthony Karatassos is president of the Association of Rooms (☎ 82

252): you might find him at his gift shop on Protopapadaki ... or at *Rooms Central* on Plateia Miaouli. Then again, you might not. If you have any problem finding accommodation, head for TeamWork Holidays.

The faded *Hotel Aktaion* (☎ 82 675), by the waterfront, has singles/doubles/triples for 4800/7500/8000 dr; some have private bathrooms.

The new *Villa Nefeli* (☎ 87 076), on Hiou, known as Market Street, has doubles with private bathroom for 8000 dr and double studios for 11,000 dr. *Rooms to Let Kimata* (☎ 82 758), between the waterfront and Plateia Kanari, has spacious doubles with private bathroom for 12,000 dr.

Rooms Dream (☎ 84 356), on the waterfront, has doubles with private bathroom for 11,000 dr. The B-class *Hotel Hermes* (☎ 83 011), Plateia Kanari, has comfortable doubles from 14,000 dr.

On the waterfront, south of the bus station and quay, is the *Hotel Diogenis* (☎ 86 301/305), a restored neoclassical building; singles/doubles with TV and minibar cost 14,000/17,000 dr.

Further along the waterfront is the neoclassical *Esperance Rooms & Studios* (☎ 81 671) with air-con and port view for 12,000 dr a double.

The luxurious *Sea Colours Apartments* (☎ 88 716 or 81 181; fax 83 508) has two-person studios for 14,000 dr and four-person apartments for 24,000 dr. To find it, descend the steps after the Church of Agios Nikolaos. Sea Colours is on the right, hovering over lovely Agios Nikolaos bay, north-east of the port.

The *Archondiko Vourlis Traditional Hotel* (☎ & fax 88 440) is a well-restored neoclassical mansion at Mavrodkordatou 5, up and around from Sea Colours Apartments. Suites with antique furniture start at 36,000 dr a double. The newly refurbished *Syrou Melathron* (☎ 86 495), also on the bay, has similar suites at the same price.

Places to Eat

Taverna Giannena, just past TeamWork Holidays, specialises in kokoretsi (lamb's liver) and spiced rolled pork, both at 1400 dr. Beneath Esperance Rooms & Studios, *Belle Amie Café Ouzeri* is good for breakfast, snacks and mezedes from 8 am to 2 am.

Café Mikalis is a good place to stop for an ouzo with all the traditional accompaniments. The waterfront is lined with daytime cafés and late-night bars such as *Cotton Club* and *Kimbakia*.

It's worth a taxi ride (or bracing walk) to go to *Taverna Charavgi* at Agiou Dimitriou 4, a continuation of Mavrokordatou. It has fair-priced grills and staples and a great view. Continue on to the *Folia Taverna*, at Athanasiou Diakou 2, which has imaginatively prepared dishes, particularly rabbit and pigeon, at reasonable prices. From town, walk up Omirou, turn right into Okaenidon, walk to its end, turn left then right into Athanasiou Diakou. The restaurant is on the left where the road curves.

If you've got a sweet tooth, don't miss the loukoumia (Turkish delight) that Syros is famous for. It's so popular that vendors race aboard ferries in the few minutes between arrival and departure. There is a *food market* on Hiou.

GALISSAS Γαλησσάς

The west-coast resort of Galissas has one of the island's best beaches – a 900m crescent of sand, shaded by tamarisk trees. Armeos, a walk round the left of the bay, is an official nudist beach.

Despite the fact that hotels and domatia are mushrooming at alarming rates here, Galissas still has a good, laid-back feel.

Places to Stay – bottom end

Syros' two camp sites are both at Galissas. The bizarrely-named *Camping the Two Hearts* (☎ 42 052/321) has most facilities – from motorcycle rental to minigolf, barbecues to bungalows. Its minibus meets the ferries. The other site is *Yianna Camping* (☎ 42 418).

Karmelina Rooms (☎ 42 320) has clean doubles which cost 11,200 dr with shared bathroom and communal kitchen. The same family owns nice apartments with doubles for 14,000 dr. The domatia are on the right of the main road coming from Ermoupolis (beyond the branch road to the beach). Close by, *Pension Blue Sky* (☎ 43 410; fax 43 411), has single/double studios for 9000/12,000 dr and four-person apartments for 16,000 dr. *Corali Rooms* (☎ 85 402), on Vassilikosis, has doubles for 12,000 dr with private bathroom and two-person apartments for 14,000 dr.

Places to Stay – middle
Hotel Benois (☎ 42 833/944/333), at the entrance to the beach, is an attractive C-class hotel. Singles/doubles/triples with private bathroom are 12,000/14,000/18,200 dr.

The A-class *Dolphin Bay Hotel* (☎ 42 924; fax 42 843) is an unmissable cluster of buildings left of the beach as you face the sea. Singles/doubles with satellite TV, private safe and other amenities are 17,000/24,000 dr.

Places to Eat
The *Café Bar* (also a minimarket), overlooking the beach, serves good, cheap meals. Three tavernas (more expensive) and a separate music bar are also in the village.

OTHER BEACHES
South of Galissas there are more beaches. All have domatia and some have hotels. The first is **Finikas**, with a small, tree-lined beach. The next, **Posidonia**, is appealing, with a sand and pebble beach shaded by tamarisk trees.

Further south, **Agathopes** has a nice tree-bordered sandy beach. On the south coast, **Megas Gialos** is tranquil with two sand beaches.

Vari, the next bay along, has a sandy beach but is more developed. In Vari, *Hotel Romantica* (☎ 61 500), *Hotel Domenica* (☎ 61 216) and *Hotel Kamelo* (☎ 61 217), all C-class, have singles/doubles for 10,000/12,000 dr.

Naxos & the Minor Islands Νάξος & τα Κουφονήσια

Give me again your empty boon,
Sweet Sleep – the gentle dream
How Theseus 'neath the fickle moon
Upon the Ocean stream
Took me and led me by the hand
To be his Queen in Athens land.

He slew the half-bull Minotaur
In labyrinthine ways.
But, threadless, had he come no more
From out my father's maze:
Yet I who taught his hands this guile
Am left forlorn on Naxos Isle.

Dionysiaca XLVII by Nonnos
(translated by Roger Lancelyn Green)

NAXOS
• *pop 14,838* • *postcode 843 00* • *area code* ☎ *0285*

It was on Naxos (**Na**xos), according to mythology, that Theseus abandoned Ariadne after she helped him in his efforts to slay the Minotaur on Crete. She didn't pine long; she was soon ensconced in the arms of Dionysos.

The island is the Cyclades' largest and most fertile, producing olives, citrus fruits, corn and potatoes. Its Mt Zeus (1010m) is the archipelago's highest peak. Rugged mountains and green valleys make it one of the most scenic of the Cycladic islands. Naxos is popular, although not as heavily visited as Mykonos, Santorini and Paros.

Organised Tours
The Naxos Tourist Information Centre (see Information section under Naxos Town) offers day tours to a secluded beach by bus (4000 dr) or caïque (up to 12,000 dr including BBQ). There are daily excursions to Santorini (9000 dr) and Mykonos (8000 dr) and frequent excursions to Delos.

Getting There & Away
Air There are two flights a day to Athens

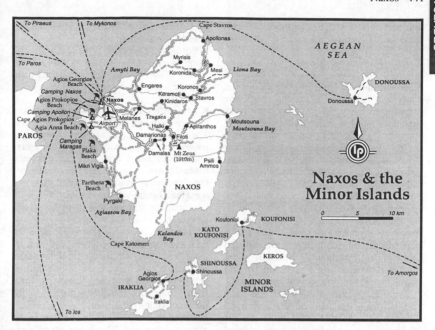

Map features (labels): To Piraeus, To Mykonos, Cape Stavros, Apollonas, AEGEAN SEA, Myrisis, Mesi, Liona Bay, DONOUSSA, Amyti Bay, Koronida, Agios Georgios Beach, Engares, Koronos, Donoussa, Camping Naxos, Keramoti, Stavros, Agios Prokopios Beach, Kinidaros, Naxos, Camping Apollon, Cape Agios Prokopios, Melanes, Tragaea, Moutsouna, Agia Anna Beach, Airport, Halki, Apiranthos, Moutsouna Bay, PAROS, Camping Maragas, Damarionas, Filoti, Plaka Beach, Damalas, Mt Zeus (1010m), Psili Ammos, Mikri Vigla, Parthena Beach, NAXOS, Pyrgaki, Agiassou Bay, Koufonisi, KOUFONISI, KATO KOUFONISI, Kalandos Bay, KEROS, Cape Katomeri, SHINOUSSA, To Amorgos, Agios Georgios, Shinoussa, MINOR ISLANDS, IRAKLIA, Iraklia, To Ios, Naxos & the Minor Islands, 0 5 10 km

(18,600 dr). Olympic Airways is represented by Naxos Tours (☎ 22 095).

Ferry Naxos has ferry connections at least twice a day to Piraeus (six hours, 4280 dr), once a day to Mykonos (1720 dr), and once a day to Paros (1400 dr), Ios (2100 dr) and Santorini (2700 dr). There are several boats a week to the Minor Islands (Iraklia and Koufonisi) and Amorgos; at least two a week to Folegandros, Sikinos and Iraklio (Crete); and one a week to Samos.

GA Ferries' *Daliana*, *Romilda*, *Milena* and *Marina* link Naxos and Paros with Piraeus, Crete, Rhodes and the Dodecanese, and with Ikaria and Samos in the North-Eastern Aegean. See the Getting There & Away section under Paros for schedules.

The Minoan Lines F/B *El Greco* leaves Crete every Thursday for Santorini, Naxos, Syros, Skiathos and Thessaloniki on the mainland, returning via the same route the following day.

Naxos' port police (☎ 23 300) are in the town hall, south of the quay.

Hydrofoil There are daily hydrofoils between Naxos, Ios (4050 dr) and Santorini (5500 dr), and between Naxos, Paros, Mykonos and Tinos. There are daily services to Rafina (7890 dr), three a week to Syros and occasional services to smaller islands. The hydrofoil representative is Passenger travel office (☎ 25 329).

Getting Around
The Airport There is no shuttle bus to the airport, but you can catch Agios Prokopios or Agia Anna-bound buses, which pass close by. A taxi to/from the airport costs 1500 dr.

Bus Frequent buses run to Agia Anna beach from Naxos town . There are five buses a day to Filoti (400 dr) via Halki (360 dr), four a day to Pyrgaki (250 dr), Apollonas and Apiranthos (550 dr) via Filoti and Halki, and two a day to Melanes (250 dr). Buses leave from the end of the wharf.

Car, Motorcycle & Bicycle You can hire cars and motorcycles as well as 21-speed all-terrain bicycles from the outlets along the waterfront in Naxos town. Pay particular attention to the small print for liability as there are frequent accidents throughout the summer. Prices for the bicycles start at 3000 dr. You'll need all the gears – the roads are steep, winding and not always in good condition. If cycling, remember that it is a very large island: from Naxos to Apollonas is 35kms.

Naxos Town

Naxos town, on the west coast, is the island's port and capital. It's a large town, divided into two neighbourhoods – Bourgos, where the Greeks lived, and Kastro, on the hill above, where the Venetian Catholics lived.

A causeway to the north of the port leads to the islet of Palatia and the unfinished Temple of Apollo, Naxos' most famous landmark. Legend holds that when İstanbul is returned to Greece, the door to the temple will miraculously appear. Naxos' northern shore is called Grotta – nicknamed Grotty by some tourists. South-west of the town is the sandy beach of Agios Georgios.

Orientation The ferry quay is at the northern end of the waterfront. The bus terminal is in front of the quay and a schedule is posted outside the bus information office to the north of the terminal.

Information There is no EOT and no tourist police. The privately owned Naxos Tourist Information Centre (☎ 24 358; fax 25 200) opposite the quay makes up for this, thanks to the inimitable English-speaking Despina.

The National Bank of Greece on the waterfront has an ATM. Next door there is a good book and newspaper shop called Zoom, and immediately adjacent, the town's best bakery and a supermarket. To reach them turn right from the quay (facing inland). The OTE is 150m further on. For the post office, turn left just beyond the OTE and take the second right.

For laundry services go to Naxos Tourist Information Centre (NTIC). It costs 2000 dr a load. NTIC and the Okeanis Hotel offer luggage storage starting at 400 dr a day.

Kastro After leaving the waterfront, turn into the winding back streets of Bourgos. The most alluring part of Naxos town is the residential Kastro, with winding alleyways and whitewashed houses. Marco Sanudo made the town the capital of his duchy and there are some handsome dwellings which were built by the Venetians, many with well-kept gardens and insignia of their original residents.

Take a stroll around Kastro during siesta time to experience its hushed, medieval atmosphere. The **archaeological museum** (signposted) is here, housed in a former school where author Nikos Kazantzakis was briefly a pupil. The contents include the usual collection of vases, torsos and funerary steles, as well as Hellenistic and Roman terracotta figurines. There are also, more interestingly, some Early Cycladic figurines. The museum is open Tuesday to Sunday from 8.30 am to 3 pm. Admission is 600 dr. Close by, **Sanudo's palace**, near the Kastro's ramparts, and the Roman Catholic **cathedral** are worth seeing.

Places to Stay – bottom end There are three camp sites near Naxos town: *Camping Naxos* (☎ 23 500), 1km south of Agios Georgios beach; *Camping Maragas* (☎ 24 552), Agia Anna beach; and *Camping Apollon* (☎ 24 417), 700m from Agios Prokopios beach. All sites have good facilities and minibuses meet the boats.

The *Dionyssos Youth Hostel* (☎ 22 331) has dorm beds for 1500 dr and is a good place to meet other travellers. Simply furnished singles/doubles are 2000/3000 dr with shared facilities and doubles/triples with bathroom are 4000/5000 dr. The hostel is signposted from Agiou Nikodemou (also known as Market St), Bourgos' main street. The recently refurbished *Okeanis Hotel*

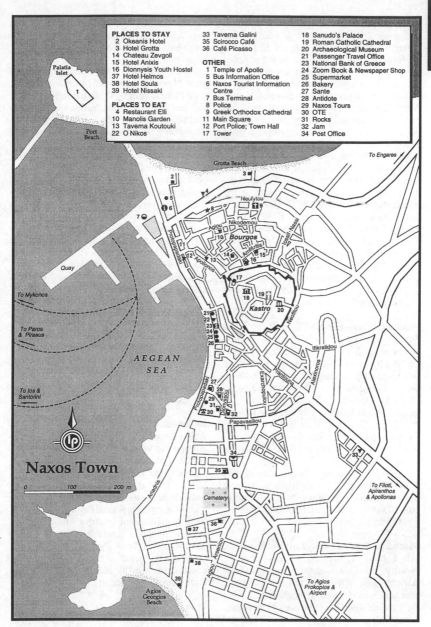

PLACES TO STAY
2 Okeanis Hotel
3 Hotel Grotta
14 Chateau Zevgoli
15 Hotel Anixis
16 Dionnysis Youth Hostel
37 Hotel Helmos
38 Hotel Soula
39 Hotel Nissaki

PLACES TO EAT
4 Restaurant Elli
10 Manolis Garden
13 Taverna Koutouki
22 O Nikos

33 Taverna Galini
35 Scirocco Café
36 Café Picasso

OTHER
1 Temple of Apollo
5 Bus Information Office
6 Naxos Tourist Information Centre
7 Bus Terminal
8 Police
9 Greek Orthodox Cathedral
11 Main Square
12 Port Police; Town Hall
17 Tower

18 Sanudo's Palace
19 Roman Catholic Cathedral
20 Archaeological Museum
21 Passenger Travel Office
23 National Bank of Greece
24 Zoom Book & Newspaper Shop
25 Supermarket
26 Bakery
27 Sante
28 Antidote
29 Naxos Tours
30 OTE
31 Rocks
32 Jam
34 Post Office

Palatia Islet

Port Beach

To Engares

Grotta Beach

Neulytou

Agiou Nikodemou

Bourgos

Iossif Nassi

Quay

To Mykonos

Protopapadaki

Apollonos

Amfitritis

Tower 17

Kastro

Neofitou

To Paros & Piraeus

AEGEAN SEA

Ifikratidou

Evarchoniou

Tramlouna

Alexinorou

To Ios & Santorini

Protopapadaki

Dionyssou

Papavasiliou

Naxos Town

0   100   200 m

Anadnis

Cemetery

To Filoti, Apiranthos & Apollonas

Agiou Arseniou

To Agios Prokopios & Airport

Agios Georgios Beach

(☎ 22 931), near the quay, has spotless rooms for 2500/4000/6000 dr with private bathroom. *Hotel Anixis* (☎ & fax 22 112), in the heart of the old town, has doubles/triples for 9000/10,000 dr. If you telephone, the owner will pick you up at the quay.

There are many domatia and hotels near Agios Georgios beach. As usual, you can barter with accommodation owners at the port, but if you can't face the stampede, head straight for Naxos Tourist Information Centre where Despina will sort you out. To get to Agios Georgios beach, turn right from the port and walk along the waterfront. At the fork, veer left. On the left, almost at the beach, is *Hotel Soula* (☎ 23 196). Nicely furnished doubles/triples here are 8000/13,000 dr with private bathroom. There are also apartments at 12,000/14,000 dr for two/three people. On the same street, the C-class *Hotel Helmos* (☎ 22 455) has cosy singles/doubles/triples for 9900/11,000/14,000 dr. Four-person apartments are 16,000 dr.

Places to Stay – middle The well-furnished *Hotel Grotta* (☎ 22 215/101) has splendid sea views. Singles/doubles/triples are 8500/12,000/14,000 dr with private bathroom. If you telephone, the owner will pick you up at the quay. The *Chateau Zevgoli* (☎ 24 525/358, 26 123 or 22 993), in Bourgos, has plush, traditionally furnished rooms for 18,000/22,000 dr. The hotel is owned by Despina from NTIC. She also has large, restored, balconied homes at 15,000/20,000 dr for two/four people.

On Agios Georgios beach, the stylish *Hotel Nissaki* (☎ 25 710) has a swimming pool, bar and restaurant. Singles/doubles cost 10,000/14,000 dr and suites for four are 25,000 dr.

Places to Eat The new *Taverna Koutouki*, just behind Apollonos, is very popular. Nearby, *Manolis Garden*, run by South African-born Vyvienne and her husband, specialises in chicken in yoghurt and wine for 1300 dr. *Scirocco Café* does great breakfasts, with prices ranging from 600 to 1400

dr, and has a good choice of Greek and vegetarian dishes. The new *Taverna Galini*, south east of the town centre, is the locals' favourite.

If you're desperate for a change, there's a great Mexican restaurant just off Arseniou. *Café Picasso*, run by Canadian-born Debbie and her husband, has burittos, tacos and quesadillas ranging from 1200 to 2300 dr. *Restaurant Elli*, by Grotto beach, has different Greek specialities every day for around 2000 dr. The best fish restaurant in town has to be *O Nikos*, where you can watch your dinner swimming around in huge tanks before you eat it. It's certainly not cheap – the average price is 9000 dr per kilo – but it's well worth a splurge.

Bakeries, grocers and fruiterers are on Agio Nikodemou. Naxos' specialities are kefalotyri cheese, citron (a liqueur made from the leaves of the grapefruit tree), raki, ouzo and fine white wine. Look for rabbit and partridge in spring.

Entertainment There are three popular late-night bars, *Sante*, *Rocks* and *Jam*, all within a stone's throw of each other, one block back from the waterfront.

The new *Antidote* bar has at least 55 different types of beer from around the world, ranging from 400 dr to 4500 dr for Belgian Trappiste.

Beaches
Agios Georgios is just a typical town beach, but you can windsurf here on water so shallow that you feel you could wade to Paros, visible in the distance. The beach becomes so crowded that you may develop an uncontrollable desire to do so. The next beach after Agios Georgios is **Agios Prokopios**, a sheltered bay, followed by **Agia Anna** – a long stretch of sand. Sandy beaches continue southwards as far as **Pyrgaki**. Domatia and tavernas are found all along this stretch of coast. Other worthy beaches are **Plaka** and **Parthena**, known locally as Virgin beach.

Tragaea Τραγαία
The lovely Tragaea region is a vast plain of

olive groves and unspoilt villages harbouring numerous little churches. **Filoti**, on the slopes of Mt Zeus, is the region's largest village. On the outskirts of the village (coming from Naxos town), a new asphalt road leads off right into the heart of the Tragaea. Following this road you will come to the isolated hamlets of **Damarionas** and **Damalas**.

The picturesque village of **Halki** has several tower houses built by aristocratic families as refuges and lookout posts in the days of pirate raids and internecine feuds. The best preserved is the Grazia Pyrgos. To reach it, turn right at the Church of Panagia Protothronis. The church itself is worth checking out for its fine frescoes. It is on the main road near the bus stop.

Apiranthos Απείρανθος

Apiranthos is a handsome, austere village of stone houses and steep, marble-paved streets. Its inhabitants are descendants of refugees who fled Crete to escape Turkish repression. On the right of the village's main thoroughfare (coming from the Naxos town-Apollonas road) is an **archaeological museum** with a small collection of local finds. It's open Tuesday to Sunday from 8.30 am to 2 pm. Admission is free. Just before the museum there is a path on your left which leads to the centre of town. It will take you past the **lace museum** and the **folklore museum**. On the left you will find *Taverna Lefteris*, where you can eat in the garden overlooking the valley. Apiranthos has no accommodation.

Apollonas Απόλλωνας

Apollonas, on the north coast, was once a tranquil fishing village but is now a popular resort. It has a small sandy beach and a larger pebble one. Hordes of day-trippers come to see the gargantuan 7th-century BC **kouros**, which lies in an ancient quarry a short walk from the village. The largest of three on the island (the other two are in the Melanes region), it is signposted to the left as you approach Apollonas on the main inland road from Naxos town. This 10.5m unfinished

statue was apparently abandoned because it cracked. Apollonas has several domatia and tavernas.

The inland route from Naxos town to Apollonas winds through spectacular mountains – a worthwhile trip. With your own transport you can return to Naxos town via the west-coast road, passing through wild and sparsely populated country with awe-inspiring sea views. Several tracks branch down to secluded beaches.

MINOR ISLANDS

Between Naxos and Amorgos is a chain of small islands variously called the Minor Islands, Back Islands and Lesser Islands. Only four of the islands have permanent populations – **Donoussa** (Δονούσα), **Koufonisi** (Κουφονήσι), **Iraklia** (Ηράκλεια) and **Shinoussa** (Σχοινούσσα).

All were densely populated in antiquity, as evidenced by the large number of graves found. In the Middle Ages, the islands were uninhabited except by pirates and goats. After independence, intrepid souls from Naxos and Amorgos reinhabited them. Now each island has a small population. Until recently, their only visitors were Greeks returning to their roots. These days they receive a few tourists, mostly backpackers looking for splendid beaches and a laid-back lifestyle.

Donoussa is the most northerly of the island group and furthest from Naxos. The others are clustered near the south-east coast of Naxos. Each has an OTE, telephone and post office, but don't depend on them for currency exchange – bring drachma with you.

The island ports have domatia and tavernas, but don't expect anything fancy. Accommodation is available at Shinoussa's inland capital (also called Shinoussa).

Getting There & Away

On Thursday the F/B *Express Santorini* sails from Piraeus to each of the Minor Islands via Paros and Naxos, continuing to Amorgos and Astypalea and returning via the same route. On Tuesday and Thursday the F/B

Skopelitis sails from Amorgos to each of the Minor Islands, continuing to Naxos and again returning via the same route. On Friday there is a ferry connection from Rafina via Andros.

On Tuesday and Friday a hydrofoil sets out from Syros, calling at Tinos, Mykonos, Paros, Naxos, Ios, Santorini, each of the Minor Islands and Amorgos, returning via the same route.

Amorgos Αμοργός

• *pop 1630* • *postcode 840 08* • *area code* ☎ *0285*
Elongated Amorgos (Amor**gos**) is the most easterly of the Cyclades. It's too far off the beaten track for package tourists but gets overrun by latter-day hippies who stay throughout the summer. It's also popular with the French, perhaps because Luc Besson's *The Big Blue* was filmed here. With rugged mountains and an extraordinary monastery clinging to a cliff, Amorgos is an enticing and worthwhile island for those wishing to venture off the well-worn Mykonos-Paros-Santorini route. It also offers excellent walking.

Amorgos has two ports, Katapola and Aegiali. The capital, Amorgos town, is north-east of Katapola.

As on Ios and Paros, be wary of cheap cocktails made from the local hooch, which can pack perfidious punches.

Getting There & Away
Ferry Most ferries stop at both Katapola and Aegiali, but check if this is the case with your ferry. A local consortium operates the F/B *Skopelitis*, which runs two services a week to Donoussa, Koufonisi, Shinoussa, Iraklia and Naxos. Both Agapitos Express and Agapitos Lines have several boats a week to Amorgos from Piraeus (4450 dr) via Paros and Naxos. Some of these boats continue as far as Astypalea (2670 dr).

Hydrofoil Three times a week, a hydrofoil from Syros to Tinos, Mykonos, Paros,

Naxos, Ios and Santorini extends its route to call at the Minor Islands (Koufonisi, Iraklia and Shinoussa) and Amorgos, before returning via the same route. On Sunday there is a hydrofoil to Rafina (8900 dr).

Getting Around
There are frequent buses from Katapola to Amorgos town, Moni Hozoviotissas, Agia Anna beach, Aegiali and Paradisi beach. There are also regular services from Aegiali to the picturesque village of Langada.

Aegialis Tours (☎ 73 107; fax 73 395), at Aegiali port, organises boat trips around the island, stopping at remote beaches for swimming (6500 dr including picnic). It also has tours of the island by bus (5000 dr).

KATAPOLA Κατάπολα
Katapola, the principal port, occupies a large bay in the most verdant part of the island. A smattering of remains from the ancient city of Minoa (a Cretan settlement) lie above the port. Amorgos has also yielded many finds from the Cycladic civilisation. The largest Cycladic figurine in the National Archaeological Museum in Athens was found in the vicinity of Katapola. The quay leads towards the central square and the waterfront is to the left.

Katapola does not have a tourist office or tourist police, but Aegialis Tours (see Getting Around) can help with all kinds of information. The regular police (☎ 71 210) are on the central square.

Places to Stay & Eat
Katapola Community Camping (☎ 71 257) is back from the northern end of the waterfront. Turn left from the quay (facing inland).

Domatia owners usually meet the ferries. *Pension Amorgos* (☎ 71 214) has spotless doubles with/without private bathroom for 8000/6000 dr. From the quay, walk past the central square and you'll see it on the right. *Pension Marousa* (☎ 71 038), just past Katapola Camping, has a beautiful garden; doubles with private bathroom cost 10,000 dr. The C-class *Hotel Minoa* (☎ 71 480/481)

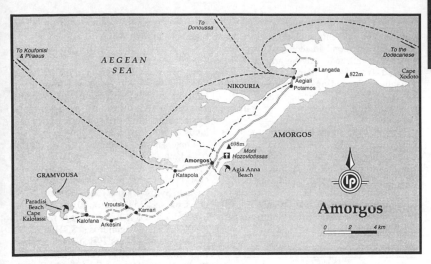

has comfortable doubles with bathroom and breakfast for 12,000 dr. The hotel is signposted from the waterfront.

A cluster of tavernas around the quay serve typical Greek fare. *Psaropoula*, near Pension Marousa, is the best for fish.

AMORGOS TOWN (HORA)

Amorgos town, also known as Hora, is a typical Cycladic village, 400m above sea level and 6km inland from Katapola. The bus stop is on a square at the beginning of the village. The post office is further along the main road, and the OTE is in a new building at the end of the village, near the high school.

There are no hotels or pensions in Amorgos town, but look for domatia signs along the main road.

AEGIALI Αιγιάλη

Aegiali is Amorgos' other port. The atmosphere is more laid-back than in Katapola and there is a good beach stretching left of the quay.

Places to Stay & Eat

As in Katapola, domatia owners meet ferries.

The C-class *Hotel Mike* (☎ 73 208), opposite the quay, was Aegiali's first hotel and opens from May to September. Doubles with private bathroom are 10,000 dr. Back from the beach, *Lakki Pension* (☎ 73 253) has immaculate singles/doubles/triples with bathroom and breakfast for 9000/10,500/ 12,600 dr and new two/four person apartments for 14,000/19,000 dr. The pension has a delightful garden, a taverna and bar.

The traditional Cycladic *Aegialis Hotel* (☎ 73 393; fax 73 395) sits between two sandy beaches and is the best on the island. All rooms have a telephone, radio and balcony with great views. The hotel has a sea-water pool, two bars and a restaurant. Singles/doubles cost 16,500/19,500 dr.

AROUND AMORGOS

A visit to the 11th-century **Moni Hozoviotissas** is unreservedly worthwhile, as much for the spectacular scenery as for the monastery itself. The dazzling white building clings precariously to a cliff face above the east coast. A few monks still live there and one will show you around. The monastery opens at 8 am, closes at 1 pm and reopens at 5 pm, but visit early (in modest

CYCLADES

dress) or you'll miss the last bus back to Aegiali. The contents include a miracle-working icon, found in the sea below the monastery – allegedly having arrived there unaided from Asia Minor, Cyprus or Jerusalem, depending on which legend you're told. It's a splendid walk to the monastery from Amorgos town, or you can take a bus.

Pebbled **Agia Anna beach**, on the east coast south of Moni Hozoviotissas, is the nearest decent beach to both Katapola and Amorgos town. It has no facilities so take water and food. **Paradisi**, on the west coast, is a delightful, unspoilt beach. **Langada** is the most picturesque of the villages inland from Aegiali – well worth a morning's respite from the beach to explore.

Paros & Antiparos
Πάρος & Αντίπαρος

PAROS
• pop 9591 • postcode 844 00 • area code ☎ 0284
Paros (**Pa**ros) is an attractive island, with softly contoured, terraced hills of vineyards, fruit trees and olive groves, culminating in Mt Profitis Ilias (770m). It is popular with backpackers and other tourists who crave style and can't afford Mykonos.

Paros is famous for its pure white marble – the Venus de Milo was created from it. Parian marble ensured the island prospered from the Early Cycladic Age onwards. Trade in marble flourished during the Hellenic and Roman periods and it was occasionally used later – Napoleon's tomb is a Parian-marble creation.

The island of Antiparos lies 1km south-west of Paros.

Getting There & Away
Air At least eight flights depart daily to/from Athens (17,100 dr). The Olympic Airways office (☎ 21 900) in Parikia is on the right side of Propona as you come from the waterfront. The airport is north of Aliki on

the island's south-west side and served by buses to and from Aliki.

Ferry Paros is the ferry hub of the Cyclades, with many connections to and from mainland Greece. It is also a regular stop for boats en route from the mainland to the Dodecanese, the North-Eastern Aegean islands of Ikaria and Samos, and Crete.

There are daily connections to Piraeus (five hours, 4260 dr), Naxos (1410 dr), Ios (2400 dr), Santorini (2900 dr) and Mykonos (1700 dr). There are at least three ferries a week to Syros (1600 dr) and Amorgos (2650 dr), six a week to Ikaria (3000 dr) and Samos (4200 dr), and at least two a week to Sikinos (1800 dr) and Folegandros (1850 dr).

The Agapitos Lines' F/B *Super Naias* runs four times a week between Piraeus, Syros, Paros, Naxos, Ios and Santorini and back, continuing once a week to Anafi, and once a week to Donoussa, Amorgos and Astypalea. The *Golden Vergina* sails twice a week from Piraeus to Paros and on to Ikaria and Samos.

The Agapitos Express' F/B *Express Olympia* plies a daily route from Santorini to Ios, Naxos, Paros and Piraeus, while the *Express Apollon* varies its route, also taking in Folegandros and Sikinos.

GA Ferries' *Milena* sails between Piraeus, Paros, Naxos, Ikaria and Samos four times a week, while the F/B *Romilda* has a weekly run from Rhodes via Symi, Tilos, Nisyros, Kos, Kalymnos, Leros and Patmos in the Dodecanese, to Naxos, Paros and Syros in the Cyclades, and on to Piraeus.

The F/B *Marina* connects the mainland with Paros and Naxos in the Cyclades and Leros, Kalymnos and Kos in the Dodecanese, while the F/B *Daliana* sails between Piraeus, Paros, Naxos, Ios, Santorini and Crete three times a week, continuing to Karpathos and Rhodes weekly.

The Minoan Lines' F/B *El Greco* and Nomicos Lines' F/B *Ariadne* offer four sailings a week between Thessaloniki, Paros, Santorini and Crete.

The port police (☎ 21 240) are back from the northern waterfront, near the post office.

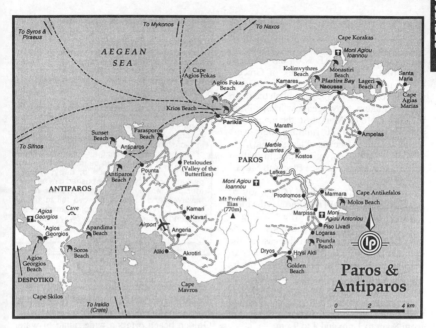

Paros & Antiparos

Hydrofoil There are daily hydrofoils to Naxos (2700 dr), Ios (4670 dr) and Santorini (5950 dr), and in the other direction to Mykonos (3280 dr) and Tinos (3350 dr), continuing to Rafina (7650 dr). There are three services a week to Syros; two to Amorgos, Iraklia, Koufonisi and Shinoussa; and one a week to Andros, Serifos and Sifnos. Strintzis Lines' *Sea Jet 1* has services to Rafina via Naxos, Paros, Mykonos, Tinos, Syros and Andros, and to Amorgos.

Getting Around
Bus There are frequent buses from the bus station in Parikia to Dryos (for Hrysi Akti) via Lefkes and Marpissa; Naoussa; Pounta (for Antiparos); and Aliki (for Petaloudes and the airport).

Car, Motorcycle & Bicycle There are numerous hire outlets all around the island. Parai Rent-a-Car-Motorcycle (☎ 21 1771), south along the waterfront in Parikia, rents cars, motorcycles and bicycles as well as tandem bikes. Paros Rent-a-Car (☎ 24 408) is north of the quay.

Taxi Boat Taxi boats leave from the quay for Antiparos and for beaches around Parikia.

Parikia Παρικία
The island's capital and port is Parikia. The waterfront conceals an attractive and typically Cycladic old quarter with a 13th- century Venetian **kastro**.

Orientation & Information The main square is straight ahead from the quay. The road on the left leads around the bay to the northern waterfront and is lined with modern hotels. The bus station is 50m left of the quay looking inland, and the post office is 150m further along on the right.

On the left, heading inland from the quay, Propona leads to the famous Church of Ekatontapyliani, which lies within a walled courtyard. The road right of the quay follows the south-west waterfront, which is lined with cafés (and is a pedestrian precinct in high season). The OTE is on the southern waterfront. The National Bank of Greece, the Commercial Bank of Greece and the regular police (☎ 23 333) are all on the main square, Plateia Mavrogenous. There is an **Internet Café** on Market St, the main commercial thoroughfare running south-west from the square (see also Places to Eat).

Kiosks on the quay give out information on domatia and hotels (see Places to Stay).

Church of Ekatontapyliani (Our Lady of the Hundred Gates) This church is the most splendid in the Cyclades. The building is actually three distinct churches. Agios Nikolaos, the largest, is in the east of the compound with lovely columns of Parian marble and carved iconostasis. The others are the Church of Our Lady and the Baptistery. Only 99 doors have been counted. It is said that when the 100th is found, İstanbul will return to Greece. Opening times are from 8 am to 1 pm and 4 to 9 pm.

Archaeological Museum This museum is behind the Church of the Ekatontapyliani, next to a school. It has some interesting reliefs and statues, but the most important exhibit is a fragment of the 3rd-century Parian Chronicle, which lists the most outstanding artistic achievements of ancient Greece. It was discovered in the 17th century by the Duke of Arundel's cleric, and most of it ended up in the Ashmolean Museum, Oxford. The museum is open daily, except Monday and public holidays, from 9 am to 3 pm. Admission is 600 dr.

Archaeological Site On the northern waterfront there is a fenced ancient cemetery dating from the 7th century BC which was excavated in 1985. Roman graves, burial pots and sarcophagi are floodlit at night. Photographs and other finds are exhibited in an attached building, but it's rarely open.

Activities The Santa Maria Diving Club

Architectural Animosity

Legend has it that St Helen, mother of Constantine the Great, had a vision of the True Cross while praying in a small church where the Ekatontapyliani now stands. She promised to build a magnificent church on the site, but died before fulfilling this promise.

Emperor Justinian authorised the construction of the church in the 6th century, commissioning Ignatius, an apprentice of Isidore of Miletus (architect of the Hagia Sophia in Constantinople), to design and build the church with Isidore acting as supervisor. The end product turned out to be magnificent, but Isidore accused Ignatius of copying his designs, and in his rage he pushed him off the roof. The tenacious Ignatius hung on to him, however, and together the two fell to their deaths. Carvings of the two protagonists can be found on the pillars of the gateway to the left of the church. ■

(☎ 094 385 307) near Naoussa and Eurodivers Odyssey Dive Centre (41 530) at Logaras both offer scuba-diving courses.

Golden beach offers a wide range of water sports such as sailing, water-skiing and windsurfing. You can also rent mountain bikes.

Organised Tours Tour agencies offer excursions around the area including Antiparos.

Places to Stay *Camping Koula* (☎ 22 081), 1km along the northern waterfront, is the most central. *Parasporos Camping* (☎ 22 268) is 2km south of Parikia. *Krios Camping* (☎ 21 705) is on Krios beach opposite the port. There are two more camp sites in Naoussa (see following section).

The Rooms Association (☎ & fax 24 528), on the quay, has information on domatia. Alternatively, you can barter with some of the owners right outside the port. For hotel details alone, call ☎ 24 555 (Parikia) or ☎ 41 333 (around the island).

For budget accommodation, your best bet is to head straight for *Rooms Mike* (☎ 22 856). It's deservedly popular with backpackers; doubles/triples cost 7000/9000 dr, with a small kitchen and a roof terrace. To get there, walk 50m left from the quay and you'll find it next to Memphis bar on Plateia Ekatontapyliani, known as central square. Around the corner, above Taverna Parikia, Mike also has self-contained studios for 8000/10,000 dr. If he's full, he'll find you alternative accommodation at similar prices.

Close by, the newly refurbished *Pension Rena* (☎ 21 427) has spotless singles/doubles/triples with private bath for 8000/12000/15000 dr. To find it, turn left from the quay and walk 200m along the waterfront, then turn right at the ancient cemetery. Around the corner, *Mariza Rooms* (☎ 22 629) has similar rooms at the same price. *Nikos Kypreos Apartments* (☎ 24 609), just behind the church, has doubles/triples for 11,000/13,000 dr. The C-class *Hotel Argonauta* (☎ 21 440), opposite the National Bank of Greece, has lovely rooms with en suite for 14,000/16,000 dr.

For something a bit more rural, *Denis Apartments* (☎ 22 466) has singles/doubles with private bathroom for 5000/9000 dr and spacious single/double/triple studios for 6000/12,000/15,000 dr. To get there, take the first major road on the right after Camping Koula, or telephone in advance to be picked up from the boat. On the waterfront, the newly refurbished *Hotel Irene* (☎ 21 476) has doubles/triples for 12,000/14,000 dr.

The fine A-class *Yria Hotel Bungalows* (☎ 24 154/158), 2.5km south of Parikia, overlooking pretty Parasporos beach, has a restaurant, bar, pool and water sports. Open from April to October, it offers singles/doubles/triples for 24,400/29,800/37,300 dr. There are also maisonettes. Take the Pounta or Aliki bus from the port and ask to be dropped off.

Places to Eat *Parikia Taverna*, first left from central square, has modestly priced and tasty daily specials. *I Trata Taverna*, near the archaeological site, has superb seafood, not least shrimp saganaki (1700 dr) and a stimulating array of mezedes, fresh fish and salads.

Cactus Mexican Restaurant, 800m along the northern waterfront, has great fajitas, tacos and enchiladas for around 2000 dr. Run by English-born Vanessa and her husband, it also has a wide variety of Greek and international fare. *Restaurant Poseidon*, signposted off the northern beach, specialises in stifado (1500 dr).

At *Restaurant Hibiscus*, near the town hall on the south-west waterfront, kleftico (1600 dr) and other specialities are cooked in a traditional wood oven. You can also get great pizzas from 1100 dr.

Half-way down Market St, *Levantes* is an interesting place, with creative international cuisine and a variety of Lebanese dishes. Inside, there is also an internet café called *Wired*. Close by, *Appollon Garden* is a classy restaurant set in a beautiful garden; chateaubriand for two costs 9000 dr.

Entertainment Most of Parikia's bars are along the south-west waterfront. *Pebbles Jazz Bar* is a good place to watch the sunset and sometimes has live music. Further south, before the road curves, is a cluster of rowdy discos. A warning that also holds for Ios and, to a lesser extent, Amorgos, is to avoid bars offering very cheap cocktails which are invariably made from the local hooch. Parikia's popular open-air cinemas are *Cine Paros*, back from the northern waterfront, and *Cinema Rex*, on the right-hand side off the road to Pounta.

Naoussa Νΰουσσα
Naoussa, on the north coast, has metamorphosed from pristine fishing village to popular tourist hang-out. To many visitors, Paros *is* Naoussa, which is fine if you just want to park up on a beach, but if you plan to explore the island by bus you're better off based in Parikia.

Naoussa is still a working harbour with piles of yellow fishing nets, brightly coloured caïques, and little *ouzeria* with rickety tables and raffia chairs. Behind the central square (where the bus terminates) it is a picturesque village, with the surface of its narrow alleyways whitewashed with fish and flower motifs.

The post office is a tedious uphill walk from the central square. To the left of the harbour, domatia and posh apartment blocks have mushroomed. Despite an incursion by package tourists, Naoussa remains relaxed and its huge serrated bay has good beaches, served by taxi boats. The best beaches are **Kolimvythres**, which has strange rocks, and the nudist **Monastiri**. **Santa Maria**, on the other side of the eastern headland, is good for windsurfing.

Organised Tours Horse lovers can enjoy a two-hour experience with Kokou Riding Center, led by a Canadian, starting at 4.15 pm from the central square. Transport to the centre by the coast is 1000 dr, and the ride costs 10,000 dr. Book with Cathy at Nissiotissa Tours (☎ 51 480), left off Naoussa's main square. The company can also organise caïque fishing trips for 2500 dr.

Places to Stay & Eat There are two camp sites. Both *Naoussa Camping* (☎ 51 595), at Kolimvythres, and *Surfing Beach* (☎ 52 013), at Santa Maria, have good facilities. The latter has a surfing and water-ski school. Minibuses from both sites meet ferries.

Voula Rooms (☎ 51 478), past the post office, is popular with backpackers; doubles/triples with shared facilities cost 7000/8500 dr. The owner speaks little English but usually meets the boats in Parikia driving a maroon Opal. Left from the bus station, towards the waterfront, *Pension Galini* (☎ 51 210) has singles/doubles with bathroom for 7000/10,000 dr. The owner also has the attractive *Spiros Apartments* at Kolimvythres beach, which cost 13,000/15,000 dr for a double/triple.

The E-class *Hotel Madaky* (☎ 51 475), off the central square, has doubles/triples for 7500/8500 dr with shared bathroom and singles/doubles with private bathroom for 10,000/12,500 dr. In the heart of Naoussa town, the *Pension Stella* (☎ 51 317) has doubles with en suite for 10,800 dr. To reach it, turn left from the central square at Café

Naoussa, then first right. It's past a small church on the left.

There is no shortage of good self-contained accommodation. Greek Australian Maria has *Sunset Apartments* (☎ 51 733), where doubles/triples cost 16,000/18,000 dr. Inland from the main square, follow the one-way system up the hill, turn right at the T-junction and it's on the left. Close by, *Scorpion Studios* (☎ 51 723) has quiet self-contained doubles/triples for 16,000/19,200 dr. Next door, *Studio Laïs* has identical rooms for the same price.

Head for the Union Office (☎ 52 158), beside the central square at the end of the bus route in Naoussa, if you need help with accommodation.

Moskonas Ouzeri, at the harbour, serves great fish; most dishes cost between 1500 and 2000 dr. *Restaurant Zorba's*, in the main square, is where the Greeks head for after catering for the tourists; it has different specialities daily from 1600 dr and is often open until 3 am. From the bus stop and square, take the first left towards the sea for the *Taverna Ouzeri Asteria* – the first restaurant established on Paros. It's cheap and authentic.

Around the Island

Marathi (Μαράθι) In ancient times, Parian marble was considered the world's finest. The **marble quarries** have been abandoned, but it's exciting to explore the three shafts by torchlight. Take the Lefkes bus and get off at Marathi village, where you'll find a signpost to the quarries.

Lefkes to Moni Agiou Antoniou Lefkes (Λεύκες), 12km south-east of Parikia, is the island's highest and loveliest village. It boasts the magnificent **Agias Trias cathedral**, as well as the **Museum of Popular Aegean Civilisation** (open in summer), an amphitheatre and an interesting library. The only accommodation is at the superior *Xenia-Lefkon Pension* (☎ 41 846) with appropriate B-class prices. In the Middle Ages, Lefkes was the island's capital. In its central square, a signpost points to a well-preserved

Byzantine paved path which leads to the village of **Prodromos**. Just below the village the path takes a sharp left which is easy to miss because there isn't a sign. Don't take the wider route straight ahead. The walk takes about an hour through beautiful countryside.

From Prodromos, it's a short walk to either **Marmara** or **Marpissa**; from Marmara, it's a stroll to the sandy beach at **Molos**. From Marpissa you can puff your way up a steep paved path to the 16th-century **Moni Agiou Antoniou** atop a 200m-high hill. On this fortified summit, Paros' Venetian rulers were defeated by the Turks in 1537 Although the monastery and its grounds are generally locked, there are breathtaking views to neighbouring Naxos. After this exertion, you'll probably feel like having a swim at the nearby east-coast resort of **Piso Livadi**.

Petaloudes (Πεταλούδες) In summer, butterflies almost enshroud the copious foliage at Petaloudes (Valley of the Butterflies) 8km south of Parikia. The butterflies are actually tiger moths, but spectacular all the same. Travel agents organise tours from both Parikia and Naoussa, or you can take the Aliki bus and ask to be let off at the turn-off to Petaloudes. Petaloudes is open in July and August from Monday to Saturday (9 am to 8 pm) and on Sunday (9 am to 1 pm and 4 to 8 pm). Admission is 500 dr. If you continue to Aliki, ask the driver to stop at the **folkloric museum**, near the airport, if it appears to be open.

Beaches Apart from the beaches already mentioned, there is a good beach at Krios, which is accessible by taxi boat (500 dr) from the capital. Paros' longest beach, Hrysi Akti (Golden beach) on the south-east coast, is popular with windsurfers. Domatia and hotels are abundant.

ANTIPAROS
• *pop 819* • *postcode 840 07* • *area code* ☎ *0284*
Antiparos was once regarded as the quiet alternative to Paros, but development is on the increase. The permanent inhabitants live in an attractive village (also called Antiparos), but it's hidden by all the tourist accommodation.

Orientation & Information
To reach the village centre, turn right from the quay, walk along the waterfront and turn left into the main street at the yellow ochre periptero. The post office is on the left. At the top of the main street, turn left for the central square. The OTE, with currency exchange and ferry information, is just beyond. There is a good bookshop and laundrette on the main street.

To reach the **kastro**, another Marco Sanudo creation, turn right at the central square and go under the stone arch. Beach bums will direct you to the island's decent beaches. Nudism is only permitted on the camp-site beach.

Cave of Antiparos
Despite previous looting of stalactites and stalagmites, the cave is still awe-inspiring. In 1673, the French ambassador Marquis de Nointel organised for Christmas Mass (enhanced by a large orchestra) to be held in the cave for 500 Parians.

In summer the cave is open daily from 10 am to 4 pm; admission is 500 dr. There are frequent buses from the village of Antiparos (600 dr one way) or you can take an excursion boat (high season only) from Antiparos village, Parikia or Pounta. From the landing stage, it's a steep 30-minute walk – or donkey ride.

Places to Stay
The island's well-equipped camp site, *Camping Antiparos* (☎ 61 221), is on a beach 800m north of the quay. Signs point the way.

Domatia are prevalent and there are several hotels. Turn right from the port for the D-class *Hotel Anarghyros* (☎ 61 204) on the left. Rates are 5000/8000 dr for singles/doubles with bathroom. The renovated *Hotel Mantalena* (☎ 61 206/365) is further along. Doubles/triples with bathroom are 10,000/12,000 dr. Next door, *Antiparos Studios* (same telephone) has good rooms for 8000/10,000 dr.

Places to Eat
The main street has many cafés. The popular *Taverna Giorgos*, on the right, serves Greek family staples and specialises in fish. Turn left at the top of the main road for *Marios Taverna* on the right. Fresh calamari is about 1300 dr. Agios Georgios, in the south, has several tavernas.

Getting There & Around
In summer, frequent excursion boats depart from Parikia on Paros for Antiparos. The trip takes 45 minutes and costs 600 dr. There is also a half-hourly car ferry from Pounta on the west coast of Paros to Antiparos (15 minutes, 150 dr; car extra). The only bus service on Antiparos runs to the cave in the centre of the island. In summer, this bus continues to Agios Georgios. Captain Yannis runs caïque trips to secluded beaches. They cost 10,000 dr for up to six people. Ask for the friendly captain at Smiles Café on the main square in Antiparos village or at the port.

Ios Ιος

• *pop 2000* • *postcode 840 01* • *area code* ☎ *0286*
Ios (**Ee**-os) is the *enfant terrible* of the Greek islands, the apogee of sun, sand, sea and sex. Non-ravers should avoid the 'village' (Ios town) from June to September.

However, Ios is working hard to clean up its image. Arriving on the island is a pleasant experience as accommodation owners are not allowed to approach you; they merely stand in a line holding signs above their heads and wait for you to talk to them (if only other islands would follow suit). Travel agents at the port offer free luggage storage to prevent backpacks from littering the area, and free use of safes to reduce thefts.

It's not only young hedonists who holiday on Ios. It's also popular with the older set –

anyone over 25 – but the two groups tend to be polarised; the young staying in the village and others at Gialos port. Ios has a tenuous claim to being Homer's burial place. His tomb is supposedly in the island's north, although no-one seems to know exactly where.

Getting There & Away
Ferry There are daily ferry connections with Piraeus (7½ to nine hours, 4700 dr), Paros (2300 dr), Naxos (2100 dr), Mykonos (2950 dr) and Santorini (1720 dr). GA Ferries' *Daliana* sails three times a week to Crete, with one service continuing to Rhodes. Ventouris Ferries' *Pegasus* does a weekly run from Piraeus to Ios and Santorini via Kythnos, Serifos, Sifnos, Folegandros and Sikinos, returning via the same route. At least twice a week the Katapoliani F/B *Paros Express* sets out from either Mykonos or Syros to Ios and Santorini via Naxos and Paros, returning by the same route. See Getting There & Away under Paros for more information.

The port police (☎ 91 264) are at the southern end of the waterfront in Gialos, just before the camp site.

Hydrofoil A daily hydrofoil service runs to and from Naxos (4045 dr), Paros (4670 dr), Mykonos (6125 dr), Tinos (6790 dr), Andros and Rafina (7900 dr).

Getting Around
In summer, crowded buses ply a route between Gialos, Ios town and Milopotas beach about every 15 minutes. Gialos and Ios town both have car and motorcycle rental firms; see the warning in the Around the Island section.

GIALOS, IOS TOWN & MILOPOTAS BEACH
The capital, Ios town (the village) is 2km inland from the port of Gialos (Γυαλός), and is also known as Hora. Milopotas beach (Μυλοπότας) is 1km east of here. Gialos beach, at the port, is quite nice. To get there, turn left at the quay. Koumbara beach, a 20-minute walk west of Gialos, is less crowded and mainly nudist. Milopotas is a superb long beach.

Orientation & Information
The bus terminal in Gialos is straight ahead from the ferry quay on Plateia Emirou. If you want to walk from Gialos to Ios town, turn left from Plateia Emirou, then immediately right and you'll see the stepped path leading up to the right after about 100m. The walk takes about 30 minutes.

The church is the main landmark in Ios town. It's uphill from the bus stop to the left. The National Bank of Greece is behind the church and has the island's only ATM. To get to the post office from the church, turn right into one of the town's main thoroughfares, pass the Ios bakery, and take the second turn left. Continue along the main road and turn left at the junction to reach the central square of Plateia Valeta. The road straight ahead from the bus stop leads to Milopotas beach.

Ios town's OTE is signposted one street before the bus station, on the road from Gialos. It's a difficult uphill walk. The office is open from 7.30 am to 3.10 pm, closed weekends and holidays. There is no EOT office, but information is available from the travel agents at the port. Plakiotis Travel (☎ 91 221), straight ahead from the quay, is very helpful.

American Express is represented in Gialos by Acteon Travel (☎ 91 343) on the main square.

There is a new hospital (☎ 91 227) 250m north-west of the quay.

Activities
Scuba Diving The Ios Diving Centre is based at Far Out Camping on Milopotas beach. Prices range from 10,000 dr for a three-hour introductory session to 85,000 dr for a Divemaster certificate.

Watersports You can take part in a wide range of activities with Maltemi Watersports (☎ & fax 91 680), situated on Milopotas beach in front of Far Out Camping. Windsurfing equipment is available for hire at many beaches.

Places to Stay – bottom end
Far Out Camping (☎ 91 468) is a slick operation, attracting up to 2000 people a night in summer. By day it is the centre of the island's action, with all but the accommodation open to everyone. It has a bar (open 24 hours), restaurant and two swimming pools as well as volleyball and basketball courts, and, of course, water-sports facilities. Charges are 1200 dr per person a site, and tent hire is 400 dr. Basic bungalows with mattresses cost 2500 dr per person. Bungalows with double and single beds cost 3500 dr per person. There's a minibus service to Ios town and Gialos.

There are two other camp sites on Ios: *Stars* (☎ 91 302), also on Milopotas beach, and the recently refurbished *Ios Camping* (☎ 91 329) in Gialos. To find the latter, turn right at Plateia Emirou and walk along the waterfront. The cost is 1200 dr per person including tent.

Backpackers who aren't camping tend to stay at the friendly *Francesco's* (☎ & fax 91 223) in the village. Dorm beds cost 2300 dr; doubles/triples are 6000/8000 dr with private bathroom and 5000/7000 dr without. It's a lively meeting place with a bar and terrace and a wonderful view of the bay. Port transfers are free. Call from the port if the van is not there.

There are lots of domatia signs on the route towards Milopotas beach from the Ios town bus stop. *Hermes Rooms* (☎ 91 471) on the right, halfway between Ios town and the beach, charges 10,000/15,000 dr for doubles/triples with bathroom. Further along is *Petradi Rooms* (☎ 91 510), offering fine doubles/triples/quads with balcony and bathroom for 6000/7500/8500 dr. There is a bar/restaurant and a terrace with views of Milopotas beach and Santorini.

Straight ahead from the quay in Gialos is *Zorba's Rooms* (☎ 91 871), with friendly owners, neat rooms and a nice courtyard. Singles/doubles/triples are 4500/9000/11,000 dr with private bathroom, 3500/7000/8500 dr without. *Irene Rooms* (☎ 91 023), signposted nearby, has balconied doubles/triples with en suite for 10,000/13,000 dr.

Hotel Poseidon (☎ 91 091) has doubles/triples for 14,000/17,000 dr and a pool. From the waterfront, turn left at the Enigma Bar and climb the steps on the left.

The *Golden Sun* (☎ 91 110), at the first bus stop on the road to Ios town, has immaculate units complete with bath and views for 7000/9000/12,000 dr.

Places to Stay – middle & top end

The lovely *Far Out Hotel* (☎ 91 446/468), on the left between Ios town and Milopotas beach, is a cluster of traditional-style, white buildings with pool. Doubles/triples are 15,000/20,000 dr with air-con. The plush B-class *Ios Palace* (☎ 91 269/224), at the end of Milopotas beach closest to Ios town, has singles/doubles/triples for 15,800/19,000/21,000 dr.

Places to Eat

At the port, the *Frog Club*, on the waterfront near Plateia Emirou, is a popular hang-out, with main courses from 1300 dr. A couple of doors along, *Waves* offers stuff resembling Indian food from 1500 dr and a variety of other dishes. *Stavados*, on the waterfront, has traditional fare from 1100 dr. The *Talisman Restaurant* on the square offers international and Mexican cuisine, while *The Octopus Tree*, on the way to Ios Camping, is a mezedes bar favoured by local fisherman.

In Ios town, *Zorba's Restaurant* is good value and friendly. *Pithari Taverna*, behind the large church, serves low-priced traditional Greek fare. Close by, the new *Taverna Lord Byron* has different specialities every day from 1500 dr. Italian foodies choose *Pinocchios*, where pizzas start at 1000 dr. Look for the signs and Pinocchio standing outside.

Restaurant Polydoros on Koumbara beach is popular. *Andoni's Restaurant & Rooms*, at Manganari beach, serves the world's best myzithra (soft ewe's milk cheese), fabulous fish and grills. Close by, at *Cristos Taverna and Rooms*, they catch their own fish. Main courses start from 1000 dr.

Entertainment

The party crowd reckons the port is dull, while the older set thinks Ios town is crazy; so take your pick.

The *Frog Club*, on the waterfront near Plateia Emirou is popular with all ages. The *Marina Bar*, overlooking Gialos beach, plays Greek music.

By day, the tiny central square in Ios town is the traditional haunt of elderly locals, swinging their worry beads to pass the time. At night there are so many party-goers that it can take 30 minutes to get from one side to the other. Surprisingly, bars in the square charge competitive prices, with a beer costing around 500 dr and (possibly dodgy) cocktails around 800 dr.

Nearby, the *Blue Note Bar* is noisy, sociable and fun, while *Kalimera* and *Funk Cafe* play acid jazz and Latin American music.

The *Dubliner Disco*, up from the bus stop, is a huge pub with reasonably priced imported drinks.

At the newly refurbished *Ios Club*, you can listen to classical music at sunset – after the sun goes down the club becomes a disco. From the town bus stop, face the port and turn left at the *Sweet Irish Dream* bar where dancers take to the tables some nights.

Other action places include the wild *Slammer Bar* and *Scorpion's Nightclub*, on the Milopotas road, which plays less frenetic dance music.

Warning There's no such thing as a free cocktail. The cheap locally brewed hooch used in mixed drinks and cocktails is bad news, particularly for the unwary. Too many young women wake up desperately regretting the night before.

AROUND IOS
The beaches and nightlife are what lure travellers to Ios. From Gialos, it's a 10-minute walk to Agia Irini for **Valmas beach**. **Psathi beach** on the north-east coast and **Kolitzani beach**, to the right of Ios town, down steps by the Scorpion Club, are popular.

Vying with **Milopotas** for best beach is **Manganari**, on the south coast, reached by excursion boats in summer from Gialos or by bus. There are domatia, including *Andoni's Restaurant* (☎ 91 483), where doubles/triples are 7000/9000 dr. *Cristos Taverna*, 200m away, has doubles for 8000 dr. The *Manganari Club Hotel* (☎ 91 200) has villas for two at 28,000 dr including breakfast and dinner.

On the way to the beach is **Moni Kalamou**, which stages a religious festival in late August and a festival of music and dance on 7 September.

Agia Theodoti beach, on the north-east coast, is more remote. Neither bus nor boat go here, so it's a three-hour trek across the island or a bumpy motorcycle ride.

Warning
Roads on the island are rough and steep. Don't hire an underpowered motorcycle or attempt to ride on unsealed roads unless you are experienced.

Folegandros
Φολέγανδρος

The happiest man on earth is the man with fewest needs. And I also believe that if you have light, such as you have here, all ugliness is obliterated.
Henry Miller

• *pop 558* • *postcode 840 11* • *area code* ☎ *0286*
Folegandros (Folegandros) is one of Greece's most enticing islands, bridging the gap between tourist traps and small depopulated islands on the brink of total abandonment. The number of visitors is increasing, but most locals still make their living from fishing and farming.

Folegandros' tourists tend to come in search of unspoiled island life and, except for July and August, the island is uncrowded and blissful. The island has several good beaches – be prepared for strenuous walking to reach some of them – and a striking landscape of cultivated terraces which gives way to precipitous cliffs.

Courses
The Cycladic School (founded on Folegandros in 1984) offers courses in drawing, painting, Greek cookery, folk dancing and hatha yoga. For further details, contact Anne and Fotis Papadopoulos (☎ 41 137), Karavostasis 840 11.

Organised Tours
Twice a week in summer, Sottovento Tourism Office (see Orientation & Information) operates day trips by caïque to hidden bays and the little-known **Hrysospilia caves** on the east coast for 5500 dr including lunch. In July and August the same company has weekly one-day trips to the neighbouring island of Sikinos (5000 dr). Commentaries are in English, French and Italian.

Getting There & Away
The F/Bs *Milos Express*, *Pegasus* and *Paros Express* each call at Folegandros a couple of times a week on their different routes from

CYCLADES

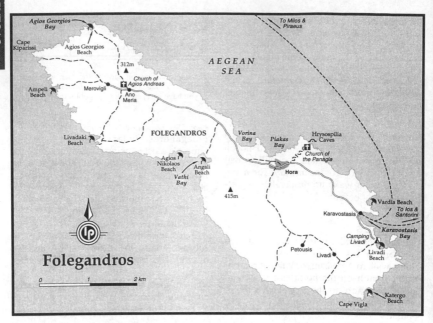

Folegandros

Piraeus through the western Cyclades before continuing to Ios and Santorini. On Monday Agapitos Express' F/B *Express Apollon* leaves Piraeus for Folegandros (nine to 10 hours, 4560 dr) and Sikinos via Paros, Naxos, Ios and Santorini, returning by the same route.

Getting Around
The local bus meets all boats and travels frequently between Hora and Ano Meria, stopping at the road leading to Angali beach. There are no taxis on the island. In July and August, daily excursion boats leave Karavostasis for Angali, Agios Nikolaos (both 2000 dr return) and Livadaki beaches (1000 dr return).

KARAVOSTASIS Καραβοστάσις
All boats dock at the small harbour of Karavostasis, on the east coast. The capital is the concealed cliff-top Hora, 4km inland.

The only other settlement is Ano Meria, 4km north-west of the Hora.

Places to Stay & Eat
Camping Livadi (☎ 41 204) is at Livadi beach, 1km from Karavostasis. Turn left on to the cement road skirting Karavostasis beach. It's 800 dr per person and 500 dr for tent hire.

Karavostasis has several domatia and hotels – look for the signs when you get off the ferry or head for the new Sottovento Tourism Office (see Orientation & Information), right in front of the quay. The C-class *Aeolos Beach Hotel* (☎ 41 205), on the beach, has immaculate singles/doubles with private bathroom for 9000/13,000 dr and suites for 18,000 dr.

Restaurant Katiallo, by the Poseidon Hotel, has one of the best reputations for top-quality traditional food. Karavostasis has two bars, *Evangelos* and *Sirma*, on the beach, which are good for snacks and mezedes.

THE HORA Χώρα
The captivating Hora is perhaps the most beautiful island capital in the Cyclades.

Orientation & Information
From the bus turnaround, facing away from the port, turn left and follow the curving road. An archway on the right leads into the kastro, the walls of which have been incorporated into dwellings. A left turn leads to three shady squares in a row. The third is the central plateia. The post office is on the left before the village on the road from the port. There is no OTE on the island but there are card phones.

There is no bank, but Maraki Travel (☎ 41 273), by the first square, exchanges currency and sells ferry tickets, as does the main Sottovento Tourism Office (☎ & fax 41 430). The office is left from the post office as you approach the Hora – by the bus stop for Ano Meria and Angali.

Folegandros doesn't have an EOT or tourist police. The regular police (☎ 41 249) are west of the central plateia.

Things to See
The Hora is an archetypal Cycladic village of aspirin-white churches and sugar-cube houses. The medieval **kastro**, a tangle of narrow streets, spanned by archways, dates from when Marco Sanudo ruled the island in the 13th century. The houses' wooden balconies are ablaze with bougainvillea, azaleas and hibiscus; and their external staircases are bedecked with potted geraniums and dozing cats.

The newer village, outside kastro, is just as pretty. On its first square are water troughs where donkeys drink. On the next square, the white circle painted on the ground is an old threshing floor. From the first bus stop, a steep path leads to the **Church of the Panagia**. The views are splendid.

Places to Stay
Pavlos' Rooms (☎ 41 232) are comfortable, converted stables on the main road, five minutes walk uphill from the village. Doubles are 13,000 dr with private bath-

room, 10,000 dr without. Rooftop sleeping space is available in summer if there are no rooms. A bus meets the boats.

There are reasonably priced domatia near the police station. The atmospheric, renovated *Hotel Kastro Danassis* (☎ 41 414) has doubles/triples with en suite for 16,000/19,000 dr. To get there, walk straight ahead from the entrance to the kastro and you'll find the hotel on the left. *Nikos Rooms* (☎ 41 055) has clean doubles with kitchen and private bathroom for 13,000 dr. Turn right at Taverna Platinis on the central square. The rooms are on the right.

The C-class *Folegandros* (☎ 41 276), where the port bus terminates, has large, well-equipped apartments priced from 22,000 dr for two people. Views don't come any better than from the top-of-the-range *Anemomilos Apartments* (☎ 41 309), by the bus station. They are built in traditional Cycladic style and furnished with pottery and antiques. There is one unit for the disabled. Rates for doubles/triples/quads are 22,000/26,000/30,000 dr.

Places to Eat
Ouzeri Folegandros is a lively place on the central square serving Greek and international main courses from 2000 dr. It is open 24 hours. Prices are similar at the traditional *Taverna Nikos*, near the police station. The *Platsa Restaurant* is one of the best on the island and has a small but exciting menu of daily specials such as tomato and cheese in filo with thick sauce for 800 dr. There are other vegetarian dishes and, in season, game. The restaurant is on the second square past the kastro.

Entertainment
The Hora may be traditional but the Folegandriots are not killjoys. Signs in town point to music bars, including a new one next to the Sottovento Tourism Office.

AROUND FOLENGANDROS
Ano Meria Ανω Μεριά
The settlement of Ano Meria stretches for several kilometres. The reason for this is that

CYCLADES

while northern Folegandros is more fertile, its open landscape was too vulnerable to pirate raids. When these threats ceased, people moved north to better farmland. Most dwellings today are surrounded by small farms. A walk from the Hora to Ano Meria is rewarded by stunning sea and cliff vistas. Visit the **folkloric museum** for 400 dr. The bus fare between the two settlements is 220 dr.

Places to Stay Ano Meria has tavernas but no hotels. Ask at a kafeneio about domatia in family homes.

Beaches

Karavostasis has a pebbled beach (nudist and mixed). For **Livadi beach**, follow the signs for Camping Livadi. The sandy and pebbled **Angali beach** has a lovely aspect but gets a bit dirty before its annual clean-up in mid-May. It has domatia and tavernas. There are other good beaches at **Agios Nikolaos** and **Livadaki**, both west of Angali. The steep path to the beach at Agios Nikolaos is only for those with strong boots and a head for heights, but it's worth it if you plan to stop for lunch: don't miss the octopus in wine sauce at *Taverna Agios Nikolaos*. **Agios Georgios** is north-west of Ano Meria. A path from Ano Meria's Church of Agios Andreas leads to Agios Georgios beach. The walk takes about an hour.

Sikinos Σίκινος

• *pop 267* • *postcode 840 10* • *area code ☎ 0286*

For years, the neighbouring islands of Sikinos (**Sik**inos) and Folegandros were regarded as remote unspoilt islands. But while Folegandros has taken off (in the nicest way) and is now on the tourist map, Sikinos remains a backwater. Perhaps Folegandros has the edge over Sikinos, with a more dramatic landscape, better beaches and a prettier capital. If, however, a quiet unspoilt island is what you're looking for, Sikinos is a better choice. The port of Alopronia, and

the capital, Sikinos town, are the only settlements – although Sikinos town comprises the contiguous villages of the hora and the kastro. The fortified **Moni Zoödohou Pigis** stands on a hill above the town.

The town has a combined post office and OTE. Alopronia and Sikinos town have domatia and tavernas with basic low-priced fare. Alopronia also has the stylish B-class *Porto Sikinos* (☎ 51 220; fax 51 220) on the beach. Rates for doubles with bathroom are 15,000 dr. This establishment is in traditional Cycladic style with a bar and restaurant.

Sikinos' main excursion is a one-hour scenic trek south-west from town to Episkopi. When ruins there were investigated by 19th-century archaeologists, the Doric columns and inscriptions led them to believe it had originally been a shrine to Apollo. But the remains are now believed to be those of a 3rd-century AD mausoleum. In the 7th century, the ruins were transformed into a church. In the 17th century, the church was greatly extended to become Moni Episkopis. The church and monastery are no longer used.

Getting There & Around

Sikinos has a similar ferry schedule to Folegandros, with the F/Bs *Pegasus, Milos Express* and *Paros Express* providing the most frequent connections with Piraeus via the Western Cyclades. Agapitos Express' F/B *Express Apollon* sails from Sikinos to Piraeus via Folegandros, Santorini, Ios, Naxos and Paros. However, this still only adds up to about four or five connections a week in high season. The local bus meets all ferries and makes several trips a day between Alopronia and Sikinos town.

Santorini (Thira)
Σαντορίνη (Θήρα)

• *pop 9360* • *postcode 847 00* • *area code* ☎ *0286*
Santorini (Santor**ree**nee), officially known as Thira, is regarded by many as the most spectacular of all the Greek islands. Thousands visit annually to gaze in wonder over the 83 sq km submerged crater, a vestige of what was probably the biggest volcanic eruption in recorded history. Although it gets crowded and is overly commercial, Santorini is unique and should not be missed.

Santorini's main port is Athinios. It's a functional place with a few eateries but no settlement as such. Buses meet all ferries and cart passengers to Fira, the capital, which teeters on the lip of the caldera, high above the sea.

History
Dorians, Byzantines and Turks occupied Santorini, as they did all other Cycladic islands, but its first inhabitants were the Minoans. Its geological peculiarities make it unique. Greece is susceptible to eruptions and earthquakes – mostly minor, but on Santorini the earth movements have been so violent as to change the shape of the island several times.

The Minoans came from Crete in 3000 BC, and their settlement at Akrotiri dates from the height of their great civilisation. The island then was circular and called Stronghyle (the Round One). Around 1450 BC, a colossal volcanic eruption caused the middle of Stronghyle to sink, leaving a caldera with high cliffs – one of the world's most dramatic geological sights. Some archaeologists have speculated that this

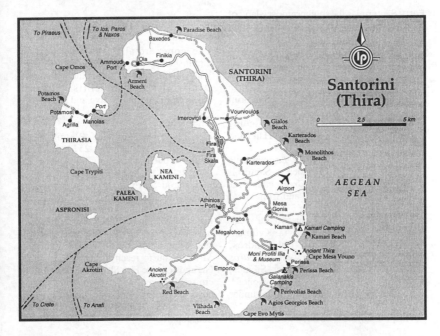

catastrophe destroyed not only Akrotiri but the whole Minoan civilisation. Another theory firing the imaginations of writers, artists and mystics since ancient times postulates that the island was part of the mythical lost continent of Atlantis.

Major eruptions and earthquakes occurred in 236 BC, 197 BC (causing Palia Kameni island to appear), 1707 (causing Nea Kameni to appear), 1711, 1866, 1870 and 1925. The last serious earthquake was in 1956, devastating the towns of Fira and Oia.

Getting There & Away

Air There are daily flights to Athens (20,200 dr) and six a week to Mykonos (13,900 dr), as well as two a week to Iraklio (13,900 dr) and four a week to Rhodes (20,400 dr). The Olympic Airways office (☎ 22 493) is in Fira, on the road to Kamari, one block east of 25 Martiou. There's no airport shuttle bus, but enthusiastic hotel and domatia staff meet flights and some return guests to the airport.

Ferry Santorini is the southernmost island of the Cyclades, and as a major tourist destination has good connections with Piraeus and Thessaloniki on the mainland, as well as with Crete and the Dodecanese. Santorini also has useful services to Anafi and Folegandros and Sikinos.

GA Ferries' *Daliana* calls in at Santorini three times a week en route from Piraeus to Crete via Paros, Naxos and Ios, continuing once a week to Kassos, Karpathos, Halki and Rhodes.

Twice a week the F/B *Milos Express* sails through the Western Cyclades to Santorini from Piraeus, and the *El Greco* calls four times a week on its way to and from Crete and Thessaloniki.

The F/B *Pegasus* sets out twice a week from Piraeus to Santorini via Kythnos, Serifos, Milos, Kimolos, Folegandros, Sikinos and Ios, and once a week the *Paros Express* sails between Folegandros, Sikinos, Santorini, Ios, Paros, Naxos and Mykonos.

See Getting There & Away sections under Paros and Rhodes for more information.

The port police (☎ 22 239) are on the west side of 25 Martiou, north of Plateia Theotokopoulou.

Hydrofoil There are daily hydrofoils to Ios (3000 dr), Naxos (5510 dr), Paros (5950 dr), Mykonos (6500 dr) and Tinos (7590 dr); one a week to Rafina (9140 dr); two a week to Syros and weekly services to Amorgos, Iraklia, Koufonisi and Shinoussa.

Getting Around

Bus In summer buses leave Fira's bus station hourly for Akrotiri, Oia and Monolithos; every 20 minutes for Kamari and Perissa. Buses leave Fira, Kamari and Perissa for the port of Athinios 1½ hours before most ferry departures.

Car, Motorcycle & Bicycle Fira has many car, motorcycle and bicycle rental firms. It's a much better way to explore the island as the buses are intolerably over-crowded in summer and you'll be lucky to get on one at all.

FIRA Φήρα

The commercialism of Fira has not diminished its all-pervasive, dramatic aura. Walk to the edge of the caldera for spectacular views of the cliffs with their multicoloured strata of lava and pumice.

Orientation

Fira's central square is Plateia Theotokopoulou. The main road, 25 Martiou, runs north to south, intersecting the square. The main drag is packed with travel agencies.

Erythrou Stavrou, the main commercial thoroughfare, is one block west of 25 Martiou. It's lined with souvenir shops, bars and restaurants. Another block west, Ypapantis runs along the crest of the caldera, with staggering panoramic views. Head north on M Nomikou to reach the cable-car station (signposted) for Fira Skala, the port used by cruise ships and some excursion boats. It costs 800 dr for a one-way cable-car trip or donkey ride; alternatively walk down the 600 steps.

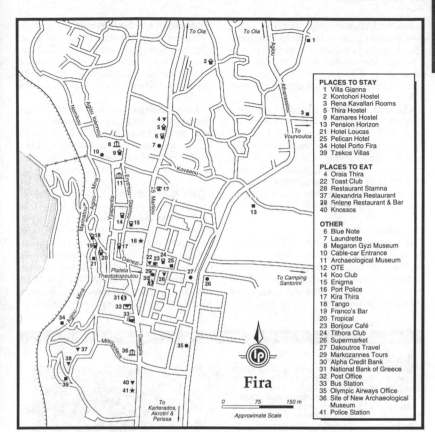

PLACES TO STAY
1 Villa Gianna
2 Kontohori Hostel
3 Rena Kavallari Rooms
5 Thira Hostel
9 Kamares Hostel
13 Pension Horizon
21 Hotel Loucas
25 Pelican Hotel
34 Hotel Porto Fira
39 Tzekos Villas

PLACES TO EAT
4 Oraia Thira
22 Toast Club
28 Restaurant Stamna
37 Alexandra Restaurant
38 Selene Restaurant & Bar
40 Knossos

OTHER
6 Blue Note
7 Laundrette
8 Megaron Gyzi Museum
10 Cable-car Entrance
11 Archaeological Museum
12 OTE
14 Koo Club
15 Enigma
16 Port Police
17 Kira Thira
18 Tango
19 Franco's Bar
20 Tropical
23 Bonjour Café
24 Tithora Club
26 Supermarket
27 Dakoutros Travel
29 Markozannes Tours
30 Alpha Credit Bank
31 National Bank of Greece
32 Post Office
33 Bus Station
35 Olympic Airways Office
36 Site of New Archaeological Museum
41 Police Station

Fira

0   75   150 m
Approximate Scale

Information

Fira doesn't have an EOT or tourist police. The regular police station (☎ 22 649) is south of Plateia Theotokopoulou, while the port police (☎ 22 239) are north of the square. Dozens of travel agencies offer tourist information. The staff at Dakoutros Travel (☎ 22 958; fax 22 686) are particularly helpful.

The bus station is on 25 Martiou, 50m south of Plateia Theotokopoulou. The post office is north of the bus station on the left. You can send email from Markozannes Tours.

The National Bank of Greece is between the bus station and Plateia Theotokopoulou. American Express is represented by Alpha Credit Bank on Plateia Theotokopoulou. Both banks have ATMs.

There is a laundrette 200m north of Plateia Theotokopoulou, underneath Pension Villa Maria on the left, and another one next to the Pelican Hotel.

Museums

Megaron Gyzi museum, behind the Catholic monastery, has local memorabilia, including fascinating photographs of Fira

CYCLADES

before and immediately after the major earthquake of 1956. In theory the museum is open Monday to Saturday from 10.30 am to 1 pm and from 5 until 8 pm; Sunday from 10.30 am to 4.30 pm (closed holidays). In practice, opening times are erratic. Entrance is 400 dr.

The **archaeological museum**, opposite the cable-car station, houses finds from Akrotiri and ancient Thira, some Cycladic figurines and Hellenistic and Roman sculpture. It's open Tuesday to Sunday from 8.30 am to 3 pm. Admission is 800 dr. At the time of writing, a new archaeological museum (beside the bus station) was nearing completion.

Organised Tours

Tour agencies operate trips to Thirasia and the nearby so-called 'burnt islands', including Palea Kameni. Reaching Palea Kameni's 'hot springs' involves a swim of about 400m (but don't be surprised if they're not actually hot when you get there).

Places to Stay – bottom end

Fira's *Camping Santorini* (☎ 22 944 or 23 203) is a superb site with many facilities, including a restaurant and pool. The cost is 1000 dr per person and 500 dr per tent. It's 400m east of Plateia Theotokopoulou. Look for the sign.

Accommodation owners meeting boats and buses are more aggressive than on any other island. Many travellers have trouble with owners of rooms in Karterados (3km south-east of Fira) who claim that their rooms are in town. Ask to see a map showing the location.

Fira has three unofficial youth hostels. The massive *Thira Hostel* (☎ 23 864), 200m north of the main square, has a variety of small dorms with up to 10 beds for 1500 dr per person, plus doubles/triples with private bath for 6000/7500 dr. *Kontohori Hostel* (☎ 22 722), 500m north of the main square, is a friendly place with satellite TV. Dorm beds are 1900 dr. The more basic *Kamares Hostel* (☎ 24 472), near the Megaro Gyzi

---

The Cats of Greece

Cats are everywhere in Greece: stalking plump pigeons around Athens' parliament house; congregating under restaurant tables in the hope of scavenging scraps; and looking cute on tourist-geared calendars and postcards. Most of the cats are strays, but sometimes you'll see a domestic cat – sporting a collar and bell – out hunting with them.

Greece is swarming with cats because the expense of having them spayed is prohibitive. Owners allow their female cats to produce litter after litter.

Although Greeks recognise that the mighty cat population keeps the rodent numbers down, the cats are still regarded as a major problem. To keep them at bay, some restaurateurs display signs requesting that patrons do not feed the cats. Other restaurant owners will discourage cats from bothering diners by feeding them leftovers themselves.

Travellers should take care when feeding the cats – although many of them are friendly, hunger can make them snatch at food with their paws, sometimes scratching or puncturing the skin. And people with a phobia about cats may feel very uneasy in a country which has so many!

Whatever Greeks and tourists feel about the cats, the population is likely to increase until the cost of desexing them comes down. ■

museum, has dorm beds for 1600 dr. All three have cheap restaurants.

Non-ravers should avoid accommodation near the main square or on the road running east to Camping Santorini. A short walk north-east of the centre of town will take you to a quiet rural area with plenty of domatia. *Rena Kavallari Rooms* charges 10,000/12,000 dr for doubles/triples, *Pension Horizon* charges 11,000/13,000 dr and *Villa Gianna* – which has a pool – charges 14,000/16,800 dr. All have a private bathroom and balcony. To book, ring Dakoutros Travel (see Information) as the owners speak no English. The same agency has a variety of accommodation in Oia on its books.

Places to Stay – middle & top end

The *Pelican Hotel* (☎ 23 113/114), right in the centre of town, has comfortable singles/doubles/triples for 20,000/25,000/30,600 dr.

Hotels perched on the caldera's edge with spectacular views are naturally more expensive. Among them, *Hotel Loucas* (☎ 22 480) has singles/doubles/triples for 20,000/28,500/34,200 dr. Close by, *Hotel Porto Fira* (☎ 22 849) has rooms for 25,500/33,000/38,000 dr. The newly built *Tzekos Villas* (☎ 22 755) is one of the best, with top-quality doubles/triples for 40,000/48,000 dr, and a pool.

Places to Eat

Fira has many tourist-trap eateries, but *Restaurant Stamna*, *Oraia Thira* and *Knossos* are all good value, with main courses from 1000 dr. The *Toast Club* is a slick fast-food operation and a favourite with backpackers, with great pasta dishes and Aussie burgers from 1000 dr.

Selene is one of the best restaurants, with creative main courses from 3700 dr. For a very special experience, head for *Alexandria*. Its enigmatic owner, the sculptor Demitrios Tsavdaridis, runs a class act. Main courses such as stuffed leg of lamb cost around 3800 dr.

Entertainment

Most of the action takes place in the square, between the Toast Club and the lively *Bonjour Café*. The *Blue Note* bar is also popular with backpackers. It has a free pool table and does a great American breakfast: 'Mama's Special' costs 1500 dr, beers cost 500 dr. Another favourite is *Tropical*, where beers cost 700 dr and cocktails 1500 dr.

Jazz buffs should head for *Kira Thira*, a funky little dive with occasional live music. Classical music-lovers can watch the sun go down at the elegant *Franco's Bar*. Close by, the newly-opened *Tango* is very upmarket; beers cost 1000 dr and cocktails are 2000 dr.

After midnight, party-goers head for the *Tithora Club* (on the steps towards Fira Skala), *Koo Club* and *Enigma*.

Backpackers hang out in the square throughout the night and can often be found at dawn still trying to sort out bedding arrangements.

There are four commercial wineries holding tastings in August, and a folkloric festival takes place at Canava Roussos Winery, near Kamari, around this time.

AROUND SANTORINI

Karterados Καρτεράδος

Karterados is a pleasant village with cheaper accommodation than Fira, providing you don't mind the 20-minute walk to town.

Places to Stay *Stavros Filitsis* (☎ 23 720), at the Taverna Neraïda, has 65 rooms to choose from. Prices are 8000/12,000 dr for doubles/triples with bathroom. Two-person apartments at a nearby beach are 12,000 to 15,000 dr. To find the Taverna Neraïda, turn left off the main approach road from Fira, and it's the last in a row of tavernas on the left.

The comfortable *Pension George* (☎ 22 351) is owned by George and his English wife, Helen. It has singles for 10,000 dr and doubles for 14,000 dr, both with private facilities. George will collect guests from Fira, the ferry port or the airport if phoned. Otherwise, walk or take a bus to the village turn-off. Follow the road and turn right after a church on your left. The pension is on the left, cloaked in bougainvillea.

Ancient Akrotiri Παλαιό Ακρωτήρι

Ancient Akrotiri was a Minoan outpost. Excavations were begun in 1967 by the late Professor Spyridon Marinatos, who was killed at the site in 1974. The dig uncovered an ancient city beneath the volcanic ash – the Aegean's best-preserved prehistoric settlement. Buildings, some three storeys high, date to the late 16th century BC. The absence of skeletons or treasures indicates that inhabitants were forewarned of the eruption and escaped. The most outstanding finds were the stunning frescoes now on display at the National Archaeological Museum in Athens. Site opening times are Tuesday to Sunday from 8.30 am to 3 pm. Admission is 1200 dr. On the way to Akrotiri, pause at the enchanting traditional settlement of **Megalohori**.

Ancient Thira Αρχαία Θήρα

Ancient Thira, first settled by the Dorians in the 9th century BC, has ruins from Hellenistic, Roman and Byzantine times. These include temples, houses with mosaics, an agora, a theatre and a gymnasium. The site has splendid views. It's open Tuesday to Sunday from 8.30 am to 3 pm. Admission is free. It takes about 30 minutes to walk to the site along the path from Perissa. If you're driving, take the road from Kamari.

Moni Profiti Ilia

Μονή Προφήτη Ηλία

This monastery crowns Santorini's highest peak, Mt Profitis Ilias (956m). Although the monastery now shares the peak with radio and TV pylons and a radar station, it's worth the trek for the stupendous views. The monastery has an interesting **folk museum**. You can walk there from Pyrgos (1½ hours) or from ancient Thira (one hour).

Oia Οία

The village of Oia was devastated by the 1956 earthquake and has never fully recovered, but it's dramatic, striking and

quieter than Fira. Built on a steep slope of the caldera, many of its dwellings nestle in niches hewn into the volcanic rock. From the bus turnaround, go left (following signs for the youth hostel), turn immediately right, take the first left, ascend the steps and walk across the central square to the main street, Nikolaou Nomikou, which skirts the caldera.

Oia is famous for its sunsets and its narrow passageways get crowded in the evenings. There are several charming commercial **galleries**, as well as a **maritime museum**, open daily except Tuesday from 10 am to 1 pm and from 4.30 to 7.30 pm.

One can swim at **Ammoudi**, the tiny port with tavernas that lies 300 steps below. There are caïques from Ammoudi to Thirasia, which seat up to six people, for about 10,000 dr.

The last bus for Fira (250 dr) leaves Oia at 9.20 pm in winter and 11 pm in summer. After that, three to four people can bargain for a shared taxi for about 2500 dr.

At the time of writing there were plans to open an EOT office in 1998. Meanwhile, you can get information and book hotels through Ecorama (☎ 71 507; fax 71 509), by the bus turnaround.

Places to Stay Oia's exceptional *youth hostel* (☎ 71 290/291/292) has dorm beds for 3000 dr (open summer only). A little further on – away from the view – there are several domatia with reasonable prices. *Irene Halari* has singles/doubles/triples with private bathroom for 4000/8000/10,000 dr. Close by, *Sunset* has similar rooms at similar prices. Next door, *Spiridula* has rooms for 5000/7000/9000 dr with shared bathroom.

Lauda Traditional Hostel (☎ 71 157), on the main street overlooking the caldera, has singles/doubles for 8000/15,000 dr and double/triple studios for 18,000/20,000 dr. *Caldera Villas* (☎ 71 285) has double/triple studios for 26,000/29,000 dr and a pool.

If you can afford to splurge anywhere, Oia is the place to do it. For traditional cave dwellings, lovingly restored, contact *Chelidonia* (☎ 71 287; fax 71 649). The office is in the centre of town; apartments for two/four people cost 25,000/32,000 dr. *Restaurant Lotza* (☎ 71 357), also on the main street, has traditional houses at similar prices. *Katikies* (☎ 71 401) is one of the best hotels and has a spectacular pool. Double rooms cost 32,000 dr, apartments for four cost 76,000 dr.

Places to Eat *Anemomylos*, at the eastern edge of the town, and *Blue Sky Taverna*, in the centre, both serve traditional food at reasonable prices. For fish, locals use *Thalami* and *O Petros*; both in the centre of town. There is no shortage of restaurants with 'the view'; *Restaurant Lotza* has main courses from 1500 dr. The most upmarket restaurant is *1800*, a restored sea captain's house complete with original furniture, serving contemporary Greek cuisine. Expect to pay 8500 dr a head including wine.

Beaches
Black-sand beaches become so hot that using a mat is essential. The best beaches are at **Kamari** and **Perissa** on the east coast, but they get very crowded. Both have sailboards, water skis and pedal boats for hire, and both have domatia, hotels and camp sites. *Kamari Camping* (☎ 31 451/453) is 1km up the main road from the beach and *Galanakis Camping* (☎ 81 343) is on Perissa beach. *Hostel Anna* (☎ 82 182, 81 943), also in Perissa, is a member of the Greek YHA. Dorm beds cost 1500 dr, double rooms cost 5000 dr and rooms for four with private bathroom cost 8000 dr. Note that the road along the beach at Kamari is for pedestrians only in summer.

Monolithos beach, further up the coast, is less crowded. North of here, the beaches are almost deserted.

THIRASIA & VOLCANIC ISLETS
Unspoilt Thirasia (Θηρασιά) was separated from Santorini by an eruption in 236 BC. Manolas has tavernas and domatia.

The uninhabited islets of **Palia Kameni** and **Nea Kameni** are still volcanically active. Daily boats go from Oia to Thirasia. Palia and Nea Kameni can be visited on excursions from Fira Skala. A day's excursion is about 4000 dr and a half-day about 3000 dr. Shop around Fira's travel agencies for the best deal.

Anafi Ανάφη

• *pop 261* • *postcode 840 09* • *area code* ☎ *0286*
Unpretentious Anafi (An**a**fee) is 30km east of showy Santorini. Until recently, tourists were a rare sight on the island and their numbers still amount to little more than a trickle. The main attractions are the slow-paced, traditional lifestyle and the lack of commercialism – an ideal place to unwind. In mythology, Anafi emerged at Apollo's command when Jason and the Argonauts were in dire need of refuge during a storm. The island's name means 'no snakes'.

Its little port is **Agios Nikolaos**, and the main town, the **hora**, is a steep 20-minute walk from the port. The hora has a post office. There are several pleasant beaches near Agios Nikolaos. The port and hora have a few domatia and tavernas. Beach camping may be tolerated. Anafi's main 'sight' is **Moni Kalamiotissas**, in the extreme east of the island near the meagre remains of a sanctuary to Apollo. The monastery is a three-hour walk from the hora.

Getting There & Away
The F/Bs *Express Apollon*, *Express Olympia* and *Super Naias* provide four services a week from Piraeus (6100 dr) via Paros, Naxos, Ios and Santorini, most of which arrive at pretty ungodly hours.

Milos & Kimolos Μήλος & Κίμολοσ

• *pop 4390* • *postcode 848 00* • *area code* ☎ *0287*
Volcanic Milos (**Mee**los), the most westerly island of the Cyclades, is overlooked by most foreign tourists. It's a pity. While the island is not as visually dramatic as the volcanic

islands of Santorini and Nisyros, Milos has some weird rock formations, hot springs, pleasant beaches and superb views.

The island's most celebrated asset, the beautiful Venus de Milo (a 4th-century statue of Aphrodite) is far away in the Louvre (having lost its arms on the way to Paris).

Since ancient times, the island has been quarried for minerals, resulting in huge gaps and fissures in the landscape. Obsidian (hard, black volcanic glass used for manufacturing sharp blades) was mined on the island and exported throughout the Mediterranean. These days about a third of

the working population is employed in the mining industry.

Phylakope, the ancient city of Milos, was one of the oldest settlements in the Cyclades. During the Peloponnesian Wars, Milos was the only Cycladic island to take Sparta's side. It paid dearly when avenging Athenians massacred all of the island's adult males and enslaved the women and children.

Getting There & Away

Air There is at least one flight a day to Athens (12,700 dr). The Olympic Airways office (☎ 22 380) is at 25 Martiou 11 in Adamas.

There are no buses to the airport, so you'll need to take a taxi (2000 dr to/from Adamas).

Ferry The F/Bs *Pegasus* and *Milos Express* are the main boats connecting Milos with the other Western Cyclades islands and Piraeus. Ferries run daily to Piraeus (seven hours, 4330 dr) and several times a week to Sifnos (1530 dr), Serifos (1650 dr) and Kythnos (2450 dr). Two services operate weekly to Folegandros and Santorini. Three times a week the *Vitsentsos Kornaros* sails from Piraeus to Milos and on to Agios Nikolaos and Sitia (Crete), and on Monday it continues to Kassos and Karpathos. A boat goes four times a day to the neighbouring island of Kimolos from Polonia, on Milos' east coast.

The port police (☎ 22 100) are on Adamas' waterfront.

Getting Around
Frequent buses leave Adamas for Plaka (via Trypiti). Six a day go to Polonia, four to Paleohori and three to Provatas.

Cars, motorcycles and mopeds can be hired along the waterfront.

ADAMAS Αδάμαντας
Although Plaka is Milos' capital, the port of Adamas has most of the accommodation. Attractive Plaka is only a 5km bus ride away (300 dr).

Orientation & Information
From Adamas' quay, turn right onto the waterfront. The post office and National Bank of Greece are all on the left. Adamas has a separate postcode from the rest of the island: 848 01. The central square, with the bus stop and taxi rank, are at the end of this stretch of waterfront. Past the square is a major crossroad. The road to the right skirts the town beach and 25 Martiou. Straight ahead is the town's main thoroughfare and the road to Plaka.

There is no EOT. Milos' municipal tourist office (☎ 22 445) is opposite the quay and open only in summer. The helpful regular police (☎ 21 378) are next to Plaka's bus station.

Organised Tours
Terry's Travel (☎ 22 640; fax 22 261), up the steps from the quay, has a range of tours. They include a sailing trip around the island (12,000 dr per person including seafood lunch), pausing at dramatic **Kleftiko** on the south-west coast to check out the caves, cliffs and islets. Milos Travel (☎ 22 000), on the waterfront, has a bus tour of the island for 3000 dr.

Places to Stay – bottom end
Adamas has no camp site and freelance camping is not tolerated. There are many domatia and pensions and, in summer, lists are given out at the tourist office on the quay, though it's still wise to book ahead in July and August.

Options include the excellent *Ethelvina's Rooms* (☎ 22 169), up from the bakery off the main square. Singles/doubles/triples, most with refrigerator and bathroom, are 9000/10,000/12,000 dr. *Hotel Semiramis* (☎ 22 117/118) has a delightful garden and doubles/triples with facilities for 14,000/16,800 dr. Walk along 25 Martiou, take the first left and the hotel is on the left. *Hotel Meltemi* (☎ 22 284) on 25 Martiou has singles/doubles/triples for 10,000/17,000/18,000 dr.

Accommodation can be hard to find if you arrive on a night ferry in the low season. The best bet is to turn right at the quay and head for the tavernas, where you can ask for assistance.

Places to Stay – middle & top end
Follow signs off 25 Martiou for *Hotel Milos* (☎ 22 087 or 21 160), which has pleasant singles/doubles/triples for 15,000/18,000/22,000 dr. The *Hotel Capitan Georgantas* (☎ 23 215/218), opposite Olympic Airways on 25 Martiou, has a bar, pool and sauna. It charges 28,000 dr for lovely air-con double suites with TV. If you're looking for something different, ask at Terry's Travel about staying at the restored windmill. It costs

30,000 dr per night and sleeps up to six people.

Places to Eat
On the waterfront, *Taverna Flisvos* is recommended. *Trapetselis Restaurant*, over-looking the town beach, serves reasonably priced fish dishes. *O Kinigos*, first right after the quay, offers good Greek staples.

PLAKA & TRYPITI Πλάκα & Τρυπητή
Plaka, 5km uphill from Adamas, is a typical Cycladic town – dazzling white and labyrinthine. It merges with the settlement of Trypiti to the south. Both have domatia.

Things to See
Milos Folklore & Art Museum The museum is housed in a 19th-century Plaka mansion. The salon has pictures, gramophones and a stove used for heating. The bedroom is filled with fascinating items, including night attire, a four-poster bed and a child's commode. A storeroom has tools for producing wine and agricultural and fishing implements. Another room displays embroidery, appliqué work, crochet and weavings.

A sign at the bus turnaround in Plaka points to the museum. It's open daily except Monday from 10 am to 1 pm.

Leaving the museum, turn left for the **Church of Panagia Korfiatissa**. From its terrace there are breathtaking views of Milos' north coast and Antimilos islet, uninhabited except for goats.

Kastro At the bus turnaround, facing Adamas (south), turn right for a path which leads to the Frankish kastro, built on the ancient acropolis. Inside the walls is the 13th-century **Church of Thalassitras**. The final battle between the ancient Melians and Athenians was fought on this hill. The kastro offers panoramic views of most of the island.

Archaeological Museum This museum is in Trypiti, on the right side of the road leading from Plaka to the much signposted catacombs. Don't miss the perfectly preserved terracotta figurine of Athena (un-

labelled) in the middle room. The room on the left has charming figurines from Phylakope. The museum is open Tuesday to Sunday from 8.30 am to 3 pm. Admission is 500 dr.

AROUND PLAKA & TRYPITI
Roman Ruins
Plaka is built on the site of ancient Milos, which was destroyed by the Athenians. It was rebuilt by the Romans, and there are some Roman ruins nearby, including Greece's only Christian **catacombs**. On the road to them, a sign points right to the well-preserved **ancient theatre**. Excavations in 1964 yielded a headless statue sculpted from Naxian marble and tiles from the theatre's original ceiling. On the track to the theatre, a Greek sign points to where a farmer found the Venus de Milo in 1820. Opposite are remains of massive Doric walls. Fifty metres further along on the cement road is a sign to the 1st-century catacombs. A passage leads to a large chamber flanked by tunnels which contained the tombs. Opening times are from 8.30 am to 3 pm, closed on Wednesday and Sunday. Admission is 500 dr.

Klima Κλήμα
The village of Klima is a short stroll from the catacombs. With your back to the catacomb ticket kiosk, turn left, then right onto a path. You'll come to the steps down to Klima after 100m. On the way there is a chapel hewn into the rock. Klima was once the port of ancient Milos, now it's a charming unspoilt fishing village skirting a narrow beach. Whitewashed buildings, with bright blue, green and red doors and balconies, have boat houses on the ground floor and the living quarters on the 1st floor. Klima's one hotel (2km from the village) is the *Hotel Panorama* (☎ 21 623), where doubles are 12,400 dr. The hotel has a restaurant.

Plathiena Beach
Plathiena is a lovely sandy beach below Plaka. On the walk to Plathiena you can detour to the tiny fishing villages of **Areti** and **Fourkovouni**. At Plaka, walk towards

the kastro path and look for the *kalderimi* (narrow alleyway) to the left. After five minutes, it forks. Veer left for Areti or right for Plathiena. If you take the Areti path, after 15 minutes you'll come to a track leading down to Areti. If you take the Plathiena path, you'll see the track down to Fourkovouni after a few minutes.

Continuing along the track, the landscape becomes quite surreal, with the intense red, orange and white volcanic rock set against deep blue summer skies. The track leads to a crossroads. A left turn leads to Plathiena, while a right leads to the other branch of the kalderimi from Plaka.

AROUND MILOS

The beaches of **Provatas** and **Paleohori**, on the south coast, are long and sandy. There are hot springs at Paleohori. **Polonia**, on the north coast, is a fishing village with a small beach and domatia.

The ancient **Phylakope** is 2km inland from Polonia. Three levels of cities have been uncovered here – Early, Middle and Late Cycladic. The islet of **Glaronisia**, off the north coast, is a rare geological phenomenon composed entirely of hexagonal volcanic stone bars.

KIMOLOS

The small island of Kimolos is perched just to the north-east of Milos. It receives few visitors, although there are domatia, four tavernas, two bakeries, a minimarket and fine beaches lying in wait.

Those who do make the effort tend to be day-trippers arriving on the boat from Polonia, on the north-eastern tip of Milos. The boat docks at the port of Psathi and it's 3km from Psathi to Kimolos town by the island's only sealed road. There's no petrol station on Kimolos – so if you're bringing a car or moped across from Milos, make sure you've got enough fuel.

Donkeys are still the principal mode of transport, and there are tracks all around the island. There are thermal springs at the settlement of **Prasa** on the north-east coast. **Beaches** can be reached by caïque from Psathi. At the centre of the island is the 350m cliff on which sits the fortress of **Paleokastro**.

Day-trippers should try the local food speciality, *lathenia*, a pizza-like dish with tomato, onion and cheese.

Getting There & Away

The F/Bs *Milos Express* and *Pegasus* call in at Kimolos four times a week en route from Piraeus (7½ hours, 4000 dr) to Milos via Serifos and Sifnos. There are daily excursion boats from Polonia on Milos (20 minutes).

Kea Κέα

• *pop 1787* • *postcode 840 02* • *area code* ☎ *0288*
Kea (**Kea**) is the closest of the Cyclades to the mainland. The island is a popular weekend escape for Athenians in summer, but remains relatively untouched by tourism. While the island appears largely barren from a distance, it has ample water and the bare hills hide fertile valleys filled with orchards, olive groves, and almond and oak trees. The main settlements are the port of Korissia, and the capital, Ioulis, 5km inland.

Getting There & Away

Ferry The F/B *Myrina Express* connects Kea with Lavrio on the mainland at least twice a day. There are two boats a week between Kea and Kythnos.

Hydrofoil In summer, there are daily hydrofoil connections to Zea Marina at Piraeus (85 minutes, 4560 dr) and to Kythnos (45 minutes, 2880 dr).

Getting Around

In theory there are frequent buses from Korissia to Vourkari (100 dr) and then from Korissia to Ioulis (250 dr). In practice, if there isn't a bus waiting for the boat, you're better off catching one of the taxis which hang about near the port and outside Ioulis. They can also be rung on ☎ 21 021/228.

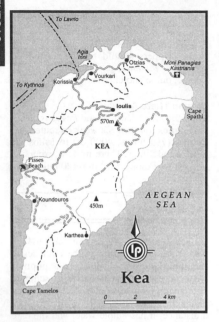

Alternatively, there are three expensive motorcycle hire outlets.

KORISSIA Κορησσία

The port of Korissia is an uninspiring place in spite of its setting on a large bay with a long, sandy beach. The tourist police (☎ 22 100) can be found one block back from the waterfront between June and September. Stefanos Lepouras, at the Flying Dolphin agency opposite the ferry and hydrofoil quay, is a good source of information about the island. He can also change money.

Places to Stay & Eat

The C-class *Hotel Karthea* (☎ 21 222) is a large concrete box at the corner of the bay with ordinary singles/doubles for 7100/8600 dr. There are better places along the road that runs behind the beach, including a couple of domatia. The *Hotel Tzia Mas* (☎ 21 305) could do with a coat of paint and a clean-up, but it has doubles that open right onto the

beach for 12,000 dr. The best rooms are at the *Hotel Korissia* (☎ 21 484), which has large, modern singles/doubles for 8000/10,000 dr; and doubles/triples with kitchen for 12,000/15,000 dr. To get there, turn right off the beach road at the creek and you'll see the hotel on the right after about 150m. The *Restaurant O Faros*, on the waterfront in Korissia, serves good fish.

IOULIS Ιουλίδα

Ioulis is a delightful higgledy-piggledy hillside town, full of alleyways and steps that beg to be explored. The bus turnaround is on a square at the edge of town. The post office is on the square. An archway leads to Ioulis proper, and the main thoroughfare (Ilia Malavazou) leads uphill to the right. The OTE is along here on the right. The pathway continues uphill and crosses a small square. Just beyond the square on the right is an agency of the National Bank of Greece, signposted above a minimarket.

Things to See

The **archaeological museum**, on the main thoroughfare, houses local finds, mostly from Agia Irini. Opening times are Tuesday to Sunday from 8.30 am to 3 pm. Admission is free.

The celebrated **Kea Lion**, carved from a huge chunk of granite in the 6th century BC, lies on the hillside an easy, pleasant 10-minute walk north-east of town. The path to the lion leads off to the left (the main path goes sharp right) about 150m past the bank. There is a sign and arrow painted on the path.

Places to Stay & Eat

The *Hotel Ioulis* (☎ 22 177) has a great location, perched on an outcrop of rock just beyond the remains of the old Venetian kastro. It has spotless singles/doubles/triples for 7000/9000/10,800 dr with shared bathroom, and doubles with private bathroom for 10,500 dr. It's worth a visit to the terrace restaurant just for the views. To get there, turn left through the archway into Ioulis and follow the signs to the kastro.

The only other option is the friendly *Hotel*

Filoxenia (☎ 22 057), a tiny place with lots of character. Singles/doubles are 5000/7000 dr with shared bathroom.

There are several decent tavernas in Ioulis. *Estiatorio I Piatsa*, just inside the archway, serves a generous plate of calamari for 1200 dr.

AROUND KEA

The beach road from Korissia leads past **Gialiskari beach** to the trendy resort of **Vourkari**, 2.5km away. Just north of Vourkari is the ancient site of **Agia Irini** (named after a nearby church), where a Minoan palace has been excavated. The road continues for another 3km to a sandy beach at **Otzias**. A dirt road continues beyond here for another 5km to the 18th-century **Moni Panagias Kastrianis**. The monastery has a commanding position and terrific views. The island's best beach, 8km south-west of Ioulis, has the unfortunate name of **Pisses**. It is long and sandy and backed by a verdant valley of orchards and olive groves.

Places to Stay

The island's camp site, *Kea Camping* (☎ 31 302), is at Pisses beach. The site has a shop, bar and restaurant. There are also domatia and tavernas here.

The island's flashest joint is *Kea Beach Hotel & Bungalows* (☎ 31 230; fax 31 234), a package hotel occupying a headland overlooking Koundouros beach, 2km south of Pisses beach. The hotel complex has a bar, restaurant, disco and swimming pool.

Kythnos Κύθνος

• *pop 1632* • *postcode 840 06* • *area code ☎ 0281*
In contrast to Kea, Kythnos (**Ki**thnos), the next island south, is virtually barren. Like Kea, it is popular mainly with Athenian holiday-makers. There is little to enthuse about on Kythnos, unless you're looking for a cure for rheumatism at the island's thermal baths. The main settlements are the port of

Merihas and the capital, Hora – also known as Kythnos. Merihas has an OTE, and there is an agency of the National Bank of Greece at Cava Kythnos travel agency. The agency also sells Flying Dolphin tickets. Hora has the island's post office and police station, as well as an OTE.

Getting There & Away

Ferry Kythnos is well served by ferries, with both the *Milos Express* and the *Pegasus* including the island on their Cycladic routes. There are boats to/from Piraeus (2½ hours, 2820 dr) five days a week. Most services from Piraeus continue to the islands of Serifos, Sifnos and Milos. The *Milos Express* presses on to Kimolos, Folegandros, Sikinos, Ios and Santorini twice a week; The F/B *Myrina Express* leaves once a week for the port of Lavrio in Attica (3½ hours, 2800 dr), stopping at Kea.

Hydrofoil In summer, hydrofoils travel to

Kythnos

Kea (45 minutes, 2880 dr) and Zea Marina at Piraeus (2¼ hours, 5750 dr) on a daily basis.

Getting Around

There are regular buses from Merihas to Dryopida (250 dr) and Hora (250 dr), occasionally continuing to Loutra. The buses supposedly meet the ferries, otherwise they leave from the turn-off to Hora in Merihas. Taxis are a better bet, providing you don't want to go anywhere at siesta time. They charge 1200 dr to Dryopida and Hora and 2000 dr to Loutra. There are two motorcycle rental outlets on the waterfront.

MERIHAS

Merihas does not have a lot going for it other than a small sand-and-pebble beach. It is, however, a reasonable base and has most of the island's accommodation. There are better beaches within walking distance north of the quay (turn left facing inland).

Places to Stay & Eat

Domatia owners meet the boats. There are plenty of rooms and studios, so you can usually barter, but if you want to stay in the town's one hotel you're better off booking ahead. *Kythnos Hotel* (☎ 32 092), up the first set of steps you come to on the way into town from the harbour, has pleasant singles/doubles/triples overlooking the harbour for 6000/8000/9000 dr. *Restaurant O Gialos*, on the waterfront, has good food and a great position with tables right on the beach.

AROUND KYTHNOS

The capital, **Hora** (also known as Kythnos), lacks the charm of other Cycladic capitals. The main reason to come here is for the walk south to **Dryopida**, a picturesque town of red-tiled roofs and winding streets that was the island's capital in the Middle Ages. It takes about 1½ hours to cover the 6km. From Dryopida, you can either walk the 6km back to Merihas or catch a bus or taxi. The **thermal baths**, in the north-east, are

reputedly the most potent in the Cyclades. The best **beaches** are on the south-west coast, near the village of Panagia Kanala.

Places to Stay

Loutra offers the only accommodation outside Merihas. There are several domatia as well as the *Hotel Porto Klaras* (☎ 31 276; fax 31 276), reportedly the best place on the island. It has doubles/triples with bathroom and kitchen facilities for 9000/11,000 dr.

Serifos Σέριφος

• *pop 1095* • *postcode 840 05* • *area code* ☎ *0281*

First impressions of Serifos (**Se**rifos) are of a barren, rocky island. On closer inspection, a few pockets of greenery turn out to be the result of tomato and vine cultivation. Serifos' port is Livadi, on the south-east coast. The island's whitewashed capital (also called Serifos) clings to a hillside 2km inland.

Getting There & Away

The F/Bs *Milos Express* and *Pegasus* sail from Piraeus to Milos via Serifos and Sifnos five days a week. Three times a week they continue to Folegandros, Sikinos, Ios and Santorini. Once a week there is a hydrofoil service to Rafina (6590 dr) via Sifnos, Paros, Mykonos, Tinos and Andros. The port police (☎ 51 470) are up steps from the quay at Livadi.

There are frequent buses between Livadi and Serifos town. Motorcycles and cars can be hired from Krinas Travel (☎ 51 488; fax 51 073), 50m from the quay.

LIVADI Λιβάδι

Attractive Livadi is at the top end of an elongated bay. From the ferry, walk to the quay's end and turn right to reach the waterfront and central square. Continue around the bay for the pleasant, shaded, sandy beach. Karavi beach, a 30-minute walk south, is the island's unofficial nudist beach. On the way is the crowded Livadakia beach. The OTE in Livadi opens only in

Serifos

AEGEAN SEA

0 1 2 km

Sykamia Beach

Platys Gialos Bay

Moni Taxiarhon

Galani

Kendarhos

To Kythnos & Piraeus

Panagia

Pirgos

SERIFOS

582m

Agios Ioannis Beach

Psili Ammos Beach

Hora

Serifos

Lia Beach

Megalo Livadi

502m

Livadi

VODI

Koutalas

Megalo Beach

Ganema

Vagia

Karavi Beach

Ambeli Beach

Cape Katano

To Milos

To Sifnos

summer. There is a new National Bank of Greece on the waterfront. There is no EOT, but Krinas Travel (see Getting There & Away) offers a wide range of tourist services.

Places to Stay
Serifos' camp site is the excellent, shady *Coralli Camping* (☎ 51 500/073), at sandy Livadakia beach. Sites cost 1300 dr per person and 650/1100 dr for small/large tents. Tent hire is available from 1700 dr. Bungalows cost 13,000/15,000 dr for doubles/triples and there is a restaurant, bar and minimarket.

The *Areti Hotel* (☎ 51 479) overlooks a pebbled beach and has doubles for 12,000 dr. To get there, walk to the end of the quay and turn left up the steps. Close by, *Naias Hotel* (☎ 51 749) has doubles/triples for 13,000/15,000 dr. On the waterfront, the *Maistrali Hotel* (☎ 51 381; fax 51 298) has good doubles with/without sea-view for 16,500/15,000 dr including breakfast. Further along, the *Asteri Hotel* (☎ 51 191) has singles/doubles/triples with en suite for 17,000/20,000/24,000 dr.

Places to Eat
Hotel Asteri Restaurant (see Places to Stay)

offers fresh produce from family farms on the menu. Near Theofilo's is the low-budget self-service *Cavo d'Oro*. *Margarita's Taverna*, at the beach, serves good Greek dishes at reasonable prices.

Moka's Restaurant, near the quay, is the place for the trendy set. It specialises in seafood, with most mains priced at about 2500 dr. The fish soup is a must at 1500 dr, while the shrimp saganaki with feta and tomatoes is worthwhile at 3000 dr. Those with a sweet tooth should check out the almond versions of baklava and other pastries that are an island speciality.

SERIFOS TOWN
Dazzling white Serifos town is one of the most striking of the Cycladic capitals. It can be reached either by bus or by walking up the steps from Livadi. More steps lead to a ruined 15th-century Venetian fortress above the village.

The post office is downhill from the bus stop. The OTE is further uphill, off the central square. There is no bank. A cobbler off the square makes fine leather shoes to order.

AROUND SERIFOS
About an hour's walk north of Livadi along a track (negotiable by moped) is **Psili Ammos beach**. There's also a path to the beach from Serifos town. Another path heads north to the pretty village of **Kendarhos** (also called Kallitsos). From here you can continue to the 17th-century fortified **Moni Taxiarhon**, which has impressive 18th-century frescoes. The walk from the town to the monastery takes about two hours, but you will need to take your own food and water as there are no facilities in Kendarhos.

Sifnos Σίφνος

• *pop 1960* • *postcode 840 03* • *area code* ☎ *0284*
Sifnos (**Seef**nos) coyly hides its assets from passing ferry passengers. At a glance, the island looks as barren as Serifos, but the port

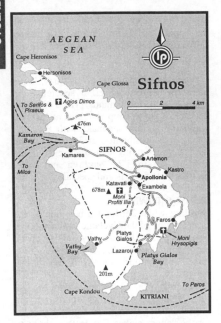

Frequent buses travel between Apollonia and Kamares, Kastro and Platys Gialos. Daily taxi boats go from Kamares to Vathy on the south-west coast. Cars can be hired from the Kamari Hotel (☎ 33 283) in Kamares, and mopeds at Apollonia's main square.

KAMARES Καμάρες

Don't judge Sifnos by the port of Kamares, which is hard to get excited about despite the fact that it has a good sandy beach. There is a tourist information office opposite the quay. The helpful staff will find accommodation for you.

Places to Stay & Eat

Domatia owners rarely meet the boats and in high season it's best to book ahead. The C-class *Stavros Hotel* (☎ 31 641), in the middle of the waterfront, has clean doubles with private bathroom for 8000 dr. The *Kamari Hotel* (☎ 33 283) has attractive doubles for 6700 dr or 8500 dr with bathroom. *Captain Andreas* and *Restaurant Simos*, on the waterfront, both serve well-prepared traditional Greek fare. Full meals with retsina cost from 2000 dr. *The Dolphins' Taverna* opposite the bus stop is also recommended.

APOLLONIA Απολλώνια

Apollonia, Sifnos' modern capital, sprawls on a plateau 5km uphill from the port. The bus stop is on the lively central square where the post office, OTE and the National Bank of Greece are located. The **Museum of Popular Art** is also here. Opening times are 6 to 10 pm daily. Admission is 200 dr.

Places to Stay & Eat

The C-class *Hotel Sophia* (☎ 31 238), north of the central square, has singles/doubles with private bathroom for 7000/9000 dr. A better option is the C-class *Hotel Sifnos* (☎ & fax 31 629) which has immaculate doubles with bathroom for 12,500 dr. From the central square (facing away from Kamares), turn right beyond the museum and right again. The hotel is on the right.

is in the island's most arid area. Explore and you'll find an attractive landscape of terraced olive groves, almond trees and oleanders. There are numerous dovecotes, whitewashed houses and chapels.

Sifniot olive oil is highly prized throughout Greece. Perhaps this has something to do with the island's reputation for producing some of the country's best chefs. Local specialities include *revithia* (baked chickpeas) and *xynomyzithra*. The island also produces superior pottery because of the quality of its clay. Many shops sell locally made ceramics.

Getting There & Around

There are five ferries a week to Milos and Piraeus (5½ hours, 3800 dr) via Serifos and Kythnos. There are three ferries a week to Folegandros, Sikinos, Ios and Santorini. There is a weekly hydrofoil to Rafina (7225 dr) via Serifos, Paros, Mykonos, Tinos and Andros.

The *Restaurant Sophia*, below the hotel of the same name, serves good food. Expect to pay about 2000 dr for a full meal and a beverage.

AROUND SIFNOS

The pretty village of **Artemon** is north of Apollonia. Not to be missed is the walled, cliff-top village of **Kastro**, 3km from Apollonia. It was the former capital, and is a magical place of buttressed alleys and whitewashed houses. The serene village of **Exambela**, south of Apollonia, is said to be the birthplace of most of Sifnos' accomplished chefs.

The resort of **Platys Gialos**, 10km south of Apollonia, has a long sandy beach, some hotels and domatia and the island's only camp site, *Camping Platys Gialos* (☎ 31

786), in an olive grove behind the beach. The spectacularly situated **Moni Hrysopigis**, near Platys Gialos, was built to house a miraculous icon of the Virgin, found in the sea by two fishermen. A path leads from the monastery to a beach with a taverna. **Vathy**, on the west coast, is a gorgeous unspoilt sandy bay with a few domatia and tavernas. There is no road access, but in summer there are taxi boats from Kamares.

Places to Stay

One of Sifnos' best hotels is *Platys Gialos Beach Hotel & Bungalows* (☎ 71 324/224) at Platys Gialos. All rooms have air-con, TV and minibar. Water sports are available from April to September, when B-class rates are charged.

Crete Κρήτη

Crete is Greece's largest and most southerly island, and arguably the most beautiful. A spectacular mountain chain runs from east to west across the island, split into three ranges: the Mt Dikti range in the east, the Mt Ida (or Mt Psiloritis) range in the centre and the Lefka Ori (white mountains) in the west. The mountains are dotted with agricultural plains and plateaus, and sliced by numerous dramatic gorges. Long, sandy beaches speckle the coastline, and the east coast boasts Europe's only palm-tree forest.

Administratively, the island is divided into four prefectures: Lassithi, Iraklio, Rethymno and Hania. Apart from Lassithi, with its capital of Agios Nikolaos, the prefectures are named after their major cities. The island's capital is Iraklio with a population of 127,600. It's Greece's fifth-largest city. Nearly all Crete's major population centres are on the north coast. Most of the south coast is too precipitous to support large settlements.

Crete is famous for its wildflowers. You'll find *Wild Flowers of Crete* by George Sfikas a comprehensive field guide, but *Flowers of Crete* by Yanoukas Iatrides may be a better bet for the layperson.

Crete is visited not only for its scenery and beaches. The island was the birthplace of Europe's first advanced civilisation, the Minoan. If you intend to spend much time at the many Minoan sites, *Palaces of Minoan Crete* by Gerald Cadogan is an excellent guide.

Crete's size and distance from the rest of Greece allowed an independent culture to evolve. Vibrant Cretan weavings can be found for sale in many of the island's towns and villages. The traditional Cretan songs differ from those heard elsewhere in Greece. Called *mantinades*, these songs are highly emotive, expressing the age-old concerns of love, death and the yearning for freedom. You will still come across a few old men wearing the traditional dress of breeches

HIGHLIGHTS

- Viewing Iraklio's archaeological museum and historical museum of Crete
- Exploring the Minoan site of Knossos
- Discovering theLassithi plateau
- Taking in the gorge between Zakros and Kato Zakros, the ancient site of Zakros, and the nearby beach
- Wandering through Hania's old quarter
- Experiencing the Samaria gorge
- Walking the scenic coastal path between Sougia and Paleohora

tucked into knee-high leather boots, and black-fringed kerchiefs tied tightly around their heads. The kerchief is making a comeback as a fashion accessory these days with young Cretans.

The attractions of Crete have not gone unnoticed by tour operators, and the island has the dubious honour of playing host to almost a quarter of Greece's tourists. The result is that much of the north coast is packed solid with hastily constructed hotels for package tourists, particularly between Iraklio and Agios Nikolaos and west of Hania.

The tour operators have also taken over several of the southern coastal villages that were once backpacker favourites. If you haven't visited Crete for a while, brace yourself for a shock. The wild and rugged west coast, however, remains relatively untouched.

If you want to avoid the crowds, the best times to visit are from April to June and from mid-September to the end of October. Winter is a dead loss outside the major population centres, as most hotel owners and restaurateurs choose to shut their establishments and recharge their batteries in preparation for the next tourist onslaught.

History

Although Crete has been inhabited since Neolithic times (7000 to 3000 BC), as far as most people are concerned its history begins with the Minoan civilisation. The glories of Crete's Minoan past remained hidden until British archaeologist Sir Arthur Evans made his dramatic discoveries at Knossos at the beginning of this century. The term Minoan was coined by Evans and derived from the King Minos of mythology. Nobody knows what the Minoans called themselves.

Of the many finds at Knossos and other sites, it is the frescoes that have captured the imagination of experts and amateurs alike. The message they communicate is of a society that was powerful, wealthy, joyful and optimistic.

Artistically the frescoes are superlative; the figures that grace them have a naturalism lacking in contemporary Cycladic figurines, ancient Egyptian artwork (which they resemble in certain respects), and the Archaic sculpture that came later. Compared with candle-smoke-blackened Byzantine frescoes, the Minoan frescoes, with their fresh, bright colours, look as if they were painted yesterday.

Gracing the frescoes are white-skinned women with elaborately coiffured glossy black locks. Proud, graceful and uninhibited, these women had hourglass figures and were dressed in stylish gowns that revealed perfectly shaped breasts. The bronze-skinned men were tall, with tiny waists, narrow hips, broad shoulders and muscular thighs and biceps; the children were slim and lithe. The Minoans also seemed to know how to enjoy themselves. They played board games, boxed and wrestled, played leap-frog over bulls and over one another, and performed bold acrobatic feats.

They were religious, as frescoes and models of people partaking in rituals testify. However, the Minoans' beliefs, like many other aspects of their society, remain an enigma. There is sufficient evidence to confirm that they worshipped bulls, but how and why

Cire Perdue

The *cire perdue* (lost wax) method of casting bronze statues was pioneered by the Cretans in preclassical times. A wax original was made and iron ducts were put into it at strategic points. These were sufficiently long to project out of the clay mould which was then put around the wax. A pouring funnel was fitted into the clay mould at a suitable place. The whole was then heated so that the wax melted and ran out through the ducts. When all the wax had escaped, the ducts were removed and the holes were plugged. Molten bronze was then poured through the funnel. When the bronze had cooled the mould was carefully chipped away.

The advantage of the cire perdue method of casting was that a high degree of detail could be achieved, and there were no joining lines on the bronze cast. The process is still used today for high-precision work.

The cire perdue method may have given rise to various legends including one which tells of Talos, a man made of bronze, who had one vein running from his neck to his leg. He was a servant of King Minos, and his duty was to help defend Crete. When the Argonauts arrived, he tried to repel them, but Medea, who had accompanied them, unplugged a pin in his ankle. He was drained of his colourless life-blood and died. ∎

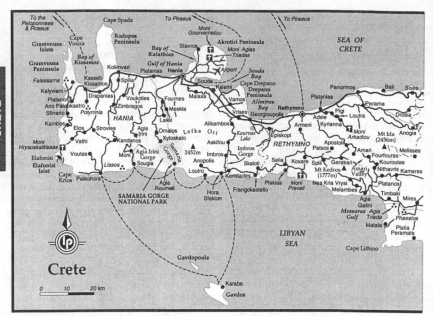

Crete

0   10   20 km

is shrouded in mystery. There is, however, a suggestion that there was a dark side to Minoan society. There are hints of human sacrifice, and of a Draconian society in which other races lived in fear.

So how much of this history is fact and how much is speculation? It is known that early in the 3rd millennium BC, an advanced people migrated to Crete and brought with them the art of metallurgy. Many elements of Neolithic culture lived on in the Early Minoan period (3000-2100 BC), but the Middle Minoan period (2100-1500 BC) saw the emergence of a society with unprecedented artistic, engineering and cultural achievements. It was during this time that the famous palace complexes were built at Knossos, Phaestos, Malia and Zakros.

The Minoans also then began producing their exquisite Kamares pottery (see the Archaeological Museum entry under Iraklio) and silverware, and became a maritime power that traded with Egypt and Asia Minor.

Around 1700 BC, all four palace complexes were destroyed by an earthquake. Undeterred, the Minoans built bigger and better palaces on the sites of the originals, as well as new settlements in other parts of the island.

Around 1500 BC, when the civilisation was at its peak, the palaces were destroyed again, signalling the start of the Late Minoan period (1500-1100 BC). This destruction was probably caused by Mycenaean invasions, although the massive volcanic eruption on the island of Santorini (Thira) may also have had something to do with it. The Knossos palace was the only one to be salvaged. It was finally destroyed by fire around 1400 BC.

The Minoan civilisation was a hard act to follow. The war-orientated Dorians, who arrived in 1100 BC, were pedestrian by comparison. The 5th century BC found Crete, like the rest of Greece, divided into city-states. The glorious classical age of

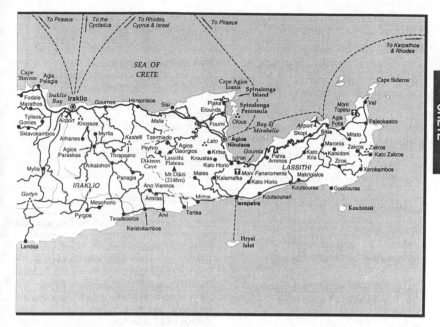

mainland Greece had little impact on Crete, and the Persians bypassed the island. It was also ignored by Alexander the Great, so was never part of the Macedonian Empire.

By 67 BC, Crete had fallen to the Romans. The town of Gortyn in the south became the capital of Cyrenaica, a province that included large chunks of North Africa. Crete, along with the rest of Greece, became part of the Byzantine Empire in 395 AD. In 1210 the island was occupied by the Venetians, whose legacy is one of mighty fortresses, ornate public buildings and monuments, and the handsome dwellings of nobles and merchants.

Despite the massive Venetian fortifications, which sprang up all over the island, by 1669 the whole of the Cretan mainland was under Turkish rule. The first uprising against the Turks was led by Ioannis Daskalogiannis in 1770. This set the precedent for many more insurrections, and in 1898 the Great Powers intervened and made the island a

British protectorate. It was not until the signing of the Treaty of Bucharest in 1913 that Crete officially became part of Greece, although the island's parliament had declared a de facto union in 1905.

The island saw heavy fighting during WWII. Germany wanted to use the island as an air base in the Mediterranean, and on 20 May 1941 German parachutists landed on Crete. It was the start of 10 days of fierce fighting that became known as the Battle of Crete. For two days the battle hung in the balance until Germany won a bridgehead for its air force at Maleme, near Hania. The Allied forces of Britain, Australia, New Zealand and Greece then fought a valiant rearguard action which enabled the British Navy to evacuate 18,000 of the 32,000 Allied troops trapped on the island. Most were picked up from the rugged southern coast around Hora Sfakion. The German occupation of Crete lasted until the end of WWII.

During the war a large active resistance

movement drew heavy reprisals from the Germans. Many mountain villages were temporarily bombed 'off the map' and their occupants shot. Among the bravest members of the resistance were the 'runners' who relayed messages on foot over the mountains. One of these runners, George Psychoundakis, wrote a book based on his experiences entitled *The Cretan Runner*.

Getting There & Away
The following section provides a brief overview of air and boat options to and from Crete. For more comprehensive information, see the relevant sections under specific town entries.

Air Crete has two international airports. The principal one is at Iraklio and there is a smaller one at Hania. In addition there is a domestic airport at Sitia. All three airports have flights to Athens. Iraklio and Hania have flights to Thessaloniki; Iraklio also has flights to Rhodes, Mykonos and Santorini; and Sitia has flights to Karpathos and Kassos.

Ferry – domestic Crete has ports at Iraklio, Hania, Agios Nikolaos, Sitia, Kastelli-Kissamos and Rethymno. The following are high-season schedules; services are reduced by about half in the low season. Direct daily ferries travel to Piraeus from Iraklio, Hania, Rethymno. There are six ferries a week from Iraklio to Santorini, and one ferry a week from Sitia via Agios Nikolaos to Piraeus, stopping at the islands of Santorini, Sikinos, Folegandros, Milos and Sifnos. Three ferries a week go to Piraeus via Santorini, Paros and Naxos, and there are three boats a week to Thessaloniki via the Cyclades and Sporades. There are also three boats a week from Iraklio to Rhodes via Karpathos, and at least two a week from Agios Nikolaos to Rhodes via Sitia, Kassos and Karpathos. Two ferries a week sail between Piraeus and Kastelli-Kissamos via Antikythira, Kythira and the Peloponnese.

Ferry – international There are two boats a

week from Iraklio to Cyprus and Israel, one via Rhodes.

Hydrofoil In summer, high-speed catamarans link Iraklio with Santorini, Ios, Naxos, Paros and Mykonos.

Getting Around
A four-lane national highway skirts the north coast from Hania in the west to Agios Nikolaos in the east, and is being extended further west to Kastelli-Kissamos. There are frequent buses linking all the major northern towns from Kastelli-Kissamos to Sitia.

Less frequent buses operate between the north-coast towns and resorts and places of interest on the south coast, via the mountain villages of the interior. These routes are Hania to Paleohora, Omalos (for the Samaria gorge) and Hora Sfakion; Rethymno to Plakias, Agia Galini, Phaestos and Matala; Iraklio to Agia Galini, Phaestos, Matala and the Lassithi plateau; Agios Nikolaos to Ierapetra; and Sitia to Ierapetra, Vaï, Kato Zakros and Paleokastro.

There is nothing comparable to the national highway on the south coast and parts of this area have no roads at all. There is no road between Paleohora and Hora Sfakion, the most precipitous part of the south coast; a boat (daily in summer) connects the two resorts via Sougia and Agia Roumeli.

As well as the bus schedules given in each section in this chapter, clapped out 'village buses' travel to just about every village which has a road to it. These buses usually leave in the early morning and return in the afternoon.

Central Crete

Central Crete is occupied by Iraklio prefecture, named after the island's burgeoning major city and administrative capital. The area's major attractions are the Minoan sites of Knossos, Malia and Phaestos. The north coast east of Iraklio has been heavily exploited by the package-tourism industry, particularly around Hersonisos.

IRAKLIO Ηραηλειο

• *pop 127,600* • *postcode 710 01* • *area code* ☎ *081*

The Cretan capital of Iraklio (Irakleeo) is a bustling modern city and the fifth largest in Greece. It has none of the charm of Hania or Rethymno, but it is a dynamic city that boasts the highest average per capita income in Greece. That wealth stems largely from its position as the island's trading capital, but also from the year-round flow of visitors who flock to Knossos.

History

The Arabs who ruled Crete from 824 to 961 AD were the first people to rule the island from the site of modern Iraklio. It was known then as El Khandak, after the moat that surrounded their fortified town, and was reputedly the slave-trade capital of the eastern Mediterranean.

El Khandak became Khandakos after Byzantine troops finally dislodged the Arabs, and then Candia under the Venetians, who ruled the island from here for more than 400 years. While the Turks quickly overran the Venetian defences at Hania and Rethymno, Candia's fortifications proved as effective as they looked – an unusual combination. They withstood a siege of 21 years before the garrison finally surrendered in 1669.

Hania became the capital of independent Crete at the end of Turkish rule in 1898, but Candia's central location soon saw it emerge as the commercial centre. Candia resumed its position as administrative centre in 1971.

The city suffered badly in WWII, when most of the old Venetian and Turkish town was destroyed by bombing.

Orientation

Iraklio's two main squares are Plateia Venizelou and Plateia Eleftherias. Plateia Venizelou, instantly recognisable by its famous Morosini fountain (better known as the Lion fountain), is the heart of Iraklio and the best place from which to familiarise

yourself with the layout of the city. The city's major intersection is a few steps south of the square. From here, 25 Avgoustou runs northeast to the harbour; Dikeosynis runs south-east to Plateia Eleftherias; Kalokerinou runs west to the Hania Gate; 1866 (the market street) runs south; and 1821 runs to the south-west. To reach Plateia Venizelou from the port, turn right, walk along the waterfront and turn left onto 25 Avgoustou.

Iraklio has three intercity bus stations. Station A, on the waterfront between the port and 25 Avgoustou, serves eastern Crete. A special bus station for only Hania and Rethymno is opposite Station A. Station B, just beyond Hania Gate, serves Phaestos, Agia Galini, Matala and Fodele. To reach the city centre from Station B walk through the Hania Gate and along Kalokerinou. For details on bus schedules, see the Iraklio Getting There & Away section.

Information

Tourist Offices The EOT (☎ 22 8225/ 6081/8203; fax 22 6020) is just north of Plateia Eleftherias at Xanthoudidou 1. The staff at the information desk are very often work-experience students from a local tourism training college. They can give you photocopied lists of ferry and bus schedules, plus a photocopied map. Opening times are Monday to Friday from 8 am to 2.30 pm. In high season they also open on Saturday and Sunday. The tourist police (☎ 28 3190) are open from 7 am to 11 pm at Dikeosynis 10.

Foreign Consulates Foreign consulates in Iraklio include:

Germany
    Zografou 7 (☎ 22 6288)
Netherlands
    Avgoustou 23 (☎ 28 3820)
UK
    Apalexandrou 16 (☎ 22 4012)

Money Most of the city's banks are on 25 Avgoustou, including the National Bank of Greece at No 35. It has a 24-hour automatic

CRETE

exchange machine, as does the Credit Bank at No 94. American Express (☎ 24 6202 or 22 2303) is represented by Adamis Travel Bureau, 25 Avgoustou 23. Opening hours are Monday to Saturday from 8 am to 2.30 pm. Thomas Cook (☎ 24 1108/9) is represented by Summerland Travel, Epimendou 30.

Post & Communications The central post office is on Plateia Daskalogianni. Coming from Plateia Venizelou, turn right off Dikeosynis opposite Hotel Petra, and you will see the post office across the square in front of you. Opening hours are 7.30 am to

8 pm, Monday to Friday; and 7.30 am to 2 pm on Saturday. In summer, there is a mobile post office at El Greco Park, just north of Plateia Venizelou, which is open from 8 am to 6 pm, Monday to Friday; and 8 am to 1.30 pm on Saturday. The OTE, on Theotokopoulou just north of El Greco Park, opens daily from 6 am to 11 pm.

Bookshops The huge Planet International Bookshop (☎ 28 1558) on the corner of Hortatson and Kidonias stocks most of the books recommended in this guide and has a large selection of Lonely Planet guides.

CRETE

PLACES TO STAY		21	Azteka Mexican	27	Buses to Knossos
9	Hotel Lena		Restaurant		& Airport
10	Vergina Rooms	35	Ta Leontaria 1922	28	Buses to Eastern
11	Hotel Rea	36	Bougatsa Serraikon		Crete
13	Hotel Mirabello	38	Loukoumades Café	30	Wash-O-Mate
14	Hotel Kastro	39	Giovanni Taverna	31	Venetian Loggia
15	Youth Hostel	45	Lakis Taverna	32	Buses to Knossos
16	Hotel Lato	46	Restaurant Ionia	34	Morosini Fountain
17	Hotel Ilaira			37	Agios Minos
18	Hotel Irini	**OTHER**			Cathedral
22	Youth Hostel	1	Venetian Fortress	40	Battle of Crete
	(Rent Rooms Hellas)	3	Historical Museum		Museum
29	Atlantis Hotel	7	Prince Travel	41	Archaeological
33	Pension Atlas	8	Grecomar Holidays		Museum
43	Astoria Hotel	19	Adamis Travel Bureau	42	EOT
		20	OTE	44	Tourist Police
PLACES TO EAT		23	Laundry Washsalon	47	Post Office
2	Ippokampos Ouzeri	24	Planet International	48	Buses to Airport
4	Garden of Deykaliola		Bookshop	49	Olympic Airways
	Taverna	25	National Bank of	50	Bembo Fountain
5	Vareladika Ouzeri		Greece	51	Apollonia Hospital
6	Katsina Ouzeri	26	Buses to Hania &	52	Kazantzakis'
12	Mythos Ouzeri		Rethymno		Grave

Laundry There are two self-service laundrettes: Laundry Washsalon, Handakos 18, and Wash-O-Mate, Merabelou 25, near the archaeological museum. Both charge 2000 dr for a wash and dry.

Luggage Storage The left-luggage office at Bus Station A charges 300 dr per day and is open from 6.30 am to 8 pm every day. Other options are Prince Travel (☎ 28 2706), 25 Avgoustou 30, which also charges 300 dr, Washsalon (see Laundry) which charges 400 dr and the youth hostel at Vyronos 5 which charges 500 dr.

Emergency The new University Hospital (☎ 39 111) at Voutes, 5km south of Iraklio, is the city's best equipped medical facility. The Apollonia Hospital (☎ 22 9713), inside the old walls on Mousourou, is more convenient.

Things to See
Archaeological Museum This outstanding museum (☎ 22 6092) is second in size and importance only to the National Archaeological Museum in Athens. If you are

seriously interested in the Minoans you will want more than one visit, but even a fairly superficial perusal of the contents requires half a day.

The exhibits, arranged in chronological order, include pottery, jewellery, figurines, and sarcophagi as well as the famous frescoes, mostly from Knossos and Agia Triada. All testify to the remarkable imagination and advanced skills of the Minoans. Unfortunately, the exhibits are not very well explained. If they were, there would be no need to part with 1500 dr for a copy of the glossy illustrated guide by the museum's director.

Room 1 is devoted to the Neolithic and Early Minoan periods. Room 2 has a collection from the Middle Minoan period. Among the most fascinating exhibits are the tiny, coloured, glazed reliefs of Minoan houses from Knossos called the 'town mosaic'.

Room 3 covers the same period with finds from Phaestos, including the famous **Phaestos disc**. The symbols inscribed on this 16cm diameter disc have not been deciphered. Here also are the famous **Kamares pottery vases**, named after the sacred cave of Kamares where the pottery was first discovered. Case 40 contains fragments of 'eggshell ware', so called because of its fragility. The four large vases in case 43 were part of a royal banquet set. They are of exceptional quality and are some of the finest examples of Kamares pottery.

Exhibits in Room 4 are from the Middle Minoan period. Most striking is the 20cm black stone **Bull's Head**, which was a libation vessel. The bull has a fine head of curls, from which sprout horns of gold. The eyes of painted crystal are extremely lifelike. Also in this room are relics from a shrine at Knossos, including two fine figurines of **snake goddesses**. Snakes symbolised immortality for the Minoans.

Pottery, bronze figurines and seals are some of the exhibits displayed in Room 5. These include vases imported from Egypt and some Linear A and B tablets. The Mycenaean Linear B script has been deciphered, and the inscriptions on the tablets displayed here have been translated

as household or business accounts from the palace at Knossos.

Room 6 is devoted to finds from Minoan cemeteries. Especially intriguing are two small clay models of groups of figures which were found in a tholos tomb. One depicts four male dancers in a circle, their arms around each other's shoulders. The dancers may have been participating in a funeral ritual. The other model depicts two groups of three figures in a room flanked by two columns. Each group features two large seated figures, who are being offered libations by a smaller figure. It is not known whether the large figures represent gods or departed mortals. On a more grisly level, there is a display of the bones of a horse. Horses, bulls and rams were sacrificed as part of Minoan worship, which had been this particular horse's fate.

The finds in Room 7 include the beautiful bee pendant found at Malia. It's a remarkably fine piece of gold jewellery depicting two

---

Linear B

The methodical decipherment of the Linear B script by English architect and part-time linguist Michael Ventris was the first tangible evidence that the Greek language had a recorded history longer than any scholar had previously believed. The decipherment demonstrated that the language disguised by these mysterious scribblings was an archaic form of Greek 500 years older than the Ionic Greek used by Homer.

Linear B was written on clay tablets that had lain undisturbed for centuries until unearthed at Knossos in Crete and later on the mainland at Mycenae, Tiryns and Pylos on the Peloponnese and at Thebes in Boeotia. The clay tablets consisting of about 90 different signs dated from the 14th to the 13th century BC and were found to be mainly inventories and records of commercial transactions. Little of the social and political life of these times can be deduced from the tablets, though there is enough to give a glimpse of a fairly complex and well-organised commercial structure.

For linguists, the script did not provide a detailed image of the actual language spoken, since the symbols were used primarily as syllabic clusters designed to give an approximation of the pronunciation of the underlying language. Typically, the syllabic cluster 'A-re-ka-sa-da-ra' is the woman's name Alexandra, but the exact pronunciation remains unknown.

Importantly, what is clear is that the language is undeniably Greek, thus giving the modern-day Greek language the second-longest recorded written history, after Chinese. The language of an earlier script, Linear A, remains to this day undeciphered. It is believed to be of either Anatolian or Semitic origin, though even this remains pure conjecture. ∎

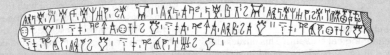

bees dropping honey into a comb. Also in this room are the three celebrated vases from Agia Triada. The **Harvester Vase**, of which only the top part remains, depicts a light-hearted scene of young farm workers returning from olive picking. The **Boxer Vase** depicts Minoans indulging in two of their favourite pastimes – wrestling and bull grappling. The **Chieftain Cup** depicts a more cryptic scene: a chief holding a staff and three men carrying animal skins. Room 8 holds the finds from the palace at Zakros. Don't miss the gorgeous little crystal vase which was found in over 300 pieces and was painstakingly put together again by museum staff. Other exhibits include a beautiful elongated libation vessel decorated with shells and other marine life.

Room 10 covers the postpalatial period (1350-1100 BC) when the Minoan civilisation was in decline and being overtaken by the warrior-like Myceaneans. Nevertheless, there are still some fine exhibits, including a child (headless) on a swing in case 143.

Room 13 is devoted to Minoan sarcophagi. However, the most famous and spectacular of these, the **sarcophagus from Agia Triada**, is upstairs in Room 14 (the Hall of Frescoes). This stone coffin, painted with floral and abstract designs and ritual scenes, is regarded as one of the supreme examples of Minoan art.

The most famous of the Minoan frescoes are also displayed in Room 14. Frescoes from Knossos include the **Procession Fresco**, the **Griffin Fresco** (from the Throne Room), the **Dolphin Fresco** (from the Queen's Room) and the amazing **Bull-Leaping Fresco**, which depicts a seemingly double-jointed acrobat somersaulting on the back of a charging bull. Other frescoes here include the two lovely **Frescoes of the Lilies** from Amnisos and fragments of frescoes from Agia Triada. There are more frescoes in Rooms 15 and 16. In room 16 there is a large wooden model of Knossos.

The museum is on Xanthoudidou, just north of Plateia Eleftherias. Opening times are Tuesday to Sunday from 8 am to 7 pm, and Monday from 12.30 to 7 pm. It closes at 5 pm from the end of October to the start of April. Admission is 1500 dr.

Historical Museum of Crete This museum (☎ 28 3219) houses a fascinating range of bits and pieces from Crete's more recent past. The ground floor covers the period from Byzantine to Turkish rule, with plans, charts, photographs, ceramics and maps. On the 1st floor is the only El Greco painting on display in Crete. Other rooms contain fragments of 13th and 14th-century frescoes, coins, jewellery, liturgical ornaments, and vestments and medieval pottery.

The 2nd floor has a reconstruction of the **library of author Nikos Kazantzakis**, with displays of letters, manuscripts and books. Another room is devoted to Emmanual Tsouderos, who was born in Rethymno and who was prime minister in 1941. There are some dramatic photographs of a ruined Iraklio in the **Battle of Crete** section. There is an outstanding **folklore collection** on the 3rd floor.

The museum, which is just back from the western waterfront, is open in summer Monday to Friday from 9 am to 5 pm and on Saturday from 9 am to 2 pm. In winter, it opens Monday to Saturday from 9.30 am to 2.30 pm. Admission is 1000 dr.

Other Attractions Iraklio burst out of its **city walls** long ago but these massive fortifications, with seven bastions and four gates, are still very conspicuous, dwarfing the concrete structures of the 20th century. Venetians built the defences between 1462 and 1562. The 16th-century **Rocca al Mare**, another Venetian fortress, stands at the end of the Old Harbour's jetty. This fortress (☎ 24 6211) is open Tuesday to Sunday from 8.30 am to 3 pm. Entry is 500 dr.

Several other notable vestiges from Venetian times survive in the city. Most famous is the **Morosini fountain** on Plateia Venizelou, which spurts water from four lions into eight ornate U-shaped marble troughs. The fountain, built in 1628, was commissioned by Francesco Morosini while he was governor of Crete. Opposite is the

CRETE

El Greco

One of the geniuses of the Renaissance, El Greco (meaning 'The Greek' in Spanish; his real name was Domeniko Theotokopoulos) was born and educated on Crete but had to travel to Spain to earn recognition.

El Greco was born in the Cretan capital of Candia (present-day Iraklio) in 1541 during a time of great artistic activity in the city. Many of the artists, writers and philosophers who fled Constantinople after it was conquered by the Turks in 1453 had settled on Crete, leading to the emergence of the Cretan school of icon painters. The painters had a formative influence upon the young El Greco, giving him the early grounding in the traditions of late Byzantine fresco painting that was to give such a powerful spiritual element to his later paintings.

Because Candia was a Venetian city it was a logical step for El Greco to head to Venice to further his studies, and he set off when he was in his early twenties to join the studio of Titian. It was not, however, until he moved to Spain in 1577 that he really came into his own as a painter. His highly emotional style struck a chord with the Spanish, and the city of Toledo was to become his home until his death in 1614. To view the most famous of his works like his masterpiece *The Burial of Count Orgaz* (1586), you will have to travel to Toledo. The only El Greco work on display in Crete is *View of Mt Sinai and the Monastery of St Catherine* (1570), painted during his time in Venice. It hangs in Iraklio's Historical Museum of Crete.

A white marble bust of the painter stands in the city's Plateia El Greco, and streets are named after him throughout the island. ■

---

three-aisled 13th-century **Basilica of San Marco**. It has been reconstructed many times and is now an exhibition gallery. A little north of here is the attractively reconstructed 17th-century **Venetian loggia**. It was a Venetian version of a gentleman's club; the male aristocracy came here to drink and gossip.

The delightful **Bembo fountain**, at the southern end of 1866, is shown on local maps as the Turkish fountain, but it was actually built by the Venetians in the 16th century. It was constructed from a hotchpotch of building materials including an ancient statue. The ornate edifice next to the fountain was added by the Turks, and now functions as a snack bar.

The former Church of Agia Ekaterini, next to Agios Minos Cathedral, is now a **museum** (☎ 24 2111) housing an impressive collection of icons. Most notable are the six icons painted by Mihail Damaskinos, the mentor of Domenikos Theotokopoulos (El Greco).

It is open Monday to Saturday from 10.30 am to 1 pm. In addition it opens on Tuesday, Thursday and Friday afternoons from 5 to 6.30 pm. Admission is 500 dr.

The **Battle of Crete Museum**, on the corner of Doukos Dofor and Hatzidaki, chronicles this historic battle through photographs, letters, uniforms and weapons. It is open daily from 9 am to 1 pm. Entrance is free.

You can pay homage to Crete's most acclaimed contemporary writer, Nikos Kazantzakis (1883-1957), by visiting his tomb at the Martinenga Bastion (the best preserved bastion) in the southern part of town. The epitaph on his grave, 'I hope for nothing, I fear nothing, I am free', is taken from one of his works.

Trekking

The Iraklio branch of the EOS (☎ 22 7609) is at Dikeosynis 53. It owns the Prinos Refuge on Mt Ida, which is reached by walking for 1½ hours along a footpath from the village of Melisses, 25km south-west of Iraklio.

Organised Tours

Iraklio's travel agents run coach tours the length and breadth of Crete. Creta Travel (☎ 22 7002), Epimendou 20-22, has a good choice. Porto Club Travel Services (☎ 28 5264), Avgoustou 20, specialises in mountain-bike tours to suit all levels.

Places to Stay – bottom end

The nearest camp sites are 26km away at Hersonisos.

Iraklio has two youth hostels. The youth hostel at Vyronos 5 (☎ 28 6281) is a clean, well-run place, where a bed in a single-sex dorm costs 1500 dr and basic doubles/triples cost 4000/5000 dr. Many people prefer the livelier atmosphere at the hostel (also called *Rent Rooms Hellas* at Handakos 24 (☎ 28 0858) where there's a roof garden and a bar. Rates are 1500 for a dorm bed and 5000/6500/8000 dr for doubles/triples/quads.

There are few domatia in Iraklio and not enough cheap hotels to cope with the number of budget travellers who arrive in high season. One of the nicest low-priced places is *Hotel Lena* (☎ 22 3280; fax 24 826), Lahana 10. The spotless, comfortable singles/doubles with shared bathrooms cost 5500/7000 dr, and doubles with private bathroom go for 7500 dr. The pleasant *Hotel Mirabello* (☎ 28 5052), Theotokopoulou 20, has clean rooms for 4500/6500 with shared bathroom, and 6000/7800 dr with private bathroom. The *Pension Atlas* (☎ 28 8989), close to Plateia Venizelou at Kantanoleon 6, has doubles with private bathroom for 6000 dr and triples with shared bathroom for 7500 dr.

Vergina Rooms (☎ 24 2739), at Hortatson 32, is a characterful turn-of-the-century house with a small courtyard and spacious high-ceilinged rooms. Doubles/triples/quads are 4500/6500/8500 dr with shared bathroom.

The *Hotel Rea*, at the junction of Hand-akos and Kalimeraki, is clean, comfortable and friendly. Singles/doubles with shared bathroom are 4000/5500 dr, while doubles/ triples with private bathroom are 6400/8200 dr.

Places to Stay – middle

Two of the cheapest C-class hotels are the *Hotel Kastro* (☎ 28 4185/5020), Theo-tokopoulou 22, where singles/doubles cost 9000/12,000 dr and the *Hotel Ilaira* (☎ 22 7103/7125), Ariadnis 1, with rates of 8800/ 11,900 dr. The more luxurious *Hotel Lato* (☎ 22 8103; fax 24 0350), at Epimendou 15, has rates of 16,800/21,600. Nearby, the *Hotel Irini* (☎ 22 6561; fax 22 6407), Ido-meneos 4, has large and airy rooms for 11,500/16,000 dr.

Places to Stay – top end

The best place in town is the A-class *Atlantis Hotel* (☎ 22 9103/4023; fax 22 6265), Igias 2. Rates are 23,000/32,000 dr and facilities include a health studio, sauna and a swimming pool. The A-class *Astoria Hotel* (☎ 22 9002; fax 22 9078), Plateia Eleftherias 11, has rates of 23,500/28,000. Facilities include a swimming pool.

Places to Eat – inexpensive

Iraklio has some excellent restaurants, and there's something to suit all tastes and pockets.

If you're after traditional taverna food, the place to look is Theodasaki, a little street between 1866 and Evans. The choices include *Lakis Taverna*, a popular spot turning out a big bowl of tasty bean stew for 750 dr. The *Restaurant Ionia*, 20m away on the corner of Evans and Giannari, serves similar food in fancier surroundings for a few drachma more.

The *Ippokampos Ouzeri*, on the waterfront just west of 25 Avgoustou, is as good as this style of eating gets. It has a huge range of mezedes on offer, priced from 400 dr. The fish dishes are especially recommended. They include grilled octopus (800 dr), calamari (800 dr) and sea urchins (900 dr). The place is always busy, so it's a good idea

CRETE

to get in early. It's closed between 3.30 and 7 pm. The stylish *Vareladika Ouzeri* on Moni Agarathou has similar fare but is a bit more expensive.

The simple little *Katsina Ouzeri*, Marineli 12, has tasty main dishes from 700 to 1200 dr. The cosy *Mythos Ouzeri*, Gianni Chroaki 14, run by two friendly brothers, offers lots of inexpensive mezedes and grilled meat and fish. Live bouzouki features on Friday and Saturday evenings.

In the charming *Garden of Deykaliola Taverna*, Kalokerinou 8, you'll soon forget you're in Crete's largest and least picturesque city. It offers a wide range of reasonably priced, imaginative mezedes and main dishes.

If you haven't yet tried loukoumades (fritters with syrup), then the *Loukoumades Café* on Dikeosynis is a good place to sample this gooey confection. For a meal on the move, try the tiny *Bougatsa Serraikon*, on Idis in the city centre. It makes excellent sweet (custard filled) or savoury (cheese filled) bougatsa for 380 dr. The more leisurely paced can while away some time people-watching at *Ta Leontaria 1922*, beside the Morosini fountain. The delicious bougatsa here costs 450 dr.

El Azteka, Psaromingou 32, serves well-prepared Mexican food which won't burn your tongue off – you can choose between mildly spiced, hot or very hot. Tacos are 600 to 1000 dr, enchiladas 1100 to 1400 dr and sangria is 800 dr a litre.

Whether or not you're self-catering, you'll enjoy a stroll up 1866 (the market street). This narrow street is always packed, and stalls spill over with produce of every description, including ornate Cretan wedding loaves. These loaves (smaller versions of the one on display at the Historical Museum of Crete) are not meant to be eaten; rather, they make an attractive kitchen decoration.

Places to Eat – expensive

The *Giovanni Taverna* is a splendid place with elegant antique furniture; in summer there is outdoor eating on a quiet pedestrian street. The food is traditional Greek, but carefully prepared with discriminating use of herbs and spices. From Plateia Venizelou walk one block up Dedalou, turn left onto Perdikari, take the first right onto Korai, and you will come to the taverna on the right. A meal for two people, including a carafe of house red, costs about 10,000 dr.

Getting There & Away

Air – domestic Olympic has at least five flights a day to Athens (20,500 dr) from Iraklio's Nikos Kazantzakis airport; three a week to Thessaloniki (27,700 dr); four a week to Rhodes (20,300 dr); three a week to Santorini (13,900 dr); and one a week to Mykonos (20,400 dr). The Mykonos service operates only between 11 June and 23 September. The Olympic Airways office (☎ 22 9191) is at Plateia Eleftherias 42.

Air Greece has one flight a day to Athens (19,600 dr), Thessaloniki (27,100 dr), and Rhodes (19,600 dr). Their office (☎ 33 0729 or 24 2357) is at Ethnikis Antistaseos 67 (off the map).

Air – international Olympic Airways has direct flights to Rome on Thursday and to Vienna on Sunday. KLM-associate Transavia flies direct between Amsterdam and Iraklio on Monday and Friday, while Lufthansa flies to Frankfurt on Saturday and Sunday. Transavia is represented by Sbokos Tours (☎ 22 9712), Dimokratias 51, and Lufthansa by Plotin Travel (☎ 24 5068), Ethnikis Antistaseos 172.

Iraklio has lots of charter flights from all over Europe. Prince Travel (☎ 28 2706), 25 Avgoustou 30, advertises cheap last-minute tickets on these flights. Sample fares include London for 28,000 dr and Munich for 41,000 dr. Grecomar Holidays (☎ 24 6672), on the first floor at Moni Agarathou 24, has flights to Paris for 46,000 dr with Air European and Zürich for 65,000 dr with Eidelvis Airline.

Bus There are buses every half-hour (hourly in winter) to Rethymno (1½ hours, 1400 dr) and Hania (2 hours, 2700 dr) from the

Rethymno/Hania bus station opposite Bus Station A. Buses leave Bus Station A for:

Destination	Duration	Fare	Frequency
Agia Pelagia	30 mins	600 dr	6 daily
Agios Nikolaos	1½ hours	1300 dr	half-hourly
Arhanes	30 mins	320 dr	12 daily
Hersonisos/ Malia	1 hour	700 dr	half-hourly
Ierapetra	2½ hours	1500 dr	7 daily
Lassithi plateau	2 hours	1300 dr	2 daily
Milatos	1½ hours	900 dr	2 daily
Sitia	3½ hours	2650 dr	6 daily

Buses leave Bus Station B for:

Agia Galini	2½ hours	1400 dr	7 daily
Anogia	1 hour	700 dr	6 daily
Fodele	1 hour	650 dr	2 daily
Matala	2 hours	1400 dr	7 daily

Taxi There are long-distance taxis (☎ 21 0102) from Plateia Eleftherias, opposite the Astoria Hotel, and Bus Station B, to all parts of Crete. Sample fares include Agios Nikolaos, 8200 dr; Rethymno, 10,500 dr; and Hania, 17,500 dr.

Ferry – domestic Minoan Lines and ANEK both operate ferries every evening each way between Iraklio and Piraeus (10 hours). They depart from both Piraeus and Iraklio between 6.30 and 7.30 pm. Fares are 6600 dr deck class and 9500 dr for second-class cabins. The Minoan Lines' boats, the F/B *Nikos Kazantzakis* and the F/B *Knossos*, are more modern and more comfortable than their ANEK rivals. ANEK, though, is a better bet for deck-class travellers. It has dorm beds with plastic-covered mattresses, while Minoan Lines has only seats.

GA Ferries has three boats a week to Santorini (four hours, 3300 dr), continuing to Paros (7½ hours, 4600 dr) and Piraeus. Two of them also stop at Naxos. GA also has three ferries a week to Rhodes (11 hours, 5900 dr) via Karpathos (3600 dr). Nomicos Lines runs three boats a week to Thessaloniki (10,700 dr) via Santorini, Paros, Mykonos,

Tinos and the Sporades. The travel agencies on 25 Avgoustou are the place to get information and buy tickets. Iraklio's port police can be contacted on ☎ 24 4912.

Ferry – international There is one boat a week from Iraklio to the Israeli port of Haifa via Limassol. Poseidon Lines ferry F/B *Sea Hamony* leaves Iraklio at 11 am on Tuesday and calls at Rhodes on the way to Limassol, Cyprus (Wednesday 11 am) and Haifa, Israel (Thursday at 6.30 am).

Getting Around
The Airport Bus No 1 goes to/from the airport every 15 minutes between 6 am and 1 am for 250 dr. It leaves the city from outside the Astoria Hotel on Plateia Eleftherias.

Bus Local bus No 2 goes to Knossos every 15 minutes from Bus Station A (20 minutes, 210 dr). It also stops on 25 Avgoustou and 1821.

Car & Motorcycle Most of Iraklio's car and motorcycle-hire outlets are on 25 Avgoustou. You'll get the best deal from local companies like Sun Rise (☎ 28 0428) at 25 Avgoustou 76, Loggeta Cars & Bikes (☎ 28 9462) at Plateia Kallergon 6, next to El Greco Park, or Ritz Rent-A-Car at the Hotel Rea (see Places to Stay), which has discounts for hotel guests. There are car-hire outlets at the airport. Loggeta also has a range of scooters and motorcycles.

Bicycle Mountain bicycles can be hired from Porto Club Travel Services (see Organised Tours).

KNOSSOS Κνωσσός
Knossos (Knos**os**), 5km from Iraklio, was the capital of Minoan Crete. Nowadays it's the island's major tourist attraction.

The ruins of Knossos were uncovered in 1900 by the British archaeologist Sir Arthur Evans. Schliemann had had his eye on the spot (a low, flat-topped mound), believing an ancient city was buried there, but had been unable to strike a deal with the local land-owner.

Evans was so enthralled by his discovery that he spent 35 years and £250,000 of his own money excavating and reconstructing sections of the palace. Some archaeologists have disparaged Evans' reconstruction, believing he sacrificed accuracy to his overly vivid imagination. However, most non-specialists agree that Sir Arthur did a good job and that Knossos is a knockout. Without these reconstructions it would be impossible to visualise what a Minoan palace looked like.

You will need to spend about four hours at Knossos to explore it thoroughly. The café at the site is expensive – you'd do better to bring a picnic along. The site (☎ 23 1940) is open every day from 8 am to 7 pm between April and October. In winter the site closes at 5 pm. Admission is 1500 dr.

History

The first palace at Knossos was built around 1900 BC. In 1700 BC it was destroyed by an earthquake and rebuilt to a grander and more sophisticated design. It is this palace that Evans reconstructed. It was partially destroyed again sometime between 1500 and 1450 BC. It was inhabited for another 50 years before it was devastated once and for all by fire.

The city of Knossos consisted of an immense palace, residences of officials and priests, the homes of ordinary people, and burial grounds. The palace consisted of royal domestic quarters, public reception rooms, shrines, workshops, treasuries and storerooms, all built around a central court. Like all Minoan palaces, it also doubled as a city hall, accommodating all the bureaucracy necessary for the smooth running of a complex society.

Until recently it was possible to enter the royal apartments, but in early 1997 it was decided to cordon this area off before it disappeared altogether under the continual pounding of feet. Extensive repairs are under way but it is unlikely to be open to the public again.

Exploring the Site

Numerous rooms, corridors, dogleg passages, nooks and crannies, and staircases prohibit a detailed walk description of the palace. However, Knossos is not a site where you'll be perplexed by heaps of rubble, trying to fathom whether you're looking at the throne room or a workshop. Thanks to Evans' reconstruction, the most significant parts of the complex are instantly recognisable (if not instantly found). On your wanders you will come across a many of Evans' reconstructed columns; most are painted deep brown-red with gold-trimmed black capitals. These, like all Minoan columns, taper at the bottom.

It is not only the vibrant frescoes and mighty columns which impress at Knossos; keep your eyes open for the little details which are evidence of a highly sophisticated society. Things to look out for are the drainage system; the placement of light wells; and the relationship of rooms to passages, porches, light wells and verandahs, which keep rooms cool in summer and warm in winter.

The usual entrance to the palace complex is across the Western Court and along the **Corridor of the Procession Fresco**. The fresco depicted a long line of people carrying gifts to present to the king; only fragments remain. A copy of one of these fragments, called the **Priest King Fresco**, can be seen to the south of the Central Court.

An alternative way to enter is to have a look at the Corridor of the Procession Fresco, but then leave it and walk straight ahead to enter the site from the northern end. If you do this you will come to the **theatral area**, a series of steps whose function remains unknown. It could have been a theatre where spectators watched acrobatic and dance performances, or the place where people gathered to welcome important visitors arriving by the Royal Road.

The **Royal Road** leads off to the west. The

The Myth of the Minotaur

King Minos of Crete invoked the wrath of Poseidon when he failed to sacrifice a magnificent white bull sent to him for that purpose. Poseidon's revenge was to cause Pasiphae, King Minos' wife, to fall in love with the animal.

In order to attract the bull, Pasiphae asked Daedalus, chief architect at Knossos and all-round handyman, to make her a hollow, wooden cow structure. When she concealed herself inside, the bull found her irresistible. The outcome of their bizarre association was the Minotaur: a hideous monster who was half-man and half-bull.

King Minos asked Daedalus to build a labyrinth in which to confine the Minotaur and demanded that Athens pay an annual tribute of seven youths and seven maidens to satisfy the monster's huge appetite.

Minos eventually found out that Daedalus had been instrumental in bringing about the union between his wife and the bull, and threw the architect and his son Icarus into the labyrinth. Daedalus made wings from feathers stuck together with wax and, wearing these, father and son made their getaway. As everyone knows, Icarus flew too close to

Theseus killing the Minotaur

the sun, the wax on his wings melted, and he plummeted into the sea off the island of Ikaria.

Athenians, meanwhile, were enraged by the tribute demanded by Minos. The Athenian hero, Theseus, vowed to kill the Minotaur and sailed off to Crete posing as one of the sacrificial youths. On arrival, he fell in love with Ariadne, the daughter of King Minos, and she promised to help him if he would take her away with him afterwards. She provided him with the ball of twine that he unwound on his way into the labyrinth and used to retrace his steps after slaying the monster. Theseus fled Crete with Ariadne. The two married, but Theseus abandoned Ariadne on the island of Naxos on his way back to Athens.

On his return to Athens, Theseus forgot to unfurl the white sail that he had promised to display to announce that he was still alive. This prompted his distraught father, Aegeus, to hurl himself to his death from the Acropolis. This, incidentally, is how the Aegean sea got its name. ■

Knossos Palace ruins

CRETE

road, Europe's first (Knossos has lots of firsts), was flanked by workshops and the houses of ordinary people. The **lustral basin** is also in this area. Evans speculated that this was where the Minoans performed a ritual cleansing with water before religious ceremonies.

Entering the **Central Court** from the north, you will pass the relief **Bull Fresco** which depicts a charging bull. Relief fres-

coes were made by moulding wet plaster, and then painting it while still wet.

Also worth seeking out in the northern section of the palace are the **giant pithoi**. Pithoi were ceramic jars used for storing olive oil, wine and grain. Evans found over 100 of these huge jars at Knossos (some were 2m high). The ropes used to move them inspired the raised patterns decorating the jars.

CRETE

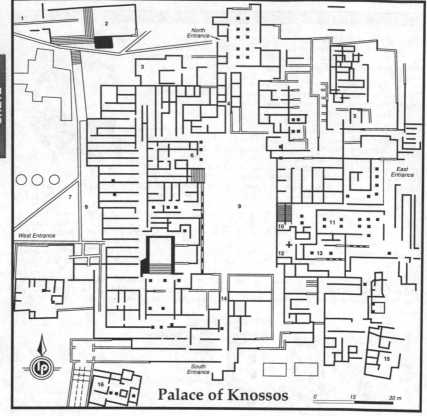

Palace of Knossos

0   15   30 m

1	Royal Road	7	Western Court	12	Water Closet
2	Theatral Area	8	Corridor of the	13	Queen's Megaron
3	Lustral Basin		Procession Fresco	14	Priest King Fresco
4	Bull Fresco	9	Central Court	15	South-East House
5	Giant Pithoi	10	Grand Staircase	16	South House
6	Throne Room	11	Hall of the Double Axes		

Once you have reached the Central Court, which in Minoan times was surrounded by the high walls of the palace, you can begin exploring the most important rooms of the complex.

From the northern end of the west side of the palace, steps lead down to the **throne room**. This room is fenced off but you can still get a good view of it. The centrepiece, the simple, beautifully proportioned throne, is flanked by the **Griffin Fresco**. Griffins were mythical beasts regarded as sacred by the Minoans.

The room is thought to have been a shrine, and the throne the seat of a high priestess, rather than a king. Certainly, the room seems to have an aura of mysticism and reverence rather than pomp and ceremony. The Minoans did not worship their deities in great temples but in small shrines, and each palace had several.

On the 1st floor of this side of the palace is the section Evans called the **Piano Nobile**, for he believed the reception and state rooms were here. A room at the northern end of this floor displays copies of some of the frescoes found at Knossos.

Returning to the Central Court, the impressive **grand staircase** leads from the middle of the eastern side of the palace to the royal apartments, which Evans called the Domestic Quarter. This section of the site is now cordoned off. Within the royal apartments is the **Hall of the Double Axes**. This was the king's megaron, a spacious double room in which the ruler both slept and carried out certain court duties. The room had a light well at one end and a balcony at the other to ensure air circulation.

The room takes its name from the double axe marks on its light well. These marks appear in many places at Knossos. The double axe was a sacred symbol to the Minoans. *Labrys* was Minoan for 'double axe' and the origin of our word 'labyrinth'.

A passage leads from the Hall of the Double Axes to the **queen's megaron**. Above the door is a copy of the **Dolphin Fresco**, one of the most exquisite Minoan artworks, and a blue floral design decorates the portal. Next to this room is the queen's bathroom, complete with terracotta bathtub and a **water closet**, touted as the first ever to work on the flush principle; water was poured down by hand.

Getting There & Away

Regular buses operate from Iraklio. See Iraklio's Getting Around section for details.

MYRTIA Μυρτιά

Myrtia (also called Varvari), 22km south of Iraklio, is making the most of being the village that spawned Crete's favourite literary son, Nikos Kazantzakis. Kazantzakis was born in Iraklio and lived most of his life overseas, but his father was born here – and the writer himself lived here for a time. The **Nikos Kazantzakis Museum**, on the central square of the village, has a collection of the writer's personal mementoes. A video show compiled from film clippings of the author's life is shown in Greek, German, French and English.

The museum is open Monday, Wednesday and weekends from 9 am to 1 pm and 4 to 8 pm, and on Tuesday and Friday from 9 am to 1 pm only. Admission costs 500 dr.

TYLISOS Τώλισος

The minor Minoan site at the village of Tylisos (**Til**isos), 13km from Iraklio, is only for the insatiable enthusiast. Three villas dating from different periods have been excavated. The site (☎ 22 6092) is open Tuesday to Sunday from 8.30 am to 2.30 pm. Admission is 500 dr. Buses from Iraklio to Anogia go through Tylisos. They also go past another Minoan site at **Sklavokambos**, 8km closer to Anogia. The ruins date from 1500 BC and were probably the villa of a district governor. Iraklio-Anogia buses pass the site.

ARHANES Αρχάνες

The attractive village of Arhanes (**Arhan**es), 16km from Iraklio, lies in the heart of Crete's principal grape-producing region. Several Minoan remains have been unearthed in the vineyards surrounding the village. The most noteworthy is the elaborate **Vathypetro Villa**, the home of a prosperous Minoan noble.

The villa complex included storerooms, where wine and oil presses, a weaving loom and a kiln were discovered. The villa is 5km from Arhanes, on the road south – look for a signpost to the right. There is no entrance fee.

Getting There & Away

It's a pleasant outing from Iraklio to Arhanes

if you have your own transport. Otherwise, there are 12 buses a day from Iraklio's Bus Station A to Arhanes (half an hour, 320 dr). There are no buses to Vathypetro, but Creta Travel in Iraklio has a tour which includes a visit to the villa.

GORTYN Γόρτυνα

The archaeological site of Gortyn (also called Gortina and Gortys) lies 46km southwest of Iraklio, and 15km from Phaestos, on the plain of Mesara. It's a vast and wonderfully intriguing site with bits and pieces from various ages strewn all over the place. The site was a settlement from Minoan to Christian times. In Roman times, Gortyn was the capital of the province of Cyrenaica.

The most significant find at the site was the massive stone tablets inscribed with the **Laws of Gortyn**, which date from the 5th century BC. The laws deal with just about every imaginable offence. The tablets are on display at the site.

The 6th-century **basilica** is dedicated to Agios Titos, who was a protege of St Paul and the first bishop of Crete.

Other ruins at Gortyn include the 2nd-century AD **praetorin**, which was the residence of the governor of the province, a **nymphaeum**, and the **Temple of Pythian Apollo**. The site (☎ 081-22 6092) is open every day from 8.30 am to 2.30 pm. Admission is 800 dr. The ruins are on both sides of the main Iraklio-Phaestos road.

PHAESTOS Φαιστός

The Minoan site of Phaestos (Fes**tos**), 63km from Iraklio, was the second most important palace city of Minoan Crete. Of all the Minoan sites, Phaestos has the most awe-inspiring location, with all-embracing views of the Mesara plain and Mt Ida. The layout of the palace is identical to Knossos, with rooms arranged around a central court.

In contrast to Knossos, Phaestos has yielded very few frescoes; it seems the palace walls were mostly covered with a layer of white gypsum. Perhaps, with such inspiring views from the windows, the inhabitants didn't feel any need to decorate

their walls. Evans didn't get his hands on the ruins of Phaestos, so there has been no reconstruction. Like the other palatial period complexes, there was an old palace here which was destroyed at the end of the Middle Minoan period. Unlike the other sites, parts of this old palace have been excavated and its ruins are partially superimposed upon the new palace.

Exploring the Site

The entrance to the new palace is by the 15m-wide **Grand Staircase**. The stairs lead to the west side of the **Central Court**. The best preserved parts of the palace complex are the reception rooms and private apartments to the north of the Central Court; excavations continue here. This section was entered by an imposing portal with half columns at either side, the lower parts of which are still *in situ*. Unlike the Minoan freestanding columns, these do not taper at the base. The celebrated Phaestos disc was found in a building to the north of the palace. The disc is in Iraklio's archaeological museum.

Getting There & Away

There are 10 buses a day from Iraklio's Bus Station B to Phaestos (two hours, 1150 dr), seven from Agia Galini (40 minutes, 380 dr) and six from Matala (30 minutes, 250 dr). Services are halved in winter.

AGIA TRIADA Αγία Τριάδα

Agia Triada (Ag**i**a Tri**a**da) is a small Minoan site 3km west of Phaestos. Its principal building was smaller than the other royal palaces but built to a similar design. This, and the opulence of the objects found at the site, indicate that it was a royal residence, possibly a summer palace of Phaestos' rulers. To the north of the palace is a small town where remains of a stoa have been unearthed.

Finds from the palace now in Iraklio's archaeological museum include a sarcophagus, two superlative frescoes and three vases: the Harvester Vase, Boxer Vase and Chieftain Cup.

The site is open Tuesday to Sunday from 8.30 am to 2.30 pm. Admission is 500 dr. The road to Agia Triada takes off to the right about 500m from Phaestos on the road to Matala. There is no public transport to the site.

MATALA Μάταλα
• pop 300 • postcode 702 00 • area code ☎ 0892

Matala (**Ma**tala), on the coast 11km south-west of Phaestos, was once one of Crete's best known hippie hang-outs.

It was the old Roman caves at the northern end of the beach that made Matala famous in the 1960s. There are dozens of them dotted over the cliff-face. They were originally tombs, cut out of the sandstone rock in the 1st century AD. In the 1960s, they were discovered by hippies, who turned the caves into a modern troglodyte city – moving ever higher up the cliff to avoid sporadic attempts by the local police to evict them. Joni Mitchell was among the visitors, and she sang the praises of life under a Matala moon in Carey.

These days, Matala is a decidedly tacky tourist resort packed out in summer and bleak and deserted in winter. The sandy beach below the caves is, however, one of Crete's best, and the resort is a convenient base from which to visit Phaestos and Agia Triada.

Orientation & Information
Matala's layout is easy to fathom. The bus stop is on the central square, one block back from the waterfront. There is a mobile post office near the beach, on the right of the main road as you come into Matala. The OTE is beyond here in the beach car park.

Places to Stay
Matala Community Camping (☎ 42 340) is a reasonable site just back from the beach. There is another camp site near Komos beach (☎ 42 596), about 4km before Matala on the road from Phaestos.

There are several pleasant options along the approach road to Matala. They include Rooms to Rent Dimitris (☎ 45 7400), where immaculate singles/doubles with bathroom go for 3000/3500 dr.

In Matala proper, walk back along the main road from the bus station and turn right at the Zafiria Hotel. This street is lined with budget accommodation. One of the cheapest places is Fantastic Rooms to Rent (☎ 45 362), on the right. The comfortable double/triple rooms cost 4500/6000 dr with private bathroom. The Pension Antonios (☎ 45 123/438), opposite, has attractively furnished rooms with bathrooms for 4000/6000/7000 dr, and double/triple apartments for 7000 dr.

The C-class Hotel Fragiskos (☎ 45 380/135), on the left as you head out of town, charges 5500/9000 dr for singles/doubles with private bathroom. It has a swimming pool.

If you don't like the sound of Matala, then **Pitsidia village**, 4.5km inland and 7km from Phaestos, is a quieter alternative. There are no hotels but plenty of rooms.

Places to Eat
Most of the restaurants in Matala are poor value. An exception is Taverna Giannis, where a huge plate of calamari, chips and salad costs 1200 dr, while a bowl of tasty lentil soup is 800 dr. Walk towards the southern headland and the taverna is on the right.

The Restaurant Mystical View, high above Komos beach about 3km from Matala, has views that live up to its name and serves good food to boot. The restaurant is signposted off the road to Phaestos.

Getting There & Away
There are seven buses a day between Iraklio and Matala (two hours, 1400 dr) and six a day between Matala and Phaestos (30 minutes, 300 dr).

MALIA Μάλια
The Minoan site of Malia (**Mal**eea) is the only cultural diversion on the stretch of coast east of Iraklio, which otherwise has surrendered lock, stock and barrel to the package tourist industry. Malia is smaller

than Knossos and Phaestos, but like them consisted of a palace complex and a town. Unlike Knossos and Phaestos, the palace was built on a flat, fertile plain, not on a hill.

The site (☎ 22 462) is 3km east of the resort of Malia, and is open Tuesday to Sunday from 8.30 am to 2.30 pm. Admission is 800 dr.

Exploring the Site

Entrance to the ruins is from the **West Court**. At the extreme southern end of this court there are eight circular pits which archaeologists think were used to store grain. To the east of the pits is the main entrance to the palace which leads to the southern end of the **Central Court**. At the south-west corner of this court you will find the **Kernos Stone**, a disc with 34 holes around its edge. Archaeologists have yet to ascertain its function.

The **central staircase** is at the north end of the west side of the palace. The **loggia**, just north of the staircase, is where religious ceremonies took place.

Getting There & Away

Any bus going to/from Iraklio along the north coast can drop you at the site.

Eastern Crete

The eastern quarter of the island is occupied by the prefecture of Lassithi, named after the quaint plateau tucked high in the Mt Dikti ranges rather than its uninspiring administrative capital of Agios Nikolaos, which is becoming something of a monument to package tourism. The main attractions, apart from the Latish plateau, are the palm forest and beach at Vaï and the remote Minoan palace site of Zakros.

AGIOS NIKOLAOS Αγιος Νικόλαος
• *pop 9000* • *postcode 721 00* • *area code* ☎ *0841*

The manifestations of package tourism gather momentum as they advance east from Iraklio, reaching their peak at Agios Nikolaos (Ayios Nikolaos). In July and August the town's permanent population is joined by 11,000 tourists. The result is that there is very little to attract the independent traveller. There is no point in attempting to squeeze into Agios Nikolaos in the peak season between July and mid-September, and the place just about closes down entirely in winter.

Orientation

The town centre is Plateia Venizelou, 150m up Sofias Venizelou from the bus station. The most interesting part of town is around the picturesque Voulismeni lake, which is ringed with tavernas and cafés. The lake is 200m from the Plateia Venizelou. Walk north-east along Koundourou and turn left at the bottom and you will come to a bridge that separates the lake from the harbour. The tourist office is at the far side of the bridge.

Once over the bridge, if you turn right and follow the road as it veers left, you will come to the northern stretch of waterfront which is the road to Elounda. Most of Agios Nikolaos' large and expensive hotels are along here. If you turn right at the bottom of Koundourou you will come to a stretch of waterfront with steps leading up to the right. These lead to the streets that have the highest concentration of small hotels and pensions.

Information

The municipal tourist office (☎ 22 357; fax 26 398) is open daily from 8.30 am to 9.30 pm from 1 April to 15 November. The tourist police (☎ 26 900), Kondogianni 34, are open 24 hours.

Money The National Bank of Greece on Plastira has a 24-hour automatic exchange machine. The tourist office also changes money.

Post & Communications The post office, 28 Oktovriou 9, is open Monday to Saturday from 7.30 am to 2 pm. The OTE is on the

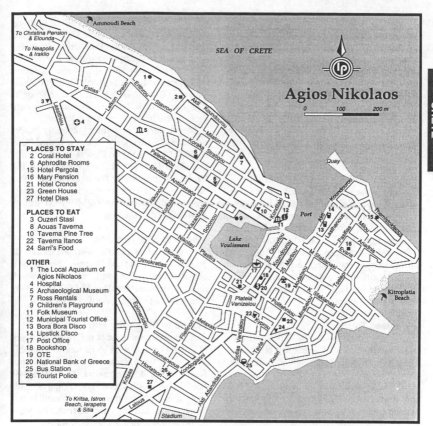

PLACES TO STAY
2 Coral Hotel
6 Aphrodite Rooms
15 Hotel Pergola
16 Mary Pension
21 Hotel Cronos
23 Green House
27 Hotel Dias

PLACES TO EAT
3 Ouzeri Stasi
8 Aouas Taverna
10 Taverna Pine Tree
22 Taverna Itanos
24 Sarri's Food

OTHER
1 The Local Aquarium of
  Agios Nikolaos
4 Hospital
5 Archaeological Museum
7 Ross Rentals
9 Children's Playground
11 Folk Museum
12 Municipal Tourist Office
13 Bora Bora Disco
14 Lipstick Disco
17 Post Office
18 Bookshop
19 OTE
20 National Bank of Greece
25 Bus Station
26 Tourist Police

corner of 25 Martiou and K Sfakianaki. It is
open daily from 7 am to 11 pm.

Bookshop There is a well-stocked English-
language bookshop at Koundourou 5.

Emergency Agios Nikolaos' general hospital (☎ 25 221) is between Lassithiou and
Paleologou.

Museums & Aquarium
The **folk museum**, next door to the tourist
office, has a well-displayed collection of
traditional handcrafts and costumes. It's
open Sunday to Friday from 10 am to 3 pm.
Admission is 250 dr.

The **archaeological museum** (☎ 24 943),
on Paleologou, is a modern building housing
a large, well-displayed collection from eastern Crete. It's open Tuesday to Sunday from
8.30 am until 2.30 pm. Admission costs
500 dr.

The **Local Aquarium of Agios Nikolaos**
(☎ 24 953), on Akti Koundourou, has interesting displays of fish and information about
diving (including PADI courses) and
snorkelling throughout Crete. It is open

Monday to Saturday from 10 am to 4 pm. Admission is 600 dr.

Beaches

The popularity of Agios Nikolaos has nothing to do with its beaches. The town beach, south of the bus station, has more people than pebbles. Ammoudi beach, on the road to Elounda, is equally uninspiring. The nearest decent beach is at Istron, 11km south-east of town. There are 14 buses a day to Istron from Agios Nikolaos.

Voulismeni Lake Λίμνη Βουλισμύνη

The lake is the subject of many stories about its depth and origins. The locals have given it various names, including Xepatomeni (bottomless), Voulismeni (sunken) and Vromolimni (dirty). The lake isn't bottomless – it is 64m deep. The 'dirty' tag came about because the lake used to be stagnant and gave off quite a pong in summer. This was rectified in 1867 when a canal was built linking it to the sea.

Organised Tours

Travel agencies in Agios Nikolaos offer coach outings to all Crete's top attractions. The Creta Travel Bureau (☎ 28 689), Akti Koundourou 3, has boat trips to Spinalonga for 4000 dr, as well as guided tours of Lato and Kritsa (4000 dr) and to the Lassithi plateau (8000 dr).

Places to Stay – bottom end

The nearest camp site to Agios Nikolaos is *Gournia Moon Camping* (☎ 0842-93 243), near the Minoan site of Gournia. It has a swimming pool, restaurant, snack bar and minimarket. Buses to Sitia can drop you off outside.

The *Green House* (☎ 22 025), Modatsou 15, is a favourite with backpackers. It is ramshackle but clean, with a lush garden. Singles/doubles are 3500/5000 dr with shared bathroom. Walk up Tavla (a continuation of Modatsou) from the bus station, and you'll find it on the right.

The *Hotel Pergola* (☎ 28 152), on Akti Themistokleous, has comfortable rooms

with private bathroom for 6000/7000 dr. *Aphrodite Rooms* (☎ 28 058), Koritsas 27, has rooms for 4000/6000 dr with shared facilities and a tiny communal kitchen. At *Mary Pension* (☎ 23 760), Evans 13, rooms with private bathroom cost 3000/6000 dr. The new *Christina Pension* (☎ 23 984 or 26 236), on the waterfront overlooking Ammoudi beach, has the same rates.

If you arrive in winter, the only places you'll find officially open are the *Hotel Cronos* (☎ 28 761) on Plateia Venizelou and the *Hotel Dias* (☎ 28 263) at Latous 6. The Cronos is marginally the better of an unexciting pair. It charges slightly more, with singles/doubles for 6000/8000 dr, or 5000/6000 dr in winter.

Places to Stay – middle

The opulent B-class *Coral Hotel* (☎ 28 363/367), on the northern waterfront, is about as up-market as places get in town. It has singles/doubles for 12,000/18,300 dr. There is a swimming pool.

Places to Stay – top end

The luxury-hotel zone is just north of Agios Nikolaos on the road to Elounda. The only hotel that's open all year is the deluxe *Minos Beach Hotel & Bungalows* (☎ 22 345/349; fax 22 548), with accommodation in seaside bungalows. A swimming pool and tennis courts are among the extras for your 25,000/30,400 dr for singles/doubles.

Places to Eat

Agios Nikolaos' waterfront tavernas are expensive – head inland for better value. *Taverna Itanos*, Kyprou 1, is a lively traditional taverna, with chicken for 950 dr and stifado for 1200 dr.

The *Ouzeri Stasi* is a bit out of the way at Lassithiou 23, but well worth the effort. It has an excellent selection of mezedes priced from 500 to 900 dr. It opens only in the evenings.

The *Taverna Pine Tree*, next to the lake, specialises in charcoal-grilled food, such as a plate of huge prawns for 1800 dr. *Aouas Taverna*, at Paleologou 50, has traditional décor and a lovely garden. A large plate of mezedes (enough for four people) is 2500 dr. The tiny *Sarri's Food*, Kyprou 15, has tasty main courses for between 900 and 1400 dr.

Entertainment

Discos and bars abound in Agios Nikolaos. *Lipstick Disco* and *Bora-Bora* are two of the most popular.

Getting There & Away

Bus Destinations of buses from Agios Nikolaos' bus station are:

Destination	Duration	Fare	Frequency
Elounda	20 mins	220 dr	19 daily
Kritsa	15 mins	220 dr	12 daily
Ierapetra	1 hour	700 dr	9 daily
Iraklio	1½ hours	1300 dr	half-hourly
Istron	30 mins	260 dr	14 daily
Kroustas	20 mins	300 dr	4 daily
Lassithi plateau	3 hours	1500 dr	2 daily
Sitia	1½ hours	1350 dr	6 daily

Ferry Agios Nikolaos has the same ferry schedule as Sitia. Ferry tickets can be bought from the Creta Travel Bureau (see Organised Tours in the Agios Nikolaos section), among others. The port police (☎ 22 312) are in the same building as the tourist office.

Getting Around

Car, Motorcycle & Bicycle You will find many car and motorcycle-hire outlets on the northern waterfront. Ross Rentals (☎ 23 407), Koundourou 10, has a huge range of brand new motorcycles, from little runabouts up to a 1300cc Harley (just 35,000 dr per day). It also has mountain bikes for 2000 dr.

GOURNIA Γουρνιά

The important Minoan site of Gournia (Gour**nya**) lies just off the coast road, 19km south-east of Agios Nikolaos. The ruins, which date from 1550 to 1450 BC, consist of a town overlooked by a small palace. Gournia's palace was far less ostentatious than the ones at Knossos and Phaestos; it was the residence of an overlord rather than a king. The town is a network of streets and stairways flanked by houses with walls up to 2m in height. Trade, domestic and agricultural implements found on the site indicate that Gournia was a thriving little community.

The site (☎ 0841-24 943) is open Tuesday to Sunday from 8.30 am to 3 pm. Admission is 500 dr. Gournia is on the Sitia and Ierapetra bus routes from Agios Nikolaos and buses can drop you at the site.

MONI FANEROMENIS

Μονή Φανερωμύνης

Just 2km before Gournia, on the Agios Nikolaos-Sitia road, a 5km road leads off right to the late-Byzantine Moni Faneromenis. If you have your own transport, a visit to the monastery is worthwhile for the stunning views down to the coast.

KRITSA Κριτσά

The village of Kritsa (Krit**sa**), perched 600m up the mountainside 11km from Agios Nikolaos, is on every package itinerary. Tourists come in bus loads to the village every day in summer. The villagers exploit these invasions to the full, and craft shops of every description line the main streets.

The tiny triple-aisled **Church of Panagia Kera** is on the right 1km before Kritsa on the Agios Nikolaos road. The frescoes that cover its interior walls are considered the most outstanding examples of Byzantine art on Crete. Unfortunately the church is usually packed with tourists. It's open Monday to Saturday from 9 am to 3 pm and Sunday from 9 am to 2 pm. Admission is 800 dr.

Kritsa doesn't have any hotels, but there are several domatia – look for the signs. There are 12 buses a day from Agios Nikolaos to Kritsa (15 minutes, 220 dr).

ANCIENT LATO Λατώ

The ancient city of Lato (La**to**), 4km north of Kritsa, is one of Crete's few non-Minoan ancient sites. Lato was founded in the 7th century BC by the Dorians and at its height was one of the most powerful cities on Crete.

CRETE

It sprawls over the slopes of two acropolises in a lonely mountain setting, commanding stunning views down to the Gulf of Mirabelo.

The city's name derived from the goddess Leto whose union with Zeus produced Artemis and Apollo, both of whom were worshipped here. Lato is far less visited than Crete's Minoan sites. It's open Tuesday to Sunday from 8.30 am to 3 pm. Entry is free.

There are no buses to Lato. The road to the site is signposted to the right on the approach to Kritsa. If you don't have your own transport, it's a pleasant walk through olive groves along this road.

Exploring the Site

In the centre of the site is a deep well which is cordoned off. Facing the Bay of Mirabello, to the left of the well are some steps which are the remains of a **theatre**.

Above the theatre was the **prytaneion**, where the city's governing body met. The circle of stones behind the well was a threshing floor. The columns next to it are the remains of a stoa which stood in the agora. There are remains of a pebble mosaic nearby. A path to the right leads up to the **Temple of Apollo**.

SPINALONGA PENINSULA
Χερσόνησος Σπιναλόγκας

Just before Elounda (coming from Agios Nikolaos), a sign points right to **ancient Olous**, which was the port of Lato. The city stood on, and around, the narrow isthmus (now a causeway) which joined the southern end of the Spinalonga peninsula to the mainland. Most of the ruins lie beneath the water, and if you go snorkelling near the causeway you will see outlines of buildings and the tops of columns. The water around here appears to be paradise for sea urchins. The peninsula is a pleasant place to stroll and there is an early Christian mosaic near the causeway.

SPINALONGA ISLAND
Νήσος Σπιναλόγκα

Spinalonga island lies just north of the Spinalonga peninsula. The island's massive

fortress was built by the Venetians in 1579 to protect Elounda and Mirabello bays. It withstood Turkish sieges for longer than any other Cretan stronghold, finally surrendering in 1715, some 30 years after the rest of Crete. The Turks used the island as a base for smuggling. Following the reunion of Crete with Greece, Spinalonga became a leper colony. The last leper died there in 1953 and the island has been uninhabited ever since. Spinalonga is still known among locals as 'the island of the living dead'.

The island is a fascinating place to explore. It has an aura that is both macabre and poignant. The **cemetery**, with its open graves, is an especially strange place. Dead lepers came in three classes: those who saved up money from their government pension for a place in a concrete box; those whose funeral was paid for by relations and who therefore got a proper grave; and the destitute, whose remains were thrown into a charnel house.

Getting There & Away

There are regular excursion boats to the island from Agios Nikolaos. Alternatively, you can negotiate with the fishermen in Elounda and Plaka (a fishing village 5km further north) to take you across. The boats from Agios Nikolaos pass Bird island and Kri-Kri island, one of the last habitats of the kri-kri, Crete's wild goat. Both of these islands are uninhabited and designated wildlife sanctuaries.

ELOUNDA Ελούντα
• *pop 1800* • *postcode 720 53* • *area code ☎ 0841*
There are magnificent mountain and sea views along the 11km road from Agios Nikolaos to Elounda (El**oon**da). The place is considerably quieter than Agios Nikolaos. It also has an attractive harbour and a sheltered lagoon-like stretch of water formed by the Spinalonga peninsula.

Orientation & Information

Elounda's post office is opposite the bus stop. From the bus stop walk straight ahead to the clock tower and church which are on the central square. There is a small OTE office next to the church. The town doesn't have a tourist office or tourist police.

Places to Stay

There's some good accommodation around, but nothing particularly cheap. *Elpis Rooms* (☎ 41 384), opposite the Church of Konstantinos, charges 7000/8000 dr for comfortable doubles/triples with private bathroom. The *Hotel Sofia* (☎ 41 482), on the seafront 100m from the town centre, has pleasantly furnished two-room apartments with kitchen for 12,000 dr among its range of options.

Getting There & Away

There are 19 buses a day from Agios Nikolaos to Elounda (20 minutes, 220 dr).

LASSITHI PLATEAU Οροπέδιο Λασιθίου
• *postcode 720 52* • *area code ☎ 0844*

The first view of the mountain-fringed Lassithi (La**sith**ee) plateau, laid out like an immense patchwork quilt, is stunning. The plateau, 900m above sea level, is a vast expanse of pear and apple orchards, almond trees and fields of crops, dotted by some 7000 windmills. These are not conventional stone windmills, but slender metal constructions with white canvas sails. There are 20 villages dotted around the periphery of the plateau, the largest of which is **Tzermiado**, with 1300 inhabitants, a bank, post office and OTE.

The plateau's rich soil has been cultivated since Minoan times. The inaccessibility of the region made it a hotbed of insurrection during Venetian and Turkish rule. Following an uprising in the 13th century, the Venetians drove out the inhabitants of Lassithi and destroyed their orchards. The plateau lay abandoned for 200 years.

Most people come to Lassithi on coach trips, but it deserves an overnight stay. Once the package tourists have departed clutching their plastic windmill souvenirs, the villages return to pastoral serenity.

Dikteon Cave Δικταίον Αντρον
Lassithi's major sight is the Dikteon cave,

just outside the village of **Psyhro** (Psi**hro**). Here, according to mythology, Rhea hid the newborn Zeus from Cronos, his offspring-gobbling father. The cave, which has both stalactites and stalagmites, was excavated in 1900 by the British archaeologist David Hogarth. He found numerous votives indicating that the cave was a place of cult worship. These finds are housed in the archaeological museum in Iraklio.

The moment you reach the parking area beneath the site, representatives from the Association of Cave Guides & Donkey Owners will be upon you. The cave guides want 2000 dr for a lantern-guided tour, while the donkey owners want the same to save you the 15-minute walk up to the cave. A guide is not essential, but a torch is. So are sensible shoes. The path to the cave is pretty rough, and the cave itself is slippery. Opening times are 10.30 am to 5 pm in summer, 8.30 am to 3 pm in winter. Admission is 800 dr.

Walk from Tzermiado to Psycho

This 90-minute walk from Tzermiado to Psycho goes through the heart of the plateau. From Tzermiado's central square take the street with the Agricultural Bank and OTE. At the end, turn right, and then first left onto a road which becomes a dirt track. Continue ahead for 1km, at the T-junction turn right, and then veer right onto the surfaced road. At the crossroads, turn left onto a rough dirt track. Turn right at the second crossroads and you will see Psycho in the distance to the left. Continue straight ahead for 1km, and at the T-junction turn left. At the road turn left to reach Psycho's central square, or continue straight ahead to reach the cave.

Places to Stay & Eat

Psyhro, the village nearest the cave, has only one place to stay, the D-class *Zeus Hotel* (☎ 31 284), where singles/doubles with private bathroom cost 5000/8000 dr. On the main street, the *Stavros* and *Platanos* tavernas serve similar fare at similar prices.

Agios Georgios, 5km away, has three accommodation options. The *Hotel Rea*

(☎ 31 209), opposite the school on the main street, has cosy rooms for 2500/4000 dr with shared bathroom. *Rent Rooms Maria*, nearby, has lovely, characterful rooms for 7000/8500 dr with private bathroom.

The *Hotel Dias* (☎ 31 207), also on the main street, has pleasant rooms for 2500/4000 dr with shared bathroom. Both hotels have restaurants.

The well-signposted *Hotel Kourites* (☎ 22 194), is Tzermiado's only accommodation. Its comfortable rooms cost 6000/8000 dr with private bathroom, breakfast included. There is free use of the hotel's bicycles.

The *Restaurant Kronio* on Tzermiado's main square has a pleasant, folksy décor. The food is excellent, but avoid the place when the tour buses call, as the waiters go into frenzy mode. *Taverna Kri-Kri*, nearby, is a good place to meet locals. The menu is limited but the food is good.

Getting There & Away

There are two buses a day from Agios Nikolaos to Lassithi (two hours, 1500 dr). It leaves Agios Nikolaos at 8.15 am and 2 pm, returning at 7 am and 2 pm. On weekends, only the morning bus from Agios Nikolaos and the afternoon bus from Lassithi operate. There are also two buses a day from Iraklio (two hours, 1300 dr), leaving at 8.30 am and 3 pm and returning at 7 am and 4.45 pm. On Sunday, only the morning service from Iraklio exists, returning at 2 pm.

All buses go through Tzermiado, Agios Georgios and Psyhro and terminate at the Dikteon cave.

SITIA Σητεία
• *pop 8000* • *postcode 72 300* • *area code* ☎ *0843*

Back on the north-coast road, Sitia (S**itee**a) is a good deal quieter than Agios Nikolaos. A sandy beach skirts a wide bay to the east of town. The main part of the town is terraced up a hillside, overlooking the port. The buildings are a pleasing mixture of new and fading Venetian architecture.

Orientation & Information

The bus station is at the eastern end of Karamanli, which runs behind the bay. The town's main square, Plateia El Venizelou – recognisable by its palm trees and statue of a dying soldier – is at the western end of Karamanli. There is a mobile tourist office in the square from May to October.

There are plenty of places to change money. The National Bank of Greece on the main square has a 24-hour automatic exchange machine.

The harbour near the square is for small boats. Ferries use the large quay further out, about 500m from Plateia Agnostou.

The post office is on Therissou. To get there from the main square, follow El Venizelou inland along the base of the hill to the next major junction. Therissou is the major road running uphill to the right. The OTE is on Kapetan Sifis, which runs uphill directly off Plateia Venizelou.

Things to See & Do

Sitia's archaeological museum (☎ 23 917) houses a well-displayed collection of local finds spanning from Neolithic to Roman times, with emphasis on the Minoan. The museum is on the left side of the road to Ierapetra. It is open Tuesday to Sunday from 8.30 am to 3 pm. Admission is 500 dr.

Sitia produces superior sultanas and a **sultana festival** is held in the town in the last week of August, during which wine flows freely and there are performances of Cretan dances.

Places to Stay – bottom end

Sitia's *youth hostel* (☎ 22 693) is at Therissou 4, on the road to Iraklio. It's a well-run hostel with hot showers and a communal kitchen and dining room. Dorm beds cost 1400 dr and doubles with shared bathroom are 3500 dr. Camping in the grounds costs 1200 per person.

Veteran backpackers who yearn for the simple domatia of yesteryear will delight in *Rooms Leventiras* (☎ 28 628 or 25 6940), although the single-storey whitewashed building will be a bit too basic for some. Singles/doubles/triples are 3000/4000/5000 dr with shared bathroom. Emerge from the bus station ticket office, turn right, take the first right and you will come to the rooms on the left.

The D-class *Hotel Arhontiko* (☎ 28 172/22 993), Kondylaki 16, is beautifully maintained and spotless. Rooms are 5000/6500 dr with shared facilities. On summer evenings, the friendly owner enjoys sharing a bottle of raki with guests on the communal terrace. Kondylaki is two streets uphill from the port. The best way to get there is to walk out towards the ferry dock along El Venizelou, turn left up Filellinon and then right into Kondylaki. The co-owned *Rooms to Let Apostolis*, an up-market domatia, at Kazantzaki 27, has the same prices. Kazantzaki runs uphill from the waterfront, one street north of the OTE.

Another attractive place is *Kazarma Rooms to Rent* (☎ 23 211), Ionias 10, where doubles with bathroom cost 8000 dr. There is a communal lounge and a well-equipped kitchen. The rooms are signposted from Patriarch Metahaki. The well-signposted *El Greco Hotel* (☎ 23 133), Arkadou 13, has more character than the town's other C-class places. Comfortable rooms with private bathroom cost 6000/9000 dr.

Places to Eat
There is a string of tavernas specialising in fish dishes along the quay side on El Venizelou. At No 189, *To Kyma* is less pretentious than most. It specialises in mezedes, priced from 500 dr, and serves excellent fried baby squid in crisp batter for 1200 dr. *Mixos Taverna*, Kornarou 117, has excellent charcoal-grilled souvlaki. Walk up Patriarch Metahaki from the waterfront, take the first left and the taverna is on the right.

The *Kali Kardia Taverna*, Foundalidhou 20, is excellent value and popular with locals. Mezedes cost from 300 to 700 dr and main dishes from 1200 to 1700 dr. Walk up Kazantzaki from the waterfront, take the second right and the taverna is on the right. *Karnagoi Tavern* which overlooks the ferry dock also has a good range of reasonably priced dishes. The galaktopoleio at Kornarou 33 specialises in fine sheep's milk

products, including fresh milk, curdled milk, delicious yoghurt and cheese.

Getting There & Away
Air Sitia's tiny airport has flights to Athens on Wednesday and Sunday (21,100 dr), and Wednesday flights to Karpathos (8400 dr) and Kassos (8400 dr). The Olympic Airways agent is Tzortzakis Travel (☎ 25 080/090), at Kornarou 146.

Bus There are five buses a day to Ierapetra (1½ hours, 1150 dr); six buses a day to Iraklio (3½ hours, 2650 dr) via Agios Nikolaos (1½ hours, 1350 dr); four to Vaï (one hour, 600 dr); and two to Kato Zakros (one hour) via Paleokastro and Zakros (one hour, 750 dr). The buses to Vaï and Kato Zakros run only between May and October; during the rest of the year, the Vaï service terminates at Paleokastro and the Kato Zakros service at Zakros.

Ferry The F/B *Vitsentzos Kornaros* leaves Sitia at 3.30 pm on Tuesday, Thursday and Sunday for Piraeus (6700 dr in deck class) via Agios Nikolaos and arrives at 6 am. The F/B *Georgios Express* leaves Sitia on Wednesday at 10 am for Karpathos (four hours, 3000 dr), Kassos (six hours, 2500 dr) and Rhodes (5600 dr). Buy ferry tickets at Tzortzakis Travel Agency (☎ 22 631 or 28 900), Kornarou 146.

Getting Around
The Airport The airport (signposted) is 1km out of town. There is no airport bus. A taxi costs about 600 dr.

Car & Motorcycle Car and motorcycle-hire outlets are mostly on the eastern waterfront near the bus station.

AROUND SITIA
Moni Toplou Μονή Τοπλού
The imposing Moni Toplou, 18km from Sitia on the back road to Vaï, looks more like a fortress than a monastery. It was often treated as such, being ravaged by both the Knights of St John and the Turks. It has an 18th-

CRETE

century icon by Ioannis Kornaros, one of Crete's most celebrated icon painters. The monastery is open from 9 am to 1 pm and from 2 to 6 pm.

The monastery is a 3km walk from the Sitia-Paleokastro road. Buses can drop you off at the junction.

Vaï Βάι

The beach at Vaï, on Crete's east coast 24km from Sitia, is famous for its palm forest.

There are many stories about the origin of these palms including the theory that they sprouted from date pits spread by Roman legionaries relaxing on their way back from conquering Egypt. While these palms are closely related to the date, they are a separate species found only on Crete.

You'll need to arrive early to appreciate the setting, because the place gets packed out in summer. It's possible to escape the worst of the ballyhoo – jet skis and all – by clambering over a rocky outcrop (to the left facing the sea) to a small secluded beach. Alternatively, you can go over the hill in the other direction to a quiet beach frequented by nudists.

There are two tavernas at Vaï but no accommodation. If you're after more secluded beaches, head north for another 3km to the ancient Minoan site of **Itanos**. Below the site are several good swimming spots. There are four buses a day to Vaï from Sitia (one hour, 600 dr).

ZAKROS & KATO ZAKROS
• *area code* ☎ 0843
The village of Zakros (Ζάκρος), 45km south-east of Sitia, is the nearest permanent settlement to the east-coast Minoan site of Zakros, which is 7km away.

Kato Zakros, next to the site, is a beautiful little seaside settlement that springs to life between March and October. If the weather is dry, there is a lovely two-hour walk from Zakros to Kato Zakros through a gorge known as the Valley of the Dead because of the cave tombs dotted along the cliffs. The gorge emerges close to the Minoan site.

Places to Stay
Zakros has domatia and one hotel, the bleak C-class *Hotel Zakros* (☎ 93 379), where doubles with private bathroom are 6500 dr. It's much better to stay at Kato Zakros, where there are four places to choose from. *Sunrise Rooms* (☎ 93 458/93 316) has singles/doubles for 5000/6000 dr; *Athena Rooms* (☎ 93 458 /93 377) has doubles with private bathroom for 8500 dr; and *Poseidon Rooms* has rooms for 5000/5500 dr with shared bathroom. All these places are at the far end of the beach road.

George's Villas (☎ 93 201/207) has spotless, beautifully furnished rooms with private bathroom and terrace. Rates are 6000/7000 dr. The villas are in a verdant setting 500m along the old road to Zakros.

Getting There & Away
There are two buses a day to Zakros (via Paleokastro) from Sitia (one hour, 750 dr). They leave Sitia at 11 am and 2 pm and return at 12.30 and 4 pm. In summer, the buses continue to Kato Zakros. The Hotel Zakros offers guests free transport to Kato Zakros.

ANCIENT ZAKROS
Ancient Zakros, the smallest of Crete's four palatial complexes, was a major port in Minoan times, with trade links to Egypt, Syria, Anatolia and Cyprus. The palace consisted of royal apartments, storerooms and workshops flanking a central courtyard.

The town occupied a low plain close to the shore. Water levels have risen over the years so that some parts of the palace complex are submerged. The ruins are not well preserved, but a visit to the site is worthwhile for its wild and remote setting. The site is open Tuesday to Sunday from 8.30 am to 3 pm. Admission is 500 dr.

Xerokambos
The tiny village of Xerokambos, the next bay south to Kato Zakros, is an unspoilt haven near several coves of inviting pale sand. Most of the domatia in Xerokambos operate only in high season, but *Villa Petrina Rent Rooms* (☎ 0843-31 115; fax 31 693) is open

all year. Its beautiful apartments cost 9000 dr per day.

There are no buses to Xerokambos. To get there from Zakros take the Kato Zakros road, and on the outskirts of Zakros turn left at the signpost for Liviko View Restaurant. This 10km dirt road to Xerokambos is only suitable for 4WD.

IERAPETRA Ιεράπετρα
• *pop 11,000* • *postcode 722 00* • *area code* ☎ *0842*

Ierapetra (Yerapetra), on the south coast, is Crete's most southerly major town. It was a major port of call for the Romans in their conquest of Egypt. After the tourist hype of Agios Nikolaos, the unpretentiousness of Ierapetra is refreshing. Ierapetra is a town whose main business continues to be agriculture, not tourism.

Orientation
The bus station is on Lasthenous, one street back from the beachfront on the eastern side of town. Emerging from the ticket office, turn right and after about 50m you'll come to a six-road intersection. There are signposts to the beach, via Patriarhou Metaxaki, and to the city centre, via the pedestrian mall section of Lasthenous.

The mall emerges after about 200m onto the central square of Plateia Eleftherias. On the left of the square is the National Bank of Greece. Turn right opposite the bank to get to the OTE, which is one block inland on Koraka.

If you continue straight ahead from Plateia Eleftherias you will come to Plateia Emmanual Kothri, where you'll find the post office at Stylianou Houta 3.

Information
There is no tourist office, but South Crete Tours (☎ 22 892), opposite the archaeological museum, can help with a map of Ierapetra. To reach it, turn right from Plateia Emmanual Kothri.

Things to See
Ierapetra's one-room **archaeological museum** is for those with a short concentra-

tion span. Pride of place is given to an exquisite statue of Demeter. Opening times are Tuesday to Sunday from 8.30 am to 3 pm. Admission is free.

If you walk south along the waterfront from the central square you will come to the **fortress**, which was built in the early years of Venetian rule and strengthened by Francesco Morosini in 1626. It's in a pretty fragile state and was closed at the time of writing. Inland from here is the labyrinthine old quarter, a delightful place to lose yourself for a while.

Beaches Ierapetra has two beaches. The main town beach is near the harbour and the other beach stretches east from the bottom of Patriarhou Metaxaki. Both have coarse, grey sand.

Places to Stay – bottom end & middle
The nearest camp sites to Ierapetra are two sites adjacent to one another on the beach at the coastal resort of Koutsounari, 7km east of Ierapetra. They are *Ierapetra Camping* (☎ 61 351) and *Koutsounari Camping* (☎ 61 213). Both sites have a restaurant, snack bar and minimarket and charge identical prices. Ierapetra-Sitia buses pass the sites.

Most of the places to stay are either near the bus station or in the old quarter. An exception is the *Katerina Hotel* (☎ 28 345) on the seafront where pleasant doubles with private bathroom are 7000 dr. To reach the hotel from the bus station, follow Patriarhou Metaxaki to the waterfront, turn right and you'll see the hotel on the right.

The *Hotel Coral* (☎ 22 842) has well-kept singles/doubles for 4000/5000 dr with private bathroom. The owner also has some rooms for 3000/4500 dr with shared bathroom, and comfortable apartments for 7000 dr. The hotel is signposted just south of the port police building on the waterfront.

The *Cretan Villa Hotel* (☎ 28 522), Lakerda 16, is a lovely, well-maintained 18th-century house with traditionally furnished rooms and a peaceful courtyard. Room rates are 6000/8000 dr with private bathroom. From the bus station walk towards

CRETE

the town centre, and take the first right, from where the hotel is signposted.

Places to Stay – top end

The best hotel in town is the B-class *Astron Hotel* (☎ 25 114; fax 25 917) at the beach end of Patriarhou Metaxaki. Rates are 12,000/17,000 dr, including breakfast.

Places to Eat

Most of the souvlaki outlets are on Kyrba. One exception is *Dionysos Restaurant Bar*, Kothi 3, which serves a generous souvlaki in pitta for 450 dr. For more sophisticated dining, try the *Restaurant Castello* – one of a string of tavernas along the waterfront in the old quarter. You'll have to go a long way to find better home-made dolmades (800 dr), and the squid cooked in its own ink (950 dr) is equally delicious.

Getting There & Away

In summer, there are nine buses a day to Iraklio (2½ hours, 1900 dr) via Agios Nikolaos (one hour, 700 dr), Gournia and Istron; eight to Makrigialos (30 minutes, 550 dr); six to Sitia (1½ hours, 1500 dr) via Koutsounari (for camp sites); six to Mirtos (30 minutes, 300 dr) and two to Ano Viannos (one hour, 750 dr).

AROUND IERAPETRA

The beaches to the east of Ierapetra tend to get crowded. For greater tranquillity, head for **Hrysi islet**, where there are good uncrowded sandy beaches. In summer an excursion boat (5000 dr) leaves for the islet every morning and returns in the afternoon. The island has three tavernas.

MIRTOS

• *pop 600* • *postcode 722 00* • *area code* ☎ *0842*

Mirtos, on the coast 17km west of Ierapetra, is a sparkling village of whitewashed houses with flower-filled balconies. Mirtos has preserved its charm, despite having become popular with independent travellers. It has a decent dark sand and pebble beach.

To get to the waterfront from the bus stop, facing south, take the road to the right passing Mertiza Studios on the right. You'll soon find your way around Mirtos which is built on a grid system.

There is no post office, bank or OTE, but Aris Travel Agency (☎ 51 017/300) on the main street has currency exchange.

Places to Stay & Eat

Despina Rent Rooms (☎ 51 343) has pleasant doubles/triples with private bathroom for 4000/5500 dr. The rooms are on the street running from the bus stop to the waterfront. *Yiannis Domatia* (☎ 51 522), next door, charges 4000/5000 dr with shared bathroom.

The *Pandora Domatia* (☎ 51 589), on the main street, has prettily furnished singles/doubles for 3500/4000 dr with shared bathroom. The superior C-class *Hotel Mirtos* (☎ 51 227) has large, well-kept rooms for 5000/7000 dr with private bathroom. *Meriza Studios* (☎ 51 208) has well-equipped studios for 8000 dr.

The *Mirtos Hotel Restaurant* is popular with both locals and tourists. The no-frills Kostos Taverna nearby has good dolmades for 900 dr and stifado for 1200 dr. The waterfront *Karavoslasi Restaurant* is more stylish, with vegetarian dishes for 900 dr and meat dishes for 1200 to 1500 dr.

Getting There & Away

There are six buses a day from Ierapetra to Mirtos (30 minutes, 260 dr). The Ano Viannos-Ierapetra bus passes through Mirtos.

MIRTOS TO ANO VIANNOS

Ano Viannos, 42km west of Mirtos, is a delightful village built on the southern flanks of Mt Dikti. The interesting **folk lore museum**, on the main street, opens daily from 9 am to 1.30 pm. Admission is 500 dr. The village's 14th-century **Church of Agios Pelagia** has fine frescos by Nikoforos Fokas. To reach the church walk up 25 Martio opposite the large church on the main street. But first ask in a kafeneia for the whereabouts of the key.

Ano Viannos has two domatia. *Taverna & Rooms Lefkas* (☎ 0895-22 719), opposite the large church, has singles/doubles for 3000/4000 dr with private bathroom. *Maria Papadimiti Rooms* (☎ 0895-22 273), opposite the museum, has rooms for 4000/5000 dr with private bathrooms.

From Ano Viannos it's 13km south to the unspoilt village of **Keratokambos**, where there's a pleasant tree-lined beach. At the coast turn left to reach *Taverna & Rooms Thoinikas* (☎ 0895-51 401), where singles/doubles with private bathroom cost 3000/6000 dr. Turn right to reach *Taverna & Rooms Kriti* (☎ 0895-51 231) where doubles/triples with private bathroom cost 5000/6000 dr.

Morning Star Taverna is the best bet for vegetarians with tasty artichoke stew for 1000 dr. *Taverna Kriti* offers excellent fish dishes and *Taverna Thoinikas* specialises in grilled food.

The turn-off for **Arvi** (population 300) is 3km east of Ano Vainnos. Arvi is bigger than Keratokambos, but only gets crowded during July and August. Hemmed in by cliffs, Arvi is a sun trap where bananas grow in abundance. The main street skirts a long sand and pebble beach. It's a 15-minute walk inland to Moni Agios Andronios.

Pension Kolibi (☎ 0895-71 250), in a quiet setting 1km west of Arvi, has immaculate doubles/triples with private bathroom for 6000/7000 dr.

Pension Gorgona (☎ 0895-71 353), on the main street, has pleasant doubles for 5400 dr with bathroom. Further west, *Hotel Ariadne* (☎ 0895-71 300) has well-kept singles/doubles for 5000/6000 dr with private bathroom. *Apartments Kyma* (☎ 0895-71 344) at the eastern end of the village has luxurious apartments for 8000 dr.

Kima Restaurant, on the main street, serves hearty Greek fare. *Taverna Diktina* features vegetarian food and *Two Dolphin's Restaurant* on the beach has good fish.

Getting There & Away
Public transport is poor. From Ano Viannos there are two buses a day to Iraklio (2½ hours, 1900 dr) and two to Ierapetra (one hour, 750 dr) via Mirtos. There is no bus service to Keratokambos or Arvi, but in term-time it may be possible to use the school buses from Ano Viannos.

With 4WD you can use the 10km coastal dirt road between Keratokambos and Arvi.

Western Crete

The western part of Crete comprises the prefectures of Hania and Rethymno, which take their names from the old Venetian cities which are their capitals. The two towns rank as two of the region's main attractions, although the most famous is the spectacular Samaria gorge. The south coast towns of Paleohora and Plakias are popular resorts.

RETHYMNO Ρέθυμνο
• *pop 24,000* • *postcode 741 00* • *area code ☎ 0831*

Rethymno (**Reth**imno) is Crete's third-largest town. The main attraction is the old Venetian-Ottoman quarter that occupies the headland beneath the massive Venetian *fortezza* (fortress). The place is a maze of narrow streets, graceful wood-balconied houses and ornate Venetian monuments; several minarets add a touch of the Orient. The architectural similarities invite comparison with Hania, but Rethymno has a character of its own. An added attraction is a beach right in town.

The approaches to the town could hardly be less inviting. The modern town has sprawled out along the coast, dotted with big package hotels attracted there by a reasonable beach.

History
The site of modern Rethymno has been occupied since Late Minoan times – the evidence can be found in the city's archaeological museum. In the 3rd and 4th centuries BC, Rithymna emerged as an autonomous state of sufficient stature to issue its own coinage.

The town prospered once more under the Venetians, who ruled from 1210 until 1645,

when the Turks took over. Turkish forces held the town until 1897, when it was taken by Russia as part of the occupation of Crete by the Great Powers.

Rethymno became an artistic and intellectual centre after the arrival of a large number of refugees from Constantinople in 1923. The city has a campus of the University of Crete, bringing a student population that keeps the town alive outside the tourist season.

Orientation

The city's old quarter occupies the headland north of Dimakopoulou, which runs from Plateia Vardinogianni on the west coast to Plateia Irön on the east (becoming Gerakari en route).

Most of the good places to eat and sleep are to be found here, while banks and government services are just to the south on the edge of the new three-quarters of town. The beach is on the eastern side of town, curving around from the delightful old Venetian harbour in the north. El Venizelou is the beachfront street. Curving parallel one block back is Arkadiou, the main commercial street.

PLACES TO STAY	23	Gounakis Restaurant	24	Historical & Folk Art
1	Lefteris Papadakis		& Bar		Museum
	Rooms	33	Taverna Ta Balkania	25	Neradjes Mosque
4	Pension Anna			29	Municipal Tourist
6	Hotel Fortezza	**OTHER**			Office
7	Rooms to Rent	2	Entrance to Fortress	30	Happy Walker
	Barbara Dolomaki	3	Archaeological	32	Porto Guora
18	Cafe Bar 67		Museum	34	Bus Station
21	Olga's Pension	8	Templum Club	35	Car Park
26	Rent Rooms Garden	9	Cretan Lines	36	OTE
27	Rooms for Rent Anda	10	Fortezza Disco	37	Credit Bank
28	Rent Rooms Sea front	12	Rimondi Fountain	38	National Mortgage
31	Youth Hostel	13	Nileas Tours		Bank
		14	Motor Stavros	39	National Bank of
PLACES TO EAT	15	Loggia		Greece
5	Taverna Pontios	16	International Press	40	Hospital
11	Taverna Kyria Maria		Bookshop	41	Olympic Airways
20	Stella's Kitchen	17	Paradise Dive Centre	42	Post Office
22	Old Town Taverna	19	Bookshop	43	EOS

CRETE

The old quarter's maze of twisting and curving streets make it an easy place to get lost. Coming from the south, the best way to approach is through the Porto Guora gate onto Ethnikis Antistaseos. This busy shopping street leads to the Rimondi fountain, the old quarter's best known landmark. The area around here is thick with cafés, restaurants and souvenir shops.

If you arrive in Rethymno by bus, you will be dropped at the new terminal at the western end of Igoum Gavriil, about 600m from Porto Guora. To get there, follow Igoum Gavriil back into the town centre. A left turn at the far end of the park will leave you facing the gate. If you arrive by ferry, the old quarter is as far away as the end of the quay.

If you are driving into town from the expressway, your final approach to the city centre is along Dimitrikaki. The parking lot opposite the park is a convenient spot to stop and check things out.

Information
Tourist Offices Rethymno's municipal tourist office (☎ 29 148) is on the beach side of El Venizelou, opposite the junction with Kalergi. It's open Monday to Friday from 8 am to 3 pm. The tourist police (☎ 28 156) occupy the same building and are open from 7 am to 10 pm every day.

Money Banks are concentrated around the junction of Dimokratias and Pavlou Kountouriotou. The National Bank is on Dimokratias, on the far side of the square opposite the town hall. The Credit Bank, Pavlou Kountouriotou 29, and the National Mortgage Bank, next to the town hall, have 24-hour automatic exchange machines.

Post & Communications The OTE is at Kountouriotou 28, and the post office is a block south at Moatsou 21.

Bookshops The International Press Bookshop, El Venizelou 81, stocks English novels, travel guides and history books. The bookshop at Souliou 43 stocks novels in English, and has a small second-hand section.

Laundry The Laundry Mat self-service laundry at Tombazi 45, next door to the youth hostel, charges 2000 dr for a wash and dry.

Things to See
The **archaeological museum** (☎ 29 975) is opposite the entrance to the fortress. The finds displayed here include an important coin collection. The museum is open Tuesday to Sunday from 8.30 am to 3 pm.

Admission is 500 dr. Rethymno's excellent **historical & folk art museum**, Vernardou 30, is open Monday to Saturday from 9 am to 1.30 pm and 5.30 to 8 pm. Admission is 400 dr.

Rethymno's 16th century **fortress** stands on Paleokastro hill, the site of the city's ancient acropolis. Within its massive walls once stood a great number of buildings, of which only a church and a mosque survive intact. The ramparts offer good views, while the site has lots of ruins to explore. The fortress is open every day from 9 am to 4.30 pm. Admission is 400 dr.

Pride of place among the many vestiges of Venetian rule in the old quarter goes to the **Rimondi fountain** with its spouting lion heads, and the 16th-century **loggia**.

At the southern end of Ethnikis Antistaseos is the well-preserved **Porto Guora** (Great Gate), a remnant of the Venetian defensive wall. Turkish legacies in the old quarter include the mosque near the Great Gate and the **Neradjes Mosque**, which was converted from a Franciscan church.

Trekking

The Happy Walker (☎ 52 920), Tombazi 56, runs a varied programme of mountain walks in the region. Most walks start in the early morning and finish with lunch. Prices start at 6500 dr per person.

Rethymno's chapter of the EOS (☎ 57 766) is at Dimokratias 12.

Diving

The Paradise Dive Centre (☎ 51 711; fax 29 503), El Venizelou 76, has activities and a PADI course for all grades of divers.

Special Events

The city's main cultural event is the annual Renaissance Festival that runs during July and August, featuring dance, drama and films as well as art exhibitions.

July is also the month of the Wine Festival, which is held in the municipal park. Admission is 750 dr.

Places to Stay – bottom end

The nearest camp site is *Elizabeth Camping* (☎ 28 694), near Myssiria beach, 3km east of Rethymno. The site has a taverna, snack bar and minimarket. An Iraklio-bound bus can drop you at the site.

The *youth hostel* (☎ 22 848), Tombazi 41, is friendly and well run with beds for 1200 dr and free hot showers. Breakfast is available and there's a bar in the evening. There is no curfew and the place is open all year.

An excellent budget choice is *Olga's Pension* (☎ 29 851 or 54 896), right in the heart of town at Souliou 57. There's a wide choice of rooms which are spread about in clusters off a network of terraces – all bursting with greenery. Prices range from basic singles for 4000 dr, up to studio rooms with kitchen for 10,000 dr. In between comes a comfortable double with shower for 6000 dr. Owners George and Stella Mihalaki speak good English and run a very friendly show.

Rooms to Rent Barbara Dolomaki (☎ 24 581), Thambergi 14, has comfortable doubles with private bathroom for 7000 dr. Double studios with a fridge and small stove cost 8000 dr.

If you're after sea views, *Lefteris Papadakis Rooms* (☎ 23 803), Plastira 26, has clean singles/doubles with private bathroom for 6000/7500 dr. *Café Bar 67* (☎ 51 283) is a tiny place on the beachfront at El Venizelou 67. The four rooms include two nice, clean doubles overlooking the town beach for 4500 dr. Also with sea views, *Rent Rooms Sea Front* (☎ 51 062 981), El Venizelou 45, has light, airy rooms with private bathroom for 4000/7000 dr.

An outstanding domatia is *Rent Rooms Garden* (☎ 26 274 or 28 586), at Nikiforou Foka 82 in the heart of the old town It's an impeccably maintained 600-year-old Venetian house with many original features and a gorgeous grape-arboured garden. Doubles/triples are 8000/10,000 dr with private bathroom. Another pleasant option on this quiet street is *Rooms for Rent Anda* (☎ 23 479), at No 33. The prettily furnished doubles/triples cost 5000/8000 dr with private bathroom.

Top: Dolphin frieze, Palace of Knossos, Crete
Bottom: Dining by the romantic Venetian harbour in Rethymno's old quarter, Crete

MARK DAFFEY

MARK DAFFEY

MICHELLE COXALL

ANN JOUSIFFE

Top Left: A trek through the Samaria gorge, Crete, is an experience to remember
Top Right: Shopfront in the beautiful Venetian quarter of Hania, Crete
Bottom Left: Vibrant colours in the Venetian quarter, Hania, Crete
Bottom Right: Blankets drying in the sun on the north coast of Crete

Right in the shadows of the fortress, *Pension Anna* (☎ 25 586), Katehaki 5, has two-person studios for 7000 dr.

Places to Stay – middle
The smartest hotel in town is the B-class *Hotel Fortezza* (☎ 55 551/552 or 23 828; fax 54 073), Melissinou 16. It has a snack bar, restaurant and swimming pool. Rates are 16,500/21,000/25,000 dr for singles/doubles/triples.

If you want to hire a villa or unit out of town, the place to ask is Nileas Tours (☎ 51 711; fax 29 503), Petihaki 22.

Places to Eat
The waterfront along El Venizelou is lined with amazingly similar tourist restaurants staffed by fast-talking waiters desperately cajoling passers-by into eating at their establishments. The situation is much the same around the Venetian Harbour, except that the setting is better and the prices higher.

To find cheaper food and a more authentic atmosphere, wander inland down the little side streets. *Taverna Kyria Maria*, Diog Mesologiou 20, behind the Rimondi fountain, is a cosy, traditional taverna that also has outdoor seating along the narrow surrounding alleyways.

Another reasonably priced place is *Old Town Taverna*, at Vernardou 31. Set menus for two with wine are 4000 dr. *Taverna Pontios* at Melissinou 34, near the Archaeological Museum, is a popular hang-out with locals. The cheese-stuffed calamari at 1200 dr is commendable.

Gounakis Restaurant & Bar, Koroneou 6, is worth visiting for its food as much as for its music (see Entertainment, below).

One of Rethymno's cheapest eateries is the untouristy *Taverna Ta Balkania*, at Igoum Gavriil 7. It's open 24 hours and is popular with local workers. *Stella's Kitchen*, Souliou 55, serves tasty low-priced snacks and full meals.

Entertainment
If your interests include drinking cheap wine and listening to live Cretan folk music,

Gounakis Restaurant & Bar is the place to go. There's music and impromptu dancing most nights.

Rethymno has no shortage of discos, most of them in the streets behind the old harbour. The *Templum Club*, at the northern end of Arkadiou, caters to the heavy-metal crowd, while the *Fortezza Disco* plays disco.

Things to Buy
Zaharias Theodorakis turns out onyx bowls and goblets on the lathe at his small workshop opposite Pension Anna on Katehaki. Prices start at 5000 dr for a small bowl.

Getting There & Away
Bus There are numerous services to both Hania (one hour, 1350 dr) and Iraklio (1½ hours, 1400 dr). There's a bus in each direction every half-hour in summer, every hour in winter. In summer there are also eight buses a day to Plakias (one hour, 850 dr); six to Agia Galini (1½ hours, 1100 dr); four to Moni Arkadiou (30 minutes, 400 dr); two to Omalos (two hours, 2250 dr) and two to Preveli (850 dr). The 8.30 am bus to Plakias continues to Hora Sfakion (two hours, 1600 dr).

Services to these destinations are greatly reduced in winter.

Ferry Cretan Lines (☎ 29 221) operates two ferries – the F/B *Arkadi* and F/B *Preveli* – between Rethymno and Piraeus. There are daily sailings in each direction, leaving Rethymno and Piraeus at 7.30 pm.

Tickets are available from the company's office at Arkadiou 250. Deck-class tickets cost 6000 dr and a berth in a tourist-class cabin is 10,000 dr.

Getting Around
Car, Motorcycle & Bicycle Most of the car-hire firms are grouped around Plateia Iroön.

Motor Stavros (☎ 22 858), Paleologou 14, has a wide range of motorcycles and also rents bicycles.

AROUND RETHYMNO

Moni Arkadiou Μονή Αρκαδίου

This 16th-century monastery stands in attractive hill country 23km south-east of Rethymno. The most impressive building of the complex is the Venetian baroque church. Its striking façade has eight slender Corinthian columns and is topped by an ornate triple-belled tower. This façade features on the 100 dr note.

In November 1866 the Turks sent massive forces to quell insurrections which were gathering momentum throughout the island. Hundreds of men, women and children who had fled their villages used the monastery as a safe haven. When 2000 Turkish soldiers staged an attack on the building, rather than surrender, the Cretans set light to a store of gun powder. The explosion killed everyone, Turks included, except one small girl. This sole survivor lived to a ripe old age in a village nearby. A bust of this woman, and the abbot who lit the gun powder, stand outside the monastery.

The monastery is open every day and entry is free. The small **museum** has an admission charge of 500 dr.

Getting There & Away There are buses from Rethymno to the monastery (30 minutes, 400 dr) at 6 and 10.30 am, noon and 2.30 pm, returning at 7 and 11.15 am, and 1.15 and 3.30 pm.

Amari Valley Κοιλάδα Αμαρίου

If you have your own transport you may like to explore the enchanting Amari valley, south-east of Rethymno, between Mts Ida and Kedros. This region harbours around 40 well-watered, unspoilt villages set amid olive groves and almond and cherry trees.

The valley begins at the picturesque village of **Apostoli**, 25km south-east of Rethymno. The turn-off for Apostoli is on the coast 3km east of Rethymno. The road forks at Apostoli and then joins up again 38km to the south, making it possible to do a circular drive around the valley; alternatively, you can continue south to Agia Galini. There is an EOS refuge on Mt Ida, a 10km walk from the small village of **Kouroutes**, 5km south of Fourfouras. For information contact the Rethymno EOS (see the Rethymno section).

RETHYMNO TO SPILI

Heading south from Rethymno, there is a turn-off to the right to the late Minoan cemetery of **Armeni** 2km before the modern village of Armeni. The main road south continues through woodland, which gradually gives way to a bare and dramatic landscape. After 18km there is a turn-off to the right for **Selia**, **Rodakino** and **Frangokastello** and, a little beyond, another turn-off right for Plakias (this turn-off is referred to as the Koxare junction or Bale on timetables). The main road continues for 9km to Spili.

SPILI

• *pop 700* • *postcode 740 53* • *area code ☎ 0832*

Spili (**Spee**lee) is a gorgeous mountain town with cobbled streets, rustic houses and plane trees. Its centre piece is a unique Venetian fountain which spurts water from 19 lion heads. Tourist buses hurtle through but Spili deserves an overnight stay.

The post office and bank are on the main street. The OTE is up a side street, north of the central square. The bus stop is just south of the square.

Places to Stay & Eat

The huge building at the northern end of town is an ecclesiastic conference centre. *Ilias Rooms* (☎ 22 417), next to it, has spotless, tastefully furnished singles/doubles for 4000/6000 dr with shared bathroom. At *Heracles Rooms* (☎ 22 111; fax 22 411), 30m further south, sparkling, beautifully furnished rooms cost 5000/8000 dr with private bathroom.

Further along, on the left, the *Costos Inn* (☎ 22 040/750), has well-kept, ornate rooms which are something of a minimalist's nightmare, with TV, radio and even bathrobes – in case you forgot to pack yours. Doubles/triples with private bathroom cost 6000/7000 dr. Further south, the pleasant singles/doubles at *Nikos Loukakis Rooms*

(☎ 22 319) cost 3000/5000 dr with private bathroom.

Taverna Stratidakis, opposite Costos Inn, serves excellent traditional Greek dishes.

Getting There & Away
Spili is on the Rethymno-Agia Galini bus route.

AROUND SPILI
Patsos & the Church of Agios Antonios
Most people come to the alluring little village of Patsos to visit the nearby **Church of Agios Antonios** in a cave above a picturesque gorge. You can drive here from Rethymno, or you can walk from Spili along a scenic 10km dirt track.

To reach the track, walk along 28 October, passing the lion fountain on your right. Turn right onto Vermopilan and ascend to the Spili-Gerakari road. Turn right here and eventually you will come to a sign for Gerakari. Take the dirt track to the left, and at the fork bear right. At the crossroads turn right, and continue on the main track for about one hour to a T-junction on the outskirts of Patsos. Turn left to get to the cave.

SPILI TO PLAKIAS
After the village of Koxare on the Plakias road, the road enters the dramatic **Kourtaliotis gorge**. After Astomatis village there is a turn-off for Moni Preveli. The road continues through Lefkogia, then passes the turn-off for Myrthios (2km) and enters Plakias.

PLAKIAS Πλακιάς
• *pop 100* • *postcode 740 602* • *area code ☎ 0832*
The south-coast town of Plakias was once a tranquil retreat for adventurous backpackers – until the package-tour operators discovered the fine beaches and dramatic mountain backdrop. It's still not a bad place to visit outside peak season and there are some good walks. A booklet of walks around Plakias is on sale at the minimarket by the bus stop.

Orientation & Information
It's easy to find your way around Plakias. One street skirts the beach and another runs parallel to it one block back. The bus stop is at the middle of the waterfront. The 30-minute path to Mythos begins just before the youth hostel.

Plakias doesn't have a bank, but Monza Travel Agency, near the bus stop, offers currency exchange. In summer there is a mobile post office on the waterfront.

Places to Stay
Camping Apollonia (☎ 31 3180), on the right of the main approach road to Plakias, has a restaurant, minimarket, bar and swimming pool. Rates are 900 dr per person and 600 dr per tent.

The excellent *youth hostel* is tucked away in the olive trees behind the town, 10 minutes walk from the bus stop – follow the yellow signs from the waterfront. Dorm beds are 1200 dr and hot showers are free. The hostel is open from 1 April until the end of October.

One of the cheapest places to stay in Plakias is *Rooms to Rent Anni & Antonis Stefanakis*. Singles/doubles with bathroom are 4000/5500 dr. To reach the rooms walk 200m straight ahead from the bus stop, follow the road around to the left and they're on the right.

Morpheas Rent Rooms (☎ 31 583), next to the bus stop, are light, airy and attractively furnished. Prices are 6000/8000 dr with private bathroom. If you're unhappy about anything, you can always try complaining to the tourist police in Rethymno – where you'll find owner Manolis working his day job.

There are some agreeable pensions tucked among the olive trees behind the town. *Pension Afrodite* (☎ 31 266) has spotless doubles/triples for 8500/9500 dr with private bathroom. Head inland at Monza Tours, turn left at the T-junction and then take the first right and you will come to the pension on the left after 100m. A right turn at the T-junction leads to *Studio Emilia* (☎ 31 302), set back in the trees to the left after 100m. It charges 5000/6000 dr for large doubles/triples upstairs with private bathroom and access to a well-equipped communal kitchen; studios downstairs cost 7000 dr.

The *Pension Paligremnos* (☎ 31 003) has a great position at the southern end of Plakias beach. Pleasant doubles with bathroom cost 6000 dr, and studio doubles are 7000 dr.

Places to Eat

Restaurant Ariadne, on the street opposite the mobile post office, is a popular place with reasonable prices. One of the best waterfront tavernas is *Taverna Christos* with a romantic terrace overlooking the sea. It has a good choice of main dishes for around 1400 dr.

Nikos Souvlaki, just inland from Monza Tours, is a good souvlaki place, where a monster mixed grill of gyros, souvlaki, sausage, hamburger and chips costs 1500 dr.

Getting There & Away

Plakias has good bus connections in summer, but virtually none in winter. A timetable is displayed on the wall outside Morpheas Rent Rooms.

Summer services include eight buses a day to Rethymno (one hour, 850 dr), two buses to Agia Galini (1½ hours, 1100 dr) and one to Hora Sfakion.

In winter there are three buses a day to Rethymno, two at weekends. It's possible to get to Agia Galini from Plakias by catching a Rethymno bus to the Koxare junction (referred to as Bale on timetables) and waiting for a bus to Agia Galini. This works best with the 12.30 pm bus from Plakias, linking with the 12.45 pm service from Rethymno to Agia Galini.

Getting Around

Odyssia (☎ 31 596), on the waterfront, has a large range of motorcycles and mountain bikes. Cars Allianthos (☎ 31 851) is a reliable car-hire outlet.

AROUND PLAKIAS
Myrthios

This pleasant village is perched on a hillside overlooking Plakias and the surrounding coast. Apart from the views, the main activity is walking, which you'll be doing a lot of unless you have your own transport.

Places to Stay & Eat Myrthios is home to the district's original *youth hostel* (☎ 31 202). A bed here costs 900 dr. Conditions are primitive but there are hot showers and kitchen facilities. There are also domatia in the village, including the comfortable *Niki's Studios & Rooms* (☎ 31 593), just below the Restaurant Panorama. Singles/doubles with private bathroom cost 3500/6000 dr, and a studio costs 8000 dr for two.

The *Restaurant Panorama* lives up to its name; it has great views. It also does good food, including vegetarian dishes and delicious desserts.

Moni Preveli Μονή Πρύβελη

The well-maintained Moni Preveli, 14km east of Plakias, stands in splendid isolation high above the Libyan sea. Like most of Crete's monasteries, it played a significant role in the islanders' rebellion against Turkish rule. It became a centre of resistance during 1866, causing the Turks to set fire to it and destroy its crops. After the Battle of Crete, many allied soldiers were sheltered here by Abbot Agathangelos before their evacuation to Egypt. In retaliation the Germans plundered the monastery. The monastery's **museum** contains a candelabra presented by grateful British soldiers after the war. Entry to the museum costs 500 dr.

The road to Moni Preveli leads past the ruins of the old monastery, a fascinating place to explore. It was a hippie hang-out in the 1970s, and they left their mark in the shape of a large marijuana leaf on one wall and a few other cosmic decorations.

Lefkogia village has domatia and tavernas, and is a pleasant base from which to explore the area.

Getting There & Away In summer, two buses a day from Rethymno to Plakias continue to Moni Preveli.

Preveli Beach Παραλία Πρέβελης

Preveli beach, at the mouth of the Kourtaliotis gorge, is one of Crete's most photographed beaches. The River Megalopotamos cuts the beach in half on its way into the Libyan sea. It's fringed with oleander bushes and palm trees and is popular with freelance campers.

A steep path leads down to it from the road to Moni Preveli. You can get to Preveli from Plakias by caïque in summer for 3000 dr return. The caïques stop at Damnoni beach (1500 dr return) on the way to Preveli.

Beaches between Plakias & Preveli

Between Plakias and Preveli beach there are several secluded coves popular with freelance campers and nudists. Some are within walking distance of Plakias, via Damnoni beach. To reach them ascend the path behind the Plakias Bay Hotel. Just before the track starts to descend turn right into an olive grove. At the first T-junction turn left and at the second turn right. Where six tracks meet, take the one signposted to the beach. Walk to the end of Damnoni beach and take the track to the right, which passes above the coves. Damnoni beach itself is pleasant out of high season, despite being dominated by the giant the Hapimag tourist complex.

AGIA GALINI Αγία Γαλήνη
• pop 600 • postcode 740 56 • area code ☎ 0832

Agia Galini (Aya Galeenee) is another picturesque little town which has gone down the tubes due to an overdose of tourism. Still, it does boast 340 days of sunshine a year, and some places do remain open out of season. It's a convenient base from which to visit Phaestos and Agia Triada, and although the town beach is mediocre, there are boats to better beaches.

Orientation & Information

The bus station is at the top of Eleftheriou Venizelou, the main street, which is a continuation of the approach road. The central square, which overlooks the harbour, is downhill from the bus station. You'll walk past the post office on the way and the OTE is on the square. There is no bank but there

are lots of travel agencies with currency exchange.

Places to Stay

Agia Galini Camping (☎ 91 386/239) is next to the beach, 2.5km east of the town. It is signposted from the Iraklio-Agia Galini road. The site is well shaded and has a restaurant, snack bar and minimarket.

Rent Rooms Pella (☎ 91 213/143) has large, clean doubles/triples with private bathroom for 5500/6000 dr. The rooms are co-owned with the Restaurant Megalonissis, near the bus stop.

The D-class *Hotel Selena* (☎ 91 273) has pleasant singles/doubles for 4500/6000 dr with private bathroom. It's open all year. To reach the hotel walk downhill from the bus station, turn left after the post office, take the second turning right and turn left at the steps. The only accommodation on the beach is *Stochos Rooms* (☎ 91 433), where stylish double/triples cost 8000/9000 dr and studios are 10,000 dr.

Rent Rooms Agapitos (☎ 91 164), on the approach road, has doubles with private bathroom for 5000 dr and large well-kept apartments for 7000 dr.

Places to Eat

The *Restaurant Megalonissis*, near the bus stop, is one of the town's cheapest restaurants, with main meals for around 1300 dr. The more up-market *Acropol Taverna*, on Vasileos Ioannis, has an extensive menu of both Greek and international dishes. A meal for two with wine costs around 6000 dr.

Getting There & Away

Bus The story is the same as at the other beach resorts: heaps of buses in summer, skeletal services in winter.

In peak season there are eight buses a day to Iraklio (2½ hours, 1400 dr), six to Rethymno (1½ hours, 1100 dr), six to Phaestos (40 minutes, 320 dr) and two a day to Plakias. You can also get to Plakias by taking a Rethymno-bound bus and changing at Koxare (Bale). To get to Matala, take an Iraklio-bound bus and change at Mires.

Taxi Boat In summer there are daily taxi boats from the harbour to the beaches of Agios Giorgios and Agios Pavlos. These beaches, which are west of Agia Galini, are difficult to get to by land. Both are less crowded than, and far superior to, the Agia Galini beach.

AROUND AGIA GALINI
Museum of Cretan Ethnology

The outstanding museum of Cretan ethnology (☎ 0892 91 394) is in the pleasant, unspoilt village of Vori, 14km from Agia Galini, just north of the main Agia Galini-Iraklio road. From 1 November to 1 March it's open Monday to Friday from 9 am to 3 pm. In summer it opens daily from 9 am to 6 pm. Admission is 500 dr.

HANIA Χανιά
• *pop 65,000* • *postcode 731 00* • *area code* ☎ *0821*

Hania (Han**ya**) is Crete's second city and former capital. The beautiful, crumbling Venetian quarter of Hania that surrounds the Old Harbour is one of Crete's best attractions. A lot of money has been spent recently on restoring the old buildings. Some of them have been converted into very fine accommodation; others now house chic restaurants, bars and shops.

The Hania district gets a lot of package tourists, but most of them stick to the beach developments that stretch out endlessly to the west. Even in a town this size many hotels and restaurants are closed from November to April.

Boats to Hania dock at the port of Souda, about 7km out of town. There are frequent buses to Hania, as well as taxis.

History

Hania is the site of the Minoan settlement of Kydonia, which was centred on the hill to the east of the harbour. Little excavation work has been done, but the finding of clay tablets with Linear B script has led archaeologists to believe that Kydonia was both a palace site and an important town.

Kydonia met the same fiery fate as most other Minoan settlements in 1450 BC, but soon re-emerged as a force. It was a flourishing city-state during Hellenistic times and continued to prosper under Roman and Byzantine rule.

The city became Venetian at the beginning of the 13th century, and the name was changed to La Canea. The Venetians spent a lot of time constructing massive fortifications to protect their city from marauding pirates and invading Turks. This did not prove very effective against the latter, who took Hania in 1645 after a siege lasting two months.

The Great Powers made Hania the island capital in 1898 and it remained so until 1971, when the administration was transferred to Iraklio.

Hania was heavily bombed during WWII, but enough of the old town survives for it to be regarded as Crete's most beautiful city.

Orientation

The town's bus station is on Kydonias, two blocks south-west of Plateia 1866, one of the city's main squares. From Plateia 1866 to the Old Harbour is a short walk north down Halidon.

The main hotel area is to the left as you face the harbour, where Akti Kountourioti leads around to the old fortress on the headland. The headland separates the Venetian port from the crowded town beach in the quarter called Nea Hora.

Zambeliou, which dissects Halidon just before the harbour, was once the town's main thoroughfare. It's a narrow, winding street, lined with craft shops, hotels and tavernas.

Information

Tourist Offices Hania's EOT (☎ 92 943; fax 92 624) is at Kriari 40, close to Plateia 1866. It is well organised and considerably more helpful than most. The opening hours are from 8 am to 3 pm weekdays. The tourist police (☎ 73 333) are on Karaïaki.

Money The National Bank of Greece on the corner of Tzanakaki and Gianari, and the Credit Bank at the junction of Halidon and Skalidi have 24-hour automatic

CRETE

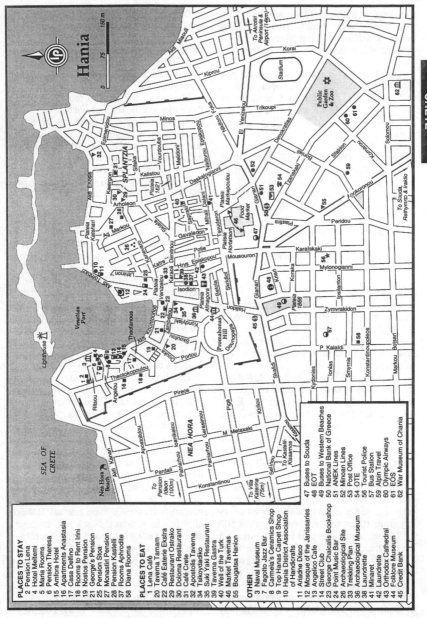

PLACES TO STAY
2 Pension Lena
4 Hotel Meltemi
5 Maria Rooms
6 Pension Theresa
15 Amfora Hotel
16 Apartments Anastasia
17 Casa Delfino
18 Rooms to Rent Irini
19 Nostos Pension
21 George's Pension
25 Pension Stoa
27 Monastiri Pension
28 Pension Kastelli
37 Rooms Aphrodite
58 Diana Rooms

PLACES TO EAT
1 Lena Café
20 Taverna Tamam
22 Café Eaterie Ekstra
29 Restaurant Ostrako
30 Dolma Restaurant
31 Café Crete
32 Apostolis Taverna
34 Tsikoudadiko
35 Suki Yaki Restaurant
39 Taverna Gastra
40 Well of the Turk
46 Market Tavernas
55 Bougatsa Hanion

OTHER
3 Naval Museum
7 Fagotto Jazz Bar
8 Carmela's Ceramics Shop
9 Top Hanas Carpet Shop
10 Hania District Association of Handicrafts
11 Ariadne Disco
12 Mosque of the Janissaries
13 Angelico Disco
14 Street Club
23 George Chaicalis Bookshop
24 Point Music Bar
26 Archaeological Site
33 Trekking Plan
36 Archaeological Museum
38 Laundrette
41 Minaret
42 Laundrette
43 Orthodox Cathedral
44 Folklore Museum
45 Credit Bank
47 Buses to Souda
48 EOT
49 Buses to Western Beaches
50 National Bank of Greece
51 ANEK Lines
52 Minoan Lines
53 Post Office
54 OTE
55 Tourist Police
57 Bus Station
59 Alpin Travel
60 Olympic Airways
61 EOS
62 War Museum of Chania

exchange machines. There are numerous places to change money outside banking hours. Most are willing to negotiate the amount of commission, so check around.

Post & Communications The central post office is at Tzanakaki 3. It is open Monday to Friday from 7.30 am to 8 pm, and on Saturday from 7.30 am to 2 pm. The OTE is next door at Tzanakaki 5. Opening times are 6 am to 11 pm every day.

Bookshops The George Chaicalis Book Shop, on Plateia Venizelou, sells English-language newspapers, books and maps.

Laundry The town has three laundries: Laundry Express, at Kanevaro 38; Laundry Fidias, at Sarpaki 6; and one at Ag Deka 18.

Luggage Storage Luggage can be stored at the bus station for 300 dr per day.

Things to See
Museums Hania's **archaeological museum** (☎ 20 334), Halidon 21, is housed in the 16th-century Venetian Church of San Francisco. The Turkish fountain in the grounds is a relic from the building's days as a mosque.

The museum houses a well-displayed collection of finds from Western Crete dating from the Neolithic to the Roman era. Exhibits include statues, pottery, coins, jewellery, three splendid floor mosaics and some impressive painted sarcophagi from the Late Minoan cemetery of Armeni. The museum is open Tuesday to Sunday from 8.30 am to 5 pm. Admission is 500 dr.

The **naval museum** has an interesting collection of model ships, naval instruments, paintings and photographs. It is open every day from 10 am to 4 pm. Admission is 500 dr. The museum is housed in the fortress on the headland overlooking the Venetian port.

Hania's interesting **folk lore museum** is at Halidon 46B. It is open Monday to Friday from 9 am to 1 pm and 6 pm to 9 pm. Admission is 500 dr. The new **war museum of Chania**, on Tzanakaki, is open Tuesday

to Saturday from 9 am to 1 pm. Admission is free.

Other Attractions The area to the east of the Old Harbour, between Akti Tombazi and Karaoli Dimitriou, is the site of **ancient Kydonia**.

The search for Minoan remains began in the early 1960s and excavation work continues sporadically. The site can be seen at the junction of Kanevaro and Kandanoleu, and many of the finds are on display in the archaeological museum.

Kydonia has been remodelled by a succession of occupiers. After ejecting the Arabs, the Byzantines set about building their *kastelli* on the same site, on top of the old walls in some places and using the same materials. It was here, too, that the Venetians first settled. Modern Kanevaro was the Corso of their city. It was this part of town that bore the brunt of the bombing in WWII.

The massive **fortifications** built by the Venetians to protect their city remain impressive today. The best preserved section is the western wall, running from the fortezza to the **Promahonas hill**. It was part of a defensive system begun in 1538 by engineer Michele Sanmichele, who also designed Iraklio's defences.

The **lighthouse** at the entrance to the harbour is the most visible of the Venetian monuments. It looks in need of tender loving care these days, but the 30-minute walk around the sea wall to get there is worth it.

You can escape the crowds of the Venetian quarter by taking a stroll around the **Splantzia quarter** – a delightful tangle of narrow streets and little plateias.

Whether or not you are self-catering you should at least feast your eyes on Hania's magnificent covered **food market**; it makes all other food markets look like stalls at a church bazar. Unfortunately, the central bastion of the city wall had to be demolished to make way for this fine cruciform creation, built in 1911.

Trekking & Mountain Climbing
Alpin Travel (☎ 53 309), in the complex at

Bonaili 11-19, offers many trekking programmes. The owner, George Antonakakis, helps run Hania's chapter of the EOS (☎ 24 647), at Tzanakaki 90, and is the guy to talk to for information about serious climbing in the Lefka Ori. George can provide information on Greece's mountain refuges, the E4 trail, and climbing and trekking on Crete. Alpin Travel is open weekdays from 9 am to 1 pm and 5.30 to 8.30 pm.

Trekking Plan (☎ 44 946), Karaoli Dimitriou 15, organises treks in the Lefka Ori. Prices for one-day treks start from 8000 dr and five-day treks cost 85,000 dr.

Mountain Biking

Trekking Plan (see Trekking) offers one-day mountain-bike tours for 10,000 dr.

Children's Activities

If your five-year-old has lost interest in Venetian architecture before the end of the first street, the place to head is the public garden between Tzanakaki and Dimokratias. There's a playground, a small zoo with a resident kri-kri (the Cretan wild goat) and a children's resource centre that has a small selection of books in English.

Places to Stay – bottom end

The nearest camp site is *Hania Camping* (☎ 31 138), 3km west of town on the beach. The site is shaded and has a restaurant, bar and minimarket. Take a Kalamaki beach bus (every 15 minutes) from the south-east corner of Plateia 1866 and ask to be let off at the camp site.

The most interesting rooms are around the Venetian harbour. But bear in mind it's a noisy area with numerous music bars. The rooms overlooking the harbour are particularly noisy, so try to get a room at the back. If you normally go to bed after 2 am it won't be an issue.

If it's character you're after, you can't do better than *George's Pension* (☎ 88 715), Zambeliou 30, in a 600-year-old house dotted with antique furniture. Singles/

doubles with shared bathroom cost 3500/6000 dr.

The *Hotel Meltemi* (92 802), next to the fortezza, charges 5000/7000 dr for rooms that are a bit special. Each of the large, airy rooms is different and has been furnished stylishly. Many have harbour views. *Maria Rooms* (☎ 71 052), next door, has large rooms for 5000/6000 dr. Warm-hearted Maria keeps the place spotless.

Rooms to Rent Irini (☎ 93 909), Theotokopoulou 9, has clean, simply furnished doubles with private bathroom for 7000 dr.

The *Monastiri Pension* (☎ 54 776) has a great setting at Ag Markou 18, right next to the ruins of the monastery of Santa Maria de Miracolioco in the heart of the old kastelli. Double rooms are fair value at 8500 dr with shared bathroom, and there's a communal kitchen. Nearby, *Pension Stoa* (☎ 46 879), at Lithinon 5, has singles/doubles for 4000/5500 dr.

If you want to hop straight out of bed and onto an early morning bus bound for the Samaria gorge, the best rooms around the bus station are at *Diana Rooms* (☎ 97 888), P Kalaïdi 33. The light, airy and clean rooms are 5000/7000 dr with private bathrooms.

At the stylish *Apartments Anastasia* (☎ 46 582), Theotokopoulou 21, well-equipped studios cost 8000 dr. *Rooms Aphrodite* on Ag Deka has two-person apartments for 8000 dr, and double rooms with shared facilities for 5000 dr.

The Nea Hora area to the west of the old town has some accommodation bargains. The area lacks the charm of the old town but is considerably quieter. *Villa Katerina* (☎ 95 183 or 98 940), Selinou 78, has a range of rooms starting with attractively furnished doubles for 6000 dr.

The well-kept *Pension Ideon* (☎ 70 132/3), on Patriarhou Ioanikeiou, is a friendly place charging 5000/6000 dr for singles/doubles. Both these places are very near Nea Hora beach.

Places to Stay – middle

Most places in this category are renovated

CRETE

Venetian houses, and there are some very stylish ones about. One of the best is *Nostos Pension* (☎ 94 740), Zambeliou 42-46, a mixture of Venetian style and modern fixtures. The 600-year-old building has been modelled into some very stylish split-level rooms/units, all with kitchen and bathroom. Rates for singles/doubles are 8000/13,000 dr.

The *Pension Theresa* (☎ 92 798), at Angelou 2, is another characterful place, with a pleasant roof garden. It charges 8000/13,000 dr for singles/doubles with bathroom. The *Pension Lena* (☎ 72 265), Theotokopoulou 60, consists of three buildings very close to one another – two Turkish and one Venetian. They are owned by friendly Lena Konstandinidi. All have beautiful, traditionally furnished rooms, and Mikis Theodorikas reputedly lodged in one of them when he was a soldier. Singles/doubles at all three are 7000/8000 dr with private bathroom.

At *Kasteli* (☎ 57 057; fax 45 314), Kanevaro 39, immaculate singles/doubles cost 6000/8000 dr, and very comfortable renovated apartments nearby cost from 10,000 dr.

Places to Stay – top end

The A-class *Amfora Hotel* (☎ & fax 93 224/226), at Parados Theotokopolou 2, is an immaculately restored mansion with rooms around a courtyard. Singles/doubles are 13,500/18,000 dr.

Nearby at Theofanous 7 is the old city's smartest accommodation, the *Casa Delfino* (☎ 93 098; fax 96 500). The Casa is the modernised former mansion of a wealthy merchant. The courtyard at the entrance features beautiful traditionally patterned cobblestones. Doubles here are 24,000 dr. A huge palatial split-level apartment, which sleeps up to four people, costs 40,000 dr.

Places to Eat – inexpensive

The two restaurants in the *food market* are good places to seek out traditional food. Their prices are almost identical. You can get a solid chunk of swordfish with chips for 1200 dr. More adventurous eaters can tuck into a bowl of garlic-laden snail and potato casserole for 1100 dr.

You'll find very similar fare at the *Doloma Restaurant*, at the western end of Kalergon. The place is a great favourite with students from the nearby Polytehnio. The *Restaurant Ostrako*, around the corner on Arholeon, is also commendable, and features live Cretan music on most summer evenings.

For a treat try the excellent bougatsa tyri (filo pastry filled with local myzithra cheese) at the *Bougatsa Hanion*, Apokoronou 37. A slice costs 450 dr and comes sprinkled with a little sugar. *Lena Café*, on Theotokopoulou, is a good place for breakfast or a snack. Homemade cheesecake is 450 dr and muesli with fruit is 850 dr.

Places to Eat – middle

The harbour is the place to go for seafood. The prices are not especially cheap – fresh seafood never is – but the setting is great. A favourite with locals is *Apostolis Taverna*, on Akti Enosis, where swordfish is 1700 dr. There are some chic places in the streets behind the harbour. The old Turkish hammam at Zambeliou 51 has been converted into the *Taverna Tamam*, where you'll find tasty soups for about 800 dr and a good range of well-prepared main dishes priced from 1700 dr. The *Café-Eaterie Ekstra*, Zambeliou 8, offers a choice of Greek and international dishes. There are set menus for 1900 dr and many vegetarian dishes.

The cosy wood-pannelled *Taverna Gastra*, on Ag Deka, is the place for carnivores to get a slice of the action. The 'farmers plate' (pork stew) is 1650 dr, and the 'butchers plate' (beef stew) is 1850 dr. Some dishes are cooked in the tavern's gastra (a traditional brick oven).

Casual nibblers should check out the *Tsikoydadiko* mezes bar at Zambeliou 31. It has a mixed plate for two for 2000 dr. The *Well of the Turk Restaurant & Bar* has a wide range of Middle Eastern dishes, as well as live music occasionally. The delicious vegetarian mezes plate is 2300 dr. The restaurant is in the heart of the old Turkish residential district of Splantzia at Sarpaki 1.

The *Suki Yaki*, through the archway at Halidon 26, is a Chinese restaurant run by a Thai family. The result is a large Chinese menu supported by a small selection of Thai favourites.

Entertainment

The *Café Crete*, Kalergon 22, is the best place in Hania to hear live Cretan music. It's a rough-and-ready joint with cheap mezedes and bulk wine, plus a lot of locals who like to reach for the instruments that line the walls once they've had a couple of drinks.

The *Ideon Adron*, next to the Suki Yaki restaurant at Halidon 26, promotes a more sophisticated atmosphere with discreet music and garden seating. *Fagotto Jazz Bar*, Angelou 16, has black-and-white photographs of jazz greats lining the walls. Sometimes there's live jazz in summer. The *Point Music Bar* on Plateia Venizelou has great sea views from its 1st-floor vantage point.

The *Angelico Café*, on the waterfront, plays rock music at a volume that renders conversation possible only for lip readers. For soul and Latin sounds try *Street Club* nearby. The bars charge very similar prices: beer is 800 dr, spirits are 1200 dr and cocktails start at 1300 dr. *Ariadne Disco* is the most central disco.

In summer there are performances of Greek folk dancing at the fortress every Monday and Thursday night at 9 pm. Tickets cost 2000 dr, 1000 dr for children.

Things to Buy

Good-quality handmade leather goods are available from shoemakers on Skridlof, where shoes cost from 8500 dr. The old town has many craft shops. Bizzarro, at Zambeliou 19, sells exquisite handmade dolls in traditional Cretan dress. The prices start at 11,000 dr. Top Hanas carpet shop, Angelou 3, specialises in old Cretan kilims that were traditional dowry gifts; prices start at 30,000 dr. Carmela's Ceramic Shop nearby sells beautiful jewellery and ceramics handcrafted by young Cretans.

The Hania District Association of Handicrafts showroom, on Akti Tombazi, has ceramics, jewellery and embroidery for sale.

Getting There & Away

Air Olympic Airways has at least three flights a day to Athens (18,600 dr) and two a week to Thessaloniki (27,700 dr). The Olympic Airways office (☎ 40 268/58 005) is at Tzanakaki 88. Air Greece also has daily flights to Athens (16,100 dr). The airport is on the Akrotiri peninsula, 14km from Hania.

Bus Buses depart from Hania's bus station for the following destinations:

Destination	Duration	Fare	Frequency
Falassarna	1½ hours	1350 dr	2 a day
Iraklio	2½ hours	2650 dr	half-hourly
Hora Sfakion	2 hours	1300 dr	4 a day
Kastelli-Kissamos	1 hour	800 dr	15 a day
Lakki	1 hour	500 dr	2 a day
Moni Agias Triadas	30 mins	400 dr	2 a day
Omalos (for Samaria gorge)	1 hour	1100 dr	4 a day
Paleohora	2 hours	1350 dr	6 a day
Rethymno	1 hour	1350 dr	half-hourly
Sougia	2 hours	1300 dr	2 a day

Ferry Ferries for Hania dock at Souda, about 7km east of town. There is at least one ferry a day to Piraeus. Minoan Lines operates the F/B *Knossos* from Souda on Monday, Wednesday and Friday at 7.45 pm, and ANEK has a boat every night at 8 pm – either the F/B *Lato* or the F/B *Lissos*. The trip costs 4900 dr for deck class and takes about 10 hours. The ANEK office (☎ 27 500) is opposite the food market, and Minoan Lines (☎ 45 911) are nearby at El Venizelou 2.

Souda's port police can be contacted on ☎ 89 240.

Getting Around

The Airport Olympic Airways buses (500 dr) leave from outside the Olympic Airways office 1½ hours before each flight.

CRETE

Bus Local buses (blue) for the port of Souda leave from outside the food market; buses for the western beaches leave from Plateia 1866.

Car, Motorcycle & Bicycle Hania's car-hire outlets include Avis (☎ 50 510), Tzanakaki 58; Budget (☎ 92 788), Karïskaki 39; and Maan (☎ 54 454), Arhontaki 10. Most motorcycle-hire outlets are on Halidon. Mountain bicycles can be rented from Trekking Plan (see Mountain Biking).

AKROTIRI PENINSULA
Χερσόνησος Ακρωτήρι

The Akrotiri (Ak**tee**ree) peninsula, to the east of Hania, has a few places of fairly minor interest, as well as being the site of Hania's airport, port and a military base. At Souda,

there is an immaculate **military cemetery**, where about 1500 British, Australian and New Zealand soldiers who lost their lives in the Battle of Crete are buried. The buses to Souda port from outside the Hania food market can drop you at the cemetery.

If you haven't yet had your fill of Cretan monasteries, there are three on the Akrotiri peninsula. The impressive 17th-century **Moni Agias Triadas** was founded by the Venetian monks Jeremiah and Laurentio Giancarolo. The brothers were converts to the Orthodox faith. The 16th-century **Moni Gourvernetou** (Our Lady of the Angels) is 4km north of Moni Agias Triada. The church inside the monastery has an ornate sculptured Venetian facade. Both of these monasteries are still in use.

The Good Oil

The olive has been part of life in the eastern Mediterranean since the beginnings of civilisation. Olive cultivation can be traced back about 6000 years. It was the farmers of the Levant (modern Syria and Lebanon) who first spotted the potential of the wild European olive *(Olea europaea)* – a sparse, thorny tree that was common in the region. These farmers began the process of selection that led to the more compact, thornless, oil-rich varieties that now dominate the Mediterranean.

Whereas most westerners think of olive oil as being just a cooking oil, to the people of the ancient Mediterranean civilisations it was very much more. It was almost inseperable from civilised life itself. As well as being an important foodstuff, it was burned in lamps to provide light, it could be used as a lubricant and it was blended with essences to produce fragrant oils.

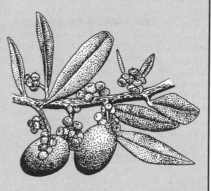

The Minoans were among the first to grow wealthy on the olive, and western Crete remains an important olive-growing area, specialising in high-quality salad oils. The region's show piece, Kolymvari cooperative, markets its extra-virgin oil in both the USA (*Athena* brand) and Britain (*Kydonia* brand).

Locals will tell you that the finest oil is produced from trees grown on the rocky soils of the Akrotiri peninsula, west of Hania. The oil that is prized above all others, however, is *agourelaio*, meaning unripe, which is pressed from green olives.

Few trees outlive the olive. Some of the fantastically gnarled and twisted olive trees that dot the countryside of western Crete are more than 1000 years old. The tree known as *dekaoktoura*, in the mountain village of Anisaraki – near Kandanos on the road from Hania to Paleohora – is claimed to be more than 1500 years old.

Many of these older trees are being cut down to make way for improved varieties. The wood is burnt in potters' kilns and provides woodturners with the raw material to produce the ultimate salad bowl for connoisseurs. The dense yellow-brown timber has a beautiful swirling grain. ■

From Moni Gourvernetou, it's a 15-minute walk on the path leading down to the coast to the ruins of **Moni Katholiko**. The monastery is dedicated to St John the Hermit who lived in the cave behind the ruins. It takes another 30 minutes to reach the sea.

There are two buses a day to Moni Agias Triadas from Hania bus station.

HANIA TO AGIA ROUMELI VIA SAMARIA GORGE

The road from Hania to the beginning of the Samaria (Samaria) gorge is one of the most spectacular routes on Crete. It heads through orange groves to the village of **Fournes** where a left fork leads to **Meskla**. The main road continues to the village of **Lakki** (**Lakee**), 24km from Hania. This unspoilt village in the Lefka Ori mountains affords stunning views wherever you look. The village was a centre of resistance during the uprising against the Turks, and in WWII.

The *Kri-Kri Restaurant & Rooms* (☎ 0821-67 316) in Lakki has comfortable singles/doubles for 4000/5000 dr with shared bathroom. The restaurant serves good-value meals.

From Lakki, the road continues to the Omalos plateau and Xyloskalo, the start of the Samaria gorge. The *Kallergi Refuge* (☎ 0821-74 560), a one-hour walk along a signposted track from the Omalos-Xyloskalo road, is a good base for trekking and climbing in the surrounding mountains. Make a reservation either through the EOS in Hania (☎ 0821-24 647), or by telephoning the refuge.

Samaria Gorge Φαράγγι της Σαμαριάς

It's a wonder that the stones and rocks underfoot haven't worn away completely, given the number of people who tramp through the Samaria gorge. Despite the crowds, a trek through this stupendous gorge is still an experience to remember.

At 18km, the gorge is supposedly the longest in Europe. It begins just below the Omalos plateau, carved out by the river that flows between the Lefka Ori and Mt Volikas. Its width varies from 150m to 3m

and its vertical walls reach 500m at their highest points. The gorge has an incredible number of wildflowers, which are at their best in April and May.

It is also home to a large number of endangered species. They include the Cretan wild goat, the kri-kri, which survives in the wild only here and on the islet of Kri-Kri, off the coast of Agios Nikolaos. The gorge was made a national park in 1962 to save the kri-kri from extinction. You are unlikely to see too many of these shy animals, which show a marked aversion to trekkers.

The gorge is open most years from mid-April until the end of October. The opening date depends on the amount of water in the gorge. Visiting hours are 6 am to 4 pm every day, and there's an entry fee of 1000 dr. Spending the night in the gorge is forbidden.

An early start helps to avoid the worst of the crowds, but during July and August even the early bus from Hania to the top of the gorge can be packed. The trek from Xyloskalo, the name of the steep wooden staircase that gives access to the gorge, to Agia Roumeli takes around six hours. Early in the season it's sometimes necessary to wade through the stream. Later, as the flow drops, it's possible to use rocks as stepping stones.

The gorge is wide and open for the first 6km, until you reach the abandoned village of Samaria. The inhabitants were relocated when the gorge became a national park. Just south of the village is a small church dedicated to Saint Maria of Egypt, after whom the gorge is named.

The gorge now narrows and becomes more dramatic until, at the 12km mark, the walls are only 3.5m apart – the famous **Iron Gates**.

The gorge ends just north of the almost abandoned village of Old Agia Roumeli. From here the path continues to the small, messy and crowded resort of Agia Roumeli, with a much-appreciated pebble beach and sparkling sea.

What to Bring Sensible footwear is essential for walking on the rocky, uneven ground. Trainers are fine. You'll also need a hat and sunscreen. There's no need to take water. While it's inadvisable to drink water from the main stream, there are plenty of springs along the way spurting delicious cool water straight from the rock. There is nowhere to buy food, so bring something to snack on.

Getting There & Away There are excursions to the Samaria gorge from every sizeable town and resort on Crete. Most travel agents have two excursions: 'Samaria Gorge Long Way' and 'Samaria Gorge Easy Way'. The first comprises the regular trek from the Omalos plateau to Agia Roumeli; the second starts at Agia Roumeli and takes you as far as the Iron Gates.

Obviously it's cheaper to trek the Samaria gorge under your own steam. Hania is the most convenient base. There are buses to Xyloskalo (one hour, 1100 dr) at 6.15, 7.30 and 8.30 am and 1.30 pm. If you intend to stay on the south coast ask for a one-way ticket (700 dr), otherwise you'll automatically be sold a return. There are also buses to Omalos from Rethymno (two hours, 2250 dr) at 6.15 and 7 am; from Kastelli-Kissamos (1½ hours, 2000 dr) at 5, 6 and 7 am; and from Paleohora (1½ hours, 1300 dr) at 6 am.

AGIA ROUMELI Αγία Ρούμελη
Agia Roumeli (Agla **Roo**melee) has little going for it, but if you have just trekked through the Samaria gorge and are too exhausted to face a journey, there is one hotel, the B-class *Hotel Agia Roumeli* (☎ 0821-91 293), where singles/doubles are 7500/ 10,500 dr with private bathroom. There are also a number of domatia where you'll pay around 6000 dr for a double.

Getting There & Away
While the gorge is open to walkers, there are frequent boats from Agia Roumeli. There are five boats a day to Hora Sfakion (one hour, 1300 dr) via Loutro (30 minutes, 700 dr). Sometimes the last boat does not call at Loutro. It connects with the bus back to Hania, leaving you in Hora Sfakion just long enough to spend a few drachma. There are also boats from Agia Roumeli to Paleohora

(1950 dr) at 3 and 4.30 pm, calling at Sougia (900 dr).

LOUTRO Λουτρό
The small but rapidly expanding fishing village of Loutro (**Loo**tro) lies between Agia Roumeli and Hora Sfakion. Loutro doesn't have a beach but there are rocks from which you can swim. There is one pension, the comfortable *Porto Loutro* (☎ 0825-91 433), which has doubles with private bathroom for 9000 dr. There are plenty of domatia and tavernas.

An extremely steep path leads up from Loutro to the village of **Anopolis**, where there are also domatia. Alternatively, you can save yourself the walk by taking the Hania-Skaloti bus which calls in at Anopolis en route. The bus leaves Hania at 2 pm and returns the following morning, calling in at Anopolis at 7.30 am.

From Loutro it's a moderate 2½-hour walk along a coastal path to Hora Sfakion. On the way you will pass the celebrated **Sweet Water beach**, named after freshwater springs which seep from the rocks. Freelance campers spend months at a time here. Even if you don't feel inclined to join them, you won't be able to resist a swim in the translucent sea. Loutro is on the Hora Sfakion-Paleohora boat route.

HORA SFAKION Χρώα Σφακίων
• *pop 340* • *postcode 730 01* • *area code* ☎ *0825*
Hora Sfakion (**Ho**ra Sfa**ki**on) is the small coastal port where the hordes of walkers from the Samaria gorge spill off the boat and onto the bus. As such, in high season it can seem like Piccadilly Circus at rush hour. Most people pause only long enough to catch the next bus out.

Hora Sfakion played a prominent role during WWII when thousands of Allied troops were evacuated by sea from the town after the Battle of Crete.

Orientation & Information
The ferry quay is at the western side of the harbour. Buses leave from the square on the eastern side. The post office and OTE are on

the square, and the police station overlooks it. There is no tourist office and no tourist police.

Places to Stay & Eat

If you do wind up staying, the options aren't so exciting. The D-class *Hotel Stavros* (☎ 91 220), up the steps at the western end of the port, has clean singles/doubles with bathroom for 4500/6000 dr. Don't expect a warm welcome though.

The *Hotel Samaria* (☎ 91 269), on the waterfront, has rooms with bathroom for 5000/7000 dr. It also has a good restaurant which turns out a tasty plate of seafood pilaf for 1200 dr.

The best rooms are at the *Hotel Xenia* (☎ 91 202/206), close to the ferry dock. Hora Sfakion is one of the few places where this government-run chain has come up with the goods. It has spacious rooms overlooking the sea from 7500/9500 dr.

Getting There & Away

Bus There are five buses a day from Hora Sfakion to Hania (two hours, 1300 dr); two to Plakias (1¼ hours, 1000 dr) via Frangokastello, leaving at 11.30 am and 5.30 pm; one to Rethymno (two hours, 1600 dr) at 7.30 pm; and one to Kastelli-Kissamos (1300 dr) which leaves at 5 pm. The 5.30 pm bus to Plakias continues to Agia Galini (2½ hours, dr).

Boat In summer there are daily boats from Hora Sfakion to Paleohora (three hours, 3300 dr) via Loutro, Agia Roumeli and Sougia. The boat leaves at 2 pm. There are also four boats a day to Agia Roumeli (one hour, 1150 dr) via Loutro (30 minutes, 700 dr).

From 1 June there are boats to Gavdos island on Friday, Saturday and Sunday. Check the schedule with the EOT in Hania.

AROUND HORA SFAKION

The road from Vrises to Hora Sfakion cuts through the heart of the Sfakia region in the eastern Lefka Ori. The inhabitants of this region have long had a reputation for fear-lessness and independence – characteristics they retain to this day. Cretans are regarded by other Greeks as being immensely proud and there are none more so than the Sfakiot.

One of Crete's most celebrated heroes, Ioannis Daskalogiannis, was from Sfakia. In 1770, Daskalogiannis led the first Cretan insurrection against Ottoman rule. When help promised by Russia failed to materialise, he gave himself up to the Turks to save his followers. As punishment the Turks skinned him alive in Iraklio. Witnesses related that Daskalogiannis suffered this excruciating death in dignified silence.

The Turks never succeeded in controlling the Sfakiots, and this rugged mountainous region was the scene of fierce fighting. The story of their resistance lives on in the form of folk tales and *rizitika* (local folk songs). One of the most popular is the *Song of Daskalogiannis*.

The village of **Imbros**, 23km from Vrises, is at the head of the beautiful 10km Imbros gorge, which is far less visited than the Samaria gorge. To get there, take any bus bound for Hora Sfakion from the north coast and get off at Imbros. Walk out of the village towards Hora Sfakion and a path to the left leads down to the gorge. The gorge path ends at the village of **Komitades**, from where it is an easy walk by road to Hora Sfakion. You can of course do the trek in reverse, beginning at Komitades. The Happy Walker organises treks through this gorge (see Rethymno, Organised Tours).

Frangokastello Φραγγοκάστελλο

Frangokastello (Frango**kas**telo) is a magnificent fortress on the coast 15km east of Hora Sfakion. It was built by the Venetians in 1371 as a defence against pirates and rebel Sfakiots, who resented the Venetian occupation as much as they did the Turkish.

It was here in 1770 that Ioannis Daskalogiannis surrendered to the Turks. In 1828 many Cretan rebels, led by Hadzi Mihalis Dalanis, were killed here by the Turks. Legend has it that at dawn on 17 May (the date of the massacre) the ghosts of Hadzi

Mihalis Dalanis and his followers can be seen riding along the beach.

The castle overlooks a gently sloping, sandy beach. Domatia and tavernas are springing up rapidly here, but it's still relatively unspoilt.

Getting There & Away The buses between Hora Sfakion and Plakias go via Frangokastello. They leave Hora Sfakion at 11.30 am and 5.30 pm.

SOUGIA Σούγια
• *pop 50* • *postcode 730 01* • *area code* ☎ *0823*

Hotels are springing up quickly in the coastal resort of Sougia, but it's still pretty small time. Sougia is at the mouth of the pretty **Agia Irini gorge**. Paleohora travel agents offer guided walks through the gorge for 4000 dr. It's easy enough to organise independently – just catch the Omalos bus from Paleohora or the Hania bus from Sougia, and get off at Agia Irini. There are a couple of beautiful **Byzantine churches** tucked away in the olive groves at the start of the gorge. The ruins of ancient **Lissos** are 1½ hours away on the coastal path to Paleohora. The path heads inland at the western end of the beach.

Sougia doesn't have a post office, OTE or bank, but you can change money at several places, including Syia Travel, on the main street, and Roxana's Office (☎ 51 362), by the bus stop.

Places to Stay
There's no camp site, but the eastern end of the long, pebbled beach is popular with freelance campers.

It seems almost every building in Sougia is a domatia or pension; even the police station has a 'rooms to rent' sign above it. At the nameless *Rooms* (☎ 51 510), opposite Syia Travel, clean, modern studios cost 6000 dr. *Rooms to Rent Irene* (☎ 51 187), further south on the main street, has comfortable singles/doubles for 5000/7000 dr with bathroom.

Further north, *Pension Captain George* (☎ 51 133; fax 51 194) has immaculate doubles/

triples with private bathroom for 7000/8000 dr. The similarly priced *Aretouca Rooms to Rent* (☎ 51 178) nearby has lovely rooms with wood-panelled ceilings. *Pension Galini* (☎ 51 178; fax 51 185), next door, has beautiful rooms with private bathroom for 5000/6000/7000 dr and studios for 7000 dr.

The very smart *Santa Irene Hotel* (☎ 51 342; fax 51 181), next to the bus stop, has studios for 8000/12,000 dr.

Places to Eat
Restaurants line the waterfront and there are more on the main street. *Oceanis*, on the sea front, has a good selection of ready-made food. *Taverna Rembetica*, on the main street, has an extensive menu; a mixed mezes plate for two is 2800 dr.

Getting There & Away
There are two buses a day from Hania to Sougia (2½ hours, 1200 dr) at 8.30 am and 1.30 pm. Buses from Sougia to Hania leave at 7 am and 3.30 pm. Sougia is on the Paleohora-Hora Sfakion boat route.

PALEOHORA Παλαιοχώρα
• *pop 2150* • *postcode 730 01* • *area code* ☎ *0823*

Paleohora (Paleeohora) was discovered by hippies back in the 60s and from then on its days as a tranquil fishing village were numbered. The resort operators have not gone way over the top – yet. The place retains a certain laid-back feel. It is also the only beach resort on Crete which does not go into total hibernation in winter.

The little town lies on a narrow peninsula with a long, curving sandy beach exposed to the wind on one side and a sheltered pebbly beach on the other. On summer evenings the main street is closed to traffic and the tavernas move onto the road. The most picturesque part of Paleohora is the narrow streets huddled around the castle.

It's worth clambering up the ruins of the 13th-century **Venetian castle** for the splendid view of the sea and mountains. From Paleohora, a six-hour walk along a scenic coastal path leads to **Sougia**, passing the ancient site of **Lissos** (five hours from

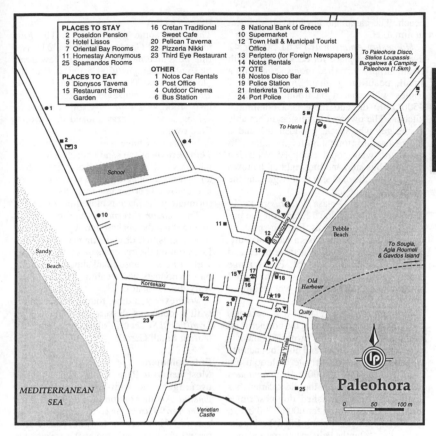

PLACES TO STAY
2 Poseidon Pension
5 Hotel Lissos
7 Oriental Bay Rooms
11 Homestay Anonymous
25 Spamandos Rooms

PLACES TO EAT
9 Dionysos Taverna
15 Restaurant Small Garden

16 Cretan Traditional Sweet Cafe
20 Pelican Taverna
22 Pizzeria Nikki
23 Third Eye Restaurant

OTHER
1 Notos Car Rentals
3 Post Office
4 Outdoor Cinema
6 Bus Station

8 National Bank of Greece
10 Supermarket
12 Town Hall & Municipal Tourist Office
13 Periptero (for Foreign Newspapers)
14 Notos Rentals
17 OTE
18 Nostos Disco Bar
19 Police Station
21 Interkreta Tourism & Travel
24 Port Police

CRETE

Paleohora

Paleohora), which was a sanctuary to Asclepius.

Orientation

Paleohora's main street, El Venizelou, runs north to south. The bus stop is opposite the Hotel Lissos. Walking south along El Venizelou from the bus stop, several streets lead off left to the pebble beach. Boats leave from the old harbour at the northern end of this beach.

At the southern end of El Venizelou, a right turn onto Kontekaki leads to the tamarisk-shaded sandy beach.

Information

The municipal tourist office (☎ 41 507) is in the town hall on El Venizelou. It is open Wednesday to Monday from 10 am to 1 pm between May and October.

The National Bank of Greece is on El Venizelou. The post office is on the road that skirts the sandy beach. The OTE is on the west side of El Venizelou, just north of Kontekaki.

Places to Stay

Camping Paleohora (☎ 41 225/120) is 1.5km north-east of the town, near the pebble beach. The camp site has a taverna but no minimarket.

Homestay Anonymous (☎ 41 509 or 42 098) is a great place for backpackers, with clean, simply furnished rooms set around a small, beautiful garden. Singles/doubles/triples with shared bathroom cost 3500/4500/5000 dr, and there is a communal kitchen. The owner, Manolis, is an amiable young guy who speaks good English and is full of useful information for travellers. To get there, walk south along El Venizelou from the bus stop and turn right at the town hall. Follow the road as it veers right, and the rooms are on the left.

The well-kept D-class *Hotel Lissos* (☎ 41 266/122), El Venizelou 12, opposite the bus stop, also has a friendly English-speaking owner called Manolis. It has a cheerful courtyard with a well-loved vegetable patch and seating beneath a grapevine. Prices range from 5500 dr for doubles with shared bathroom to 10,000 dr for well-equipped studios.

Oriental Bay Rooms (☎ 41 076) occupies the large modern building at the northern end of the pebble beach. The owner, Thalia, is a very cheerful woman and the immaculate singles/doubles with private bathroom are good value at 4000/6000 dr. *Spamandos Rooms* (☎ 41 197), in the old quarter, has spotless, nicely furnished doubles/triples with private bathroom for 6000/7000 dr. To get there walk south along Einai Yrela take the first left after the Pelican taverna and then the first right. After 60m turn left and the rooms are on the right.

Out of season, it's worth looking for a deal at one of the places offering self-catering apartments along the sandy beach on the other side of town. The *Poseidon Pension* (☎ 41 374/115) has cosy rooms for 5000/6000 dr with private bathroom, and studios for 7000/9000 dr.

Stelios Loupassis Bungalows (☎ 41 744) has well-equipped bungalows, which sleep up to four people for 15000 dr, and double/triple rooms with private bathroom for 6000/7200 dr. The bungalows overlook the beach on the way to Camping Paleohora.

Places to Eat

There are some good eateries. The *Restaurant Small Garden* behind the OTE is a fine little taverna that turns out a few treats like wild asparagus (600 dr) as well as the old favourites. The very popular *Dionysos Taverna*, on El Venizelou, also serves cheap, tasty food. *Pizzeria Niki*, on Kontekaki, serves superior pizzas cooked in a wood-fired oven.

Vegetarians have a treat in store at the *Third Eye*, near the sandy beach. The menu includes curries and a range of Asian dishes, all at very reasonable prices. You can eat well and enjoy a beer for less than 2000 dr. Unfortunately the place is closed in winter.

The *Pelican Taverna* has a prime position overlooking the old harbour. A plate of small fried fish is 900 dr and calamari is 1200 dr. Look out for the taverna's mascot – a pelican with attitude, whose pranks include landing on car bonnets and stealing food from unwary diners' plates.

Wherever you dine, round your meal off with a delicious dessert from the *Cretan Traditional Sweet Café* almost opposite Restaurant Small Garden.

Entertainment

Most visitors to Paleohora spend at least one evening at the well-signposted *outdoor cinema*. Another option for a night out is the *Paleohora Disco*, next to Camping Paleohora 1.5km north of town. If you've seen the movie and don't fancy the trek to the disco, try the *Nostos Night Club* right in town, between El Venizelou and the Old Harbour.

Getting There & Away

Bus In summer there are five buses a day to Hania (two hours, 1350 dr); in winter there are three – 7.30 am, noon and 3.30 pm. There's an extra daily service to Hania that goes on the back roads through the mountain villages and takes three hours. This bus leaves Paleohora at 6 am, and returns at 1.30 pm. In summer, this service goes via Omalos (1½ hours, 1300 dr) to cash in on the Samaria gorge trade.

Boat In summer there are daily boats from Paleohora to Hora Sfakion (three hours, 3300 dr) via Sougia (one hour, 900 dr), Agia Roumeli (two hours, 1950 dr) and Loutro (2½ hours, 2600 dr). The boat leaves Paleohora at 8.30 am, and returns from Hora Sfakion at 2 pm.

There is another boat operating only as far as Agia Roumeli via Sougia. It leaves Paleohora at 8 am and Agia Roumeli at 4.30 pm. This boat does the trip in half the time for the same fare. Between mid-April and mid-October, this service keeps going to the island of Gavdos (2½ hours, 2850 dr) three times a week. Tickets for all of these boats can be bought at Interkreta Tourism & Travel (☎ 41 393/888; fax 41 050), Kontekaki 4.

Getting Around
Car, Motorcycle & Bicycle All three can be hired from Notos Rentals (☎ 42 110), on El Venizelou and by the sandy beach.

Excursion Boat The M/B *Elafonisos* gets cranked into action in mid-April ferrying people to the west coast beach of Elafonisi (one hour, 1300 dr). The service builds up from three times a week to twice daily in July, August and September, when boats leave at 9 and 11 am. Twice a week there are boats running day trips to Anydri beach (5000 dr, children 3500 dr), calling at ancient Lissos and Sougia on the way.

AROUND PALEOHORA
Gavdos Island Νήσος Γαώδος
Gavdos island (**Gav**dos, population 50), in the Libyan sea, 65km from Paleohora, is the most southerly place in Europe. The island has three small villages and pleasant beaches. There is a post office, OTE, one police officer and one doctor. Gavdos is an excellent choice for those craving isolation and peace. The best source of information about the island is Interkreta Tourism & Travel in Paleohora.

There are no hotels but several of the locals let rooms, and there are tavernas. There is no official camp site but camping freelance may be tolerated. Fishermen from Gavdos take tourists to the remote, uninhabited island of Gavdopoula.

Getting There & Away A small post boat operates between Paleohora and Gavdos on Monday and Thursday all year, weather permitting. It leaves Paleohora at 8 am and takes about four hours (2550 dr). It returns almost immediately. From 15 April until 15 October, the daily boats to Agia Roumeli continue to Gavdos three times a week. These boats do the journey in 2½ hours and charge the same. They leave Gavdos at 3 pm. There are also boats from Hora Sfakion to Gavdos on Friday, Saturday and Sunday.

Elafonisi Ελαφονήσι
It's hard to understand why people enthuse so much about Elafonisi, at the southern extremity of Crete's west coast, but the place is absolutely packed with day-trippers in summer. The beach is ordinary and generously littered. Opposite the beach, through about 100m of knee-deep water, is Elafonisi islet. The beaches here are popular with freelance campers. There is one small hotel/taverna 500m from the beach which opens only in summer, when there are also three *cantinas* operating on the beach.

There are two boats a day from Paleohora (one hour, 1140 dr) in summer, as well as daily buses from Hania (2½ hours, 1500 dr) and Kastelli-Kissamos (1½ hours, 900 dr). The buses leave Hania at 7.30 am and Kastelli-Kissamos at 8.30 am, and both depart from Elafonisi at 4 pm. The final section of road from Hrysoskalitissas to the beach is very rugged.

Moni Hrysoskalitissas
Μονή Χρυσοσκαλίτισσας
Moni Hrysoskalitissas (**Mo**nee Hrisoskal**ee**tissas), 5km north of Elafonisi, is inhabited by two nuns. It's a beautiful monastery perched on a rock high above the sea. Hrysoskalitissas means 'golden staircase' and the name derives from a legend which claims that one of the 90 steps leading up from the sea to the monastery is made of gold. There are tavernas and domatia in the

CRETE

vicinity. The buses to Elafonisi drop passengers here.

KASTELLI-KISSAMOS

Καστελ- Κισσαμου
• *pop 3000* • *postcode 734 00* • *area code* ☎ *0822*
If you find yourself in the north-coast town of Kastelli-Kissamos, you've probably arrived by ferry from the Peloponnese or Kythira. While there isn't anything particularly remarkable about Kastelli- Kissamos itself, it serves as a good base from which to explore Crete's west coast.

A fair amount of confusion surrounds the name of the town. In antiquity, its name was Kissamos, the main town of the province of the same name. When the Venetians came along and built a castle here, the place became known as Kastelli. The name persisted until 1966 when authorities decided that too many people were confusing this Kastelli with Crete's other Kastelli, 40km south-east of Iraklio. The official name reverted to Kissamos, and that's what appears on bus and shipping schedules. Local people still prefer Kastelli, and many books and maps agree with them. An alternative that is emerging is to combine the two into Kastelli-Kissamos, which leaves no room for misunderstanding.

Orientation & Information

The port is 3km west of town. In summer a bus meets the boat, otherwise a taxi costs 800 dr. The bus station in Kastelli-Kissamos is to the north of the main road. The town centre is closer to the sea. With your back to the bus-station office, turn left and then take the first left onto Amerikas. Take the second right into Skalidi to reach the central square.

The post office is on the north side of the main road, beyond the bus station. The OTE is further along this road on the right. The National Bank of Greece is just east of the bus station. Kastelli-Kissamos has no tourist office.

Places to Stay

There are three camp sites to choose from. *Camping Kissamos* (☎ 23 444/322), close to the city centre, is convenient for the huge

supermarket next door and for the bus station, but not much else. It's got great views of the olive-processing plant next door.

A much better choice is *Camping Mithimna* (☎ 31 444/445), 6km west of town. It's an excellent shady site near the best stretch of beach. Facilities include a restaurant, bar and shop. It charges 900 dr per person and 600 dr per tent. It also has rooms to rent nearby. Getting there involves either a 4km walk along the beach, or a bus trip to the village of Drapania – from where it's a pleasant 15-minute walk through olive groves to the site.

Camping Nopigia (☎ 31 111) is another good site, 2km west of Camping Mithimna. The only drawback is that the beach is no good for swimming. It makes up for that with a swimming pool.

Back in town, one of the best deals is *Koutsounakis Rooms* (☎ 23 416), on the central square. The spotless singles/doubles are 5000/8000 dr with private bathroom. Opposite, the C-class *Hotel Castell* (☎ 22 140) has similar prices. *Argo Rooms for Rent* (☎ 23 563/322), Plateia Teloniou, has spacious rooms for 5000/7000 dr with private bathroom. From the central square, walk down to the seafront, turn left, and you will come to the rooms on the left. The C-class *Hotel Kissamos* (☎ 22 086), west of the bus station on the north side of the main road, has rooms with private bathroom for 5500/7700 dr, including breakfast.

Places to Eat

The *Argo Seafood Restaurant*, opposite the Argo rooms, has a good setting overlooking the beach and serves well-prepared food. For local colour go to the no-frills *Restaurant Macedonas* where an excellent meal of crisply fried whitebait and Greek salad costs 1500 dr. From the central square walk towards the sea, take the first left and the restaurant is on the left.

Getting There & Away

Bus There are 17 buses a day to Hania (one hour, 800 dr), where you can change for Rethymno and Iraklio. Buses for Omalos (for the Samaria gorge, 2000 dr) leave at 5, 6 and 7 am; for Elafonisi (1000 dr) via Moni Hrysoskalitissas at 8.30 am; and for Falassarna (500 dr) at 10 and 11 am and 5 pm.

Ferry Golden Ferries Maritime operates the F/B *Maria* on a route that takes in Antikythira and Kythira (five hours, 3500 dr), Neopoli (six hours, 3600 dr) and Gythio (nine hours, 4300 dr). It leaves Kastelli-Kissamos at 8 am on Sunday and 5 pm on Thursday. Other services from Kastelli-Kissamos are to Kalamata and Gythio. Both the Miras agent Horeftakis Tours (☎ 23 250), and the ANEK Office (☎ 22 009 or 24 030) are on the south side of Skalidi, east of the central square.

Getting Around
Motorcycles can be hired from Rent From Antony (☎ 22 909). Walk eastwards along the main road, take the second turn left after the post office and the outlet is on the right. There are several car-hire outlets along Skalidi.

AROUND KASTELLI-KISSAMOS
Falassarna Φαλασάρνα
Falassarna, 16km to the west of Kastelli-Kissamos, was a Cretan city-state in the 4th century BC. There's not much to see, and most people head to Falassarna for its superb beach, which is long and sandy and interspersed with boulders. There are several domatia at the beach. In summer there are three buses a day from Kastelli-Kissamos to Falassarna (550 dr) as well as buses from Hania (1350 dr).

Gramvousa Peninsula
Χερσόνησος Γραμβούσας
North of Falassarna is the wild and remote Gramvousa peninsula. There is a wide track, which eventually degenerates into a path, along the east coast side to the sandy beach of **Tigani**, on the west side of the peninsula's narrow tip. The beach is overlooked by the two islets of Agria (wild) and Imeri (tame) Gramvousa. To reach the track, take a westbound bus from Kastelli-Kissamos and ask

to be let off at the turn-off to the right for the village of Kalyviani (5km from Kastelli-Kissamos). Kalyviani is a 2km walk from the main road. The path begins at the far end of the main street. The shadeless walk takes around three hours – wear a hat and take plenty of water.

You don't have to inflict this punishment upon yourself to see the beautiful peninsula. In summer there are daily cruises around the peninsula in the *Gramvousa Express*. The boat leaves the port at 9 am and returns at 6 pm. The cost is 5000 dr.

Ennia Horia Εννιά Χωριά
Ennia Horia (nine villages) is the name given to the highly scenic mountainous region south of Kastelli-Kissamos, which is renowned for its chestnut trees. If you have your own transport you can drive through the region en route to Moni Hrysoskalitissas and Elafonisi or, with a little back-tracking, to Paleohora. Alternatively, you can take a circular route, returning via the coast road. The village of **Elos** stages a chestnut festival on the third Sunday of October when sweets made from chestnuts are eaten. The road to the region heads inland 5km east of Kastelli-Kissamos.

Polyrrinia Πολυρρηνία
The ruins of the ancient city of Polyrrinia (Poleere**nee**a) lie 7km south of Kastelli-Kissamos, above the village of Ano Paleokastro (sometimes called Polyrrinia). It's a steep climb to the ruins but the views are stunning. The city was founded by the Dorians and was continuously inhabited until Venetian times. There are remains of city walls, and an aqueduct built by Hadrian. It's a scenic walk from Kastelli-Kissamos to Polyrrinia, otherwise there is a very infrequent bus service – ask at Kastelli-Kissamos' bus station.

To reach the Polyrrinia road, walk east along Kastelli-Kissamos' main road, and turn right after the OTE.

Ano Paleokastro has one taverna, the *Taverna Odysseos*, but no accommodation.

Dodecanese Δωδεκάνησα

Strung along the coast of western Turkey, the Dodecanese (Do-de-**ka**-nis-a) archipelago is much closer to Asia Minor than to mainland Greece. Because of their strategic and vulnerable position these islands have encountered an even greater catalogue of invasions and occupations than the rest of Greece.

The name means 'Twelve Islands', but a glance at the map confirms that the group has quite a few more. The name originated in 1908 when 12 of the islands united against the newly formed Young Turk-led Ottoman parliament which had retracted the liberties the Dodecanese had been granted under the sultans. The Dodecanese islanders enjoyed greater autonomy than did the rest of Greece under the sultans, and they paid fewer taxes.

The 12 islands were Rhodes, Kos, Kalymnos, Karpathos, Patmos, Tilos, Symi, Leros, Astypalea, Nisyros, Kassos and Halki. The islands' vicissitudinous history has endowed them with a wealth of diverse archaeological remains, but these are not the islands' only allurements. The highly developed resorts of Rhodes and Kos have beaches and bars galore, while Lipsi and Tilos have appealing beaches, but without the crowds. The far-flung islands of Agathonisi, Arki, Kassos and Kastellorizo await Greek island aficionados in pursuit of traditional island life, while everyone boggles at the extraordinary landscape that geological turbulence has created on Nisyros.

History

The Dodecanese islands have been inhabited since pre-Minoan times; by the Archaic period Rhodes and Kos had emerged as the dominant islands of the group. Distance from Athens gave the Dodecanese considerable autonomy and they were, for the most part, free to prosper unencumbered by subjugation to imperial Athens. Following Alexander the Great's death, Ptolemy I of Egypt ruled the Dodecanese.

HIGHLIGHTS

- Exploring the medieval city of Rhodes
- Enjoying the nightlife on Kos
- Discovering the volcanic craters of Nisyros
- Trekking on Tilos

The Dodecanese islanders were the first Greeks to become Christians. This was through the tireless efforts of St Paul, who made two journeys to the archipelago, and through St John, who was banished to Patmos where he had his revelation.

The early Byzantine era was fortuitous for the islands, but by the 7th century AD they were plundered by a string of invaders. By the early 14th century it was the turn of the crusaders – the Knights of St John of Jerusalem, or Knights Hospitallers. The Knights eventually became rulers of almost all the Dodecanese, building mighty fortifications, but not mighty enough to keep out the Turks in 1522.

The Turks were ousted by the Italians in 1912 during a tussle over possession of Libya. Inspired by Mussolini's vision of a

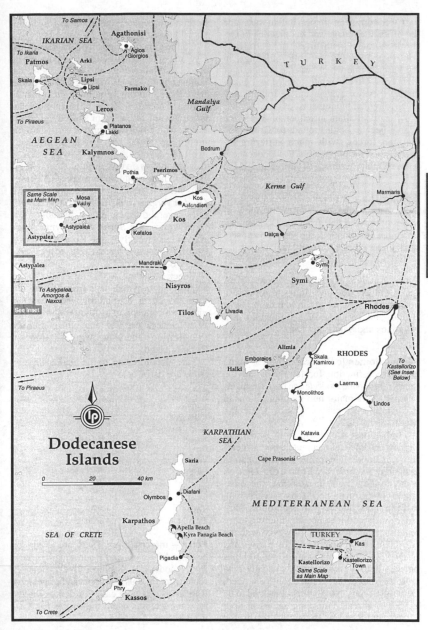

Dodecanese
Islands

vast Mediterranean empire, Italian was made the official language and the practice of Orthodoxy was prohibited. The Italians constructed grandiose public buildings, in the Fascist style which was the antithesis of archetypal Greek architecture. More beneficially, they excavated and restored many archaeological monuments.

After the Italian surrender of 1943, the islands became battle grounds for British and German forces, with much suffering inflicted upon the population. The Dodecanese were formally returned to Greece in 1947.

Getting There & Away

This section contains a brief overview of travel options to and from the Dodecanese. For more information, see the relevant sections under entries on individual islands.

Air Astypalea, Karpathos, Kassos, Kos, Leros and Rhodes have flights to Athens. In addition, Rhodes has flights to Iraklio, Hania (Crete) and Thessaloniki and in summer to Mykonos and Santorini (Thira).

Ferry – domestic Rhodes, as well as being a major destination for ferries plying the routes through the Dodecanese from the mainland, is also a major hub for connections to Kastellorizo, Karpathos, Kassos, Crete and Marmaris in Turkey.

The shortest round trip from Rhodes to Piraeus and back takes about 28 hours, therefore it is impossible for the ferry companies to operate a simple, predictable timetable on a day-by-day basis. In addition, the other islands in the chain need ferry services with differing frequencies, so the routes vary enormously and it can be bewildering to try to fathom out the system. However, with the two main ferry companies, GA Ferries and DANE Sea Lines, operating about 10 boats on a 24-hour-a-day basis, it is usually possible to make the connection you need. Departure times in both directions tend to be geared to an early morning arrival at both Piraeus and Rhodes. This means that island hopping in between can involve some antisocial hours.

Connecting from the Dodecanese to the Cyclades can be difficult. It is possible to reach Astypalea from the Dodecanese and connect with ferries serving the Cyclades from there, but this is more by luck than by design. The F/B *Daliana* sails from Rhodes twice a week to Santorini and on to Ios and Paros, with either three or five stops en route including Crete, but this is a long way around. Samos, in the North-Eastern Aegean, offers a very useful connection via Ikaria to Naxos and Paros on the GA Ferries ship *Milena*, and on the Agapitos Lines' *Golden Vergina*. DANE Sea Lines F/B *Leros* plies several different routes, including Kos to Mykonos and Syros via Kalymnos and Astypalea (weekly) and Kos, Kalymnos, Leros, Patmos and across to Naxos and Paros (every other week).

Check also the LANE Lines F/B *Vitsentsos Kornaros*, which sails from Piraeus via Crete as far as Karpathos, where you can pick up a connection to Rhodes and the rest of the Dodecanese. For more information see the Getting There & Away section for Rhodes island.

Fares from Piraeus to the Dodecanese islands are listed below:

Astypalea	6130 dr
Halki	8400 dr
Kalymnos	6200 dr
Karpathos	7040 dr
Kassos	6960 dr
Kos	6800 dr
Leros	5770 dr
Lipsi	6500 dr
Nisyros	6780 dr
Patmos	6100 dr
Rhodes	7940 dr
Symi	7580 dr
Tilos	6780 dr

Ferry – international There are excursion boats to Marmaris and Bodrum (in Turkey) from Rhodes and Kos respectively. Boats en route from Piraeus to Cyprus and Israel have Rhodes as a port of call. For details see the relevant sections under the entries for these islands.

Getting Around

Air Inter-island flights connect Rhodes with Kos, Kastellorizo, Karpathos and Kassos, and Karpathos with Kassos.

Ferry Island hopping within the Dodecanese is fairly easy as the principal islands in the group have daily connections by either regular ferries or excursion boats. The more remote islands do not have daily boats and a few are totally dependent on the F/B *Nissos Kalymnos*, although even this ferry does not call at Arki. The F/B *Nissos Kalymnos* operates out of Kalymnos and plies up and down the chain, calling in at most of the islands, at least twice a week. Karpathos and Kassos are not included on its route. See the Getting There & Away sections for Kalymnos and Rhodes island for details of its schedule.

For further information regarding travel between the Dodecanese islands, see the relevant sections on individual islands.

Rhodes Ρόδος

Rhodes (**Ro**-dos), the largest by far of the Dodecanese islands, with a total population of 98,181, is the number-one package-tour destination of the group. With 300 days of sunshine a year, and an east coast of virtually uninterrupted sandy beaches, it fulfils the two prerequisites of the sun-starved British, Scandinavians and Germans, who make up the majority of its visitors.

However, an aversion to mass tourism does not necessarily mean you should avoid Rhodes, for beaches and sunshine are not its only attributes. Rhodes is a beautiful island with unspoilt villages nestling in the foothills of its mountains. Its landscape varies from arid and rocky around the coast to lush and forested in the interior.

The old town of Rhodes is the largest inhabited medieval town in Europe, and its mighty fortifications are the finest surviving example of defensive architecture of the time.

To water-sports buffs, Rhodes will seem like heaven with the gate shut. Almost every sport is available. Windsurfing is best on the west coast and water-skiing on the east. Equipment is widely available for hire on both coasts.

Lawrence Durrell lived in Rhodes during the late 1940s and wrote his book *Reflections on a Marine Venus* as a companion to the island.

History & Mythology

As is the case elsewhere in Greece, the early history of Rhodes is interwoven with mythology. The sun god Helios chose Rhodes as his bride and bestowed upon her light, warmth and vegetation. Their son, Cercafos, had three sons, Camiros, Ialyssos and Lindos, who each founded the cities that were named after them.

The Minoans and Mycenaeans had outposts on the islands, but it was not until the Dorians arrived in 1100 BC that Rhodes began to exert power and influence. The Dorians settled in the cities of Kamiros, Ialyssos and Lindos and made each an autonomous state. They utilised trade routes to the East which had been established during Minoan and Mycenaean times, and the island flourished as an important centre of commerce in the Aegean. Largely through expediency and connivance, Rhodes continued to prosper until Roman times.

Rhodes was allied to Athens in the Battle of Marathon (490 BC), in which the Persians were defeated. By the time of the Battle of Salamis (480 BC), it had shifted to the Persian side. However, after the unexpected Athenian victory at Salamis, Rhodes hastily became an ally of Athens again, joining the Delian League in 478 BC. After the disastrous Sicilian Expedition (416-412 BC), when after four years of fighting at Syracuse all the Athenian soldiers were either killed or dead from starvation, Rhodes revolted against Athens and formed an alliance with Sparta, which it aided in the defeat of the Athenians in the Peloponnesian Wars.

In 408 BC, the cities of Kamiros, Ialyssos and Lindos consolidated their powers for

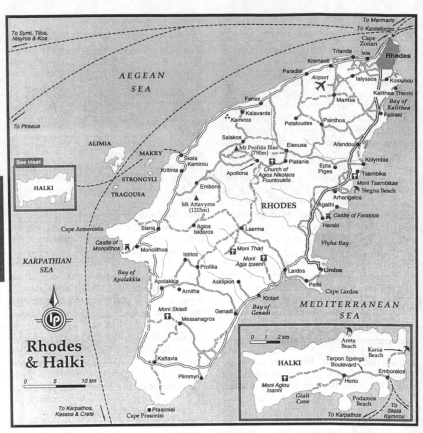

Rhodes
& Halki

mutual protection and expansion by co-founding the city of Rhodes. The architect Hippodamos, who came to be regarded as the father of town planning, planned the city. It was one of the most harmonious cities of antiquity, divided into four distinct parts: the acropolis, agora, harbour and residential quarter, with wide, straight streets connecting them. Rhodes now became Athens' ally again, and together they defeated Sparta at the battle of Knidos, in 394 BC. Rhodes then joined forces with Persia in a battle against Alexander the Great. However, when Alexander the Great demonstrated invin-

cibility, Rhodes hastily allied itself with him. In the skirmishes following Alexander's death, Rhodes sided with Ptolemy.

In 305 BC, Antigonus, one of Ptolemy's rivals, sent his son, the formidable Demetrius Poliorketes (the Besieger of Cities), to conquer the city. Rhodes managed to repel Demetrius after a long siege. To celebrate this victory, the 32m-high bronze statue of Helios Apollo (Colossus of Rhodes), one of the Seven Wonders of the Ancient World, was built. The statue was traditionally thought to have straddled Mandraki harbour but this is now refuted. Whatever the case, it only stood for 65 years before collapsing during an earthquake. It lay abandoned until 653 AD when it was chopped up by the Saracens, who sold it to a merchant in Edessa (in modern-day Turkey). The story goes that after being shipped to Syria, it took almost 1000 camels to convey it to its final destination.

After the defeat of Poliorketes, Rhodes knew no bounds. It built up the biggest navy in the Aegean and its port became a principal Mediterranean trading centre. The arts also flourished, and the Rhodian school of sculpture supplanted that of Athens as the foremost in Greece. Its most esteemed sculptor was Pythocretes, whose works included the Victory of Samothrace, and the relief of the trireme (warship) at Lindos.

When Greece became the battleground upon which Roman generals fought for leadership of the empire, Rhodes allied itself with Julius Caesar. After Caesar's assassination in 44 BC, Cassius besieged Rhodes, destroying its ships and stripping the city of its artworks, which were then taken to Rome. This marked the beginning of Rhodes' decline. In 70 AD, Rhodes became part of the Roman Empire.

In 155 AD, Rhodes city was badly damaged by an earthquake, and in 269 AD the Goths invaded, rendering further damage. When the Roman Empire split, Rhodes became part of the Byzantine province of the Dodecanese. Raid upon raid followed. First it was the Persians in 620, then the Saracens in 653; the Turks followed. When the crusaders seized Constantinople, Rhodes was given independence. Later the Genoese gained control. The Knights of St John arrived in Rhodes in 1309 and ruled for 213 years until they were ousted by the Ottomans. Rhodes suffered several earthquakes during the 19th century, but greater damage was rendered in 1856 by an explosion of gunpowder which had been stored and forgotten – almost 1000 people were killed and many buildings were wrecked. In 1947, after 35 years of Italian occupation, Rhodes became part of Greece along with the other Dodecanese islands.

Getting There & Away

Air Olympic Airways has at least four flights a day to Athens (23,100 dr), two a day to Karpathos (12,100 dr), one a day to Kassos (12,200 dr), three a week to Kastellorizo (10,600 dr), four a week to Iraklio (20,300 dr), three a week to Santorini (20,400 dr), two a week to Kos (13,200 dr) and two a week to Thessaloniki (29,900 dr). Every Sunday there is a flight to Mykonos (20,400). The Olympic Airways office (☎ 24 571/572/573) is at Ierou Lohou 9.

Air Greece has two flights a day to Athens (19,100 dr), three flights a week to Iraklio (17,100 dr) and four a week to Thessaloniki (25,000). Triton Holidays (☎ 21 690; fax 31 625), Plastira 9, is the agent for Air Greece. The airport is 16km south-west of the city near Paradisi.

Ferry – domestic Rhodes is the ferry hub of the Dodecanese. The following was the schedule at the time of writing, but the EOT and the municipal tourist office in Rhodes city have up-to-date schedules.

GA Ferries operates a weekly timetable. The F/B *Rodanthi* leaves Rhodes on Saturday at 9 am and Tuesday at 4 pm for Piraeus (15 hours) via Kos (3½ hours) and Kalymnos (5 hours). On Thursday at 4 pm it leaves Rhodes for Kos (3½ hours), Kalymnos (5 hours), Leros (6¾ hours), Patmos (8¼ hours) and Piraeus (17¾ hours).

The F/B *Romilda* leaves Rhodes on Wednesday at 9 pm for Symi (1¼ hours), Tilos (3 hours), Nisyros (4¼ hours), Kos (5¾ hours), Kalymnos (7 hours), Leros (8¾ hours), Lipsi (10 hours), Patmos (11 hours), Naxos (15½ hours), Paros (17 hours), Syros (18¾ hours) and Piraeus (23¾ hours).

The F/B *Marina* leaves Rhodes on Monday at 8 pm for Kos (3½ hours), Kalymnos (5 hours) and Piraeus (15½ hours). On Wednesday and Friday it departs from Rhodes at 4 pm for Kos (3½ hours), Kalymnos (5 hours), Leros (6¾ hours), Patmos (8¼ hours) and Piraeus (17¾ hours). At 7 am on Sunday it sets out from Kos for Kalymnos (1 hour), Leros (2¾ hours), Patmos (4¼ hours), Naxos (8¼ hours), Paros (9¾ hours and Piraeus (15½ hours).

The F/B *Daliana* has two different routes. On Saturday at 8 pm it leaves Rhodes for Karpathos (4¾ hours), Kassos (6¼ hours), Crete (11¾ hours), Santorini (16¾ hours), Ios (18¾ hours),

Paros (21¼ hours) and Piraeus (27 hours). On Wednesday at 10 pm it leaves Rhodes for Halki (2 hours), Diafani (4½ hours) and Pigadia (5½ hours) on Karpathos, then Kassos (7¼ hours), Crete (12¾ hours), Santorini (22 hours), Ios (23¾ hours), Paros (25 hours) and Piraeus (32¾ hours).

DANE Sea Lines operates a complicated schedule with boats running different routes on different days, on a fortnightly timetable. On the first Tuesday of the timetable, the F/B *Rodos* leaves Rhodes for Kos (3¾ hours), Kalymnos (5¼ hours), and Piraeus (16¼ hours). On the first Thursday and Saturday, and on the following Wednesday, Friday and Sunday, it leaves at 2 pm for Kos (3¾ hours), Kalymnos (5 hours), Leros (8½ hours), Patmos (10 hours) and Piraeus (17½ hours).

The F/B *Patmos* leaves Rhodes at 5 pm on the first Wednesday and Sunday of the timetable, and the following Tuesday and Thursday, for Kos (3½ hours) and Piraeus (14½ hours). On the first Friday, and on Saturday the following week, it leaves Rhodes at 11 am for Kos (3½ hours), Samos (7½ hours) and Thessaloniki (23½ hours).

The F/B *Leros* leaves Rhodes at noon every Monday for Symi (1¼ hours), Tilos (3½ hours), Nisyros (5 hours), Kos (6¾ hours), Leros (7¾ hours), Lipsi (9 hours), Patmos (10 hours) and Piraeus (19¾ hours).

The F/B *Ialysos* operates on five different routes: on the first Wednesday and every Sunday it leaves Rhodes at noon for Kos (3½ hours), Kalymnos (4¾ hours), Leros (6¾ hours), Patmos (8¼ hours) and Piraeus (18 hours). Alternating between Friday and Tuesday, at noon it sets out for Symi (1½ hours), Tilos (3½ hours), Nisyros (5 hours), Kos (6½ hours), Kalymnos (7¾ hours), Leros (9¼ hours), Patmos (10¾ hours) and Piraeus (20½ hours). On the second Wednesday it departs Rhodes at 7 pm for Kos (3¼ hours), Kalymnos (5¾ hours) and Piraeus (16½ hours). On Friday in week two, it leaves at 1 pm for Symi (1½ hours), Tilos (3¾ hours), Nisyros (5¼ hours), Kos (7¼ hours), Astypalea (11 hours) and Piraeus (21¼ hours). Every other Sunday it leaves Rhodes at 8 am for an 8¼ hour round trip to Kastellorizo.

Smaller independent boats chug around the island groups without connecting with mainland Greece. The F/B *Nissos Kalymnos* leaves Kalymnos on Monday and Friday at 7 am for Nisyros, Tilos, Symi, Rhodes, Kastellorizo and back to Rhodes. At 9 am on Tuesday it leaves Rhodes for Symi, Tilos, Nisyros, Kos, Kalymnos, Astypalea and back to Kalymnos. On Saturday it returns to Kalymnos via Symi, Tilos, Nisyros and Kos. At 7 am on Wednesday and Sunday it sets out from Kalymnos for Leros, Lipsi, Patmos, Agathonisi and Samos, returning by the same route. On Thursday it does a round trip to Astypalea, setting out at 7 am.

Fares from Rhodes to other Dodecanese islands are as follows:

Halki	1920 dr
Kalymnos	4060 dr
Karpathos	4980 dr
Kassos	4750 dr
Kastellorizo	3300 dr
Kos	3290 dr
Leros	4420 dr
Lipsi	5000 dr
Nisyros	2700 dr
Patmos	5250 dr
Symi	1550 dr
Tilos	2670 dr

Ferry & Hydrofoil – international The following are schedules for international ferries from Rhodes:

Cyprus & Israel Poseidon Lines and Salamis Lines both operate boats that sail from Piraeus to Rhodes, and on to Cyprus (Limassol) and Israel (Haifa). From Rhodes to Cyprus takes 15 hours, with a further 19½ hours to Haifa. The boats leave Rhodes on Tuesday and Friday. See Getting There & Away in the Piraeus section of the Athens chapter for more information. Buy tickets from Kydon Agency (☎ 23 000, 75 268), Ethelondon Dodekanision between Amerikis and Makariou, new town, Rhodes city, or Kouros Travel (☎ 24 377, 22 400), Karpathou 34, new town, Rhodes city. Immigration and customs are on the quay.

Turkey One ferry shuttles between Rhodes and Marmaris (Turkey) twice a day, seven days a week. It leaves Rhodes at 8 am and 3 pm, setting out from Marmaris for the return run at 10 am and 4 pm. The crossing takes one hour. In addition, small Turkish car ferries run between Rhodes and Marmaris daily (except Sunday) between April and October and less frequently in winter. Prices vary, so shop around.

Hydrofoils also go to Marmaris daily

(weather permitting) from April to October, and are currently cheaper, costing 12,000/19,000 dr one way/return. You can buy tickets from Triton Holidays (☎ 21 657; fax 31 625), Plastira 9 (between Mandraki and Makariou, new town, Rhodes city), to whom you must submit your passport on the day before your journey.

Hydrofoil – domestic The Dodecanese Hydrofoil company (☎ 24 000), Neoriou Square 6, new town, Rhodes city, is situated on the quay near the Kontiki restaurant, and has three craft that service the Dodecanese. These operate from April to October, but schedules vary depending on demand and the weather. There are daily shuttle services to and from Kos (two hours, 6665 dr, early morning and late afternoon both ways) as well as various other itineraries through the islands, and on to Samos in the North-Eastern Aegean.

Samos Hydrofoils operates out of Samos, serving the North-Eastern Aegean islands and Kuşadası in Turkey, as well as the Dodecanese islands as far south as Kos. From Samos there are good connections to the Cyclades.

At the time of writing, a third company – Union Hydrofoils – was planning to launch a new service.

Fares from Rhodes to other Dodecanese islands are as follows:

Astypalea	8550 dr
Halki	3720 dr
Kalymnos	8300 dr
Kos	6750 dr
Leros	9000 dr
Nisyros	5600 dr
Patmos	10,300 dr
Symi	2980 dr
Tilos	5500 dr

Excursion Boat There are excursion boats to Symi (4000 dr return) and Lindos (4000 dr return) every day in summer, leaving Mandraki, Rhodes city, at 9 am and returning at 6 pm. You can buy tickets at most travel agencies but it is better to buy directly from the tables set up at Mandraki since you can

bargain and also see the boat you will be going on. Look for shade and the size and condition of the boat, as these vary greatly. You can buy an open return if you wish to stay over on Symi, or you can buy a one-way ticket to Lindos and return by bus or taxi – many people find the return by boat a boring and hot three hours.

Caïque For information about caïques to Halki from Rhodes, see the Getting There & Away section for Halki.

Getting Around

The Airport Each day 21 buses travel between the airport and Rhodes city's west side bus station (300 dr). The first one leaves Rhodes city at 6 am and the last one at 11 pm. From the airport the first one leaves at 5.55 am and the last one at 11.45 pm.

Bus Rhodes city has two bus stations. From the east side bus station on Plateia Rimini there are 18 buses a day to Faliraki (300 dr), eight to Kolymbia (550 dr), 10 to Lindos (900 dr), five to Genadi (1100 dr) via Lardos, and three to Psinthos (400 dr).

From the west side station next to the New Market there are 16 buses a day to Kalithea Thermi (300 dr), 11 to Koskinou (300 dr), five to Salakos (700 dr), one to ancient Kamiros (850 dr), one to Monolithos (1300 dr) via Skala Kamirou, and one to Embona (900 dr). Both the EOT and municipal tourist office give out schedules.

Car & Motorcycle You'll be tripping over independent car and motorcycle rental outlets in Rhodes city's new town, particularly on and around 28 Oktovriou. Try several and bargain even in season because the competition is fierce.

Taxi Rhodes city's main taxi rank is east of Plateia Rimini. Meters start at 200 dr and then the cost is approximately 120 dr per km. There are two zones on the island for taxi meters: zone one is Rhodes city and zone two (slightly higher) is everywhere else. Rates are slightly higher between midnight and 6

DODECANESE

am. Rip-offs are rare but if you think you have been ripped off take the taxi number and go to the tourist police.

Bicycle The Bicycle Centre (☎ 28 315), Griva 39, Rhodes city, is an excellent bicycle-hire outlet. Daily rates are 800 dr for three-speed bikes and 1200 dr for mountain bikes.

RHODES CITY
• *pop 43,500* • *postcode 851 00* • *area code* ☎ *0241*
The heart of Rhodes city is the old town, enclosed within massive walls. Much of the

new town to the north is a monument to package tourism; however, it does have several places of interest to visitors.

Orientation
The old town is a mesh of Byzantine, Turkish and Latin architecture with quiet, twisting alleyways punctuated by large, lively squares. Sokratous, which runs east to west, and its easterly continuation, Aristotelous, make up the old town's bustling main commercial thoroughfare. The old town's two main squares are also along here: Plateia Martyron Evreon, with a fountain decorated

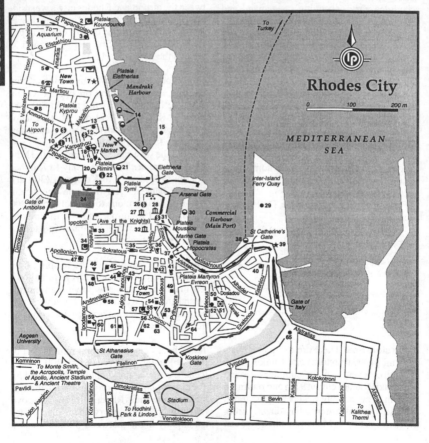

with bronze sea horses, at the eastern end of Aristotelous; and Plateia Hippocrates, with the distinctive Castellania fountain, at the eastern end of Sokratous. Acquainting yourself with Sokratous and these two squares will help somewhat with orientation, but getting lost in Rhodes' old town is almost inevitable and part of the fun of exploring the place. Further north, parallel to Sokratous, is Ippoton (Avenue of the Knights), which was the main medieval thoroughfare.

The commercial harbour, for international ferries and large inter-island ferries, is east of the old town. Excursion boats, small ferries, hydrofoils and private yachts use Mandraki harbour, to the north of the commercial harbour. When you buy a ferry ticket check which harbour the ferry is leaving from.

In Mandraki the two bronze deer (a doe and a stag) on stone pillars mark the supposed site of the Colossus of Rhodes. Mandraki's grandiose public buildings are relics of Mussolini's era. The main square of the new town is Plateia Rimini, which is just north of the old town. The tourist offices, bus stations and main taxi rank are on or near this square. If you arrive by ferry, the square is just a short walk from Mandraki, but further from the commercial harbour.

There are eight gates into the old town. From Plateia Rimini enter through the Eleftheria Gate. Once through the gate, walk south to get to Sokratous. From the commercial harbour, enter through St Catherine's Gate. This is a narrow pedestrian gate behind the ticket offices opposite the harbour entrance.

DODECANESE

PLACES TO STAY
1 Hotel International
33 Maria's Rooms
40 Hotel Kava d'Oro
44 Rodos Youth Hostel
45 Mike and Mama's Pension
49 Pension Rena; Taverna Kostas
50 Hotel Spot
53 Niki's Rooms to Let
54 Hotel Tehran
59 S Nikolis Hotel & Apartments
61 Pink Elephant
62 Pension Andreas
63 Pension Minos

PLACES TO EAT
16 Patisseries
36 Alexis Restaurant
41 Mythos Café Bar
42 Yiannis Taverna
43 Cleo's Italian Restaurant
46 Diafani Garden Restaurant
55 Popeye Bar & Grill
56 Le Bistrot des Tropiques
60 Ancient Agora Garden Resaurant & Bar

64 Le Bistrot de L'Auberge

OTHER
2 Mosque of Murad Reis
3 National Theatre
4 Post Office
5 Olympic Airways Office
6 OTE
7 Port Police
8 Rhodos Tours
9 National Bank of Greece
10 Tourist Police
11 EOT
12 Alpha Credit Bank
13 Triton Holidays
14 Departure Points for Hydrofoils, Diving and Excursion Boats
15 Dodecanese Hydrofoil Company
17 Bus Station (West Side)
18 Kouros Travel
19 Luggage Storage
20 Bus Station (East Side)
21 Taxi Rank
22 Rhodes Municipal Tourist Office

23 Son et Lumière
24 Palace of the Grand Masters
25 Temple of Aphrodite
26 Commercial Bank of Greece
27 Museum of the Decorative Arts
28 Byzantine Museum
29 Customs Office
30 Departure Point for F/B Nissos Kalymnos
31 National Bank of Greece (Old Town)
32 Archeological Museum
34 Mosque of Süleyman
35 Funky Old Greek Café
37 Castellania Fountain
38 Departure Point for Boats to Turkey
39 Port Police
47 Turkish Library
48 Turkish Bath
51 Synagogue
52 Waterhoppers Diving Centre
57 Mosque of Retjep Pasha
58 Folk Dance Theatre
65 YAR Maritime Centre
66 Rock Style Internet Café

Most of the old town is off limits to motorists but there are car parks on the periphery. Most budget accommodation for independent travellers is in the old town. Many hotels in the new town are block-booked by tour companies. However, they may have rooms available on any given day, but this is more likely in low season.

Information
Tourist Offices The EOT (☎ 23 255/655) is on the corner of Makariou and Papagou. The staff give out brochures and a map of the city, and will assist in finding accommodation. Opening times are Monday to Friday from 7.30 am to 3 pm. In summer the same service is provided by Rhodes' municipal tourist office (☎ 35 945), on Plateia Rimini. Opening times are from 8 am to 8 pm Monday to Saturday and 8 am to noon on Sunday. It is closed in winter. From either of these offices you can pick up a copy of the *Rodos News*, a free English-language newspaper.

Tourist Police The tourist police (☎ 27 423) are next door to the EOT. The police here see their job as having to do with crime against tourists rather than tourist information and are perhaps not as helpful as the tourist police in other parts of Greece.

Foreign Consulates Foreign consulates in Rhodes include:

Germany
    Parodos Isiodou 12 (☎ 63 730)
Netherlands
    Alexandrou Diakou 27 (☎ 31 571)
Turkey
    Iroön Politechniou 12 (☎ 23 362)
UK
    Amerikis 111 (☎ 27 247)

Money The main National Bank of Greece and the Alpha Credit Bank are on Plateia Kyprou. In the old town there is a National Bank of Greece and a Commercial Bank of Greece on Plateia Moussiou. All have ATMs. Opening times are Monday to Thursday from 8 am to 2 pm, Friday from 8 am to 1.30 pm.

American Express (☎ 21 010) is repre-sented by Rhodos Tours, Ammohostou 18. There is a Thomas Cook *bureau de change* (☎ 35 672) at Venizelou Sofi 6.

Post & Telecommunications The main post office is on Mandraki. Opening times are Monday to Friday from 7.30 am to 8 pm, Saturday from 7.30 am to 2 pm and Sunday from 9 am to 1.00 pm. Rhodes' postcode is 851 00. The OTE is at Amerikis 91. It is open daily from 7 am to 11 pm.

There is an internet café, *Rock Style*, at Dimokratias 7, just south of the old town.

Bookshops The Academy Bookstore, at Dragoumi 7, and Moses Cohn, at Themeli 83D, both stock foreign-language books.

Laundry Rhodes has two self-service laundrettes: Lavomatique, 28 Oktovriou 32, and Express Servis, Dilberaki 97 (off Orfanidou). Both charge around 1400 dr a load.

Luggage Storage The New Market Pension on Plateia Rimini has luggage storage for 500 dr a day (8 am to 8 pm) or 1000 dr a night (8 pm to 8 am).

Emergency Rhodes' general hospital (☎ 25 580) is at Papalouka, just north-west of the old town. For emergency first aid and the ambulance service you should telephone ☎ 25 555 or 22 222.

Old Town
The town is divided into two parts. In medieval times the Knights of St John lived in the Knights' Quarter and the other inhabitants lived in the Hora. The 12m-thick city walls are closed to the public, but on Tuesday and Saturday at 2.45 pm you can take a guided walk along them starting at the courtyard of the Palace of the Grand Masters (1200 dr). As well as seeing the old town's sights, take time to wander in the maze of narrow, vaulted side streets to relish the medieval aura.

Knights' Quarter The Knights of St John were a religious order of the church of Rome

Top Left: The magnificent 4th-century Palace of the Grand Masters, Rhodes, Dodecanese
Top Right: An ornately cobbled path in Rhodes town, Dodecanese
Bottom: View over Symi Harbour, Symi, Dodecanese

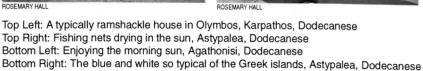

Top Left: A typically ramshackle house in Olymbos, Karpathos, Dodecanese
Top Right: Fishing nets drying in the sun, Astypalea, Dodecanese
Bottom Left: Enjoying the morning sun, Agathonisi, Dodecanese
Bottom Right: The blue and white so typical of the Greek islands, Astypalea, Dodecanese

founded in Amalfi in the 11th century. They went to Jerusalem initially to minister to the pilgrims who arrived there, but soon extended their duties to tending the poor and sick of the Holy Land. Over the years they became increasingly militant, joining forces with the Knights Templars and the Teutonic Knights of St Mary in battles against infidels.

The Knights of St John were expelled from the Holy Land with the fall of Jerusalem. They went first to Cyprus and then to Rhodes, where they arrived in 1309. Through some wheeling and dealing with the island's ruling Genoese admiral, Viguolo de Viguoli, they became the possessors of Rhodes, transforming it into a mighty bulwark that stood at the easternmost point of the Christian West safeguarding it from the Muslim infidels of the East. The knights withstood Muslim offensives in 1444 and 1480, but in 1522 Sultan Süleyman the Magnificent staged a massive attack with 200,000 troops. After a long siege the 600 knights, with 1000 mercenaries and 6000 Rhodians, surrendered – hunger, disease and death having taken their toll.

An appropriate place to begin an exploration of the old town is the imposing cobblestone **Avenue of the Knights**, which was where the knights lived. The knights were divided into seven 'tongues' or languages, according to their place of origin – England, France, Germany, Italy, Aragon, Auvergne and Provence – and each group was responsible for protecting a section of the bastion. The Grand Master, who was in charge, lived in the palace, and each tongue was under the auspices of a bailiff. The knights were divided into soldiers, chaplains and ministers to the sick.

To this day the street exudes a noble and forbidding aura, despite modern offices now occupying most of the inns. Its lofty buildings stretch in a 600m-long unbroken wall of honey-coloured stone blocks, and its flat façade is punctuated by huge doorways and arched windows. The inns reflect the Gothic styles of architecture of the knights' countries of origin. They form a harmonious whole in their bastion-like structure, but on closer inspection each possesses graceful and individual embellishments.

First on the right, at the eastern end of the Avenue of the Knights, is the **Inn of the Order of the Tongue of Italy** (1519); next to it is the **Palace of Villiers de l'Île Adam**. After Sultan Süleyman had taken the city, it was Villiers de l'Île who had the humiliating task of arranging the knights' departure from the island. Next along is the **Inn of France**, the most ornate and distinctive of all the inns. On the opposite side of the street is a wrought-iron gate in front of a Turkish garden. Back on the right side is the **Chapelle Française** (Chapel of the Tongue of France), embellished with a statue of the Virgin and Child. Next door is the residence of the Chaplain of the Tongue of France. Across the alleyway is the **Inn of Provence**, with four coats of arms forming the shape of a cross, and opposite is the **Inn of Spain**.

On the right is the magnificent 14th-century **Palace of the Grand Masters** (☎ 23 359). It was destroyed in the gunpowder explosion of 1856 and the Italians rebuilt it in a grandiose manner, with a lavish interior, intending it as a holiday home for Mussolini and King Emmanuel III. It is now a museum, containing sculpture, mosaics taken from Kos by the Italians, and antique furniture. The palace is open Tuesday to Sunday from 8.30 am to 3 pm. Admission is 1200 dr.

The **archaeological museum** (☎ 27 657), Plateia Moussiou, is housed in the 15th-century knights' hospital, a splendid structure built around a courtyard. Its infirmary had beds for 100 patients.

The museum's most famous exhibit is the exquisite Parian marble statuette, the *Aphrodite of Rhodes*, a 1st-century BC adaptation of a Hellenistic statue. It depicts the love goddess newly emerged from the sea, kneeling, and holding up her long hair to dry in the sun. Less charming, to most people, is the 4th-century BC *Aphrodite of Thalassia* in the next room. However, Lawrence Durrell was so enamoured by this statue that he named his *Reflections on a Marine Venus* after it. Also in this room is the 2nd-century

BC marble *Head of Helios*, unearthed from near the Palace of the Grand Masters where a Temple of Helios once stood. The head belonged to a statue in the temple's pediment which depicted the sun god riding a chariot in the sky. Another renowned exhibit is the beautiful, well-preserved 4th-century BC grave stele found at Kamiros, which depicts Crito bidding farewell to her mother, Timarista. In the same room are two 6th-century BC kouroi statues, also found at Kamiros. Other exhibits include small statues from various periods, gravestones of the knights and small grave steles from the Roman period. The museum is open Tuesday to Sunday from 8.30 am to 3 pm. Admission is 800 dr.

Across the square from the archaeological museum, the 11th-century **Church of the Virgin** of the Castle was enlarged by the knights and became their cathedral. It is now the **Byzantine Museum**, with Christian artworks. It is open Tuesday to Sunday from 8.30 am to 3 pm. Admission is 500 dr.

Further north, on the opposite side, the **Museum of the Decorative Arts** houses an interesting collection of pottery, furniture and costumes from around the Dodecanese. Opening times are Tuesday to Sunday from 8.30 am to 3 pm. Admission is 600 dr. On Plateia Simi, there are the remains of a 3rd-century BC **Temple of Aphrodite**, one of the few ancient ruins in the old town.

Hora Until this century, Rhodes had a large Jewish population who lived in the southeast district of Hora. During the Nazi occupation most of these Jews were transported to Auschwitz, never to return. The synagogue on Dosiadou has a plaque commemorating the tragedy. The remaining Jews still worship here and it is usually open in the morning. Close by, Plateia Martyron Evreon (Square of the Jewish Martyrs) also commemorates these Jews.

The Hora also has many Ottoman legacies. During Turkish times the churches were converted to mosques, and many more were built from scratch. Most are now dilapidated. The most important one is the pink-domed **Mosque of Süleyman**, at the top of Sokratous. It was built in 1522 to commemorate the Ottoman victory against the knights. It was rebuilt in 1808. Opposite is the 18th-century **Turkish library** where many Islamic manuscripts are kept. It is sometimes open to the public – check the times on the notice outside.

The 18th-century **Turkish bath**, on Plateia Arionos, offers a rare opportunity to have a Turkish bath in Greece. It is open on Tuesday from 1 pm to 7 pm, on Wednesday, Thursday and Friday from 11 am to 7 pm and on Saturday from 8 am to 6 pm. Entry is 500 dr.

New Town
The **Acropolis of Rhodes** (on Monte Smith) was the ancient Hellenistic city of Rhodes. The hill it stands on is named after the English admiral Sir Sydney Smith who kept watch here for Napoleon's fleet in 1802. Competitions were held in preparation for the Olympic Games in the restored 2nd-century **stadium**. The adjacent **theatre** is a reconstruction of one used for lectures by the School of Rhetoric. Steps above here lead to the **Temple of Pythian Apollo**, with four re-erected columns. From here there are superb views and you can catch some particularly good sunsets. The site is an open one. You can take city bus No 5, or walk there along Diagoridon.

North of Mandraki, at the eastern end of G Papanikolaou, is the graceful **Mosque of Murad Reis**. In its grounds are a **Turkish cemetery** and the small Villa Cleobolus, where Lawrence Durrell lived in the 1940s.

The **aquarium** is housed in a fine red-and-cream Italianate building at the island's northernmost point. Its exhibits include all things aquatic and some oceanography instruments. Opening times are 9 am to 9 pm daily. Admission is 600 dr.

The town **beach** begins north of Mandraki and continues around the island's northernmost point and down the west side of the new town. The best spot is on the northernmost point since you get both a breeze and calm water and it's not quite as crowded. Another good spot in calm weather is at the south-west end of the beach.

Rodini Park, 3km south of the town, is a pleasant shady park with pine, cypress and maple trees, streams, ponds and peacocks. It's believed to have been the site of the Rhodes School of Rhetoric. The city bus No 3 goes there.

Activities
Scuba Diving Two diving schools operate out of Mandraki: the Waterhoppers Diving Centre (☎ & fax 38 146), Pericleous 29, and Dive Med Centre (☎ 33 654; fax 23 780). Both offer a range of courses including a One Day Try Dive for 11,000 dr. They also have a wide range of equipment for hire, advanced courses and night dives for certified divers. You can get information from the Waterhopper boat, MV *Kouros*, and the Dive Med Centre's boats *Pheonix*, *Free Spirit* and *Aurora*, at Mandraki. Alternatively, check out the **divers' bar** at a pub where divers hang out called *Shooters* at Apolloniou 61, north-west of the old town. Diving takes place at Kalithea Thermi (currently the only area around Rhodes where diving is legal).

Yachting You can hire yachts from the YAR Maritime Centre (☎ 22 927; fax 23 393), Vyronos 1. For more information about yachting contact the Rodos Yacht Club (☎ 23 287).

Windsurfing The Fun Surf Center (☎ 95 819), Ialysos Beach, Ixia (6km from Rhodes city), has hourly, daily and weekly rental of sailboards. There are many other rental outlets around the coast.

Tennis Many of the large hotels have tennis courts open to non-guests. The Rhodes Tennis Club (☎ 25 705) is on the waterfront north of Mandraki.

Greek Dancing Lessons The Nelly Dimoglou Dance Company (☎ 20 157/29 085), at the Folk Dancing Theatre on Andronikou, gives Greek dancing lessons.

Organised Tours
If your time on Rhodes is limited then Triton Holidays (☎ 21 690; fax 31 625), Plastira 9, Mandraki, has a wide range of tours. You can fax them for specialist advice on any of the islands and Turkey before you even leave home and they'll fax you back free of charge.

Places to Stay – bottom end
The old town of Rhodes is well supplied with accommodation so even in high season you should be able to find somewhere. The unofficial *Rodos Youth Hostel* (☎ 30 491), Ergiou 12, charges 1500 dr per person. There is a kitchen for self-caterers and during the summer there are BBQ facilities.

The exceptionally friendly *Pension Andreas* (☎ 34 156, fax 74 285), Omirou 28D, has clean, pleasant doubles with shared bathroom for 8000 dr, triples with private bathroom for 12,000 dr, and a terrace bar with terrific views. Close by, *Pension Minos* (☎ 31 813), at Omirou 5, has spotless, spacious rooms for 8000/10,000 dr and a roof garden with views of almost the entire old town.

Mike and Mama's Pension (☎ 25 359), Menekleous 28, has singles/doubles/triples for 4000/5000/6000 dr with shared bathroom.

Pension Rena (☎ 26 217), Pythagora 55, has tidy doubles for 6000 dr with shared bathroom.

Maria's Rooms (☎ 20 730), just off Sokratous, has doubles/triples for 6000/9000 dr with shared bathroom. *Hotel Spot*, (☎ 34 737), Perikleous 21, has singles/doubles/ triples for 7500/8000/9000 dr with private bathroom. *Hotel Tehran* (☎ 27 594), Sofokleous 41b, overlooking Plateia Sofokleous, has tidy doubles/triples for 6000/8000 dr with private bathroom. Just off this square, *Niki's Rooms to Let* (☎ 25 115), Sofokleous 39, has spacious, rooms for 7000/8500/ 12,000 dr.

The D-class *Hotel Kava d'Oro* (☎ 36 980), Kistiniou 15, is in an 800-year-old house close to the commercial harbour and has a bar. Rates are 6000/7000/10,000 dr with private bathroom.

Places to Stay – middle

The *Pink Elephant* (☎ & fax 22 469), Irodotou 42, has doubles with private bathroom for 14,000 dr, doubles/triples for 11,000/15,000 dr without.

Hotel International (☎ 24 595), in the new town at Kazouli 12 is good value, with singles/doubles at 7000/10,000 dr with private bathroom.

Places to Stay – top end

The *S Nikolis Hotel & Apartments* (☎ 34 561, 36 238; fax 32 034), Ippodamou 61, is the old town's most luxurious accommodation. It has a large garden and a roof terrace with terrific views. The rooms, which really are top quality, cost 18,000/28,000/33,600 dr, including breakfast. Well-equipped apartments sleep two/three/four people and cost 22,200/26,000/30,000 dr; there are also huge double/triple suites at 35,000/42,000 dr.

If you can't get into S Nikolis Hotel, the pricey *Grand Hotel Astir Palace* (☎ 26 284) on Akti Miaouli has a bar, restaurant and swimming pools. Rates are 25,000/35,300 dr for singles/doubles, and 62,000 dr for suites.

At the suburb resort of Ixia, which is 6km south-west of Rhodes city, the A-class *Cosmopolitan Hotel* (☎ 35 373) has singles/doubles/triples for 15,500/25,000/34,375 dr.

The deluxe-category *Rodos Palace* (☎ 25 222, 26 222; fax 25 350), also at Ixia, is a vast place with loads of amenities. Singles/doubles cost 32,250/44,150 dr.

You can get discounts of up to 30% on the more expensive hotels if you book through Triton Holidays (see Organised Tours).

Places to Eat – inexpensive

Enthusiastic touting and displays of tacky photographs of food seem to be the order of the day at many restaurants in Rhodes, with the enthusiasm of the touts not reflected in the quality of the food. However if you hunt around you will find good-value places.

In the old town, *Yiannis Taverna*, Appellou 41, is popular with locals and is also good value. Stifado is 1200 dr and souvlaki is 1600 dr. *Taverna Kostas*, underneath Pension Rena at Pythagora 62, is also commendable,

with souvlaki for 1600 dr and swordfish for 2300 dr. One of the cheapest places to eat is *Mike's*, with souvlaki and calamari both at 1000 dr. There's no name outside and the street isn't marked, but find Castellania fountain and it's the tiny street running parallel south of Sokratous. *Diafani Garden Restaurant*, opposite the Turkish bath, serves gratifying, reasonably priced dishes, 'cooked from the heart', as the owner says in German.

If you're sick to death of Greek food by now, *Le Bistrot de L'Auberge*, in a medieval house at Praxitelous 21, serves terrific French dishes, with main courses costing around 1800 dr. *Le Bistrot des Tropiques*, Omirou 22, has Afro/Asian/Caribbean food. Most people choose a selection of starters (from 700 dr) rather than a main course.

In the new town, *India Restaurant* (☎ 38 395), at Konstantopedos 16, has a fantastic selection of Indian food. It's directly opposite the new *Kringlans Swedish Bakery* on Dragoumi street. Reservations are recommended.

The *Popeye Bar & Grill* (see the following Entertainment section), Plateia Sofokleous, serves inexpensive snacks and barbecued meat dishes. Appropriately, this is a good place to find work on a yacht.

For a good cappuccino in Rhodes city, head for *Mythos Café Bar*, Evripidou 13-15, near the Castellania fountain. The *food market* opposite Plateia Rimini has numerous fast-food outlets and fruit and vegetable stalls.

If you just have to have some English food, *Mollye's*, at Ionos Dragoumi 25, is reasonably priced.

South of the old town, *To Steno*, Agion Anargiron 29, near the church, is popular with locals.

The suburb resort of Ixia has two restaurants of note. *Tzaki Taverna*, on the main road just after the Ialissos beach turn-off, has around 30 different mezedes ranging from 550 to 850 dr and good barrel wine. There's live bouzouki music every evening. Despite the name, *Le Jardin*, just before the beach turn-off, serves traditional Greek fare like moussaka for 1200 dr and giouvetsi (a casserole of lamb or veal and pasta) for 2000 dr.

Places to Eat – moderate
The atmospheric stone-walled, wooden-beamed *Ancient Agora Garden Restaurant and Bar* on Omirou 70, built on the site of the original market, has a good range of main courses from 1000 dr.

Cleo's Italian Restaurant, Agiou Fanouriou 17, is a sophisticated place with a cool, elegant interior and a quiet courtyard. Set menus cost around 4000 dr. *Alexis Restaurant*, on Sokratous, is a first-rate seafood restaurant, where you'll pay around 6000 dr for a meal with wine.

Feverish touting reaches its acme at the people-watching pâtisseries bordering the New Market. Nevertheless, they're convivial meeting places with a vast choice of cakes. Coffee and cake costs a pricey 1200 to 1500 dr.

Places to Eat – expensive
Palia Istoria (☎ 32 421), 108 Mitropoleos, south of the old town, is popular with well-healed locals. It has a large, imaginative menu which includes delicious and unusual mezedes such as scallops with mushrooms, and artichokes in nutmeg sauce. Expect to pay 6000 to 8000 dr for a meal with wine. Reservations are recommended.

Entertainment
In the grounds of the Palace of the Grand Masters, the *son et lumière* (☎ 21 922), depicting the Turkish siege, is superior to most such efforts. The entrance is on Plateia Rimini and admission is 1000 dr. A noticeboard outside gives the times for performances in English, or you can check with the EOT.

The Nelly Dimoglou Dance Company gives first-rate performances at the *Folk Dance Theatre* (☎ 29 085/20 157) on Andronikou. Performances are nightly except Saturday from May to October and begin at 9.20 pm. Admission is 3500 dr.

There are classical music recitals at the *National Theatre* (☎ 29 678).

The *Popeye Bar & Grill* (see also Places to Eat) is a lively bar with a dart board and pool table. Beers cost 450 to 600 dr and cocktails are 800 dr.

For the best Greek coffee in town and a game of backgammon or chess, head for the fantastically funky old café at Sokratous 76.

The new town has a plethora of discos and bars – over 600 at last count and rising. The two main areas are called Top Street and the Street of Bars. Top Street is Alexandrou Diakou and the Street of Bars is Orfanidou, where a cacophony of western music blares from every establishment; just take your pick. Quieter than most is the *Red Lion*, Orfanidou 9, with the relaxed atmosphere of a British pub. Proprietors Ron and Vasilis will gladly answer any of your questions about Rhodes for the price of a drink. Beers cost from 550 dr and cocktails are 1000 dr. For live rock 'n' roll, try *Sticky Fingers* at Zervou 6.

Things to Buy
Good buys in Rhodes old town are gold and silver jewellery, leather goods and ceramics. However, leather goods are less expensive in Turkey. Look around and be discriminating – it's quite acceptable to haggle.

Getting There & Away
See the Getting There & Away and Getting Around sections for Rhodes island at the beginning of the Rhodes section.

Getting Around
Local buses leave from Mandraki. Bus No 2 goes to Analipsi, No 3 to Rodini, No 4 to Agios Dimitrios and No 5 to Monte Smith. Buy tickets at the kiosk on Mandraki.

EASTERN RHODES
Rhodes' best beaches are on the east coast. Frequent buses go down the coast as far as Lindos, but some of the beaches are a bit of a trek from the main road where the bus stops are.

Kalithea Thermi, 10km from Rhodes city,

is a derelict Italian-built spa. The frequent buses from Rhodes city stop on the main road opposite the short turn-off to the spa.

Walk through a colonnade to a large domed building with tiny blue-glassed star-shaped windows. Surrounding it are more buildings with crumbling colonnades, pebble-mosaic floors and domed ceilings. There is a small beach in an inlet which is used by Rhodes' diving schools (see Activities in the Rhodes city section). There's good snorkelling from the rocks to the left of here, and snorkelling gear for hire. To the right there's a small sandy beach (with a snack bar) reached along a track through pines, which veers right from the turn-off to the spa.

Kalithea is currently being restored with funds awarded to Greece under the Delors II Regional Development Programme.

Faliraki beach, 5km further south, is the island's premier resort and comes complete with high-rise hotels, fast-food joints and bars. Although the main stretch of beach is crowded, the bay at the extreme southern end is uncrowded and popular with nude bathers. **Aqua Adventure** (Greece's longest water slide) is located between the Sun Palace and Calypso hotels at the northern end of the beach. The bus stop is close to the beach. *Faliraki Camping* (☎ 85 358) has a restaurant, bar, minimarket and swimming pool.

At Kolymbia, 10km south of Faliraki, a right turn leads in over 4km of pine-fringed road to the **Epta Piges** (Seven Springs), a verdant beauty spot, where a small lake fed by springs can be reached either along a path or through a tunnel. There are no buses here, so take a Lindos bus and get off at the turn-off. With your own transport you can continue for another 9km to **Eleousa** on the slopes of Profitis Ilias, and then another 3km to the **Church of Agios Nikolaos** at Fountouklis, which has fine Byzantine frescoes. A dirt road continues to Salakos (see Inland Rhodes).

Back on the coast, **Kolymbia** and **Tsambikas** are good but crowded beaches. A steep road (signposted) leads in 1.5km to **Moni Tsambikas**, from where there are terrific

views. It is a place of pilgrimage for childless women. On 18 September, the monastery's festival day, they climb up to it on their knees and pray to conceive.

Arhangelos, 4km further on and inland, is a large agricultural village with a long tradition of carpet weaving and hand-made goatskin boots production, both of which are being overtaken by tourism as the major money-earner. Just before Arhangelos there is a turn-off to **Stegna beach**, and just after to the lovely sandy cove of **Agathi**; both are reasonably quiet. The **Castle of Faraklos** above Agathi was a prison for recalcitrant knights and the island's last stronghold to fall to the Turks. The fishing port of **Haraki**, just south of the castle, has a pebbled beach and good fish tavernas. There are more beaches between here and Vlyha Bay, 2km from Lindos.

Lindos Λίνδος
• *pop 900 • postcode 851 07 • area code* ☎ *0244*
Lindos village, 47km from Rhodes, lies below the Acropolis and is an immaculate showpiece of dazzling-white 17th-century houses, many with ornate lintels and doors, and courtyards with black-and-white *hohlakia* (pebble mosaics) floors. Once the dwellings of wealthy admirals, many have been bought and restored by foreign celebrities. The main thoroughfares are lined with tourist shops, cafés and bars, so you need to explore the labyrinthine alleyways to fully appreciate the place.

The 15th-century **Church of Agia Panagia** on Acropolis is festooned with 18th-century frescoes of saints, and has lots of elaborately carved wood.

Orientation & Information The town is pedestrianised. All vehicular traffic terminates on the central square of Plateia Eleftherias, from where the main drag, Acropolis, begins. The donkey terminus is a little way along here.

The municipal tourist information office (☎ 31 900/288/227) is on Plateia Eleftherias. It is open daily from 9 am to 10 pm. Pallas Travel (☎ 31 494, fax 31 595) and Lindos

Sun Tours (☎ 31 333), both on Acropolis, have a room-letting service. The latter also has a car and motorcycle-rental facility with good rates out of high season. For delicious home-made ice cream, head for Gelo Blu, 50m beyond Pallas Travel.

The Commercial Bank of Greece is right by the donkey terminus and has an ATM. The National Bank of Greece is on the street opposite the Church of Agia Panagia. Turn right at the donkey terminus for the post office. There is no OTE but there are cardphones on Plateia Eleftherias and the Acropolis.

The privately owned Lindos Lending Library, on Acropolis, is well stocked with English books. It no longer lends them, but prices range from 200 to 1500 dr and you can sell them back for half the price towards another book. It also has a laundrette, with service washes costing 1800 dr per load, and it rents out fans for 2000 dr a week.

The Acropolis of Lindos Lindos is the most famous of the Dodecanese ancient cities, but with 500,000 visitors a year it's just a bit *too* famous.

Lindos was the most important Doric settlement because of its excellent vantage point and good harbour. It was first established around 2000 BC and is a conglomeration of ancient, Byzantine, Frankish and Turkish remains.

After the founding of the city of Rhodes, Lindos declined in commercial importance, but remained an important place of worship. The ubiquitous St Paul landed here en route to Rome. The Byzantine fortress was strengthened by the knights, and also used by the Turks.

The Acropolis of Lindos is spectacularly perched atop a 116m-high rock. It's about a 10-minute climb to the well-signposted entrance gate. Once inside, a flight of steps leads to a large square. On the left (facing the next flight of steps) is a trireme (warship) hewn out of the rock by the sculptor Pythocretes. A statue of Hagesandros, priest of Poseidon, originally stood on the deck of the ship. At the top of the steps ahead, you enter the acropolis by a vaulted corridor. At the other, side-turn sharp left through an enclosed room to reach a row of storerooms on the right. Opposite here is another rostrum. The stairway on the right leads to the remains of a 20-columned **Hellenistic stoa** (200 BC). The Byzantine **Church of Agios Ioannis** is to the right of this stairway. The wide stairway behind the stoa leads to a 5th-century BC propylaeum, beyond which is the 4th-century **Temple to Athena**, the site's most important ancient ruin (at the time of writing encased in scaffolding). Athena was worshipped on Lindos as early as the 10th century BC, so this temple has replaced earlier ones on the site. From its far side there are splendid views of Lindos village and its packed beach, and St Paul's Beach, in an almost circular harbour.

Donkey rides to the acropolis cost 1000 dr one way. The site is open Tuesday to Sunday from 8.30 am to 4.30 pm. Admission is 1200 dr.

Places to Stay Accommodation is expensive and reservations are essential in summer. The following options are not entirely monopolised by tour groups. *Fedra Rooms to Rent* (☎ 31 286), along the street opposite the Church of Agia Panagia, has doubles/triples for 8000/9600 dr with private bathroom.

Pension Electra (☎ 31 266) has a roof terrace with superb views and a beautiful shady garden; doubles with shared bathroom cost 9000 dr, and double/triple studios cost 14,000/16,000 dr. *Pension Katholiki* (☎ 31 445) next door has doubles with shared bathroom for 9000 dr. To get there, follow the signs to the Acropolis but don't turn right at *Restaurant Aphrodite* – carry on towards the sea.

Getting There & Away There are at least 10 buses a day to and from Lindos from Rhodes city (900 dr). There are six buses a day to and from Genadi and Lindos via Pefkos and Lardos (400 dr).

There are daily excursion boats from

Mandraki in Rhodes city (see the Getting Around section for Rhodes city).

WESTERN RHODES

Western Rhodes is more green and forested than the east coast, but it's more exposed to winds so the sea tends to be rough, and the beaches are mostly of pebbles or stones. Nevertheless, tourist development is rampant, almost to the airport, and consists of the suburb resorts of Ixia, Trianda and Kremasti. Paradisi, despite being next to the airport, has retained some of the feel of a traditional village. If you are on Rhodes between flights or have an early morning flight you may consider staying here. There are several *domatia* options and decent restaurants on the main street.

Ialyssos Ιαλυσσός

Like Lindos, Ialyssos, 10km from Rhodes, is a hotchpotch of Doric, Byzantine and medieval remains. The Doric city was built on Filerimos hill, which was an excellent vantage point, and so attracted successive invaders. The only ancient remains are the foundations of a 3rd-century BC temple and a restored 4th-century BC fountain. Also at the site are the restored **Monastery of Our Lady** and the **Chapel of Agios Georgios**.

The ruined fortress was used by Süleyman the Magnificent as his headquarters during his siege of Rhodes city. The site is open Tuesday to Sunday from 8.30 am to 3 pm. Admission is 800 dr.

Getting There & Away No buses go to ancient Ialyssos. The airport bus stops at Trianda, on the coast. Ialyssos is 5km inland from here.

Kamiros Κάμειρος

Many people believe this is Rhodes' best ancient site. The extensive ruins of the ancient city of Kamiros stand on a hillside above the west coast, 34km from Rhodes city. It was a city built by the Dorians and produced figs, oil and wine. It reached its height in the 6th century BC, but by the 4th century BC it had been superseded by the city of Rhodes, and was almost totally destroyed by earthquakes in 226 and 142 BC. The site was first excavated in 1929 after locals unearthed an ancient grave. The layout of the ancient city is easily discernible.

From the entrance, walk straight ahead and down the steps. The semi-circular rostrum on the right is where officials made speeches to the public. Opposite are the remains of a **Doric temple** with one standing column. The area next to it, with a row of intact columns, was probably where the public watched priests performing rites in the temple. Ascend the wide stairway to the ancient city's main street. Opposite the top of the stairs is one of the best preserved of the **Hellenistic houses** that flanked the east side of the street. Walk along the street, ascend three flights of steps, and continue straight ahead to reach the ruins of the 3rd-century **great stoa**, which had a 206m portico supported by two rows of Doric columns. It was built on top of a huge 6th-century cistern which supplied the houses with rainwater through an advanced drainage system. Behind the stoa, at the city's highest point, stood the **Temple to Athena**. From here there are terrific views inland to Mt Profitis Ilias and Mt Attavyros.

The site is open Tuesday to Sunday from 8.30 am to 3 pm. Admission is 800 dr. Buses from Rhodes city to Kamiros stop on the coast road. The site is 1km inland from here.

Kamiros to Monolithos Μονόλιθος

Skala Kamiros, 16km south of Kamiros, is touted as an 'authentic fishing village' so it's very much on the tour-bus circuit and only worth a visit to get a caïque to Halki (see the Getting There & Away section for Halki). The road south from here to Monolithos has some of the island's most impressive scenery. From Skala Kamiros the road winds uphill with great views across the sea to Halki and the islets of Alimia, Makry, Strongyli and Tragousa. This is just a taste of what's to come at the ruined 16th-century **Castle of Kastellos** that's reached along a rough road from the main road, 2km beyond Skala Kamiros. Eight km further along there is a left fork to Embona (see The Interior). The main road continues for another 9km to **Siana**, a picturesque village below Mt Akramytis (825m), famed for its honey and *souma*, a local firewater.

Five km beyond Siana, the village of Monolithos has the spectacularly sited **Castle of Monolithos** perched on a sheer 240m rock and reached along a dirt track. Continuing along this track, at the fork bear right for **Moni Georgiou** and left for the very pleasant shingled **Fourni beach**. Monolithos has rooms to rent and the *Hotel Thomas* (π 0246-61 291) with singles/doubles for 6000/8000 dr The post code for Monolithos is 85 104.

SOUTHERN RHODES
South of Lindos, Rhodes becomes progressively less developed (see the Getting There & Away sections for Rhodes city and Lindos for information about buses to the region). **Pefki**, 2km south of Lindos, was once well and truly off the beaten track, but is now package-tourist territory. However, it's still possible to get out of earshot of other tourists, away from the main beach.

Lardos Λάρδος
Lardos is a pleasant village 6km west of Lindos and 2km inland from Lardos beach. Lardos Tours (π 0244-44 069), on the central square, has a room-finding service. The post code for Lardos is 85 109.

Around Lardos
There are two monasteries near the village worth seeing. From Lardos you can walk (or drive) to **Moni Agia Ipseni** (Monastery of Our Lady) through hilly, green countryside. Begin from the central square and with the Tourist Information Office on your right, walk along the road ahead and after 300m, turn sharp right. This road leads in 4km to the monastery.

The well-watered village of **Laerma** is 12km north-west of Lardos. From here it's another 5km (signposted) to the beautifully sited 9th-century **Moni Thari**, which was the island's first monastery and has recently

been re-established as a monastic community. It contains some fine 13th-century frescoes.

Genadi Γεννάδι
• *postcode 851 09 • area code* π *0244*
Genadi, 13km south of Lardos, is another burgeoning resort, but inland from the central square and main street it's an unspoilt agricultural village. At the crossroads turn left to reach the long pebble and sand beach, and right to reach the village.

Genadi's main street is to the right (facing inland) of the central square. There is no tourist information office, but Pallas Travel (π 43 340), on the central square, organises excursions and has a room-finding service. The post office is on the right side of the main street. The OTE is on the right, just before the central square.

Places to Stay & Eat *Tina's Studios* (π 43 204), off the main street, has modern double studios for 8000 dr. *Carrera Rooms* (π 43 340) has similar studios for around the same price; turn right at the crossroads and the rooms are on the right. The spacious *Betty Studios & Apartments* (π 43 020), 20m along the main street, has double/triple studios for 8600/10,000 dr and four-person apartments for 11,800 dr.

There are several restaurants along the main street. The nicest beach restaurant is *Restaurant Antonis* at the bottom of the beach road.

Around Genadi
Four km north of Genadi, **Kiotari** beach has recently been subjected to rampant development, but with a bit of leg work secluded parts can still be found. **Asklipion**, 4km inland, is an unspoilt village with the ruins of yet another castle and the 11th-century **Church of Kimisis Theotokou**.

Genadi to Prasonisi
Γεννάδι – Πρασονήσι
From Genadi an almost uninterrupted beach of pebbles, shingle and sand dunes extends down to **Plimmyri**, 11km south. Between the

DODECANESE

two, and south of Plimmyri, it's easy to find deserted beaches.

From Plimmyri the main road continues to **Kattavia**, Rhodes' most southerly village. The 11km dirt road north to Messanagros winds through some terrific scenery. From Kattavia there's a rough 10km road south to the remote **Prasonisi** (Green Island), the island's southernmost point, joined to Rhodes by a narrow sandy isthmus with rough sea on one side and calm water on the other. There are two tavernas that operate in high season. There is no formal accommodation but many people simply pitch a tent on the surrounding land.

South of Monolithos

On the west coast the beaches south of Monolithos are prone to strong winds. From Apolakkia, an unremarkable village 10km south of Monolithos, a road crosses the island to Genadi, passing through the unspoilt villages of Arnitha, Profilias, Istrios and Vati. Seven km south of Apolakkia a turn-off to the left leads up to the 18th-century **Moni Skiadi**. It's a lovely, serene place with terrific views down to the coast, and there is free basic accommodation for visitors.

The coast road beyond this turn-off is unsurfaced and runs close to the sea before veering inland for Kattavia.

THE INTERIOR

Roads that cross the island between the east and west coasts have great scenery and very little traffic. If you have transport then they're well worth exploring.

Petaloudes Πεταλούδες

Petaloudes (Valley of the Butterflies), one of the 'must sees' on the package-tour itinerary, is reached along a 6km turn-off from the west coast road, 2.5km beyond Paradisi.

The butterflies (*Callimorpha quadripunctarea*) are lured to this gorge of rustic footbridges, streams and pools by the scent of the resin exuded by the styrax trees. Regardless of what you may see other tourists doing, do not make any noises to disturb the butterflies; their numbers are declining rapidly, largely due to noise disturbance. Petaloudes is open daily from 7.50 am to 5 pm from 1 May to 10 October; admission is 600 dr. There are buses to Petaloudes from Rhodes city.

Around Petaloudes

From Petaloudes a 2km dirt track leads to the 18th-century **Moni Kalopetras** built by Alexander Ypsilantas, the grandfather of the Greek freedom-fighter.

Also from Petaloudes, a new 5km road leads to Psinthos, a pleasant village where *Artemidis Restaurant & Rooms* (☎ 0246-51 735) serves tasty traditional Greek fare and has a swimming pool to boot. Double rooms above the restaurant cost 7000 dr. Psinthos can also be reached by a good road inland from the east coast.

Salakos & Mt Profitis Ilias

Σάλακος & Όρος Προφήτης Ηλίας
Salakos is an attractive village below Mt Profitis Ilias (790m) reached along an 8km turn-off, 30km along the west-coast road. From the village, a path leads almost to Mt Profitis Ilias' summit. Walk along Salakos' main road towards the mountains; at the curve, 60m beyond the Hotel Nymphi, turn left, and after 50m take a path to the right signposted 'Profitis Ilias'. After climbing for about 40 minutes the path levels out and proceeds through woodland towards a peak with OTE satellite dishes. After a gentle ascent, turn left at a dirt track to reach an asphalt road and the defunct Alpine-style Elafos Hotel. The café opposite is often open.

Places to Stay & Eat *Hotel Nimfi* (☎ 0246-22 206/346) in Salakos has doubles for 7500 dr. It has a restaurant and there are two tavernas on the central square.

Beyond Salakos

Six km beyond Salakos the road forks. The left fork leads to the aforementioned Elafos Hotel from where a dirt road continues to the Byzantine **Church of Agios Nikolaos**

Fountouklis, and Eleousa (see the Eastern Rhodes section).

The right fork leads to **Embonas** on the slopes of Mt Attavyros (1215m), the island's highest mountain (see Western Rhodes). Embonas is, unfortunately, touted as a 'traditional mountain village' and visited by many tourist buses. It's also renowned for its wine and is surrounded by vineyards. The wine produced is the dry white *Villaré*. It costs around 1800 dr a bottle and is produced at the **Emery Winery** (☎ 0246-29 111), where there's free wine tasting on weekdays until 3 pm. **Agios Isidoros**, 14km south of Embona, is a lovely unspoilt village to which you can detour en route to Siana (see the Western Rhodes section).

Halki Χάλκη

• *pop 281* • *postcode 851 10* • *area code ☎ 0241*

Halki (**Hal**-kee) is a small island 16km off the west coast of Rhodes. It has escaped the tourist development of its large neighbour; however, much of the accommodation is monopolised by Laskarina for package tourists who want a holiday on an untouristy island. It's a barren, rocky island with a severe water shortage. The population has been greatly reduced by emigration. Many islanders moved to Tarpon Springs, Florida, where they have established a sponge-fishing community.

Getting There & Away
Ferry On Wednesday at 5.30 pm the F/B *Daliana* arrives at Halki from Piraeus, Syros, Paros, Naxos, Ios, Santorini, Iraklio, Kassos and Karpathos and then departs for Rhodes. At midnight it arrives back at Halki from Rhodes, and takes the same route back to Piraeus. Also see the Getting There & Away section for Rhodes island.

Hydrofoil On Wednesday at 10.40 am a hydrofoil arrives from Kalymnos, Kos, Nisyros and Tilos. It then sets out for Rhodes, returning to Halki at 7.10 pm, and takes the same route back to Kalymnos.

Caïque There is a caïque running from Skala Kamiros on Rhodes' west coast to and from Halki. The boat leaves Skala Kamiros every day (except Sunday) at 2.30 pm. On Sunday it leaves at 9 am. The cost is 1300 dr. To get to Skala Kamiros from Rhodes city take the 1.15 pm Monolithos bus from the west side bus station.

Caïques from Halki to Skala Kamiros leave at 5.30 am to connect with the Rhodes city bus which arrives at Skala Kamiros at 7.30 am. The return caïque to Halki departs at 2.30 pm. There is no bus on Sunday; the Sunday boat leaves Halki at 4 pm.

Getting Around
Halki has no cars, buses or taxis. There are excursions to the island's beaches and to the nearby uninhabited islet of Alimia which has good beaches.

EMBOREIOS Εμπορειός
Halki has only one settlement, the attractive little port town of Emboreios, consisting of imposing mansions, many now derelict. The town's most prominent building is the Agios Nikolaos church, with the tallest belfry in the Dodecanese.

Orientation & Information
The ferry quay is in the middle of the harbour. There is one road out of Emboreios, incongruously named Tarpon Springs Boulevard for the ex-Halkiots in Florida, who financed its construction. It begins behind the post office and passes Podamos, the island's only sandy beach.

There is a small tourist information kiosk between the post office (opposite the quay) and the war memorial. The staff will help you to find accommodation.

There is no OTE, but the minimarket behind the waterfront war memorial does have a metered telephone.

Places to Stay
The nicest place to stay is the *Captain's*

House (☎ 45 201), a beautiful 19th-century mansion with period furniture and a tranquil tree-shaded garden. It is owned by a retired Greek sea captain and his British wife, Christine. Rates are 7000 dr a double with private bathroom. To reach the Captain's House, walk through the church grounds and out at the other side. Turn left and then immediately turn to the right along a narrow alleyway. At the fork bear left and you will come to seven stone steps to the left. The Captain's House is at the top of these on the right.

Pension Cleanthi (☎ 45 334), on the road to Podamos beach, has modern doubles with private bathroom for 7000 dr and two/four-person studios for 7000/12,000 dr.

Places to Eat

Several tavernas line the waterfront. *Omonoias Taverna*, to the right of the port as you face inland, and *Ioannis Taverna*, at the far left of the waterfront, are both popular. There is also a good taverna on Podamos Beach.

AROUND HALKI
Horio Χωριό
Horio, a 30-minute walk along Tarpon Springs Boulevard from Emboreios, was the 'pirate-proof' inland town. Once a thriving community of 3000 people, it's now derelict and uninhabited. A path leads from Horio's churchyard to a Knights of St John castle. From Horio, if you take the left fork of Tarpon Springs Boulevard, and then take the first turn right onto a stony track, in about 30 minutes you will reach the secluded cove of **Giali**, which has a stony, often wave-lashed beach.

Moni Agiou Ioanni Μονή Αγίου Ιωάννη
This monastery is a two-hour walk from Horio. There are no monks here now, but the shepherd-cum-caretaker, Dimitris, lives here with his family. Free beds are available for tourists, but you must take your own food and water. Take the right fork of Tarpon Springs Boulevard. There are fine views of many Dodecanese islands and Turkey.

Karpathos Κάρπαθος

• *pop 5323* • *postcode 857 00* • *area code* ☎ *0245*
The elongated island of Karpathos (**Karpa-thos**), midway between Crete and Rhodes, is traversed by a mountain range which runs north-south. For hundreds of years the north and south parts of the island were isolated from one another and so they developed independently. It is even thought that the northerners and southerners have different ethnic origins. The northern village of Olymbos is of endless fascination to ethnologists for the age-old customs of its inhabitants. Karpathos has rugged mountains, numerous beaches and unspoilt villages, and despite having charter flights from northern Europe, it has not, so far, succumbed to the worst excesses of mass tourism.

Karpathos has a relatively uneventful history. Unlike almost all other Dodecanese islands, it was never under the auspices of the Knights of St John. It is a wealthy island as it receives more money from emigrants living abroad (mostly in the USA) than any other Greek island.

Getting There & Away
Air There are three flights a week to Athens (24,700 dr), four a week to Kassos (6000 dr) and four a day to Rhodes (12,100 dr). There is a flight on Wednesday to Sitia on Crete (11,500 dr). The Olympic Airways office (☎ 22 150/057) is on the central square in Pigadia. The airport is 18km south-west of Pigadia.

Ferry Karpathos has two ports: Pigadia (Karpathos port) and Diafani, to the north of the island. At 2.20 pm on Wednesday the F/B *Daliana* arrives at Pigadia from Piraeus, Syros, Paros, Naxos, Ios, Santorini, Iraklio and Kassos, and then departs for Diafani, Halki and Rhodes. At 2.50 am on Thursday it arrives back at Diafani from Halki and Rhodes, and takes the same route back to Piraeus. Also see the Getting There & Away section for Rhodes island.

At 2.20 pm on Saturday the F/B *Vitsentsos Kornaros* arrives at Pigadia from Piraeus, Milos, Agios Nikolaos, Sitia and Kassos. At 9.30 am on Sunday it departs for Piraeus via the same route. See the Getting There & Away section for Rhodes island, the Getting There & Away section for Sitia (Crete) and the Getting There & Away section for Iraklio for their schedules.

Getting Around

The Airport In 1997 there was no airport bus, but check with the Olympic Airways office whether this is still the case. A taxi from Pigadia to the airport costs a hefty 2500 dr.

Bus Pigadia is the transport hub of the island. A schedule is pinned up at the bus station. There are four buses a day to Amopi (300 dr), four a day to Pyles (380 dr) via Aperi (300 dr), Volada (300 dr); and Othos (300 dr); two a day to Finiki (380 dr) via Menetes (300 dr) and Arkasa (380 dr); and only two a week to Lefkos (in 1997 on a Monday and Thursday). There is no bus between Pigadia and Olymbos or Diafani.

Car & Motorcycle Next door to the post office (on the corner of 28 Oktovriou and Georgiou Loïzou in Pigadia) is a reliable, reasonably priced car and motorcycle-rental outlet called By Circle (☎ 22 690/489). The 21km road from Spoa to Olymbos is unsurfaced but driveable. However, check on its current condition with the tourist police before setting off and make sure you know where the petrol stations are – they're few and far between.

Taxi The taxi rank (☎ 22 705) is on Dimokratias, just around the corner from Karpathou. A price list is displayed.

Excursion Boat In summer there are daily excursion boats from Pigadia to Diafani for 5200 dr return. There are also frequent boats to the beaches of Kyra Panagia and Apella for 2500 dr. Tickets can be bought from Karpathos Travel in Pigadia.

PIGADIA Πηγάδια

Pigadia (population 1300) is the island's capital and main port. It's a modern town, pleasant enough, but without any eminent buildings or sites. The town is built on the edge of Vronti bay, a 4km-long sandy beach where you can rent jet skis (two people 5000 dr) and water skis (4000 dr). On the beach are the remains of the early Christian basilica of Agia Fotini.

Orientation & Information

From the quay, turn right and take the left fork onto Apodimon Karpathou, Pigadia's main thoroughfare, which leads to the central square of Plateia 5 Oktovriou.

Pigadia has no EOT. The tourist police (☎ 22 218) are next door to the post office which is on the corner of 28 Oktovriou and Georgios Loïzouon Georgios Loïzou. The most helpful of the travel agencies is Karpathos Travel (☎ 22 148/754), on Dimokratias.

The OTE is on Ethnikis Anastasis. The National Bank of Greece is on Apodimon Karpathou. The bus station is one block up from the waterfront, on Dimokratias. There's a laundrette – Laundro Express – on Mitr Apostolou. Carol's Corner Shop,

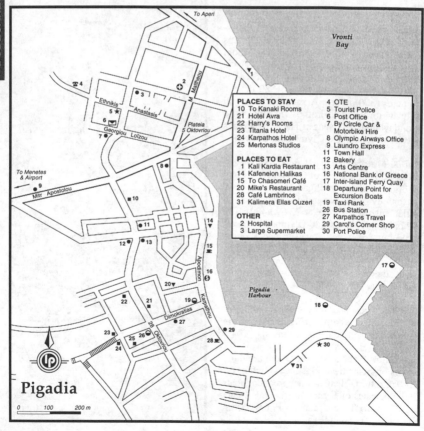

PLACES TO STAY
10 To Kanaki Rooms
21 Hotel Avra
22 Harry's Rooms
23 Titania Hotel
24 Karpathos Hotel
25 Mertonas Studios

PLACES TO EAT
1   Kali Kardia Restaurant
14 Kafeneion Halikas
15 To Chasomeri Café
20 Mike's Restaurant
28 Café Lambrinos
31 Kalimera Ellas Ouzeri

OTHER
2   Hospital
3   Large Supermarket
4   OTE
5   Tourist Police
6   Post Office
7   By Circle Car & Motorbike Hire
8   Olympic Airways Office
9   Laundro Express
11 Town Hall
12 Bakery
13 Arts Centre
16 National Bank of Greece
17 Inter-island Ferry Quay
18 Departure Point for Excursion Boats
19 Taxi Rank
26 Bus Station
27 Karpathos Travel
29 Carol's Corner Shop
30 Port Police

Pigadia

on Apodimon Karpathou, sells new and second-hand books.

Places to Stay

There's plenty of accommodation and owners meet the boats. The E-class *Hotel Avra* (☎ 22 388/485/528), on 28 Oktovriou, has comfortable doubles for 7000 dr with private bathroom and 5600 dr without. *Harry's Rooms* (☎ 22 188), just off 28 Oktovriou, has spotless singles/doubles with shared bathroom for 4000/5000 dr. Further along 28 Oktovriou, just beyond the Karpathos Arts Centre, *To Kanaki Rooms* (☎ 22 908) has pleasant doubles for 6000 dr with private bathroom.

The C-class *Karpathos Hotel* (☎ 22 347) has light, airy rooms for 6000/6500 dr with private bathroom. Opposite, the C-class *Titania Hotel* (☎ 22 144) has spacious, nicely furnished rooms for 7000/8000/9600 dr. The rooms at the C-class *Panorama Hotel* (☎ 22 739), on the edge of town, have white stucco walls and traditional furniture. Singles/doubles cost 6000/8000 dr. Walk to the end of Matheou and continue straight ahead. Turn right at the first crossroads, left at the second and the hotel is on the left.

Mertonas Studios (☎ 22 622, 31 396) has lovely, tastefully furnished studios, managed by the warm and friendly Eva Angelos. Rates for doubles/triples are 10,000/12,000 dr, and four-person studios are 14,500 dr. Take the first left after Café Lambrinos, turn right at the T-junction, take the first left, and the studios are on the right.

Places to Eat

Pigadia is well supplied with good restaurants. *Mike's Restaurant*, just off Apodimon Karpathou, is excellent. A meal of lamb stew, Greek salad and retsina costs 2500 dr.

The popular *Kafeneion Halikas* is open all day for drinks, but only serves meals in the evenings. The menu is limited; quite often it's only stifado (1600 dr) and green beans (650 dr), but both are delicious. It's a crumbling white building, just beyond the National Bank of Greece on Apodimon Kar-

pathou. The *Kali Kardia Restaurant*, on the western side of town overlooking the beach at the beginning of Vronti bay opposite the Hotel Atlantic, serves freshly caught fish and inexpensive meat dishes.

The guys who run the atmospheric *Kalimera Ellas Ouzeri*, near the quay, come from Thessaloniki, Greece's gastronomic epicentre, and this is reflected in the delectable mezedes they serve. A mixed mezes plate is 1200 dr.

For a cheap breakfast try *Café Lambrinos*, on Apodimon Karpathou, where an English breakfast with fruit juice and tea or coffee is 900 dr. *To Chasomeri Café*, further along Apodimon Karpathou, on the opposite side, has tasty, filling sandwiches. The *bakery* is opposite the Arts Centre.

SOUTHERN KARPATHOS
Amopi

The island's premier holiday resort, Amopi, is 8km from Pigadia. It's not especially attractive but has two bays of golden sand and translucent sea, and pebbled coves nearby. There are four buses a day from Pigadia.

Places to Stay & Eat Amopi is a scattered place without any centre or easily identifiable landmarks, so ask the bus or taxi driver to drop you off at whichever establishment you decide to check. The cheapest place is *Amopi Beach Rooms* (☎ 22 723) where singles/doubles with shared bathroom cost 4000/6500 dr.

Votsalakia Rooms & Restaurant (☎ 22 204) has attractively furnished doubles/triples for 6000/8000 dr. *Four Seasons Studios* (☎ 22 116) has equally commendable doubles with private bathroom for 7000 dr. *Hotel Sophia* (☎ 22 078) has doubles/triples for 7000/8500 dr, and *Kastelia Bay Hotel* (☎ 22 678) has light, airy singles/doubles/triples for 8000/9000/10,800 dr.

Menetes Μενετές

Menetes is perched on a sheer cliff 8km above Pigadia. It's a picturesque, unspoilt village with pastel-coloured neoclassical

DODECANESE

houses lining its main street. Behind the main street are narrow, stepped alleyways that wind between more modest whitewashed dwellings. The village has a little **museum** on the right coming from Pigadia. The owner of Taverna Manolis, one block back from the main road, has the key and will open it up for you.

Places to Stay & Eat Menetes has only one place to stay: the *domatia* of friendly Greek-American Mike Rigas (☎ 81 269/255), in a traditional Karpathian house with a garden of figs and grapes. Doubles with shared bathroom are 4700 dr and triples with private bathroom are 5500 dr. Coming from Pigadia, the rooms are 150m down a cement road (signposted 'Lai') veering off to the right, just beyond the museum. *Taverna Manolis* serves decent, inexpensive food.

Arkasa Αρκάσα

Arkasa, 9km further on, is metamorphosing from traditional village to holiday resort. The old village straddles a ravine, and most of the resort development is north of here. If you turn right at the T-junction you will come to the authentic village square.

A turn-off left, just before the ravine, leads after 500m to the remains of the 5th-century Basilica of Agia Sophia. Two chapels stand amidst mosaic fragments and columns; one is built over a well-preserved section of mosaic. There's a nice beach just south of the ruins.

Places to Stay & Eat *Pension Philoxena* (☎ 61 341), on the left before the T-junction, has very clean singles/doubles/triples for 3500/4500/5000 dr. *Elini Rooms* (☎ 61 248), on the left along the road to Finiki, has attractive double apartments for 7000 dr.

Taverna Petaluda, on Arkasa's central square, is very good value.

Finiki Φοινίκι

Turn left at the T-junction in Arkasa to reach the serene fishing village of Finiki, 2km away. The little sculpture at the harbour com-memorates the heroism of seven local fishers during WWII – locals will tell you the story.

Places to Stay & Eat *Fay's Paradise* (☎ 61 308), just up from the harbour, has lovely studios that cost 5000/6000/7000 dr. *Finiki View Hotel* (☎ 61 309/400), on the right coming from Arkasa, has spacious doubles for 7000 dr and a swimming pool and bar.

Locals come from all over the island to eat the very fresh fish at *Dimitrios Fisherman's Taverna*, opposite Fay's Paradise. Lobster is 7400 a kg, and swordfish is 2200 dr a portion.

Lefkos Λεύκος

Lefkos, 13km north of Finiki, is a burgeoning resort with three superb sandy beaches. In summer it gets crowded, but at other times it still has a rugged, off-the-beaten-track feel about it. It's 2km from the coast road.

Places to Stay & Eat At *O Nikos Rooms* (☎ 71 003), on the left halfway down the turn-off, tidy doubles cost 5000 dr. Further down on the right, the sparkling *Imeri Rooms* (☎ 71 375) has doubles/triples for 4000/5500 dr with private bathroom. Enquire at *Small Paradise Taverna & Rooms* (☎ 71 171/184), further down the road, about its Sunset Studios which overlook a beach. Doubles/triples cost 8000/9000 dr. All of these places have tavernas.

Getting There & Away There are three buses a week to Lefkos and a taxi costs 7000 dr, but telephone the rooms' proprietors and they may be able to arrange a lift from Pigadia, providing you intend staying with them, of course! Hitching is dicey as there is not much traffic. Backpackers sometimes do the four-hour walk to and from Pyles, which has a bus connection with Pigadia (see Mountain Villages).

East-Coast Beaches

The fine east-coast beaches of **Ahata**, **Kyra Panagia** and **Apella** can be reached along dirt roads off the east-coast road, but are most easily reached by excursion boat from

Pigadia. Only Kyra Panagia has accommodation facilities and tavernas.

Mesohori & Spoa Μεσοχώ & Σπόα
Mesohori, 4km beyond the turn-off for Lefkos, is a pretty village of whitewashed houses and stepped streets. Spoa village, 5km further on along a dirt road, is at the beginning of the 21km dirt road to Olymbos. It overlooks the east coast and has a track down to Agios Nikolaos beach.

Mountain Villages
Aperi, Volada, Othos and Pyles, the well-watered mountain villages to the north of Pigadia, are largely unaffected by tourism. None has any accommodation, but all have tavernas and kafeneia. Othos and Pyles are within walking distance from Volada.

Aperi was the island's capital from 1700 until 1892. Its ostentatious houses were built by wealthy returning émigrés from the USA. Like Aperi, Volada has an air of prosperity.

Othos (altitude 510m) is the island's highest village. Its small ethnographic museum is on the right as you enter the village from Volada. Yiannis Hapsis, a local artist, has the key and gives guided tours. If you would like to see Yiannis' work, his studio is on the right 200m beyond the museum.

From Othos the road winds downhill with good views over to Kassos. Pyles is a gorgeous village of twisting, stepped streets, pastel houses and citrus groves. It clings to the slopes of Mt Kali Limni (1215m); the Dodecanese's second-highest peak. Good cheese and honey are produced here.

A turn-off left is the new road to the west coast. Walk straight through Pyles to reach the old unsurfaced road which descends through a fragrant pine forest to the coast. The walk takes about one hour. The track emerges 500m south of Adia where there is a taverna and rooms to rent. Lefkos is 13km further north and Finiki is 5km south.

NORTHERN KARPATHOS
Diafani & Olymbos Διαφάνι & Ολυμπος
Diafani is Karpathos' small northern port.

There's no post office or bank, but the Nikos Travel Agency (☎ 51 410), on the waterfront, has a currency-exchange service. There's no OTE but there are cardphones.

Clinging to the ridge of barren Mt Profitis Ilias, 4km above Diafani, Olymbos (population 340) is a living museum. Women wear bright, embroidered skirts, waistcoats and headscarves, and goatskin boots. The interiors of the houses are decorated with embroidered cloth and their façades feature brightly painted ornate plaster reliefs. The inhabitants speak in a vernacular which contains some Doric words, and the houses have wooden locks of the kind described by Homer. Olymbos is a matrilineal society – a family's property passes down from the mother to the first-born daughter. The women still grind corn in windmills and bake bread in outdoor communal ovens.

Olymbos, alas, is no longer a pristine backwater caught in a time warp. Nowadays hordes of tourists come to gape, and tourist

Woman in traditional dress

shops are appearing everywhere. However, Olymbos is still a fascinating place, and accommodation and food are inexpensive.

The bus stops at the beginning of the village. Continue ahead along the main street to reach the central square.

Walk from Olymbos to Avlona The village of Avlona is deserted in winter, but has a small population of farmers in summer. Face the beginning of the row of windmills behind Olymbos village and go down the steps to their right, passing the windmill museum on your left. At the yellow-and-green house on the left continue straight ahead along a cement track to more steps, then a stony path. After about 10 minutes you'll pass a white church on the right. After this, cross a river bed and take the ascending path straight ahead. When the path levels out, climb the poorly defined path to the left of a ruined stone house. At the top, take the path to the left, which soon veers slightly right. To the right you will see some terraces, the river bed and the Diafani-Olymbos road.

About 30 minutes out of Olymbos the path crosses the top of a ravine. You are heading for the white, red-domed **Moni Agiou Konstantinou**, ahead in the distance. In another 15 to 20 minutes the path veers slightly right and soon crosses the top of another ravine. Clamber over some rocks and veer left to go around a terraced ravine. You will reach the monastery 80 or 90 minutes after leaving Olymbos. Turn left onto the dirt road in front of the monastery (a right turn leads to the Diafani-Olymbos road). Ignore the right fork and stay on the main (downhill) track. Soon Avlona's pastel-coloured houses and neat terraces will appear. Return along the dirt road and you'll reach the Diafani-Olymbos road after about 30 minutes. The views along this road are stunning, with Olymbos and Mt Profitis Ilias to the right, and Diafani far below to the left.

The **Church of Agios Ioannis** at Vourgounta, a deserted village north of Avlona, is the scene of a lively four-day festival which begins on 29 August.

Places to Stay There's an unofficial camping ground at Vananda beach, 30 minutes walk (signposted) north of Diafani. The *Golden Beach Hotel* (☎ 51 315), opposite the quay in Diafani, has singles/doubles/triples for 3500/4500/5500 dr with shared bathroom. *Pension Glaros* (☎ 51 259/216), back from the quay to the left, has rooms for the same price.

Just off the main street in Olymbos, the clean, simply furnished rooms at *Pension Olymbos* (☎ 51 252) cost 3500/4500/5000 dr with shared bathroom. Just beyond the bus turnaround, *Mike's Rooms* (☎ 51 304) cost 4000 dr a double.

Hotel Aphrodite (☎ 51 307/454), just off the central square, has immaculate doubles/triples for 5000/6000 dr with private bathroom.

Places to Eat In Diafani the *Golden Beach Taverna* and *Taverna Anatoli* are both good.

Makarounis (handmade noodles mixed with grated cheese and onions and fried) is a speciality of Olymbos, served at all the restaurants. You'll eat well at *Olymbos Taverna*, below Pension Olymbos, at *Mike's Taverna*, directly below his rooms, and also at *Parthenonas Restaurant*, on the central square.

Getting Around A bus meets the excursion boats from Pigadia at Diafani and transports people up to Olymbos.

From Diafani, excursion boats go to nearby beaches and occasionally to the uninhabited islet of Saria where there are some Byzantine remains.

Kassos Κάσσος

• *pop 1088* • *postcode 858 00* • *area code* ☎ *0245*
Kassos (**Ka**-sos), 11km south of Karpathos, is a rocky little island with prickly pear trees, sparse olive and fig trees, drystone walls, and sheep and goats. It is one of the least visited islands of the Dodecanese. If you tell Kar-

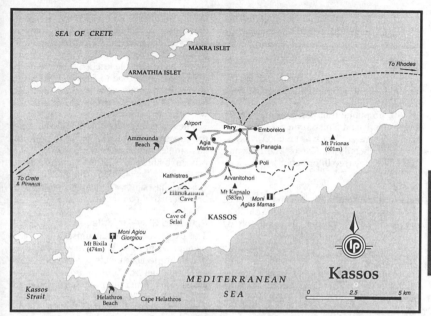

parthians you're off to Kassos they'll tell you to take your knitting. However, even if you don't knit there's more to do on Kassos than contemplating your navel. It's the perfect island to see something of traditional Greek life, and it's also a great island for walking.

History

Despite being diminutive and remote, Kassos has an eventful and tragic history. During Turkish rule it flourished, and by 1820 it had 11,000 inhabitants and a large mercantile fleet. Mohammad Ali, the Turkish governor of Egypt, regarded this fleet as an impediment to his plan to establish a base on Crete from which to attack the Peloponnese and quell the uprising there. So, on 7 June 1824, Ali's men landed on Kassos and killed around 7000 inhabitants. This massacre is commemorated annually on the anniversary of the slaughter and Kassiots return from around the world to participate.

During the late 19th century, many Kas-

siots emigrated to Egypt and around 5000 of them helped build the Suez Canal. In this century many have emigrated to the USA.

Getting There & Away

Air There are daily flights to Rhodes (12,200 dr) and four a week to Karpathos (6000 dr). The Wednesday afternoon flight to Karpathos continues on to Sitia (10,700 dr) and Athens (24,700 dr). The Olympic Airways office (☎ 41 444) is on Kritis.

Ferry Kassos has the same ferry schedule as Pigadia (Karpathos); the F/B *Daliana* and the F/B *Vitsentsos Kornaros* are the only ferries that use the island as a port of call. See the Getting There & Away section for Rhodes island and the Getting There & Away section for Karpathos for their schedules.

Excursion Boat There are excursion boats from Karpathos to Kassos on Sunday in summer (6000 dr). In summer there are excursion boats from Phry to the uninhabited Armathia islet (2000 dr return) where there are sandy beaches.

Getting Around

There is no longer a bus on the island, but the airport is only 600m along the coast road from Phry.

With no public transport you may prefer to give the island a miss, unless you're into hiking. There are just two taxis on Kassos. For further details ask Kassos Maritime and Travel Agency (see Information).

PHRY Φρυ

Phry is the island's capital and port. The town's focal point is the picturesque old fishing harbour of Bouka. The suburb of Emboreios is 1km east of Phry.

Orientation

Turn left at the quay to reach Bouka and the Church of Agios Spyridon. Veer left towards the church, follow the road right, and then take the first left which leads to Kritis, Phry's main street. Turn left to reach the waterfront and the central square of Plateia Iroön Kassou. To reach Emboreios, turn right at the waterfront. The Poli turn-off is 120m along the Emboreios road.

Information

Kassos does not have an EOT or tourist police, but Emmanuel Manousos, at Kassos Maritime and Travel Agency (☎ 41 495 or 41 323), Plateia Iroön Kassou, is helpful and speaks English.

The National Bank of Greece is represented by the supermarket at the beginning of Kritis. From the waterfront, take the first turn left along Kritis to reach the post office. The OTE is behind Plateia Dimokratias – you'll see the huge satellite dishes.

The port police (☎ 41 288) are behind the Church of Agios Spyridon. The police (☎ 41 222) are just beyond the post office, on the opposite side.

Places to Stay – bottom end

All of the island's accommodation (and there's not that much) is in Phry, except for the rooms at Moni Agiou Giorgiou (see Walks to Monasteries). *Ketty Markous* (☎ 41 613/498/216) rents doubles for 8000 dr with shared bathroom and kitchen. They're on the right side of the road to Emboreios. Further along, on the opposite side, *Elias Koutlakis Rooms* (☎ 41 363), costs 8000 dr a double with private bathroom.

The *Anessis Hotel* (☎ 41 234/201), above the supermarket which represents the bank, has singles/doubles for 4500/8000 dr with private bathroom. The *Anagennisis Hotel* (☎ 41 495; fax 41 036), on Plateia Iroön Kassou, has singles/doubles for 4200/6500 dr with shared bathroom.

Places to Stay – middle

The owner of the Anagennisis Hotel, Emmanuel Manousos, also has well-equipped double/triple apartments for 12,000/14,500 dr. Emmanuel's brother, Georgios Manousos (☎ 41 047), rents luxurious apartments for 12,000/16,000/20,000 dr. These are on the right side of Kritis, 160m from the waterfront.

Places to Eat

There are several restaurants in Phry, two in Emboreios and one in Agia Marina. *Kassos Restaurant* on Plateia Dimokratias is run by a women's co-operative and is one of Phry's nicest places to eat. *Taverna Emborios* is the better of Emborios' two options. Phry is well supplied with supermarkets.

AROUND KASSOS

Kassos' best beach is the isolated, pebbled cove of **Helathros**, reached along a turn-off from the Agios Georgios road (see Walks to Monasteries). The beach has no facilities. The mediocre **Ammounda** beach, just beyond the airport, is the nearest to Phry.

You can walk from Phry to all of the other villages. **Agia Marina**, 1km south-west of Phry, is a pretty village with a gleaming white-and-blue church. On 17 July the Festival of Agia Marina is celebrated here. From Agia Marina the road continues to verdant **Arvanitohori**, with fig and pomegranate trees and gardens replete with frangipani and bougainvillea.

Poli, 3km south-east of Phry, is the former capital, built on the ancient acropolis. **Panagia**, between Phry and Poli, has fewer than 50 inhabitants. Its once grand sea captains' and ship-owners' mansions are now derelict.

Walks to Monasteries

The island has two monasteries: **Moni Agias Mamas** and **Moni Agiou Giorgiou**. The uninhabited Moni Agias Mamas on the south coast is a 1½-hour walk from Phry. Take the Poli road and just before the village turn left (signposted 'Agia Mamas'). The road winds uphill through a dramatic, eroded landscape of rock-strewn mountains, crumbling terraces and soaring cliffs. Eventually a sharp turn right (it's signposted 'Agia Mamas') descends to the blue-and-white, red-domed monastery.

Moni Agiou Giorgiou is a 2½-hour walk from Arvanitohori. Take the dirt road south (with a little white church at its start) from the Avantohori-Agia Marina road. In 15 minutes you will see a house on the right. The **cave of Selai** is supposedly on the hill above here, but is hard to find. Continue along the road to a fork. Bear left for Helathros beach, or take the right (uphill) fork to reach the sparkling white monastery. There are no monks, but there is a resident caretaker for most of the year, and basic (free) accommodation for visitors.

Kastellorizo (Megisti)
Καστελλόριζο

• *pop 275* • *postcode 851 11* • *area code* ☎ *0241*

Tiny, rocky Kastellorizo (Kastelorizo), a mere speck on the map, is 118km east of Rhodes, its nearest Greek neighbour, and only 2.5km from the southern coast of Turkey. Its official name is Megisti (the biggest), for it is the largest of a group of 14 islets. The island's remoteness has so far ensured that its tourism is low-key. There are

no beaches, but there are rocky inlets from where you can swim and snorkel in a crystal-clear sea.

The island featured in the Oscar-winning, Italian film *Mediterraneo* (1991) which was based on a book by an Italian army sergeant. *Castellorizo: An Illustrated History of the Island & Conquerors* by Nicholas G Pappas was published in Australia in 1994. The Australian author's parents originated from Kastellorizo.

History

The ghost town you see today is made all the more poignant by an awareness of the island's past greatness. Due to its strategic position, Dorians, Romans, crusaders, Egyptians, Turks, Venetians and pirates have all landed on its shores. The 20th century has been no less traumatic, with occupations by the French, British and Italians.

In 1552, Kastellorizo surrendered peacefully to the Turks and so was granted special privileges. It was allowed to preserve its language, religion and traditions. Its cargo fleet became the largest in the Dodecanese and the islanders achieved a high degree of culture and education.

Kastellorizo lost all strategic and economic importance after the 1923 population exchange (a condition of the Treaty of Lausanne). In 1928 it was ceded to the Italians, who severely oppressed the islanders; in contrast, Turkish rule must have seemed like the good old days. Many islanders emigrated to Perth, Australia, where today some 10,000 of them live. They call themselves 'Kassies' and refer to their homeland as 'The Rock'.

During WWII, Kastellorizo suffered severe bombardment, and English commanders ordered the few remaining inhabitants to abandon their island. They fled to Cyprus, Palestine and Egypt, but were not allowed to take any belongings with them. In October 1945, 300 islanders boarded the Australian ship *Empire Control* to return to Kastellorizo. Tragically, the ship burst into flames and 35 people lost their lives. Two months later the remaining refugees returned to their island to find that most of their houses had been destroyed by bombings and the remaining ones had been ransacked by the occupying troops. Not surprisingly, more islanders emigrated. Most of the houses that escaped the bombing in WWII stand empty. Despite this gloomy picture Kastellorizo's waterfront is very lively.

Getting There & Away
Air In July and August there are daily flights to and from Rhodes (10,600 dr including tax), and at other times there are three a week. You can buy tickets from Dizi Tours & Travel in Kastellorizo town.

Ferry The F/B *Nissos Kalymnos* leaves Rhodes at 5 pm on Monday and Friday, arriving in Kastellorizo at 11 pm. At 11.15 pm it heads back for Rhodes. The F/Bs *Romilda* and *Ialysos* call in once a week, on Saturday and Sunday respectively. See the Getting There & Away section for Rhodes island for further details.

Excursion Boat to Turkey It is possible to visit Turkey from Kastellorizo on a day trip (5000 dr). Islanders get supplies from

Turkey so you may be able to get a free lift with someone. Ask around.

Getting Around
There is one bus on the island, which is used solely to transport people to and from the airport (500 dr).

KASTELLORIZO TOWN
Kastellorizo town is the only settlement. Built around a U-shaped bay, its waterfront is skirted with imposing spruced-up three-storey mansions with wooden balconies and red-tiled roofs. However, this alluring contrasts with backstreets of abandoned and derelict houses overgrown with ivy, crumbling stairways and stony pathways winding between them.

Orientation & Information
The quay is at the eastern side of the bay. The central square, Plateia Ethelonton Kastellorizou, abuts the waterfront almost halfway round the bay, next to the yachting jetty. The suburbs of Horafia and Mandraki are to the east of the bay.

The post office and police station (☎ 49 333) are on the bay's western side. There is no OTE but there are cardphones. The National Bank of Greece is represented by Taverna International, on the waterfront beyond the central square. The port police (☎ 49 333) are at the eastern tip of the bay.

Dizi Tours & Travel (☎ & fax 49 240) is the island's only travel agency. Here you can buy Olympic Airways tickets, exchange travellers' cheques and get cash advances on American Express, MasterCard and Visa card. You can also exchange travellers cheques and foreign currency at Hotel Megisti.

Things to See & Do
Knights of St John Castle This castle stands above the quay. A metal staircase leads to the top from where there are splendid views of Turkey. The **museum** within the castle houses a well-displayed eclectic collection. Opening times – in theory at least – are Tuesday to Sunday from 7.30 am to 2.30 pm; entry is free. Beyond the museum, steps

DODECANESE

lead down to a coastal pathway, from where there are more steps up the cliff to a **Lycian tomb** with a Doric façade. There are several of these along the Anatolian coast, but this is the only known one in Greece.

Walk to Moni Agiou Georgiou, Paleo-kastro & Moni Agias Triadas Take the airport road out of Kastellorizo town and turn left onto the upper road to Horafia. Take the right fork on the outskirts of Horafia and a rough, indistinct path 6m along here on the right leads to the steps up to Moni Agiou Georgiou. At the top, the path straight ahead leads to the monastery. About 15m along this path look for a bomb shell to the right, then 30m further on look for a path to the right. This is the path to Paleokastro. Several paths crisscross one another hereabouts, but the correct path is the widest, and flanked by two rows of rocks.

After seeing the monastery, return to the Paleokastro path. After 15 minutes walking, go through a gate and turn left (right descends to Moni Agias Triadas). After a few metres take the path to the right, and after another five minutes take the right fork. Continue along this path, ignoring a turn-off left. The island's highest hill, Vikla (273m), with a white military look-out post on its summit, is on the right. If you ascend here you will be welcomed by the soldiers. Perhaps a breathless tourist enthusing about the views relieves the monotony of scanning the Turkish coast through binoculars. Continuing along the path below, you will soon see Paleokastro ahead. After passing between two churches continue to a stepped path and turn left to arrive at Paleokastro – a right turn leads down to the airport road.

Paleokastro was the island's ancient acropolis. Within its Hellenistic walls are three churches, an ancient tower and a cistern with roughly hewn steps. From Paleokastro descend the stepped path to the airport road, then turn right to reach Moni Agias Triadas and Kastellorizo town.

Walk to Moni Agiou Stefanou Moni Agiou Stefanou overlooks a bay on the north coast,

about 45 minutes walk away from Kastellorizo town. Walk towards the post office, along the track parallel to the western waterfront. Then 18m before the post office take a narrow path veering left. Go through a gate and continue along the path ahead. The little white monastery is usually locked but the walk is worthwhile for the views. A path leads down to the bay.

Organised Tours
Excursion boats go to the **islet of Ro**, Agios Georgios and Strogyli islets and the spectacular **Blue cave** (Parasta), which derives the name from its brilliant-blue water caused by refracted sunlight. All of these trips cost around 5000 dr.

Places to Stay – bottom end
If you are not offered a room when you disembark, the following co-owned budget options are OK and charge around 5000 dr a double. *Rooms Kastraki* (☎ 49 324) and *Pension Barbara* (☎ 49 295) are both along the street to Horafia and Mandraki, beside the white-arched building; and *Rooms O Paradeisos* (☎ 49 074) is further around the bay, behind Plateia Australias.

The *Pension Kristallo* (☎ 49 209), behind and to the right of the central square, has cosy, clean doubles for 5000 dr with shared

---

The Woman of Ro
The islet of Ro, one of Kastellorizo's 13 satellites, has been immortalised along with its last inhabitant, Despina Achladioti, alias the Woman of Ro, who died in 1982. Despina and her shepherd husband were the only inhabitants of Ro. When her husband died, Despina remained alone on the island, staunchly hoisting the Greek flag every morning, and lowering it in the evening, in full view of the Turkish coast. The Woman of Ro has become a symbol of the Greek spirit of indomitability in the face of adversity. There are excursion boats to the islet; look for signs along the waterfront at Kastellorizo town. There is a bust of the Woman of Ro on Plateia Horafia. ■

bathroom. The owner of Lazarakis Restaurant (☎ 49 370/365/357), on Plateia Ethelonton Kastellorizou, rents very pleasant singles/doubles/triples with private bathroom for 5000/6000/7200 dr, and double/triple studios for 8000/9000 dr. Beyond here, *Sydney Rooms* (☎ 49 302), above the Sydney Restaurant, has rates of 4000/7000 dr for singles/doubles with shared bathroom. The owner, Angelo, also has some lovely double rooms with private bathroom for 10,000 dr.

Pension Castelo, behind the central square, has doubles for 7000 dr and two-bedroom family apartments for 12,000 dr.

Places to Stay – middle

The traditionally furnished *Karnayo Apartments* (☎ & fax 49 266), in a beautifully restored red-and-ochre mansion near the top of the harbour's west side, has rates of 15,000/20,000 dr for two/four people.

Further around, the island's only hotel, the B-class *Hotel Megisti* (☎ 49 272) charges 9,500/15,000/19,500 dr. It is run by Nektarios Karavelatzis, who owns Karnayo Apartments. *Krystalls Apartments* (☎ 49 363; fax 49 368), co-owned with Taverna International, has doubles/triples for 16,000/19,200 dr.

Places to Eat

Restaurant Oraia Megisti, on Plateia Ethelonton Kastellorizou, is excellent. A meal of lamb cutlets and chips, green salad and retsina here costs 2500 dr. *Restaurant Eftychia*, opposite, is also highly commendable and has similar prices. Beyond the square, *Restaurant Sydney* is popular and *Taverna International* is a decent café.

Restaurant Platania, on Plateia Horafian, is a nice unpretentious place, which appeared in the film *Mediterraneo*.

Lazarakis Restaurant and *Restaurant Mavros*, opposite the jetty, are the yachties' haunts. They excel in seafood, but are quite expensive. The *ouzeri* behind the white-arched building is a favourite haunt of locals and serves inexpensive food.

Tilos Τήλος

• *pop 279* • *postcode 850 02* • *area code* ☎ *0241*

Tilos (**Tee**-los) lies 65km west of Rhodes. With good, uncrowded beaches, two abandoned, evocative villages, a well-kept monastery at the end of a spectacularly scenic road, and its authentic Greek island image intact, Tilos, remarkably, is still little visited. It's a terrific island for walkers, with vistas of high cliffs, rocky inlets and sea, and valleys of cypress, walnut and almond trees, and bucolic meadows with well-fed cattle.

Tilos' agricultural potential is not utilised, since, rather than work the land for a pittance, young Tiliots prefer to leave for the mainland or emigrate to Australia or the USA.

There are two settlements: the port of Livadia, and Megalo Horio, 8km to the north.

History

Bones of mastodons – midget elephants that became extinct around 4600 BC – were found in a cave on the island in 1974, and Irini, one of the greatest of ancient Greece's female poets, lived on Tilos in the 4th century BC.

Elephants and poetry apart, Tilos' history followed the same catalogue of invasions and occupations as the rest of the archipelago.

Getting There & Away

Ferry Tilos is well served by ferries. Between them, the *Rodanthi*, *Romilda*, *Ialysos* and *Nissos Kalymnos* pass through at least 10 times a week. See the Getting There & Away section for Rhodes island for details of their schedules.

Hydrofoil On Wednesday a hydrofoil from Kalymnos via Kos and Nisyros arrives at Tilos at 9.40 am, then continues to Halki and Rhodes. It follows the same route back, arriving at Tilos at 8 pm and continuing to Kos. On Sunday there is a morning hydrofoil from

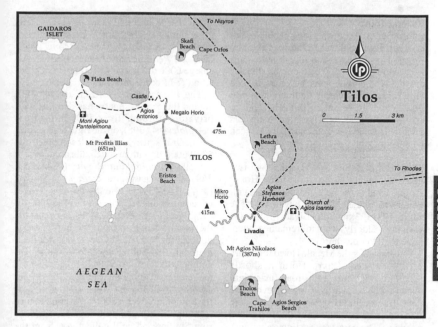

Kos via Rhodes to Tilos, returning late afternoon through Rhodes and Kos to Kalymnos. From Rhodes to Tilos costs 5500 dr.

Excursion Boat At the time of writing only one boat was licensed to do trips. The *Espiros* can take a maximum of 25 people and does a BBQ once a week on Skafi beach (5500 dr). If there are enough people, the owner does trips around the island (5000 dr), but most days he just takes people to Lethra beach.

Getting Around
Tilos' public transport is a white van, which goes from Livadia to Megalo Horio (500 dr) and Eristos beach (700 dr) on weekdays only. There are three motorcycle-rental outlets in Livadia.

LIVADIA Λιβάδια
Livadia skirts around a large bay with a long pebble beach on the island's east coast. All

the tourist facilities, as well as most of the accommodation, are here.

Orientation & Information
From the quay, turn left, ascend the steps beside Stefanakis Travel, and continue ahead to the central square. To reach the beach, walk across the square and straight ahead; a turn to the left along here leads to the three adjacent domatia on the beach. Continuing straight ahead, the road curves and turns right, passing the Church of Agios Nikolaos, to skirt the beach.

The post office and OTE are on the central square. The port police (☎ 44 322) and the regular police (☎ 44 222) share the white Italianate building at the quay. Tilos has no EOT but the staff at both Stefanakis Travel (☎ 44 310/360/384) and Tilos Travel Agency (☎ 44 259), opposite the quay, are helpful. The Friends of Tilos Association is run from Sophia's Taverna, where you can pick up a copy of FOTA News.

Walking Tours
Lethra Beach Lethra is a long pebble beach an hour's walk from Livadia. Take the Megala Horio road and in five minutes turn right onto a dirt road, which climbs steadily above Livadia Bay. This becomes a path which eventually dips as Lethra comes into view. Above the beginning of the beach take a path which veers right for 20m, then veers left down to a ravine. Turn right here to reach the beach.

Mikro Horio Before WWII, Tilos had two villages, Megala Horio and Mikro Horio. No-one lived at the port because it was vulnerable to pirates. People began to leave Mikro Horio, 3km from Livadia, after the war. One elderly woman remained there alone until her death in 1974.

Two km along the Megala Horio road, turn left (signposted 'Mikro Horio'); shortly after, turn right onto a dirt road (also signposted). The village is a lonely, evocative place. Hawks circle overhead and lizards run for cover as you wander along the overgrown pathways. There is a bar (see Entertainment), and two churches that are overlooked by a ruined tower.

Gera Gera, high above Tilos' east coast, was the summer settlement of Mikro Horio. The path begins 120m beyond Marina Beach Rooms (see Places to Stay). After a 20-minute walk the path passes the Church of Agios Ioannis, and about one hour later Gera's derelict wooden-roofed houses appear on the left.

Places to Stay
Livadia now has masses of domatia. The information kiosk at the harbour is open whenever a ferry arrives and has photographs and prices of accommodation. Freelance camping is permitted on the beaches – Plaka beach is good if you have your own transport, but there are no facilities and you will need to take your own drinking water. Eristos beach is better and has a small facilities block, but there is a charge of 500 dr per tent.

On the beach in Livadia there are three good domatia. They are *Rooms to Rent O Spiros* (☎ 44 339), *Paraskevi Rooms* (☎ 44 280) and *Pension Paradise* (☎ 44 341). All charge 6000 dr for double rooms (see Orientation & Information).

The E-class *Hotel Livadia* (☎ 44 202), behind the central square, has doubles with private bathroom for 6500 dr. *Pension Perigiali* (☎ 44 398), on the right just beyond the central square, has singles/doubles for 5000/6000 dr with private bathroom.

Both *Casa Italiana Rooms* (☎ 44 253/ 259) at the quay and *Stefanakis Studios* (☎ 44 310/439) above Stefanakis Travel have immaculate double studios for 7500 dr.

Studio Golden Beach (☎ 44 257), just off the beach road 1km from the harbour, has doubles for 7000 dr. If George doesn't meet the boat, find him at the café in the square and he will transport your luggage. Just off the main road going out of town, *Panorama Studios* (☎ 44 365) has a spectacular view of the bay. Doubles cost 8000 dr. To find it, turn right up the hill just past the Eden Café, or ring Stellios and he'll collect you from the ferry. *Manos Hagifundas Studios* (☎ 44 259), past Sophia's Taverna on the beach road, has doubles for the same price. Telephone in advance and Manos will meet the boat; alternatively, you'll find him in Taverna Blue Sky.

The well-signposted, C-class *Hotel Irini* (☎ 53 293) has tastefully furnished doubles for 12,000 dr. *Hotel Eleni* (☎ 44 062), 400m along the beach road, has double studios for the same price. *Marina Beach Rooms* (☎ 44 064) on the bay's eastern side, 1km from the quay, has immaculate but small rooms with sea-view balconies; doubles are 9000 dr.

Places to Eat
Kostas Café, next to Stefanakis Travel, is a popular drinking haunt. 'Drinks to blow your head off and drinks to make you cry over lost opportunities', said a friendly expatriate. You can also get pizzas and sandwiches. *Sophia's Taverna*, 20m along the beach road, serves delicious, low-priced food. *Restaurant Irini* nearby and *Taverna Blue Sky* at

the quay are also good. *Kafeneion Omonoias*, next to the post office, is a favourite place for breakfast. Tilos is well supplied with supermarkets.

Entertainment

La Luna at the quay and *Kafeneion Livadi* on the beach road are the local hot spots. In summer the *Mikro Horio* disco is open till 4 am.

MEGALO HORIO Μεγάλο Χωριό

Megalo Horio (population 150) is a serene whitewashed village. Crowning it is a ruined **knights' castle** which has an intact gateway, and a small chapel with frescoes. The village's main street deteriorates to a path, which passes a concrete cistern on the left then climbs steeply to the castle.

Places to Stay & Eat

Megalo Horio has three places to stay. *Pension Sevasti* (☎ 44 237), just beyond the Eristos beach turn-off, has singles/doubles for 3500/5000 dr. *Milou Rooms and Apartments* (☎ 44 204) are in the village, and *Elefantakia Studios* (☎ 44 242/213), next door, have doubles for 7000 dr. *Kali Kardia Taverna*, next to Pension Sevasti, is good value.

AROUND MEGALO HORIO

Just before Megalo Horio, a turn-off to the left leads after 2.5km to **Eristos beach** – a mixture of gritty sand and shingle, with a mobile snack bar in summer. A signposted turn-off to the right from this road leads to **Agios Antonios beach**. **Plaka beach**, 3km further west, is dotted with trees.

The 18th-century **Moni Agiou Panteleimona** is 5km beyond here along a scenic road. It is uninhabited but well-maintained, with fine 18th-century frescoes. The island's minibus driver takes groups of visitors here on Sunday. A three-day festival takes place at the monastery, beginning on 25 July.

Places to Stay

The accommodation options are *Tropicana Taverna & Rooms* (☎ 44 223) on the Eristos

road, with doubles/triples for 5000/6500 dr, and *Nausika Taverna & Rooms* to the left of Eristos beach (signposted), where rates are 4500/6500 dr.

The immaculate D-class *Hotel Australia* (☎ 44 296) overlooks Agios Antonios beach. Rates are 7000/8000 dr for doubles/triples with private bathroom.

Nisyros Νίσυρος

• pop 913 • postcode 853 03 • area code ☎ 0242
Nisyros (**Neesceros**), with lush vegetation combined with dramatic landscaping resembling the moon, is one of the strangest and most beautiful of all Greek islands. The nucleus of the island is a dormant volcano. This creates a curious anomaly whereby the island, although waterless, is fertile. The mineral-rich earth holds moisture and yields olives, vines, figs, citrus fruit and almonds.

It attracts a lot of day-trippers from Kos, but a relatively small number of overnight visitors.

The island's settlements are Mandraki, the capital; the fishing village of Pali; and the crater-top villages of Emboreios and Nikea.

The island's population has not suffered the drastic depletion of other small islands because some of its men earn a living quarrying pumice.

Getting There & Away

Ferry & Hydrofoil Between them, the ferry boats *Rodanthi, Romilda, Leros, Ialysos* and the *Nissos Kalymnos* call at Nisyros at least eight times a week. See the Getting There & Away section for Rhodes island for further details.

On Wednesday a hydrofoil from Kalymnos via Kos arrives at Nisyros at 8.50 am, continuing via Tilos and Halki to Rhodes. The same hydrofoil leaves Rhodes at 6 pm, calling at Halki and Tilos before arriving at Nisyros at 8.50 pm and continuing to Kos. On Sunday a hydrofoil from Rhodes via Kos arrives at Nisyros at 11.05 am, leaving at

DODECANESE

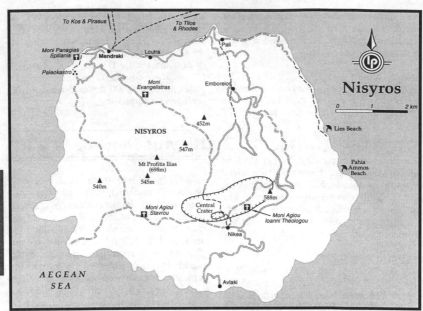

4.50 pm to return to Kos and Rhodes. From Rhodes to Nisyros costs 6500 dr.

Excursion Boat In summer there are daily excursion boats from Kardamena, Kefalos and Kos town on Kos.

Getting Around
Bus There are at least two buses every day to the volcano (1000 dr), five to Pali and two on weekdays only to Nikea and Emboreios. The bus terminal is at the quay, where a schedule is displayed outside Polyvotis Tours.

Motorcycle There are three motorcycle-rental outlets on Mandraki's main street.

Taxi There are two taxi companies: Bobby's Taxi (☎ 31 360) and Irene's Taxi (☎ 31 474). Tariffs to the following destinations are: the volcano (2500 dr), Emboreios (2500 dr), Nikea (3000 dr) and Pali (1200 dr).

Taxi Boat There are occasional taxi boats to the pumice-stone islet of Giali where there is a good sandy beach (1500 dr return).

MANDRAKI Μανδράκι
Mandraki is the attractive port and capital of Nisyros. Its two-storey houses have brightly painted wooden balconies. Some are whitewashed but many are painted in bright colours, predominantly ochre and turquoise. The web of streets huddled below the monastery and the central square are especially charming.

Orientation & Information
To reach Mandraki's centre, walk straight ahead from the quay. At the fork bear right; the left fork leads to Hotel Porfyris. Beyond here a large square adjoins the main street, which proceeds to Plateia Aristotelous Fotiadou, then continues diagonally opposite, passing the town hall. Turn left at the

T-junction for the central square of Plateia Elikiomini.

The post office, port police (☎ 31 222) and the regular police share premises opposite the quay. Both the OTE and the National Bank of Greece representative are on the right side of the main street. Nisyros has no EOT or tourist police. The staff at Enetikon Travel (☎ 31 180; fax 31 168) on the main street are particularly helpful. They also have a good library of used books.

Things to See

Mandraki's greatest tourist attraction is the cliff-top 14th-century **Moni Panagias Spilianis** (Virgin of the Cave) which is crammed with ecclesiastical paraphernalia. Opening times are 10.30 am to 3 pm daily, and admission is free. Turn right at the end of the main street, after the church turn left, and the steps up to the monastery are on the right. On the way up is the **Historical & Popular Museum**. Opening times are erratic, but there's no admission fee.

The impressive ancient acropolis of **Paleokastro** (Old Kastro), above Mandraki, has well-preserved Cyclopean walls built of massive blocks of volcanic rock. Follow the route signposted 'kastro', just beyond the monastery turn-off. This eventually becomes a path. At the road turn right and the kastro is on the left.

Koklaki is a beach of black stones. Its 'Heath Robinson' house was built by a local artist. To get there, walk along the road past hotel Nisiros, go up the steps and turn right onto a path.

Places to Stay

Mandraki has a fair amount of domatia but, unusually, owners do not meet the ferries. Just walk down the main street to find them. There is no camping ground.

If you turn left from the quay, pleasant options include *Hotel Romantzo* (☎ 31 340), with singles/doubles/triples for 4000/5000/7000 dr; and the *Three Brothers Hotel* (☎ 31 344) opposite, with rooms for 5000/6000/7300 dr. Next door, *Xenon Hotel* (☎ 31 011) has rooms for 5000/7500/8500. The C-class

Haritos Hotel (☎ 31 322/122), further along on the right, has comfortable rooms for 6000/8000/10,000 dr. Beyond here, also on the right, *Mire Mare Apartments* (☎ 31 100) has singles/doubles/triples for 6000/10,000/14,000 dr.

The C-class *Hotel Porfyris* (☎ & fax 31 376), with a swimming pool, has singles/doubles for 7000/10,000 dr (see Orientation).

Places to Eat

Both the waterfront on the way to the central square and the square itself are lined with tavernas. *Taverna Nisyros*, just off the main street, is a cheap and cheerful little place. A little further on, *Tony's Tavern* does great breakfasts for 800 dr and a superb T-bone steak for 1300 dr. Nisyros-born Tony spent 28 years living in Melbourne, Australia, before returning in 1991. *Restaurant Irini*, on the central square, is also good. A van comes daily from Pali's bakery to sell pies and bread. Be sure to try the non-alcoholic local beverage called soumada, made from almond extract.

Entertainment

At night, the *Cactus Bar*, near Hotel Porfyris, is the favourite haunt of young islanders. It plays both Greek and international music. *Bar Vavel*, on the main street, is favoured by the slightly older set.

AROUND NISYROS
Loutra Λουτρά
Loutra, 2km east of Mandraki, has a thermal spa, with two spa buildings. One is derelict, but you can wander around the crumbling interior. The other still functions. If you fancy taking a curative dip you'll need a quick health-check at the clinic (☎ 31 217) near Hotel Porfyris first. The spa's well-worn *Loutra Restaurant* is surprisingly good.

The Volcano

Nisyros is on a volcanic line which passes through the islands of Aegina, Paros, Milos, Santorini, Nisyros, Giali and Kos. The island originally culminated in a mountain of 850m, but the centre collapsed 30,000-40,000 years ago after three violent eruptions. Their legacy is the white and orange pumice stones which can still be seen on the northern, eastern and southern flanks of the island, and the large lava flow which covers the whole south-west of the island around Nikea village. The first eruption partially blew off the top of the ancestral cone, but the majority of the sinking of the central part of the island came about as a result of the removal of magma from within the reservoir underground.

Another violent eruption occurred in 1422 on the western side of the caldera depression, but this, like all others since, was hydrothermal, emitting steam, gases and mud, but no lava. The islanders' name for the volcano is Polyvotis, because the Polyvotis crater on the western side of the caldera floor was the site of the eruptions in 1873, 1874 and 1888, and it is still the most active one today.

There are five craters in Lakki. A path descends into the largest one, Stefanos, where you can examine the multicoloured fumaroles, listen to their hissing and smell their sulphurous vapours. The surface is soft and hot, making sturdy footwear essential.

If you come to the crater by bus you'll be with hordes of day-trippers, which detracts from the extraordinary sight. Also, the bus does not allow you long enough to wander around and savour a glass of soumada from the café near Stefanos. It's a good idea to walk either to or from the crater.

Walk from the Volcano to Mandraki via Moni Agiou Stavrou With your back to the café, walk straight ahead. Turn left at the crater, and half way around take the path that veers left up to a track. Turn right onto the track and continue ahead to reach Moni Agiou Stavrou in about 40 minutes. Shortly after the monastery, bear left at a fork. After about 40 minutes the track turns sharp left. In another 40 minutes you will reach a road, from where it's just a short walk to Mandraki along the path opposite.

Emboreios & Nikea Εμπορειός & Νίκαια
Emboreios and Nikea perch on the volcano's rim. From each, there are stunning views down into the caldera. Only 20 inhabitants linger on in Emboreios. You may encounter a few elderly women sitting on their doorsteps crocheting, and their husbands at the kafeneio. However, generally, the winding, stepped streets are empty, the silence broken only by the occasional braying of a donkey or the grunting of pigs. A stepped *kalderimi* (cobbled footpath), beginning on the left side of the road coming from Emboreios, leads to Pali. Halfway down you will come to the road again. Turn left and after 2km you will rejoin the kalderimi (recognisable by concrete steps).

In contrast to Emboreios, picturesque Nikea, with 50 inhabitants, buzzes with life. It has dazzling white houses with vibrant gardens and a central square with a lovely pebble mosaic. The bus terminates on Plateia Nikolaou Hartofili. Nikea's main street links the two squares.

The steep path down to the volcano begins from Plateia Nikolaou Hartofili. It takes about 40 minutes to walk it one way. Near the beginning you can detour to **Moni Agiou Ioanni Theologou**.

Places to Stay & Eat Emboreios has no accommodation for tourists and no tavernas – only one kafeneio.

Nikea's only accommodation is a *Community Hostel*, on Plateia Nikolaou Hartofili, which is managed by Panayiotis Mastromihalis (☎ 31 285), the owner of Nikea's only taverna, near Plateia Nikolaou Hartofili. Doubles cost 3000 dr.

Pali Πάλοι
The island's best beaches are at Pali, 4km east of Mandraki, and Lies, 5km further on. Pali's C-class *Hotel Hellenis* (☎ 31 453) has doubles for 7000 dr with private bathroom. Paraskevi, the owner, serves up delectable dishes in the adjoining restaurant. Her shepherd husband, the charismatic Manolis, sometimes plays the lyre in the taverna. The

Afrodite Taverna next door is also good. There are quite a few domatia.

Astypalea Αστυπάλαια

• *pop 1073* • *postcode 859 00* • *area code* ☎ *0243*
Astypalea (Asti**pal**eea), the most westerly island of the archipelago, is geographically and architecturally more akin to the Cyclades. The island's two land masses are joined by a narrow isthmus.

With its wonderfully picturesque hilltop Hora, bare, gently contoured hills, high mountains, green valleys and sheltered coves, it's surprising Astypalea does not get more foreign tourists. It is, however, popular with urban Greeks.

Getting There & Away
Air There are six flights a week from Astypalea to Athens (19,100 dr). Astypalea Tours (see Information) is the agent for Olympic Airways.

Ferry Lying between the Cyclades and the Dodecanese, Astypalea is the most easterly

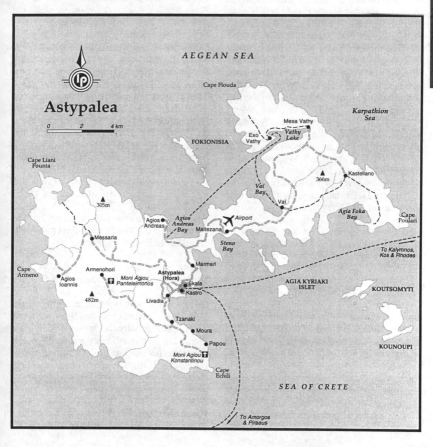

destination of some Cyclades services, and the most westerly of the Dodecanese services.

The F/B *Nissos Kalymnos* departs Rhodes at 9 am on Tuesday for Symi, Tilos, Nisyros, Kos, Kalymnos and Astypalea, returning to Kalymnos. On Thursday it leaves Kalymnos at 7 am for a round trip to Astypalea (two hours, 2250 dr each way). Contact Central Agency (☎ 29 612) on Kalymnos for the ferry's current schedule.

Ferries sail twice a week to and from Piraeus via the Cyclades islands (16 hours): one goes via Syros, Paros, Naxos, Donoussa, Katapola (Amorgos) and Aegiali (Amorgos) to Astypalea; the other sails via Paros, Naxos, Iraklia, Shinoussa, Koufonisi, Donoussa, and both ports on Amorgos.

The only ferry making a through-connection from Piraeus to the Dodecanese and Rhodes via Astypalea is the F/B *Ialysos*, leaving Piraeus at 1 pm every other Thursday and returning from Rhodes at 1 pm the following day.

Check the times of the ferries running to and from Astypalea with the port police or a travel agent as they are likely to change. See also the Getting There and Away sections in Rhodes and the Cyclades.

Paradise Travel (☎ 61 224) beneath the Paradissos Hotel and Astypalea Tours (see Information) sell ferry tickets.

Hydrofoil Between June and September there is one hydrofoil a week plying its way on a round trip from Rhodes (5 hours, 8550 dr) to Astypalea via Symi, Kos and Kalymnos.

Getting Around
Bus From Skala the bus travels several times a day to Hora and Livadia (200 dr), and from Hora and Skala to Maltezana (300 dr) via Marmari.

Excursion Boat In summer there are daily excursion boats to the island's less accessible beaches and to Agia Kyriaki islet (2000 dr). Tickets can be bought from the stalls by the boats.

ASTYPALEA TOWN
Astypalea town, the capital, consists of the port of Skala and the hilltop district of Hora, crowned by a fortress. Skala has a friendly pelican, Carlos, who blew in one windy day in 1992. He landed on his feet, it seems, for the local fishers throw him lots of tasty tit-bits.

Hora has narrow streets of dazzling-white cubic houses with brightly painted wooden balconies, doors and banisters, some of which are ornately carved. A line of windmills completes the picture.

Orientation & Information
From Skala's quay, turn right to reach the waterfront. The steep road to Hora begins beyond the white Italianate building. In Skala the waterfront road skirts around a beach and then veers right to continue along the coast to Marmari and beyond. The post office is at the top of the Skala-Hora road. The OTE has moved to a new building close to the waterfront's Hotel Paradissos. The National Bank of Greece representative is at the Aegean Hotel, a little way up the Skala-Hora road, but at last the island has its own 'real' bank complete with ATM: the Commercial Bank on the waterfront.

A municipal tourist office adjoins the quay-side café. Astypalea Tours (☎ 61 571/572, fax 61 328), below Vivamare Apartments, has a room-finding service. The police (☎ 61 207) and port police (☎ 61 208) are in the Italianate building.

Castle
During the time of the Knights of St John, Astypalea was occupied by the Venetian Quirini family who built the imposing castle. In the Middle Ages everyone lived within its walls, but gradually the settlement outgrew them. The last inhabitants left in 1948 and the stone houses are now in ruins. Above the entrance is the Church of Our Lady of the Castle and within the walls is the Church of Agios Giorgios.

Places to Stay
There is no shortage of domatia and the

owners meet the boats. *Hotel Australia* (☎ 61 338), on the waterfront where the road veers right, has well-kept doubles/triples for 6000/7200 dr, and a friendly Greek-Australian owner. Further along are *Karlos Studios* (☎ 61 330), with rates of 5500/6600 dr, and *Hotel Vengalis* (☎ 61 281/114), where rooms are 6500/7800 dr and studios are 9000/10,800 dr. *Hotel Aegeon* (☎ 61 236), on the left side of the Skala-Hora road, has singles/doubles for 4500/6000 dr. The ageing but well-maintained *Hotel Paradissos* (☎ 61 224/256) has comfortable singles/doubles/triples with private bathroom for 6000/7000/8000 dr. *Vivamare Apartments* (☎ 61 571/572), a little way up the Skala-Hora road, located on the right, has double/triple/quad studios for 11,000/13,000/17,000 dr.

Camping Astypalea (☎ 61 338) is 3km east of Skala.

Places to Eat
Restaurant Australia, below Hotel Australia, is popular. *Dimitrios Restaurant* on the Skala-Hora road and *Vicki's*, near the quay, are also commendable. Astypalea's *bakery* is opposite Dimitrios Restaurant. There is a *supermarket* on the waterfront, and another next to the post office in Hora.

LIVADIA Λιβάδια
The little resort of Livadia lies in a fertile valley 2km from Hora. Its beach is the best on the island, but also the most crowded. Quieter beaches can be found further south at **Tzanaki**, the island's unofficial nudist beach, and at Agios Konstantinos (see Walks to Moni Agiou Konstantinou & Moni Agiou Panteleimonos below).

Walks to Moni Agiou Konstantinou & Moni Agiou Panteleimonos
From the far end of the waterfront, continue along the road as it rises above the coast. After a 30-minute walk, a track turns inland to the right for Agiou Panteleimonos. This hilly walk takes about one hour. Continuing on the road straight ahead you will soon reach Moni Agiou Konstantinou and the beach of Agios Konstantinos.

Places to Stay & Eat
There's plenty of accommodation in Livadia. A sign at the end of the beach road points to *Jim Venetos Studios & Apartments* (☎ 61 490/150) which is one of the nicest places. Double studios cost 7000 dr and four-person apartments are 12,000 dr. Tavernas line the beach road.

OTHER BEACHES
Two km north-east of Skala, **Marmari** has three bays with pebble-and-sand beaches. **Maltezana** is 7km beyond here in a fertile valley on the isthmus. It's a scattered, pleasantly laid-back settlement, but its two beaches are grubby. There are some remains of Roman baths with mosaics on the settlement's outskirts.

The road from Maltezana is OK as far as **Vaï**, but it's atrocious beyond here. **Mesa Vathy** is a fishing hamlet with a beach at the end of a narrow inlet. It takes about 1½ hours to walk here from Vaï. From Mesa Vathy a footpath leads to **Exo Vathy**, another hamlet with a beach.

Places to Stay & Eat
There are plenty of accommodation options in Maltezena, but many only operate during the summer. There is a domatia at Exo Vathy, but check with Astypalea Tours in Astypalea town whether it's operating.

Getting There & Away
The bus travels between Skala and Maltezana several times a day. In summer, Gournas Tours run excursion boats to Exo Vathy. There is also a daily excursion boat from Vaï.

Symi Σύμη

• *pop 2332* • *postcode 856 00* • *area code* ☎ *0241*
Symi (**See**-mi) lies in the straits of Marmara, 24km north of Rhodes, its nearest Greek

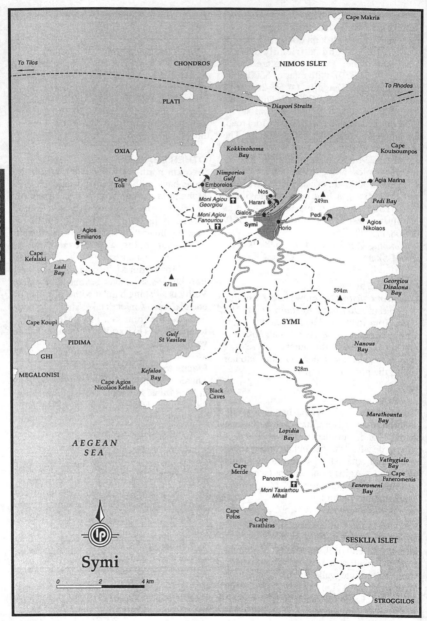

To Tilos

CHONDROS

NIMOS ISLET

Cape Makria

PLATI

Diapori Straits

To Rhodes

OXIA

Kokkinohoma Bay

Cape Koutsoumpos

Cape Toli

Nimporios Gulf
Emboreios

Nos

Agia Marina

Moni Agiou Georgiou

Harani

249m

Pedi Bay

Moni Agiou Fanouriou

Gialos

Symi

Pedi

Agios Nikolaos

Horio

Agios Emilianos

Cape Kefalaki

Ladi Bay

471m

Georgiou Disalona Bay

594m

SYMI

Cape Koupi

PIDIMA

Gulf St Vasilou

Nanous Bay

GHI

Kefalos Bay

528m

MEGALONISI

Cape Agios Nicolaos Kefalis

Black Caves

Marathounta Bay

Lopidia Bay

AEGEAN SEA

Vathygialo Bay

Cape Merde

Panormitis

Cape Faneromenis

Moni Taxiarhou Mihail

Faneromeni Bay

Cape Potos

Cape Parathiras

SESKLIA ISLET

Symi

0   2   4 km

STROGGILOS

neighbour, and only 10km from the Turkish peninsula of Dorakis. The island has a scenic interior of jagged rocks, interspersed with pine and cypress woods. It has a deeply indented coast with precipitous cliffs, and numerous small bays with pebbled beaches, which are best reached by excursion boats or on organised walks (see the Getting Around section for Symi). Symi suffers from a severe water shortage.

Symi gets an inordinate number of day-trippers from Rhodes. Most of them don't venture any further than the restaurants, bars and tourist shops on Gialos' waterfront; only a few make it as far as Nos beach.

History
Symi has a long tradition of both sponge diving and shipbuilding. During Ottoman times it was granted the right to fish for sponges in Turkish waters. In return Symi supplied the sultan with first-class boat builders and top-quality sponges.

These factors, and a lucrative shipbuilding industry, brought prosperity to the island. Gracious mansions were built and culture and education flourished. By the turn of the century the population was 22,500 and the island was launching some 500 ships a year. The Italian occupation, the introduction of the steamship and Kalymnos' rise as the Aegean's principal sponge producer put an end to Symi's prosperity.

On 8 May 1945, the treaty surrendering the Dodecanese islands to the Allies was signed on Symi.

Getting There & Away
Ferry & Hydrofoil Symi is served by the ferry boats *Romilda*, *Leros*, *Ialysos* and *Nissos Kalymnos*. Every Saturday a hydrofoil departs Rhodes at 8 am, arriving on Symi at 8.50 am before leaving for Kos, Kalymnos and Astypalea. It returns to Symi at 7.30 pm and heads back for Rhodes. See the Getting There & Away section for Rhodes island for further details.

Excursion Boat There are daily excursion boats running between Symi and Rhodes'

Mandraki harbour. The Symi-based and cooperatively owned boats *Symi I* and *Symi II* are the cheapest.

Getting Around
Bus & Taxi A 20-seater van makes frequent runs between Gialos and Pedi beach (via Horio). Check the current schedule with Symi Tours. The bus stop and taxi rank (☎ 72 666) are on the left side of the harbour.

Excursion & Taxi Boat Symi Tours (☎ 71 307) has truck (7500 dr) and boat (5000 dr including BBQ) trips to the monastery, and to Sesklia islet. Taxi boats do trips to many of the island's beaches.

SYMI TOWN
Symi town is a Greek treasure. Neoclassical mansions in a harmonious medley of colours are heaped up the steep hills which flank its U-shaped harbour. Behind their strikingly beautiful façades, however, many of the buildings are derelict. The town is divided into two parts: Gialos, the harbour, and Horio, above, crowned by the kastro (castle).

Symi town's beach is the crowded, minuscule Nos beach. Turn left at the quay's clock tower to get there. Emboreios beach, further on, is preferable (see Walk to Emboreios).

The **Symi Maritime Museum**, behind the central square, is open Tuesday to Sunday from 10 am to 2 pm. Admission is 500 dr.

Orientation
Facing inland, the quay-side skirts around the right side of the harbour. Inter-island ferries dock at the tip of the quay, and excursion boats from Rhodes dock further in. Excursion boats to Symi's beaches leave from the top of the opposite side. The central square is behind the top of the harbour's right side. The smaller Plateia tis Skalas is near the top of the left side. Kali Strata, a broad stairway, leads from here to Horio.

Information
There is no EOT, but information is available from travel agents. Nikos Sikalos at Symi Tours (☎ 71 307) is particularly helpful.

There is an additional Symi Tours office next to Dallaras Restaurant in Horio.

The post office, police (☎ 71 111) and port police (☎ 71 205) can both be found in the large white building next to the clock tower. To reach the OTE take the road by the left side of the central square and look for a sign pointing left. The National Bank of Greece is at the top of the harbour. The Ionian Bank is next to Pension Katerinettes on the waterfront.

Horio Χωριό

Horio consists of narrow, labyrinthine streets crossed by crumbling archways. As you approach the kastro, the once-grand 19th-century neoclassical mansions give way to small, modest stone dwellings of the 18th century.

At the top of Kali Strata continue straight ahead. At the top of the street turn right and follow the blue arrows to the **Museum of Symi**, which has archaeological and folklore exhibits. Opening times are Tuesday to Sunday from 10 am to 2 pm. Admission is 500 dr. If you turn right at the museum and then right again you will see the first of the arrows that point to the **castle**. The castle incorporates blocks from the ancient acropolis, and the Church of Megali Panagia is within its walls.

Organised Tours

Symi Tours (see Information) has multilingual guides leading walks around the island. Enquire about these at the Poseidon excursion boat at the top of the harbour's left side.

Places to Stay – bottom end

There is a dearth of budget accommodation on Symi, but where vacancies occur the owners meet the boats. There are, however, some eminently attractive hotels in the mid-price range.

Two basic cheapies are the *Hotel Glafkos* (☎ 71 358), to the left of the central square, with doubles/triples for 6500/7800 dr, and *Aigli Rooms* (☎ 71 454/392), just off Plateia tis Skala, with singles/doubles/triples for 4500/6500/7800 dr.

Hotel Kokona (☎ 71 549/451), opposite the large church behind the harbour, has comfortable rooms with private bathroom for 6000/8500/10,000 dr.

Pension Katerinettes is housed in the former town hall where the treaty granting the Dodecanese to the Allies was signed. Some of its rooms have magnificent painted ceilings. Doubles here cost 9500 dr. The pension is managed by Sunny Land Ltd Tourist & Travel Agency (☎ 71 320; fax 71 413) nearby. If you do have trouble finding accommodation, Sunny Land has a room-finding service.

Places to Stay – middle

In Horio, the B-class *Hotel Village* (☎ 71 800; fax 71 802) has comfortable, carpeted doubles/triples for 12,000/15,000 dr.

Hotel Nireus (☎ 72 400/403; fax 72 404) has elegant, traditional double/triple rooms for 16,000/19,300 dr and double/triple suites for 20,000/24,200 dr. Turn left at the clock tower (facing the sea) and the hotel is on the left. Further along, the A-class *Hotel Aliki* (☎ & fax 71 665) is another traditional-style hotel. Singles/doubles/triples are 10,000/14,000/18,000 dr.

The *Opera House Hotel* (☎ 72 034; fax 72 035), well signposted from the harbour, is a cluster of buildings in a peaceful garden. Spacious double/triple studios are 16,000/18,000 dr.

Places to Eat

Many of Gialos' restaurants are mediocre, catering for day-trippers. Exceptions are *Vigla Restaurant* and *Vassilis Restaurant*, both at the top of the harbour; *O Meraklis Taverna*, two blocks back; and *Taverna Neraida*, beyond Hotel Glafkos. The new *Ouzeri Demitrios*, near the bus stop, is popular with locals.

Restaurant Les Katerinettes, below the pension, has an extensive range of well-prepared dishes at reasonable prices. Several supermarkets are dotted around.

In Horio try *Dallaras Restaurant*, *Taverna Georgios* or *Taverna Panorama*, all on the left at the top of Kali Strata.

AROUND SYMI
Walk from Gialos to Emboreios

This is an easy, scenic walk along a paved Byzantine path. Walk along the road by the left side of the central square, and continue straight ahead. At the fork bear right and go uphill, passing a cemetery and a monastery on either side. When the cement road turns right, take the dirt track to its left, which soon becomes a paved path passing between stone walls. After Moni Agiou Georgiou, the path drops down to Kokkinohoma bay. Turn left to reach Emboreios, or right to return to Gialos along the coast road.

Walk from Gialos to Moni Agiou Fanouriou

Walk along the road by the left side of the central square and continue straight ahead. When the road begins to ascend, turn left for the Hotel Grace. At the fork bear right and continue uphill, passing behind the hotel. Follow this cobblestone track up the steps, and then to the left at the top. Continue to a wooden gate beyond which the path winds up to the monastery.

Pedi Πέδι

Pedi is a little fishing village and burgeoning holiday resort in a fertile valley 2km downhill from Horio. It has some sandy stretches on its narrow beach.

Places to Stay & Eat Like in Symi town, accommodation in Pedi is hard to find. You could try *Gallini Hotel* (☎ 71 385), inland from the jetty, where double apartments are 9000 dr. The large *Pedi Beach Hotel* (☎ 71 870/276) has singles/doubles/triples for a pricey 10,000/13,400/ 18,000 dr.

Taverna Kamares, on the waterfront, serves tasty Greek fare.

Moni Taxiarhou Mihail

Μονή Ταξιάρχου Μιξαήλ

The large white Moni Taxiarhou Mihail (Monastery of Michael of Panormitis) in the almost circular bay of Panormitis is Symi's principal sight, so it's the stopping-off point for many of the day-trippers from Rhodes. A monastery was first built here in the 5th or 6th century, but the present building, with an imposing bell tower, dates from the 18th century. The **katholikon** contains an intricately carved wooden iconostasis, frescoes, and an icon of St Michael which supposedly appeared miraculously where the monastery now stands. St Michael is the patron saint of Symi, and protector of sailors.

The monastery complex comprises a museum, restaurant and basic guest rooms. Beds cost 2000 dr; you cannot make a reservation, but, except in July and August, you will have no difficulty getting a bed.

Kos Κως

• *pop 26,379* • *postcode 853 00 (Psalidi 852 00)*
• *area code ☎ 0242*

Kos is the third-largest island of the Dodecanese and one of its most well-watered and fertile. It lies only 5km from the Turkish peninsula of Bodrum. It is second only to Rhodes in both its wealth of archaeological remains and its tourist development, with most of its beautiful beaches wall-to-wall with sun beds and parasols. It's a long, narrow island on a north-east–south-west axis, with a mountainous spine.

Pserimos is a small island between Kos and Kalymnos. It has a good sandy beach, but unfortunately becomes overrun with day-trippers from both of its larger neighbours.

History

Kos' fertile land attracted settlers from the earliest times. So many people lived here by Mycenaean times that it was able to send 30 ships to the Trojan War. During the 7th and 6th centuries BC, Kos flourished as an ally of the powerful Rhodian cities of Ialyssos, Kamiros and Lindos. In 477 BC, after suffering an earthquake and subjugation to the Persians, it joined the Delian League and flourished once more.

Hippocrates (460-377 BC), the father of

DODECANESE

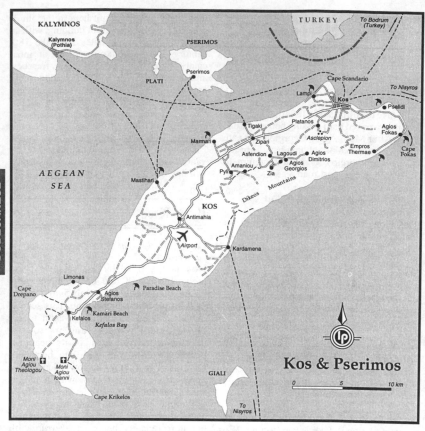

Kos & Pserimos

medicine, was born and lived on the island. After Hippocrates' death, the Sanctuary of Asclepius and a medical school were built, which perpetuated his teachings and made Kos famous throughout the Greek world.

Ptolemy II of Egypt was born on Kos, thus securing it the protection of Egypt, under which it became a prosperous trading centre. In 130 BC, Kos came under Roman domination, and in the 1st century AD it was put under the administration of Rhodes, with which it came to share the same vicissitudes, right up to the tourist deluge of the present day.

Getting There & Away

Air There are at least two flights a day to Athens (19,800 dr) and three flights a week to Rhodes (13,200 dr). The Olympic Airways office (☎ 28 330/331/332) is at Vasileos Pavlou 22, in Kos town.

Ferry – domestic Kos is one of the better served of the Dodecanese islands, with the F/Bs *Rodanthi*, *Romilda*, *Marina*, *Rodos*, *Patmos*, *Ialysos* and *Nissos Kalymnos* all calling in regularly, and offering good connections throughout the islands, including daily services to Rhodes (3300 dr) and

Piraeus (6800 dr). The F/B *Leros* offers a useful connection to Mykonos in the Cyclades, leaving every Sunday at 1 pm (11 hours). See the Getting There & Away sections for the Dodecanese and Rhodes island for further details.

Ferry – international There are daily ferries in summer from Kos town to Bodrum (ancient Halicarnassus) in Turkey. Boats leave at 8.30 am and return at 4 pm. The journey takes one hour and costs 13,000 dr return (which includes the Turkish port tax). Many travel agents around Kos town sell tickets.

Hydrofoil Kos is served by both the Dodecanese Hydrofoil Company and Samos Hydrofoils. In high season there are daily shuttles, morning and evening, to and from Rhodes, (two hours, 6670 dr), with good connections to all the major islands in the group, as well as Samos, Ikaria and Fourni in the North-Eastern Aegean. From Samos you can easily connect with the Cyclades. Information and tickets are readily available from the many travel agents.

Excursion Boat From Kos town there are many boat excursions, both around the island and to other islands. Some examples of return fares include the following: Kalymnos (3000 dr); Pserimos, Kalymnos and Plati (6000 dr); and Nisyros and Giali (5500 dr). There is also a daily excursion boat from Kardamena to Nisyros (3000 dr return) and from Mastihari to Pserimos and Kalymnos.

Getting Around
The Airport An Olympic Airways bus (1000 dr) leaves the Olympic Airways office two hours before each flight. The airport is 26km south-west of Kos town, near the village of Antimahia, and is poorly served by public transport, though buses to and from Kardamena and Kefalos do stop at the roundabout nearby. Many travellers choose to share a taxi into town (4000 dr).

Bus The bus station is just west of the Olympic Airways office. There are five buses a day

to Tigaki (270 dr); three to Mastihari (420 dr); four to Kardamena (470 dr); four to Pyli (270 dr); three to Kefalos (650 dr) via Paradise, Agios Stefanos and Kamari beaches; and two to Zia (270 dr). There are frequent local buses to the Asclepion, Lampi and Agios Fokas from Akti Kountouriotou.

Car & Motorcycle There are numerous car, motorcycle and moped-rental outlets.

Bicycle On Kos you'll be tripping over bikes to rent. The price range is between 700 dr for an old bone-shaker to 1000 dr for a top-notch mountain bike.

Excursion Boat These boats line the southern side of Akti Kountouriotou in Kos town and make trips around the island.

KOS TOWN
Kos town, on the north-east coast, is the capital of the island and the main port. The old town of Kos was destroyed by an earthquake in 1933; but the new town, although modern, is picturesque and lush, with palms, pines, oleander and hibiscus sprouting everywhere. The Castle of the Knights dominates the port, and Hellenistic and Roman ruins are strewn everywhere.

Orientation
The ferry quay is north of the castle. Excursion boats dock on Akti Kountouriotou to the south-west of the castle. To get to the central square of Plateia Eleftherias walk up Vasileos Pavlou from Akti Kountouriotou. Kos' so-called Old Town is Ifestou. Its souvenir shops, jewellers and boutiques, however, denude it of any old-world charm. South-east of the castle, the waterfront is called Akti Miaouli. It continues as Vasileos Georgiou and then G Papandreou, which leads to the beaches of Psalidi, Agios Fokas and Empros Thermae.

Information
Kos' municipal tourist office (☎ 24 460, 28 724; fax 21 111) is on Vasileos Georgiou. The staff are efficient and helpful. From May

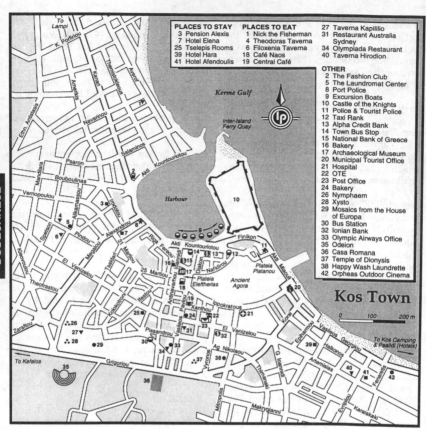

PLACES TO STAY
3 Pension Alexis
7 Hotel Elena
25 Tselepis Rooms
39 Hotel Hara
41 Hotel Afendoulis

PLACES TO EAT
1 Nick the Fisherman
4 Theodoras Taverna
6 Filoxenia Taverna
18 Café Naos
19 Central Café

27 Taverna Kapililio
31 Restaurant Australia
    Sydney
34 Olympiada Restaurant
40 Taverna Hirodion

OTHER
2 The Fashion Club
5 The Laundromat Center
8 Port Police
9 Excursion Boats
10 Castle of the Knights
11 Police & Tourist Police
12 Taxi Rank
13 Alpha Credit Bank
14 Town Bus Stop
15 National Bank of Greece
16 Bakery
17 Archaeological Museum
20 Municipal Tourist Office
21 Hospital
22 OTE
23 Post Office
24 Bakery
26 Nymphaem
28 Xysto
29 Mosaics from the House
    of Europa
30 Bus Station
32 Ionian Bank
33 Olympic Airways Office
35 Odeion
36 Casa Romana
37 Temple of Dionysis
38 Happy Wash Laundrette
42 Orpheas Outdoor Cinema

Kos Town

to October the office is open every day from 8 am to 9 pm. Both the tourist police (☎ 22 444) and regular police (☎ 22 222) are in the large yellow building opposite the quay. The port police (☎ 28 507) can be found on the corner of Akti Kountouriotou and Megalou Alexandrou.

The post office is on El Venizelou and the OTE is close by at Vyronos 6.

Both the National Bank of Greece, on Antinavarhou Ioannidi, and the Ionian Bank, on El Venizelou, have ATMs. The Alpha Credit Bank on Akti Kountouriotou has a 24-hour automatic exchange machine.

To get to the bus station walk up Vasileos Pavlou and turn right at the Olympic Airways office.

The hospital (☎ 22 300) is at Ippokratous 32.

Kos Town's laundrettes are Happy Wash at Mitropolis 20, and the Laundromat Center at Alikarnassou 124.

Archaeological Museum

The archaeological museum (☎ 28 326), on Plateia Eleftherias, has a fine 3rd-century AD mosaic in the vestibule and many statues from various periods. The most renowned is the statue of Hippocrates. The museum is open Tuesday to Sunday from 8.30 am to 3 pm. Admission is 800 dr.

Archaeological Sites

Two factors contributed to Kos having such a wealth of archaeological sites. One was the earthquake of 1933 which revealed the ruins and the other was the presence of the Italians who carried out excavations and restoration work.

The **ancient agora** is an open site south of the castle. A massive 3rd-century BC stoa, with some reconstructed columns, stands on its western side. On the north side are the ruins of a **Shrine of Aphrodite, Temple of Hercules** and a 5th-century **Christian basilica**. There is no admission charge.

North of the agora is the lovely cobblestone Plateia Platanou where you can pay your respects to the **Hippocrates Plane Tree**. Under this tree, according to the EOT brochure, Hippocrates taught his pupils. Plane trees don't usually live for more than 200 years – so much for the power of the Hippocratic oath – though in all fairness it is certainly one of Europe's oldest. This once-magnificent tree is held up with scaffolding, and looks to be in its death throes. Beneath it is an old sarcophagus which the Turks converted into a fountain. Opposite the tree is the well-preserved 18th-century **Mosque of Gazi Hassan Pasha**, its ground floor loggia now converted into souvenir shops.

From Plateia Platanou a bridge leads across Finikon (aptly called the Avenue of Palms) to the **Castle of the Knights**. Along with the castles of Rhodes city and Bodrum, this impregnable fortress was the knights' most stalwart defence against the encroaching Ottomans. The castle, which had massive outer walls and an inner keep, was built in the late 1300s. It was damaged by an earthquake in 1495 and restored by the Grand Masters d'Aubusson and d'Amboise (each a master of a 'tongue' of knights) in the 16th century. The keep was originally separated from the town by a moat, which is now Finikon. Many blocks of stone and marble from ancient buildings were used in its construction. Opening times are Tuesday to Sunday from 8.30 am to 3 pm. Admission is 800 dr.

The other ruins are mostly in the southern part of the town. Walk along Vasileos Pavlou to Grigoriou and cross over to the restored **Casa Romana**, an opulent 3rd-century Roman villa which was built on the site of a larger 1st-century Hellenistic house. It is open Tuesday to Sunday from 8.30 am to 2.54 pm. Admission is 800 dr. Opposite here are the scant ruins of the 3rd-century **Temple of Dionysos**.

Facing Grigoriou, turn right to reach the **western excavation** site. Two wooden shelters at the back of the site protect the 3rd-century mosaics of the **House of Europa**. The best preserved mosaic depicts Europa's abduction by Zeus in the guise of a bull. In front of here an exposed section of the Dekumanus Maximus (the Roman city's main thoroughfare) runs parallel to the modern road, then turns right towards the **nymphaeum**, which consisted of once lavish public latrines, and the **xysto**, a large Hellenistic gymnasium, with some restored columns. On the opposite side of Grigoriou is the restored 3rd-century **odeion**.

Places to Stay – bottom end

Camping Kos' one camping ground is *Kos Camping* (☎ 23 910/275), 3km along the eastern waterfront. It's a well-kept, shaded site with a taverna, snack bar, minimarket, kitchen and laundry. Rates are 1400 dr per person and 700 dr per tent.

Hotels Your best bet is to head straight for the convivial *Pension Alexis* (☎ 28 798, 25 594), at Irodotou 9 (the entrance is in Omirou). Clean singles/doubles/triples with shared bathroom cost 4000/6500/8000 dr. The friendly English-speaking Alexis promises never to turn anyone away, and he's a mine of information. A little further east, his other hotel, the *Hotel Afendoulis*, Evripilou 1, (☎ 25 321; fax 25 797) has spotless, tastefully furnished singles/doubles/triples with private bathroom for 6000/9000/11,000 dr. Both places are open from April through

October. Laundry for guests costs 1000 dr a load.

Other commendable budget options include the D-class *Hotel Elena* (☎ 22 740), Megalou Alexandrou 7, where doubles/triples with private bathroom are 6000/7000 dr, and *Tselepis Rooms* (☎ 28 896, 23 925), Metsovou 8, where rooms cost 7500/9000 dr with private bathroom.

At the other end of town the D-class *Hotel Hara* (☎ 22 500, 23 198), Halkonos 6, is a clean, well-maintained hotel, with singles/doubles/triples with private bathroom for 6500/8500/9800 dr.

Places to Stay – middle

The B-class *Theodorou Beach* (☎ 23 363/364), on G Papandreou (off the map), has a cool, spacious interior and nicely furnished rooms. Rates are 11,000/14,000/16,800 dr for singles/doubles/triples with private bathroom.

Places to Stay – top end

Most of Kos' top-end hotels are on the beaches to either side of Kos town. The luxurious *Kipriotis Village* (☎ 27 640) at Psalidi, 4km east of town, has singles/doubles/triples for 40,000/49,000/ 66,150 dr. Apartments for up to three people cost 50,000 dr. The A-class *Platanista Hotel* (23 749 or 25 452), also at Psalidi, is an architecturally interesting crenellated building. Singles/doubles/triples are 20,200/ 25,800/31,500 dr.

Places to Eat

The restaurants lining the central waterfront are generally expensive and poor value. *Taverna Hirodion* at Artemisias 27 serves good food and has a highly entertaining menu, featuring dishes such as Godfish (1500 dr), Humbergers (1200), Gordon Blu (1600 dr) and Jack potato (350 dr). *Taverna Kapilio*, in Diagoras Square, is very popular, with main courses starting at 1000 dr. The *Olympiada Restaurant*, behind the Olympic Airways office, and *Restaurant Australia Sydney*, on Vasileos Pavlou, are unpreten-

tious places serving reasonably priced, tasty food.

Filoxenia Taverna, on the corner of Pindou and Alikarnassou, has a good reputation for traditional home-cooked food. The pleasant *Theodoras Taverna*, on Pindou, is also popular with locals; a 'Greek Plate' is 1200 dr. For a fishy feast head for *Nick the Fisherman* on Averof.

Café Naos, housed in a former mosque opposite the market at Plateia Eleftherias, and the *Central Café*, Vasileos Pavlou 17, are popular meeting places for both locals and tourists. There are *bakeries* on Antinavarthou Ioannidi and Vasileos Pavlou.

Entertainment

Kos has two streets of bars, Diakon and Nafklirou, that positively pulsate in high season. The best disco in town is the *Fashion Club* at Kanari 2, open from 10.30 pm. Entry is 2000 dr. *Orfeus* is an outdoor cinema on Vasileos Georgiou (open summer only).

AROUND KOS TOWN
Asclepion Ασκληπιείον

The Asclepion (☎ 28 763), built on a pine-covered hill 4km south-west of Kos town, is the island's most important ancient site. From the top there is a wonderful view of Kos town and Turkey. The Asclepion consisted of a religious sanctuary to Asclepius, the god of healing, a healing centre, and a school of medicine, where the training followed the teachings of Hippocrates.

Hippocrates was the first doctor to have a rational approach to diagnosing and treating illnesses. Until 554 AD people came from far and wide to be treated here, as well as for medical training.

The ruins occupy three levels. The propylaea, the Roman-era public baths and the remains of guest rooms are on the first level. A wide staircase leads to the next level in the middle of which is a 4th-century BC **altar of Kyparissios Apollo**. West of this is the first **Temple of Asclepius**, which was built in the 4th century BC. To the east is the 1st-century BC **Temple to Apollo**; seven of its graceful columns have been re-erected. In the middle of the third level are the remains of the once magnificent 2nd-century BC **Temple of Asclepius**, the most important building of the Asclepion. The site is open from 8.30 am to 3 pm. Admission is 800 dr.

Getting There & Away Frequent buses go to the site, but it is pleasant to cycle or walk there via the village of Platanos, where many of the inhabitants are of Turkish origin. The village has a mosque, Turkish and Jewish cemeteries, and Taverna Arap serves good traditional Greek/Turkish fare.

AROUND THE ISLAND
The island's main road runs south-west from Kos town with turn-offs for the mountain villages and the resorts of Tigaki and Marmari. Between Kos town and Marmari a network of quiet roads, ideal for cycling, wind through flat, agricultural land.

Antimahia (near the airport) is a major crossroads with two large roundabouts. A worthwhile detour is to the **Castle of Antimahia** along a turn-off to the left, 1km before Antimahia. There's a ruined settlement within its well-preserved walls.

From Antimahia there are turn-offs to Mastihari and Kardamena. The trans-island road continues to Kefalos, the largest village in the south and gateway to the southern peninsula.

The nearest decent beach to Kos town is the crowded **Lampi beach**, 4km to the north. Further round the coast, **Tigaki**, 11km from Kos town, has an excellent, long, pale-sand beach. **Marmari beach**, 4km west of Tigaki, is slightly less crowded.

G Papandreou in Kos town leads to the three crowded beaches of **Psalidi**, 3km away; **Agios Fokas**, 7km; and **Empros Thermae**, 11km from Kos town. The latter has hot mineral springs which warm the sea.

Kardamena, 27km from Kos town, and 5km south of Antimahia, is an over-developed, tacky resort best avoided, unless you want to take an excursion boat to Nisyros (see the Getting There & Away section for Kos island).

Mastihari Μαστιξά
Mastihari, 30km from Kos town, retains some charm, despite recent development. It has a good sandy beach and secluded spots can be found at its extreme western end. From here there are excursion boats to Kalymnos and the small island of **Pserimos**. Buy tickets from Mastahari Travel (☎ 51 292), just inland from the *Kali Kadia* restaurant.

Orientation & Information The road from Antimahia terminates at the central square at Mastihari's waterfront. There is a mobile post office but no OTE.

Places to Stay & Eat There's loads of accommodation in Mastihari. *Fessatas Rooms to Rent* (☎ 59 005) has doubles for 5000 dr. Walk up the road by the Kali Kardia Restaurant, take the third turn to the right and the rooms are on the left. Walk inland along the main road to *Rooms to Rent Anna* (☎ 59 041), on the left, where doubles are 6000 dr. Further up on the right, *Pension Elena* (☎ 59 010) has doubles for 5500 dr. Next door, *Rooms to Let David* (☎ 59 122) has doubles for 7000 dr. The *Kali Kardia Restaurant*, on the central square, is a popular eating place.

Kamari & Kefalos Καμάρι & Κέφαλος
From Antimahia the main road continues south-west to the huge Kefalos bay, fringed by a 5km stretch of sand-and-pebble beaches which, although not isolated, are less crowded than most on Kos. The first is the lovely sandy Paradise beach reached down a track from the main road. The next, Agios Stefanos, is taken up by a vast Club Med complex. However, the beach, reached along a short turn-off from the main road, is still worth a visit to see the island of Agios Stefanos (named after its church), which is within swimming distance; and the ruins of two 5th-century basilicas to the left of the beach as you face the sea. The beach continues to Kamari.

Kefalos, 43km south of Kos town, is the sprawling village perched high above Kamari beach. It's a pleasant place with few concessions to tourism. The central square, where the bus terminates, is at the top of the 2km road from the coast.

Places to Stay Most of the accommodation options lining Kefalos bay are monopolised by tour groups, but *Petros and Maria Rooms* (☎ 71 306), is a good option. Situated on the main road 50m from the Agios Stefanos bus stop, its only downside is the 15-minute walk from the port. It has a beautiful garden and doubles/triples with private bathroom cost 5000/6000 dr. Maria also has three apartments in the port for the same price.

You could also try *Rooms Agios Stefanos* (☎ 71 423), opposite Kastri island, where doubles with private bathroom are 5500 dr, or *Studios Soula* (☎ 71 276/176), further south near the Kamari fishing quay, where double studios cost 8000 dr.

Walks from Kefalos to Moni Agiou Theologou & Moni Agiou Ioanni

The southern peninsula has the island's most wild and rugged scenery. Moni Agiou Theologou is on the east coast, 4km away, and Moni Agiou Ioanni is at the end of the road, 7km south of Kefalos.

Leave Kefalos by the road signposted to both monasteries. Presently you will come to a driveable dirt track to the right, signposted as 'Moni Agiou Theologou'. Take this track, ignore all turn-offs, and you will reach a fork in about 30 minutes. Bear right and you will soon reach the commendable Restaurant Agiou Theologou, near a sand-and-pebble beach. Continue along the track to reach the monastery.

To get to Moni Agiou Ioanni, continue along the main road. After about 45 minutes the road curves and a dirt track ahead leads to the monastery, while the road continues to the hilltop OTE dishes.

Mountain Villages

Several attractive villages are scattered on the northern slopes of the green and wooded alpine-like Dikeos mountain range. At **Zipari**, 10km from the capital, a road to the left (coming from Kos town) leads to **Asfen-**dion. From Asfendion, a turn-off to the left leads to the pristine hamlets of **Agios Georgios** and **Agios Dimitrios**. The road straight ahead leads to the village of **Zia**, which is touristy but worth a visit for the surrounding countryside and some great sunsets. But it's not just a pretty place: it has the highly commendable Taverna Olympia, 70m uphill from the central square, where a 'Greek Plate' costs 1600 dr.

Lagoudi is a small, unspoilt village to the west of Zia. From here you can continue to **Amaniou** (just before modern Pyli) where there is a left turn to the ruins of the medieval village of **Pyli**, overlooked by a ruined castle.

Kalymnos Κάλυμνος

• *pop 18,200* • *postcode 852 00* • *area code ☎ 0243*
Kalymnos (**Ka**limnos), only 2.5km south of Leros, is a mountainous, arid island, speckled with fertile valleys. Kalymnos is renowned as the 'sponge-fishing island', but with the demise of this industry it has begun to exploit its tourist potential. However, out of high season its coast is still relatively uncrowded.

Kalymnos hit the Greek headlines in 1995 when local fisherman Antonis Hatziantoniou looked into his net on New Year's Eve and saw a beautiful 2m-high bronze statue of a woman. No, he hadn't been overindulging in New Year celebrations. Archaeologists think his priceless 'catch' may be the work of the renowned 4th-century-BC sculptor Praxiteles. The statue is presently in Athens for evaluation. Theoretically a museum is to be built on Kalymnos to house it; needless to say it hasn't happened yet, but at least Antonis was suitably rewarded.

Getting There & Away

Air At the time of writing, Kalymnos' airport was due to open at the end of 1997, as it was in 1996 and 1995. The EOT will tell you if flights are operating, but don't hold your breath.

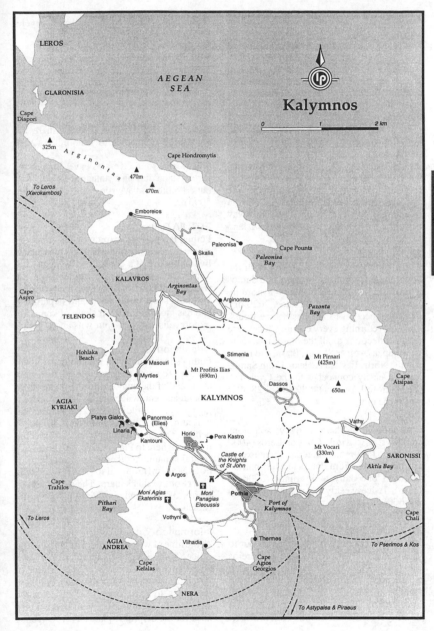

DODECANESE

Kalymnos

Ferry The F/B *Nissos Kalymnos* is based on Kalymnos and runs an important service connecting most of the major islands in the chain, as well as the more outlying islands such as Astypalea and Kastellorizo, and Samos in the North-Eastern Aegean. It operates five different daytime routes seven days a week, setting out each morning from either Kalymnos or Rhodes.

The F/Bs *Rodanthi*, *Romilda*, *Marina*, *Rodos*, and *Ialysos* all call regularly and offer good connections throughout the islands, including daily services to Rhodes (4060 dr) and Piraeus (6200 dr). The F/B *Leros* offers a useful connection to Mykonos in the Cyclades, leaving every Sunday at 2.15 pm (9¾ hours). See the Getting There & Away sections for Dodecanese and Rhodes island for further details.

Hydrofoil Kalymnos is served by both the Dodecanese Hydrofoil Company and Samos Hydrofoils. In high season there is a morning service daily to Kos (35 minutes, 2620 dr), with a connection to Rhodes, (three hours, 8055 dr), returning every evening. There are good connections to all the major islands in the group, as well as Samos, Ikaria and Fourni in the North-Eastern Aegean. From Samos you can easily connect with the Cyclades. The Hydrofoil Agency (☎ 29 886 or 28 502) is near the quay.

Excursion Boat There are daily excursions from Myrties to Xirokambos on Leros (4000 dr return). In summer there are three excursion boats a day from Pothia to Mastihari on Kos, and one daily to Pserimos (3000 dr return). Twice-weekly excursions to Turkey cost 6000 dr.

Getting Around
Bus In summer there is a bus on the hour to Masouri (250 dr) via Myrties; to Emboreios (300 dr) on Monday, Wednesday and Friday at 9 am and 3.15 pm; to Vathy (300 dr) from Monday to Saturday at 6.30 am, 1.30 and 5 pm, and on Sunday at 7.30 am, 1.30 and 5 pm. Buy tickets from *Themis Mini Market.*

Motorcycle There are several motorcycle-hire outlets along Pothia's waterfront.

Taxi Shared taxis are an unusual feature of Kalymnos that cost around twice as much as buses. A tariff is displayed at the taxi rank on Plateia Kyprou. These taxis can also be flagged down en route.

Excursion Boat From Myrties there are daily excursion boats to Emboreios (2000 dr).

Day trips to the Kefalas cave, impressive for its stalactites and stalagmites, run from both Pothia and Myrties and cost around 5000 dr.

POTHIA Πόθια
Pothia, the port and capital of Kalymnos, is where the majority of the island's inhabitants live. Although it's considerably bigger and noisier than most island capitals, it's not without charm. However, a word of warning! Pothia is short in the pavement department and has more than its fair share of kamikaze motorcyclists – keep your wits about you.

Orientation
Pothia's ferry quay is at the southern side of the bay. To reach the town centre, turn right at the end of the quay. Follow the waterfront around and you will come to the two matching municipal buildings flanking the nautical museum. The Cathedral of Agios Hristos is behind. The main thoroughfare of Venizelou runs from here to Plateia Kyprou, the town's central square. Another busy street, Patriarhou Maximimou, also runs from the waterfront to this square. The settlement of Horio, 3km inland, is the island's former capital.

Information
At the time of writing, the tourist information office (☎ 23 140, open summer only) was housed in a small kiosk behind the statue of Poseidon, 200m north of the quay, but there are 'plans' to build a new EOT office on the quay itself. Out of season, your best bet is to head for the helpful Aquanet Travel Agency

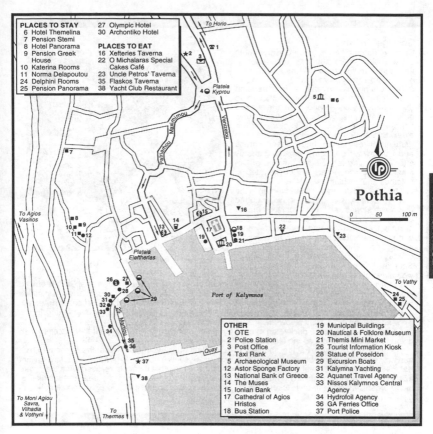

PLACES TO STAY
6 Hotel Themelina
7 Pension Stemi
8 Hotel Panorama
9 Pension Greek
   House
10 Katerina Rooms
11 Norma Delapoutou
24 Delphini Rooms
25 Pension Panorama
27 Olympic Hotel
30 Archontiko Hotel

PLACES TO EAT
16 Xefteries Taverna
22 O Michalaras Special
   Cakes Café
23 Uncle Petros' Taverna
35 Flaskos Taverna
38 Yacht Club Restaurant

To Horio
To Agios Vasilios
Plateia Kyprou
Pothia
Plateia Eleftherias
To Agios Vasilios
Port of Kalymnos
To Vathy
0   50   100 m
To Moni Agiou Savra, Vlihadia & Vothyni
To Thermes
Quay

DODECANESE

OTHER
1 OTE
2 Police Station
3 Post Office
4 Taxi Rank
5 Archaeological Museum
12 Astor Sponge Factory
13 National Bank of Greece
14 The Muses
15 Ionian Bank
17 Cathedral of Agios
   Hristos
18 Bus Station
19 Municipal Buildings
20 Nautical & Folklore Museum
21 Themis Mini Market
26 Tourist Information Kiosk
28 Statue of Poseidon
29 Excursion Boats
31 Kalymna Yachting
32 Aquanet Travel Agency
33 Nissos Kalymnos Central
   Agency
34 Hydrofoil Agency
36 GA Ferries Office
37 Port Police

(☎ 22 036, fax 28 329), 50m north of the quay.

Plateia Kyprou, the main square, is 250m north of the quay. The post office, the OTE and police are just north of the square.

The National Bank of Greece is at the bottom of Patriarhou Maximimou, and the Ionian Bank is 100m further east along the front. Both have ATMs.

The police (☎ 22 100) are north of Plateia Kyprou and the port police (☎ 29 304) are at the beginning of the quay.

The bus station is just south of the cathedral.

Archaeological Museum

The archaeological museum (☎ 23 113), east of Plateia Kyprou, is housed in a neoclassical mansion which once belonged to a wealthy sponge merchant, Mr Vouvalis. In one room there are some Neolithic and Bronze Age objects. Other rooms are reconstructed as they were when the Vouvalis family lived here. The museum is open Tuesday to Sunday from 10 am to 2 pm. Admission is free.

The **Nautical & Folklore Museum** is in the centre of the harbour, flanked by the two municipal buildings. It is open daily from 8 am to 2 pm. Entry is 500 dr.

Sponge Fishing

Sponge fishing has occupied Kalymniots since ancient times and was, until recently, their major industry. As well as the obvious one, sponges have had many uses throughout history – everything from padding in armour to tampons. For hundreds of years the sponges were fished from the waters around Kalymnos, but as the industry grew, fishermen were forced to venture further away. By the 19th century, divers sailed such great distances that they had to spend months at a time away from home, departing shortly after Easter and returning at the end of October. These two events were celebrated in religious and secular festivals.

Until the first diving suit was invented in the late 19th century, sponge divers were weighed down with stones and had to hold their breath under water. The early diving suits were made of rubber and canvas and were worn with a huge bronze helmet joined to an air pump by a long hose. This contraption enabled divers to stay under the water for much longer. Sponge diving was perilous work and those who didn't die young were often paralysed by the bends.

For many years fishing fleets dived for sponges off the Libyan coast, but Moamar al Gadaffi proved an unwelcoming host, exacting an exorbitant tax from the divers. Nowadays, the few remaining sponge-gatherers wear oxygen tanks and work much closer to home, in the north-eastern Aegean and around Crete. The demise of the sponge industry has been caused by overfishing in the Aegean and the availability of low-priced synthetic sponges.

Greeks are not ones to decline an excuse for feasting and celebration, even if the reasons for so doing have disappeared, so the festivals have been preserved.

At the Astor Sponge Factory, behind Plateia Eleftherias, you can watch the process which transforms a disgusting black object into a nice pale-yellow sponge. It goes without saying that Kalymnos is one of the best places in Greece to buy sponges, but if people realised what they were actually buying they might think again. The black objects retrieved from the sea are colonies of micro-organisms living in their fibrous waste products, which are then boiled alive and bleached in acid. Anyone for a bath? ■

Activities

Scuba Diving For information on the Kalymnos Diving Centre contact Aquanet (see Information). A one-day course to certificate standard costs 11,000 dr.

Yachting You can hire yachts from Kalymna Yachting (☎ 24 083/4, fax 29 125), 50m north from the quay.

Places to Stay

Domatia owners meet the ferries. Two pleasant budget choices are the *Pension Greek House* (☎ 29 559 or 23 752), where cosy wood-panelled singles/doubles/triples with private bathroom and kitchen facilities cost 5000/6000/7200 dr, and directly up the hill behind it, *Katerina Rooms* (☎ 22 186), where doubles/triples with shared bathroom cost 4000/5000 dr. Next door, the C-class *Hotel Panorama* (☎ 23 138) has doubles/triples for 9000/11,000 dr. From the port area, go up Patriarhou Maximimou and take the first turn left. Where the road ends at a T-junction, turn right and then left. At the Astor Sponge Factory turn right and you'll see the Pension Greek House on the left.

Norma Delapoutou rents well-kept

domatia (☎ 24 054 or 48 145) in her house behind the Astor Sponge Factory, which is owned by her brother. Doubles with shared bathroom, kitchen and verandah are 5000 dr.

Pension Stemi (☎ 28 361) has clean, modern rooms with balconies. Doubles/ triples with shared bathroom cost 6000/7000 dr. Turn right at the aforementioned T-junction and continue straight ahead to a large square (used as a car park) on the left. Walk across here, ascend the steps, and the pension is at the top on the left.

Two pleasant neighbouring options 400m along the road to Vathy are *Delphini Rooms* (☎ 29 087), where doubles are 5000 dr, and the *Pension Panorama* (☎ 29 249), where rooms cost 4000/5500/7000 dr.

Back in town, the more up-market *Olympic Hotel* (☎ 28 801/2/3), just north of the quay, has rooms for 7,000,11,000/13,000 dr.

The *Hotel Themelina* (☎ 22 682), by the well-signposted archaeological museum, is a 19th-century mansion with swimming pool. The spacious, traditionally furnished singles/doubles/triples cost 5000/9,000/ 12,000 dr with private bathroom. In summer the mansion is booked by tour operators, but there are 30 modern rooms around the pool for the same price.

The *Archontiko Hotel* (☎ & fax 24 149), at the top of the quay, is a new hotel in a renovated turn-of-the-century mansion. The immaculate rooms go for a reasonable 5000/7000/9000 dr.

Places to Eat

The *Xefteries Taverna*, just off Venizelou, is almost a century old and serves delicious, inexpensive food; ask for a menu and you'll be taken into the domestic kitchen to choose from the pots. Of the fish tavernas on the western waterfront, *Uncle Petros' Taverna* is the one favoured by locals. The well-worn, cavernous *Yacht Club Restaurant*, behind the port police, serves inexpensive fare. *Flaskos Taverna*, near the quay, is a good place for a quick meal if you're waiting for a ferry.

O Michalaras Special Cakes Café serves galaktoboureko, a speciality of Kalymnos. A generous slice of this gooey confection is 450 dr. The *Themis Mini Market* is well stocked.

The Muses, an impressive bar housed in a neoclassical building, was established as a reading room during the Ottoman Empire by islanders striving to preserve their culture.

AROUND POTHIA
Castle of the Knights of St John & Pera Kastro

The ruined Castle of the Knights of St John (or Castle Hrysoherias) looms to the left of the Pothia-Horio road. The following walking route avoids Pothia's heavy traffic. Follow the directions to Pension Stemi (see Places to Stay). At the pension, turn right. Soon the road turns right, then left, and then left again. Then it ascends. Beyond the cream, red-domed church on the left, follow the road as it turns right, then take the first turn left, and you will see three windmills ahead. Continue ahead then take the road signposted 'Vothyni and Vlihadia'. Bear right at the fork to reach the steps up to the castle.

You can take a short cut to the main Pothia-Horio road, from where you can walk to Pera Kastro. Descend the steps at the opposite side of the castle from where you entered. Clamber down the hillside, with the windmills on your right, and descend the steps to the main road. Turn left and in about 30 minutes you will come to a roundabout in Horio. Turn right here, at the fork bear left, then immediately bear right at three forks and take the first turning left. Continue straight ahead, passing a kafeneio on the left. At the top of the hill a sign points to the kastro. Follow this for 15m then take the steps on the left. It's a strenuous climb up to the kastro, but the splendid views make it worthwhile. Pera Kastro was a 'pirate-proof' village inhabited until the 18th century. Within the crumbling walls are the ruins of stone houses and six tiny well-kept white churches.

Moni Agiou Savva, Vlihadia & Vothyni

Moni Agiou Savra stands above Pothia, on the left as you face inland. A large cement cross stands nearby. Climb up the stepped streets on the left side of the harbour, then take the road signposted 'Vothyni and Vlihadia'. After 700m, a turn-off to the right leads to the monastery. You can enter the monastery but a strict dress code is enforced, so wear long sleeves and long trousers or skirts.

The main road continues to the inland village of Vothyni and the sleepy coastal hamlet of Vlihadia, which has two nice, tree-shaded beaches.

Panormos Πανόρμος
A tree-lined road continues from Horio to Panormos (also called Elies), a pretty village 5km from Pothia. Its pre-war name of Elies (olives), derived from its abundant olive groves which were destroyed in WWII. An enterprising post-war mayor planted abundant trees and flowers to create beautiful panoramas wherever one looked – hence its present name. The beaches of Kantouni, Linaria and Platys Gialos are all within walking distance.

Places to Stay & Eat *Pension Grazella* (☎ 47 314/346) has comfortable double rooms for 5000 dr, double studios for 7000 dr and five-person apartments for 14,000 dr. Popi attends the lovely garden while her husband, the dynamic English-speaking Manalos, enlightens guests on the delights of Kalymnos. The pension is signposted from the main road. The *Marinos Restaurant*, on the main road, is the best eating place hereabouts.

Just outside Panormos, on the road to Myrties, *Hotel Kamari* (☎ 47 278) has 18 rooms and a great view. Singles/doubles/triples cost 5000/6000/7000 dr.

VATHY Βαθύς
Vathy, 8km north-east of Pothia, is one of the most beautiful and peaceful parts of the island. Vathy means 'deep' in Greek and refers to the slender fjord which cuts through high cliffs into a fertile valley, where narrow roads wind between citrus orchards. There is no beach at Vathy's harbour, called Rena, but

excursion boats take tourists to quiet coves nearby.

Places to Stay & Eat
Vathy has two places to stay, both at Rena. To the left as you face the sea, the C-class *Hotel Galini* (☎ 31 241), has immaculate doubles/triples for 6500/7500 dr with private bathroom and balcony. *Pension Manolis* (☎ 31 300), above the right side of the harbour, has beautiful singles/doubles/triples for 5000/6000/7200 dr with private bathroom. There is a communal kitchen and terraces surrounded by a garden full of fruit trees and flowers. The English-speaking Menelaos is a tour guide and very knowledgeable about the area.

The *Harbour Taverna* serves excellent seafood.

MYRTIES Μυρτιές
The road continues to the west coast with stunning views of Telendos islet as it winds down into package-tourist territory beginning at Myrties. From Myrties there is a daily caïque to Xirokambos on Leros (see the Getting There & Away section for Kalymnos).

Places to Stay & Eat *Pension Mikes* (☎ 47 677/318), on the final bend before Myrties, has well-kept doubles/triples for 6500/7500 dr. The C-class *Delphini Hotel* (☎ 47 514), on the right beyond the jetty, has singles/doubles/triples with private bathroom for 5500/8000/9600 dr. The restaurant by the quay has decent food.

TELENDOS ISLET Νήσος Τέλενδος
The lovely, tranquil and traffic-free islet of Telendos (**Tel**-en-dos), with a little quay-side hamlet, was part of Kalymnos until they were separated by an earthquake in 554 AD.

If you turn right from the quay you will pass the ruins of a basilica. Further on, beyond the On the Rocks Café, there are several pebble-and-sand beaches. To reach Hohlaka beach, turn left from the quay and then right at Zorba's Restaurant.

Places to Stay & Eat

Telendos has several domatia. All have pleasant, clean rooms with private bathroom. Opposite the quay, *Pension & Restaurant Uncle George* (☎ 47 502, 23 855) has singles/doubles for 3000/5000 dr. Next door at *Pension Rita* (☎ 47 914) the rates are the same and there are also double studios for 7000 dr. *Nicky Rooms* (☎ 47 584), to the left of the quay, has doubles for 4000 dr and *Galanommatis Fotini Rooms* (☎ 47 401), to the right of the quay, has doubles for 5000 dr.

Port Potha Hotel (☎ 47 321; fax 48 108), beyond On the Rocks Café, has rates of 6000/7000/8400 dr. The *Restaurant Uncle George* serves good seafood.

Entertainment

At the trendy *On the Rocks Café* you can hear both Greek and international music. If you can't drag yourself away from the fun to catch the last caïque back to Myrties, then George, the friendly Greek-Australian owner, will take you back in his boat free of charge.

Getting There & Away

Frequent caïques leave Myrties for Telendos (500 dr return) between 8 am and 11 pm.

MYRTIES TO EMBOREIOS

Myrties blends almost imperceptibly with **Masouri**, a nondescript package-tourist resort. The road continues through spectacular scenery to the fishing villages of **Arginontas** and **Skalia**. Both have beaches, tavernas and rooms to rent.

Walk from Skalia to Paleonisa

This one-hour walk crosses the island to the remote east-coast hamlet of Paleonisa where several families live on amidst the ruins. There are tremendous sea and mountain vistas along the way. From Skalia, walk north along the coast road, and after 500m you will come to a white church on the left. Take the dirt road opposite which winds steeply uphill. At the top take the narrow path straight ahead which leads to

Paleonisa's ruined houses and abandoned terraces.

EMBOREIOS Εμπορειός

The west-coast road continues to Emboreios, where there's a very pleasant tree-shaded pebble beach, which only gets crowded in July and August. One of the nicest places to stay is *Harry's Apartments* (☎ 47 434/922) where modern double/triple apartments cost 9000/10,800 dr. Harry is a dedicated chef and his adjoining *Paradise Restaurant* has a good reputation around the island.

Leros Λέρος

• *pop 8059* • *postcode 854 00* • *area code* ☎ *0247*

An infamous psychiatric institution, shabby Mussolini-inspired public buildings, a heavy military presence and, during the junta years, a prison for political dissidents, have saddled Leros (**Le**-ros) with an almighty image problem. However, offsetting these flaws is the island's gentle, hilly countryside dotted with small holdings and huge, impressive, almost-landlocked bays, which look more like lakes than open sea.

Lakki is the main port of Leros, but smaller ferries and some excursion boats use Agia Marina port, and the caïque from Myrties on Kalymnos docks at Xirokambos. Platanos is the capital of Leros. Lakki is one of the best natural harbours in the Aegean; during their occupation of the Dodecanese the Italians chose it as their principal naval base in the eastern Mediterranean.

Getting There & Away

Air There is at least one flight a day to Athens (20,100 dr) in summer, and four a week in winter. The Olympic Airways office (☎ 22 844, 24 144) is in Platanos, just before the turn-off for Panteli. The airport is in the north of the island at Partheni.

Ferry The F/Bs *Nissos Kalymnos*, *Marina*, *Romilda*, *Rodanthi*, *Ialysos*, *Leros* and *Rodos* all call here on a frequent basis, connecting

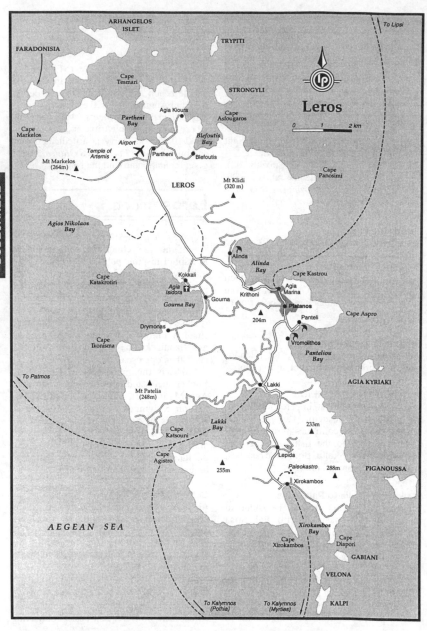

Leros with the major islands in the group: Rhodes (4420 dr), and Piraeus (5770 dr). For details of their schedules see the Getting There & Away section for the Dodecanese and Rhodes island.

Tickets can be bought at either Kastis or Leros travel agencies. The telephone number of the port police in Lakki is ☎ 22 224.

Hydrofoil In summer there are hydrofoils every day to Patmos (45 minutes, 3070 dr), Lipsi (2700 dr), Samos (6500 dr), Kos (one hour, 4050 dr) and Rhodes (3¼ hours, 9000 dr); and one a week to Agathonisi (4320 dr) via Patmos and Fourni (4600 dr). Hydrofoils leave from Agia Marina. Tickets can be bought from Kastis Travel.

Excursion Boat The caïque leaves Xirokambos every day at 7.30 am for Myrties on Kalymnos (1500 dr, one way). In summer the Lipsi-based *Anna Express* and *Captain Makis* (both 3800 dr return) make daily trips between Agia Marina and Lipsi.

Getting Around
Bus The hub for Leros' buses is Platanos. There are four buses a day to Partheni via Alinda and six buses to Xirokambos via Lakki. Check the current schedule with a travel agent.

Car, Motorcycle & Bicycle There is no shortage of outlets around the island.

Activities
Scuba Diving The Diving Club (☎ 23 502) is based in Xirokambos, in the south of the island. Seven-day diving courses cost around 80,000 dr (inclusive).

Boating You can hire motorboats, pedal boats and canoes from Alinda Seasport (☎ 24 584), on the waterfront.

LAKKI Λακκί
If you arrive on one of the large inter-island ferries, you'll disembark at Lakki. The grandiose buildings and wide tree-lined boulevards dotted around the Dodecanese

reach their apogee here, for Lakki was built as a Fascist showpiece during the Italian occupation.

Places to Stay & Eat
If you must stay here the D-class *Miramare Hotel* (☎ 22 469), signposted from the waterfront, has single/double/triple rooms for 5000/5500/6600 dr with private bathroom. *Taverna O Sotos*, next to the well-signposted post office, serves hearty Greek fare.

PLATANOS Πλάτανος
Platanos, the capital of Leros, is 3km north of Lakki. It's a picturesque little place which spills over a narrow hill pouring down to the port of Agia Marina to the north, with Panteli to the south, both within walking distance. On the east side Platanos, houses are stacked up a hillside topped by a massive castle. To reach the castle you can either climb up 370 steps, or walk or drive 2km along an asphalt road. It is usually – but not necessarily – open from 8 am to noon; entry is 200 dr. A few grand neoclassical mansions have recently been restored on Xarami.

Orientation & Information
In Platanos the focus of activity is the lively central square of Plateia N Poussou. Xarami links this square with Agia Marina. The post office and OTE share premises on the right side of Xarami. The National Bank of Greece is on the central square. There is no ATM. The police station (☎ 22 222) is in Agia Marina; turn left from Xarami and it's on the right. The bus station and taxi rank are both on the Lakki-Platanos road, just before the central square.

Leros has no EOT or tourist police. Laskarina Tours (☎ 23 550/24 550, fax 24 551), at the Elefteria Hotel, and Kastis Travel & Tourist Agency (☎ 22 140) near the quay in Agia Marina, are very helpful.

Organised Tours
Laskarina Tours organises trips around the island (3500-5500 dr).

DODECANESE

Places to Stay

The *Pension Platanos* (☎ 22 608), on the central square, has well-kept and comfortable singles/doubles/triples with private bathroom for 4000/6000/7000 dr. The western-style café underneath dominates the square; it does great coffee and toasted sandwiches. The C-class *Elefteria Hotel* (☎ 23 550/145), near the taxi rank, has lovely rooms for 5000/6000/7500 dr with private bathroom.

AROUND PLATANOS

The port of **Agia Marina** is very pretty and has a more authentic ambience than the resort of Alinda to the north. Walking in the other direction from Platanos, you'll arrive at **Panteli**, a little fishing village-cum-resort with a sand-and-shingle beach.

Just outside of Platanos, beyond the turn-off for Panteli, a road winds steeply down to **Vromolithos** where there's a good shingle beach, superior to Pendali's.

Places to Stay

Kapiniris Miltos Rooms (☎ 22 750), just beyond the police station in Agia Marina, has spacious doubles/triples for 5000/6000 dr.

In Panteli, the waterfront *Pension Roza* (☎ 22 798) has doubles/triples for 3500/5500 dr with shared bathroom and doubles with private bathroom for 4000 dr. A bit further along, *Rooms to Rent Kavos* (☎ 23 247, 25 020) has rates of 6000/6500 dr and studios for 8000 dr. The *Pension Happiness* (☎ 23 498), on the left of the road down from Platanos, has modern, sunny rooms with private bathroom for 7000/8500 dr. There are domatia in Vromolithos.

Places to Eat

There are several tavernas at Agia Marina; the best two are on the right as you hit the waterfront.

In Panteli, *Zorbas* and *Psarapoula*, next door to each other on the waterfront, are the most popular tavernas. There are two tavernas on the beach at Vromolithos.

Entertainment

Agia Marina is the heart of the island's nightlife, with three late-night music bars: *Meltemi Bar*, *La Playa Bar* and *Apocalypsos*.

In Panteli, head for *Savana Bar*, run by two English guys, Simon and Peter. It is open from mid-afternoon till late and has a great music policy: you can choose what you want.

KRITHONI & ALINDA Κριθώνι & Αλίνδα

Krithoni and Alinda are contiguous resorts on the wide Alinda bay, 3km north-west of Agia Marina. On Krithoni's waterfront there is a poignant, well-kept **war cemetery**. After the Italian surrender in WWII, Leros saw fierce fighting between German and British forces. The cemetery contains the graves of 179 British, two Canadian and two South African soldiers.

Alinda, the island's biggest resort, has a long crescent of tree-shaded sand-and-gravel beach, and fine views over to Agia Marina and Platanos. If you walk beyond the development you'll find some quiet coves.

Places to Stay

The following recommendations all have private bathrooms. Krithoni's *Hotel Costantinos* (☎ 22 337/904), on the right coming from Agia Marina, has comfortable doubles for 6000 dr. A bit further along, the new B-class *Krithoni Palace Hotel* (☎ 25 120; fax 24 680), complete with bars, restaurant and swimming pool, has singles/doubles/triples for 10,000/15,000/20,000 dr and suites for 45,000 dr. Just beyond the war cemetery, a road veers left to *Hotel Gianna* (☎ 23 153, 24 135) which has nicely furnished rooms for 3000/5000/6200 dr. The sparkling, pine-furnished *Studios & Apartments Diamantis* (☎ 22 378, 23 213), behind the cemetery, has rates of 5000/6000/7000 dr.

Papafotis Pension (☎ 22 247), in a cul-de-sac at the northern end of Alinda, has light, airy rooms for 3000/5000/7000 dr.

Places to Eat

Grilled food is the speciality of *To Fanari*, a restaurant on the left 10 minutes walk along the signposted Alinda-Partheni road. An excellent meal of grilled chicken, chips, Greek salad and retsina costs 2400 dr. Alinda's waterfront *Finikas Taverna* has an extensive menu of well-prepared Greek specialities; mezedes are 600 to 900 dr and souvlaki is 1600 dr. The *Alinda Restaurant*, at the front of the Alinda Hotel, is also highly recommended.

GOURNA Γούρνα
The wide bay of Gourna, on the west coast, has a similar beach to Alinda, but it is less developed. To get there, take the Alinda-Partheni road and then the first turn-off left. At the northern side of the bay, the chapel of **Agia Isidora** is on an islet reached by a causeway – it's a wonderfully tranquil spot, reached along the third turn-off left from the Alinda-Partheni road.

NORTHERN LEROS
Partheni is a scattered settlement north of the airport. Despite having a large army camp, it's an attractive area of hills, olive groves, fields of bee hives and two large bays.

Artemis, the goddess of the hunt, was worshipped on Leros in ancient times. Just before the airport there's a signposted turn to the left that leads to the **Temple of Artemis**. A dirt track turns right 300m along it. Where the track peters out, clamber up to the left. You will see the little derelict Chapel of Agia Irini where locals still tend the altar. There's little in the way of ancient ruins but it's a strangely evocative, slightly eerie place.

Further along the main road there is a turn to the right to **Blefoutis bay** which has a shaded sand-and-pebble beach and the popular *Taverna Artemi*. Beyond this turn-off, the main road skirts around **Partheni bay** and its poor beach. However, if you continue straight ahead and turn right at the T-junction, go through a gate to pass the chapel of Agia Kioura, then go through another gate and bear right, you will come to a secluded pebbled cove.

XIROKAMBOS Ξερόκαμπος
Xirokambos bay, in the south of the island, is a low-key resort with a gravel-and-sand beach and some good spots for snorkelling. Just before the camping ground, on the opposite side, a signposted path leads up to the ruined fortress of **Paleokastro**.

Places to Stay & Eat
Leros' one camping ground is Xirokambos' *Camping Leros* (☎ 23 372), on the right coming from Lakki. It's pleasant and shaded, with a restaurant and bar.

Further along on the left is *Michael Yianoukas Rooms* (☎ 23 148), which has doubles with shared bathroom for 3500 dr and double/triple apartments for 5000/7500 dr. For eating, there is a taverna opposite the camping ground, a nameless psistaria further along the road and a taverna on the beach.

Patmos Πάτμος

• *pop 2663* • *postcode 855 00* • *area code* ☎ *0247*
Patmos (**Pat**-mos) is a place of pilgrimage for both Orthodox and western Christians, for it was here that St John wrote his divinely inspired revelation (the Apocalypse). Once a favourite venue for the pious and hippies wishing to tune into its spiritual vibes, Patmos is now just as popular with sun and sea worshippers. The only remaining vestiges of the island's former isolation are the many signs (often ignored) that forbid topless and nude bathing. If it's contemplation or tranquillity you're after, then stay on the ferry until it gets to Lipsi or Agathonisi, or take the caïque to Arki.

History
In AD 95, St John the Divine was banished to Patmos from Ephesus by the pagan Roman Emperor Dominian. While residing in a cave on the island, St John wrote the *Book of Revelations*. In 1088 the Blessed Christodoulos, an abbot who came from Asia Minor to Patmos, obtained permission from the Byzantine Emperor Alexis I Comnenus to build a monastery to commemorate St John. Pirate raids necessitated powerful

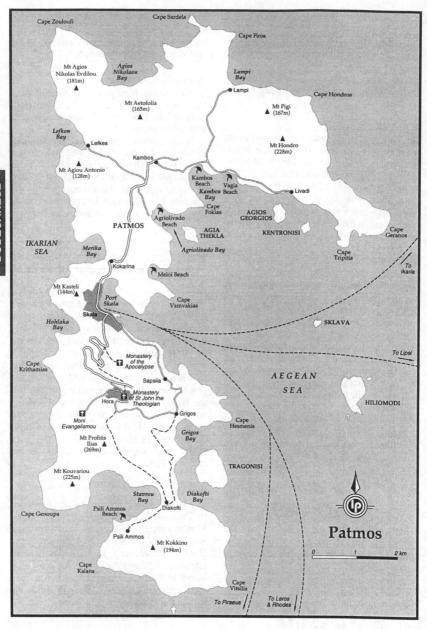

Patmos

fortifications, so the monastery looks like a mighty castle.

Under the Duke of Naxos, Patmos became a semiautonomous monastic state, and achieved such wealth and influence that it was able to stand indomitable against Turkish oppression. In the early 18th century, a school of theology and philosophy was founded by Makarios Kalogheras and it flourished until the 19th century. Gradually the island's wealth polarised into secular and monastic entities. The secular wealth was acquired through shipbuilding, an industry which diminished with the arrival of the steam ship.

Getting There & Away

Ferry Patmos has good ferry connections, with the F/Bs *Nissos Kalimnos*, *Marina*, *Rodanthi*, *Romilda*, *Ialysos*, *Leros* and *Rodos* all calling regularly. There are daily services to and from Rhodes (5250 dr) via Leros, Kalymnos, and Kos, and to and from Piraeus (6100 dr). See the Getting There & Away sections for the Dodecanese and Rhodes island for details.

Hydrofoil There are daily hydrofoils to Rhodes (10,280 dr), via Kalymnos (4620 dr) and Kos (5560 dr), and to Fourni, Ikaria and Samos in the North-Eastern Aegean. Every Saturday, a hydrofoil sails to and from Agathonisi.

Excursion Boat In summer the Lipsi-based *Anna Express* and *Captain Makis* (both 3800 dr return) sail to Patmos every day (see also the Getting There & Away section for Lipsi island). Daily Patmos-based excursion boats go to Marathi, and the caïque *Delfini* does frequent trips to Arki. If you can't see the *Delfini* at Skala's quay, call ☎ 31 995/371 for information.

Getting Around

Bus From Skala there are seven buses a day to Hora (190 dr), five to Grikos (200 dr) and four to Kambos (190 dr). There is no bus service to Lampi.

Motorcycle Theo & Giorgio Motorcycles for Rent (☎ 32 997), opposite the excursion boats, is a reliable outlet. Motorcycles are 2000 to 3500 dr a day and 18-speed mountain bikes are 1200 dr.

Taxi From Skala's taxi rank, tariffs are: Meloi 800 dr, Lampi 1500 dr, Grigos 1200 dr and Hora 1000 dr.

Excursion Boat These go to all the island's beaches from Skala, leaving about 11 am and returning about 4 pm.

SKALA Σκάλα

All boats dock at the island's port and capital of Skala. The town sprawls around a large curving bay. It's quite a glitzy place, pandering to the passengers of the many visiting cruise ships. Although it's very busy and not especially attractive, it's a convenient place to stay as it's the public-transport hub and has all the tourist facilities and plenty of accommodation.

Orientation

Facing inland from the quay, turn right to reach the main stretch of waterfront where excursion boats and yachts dock. The right side of the large, white Italianate building opposite the quay overlooks the central square. To reach the road to Hora, turn left at the quay and right at Taverna Grigoris.

Information

Patmos' municipal tourist office (☎ 31 666/235/058, open summer only), post office and police station are all in the large, white Italianate building. The tourist office entrance is at the back of the building, the post office is at the right side, and the police are at the front. Patmos' port police (☎ 31 231) are behind the large quay's cafeteria/passenger-transit building. The bus terminal is at the large quay and the taxi rank (☎ 31 225) is opposite the post office.

Astoria Travel (☎ 31 205, fax 31 975), on the waterfront near the quay, is very helpful if you need information.

The National Bank of Greece is on the

DODECANESE

central square. Its ATM is in front of the post office. Inland from the central square is another smaller square; the OTE is on the left side of the road which proceeds inland from here. The hospital (☎ 31 211) is 2km along the road to Hora.

Swan Dry Cleaners & Laundry is up the little street behind the main square. There is another laundrette just past *Pension To Akteon*.

Activities
Water Sports You can hire pedal boats and canoes and book water-skiing at *Hellen's Place* on Agriolivado Beach.

Places to Stay – bottom end
In Skala, enthusiastic domatia owners don't wait for passengers to disembark – they rush onto the ferry and almost knock over prospective customers.

If you are not scooped up by a domatia owner, there are several budget places along Hora road. *Pension Sofia's* (☎ 31 876), 250m up on the left, has doubles/triples with private bathroom and balcony for 4000/6000 dr. Further up, *Pension Maria Paskeledi* (☎ 32 152) has singles/doubles/triples with shared bathroom for 3500/6000/8000 dr.

The D-class *Hotel Rex* (☎ 31 242), on a narrow street opposite the cafeteria/passenger-transit building, has rooms for 5200/6700/7500 dr with private bathroom.

If you turn right at the quay and walk along the waterfront, *Pension Akteon* (☎ 31 187) has immaculate self-contained studios at 4000/8000/9600 dr for singles/doubles/triples. *Pension Sydney* (☎ 31 689) has rooms for 4000/7000/10,000 dr with private bathroom. The nearby *Pension Avgerinos* (☎ 32 118), run by the same family, has doubles with superb views and private bathroom for 7000 dr. Turn left 100m past the cemetery; the Sydney is on the left and the Avgerinos is opposite.

Katina Michenni Rooms (☎ 31 327) has spotless doubles/triples for 7000/8500 dr. Ornaments and rugs add a homely touch, and there are excellent views of Skala and Hora from the communal veranda. Take the left fork 30m beyond the turn-off for Pension Sydney, turn right opposite the circular traffic mirror, and the rooms are in the last house on the right.

Further along the coast road, the C-class *Hotel Hellinos* (☎ 31 275) has immaculate doubles/triples for 7000/8500 dr with private bathroom. Co-owned with the hotel are some attractive domatia for 6000/7000 dr with shared bathroom.

Yvonne Studios (☎ 32 466, 33 066) are beautifully furnished apartments overlooking Hohlaka bay. Doubles/triples are 8000/9500 dr. Enquire about them at Yvonne's Tourist Shop, near O Pantelis Taverna.

Places to Stay – middle
Hotel Chris (☎ 31 403) has singles/doubles/triples for 6000/10,000/12,000 dr. Turn right at the quay and it's on the waterfront. The C-class *Hotel Effie* (☎ 31 298) has rooms for 8000/11,600/14,500 dr. Turn left after Hotel Chris and it's 120m up on the right.

The C-class *Hotel Delfina* (☎ 32 060; fax 32 061), to the left of the quay, has immaculate rooms for 8000/11,000/12,300 dr. Next door, the *Captain's House* (☎ 31 793) has rates of 7000/14,000/15,000 dr. Around the corner, *Hotel Byzance* (☎ 31 052/663) charges 8100/12,300/15,300 dr. Triple apartments are 17,000 dr and four-person apartments are 20,400 dr.

Skala's best hotel is the B-class *Hotel Skala* (☎ 31 343, fax 31 747), on the waterfront. Rates are 12,500/18,000/22,350 dr, including breakfast, and there's a swimming pool. (For Patmos' most luxurious hotel see the Kambos section.)

Places to Eat – inexpensive
For excellent seafood at reasonable prices, try *Hiliomodi Ouzeri*, 50m up the Hora road on the left. *Grigoris Taverna*, on the corner of the Hora road, and *O Pantelis Taverna*, behind the waterfront Café Bar Arion, are also popular.

Polar Galateria, just inland from the square, is good for sweet and savoury pies and pastries as well as ice cream. There are two excellent *bakeries* on the square; both sell cakes, cookies and pies, as well as bread. Two well-signposted *fruit and vegetable markets* are close by.

Places to Eat – moderate
The Old Harbour, on a 1st-floor terrace just past Hotel Chris, is Skala's best restaurant. Chateaubriand for two costs 5,600 dr.

Entertainment
The waterfront *Café Bar Arion* is a popular haunt of trendy young locals. For nightlife, try *Music Club 2000*, just past Argo petrol station on the other side of the bay. You can dance until 5 am and it has an outdoor swimming pool. Another hot spot is *Consolatos Dancing Bar*, to the left of the quay. Entrance is 1000 dr (first drink free).

MONASTERIES & HORA
The immense Monastery of St John the Theologian, with its buttressed grey walls, crowns the island of Patmos. A 4km asphalt road leads in from Skala to the monastery, but many people prefer to walk up the Byzantine path. To do this, walk up the Skala-Hora road and take the steps to the right at the far side of the football field. The path begins opposite the top of these steps.

A little way along, a dirt path to the left leads through pine trees to the **Monastery of the Apocalypse**, built around the cave where St John received his divine revelation. In the cave you can see the rock which the saint used as a pillow, and the triple fissure in the roof, from which the voice of God issued, and which supposedly symbolises the Holy Trinity. Opening times are 8.00 am to 1.00 pm daily, and from 4 to 6 pm on Tuesday, Thursday and Sunday.

To rejoin the Byzantine path, walk across the monastery's car park and bear left onto the (uphill) asphalt road. After 60m, turn sharp left onto an asphalt road, and almost immediately the path veers off to the right. Soon you will reach the main road again. Cross straight over and continue ahead to reach Hora and the **Monastery of St John the Theologian**. The finest frescoes of the monastery are those in the outer narthex, which depict significant events in St John's life. The priceless contents in the monastery's treasury include icons, ecclesiastical ornaments, embroideries and pendants made of precious stones. Opening times are the same as for the Monastery of the Apocalypse. Admission to the treasury is 1000 dr.

Huddled around the monastery are the immaculate whitewashed houses of **Hora**, many with handsome wooden doors. The houses are a legacy of the island's great wealth of the 17th and 18th centuries. Some of them have been bought and renovated by wealthy Greeks and foreigners.

Places to Eat – inexpensive
Vagelis Taverna, on the central square, with a garden at the back, is deservedly popular.

Places to Eat – moderate
The elegant *Patmian House* (☎ 31 180), in a restored mansion, is the island's undisputed restaurant par excellence. There's a large choice of superb mezedes: the little spinach and cheese pies are especially good. The fillet steak is also commendable. Expect to pay between 5000 and 7000 dr for a three-course meal with wine. Reservations are recommended.

NORTH OF SKALA
The pleasant, tree-shaded **Meloi beach** is just 2km north-east of Skala, along a turn-off from the main road.

Two km further along the main road there's a turn-off right to the sandy and relatively quiet **Agriolivado beach**. The main road continues to the inland village of **Kambos** and then descends to the shingle beach from where you can walk to the secluded **Vagia beach**. The main road ends at **Lampi**, 9km from Skala, where there is a beautiful beach of multicoloured stones.

Places to Stay – bottom end
Next to the well-signposted Taverna Meloi there is a basic *domatia* (☎ 31 213) where doubles are 4000 dr with shared bathroom. The owners do not speak English so

DODECANESE

telephone Taverna Meloi (☎ 31 888) to enquire about them.

At Kambos, the owners of George's Place Snack Bar (see Places to Eat) work as an unofficial room-letting agency, so if you pop in they will put you in touch with a local domatia owner. At Lampi, *Delfini Rooms* (☎ 31 951), at Delfini Taverna, has doubles with private bathroom for 6000 dr.

Stefanos Camping (☎ 31 821), at Meloi, is a good camping ground, with bamboo-shaded sites, minimarket, café bar and motorcycle-rental facilities. The rates are 1200 dr for an adult (tent included). Buses don't go to Meloi; a taxi from Skala will cost 700 dr.

Places to Stay – top end
Patmos has two luxury hotels. *Porto Scoutari* (☎ 33 124/5, fax 33 175), overlooking Meloi Bay, has doubles/triple studios for 26,000/30,000 dr. In Kambos, *Patmos Paradise* (☎ 32 624) has a restaurant, tennis courts, sauna and swimming pool. Rates for singles/doubles/triples are 19,000/24,000/47,000 dr.

Places to Eat
The excellent *Taverna Meloi* has a large menu of traditional Greek dishes and is open all day. *George's Place Snack Bar*, on Kambos beach, is a good place to hang out. *Ta Kavurakia* is commendable for Greek fare. Of the two restaurants on Lampi beach, *Leonidas* has the edge. It specialises in fish dishes but the saganaki is also very good.

SOUTH OF SKALA
Grikos, 4km south-east of Skala, is a rather lifeless resort with a sandy beach. Further south, the long, sandy, tree-shaded **Psili Ammos** is the island's best, and the unofficial nudist beach. The easiest way to get there is by excursion boat.

Most of the accommodation in Grikos is monopolised by tour groups. Try the *Restaurant O Stamatis and Rooms* (☎ 31 302), by the beach, which has comfortable doubles with private bathroom for 8000 dr. Psili

Ammos has a seasonal taverna, but no accommodation.

Lipsi Λειψοί

• pop 606 • postcode 850 01 • area code ☎ 0247

Lipsi (Li-**psee**), 12km east of Patmos and 11km north of Leros, is an idyllic little island. The cheery inhabitants busy themselves with fishing, agriculture, animal husbandry and keeping happy the relatively small number of tourists who venture here. The picturesque port town of Lipsi is the only settlement. Around the coast are good beaches. Lipsi produces good cheeses and a potent wine known as Lipsi Black (see Kohlakoura in Walks to the Beaches from Lipsi Town).

Getting There & Away
Ferry The F/B *Leros* calls in at Lipsi on Monday nights on its way through the Dodecanese to Rhodes, stopping at all the main islands. On Tuesday evening it stops at Lipsi on its journey back to Piraeus. The F/B *Romilda* calls at Lipsi twice a week on a route that connects most of the Dodecanese islands with Naxos, Paros and Syros in the Cyclades and Piraeus on the mainland. The F/B *Nissos Kalymnos* also calls twice a week. See the Getting There & Away section for the Dodecanese and Rhodes island for details.

Hydrofoil In summer, hydrofoils call at Lipsi at least twice a day (except Monday) on their routes north and south between Samos, in the North-Eastern Aegean, and Kos. On Saturday the route includes Agathonisi.

Excursion Boat The *Captain Makis* and *Anna Express* do daily trips in summer to Agia Marina on Leros and to Skala on Patmos (both 3800 dr return). Various excursion boats do trips to Lipsi's beaches and to the uninhabited White Islands (1000 dr). *Black Beauty* and the new *Margarita* do daily excursion boat trips to Arki and Marathi (2000 dr return).

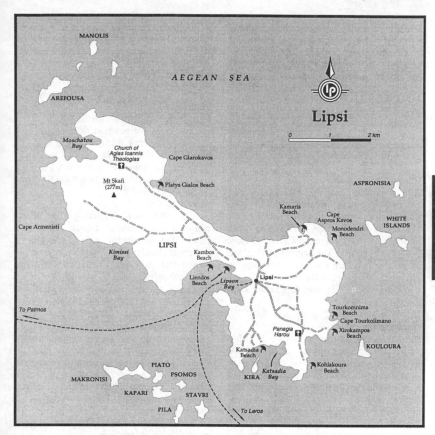

Getting Around

Motorcycle There are several motorcycle-rental outlets.

Taxi Lipsi's 'taxis' are two new minibuses. They make trips to the island's beaches for around 400 dr per person.

LIPSI TOWN
Orientation

All boats dock at Lipsi town, where there are two quays. The Lipsi-based *Anna Express* and *Captain Makis* dock at the small quay.

All other boats and ferries dock at the large quay.

From the large quay, facing inland, turn right. Continue along the waterfront to the large Plateia Nikiforias, which is just beyond the Calypso Hotel. The small quay is opposite this hotel. Ascend the wide steps at the far side of Plateia Nikiforias and bear right to reach the central square. The left fork leads to a second, smaller square.

Information

The municipal tourist office (☎ 41 288) is on the central square, but you may find Lipsi's two privately owned tourist offices more helpful. Paradise Travel (☎ 41 120, fax 41 110) is at the base of the wide steps and Lipsos Travel (☎ 41 225, fax 41 215), run by Anna Rizos, an Englishwoman, is signposted from the top of these steps. The post office and OTE are on the central square. Lipsi doesn't have a bank, but Eureka Travel changes money and cashes Eurocheques. The police (☎ 41 222) are in the large white building opposite Eureka Travel. Lipsi uses Leros' port police (☎ 22 224).

Things to See & Do

Lipsi's **museum** is on the central square. Its underwhelming exhibits include pebbles and plastic bottles of holy water from around the world. Admission is free, but opening times are erratic. To the right of the wide steps there is a **carpet factory**. The handwoven carpets are not for sale here but you can wander in and see them being made.

The town beach of **Liendos** is a short walk from the waterfront.

Places to Stay

The D-class *Hotel Calypso* (☎ 41 242) has comfortable doubles/triples for 8000/9000 dr with private bathroom and there is a supermarket next door. *Rena's Rooms* (☎ 41 363), owned by Greek-Americans John and Rena Paradisos (of Eureka Travel), are spotless, beautifully furnished and spacious. Doubles/triples are 8000/9000 dr with private bathroom. There is a communal refrigerator and gas ring, and a terrace overlooking Liendos beach. Turn right from the large quay (left from the small quay) and take the signposted road to Liendos. The rooms are up here on the left.

Rooms Galini (☎ 41 212), opposite the large quay, have lovely, light rooms with bathroom, refrigerator, gas ring and balcony. Doubles/triples are 8000/9000 dr. Nearby, above Cafeteria Fotina, *Panorama Studios* (☎ 41 235) are equally agreeable and the rates are the same.

Flisvos Pension (☎ 41 261), beyond the carpet factory, has singles/doubles/triples for 5000/7000/9000 dr. *Barbarosa Studios*

(☎ 41 092/312), next door to Lipsos Travel, has spacious, well-equipped double/ triple/quad studios for 10,000/12,000/ 14,200 dr. The same family has doubles with shared bathroom for 6500 dr.

The new A-class *Aphrodite Hotel* (☎ 41 394), overlooking Liendos beach, has luxurious double studios for 15,000 dr and four-person apartments for 25,000 dr.

Lipsi does not have an official camping ground, but there is free camping at Katsadia beach (see Katsadia in the Walks to the Beaches from Lipsi Town section). There are no facilities, but there are two good tavernas.

Places to Eat

Taverna Vasileia Kali Kardia, at the beginning of the Liendos beach road, and *Restaurant Barbarosa*, around the corner, are good choices. The *Fish Restaurant*, between the two quays, serves (surprise, surprise) only seafood. The trendy *Rock Coffee Bar & Ouzeri*, next door, serves a mixed mezes plate for 1200 dr. The *Dolphin Taverna*, behind Plateia Nikiforias, also serves well-prepared seafood.

Lipsi's shady, traffic-free square, with two inexpensive kafaneia, is a lovely spot for breakfast. On the small square there's a *fast-food outlet*, a *supermarket*, a *fruit and vegetable shop* and *O Mylos Café*, which has good pies and cakes. The *bakery* is just off the central square.

The new *Oceanis* café at the port is a good place to wait for the ferry.

Entertainment

'Away from it all' Lipsi town now has a disco – the *Scorpion Night Club*. Evenings here begin with international music but Greek music gradually takes over, with locals giving tourists impromptu lessons in Greek dancing.

WALKS TO THE BEACHES FROM LIPSI TOWN

Kambos & Platys Gialos

Κέμος & Πλατύς Γιαλός
Beyond Liendos beach the road forks; bearing left, you will arrive at Kambos beach. If

you take the right fork, after about 40 minutes you will arrive at Platys Gialos, a lovely sandy beach with a decent taverna.

Katsadia Κατσάδια

Walk inland along the road by the cafeteria next to Restaurant Manolis and take the first turn to the right signposted 'Katsadia'. Continue straight ahead, and after passing a church on the right, take the left fork and pass another church on the right. Continue along this track and at the top of a short, steep hill turn left (signposted 'Katsadia'). Soon you will see Katsadia bay. Go straight ahead then turn sharp right, passing another church on the left, to reach the sand-and-pebble beach.

There is free camping beside *Dilaila Restaurant*, and *Kampieris Restaurant* has some basic double rooms for 2000 dr.

Kohlakoura Κοχλακούρα

Walk inland along the road by the cafeteria next to Restaurant Manolis, and take the second turn to the right signposted 'Kohlakoura'. At the fork bear right, and at the crossroads continue straight ahead. A turn-off to the right along this road leads to the **Church of Panagia Harou** (The Virgin of Death), where, according to tradition, dried flowers are resurrected on 24 August, the church's festival day. Take the next turn to the right along the road (which veers left) onto a dirt track. You will pass **Dimitris Makris' vineyard** where you can buy Lipsi Black wine (bring a container). The track becomes cement at the end of a low stone wall. Turn left here to arrive at the pebble beach of Kohlakoura. There are no facilities.

Monodendri (One Tree) Μονοδένδρι

At the small square, face Milos Café, turn right and take the second turn to the left. Continue along this road, passing the high school on the left. At the fork bear right and keep on this track, ignoring two turnings right by a church. Soon the White Islands come into view ahead. At the next fork bear right. Continue ahead going downhill for a while, then, after going gently uphill, ignore the left turn, and continue straight ahead for

another 250m. Then take a narrow path which veers uphill to the left. You will soon see the single tree of Monodendri (which means 'one tree') down to the left. It stands on a rocky peninsula, the neck of which is pebbled; this is an unofficial nudist beach. There are no facilities.

Kimissi Κοίμηση

This walk to Kimissi bay, on the south-west coast, is the most scenic on the island. A hermit monk lives here beside the little **Church of Our Lady**; behave appropriately with respect for his peace and holiness. In Ottoman times monks hid in a cave here, choosing death from starvation rather than capture by the Turks. A casket in the church contains their bones.

Take the Platys Gialos road. A rough track dissects the road 300m beyond the fork. Take the track that veers left and goes uphill by a stone wall. Go through a wooden gate and continue ahead and uphill. Eventually the path levels out high above the east coast. Go through another gate and continue ahead, veering slightly left. Continue to the **Church of the Virgin of the Cross**, and pass in front of it. Soon you will see a stony track down to the right. Keep going ahead to reach this track at its summit. Turn left onto it and descend to Kimissi. You can return by this track to the Platys Gialos-Lipsi road.

Arki & Marathi
Αρκοί & Μαράθι

ARKI
• *pop 50* • *postcode 850 01* • *area code ☎ 0247*
Tiny Arki, 5km north of Lipsi, is hilly, with shrubs but few trees. Its one settlement, the little port on the west coast, is also called Arki. Islanders make a meagre living from fishing.

There is no post office, OTE, policeman or doctor on the island. An islander said they were promised a bi-monthly visit from a doctor in 1994, but in practice this rarely

AEGEAN SEA

Arki & Marathi Islets

0   1   2 km

ARKI

Church of
Arki Metamorphosis

MARATHI

Tiganakia
Bay

To Patmos

To Lipsi

Places to Stay & Eat
Arki has three tavernas, two of which also rent rooms. *Taverna Arki Katsavidis* (☎ 32 371), opposite the quay, has doubles/triples for 5500/6600 dr. To the right, *O Tripos Taverna* (☎ 32 230) has singles/doubles/ triples for 4000/5500/7200 dr. The owner, Manolis, speaks good English. Close by, another eating option is the new *Taverna Mihalis Kavoura*.

Getting There & Away
No inter-island ferries call in at Arki. In summer the Lipsi-based excursion boats go there and the caïque *Delfini* does frequent trips from Patmos (3000 dr return). There is also the possibility of 'hitching' a lift on a fishing boat or yacht, though this is not common practice and shouldn't be taken for granted.

MARATHI
Marathi is the largest of Arki's satellite islets. Before WWII it had a dozen or so inhabitants, but is now uninhabited. However, it has two seasonal tavernas, both of which rent rooms. *Taverna Pantelis* (☎ 32 609/32 759) and *Taverna Mihalis* (☎ 31 805/31 580) have comfortable doubles for 6000 dr and decent food. Pantelis and his wife, Katina, speak very good English. The island has a superb beach.

Getting There & Away
Excursion Boat In summer the Lipsi-based *Black Beauty* and *Margarita* do trips to Marathi. You may be able to get a lift on a fishing boat from Arki.

happens. 'We have been forgotten' he bemoaned. One gets the feeling that this applies to all aspects of Arki.

Away from its little settlement, the island seems almost mystical in its peace and stillness. On the other hand, some people find it just plain dull.

Things to See & Do
Walk to the **Church of Metamorphosis** for superb views of Arki and its surrounding islets. Facing inland at the quay, turn right and then left after O Tripas Taverna. Ignore the cement road to the right, and take the path straight ahead. At the fork, by a telegraph pole, bear right and go through a metal gate. Turn right and climb up to a stone wall. Then turn left onto a path up to a wooden gate, beyond which is the church. Its key is kept under a stone slab to the right of the door.

Beyond the red-domed church, to the left of the port (facing the sea), there are two mediocre, dirty beaches. There are several other beaches around the coast. **Tiganakia bay**, which has incredibly blue water, is a superb place for swimming. It's easily reached by boat but it's possible to walk there along goat tracks; ask locals for directions.

Agathonisi Αγαθονήσι

• *pop 112* • *postcode 850 01* • *area code* ☎ *0247*
Agathonisi (Agathonisi) is the most northerly island of the archipelago. It's a little gem, still only visited by adventurous backpackers and yachties. There are three villages: the port of Agios Giorgios, Megalo Horio and Mikro Horio, all less than 1km

apart. The island is hilly and covered with thorn bushes.

Getting There & Away
Ferry & Hydrofoil The F/B *Nissos Kalymnos* calls at Agathonisi on its route north to Samos, and again on its route south to Patmos, Lipsi, Leros and Kalymnos, twice a week, on Wednesday and Sunday. The twice-weekly supply boat from Samos also takes passengers, but its schedule is subject to change – check with the police officer or locals. A hydrofoil running to and from Samos, Patmos, Lipsi, Leros, Kalymnos and Kos calls in on Saturday.

Getting Around
There is no public transport, but it takes less than 15 minutes to walk from Mikro Horio to Megalo Horio or Agios Giorgios. If you don't want to walk you can usually get a lift fairly easily.

AGIOS GIORGIOS Άγιος Γεάργιος
Agios Giorgios is a delightful little place with just enough waterfront activity to stop you sinking into a state of inertia. It has a pebble beach and Spilia beach, also pebbled, is close by, reached along the track around the far side of the bay.

Orientation & Information
Boats dock at Agios Giorgios from where cement roads ascend right (facing inland) to Megalo Horio and left to Mikro Horio. There is no post office or bank or OTE, but there are cardphones.

There is no tourist information office. The one police officer, who is also the port police officer, has an office in the white building at the beginning of the Megalo Horio road.

Places to Stay
Agios Giorgios has three pensions: *Pension Maria Kamitsa* (☎ 23 650/690), *Theologis Rooms* (☎ 23 692/687) next door, and *George's Pension* (☎ & fax 24 385) behind them. All charge 7000 dr for doubles with private bathroom. George and his wife Sabine are among the few people on the

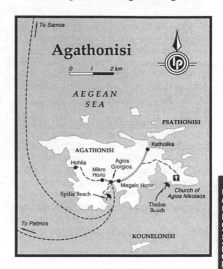

island who speaks English. Sabine also speaks German.

Places to Eat
There are several eateries in Agios Giorgios, but out of high season the only place likely to be open is *George's Taverna* below the pension, where the octopus stifado is magnificent.

AROUND AGATHONISI
Megalo Horio Μεγάλο Χωριό
Megalo Horio, Agathonisi's biggest village, has one domatia, *Mrs Katsoulieri's Rooms to Rent* (☎ 24 385). *Restaurant I Eireni* and the kafeneio/pantopoleio, both on the central square, serve inexpensive meals.

Walk from Megalo Horio to Katholika
Katholika is an abandoned fishing hamlet 40 minutes walk from Megalo Horio. En route you can detour to a lookout point. From the central square turn right at Restaurant I Eireni to reach a cement road. Walk 300m beyond the baseball field and turn left, and then right, to reach an army lookout hut, from where there are tremendous views over to Samos and Turkey's Meandros estuary.

From the hut look half-left and you will see two large olive trees – proceed towards these, then walk towards the long, narrow island of Psathonisi. Ahead and half-right you will soon see an oblong enclosure; walk to this and turn right. At the road, turn left for Katholika.

Walk from Megalo Horio to the Church of Agios Nikolaos & Tholos Beach
Leave Megalo Horio on the Katholika road. After about 30 minutes, turn right onto a dirt road. At the stone building go through a wooden gate, continue along the track and through a metal gate. At the fork bear right to get to Tholos beach. To get to the Church of Agios Nikolaos bear left and, almost immediately, take an indistinct stony path to the left and you will soon glimpse the church. The key is kept under a stone to the right of the door.

Walk from Mikro Horio to Hohlia
Hohlia is a bay on the west coast of Agathonisi, about one hour's walk from Mikro Horio. There's no beach but you can swim from the rocks. Leave Mikro Horio by the dirt road; when it turns right you will see ahead of you a dip between two hills – Hohlia lies beyond here. Just before the track narrows to pass between two stone walls, take the path which veers off to the right and then skirts around the stone walls and an animal enclosure before ascending steeply. Keep close to the stone wall on the left as it continues to the bay.

North-Eastern Aegean Islands
Τα Νησιά του Βορειοανατολικού Αιγαίου

The islands of the North-Eastern Aegean islands are grouped together more for convenience than for any historical, geographical or administrative reason. Apart from Thasos and Samothraki, they are, like the Dodecanese, much closer to Turkey than to the Greek mainland, but unlike the Dodecanese they are not close to one another. This means island-hopping is not the easy matter it is within the Dodecanese and Cyclades, although, with the exception of Thasos and Samothraki, it is possible.

These islands are less visited than either the Dodecanese or the Cyclades. Scenically, they also differ from these groups. Mountainous, green and mantled with forests, they are ideal for hiking but most are also blessed with long stretches of delightful beaches.

Although historically diverse, a list of the islands' inhabitants from far-off times reads like a who's who of the ancient world. Some of the North-Eastern Aegean islands also boast important ancient sites. All of them became part of the Ottoman Empire and were then reunited with Greece after the Balkan Wars in 1912.

There are seven major islands in the group: Chios, Ikaria, Lesvos (Mytilini), Limnos, Samos, Samothraki and Thasos. Fourni near Ikaria, Psara and Inousses near Chios, and Agios Efstratios near Limnos are small, little-visited islands in the group.

Accommodation throughout the island chain tends to be a little more expensive than on some of the more touristed islands, but bear in mind that the high season (July to August) prices quoted in this chapter are anywhere from 30% to 50% cheaper out of season.

Getting There & Away
Following is an overview of travel options

to/from and between the islands of the North-Eastern Aegean. Also see the entries at the beginning of sections on individual islands.

HIGHLIGHTS

- Watching the abundant migratory birdlife of Lesvos, popular with birders from all over Europe
- Exploring the Levantine-looking Mastihohoria (mastic villages), of Pyrgi and Mesta in southern Chios
- Walking in the lush, sub-tropical Samos – a paradise for lovers of nature
- Investigating the mystical Sanctuary of the Great Gods on remote and ecologically conscious Samothraki
- Experiencing the solitude of quirky Ikaria – an Aegean island still awaiting 'discovery' and in no hurry to achieve it
- Relaxing on volcanic Limnos – much loved by travellers longing for space, solitude and sandy beaches
- Taking in the scent of thickly forested Thasos – redolent of pine and thyme. Easy to get to – easy lifestyle

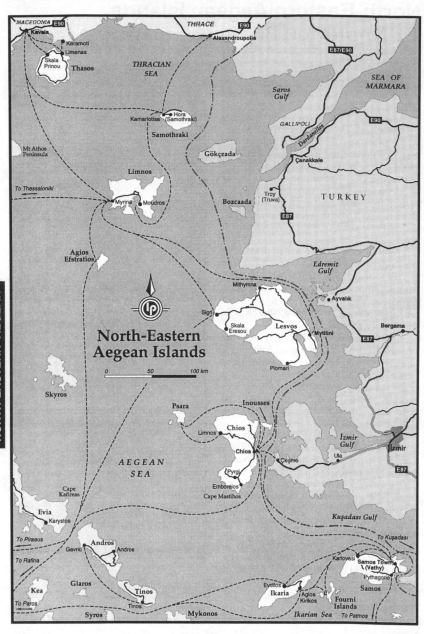

Air Samos, Chios, Lesvos, Limnos and Ikaria have air links with Athens. In addition, Samos, Chios, Lesvos and Limnos have flights to Thessaloniki.

Ferry – domestic Chios, Samos, Lesvos and Ikaria have daily connections with Piraeus. Some of the ferries from Samos and Ikaria to Piraeus go via any combination of Mykonos, Naxos, Paros, Tinos or Syros. Limnos has three connections a week with Piraeus, Rafina and Kavala. Chios and Lesvos have two connections a week with Thessaloniki, and Limnos has one. Agios Efstratios is linked to both Rafina and Limnos.

Thasos and Samothraki have no connections with Piraeus, but Samothraki is linked to Limnos by both ferry and occasional summer hydrofoil. Thasos has daily ferry connections with Kavala and Keramoti, both in Macedonia. There are daily connections between Samothraki and Alexandroupolis in Thrace and in summer there is a connection with Kavala twice or three times a week (depending on demand). Alexandroupolis is also linked to Rhodes via a weekly service that takes in most of the other islands en route.

An excursion boat connects Samos with Patmos in the Dodecanese every day in summer. The F/B *Nissos Kalymnos* links Samos (Pythagorio) twice a week with the Dodecanese islands of Agathonisi, Lipsi, Patmos, Leros, Kalymnos, Kos, Nisyros, Tilos, Symi and Rhodes.

Ferry – international In summer there are daily ferries from Samos to Kuşadası (for Ephesus) and from Chios to Çeşme, both in Turkey. The Lesvos to Ayvalık link is currently unconfirmed.

Hydrofoil In summer there are regular hydrofoil links between Kavala and Thasos and some hydrofoils between Alexandroupolis, Samothraki and Limnos. Hydrofoils also operate out of Samos west towards Ikaria and south towards the Dodecanese.

Getting Around
Air Lesvos is connected to both Limnos and Chios by local flights.

Ferry There are daily ferries between Ikaria and Samos, Chios and Lesvos; ferries three times a week between Lesvos and Limnos; and twice a week between Chios and Samos.

Samos Σάμος

Samos (Samos; population 32,000), the most southerly island of the group, is the closest of all the Greek islands to Turkey, from which it is separated by the 3km-wide Mykale straits. The island is the most visited of all the North-Eastern Aegean group. Charter flights of tourists descend on the island from many northern European countries. Try to avoid Samos in July and August when rooms are hard to come by.

Despite the package tourists, Samos is still worth a visit: forays into its hinterland are rewarded with unspoilt villages and mountain vistas. In summer the humid air is permeated with heavy floral scents, especially jasmine. This, and the prolific greenery of the landscape, lend Samos an exotic and tropical air. Orchids are grown here for export and an excellent table wine is made from the locally grown Muscat grapes.

Samos has three ports: Samos town (Vathy) and Karlovasi on the north coast, and Pythagorio on the south coast.

History
The first inhabitants of Samos, the Pelasgian tribes, worshipped Hera, whose birthplace was Samos. Pythagoras was born on Samos in the 6th century BC. Unfortunately, his life coincided with that of the tyrant Polycrates, who in 550 BC deposed the Samian oligarchy. As the two did not see eye to eye, Pythagoras spent much of his time in exile in Italy. Despite this, Samos became a mighty naval power under Polycrates, and the arts and sciences also flourished. 'Big is

NORTH-EASTERN AEGEAN

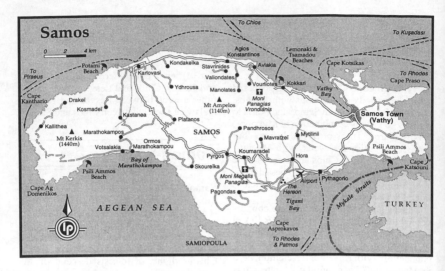

beautiful' seems to have been Polycrates' maxim: almost every construction and artwork he commissioned appears to have been ancient Greece's biggest. The historian Herodotus wrote glowingly of the tyrant's achievements, stating that the Samians had accomplished the three greatest projects in Greece at that time: the Sanctuary of Hera (one of the Seven Wonders of the Ancient World), the Evpalinos Tunnel, and a huge jetty.

After the decisive Battle of Plataea (479 BC), in which Athens had been aided by the Samians, Samos allied itself to Athens and returned to democracy. In the Battle of Mykale, which took place on the same day as the Battle of Plataea, the Greek navy (with many Samian sailors) defeated the Persian fleet. However, during the Peloponnesian Wars, Samos was taken by Sparta.

Under Roman rule Samos enjoyed many privileges, but after successive occupations by the Venetians and Genoese it was conquered by the Turks in 1453. Samos played a major role in the uprising against the Turks in the early 19th century, much to the detriment of its neighbour, Chios (see Chios' History section).

Trekking

Samos is a popular place for rambling, or even more demanding mountain treks. Its natural fecundity and appealing combination of mountains and sea make it a popular destination for walkers from all over Europe. There are two excellent publications that you might wish to consult, should you be planning a hike on Samos. Lonely Planet's *Trekking in Greece* by Marc Dubin has some excellent descriptions of hikes. Brian and Eileen Anderson's *Landscapes of Samos*, a pocket guide to walks on the island is also good. Written in exquisitely twee British English, it contains descriptions for over 20 walks. The book is available in Vathy for around 4500 dr.

Getting There & Away

Air There are at least three flights a day from Samos to Athens (16,100 dr) and two flights a week to Thessaloniki (23,700 dr). The Olympic Airways office (☎ 27 237) is on the corner of Kanari and Smyrnis in Samos town. There is also an Olympic Airways office (☎ 61 213) on Lykourgou Logotheti in Pythagorio. The airport is 4km west of Pythagorio.

Ferry – domestic Samos is the transport hub of the North-Eastern Aegean, with ferries to the Dodecanese and Cyclades as well as to the other North-Eastern Aegean islands. Schedules are subject to seasonal changes, so consult any of the ticket offices for the latest versions. ITSA Travel (☎ 23 605; fax 27 955) is the closest agency to the ferry terminal in Samos town and covers most destinations. They will also store your luggage for free whether you buy a ticket or not. Ask for Dimitris Sarlas. The following summary will give you some idea of the ferry options from Samos during summer.

Piraeus There are one to two ferries daily to Piraeus (13 hours, 5680 dr) which usually call in at Ikaria.

Other North-Eastern Aegean Islands There are two to three ferries daily to Ikaria (2½ hours, 1850 dr); one a day to Fourni (two hours, 1650 dr); three a week to Chios (four hours, 2480 dr); one a week to Lesvos (seven hours, 3400 dr); one a week to Limnos (11 hours, 5800 dr); one a week to Alexandroupolis (20 hours, 7100 dr) and one a week to Kavala (20 hours, 7200 dr).

Cyclades Daily ferries go to Naxos and/or Paros (6½ hours, 3660 dr) with connections to Mykonos, Ios, Santorini (Thira) and Syros.

Dodecanese There are about five ferries per week to Patmos (2½ hours, 2200 dr) and one per week to Leros (3½ hours, 2400 dr), Kalymnos (four hours, 3200 dr), Kos (5½ hours, 3400 dr) and Rhodes (nine hours, 5700 dr).

Ferry – international In summer two ferries go daily from Samos town to Kuşadası (for Ephesus) in Turkey. From November to March there are one to two ferries a week. Tickets cost around 5000/9000 dr one way/return (plus 5000 dr Greek port tax and US$10 Turkish port tax – payable upon arrival). Competition for ticket sales is intense in Samos town, so shop around. Samina

Tours (☎ 28 841; fax 23 616) at Themistokli Sofouli 67 currently offers the best deal, but try Samos Tours (☎ 27 715; fax 28 915) or the aforementioned ITSA Travel to see if it will match prices.

Bear in mind that the ticket office will require your passport in advance for port formalities. Turkish visas are currently required for US, UK, Irish and Italian citizens, but are issued on arrival in Turkey for US$20.

Hydrofoil – domestic In summer hydrofoils link Pythagorio twice a day with Patmos (one hour, 3500 dr), Leros (two hours, 4700 dr), Kos (3½ hours, 6000 dr) and Rhodes (6½ hours, 12,400 dr). There is also one service a week from Samos town to Fourni (1¾ hours, 3100 dr) and Ikaria (2¼ hours, 3700 dr). Schedules are subject to frequent changes, so contact the tourist office in Pythagorio or the port police (☎ 61 225) for up-to-date information.

Hydrofoil – international A hydrofoil now plies three times a week between Vathy and Kuşadası (30 minutes, 10,000 dr) in Turkey. It departs at 8.30 am and returns from Kuşadası at 5 pm. The return fare is 13,000 dr. Return and one-way fares include the exorbitant 5000 dr port tax for Greece. An additional Turkish port tax of US$10 is also payable upon arrival in Turkey.

Excursion Boat In summer there are excursion boats three times a week between Pythagorio and Patmos (9000 dr) leaving at 7.30 am. Daily excursion boats also go to the little island of Samiopoula for 8000 dr including lunch.

Getting Around
The Airport There are no Olympic Airways buses to the airport. A taxi from Samos town should cost about 2400 dr. Alternatively, you can take a local bus to Pythagorio and a taxi to the airport from there for about 1000 dr.

Bus Samos has an adequate bus service which continues till about 8 pm in summer.

There are 13 buses a day from Samos town to both Kokkari (20 minutes, 240 dr) and Pythagorio (25 minutes, 280 dr); eight to Agios Konstantinos (40 minutes, 400 dr); seven to Karlovasi (via the north coast, one hour, 780 dr); six to the Hereon (25 minutes, 420 dr); five to Mytilinii (20 minutes, 260 dr); three to Psili Ammos beach on the east coast (20 minutes, 260 dr); and two to Ormos Marathokampou and Votsalakia (two hours, 1120 dr).

In addition to frequent buses to Samos town there are six buses from Pythagorio to the Hereon and two to both Mytilinii and Karlovasi.

Car & Motorcycle Samos has many car-rental outlets. They include Hertz (☎ 61 730), Lykourgou Logotheti 77, and Europcar (☎ 61 522), Lykourgou Logotheti 65, both in Pythagorio. There are also many motorcycle hire outlets on Lykourgou Logotheti. Many larger hotels can arrange motorcycle or car hire for you.

Taxi From the taxi rank (☎ 28 404) on Plateia Pythagora in Samos town, tariffs are: Kokkari 1800 dr, Pythagorio 2000 dr, Psili Ammos 1700 dr, Avlakia 2100 dr, the airport 2400 dr, and the Hereon 2700 dr.

SAMOS TOWN (VATHY)
• *pop 5790* • *postcode 831 00* • *area code* ☎ *0273*
The island's capital is the large and bustling Samos town, also called Vathy (Βαθύ), on the north-east coast. The waterfront is crowded with tourists who rarely venture to the older and extremely attractive upper town of Ano Vathy where 19th-century red-tiled houses perch on a hillside. The lower and newer town is strung out along Vathy bay and it is quite a walk from one end to the other.

Orientation
From the ferry terminal (facing inland) turn right to reach the central square of Plateia Pythagora on the waterfront. It's recognisable by its four palm trees and statue of a lion. A little further along and one block inland are the shady municipal gardens with a pleasant outdoor café. The waterfront road is called Themistokleous Sofouli.

Information
The municipal tourist office (☎ 28 530) is just north of Plateia Pythagora in a little side street, but it only operates during the summer season. The staff will assist in finding accommodation. The tourist police (☎ 27 980) are in the same building as the regular police at Themistokleous Sofouli 129 on the south side of the waterfront. The port police (☎ 27 318) are just north of the quay and one block back from the waterfront.

The National Bank of Greece is on the waterfront just south of Plateia Pythagora and the Commercial Bank is on the east side of the square.

The island's bus station (KTEL) is just back from the waterfront on Ioannou Lekati. The post office is on Smyrnis, four blocks from the waterfront. The OTE is on Plateia Iroön, behind the municipal gardens.

The taxi rank (☎ 28 404) is on Plateia Pythagora. Samos' general hospital (☎ 27 407) is on the waterfront, north of the ferry quay.

Things to See
Apart from the charming old quarter of Ano Vathy, which is a peaceful place to stroll, and the municipal gardens, which are a pleasant place to sit, the main attraction of Samos town is the **archaeological museum** (☎ 27 469). Many of the fine exhibits in this well laid out museum are a legacy of Polycrates' time. They include a gargantuan *kouros* statue (4.5m) which was found in the Hereon (Sanctuary of Hera). In true Polycrates fashion it was the largest standing kouros ever produced. The collection also includes many more statues, mostly from the Hereon, bronze sculptures, steles and pottery. The museum is east of the municipal gardens. Opening times are Tuesday to Sunday from 8.30 am to 3 pm. Admission is 800 dr, 400 dr for students.

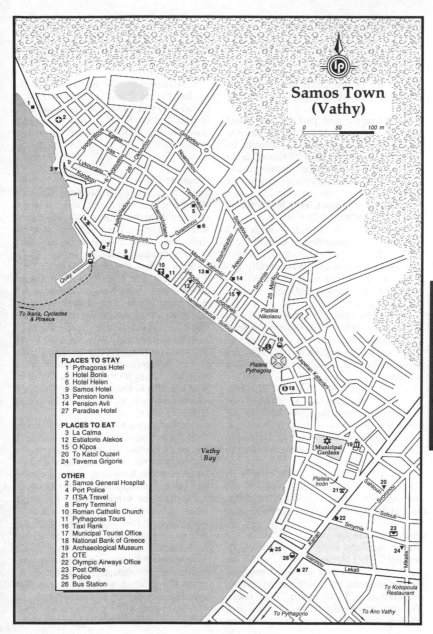

Samos Town
(Vathy)

0   50   100 m

To Ikaria, Cyclades
& Piraeus

Vathy
Bay

PLACES TO STAY
1 Pythagoras Hotel
5 Hotel Bonis
6 Hotel Helen
9 Samos Hotel
13 Pension Ionia
14 Pension Avli
27 Paradise Hotel

PLACES TO EAT
3 La Calma
12 Estiatorio Alekos
15 O Kipos
20 To Katoï Ouzeri
24 Taverna Grigoris

OTHER
2 Samos General Hospital
4 Port Police
7 ITSA Travel
8 Ferry Terminal
10 Roman Catholic Church
11 Pythagoras Tours
16 Taxi Rank
17 Municipal Tourist Office
18 National Bank of Greece
19 Archaeological Museum
21 OTE
22 Olympic Airways Office
23 Post Office
25 Police
26 Bus Station

To Kotopoula
Restaurant

To Pythagorio   To Ano Vathy

Places to Stay – bottom end

Samos does not have a camp site. Don't listen to touts who may accost you as you disembark from the ferry – especially if you are offered a 'private refrigerator'. They may try to tell you that places listed here are closed or 'unsuitable'. It's a scam – ignore them.

The cheapest and perhaps homeliest places to stay are the domatia of the *Pension Ionia* (☎ 28 782), on Manoli Kalomiri. Its clean and pretty rooms cost 2500/3500 dr for singles/doubles with shared bathroom and 4000/5000 dr for doubles/triples with private bathroom. To get there from the quay, turn right onto the waterfront, left at Stamatiadou, then left into Manoli Kalomiri.

Close by, the traditional *Pension Avli* (☎ 22 939) is a former Roman Catholic convent, built around a lovely courtyard (avli). The rooms are spacious and tastefully furnished. Rates are between 5000 and 7000 dr for doubles with private bathroom, depending on the season.

The C-class *Pythagoras Hotel* (☎ 28 422; fax 27 955), 800m to the left from the ferry arrival point, is an excellent budget option. Clean and simply furnished singles/doubles go for 4000/5000 dr. Ask for a room with a sea view.

The C-class *Hotel Helen* (☎ 22 866), Grammou 2, has cosy rooms with fitted carpets and attractive furniture. Doubles are 7000 dr with private bathroom. Turn right from the quay, and left just before the Roman Catholic church, veer right at the intersection and the hotel is on the right.

Close by is the C-class *Hotel Bonis* (☎ 28 790; fax 22 501) with large rooms and TV. Single/double rooms cost 6000/8200 dr including breakfast. This place is open all year.

Places to Stay – middle

The nearest hotel to the quay is the grand-looking C-class *Samos Hotel* (☎ 28 377; fax 23 771). It is well kept with a spacious and elegant cafeteria, bar, snack bar, restaurant, breakfast room, TV room and billiard room. The comfortable rooms have fitted carpets, balcony, telephone and private bathroom.

Rates fluctuate from 7800 to 10,000 dr for singles and 9200 to 12,600 dr for doubles depending on season. On leaving the quay turn right and you'll come to the hotel on the left.

Very handy for the bus station is the modern C-class *Paradise Hotel* (☎ 23 911; fax 28 754) with a snack bar, pool and comfortable doubles for 11,000 dr. In the high season it is likely to be booked out by tour groups.

Places to Eat

Samos town has a good selection of eateries. When dining out on Samos don't forget to sample the Samian wine, extolled by Byron. Just one street back from the waterfront is *Estiatorio Alekos* at Lykourgou Logotheti 49, serving ready-made staples and made-to-order dishes at around 2000 dr for a decent meal. The food at *To Katoï Ouzeri*, also known as Why Not, is superlative and moderately priced. The modern, tastefully decorated ouzeri is tucked away on a little side street behind the municipal gardens.

Greeks escape the tourists and head for the *Kotopoula* restaurant (off map) hidden away in the backstreets. Follow Ioannou Lekati inland for about 800m until you find it on your left. Chicken is the speciality, but their scrumptious mezedes can be had for around 600 dr a pop.

Another commendable place is *Taverna Grigoris* on Smyrnis, near the post office. If you are here between 8.30 and 9.30 pm your table number may be drawn out of a hat, in which case you'll eat free. This is a reasonably priced restaurant and is open all day.

For live neo kyma (1960s new wave) music and maybe some dancing, seek out *O Kipos*, just off Lykourgou Logotheti (entry is from the next street up to the north) in a garden setting. The food is commendable; try a splendid Samena Golden white wine with it. For a romantic, night-time ambience, try *La Calma* which overlooks the sea. The seductive views and tasty food complement each other perfectly. Prices at these last two places are somewhat more upmarket.

PYTHAGORIO Πυθαγόρειο
• *pop 1400* • *postcode 831 03* • *area code* ☎ *0273*

Pythagorio, on the south-east coast of the island, is 14km from Samos town. Today, it's a crowded and rather twee tourist resort, but it's a convenient base from which to visit Samos' ancient sites.

Pythagorio stands on the site of the ancient city of Samos. Although the settlement dates from the Neolithic Age, most of the remains are from Polycrates' time (around 550 BC). The mighty jetty of Samos projected almost 450m into the sea, protecting the city and its powerful fleet from the vagaries of the

Aegean. Remains of this jetty lie below and beyond the smaller modern jetty, which is on the opposite side of the harbour to the quay. The town beach begins just beyond the jetty. All of the boats coming from Patmos, and other points south of Samos, dock at Pythagorio.

Orientation

From the ferry quay, turn right and follow the waterfront to the main thoroughfare of Lykourgou Logotheti, a turn-off to the left. Here there are supermarkets,

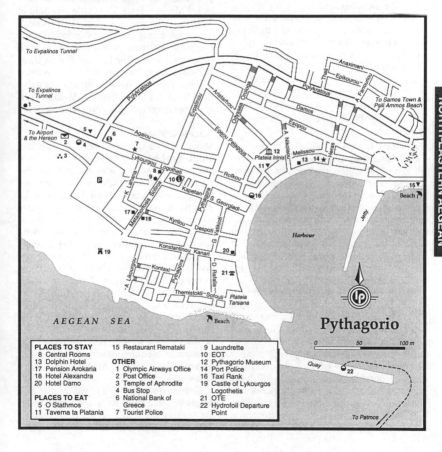

Pythagorio

PLACES TO STAY	15 Restaurant Remataki	9 Laundrette
8 Central Rooms		10 EOT
13 Dolphin Hotel	OTHER	12 Pythagorio Museum
17 Pension Arokaria	1 Olympic Airways Office	14 Port Police
18 Hotel Alexandra	2 Post Office	16 Taxi Rank
20 Hotel Damo	3 Temple of Aphrodite	19 Castle of Lykourgos
	4 Bus Stop	Logothetis
PLACES TO EAT	6 National Bank of	21 OTE
5 O Stathmos	Greece	22 Hydrofoil Departure
11 Taverna ta Platania	7 Tourist Police	Point

greengrocers, bakers, travel agents and numerous car, motorcycle and bicycle-hire outlets. The central square of Plateia Irinis is on the waterfront just beyond here.

Information

The municipal tourist office (☎ 61 389; fax 61 022) is on the south side of Lykourgou Logetheti. The English-speaking staff are particularly friendly and helpful and give out a town map, bus timetable and information about ferry schedules. They also have a currency exchange. The tourist police (☎ 61 100) are also on Lykourgou Logetheti, to the left of the tourist office.

The post office and the National Bank of Greece are both on Lykourgou Logotheti. The OTE is on the waterfront near the quay. The bus station (actually a bus stop) is on the south side of Lykourgou Logotheti. There is a taxi rank (☎ 61 450) on the corner of the waterfront and Lykourgou Logotheti. There is a self-service laundrette on Metamorfosis Sotiros, close to Lykourgou Logotheti.

Evpalinos Tunnel Ευπαλίνειο Ορυγμα

The 1034m-long Evpalinos Tunnel, completed in 524 BC, is named after its architect. It penetrated through a mountainside to channel gushing mountain water to the city. The tunnel is, in effect, two tunnels: a service tunnel and a lower water tunnel which you can see at various points along the narrow walkway. The diggers began at each end and managed to meet in the middle, an achievement of precision engineering that is still considered remarkable.

In the Middle Ages the inhabitants of Pythagorio used the tunnel as a hide-out during pirate raids. The tunnel is fun to explore, though access to it is via a very constricted stairway. If you are tall, portly, or suffer from claustrophobia, give it a miss! Opening times are 9 am to 2 pm every day except Monday. Entry is 500 dr, or 300 dr for students. The tunnel is most easily reached from the western end of Lykourgou Logotheti, from where it is signposted. If you arrive by road, a sign points you to the

tunnel's southern mouth as you enter Pythagorio from Samos.

Other Attractions

Walking east on Polykratous from the town centre, a path off to the left passes traces of an ancient theatre. The Evpalinos Tunnel can also be reached along this path – take the left fork after the theatre. The right fork leads up to **Moni Panagias Spilianis** (Monastery of the Virgin of the Grotto). The ancient city walls extend from here to the Evpalinos Tunnel.

Back in town are the remains of the **Castle of Lykourgos Logothetis**, at the southern end of Metamorfosis. The castle was built in 1824 and became a stronghold of Greek resistance during the War of Independence. The small **Pythagorio Museum** (☎ 61 400) in the town hall at the back of Plateia Irinis has some finds from the Hereon. It is open Sunday, Tuesday, Wednesday and Thursday from 9 am to 2 pm and on Friday and Saturday from noon to 2 pm. Admission is free.

Places to Stay

Many of Pythagorio's places to stay are block-booked by tour companies. Two pleasant and quiet places for independent travellers are opposite one another on Metamorfosis. The *Pension Arokaria* (☎ 61 287) has a cool and leafy garden; the lovely owner charges 6500/8500 dr for doubles/triples. The D-class *Hotel Alexandra* (☎ 61 429), just opposite, charges 7000 dr for a double with private bathroom. Another option is *Central Rooms* (☎ 61 032) near the corner of Lykourgou Logotheti and Metamorfosis. Don't be put off by the entrance and stairway, which look like the Gate to Hades – the rooms are clean and comfortable. The rate is 6000/7200 dr for doubles/triples with private bathroom. The manager is a courteous elderly man called Steven who lived in Australia for many years.

Coming from the quay, one of the first hotels you will come to on the waterfront is the C-class *Hotel Damo* (☎ 61 303; fax 61 745), which is near the OTE. The agreeable studios here are 11,000/13,200 dr for two to three people and the rooms are fully self-contained. Further around the waterfront, beyond the main intersection, is the C-class *Dolphin Hotel* (☎ 61 205; fax 61 842), with spotless and cosy wood-panelled rooms for 8650/11,350 dr with private bathroom.

Places to Eat

One of the cheapest eateries is the quaint ouzeri *O Stathmos* on Lykourgou Logotheti, close to the junction with the main road from Samos. *Restaurant Remataki*, at the beginning of the beach, has an imaginative menu of carefully prepared, delicious food. Try a meal of various mezes for a change: revithokeftedes (chick-pea patties), piperies Florinis (Florina peppers) and gigantes (lima beans) make a good combination. Main courses start from around 1000 dr. *Taverna ta Platania* is on Plateia Irinis, opposite the museum, and away from the more expensive waterfront eateries.

AROUND PYTHAGORIO

Hereon Ηραίον

The Sacred Way, once flanked by thousands of statues, led from the city to the Hereon. The Hereon was a sanctuary to Hera, built at the legendary place of her birth, on swampy land where the River Imbrasos enters the sea. There had been a temple on the site since Mycenaean times, but the one built in the time of Polycrates was the most extraordinary: it was four times the size of the Parthenon. As a result of plunderings and earthquakes only one column remains standing, although the extent of the temple can be gleaned from the foundations. Other remains on the site include a stoa, more temples and a 5th-century basilica. The site (☎ 95 277) is on the coast 8km west of Pythagorio. Opening times are Tuesday to Sunday from 8.30 am to 2.30 pm. Admission is 800 dr, 400 dr for students. It's free on Sunday.

Mytilinii Μυτιληνιοί

The fascinating **paleontology museum** (☎ 52 055), on the main thoroughfare of the inland village of Mytilinii, between

Pythagorio and Samos town, houses bones and skeletons of prehistoric animals. Included in the collection are remains of animals that were the antecedents of the giraffe and elephant. The museum is open Monday to Saturday from 9 am to 2 pm and 5 to 7 pm; on Sunday it opens from 10.30 am to 2.30 pm. Admission is 500 dr, free on Sunday.

Beaches

Back on the coast, sandy **Psili Ammos** (not to be confused with a beach of the same name near Votsalakia) is the finest beach near Pythagorio. This gently sloping beach is ideal for families and is popular, so be there early to grab your spot. The beach can be reached by excursion boat (2500 dr) from Pythagorio, leaving each morning at 9 am and returning at 4 pm. There are also buses from Samos town.

There are a couple places to stay at Psili Ammos. *Elena Apartments* (☎ 23 645; fax 28 959), right on the beach, has spacious self-contained double/quad apartments for 8000/15,000 dr for bookings of at least a few days. Nearby, *Appartments Psili Ammos* (☎ 25 140) have self-contained rooms for two to three people for between 7000 and 9000 dr. There are four eating places, of which *Restaurant Psili Ammos* and the more intimate *Sunrise* – commendable for its classy choice of ambient music – are both favourably located overlooking the beach.

SOUTH-WEST SAMOS

The south-west coast of Samos remained unspoilt for longer than the north coast, but in recent years a series of resorts have sprung up alongside the best beaches. **Ormos Marathokampou**, 50km from Samos town, has a pebble beach. From here a road leads 6km to the inland village of **Marathokampos**, which is worth a visit for the stunning view down to the immense Bay of Marathokampos. **Votsalakia**, 4km west of Ormos Marathokampou and known officially as Kampos, and **Psili Ammos** (not to be confused with the Psili Ammos beach near Pythagorio), 2km beyond, have long, sandy beaches. There are many domatia and tavernas on this stretch of coast. The best taverna of an otherwise uninspiring bunch is *Ta Votsalakia*, with tables overlooking the beach.

With your own transport you may like to continue on the dirt road from Psili Ammos which skirts Mt Kerkis, above the totally undeveloped and isolated west coast. The road passes through the village of **Kallithea**, and continues to **Drakeï** where it terminates.

WEST OF SAMOS TOWN

The road which skirts the north coast passes many beaches and resorts. The fishing village of **Kokkari**, 10km from Samos town, is also a holiday resort with a pebble beach. The place is fairly popular with tourists, but it is exposed to the frequent summer winds and for that reason is popular with windsurfers. Rooms, studios and tavernas abound, all offering much the same quality.

Beaches extend from here to **Avlakia**, with **Lemonaki** and **Tsamadou** beaches being the most accessible for walkers staying in Kokkari. Clothing is optional at these two pebbly, secluded beaches. Continuing west, beyond Avlakia, the road is flanked by trees, a foretaste of the alluring scenery encountered on the roads leading inland from the coast. A turn-off south along this stretch leads to the delightful mountain village of **Vourliotes**, from where you can walk another 3km to **Moni Panagias Vrondianis**. Built in the 1550s, it is the island's oldest extant monastery; a sign in the village points the way.

Continuing along the coast, just before the little resort of Agios Konstantinos, a 5km road winds its way up the lower slopes of Mt Ampelos through thick, well-watered woodlands of pine and deciduous trees, to the gorgeous village of **Manolates**. The area is rich in bird life, with a proliferation of nightingales, warblers and thrushes. There are no buses to Manolates so you'll have to find your own way (Agios Konstantinos is the nearest bus stop). In the village there are many old houses built of stone with projecting balconies. The surfaces of the narrow streets and idyllic little squares are decorated with whitewashed floral designs. There is also a sizeable community of well-fed and slightly aristocratic cats. The Samians say that if you have not visited either Vourliotes or Manolates, then you have not seen Samos.

Back on the coast, the road continues to the quiet resort of **Agios Konstantinos**. Beyond here it winds through rugged coastal and mountain scenery to the town of **Karlovasi**, Samos' second port. The town consists of three contiguous settlements: Paleo (old), Meson (middle) and Neo (new). It once boasted a thriving tanning industry, but now it's a lacklustre town with little of interest for visitors. The nearest beach is the sand-and-pebble **Potami**, 2km west of town.

Places to Stay

Despite the onset of package tourism, Kokkari still has many accommodation options for independent travellers. In the high season an EOT (☎ 92 217) operates in the village and they will assist in finding accommodation. The bus stops on the main road at a large stone church; the EOT is a little way down the street opposite the church.

The *Pension Eleni* (☎ 92 317) has immaculate, tastefully furnished rooms for 7000 dr a double with private bathroom. From the large stone church in Kokkari, continue along the main road; at the T-junction veer left and, 50m along on the left, next to the Dionyssos Garden restaurant, you will see a sign pointing to the pension. There are many more domatia, apartments and small hotels along this stretch of road, which is just one block back from the waterfront.

Further west along the coast road, close to a beach, are the *Calypso Rooms to Rent* (☎ 94 124), named after their friendly and kind owner. The rooms are well kept and surrounded by a gorgeous garden. Rates are 6000 dr for doubles with private bathroom and use of a communal kitchen. Coming from Kokkari, turn right opposite the turn-off for Manolates (signposted) and you will come to a sign pointing right to the rooms. There are more domatia in this area. The bus stop is just before the Manolates turn-off. There are as yet no pensions or hotels in Manolates. In the meantime a limited number of beds are available in private homes. Ask about these in the *kafeneia* and tavernas.

If you get stuck in Karlovasi there are several budget hotels and domatia (☎ 32 133) with doubles for 5500 dr. This accommodation is signposted from the central square where the bus terminates.

Places to Eat

There are many reasonably priced restaurants in Kokkari all offering 'English menus' and the usual range of bland tourist fare. No one place stands out.

Paradisos Restaurant, at the turn-off to Manolates, serves delectable dishes; a full meal with wine or beer will cost around 2200 dr. *Alpha Snack Bar*, on the tiny central square in Manolates, serves low-priced tasty food. There are also a couple of small but pleasant eateries on the edge of the village.

Ikaria & the Fourni Islands Ικαρία & οι Φούρνοι

Ikaria (Ikaria; 9000), lying west of Samos, is a rocky and mountainous island. Like Samos it is also fertile, with an abundance of cypress trees, pine forests, olive and fruit trees – Ikarian apricots are especially luscious. At present the island's tourism is low-key, but Ikaria is slowly being 'discovered' by Germans seeking a quiet alternative. Ailing Greeks have visited Ikaria since ancient times because of its therapeutic radioactive springs which they believe to be the most efficacious in Europe. One spring is so highly radioactive it was deemed unsafe and forced to close.

The name Ikaria originates from the mythical Icarus (see The Myth of the Minotaur aside under Central Crete in the Crete chapter); another myth ascribes the island as the birthplace of Dionysos. Ikaria has two ports,

Agios Kirykos on the south coast, and Evdilos on the north coast. The island's best beaches are on the north coast, west of Evdilos.

Ikaria is a bit of an oddity as a tourist destination. Long neglected by mainland Greece and used as a dumping ground for left-wing political dissidents by various right-wing governments, Ikaria and Ikarians have a rather devil-may-care approach to things, including tourism. The islanders, while welcoming tourists, are taking a slow approach to cultivating the tourist dollar. The result is that Ikaria is an island that may take a bit of getting used to at first, but will surely remain long in your memory.

Getting There & Away

Air In summer there are five flights a week to Athens (16,100 dr) departing at 8.40 am. The Olympic Airways office (☎ 22 214) is in Agios Kirykos, though tickets can also be bought from Blue Nice Agency (☎ 31 990; fax 31 752) in Evdilos. There is a private airport bus to/from Agios Kirykos (1000 dr).

Ferry All ferries which call at Ikaria's two ports of Evdilos and Agios Kirykos are on the Piraeus-Samos route. In general there are departures every day from Agios Kirykos and three to four times a week from Evdilos. Sample fares are Piraeus (nine hours, 4450 dr); Samos (three hours, 1900 dr); Mykonos (three hours, 2740 dr); and Tinos (four hours, 2750 dr). Tickets can be bought at Dolihi Tours Travel Agency (☎ 71 474; fax 22 346) in Agios Kirykos or from Rostas and Blue Nice agencies in Evdilos (see Evdilos for details).

Chios-based Miniotis Lines also runs a couple of small boats leaving at 4 pm on Monday and Friday up to Chios (8½ hours, 4500 dr) from Agios Kirykos via Fourni (one hour, 1200 dr) and Samos.

Hydrofoil Ikaria and Fourni islands are linked with Samos by fairly frequent summer services and twice weekly connections to Patmos and weekly connections to Rhodes. Sample rates are Patmos (one hour, 3460 dr); Samos (1¼ hours, 4025 dr); Kos

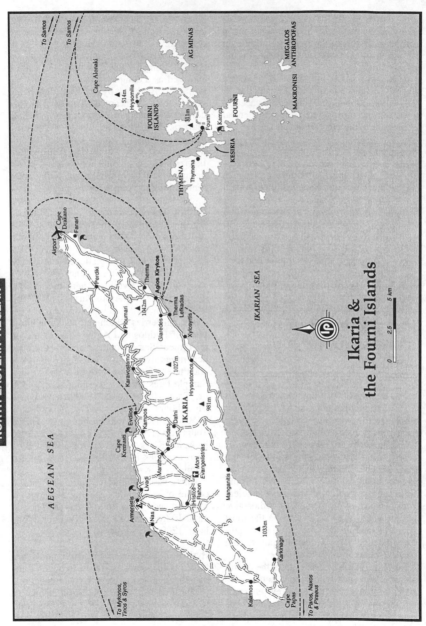

Ikaria &
the Fourni Islands

(2½ hours, 7000 dr); Rhodes (six hours, 11,200 dr). Check with Dolihi Tours (see above) for the latest schedules and prices.

Caïque A caïque leaves Agios Kirykos on Monday, Wednesday and Friday at 1 pm for Fourni, the largest island in the miniature Fourni archipelago. The caïque calls at Fourni's main settlement, where there are domatia and tavernas. Tickets cost 700 dr one way.

Getting Around

Bus Ikaria's bus services are almost as mythical as Icarus, but they do exist. In summer a bus leaves Evdilos for Agios Kirykos every day at 8 am and returns to Evdilos at noon, or thereabouts; otherwise it leaves on Monday, Wednesday and Friday. There should also be a 'tourist' bus leaving Agios Kirykos for Armenistis at 4 pm each day in summer. Check to be on the safe side. The trip takes about 1½ hours and costs 800 dr.

Buses to the villages of Hristos Rahon (near Moni Evangelistrias), Xylosyrtis and Hrysostomos from Agios Kirykos are more elusive and depend mainly on the whims of the local drivers. It is usually preferable to share a taxi with locals or other travellers for long-distance runs.

Car & Motorcycle Cars can be rented from Dolihi Tours Travel Agency (☎ 71 474; fax 22 346), Rent Cars & Motorcycles DHM (☎ 22 426) in Agios Kirykos, and Marabou Travel (☎ 71 460) at Armenistis.

Taxi Boat In summer there are daily taxi boats from Agios Kirykos to Therma and to the sandy beach at Fanari on the northern tip of the island.

AGIOS KIRYKOS Αγιος Κήρυκος
• *pop 1800* • *postcode 833 00* • *area code* ☎ *0275*

Agios Kirykos is Ikaria's capital and main port. It's a pleasant, relaxed little town with a tree-shaded waterfront flanked by several kafeneia. Beaches in Agios Kirykos are stony; the pebbled beach at Xylosyrtis, 7km

to the south-west, is the best of a mediocre bunch of beaches near town.

Orientation & Information

To reach the central square from the quay, turn right and walk along the main road. The National Bank of Greece is on this square and has an ATM. As you walk away from the quay, turn left on the central square and you will come to the post office and OTE on the left.

The regular police (☎ 22 222) and port police (☎ 22 207) share a building in the eastern part of town. Continue along the waterfront from the central square and go up the six steps; continue up the next flight of steps and at the top you will see the police building on the right. The bus stop is just west of the central square.

Ikaria does not have an EOT or tourist police. A good unofficial source of information is Vassilis Dionissos, a charismatic fellow who owns the village store in the north-coast village of Kampos (see the Kampos section).

At the bottom of the steps which lead to Agios Kirykos' police building you will find Dolihi Tours Travel Agency. The staff here have information about bus and boat schedules, and can also arrange accommodation.

Radioactive Springs

The radioactive springs are between the Hotel Akti and the police building. A dip costs 700 dr and supposedly cures a multitude of afflictions including arthritis, rheumatism, skin diseases and infertility. There are more hot springs at Therma, 3km north-east of Agios Kirykos. This thriving spa resort has many visitors in summer.

Archaeological Museum

Agios Kirykos' small archaeological museum houses many local finds. Pride of place is given to a large, well-preserved stele (500 BC) depicting in low relief a mother (seated) with her husband and four children. The stele was discovered some years ago during the building of a school in a nearby village. It took a court case to prize the stele from the possessive clutches of the school.

The museum's opening times are generally 10 am to 2 pm, but don't bet on it. Entry is free. The museum is west of the quay and is well signposted.

Places to Stay – bottom end

One of the cheapest places to stay in Agios Kirykos is the E-class *Hotel Akti* (☎ 22 694; fax 22 346). The tidy rooms cost 5500/7500 dr for singles/doubles with private bathroom. The pension has great sea views from its appealing garden. To reach it, turn right facing Dolihi Tours, go up the steps to the left and follow the signs.

Pension Maria-Elena (☎ 22 835; fax 71 331) has impeccable rooms. Rates are 8000/9600 dr for doubles/triples with private bathroom. From the quay turn left at the main road, take the first right, and then first left into Artemidos – the pension is along here on the right.

Places to Stay – middle

Agios Kirykos' best-appointed hotel is the C-class *Hotel Kastro* (☎ 23 480; fax 23 700). The rooms are beautifully furnished and have a telephone, three-channel music system, private bathroom and balcony. Rates are 8000/10,000 dr for singles/doubles, including breakfast. On a clear day you can see the islands of Amorgos, Naxos, Fourni, Patmos, Samos, Arki and Lipsi from the communal terraces. The hotel is opposite the police building.

Places to Eat

Agios Kirykos has a number of restaurants, snack bars, ouzeria and kafeneia. *Taverna Klimataria* serves good grilled meats in a neat little courtyard hidden away in the backstreets and is open all year. A decent-sized pork chop should be about 1300 dr and it will taste even better with a small bottle of Samaina Sec from Samos. On the main square is *Restaurant Dedalos* which offers delicious fresh fish. Their draught wine is highly recommended.

Further along the waterfront you cannot miss the looming *Ta Adelfia Restaurant* that serves pretty standard fare. *Filoti Pizzeria Restaurant* is one of the town's best regarded restaurants. Apart from pizza and pasta, there are good souvlaki and chicken dishes. The restaurant can be found at the top of the cobbled street that leads from the butcher's shop.

If you feel like a brisk walk and fancy a change of scenery, try the nifty little taverna *To Tzaki* in the village of Glaredes, about 4km west of Agios Kirykos.

AGIOS KIRYKOS TO THE NORTH COAST

The island's main north-south asphalt road begins a little west of Agios Kirykos and links the capital with the north coast. As the road climbs up to the island's mountainous spine there are dramatic mountain, coastal and sea vistas. The road winds through several villages, some with traditional stone houses topped with rough-hewn slate roofs. It then descends to the island's second port of Evdilos, 41km by road from Agios Kirykos.

This journey is worth taking for the views, but if you are based in Agios Kirykos and want to travel by bus you will more than likely have to stay overnight in Evdilos or Armenistis. A taxi back to Agios Kirykos will cost 5000 dr. Hitching is usually OK, but there is not that much traffic.

EVDILOS Εύδηλος

• *pop 440* • *postcode 833 00* • *area code* ☎ *0275*

Evdilos, the island's second port, is a small, dusty fishing village. Like Agios Kirykos it's a pleasant and relaxing place, but you may prefer to head further west to the island's best beaches. There is, nonetheless, a reasonable beach to the east of Evdilos. Walk 100m up the hill from the square and take the path down past the last house on the left.

Places to Stay – bottom end

For a quiet stay upon arrival in Evdilos you might consider making the 3km (40-minute) walk to Kampos (see West of Evdilos) where there are domatia, an excellent beach and a couple of restaurants. The nearest and cheapest accommodation option in Evdilos is the *pension* of Ioannis Spanos (☎ 31 220). The rooms are centrally located just back from the main square. Reasonable singles/doubles are 4500/6000 dr.

Facing the sea from the middle of the waterfront, the plush-looking building on the far right with black wrought-iron balconies is the *domatia* belonging to Spyros Rossos (☎ 31 518). Rates are 7000 dr for a double with private bathroom.

Places to Stay – middle

Evdilos has two good-quality hotels. The B-class *Hotel Atheras* (☎ 31 434; fax 31 926) is a breezy, friendly place with modern rooms with balconies. There is also a small pool and bar. Singles/doubles go for 10,000/12,000 dr in the high season. At the top of the hill is the small B-class *Hotel Evdoxia* (☎ 31 502; fax 31 571) with double rooms for 11,000 dr, if you don't mind the petty house rules. There is a minimarket with basic provisions, a laundry service, money exchange and restaurant (see Places to Eat) and it's open all year.

Places to Eat

In season, there are a number of eateries to choose from, including the fairly obvious *Souvlarhio* with its blue cane chairs. Try their tasty Ikarian specialities soufiko or mayirio – pan-simmered concoctions of the season's first vegetables. The *Kavos Restaurant* on the east side of the little harbour is open all day for lunch and dinner. However, avoid the nearby *To Steki* restaurant (for want of a better word) if you are planning to eat.

For food with a view, the *Hotel Evdoxia Restaurant* is a good meeting place for travellers. The food is home-cooked and you can even order your favourite dish if you are staying at the hotel. Otherwise you will pay about 1500 dr for a meat dish and wine.

WEST OF EVDILOS

Kampos Κάμπος

• *pop 127* • *postcode 833 01* • *area code* ☎ *0275*

Kampos, 3km west of Evdilos, is an unspoilt little village with few concessions to tourism. Although it takes some believing, sleepy little Kampos was the island's ancient capital of Oinoe (etymologically derived from the Greek word for wine). The name comes from the myth that the Ikarians were the first people to make wine. In ancient times Ikarian wine was considered the best in Greece, but a phylloxera outbreak in the mid-60s put paid to many of the vines. Production is now low-key and mainly for local consumption. Ancient coins found in the vicinity of Kampos have a picture of Dionysos, the wine god, on them. Kampos' sandy beach is excellent and easily accessible.

Ancient coin depicting Dionysos, the wine god

Information The irrepressible Vassilis Dionissos, who speaks English, is a fount of information on Ikarian history and walking in the mountains. You will often find him in his gloomy but well-stocked village store – on the right as you come from Evdilos. The village's post box is outside this shop and inside there is a metered telephone. There is also a cardphone nearby.

NORTH-EASTERN AEGEAN

Things to See As you enter Kampos from Evdilos, the ruins of a **Byzantine palace** (strictly speaking a *kyvernio*, or governor's house) can be seen up on the right. In the centre of the village there is a small **museum** housing Neolithic tools, geometric vases, fragments of classical sculpture, small figurines and a very fine 'horse head' knife sheath, carved from ivory.

Next to the museum is the 12th-century **Agia Irini**, the island's oldest church. It is built on the site of a 4th-century basilica, and columns standing in the grounds are from this original church. Agia Irini's supposedly fine frescoes are currently covered with whitewash, because of insufficient funds to pay for its removal. Vassilis Dionissos has the keys to both the museum and church.

The village is also a good base for mountain walking. A one-day circular walk along dirt roads can be made, taking in the village of **Dafni**, the remains of the 10th-century Byzantine **Castle of Koskinas**, and the villages of **Frandato** and **Maratho** and a cave at **Mikropouli** which can be difficult to find: ask Vassilis Dionissos if you get stuck. Take a torch if you plan to enter it.

Places to Stay & Eat There are a couple of domatia in Kampos, the best of which is owned by – you guessed it – Vassilis Dionissos (☎ 31 300/688) and his brother Yiannis, who create a wonderful family atmosphere for their guests. The very pleasant rooms are between 4000 and 6000 dr for doubles with private bathroom. The optional enormous breakfasts are something to be experienced and are accompanied by tasteful Greek music. Coming from Evdilos take the dirt road to the right from near the cardphone and follow it round to the blue-and-white building on your left. Alternatively, make your presence known at the village store.

Vassilis often cooks delicious fish or lobster dishes for his guests and his original pitta recipe is exquisite. Otherwise, there is a moderately priced taverna in the village, the *Klimataria*, and a summer taverna, the *Oinoi*, on Kampos' sandy beach about 300m past Vassilis Dionissos' place.

Armenistis Αρμενιστής
• *pop 70* • *postcode 833 01* • *area code* ☎ *0275*
Armenistis, 15km west of Evdilos, is the island's largest resort with two beautiful long beaches of pale golden sand, separated by a narrow headland. Although places to stay are springing up quickly here, it's still visited predominantly by independent travellers. Marabou Travel (☎ 71 460; fax 71 325), on the road which skirts the sea, organises walking tours and jeep safaris on the island. Just east of Armenistis a road leads inland to **Moni Evangelistrias**.

From Armenistis a 3.5km dirt road continues west to the small and secluded pebbled beach of **Nas** at the mouth of a stream. This is Ikaria's unofficial nudist beach. Behind the beach are some scant remains of a **temple of Artemis**. Nas has in recent times begun to witness a mini-boom with no less than 45 beds available and a choice of five tavernas to eat at.

Places to Stay – bottom end Ikaria's only camp site is the rather scrawny *Armenistis Camping* (☎ 71 250), on the beach at Armenistis. Facilities are fairly minimal though the owners are planning expansions and renovations. It opens about mid-June and they charge 1500 dr for two persons with a tent.

One of the cheapest places to stay in Armenistis is *Rooms Ikaros* (☎ 71 238) – rates are 4000 dr for a double with shared bathroom, or 5000 dr with private bathroom. The elderly owner, Dimitris Hroussis, speaks a little English and is kind and friendly. The place is signposted as you enter the village. Above the Pashalia restaurant are the *domatia* (☎ 71 302) belonging to the restaurant. Clean and modern doubles with private bathroom and most with sea-view balconies go for between 4000 and 7000 dr according to season.

At the approach to the village, before the road forks, you will see *Rooms Fotinos* (☎ 71 235) on the left. The rooms are light, airy and beautifully furnished. Rates are 7000/8400 dr for doubles/triples with private bathroom.

The Artemis Taverna at Nas serves as a *pension* (☎ 71 485) with small, but neat double rooms with a bathroom for 6000 dr and without for 5000 dr. *Pension Thea* (☎ 71 491), also at Nas, is newer, but the rooms are a bit sterile and more exposed to the sun. Still, they have a fridge, a sea view and go for 7000 dr for a double, 6000 dr if they are not busy.

Places to Stay – middle One of Armenistis' better hotels is around to the west of the village. The C-class *Cavos Bay Hotel* (☎ 71 381; fax 71 380) has a cool and inviting interior. The stucco-walled rooms open out onto a large private terrace overlooking a rocky seascape. The hotel has a large restaurant and bar and a sea water swimming pool built into the rocks. Depending on the season, rates range from 6000 to 11,000 dr for singles and 7500 to 13,000 dr for doubles, breakfast included.

The most exquisite accommodation on the island, however, is the Cycladic-inspired *pension* (☎ 71 310) belonging to Dimitris Ioannidopoulos, known as *o yermanos* (the German) because of his many years of residence in that country. The individual studios and apartments spill down a hillside which overlooks the sea amid a riotous profusion of flowers and plants. They are 700m west of Armenistis. A small studio for two people with private patio goes for 9000 dr while a fully equipped two to three person apartment complete with music system and enormous patio goes for a very reasonable 10,500 dr. Bookings are absolutely essential. Phone or fax ☎ (49) 89-690 1097 in Germany during the winter months for reservations.

Places to Eat There are three restaurants along the Armenistis harbourside: *To Symposio*, *Kafestiatorio o Ilios* and *To Mouragio* – take your pick, though the Symposio is probably more popular.

Further back up the hill the *Pashalia Taverna* offers prompt service and a variety of ready-made dishes; try the filling veal yiouvetsi in a clay pot for about 1300 dr.

Directly opposite and below the Pashalia is the folksy *Delfini* restaurant offering great grilled souvlaki to complement the view over the water. Wherever you eat, see if you can get to taste some of the locally made light but potent wine.

Handy for the camp site and the beach is the *Atsahas* taverna 2km east of Armenistis. The views are great and the food is pretty reasonable, priced in the mid-range – though service is very slow.

Nas has five tavernas of which the *Astra* and the *Artemis Taverna* do the briskest trade. Prices are pretty reasonable.

FOURNI ISLANDS Οι Φούρνοι
• *pop 1030* • *postcode 0275* • *area code* ☎ 834 00

The Fourni islands are a miniature archipelago lying between Ikaria and Samos. Two of the islands are inhabited: Fourni and Thymena. The capital of the group is Fourni town (also called Kampos), which is the port of Fourni island. Fourni has one other village, tiny Hrysomilia, which is 10km north of the port; the island's only road connects the two. The islands are mountainous and a good number of beaches are dotted around the coast.

The telephone number of Fourni's port police is ☎ 51 207.

Fourni is the only island with accommodation for tourists and is ideal for those seeking a quiet retreat. Other than the settlement of Fourni itself and a beach over the headland to the south at **Kampi**, the island offers little else besides eating, sleeping and swimming. Most of the islanders make a living from fishing, sending their catch to the Athens fish market.

There are several domatia and tavernas in Fourni town, but no accommodation in Hrysomilia. *Snack Bar-Pension Palladio* (☎ 51 436) is one option for meals.

Taverna Nikos or *Psarotaverna tou Miltou* on the waterfront will keep you amply supplied with fresh fish.

See the Ikaria Getting There & Away section for information about how to get to Fourni.

Chios Χίος

Chios (Hios), like its neighbours Samos and Lesvos, is a large island covering 859 sq km. It is separated from the Turkish peninsula of Karaburun by the 8km-wide Chios straits. It is a verdant island, although in recent years fires have destroyed many of its forests.

A large number of highly successful ship owners come from Chios and its dependencies, Inousses and Psara. This, and its mastic production, have meant that Chios has not needed to develop a tourist industry. In recent years, however, package tourism has begun to make inroads, although nothing like on the scale of what's happening in Samos.

History

In ancient times, Chios, like Samos, excelled in the arts, which reached their peak in the 7th century BC when the Chios school of sculpture produced some of Greece's most eminent sculptors of the time. The technique of soldering iron was invented in this school. During the Persian Wars, Chios was allied to Athens, but after the Battle of Plataea it became independent and prospered, because it didn't have to pay the annual tribute to Athens.

In Roman times Chios was invaded by Emperor Constantine, who helped himself to its fine sculptures. After the fall of Byzantium the island fell prey to attacks by pirates, Venetians, Catalans and Turks. It revived somewhat under the Genoese, who took control in the 14th century. However, it was recaptured by the Turks in 1566 and became part of the Ottoman Empire.

In the 19th century, Chios suffered two devastations. In 1822 the Samians cajoled the people of Chios into assisting them in an uprising against Ottoman rule. The Turks retaliated by sacking Chios, killing 25,000 of its inhabitants and taking almost twice that number into slavery. The massacre was the subject of Victor Hugo's poem *L'Enfant de Chios* and Eugene Delacroix's painting *Le Massacre de Chios* (in the Louvre). In 1881 the island suffered a violent earthquake which killed almost 6000 people, destroyed many of the buildings in the capital and caused considerable damage throughout the island.

Chios is one of a number of places around the Mediterranean that lay claim to being Homer's birthplace. The island is also in the running for the birthplace of Christopher Columbus. Ruth G Durlacher-Wolper, director of the New World Museum in San Salvador, has researched the life of the great seafarer, and in a 1982 report she hypothesised that he was born on Chios and that the island may have been his point of departure to the New World.

Getting There & Away

Air Chios has on average five flights a day to Athens (14,600 dr); two a week to Thessaloniki (21,100 dr); and two flights a week to Lesvos (10,200 dr). The Olympic Airways office (☎ 0271-20 359) is on Leoforos Egeou in Chios town. The airport is 4km from Chios town. There is no Olympic Airways bus, but a taxi to/from the airport should cost about 800 dr.

Ferry – domestic In summer there are two ferries a day to Piraeus (eight hours, 4820 dr); one a day to Lesvos (three hours, 2900 dr); and one a week to Kavala (16 hours, 6360 dr) and Thessaloniki (18 hours, 7230 dr), both via Limnos (five hours, 4550 dr). Tickets for these routes can be bought from the Maritime Company of Lesvos (NEL) office (☎ 0271-23 971; fax 41 319), on Leoforos Egeou, in Chios town.

The smaller Miniotis Lines (☎ 0271-24 670; fax 25 371) runs three small boats to Karlovasi and Vathy, both on Samos; and then on to Fourni (7½ hours, 4200 dr) and Ikaria (8½ hours, 4500 dr). They also have three boats a week to Psara (3½ hours, 1900 dr). The *Oinoussai II* is another small local boat that runs to and from Oinousses twice a week (1¼ hours, 800 dr).

In addition, there is another service once a week southwards to Samos (three hours,

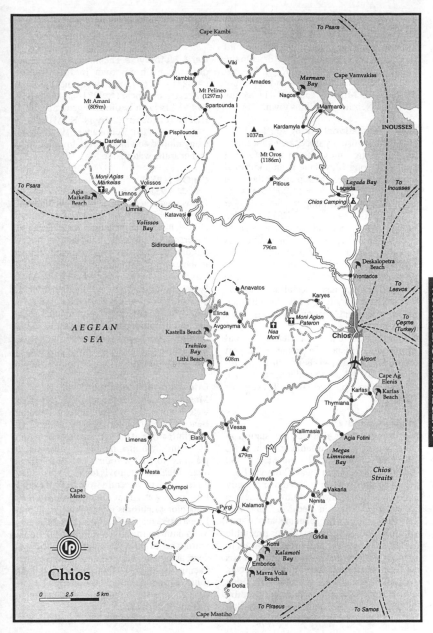

2640 dr) and Rhodes (14 hours, 6770 dr); and northwards to Lesvos (three hours, 2950 dr), Limnos (9½ hours, 4630 dr) and Alexandroupolis (14 hours, 5950 dr). On the southern leg the boat, the *C/F Romilda*, continues on to Crete. For tickets and departure details contact Miniotis Tours (☎ 41 073; fax 41 468) at Neorion 23, Chios town.

Ferry – international During April and October there are usually three ferries a week to Çeşme, leaving Chios at 8 am and returning at 6 pm. During May there is an additional sailing and from July to September there are daily sailings. The fare is 14,000/18,000 dr one way/return (including the 5000 dr port tax). A Turkish port tax of US$10 is also payable upon arrival in Çeşme. The cost for a small car is 11,000 dr, a motorcycle is 11,000 dr, a moped is 7000 dr and a bicycle is 4000 dr. Further information and tickets can be obtained from Miniotis Tours (see above). There are also special daily excursion rates which often work out cheaper. Check with local agencies offering such trips.

Bear in mind that the ticket office will require your passport in advance for port formalities. Turkish visas are currently required for US, UK, Irish and Italian citizens, but are issued on arrival in Turkey for US$20.

Getting Around

Bus From the long-distance bus station in Chios town there are, in summer, eight buses a day to Pyrgi (600 dr), five to Mesta (800 dr) and six to Kardamyla (700 dr) via Langada; take this bus for the camp site. Only one or two buses a week do the journey to Anavatos (470 dr) via Nea Moni and Avgonyma – check the schedule at the bus station, or ask for a copy of the bus timetable in English. There are fairly regular buses to the main beaches of Emborios, Komi, Nagos and Lithi and extra excursion buses to Nea Moni and Anavatos are scheduled on Tuesdays. Buses to Karfas beach are serviced by the blue (city) bus company. A detailed English-language bus timetable appears in the back pages of the free *Chios Summertime*, available at the EOT office.

Car & Motorcycle The numerous car-rental outlets in Chios town include Budget (☎ 0271-41 361), on Psyhari, near the post office and Europcar (☎ 0271-41 031; mobile 094 517 141) on Leoforos Egeou 56. Chios' ELPA representative is K Mihalakis (☎ 0271-22 445), Rodokanaki 19. There are many moped and motorcycle-hire outlets on and near the waterfront.

CHIOS TOWN
• *pop 22,900* • *postcode 821 00* • *area code* ☎ *0271*
Chios town, on the east coast, is the island's port and capital. It's a large town, home to almost half of the island's inhabitants. Its waterfront, flanked by unattractive modern buildings and trendy coffee shops, is noisy in the extreme with an inordinate amount of cars and motorcycles careering up and down. However, things improve considerably once you begin exploring the backstreets. The atmospheric old quarter, with many Turkish houses built around a Genoese castle, and the lively market area, are both worth a stroll. Chios town doesn't have a beach; the nearest one is the sandy beach at Karfas, 6km south.

Orientation & Information
Most ferries dock at the northern end of the waterfront at the western end of Neorion. Bear in mind that ferries from Piraeus (to Mytilini) arrive at the very inconvenient time of 4 am – worth remembering if you are planning to find a room. The old Turkish quarter (called Kastro) is to the north of here. To reach the town centre from the ferry quay, follow the waterfront round to your left and walk along Leoforos Egeou. Turn right onto Kanari to reach the central square of Plateia Vounakiou (formerly called Plastira). To the north-west of the square are the public gardens, and to the south-east is the market area. Facing inland, the bus station for local buses (blue) is on the right side of the public gardens and the station for long-distance buses (green) is on the left.

Continuing along the waterfront, the next

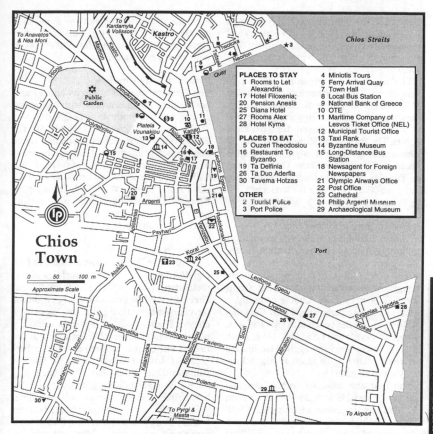

PLACES TO STAY
1 Rooms to Let
   Alexandria
17 Hotel Filoxenia;
20 Pension Anesis
25 Diana Hotel
27 Rooms Alex
28 Hotel Kyma

PLACES TO EAT
5 Ouzeri Theodosiou
16 Restaurant To
   Byzantio
19 Ta Delfinia
26 Ta Duo Aderfia
30 Taverna Hotzas

OTHER
2 Tourist Police
3 Port Police
4 Miniotis Tours
6 Ferry Arrival Quay
7 Town Hall
8 Local Bus Station
9 National Bank of Greece
10 OTE
11 Maritime Company of
   Lesvos Ticket Office (NEL)
12 Municipal Tourist Office
13 Taxi Rank
14 Byzantine Museum
15 Long-Distance Bus
   Station
18 Newsagent for Foreign
   Newspapers
21 Olympic Airways Office
22 Post Office
23 Cathedral
24 Philip Argenti Museum
29 Archaeological Museum

NORTH-EASTERN AEGEAN

turn after Kanari is Roïdou. Turn right here and then first left into Rodokanaki. The post office is two blocks along here on the right. Facing inland, take the first right along Kanari and you'll see the OTE on the left. Most banks, including the National Bank of Greece, are between Kanari and Plateia Vounakiou. There is an ATM halfway along Aplotarias.

The municipal tourist office (☎ 44 389; fax 44 343) is at Kanari 18. The helpful staff give information on accommodation, bus and boat schedules. The magazine *Chios Summertime* is available here. Opening hours are 7 am to 2.30 pm and 7.30 to 9 pm on weekdays and from 10 am to 1 pm on Saturday. The tourist police (☎ 44 428) and the port police (☎ 44 432) are at the eastern end of Neorion.

Museums

Chios town's most interesting museum is the **Philip Argenti Museum** (☎ 23 463), in the same building as the **Koraïs Library**, one of the country's largest libraries. The museum, which is on Koraïs near the cathedral, contains exquisite embroideries, traditional costumes and portraits of the wealthy Argenti family. The museum and the library are open from 8 am to 2 pm Monday to Thursday and on Friday from 5 to 7 pm. On Saturday they open from 8 am to 12.30 pm. Admission is free.

The town's other museums are not so compelling. The **archaeological museum** (☎ 26 664), on Polemidi, contains sculptures, pottery and coins. However, at the time of writing, it was closed for structural repairs. The **Byzantine Museum** (☎ 26 866) is housed in a former mosque, the Medjitie Djami, on Plateia Vounakiou. Opening times are Tuesday to Sunday from 10 am to 1 pm. Entry is 500 dr, or 300 dr for students.

Places to Stay – bottom end

With over 30 domatia to choose from, budget accommodation is plentiful in Chios town. Get a copy of *Chios Summertime* from the tourist office for a full listing. Be aware though, accommodation in central Chios town can be very noisy. Choose carefully.

Chios has one camp site, *Chios Camping* (☎ 74 111), on the beach at Agios Isidoros, between Sykiada and Langadas, 14km north of Chios town. The site has good facilities, a bar and restaurant. To reach it take a Kardamyla or Langadas bus.

The best and most welcoming domatia option is *Rooms Alex* (☎ 26 054) at Livanou 29. Alex has six rooms which go for 5500/6500 dr without/with bathroom. There is a relaxing roof garden, festooned with flags and Alex will meet your boat, or come to pick you up, if you call him. He will also help you with car or bike rentals and fill you in on what you need to know about Chios.

The D-class *Hotel Filoxenia* (☎ 26 559) is signposted from the waterfront and is near the Restaurant To Byzantio. The unadorned but clean singles/doubles cost 5000/6000 dr with shared bathroom or 5500/7500 dr with private bathroom.

Pension Anesis (☎ 44 801; fax 44 803), at Vasilikari 2, has B-class singles/doubles for 6000/8000 dr. To reach this place, follow Aplotarias from the main square and you will see it on your right.

In the old quarter *Rooms to Rent Alexandria* (☎ 41 815), on Theotoka, has agreeable doubles/triples for 5500/6600 dr with shared bathroom.

Places to Stay – middle

The *Pension Anesis* (described above) also has A-class doubles/triples with bathroom, air-con and fridge for 9000/12,000 dr.

The C-class *Diana Hotel* (☎ 44 180; fax 26 748) on El Venizelou is a good mid-range hotel aimed primarily at the Greek business market. Single/double rates here are 9800/14,100 dr including breakfast. The C-class *Hotel Kyma* (☎ 44 500; fax 44 600) occupies a turn-of-the-century mansion and has lots of character. Rates are 12,500/16,000 dr with breakfast.

Places to Eat

Restaurant To Byzantio, on the corner of Rali and Roïdou, is a bright, cheerful and unpretentious place which serves traditional Greek fare at low prices. Right opposite the ferry disembarkation point on Neorion is *Ouzeri Theodosiou*, an old-style and very popular establishment. Wedged next to the fish wharf, on the northern arm of the harbour, is *Iakovos Taverna*, selling the freshest fish available. Blink and you'll miss it – there's no sign indicating its existence. Be here before 8.30 pm or you won't get a table.

Ta Delfinia, on the waterfront, is a bit touristy (with photo menus), but the food and service are good and it's the best place to watch street life. Main dishes start at around 1200 dr. Opposite Rooms Alex at Livanou 38 is *Ta Duo Aderfia* with a pleasant walled garden. Try the special spare ribs in BBQ sauce for around 1400 dr.

Finally, *Taverna Hotzas* (open evenings only) at the southern end of town is a bit of an institution, with cats, hens and ducks wandering around the garden. To get here, walk up Aplotarias and turn right at the fork along Stefanou Tsouri; follow it until you come across the restaurant.

CENTRAL CHIOS

North of Chios town is an elongated beachside suburb leading to **Vrontados** where you can sit on the supposed stone chair of Homer, the Daskalopetra, though it is quietly accepted that it is unlikely to have been used by Homer himself. It is a serene spot though, and it would not be hard to imagine Homer and his acolytes reciting epic verses to their admiring followers.

Immediately south of Chios town is a warren of walled mansions, some restored, others crumbling, called the **Kampos**. This was the preferred place of abode of wealthy Genoese and Greek merchant families from the 14th century onwards. It's easy to get lost here so keep your wits about you – the free Chios map from the EOT is helpful. You are also better off touring the area by bike or moped, since it is fairly extensive. Chios' main beach resort **Karfas** is here too, 7km south of Chios town. It's an OK beach with some moderate development and some A-class hotels; if you like your beaches quiet, look elsewhere.

In the centre of the island is the 11th-century Nea Moni. This large monastery stands in a beautiful mountain setting, 14km from Chios town. Like many monasteries in Greece it was built to house an icon which appeared miraculously. The icon in question was of the Virgin Mary and it materialised before the eyes of three shepherds. In its heyday the monastery was one of the richest in Greece and the most pre-eminent artists of Byzantium were commissioned to create the mosaics in its *katholikon*.

During the 1822 atrocities (see History at the start of the Chios section) the buildings were set on fire and all the resident monks were massacred. There is a macabre display of their skulls in the ossuary at the monastery's little chapel. In the earthquake of 1881 the katholikon's dome caved in, causing quite a lot of damage to the mosaics. Nonetheless, these mosaics still rank among the most outstanding examples of Byzantine art in Greece. They are esteemed for the striking contrasts of their vivid colours and the fluidity and juxtapositions of the figures. A few nuns live at the monastery. Opening times are from 8 am until 1 pm and 4 to 8 pm daily. Admission is free. The bus service to the monastery is poor, but travel agents in Chios town have excursions here and to the village of Anavatos.

Ten km from Nea Moni, at the end of a road that leads to nowhere, stands the forlorn ghost village of **Anavatos**. Its abandoned grey-stone houses stand as lonely sentinels to one of Chios' great tragedies. Nearly all the inhabitants of the village perished in 1822 and today only a small number of elderly people live there, mostly in houses at the base of the village.

Anavatos is a striking village, built on a precipitous cliff which the villagers chose to hurl themselves over, rather than be taken captive. Narrow, stepped pathways wind between the houses to the summit of the village.

Avgonyma, further back along the road, is only slightly more populated than Anavatos, but lacks the drama of its neighbour.

The beaches on the mid-west coast are not spectacular, but they are quiet and generally undeveloped. **Lithi beach**, the southernmost, is popular with weekenders and can get busy.

SOUTHERN CHIOS
Southern Chios is dominated by medieval villages that look as though they were transplanted from the Levant rather than built by Genoese colonisers in the 14th century. The rolling, scrubby hills are covered in low mastic trees that for many years were the main source of income for these scattered settlements.

There are some 20 Mastihohoria (mastic villages); the two best preserved are Pyrgi and Mesta. As mastic was a highly lucrative commodity in the Middle Ages, many an invader cast an acquisitive eye upon the villages, necessitating sturdy fortifications. (The archways spanning the streets were to prevent the houses from collapsing during earthquakes.) Because of the sultan's fondness for mastic chewing gum, the inhabitants of the Mastihohoria were spared in the 1822 massacre.

Gum Mastic

Gum mastic comes from the lentisk bush, and conditions in southern Chios are ideal for its growth. Many ancient Greeks, including Hippocrates, proclaimed the pharmaceutical benefits of mastic. Ailments it was claimed to cure included stomach upsets, chronic coughs and diseases of the liver, intestines and bladder. It was also used as an antidote for snake bites. During Turkish rule Chios received preferential treatment from the sultans who, along with the ladies of the harem, were hooked on chewing gum made from mastic – try the stuff and you will no doubt wonder why.

Until recently, mastic was widely used in the pharmaceutical industry, as well as in the manufacture of chewing gum and certain alcoholic drinks, particularly arak, a Middle Eastern liqueur. In most cases mastic has now been replaced by other products. However, mastic production may yet have a future. Some adherents of alternative medicine claim that it stimulates the immune system and reduces blood pressure and cholesterol levels. Chewing gum made from mastic can be bought on Chios, under the brand name Elma. ■

Pyrgi Πυργί

The largest of the Mastihohoria, and one of the most extraordinary villages in the whole of Greece, is Pyrgi (population 1300), 24km south-west of Chios town. The vaulted streets of the fortified village are narrow and labyrinthine. However, what makes Pyrgi unique are the façades of its buildings, decorated with intricate grey and white designs. Some of the patterns are geometric and others are based on flowers, leaves and animals. The technique used, called *xysta*, is achieved by coating the walls with a mixture of cement and black volcanic sand, painting over this with white lime, and then scraping off parts of the lime to reveal the matt grey beneath, using the bent prong of a fork.

From the main road, a fork to the right (coming from Chios town) leads into the heart of the village and the central square. The little 12th-century **Church of Agios Apostolos**, just off the square, is profusely decorated with well-preserved 17th-century frescoes. Ask at the taverna or *kafeneio* for the whereabouts of the church's caretaker, who will open it up for you. The façade of the larger church, on the opposite side of the square, has the most impressive xysta of all the buildings in the village.

Places to Stay & Eat The *Women's Agricultural Co-operative of Chios* (☎ 72 496) rents a number of traditionally furnished rooms in private houses throughout Pyrgi. Rates are

around 5000 to 7000 dr for doubles, depending on the season. The cooperative's office is near the central square of Pyrgi and is signposted. On the edge of the village are the very pleasant *Rooms to Let Nikos* (☎ 72 425), with doubles for 6500 dr. This includes the use of a kitchen and fridge.

The little taverna *I Manoula* on the central square (on the right as you face the large church) is your main eating option, or else the upstairs *Snack Bar* on the square can probably rustle up a few *mezedes* or a snack for you.

Emboreios (Εμπορειός)

Six km to the south of Pyrgi, Emboreios was the port of Pyrgi in the days when mastic production was big business. These days Emboreios is a quiet holiday resort for people who like to relax. As you come from Chios town, a signpost points left to Emboreios, just before you arrive at Pyrgi.

There are three tavernas, the *Neptune* with the most prominent position, and to the side the *Ifestio* and the *Porto Emborios*, the latter with a marginally better ambience. If you want to stay here, call *Studio Apartments Vasiliki* (☎ 71 422), or *Themis Studios* (☎ 71 810).

Mavra Volia beach is at the end of the road and has unusual black volcanic pebbles as its main attraction. There is another more secluded beach, just over the headland along a paved track.

Mesta (Μεστά)

Continuing on the main road from Pyrgi you will reach the mastic village of **Olympoi** after 5km. It's less immediately attractive than its two neighbours but still worth a brief stop.

Mesta, 5km further on, has a very different atmosphere than that created by the striking visual impact of Pyrgi and should be on any visitor's itinerary. The village is exquisite and is completely enclosed within massive fortified walls. Entrance to the maze of streets is via one of four gates. This method of limiting entry to the settlement and its disorienting maze of streets and tunnels is a prime example of 14th century defence architecture, as protection against pirates and marauders. The labyrinthine cobbled streets of bare stone houses and arches have a melancholy aura.

The village has two churches of the Taxiarhes (archangels): the older one dates from Byzantine times and has a magnificent 17th-century iconostasis; the second one, built in the 19th century, has very fine frescoes.

Orientation Buses stop on Plateia Nikolaou Poumpaki, on the main road outside Mesta. To reach the central square of Plateia Taxiarhon, with your back to the bus shelter, turn right, and then immediately left, and you will see a sign pointing to the centre of the village.

Places to Stay Many of the rooms in Mesta belong to the Pyrgi Women's Co-operative, and prices are similar. One place to start is the accommodation belonging to *Despina Syrimis* (☎ 76 494). The room (7500 dr) will sleep up to four people, and has a kitchen and private bathroom. It is difficult to find but Despina speaks English so you could telephone her; otherwise you can find her in the central square's Mesaionas Restaurant where she works. Alternatively, you can approach the owner of the Morias sta Mesta restaurant (see Places to Eat) and he will organise something for you.

Places to Eat There are two restaurants on the Plateia Taxiarhon and both conduct their business in romantic courtyard settings. Dionysios Karambelas, the affable owner of *Restaurant O Morias Sta Mesta* and originally from the Peloponnese (hence the name of the restaurant – Morias is the old name for the Peloponnese), will provide you with some superb country cooking. Ask to try hortokeftedes (vegetable patties) and an unusual wild green, kritamos, that grows by the sea. You should also ask for a glass of souma, an ouzo made from figs.

Next door, the *Mesaionas Restaurant* will provide you with equally good food should Dionysios' place be full.

NORTHERN CHIOS

Northern Chios is characterised by its craggy peaks (Mt Pelineo, Mt Oros and Mt Amani), deserted villages and scrawny hillsides once blanketed in rich pine forests. The area is mainly for the adventurous and those not phased by tortuous roads. Public transport up here is poor; you will need a reasonably-powered motorcycle to get around.

Volissos is the main focus for the villages of the north-western quarter. Reputedly Homer's place of birth, it is today a somewhat crumbling settlement, capped with an impressive Genoese fort. Volissos' port is **Limnia**, which is a workaday fishing harbour. It's not especially appealing, but has a welcoming taverna. You can continue to **Limnos**, 1km away, where caïques sometimes leave for Psara. The road onwards round the north end is very winding and passes some isolated villages.

On the eastern side a picturesque road leads out of **Vrontados** through a landscape that is somewhat more visitor-friendly than the western side. Pretty **Langada** is the first village, wedged at the end of a bay looking out towards Inousses. Next are **Kardamyla** and **Marmaro**, the two main settlements, though coastal Marmaro is not geared for tourism and is mercilessly exposed to the summer meltemi that howl through its narrow bay.

Most people go no further than the beach at **Nagos**, which is not bad, though still exposed to the vagaries of the winds – as is all the north coast. The road onwards winds upwards, skirting craggy Mt Pelineo. The scenery is green enough, but settlements are fewer and more remote. **Amades** and **Viki** are two villages you will traverse before hitting the last village, **Kambia**, perched high up on a ridge overlooking bare hillsides and the sea far below. From here a mostly sealed road leads you round Mt Pelineo, past a futuristic phalanx of 10 huge wind-driven generators on the opposite side of the valley, back to the cross-island route near Volissos.

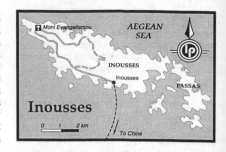

Inousses Οινούσσες

Off the north-eastern coast of Chios lie nine tiny islets, collectively called Inousses. Only one of these, also called Inousses, is inhabited. Those that live here permanently make their living from fishing and sheep farming. The island has three fish farms and exports small amounts of fish to Italy and France. Inousses is hilly and covered in scrub and has good beaches.

However, these facts apart, this is no ordinary Greek island. Inousses may be small, but it is the ancestral home of around 30% of Greece's ship owners. Most of these exceedingly wealthy maritime barons conduct their businesses from Athens, London and New York, but in summer return with their families to Inousses where they own luxurious mansions.

There is a rumour that these ship owners offer financial incentives to discourage people from opening tavernas or domatia on the island, because they don't want to attract foreign tourists. It may not be possible to vouch for the truth of this but certainly tourism is not encouraged on the island: no domatia owners come to meet the boat, there are no domatia signs and wandering around the streets fails to bring offers of accommodation. Several islanders have stated that Inousses has a few domatia, but they are vague as to their whereabouts.

On a more positive note – and if these

quirks have not discouraged you from going to Inousses – the island has a picturesque town of neoclassical mansions; superb beaches; lots of opportunities for walking; stunning vistas and no package tourists – in fact not many tourists at all. In Inousses town there is a large naval boarding school. If you visit during term time you may well encounter the pupils parading around town to bellowed marching orders.

Getting There & Away
The island is served only by the local ferry boat *Oinoussai II*, which plies daily between the island and Chios town. It leaves Chios town at 2 pm and Inousses at 9 am. Purchase tickets on board for 700 dr (one way). The trip takes about one hour. In summer there are sometimes excursion boats from Chios town to the island. Enquire about these at one of the travel agencies in Chios town.

Getting Around
Inousses has no public transport, but there is one taxi.

INOUSSES TOWN
• *pop 640* • *postcode 821 01* • *area code* ☎ *0271*
The island has one settlement, the little town which is also called Inousses. To reach the centre of town from the boat quay, facing inland turn left and follow the waterfront to Plateia Antoniou P Laimou; veer slightly right here, and you will immediately come to Plateia T Naftisynis; veer right once again and you will see ahead the Restaurant &

Kafeneio Pateronissa. Facing this establishment turn right and ascend the steps.

If you turn left at the Restaurant Pateronissa and then take the first right into Konstantinou Antonopoulou you will come to the National Bank of Greece which, one can surmise, is kept very busy. Next door to the bank is a combined post office and OTE.

There are no EOT or tourist police on the island. The regular police (☎ 55 222) are at the top of the steps which lead to the town centre.

Maritime Museum

This museum is between the Restaurant Pateronissa and the National Bank of Greece. It opened in 1990 and the benefactors were wealthy ship owners from the island. Many island families donated nautical memorabilia, which includes *objets d'art*, photographs, models of early ships, cannons and nautical instruments.

The museum keeps very erratic opening times. If you find it closed (which is highly likely), ask around and someone may open it up for you.

Places to Stay

There is no camp site on the island and camping freelance would definitely be frowned upon. For domatia, ask at one of the restaurants or kafeneia. Good luck!

Inousses' one hotel is the comfortable, but pricey, C-class *Hotel Thalassoporos* (☎ 55 475), at the top of the steps which lead to the town centre. Rates are 6000/9000 dr for singles/doubles with private bathroom. These prices drop to 5000/7000 dr in the low season. It's unlikely ever to be full, but just in case, phone ahead in July and August.

Places to Eat

Of Inousses' three restaurants, the *Restaurant Pateronissa* has been established the longest. The food is reasonably priced and well prepared.

The town has three *pantopoleia*: one is near the Restaurant Pateronissa and the other two are in the centre of town on the road

which leads up to the prominent Agios Nikolaos church.

ISLAND WALK

This is a three-hour circular walk. Although most of the walk is along a narrow cement road, you are unlikely to meet much traffic. Take plenty of water and a snack with you as there are no refreshments available along the way. Also take your swimming gear as you will pass many of the island's beaches. You will also pass the Moni Evangelismou in the west of the island.

Just beyond the maritime museum you will see a signpost to **Moni Evangelismou**. This will take you along the cement road which skirts the west coast. Along the way you will pass several inviting beaches and coves. Only **Apiganos beach** is signposted, but there are others which are easily accessible from the road. After about one hour the road loops inland, and a little further along is the entrance to the palatial Moni Evangelismou, surrounded by extensive grounds.

Within the convent is the mummified body of Irini Pateras, daughter of the late Panagos Pateras, a multimillionaire ship owner. Irini became a nun in her late teens and died in the early 1960s when she was 20. Her distraught mother decided to build the convent in memory of her daughter. In the Greek Orthodox religion, three years after burial the body is exhumed and the bones cleaned and reburied in a casket. When Irini's body was exhumed it was found to have mummified rather than decomposed; this phenomenon is regarded in Greece as evidence of sainthood. Irini's mother is now abbess of the convent, which houses around 20 nuns. Only women may visit the convent and of course they must be appropriately (modestly) dressed.

Continuing along the cement road, beyond the entrance to the convent, you will come to two stone pillars on the left. The wide path between the pillars leads in 10 minutes to an enormous white cross which is a memorial to St Irini. This is the highest point of the island and commands stunning views over to northern Chios and the Turkish peninsula of Karaburun. About 20 minutes further along, the cement road gives way to a dirt track. Continue straight ahead to reach Inousses town.

Psara Ψαρά

• *pop 500* • *postcode 821 04* • *area code* ☎ *0274*
Psara (Psara) lies off Chios' north-west coast. The island is 9km long and 5km wide and is rocky with little vegetation. During Ottoman times Greeks settled on this remote island to escape Turkish oppression. By the 19th century, many of these inhabitants, like those of Chios and Inousses, had become successful ship owners. When the rallying cry for self-determination reverberated through the country, the Psariots zealously took up arms and contributed a large number of ships to the Greek cause. In retaliation the Turks stormed the island and killed all but 3000 of the 20,000 inhabitants. The island never regained its former glory and today all of the inhabitants live in the island's one settlement, also called Psara.

Places to Stay & Eat
Like Inousses, Psara sees few tourists. The old parliament building has been converted into an *EOT Guesthouse* (☎ 61 293). Doubles with shared bathroom are 6000 dr and with private bathroom, 7000 dr. Information may be obtained by either telephoning the guesthouse or ringing ☎ 27 908 in Lesvos. There are also domatia in Psara.

There are a small number of eating places on the island.

Getting There & Away
Ferries leave Chios town for Psara at 7 am three times a week. Check with a local agent for current departure days since these may change from year to year.

Lesvos (Mytilini)
Λέσβος (Μυτιλήνη)

Lesvos (Lesvos, population 88,800) is the third-largest island in Greece, after Crete and Evia. It lies north of Chios and south-east of Limnos. The island is mountainous with two bottleneck gulfs penetrating its south coast. The south and east of the island are fertile, with numerous olive groves. Lesvos produces the best olive oil in Greece and has many olive-oil refineries. In contrast to the south and east, the west has rocky and barren mountains, creating a dramatic moonscape.

Lesvos is becoming a popular package-holiday destination, but is large enough to absorb tourists without seeming to be over-run. Most Greeks call the island Mytilini, which is also the name of the capital.

History
In the 6th century BC, Lesvos was unified under the rule of the tyrant Pittakos, one of ancient Greece's Seven Sages. Pittakos succeeded in resolving the long-standing animosity between the island's two cities of Mytilini and Mithymna. This new-found peace generated an atmosphere conducive to creativity, and Lesvos became a centre of artistic and philosophical achievement. Terpander, the musical composer, and Arion, the poet, were both born on Lesvos in the 7th century BC.

Arion's works influenced the tragedians of the 5th century BC such as Sophocles and Euripides. Sappho, one of the greatest poets

Psara

0   2   4 km

▲546m

AEGEAN SEA   PSARA

Psara

ANTIPSARA

To Chios

DIMITRI GATZOURAS

ROSEMARY HALL

PAUL HELLANDER

Top Left: Two girls dressed in their finest in Olymbos, Karpathos, Dodecanese
Top Right: The Church of the Taxiarhs in Mesta, Chios, North-Eastern Aegean islands
Bottom: Restored windmills grace a harbour on Chios, North-Eastern Aegean islands

CORINNE SIMCOCK

DAVID HALL

Top: Brightly painted fishing boats in Samos town's harbour, North-Eastern Aegean islands
Bottom: Sanctuary of the Great Gods, Samothraki, North-Eastern Aegean islands

Sappho

Sappho is renowned chiefly for her poems that speak out in favour of lesbian relationships, though her range of lyric poetry extends beyond works of an erotic nature. She was born in 630 BC in the town of Eresos on the western side of Lesvos. Little is known about her private life other than that she was married, had a daughter and was exiled to Sicily in about 600 BC. Only fragments remain of her nine books of poems, the most famous of which are the marriage songs. Among her works were hymns, mythological poems and personal love songs. Most of these seem to have been addressed to a close inner-circle of female companions. Sappho uses sensuous images of nature to create her own special brand of erotic lyric poetry. It is a simple yet melodious style, later copied by the Roman poet Catullus. Lesvos, and Eresos in particular, are today the targets of many visits by lesbians paying homage to Sappho. ■

The Lesvos-born poet Sappho

of ancient Greece, was born on Lesvos almost a century later. Unfortunately little of her poetry is extant, but what remains reveals a genius for combining passion with simplicity and detachment, in verses of great beauty and power. In the 4th century BC, Aristotle and Epicurus taught at an exceptional school of philosophy which flourished on Lesvos.

On a more prosaic level, Lesvos suffered at the hands of invaders and occupiers to the same extent as all other Greek islands. In 527 BC the Persians conquered the island, but in 479 BC it was captured by Athens and became a member of the Delian League. In the following centuries the island suffered numerous invasions, and in 70 BC it was conquered by Julius Caesar. Byzantines, Venetians, Genoese and Turks followed.

However, through all these vicissitudes the arts retained a high degree of importance. The primitive painter Theophilos (1866-1934) and the Nobel prize-winning poet Odysseus Elytis were both born on Lesvos. The island is to this day a spawning ground for innovative ideas in the arts and politics, and is the headquarters of the University of the Aegean.

Trekking

Lesvos has an admirably well-organised and well-publicised set of trekking trails in the north and south of the island. These are marked with colour-coded, easy-to-spot signs and cover a wide variety of landscapes. Get a copy of the booklet *Trekking Trails on Lesvos* from the Tourism Directorate of the North Aegean, PO Box 37, Mytilini GR-811 00, or from any good EOT office. These walks can be taken in sections, or over a few days, stopping off along the way wherever appropriate. They are a mixture of dirt vehicle tracks and walking-only trails. The four trails are:

Itinerary 1: Vatera to Gera This is a longish trail that leads from the beach enclave of Vatera over some of Lesvos' finest forest and mountain scenery to Gera on the gulf of the same name. This trail is marked by a sign with a yellow circle.

Itinerary 2: Petra to Lapsarna This route takes you along the north coast of Lesvos from the resort of Petra to Lapsarna in the far west mainly along walking-only trails. This is a beautiful walk for beachcombers. The trail is marked by a sign with a yellow square.

Itinerary 3: Kapi to Sykamia This route circles Mt Lepetymnos in northern Lesvos and traverses ravines covered with olive groves, poplar and oak trees and passes

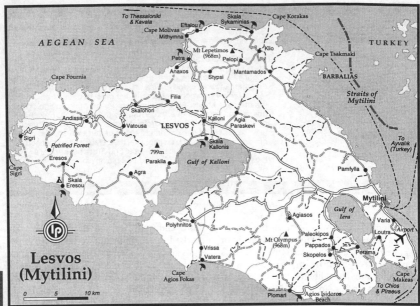

through a number of villages. This route is marked by a sign with a yellow triangle.

Itinerary 4: Sigri-Eresos This route crosses the barren landscape of south-western Lesvos between the two villages of Sigri and Eresos and follows the old road all the way, skirting the forest of petrified trees. This is an easy day trek. This route is marked by a sign with a yellow oblong.

Books Lonely Planet's *Trekking in Greece* walking guide by Marc Dubin has a description of the hike around Mt Lepetymnos (Itinerary 3) on pages 345 to 349.

If you read Greek, there is also a detailed guide to trekking called Περπατώντας τη Λέσβο (Trekking in Lesvos) by a local authority called Makis Axiotis. The book is currently out of print, though it may have reappeared by the time you read this.

Bird-Watching

Bird-watching – or 'birding', as the experts call it – is big business in Lesvos. The island is the transit point and home to over 279 species of birds ranging from raptors to waders. As a result, Lesvos is attracting an ever-increasing number of visitors – both human and feathered – particularly in spring. There are four main observation areas centred on Eresos, Petra, Skala Kallonis and Agiasos.

The major aim of birders seems to be spotting the elusive cinereous bunting and Kruper's nuthatch. At any rate it is a growing and popular activity – birders seem to be more numerous than birds at times.

A folksy and detailed handbook to the hobby is Richard Brooks' *Birding in Lesbos*, which retails for a fairly steep 5700 dr on Lesvos, but is probably the most authoritative – and entertaining – book on the topic. Fax 44-1328-878 632 for further distribution details.

Getting There & Away

Air There are three flights a day from Lesvos to Athens (15,800 dr); one a day to Thessaloniki (19,600 dr); and daily flights to Limnos (12,700 dr). There are two flights a week to Chios (10,200 dr). Note that Lesvos is always referred to as Mytilini on air schedules. The Olympic Airways office (☎ 0251-28 659) in Mytilini is at Kavetsou 44. (Kavetsou is a southerly continuation of Ermou.) The airport is 8km south of Mytilini. A taxi to/from the airport will cost about 1000 dr.

Ferry – domestic In summer there is at least one ferry a day to Piraeus (12 hours, 5820 dr) via Chios and some direct services (10 hours); three a week to Kavala (11 hours, 5430 dr) via Limnos; and two a week to Thessaloniki (13 hours, 7120 dr) via Limnos. Ferry ticket offices line the eastern side of Pavlou Kountouriotou, in Mytilini. Get tickets for the above destinations from the Maritime Company of Lesvos (NEL) (☎ 0251-28 480; fax 28 601), Pavlou Kountouriotou 67.

In addition, there is an independent service once a week southwards to Chios (3½ hours, 2875 dr); Samos (seven hours, 3560 dr); Kos (12 hours, 4420 dr) and Rhodes (16 hours, 6500 dr); and northwards to Limnos (5½ hours, 3690 dr) and Alexandroupolis (10½ hours, 4500 dr). On the southern leg the C/F Romilda continues on to Crete. For tickets and departure details contact Picolo Travel (☎ 0251-27 000; fax 42 042), at Pavlou Kountouriotou 73a.

The port police (☎ 0251-28 827) are next to Picolo Travel on the east side of Pavlou Kountouriotou.

Ferry – international Ferry services to Ayvalik in Turkey were under a cloud as of mid-1997. They may or may not be running by the time you read this. In any case, planned fares would be 17,000 dr for both one-way and return tickets. A small car would cost 14,000 dr. Call ☎ 093-440 091 (mobile) for the latest news. Turkish ferries from Ayvalik to Mytilini *are* running, but

you cannot buy a ticket on a Turkish boat from Greece. Such is the nature of local politics.

Getting Around

Bus Lesvos' transport hub is the capital, Mytilini. In summer, from the long-distance bus station there are three buses a day to Skala Eresou (2½ hours, 1850 dr) via Eresos. There are five buses a day to Mithymna (1¾ hours, 1250 dr) via Petra, and two buses to Sigri (2½ hours, 1850 dr). There are no direct buses between Eresos, Sigri and Mithymna. If you wish to travel from one of these villages to another, change buses in the town of Kalloni, which is 48km from Eresos and 22km from Mithymna. There are five buses a day to the south-coast resort of Plomari (1¼ hours, 800 dr).

Car & Motorcycle There are many car-hire outlets in Mytilini. They include Troho Kinisi (☎ 0251-41 160; mobile 093 237 900), which operates from the Erato Hotel just south of the Olympic Airways office, and Lesvos Car (☎ 0251-28 242), Pavlou Kountouriotou 47. Many motorcycle-rental firms are along the same stretch of waterfront. You will, however, be better off hiring a motorcycle or scooter in Mithymna or Skala Eresou, since Lesvos is large and an underpowered two-wheeler is not really a practical mode of transport for getting around the island.

MYTILINI Μυτιλήνη
• pop 23,970 • postcode 811 00 • area code ☎ 0251
Mytilini, the capital and port of Lesvos, is a large workaday town. If you are enthralled by pretty and sparkling towns like Mykonos and Paros then you won't necessarily find the same ambience in Mytilini. However, this town has its own attractions including a lively harbour and nightlife, its once grand 19th-century mansions (which are gradually being renovated), and its jumbled streets.

Mytilini won't enthral sun, sea and sand lovers: the town beach is mediocre, crowded and what's more you have to pay to use it (adults, 200 dr; children, 100 dr). However,

PLACES TO STAY
2 Salina's Garden Rooms
3 Thalia Rooms
4 Pelagia Koumiotou Rooms
10 Pension Iren
14 Sappho Hotel
16 Hotel Lesvion

PLACES TO EAT
1 Ermis Ouzeri
6 Music Café
7 I Psatha
8 Ta Stroggylia
9 Ta Asteria
13 Restaurant Averof
20 Taverna Boudroumi
28 Stratos Psarotaverna

OTHER
5 Entrance to Fortress
11 Hot Spot
12 Bus Station for Local Buses
15 National Bank of Greece
17 Iguana Café
18 Byzantine Museum
19 Picolo Travel
21 Archaeological Museum
22 Port Police
23 Currency-Exchange Machine
24 EOT & Tourist Police
25 OTE
26 Post Office
27 Public Theatre
29 Bus Station for
Long-Distance Buses
30 Olympic Airways Office

Mytilini

you will appreciate Mytilini if you enjoy seeking out traditional kafeneia and little backstreet *ouzeria*, or if you simply take pleasure in wandering through unfamiliar towns.

The northern end of Ermou, the town's main commercial thoroughfare, is a wonderful ramshackle street full of character. It has old-fashioned *zaharoplasteia*; grocers; fruit and vegetable stores; bakers; and antique, embroidery, ceramic and jewellery shops. (The latter four are there for the benefit of discerning locals rather than spendthrift tourists.)

Orientation

Mytilini is built around two harbours (the north and south) which occupy both sides of a promontory and are linked by the main thoroughfare of Ermou. East of the harbours is a large fortress surrounded by a pine forest. All passenger ferries dock at the southern harbour. The waterfront here is called Pavlou Kountouriotou and the ferry quay is at its southern end. The northern harbour's waterfront is called Navmahias Ellis.

Information

The EOT and tourist police (☎ 22 776) share

the same office at the entrance to the quay. Banks, including the National Bank of Greece with an ATM, can be found on Pavlou Kountouriotou. There is also an ATM at the Mortgage Bank on this street, not too far from the ferry terminal. The post office is on Vournazon, which is west of the southern harbour. The OTE is on the same street just west of the post office.

Things to See

Mytilini's imposing **castle**, with its well-preserved walls, was built in early Byzantine times and renovated in the 14th century by Fragistco Gatelouzo. It was enlarged by the Turks. The surrounding pine forest is a pleasant place for a picnic. The castle is open daily from 8.30 am to 3 pm. Admission is 500 dr; 300 dr for students.

The **archaeological museum** (☎ 22 087) is housed in a neoclassical mansion one block north of the quay and has impressive finds from Neolithic to Roman times. Opening times are Tuesday to Sunday from 8.30 am to 2.30 pm. Admission is 500 dr.

The dome of the **Church of Agios Therapon** can be spotted from almost anywhere on the southern waterfront. The church has a highly ornate interior with a huge chandelier, an intricately carved iconostasis and priest's throne, and a frescoed dome. The **Byzantine Museum** (☎ 28 916) in the church's courtyard houses some fine icons. The museum is open from Monday to Saturday from 10 am to 1 pm. Admission is 300 dr.

Whatever you do, don't miss the **Theophilos Museum** (☎ 41 644), which houses the works of the prolific primitive painter Theophilos, who was born on Lesvos. Several prestigious museums and galleries around the country now proudly display his works. However, he lived in abject poverty painting the walls of kafeneia and tavernas in return for sustenance. The museum is open Tuesday to Sunday from 9 am to 1 pm and 4.30 to 8 pm. Admission is 500 dr.

The **Teriade Museum** (☎ 23 372), next door, commemorates the artist and critic Stratis Eleftheriadis (he Gallicised his name to Teriade) who was born on Lesvos but lived and worked in Paris. It was largely due to Teriade's efforts that Theophilos' work gained international renown. On display are reproductions of Teriade's own illustrations and his collection of works by 20th-century artists, including such greats as Picasso, Chagall and Matisse. The museum is open Tuesday to Sunday from 9 am to 2 pm and 5 to 8 pm. Admission is 250 dr.

These museums are 4km from Mytilini in the village of **Varia** where Theophilos was born. Take a local bus from the bus station at the northernmost section of Pavlou Kountouriotou.

Places to Stay – bottom end

In Mytilini, domatia owners belong to a co-operative called *Sappho Self-Catering Rooms in Mytilini*. There are 22 establishments; if any of the ones recommended are full or don't suit, the owner will direct you to another. Most of these domatia are in little side streets off Ermou, near the northern harbour. The nearest to the quay is *Iren* (☎ 22 787), Komninaki 41. The clean and simply furnished doubles/triples cost 5500/6750 dr with breakfast. Komninaki is one block behind the eastern section of Pavlou Kountouriotou. *Salina's Garden Rooms* (☎ 42 073), Fokeas 7, are cosy and clean with a delightful garden. Rates are 6500 dr for a double with private bathroom and 6000 dr without. The rooms are signposted from the corner of Ermou and Adramytiou.

Coming from Ermou, if you turn right opposite Salina's rooms you will reach *Thalia Rooms* (☎ 24 640), at Kinikiou 1. The pleasant doubles/triples in this large family house are 6000/7200 dr with private bathroom. *Pelagia Koumiotou Rooms* (☎ 20 643), Tertseti 6, near the castle, are lovely rooms in an old family house. Rates are 5400/7000 dr for doubles/triples with shared bathroom. Walk along Mikras Asias and turn left into Tertseti; the rooms are on the right.

Places to Stay – middle

There are several hotels on the southern

waterfront, but you will pay more at these than in the domatia. The C-class *Sappho Hotel* (☎ 22 888), on the north-west section of Pavlou Kountouriotou, has rates of 7700/12,000 dr for singles/doubles/triples with private bathroom. The more luxurious B-class *Hotel Lesvion* (☎ 22 037; fax 42 493), just two doors away, has singles/doubles for 10,000/17,500 dr which can usually be negotiated for a better deal.

Places to Eat
You will eat well on Lesvos whether you enjoy fish dishes, traditional Greek food, international cuisine or vegetarian meals, and Mytilini is no exception. You might wish to avoid the restaurants on the western section of the southern waterfront where the waiters tout for customers. These restaurants are atypical of Mytilini as they pander to tourists and serve bland, overpriced food.

The small, mildly ramshackle but delightfully atmospheric *Ermis Ouzeri* has yet to be discovered by the mass tourist crowd. It is at the north end of Ermou on the corner with Kornarou. Its interior is decorated with scattered antiques, old watercolour paintings and old black and white photos of previous clients. Chickpeas, salad, fried peppers and a beer should cost you about 2200 dr.

The *Restaurant Averof*, in the middle of the southern waterfront, is a no-nonsense traditional restaurant serving hearty Greek staples, while *Ta Asteria* on the opposite side of the harbour is slightly more up-market and serves similar food for slightly higher prices.

The small, friendly ouzeri-style *Ta Stroggylia* at Komninaki 9 has wine barrels and good food at reasonable prices. If you want meat dishes, check out *I Psatha* (winter only) on Methodiou, off Ermou. There is an old jukebox that actually works. For top fish dishes, go to *Stratos Psarotaverna* at Fanari, at the bottom end of the main harbour. It is more up-market in prices. Tables from all the surrounding restaurants take over the road in summer.

Another place serving high-quality Greek dishes is *Taverna Boudroumi*. The restaurant is set back from the southern end of Komninaki and is a bit difficult to find – look for a stone building with black wrought-iron wall lamps at the entrance.

Entertainment
The *Music Café*, on the corner of Mitropoleos and Vernardaki, is a hip place – arty without being pretentious. Drinks are in the mid-price range rather than cheap, but worth it for the terrific atmosphere. Tapes of jazz, blues and classical music are played, and there is live music on Wednesday evenings – usually jazz. The café is open from 7.30 am to 2 am. Another couple of 'in' places are the *Iguana Café* on the west side of the harbour and the *Hot Spot* on the east side. Both are popular with students and you can borrow board games.

For disco life with a difference, head out to *Quebrancho*, an old converted tannery, replete with original machinery. It is 5km north of Mytilini, just before Panagiouda.

Getting There & Away
Mytilini has two bus stations: the one for long-distance buses is just beyond the southwestern end of Pavlou Kountouriotou; the bus station for buses to local villages is on the northernmost section of Pavlou Kountouriotou. For motorists, there is a large free-parking area just south of the main harbour.

NORTHERN LESVOS
Northern Lesvos is dominated both economically and physically by the exquisitely preserved traditional town of Mithymna, a town of historical, and modern, importance in Lesvos' commercial life. Its neighbouring beach resort of Petra, 6km south, receives low-key packaged tourism and the villages surrounding Mt Lepetymnos are authentic, picturesque and worth a day or two of exploration.

Mithymna Μήθυμνα
• *pop 1333* • *postcode 811 08* • *area code* ☎ *0253*
Although this town has officially reverted to its ancient name of Mithymna (Methymna) most locals still refer to it as Molyvos. It is

62km from Mytilini and is the principal town of northern Lesvos. The one-time rival to Mytilini, picturesque Mithymna is nowadays the antithesis of the island capital. Its impeccable stone houses with brightly coloured shutters reach down to the harbour from a castle-crowned hill. Its two main thoroughfares of Kastrou and 17 Noemvriou are winding, cobbled and shaded by vines. In contrast to Mytilini, Mithymna's pretty streets are lined with souvenir shops.

Orientation & Information From the bus stop, walk straight ahead towards the town. Where the road forks, take the right fork into 17 Noemvriou, which is the main street of Mithymna. Along here, at the top of the hill, the road forks again; the right fork is Kastrou and the post office is along here on the left. The left fork is a continuation of 17 Noemvriou.

The National Bank of Greece is on the left, just past the bus stop and sports an ATM.

There is a small tourist information office (☎ 71 347/069) on the left, between the bus stop and the fork in the road.

Things to See & Do One of the most pleasant things to do in Mithymna is to stroll along its gorgeous streets. If you have the energy, the ruined 14th-century **Genoese castle** is worth clambering up to for fine views of the coastline and over the sea to Turkey. From this castle in the 15th century, Onetta d'Oria, wife of the Genoese governor, repulsed an onslaught by the Turks by putting on her husband's armour and leading the people of Mithymna into battle. In summer the castle is the venue for a drama festival; ask for details at the tourist office.

The beach at Mithymna is pebbled and crowded, but in summer excursion boats leave daily at 10 am for the superior beaches of Eftalou, Skala Sykaminias, Petra and Anaxos.

Places to Stay – bottom end The excellent and refreshingly shady camp site *Camping Mithymna* (☎ 71 169/079) is 1.5km from town and signposted from near the tourist

office. It opens in early June, though you can usually camp if you arrive a little earlier than that. One person with a tent will cost 1350 dr.

There are over 50 official domatia in Mithymna; most consist of only one or two rooms. All display domatia signs and most are of a high standard. The tourist booth near the bus stop will help you if you can't be bothered looking; otherwise, the best street to start is 17 Noemvriou. Among the first signposted rooms you will come to are those of the *Nassos Guest House* (☎ 71 022), leading off to the right. The rooms are simply furnished and most have a panoramic view. The cost is 6000 dr.

A beautifully restored stone building houses the *domatia* of Myrsina Baliaka (☎ 71 414). From the bus stop walk towards the town and take the second right into Myrasillou, by the card phone. The domatia are 50m on your right. Look out for the prominent green shutters. A double will cost around 7000 dr.

Places to Stay – middle A pleasant C-class hotel that won't totally blow the budget is the *Hotel Eftalou* (☎ 71 713; fax 71 791) among the cluster of small, low-key resort hotels on the road out to Eftalou. A comfortable double room goes for 10,000 dr in the low season and 13,000 dr in the high season. There's a swimming pool and restaurant to boot.

Nearby are the secluded *Eftalou Villas* (☎ 22 662; fax 26 535), each with a different name and sleeping from four to eight people. A villa for four ranges in price from 14,000 to 17,000 dr, depending on the season.

Places to Eat The streets 17 Noemvriou and Kastrou have a wide selection of restaurants serving typical Greek fare. Look out for *Nassos*, *Gatos*, the *Asteria tis Molyvou* and *To Chani*, most of which have fine views over the sea. For more of a fishing-village ambience, head down to the far end of the little harbour where there is a clutch of eating places, the best of which is the Australian-Greek *Captain's Table*. Their mezedes are exquisite: try adjuka – a Ukrainian-inspired

NORTH-EASTERN AEGEAN

spicy aubergine dip – or their unique spinach salad. There is live bouzouki music three nights a week and Melinda and her husband Theodoros will make you more than welcome.

Petra Πέτρα
• postcode 811 09 • area code ☎ 0253

Petra, 5km south of Mithymna, is a popular coastal resort with a long sandy beach shaded by tamarisk trees. Despite tourist development it remains an attractive village retaining some traditional houses. Looming over the village is an enormous, almost perpendicular rock which looks as if it's been lifted from Meteora in Thessaly; Petra means 'rock'. The rock is crowned by the 18th-century Panagia Glykophilousa (Church of the Sweet Kissing Virgin). You can reach it by climbing up the 114 rock-hewn steps – worth it for the view. Petra, like many settlements on Lesvos, is a 'preserved' village. It has not and will not make any concessions to the concrete monstrosities that have characterised tourist development elsewhere in Greece.

Petra has a post office, OTE, bank, medical facilities and bus connections.

Places to Stay Your best bet for accommodation in Petra is to head straight for Greece's first Women's Agricultural Tourism Collective (☎ 41 238; fax 41 309) which began here in 1985 and is still going strong. The women can arrange for you to stay with a family in the village; you will pay around 4000/6000 dr for a single/double. Their office is on the central square – signposted from the waterfront.

Of the cluster of small pensions at the western end of Petra's waterfront, *Studio Niki* (☎ 41 601) is a good bet. Neat doubles/triples with kitchenette go for around 8000 dr. Studio Niki, like most pensions nearby, works mainly with packaged groups, so it is a good idea to ring beforehand if planning to arrive in peak season.

Places to Eat The *Syneterismos* restaurant has moussaka and Greek salad for about

1800 dr. There's a gamut of eateries along the waterfront, all pandering to the tourist and Greek palate alike. *To Tyhero Petalo*, towards the eastern end, has attractive décor and sells ready-made food for around 1200 dr for a main course dish. The *Pittakos Ouzeri* is a bit more like the genuine article and is still on the seafront, while in the backstreet you might look out for the *Koutouki*, which is popular with locals.

WESTERN LESVOS

Western Lesvos is quite different from the rest of the island and this becomes apparent almost immediately as you wind westward out of Kalloni. The landscape becomes drier and barer and there are fewer settlements, though when they do appear they look very tidy and their red-tiled roofs add vital colour to an otherwise mottled green-brown landscape. The far western end is almost devoid of trees other than the petrified kind. Here you will find Lesvos' 'petrified forest' on a windswept and barren hillside. One resort, a remote fishing village and the birthplace of Sappho are what attract people to western Lesvos.

Eresos & Skala Eresou
• postcode 881 05 • area code ☎ 0253

Eresos, 90km from Mytilini, is a traditional inland village. It is reached via the road junction just after the hillside village of Andissa. The road leading down to Eresos, through what looks like a moonscape, belies what is ahead. Beyond the village of Eresos a riotously fertile agricultural plain leads to Eresos' beach annexe, Skala Eresou, which is 4km beyond on the west coast. It is a popular resort linked to Eresos by an attractive, very straight tree-lined road.

Skala Eresou is built over ancient Eresos where Sappho (628-568 BC) was born. Although it gets crowded in summer it has a good laid-back atmosphere. It is also a popular destination for lesbians who come on a kind of pilgrimage in honour of the poet. If you're a beach freak you should certainly visit – there is almost 2km of fine silvery-brown sand.

Orientation & Information From the bus turnaround at Skala Eresou, walk towards the sea to reach the central square of Plateia Anthis & Evristhenous abutting the waterfront. The beach stretches to the left and right of this square. Turn right at the square onto Gyrinnis and just under 50m along you will come to a sign pointing left to the post office; the OTE is next door. Neither Skala Eresou nor Eresos have a bank but there is a prominent automatic exchange and ATM for visitors' convenience.

There is no EOT or tourist police, but Exeresis Travel (☎ 53 044), 200m to the right of the bus station (facing the sea), is helpful. The staff here can arrange car, motorcycle and bicycle hire; and treks on foot and on horses and donkeys. They also have a currency exchange.

Archaeological Museum Eresos' archaeological museum houses archaic, classical and Roman finds including statues, coins and grave steles. The museum, which is in the centre of Skala Eresou, stands near the remains of the early Christian Basilica of Agios Andreas. Opening times are Tuesday to Sunday from 8.30 am to 3 pm. Admission is free.

Petrified Forest of Sigri 'Petrified forest' is the EOT's hyperbolic description of the scattering of ancient tree stumps near the village of Sigri, on the west coast, north of Skala Eresou. Experts reckon the petrified wood is at least 500,000, but possibly 20 million, years old. If you're intrigued, the forest is easiest reached as an excursion from Skala Eresou; enquire at Exeresis Travel. If you're making your own way, the turn-off to the forest is 7km before the village of Sigri. It is signposted.

Places to Stay There is an official free *camp site* at the western end of the beach at Skala Eresou; to reach it turn right at the waterfront. The site has cold showers and toilets, but as the upkeep is minimal the latter get pretty filthy when the site is crowded.

Bear in mind that this camp site is used predominantly by lesbians.

There are a few domatia in Eresos but most people head for Skala Eresou, where there are a number of domatia, pensions and hotels. *Rooms to Let Katia* (☎ 53 148), at the eastern end of the waterfront, has comfortable singles/doubles with a view for 6100/9500 dr.

C-class *Sappho the Eressia* (☎ 53 233; fax 53 174) is a small hotel on the waterfront with singles/doubles for 6000/8000 dr. The only problem here is that it can be noisy.

Skala Eresou's best hotel is the C-class *Hotel Galini* (☎ 53 137; fax 53 155). Its light and airy rooms cost 6500/8500 dr for singles/doubles/triples with private bathroom. The hotel has a comfortable TV room-cum-bar and an outside terrace under a bamboo shade. It is clearly signposted.

Places to Eat The shady promenade offers many eating options, most with beach and sea views across to Chios and Psara. The *Gorgona* restaurant with its stone-clad façade is as good a place to start as any. Tasty, stuffed courgettes in lemon sauce, Greek salad and a small bottle of retsina cost 2500 dr.

Yamas (☎ 53 693) is a Canadian-run pancake and snack joint run by expats Nick and Linda. Here you can get home-made North American cooking, chocolate cake and cool beer. You can also listen to 70s music, and the occasional jam takes place when the mood takes over. Bikes can be hired here.

Bennett's International & Vegetarian Restaurant is an English-run establishment, with a good menu selection, including vegetarian, at the eastern end of the waterfront. Prices are much like the Gorgona's.

SOUTHERN LESVOS

Southern Lesvos is dominated by 968m Mt Olympus. Pine forests decorate its flanks, though in recent years fires have ravaged large sections – particularly the steep slopes

NORTH-EASTERN AEGEAN

north of the resort town of **Plomari**. A large, traditional village, popular with visitors, Plomari also has a laid-back beach settlement.

If you are touring this part of the island, you will almost certainly want to visit the large village of **Agiasos** on the northern flank of Mt Olympus. This village features prominently in most local tourist publications and is a popular day-trip destination. Agiasos is very picturesque but not tacky, with artisan workshops making anything from handcrafted furniture to pottery. Its winding, cobbled streets will eventually lead you to the church of the Panagia Vrefokratousa with its Byzantine Museum and Popular Museum in the courtyard.

A couple of restaurants near the bus stop are your best bet for eating in Agiasos. One is the *Anatoli* and the other is a nameless *psistaria* owned by Grigoris Douladellis.

Plomari on the south coast is a cramped and crumbling resort. It is not so exciting, but is very popular with Scandinavian tourists who are lured by cheap accommodation, but end up paying for it with expensive food. Most people stay at **Agios Isidoros** 3km to the east where there is a narrow, overcrowded beach.

A far superior option is the low-key family resort of **Vatera** over to the east and reached via the inland town of **Polyhnitos**. This relaxing oasis has a very good, clean 9km-long beach, a sprinkling of widely scattered hotels, domatia and restaurants.

There is one camp site here: *Camping Dionysos* (☎ 0252-61 151; fax 61 155). It's quite good, if somewhat small, but has a pool, minimarket, restaurant and cooking facilities. It is set back about 100m from the beach. Camping costs are about 1500 dr for a tent and one person. The site is open from 1 June to 30 September.

Your best eating and accommodation option by far is the modern C-class *Hotel Vatera Beach* (☎ 0252-61 212; fax 61 164) with its American-Greek owners Barbara and George Ballis. They provide a relaxed environment and good Greek home cooking. A double room ranges in price from 11,200

to 15,500 dr depending on the season. You can also book by e-mail: hovatera@compulink.gr.

Limnos Λήμνος

There is a saying on Limnos that when people come to the island they cry twice: once when they arrive and once when they leave. Limnos' appeal is not immediate; it's charm slowly but surely captivates.

The deeply penetrating Moudros bay almost severs the island in two. The landscape of Limnos lacks the imposing grandeur of the forested and mountainous islands and the stark beauty of the barren and rocky ones. Gently undulating, with little farms, Limnos has a unique and understated appeal. In spring vibrant wildflowers dot the landscape, and in autumn purple crocuses sprout forth in profusion. Large numbers of flamingoes grace the lakes of eastern Limnos and the coastline boasts some of the best beaches in the North-Eastern Aegean group. The island is sufficiently off the beaten track to have escaped the adverse effects of mass tourism.

History

Limnos' position near the straits of the Dardanelles, midway between the Mt Athos peninsula and Turkey, has given it a traumatic history. To this day it maintains a large garrison, and jets from the huge air base loudly punctuate the daily routine.

Limnos had advanced Neolithic and Bronze Age civilisations, and during these times had contact with peoples in western Anatolia, including the Trojans. In classical times the twin sea gods, the Kabeiroi, were worshipped at a sanctuary on the island, but later the Sanctuary of the Great Gods on Samothraki became the centre of this cult.

During the Peloponnesian Wars, Limnos sided with Athens and suffered many Persian attacks. After the split of the Roman Empire in 395 AD it became an important outpost of Byzantium. In 1462 it came under the

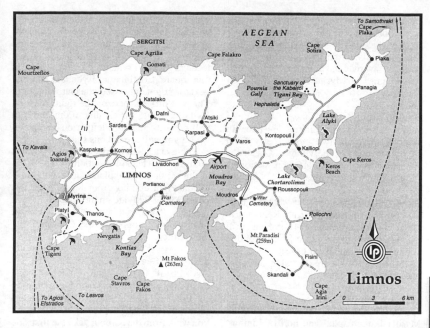

domination of the Genoese who ruled Lesvos. The Turks succeeded in conquering the island in 1478 and it remained under Turkish rule until 1912. Moudros bay, on Limnos, was the Allies' base for the disastrous Gallipoli campaign in WWI.

Getting There & Away

Air In summer there are daily flights to Limnos from Athens (13,900 dr) and Thessaloniki (14,100 dr); and daily flights from Lesvos (12,700 dr). The Olympic Airways office (☎ 0254-22 214) is on Nikolaou Garoufallidou, opposite the Hotel Paris, in Myrina.

The airport is 22km east of Myrina. An Olympic Airways bus from Myrina to the airport (1000 dr) connects with all flights.

Ferry In summer there are four ferries a week to Kavala from Limnos (five hours, 3200 dr); four a week to Rafina (10 hours, 4700 dr), all via Agios Efstratios (1½ hours, 1600 dr); and

two of them via Sigri in Lesvos (six hours, 3000 dr). There is also one boat a week to Chios (11 hours, 4600 dr); three to Piraeus via Lesvos and Chios and one to Piraeus directly (13 hours, 6050 dr); and one a week to Thessaloniki (seven hours, 4200 dr).

There is a boat to Alexandroupolis (seven hours, 3000 dr), via Samothraki (three hours, 1600 dr) on Tuesdays from the inconvenient port of Moudros.

Aiolis, a small local ferry, does the run to Agios Efstratios (2½ hours, 1600 dr) twice a week on Monday and Friday. Tickets can be bought at Myrina Tourist & Travel Agency (☎ 0254-22 460; fax 23 560), next door to the Hotel Aktaion, in Myrina.

Hydrofoil Hydrofoil services to and from Alexandroupolis, via Samothraki, are notoriously unpredictable in their scheduling. Check with Myrina Tourist & Travel Agency; some services may run during summer.

Excursion Boat In July and August the *Aiolis* does a couple of extra day returns per week to the small island of Agios Efstratios. The island is untouristy and has several beaches, tavernas and domatia. For information enquire at Myrina Tourist & Travel Agency.

Getting Around

Bus Bus services on Limnos are poor. In summer there are two buses a day from Myrina to most of the villages. Check the schedule (only in Greek) at the bus station on Plateia Eleftheriou Venizelou.

Car & Motorcycle In Myrina, cars and jeeps can be rented from Myrina Rent a Car (☎ 0254-24 476; fax 22 484) on Kyda near the waterfront. Prices range from 10,000 to 15,000 dr for a small car or jeep depending on the season. There are several motorcycle-hire outlets on Kyda.

MYRINA Μύρινα
• *pop 4340* • *postcode 814 00* • *area code* ☎ *0254*

Myrina is the capital and port of Limnos. Surrounded by massive hunks of volcanic rock, it is not immediately perceived as a picturesque town, but it is animated, full of character and unfettered by establishments pandering to tourism.

The main thoroughfare of Kyda is a charming paved street with clothing stores, traditional shops selling nuts and honey, old-fashioned kafeneia and barber shops – the latter are testimony to the island's military presence. As you wander along the side streets you'll see (interspersed with modern buildings) little whitewashed stone dwellings, decaying neoclassical mansions and 19th-century wattle-and-daub houses with overhanging wooden balconies. A Genoese castle looms dramatically over the town.

Orientation & Information

From the end of the quay turn right onto Plateia Ilia Iliou. Continue along the waterfront passing the Hotel Lemnos and the town hall. A little further along you will see the Hotel Aktaion, set back from the waterfront. Turn left here, then immediately veer half-left onto Kyda. Proceeding up here you will reach the central square where the National Bank of Greece and the OTE are located. The taxi rank (☎ 23 033) is also on this square. Continue up Kyda and take the next turn right onto Nikolaou Garoufallidou. The post office is here on the right. Back on Kyda, continue for another 100m and you will come to Plateia Eleftheriou Venizelou where you will see the bus station.

There is a small tourist information kiosk on the quay. The police station (☎ 22 201) is at the far end of Nikolaou Garoufallidou – on the right coming from Kyda. The port police (☎ 22 225) are on the waterfront near the quay. There is a laundrette on Nikolaou Garoufallidou, opposite the Olympic Airways office.

Things to See & Do

As with all Greek-island castles, the one towering over Myrina is worth climbing up to. From its vantage point there are magnificent views over the sea to Mt Athos. As you walk from the harbour, take the first side street to the left by an old Turkish fountain. An inconspicuous sign here points you to the castle.

Myrina has a lovely long sandy beach right in town. It stretches north from the castle and can be reached by walking along Kyda from the harbour, and taking any of the streets off to the left. The first part of the beach is known as **Romeïkos Yialos** and the northern end, just before Akti Marina Hotel resort, is known as **Riha Nera**.

Myrina's **archaeological museum**, which is housed in a neoclassical mansion, is worth a visit. It contains finds from all the three sites on Limnos; and from an unusual archaeological dig in the grounds of the Porto Myrina Palace as well. The museum overlooks the beach, next to the Hotel Castor. It's open from 8.30 am to 3 pm, Tuesday to Sunday. Admission is 500 dr.

Organised Tours

In the absence of a decent bus service, Theodoros Petridis Travel Agency (☎ 22

039; fax 22 129) organises daily bus excursions around the island. These include a visit to ancient Poliochni, Hephaistia and Sanctuary of the Kabeiroi. There is also a swimming stop and lunch break at Moudros. The agency also organises round-the-island boat trips which again include stops for swimming and lunch. The cost of each of these excursions is 3000 dr. Lunch is not included in the price.

Places to Stay – bottom end

Limnos doesn't have any official camp sites. There is an information board with a map of the island and the names and telephone numbers of all domatia and hotels in Limnos on the harbourfront square. Really budget accommodation is thin on the ground in Myrina.

The D-class *Hotel Aktaion* (☎ 22 258), on the waterfront, is the town's cheapest hotel and not really all that appealing. Nonetheless, the singles/doubles are clean enough and cost 6200/10,600 dr. The *Hotel Paris* (☎ 24 927) is a more pleasant option, with rates of 10,000/14,000 dr for doubles/triples. The hotel is on Nikolaou Garoufallidou, opposite the Olympic Airways office.

The neoclassical *Apollo Pavillion* (☎ 23 712) on Frynis, with friendly English-speaking owners, has spacious and clean rooms with a variety of accommodation options. Backpacker basement rooms cost 3500 dr per person. Studios with private bathroom and kitchen cost 10,000/12,500 dr for doubles/triples. Two-room apartments with kitchens are 20,000 dr for four to five people. Walk along Nikolaou Garoufallidou from Kyda and you will see the sign 150m along on the right.

The breezy, well-appointed rooms of *Poseidon Domatia* (☎ 23 982; fax 23 982) are close to the beach near the museum. Each room has a small kitchen, TV and private bathroom and there is a small bar and breakfast room for guests. Doubles/triples go for 14,500/16,500 dr in high the season.

Places to Stay – middle

The B-class *Hotel Castro* (☎ 22 772; fax 22 784) is built in neoclassical style. The carpeted rooms have balcony, telephone, three-channel music, TV and air-conditioning. Rates are 12,000/18,000 dr for singles/doubles with breakfast. The hotel has a snack bar and TV room and it overlooks the beach. It is in the middle of Romeïkos Yialos.

The tastefully furnished, self-contained accommodation of *Afroditi Apartments* (☎ 23 489) is set back 200m from Riha Nera beach. Doubles/triples, some with air-con, are 16,000/19,200 dr.

Places to Eat

Restaurants are of a high standard on Limnos. There are several fish restaurants around the waterfront. Locals give top marks to *Taverna Glaros*, which probably has the best harbourside location, but somewhat expensive prices. By the ferry quay is the *Avra* restaurant; handy if you are waiting for a boat to leave.

Half-way along Kyda is the small, unassuming but very pleasant *O Platanos Taverna*, on the left as you walk from the waterfront. It is on a small square under a couple of huge plane trees and makes an attractive alternative to the waterfront establishments. Moussaka, salad, chips and local retsina should cost around 2500 dr.

Finally, the posh-looking *Filoktetes* restaurant, 200m inland from Riha Nera beach has – unusually for Greece – an access ramp and toilet for disabled diners. The food is excellent and marginally cheaper than the harbourside joints. It is open for lunch and dinner and offers a range of ready-made dishes.

AROUND THE ISLAND
Western Limnos

North of Myrina is the five-star mega resort *Porto Myrina Palace* on the south side of pristine Aspakas bay. Turn left just past the little village of **Kaspakas** and a narrow road will lead you down to the beach of **Agios Ioannis**. The beach is pleasant enough, but Agios Ioannis consists of a few desultory fishing shacks, scattered beach houses and a couple of tavernas, one of which has its tables set out in the embrace of a large volcanic rock.

Inland from Kaspakas, the barren hilly landscape dotted with sheep and rocks (particularly on the road to Katalako via Sardes and Dafni) reminds you more of the English Peak District than an Aegean island. The villages themselves have little to cause you to pause and you will certainly be an object of curiosity if you do. There is a remote and completely undeveloped beach at Gomati on the north coast and it can be reached by a good dirt road from Katalako.

Heading 3km south from Myrina you will reach one of Limnos' best beaches, below the village of **Platy**. To get to Platy beach follow the signs out of Myrina for Platy and Thanos, but turn right just before the cemetery. Look out for the signs to the resorts of Villa Afroditi and Lemnos Village.

As well as the clubby, exclusive and English-owned Lemnos Village Resort Hotel, Platy beach has a few reasonably priced budget places to stay. In Platy village are the *Filoxenia Domatia* (☎ 24 211; fax 23 545) owned by Greek-Australians Andreas and Konstantina Sarmonikas. The large, airy rooms with kitchenette have a great view and there is a guest common room downstairs. Doubles/triples go for 9000/11,000 dr.

The *Anastasia domatia* (☎ 24 127) are simply furnished with fridge, kitchenette and bathroom. Rates are 8000 dr a double. The rooms are on the left side of the road which leads from Platy village to the beach. Behind *Jimmy's Taverna* on the beach itself you will find some more, somewhat cramped, *domatia* (☎ 24 142). Ask at Jimmy's for details. There are also other unofficial domatia in the village.

Apart from Jimmy's Taverna, the best food to be had is in Platy village itself, where the *Zimbabwe* restaurant and the striking blue and white *Kalouditsa* taverna vie for clientele by spilling out across two squares next to each other.

Back on the beach road, if you continue along the now dirt road, past the Lemnos Village Resort Hotel, you will come to a sheltered sandy cove with an islet in the bay.

The beach here will probably be less crowded than Platy. **Thanos beach** is the next bay around from Platy; it is also less crowded, and long and sandy. To get there, continue on the main road from Platy village to Thanos village, where a sign points to the beach.

Central Limnos

Central Limnos is flat and agricultural with wheat fields, small vineyards, and cattle and sheep farms. There is also the island's huge air-force base, which is ominously surrounded by endless barbed-wire fences. The muddy and bleak Moudros bay cuts deep into the interior, with **Moudros**, Limnos' second town in size, positioned on the eastern side of the bay. Moudros does not offer much for the tourist other than an arrival and departure point for ferries from/to Samothraki and Alexandroupolis. There are a couple of small hotels with tavernas on the waterfront, but the harbour has none of the picturesque qualities of Myrina's.

One km out of Moudros on the road to Roussopouli, you will come across the **East Moudros Military Cemetery** where Commonwealth soldiers from the Gallipoli campaign are buried. Limnos, with its large protected anchorage, was occupied by a force of Royal Marines on 23 February 1915 and became the principal base for this ill-fated campaign. A metal plaque, just inside the gates, gives a short history of the Gallipoli campaign. A second Commonwealth cemetery, the **Portianos Military Cemetery**, is at Portianos, about 6km south of the village of Livadohori on the trans-island highway. The cemetery is not as obvious as the Australian-style blue and white street sign sporting the name Anzac St. Follow Anzac Street to the church and you will find the cemetery off a little lane behind the church.

Eastern Limnos

Eastern Limnos has three archaeological sites. The Italian School of Archaeologists has uncovered four ancient settlements at

Poliochni, on the island's east coast. The most interesting was a sophisticated pre-Mycenaean city, which predated Troy VI (1800-1275 BC). The site is well laid-out with colour-coded maps to show the so-called Blue, Green, Red and Yellow periods of settlement and there are good descriptions in Greek, Italian and English. However, there is nothing of really earth-shattering interest to be seen – not surprising for such an ancient site – and it's probably of greater interest to archaeological buffs than casual visitors.

The second site is that of the **Sanctuary of the Kabeiroi** (Ta Kaviria) in north-eastern Limnos on the shores of remote Tigani bay. This was originally a site for the worship of Kabeiroi gods predating those of Samothraki (see Sanctuary of the Great Gods, Samothraki, later in this chapter). There is little of the Sanctuary of Samothraki's splendour, but the layout of the site is obvious and excavations are still being carried out.

The major site, which has 11 columns, is that of a Hellenistic sanctuary. The older site is further back and is still being excavated. Of additional interest is the cave of Philoctetes, the hero of the Trojan war, who was abandoned here while a gangrenous leg (a result of snakebite) healed. The sea cave can be reached by a path that leads down from the site.

You can reach the sanctuary easily if you have your own transport via a fast new road that was built for the multimillion-drachma (and now white elephant) tourist enclave, Kaviria Palace. The turn-off is about 5km to the left, after the village of **Kontopouli**. From Kontopouli itself you can make a detour to the third site, along a rough dirt track to **Hephaistia** (Ta Ifestia), which was once the most important city on the island. Hephaestus was the god of fire and metallurgy and, according to mythology, was thrown here from Mt Olympus by Zeus. The site is widely scattered over a scrub-covered, but otherwise desolate, small peninsula. There is not much to see of the ancient city other than some low walls and a partially excavated theatre. Excavations are still under way. All three sites are open from 9 am to 3.30 pm and entry is, so far, free.

The road to the northern tip of the island is worth exploring. There are some typical Limnian villages in the area and the often deserted beach at **Keros** is popular with windsurfers. From the cape at the north-eastern tip of Limnos you can see the islands of Samothraki and Imvros (Gökçeada) in Turkey.

Agios Efstratios Αγιος Ευστράτιος

• *pop 290* • *postcode 815 00* • *area code* ☎ *0254*

This little-known island, called locally Aï-Stratis, deservedly merits the title of perhaps the most isolated island in the Aegean. Stuck more or less plumb centre in the North Aegean some distance from its nearest neighbour Limnos, it has few cars and fewer roads, but a steady trickle of curious foreign island-hoppers seeking to find some peace and quiet.

Sent for enforced peace and quiet were large numbers of political exiles before and after WWII. Among the exiled guests were such luminaries as composer Mikis Theodorakis and poets Kostas Varnalis and Giannis Ritsos.

The little village of Aï-Stratis was once picturesque, but in the early hours of the morning of 21 February 1968 a violent earthquake, with its epicentre in the seas between Limnos and Aï-Stratis, virtually destroyed the vibrant village in one fell swoop. Many people emigrated as a result and there are now large numbers of islanders living in Australia and elsewhere.

Ham-fisted intervention by the then ruling junta saw the demolition of most of the remaining traditional homes and in their place, cheaply built concrete boxes were erected to house the islanders. Needless to say, the islanders are still pretty miffed almost 30 years after the event, and the

NORTH-EASTERN AEGEAN

remaining hillside ruins stand silent sentinel over a rather lacklustre village today.

Still, if you yearn for serenity, traffic-free bliss and enjoy walking, Aï-Stratis is a great place to visit. It has some great beaches – though most are only accessible by caïque – ample accommodation, simple island food and a surprisingly busy nightlife scene.

There is a post office, one card phone and one metered phone for the public.

Beaches

Apart from the fairly reasonable dark, volcanic sand village beach, the nearest beach worth making the effort to visit is **Alonitsi beach** on the north-east side of the island. It is a long, totally undeveloped, pristine strand and it can be all yours if you are prepared to walk the 90 minutes to reach it. To get there take the little track from the north-east side of the village, starting by a small bridge, and follow it upwards towards the power pylons. Halfway along the track splits; take the right track for Alonitsi, or the left track for the **military lookout** for great views. **Lidario beach** on the west side can be reached – with difficulty – on foot, but is better approached by sea, if you can get someone to take you there.

Places to Stay & Eat

Accommodation options in Agios Efstratios are now pretty good. There is no hotel on the island but there are currently about 100 beds available and you will always find somewhere to stay unless you turn up at the height of the summer season without a reservation. The spotless and airy *Xenonas Aï-Strati* (☎ 93 329) run by Julia and Odysseas Galanakis has doubles/triples ranging in price from 4000 to 9000 dr, depending on facilities and the season. The rooms are in one of the few buildings that survived the earthquake on the north-eastern side of the village. The *domatia* of Malama Panera (☎ 93 209) on the south side of the village are equally well-appointed with similar prices. There are also other unofficial domatia available. Ask at the little convenience store, if you get stuck. The

community fax machine (93 210) will receive faxes and pass them on if you want to fax a booking.

For eating you have the choice of the fairly obvious community-run *Thanasis Taverna* which overlooks the harbour, or *Tasos Ouzeri* diagonally opposite. At the far south end of the waterfront is the *Taverna tou Antoni* which opens in the summer, when Antonis feels like it. All places are fairly inexpensive, though fish still tends to be a bit on the steep side.

Getting There & Away

Agios Efstratios is on the Kavala-Rafina ferry route, which includes Limnos. There are four services a week to Rafina (8½ hours, 4000 dr) and another four in the other direction to Limnos (1½ hours, 1600 dr) and Kavala (6½ hours, 4500 dr). In addition, the small local ferry *Aiolis* putters to and from Limnos twice a week on Mondays and Fridays. On the off-days, during summer, *Aiolis* does a more or less daily excursion run from Limnos. The harbour is, however, exposed to the west winds and ferry services are often cancelled or delayed because of bad weather.

Samothraki Σαμοθράκη

The egg-shaped island of Samothraki (Samothráki, population 2800) is 32km south-west of Alexandroupolis. Scenically it is one of the most awe-inspiring of all Greek islands. It is a small island, but a great deal of diverse landscape is packed into its 176 sq km. Its natural attributes are dramatic, big and untamed, culminating in the mighty peak of Mt Fengari (1611m), the highest mountain in the Aegean. Homer related that Poseidon watched the Trojan War from Mt Fengari's summit.

The jagged boulder-strewn Mt Fengari looms over valleys of massive gnarled oak and plane trees, thick forests of olive trees, dense shrubbery and damp, dark glades where waterfalls plunge into deep, icy pools.

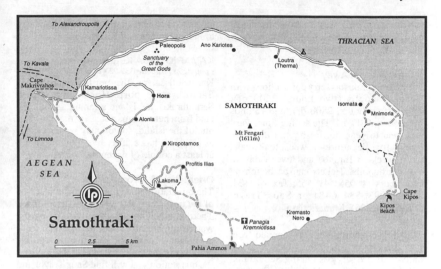

On the gentler, western slopes of the island there are corn fields studded with wildflowers. Samothraki is also rich in fauna: its springs are the habitat of a large number of frogs, toads and turtles; in its meadows you will see swarms of butterflies and may come across the occasional lumbering tortoise. On the mountain slopes there are an inordinate number of bell-clanking goats. The island's beaches, with one exception, are stony or pebbly.

Samothraki's ancient site, the Sanctuary of the Great Gods, at Paleopolis, is one of the most evocative ancient sites in Greece. Historians have been unable to ascertain the nature of the rites performed here, and its aura of potent mysticism prevails over the whole island.

Samothraki is relatively difficult to reach and does not have any package tourism. It does, however, attract a fair number of Greek holiday-makers in July and August, so you may have some difficulty finding a room then. With the exception of the Xenia Hotel, all of Samothraki's hotels were built in the 1980s and were designed to a high standard with sensitive regard to the environment. All are extremely pleasant places to stay but none falls into the budget category. This doesn't mean budget travellers are not welcome or catered for as there are a fair number of domatia and two camp sites.

History

Samothraki was first settled around 1000 BC by Thracians who worshipped the Great gods, a cult of Anatolian origin. In 700 BC the island was colonised by people from Lesvos, who absorbed the Thracian cult into the worship of the Olympian gods.

This marriage of two cults was highly successful and by the 5th century BC Samothraki had become one of Greece's major religious centres, attracting prospective initiates from far and wide to its Sanctuary of the Great Gods. Among the luminaries initiated into the cult were King Lysander of Sparta, Philip II of Macedon and Piso, Julius Caesar's father-in-law. One famous visitor who did not come to be initiated was St Paul, who dropped in en route to Philippi.

The cult survived until paganism was outlawed in the 4th century AD. After this the island became insignificant. Falling to the Turks in 1457 it united with Greece, along with the other North-Eastern Aegean islands, in 1912. During WWII Samothraki was occupied by the Bulgarians.

Getting There & Away
Ferry Samothraki has ferry connections with Alexandroupolis (two hours, 2200 dr); Kavala (four hours, 2800 dr); and Limnos (3½ hours, 2400 dr). The sailing times vary from year to year, but in summer there are usually five departures a week to Kavala, two a week to Limnos and two a day to Alexandroupolis. Tickets can be bought at Niki Tours (☎ 0551-41 465; fax 41 304; mobile 093 534 648) or Saos Travel (☎ 0551-41 505), Kamariotissa.

Hydrofoil Hydrofoil services operate from Samothraki from 1 May to 31 October. Currently there are services linking Samothraki with Limnos, Thasos, Halkidiki (Stavros), Kavala, Maronia, Porto Lagos and Alexandroupolis. For departure details contact Niki Tours in Kamariotissa or the office for the *Thraki III* hydrofoil (☎ 0551-41 100; fax 0551-230 200) which is near Budget car rentals. Ticket prices are roughly twice as much as the equivalent ferry ticket.

Getting Around
Bus In summer there are at least nine buses a day from Kamariotissa to Hora and Loutra (Therma), via Paleopolis. Some of the Loutra buses continue to the nearby camp sites. There are four buses a day to Profitis Ilias (via Lakoma). A bus schedule is displayed in the window of Saos Travel, Kamariotissa.

Car & Motorcycle Cars and small jeeps can be rented from Niki Tours (☎ 0551-41 465; fax 41 304) and Budget (☎ 0551-41 100). A 4WD jeep, recommended for Samothraki, costs about 18,000 dr per day, whereas a small car will cost about 12,000 dr. motorcycles can be rented from Rent A Motor Bike, opposite the ferry quay

Excursion Boat Depending on demand, caïques do trips from the Kamariotissa jetty to Pahia Ammos and Kipos beaches.

KAMARIOTISSA Καμαριώτισσα
• *pop 826* • *postcode 680 02* • *area code* ☎ *0551*
Kamariotissa, on the north-west coast, is Samothraki's port. Hora (also called Samothraki), the island's capital, is 5km inland from here. Kamariotissa is the transport hub of the island, so you may wish to use it as a base. It has a fairly lively nightlife and at least a couple of decent restaurants.

Orientation & Information
The bus station is on the waterfront just east of the quay (turn left when you disembark). There is a National Bank of Greece on the waterfront, but no post office or OTE; these are in Hora. There is no EOT or tourist police and the regular police are in Hora. Opposite the bus station you will find Saos Travel and Niki Tours, both of which are reasonably helpful. The port police (☎ 41 305) are on the eastern waterfront at Kamariotissa.

Places to Stay
Domatia owners often meet ferries in Kamariotissa, but domatia are easy to find in the compact port. Otherwise, the *Hotel Kyma* (☎ 41 263), at the eastern end of the waterfront, has comfortable singles/doubles for 5000/6000 dr with shared bathroom and 5500/6500 dr with private bathroom. Further along the waterfront, the C-class *Niki Beach Hotel* (☎ 41 545) is airy and spacious. Room rates here are a touch pricey at 10,000/14,000 dr for singles/doubles with private bathroom. The hotel is at the eastern end of the waterfront.

Behind the Niki Beach is Samothraki's most luxurious hotel, the B-class *Aeolos Hotel* (☎ 41 595; fax 41 810), where singles/doubles cost 10,000/15,000 dr with breakfast. The hotel has a swimming pool and a commanding position on a hill overlooking the sea.

Places to Eat
Samothraki used to have a negative reputation for its culinary offerings, but things have

improved considerably. The *Horizon* is one of Kamariotissa's better restaurants. Main courses include chicken casserole for 1000 dr; meatballs, moussaka and souvlaki are all 1200 dr. The restaurant is just back from the waterfront on the left side of the road which leads up to Hora. At the eastern end of the waterfront the *Klimitaria Restaurant* serves an unusual speciality called gianiotiko for 1600 dr. This is a dish of diced pork, potatoes, egg and other goodies baked in the oven.

HORA Χώρα

Hora, concealed in a fold of the mountains above Kamariotissa, is one of the most striking of Greek-island villages. The crumbling red-tiled houses – some of grey stone, others whitewashed – are stacked up two steep adjacent mountainsides. The twisting cobbled streets resound with cockerels crowing, dogs barking and donkeys braying, rather than the ubiquitous roar of motorcycles and honking of car horns. The village is totally authentic with no concessions to tourism. The ruined castle at the top of the main thoroughfare is fascinating to explore and from its vantage point there are sweeping vistas down to Kamariotissa. It is an open site with free entrance.

Orientation & Information

To get to Hora's narrow winding main street, follow the signs for the kastro from the central square where the bus turns around. Here on the main street, which is nameless (as are all of Hora's streets; houses are distinguished by numbers), are the OTE, the Agricultural Bank and the post office.

The police (☎ 0551-41 203) are next to the ruined castle at the top of Hora's main street. A little way up the main street, on the right, a fountain gushes refreshing mountain water.

Walk from Hora to Paleopolis

It takes between 45 minutes and one hour to walk along a dirt road from Hora to Paleopolis (Sanctuary of the Great Gods). On this walk there are tremendous views of Fengari to the right and rolling hills, corn fields and the sea to the left. To get to the road, walk up to the castle ruins in Hora and take the dirt road which leads down to the right. Alternatively, you can start the walk from the road just below the bus stop.

Follow the main track all the way down and around and look out for the Kastro Hotel to your left as you come over the rise. Bear right along a smaller track as you come down the hill and you will eventually come across the museum and ancient site. You can negotiate this road in car (4WD recommended, though). Keep going straight down the hill until you hit the main road.

Places to Stay & Eat

There are no hotels in Hora. There are two reasonably priced *pensions* just off the central square but the best places to stay in Hora are *rooms* in private houses. Almost all of these are unofficial and do not display signs. If you ask in one of the kafeneia you will be put in touch with a room owner.

There is a *psistaria* on the square where the bus stops, and *Taverna Kastro* on the central square. Both places serve food catering for local tastes rather than for tourists. Ask for fish, if they have it. Bear in mind that these places may well be closed out of season.

SANCTUARY OF THE GREAT GODS

Το Ιερό των Μεγάλων Θεών

The Sanctuary of the Great Gods, next to the little village of Paleopolis, is 6km north-east of Kamariotissa. The extensive site, lying in a valley of luxuriant vegetation between Mt Fengari and the sea, is one of the most magical in the whole of Greece. The Great gods were of greater antiquity than the Olympian gods worshipped in the official religion of ancient Greece. The principal deity, the Great Mother (Alceros Cybele), was worshipped as a fertility goddess.

When the original Thracian religion became integrated with the state religion, the Great Mother was merged with the Olympian female deities Demeter, Aphrodite and Hecate. The last of these was a mysterious goddess, associated with darkness, the

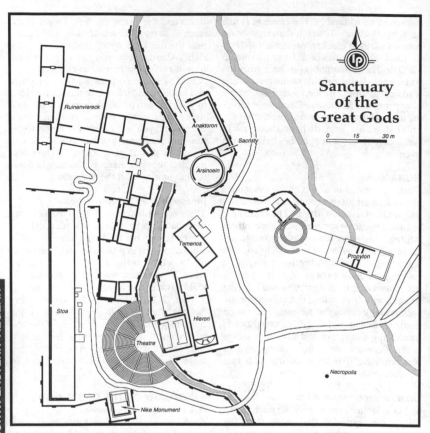

underworld and witchcraft. Other deities worshipped here were the Great Mother's consort, the virile young Kadmilos (god of the phallus), who was later integrated with the Olympian god Hermes; and the demonic Kabeiroi twins, Dardanos and Aeton, who were integrated with Castor and Pollux (known as the Dioscuri), the twin sons of Zeus and Leda. These twins were invoked by mariners to protect them against the perils of the sea. The formidable deities of Samothraki were venerated for their immense power. In comparison, the Olympian gods were a frivolous and fickle lot.

Initiates were sworn on punishment of death not to reveal what went on at the sanctuary. Consequently, there is only very flimsy knowledge of what these initiations involved. All that has been gleaned from archaeological evidence is that there were two initiations, a lower and a higher. In the first initiation, gods were invoked to bring about a spiritual rebirth within the candidate. In the second initiation the candidate was absolved of transgressions. There was no prerequisite for initiation – it was available to anyone and everyone.

The site's most celebrated relic, the

Winged Victory of Samothrace, was found by Champoiseau, the French consul, at Adrianople (present-day Edirne in Turkey) in 1863. Sporadic excavations followed in the late 19th and early 20th centuries, but did not begin in earnest until just before WWII, when the Institute of Fine Arts, New York University, under the direction of Karl Lehmann and Phyllis Williams Lehmann, began digging. The site is open Tuesday to Sunday from 8.30 am to 3 pm. Admission is 500 dr, but is free on Sunday and public holidays.

Exploring the Site

The site is labelled in both Greek and English. If you take the path which leads south from the entrance you will arrive at the rectangular **anaktoron**, on the left. At the southern end was a **sacristy**, an antechamber where candidates put on white gowns ready for their first (lower) initiation. The initiation ceremony took place in the main body of the anaktoron. Then one at a time each initiate entered the holy of holies, a small inner temple at the northern end of the building, where a priest instructed them in the meanings of the symbols used in the ceremony. Afterwards the initiates returned to the sacristy to receive their initiation certificate.

The **arsinoein**, which was used for sacrifices, to the south-west of the anaktoron, was built in 289 BC and was then the largest cylindrical structure in Greece. It was a gift to the Great gods from the Egyptian queen Arsinou. To the south-east of here you will see the **sacred rock**, the site's earliest altar, which was used by the Thracians.

The initiations were followed by a celebratory feast which probably took place in the **temenos**, to the south of the arsinoein. This building was a gift from Philip II. The next building is the prominent Doric **hieron**, which is the most photographed ruin on the site; five of its columns have been reassembled. It was in this temple that candidates received the second initiation.

On the west side of the main path (opposite the hieron) are a few remnants of a **theatre**. Nearby, a path ascends to the **Nike monument** where the magnificent Winged

Winged Victory of Samothrace

Victory once stood. The statue was a gift from Demetrius Poliorcetes (the 'besieger of cities') to the Kabeiroi for helping him defeat Ptolemy II in battle. To the north-west of here are the remains of a massive **stoa**, which was a two-aisled portico where pilgrims to the sanctuary sheltered. Names of initiates were recorded on its walls. North of the stoa are the ruins of the **ruinenviereck**, a medieval fortress.

Retrace your steps to the Nike monument and walk along the path leading east; on the left is a good plan of the site. The path continues to the southern **necropolis** which is the most important ancient cemetery so far found on the island. It was used from the Bronze Age to early Roman times. North of the cemetery was the **propylon**, an elaborate Ionic entrance to the sanctuary; it was a gift from Ptolemy II.

Museum

The site's museum is well laid out, with English labels. Exhibits include terracotta

NORTH-EASTERN AEGEAN

figurines, vases, jewellery and a plaster cast of the Winged Victory. It's open Tuesday to Sunday from 9 am to 3 pm. Admission is 500 dr and is free on Sunday and public holidays.

Places to Stay & Eat

There are several domatia at Paleopolis, all of which are signposted from near the museum. The B-class *Xenia Hotel* (☎ 0551-41 230; fax 41 166) near the museum was built in 1952 to provide accommodation for archaeologists. Although clean, cool and comfortable, it lacks the sophistication of Samothraki's newer hotels. Doubles cost 10,800 dr with private bathroom.

Just west of Paleopolis, above the coast road, is the C-class *Kastro Hotel* (☎ 0551-41 001; fax 41 000), the island's newest hotel. The rooms are simply and tastefully furnished and rates are 11,000/14,000 dr for singles/doubles, including breakfast. The hotel has a swimming pool. There is at least one taverna at Paleopolis but both hotels have a restaurant and bar. If you have your own transport there are some other eating places to choose from along the road towards Loutra (Therma).

AROUND THE ISLAND

Loutra (Therma) Λουτρά (Θερμά)

Loutra, also called Therma, is 14km east of Kamariotissa and a short walk inland from the coast. It's in an attractive setting with a profusion of plane and horse-chestnut trees, dense greenery and gurgling creeks. While not an authentic village, it is the nearest Samothraki comes to having a holiday resort. Many of its buildings are purpose-built domatia, and most visitors to the island seem to stay here.

The village takes both its names from its therapeutic, sulphurous, mineral springs. Whether or not you are arthritic you may like to take a thermal bath here. The baths are in the large white building on the right as you walk to the central square from the bus stop. Opening times are 6 to 11 am, and 5 to 7 pm. Admission is 450 dr.

Places to Stay

Samothraki has two official camp sites; both are near Loutra, and both are signposted 'Multilary Campings'. Rest assured, the authorities mean municipal camp sites and not military camp sites. The first *Multilary Camping* (☎ 41 784) is to the left of the main road, 2km beyond the turn-off for Loutra, coming from Kamariotissa. The site is very spartan, with toilets and cold showers but no other amenities. The charges are 500 dr per person and 400 dr per tent. The second *Multilary Camping* (☎ 41 491) is 2km further along the road. It has a mini-market, restaurant and hot showers, but is still a rather scrappy and dry camp site. It charges 800 dr per person, 600 dr per tent. Both sites are open only during June, July and August.

Domatia owners meet the buses at Loutra. If you can afford something more expensive, then Loutra has two lovely hotels. The C-class *Mariva Bungalows* (☎ 98 230) are set on a hillside in a secluded part of the island, near a waterfall. The spacious doubles cost 12,000 dr with private bathroom. To reach the hotel take the first turn left along the road which leads from the coast up to Loutra. Follow the signs to the hotel which is 600m along this road.

The B-class *Kaviros Hotel* (☎ 98 277; fax 98 278) is bang in the middle of Loutra, just beyond the central square. It is a very pleasant family-run hotel with singles/doubles for 10,000/11,000 dr. The hotel is surrounded by a pretty garden.

Places to Eat

In Loutra there are a number of restaurants and tavernas scattered throughout the upper and lower village. There is not a lot to choose between them, but chopping and changing may be part of the fun. In the upper village try the *Paradisos Restaurant* which plies its trade under a huge plane tree with its welcome shade on a hot day. Take the road to the right from the bus stop to find it. The *Fengari Restaurant*, signposted from near the bus stop, cooks its food in traditional Samothraki ovens and is hidden away on a backstreet.

Fonias River

Visitors to the north coast should not miss the walk along the Fonias river to the **Vathres** rock pools. The walk starts at the bridge over the river 4.7km east of Loutra – the track being over-optimistically signposted as a vehicular road. After an easy 40-minute walk along a fairly well-marked track you will come to a large rock pool fed by a dramatic 12m waterfall. The pool water is pretty cold but very welcome on a hot day. Locals call the river the 'Murderer' – winter rains can transform the waters into a raging torrent.

Pahia Ammos

The gods did not over-endow Samothraki with good beaches. However, its one sandy beach, **Pahia Ammos**, on the south coast, is superb. You can reach this 800m stretch of sand by walking along an 8km winding dirt road from Lakoma. In summer there are caïques from Kamariotissa to the beach. Around the headland is the equally superb **Vatos beach**, used mainly by nudists.

Opposite Pahia Ammos, on a good day, you can see the mass of the former Greek island of Imvros (Gökçeada), which was ceded to the Turks under the Treaty of Lausanne in 1923.

There is now a restaurant and domatia at Pahia Ammos, but bookings are recommended for July and August, since there are only six rooms which go for 8000 dr each. Call *Taverna Pahia Ammos* (☎ 94 235), or write to Nikolaos Kapelas, Profitis Ilias, Samothraki. You will probably be able to camp (unofficially) at Pahia Ammos too.

Samothraki's other decent beach is the pebbled **Kipos beach** on the south-east coast. It can be reached on the unsealed road which is the easterly continuation of the road skirting the north coast. However, there are no facilities here other than a shower and a freshwater fountain, and there is no shade. It also pales in comparison to Pahia Ammos beach.

Kipos beach can also be reached by caïque from Kamariotissa.

Other Villages

The small villages of **Profitis Ilias**, **Lakoma** and **Xiropotamos** in the south-west, and **Alonia** near Hora, are serene unspoilt villages all worth a visit. The hillside Profitis Ilias, with many trees and springs, is particularly delightful and has several tavernas of which the *Vrahos* is famous for its delicious roast kid. Asphalt roads lead to all of these villages.

Thasos Θάσος

Thasos (Thasos, population 13,300) lies 10km south-east of Kavala. It is almost circular in shape and although its scenery is not as awesome as Samothraki's it has some pleasing mountain vistas. The EOT brochures tout it as the 'emerald isle', but like so many other Greek islands it has suffered bad fires which have destroyed much of its forest. The main attractions of Thasos are its excellent beaches and the many archaeological remains in and around the capital of Limenas. A good asphalt road goes around the island so all the beaches are easily accessible.

There are still enough rooms for everyone even in the high season and Thasos has no less than eight camp sites dotted around its coast. A notice opposite the bus station in Limenas lists the town's hotels, and also, very helpfully, indicates which hotels remain open in the winter. If only all Greek islands did this.

History

Thasos has been continuously inhabited since the Stone Age. Its ancient city was founded in 700 BC by Parians, led there by a message from the Delphic oracle. The oracle told them to 'Find a city in the Isle of Mists'. From Thasos, the Parians established settlements in Thrace where they mined for gold in Mt Pangaion.

Gold was also mined on Thasos, and the islanders were able to develop a lucrative export trade based on ore, marble, timber and

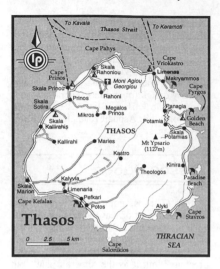

Thasos

with the other islands of the group, Thasos was united with Greece. Like Samothraki, Thasos was occupied by Bulgaria in WWII.

In recent years Thasos has once again struck 'gold'. This time it's 'black gold', in the form of oil which has been found in the sea around the island.

Getting There & Away

Ferry There are ferries every hour between Kavala, on the mainland, and Skala Prinou (1½ hours, 650 dr). There is only one ferry a day between Kavala and Limenas. Ferries direct to Limenas leave every hour or so in summer (40 minutes, 330 dr) from Keramoti, 46km south-east of Kavala.

Hydrofoil There are six hydrofoils every day between Limenas and Kavala (30 minutes, 1500 dr).

Getting Around

Bus Limenas is the transport hub of the island. There are many buses a day to Limenaria (via the west-coast villages) and to Golden beach via Panagia and Potamia. There are six buses to Theologos and three to Alyki. Six buses a day journey in a clockwise direction all the way around the island. The cost of a complete two-hour circuit of the island by bus is 1900 dr.

Car, Motorcycle & Bicycle Cars can be hired from Avis Rent a Car (☎ 0593-22 535) on the central square in Limenas. They also have offices in Skala Prinou (☎ 0593-71 202) and Potamia (☎ 0593-61 506). You can hire motorcycles and mopeds from Billy's Bikes (☎ 0593-22 490), opposite the foreign-language newspapers' agency, and bicycles from Babi's Bikes (☎ 0593-22 129), which is on a sidestreet between 18 Oktovriou and the central square in Limenas.

Excursion Boat The *Eros 2* excursion boat does daily trips around the island, with stops for swimming and a barbecue. The boat leaves from the old harbour at 9.30 am and returns at 5.30 pm. The price is 5000 dr. There are a couple of water taxis running

wine, as well as gold. As a result Thasos built a powerful navy, and culture flourished. Famous ancient Thassiots included the painters Polygnotos, Aglafon Aristofon and the sculptors Polyclitos and Sosicles. The merchants of Thasos traded with Asia Minor, Egypt and Italy.

After the Battle of Plataea, Thasos became an ally of Athens, but war broke out between the two cities when Athens attempted to curtail Thasos' trade with Egypt and Asia Minor. The islanders were defeated and forced into becoming part of the Delian League; the heavy tax imposed crippled its economy. Thasos' decline continued through Macedonian and Roman times. Heavy taxes were imposed by the Turks, many inhabitants left the island and during the 18th century the population dropped from 8000 to 2500.

Thasos was revived in the 19th century when Mohammed Ali Pasha of Egypt became governor of Kavala and Thasos. Ali allowed the islanders to govern themselves and exempted them from paying taxes. The revival was, however, short-lived. The Egyptian governors who superseded Ali Pasha usurped the island's natural resources and imposed heavy taxes. In 1912, along

regularly to Hrysi Ammoudia and Makryammos beaches.

LIMENAS Λιμένας

• *pop 2600* • *postcode 640 04* • *area code* ☎ *0593*
Limenas, on the north-east coast, is the main port and capital of the island. Confusingly, it is also called Thasos town and Limin. The island's other port is Skala Prinou on the west coast. Limenas is built on top of the ancient city, so ruins are scattered all over the place. It is also the island's transport hub, with a reasonable bus service to the coastal resorts and villages.

Orientation & Information

The quay for both ferries and hydrofoils is at the centre of the waterfront. The central square is straight ahead from the waterfront. The main thoroughfare through the town is 18 Oktovriou, which is parallel to the waterfront and north of the central square. Turn left into 18 Oktovriou from

the quay to reach the OTE on the right. Take the next turn right into Theogenous and the second turn right to reach the post office, which is on the left.

The National Bank of Greece is on the waterfront opposite the quay and has both an automatic exchange and teller machine. The newsagent on Theogenous sells English-language newspapers.

The bus station is on the waterfront; to reach it turn left from the quay. To reach the town's picturesque small harbour turn left from the quay and walk along the waterfront. The crowded town beach begins at the end of the western waterfront.

Street name signs are a bit of a novelty in Limenas, so don't be surprised if you can't find one.

There is no EOT on Thasos, but the helpful tourist police (☎ 22 500) are on the waterfront near the bus station. They will assist in finding accommodation if necessary.

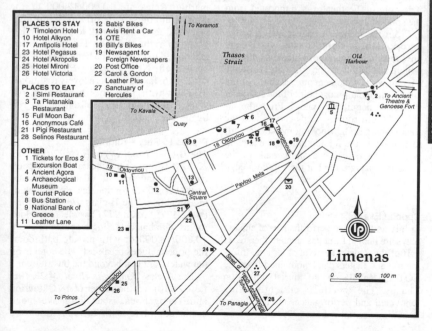

PLACES TO STAY
7 Timoleon Hotel
10 Hotel Alkyon
17 Amfipolis Hotel
23 Hotel Pegasus
24 Hotel Akropolis
25 Hotel Mironi
26 Hotel Victoria

PLACES TO EAT
2 I Simi Restaurant
3 Ta Platanakia Restaurant
15 Full Moon Bar
16 Anonymous Café
21 I Pigi Restaurant
28 Selinos Restaurant

OTHER
1 Tickets for Eros 2 Excursion Boat
4 Ancient Agora
5 Archaeological Museum
6 Tourist Police
8 Bus Station
9 National Bank of Greece
11 Leather Lane

12 Babis' Bikes
13 Avis Rent a Car
14 OTE
18 Billy's Bikes
19 Newsagent for Foreign Newspapers
20 Post Office
22 Carol & Gordon Leather Plus
27 Sanctuary of Hercules

Limenas

0   50   100 m

NORTH-EASTERN AEGEAN

Things to See & Do

Thasos' **archaeological museum** is next to the ancient agora at the small harbour. The most striking exhibit is a very elongated 6th-century *kouros* statue which stands in the foyer. It was found on the acropolis of the ancient city of Thasos. Other exhibits include pottery and terracotta figurines and a large well-preserved head of a rather effeminate-looking Dionysos. The ancient city of Thasos was excavated by the French School of Archaeology, so the museum's labelling is in French and Greek.

The **ancient agora** next to the museum was the bustling marketplace of ancient and Roman Thasos – the centre of its civic, social and business life. It's a pleasant, verdant site with the foundations of stoas, shops and dwellings. Entrance is free.

The **ancient theatre**, in a lovely wooded setting, has been fitted with wooden seats (now a bit dilapidated), and performances of ancient dramas are staged here annually, though the theatre is currently undergoing renovation. The theatre is signposted from the small harbour.

From the theatre a path leads up to the **acropolis of ancient Thasos** where there are substantial remains of a medieval fortress which was built on the foundations of the ancient walls which encompassed the entire city. From the topmost point of the acropolis there are magnificent views. From the far side of the acropolis, steps carved into the rock (with a dodgy-looking metal handrail) lead down to the foundations of the ancient wall. From here it's a short walk to the Limenas-Panagia road at the southern edge of town.

Special Events

In July and August, performances of ancient plays are held at Limenas' ancient theatre, as part of the Kavala Festival of Drama. Information and tickets can be obtained from the EOT in Kavala or the tourist police on Thasos. The theatre is currently being renovated and performances are not due to re-commence until about 1999.

Places to Stay – bottom end

The nearest camp site to Limenas is *Nysteri Camping* (☎ 23 327), just west of the town. With the exception of the camp site on Golden beach all of Thasos' other camp sites are on the west and south-west coasts.

Limenas has many reasonably priced domatia. If you are not offered anything when you arrive, then look for signs around the small harbour and the road to Prinos.

Close to the waterfront is the very pleasant and clean C-class *Hotel Alkyon* (☎ 22 148). Singles/doubles will cost about 6500/8600 dr. Take a back room if you prefer less noise from street life. The hotel also has a snack bar where tea is the speciality; the co-owner is English. The *Hotel Akropolis* (☎ 22 488), one block south of the central square, is a very well-maintained turn-of-the-century mansion, with a lovely garden. The beautifully furnished rooms cost 9000/11,800 dr for doubles/triples with private bathroom.

The *Hotel Mironi* (☎ 23 256; fax 22 132) is modern and spacious with lots of cool marble. Rates are 10,000/12,000 dr for singles/doubles with private bathroom. From the ferry quay walk to 18 Oktovriou and turn right and then left on the road signposted to Prinos. The hotel is along here on the left. Next door, the *Hotel Victoria* (☎ 22 556; fax 22 132) is a lovely traditional place which has doubles/triples for 9000/12,000 dr. Both establishments are run by the same owner.

Places to Stay – middle

The B-class *Hotel Pegasus* (☎ 22 061; fax 22 373) is a pleasant choice. It has a pool, restaurant and bar. Its quality rooms are 14,000/16,000 dr for doubles/triples, including breakfast. The B-class *Timoleon Hotel* (☎ 22 177; fax 23 277) has clean spacious rooms with balcony. Single/double rates are 10,800/14,000 dr with private bathroom; the price includes breakfast. The hotel is on the waterfront just beyond the bus station.

The A-class *Amfipolis Hotel* (☎ 23 101; fax 22 110), on the corner of 18 Oktovriou and Theogenous, is an attractive mock castle complete with turrets. Rates are

13,700/18,700 dr including a buffet breakfast. The hotel has a swimming pool.

Places to Eat & Drink
Limenas has a good selection of restaurants serving well-prepared food. *I Pigi Restaurant*, on the central square, is an inviting, unpretentious restaurant next to a spring. The food is good and the service friendly and attentive. Try stifado (stew in tomato sauce), mussel saganaki or swordfish.

The old harbour, and the area just beyond it along the beach, boasts no less than eight restaurants. They all cater primarily to the tourist trade and feature multilingual menu cards. The first two, *Ta Platanakia* and *I Simi*, are convenient and slightly more down-market than the other establishments. The food is good at both restaurants and the prices aren't too bad. Reckon on about 2200 dr for a meal with beer or wine.

The very good *Selinos Restaurant* is a little out of town, but is worth a visit. Check out a couple of their specialities: kolokythokeftedes (zucchini rissoles), ohtapodi krasato (octopus in wine) or mydia saganaki (mussels in sauce). Prices are mid-range. Walk inland from the central square and the restaurant is a little way beyond the Sanctuary of Hercules. The taverna is only open in the evening.

The *Anonymous Café*, next to Leather Lane on 18 Oktovriou, serves English-style snacks and Guinness in a can (and many other beers) to a background of eclectic music. Two doors along is another popular watering hole, the *Full Moon*, which has an Australian owner.

Things to Buy
Limenas has two excellent leather shops, both of which sell high-quality leather bags. They are Carol & Gordon Leather Plus on the central square, and Leather Lane on 18 Oktovriou. The latter also has a used-book exchange (with mostly English and German titles).

EAST COAST
The neighbouring hillside villages of **Pan-** agia and **Potamia** are quite touristy but picturesque. Both are 4km west of Golden beach. The Greek-American artist Polygnotos Vagis was born in Potamia in 1894 and some of his work can be seen in a small museum in the village next to the main church. It is open from Tuesday to Saturday from 9 am to 1 pm and 6 to 9 pm and on Sunday and holidays from 10 am to 2 pm. (The municipal museum in Kavala also has a collection of Vagis' work.)

The long and sandy **Golden beach** is the island's best beach and roads from both Panagia and Potamia lead down to it. These roads are very pleasant to walk along, but if you prefer, the bus from Limenas calls at both villages before continuing to the southern end of the beach.

The next beach south is at the village of **Kinira**, and just south of here is the very pleasant **Paradise beach**. The little islet just off the coast here is also called Kinira. **Alyki**, on the south-east coast, consists of two quiet beaches back to back on a headland. The southernmost beach is the better of the two. There is a small archaeological site near the beach and a marble quarry. The road linking the east side with the west side runs high across the cliffs, providing some great views of the bays at the bottom of the island. With only a few breaks, the island circuit (110km) can be completed by motorcycle in about 3½ hours.

Places to Stay & Eat
Hrysi Ammoudia (☎ 0593-61 472), on Golden Beach, is the only camp site on this side of the island and is only a stone's throw from the inviting water. Facilities are good and include a minimarket. The *Hotel Emerald* (☎ 0593-61 979), on Golden beach, has self-contained studios for two to four persons for 11,400 to 14,000 dr.

In Panagia, *Hotel Elvetia* (☎ 0593-61 231) has pleasant doubles costing 10,900 dr. With your back to the fountain in the central square of Panagia (where the bus stops), turn left and take the first main road to the left and the hotel is on the left. Just beyond here on the right, the *Hotel Hrysafis* (☎ 0593-61 451) has singles and doubles for 9500 dr with private bathroom. There are domatia at both Kinira and Alyki.

There are reasonably priced restaurants in Panagia. *Restaurant Vigli*, overlooking the northern end of Golden beach, has superb views and food and offers live music on Thursday evenings. There are tavernas on the beach at Kinira and Alyki.

WEST COAST

The west coast consists of a series of seaside villages with Skala (by the sea) before their names. Roads lead from each of these to inland villages with the same name (minus the 'skala'). Beaches along the west coast are uniformly pebbly and exposed. Travelling from north to south the first village is **Skala Rahoniou**. This is Thasos' latest development, having recently been discovered by the package-tour companies. It has an excellent camp site and the inland village of Rahoni remains unspoilt. Just before Rahoni there is a turn-off left to Moni Agiou Georgiou.

Skala Prinou, the next coastal village, and Thasos' second port, is crowded and unattractive. **Skala Sotira** and **Skala Kallirahis** are more pleasant and both have small beaches. Kallirahi, 2km inland from Skala Kallirahis, is a peaceful village with steep narrow streets and old stone houses. It has a large population of skinny, anxious-looking cats and, judging by the graffiti and posters, a lot of communists.

Skala Marion is a delightful fishing village and one of the least touristy places around the coast. It was from here, earlier this century, that the German Speidel Mining Company exported iron ore from Thasos to Europe. There are beaches at both sides of the village, and between here and Limenaria there are stretches of uncrowded beach.

Limenaria (42km from Limenas) is Thasos' second-largest town and a very crowded resort with a narrow sandy beach. The town was built in 1903 by the Speidel Metal Company. There are slightly less crowded beaches around the coast at **Pefkari** and **Potos**. From Potos a scenic 10km road leads inland to **Theologos** which was the capital of the island in medieval and Turkish times. This is the island's most beautiful village and the only mountain settlement served by public transport. The village houses are of whitewashed stone with slate roofs. It's a serene place, still unblemished by mass tourism.

Places to Stay

Camping Perseus (☎ 0593-81 242), at Skala Rahoniou, is an excellent, grassy camp site in a pretty setting of flowers and olive and willow trees. The cook at the site's taverna will prepare any Greek dish you wish if you place your order a day in advance. The EOT-owned *Camping Prinos* (☎ 0593-71 171), at Skala Prinou, is well maintained with lots of greenery and shade and is about a kilometre or so south of the ferry quay.

The next camp site, *Camping Daedalos* (☎ 0593-71 365), is just north of Skala Sotira. It has a minimarket, restaurant and bar. The next site, *Pefkari Camping* (☎ 0593-51 190), at Pefkari beach, is a nifty site south of Limenaria but requires a minimum three-night stay. Look carefully for the sign; it is not so obvious. All sites charge around 850 dr per person and 650 dr per tent.

All of the seaside villages have hotels and domatia and the inland villages have rooms in private houses. For information about these enquire at kafeneia. The single/double *domatia* of Stelios Kontogeorgiadis, overlooking the harbour at Skala Marion, are clean and attractive and cost 5000/6000 dr for singles/doubles with shared bathroom and kitchen.

Places to Eat

All of the coastal villages have tavernas. *Taverna Drosia*, in Rahoni, features live bouzouki music on Friday and Saturday evenings. *Taverna Orizontes*, first on the left as you enter Theologos, features rembetika nights. *Taverna Kleoniki*, on the main street in Theologos, has an outdoor terrace with wonderful views of the surrounding mountains.

Ionian Islands Τα Επτάνησα

The Ionian group consists of seven main islands anchored in the Ionian sea – Corfu, Paxi, Kefallonia, Zakynthos, Ithaki, Lefkada and Kythira; this last one is more accessible from the Peloponnese. The islands differ from other island groups and, geographically, are less quintessentially Greek. More reminiscent of Corfu's neighbour Italy, not least in light, their colours are mellow and green compared with the stark, dazzling brightness of the Aegean. These islands receive a great amount of rain and consequently, the vegetation, with the exception of the more exposed Kythira, is more luxuriant. Corfu has the nation's highest rainfall. Overall, vegetation combines elements of the tropical with forests that could be northern European: exotic orchids with wild flowers emerging below spring snowlines and eucalypts and acacias sharing soil with plane, oak and maple trees. The islands do not experience the meltemi, and as a result they can be extremely hot in summer.

The culture and cuisine of each Ionian island is unique and differs from the Aegean islands and Crete. Influences from Mediterranean Europe and Britain have also been stronger yet have developed with special individuality on each island.

Accommodation prices in this chapter are for the high season (July and August). They are lower at other times.

History & Mythology

The origin of the name Ionian is obscure but is thought to derive from the goddess Io. Yet another one of Zeus' countless paramours, Io, while fleeing the wrath of a jealous Hera, happened to pass through the waters now known as the Ionian sea.

If we are to believe Homer, the islands were important during Mycenaean times; however, no magnificent palaces or even modest villages from that period have been revealed, although Mycenaean tombs have been unearthed. Ancient history lies buried

HIGHLIGHTS

- Exploring the fine Venetian buildings and narrow streets of Corfu's old town
- Discovering the half-derelict village of Old Perithia in northern Corfu
- Viewing ancient olive groves of Paxi
- Visiting the traditional, unspoilt villages and fine pebble beaches of Meganisi
- Relaxing on the white sand beach of Myrtos on Kefallonia
- Exploring the fishing villages of Frikes and Kioni on Ithaki

beneath tonnes of earthquake rubble. Seismic activity has been constant on all Ionian islands, including Kythira.

According to Homer, Odysseus' kingdom consisted not only of Ithaca (Ithaki) but also encompassed Kefallonia, Zakynthos and Lefkada. Ithaca has long been controversial. Classicists and archaeologists in the 19th century concluded that Homer's Ithaca was modern-day Ithaki, his Sami was Sami on Kefallonia, and his Zakynthos was today's Zakynthos, which sounded credible. But early this century German archaeologist Wil-

helm Dorpfeld put a spanner in the works by claiming that Lefkada was ancient Ithaca, modern Ithaki was ancient Sami and Kefallonia was ancient Doulichion. His theories have now fallen from favour with everyone except the people of Lefkada.

By the 8th century BC, the Ionian islands were in the clutches of mighty Corinth, which regarded them of value as stepping stones on the route to Sicily and Italy. A century later, Corfu staged a successful revolt against Corinth, which was allied to Sparta, and became an ally of Sparta's archenemy, Athens. This alliance provoked Sparta into challenging Athens, thus precipitating the Peloponnesian Wars. The wars left Corfu depleted as they did all participants and Corfu became little more than a staging post for whoever happened to be holding sway in Greece. By the end of the 3rd century, Corfu, along with the other Ionian islands, had become Roman. Following the decline of the Roman Empire, the islands saw the usual waves of invaders that Greece suffered. After the fall of Constantinople, the islands became Venetian.

Corfu was never part of the Ottoman Empire. Paxi, Kefallonia, Zakynthos, Ithaki and Kythira were variously occupied by the Turks, but the Venetians held them longest. The exception was Lefkada, which was Turkish for 200 years. The Ionian islands fared better under the Venetians than their counterparts in the Cyclades. They benefited culturally through contact with Italy and the tradition of icon-painting was allowed to continue. In Turkish-occupied Greece, icon-painting was driven underground as Islamic law prohibited portrayal of the human form.

Venice fell to Napoleon in 1797. Two years later in the Treaty of Campo Formio, the Ionian islands were allotted to France. In 1799 Russian forces wrested the islands from Napoleon, but by 1807 they were his again. By then, the all-powerful British couldn't resist meddling. As a result, in 1815, after Napoleon's downfall, the islands became a British protectorate under the jurisdiction of a series of Lords High

Commissioner. These reportedly ranged from being eccentric to downright nutty.

British rule was oppressive but, on a more positive note, the British constructed roads, bridges, schools and hospitals, established trade links and developed agriculture and industry. However, the fervour of nationalism in the rest of Greece soon reached the Ionian islands.

The call for enosis (union with Greece) was realised in 1862 when Britain relinquished the islands to Greece. In WWII the Italians invaded Corfu as part of Mussolini's plan to resurrect the mighty Roman Empire. Italy surrendered to the Allies in September 1943 and, in revenge, the Germans massacred thousands of Italians who had occupied the island. The Germans also sent some 5000 Corfiot Jews to Auschwitz.

A severe earthquake shook the Ionian islands in 1953. It did considerable damage, particularly on Zakynthos and Kefallonia.

Getting There & Away
Air Corfu, Kefallonia, Zakynthos and Kythira have airports. Corfu has a weekly Olympic Airways scheduled flight to/from Geneva. In addition, many charter flights to Corfu come from northern Europe and the UK. Kefallonia and Zakynthos also receive flights. These islands have frequent flights to Athens.

Bus Lefkada is joined to the mainland by a causeway and can be reached by bus from Athens as well as Patras. Buses go from Athens and Thessaloniki to Corfu and from Athens to Kefallonia and Zakynthos.

Ferry – domestic The Peloponnese has several ports of departure for the Ionian islands: Patras for ferries to Kefallonia, Ithaki, Paxi and Corfu; Kyllini for ferries to Kefallonia and Zakynthos, and Monemvasia, Neapoli and Gythio for Kythira which is also served from Crete. Epiros has one port, Igoumenitsa, for Corfu; and Sterea Ellada has two, Astakos for Ithaki and Kefallonia, and Mytikas for Lefkada.

Ferry – international From Corfu, ferries depart for Brindisi, Bari, Ancona, Trieste and Venice in Italy. At least three times weekly, a ferry goes from Kefallonia to Brindisi via Igoumenitsa and Corfu. In July and August this ferry also calls at Zakynthos and Paxi.

Corfu Κέρκυρα

• *pop 107,600* • *postcode 491 00*
• *area code* ☎ *Central Corfu & Corfu town 0661; south of Gardiki and Messonghi 0662; north of Paleokastritsa and Ipsos 0663*

Corfu is the second-largest, greenest Ionian island and the best known. In Greek, the island is called Kerkyra (**Ker**keera). It was Homer's 'beautiful and rich land', and Odysseus' last stop on his journey home to Ithaca. Shakespeare reputedly used it as a background for *The Tempest*. This century, the Durrell brothers, among others, have extolled its virtues. With its beguiling landscape of vibrant wild flowers and slender cypress trees rising out of shimmering olive groves, Corfu is considered by many as Greece's most beautiful island. With the highest rainfall, it's also the nation's major vegetable garden and produces scores of herbs. The mountain air is heavily scented. In autumn, the night sky over the sea is a spectacular sight.

Getting There & Away
Air Corfu has at least three flights to Athens every day (19,200 dr). There are flights to Thessaloniki on Monday, Thursday and Saturday (19,600 dr). The Olympic Airways office (☎ 38 694/695/696; fax 36 634) is at Polyla 11, Corfu town.

Bus Two daily buses go to Athens (11 hours, 8600 dr including ferry), at 8.30 am and 6.30 pm, and one to Thessaloniki (8100 dr). Tickets must be bought in advance.

Ferry – domestic From Corfu, hourly ferries go to Igoumenitsa (1½ hours, 1400 dr). One daily ferry goes to Paxi (two hours, 1900

Corfu

dr). In summer, a fast boat, the Pegasus, takes 90 minutes (2800 dr). This boat leaves from the old port. For details on ferries to Patras, see the following section. Corfu's port police can be contacted on ☎ 32 655.

Ferry – international Corfu is on the Patras-Igoumenitsa ferry route to Italy (Brindisi, Bari, Ancona, Trieste, Venice). About six ferries a day go to Brindisi (9½ hours). Some go direct from Igoumenitsa, but others go via Corfu (10 hours), where some lines allow a free stopover.

At least one ferry a day goes to Bari and Ancona, and one daily goes to Venice (30 hours) in summer.

Brindisi-bound ferries leave Corfu's new port between 8.30 and 9.30 am. For ticket prices see the Igoumenitsa Getting There & Away section in the Northern Greece chapter. Agencies selling tickets are mostly on Xenofondos Stratigou. Shop around for the best deal. You can take one of the frequent international ferries to Patras (10 hours, 5000 dr), daily in summer.

Getting Around

The Airport There is no Olympic Airways

Coast near Alykes, Zakynthos, Ionian islands

ROSEMARY HALL

ROSEMARY HALL

ROSEMARY HALL

ROSEMARY HALL

DAVID HALL

Top: Yachts moored in tranquil waters off Porto Spillia, Meganisi, Ionian islands
Middle: Narrow lanes and rustic dwellings in Corfu, Ionian islands
Bottom: The end of the bay, Skopelos town, Sporades islands

shuttle bus between Corfu town and the airport. Bus No 3 from Plateia San Rocco stops on the main road 500m from the airport.

Bus Destinations of buses (green-and-cream) from Corfu town's long-distance bus station are as follows:

Destination	Duration	Fare	Frequency
Agios Stefanos (via Sidhari)	1½ hours	750 dr	5 daily
Glyfada (via Vatos)	45 mins	300 dr	4 daily
Kassiopi (via Loutses)	1 hour	600 dr	4 daily
Kavos (via Lefkimmi)	1½ hours	750 dr	8 daily
Messongi	45 mins	360 dr	4 daily
Paleokastritsa	45 mins	400 dr	6 daily
Pyrgi (via Ipsos)	30 mins	260 dr	4 daily
Roda (via Aharavi)	1½ hours	600 dr	4 daily
Agios Gordios (via Sinarades)	45 mins	260 dr	4 daily

Numbers and destinations of buses (dark blue) from the bus station at Plateia San Rocco, Corfu town, are:

Destination	Bus No	Duration	Frequency
Ahillion (via Gastouri)	No 10	20 mins	6 daily
Afra	No 8	30 mins	8 daily
Agios Ioannis (via Pelekas)	No 11	30 mins	9 daily
Kastellani (via Kourmades)	No 5	25 mins	14 daily
Kontokali (via Gouvia & Dassia)	No 7	30 mins	hourly
Perama (via Benitses)	No 6	30 mins	12 daily
Potamos (via Evropouli & Tembloni)	No 4	45 mins	12 daily

The local-bus flat fare is 190 dr. Tickets can be bought on board or on Plateia San Rocco.

Car, Motorcycle & Bicycle Car-hire companies in Corfu town include Autorent (☎ 44 623/624/625), Xenofondos Stratigou 34; Avis (☎ 24 042), Ethnikis Antistaseos 42; Budget (☎ 22 062), Donzelot 5; and Europcar (☎ 46 931/932/933), Xenofondos Stratigou 32. Motorcycle-hire outlets are on Xenofondos Stratigou and Avramiou. Mountain bicycles can be hired from Charitos Travel Agency (☎ 44 611/620; fax 36 825), Arsenou 35.

CORFU TOWN
• *pop 36,000* • *postcode 491 00* • *area code* ☎ *0661*
The island capital is Corfu town (Kerkyra), built on a promontory. It's a gracious medley of numerous occupying influences, which never included the Turks. The Spianada (esplanade) is green, gardened and boasts Greece's only cricket ground, a legacy of the British. After a match, spectators may join players in drinking ginger beer made to an old Victorian recipe or, typically, tea or gin and tonic.

The Liston, a row of arcaded buildings flanking the north-western side of the Spianada, was built during the French occupation and modelled on Paris' Rue de Rivoli. The buildings function as up-market cafés, lamplit by night. Georgian mansions and Byzantine churches complete the picture. The Venetian influence prevails, particularly in the enchanting old town, wedged between two fortresses. Narrow alleyways of 18th-century shuttered tenements in muted ochres and pinks are more reminiscent of Venice or Naples than Greece.

Orientation
The town is separated into northern and southern sections. The old town is in the northern section between the Spianada and the New Fortress. The Palaio Frourio (Old Fortress) is east of the northern section and projects out to sea, cut off from the town by a moat. The Neo Frourio (New Fortress) is west. The Spianada separates the Old Fortress from the town. The southern section is the new town.

The old port is north of the old town. The

IONIAN ISLANDS

Herbs

Wherever the land in Greece is uncultivated and denuded of trees, vegetation has degenerated to a tangle of shrubs, bushes and a profusion of herbs. The most common herbs in Greece are basil, rosemary, thyme, oregano, sage, bay, dill and garlic, but many others can be found. The evocative, all-pervading aroma of these herbs is something which lingers in the memory for a long time.

Herbs, more than any other ingredient, used wisely and in moderation, can transform a mundane dish into a gourmet feast.

Tourist-orientated shops selling traditional products, including dried herbs, are springing up all over Greece, but you will find the same herbs at a lower price in street markets and supermarkets. Dried herbs are a poor substitute for freshly picked ones, but if you must use them they keep best in a cool, dark cupboard. They can be reconstituted in lemon juice, for use in salads. Greeks often go to nearby hills, or patches of wasteland in towns, to pick fresh herbs as they need them.

Since ancient times herbs have been used in Greece for medicinal purposes. This custom continues today, particularly in rural areas. Oregano, a member of the marjoram family, but with a more pungent flavour, is the most widely used herb in Greek cooking. It is an important ingredient in tomato sauce and many oven-baked dishes. Finely chopped oregano is sprinkled on souvlaki, salads and fetta cheese.

Basil is not used much in cooking in Greece, but is sprinkled on salads, especially tomatoes. Almost every house will have a pot of basil on the balcony, as it makes an excellent insect repellent. A basil infusion is said to aid digestion, act as a mild laxative and prevent travel sickness.

Rosemary is a sweet-scented, strong-tasting herb which the Greeks sprinkle liberally on roast meat, particularly lamb. The Greeks don't use thyme much in cooking, but put it to a variety of other uses. The infusion is used as a cure for coughs, sleeplessness and bathing sore eyes. It is sometimes hung in wardrobes as a moth repellent – it certainly smells better than mothballs. Both rosemary and thyme make excellent honey. Sage is another herb not used much in cooking, but a sage infusion is said to cure headaches.

Bay leaves are widely used to flavour stews and soups. Dill is a highly aromatic herb and both the leaves and seeds are used in cooking. Chopped fresh dill leaves are used in salads, and are an important ingredient in tzatziki. Dill also goes well with fish and potatoes. Dill infusions are taken as a digestive aid, and the seeds are chewed to sweeten the breath, which is just as well because another ingredient, garlic, is widely used in Greece. *Skordalia*, a strong garlic sauce, is served with fried cod. Garlic is also used in many baked dishes, as well as being an essential ingredient in tzatziki. It is said to aid digestion, build up immunity to colds and lower blood pressure.

Cinnamon is sprinkled on *rizogalo* (rice pudding) and sliced apple, and is an ingredient in *stifado* (meat stewed with onions). Chamomile infusions are widely used for medicinal purposes; they are said to aid digestion, calm nerves and prevent colds.

If you've enjoyed your holiday in Greece, then hope that someone will give you some basil, because a parting gift of this herb, according to the Greeks, ensures that you will return. ■

new port is west. Between them is the hulking New Fortress. The long-distance bus station is on Avramiou, inland from the new port. The local bus station is on Plateia San Rocco. Local buses serve the town and nearby villages.

Information

Tourist Offices The EOT (☎ 37 520/640; fax 30 298) is on Rizospaston Voulefton. The tourist police (☎ 30 265) are at Samartzi 4, near Plateia Solomou.

Money The National Bank of Greece is at the junction of Voulgareos and G Theotoki. It has a 24-hour cash exchange machine as does the Commercial Bank opposite the new port, and many others. American Express is represented by Greek Skies Tours (☎ 32 469 or 30 883) at Kapodistriou 20a.

Post & Communications The post office is on Alexandras. It is open Monday to Friday from 7.30 am to 8 pm; on Saturday from 7.30 am to 2 pm; and on Sunday from 9 am to 1.30 pm. The OTE at Mantzarou 9 is open from 6 am to midnight daily.

Bookshops The Xenoglossa Bookshop, Markora 45, stocks English-language books including novels and a few travel guides.

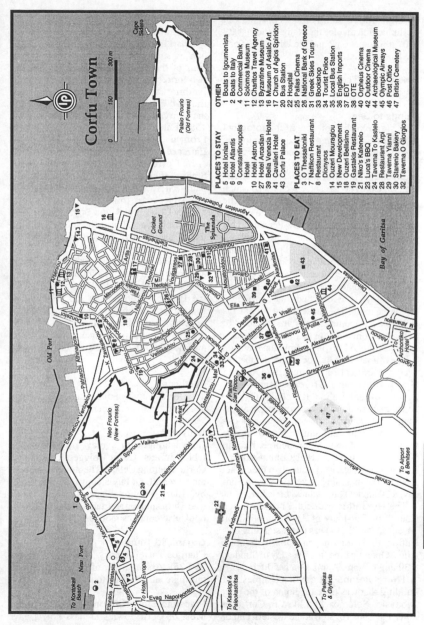

Corfu Town

0   150   300 m

Palaio Frourio
(Old Fortress)

Cape Sidero

PLACES TO STAY
5   Hotel Ionian
6   Hotel Atlantis
9   Constantinoupolis Hotel
10   Hotel Astron
27   Hotel Arcadian
39   Bella Venezia Hotel
41   Cavalieri Hotel
43   Corfu Palace

PLACES TO EAT
3   O Thessaloniki
7   Naftikon Restaurant
8   Restaurant Dionysos
14   Ouzeri Mouraglou
15   New Development
18   Ouzeri Belissimo
19   Gastakis Restaurant
21   Niko's Kafeneio
23   Luca's BBQ
24   Taverna To Kastelo
28   Restaurant Arpi
29   Taverna Yianni
30   Starenio Bakery
32   Taverna O Giorgios

OTHER
1   Boats to Igoumenista
2   Boats to Italy
4   Commercial Bank
11   Solomos Museum
12   Charitos Travel Agency
13   Byzantine Museum
16   Museum of Asiatic Art
17   Church of Agios Spiridon
20   Bus Station
22   Hospital
25   Pallas Cinema
26   National Bank of Greece
31   Greek Skies Tours
33   Bookshop
34   Tourist Police
35   Local Bus Station
36   English Imports
37   EOT
38   OTE
40   Orpheus Cinema
42   Outdoor Cinema
44   Archaeological Museum
45   Olympic Airways
46   Post Office
47   British Cemetery

Neo Frourio
(New Fortress)

Old Port

New Port

Bay of Garitsa

IONIAN ISLANDS

Foreign Consulates Foreign consulates in Corfu include that for the Netherlands (☎ 39 900) at Idromenon 2 and the UK (☎ 30 055) at Menekratous 1.

Emergency The Corfu General Hospital (☎ 45 811) is on I Andreadi.

Things to See

The star exhibit of the **archaeological museum** is the Gorgon Medusa sculpture, one of the best preserved pieces of Archaic sculpture in Greece. It was part of the west pediment of the 6th-century Temple of Artemis at Corcyra (the ancient capital), which stood on the peninsula south of the town. The petrifying Medusa is depicted in the instant before she was beheaded by Perseus. This precipitated the birth of her sons, Chrysaor and Pegasus (the winged horse), who emerged from her headless body.

Also impressive is the 7th-century crouching lion, found near the Tomb of Menecrates. Archaeologists ascertained that it stood on top of the tomb. The museum (☎ 30 680) is at Vraili 5. Opening times are Tuesday to Saturday from 8.45 am to 3 pm and Sunday from 9.30 am to 2.30 pm. Admission is 800 dr.

The **museum of Asiatic art** houses the impressive collection, bequeathed by the Greek diplomats Grigoris Manos and Nikolaos Hatzivasiliou. It includes Chinese and Japanese porcelain, bronzes, screens, sculptures, theatrical masks, armour, books and prints. The museum is housed in the Palace of St Michael & St George, built in 1819 as the British Lord High Commissioner's residence The palace is just north of the cricket ground. The museum is open Tuesday to Sunday, 8.30 am to 3 pm. Admission is free.

The **Byzantine museum**, housed in the Church of Our Lady of Antivouniotissa on Arseniou (☎ 38 313) has an outstanding collection of Byzantine and post-Byzantine icons. Opening times are Tuesday to Sunday, 8.30 am to 3 pm. Admission is 500 dr.

The **Solomos museum** occupies the building that was once the home of the poet Dionysios Solomos who lived in Corfu for 30 years. Look for sign at the western end of Arseniou. It is open daily from 9.30 to 2pm; admission is 200 dr.

Apart from the pleasure of wandering the narrow streets of the old town and the gardens of the Spianada, you can explore the two fortresses, Corfu town's most dominant landmarks. The promontory on which the **Neo Frourio** stands was first fortified in the 12th century. Existing remains date from 1588. Entrance is 400 dr. The ruins of **Palaio Frourio** date from the mid-12th century. Entrance is 800 dr. Both are open all day.

In Corfu, many males are christened Spyros after the island's miracle-working patron St Spyridon. His mummified body is in a silver glass-fronted coffin in the 16th-century **Church of Agios Spyridon** on Odos Agios Spiridonos. It is paraded on Palm Sunday, Easter Sunday, 11 August and the first Sunday in November.

The well-kept, tranquil **British cemetery**, at the northern end of Kolokotroni, has been a fitting resting-place for British expats from the British occupation to the present day. Many fine trees and flowers, including wild orchids, grow here. George Psaila, the cemetery's resident gardener since 1944, was awarded the MBE in 1988 for conscientious service.

Festivals

The Corfu festival of dance and music is held in August and September.

Activities

Go yachting with a crew or bareboat in fabled waters. Corfu's biggest charterer is Corfu Yachting Centre, Theotokou 120, near the new port. Or buy a copy of *Corfu Walks* by Hilary Whitton Piapeti, at Xenoglossa (see Bookshops), and take to the hills. The book also contains mountain-bike tours.

Organised Tours

Charitos Travel Agency (☎ 44 611/620; fax 36 825), Arseniou 35, offers coach, mountain-bike and walking tours.

Places to Stay – bottom end

Most of Corfu town's D-class hotels have

closed resulting in a shortage of budget accommodation. There are no EOT-approved domatia but locals who unofficially let rooms often meet the boats – you may strike lucky. Be wary of booking rooms for Greece in advance in Italy before arrival. A few unscrupulous agencies may suggest your preferred choice is closed or full – and reap a tidy commission from the places booked through them.

The *Hotel Europa* (☎ 39 304), on Neos Limin, is the town's only D-class hotel. It has little to recommend it other than being near the new port. Singles/doubles cost 5500/6000 dr with shared bathroom and doubles with private bathroom are 7000 dr. A sign points to the hotel at the western end of Xenofondos Stratigou. The *Hotel Ionian* (☎ 30 628), Xenofondos Stratigou 46, is the cheapest C-class with reasonable singles/doubles for 7500/10,200 dr.

If you have transport, or don't mind a short ride on the No 7 bus, you may consider one of the following options on the north-west coast road, 4km from Corfu town. The area is noisy, but the recommendations are superior to anything comparably priced in town. *Angelos Athanasiou Domatia* (☎ 34 091/24 433) has clean, comfortable double/triple studios for 10,900/11,500 dr. The rooms are 60m north-west of the Sunset Hotel, on the opposite side. A little further along, *Linda Cheimariou Rooms* (☎ 28 479), has well-kept doubles with shared bathroom for 6000 dr.

Places to Stay – middle

The *Hotel Arcadian* (☎ 37 670/671; fax 45 087), Kapodistriou 44, has small, comfortable singles/doubles for 13,000/17,000 dr, including breakfast. The *Hotel Atlantis* (☎ 35 560/561/562), on Xenofondos Stratigou, has pleasant rooms for 14,900/17,900/21,650 dr.

The C-class *Hotel Archontiko* (☎ & fax 38 294), M Athanasiou 61, occupies a 19th-century neoclassical building with many original features. The charming rooms cost 10,000/12,500/14,000 dr.

The refurbished C-class *Hotel Constantinopoulis* (☎ 48 716/717), Zavitsianou 3,

reincarnated from a shabby, backpacker's favourite into a splendid art-nouveau hostelry, has rates of 12,500/18,600/23,200 dr. Nearby, the B-class *Hotel Astron* (☎ 39 505/986), Donzelot 15, has a neoclassical ambience and room rates of 13,500/18,000/22,500 dr.

The B-class *Bella Venezia Hotel* (☎ 46 5000/44 290), Zambeli 4, is another impressive neoclassical style hotel. Rates are 15,400/18,500/21,000 dr.

Places to Stay – top end

The A-class *Cavelieri Hotel* occupies a 300-year-old building at Kapodistriou 4, and has an interior of classical elegance. Singles/doubles cost 30,000/35,000 dr and family suites cost 40,000 dr.

The *Corfu Palace* (☎ 39 485; fax 31 749), on Dimokratias, is the town centre's only deluxe hotel, the choice of Prince Rainier and the late Princess Grace. It has two bars, two restaurants and pools. Rates are 39,000/53,000 dr.

Places to Eat – inexpensive

As it was not conquered by the Turks, Corfu maintains a distinctive cuisine influenced by other parts of Europe, including Russia. (See the food section in Facts for the Visitor).

There are several low-priced eateries near the new port. Both the tiny *O Thessaloniki*, on Xenofondos Stratigou, and *Luca's BBQ*, on Avramiou, serve low-priced succulent spit-roast chicken.

Taverna To Kastelo, on Desilla, offers tasty ready-prepared meals. Join locals at lunchtime to watch the comings and goings at the food market.

There's a cluster of atmospheric restaurants at the southern end of the old town. *Taverna O Georgos*, on Guilford, serves reasonably priced mezedes and main courses at outdoor tables under a grapevine. The cosy *Taverna Yianni* on Idromenon has similar food and prices. Nearby, *Restaurant Arpi* on Giotopolou is a classy little place with pastitsada for 1800 dr and sofrito for 1500 dr.

Further north, most eateries are touristy and down-market, but there are exceptions.

IONIAN ISLANDS

Gistakis Restaurant, Solomou 20, serves delicious food. *Naftikon Restaurant*, N Theotoki 152, has fair prices and Corfiot food. *Restaurant Dionysos*, on Dona, is also commendable. At *Ouzeri Bellisimo*, N Theotoki, a tasty mezedes plate costs 1500 dr.

The owner of *Niko's Kafeneio*, Avramiou 100, deserves a medal for serving excellent cappuccino for 350 dr. Other drinks are also low-priced. *Starenio Bakery*, Guilford 51, sells delicious home-made pies and bread.

Places to Eat – moderate

Indulge in a little people-watching at one of the cafés on the Liston. You will pay around 1200 dr for coffee and cake.

Mouraglou Ouzeri, on Arseniou, has a large range of mezedes. The small mixed fish plate (2670 dr) and a few vegetable mezedes is an enjoyable meal for two. The *new development*, east of Arseniou, is a refurbishment of a popular turn-of-the-century bathing spot. There's an up-market café and restaurant at the water's edge.

Entertainment

Corfu town has two indoor cinemas; the *Pallas*, on Theotoki, and the *Orpheus* on Aspioti. A little further south of the latter, there's an outdoor cinema.

The old town has many bars, but discos are on the coast road, 2km north-west of the new port on a street known as 'disco strip'.

AROUND CORFU
North of Corfu Town

Most of the coast of northern Corfu is package-tourist saturated, and thoroughly de-Greeked. Camp sites along the north-east coast include: *Karda Beach* (☎ 0661-93 595) and *Kormarie* (☎ 0661-93 587) at Dassia; *Kerkira Camping* (☎ 0661-93 246) and *Ipsos Ideal* (☎ 0661-93 243) at Ipsos; and *Paradise Camping* (☎ 0661-93 282) at Pyrgi.

The **Shell Museum** (☎ 0661-99340), at Gouvia, reputedly contains the best private shell collection in Europe. It is open daily from 9 am to 10 pm. Entrance is 500 dr.

At **Pyrgi**, 16km north of Corfu town, a road continues around the base of **Mt Pantokrator** (906m), the island's highest peak. At this point, where the island protrudes as if to accommodate the mountain, the 2000m mountains of Albania are less than 2km away. The writers Lawrence and Gerald Durrell spent their idyllic childhoods in this region. Back at Pyrgi, another road snakes inland over the western flank of the mountain to the north coast. A detour can be made to the picturesque village of **Strinila** from where an unsurfaced road leads through stark terrain to the summit, Moni Pantokrator and stupendous views.

The coast road continues to the large resort of Kassiopi, 36km from Corfu town, overlooked by a ruined fortress.

The **Church of Our Lady of Kassiopi** stands on what may have been the site of the Roman Temple of Jupiter, where the Emperor Nero is supposed to have sung while accompanying himself on the lyre. Beyond Kassiopi is a turn-off for the fascinating, half-derelict and almost abandoned village of **Old Perithia**, high up on Mt Panokrator. No buses go there. There are paths to the summit of Mt Panokrator from Strinila and Old Perithia. Only experienced walkers should attempt the trek.

The coast road continues to the resort of **Roda**, with a camp site *Roda Beach* (☎ 0663-63 120). Just east of Sidhari you can walk south along a footpath by the River Typhlos, a habitat for terrapins, herons and egrets. Sidhari is a tacky resort, but its sandy beach is ideal for children as the sea is shallow for a long way out. Peroulades, 3km west of Sidhari, is less developed and there's a track to beautiful Cape Drastis.

Agios Stefanos, further around the coast, is still quite pleasant out of high season. It has a long sandy beach and is a good spot for windsurfing. *San Stefanos Golden Beach Hotel* (☎ 0663-51 053/154), by the bus stop, has comfortable single/double rooms and studios for 5500/7000 dr.

South of Corfu Town

The Kanoni peninsula, 4km from Corfu

town, was the site of the ancient capital but little has been excavated. **Mon Repos Villa**, at its north-east tip was Prince Philip's birthplace. The beautiful wooded grounds are open daily from 8am to 8 pm. Opposite the entrance are two excavation sites, both closed to the public. One is the ruins of the 5th-century **Basilica of Agia Kerkira**, built on the site of a 5th-century BC temple. You can walk to the **Kardaki Spring** from Analypsi nearby.

Just off the southern tip of Kanoni are two pretty islets. On one is **Moni Vlahernas**, reached by a causeway. On the other, **Mouse Island**, where there is a 13th-century church. Caïques ply back and forth from the top of the Kanoni peninsula.

In the centre of the island are the delightful, unspoilt villages of **Kastellani**, **Kamara** and **Agios Prokopios**.

The coast road continues south with a turn-off to the **Ahillion Palace** (☎ 0661-56 245/251), near the hillside village of Gastouri. In the 1890s it was the summer palace of Austria's Empress Elizabeth. King Otho of Greece was her uncle. She dedicated the villa to Achilles. The beautifully landscaped garden is guarded by kitsch statues of the empress' other mythological heroes.

The palace is an astonishing farrago of excessive elements of styles fashionable in the late 19th century. After the empress' assassination, the palace was bought by Kaiser Wilhelm II. It is open Monday to Sunday from 11 am to 4 pm. Admission is 700 dr.

The resort of **Benitses** is the playground of holiday hooligans (ie British lager louts). If you can fight your way through them, head for the ruins of a 3rd-century AD Roman villa, inland. It's also an agreeable 30-minute walk to an old waterworks, built during the time of the British protectorate. **Messongi**, 20km south of Corfu town, is only marginally quieter. **Kavos**, near the southern tip of the island, vies with Benitses for crowds and rowdiness.

The West Coast

Corfu's best beaches are on the west coast. **Paleokastritsa**, 26km west of Corfu, is the coast's largest resort. Built around sandy and pebbled coves with a green mountain backdrop, it's incredibly beautiful. Once paradisiacal, it's been the victim of rampant development. **Moni Theotokou** perches on the rocky promontory at Paleokastritsa, above the shimmering turquoise sea. The monastery was founded in the 13th century but the present building dates from the 18th century. A small museum contains icons. It is open from 7 am to 1 pm and 3 to 8 pm. Admission is free but a donation is expected.

Paleokastritsa Camping (☎ 0663-41 104) is on the main approach road to the resort. The bus will drop you at the entrance. The resort also has many hotels and domatia.

From Paleokastritsa a path ascends to the unspoilt village of **Lakones**, 5km inland. Walk back along the approach road and you will come to a signposted footpath on the left. Climb the steps and at the fork go right. At the asphalt road turn left. After 40m take the narrow path on the right which leads to Lakones.

There are superb views along the 6km road west to **Makrades** and **Krini**. The restaurants along the way extol the views from their terraces. At one, the Belle Vista, the Kaiser, Tito and Nassau reputedly dined. Further west, Golden Fox Restaurant & Apartments (☎ 0663-41 381/409) serves excellent charcoal-grilled dishes. Its immaculate studios cost 10,900 dr.

From Krini you can explore the ruins of the 13th-century Byzantine fortress of **Angelokastro** where the inhabitants of Paleokastritsa took refuge from attackers. A long-distance bus goes twice daily to Krini from Corfu Town.

Further south, the beach at **Ermones** is near **Corfu Golf Course**, the largest in Europe. Hilltop **Pelekas**, 4km away, is renowned for its spectacular sunsets. It's as busy as the coast, but with young independent travellers, rather than package tourists. Pelekas is close to three sandy beaches, **Glyfada** and **Pelekas**, and **Myrtiotissa**, an unofficial nudist beach. There is a free bus from Pelekas to the first two. *Alexandros Pension* (☎ 0661-94 215) on the road signposted 'sunset' has pleasant doubles for 7000 dr with private bathroom. A bit further along, *Rooms to Let Thomas* (☎ 0661-94 491), has clean, comfortable singles/doubles with private bathroom for 4000/8000 dr, and doubles with shared bathroom for 6000 dr.

The stylish, neoclassical *Pelekas Sunset Hotel* (☎ 0661-94 230), further up this road, has beautiful singles/doubles for 15,000/17,000 dr. Near the central square, the bougainvillea-smothered *Pension Tellis & Briditte* (☎ 0661-94 326) near the central square has pleasant doubles for 6000 dr with private bathroom. The nearest camp site is *Vatos Camping* (☎ 0661-94 505) near the village of Vatos.

Agios Gordios beach, 8km south of Glyfada, lies beneath the quite extraordinary *Pink Palace* (☎ 0661-53 103/104), a pink-painted, pleasure complex charging 5000 dr for a room with shared bathroom, cooked breakfast, three-course dinner and use of a pool, volleyball and basketball courts, disco and bar. Facilities include a pool-sized jacuzzi, gym, indoor games and a range of water sports. Magda, sister of the owner, meets the boats from 1 March to 30 November.

Over 25s may prefer *Mires House* (☎ 0661-53 378), just back from the long sandy beach, where nicely furnished doubles cost 7000 dr and studios are 8000 dr. The *Calypso Diving Centre* (☎ 0661-53 101), on the beach, offers PADI courses.

There are three long-distance buses a day to Agios Gordios, via Sinarades.

At Sinarades, 4km from Agios Gordios, the **Folk Museum of Central Corfu** occupies a 19th century house. It is open Tuesday to Sunday from 9.30 am to 3 pm.

The main road south continues to **Agios Mattheos**, a pleasant village overlooked by a pine-clad mountain. It's a one-hour walk to the mountain's Moni Pantokrator, from where a path leads to the summit and awe-inspiring views.

Freshwater **Lake Korission**, a little further south, is a habitat for waders. The long stretch of inviting sand and dunes between the lake and sea continues to Issos. This is one of the least spoilt stretches of Corfu's coast, but it's back to rampant development at Agios Georgios.

Paxi & Antipaxi Παξοί & Αντίπαξοι

PAXI
• *pop 2200* • *postcode 490 82* • *area code ☎ 0662*

Paxi, 10km long and 4km wide, is the smallest main Ionian island. It has a captivating landscape of dense, centuries-old olive groves, snaking limestone walls, derelict farmhouses and abandoned stone olive presses – olives are now pressed mechanically. The olive trees have amazingly twisted, gnarled and hollowed trunks, which gives them the look of sinister, ancient monsters. Walking through the olive groves at dusk is quite eerie.

Paxi has escaped the mass tourism of Corfu and caters for small, discriminating tour companies. There's a shortage of accommodation for independent travellers but outside the high season you'll find somewhere.

Many tourists come on day trips from Corfu and mainland Parga, but they tend to stick to the waterfront at Gaios. There are three coastal settlements – Gaios, Loggos and Lakka, and a few inland villages.

Getting There & Away
At least one regular ferry a day connects Paxi and Corfu (2½ hours, 1600 dr). Daily excursion boats also come from Corfu and Parga on the mainland. Paxi's port police can be contacted on ☎ 31 222. Ferries dock at Gaios' port 1.5km north of the central square. The bus doesn't go there and a taxi costs 500 dr. Excursion boats dock by the central square.

Ferry – international In July and August a ferry goes two or three times a wee k from Paxi to Brindisi, via Igoumenitsa and Corfu.

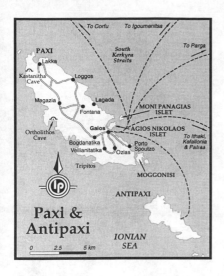

PAXI
To Corfu To Igoumenitsa
South Kerkyra Straits
To Parga
Lakka
Kastanitha Cave
Loggos
Magazia
Lagada
Fontana
MONI PANAGIAS ISLET
Ortholithos Cave
Gaios
AGIOS NIKOLAOS ISLET
Bogdanatika
Porto Spoutzo
To Ithaki, Kefallonia & Patras
Vellianitatika
Ozias
Tripitos
MOGGONISI
ANTIPAXI

Paxi & Antipaxi
IONIAN SEA
0 2.5 5 km

Getting Around
The island's bus links Gaios and Lakka via Loggos up to five times a day.

Motorcycles can be hired from *Makris Motorcycles* (☎ 32 031), on Gaios' waterfront.

Gaios Γάιος
Gaios, on a wide, east coast bay, is the island's capital. It's an attractive place with crumbling 19th-century red-tiled pink, cream and whitewashed buildings. The fortified Agios Nikolaos islet almost fills its harbour. Moni Panagias islet, named after its monastery, lies at the entrance to the bay. On 15 August, a lively festival ends with dancing in Gaios' central square.

Orientation & Information The main square abuts the central waterfront. The main street of Panagioti Kagka runs inland from here to another square where you'll find the bus station. The post office is just beyond here and the OTE is next door. There is no tourist office but the staff at Paxos Magic Holidays (☎ 32 269), on Panagioti Kagka, are helpful.

Things to See & Do The excellent **Cultural**

Museum of Paxi, on the waterfront, has a well-displayed eclectic collection. Don't miss the mind-boggling stirrups hanging from a four-poster bed – a 19th century sex-aid to facilitate love-making. The museum is open from 11 am to 1.30 pm and 7 to 10 pm every day. Admission is 500 dr.

Paxos Magic Holidays organises guided walks for 4000 dr. They also sell a book of walks titled *Exploring Paxos & Antipaxos*.

Take your child along to the Hullabaloo Holiday Club. Activities include nature walks, art & craft and outdoor games. Information is available from Paxos Magic Holidays.

Places to Stay There are no camp sites and wild camping is forbidden. The large *San Giorgio Rooms to Rent* (☎ 32 223), above the waterfront, 150m north of the central square, has well-kept doubles with shared bathroom for 6000 dr, studios for 8000 dr and apartments for 12,000 dr.

At *Georgia Domatia* doubles cost 8000 dr with private bathrooms. Make enquiries at *Makris Motorcycles* (see Getting Around). At *Magda's Domatia* (☎ 32 573), up the hill opposite the bus station, doubles/triples are 6000/8000 dr with shared bathroom.

Roula Apartments (☎ 32 030/650) has clean, comfortable studios for 15,000 dr and four-person apartments for 28,000 dr. Alekos, the owner, will give you a discount out of season. You'll find him at Giasemi café on Panagioti Kagka.

The B-class *Paxos Beach* (☎ 31 211/333; fax 31 166) is a bungalow complex, overlooking the sea, 1.5km south-east of Gaios. The tastefully furnished doubles cost 29,000 dr (half-board) in high season. The complex has a tennis court, beach, bar and restaurant.

Places to Eat *Giasemi Café*, on Panagioti Kagka, has excellent cappuccino for 350 dr, and low-priced alcohol and snacks.

Gaios' best restaurant, by far, is *O Kakaletzos*, opposite the well-signposted Paxos Club, just west of Gaios. It serves a wide range of ready-cooked dishes and grilled food.

Around Paxi

Paxi's gentle east coast has small, pebble beaches, while the west coast has awesome vistas of precipitous cliffs, punctuated by several grottos, only accessible by boat. You can walk to **Tripitos**, a high cliff, from where there are stunning views of AntiPaxi. From the village of Ozias, 2km south of Gaios, walk westwards along the road and turn left at Villa Billy's. Stay on the main track and just before it ends turn right onto a narrow path which leads to Tripitos.

Loggos, 10km north of Gaios, is a small fishing village-cum-resort with several beaches nearby. Most of the accommodation is monopolised by tour companies, but *Babis Dendias* (☎ 31 597) rents studios for 15,000 dr. Inquire at his pantopoleio (general store), 20m beyond the bus stop.

Lovely **Lakka** lies at the end of a deep, narrow bay on the north coast. If you would like to stay, contact *Routsis Holidays* (☎ 31 807/31 162/138; fax 31 161), on the waterfront. The helpful owners are the agents for many rooms in and around Lakki.

The islet of **Mogonissi**, joined by a causeway to the southern tip of Paxi, has a small sand beach and a taverna.

ANTIPAXI

Diminutive Antipaxi, 2km south of Paxi, is covered with grapevines from which notable wine is produced. Its beaches are superb. It has tavernas, but no accommodation. In summer, small boats ply frequently between Gaios and Antipaxi.

Lefkada, Meganisi & Kalamos Λευκάδα, Μεγανήσι & Κάλαμος

LEFKADA

• *pop 21,100* • *postcode 311 00* • *area code* ☎ *0645*
Lefkada (Lef**kad**ha) is the fourth-largest island in the Ionian group. Joined to the mainland by a narrow isthmus until the occupying Corinthians dug a canal in the 8th

Vineyards are a common sight on Antipaxi

century BC, its 25m strait is spanned from the mainland by a causeway. Lefkada has 10 satellite islets – Meganisi, Kalamos, Kastos, Madouri, Skorpidi, Skorpios, Sparti, Thilia, Petalou and Kythros.

Lefkada is mountainous with two peaks over 1000m. It is also fertile, well-watered by underground streams, with cotton fields, acres of dense olive groves, vineyards, fir and pine forests. Once a very poor island, Lefkada's beauty is also in its people, who display intense pride in their island. Many of the older women wear traditional costume. An International Festival of Literature & Art is held in the last two weeks of August.

Getting There & Away

Air Lefkada has no airport but Aktion, near Preveza on the mainland, is a 30-minute bus journey away. Daily flights to Athens are 12,800 dr. Lefkada's Olympic Airways office (☎ 22 881) is at Dorpfeld 1. Preveza's (☎ 0682-28 674) is on Spiliadou 5.

Bus From Lefkada town there are four buses a day that go to Patras (3050 dr), Athens (5½ hours, 5700 dr) and Aktion airport (30 minutes, 350 dr).

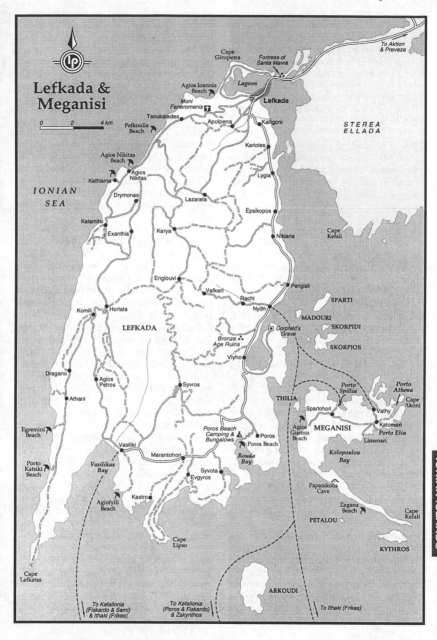

Lefkada & Meganisi

0   2   4 km

IONIAN SEA

STEREA ELLADA

Cape Giropetra
Fortress of Santa Mavra
Lagoon
To Aktion & Preveza
Agios Ioannis Beach
Lefkada
Moni Faneromenis
Apolpena
Tsoukalades
Kalligoni
Pefkoulia Beach
Kariotes
Agios Nikitas Beach
Lygia
Kathisma
Agios Nikitas
Drymonas
Lazarata
Epsikopos
Kalamitsi
Karya
Nikiana
Exanthia
Cape Kefali
Englouvi
Valkeri
Perigiali
Rachi
Komili
Hortata
Nydri
SPARTI
MADOURI
SKORPIDI
Dorpfeld's Grave
SKORPIOS
LEFKADA
Bronze Age Ruins
Vlyho
Dragano
Agios Petros
Syvros
THILIA
Porto Spillia
Porto Athena
Spartohori
Cape Akoni
Vathy
Athani
Agios Giannis Beach
MEGANISI
Katomeri
Porto Elia
Egremini Beach
Poros Beach Camping & Bungalows
Poros
Poros Beach
Limenari
Porto Katsiki Beach
Vasiliki
Marantohori
Rouda Bay
Kolopoulou Bay
Vasilikas Bay
Syvota
Evgyros
Papanikolis Cave
Agiofylli Beach
Kastro
Zagana Beach
Cape Kefali
PETALOU
Cape Lipso
KYTHROS
Cape Lefkatas
ARKOUDI
To Kefallonia (Fiskardo & Sami) & Ithaki (Frikes)
To Kefallonia (Poros & Fiskardo) & Zakynthos
To Ithaki (Frikes)

IONIAN ISLANDS

Ferry From Vasiliki, at least two ferries a day go to Sami (1890 dr) on Kefallonia via Fiskardo (810 dr) and Frikes (860 dr) on Ithaki in high season. In summer one ferry leaves daily from Nydri for Fiskardo on Kefallonia, via the islet of Meganisi. In summer another goes daily to Frikes on Ithaki.

You can contact Lefkada's port police on ☎ 22 322.

Getting Around

Bus From Lefkada town, frequent buses go to Karya and Vlyho via Nydri. Four go daily to Vasiliki and two a day go to Poros. Other villages are served by one or two buses a day.

Car & Motorcycle Cars can be hired from Europcar (☎ 25 726), Stratigou Mela 7, among others, and motorcycles from Motorcycle Rental Santas (☎ 23 947), on Aristotelis Valoritis. At the top of Ioannou Mela, turn right.

Lefkada Town

• *pop 6800* • *postcode 311 00* • *area code* ☎ *0645*

Lefkada town, the island's capital and port, is built on a promontory at the south-east corner of a salty lagoon, which is used as a fish hatchery. The town was devastated by earthquakes in 1867 and 1948. Damage in the 1953 earthquake was minimal. After 1948, many houses were rebuilt in a unique style, with upper floors of painted sheet metal or corrugated iron that is strangely attractive, constructed in the hope they would withstand future earthquakes. The belfries of churches are made of metal girders – another earthquake precaution.

Lefkada Town is a popular anchorage for yachties, but package tourism is mostly concentrated along the east coast.

Orientation From the bus station on the eastern waterfront walk back towards the beginning of the causeway road, turn left at the first major road, and left again at the Nirikos Hotel on to Dorpfeld, the town's animated main thoroughfare. This street is named after the 19th-century archaeologist Wilhelm Dorpfeld who is held in high esteem for postulating that Lefkada, not Ithaki, was the home of Odysseus. Dorpfeld leads to Plateia Agiou Spyridonos, the main square where locals enjoy *soumadia* (an almond drink), during the evening volta (stroll). After the square the thoroughfare's name changes to Ioannou Mela.

Information There is no tourist office on Lefkada. The tourist police (☎ 26 450) are in the same building as the regular police on Dimitriou Golemi. The National Bank of Greece and the post office are on the east side of Ioannou Mela. Take the second right after the bank onto Mitropolis for the OTE. Veer right on to Zambelou and the OTE is on the left.

Things to See The **folkloric museum**, was temporarily closed in mid-1997. Check with locals if it has reopened. The **phonographic museum** has a collection of venerable gramophones and memorabilia and sells tapes of old Greek songs. It's signposted from Ioannou Mela.

Lefkada's library, at Skiadaresis 1, has books about Lefkada in many languages. The ground-floor art gallery has changing exhibitions. It's open daily between 7 and 9 pm. There's a small **archaeological museum** at Pefaneromenis 21 which runs almost parallel to Ioannou Mela. It is open Tuesday to Sunday from 9 am to 1 pm.

The 14th-century Venetian **Fortress of Santa Mavra** is on the mainland. **Moni Faneromenis**, 3km west of town, was founded in 1634, destroyed by fire in 1886 and rebuilt. Inhabited by a few monks and nuns, its church can be visited. Views of the lagoon and town are worth the ascent. West of the lagoon, past windmills, is **Agios Ioannis beach** where, at sunset, clouds are neon-lit islands in the sky. The nearest beaches to town are at the northern side of the lagoon, about a 2km walk away.

Eastern coastal beaches are pebbled, while most on the west are white sand. Lefkada is famous for its embroideries. A small museum is at **Karya**, the island's core, west of **Nikiana**.

Places to Stay The nearest camp site to Lefkada town is *Kariotes Beach Camping* (☎ 71 103), on the east coast, 5km away. *Episkopos Camping* (☎ 23 043, 92 410 or 71 388), is 3km further south. See the Around the Island section for Lefkada's other camp sites. Lefkada also has farm-holiday accommodation in eight different locations.

The D-class *Hotel Byzantio* (☎ 21 315), Dorpfeld 4, has clean, well-kept doubles/ triples for 8000/10,000 dr with shared bathroom. The C-class *Hotel Santa Maura* (☎ 22 342), nearby, has pleasant singles/ doubles for 8500/12,100 dr.

The comfortable B-class *Hotel Niricos* (☎ 24 132/133), on the corner of the waterfront and Dorpfeld, has singles/ doubles for 9200/12,700 dr (half-board). Close by, the palatial, port-facing B-class *Hotel Lefkas* (☎ 23 916/917), Panagou 2, has rates of 15,500/20,000 dr with breakfast.

Places to Eat *Karaboulia's Restaurant* on the eastern waterfront offers traditional fare with flair. The intimate *Eitichia Taverna* has hearty, inexpensive food. The walls are graced by watercolours by Pagagos. Facing inland, turn left at the fountain on Dorpfeld to find the taverna. *Regantos Taverna* is another atmospheric little place with good food. A meal of stuffed eggplant, Greek salad and soft drink costs

1500 dr. To reach the taverna, turn right at the central square. An anchored boat on the eastern waterfront serves as a music bar on summer evenings.

Around the Island
Not long ago Nydri, 16km south of Lefkada Town, was a sleepy fishing village, but it fell hook, line and sinker to the lure of the tourist trade. Now it's a busy, commercialised but fun town from where one you cruise around the islets of **Madouri**, **Sparti**, **Skorpidi** and **Skorpios**, for 2500 dr or 6000 dr if a barbecue and unlimited drinks are included.

The family-owned Madouri islet, where the Greek poet Aristotelis Valoritis (1824-79) spent his last 10 years, is off-limits. But it's usually possible to land on Skorpios, where Ari, sister Artemis and children Alexander and Christina Onassis are buried in a cemetery visible from the sea. You can swim off a sandy beach if Christina's daughter Athina is not holidaying there.

If you would rather explore the islets independently, boats can be hired from *Trident Travel Agency* (☎ & fax 92 037) on the main street. Motorboats cost 10,000 dr a day and sailing dinghies are 8000 dr. The agency also has motorcycle and car hire and a room-finding service.

Shipping Magnates
The most famous of all shipping magnates is undoubtedly the Turkish-born Greek Aristotle Socrates Onassis, who was born in Smyrna (now İzmir) in 1906, the son of a tobacco merchant. At the age of 16 his family fled from Turkish hostility to Athens. The following year he arrived in Buenos Aires with a total of $60 and worked as a telephone operator by night while building up his own tobacco business during the day.

At the age of 25 he was already a millionaire and the following year he began what became the world's largest independent shipping line, investing in six Canadian freighters in the midst of a serious recession and putting them into service as the market recovered. Onassis was one of the pioneers of supertankers in the 1950s, and he was awarded the contract to operate the Greek national airline, Olympic Airways, which started in 1957. At 62 he married President Kennedy's widow, Jacqueline. He died in 1975. ∎

IONIAN ISLANDS

The owner, friendly Helen Morgan, is from Ireland.

Windsurfing, water-skiing, parasailing and sailing (bare-boating with licence or crewed yachts) out of Nydri can be organised by Nikos Thermes' Sport Boat Charter, Perigiali (☎ 92 431). Englishman Andy Fenna runs the island's only PADI School of Diving (☎ 92 286) from Nydri.

On the waterfront, *Nick the Greek* was one of Jackie Onassis' favourite eateries. Home-style food is served and a huge 3500-dr seafood platter can be shared.

The quiet village of **Vlyho** is 3km south of Nydri. Beyond here, a road leads to a peninsula where Wilhelm Dorpfeld is buried. There are Bronze Age ruins, just to the west of the Nydra-Vlyho road, which he excavated, leading him to believe Lefkada was Homer's Ithaca.

Desimi Beach Camping (☎ 95 223) is south of the peninsula. Further south and then west is **Vasiliki**. Detour to *Poros Beach Camping & Bungalows* (☎ 95 452) by turning left 5km south of Vlyho, near the village of **Poros**. Its pebbled beach is on **Rouda bay**.

Vasiliki is a pretty fishing village with both sand and pebbled beaches. It's purported to be *the* best windsurfing location in Europe.

You can rent surf boards from *Club Vas* (☎ 31 588) and instruction for all levels, including beginners, is available. It's crowded in summer so prepare to commute.

Caïques take visitors from Vasiliki to swim at the best sand beaches on the west coast, which include **Porto Katsiki**, **Egremini**, and **Kathisma**. All are signposted on the west coast off the road leading to the island's south-west promontory. A boat will also take you to the unspoiled **Agiofylli beach**. A Sanctuary to Apollo once stood at **Cape Lefkatas**.

From this high-cliffed cape, Sappho supposedly leapt, distraught over her unrequited love for Phaon. This seems to have set a precedent for further suicides throughout the ages; however, most people now come here to see dramatic sunsets.

MEGANISI
• pop 1250 • postcode 310 83 • area code ☎ 0645

Meganisi has the largest population of Lefkada's three inhabited satellite islets, but like many small Greek islands it has suffered population depletion.

It's a tranquil islet with a lovely, verdant landscape and deep bays of turquoise water, fringed by pebbled beaches. It's visited primarily by yachties and is untouched by package tourist operators. It has three settlements; the capital of Spartohori, the port of Vathy and the village of Katomeri.

Getting There & Away
There's a ferry at least once a day from Porto Spillia and Vathy to Kefallonia (Fiskardo), Ithaki (Frikes) and Lefkada (Nydri).

Getting Around
A minibus meets boats at both ports and takes passengers to Spartohori and Katomeri.

Spartohori
Spartohori, with narrow, winding lanes and pretty flower-bedecked houses, perches on a plateau above Porto Spillia.

Boats dock at Porto Spillia. No one lives here but there are several tavernas. A 1km road ascends steeply to Spartohori or you can walk there up steps. To reach Spartohori's main street and central square turn right at Tropicana Pizzeria. The island's only post office is at Vathy.

One of the island's best beaches is Agios Giannis, a long stretch of small pebbles, 3km south-west of Spartohori.

Other good beaches are on the island's tapering southern tail. In summer, the owner of Taverna Lakis (see Places to Eat) takes visitors there in his boat.

Places to Stay There are no official camp sites but wild camping is tolerated.

The owner of Chicken Billy's Psistaria (☎ 51 442) plans to open some low-priced domatia in 1998. Beyond the central square, just before the main street curves left, turn right, and Chicken Billy's is on the right.

Kostas rooms (☎ 51 372) are clean and well-kept with shared bathroom and communal kitchen. Doubles/triples are 6000/8000 dr. Take the street signposted to Agios Giannos and the rooms are on the right.

The immaculate *Studios For Rent Argiri* (☎ 51 502; fax 24 911) has rates of 10,000/12,000 dr for double/triple studios. Make enquiries at Oasi Bar, opposite Chicken Billy's.

Places to Eat *Tropicana Pizzeria* has pizzas for 1000 dr and stunning views of Skorpios – old Ari certainly knew where to buy an island.

Taverna Lakis offers tasty Greek fare and features Greek evenings. When things really get going, Mamma Lakis, who is no spring chicken, dances with a table on her head. In its hey-day, *Chicken Billy's* was visited by Christina Onassis – her photograph is on the wall to prove it. It serves delectably tender, low-priced chicken.

Around Meganisi
Vathy is the island's second port. The post office is on the waterfront near the quay. Further round there's a children's playground. Beyond here, the road climbs to Katomeri, 700m away.

There are no EOT-approved domatia in Vathy or Katomeri, but locals let rooms unofficially – ask around. *Risko Gelateria*, next to the post office, has a large menu which includes delicious cakes, made by friendly English-speaking Kiki.

There are several beaches near **Katomeri**. At Porto Elia beach, *Porto Elia Rooms* (☎ 51 341), owned by English-speaking Fatos Katopodis, are lovely studios costing 12,000 dr.

The well-signposted *Hotel Meganisi* (☎ 51 240/639) has spotless, modern singles/doubles for 8000/13,000 dr with private bathroom. Its restaurant serves tasty traditional dishes.

Restaurant Niagas, at Porto Athina beach, serves well-prepared, freshly caught fish.

KALAMOS
• *pop 400* • *postcode 311 00* • *area code* ☎ *0646*
Beautiful, mountainous and well-wooded, Kalamos is the second largest of Lefkada's satellite islets. It has two settlements, the port of Kalamos, on the south-east coast, where most of the inhabitants live, and the north-coast village of Episkopi, 8km away. Most of the houses in Episkopi are derelict and only 20 inhabitants remain. Kefali, 8km south-west of Kalamos, was abandoned after the 1953 earthquake, but its church is well-kept.

Until the 1950s Kalamos had a much larger population. During the War of Independence many of the Greeks who escaped the siege of Messolongi came to live on the island. In WWII it sheltered a fleet of allied ships which sailed during the night to Albania. Since the 1950s many of its inhabitants have moved to Athens or emigrated to America or Australia. The islanders who remain are mostly elderly. They are a dignified and proud people, many of them have returned to enjoy a peaceful retirement after living abroad for many years. These factors should be foremost in the minds of anyone visiting the island.

A few adventurous yachties sail into Kalamos port, but it is extremely unusual for any other type of tourist to turn up.

Kalamos village is built on a steep hillside. Its narrow lanes wind between well-kept little houses with pretty gardens. There's a post office in the village and a cardphone on the waterfront.

The beautiful long, pebbled **Agra Pedia beach** is a short walk away; locals will direct you.

There is only one place to stay, *Dionisis Lezentinos Rooms* (☎ 91 238/279), just back from the waterfront in Kalamos. Basic, but clean doubles/triples are 5000/6000 dr. A reservation is essential in July and August. There are several restaurants on the waterfront. *Restaurant O Zefirros* is owned by a friendly couple. The food they serve is delicious and reasonably priced.

Infrequent ferries serve Kalamos from Lefkada. A caïque leaves Mytikas on the

IONIAN ISLANDS

mainland every morning around 11 am for Kalamos.

Kefallonia & Ithaki
Κεφαλλονιά & Ιθάκη

KEFALLONIA
• *pop 32,500* • area code ☎ *0671*

Kefallonia, the largest of the Ionian islands, has rugged, towering mountains. The highest, Mt Enos, is the Mediterranean's only mountain with a unique fir forest species, *Abies kefallia*. While not as tropical as Corfu, Kefallonia has many species of wild flowers, including orchids and, when you approach it by sea on a windy summer's day, the scents of thyme, oregano, bay leaves and flowers will reach you before you land. The island receives package tourists, but not on the same scale as Corfu and Zakynthos. It is also a nesting ground for loggerhead turtles, which lay their eggs on southern beaches in June. Turtle numbers ashore have remained stable, unlike on Zakynthos. A Marine Turtle Project monitors the turtles. If

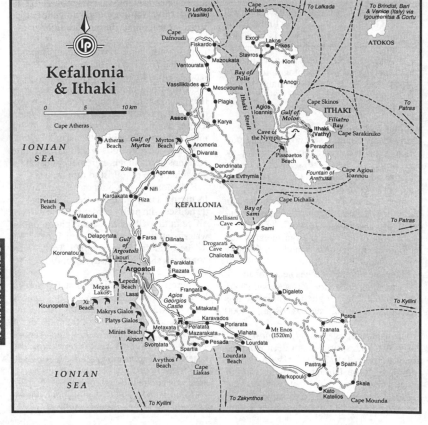

The Mediterranean Monk Seal

The Mediterranean monk seal is the rarest of all the seal species and one of the six most endangered mammals in the world. It belongs to the same genus as the Hawaiian and Caribbean monk seals. The latter is now believed to be extinct, since none has been sighted since the 1950s.

Monk seals (*Monachus monachus*) have been in existence for around 15 million years, and in ancient times were so abundant that Homer wrote of herds of them lying on beaches. There is also mention of them in the works of Plutarch, Pliny and Aristotle. It is estimated that in the 15th century around 5000 of the seals lived around the coasts of Spain, France, Portugal, Italy, Albania, Egypt, Israel, Turkey, Algeria and the Lebanon. Numbers have declined drastically in the last 100 years and the present population is between 400 and 500 individuals, about half of which live in Greece. There are small numbers in Madeira and Italy, but the second-largest colony lives in the Atlantic, off the coast of north-west Africa, entirely cut off from the rest.

In the past the seals were hunted for their skin and oil, and were killed by fishers because they ate the fish caught in nets. Nowadays they are threatened by marine pollution, oil spills and the numerous pesticides that end up in the sea. However, the greatest threat comes from disturbance by humans. Before the days of mass tourism the seals would haul themselves onto gently sloping sandy beaches to give birth, where they and their young were safe from rough waves. Then, as remote beaches became exploited by the tourist industry, the seals abandoned them and resorted to quiet coastal caves fronted by a patch of sand. However, these caves are now also becoming tourist attractions. Unfortunately, the births take place between May and November which coincides with the tourist season. A seal usually only has one pup at a time. The pup remains on land until it is weaned six to eight weeks later. If a female is frightened by the presence of tourists she may miscarry or abandon her helpless pup.

Tourism has driven the monk seal from Sardinia, Sicily and Corsica. To prevent the same happening in Greece it is imperative that tourists do not visit remote sea caves – the last safe refuge of the seal. If the necessary measures are not taken the species could become extinct within 25 years. If you are lucky enough to see a monk seal, keep a distance from it and keep quiet, to make your presence felt as little as possible.

The Hellenic Society for the Study & Protection of the Monk Seal (☎ 01-364 4164), Solomnou 35, Athens 10682, has a seal-rescue centre on Alonnisos, and the WWF funds a seal-watch led by Dimitris Panos (☎ 0671-31 114) at Fiscardo, Kefallonia. ∎

you would like more details, write to Marine Turtle Project, Care for the Wild, 1 Ashfolds, Horsham Rd, Rusper, West Sussex RH12 4QX, UK. Monk seals may also be seen on the north-west coasts of Kefallonia and Ithaki.

Kefallonia's capital is Argostoli but the main port is Sami. As the island is so big and mountainous, travelling between towns is time consuming.

In summer there are art exhibitions in major towns. In August and September an international choral festival is held in Argostoli and Lixouri.

Getting There & Away

Air There is at least one flight a day from Kefallonia to Athens (16,900 dr). The Olympic Airways office (☎ 28 808/881) in Argostoli is at Rokou Vergoti 1.

Ferry Kefallonia has seven ports (the telephone numbers of the port police are in brackets): Sami (☎ 0674-22 031), Argostoli (☎ 0671-22 224), Poros (☎ 0674-72 460), Lixouri (☎ 0671-91 205), Pesada, Fiskardo (0674-41 400) and Agia Evthymia (0674-61 207).

Domestic From Fiskardo, at least two ferries a day leave for Vasiliki (800 dr) on Lefkada. At least one a day goes from Sami to Patras (2½ hours, 3100 dr). From Poros (90 minutes), and Argostoli (2¾ hours, 2700 dr), at least two ferries ply daily to Kyllini in the Peloponnese. From Agia Evthymia, at least one ferry goes daily to Vathy on Ithaki and Astakos on the mainland. From Pesada, near Spartia, there is a high-season service to Skinari on Zakynthos. Daily ferries go from Fiskardo to Ithaki (Frikes) and Lefkada (Nydri) via Meganisi. In summer, small boats leave Sami at 6.30 am to go to Fiskardo via Pissoaetos on Ithaki. From Fiskardo they continue to Vasiliki on Lefkada to return to Kefallonia later in the day. Frequent ferries take 30 minutes to reach Lixouri from Argostoli. The 290-dr tickets are sold on board. In the high season, daily ferries connect Fiskardo with Sami.

International A daily ferry leaves Sami for Italy's Brindisi, via Igoumenitsa and Corfu. In high season two or three ferries a week leave Sami for Bari and Venice, via Igoumenitsa and Corfu.

Getting Around

The Airport The airport is 9km south of Argostoli. There is no airport bus. A taxi costs 2000 dr.

Bus From Argostoli, frequent buses go to Platys Gialos and Sami, three daily to Poros (750 dr), via Peratata, Vlahata and Markopoulo, two a day to Skala (650 dr) and two a day to Fiskardo (850 dr). But in the off season, only one return service daily connects Fiskardo with Argostoli. Daily return buses leave Athens' A terminal for Argostoli (eight hours via ferry to Poros, 7150 dr).

Car & Motorcycle Cars can be hired from Ainos Tours (☎ 22 333), Georgiou Vergoti 14 and motorcycles from Sunbird Motor Rent (☎ 23 723), in Argostoli on the waterfront. Vehicle hire is recommended off season because of the infrequency of buses.

Argostoli Αργοστόλι
• pop 7300 • postcode 281 00 • area code ☎ 0671

Argostoli, unlike Zakynthos town, was not restored to its former Venetian splendour after the 1953 earthquake. It's a modern, lively port set on a peninsula. Its harbour is divided from Koutavos lagoon by a British-built causeway connecting it with the rest of Kefallonia. There is a colourful, fresh-produce market on the waterfront on Saturday morning. The town's closest sandy beaches are **Makrys Gialos** and **Platys Gialos**, 5km south. The island's most expensive accommodation is here, although domatia can be found.

Orientation & Information The bus station (☎ 22 276) is on the waterfront near the causeway. The post office is on Diad Konstantinou and the OTE is on Georgiou Vergoti. Plateia Valianou is the huge palm-treed central square up from the waterfront off 21 Maiou. The National Bank of Greece is one block back from the southern end of the waterfront. The National Mortgage Bank on the waterfront has a 24-hour cash exchange machine. The ferry quay is at the waterfront's northern end. The EOT (☎ 22 248) is on the waterfront, south of the quay.

Things to See The **archaeological museum** (☎ 28 300), on Rokou Vergoti, has a small collection of island relics including Mycenaean finds from tombs. Opening times are Tuesday to Sunday from 8.30 am to 3 pm. Admission is 500 dr.

The **historical & cultural museum** (☎ 28 835), further up Rokou Vergoti, has a collection of traditional costumes, furniture and tools, items which belonged to British occupiers, and photographs of pre-earthquake Argostoli. The museum is open Monday to Saturday from 9am to 2 pm. Admission is 500 dr.

Argostoli's new **municipal theatre**, on Georgiou Vergoti, was inaugurated by the late Melina Merkouri. There's a ground floor art gallery.

Organised Tours The KTEL organises

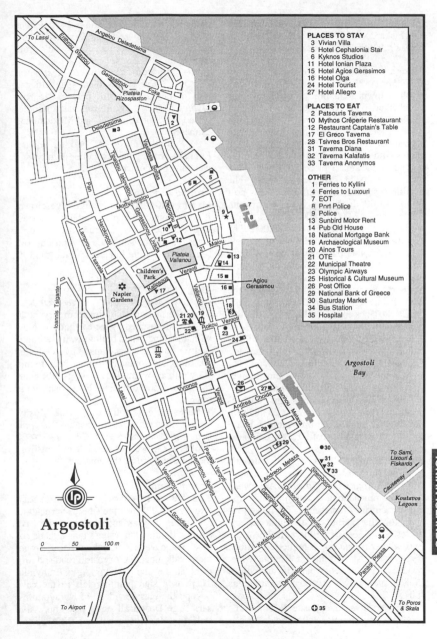

PLACES TO STAY
3 Vivian Villa
5 Hotel Cephalonia Star
6 Kyknos Studios
11 Hotel Ionian Plaza
15 Hotel Agios Gerasimos
16 Hotel Olga
24 Hotel Tourist
27 Hotel Allegro

PLACES TO EAT
2 Patsouris Taverna
10 Mythos Crêperie Restaurant
12 Restaurant Captain's Table
17 El Greco Taverna
28 Tsivres Bros Restaurant
31 Taverna Diana
32 Taverna Kalafatis
33 Taverna Anonymos

OTHER
1 Ferries to Kyllini
4 Ferries to Luxouri
7 EOT
8 Port Police
9 Police
13 Sunbird Motor Rent
14 Pub Old House
18 National Mortgage Bank
19 Archaeological Museum
20 Ainos Tours
21 OTE
22 Municipal Theatre
23 Olympic Airways
25 Historical & Cultural Museum
26 Post Office
29 National Bank of Greece
30 Saturday Market
34 Bus Station
35 Hospital

Argostoli

0   50   100 m

IONIAN ISLANDS

tours to the Drogarati cave, Melisani lake and Fiskardo for 4500 dr, and to Ithaki for 6500 dr. Inquire at the bus station.

Places to Stay The pleasant *Argostoli Camping* (☎ 23 487) is on the coast, 2km north of town. Relaxing farm holidays can be taken at 16 village locations.

The D-class *Hotel Allegro* (☎ 22 268 or 28 684), Andrea Choida 2, has doubles with shared bathroom for 8000 dr and doubles/triples with bathroom for 10,600/17,000 dr.

One of the nicest places is *Vivian Villa* (☎ 23 396; fax 28 670), Deladetsima 9. The beautiful, spotless double/triple rooms cost 9000/11,000 dr with private bathroom. Studios cost 12,000/14,800 dr and a large, well-equipped apartment costs 20,000. The friendly owners spent many years in New Zealand. Another pleasant option is *Kyknos Studios* (☎ 23 398), M Geroulanou 4, where doubles are 12,000 dr.

There's a string of C-class hotels along the waterfront. The *Hotel Cephalonia Star* (☎ 23 180), has comfortable air-con singles/doubles for 9000/16,500 dr. At the *Hotel Tourist* (☎ 22 510) rates are 10,000/ 17,000 dr and at the *Hotel Olga* (☎ 24 981) they are 12,000/16,500 dr. The *Hotel Agios Gerasimos* (☎ 28 697), Agiou Gerasimou 6, has cosy rooms for 9500/11,000 dr.

Argostoli's best hotel is the marble-decorated *Hotel Ionian Plaza* (☎ 25 581), on the central square. Comfortable air-con suites with breakfast cost 10,500/16,500 dr.

Places to Eat & Drink The waterfront's neighbouring restaurants *Taverna Diana*, *Taverna Kalafatis* and *Taverna Anonymos* are all commendable. Kefallonia has a distinctive cuisine, represented by meat pies and skordalia (garlic sauce) which accompanies fish. Greeks find these dishes at the *Patsouras Taverna* opposite the ferry quay. Ask for the island's famed Robola wine, which is expensive but wonderful and comes from grapes grown in stony, mountainous soil.

El Greco Taverna, opposite the children's park, is also popular with locals. Well-

prepared cod with skordalia is 1450 dr. The old-fashioned *Tsivres Bros Restaurant*, just off the waterfront, serves filling goat's broth for 900 dr.

Off the central square, *Restaurant Captain's Table* serves pies, spaghetti and fish dishes at medium prices. Nearby, *Mythos Crêperie Restaurant* has a middle-priced selection of crêpes and Mexican and Chinese dishes.

At *Pub Old House*, off the main square, English-speaking expats gather nightly, and welcome newcomers.

Around Argostoli

Lixouri is Kefallonia's second-largest town. It's an unremarkable place but has ecclesiastical exhibits in its museum in a restored mansion. To the south are several unspoilt beaches, including Lepeda and red-sand Xi beach.

Sami Σάμη
• *pop 1000* • *postcode 280 82* • *area code ☎ 0674*
Sami, the main port, 25km from Argostoli, was also devastated by the earthquake. Now with undistinguished buildings, its setting is pretty, nestled in a bay, flanked by steep hills. Classical and Roman ruins have been found. It's worth an overnight stay to visit the near-by caves. A post office, OTE and bank are in town.

Buses for Argostoli meet ferries. Mostly, domatia owners meet the boats. The well-kept *Karavomilos Beach Camping* (☎ 22 480) is 800m west of Sami. Turn left from the quay and follow the coast.

Around Sami

The **Mellisani cave** is a subterranean seawater lake. When the sun is overhead its rays shine through an opening in the cave ceiling, lighting the water's many shades of blue. The cave is 2.5km from Sami. To get there walk along the Argostoli road and turn right at the signpost for Agia Evthymia. There is a sign pointing left to the cave beyond the seaside village of Karavomilos. The large **Drogarati cave** has impressive stalactites. It's signposted from the Argostoli road, 4km from Sami. Both caves are open all day and charge 700 dr.

Agia Evthymia, 10km north of Sami, is a picturesque fishing village with a pebbled beach. A daily ferry leaves from here to Ithaki and Astakos.

Fiskardo Φισκάρδο
• *pop 300* • *postcode 280 84* • *area code* ☎ *0674*

Fiskardo, 50km north of Argostoli, was the only village not devastated by the 1953 earthquake. Framed by cypress-mantled hills, with fine Venetian buildings, it's a delightful place. A Roman cemetery and Mycenaean pottery have been found here. It's a popular place, especially with yachties, but it's pleasant outside high season.

The bus will drop you off on the road which by-passes Fiskardo. Walk across the car park, descend the steps to the left of the church and continue ahead to Fiskardo's central square and waterfront.

You can get to Fiskardo by ferry from Lefkada and Ithaki or by bus from Argostoli.

Places to Stay & Eat You're unlikely to find accommodation in high season. At others times it's OK, but prices are high.

At *Regina's Rooms* (no telephone) doubles/triples are 9000/11,000 dr with shared bathroom, and new studios are 12,000/15,000 dr. *John Paligisianos Rooms* (☎ 41 304), opposite, has rates of 7000/8500 for rooms with shared bathroom. To get to these from the bus stop, cross the car park, turn left at the church, turn left again, and look for the signs.

The rooms at *Tselenti Domatia* (☎ 41 204), just back from and west of the central square, are tastefully furnished, but are a pricey 15,000/18,000 dr. The *Philoxenia Traditional Settlement* (☎ 41 410; fax 41 319) occupies a lovely 19th-century house near the square. Room rates are 18,000/19,000 dr. Further around the waterfront, *Nefili Studios*, has immaculate self-contained units and great sea views. Rates are 25,000 dr.

The *Captain's Cabin Taverna* and *Taverna Nicolas* are both commendable and reasonably priced.

Around Fiskardo
Assos village is a gem of white-washed and pastel houses, straddling the isthmus of a peninsula on which stands a Venetian fortress. Assos was damaged in the 1953 earthquake but sensitively restored with the help of a donation from the city of Paris. There's an outstanding white sandy beach at **Myrtos**, 3km south of Assos. If you explore by boat, you'll find nearby hidden coves between tall limestone cliffs.

Southern Kefallonia
Kastro, above the village of Peratata, 9km south-east of Argostoli, was the island's capital in the Middle Ages. Ruined houses stand beneath the 13th-century castle of Agios Georgios, which affords magnificent views.

Peratata has domatia as has **Vlahata**, a pleasant village east along the road which branches to **Lourdata beach** where you can go horse-riding. On a scenic 2½ hour circular walk from Lourdata, you pass thickets, orchards and olive groves with flowers and birds, and return along the coast. A free Lourdata trail walk guide is available from the EOT in Argostoli.

At **Metaxata**, palms appear incongruous against white winter slopes of Mt Enos. No wonder Byron found inspiration. Near it, the 13th-century **Moni Agiou Andreou** has restored frescoes from the 14th to 16th century. Nearby are some Mycenaean tombs, discovered in 1993. There are more tombs at **Mazarakata**.

At **Markopoulo** an extraordinary event creeps up on 15 August (the Feast of the Assumption). The village church becomes infested with harmless snakes with crosses on their heads. They are said to bring good luck.

Poros is overdeveloped but has a nice pebbled beach. **Skala**, on the southern tip, is a preferable resort with a large, fine gravel beach. There are domatia and hotels.

ITHAKI
• *pop 3100* • *postcode 283 00* • *area code* ☎ *0674*

Ithaki (ancient Ithaca) was Odysseus' long-lost home, the island where the stoical Penelope sat patiently, weaving a shroud for her father-in-law. She told her suitors, who believed Odysseus was dead, that she would choose one of them once she had completed the shroud. Cunningly, she unravelled it every night in order to keep her suitors at bay, as she awaited Odysseus' return. Less well known is that Ithaki, lying amidst the tourist ghettos of the Ionian islands, remains relatively unspoilt.

Ithaki is separated from Kefallonia by a strait, only two to 4km wide. The island has a harsh precipitous east coast and a soft green west coast. The interior is mountainous and rocky with pockets of pine forest, stands of cypresses, olive groves and vineyards.

Getting There & Away

From Ithaki there are daily ferries to Patras, to Vasiliki on Lefkada via Fiskardo on Kefallonia, and to Sami and Agia Evthymia on Kefallonia. In high season, a daily ferry sails from Frikes (Ithaki) to Fiskardo, Meganisi and Nydri. The telephone number of Ithaki's port police is ☎ 32 909.

Getting Around

The island's one bus runs two or three times a day to Kioni (via Stavros and Frikes) from Vathy.

Ithaki Town Ιθύκη Χορα

• pop 1800 • postcode 283 00 • area code ☎ 0674

Ithaki town (Vathy Βαθυ) is small with a few twisting streets, a central square, nice cafés and restaurants and a few tourist shops, grocers and hardware stores. Old mansions rise up from the seafront.

Orientation & Information The ferry quay is on the west side of the bay. To reach the central square of Plateia Efstathiou Drakouli, turn left and follow the waterfront. The main thoroughfare, Kallinikou, is parallel to, and one block inland from, the waterfront.

Ithaki has no tourist office. The tourist police (☎ 32 205) are on Evmeou, which runs south from the middle of the waterfront. The National Bank of Greece is just southwest of the central square. The post office is on the central square and the OTE is further around the waterfront.

Things to See The town's **archaeological museum** is on Kallinikou. It is open Tuesday to Sunday from 8.30 am to 3 pm. Entrance is free. The **nautical and folklore museum** is housed in an old generating station. Ithaki was the first place in Greece to have electricity, thanks to the generosity of George Drakoulis, a wealthy Ithakan shipowner. The museum, behind the Agricultural Bank, is open Monday to Friday from 9.30 am to 1.30 pm and 6 to 9 pm.

A summer music & theatre festival is held in Ithaki town.

Places to Stay *Andriana Kouloupi Domatia* (☎ 32 387), just south of the quay, has agreeable single/double rooms for 5000/6600 dr with shared bathroom, and doubles/triples with private bathroom for 8000/10,000 dr. At *Vasiliki Vlassopoulou Domatia* (32 119) pleasant doubles with bathroom cost 7000 dr. Turn left from the quay and right at the town hall, take the steps ahead, and you will see the domatia sign.

Just off the eastern waterfront, *Dimitrios Maroudes Rooms & Apartments* (☎ 32 751), signposted 180m beyond the OTE, has clean doubles/triples for 7000/10,000 dr and four-person apartments for 14,000 dr.

The *Hotel Odysseus* (☎ 32 381), on the western waterfront, has pleasant doubles for 9000 dr. The B-class *Hotel Mentor* (☎ 32 433/293), near the OTE, has a bar, restaurant and roof garden. The attractive rooms cost 11,000/13,000/16,000 dr.

Places to Eat *Taverna Trehantiri*, a long-established place west of the central square, serves quality traditional Greek dishes. The classy *Sirens Yacht Club Restaurant & Bar*, nearby, has old photos of Vathy on its walls.

The imaginative menu includes shrimps with lemon and mushroom sauce for 1700 dr. *Restaurant Kantoyni*, on the waterfront, excels in reasonably priced fish dishes.

Young locals meet at the stylish *Dracoulis Café* in a waterfront mansion, which was the home of George Drakoulis. Try the sweet, gooey ravani, the local speciality, at one of the waterfront's zaharoplasteia.

Around Ithaki

Ithaki has a few sites associated with Homer's *Odyssey*. Though none is impressive, you may enjoy (or endure) the scenic walks to them. The most renowned is the **Fountain of Arethusa**, where Odysseus' swineherd, Eumaeus, brought his pigs to drink and where Odysseus, on his return to Ithaca, went to meet him disguised as a beggar after receiving directions from the goddess Athena. Lesser mortals have to deal with inadequate signposting. The walk takes between 1½ to two hours, depending on your stamina.

Take Evmeou which leads south from town and becomes an uphill track. After about an hour, you'll see a sign pointing left to the fountain. It indicates a narrow downhill footpath, which almost disappears at one point and would probably be rejected by any self-respecting mountain goat. Eventually, you'll see a big rocky crag above a spring. This is the Koraka (raven's) crag (mentioned in the *Odyssey*). Take plenty of water as the spring shrinks in summer.

A shorter trek is to the **Cave of the Nymphs**, where Odysseus concealed the splendid gifts of gold, copper and fine fabrics that the Phaeacians had given him. Below the cave is the Bay of Dexia, thought to be ancient Phorkys where the Phaeacians disembarked and laid the sleeping Odysseus on the sand. The cave is signposted from the town. The location of Odysseus' palace has been much disputed and archaeologists have been unable to find conclusive evidence. Schliemann erroneously believed it was near Vathy whereas present-day archaeologists speculate it was on a hill near Stavros.

Anogi, 14km north of Vathy, was the old capital. Its church of Agia Panagia has beautiful frescos. Ask at the neighbouring *kafeneio* for the key.

At the village of **Stavros**, 17km north-west of Ithaki town, there's a small **archaeological museum**. It's open Tuesday to Sunday from 9.30 am to 2 pm. Admission is free.

Villa St Ilias (☎ 31 751), near the museum, has lovely rooms with private bathroom for 11,000 dr. From Stavros it's 1km to the **Bay of Polis**, which has a stony beach.

Frikes, 1.5km in the opposite direction, is a charming fishing village with wind-swept cliffs. *Kiki Travel Agency* (☎ 31 726; fax 31 387), owned by helpful Angelika Digaletou, has a range of services including moped hire. The *Kiki Domatia* has tastefully furnished, spotless doubles for 12,000 dr with private bathroom. *Raftopolos Rooms* (☎ 31 733), 1km away, in a quiet rural setting, has clean doubles/triples for 7000/8400 dr. Inquire about these at the Restaurant Ulysses.

The well-kept, C-class *Hotel Nostos* (☎ 31 644/716), in lovely verdant countryside, behind the village, has spacious, modern singles/doubles for 11,000/16,000 dr and friendly helpful owners.

Symposium Restaurant, owned by two friendly sisters, serves imaginative fare including local dishes from the their grandmother's recipes. Tuna *savoro* (tuna with raisins and garlic) costs 1450 dr. The Hotel Nostos Restaurant serves tasty Greek fare and delicious desserts.

Attractive **Kioni**, 4km south-east of Frikes, is a popular yacht anchorage. There are pebbled coves between these villages.

Kioni's cheapest accommodation is *Kostas Kallinikos Domatia* (☎ 31 580, high above the south side of the bay. Doubles with private bathroom cost 7000 dr At the immaculate *Maroudas Apartments* (☎ 31 691), opposite the doctor's surgery, double/triple studios are 11,000/16,000 dr. Nearby, the well-maintained, beautifully furnished *Dellaportes Apartments*, have double studios for 12,000 dr and four-person apartments for 18,000 dr.

Zakynthos Ζάκυνθος

• *pop 32,560* • *postcode 291 00* • *area code* ☎ *0695*
The island of Zakynthos (**Zak**eenthos) has
inspired many superlatives. The Venetians
called it Fior' di Levante (flower of the
orient). The poet Dionysios Solomos wrote
'Zakynthos could make one forget the
Elysian Fields'. Indeed, it is an island of
exceptional natural beauty and outstanding
beaches.

Unfortunately Zakymthos' coastline has
been the victim of the most unacceptable
manifestations of package tourism. Even
worse, tourism is endangering the loggerhead turtle *(Caretta caretta)* and the
Mediterranean monk seal (Monachus
monachus).

Getting There & Away
Air There is one daily flight from Zakynthos
to Athens (16,400 dr). The Olympic Airways

office (☎ 28 611) in Zakynthos town is at
Alexandrou Roma 16. You can call the airport on ☎ 28 322.

Bus There are up to five buses a day from
Zakynthos town to Patras (3½ hours, 2800 dr),
and there are also three to Athens (seven hours,
5850 dr).

Ferry Depending on the season, between
three and seven ferries a day operate from
Zakynthos town to Kyllini, in the Peloponn-
nese (1½ hours, 1470 dr).

From Skinari, one ferry a day goes to
Pesada on Kefallonia, in the high season
only. There is no bus from Pesada to
anywhere else on Kefallonia. Check with
the port police (☎ 42 417) for the times of
the high-season crossing from Zakynthos
town to Nydri, on Lefkada.

Getting Around
The Airport There is no shuttle service be-

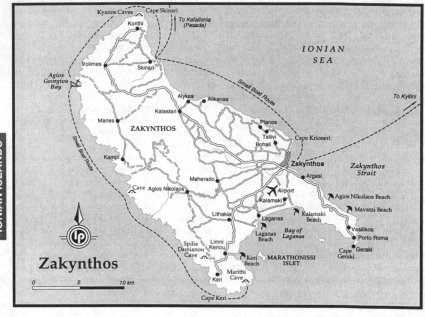

tween Zakynthos town and the airport, 6km to the south-west. A taxi costs 1200 dr.

Bus Frequent buses go from Zakynthos town to Alykes (260 dr), Tsilivi (210 dr), Argasi (210 dr) and Laganas. Bus services to other villages are poor, one or two a day. Check the current schedule at the bus station.

Car & Motorcycle A reliable motorcycle and car-hire outlet is Moto Stakis, at Demokratias 3, Zakynthos town.

ZAKYNTHOS TOWN
• *pop 10,250* • *postcode 291 00* • *area code ☎ 0695*

Zakynthos town is the capital and port of Zakynthos. The town was devastated by the 1953 earthquake but was reconstructed with its former layout preserved in wide arcaded streets, imposing squares and gracious neoclassical public buildings. Unless you saw the beautiful pre-earthquake town, you should be impressed.

Orientation & Information
The central Plateia Solomou is on the waterfront of Lombardou, opposite the ferry quay. Another large square, Plateia Agiou Markou, is nearby. The bus station is on Filitia, one block back from the waterfront and south of the quay. The main thoroughfare is Alexandrou Roma, parallel to the waterfront several blocks inland.

Zakynthos town has no tourist office. The helpful tourist police (☎ 27 367) are at Lombardou 62.

The National Bank of Greece is just west of Plateia Solomou. The post office is at Tertseti 27, one block west of Alexandrou Roma. The OTE is on Plateia Solomou. Zakynthos' hospital (☎ 22 514) is west of town.

Museums
The **Museum of Solomos** is dedicated to Dionysios Solomos (1798-1857), who was born on Zakynthos. His work, *Hymn to Liberty*, became the stirring Greek national anthem. Solomos is regarded as the father of modern Greek poetry, because he was the first Greek poet to use demotic Greek, rather than katharevousa. This museum houses a collection of memorabilia associated with his life, as well as displays pertaining to the poets Andreas Kalvos (1792-1869) and Ugo Foskolo (1778-1827), who were also born on Zakynthos. The museum is on Plateia Agiou Markou. Opening times are 9 am to 2 pm every day. Entrance is free.

The **neo-Byzantine museum**, on Plateia Solomou, houses an impressive collection of ecclesiastical art which was rescued from churches razed in the earthquake. Opening times are Tuesday to Sunday from 8.30 am to 3 pm.

Churches
At the southern end of town, the **Church of Agios Dionysios** is named after the island's patron saint and contains the saint's relics in a silver coffer. This is paraded around the streets during the festivals held in his honour on 24 August and 17 December. The church has notable frescoes.

The 16th-century **Church of Agios Nikolaos**, on Plateia Solomou, was built in Italian Renaissance style. Partially destroyed in the earthquake, it has been carefully reconstructed.

Organised Tours
The KTEL has a 'round Zakynthos island' tour which costs 2500 dr. Inquire at the bus station. Boat tours which visit Langadas and the blue cave should be avoided as they disturb the loggerhead turtles and monk seals.

Places to Stay – bottom end
The nearest camp site to Zakynthos town is *Zante Camping* (☎ 61 710) at Tsilivi, 5km away while 8km south-west of the port is *Camping Laganas* (☎ 22 292) at Agios Sostis.

The clean, nameless *rooms* (☎ 26 012), at Alexandrou Roma 40, are 5000/7000 dr. *Athina Rooms* (☎ 45 194), Tzoulati 29, are simply furnished singles/doubles for 5000/6000 dr with shared bedroom. The D-class *Hotel Ionian* (☎ 42 511), Alexandrou Roma 18, has rates of 6000/10,000 dr.

IONIAN ISLANDS

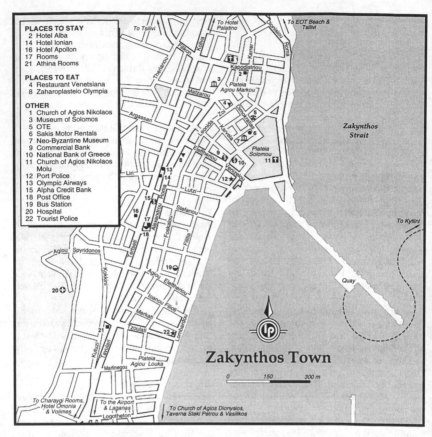

PLACES TO STAY
2 Hotel Alba
14 Hotel Ionian
16 Hotel Apollon
17 Rooms
21 Athina Rooms

PLACES TO EAT
4 Restaurant Venetsiana
8 Zaharoplasteio Olympia

OTHER
1 Church of Agios Nikolaos
3 Museum of Solomos
5 OTE
6 Sakis Motor Rentals
7 Neo-Byzantine Museum
9 Commercial Bank
10 National Bank of Greece
11 Church of Agios Nikolaos Molu
12 Port Police
13 Olympic Airways
15 Alpha Credit Bank
18 Post Office
19 Bus Station
20 Hospital
22 Tourist Police

Zakynthos Strait

Zakynthos Town

0   150   300 m

The pleasant *Charaygi Rooms* (☎ 23 629), Xanthopoulou 4, has doubles/triples with private bathroom for 8000/9000 dr. Opposite, the *Hotel Omonia* (☎ 22 113), has rates of 9000/11000 dr. Xanthopoulou is off the map. Walk south along Alexandrou Roma, at the fork take Agios Lazarou and Xanthopoulou is 250m along on the left.

Places to Stay – middle
The B-class *Hotel Alba* (☎ 26 641), 1 Ziva 38, is good value with rates of 9,000/10,00/15,000 dr. The B-class *Hotel Palatino* (☎ 45 400), on the corner of Kolokotroni and Koliva, has neoclassical style with comfortable modern rooms. Rates are 12,500/14,800/17,500 dr.

Places to Eat
Cafés featuring madelato, a local nougat sweet, are on Alexandrou Roma. The traditional *Zaharoplasteio Olympia* has sheep yoghurt and rice pudding. *Venetsiana Restaurant* is the best restaurant on the central square.

The untouristy *Taverna To Steki Petrou*, 150m south of Agios Dionysios, serves delicious, reasonably priced food.

AROUND ZAKYNTHOS

Loggerhead turtles come ashore to lay their eggs on the golden sand beaches of the huge Bay of Laganas, on Zakynthos' south coast. Laganas is a highly developed, taçky resort, **Kalamaki** is not much quieter and even **Geraki**, where the highest number of turtles lay their eggs, has not been spared water sports. The turtles also nest on nearby **Marathonissi** islet. You may decide to avoid these beaches for the turtles' sakes and to bypass the commercialism.

Vassilikos and **Porto Roma**, south of Zakynthos town, have crowded, sand beaches but are less developed than those of Laganas. The best beach north of Zakynthos town is at **Alykes**.

You can escape from the tourist hype by visiting inland farming villages. The village of **Maherado** has the impressive 14th-century church of Agia Mavra. **Agios Nikolaos** is an attractive village. The drive north from here to **Maries** is through splendid hilly country.

Waterfront dining is common in the Ionians

Kythira & Antikythira
Κύθηρα & Αντικύθηρα

KYTHIRA

• *pop 3100* • *postcode 801 00 & 802 00* • *area code* ☎ *0735*

The island of Kythira (**Ki**thi-ra), south-west of Neapoli, is about 30km long and 18km wide. Its north-east coast faces the sometimes turbulent meeting of the Ionian and Aegean seas. This anomalous island of 600 churches is geographically an extension of the Peloponnese, historically part of the Ionian archipelago and administered from Piraeus.

Kythirs survives economically mainly on remittances from many islanders who have emigrated to 'big Kythira', as these expats call Australia. Kythira supplied Australia with its first Greek settlers during the1850s gold-rush days when sailors jumped ship.

Mythology records the island was the birthplace of Aphrodite, who rose magnificent from the foam where Zeus had thrown Cronos' sex organ after castrating him. The goddess of love then re-emerged in Cyprus, so both islands haggle over her birthplace.

Until recently, Kythira was little visited by foreign tourists because of uncertain shipping schedules and local indifference to tourism. The military junta exiled political dissidents to the island, so no visitor information was available. The EOT has begun encouraging tourists to visit Kythira but it's still unspoiled. However, don't turn up in high season without a reservation, as accommodation, particularly in the low-budget range, is not abundant. Domatia owners, unusually, don't meet boats.

Kythira's plateau of rolling hills is above high cliffs. Once denuded of timber, Kythira is responding to a pine re-afforestation programme. The two ports are Agia Pelagia on the north-east coast and Kapsali in the south below the capital, Hora (also called Kythira). The island's main road cuts through the centre, joining the ports and several settlements between.

IONIAN ISLANDS

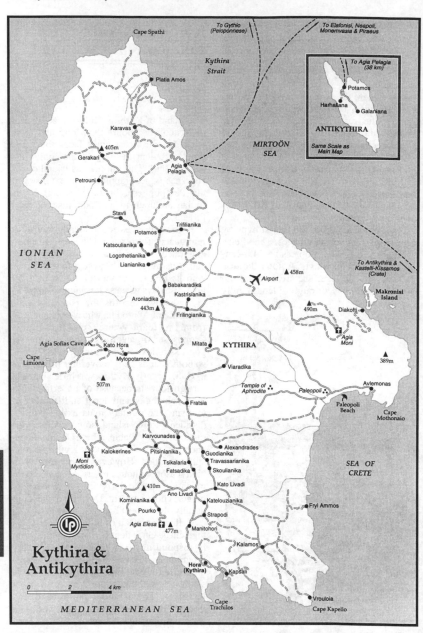

IONIAN ISLANDS

Kythira & Antikythira

0   2   4 km

Getting There & Away

Air There is at least one flight a day to Athens (50 minutes, 13,400 dr). The Olympic Airways office (☎ 33 362) is on the central square in Potamos. Book also at Conomos Travel, (☎ 33 490/890) in Agia Pelagia or Kythira Travel (☎ 31 390) in Hora. The airport is 10km east of Potamos.

Ferry The F/B *Maria* sails from Agia Pelagia to Neapoli (1600 dr) on Tuesday, Friday and Sunday and to Gythio on Monday, Wednesday and Sunday (1510 dr). Schedules and times are often subject to delays so check at Agia Pelagia's Conomos Travel, which sells ferry and hydrofoil tickets.

In summer, caïques connect Agia Pelagia with Elafonisi. Ask the port police (☎ 33 280) at Agia Pelagia on the waterfront.

Hydrofoil In summer, there are four hydrofoils a week from Agia Pelagia to Piraeus (five hours, 9000 dr) via Monemvasia, Spetses and Nydri.

Getting Around

Bus Kythira's bus service is deplorable. In summer, a bus leaves Agia Pelagia at 8 am, stopping at all the main-road villages and arrives at Kapsali at 9.30 am to begin the return trip at 11.30 am. In school terms, buses are more frequent but are monopolised by children. On Sunday, buses usually operate between Agia Pelagia and Potamos and Hora and Potamos. There is no airport bus. Not surprisingly, Kythira has many taxis. Hitching is fairly easy.

Car & Motorcycle Panayiotos, at Moto Rent (☎ 31 600) on Kapsali's waterfront, rents cars, jeeps, mopeds and motorcycles.

Agia Pelagia Αγία Πελαγία
• *pop 280 • postcode 802 00 • area code ☎ 0735*
Kythira's northern port of Agia Pelagia is a simple, friendly waterfront village strung to the right of the quay. At the top of the quay is a room-finding office (no telephone) operating in high season. Lia at Conomos

Travel, opposite the quay, happily assists newcomers.

Pebbled beaches are to either side of the quay. To the left of the quay, behind an outcrop, is a secluded, red-sand beach.

Places to Stay – bottom end One of Agios Pelagia's cheapest places was *Pari Gerakiti's Rooms* (☎ 33 462), but when we visited it was temporarily closed. Ask at the room-finding office if it has reopened. Opposite the quay above the Faros Taverna, *Alexandra Megalopoulou's Rooms* (☎ 33 282) are tidy, simply furnished and with bathroom for 7700 dr a double. The welcoming D-class *Hotel Kytherea*(☎ 33 321), owned by helpful Angelo from Australia, has very comfortable, spotless singles/doubles with bathroom for 7000/1200 dr. There are big discounts out of high season.

Places to Stay – middle The *Hotel Romantica* (☎ 33 834; fax 33 915) has charming self-contained apartments for four (23,000 dr) and double air-con studios for 17,000 dr. Turn right from the quay and look for the sign.

Places to Stay – top end The attractive *Filoxenia Apartments* (☎ 33 100) each have a bedroom, lounge and kitchen. Rates for doubles/quads are 15,000/20,000 dr. Two-bedroom units for four/six people are 22,000/26,000 dr. Turn left then right from the quay. Another splendid place is *Venardos Hotel* (☎ 34 205; fax 33 850) where singles/doubles/triples are 14,000/18,000/ 22,000 dr.

Kythira's sole A-class hotel, *Hotel Marou* (☎ 33 466/496), with the island's only tennis court, a bar, snack bar, laundry and a wheel-chair-accessible unit, is above the north-west end of the village. Doubles are 22,000 dr.

Places to Eat & Drink *Faros Taverna* serves good, economical Greek staples. To the far right, *Ouzeri Moustakias*, offers food ranging from snacks to seafood. *Sempreviva Patisserie* serves wickedly delicious Greek cakes and jugs of freshly brewed coffee.

High above the harbour, *Agia Pelagia Café* is another tempting patisserie.

Potamos Ποταμος

• *pop 680* • *postcode 802 00* • *area code* ☎ *0735*

Potamos, 10km from Agia Pelagia, is the island's commercial hub. On Sunday it magnetises almost every islander to market. The National Bank of Greece is on the central square. The post office and police are south of the central square, and the OTE is 150m north. The only hotel is *Hotel Porfyra* (☎ 33 329). Self-contained units surround an internal courtyard. Doubles/triples/quads are 11,500/14,000/16,000 dr.

Taverna Panaretos, on the central square, serves well-prepared international and Greek dishes.

Mylopotamos Μυλοπόταμος

• *postcode 802 00* • *area code* ☎ *0735*

Mylopotamos is an alluring, verdant village. Its central square is flanked by a much-photographed church and kafeneio. Stroll to the **Neraïda** (water nymph) waterfall. From the square, continue along the road and take the right fork. After 100m, a path on the right leads to the waterfall. It's magical, with luxuriant greenery and mature, shady trees.

To reach the abandoned **kastro** of Mylopotamos, take the left fork after the church and follow the sign for Kato Hora (lower village). The road leads to the centre of Kato Hora, from where a portal with the insignia of St Mark leads into the spooky kastro, with derelict houses and well-preserved little churches (locked).

The **Cave of Agia Sofias** was first explored by the famous speleologists Ioannis and Anna Patrochilos, who also discovered the Diros cave in the Peloponnese. In the 12th century, the cave was converted into a chapel and dedicated to Agia Sophia. Legend says she visited the cave with her daughters Pistis, Elpis and Agape (Faith, Hope and Charity). The cave is reached by a 2km road and a steep path from Mylopotamos. Irregular opening times are pinned on a signpost to the cave beyond Mylopotamos'

square. Admission is 500 dr and includes a guided tour.

Hora Χορα

• *pop 550* • *postcode 801 00* • *area code* ☎ *0735*

Hora (Kythira Κύθηρα), the pretty capital, with white, blue-shuttered houses, perches on a long slender ridge 2km uphill from Kapsali. The central square, planted with hibiscus, bougainvillea and palms, is Plateia Dimitriou Stati. The main street runs south of it. The post office is on the left, at its southern end. For the OTE, climb the steps by the side of Kythira Travel on the central square.

The National Bank of Greece is on the central square. The police station (☎ 31 206) is near the kastro.

Hora has no tourist office or tourist police but English-speaking Panayiotis offers information to tourists at his Moto Rent office (☎ 31 600) on Kapsali's waterfront.

Things to See Hora's **Venetian kastro** is at the southern end of town. If you walk to its southern extremity, passing the Church of Panagia, you will come to a sheer cliff. From here there is a stunning view of Kapsali and beyond.

The town's **museum** is north of the central square. It features gravestones of British soldiers and their infants who died on the island in the 19th century. (Hora was part of Britain's Ionian Protectorate from 1815 to 1864.) A large stone lion is exhibited and a sweet terracotta figurine of a woman and child. The museum is open Tuesday to Saturday from 8.45 am to 3 pm and Sunday from 8.30 am to 2.30 pm. Admission is free.

Places to Stay – bottom end Hora's cheapest accommodation is *Georgiou Pissi Rooms* (☎ 31 070/210), where doubles are 6000 dr with shared bathroom. Walk south along the main street and look for the sign on the left.

The *Castello Rooms* (☎ 31 869) are spacious, and have kitchens, bathrooms and terraces with breathtaking views. Rates are 9000 dr a double. There's a sign at the southern end of the main street. *Papadonicos Rooms* (☎ 31 129), a bit further south, has pleasant double studios for 9000 dr. *Belvedere Apartments* (☎ & fax 31 761), just beyond the turn-off for Kapsali, features attractive apartments for 12,000 dr. It has terrific views of Kapsali.

Places to Stay – middle The B-class *Hotel Margarita* (☎ 31 711/014; fax 31 325), on the main street, is a renovated 19th-century mansion. Rates are 15,200/19,300/26,000 dr for singles/doubles/triples with breakfast. Air-con rooms have TV and telephone.

Places to Eat On the main street, *Zorba's Taverna* offers tasty grilled food. Nearby, *Merrato Crêperie* is a hip place serving savoury and sweet crêpes. *Veggero Café* serves summer evening snacks on the central square in summer.

Kapsali Καψάλι
• *pop 70* • *postcode 801 00* • *area code* ☎ *0735*
Kapsali is an appealing village with two beaches separated by a headland. The larger beach is skirted by the road to Hora. A third beach is secluded. To get there from the Hora road, take the first left along a dirt track from where steps descend to the beach. An inland road and one parallel to the waterfront is also signposted to Hora. The two merge outside Kapsali. Canoes (500 dr per hour), pedal boats and surf boards (both 1000 dr per hour) and water-skis (3000 dr per hour) can be hired from Panayiotis at Moto Rent, on the waterfront. Kapsali's port police (☎ 31 222) are next door.

Places to Stay Kythira's one camp site, *Camping Kapsali* (☎ 31 580), is pine-shaded and open in summer only. The site is 400m from Kapsali's quay and signposted from the inland road to Hora.

Irene Megaloudi's Rooms (☎ 31 340), has clean doubles/triples with bathroom for 9000/11,000 dr. At *Poulmendis Rooms* (☎ 31 451), clean, pleasant rooms with bathroom cost 12,000/15,000 dr. For a splurge try *Riga's Apartments* (☎ 31 265/365; fax 31 365). The accommodation, in a cluster of white terraced buildings, ranges from beautifully furnished double studios for 20,000 dr to two-bedroomed maisonettes for 35,000 dr. All of these recommendations overlook the large beach

Places to Eat At the large beach, *Restaurant Vensianiko* serves a wide range of local dishes, pasta and crêpes, and the lively *Mezedoleon Hydragogion* specialises in fish and mezedes.

Around Kythira
If you have transport, a tour round the island is rewarding. The monasteries of Agia Moni and Agia Elesa, are mountain refuges with superb views. Moni Myrtidion is a beautiful monastery surrounded by trees. From Hora, drive north-east to the picturesque village of **Avlemonas** via **Paleopoli** with its wide, pebbled beach. Here, archaeologists spent years searching for temple evidence of Aphrodite's birthplace. *Skandela Taverna*, at Paleopoli, has new owners, the Greek-English Hill family. It promises to be quite a place, with an extensive menu and live music most evenings.

ANTIKYTHIRA
• *pop 70* • *postcode* • *area code* ☎ *0735*
The tiny island of Antikythira, 38km southeast of Kythira, is the most remote island in the Ionian group. It has only one settlement (Potamos), one doctor, one police officer, one teacher (with five pupils), one metered telephone and a monastery. It has no post office or bank. The only accommodation for tourists is 10 basic rooms in two purpose-built blocks, open in summer only. Potamos has a kafeneio and taverna.

The F/B *Theseus* calls at least weekly in the early hours on the way to Crete, returning the same day to Kythira, Gythio, Neapoli and Monemvasia. If the sea is choppy, the ferry does not stop, so this is not an island for tourists on a tight schedule. Check conditions in Piraeus if you intend to come direct or with Conomos Travel in Kythira's Agia Pelagia.

Evia & the Sporades
Εύβοια & οι Σποράδες

Evia, Greece's second-largest island, is so close to the mainland historically, physically and topographically that one tends not to regard it as an island at all. Athenians regard Evia as a convenient destination for a weekend break, so consequently it gets packed. Except for the resort of Eretria, however, it is not frequently visited by foreign tourists.

The Sporades lie to the north and east of Evia and to the east and south-east of the Pelion peninsula, to which they were joined in prehistoric times. With their dense vegetation and mountainous terrain, they seem like a continuation of this peninsula. There are 11 islands in the archipelago, four of which are inhabited: Skiathos, Skopelos, Alonnisos and Skyros. The first two have a highly developed tourist industry, whereas Alonnisos and Skyros, although by no means remote, are far less visited and retain more local character.

Getting There & Away

Air Skiathos airport receives charter flights from northern Europe and there are also domestic flights to Athens. Skyros airport has domestic flights to Athens and occasional charter flights from the Netherlands and Switzerland.

Bus From Athens' Terminal B bus station there are buses every half-hour to Halkida from 5.45 am to 9.45 pm (1½ hours, 1250 dr); six a day to Kymi from 6 am to 7 pm (3½ hours, 2750 dr); and three a day to Edipsos (for Loutra Edipsou; 3½ hours, 2600 dr). From the Mavromateon terminal in Athens, there are buses every 45 minutes to Rafina (for Karystos and Marmari; one hour, 500 dr).

Train There are hourly trains each day from Athens' Larisis station to Halkida. The jour-

HIGHLIGHTS

- The changing tides of the Evripous channel in Evia that baffled Aristotle
- Skiathos' golden beaches – reputedly the best in Greece
- The labyrinthine streets of picturesque Skopelos town
- Delightfully quirky Skyros – Greece's hidden island treasure
- The marine life of Alonnisos' northern satellite islands
- Nature walks on green and clean Skopelos
- Getting back to nature on unspoilt, ecotouristy Alonnisos

ney takes 1½ hours and costs 1100 dr. The Halkida train station is on the mainland side of the bridge. To get there, walk over the bridge, turn left and you will find Leoforos Venizelou, Halkida's main drag, off to the right.

Ferry There are six ferry crossings from the mainland to Evia. They are from north to south: eight a day from Glyfa to Agiokambos

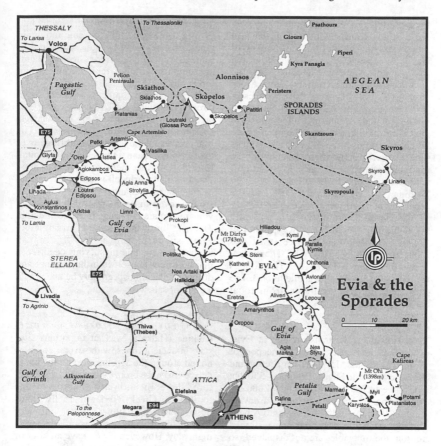

Evia & the Sporades

(30 minutes, 330 dr); 12 a day from Arkitsa to Loutra Edipsou (one hour, 650 dr); every half-hour from Oropou to Eretria (30 minutes, 240 dr); five a day from Agia Marina to Nea Styra (40 minutes, 540 dr); three a day from Rafina to Marmari (1¼ hours, 1230 dr); and two a day from Rafina to Karystos (one hour, 1630 dr).

Mainland ports serving Skiathos, Skopelos (Glossa and Skopelos town) and Alonnisos are Volos and Agios Konstantinos, in the Thessaly and Sterea Ellada regions, respectively. In summer, there are some services from Thessaloniki. Buses run hourly from Athens' Terminal B bus station to Agios Konstantinos (2½ hours, 2650 dr).

Note that Skopelos has two ports – Glossa and Skopelos town. All ferries stop at Skopelos town and almost all at Glossa. To complicate matters further, the port referred to on timetables as Glossa is not Glossa at all but Loutraki; Glossa is a village 3km uphill from the port.

Skyros, to the south-east of the other Sporades islands, is served in summer by at least two ferries daily from Kymi in Evia (two hours, 1900 dr) and one ferry a week from the Sporades islands (five hours, 4600 dr).

Hydrofoil There are hydrofoils every day from Agios Konstantinos and Volos (via Platanias on the Pelion peninsula) to Skiathos, Glossa (Skopelos), Skopelos town and Alonnisos. Seven times a week the hydrofoil from Volos continues from Alonnisos to Skyros. There are daily services in summer from Thessaloniki to Skiathos, Skopelos and Alonnisos, sometimes via ports in Halkidiki and the Pelion peninsula. There are also a number of hydrofoil services linking ports in northern Evia with the Sporades islands and Agios Konstantinos, and there is one hydrofoil a week from Stylida, east of Lamia, to Evia and the Sporades and a further service to Volos.

The summer hydrofoil timetable is usually available in late April. For your copy contact Ceres Hydrofoil Joint Service (☎ 01-428 0001; fax 01-428 3526), Akti Themistokleous 8, Piraeus GR-185 36. The Athens office (☎ 01-324 4600) is at Filellinon 3. The timetable is also available from local hydrofoil booking offices.

Bus Halkida is the transport hub of Evia. There are nine buses a day to the port of Kymi (2½ hours, 1500 dr) via Eretria and Kymi town; six to Steni (45 minutes, 550 dr); and three to Karystos (3½ hours, 2000 dr) via Eretria. There are four buses a day to Limni (2½ hours, 1400 dr). Buses to Athens run almost half-hourly. For some strange reason, the timetables are not displayed, so be prepared for communication problems unless you speak Greek.

Getting Around
Hydrofoil In summer there are daily hydrofoils from Halkida to Loutra Edipsou (one hour, 4310 dr) via Limni.

Evia Εύβοια

Evia (Evia) will probably never be a prime destination for foreign tourists, but if you're based in Athens with a few days to spare, and (preferably) your own transport, a foray into Evia is worthwhile for its scenic mountain roads, pristine inland villages, and a look at some resorts which cater for Greeks (including one for ailing Greeks), rather than foreign tourists.

A mountainous spine runs north-south through the island; the east coast consists of precipitous cliffs, whereas the gentler west coast has a string of beaches and resorts. The island is reached overland by a bridge over the Evripous channel to the island's capital, Halkida. At the mention of Evia, most Greeks will eagerly tell you that the current in this narrow channel changes direction around seven times a day, which it does, if you are prepared to hang around to watch it. The next bit of the story, that Aristotle became so perplexed at not finding an explanation for this mystifying occurrence that he threw himself into the channel and drowned, can almost certainly be taken with a grain of salt.

HALKIDA Χαλκίδα
• *pop 45,000* • *postcode 341 00* • *area code* ☎ *0221*
Halkida (Halkída) was an important city-state in ancient times, with several colonies dotted around the Mediterranean. The name derives from the bronze which was manufactured here in antiquity (halkos means 'bronze' in Greek). Today it's a lively industrial and agricultural town, but with nothing of sufficient note to warrant an overnight stay. However, if you have an hour or two to spare between buses, then have a look at the **archaeological museum**, Leoforos Venizelou 13, it's worth a mosey around. It houses finds from Evia's three ancient cities of Halkida, Eretria and Karystos, including a chunk from the pediment of the Temple of Dafniforos Apollo at Eretria. The museum is open Tuesday to Sunday from 8.30 am to 3 pm. Admission is 500 dr. The phone number of the Halkida tourist police is ☎ 83 333.

CENTRAL EVIA
Steni Στενή
• *pop 1300* • *postcode 340 03* • *area code* ☎ *0228*
From Halkida it's 31km to the lovely moun-

tain village of Steni, with gurgling springs and plane trees. The village has two hotels, both C class. The *Hotel Dirfys* (☎ 51 217) has singles/doubles for 4500/8000 dr. The *Hotel Steni* (☎ 51 221; fax 51 325) has singles/doubles for 7000/10,000 dr with private bathroom.

For a meal, look for the *Sakaflias* restaurant on the main square. Try *tiganopsomo*, a kind of pan-fried cheese pie, and their house-rosé. It shouldn't cost you more than 1500 dr.

Steni is the starting point for the climb up **Mt Dirfys** (1743m), Evia's highest mountain. The EOS-owned *Dirfys Refuge* (☎ 51 285), at 1120m, can be reached along a 9km dirt road, or after a two-hour walk along a forest footpath. From the refuge it's two hours to the summit. For further information contact the EOS (☎ 0221-25 230), Angeli Gyviou 22, Halkida.

A partially sealed road continues from Steni to **Hiliadou**, on the north coast, where there is a fine beach.

Kymi Κύμη
• *pop 3850* • *postcode 340 03* • *area code* ☎ *0222*
Kymi is a picturesque town built on a cliff 250m above the sea. The port of Kymi (called Paralia Kymis), 4km downhill, is the only natural harbour on the precipitous east coast, and the departure point for ferries to Skyros.

The **folklore museum**, on the road to Paralia Kymis, has an impressive collection of local costumes and memorabilia, including a display commemorating Kymi-born Dr George Papanikolaou, who found fame as the inventor of the Pap smear test. Opening times are 10 am to 1 pm and 5 to 7.30 pm daily.

Paralia Kymis has two hotels: the C-class *Hotel Beis* (☎ & fax 22 604) has singles/doubles for 8000/10,000 dr; and the C-class *Hotel Corali* (☎ 22 212; fax 23 353) has singles/doubles for 6600/9900 dr. This hotel is set back from the main road up a steep hill on the south side of Paralia Kymis. There are some rooms to be had in Kymi itself, on the left along the main Halkida road.

NORTHERN EVIA
From Halkida a road heads north to **Psahna**, the gateway to the highly scenic mountainous interior of northern Evia. The road climbs through pine forests to the beautiful agricultural village of **Prokopi**, 52km from Halkida. The inhabitants are descendants of refugees who came from Prokopion (present day Ürgüp) in Turkey in 1923, bringing with them the relics of St John the Russian. On 27 May (St John's festival), hordes of pilgrims come to worship his relics in the Church of Agios Ioannis Rosses.

At **Strofylia**, 14km beyond Prokopi, a road heads south-west to **Limni**, a pretty (but crowded) fishing village with whitewashed houses and a beach. With your own transport or a penchant for walking, you can visit the 16th-century **Convent of Galataki**, 8km south-east of Limni. Its katholikon (main church) has fine frescoes. Limni has a limited number of places to stay, with only two hotels and some domatia. There's one camp site, *Rovies Camping* (☎ 71 120), on the coast, 13km north-west of Limni.

The road continues to the sedate spa resort of **Loutra Edipsou** (119km from Halkida) whose therapeutic sulphur waters have been celebrated since antiquity. Many luminaries, including Aristotle, Plutarch, Strabo and Plinius sang the praises of these waters. The waters are reputed to cure many ills, mostly of a rheumatic, arthritic or gynaecological nature. Today the town has the most up-to-date hydrotherapy-physiotherapy centre in Greece. If you're interested, contact any EOT or the EOT Hydrotherapy-Physiotherapy Centre (☎ 23 500), Loutra Edipsou. Even if you don't rank among the infirm you may enjoy a visit to this resort with its attractive setting, a beach, many domatia and hotels.

SOUTHERN EVIA
Eretria Ερέτρια
• *pop 5000* • *340 08 postcode* • *area code 0211*☎
Heading east from Halkida, Eretria is the first major place of interest. Ancient Eretria was a major maritime power and also had an eminent school of philosophy. The city was

destroyed in 87 AD during the Mithridatic War, fought between Mithridates (king of Pontos) and the Roman commander Sulla. The modern town was founded in the 1820s by islanders from Psara fleeing the Turkish. It has metamorphosed from Evia's major archaeological site into a tacky resort patronised by British package tourists.

Things to See From the top of the **ancient acropolis**, at the northern end of town, there are splendid views over to the mainland. West of the acropolis are the remains of a palace, temple, and a theatre with a subterranean passage which was used by actors. Close by, the **Museum of Eretria** (☎ 62 206) contains well-displayed finds from ancient Eretria. Opening times are Tuesday to Sunday from 8.30 am to 3 pm. Admission is 500 dr. In the centre of town are the remains of the **Temple of Dafniforos Apollo** and a mosaic from an ancient bath.

Places to Stay Eretria has loads of hotels and domatia, and *Eva Camping* (☎ 61 081) is at Malakonda, 5km west along the coast. *Milos Camping* (☎ 60 360) is 1km west of Eretria town.

Karystos Κάρυστος
• *pop 4500* • *postcode 340 01* • *area code* ☎ *0224*

Continuing east from Eretria, the road branches at Lepoura: the left fork leads to Kymi, the right, to Karystos (Karystos). Set on the wide Karystian bay, below Mt Ohi (1398m), Karystos is the most attractive of southern Evia's resorts. The town was designed on a grid system by the Bavarian architect Bierbach, who was commissioned by King Otho. If you turn right from the quay you will come to the remains of a 14th-century Venetian castle, the **Bourtzi**, which has marble from a temple dedicated to Apollo incorporated into its walls. Beyond this there is a sandy beach. There is also a beach at the other end of the waterfront.

Places to Stay Look for domatia signs along the waterfront, or there are three easy-to-find hotels also on the waterfront. The D-class

Hotel Als (☎ 22 202) is opposite the ferry quay with singles/doubles for 5000/7000 dr. The ageing *Hotel Galaxy* (☎ 22 600; fax 22 463) is at the west end of Kriezotou, on the corner with Omirou. Their rates are 7200/10,300 for singles/doubles. The pleasant *Hotel Karystion* (☎ 22 391; fax 22 727) is at Kriezotou 2, just beyond the Bourtzi. It has singles/doubles for 8200/11,800 dr, including breakfast.

Around Karystos
The ruins of **Castello Rossa** (red castle), a 13th-century Frankish fortress, are a short walk from **Myli**, a delightful, well-watered village 4km inland from Karystos. The aqueduct behind the castle once carried water from the mountain springs and a tunnel led from this castle to the Bourtzi in Karystos. A little beyond Myli there is an **ancient quarry** scattered with fragments of the once prized Karystian marble.

With your own transport you can explore the sleepy villages nestling in the southern foothills of Mt Ohi. The rough road winds through citrus groves and pine trees high above the south coast. From **Platanistos**, a charming village named for its plane trees, a 5km dirt road (driveable) leads to the coastal village of **Potami** with its sand and pebble beach. The 'main road' continues to the east coast.

Skiathos Σκιάθος

• *pop 4100* • *postcode 370 02* • *area code* ☎ *0427*

The good news is that much of the pine-covered coast of Skiathos (Skiathos) is blessed with exquisite beaches of golden sand. The bad news is that the island is overrun with package tourists – at least in August – and is very expensive. Despite the large presence of sun-starved northern Europeans, and the ensuing tourist excess, Skiathos is still a pretty island and not surprisingly one of Greece's premier resorts.

The island has only one settlement, the

Skiathos

AEGEAN SEA

To Thessaloniki

Skopelos Strait

Cape Kastro

Lalaria Beach

Kastro

Skotini Spilia
Galazia Spilia

Cape Ag Sozon

Moni Agiou Haralambou

Cape Kefala

Moni Evangelistrias

Skiathos Strait

Skiathos

Kechrias Bay

Airport

Xanemos Camping

ASPRONISOS

Mikri Aselinos Beach

Megali Aselinos Beach

SKIATHOS

Skiathos

Skiathou Bay

Aselinos Camping

Moni Panagias Kounistras

Bourtzi

Cape Gournes
Mandraki Beach

Ftelias Bay

Mytikas Beach

Cape Plakes

Cape Pounta

To Skopelos, Alonnisos, Skyros & Kymi

Cape Ag Elenis

Lazos Camping

MARAGOS

ARGOS

Koukounaries Camping

Kolios

Nostos Beach

Krassa Beach (Banana Beach)

Koukounaries Beach
Koukounaries Strofilias Bay

Troulos

Platanias Beach

Kolios Beach

Cape Tourkovigia

Troulos Beach

Cape Tsimokokalo

Vromolimnos Beach

TSOUGRIA

To Volos & Agios Konstantinos

Cape Kalamaki

TSOUGRIAKI

0   1   2 km

port and capital of Skiathos town, on the south-east coast. The rest of the south coast is one long chain of holiday villas and hotels. The north coast is precipitous and less accessible. Most people come to the island for the beaches and nightlife – if you've come for anything else you may want to depart quickly.

Getting There & Away

Air As well as the numerous charter flights from northern Europe to Skiathos, during summer there are up to five flights a day to Athens (15,300 dr). The Olympic Airways

office (☎ 22 200) is in Skiathos town on the right side of Papadiamanti walking inland.

Ferry In summer, there are three to four ferries daily from Skiathos to Volos (three to four hours, 2300 dr); two to Agios Konstantinos (3½ hours, 3000 dr); four to six a day to Alonnisos (two hours, 1450 dr) via Glossa (Skopelos); and Skopelos town (1½ hours, 1300 dr). One ferry a week sails from Skiathos to Kymi (five hours, 4600 dr). There are also three boats a week from Skiathos to Thessaloniki (5½ to seven hours, 3500 dr) in July and August. There are many

SPORADES

agencies on the waterfront selling ferry tickets. The port police can be contacted on ☎ 22 017.

Hydrofoil In summer, there is a bewildering array of hydrofoils from Skiathos and around the Sporades in general. Among the main services, there are three or four hydrofoils daily from Skiathos to Volos (1¼ hours, 5515 dr), and eight or 10 to Alonnisos (one hour, 3340 dr) via Glossa (Skopelos) and Skopelos town (35 minutes, 2540 dr). There are also two or three daily hydrofoils to Agios Konstantinos (1½ hours, 6580 dr). Three to five times a week there is a hydrofoil to Skyros (2¼ hours, 8120 dr) and Kymi (three hours, 10,055 dr). Five or six hydrofoils a week go to Thessaloniki (3½ hours, 9,500 dr). In addition, there are also services to the Pelion peninsula, Halkidiki, various ports in northern Evia and to Stylida near Lamia. Hydrofoil tickets may be purchased from Skiathos Holidays (☎ 22 018; fax 22 771) in the middle of the new harbour waterfront.

Getting Around

Bus Crowded buses leave Skiathos town for Koukounaries beach (30 minutes, 300 dr) every half-hour between 7.30 am and 10.30 pm. The buses stop at all the access points to the beaches along the south coast. A couple of buses connect for passengers going to Megali Aselinos beach, on the north coast.

Car & Motorcycle Car-hire outlets include Autorent (☎ 21 797) and Eurocar (☎ 21 124), both of which are on the waterfront. There are heaps of motorcycle-hire outlets along the waterfront in Skiathos town.

Excursion Boat As well buses, excursion boats go to most of the south-coast beaches. Trips around the island cost 3500 dr and include a visit to Kastro, Lalaria beach, and the three caves of Halkini Spilia, Skotini Spilia and Galazia Spilia, which are only accessible by boat. Excursion boats leave from the old harbour.

SKIATHOS TOWN

Skiathos town, with its red-roofed, whitewashed houses is built on two low hills. It is picturesque enough, although it's not as pretty as Skopelos or Skyros towns. The islet of Bourtzi (reached by a causeway) between the two harbours is covered with pine forest. Inevitably, hotels, souvenir shops, travel agents and bars dominate the waterfront and main thoroughfares.

Orientation

The quay is in the middle of the waterfront, just north of Bourtzi islet. To the right (as you face inland) is the straight, new harbour; to the left, and with more character, is the curving old harbour used by local fishers and excursion boats. The main thoroughfare of Papadiamanti strikes inland from opposite the quay. The central square of Plateia Trion Ierarhon is just back from the middle of the old harbour and has a large church in the middle.

Information

The tourist police (☎ 23 172) is opposite the regular police about halfway along Papadiamanti, next to the high school. It operates from 8 am to 9 pm every day during the summer season.

The post office and OTE are on the right side of Papadiamanti, and the National Bank of Greece is on the left. The bus terminus is at the northern end of the new harbour. There are several ATMs and a couple of automatic exchange machines around town. Mare Nostrum Holidays (☎ 21 463) at Papadiamanti 21 represents American Express. They will exchange travellers cheques without deducting a commission.

Museum

Skiathos was the birthplace of the Greek short-story writer and poet, Alexandros Papadiamantis, as well as the novelist Alexandros Moraïtidis. Alexandros Papadiamantis' house is now a museum with a small collection documenting his life.

The museum's opening times are 9 am to 1 pm and 5 to 8 pm; it's closed on Monday.

It is just off the right side of Papadiamanti coming up from the harbour. Entry is 250 dr.

Organised Tours
Various local operators run excursion-boat trips around the island. See the Getting Around section for Skiathos island.

Places to Stay – bottom end
Skiathos has four camp sites: *Koukounaries Camping* (☎ 49 250), at the east end of the beach of the same name; *Lazos Camping* (☎ 49 206), at Kolios beach, 7km south-west of Skiathos town (take the Koukounaries beach bus from Skiathos town); *Aselinos Camping* (☎ 49 312), on the north coast, at Megali Aselinos beach; and *Xanemos Camping*, close to the airport. Of the four, Koukounaries Camping is the best. Xanemos Camping is too close to the airport for comfort.

Most accommodation is booked solid by package-tour operators from July to the end of August, when prices are often double those of low season. Outside these months you may be offered a room when you get off the ferry – if not, look for domatia signs up Papadiamanti and around Plateia Trion Ierarhon. If you're brave enough to arrive during the summer rush, then just about any travel agent will endeavour to fix you up with accommodation. Worth trying are Alkyon Travel (☎ 22 029), at the bottom of Papadiamanti; Meridian (☎ 21 309), Papadiamanti 8; or Mare Nostrum Holidays (☎ 21 463), Papadiamanti 21.

The E-class *Hotel Karafelas* (☎ 21 235) is one of the town's best-value hotels. The comfortable singles/doubles are 5000/6000 dr (low season), or 8000/11,000 dr (high season) with private bathroom. The hotel is at the far end of Papadiamanti, on the left. Also worth a try is the slightly more expensive E-class *Australia Hotel* (☎ 22 488), which has tidy singles/doubles for 6500/8700 dr (low season) and 12,500/15,100 dr (high season) with private bathroom. Walk up Papadiamanti to the post office, turn right and take the first left.

If you would like a pleasant and quiet domatio within walking distance of Skiathos town (1.5km), try *Villa Meroulas* (☎ 21 154). This place has comfortable rooms with large balconies and is set back from the Koukounaries road among olive groves. A double room here costs 9000 to 14,000 dr, depending on the season.

Places to Stay – middle
The C-class *Hotel Morfo* (☎ 21 737; fax 23 222) has nicely furnished doubles/triples for 9000/1000 dr (low season), or 12,000/14,000 dr (high season) with private bathroom. From the waterfront take M Ananiou (parallel, and to the right of, Papadiamanti), and you'll come to the hotel on the left.

For a very central location with a great waterfront view, try the C-class *Hotel Akti* (☎ 22 024). Airy singles/doubles go for 8000/10,000 dr in low season and 14,000/18,000 in high season. The roomy four-person penthouse apartment on the top floor goes for 20,000 and 30,000 dr accordingly. Book ahead if you can.

Places to Stay – top end
Most of the island's top-end hotels are on the coast to the west of Skiathos town. The A-class *Hotel Paradise* (☎ & fax 21 939), 3km west of town, is one of the newest and smallest of these hotels. It has tastefully furnished air-con rooms and a restaurant and bar. Doubles are 20,700 dr (low season).

The A-class Nostos Bungalows (☎ 22 420; fax 22 525) is a well-designed bungalow complex at Nostos beach, 5km west of town. The complex has bars, a restaurant, taverna, pool and tennis court. Bungalows sleeping up to four cost 27,000 dr. The Atrium Hotel (☎ 49 345; fax 49 444) is an attractive place with a bar, restaurant, pool and gymnasium. Doubles/triples are 15,000/20,000 dr in low season and 20,000/36,500 dr in high season. The hotel is 7km west of town.

Places to Eat
The good news is that there is a wide choice of eateries in Skiathos; the bad news is that

SPORADES

they all tend to gear their cuisine to the tourist trade and they are more expensive than elsewhere. Finding some real Greek cuisine is a matter of trial and error. There is a swathe of restaurants just down from Plateia Trion Ierarhon, overlooking the old harbour. Of these, *Taverna Stamatis* does a good job and seems to draw most of the customers. The service is fast and the food is good and reasonably Greek. Expect to pay in excess of 2500 dr for a feed.

Taverna Ouzeri Kambourelis on the waterfront of the old harbour also rates well and *Psarotaverna to Aigaio* has reasonable prices and ready-made dishes as well as fish, but is in a less attractive location on the new harbour front. Two restaurants close to each other and away from the main tourist traps are the *Mesogia* and the *Alexandros*. Both are signposted from Polytehniou (parallel to, and to the left of Papadiamanti from the waterfront). Prices are still in the 2500 dr range for a decent meal, but the tables spill out onto the narrow streets, making a change from the rush of the waterfront.

Entertainment

Scan Papadiamanti and Polytehniou and see which disco or bar takes your fancy. The *Adagio Bar* is one of the most civilised, playing classical music and jazz. Walk up Papadiamanti, turn right at the post office and it's on the left. In contrast, the *Banana Bar*, on Polytehniou, is patronised by tourists from the UK. *Borzoï* and *Spartacus* play both Greek and non-Greek music. Both are on Polytehniou. The *Kentavros Bar*, one of Skiathos' more established joints, promises rock, funky soul, acid jazz and blues, and gets the thumbs up from local expats. It's in view of the Papadiamantis museum.

AROUND SKIATHOS
Beaches

With some 65 beaches to choose from, beach-hopping on Skiathos can become a full-time occupation. Many are only accessible by caïque and the ones that are more easily accessible tend to get crowded.

Buses ply the south coast stopping at the beaches access points. The ones nearest town are extremely crowded; the first one worth getting off the bus for is the pine-fringed, long and sandy **Vromolimnos beach**, which has been awarded an EU blue flag for cleanliness. **Platanias** and **Troulos**, the next two beaches along, are also good but both, alas, are very popular. The bus continues to **Koukounaries beach**, backed by pine trees and a lagoon and touted as the best beach in Greece. Nowadays it's best viewed from a distance from where the wide sweep of pale gold sand does indeed look beautiful.

Krassa beach, at the other side of a narrow headland, is more commonly known as **Banana beach**, because of its curving shape and soft yellow sand. It is nominally a nudist beach, though the skinny dippers tend to disappear to **Little Banana beach** around the corner if things get too crowded. It has two or three *cantinas*. The north coast's beaches are less crowded but exposed to the meltemi.

From Troulos a road heads north to sandy **Megali Aselinos beach** (with a camp site). Turn left onto a dirt road to reach this beach. A right fork from this road leads to **Mikri Aselinos beach**. **Lalaria**, on the northern coast, is a striking beach of pale grey pebbles, and is featured in most of the tourist brochures depicting Skiathos. It is most easily reached by excursion boat from Skiathos town.

Kastro Κάστρο

Kastro, perched dramatically on a rocky headland above the north coast, was the fortified pirate-proof capital of the island from 1540 to 1829. It consisted of some 300 houses and 20 churches and the only access was by a drawbridge. Except for two churches, it is now in ruins. Access is by steps, and the views from Kastro are tremendous. Excursion boats do the trip to the beach below Kastro, from where it's an easy clamber up to the ruins.

Moni Evangelistrias
Μονή Ευαγγελίστριας

The 18th-century Moni Evangelistrias is the most appealing of the island's monasteries.

It is in a delightful setting, poised above a gorge, 450m above sea level, and surrounded by pine and cypress trees. The monastery, like many in Greece, was a refuge for freedom fighters during the War of Independence, and the islanders claim the first Greek flag was raised here in 1807.

The monastery is an hour's walk from town or you can drive here. It's signposted off the Skiathos town ring road, close to the turn-off to the airport.

Skopelos Σκόπελος

• *pop 5000* • *postcode 370 03* • *area code* ☎ *0424*
Skopelos (Skopelos) is less commercialised than Skiathos, but following hot on its trail. Like Skiathos, the north-west coast is exposed, with high cliffs. The sheltered south-east coast harbours many beaches but, unlike Skiathos, most are pebbled. The island is heavily pine-forested and has vineyards, olive groves and fruit orchards. There are two large settlements: the capital and main port of Skopelos town on the east coast; and the lovely unspoilt hill village of Glossa, the island's second port, 3km north of Loutraki on the west coast.

Skopelos has yielded an exciting archaeological find. In ancient times the island was an important Minoan outpost ruled by Staphylos, who, according to mythology, was the son of Ariadne and Dionysos. *Staphylos* means grape in Greek and the Minoan ruler is said to have introduced wine-making to the island. In the 1930s a tomb containing gold treasures, and believed to be that of Staphylos, was unearthed at Staphylos, now a resort.

Getting There & Away
Ferry Skopelos' second port is called Glossa. However, boats actually depart from Loutraki, on the coast. Glossa is 3km inland. In summer there are three ferries a day from Glossa and Skopelos town to Alonnisos (30 minutes, 950 dr); four to Volos (4½ hours, 2800 dr); two to Agios Konstantinos (4½

hours, 3500 dr); and four or five to Skiathos (1½ hours, 1300 dr). In addition, there is one boat a week to Kymi (3½ hours, 4100 dr) and three a week to Thessaloniki (six hours, 3700 dr). The times given are for Skopelos town; Glossa is one hour less. Tickets are available from Lemonis Agents (☎ 23 055; fax 22 363). The telephone number of Skopelos' port police is ☎ 22 180.

Hydrofoil Like Skiathos, Skopelos is linked to a large number of destinations by hydrofoil. Among the main services during the summer period are the following: eight or nine per day to Alonnisos (20 minutes, 2010 dr); 10 or 12 a day to Skiathos (one hour, 2540 dr); five a day to Volos (two hours 20 minutes, 6610 dr); three a day to Agios Konstantinos (2½ hours, 7920 dr); four or six a week to Skyros (two hours 20 minutes, 7040 dr); and one a day to Thessaloniki (4¾ hours, 9500 dr). Cheaper return fares apply on most of these services. In addition, there are also services to the Pelion peninsula, Halkidiki, to various ports in Evia and to Stylida, which is near Lamia. Hydrofoil tickets may be purchased from Madro Travel in Skopelos town (☎ 22 145; fax 22 941).

Getting Around
Bus There are eight buses a day from Skopelos town all the way to Glossa/Loutraki (one hour, 700 dr), a further three that go only as far as Milia (35 minutes, 480 dr) and another two that go only as far as Agnontas (15 minutes, 210 dr).

Car & Motorcycle There are a fair number of rental outlets for cars and motorcycles, mostly at the eastern end of the waterfront. Among them is Motor Tours (☎ 22 986), on the waterfront near the Hotel Eleni.

SKOPELOS TOWN
Skopelos town is one of the most captivating of the island's towns. It skirts a semicircular bay and clambers in tiers up a hillside, culminating in a ruined fortress. Dozens of churches are interspersed among tall,

dazzling-white houses with brightly shuttered windows and flower-adorned balconies. Traditionally, roofs in Skopelos town were tiled with beautiful rough-hewn bluestone, but these are gradually being replaced with mass-produced red tiles.

Orientation

Skopelos town's quay is on the west side of the bay. From the ferry, turn left to reach the bustling waterfront lined with cafés, souvenir shops and travel agencies. The bus station is to the left of the quay, at the end of the excursion-boat moorings.

Information

The post office lurks in an obscure alleyway: walk up the road opposite the bus station, take the first left, the first right and the first left and it's on the right. To reach the OTE turn left at the quay, right at the Armoloï craft shop and you'll come to it on the left at the first crossroad.

The National Bank of Greece is on the waterfront near the quay. It has an ATM and an automatic exchange machine. To reach Skopelos' laundrette go up the street opposite the bus station, turn right at Platanos Taverna and it's on the left.

There is no tourist office or tourist police on Skopelos. The regular police station (☎ 22 235) is above the National Bank. Go up the steps to the right of the bank, turn left and the entrance is on the left.

Museum

Strolling around town and sitting at the waterside cafés will probably be your chief occupations in Skopelos town, but there is also a small **folk-art museum** on Hatzistamati. It is open daily from 7 am to 10 pm and admission is free. Walk up the steps to the left of the pharmacy on the waterfront, take the first right, the first left, the first right and it's on the right.

Places to Stay – bottom end

Skopelos town is still a place where you have a good chance of renting a room in a family house. People with rooms to offer meet the ferries, but be aware that many of these rooms are in the labyrinthine streets high above the waterfront, so getting to them initially, and finding them again afterwards, tests stamina and powers of orientation to the limit.

One of the most pleasant domatia is *Pension Soula* (☎ 22 930). This lovely place is owned by an elderly couple who don't speak English but are very hospitable. The rates are 8000/10,000 dr for doubles/triples with private bathroom; there is a communal kitchen and a tranquil garden. To find the pension, turn left at the Hotel Amalia and follow this road, bearing right after about 200m. You will find the house on your right.

The domatia of *Marigoula Abelakia* (☎ 22 662) at Tria Platania are in a pleasant garden setting 10 minutes walk from the waterfront. Apart from the garden, you get a BBQ area and the private church of Agios Fanourios thrown in for good luck. Doubles are 10,000 dr and triples are 14,000 dr.

There are no camp sites on Skopelos.

Places to Stay – middle

The wooden-floored rooms of pension *Kyr Sotos* (☎ 22 805; fax 23 668), in a lovely old building in the middle of the waterfront, are delightful and very popular with visitors. There's a little courtyard, a communal kitchen and a fridge for guests' use, and each well-appointed room is different. Doubles/triples are 8,800/14,600 dr respectively.

In a prime location overlooking all the waterfront action is the C-class *Hotel Adonis* (☎ 22 231). Its comfortable and homely doubles/triples (a couple with large balconies overlooking the street) go for 15,000/20,000 dr.

Places to Stay – top end

The B-class *Dolphin Hotel* (☎ 23 015; fax 23 016) is a striking pastel-coloured building with an ultramodern, luxurious interior and an extensive garden with a swimming pool and an ornamental pond. The rooms have a minibar, telephone, radio and balcony. Single/double rates are 16,300/22,000 dr. Apartments for three or four people cost 28,000 dr.

All accommodation prices quoted here cost considerably less out of high season.

Places to Eat

There are a large number of restaurants in Skopelos town and the quality is somewhat better than that on Skiathos. The following are among the better ones. *O Platanos* is cheap, basic and popular. Its speciality is souvlaki. You will find it if you follow the instructions for finding the post office. It has tables underneath a large plane tree.

There are two reasonable Greek restaurants next to each other on the waterfront near the ferry quay. The *Klimataria* and the *Molos* serve a range of good food and are in the mid-price range.

Two more expensive, but very pleasant restaurants catering mainly for better-heeled visitors are the *Taverna Finikas* and the *Taverna Alexander*. Look for the signs to this first place from the OTE. It has a varied cuisine and the restaurant is set round an enormous palm tree. In the Taverna Alexander, apart from good food, you get to eat in a walled garden. Follow the signs from the OTE.

SPORADES

For a special treat in summer only, head to the *Ouzeri Anatoli* high up above the town. Here in summer, from 11 pm onwards, you will hear rembetika music sung by Skopelos' own rembetis Georgos Xindaris. To get there by road, turn right at the road junction as you head out of town and follow the ring road to the end. To walk there via the shortest route, take the street to the immediate right from the Commercial Bank and follow it more or less to its conclusion, heading upwards and passing a well on your way. Ask if you lose your way – getting lost is half the fun.

Entertainment

The *Platanos Jazz Club*, opposite the quay, is a long-time favourite hang-out with backpackers. New-age music is played at breakfast time; jazz and blues in the evenings. The *Ano Kato* music club is one of the liveliest places for disco music. It's 100m along the road leading left from the Platanos restaurant.

GLOSSA Γλώσσα

Glossa, Skopelos' other major settlement, is another whitewashed delight and considerably quieter than the capital. It manages to combine being a pristine Greek village with having most of the amenities that visitors require.

The bus stops in front of a large church at a T-junction. Facing the church, the left road winds down to Loutraki and the right to the main thoroughfare of Agiou Riginou. Along here you'll find a bank and a shop with a metered telephone.

Skopelos' beaches are just as accessible by bus from Glossa as they are from Skopelos town; Milia, the island's best beach, is actually closer to Glossa. There are also places to stay and tavernas at Loutraki, but it's an uninteresting and unattractive place.

Places to Stay & Eat

In summer, if accommodation gets tight in Skopelos town, you can try the *Hotel Atlantes* (☎ 33 223), at the T-junction in Glossa. The clean, attractive single/double/triple rooms are 6500/7500 dr. Just before you enter Glossa, you will find *Rooms Kerasia* (☎ 33 373) in a newish building set back from the road to the left. Rates here are around 7000 dr a double. Glossa also has a few other rooms in private houses – enquire at kafeneia.

Taverna Agnanti serves well-prepared, reasonably priced Greek fare. It's on the left side of Agiou Riginou as you walk from the T-junction. Just before you enter Glossa from Skopelos you'll find the *Kali Kardia* taverna, which has excellent views down to the sea.

AROUND SKOPELOS
Monasteries

Skopelos has many monasteries, several of which can be visited on a scenic, although quite strenuous, one-day trek from Skopelos town. Facing inland from the waterfront, turn left and follow the road which skirts the bay and then climbs inland (signposted Hotel Aegeon). Continue beyond the hotel and you will come to a fork. Take the left fork for the 18th-century **Moni Evangelismou** (now a convent). From here there are breathtaking views of Skopelos town, 4km away. The monastery's prize piece is a beautiful and ornately carved and gilded iconostasis in which there is an 11th-century icon of the Virgin Mary.

The right fork leads to the uninhabited 16th-century **Moni Metamorfosis**, which is the island's oldest monastery. From here the track continues to the 18th-century **Moni Prodromou** (now a nunnery), 8km from Skopelos town.

Walking Tours

There is a useful English-language walking guide to Skopelos called *Sotos Walking Guide*, by Heather Parsons. It lists 21 different walking itineraries around Skopelos town and Glossa. The hand-drawn sketches and maps are a bit rough, but the suggestions for walking tours of the island are excellent. It costs 2000 dr and is available in waterfront stores selling books.

Beaches

Skopelos' beaches are almost all on the sheltered south-west and west coasts. All the buses stop at the beginning of paths which lead down to them. The first beach along is the crowded sand and pebble **Staphylos beach** (site of Staphylos' tomb), 4km southeast from Skopelos town. There is a welcoming taverna here with romantic views when there is a full moon. From the eastern end of the beach a path leads over a small headland to the quieter **Velanio beach**, the island's official nudist beach. **Agnontas**, which is 3km west of Staphylos, has a small pebble beach and from here caïques sail to the superior and sandy **Limnonari beach** (you can also walk here along a path from Agnontas, or along a track from the main road). There are three waterside tavernas at Agnontas. From Agnontas the road cuts inland through pine forests and re-emerges at sheltered **Panormos beach**. The next beach along, **Milia**, is considered the island's best – a long swathe of tiny pebbles.

All of these beaches have tavernas or *cantinas*, and there are hotels and domatia at Staphylos, Limnonari, Panormos and Milia. However, the comfortable ones at Limnonari (☎ 23 046) are a little more secluded and the beach is smaller and less likely to be crowded. Domatia hare cost 14,000 dr for a double.

Alonnisos Αλόννησος

• *pop 3000* • *postcode 370 05* • *area code* ☎ *0424*

Alonnisos (Alonnisos) is still a serene island despite having been ferreted out by 'high-quality' package-tour companies. Package tourism would no doubt have taken off in a bigger way had the airport (erroneously and optimistically shown on island maps) materialised. This project was begun in the mid-1980s, but the rocks of Alonnisos proved unyielding and the politics Byzantine, making the construction of a runway impossible.

Alonnisos once had a flourishing wine industry, but in 1950 the vines were struck with disease and, robbed of their livelihood, many islanders moved away. Fate struck another cruel blow in 1965 when a violent earthquake destroyed the hilltop capital of Alonnisos town (now called Old Alonnisos or Hora). The inhabitants abandoned their hilltop homes and were subsequently rehoused in hastily assembled concrete dwellings at Patitiri. In recent years many of the derelict houses in the capital have been bought for a song from the government and renovated by northern Europeans.

Alonnisos is a green island with pine and oak trees, mastic and arbutus bushes, and fruit trees. The west coast is mostly precipitous cliffs but the east coast is speckled with pebbled beaches. The water around Alonnisos has been declared a marine park, and is consequently the cleanest in the Aegean. Every house has a cesspit, so no sewage enters the sea.

Getting There & Away

Ferry There are two or three daily ferries from Alonnisos to Volos (six hours, 3200 dr); four to five a day to both Skopelos town (30 minutes, 900 dr) and Skiathos (two hours, 1450 dr); and one a day to Agios Konstantinos (six hours, 3850 dr). In addition, there is one ferry a week to Kymi (2¼ hours, 3800 dr) and one or three a week to Thessaloniki via Skiathos (6½ hours, 2500 dr). Tickets can be purchased from Alonnisos Travel (☎ 65 198; fax 65 511). The port police (☎ 65 595) are on the left side of Ikion Dolopon in Patitiri.

Hydrofoil As with Skiathos and Skopelos, there are a large number of connections in summer. The more important ones are as follows: two or three services a day to Volos (2½ hours, 7285 dr); seven or 11 a day to both Skopelos town (20 minutes, 2010 dr) and Skiathos (40 minutes, 3340 dr); two or three a day to Agios Konstantinos (2½ hours, 8475 dr); one or two a day to Skyros (1¼ hours, 6765 dr); and one a day to Thessaloniki (5¼ hours, 11,020 dr).

Cheaper return fares apply on most of

these services. In addition, there are also services to the Pelion peninsula, Halkidiki, various ports in Evia and to Stylida near Lamia. Hydrofoil tickets may be purchased from Ikos Travel (☎ 65 320; fax 65 321) in Patitiri.

Getting Around

If you'd prefer to leave the travel arrangements up to someone else, Ikos Travel in Patitiri operates various excursions. See Organised Tours under the Patitiri entry.

Bus In summer, Alonnisos' one bus plies more or less hourly between Patitiri (from opposite the quay) and Old Alonnisos. The ticket costs 200 dr each way.

Motorcycle There are several motorcycle-hire outlets on Pelasgon, in Patitiri. Alonissos does not have many surfaced roads, so exercise extra caution when venturing away from the main settlements.

Taxi Boat The easiest way to get to the east-coast beaches is by the taxi boats that leave from the quay in Patitiri every morning.

SPORADES

PATITIRI Πατητήρι

Patitiri sits between two high sandstone cliffs at the southern end of the east coast. Not surprisingly, considering its origins, it's not a traditionally picturesque place, but it nevertheless makes a convenient base and has a very relaxed atmosphere.

Orientation

Finding your way around Patitiri is easy. The quay is in the centre of the waterfront and two roads lead inland. Facing away from the sea, turn left and then right for Pelasgon or right and then left for Ikion Dolopon.

Information

There is no tourist office or tourist police. The regular police (☎ 65 205) are just east of the southern end of Ikion Dolopon, as is The National Bank of Greece.

The post office is on the right side of Ikion Dolopon and the OTE is on the waterfront to the right of the quay. There is a laundrette on the left side of Pelasgon.

Walk to Old Alonnisos

From Patitiri to Old Alonnisos a delightful path winds through shrubbery and orchards. Walk up Pelasgon and, 40m beyond Pension Galini, a Euronature sign sporting the grand title of 'Ecological Cultural Hiking Trail' indicates the start of the path to Old Alonnisos. Take this path and after 10 minutes turn right at a water tap, which may not be functioning. After about 15 minutes the path is intersected by a dirt road. Continue straight ahead on the path and after about 25 minutes you will come to the main road. Walk straight along this road and you will see Old Alonnisos ahead.

If you are coming from Old Alonnisos the start of the track is not yet marked with a sign. Notwithstanding, walk down the main road to Patitiri for about 350m and look for a short, concrete OTE obelisk on the left. The trail starts here on the opposite side of the road.

Organised Tours

Ikos Travel (☎ 65 320; fax 65 321), opposite the quay, has several excursions. These include: Kyra Panagia, Psathoura and Peristera islets (7000 dr, including a picnic on a beach, snacks and drinks) and a round-the-island excursion (6500 dr).

They also organise four guided walking tours along the back tracks of Alonnisos and then usually down to a beach for a picnic lunch and a swim. Stout walking shoes, trousers and a long-sleeved shirt are recommended. Ikos travel, or your guides Chris and Julia, will provide you with a locally produced, but very detailed walking map.

Places to Stay – bottom end

Alonnisos has two camp sites. The nearest one to the port is the semi-official *Camping Rocks* (☎ 65 410). Don't be put off by the name; it doesn't refer to the site's surface but to the nearest rocky beach (a nudist beach). The site is a 700m uphill slog from the quay (turn left at the Enigma Disco on Pelasgon); however, the owner meets all the ferries in his jeep. The other site is *Ikaros Camping* (☎ 65 258), on Steni Vala beach.

Accommodation standards are good on Alonnisos (and cheaper than on Skiathos and Skopelos) and, except for the first two weeks of August, you shouldn't have any difficulty finding a room. The Rooms to Let service (☎ 65 577), opposite the quay, will endeavour to find a room for you on any part of the island.

The *domatia* of Eleni Alexiou (☎ 65 149) are a pleasant place to stay in Alonnisos. If you call ahead, you will be met at the quay. Rates are 7000/8400 dr for doubles/triples. The rooms are high up and a bit back from the harbour. Ask at Rooms to Let for more detailed instructions on how to get there. Along Pelasgon, on the left at No 27, are the prettily furnished *domatia* of Magdelini Bassini (☎ 65 451). They cost 8000/9600 dr for doubles/triples with private bathroom. *Pension Galini* (☎ 65 573; fax 65 094) is beautifully furnished and has a fine flower-festooned terrace. Doubles/triples are 8000/9500 dr with private bathroom, and well-equipped apartments for five/six people are

14,000/17,000 dr. The pension can be found on the left, 400m up Pelagson.

Eleni Athanasiou (☎ 65 240) rents lovely rooms in a sparkling white, blue-shuttered building high above the harbour. Rates are 7500/8500 dr for doubles/triples with private bathroom, and five-person apartments are 15,500 dr. The rooms are reached by taking the first left off Ikion Dolopon and following the path upwards until you come across them on your right. The C-class *Alkyon Guest House* (☎ 65 220; fax 65 195), on the waterfront, has comfortable singles/doubles for 9730/13,500 dr with private bathroom. The entrance is from Ikion Dolopon.

The attractive rooms in the C-class *Liadromia Hotel* (☎ 65 521) have stucco walls, stone floors, balcony and traditional carved-wood furniture. Walk inland up Ikion Dolopon and take the first turn right, follow the road around and the hotel is on the left. Doubles are 10,000 dr.

Places to Stay – middle

Alonnisos' classiest hotel is the C-class *Galaxy Hotel* (☎ 65 254; fax 65 110), where luxurious single/double rooms with balcony cost 9500/12,500 dr. The hotel is built on a hill to the left of the bay if you're facing inland. Turn left at the port and beyond the waterfront tavernas take the steps up to the right; turn left at the top to reach the hotel.

Places to Eat

If you feel you can't stomach another moussaka, pastitsio or souvlaki, then Alonnisos will come as a revelation, for the island has some top-notch eateries. Most specialise in imaginatively prepared fish dishes. At *To Kamaki Ouzeri*, on the left side of Ikion Dolopon, try mussels in cream sauce or other delicious saganaki (ie 'cooked in a small frying pan') dishes.

Another superlative little ouzeri is *Ouzeri Lefteris*, on the right side of Pelagson, which offers stuffed cuttlefish as well as lobster with tomatoes and peppers. The *Argo Restaurant* has wonderful views of the sea from its terrace and the food is good, with main

meals for about 1900 dr. Face the sea, walk to the extreme left of the harbour and the restaurant is signposted. The waterfront restaurants are all much of a muchness: take your pick and hope for the best.

OLD ALONNISOS

Nowadays, Old Alonnisos (Hora) has a strange appearance. Its narrow streets are made of mud and stone, but it is dominated by highly renovated stone villas. These dwellings are owned by wealthy northern Europeans hankering after the simple life.

Old Alonnisos is a tranquil, picturesque place with lovely views. From the main road just outside Old Alonnisos a path leads down to Vrysitsa beach, and paths lead south to Vythisma and Marpounda beaches.

Places to Stay

There are no hotels in Old Alonnisos, but there are a few domatia. One agreeable place is the *Rooms & Studios* of John Tsoukanas (☎ 65 135), with rates of 5000/8000/11,000 dr for singles/doubles/triples with private bathroom. The triple rooms have a kitchen. Rooms & Studios is on the central square of Plateia Hristou, which is named after its 17th-century church. Nearby is the newer *Fadasia House* (☎ 65 186) with lovely rooms for 8000 dr and a studio with fridge and cooker for 12,000 dr. There is also a little snack bar and garden.

Places to Eat

Old Alonnisos has three newish tavernas, all close to the bus stop. All are good, but the one with the best view is the *Taverna Aloni*, which will do you calamari, chips, salad and retsina for around 2300 dr. Take the right fork at the bus stop to get to it. In the village itself, the *Paraport taverna* also has great views towards the south side of the island.

AROUND ALONNISOS
Beaches

Most of Alonnisos' beaches are on the east coast. Apart from the Patitiri-Old Alonnisos road, the only road is one which goes north to the tip of the island. It is driveable all the way but only has tarmac for a few km out of Patitiri. Dirt tracks lead off the road to the beaches.

The first beach is the gently shelving **Hrysi Milia beach**. The next beach up is **Kokkinokastro**. Kokkinokastro is the site of the ancient city of Ikos (once the capital) and there are remains of city walls and a necropolis under the sea.

Steni Vala is a small fishing village with a permanent population of 30 and a good beach. There are three tavernas and 30-odd rooms in domatia, as well as the *Ikaros Camping* camp site. **Kalamakia**, further north, has a good beach, rooms and tavernas. **Agios Dimitrios beach**, further up, is an unofficial nudist beach.

ISLETS AROUND ALONNISOS

Alonnisos is surrounded by seven uninhabited islets, all of which have rich flora and fauna. The largest remaining population of the monk seal *(Monachus monachus)*, a Mediterranean sea mammal faced with extinction, lives in the waters around the Sporades. These factors were the incentive behind the formation of the marine park in 1983. The park encompasses the sea and the islets around Alonnisos. Its research station is on Alonnisos, near Gerakas cove.

Piperi, to the north-east of Alonnisos, is a refuge for the monk seal and it is forbidden to set foot there without a licence to carry out research.

Gioura, also north-east of Alonnisos, has many rare plants and a rare species of wild goat. **Skantzoura**, to the south-east of Alonnisos, is the habitat of falcons and the rare Aegean seagull. **Peristera**, just off Alonnisos' east coast, has several sandy beaches and the remains of a castle.

Kyra Panagia also has good beaches and two abandoned monasteries. **Psathoura** has the submerged remains of an ancient city and the brightest lighthouse in the Aegean. Both of these islands are to the north of Alonnisos. The seventh islet is tiny **Adelphi**, between Peristera and Skantzoura.

Skyros Σκύρος

• pop 2800 • postcode 340 07 • area code ☎ 0222

Skyros (Skýros) is some distance from the rest of the group and differs from them topographically. Almost bisected, its northern half has rolling, cultivated hills and pine forests, but the south is barren and rocky and is largely uninhabited.

There are only two settlements of any worth on the island: the small port of Linaria, and Skyros town, the capital, 10km away on the east coast. Skyros is visited by poseurs rather than package tourists – and as many of these are wealthy young Athenians as foreigners. Skyros also has quite a different atmosphere from other islands in this region, reminding you more of the Cyclades than the Sporades, especially the stark, cubist architecture of Skyros town.

Some visitors come to Skyros to attend courses at the Skyros Institute, a centre for holistic health and fitness. See Skyros town for details.

Skyros' factual history was mundane in comparison to its mythological origins until Byzantine times, when rogues and criminals from the mainland were exiled on Skyros. Rather than driving away invading pirates, these opportunist exiles entered into a mutually lucrative collaboration with them.

The exiles became the elite of Skyriot society, furnishing and decorating their houses with elaborately hand-carved furniture, plates and copper ornaments from Europe, the Middle East and Far East. Some of these items were brought by seafarers and some were simply looted by pirates from merchant ships.

Those people on the island before the mainland exiles arrived soon began to emulate the elite in their choice of décor, so local artisans cashed in by making copies of the furniture and plates, a tradition which continues to this day. Almost every Skyriot house is festooned with plates, copperware and hand-carved furniture.

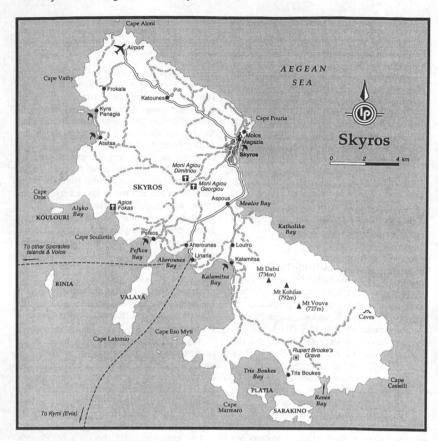

Other traditions also endure. Many elderly Skyriot males still dress in the traditional baggy pantaloons and *trohadia* (multi-thonged footwear unique to the island). The Skyros Lenten Carnival is Greece's weirdest and most wonderful festival, and is the subject of Joy Coulentianou's book *The Goat Dance of Skyros*. See the Skyros Carnival aside in this chapter.

Another special feature of Skyros which shouldn't go unmentioned, although it will probably go unseen, is the wild Skyrian pony, a breed unique to Skyros. The ponies used to roam freely in the southern half of the island, but are now almost extinct. The only ones you are likely to see are tame ones that people sometimes keep as domestic pets in their gardens.

Finally, Skyros was the last port of call for the English poet Rupert Brooke (1887-1915), who died of septicaemia at the tender age of 28 on a ship off the coast of Skyros in 1915, en route to Gallipoli.

Getting There & Away

Air In summer there are five flights a week, Monday to Friday, between Athens and

Skyros Carnival

In this pre-Lenten festival, which takes place on the last two Sundays before *Kathara Deftera* (Clean Monday – the first Monday in Lent), young men don goat masks, hairy jackets and dozens of copper goat bells. They then proceed to clank and dance around town, each with a partner (another man), dressed up as a Skyriot bride but also wearing a goat mask. Women and children also wear fancy dress. During these revelries there is singing and dancing, performances of plays, recitations of satirical poems and drinking and feasting. These riotous goings-on are overtly pagan, with elements of Dionysian festivals, goat worship (in ancient times Skyros was renowned for its excellent goat meat and milk), and the cult of Achilles, the principal deity worshipped here. The transvestism evident in the carnival may derive from the fact that Achilles hid on Skyros dressed as a girl to escape the oracle's prophecy that he would die in battle at Troy. ∎

Skyros (50 minutes, 13,900 dr) and two a week in the low season. Olympic Airways is represented by Skyros Travel & Tourism Agency, in Skyros town.

Ferry & Hydrofoil There are ferry services at least twice a day in summer, provided by the F/B *Lykomidis* to/from the port of Kymi (Evia) and Skyros (two hours, 1900 dr). Three hydrofoils a week go to Volos (4¼ hours, 13,140 dr) via Alonnisos (1¼ hours 6765 dr), Skopelos town (2 hours, 7045 dr), Glossa (Skopelos) and Skiathos (2¼ hours, 8120 dr), and one a week to Kymi (45 minutes, 4495 dr).

You can buy ferry tickets from Lykomidis Ticket Office (☎ 91 789; fax 91 791), on Agoras in Skyros town. Hydrofoil tickets can be bought at Skyros Travel & Tourism. There are also ferry and hydrofoil ticket offices at Linaria. The port police telephone number is ☎ 91 475.

Skyros Travel & Tourism also sells tickets for the Kymi-Athens bus (3½ hours, 2750 dr) which meets the ferry boat on arrival at Kymi.

Getting Around

In addition to the options listed here, it is also possible to join a boat trip to sites around the island. See Organised Tours under the Skyros town entry.

Bus There are five buses a day from Skyros town to Linaria (210 dr), and Molos (via Magazia). Buses for both Skyros town and Molos meet the boats and hydrofoils at Linaria. Bus services to Kalamitsa, Pefkos and Atsitsa are organised on an ad hoc basis during summer. See Skyros Travel & Tourism for full details.

Car & Motorcycle Cars and 4WD vehicles can be rented from Skyros Travel & Tourism Agency (see Organised Tours under Skyros town). A car goes for between 10,000 and 12,000 dr and a 4WD for between 17,000 and 19,000 dr. Cheap & Nice Motorbikes (☎ 92 022) rent motorcycles. To find the outlet, walk north and take the second turn right past Skyros Travel & Tourism Agency. Look for the prominent sign. Giannakakis Bikes also rent out motorcycles. Their office is at the Elinoil petrol station 150m down the road from the Nefeli hotel.

SKYROS TOWN

Skyros' capital is a striking, dazzling white town of flat-roofed Cycladic-style houses draped over a high rocky bluff, topped by a 13th-century fortress and the monastery of Agios Georgios. It is a gem of a place and a wander around its labyrinthine, whitewashed streets is more than likely to produce an invitation to admire a traditional Skyrian house by its proud and hospitable owner.

Orientation

The bus terminal is at the southern end of town on the main thoroughfare of Agoras, an animated street lined with tavernas, snack bars and grocery shops, and flanked by narrow winding alleyways. To reach the central square of Plateia Iroön walk straight ahead up the hill.

Walk along Agoras, beyond Plateia Iroön,

and eventually you will come to a fork in the road. The right fork leads up to the fortress and Moni Agiou Georgiou (with fine frescoes), from where there are breathtaking views. The left fork leads to Plateia Rupert Brooke, which is dominated by a disconcerting, bronze statue of a nude Rupert Brooke. The frankness of the statue caused an outcry among the islanders when it was first installed in the 1930s. From this square a cobbled, stepped path leads in 15 minutes to **Magazia beach.**

Information

Skyros does not have tourist police, but has a tourist office (☎ & fax 92 789) 50m along the road opposite the Glaros restaurant. The office is open from 7.30 am to 2 pm and 7 pm to 10 pm. The regular police (☎ 91 274) are just beyond Cheap & Nice Motorbikes (see the Skyros island Getting Around section).

The National Bank of Greece is on Agoras, a little way up from the bus terminal on the left, and sports an ATM.

To get to the post office, take the first turn right after the bus terminal and it's on the left. The OTE is opposite the police station, a little way back towards Linaria, on the right as you walk from the bus terminal.

Museums

Skyros town has three museums. The **archaeological museum** features an impressive collection of artefacts from Mycenaean to Roman times, as well as a traditional Skyrian house interior, transported in its entirety from the home of the benefactor. It is open Tuesday to Sunday from 8.30 am to 3 pm. Admission is 500 dr.

The **Faltaïts Museum** is a private museum housing the outstanding collection of a Skyriot ethnologist, Manos Faltaïts. The collection includes costumes, furniture, books, ceramics and photographs. Daily opening times are 10 am to 1 pm, and 5.30 to 8 pm. Admission is free. Both museums are just off Plateia Rupert Brooke.

The little-known **Traditional Skyrian House** is just what its name implies. It's

difficult to find, but worth the effort. Take the steps which lead up to the fortress. When you come to a crossroad with house No 992 on your right, turn left and the museum is a little way along on the left. It's open Monday to Saturday from 11 am to noon and 6 to 8 pm. Admission is 400 dr.

Courses

The Skyros Institute runs courses on a whole range of subjects, from yoga and dancing, to massage and windsurfing. The emphasis is on learning to develop a holistic approach to life. There is a branch in Skyros town, but the main 'outdoor' complex is at Atsitsa beach, on the west coast. For detailed information on their fortnightly programmes contact the Skyros Centre (☎ 0171-267 4424/284 3065; fax 0171-284 3063), 92 Prince of Wales Rd, London NW5 3NE, UK. Their email address is skyros@easynet.co.uk.

Organised Tours

Skyros Travel & Tourism Agency (☎ 91 600; fax 92 123), on the left, north of the central square, runs a boat excursion to Sarakino islet and the sea caves of Pendekali and Gerania. The excursion costs 5500 dr. Ask for manager Lefteris Trakos.

From June to mid-September another independent excursion is run on Monday and Thursday to Tris Boukes Bay and the sea caves. The cost is 6000 dr. Call ☎ 96 472 for bookings.

Places to Stay – bottom end

Whilst there is a dearth of organised hotel-style rooms in Skyros town, there are many rooms (decorated with traditional plates) to rent in private houses; the owners meet the buses from Linaria.

The cheapest hotel is the E-class *Hotel Eleni* (☎ 91 738), next to the post office, with tidy singles/doubles for 4000/8000 dr with bathroom. The luxurious *Lykomedes House* (☎ 91 697) has spacious rooms with terraces affording fine hill vistas. There is an ultramodern communal kitchen and dining area; doubles are 10,000 dr. Walk north along Agoras and take a sharp left at the Flying

Dolphin Agency, then turn right at the Pegasus Restaurant, and the rooms are a little beyond Kabanera Restaurant, on the left.

Maria Emmanouil-Fregadi (☎ 91 582) has a couple of traditional *domatia* to rent. She also has a wonderful traditional home of her own, including a 300-year-old loom. Her house is to the left of the Megali Strata – the little street leading to Plateia Rupert Brooke. Ask for directions once you are within shouting distance.

Places to Stay – middle

Moraïtis Houses (☎ 91 123) is a small number of delightful apartments in one of the nicest parts of town, high up above the town centre. A traditional double room here goes for 13,000 dr. Contact Skyros Travel & Tourism for bookings and directions.

The C-class *Hotel Nefeli* (☎ 91 964; fax 92 061) is one of the best hotels in Skyros town. The lovely rooms have enlarged B&W photographs depicting traditional Skyrian life. Rates are 17,000/19,000 dr for doubles/triples. The hotel is on the left just before you enter Skyros town.

The same hotel can organise your stay in *Skyriana Spitia*, an apartment complex made up of new, self-contained units in traditional Skyrian style. It costs 21,600/26,800 dr for an apartment for two to four people in low/high season, including breakfast – a good deal for a group of four people.

Places to Eat

With a few exceptions, Skyros town lacks memorable eating establishments The most exceptional is *Kristina's Restaurant*, set in a delightful walled garden. Kristina is an Australian who conjures up delectable local and international dishes. The kaseri and sac cheeses (local specialities), chicken fricassee and cheesecake are recommended. The restaurant is closed on Sunday. Walk south along the main street, beyond the OTE where the road forks, continue straight ahead, bear right and the restaurant is on the left.

The unpretentious *Glaros Restaurant*, on Agoras, near the central square, serves the best Greek food in town. The restaurant is to

the right of the *Simposio* ouzeri and its sign is only in Greek. However, rumour has it that it may turn into a cafeteria.

For sweet-toothed travellers The *Sweets Workshop*, on Agoras, has a vast array of mouth-watering traditional cakes, chocolates, nuts and Turkish delight.

Entertainment

The popularity enjoyed by particular bars in Skyros is ephemeral, but flavours of the month at the time of research were the stylish *Artistico*, the *Apokalypsis*, *Kalipso* and the *Renaissance Pub*, all on or just off Agoras. *Borio*, just south of Skyros town, was an 'in' disco. At Linaria *To Kastro* is another 'in' disco club, as is *O Kavos* for drinks and evening gossip. Both overlook the harbour.

MAGAZIA & MOLOS Μαγαζιά & Μώλος

The resort of Magazia is at the southern end of a splendid long sandy beach, a short distance east of Skyros town; quieter Molos is at the northern end, although there is not much to physically distinguish the two communities these days.

Places to Stay – bottom end & middle

Skyros has one camp site, *Skyros Camping* (☎ 92 458), at Magazia. It's a scruffy, run-down place with a few thirsty-looking olive trees offering shade. Freelance campers stake out without hassle at Atsitsa among the pines, and at nearby Kyra Panagia, both on the west coast (see Around Skyros).

Efrosyni Varsamou Rooms (☎ 91 142), above the family ceramics shop in Magazia, are spacious and beautifully furnished. Rates are 9600/11,000 dr for doubles/triples. If you're walking, go down the cobbled path from Skyros town, turn right at the bottom, and then right at the camp site (signposted Magazia and the Xenia Hotel) and the rooms are on the left. If you take the bus, get off at the camp site.

If you turn left at the Xenia Hotel, in just under 150m you will come to the *Alekos domatia* (☎ 91 828), on the right overlooking the beach. Pleasant and comfortable doubles/triples are 12,000/14,000 dr with private bathroom.

At Molos, the *Motel Hara* (☎ 91 763) has clean, pine-furnished doubles/triples for 11,000/13,200 dr. It also has some newer self-contained apartments. If you arrive by bus look for the motel on the right. *Angela's Bungalows* (☎ 91 764; fax 92 030), set in a lovely garden, has clean, spacious singles/doubles/triples with bathroom, balcony and telephone for 10,000/13,000/15,600 dr, including breakfast. The bungalows are signposted from the Molos bus terminal. The C-class *Hotel Paradise* (☎ 91 220; fax 92 030), next to the bus terminal, is an attractive hotel with cream marble floors and white walls. Rates here are 12,000/14,400 dr for doubles/triples.

Places to Stay – top end

The island's most luxurious hotel is the A-class *Skyros Palace* (☎ 91 994; fax 92 070), a complex of attractive apartments, which stand in splendid isolation just north of Molos. The apartments have air-con, verandahs and music channels. The complex has a café, bar, restaurant, TV lounge and swimming pool, and is 50m from a good beach. Mosquitoes can be a problem here: ask for a mosquito zapper. Singles/doubles go for 14,000/18,900 dr in high season.

Things to Buy

A good selection of ceramics is on sale at Efrosyni Varsamou's shop below the domatia of the same name at Magazia (see Places to Stay). It's hard to imagine any non-Skyriot wanting to wear the multithonged *trohadia*, but maybe they'd appeal to someone with a foot fetish who is into bondage. They can be bought at the Argo Shop, on the street which leads to Plateia Rupert Brooke.

AROUND SKYROS
Beaches

At **Atsitsa**, on the west coast, there's a tranquil pebble beach shaded by pines. The beach attracts freelance campers and there's the main outdoor centre of the Skyros Institute and a taverna with domatia here. Just to the north is the even less crowded beach of **Kyra Panagia** (also with freelance campers). At **Pefkos**, 10km south-east of Atsitsa, there is another good but small beach and a taverna. If you don't have transport take a Skyros town-Linaria bus and ask to be let off at the turn-off. It's a 3km walk from there to the beach. Further east, the pebble-and-sand beach at **Kalamitsa** is rated as one of the island's best.

Rupert Brooke's Grave

Rupert Brooke's well-tended grave is in a quiet olive grove just inland from Tris Boukes bay in the south of the island. The actual grave is poorly marked with a rough wooden sign in Greek on the roadside, but you can hardly miss it. The gravestone is inscribed with some verses of Brooke's among which is the following apt epitaph:

> If I should die think only this of me:
> That there's some corner of a foreign field
> That is forever England.

No buses go to this corner of the island. However, you can take an excursion boat to Sarakino islet, or drive or walk along a good, graded scenic road from Kalamitsa, built for the Greek navy, which now has a naval station on Tris Boukes bay.

If you walk it will take about 1½ hours; take food and water. If you have come this far with the aim of getting to the sea, you will have to turn back since the area further down the hill is a restricted and the road onwards is closed.

Language Guide

The Greek language is probably the oldest European language, with an oral tradition of 4000 years and a written tradition of approximately 3000 years. Its evolution over the four millennia was characterised by its strength during the golden age of Athens and the Democracy (mid-5th century BC); its use as a lingua franca throughout the Middle Eastern world, spread by Alexander the Great and his successors as far as India during the Hellenistic period (330 BC to 100 AD); its adaptation as the language of the new religion, Christianity; its use as the official language of the Eastern Roman Empire; and its eventual proclamation as the language of the Byzantine Empire (380-1453).

Greek maintained its status and prestige during the rise of the European Renaissance and was employed as the linguistic perspective for all contemporary sciences and terminologies during the period of Enlightenment. Today, Greek constitutes a large part of the vocabulary of any Indo-European language, and much of the lexicon of any scientific repertoire.

The modern Greek language is a southern Greek dialect which is now used by most Greek speakers both in Greece and abroad. It is the result of an intralinguistic influence and synthesis of the ancient vocabulary combined with lexemes from Greek regional dialects – namely Cretan, Cypriot and Macedonian.

Greek is spoken throughout Greece by a population of around 10 million, and by some five million Greeks who live abroad.

Stress

All Greek words of two or more syllables have an acute accent which indicates where the stress falls. For instance, άγαλμα (statue) is pronounced **a**ghalma, and αγάπη (love) is pronounced agh**a**pi. Bold letters indicate where stress falls.

Note 'dh' is pronounced as 'th' in then; 'gh' is a softer, slightly gutteral version of 'g'.

Greetings & Civilities
Hello.
y**a**sas	Γειά σας.
y**a**su (informal)	Γειά σου.

Goodbye.
and**i**o	Αντίο.

Good morning.
kalim**e**ra	Καλημέρα.

Good afternoon.
h**e**rete	Χαίρετε.

Good evening.
kalisp**e**ra	Καλησπέρα.

Good night.
kalin**i**hta	Καληνύχτα.

Please.
parakal**o**	Παρακαλώ.

Thankyou.
efharist**o**	Ευχαριστώ.

Yes.
ne	Ναι.

No.
ohi	Οχι.

Sorry. (excuse me, forgive me)
sighn**o**mi	Συγγνώμη.

How are you?
ti k**a**nete?	Τι κάνετε;
ti k**a**nis? (informal)	Τι κάνεις;

Well, thanks.
kal**a** efharist**o**	Καλά ευχαριστώ.

Essentials
I (don't) understand.
(Dhen) katalav**e**no	(Δεν) καταλαβαίνω.

Do you speak English?
mil**a**te anglika?	Μιλάτε Αγγλικά;

Where is ...?
pou **i**ne ...?	Πού είναι ...;

How much?
p**o**so k**a**ni?	Πόσο κάνει;

Greek Alphabet & Pronunciation

Greek		Pronunciation Guide	Example		
Α α	a	like the *a* in 'father'	αγάπη	a-GHA-pi	love
Β β	v	as in 'vine'	βήμα	VI-ma	step
Γ γ	gh	like a rough *g*	γάτα	GHA-ta	cat
	y	as in 'yes'	για	ya	for
Δ δ	dh	as in 'there'	δέμα	DHE-ma	parcel
Ε ε	e	as in 'egg'	ένας	E-nas	one (m)
Ζ ζ	z	as in 'zoo'	ζώο	ZO-o	animal
Η η	i	as in 'feet'	ήταν	IT-an	was
Θ θ	th	as in 'throw'	θέμα	THE-ma	theme
Ι ι	i	as in 'feet'	ίδιος	I-dhy-os	same
Κ κ	k	as in 'kite'	καλά	ka-LA	well
Λ λ	l	as in 'leg'	λάθος	LA-thos	mistake
Μ μ	m	as in 'man'	μαμά	ma-MA	mother
Ν ν	n	as in 'net'	νερό	ne-RO	water
Ξ ξ	x	as in 'ox'	ξύδι	KSI-dhi	vinegar
Ο ο	o	as in 'hot'	όλα	O-la	all
Π π	p	as in 'pup'	πάω	PA-o	I go
Ρ ρ	r	as in 'road'	ρέμα	RE-ma	stream
		a slightly trilled *r*	ρόδα	RO-dha	tyre
Σ σ, ς	s	as in 'sand'	σημάδι	si-MA-dhi	mark
Τ τ	t	as in 'tap'	τόπι	TO-pi	ball
Υ υ	i	as in 'feet'	ύστερα	IS-ter-a	after
Φ φ	f	as in 'find'	φύλλο	FI-lo	leaf
Χ χ	h	like the *ch* in the Scottish loch, or	χάνω	HA-no	I lose
		like a rough *h*	χέρι	HE-ri	hand
Ψ ψ	ps	as in 'lapse'	ψωμί	pso-MI	bread
Ω ω	o	as in 'hot'	ώρα	O-ra	time

When?
pote? — Πότε;

Where are the toilets?
pou ine i toualetez? — Πού είναι οι τουαλέτες;

Help!
voithya! — Βοήθεια!

Go away!
fiye! — Φύγε!

Police!
astynomia! — Αστυνομία!

There's been an accident.
eyine atihima — Εγινε ατύχημα.

Small Talk

What is your name?
pos sas lene? — Πώς σας λένε;

My name is ...
me lene ... — Με λένε ...

Where are you from?
apo pou iste? — Από πού είστε;

I'm from ...
ime apo ... — Είμαι από ...

Australia
afstralia — Αυστραλία

England
anglia — Αγγλία

New Zealand
nea zilandhia — Νέα Ζηλανδία

America
ameriki — Αμερική

How old are you?
poson hronon iste? — Πόσων χρονών είστε;

Combinations of Letters

The combinations of letters shown here are pronounced as follows:

Greek	Pronunciation Guide		Example		
ει	i	as in 'feet'	είδα	I-dha	I saw
οι	i	as in 'feet'	οικόπεδο	i-KO-pe-dho	land
αι	e	as in 'bet'	αίμα	E-ma	blood
ου	u	as in 'mood'	πού	pou	who/what
μπ	b	as in 'beer'	μπάλα	BA-la	ball
	mb	as in 'amber'	κάμπος	KAM-bos	forest
ντ	d	as in 'dot'	ντουλάπα	dou-LA-pa	wardrobe
	nd	as in 'bend'	πέντε	PEN-de	five
γκ	g	as in 'God'	γκάζι	GA-zi	gas
γγ	ng	as in 'angle'	αγγελία	an-ge-LI-a	classified
γξ	ks	as in 'minks'	σφιγξ	sfinks	sphynx
τζ	dz	as in 'hands'	τζάκι	DZA-ki	fireplace

The pairs of vowels shown above are pronounced separately if the first has an acute accent, or the second a dieresis, as in the examples below:

γαϊδουράκι	ga-i-dhou-RA-ki	little donkey
Κάιρο	KA-i-ro	Cairo

Some Greek consonant sounds have no English equivalent. The υ of the groups αυ, ευ and ηυ is generally pronounced *v*.
The Greek question mark is represented with the English equivalent of a semicolon ;.

I'm ... years old.
ime ... hronon   Είμαι ... χρονών.

Getting Around

How do I get to ...?
*pos tha pao
sto/sti ...?*   Πώς θα πάω
στο/στη ...;
I'd like ...
tha ithela ...   Θα ήθελα ...

a return ticket
*isitirio me
epistrofi*   εισιτήριο με
επιστροφή
two tickets
dhio isitiria   δυο εισιτήρια
a student's fare
fititiko isitirio   φοιτητικό εισιτήριο

first class
proti thesi   πρώτη θέση
economy
touristiki thesi   τουριστική θέση

train station
sidhirodhromikos stathmos
σιδηροδρομικός σταθμός
timetable
dhromologio   δρομολόγιο

What time does the
boat leave/arrive?
*ti ora fevyi/ftani
to karavi?*   Τι ώρα φεύγει/φτάνει
το καράβι;

plane   *aeroplano*   αεροπλάνο
boat   *karavi*   καράβι

bus (city)   *astiko*   αστικό
bus (intercity) *leoforio*   λεωφορείο
train   *treno*   τραίνο
taxi   *taxi*   ταξί

Where can I hire a
car?
  pou boro na   Πού μπορώ να
  nikiaso ena   νοικιάσω ένα
  aftokinito?   αυτοκίνητο;

Directions
I am lost.
  eho hathi   Εχω χαθεί.
Where is ...?
  pou ine ...?   Πού είναι...;
Is it near?
  ine konda?   Είναι κοντά;
Is it far?
  ine makria?   Είναι μακριά;

straight ahead *efthia*   ευθεία
left   *aristera*   αριστερά
right   *dexia*   δεξιά
behind   *piso*   πίσω
far   *makria*   μακριά
near   *konda*   κοντά
opposite   *apenandi*   απέναντι

Can you show me
on the map?
  borite na mou to   Μπορείτε να μου το
  dhixete sto harti? δείξετε στο χάρτη;

Useful Signs
ΕΙΣΟΔΟΣ   ENTRY
ΕΞΟΔΟΣ   EXIT
ΩΘΗΣΑΤΕ   PUSH
ΣΥΡΑΤΕ   PULL
ΓΥΝΑΙΚΩΝ   WOMEN (toilets)
ΑΝΔΡΩΝ   MEN (toilets)
ΝΟΣΟΚΟΜΕΙΟ   HOSPITAL
ΑΣΤΥΝΟΜΙΑ   POLICE
ΑΠΑΓΟΡΕΥΕΤΑΙ   PROHIBITED
ΕΙΣΙΤΗΡΙΑ   TICKETS

Around Town
I'm looking for ...
  psahno ...   Ψάχνω ...

I want to exchange
some money.
  thelo na ex-   Θέλω να
  aryiroso lefta   εξαργυρώσω λεφτά.

bank   *trapeza*   τράπεζα
the ...   *tin ...*   την ...
  embassy   *presvia*   πρεσβεία
market   *aghora*   αγορά
museum   *musio*   μουσείο
police   *astynomia*   αστυνομία
post office   *tahydhromio*   ταχυδρομείο
beach   *paralia*   παραλία
castle   *kastro*   κάστρο
church   *ekklisia*   εκκλησία
ruins   *arhea*   αρχαία

Accommodation
Where is ...?
  pou ine ...?   Πού είναι ...;
I'd like ...
  thelo ena ...   Θέλω ένα ...

a cheap hotel
  ena ftino   ένα φτηνό ξενοδοχείο
  xenodohio
clean rooms
  kathara dhomatia καθαρά δωμάτια
a good hotel
  ena kalo   ένα καλό
  xenodohio   ξενοδοχείο
a camp site
  ena kamping   ένα κάμπιγκ

single   *mono*   μονό
double   *dhiplo*   διπλό
room   *dhomatio*   δωμάτιο
with bathroom *me banio*   με μπάνιο
key   *klidhi*   κλειδί

How much is it ...?
  poso kani ...?   Πόσο κάνει ...;
per night
  ti vradhya   τη βραδυά
for ... nights
  ya ... vradhyez για ... βραδυές

Is breakfast
included?
symberilamvani — Συμπεριλαμβάνει
ke proino? — και πρωϊνό;
Can I see it?
boro na to dho? — Μπορώ να το δω;
Where is the
bathroom?
pou ine to banio? — Πού είναι το
μπάνιο;
It's expensive.
ine akrivo — Είναι ακριβό.
I'm leaving today.
fevgho simera — Φεύγω σήμερα.

Food

breakfast	proino	πρωϊνό
lunch	mesimvrino	μεσημβρινό
dinner	vradhyno	βραδυνό
beef	vodhino	βοδινό
bread	psomi	ψωμί
beer	byra	μπύρα
cheese	tyri	τυρί
chicken	kotopoulo	κοτόπουλο
Greek coffee	ellinikos kafes	ελληνικός καφές
iced coffee	frappe	φραππέ
lamb	arni	αρνί
milk	ghala	γάλα
mineral	metalliko	μεταλλικό
water	nero	νερό
tea	tsai	τσάι
wine	krasi	κρασί

I'm a vegetarian.
ime hortofaghos — Είμαι χορτοφάγος.

Shopping

How much is it?
poso kani? — Πόσο κάνει;
I'm just looking.
aplos kitazo — Απλώς κοιτάζω.
I'd like to buy …
thelo — Θέλω
n'aghoraso … — ν'αγοράσω …
Do you accept
credit cards?
pernete pistotikez — Παίρνετε πιστωτικές
kartez? — κάρτες;

Could you lower
the price?
borite na mou — Μπορείτε να μου
kanete mya — κάνετε μια
kaliteri timi? — καλύτερη τιμή;

Time & Dates

What time is it?
ti ora ine? — Τι ώρα είναι;
It's … — ine … — είναι …

1 o'clock	mia i ora	μία η ώρα
2 o'clock	dhio i ora	δύο η ώρα
7.30	efta ke misi	εφτά και μισή
am	to proi	το πρωί
pm	to apoyevma	το απόγευμα

Sunday	kyriaki	Κυριακή
Monday	dheftera	Δευτέρα
Tuesday	triti	Τρίτη
Wednesday	tetarti	Τετάρτη
Thursday	pempti	Πέμπτη
Friday	paraskevi	Παρασκευή
Saturday	savato	Σάββατο

January	ianouarios	Ιανουάριος
February	fevrouarios	Φεβρουάριος
March	martios	Μάρτιος
April	aprilios	Απρίλιος
May	maïos	Μάιος
June	iounios	Ιούνιος
July	ioulios	Ιούλιος
August	avghoustos	Αύγουστος
September	septemvrios	Σεπτέμβριος
October	oktovrios	Οκτώβριος
November	noemvrios	Νοέμβριος
December	dhekemvrios	Δεκέμβριος

today	simera	σήμερα
tonight	apopse	απόψε
nowt	ora	τώρα
yesterday	hthes	χθες
tomorrow	avrio	αύριο

Numbers & Amounts

0	midhen	μηδέν
1	enas	ένας (m)
	mia	μία (f)
	ena	ένα (n)
2	dhio	δύο

3	*tris*	τρεις (m & f)
	tria	τρία (n)
4	*teseris*	τέσσερεις (m & f)
	tesera	τέσσερα (n)
5	*pende*	πέντε
6	*exi*	έξη
7	*epta*	επτά
8	*ohto*	οχτώ
9	*enea*	εννέα
10	*dheka*	δέκα
20	*ikosi*	είκοσι
30	*trianda*	τριάντα
40	*saranda*	σαράντα
50	*peninda*	πενήντα
60	*exinda*	εξήντα
70	*evdhominda*	εβδομήντα
80	*oghdhonda*	ογδόντα
90	*eneninda*	ενενήντα
100	*ekato*	εκατό
1000	*hilii*	χίλιοι (m)
	hiliez	χίλιες (f)
	hilia	χίλια (n)

one million
   ena ekatomyrio   ένα εκατομμύριο

Health

I need a doctor.
   hriazome yatro   Χρειάζομαι ιατρό.

I want something
for ...
   thelo kati ya ...   Θέλω κάτι για ...

insect bites
   tsimbimata apo   τσιμπήματα από
   endoma   έντομα
travel sickness
   naftia taxidhiou   ναυτία ταξιδιού
diarrhoea
   dhiaria   διάρροια

aspirin
   aspirini   ασπιρίνη
condoms
   profylaktika   προφυλακτικά
   (kapotez)   (καπότες)
contact lenses
   faki epafis   φακοί επαφής
medical insurance
   yatriki asfalya   ιατρική ασφάλεια

Can you take me to
hospital?
   borite na me pate   Μπορείτε να με πάτε
   sto nosokomio?   στο νοσοκομείο;

Glossary

Achaean Civilisation – see *Mycenaean civilisation*

acropolis – highest point of an ancient city

AEK – Athens football club

agia (f), **agios** (m) – saint

agora – commercial area of an ancient city; shopping precinct in modern Greece

amphora – large two-handled vase in which wine or oil was kept

ANEK – Anonymi Naftiliaki Eteria Kritis; main shipping line to Crete

Archaic period (800-480 BC) – period in which the city-states emerged from the 'dark age' and traded their way to wealth and power; the city-states were unified by a Greek alphabet and common cultural pursuits, engendering a sense of national identity; also known as the Middle Age

architrave – part of the *entablature* which rests on the columns of a temple

arhontika – 17th and 18th-century AD mansions which belonged to archons, the leading citizens of a town

Arvanites – Albanian-speakers of north-western Greece

Asia Minor – the Aegean litoral of Turkey centred around İzmir but also including İstanbul; formerly populated by Greeks

askitiria – mini-chapels; places of solitary worship

baglamas – miniature bouzouki with a tinny sound

basilica – early Christian church

bouleuterion – council house

bouzouki – stringed lute-like instrument associated with rembetika music

bouzoukia – 'bouzoukis'; used to mean any nightclub where the bouzouki is played and low-grade blues songs are sung; see *skyladika*

buttress – support built against the outside of a wall

Byzantine Empire – characterised by the merging of Hellenistic culture and Christianity and named after Byzantium, the city on the Bosporus which became the capital of the Roman Empire in 324 AD; when the Roman Empire was formally divided in 395 AD, Rome went into decline and the eastern capital, renamed Constantinople after Emperor Constantine I, flourished; the Byzantine Empire dissolved after the fall of Constantinople to the Turks in 1453

capital – top of a column

cella – room in a temple where the cult statue stood

choregos – wealthy citizen who financed choral and dramatic performances

chryselephantine statue – ivory and gold statue

city-states – states comprising a sovereign city and its dependencies; the city-states of Athens and Sparta were famous rivals

classical Greece – period in which the city-states reached the height of their wealth and power after the defeat of the Persians in the 5th century BC; ended with the decline of the city-states as a result of the Peloponnesian Wars, and the expansionist aspirations of Philip II, King of Macedon (ruled 359-336 BC), and his son, Alexander the Great (ruled 336-323 BC)

Corinthian – order of Greek architecture recognisable by columns with bell-shaped *capitals* with sculpted elaborate ornaments based on acanthus leaves

cornice – the upper part of the *entablature*, extending beyond the frieze

crypt – lowest part of a church, often a burial chamber

Cycladic civilisation (3000-1100 BC) – civilisation which emerged following the settlement of Phoenician colonists on the Cycladic islands

cyclopes – mythical one-eyed giants

dark age (1200 - 800 BC) – period in which Greece was under *Dorian* rule

delfini – dolphin; common name for hydrofoil

diglossy – the existence of two forms of one language within a country; has existed in Greece for most of its modern history

dimarhio – town hall

Dimotiki – demotic Greek language; the official spoken language of Greece

domatio (s), **domatia** (pl) – room; a cheap accommodation option available in most tourist areas

Dorians – Hellenic warriors who invaded Greece around 1200 BC, demolishing the city-states and destroying the Mycenaean civilisation; heralded Greece's 'dark age', when the artistic and cultural advancements of the Mycenaeans and Minoans were abandoned; the Dorians later developed into land-holding aristocrats which encouraged the resurgence of independent city-states led by wealthy aristocrats

Doric – order of Greek architecture characterised by a column which has no base, a *fluted* shaft and a relatively plain capital, when compared with the flourishes evident on *Ionic* and *Corinthian* capitals

ELPA – Elliniki Leshi Periigiseon & Aftokinitou; Greek motoring and touring club

ELTA – Ellinika Tahydromia; Greek post office

entablature – part of a temple between the tops of the columns and the roof

EOS – Ellinikos Orivatikos Syllogos; Greek alpine club

EOT – Ellinikos Organismos Tourismou- national tourism organisation which has offices in most major towns

Epitaphios – picture on cloth of Christ on his bier

estiatorio – restaurant serving ready-made food as well as à la carte dishes

ET – Elliniki Tileorasi; state television company

evzones – famous border guards from the northern Greek village of Evzoni; they also guard the Parliament building

Filiki Eteria – friendly society; a group of Greeks in exile; formed during Ottoman rule to organise an uprising against the Turks

fluted – vertical indentations on the shaft of some columns

frappé – iced coffee

frieze – part of the *entablature* which is above the *architrave*

galaktopoleio (s), **galaktopoleia** (pl) – a shop which sells dairy products

Geometric period (1200-800 BC) – period characterised by pottery decorated with geometric designs; sometimes referred to as Greece's 'dark age'

GESEE – Greek trade union association

giouvetsi – casserole of meat and pasta

Hellas, Ellas or **Ellada** – the Greek name for Greece

Helots – original inhabitants of Lakonia whom the Spartans used as slaves

hora – main town (usually on an island)

ikonostasis – altar screen embellished with icons

Ionic – order of Greek architecture characterised by a column with truncated flutes and capitals with ornaments resembling scrolls

kafeneio (s), **kafeneia** (pl) – traditionally a male-only coffee house where cards and backgammon are played

kafeteria – up-market kafeneio, mainly for younger people

kalderimi – cobbled footpath

kasseri – mild, slightly rubbery sheep's milk cheese

kastro – walled-in town

Katharevousa – purist Greek; very rarely used these days

katholikon – principal church of a monastic complex

kefi – an undefinable feeling of good spirit, without which no Greek can have a good time

KKE – Kommounistiko Komma Elladas; Greek communist party

Koine – Greek language used in pre-Byzantine times; the language of the church liturgy

kore – female statue of the Archaic period; see *kouros*

kouros – male statue of the Archaic period,

characterised by a stiff body posture and enigmatic smile

KTEL – Kino Tamio Ispraxeon Leoforion; national bus cooperative; runs all long-distance bus services

Kypriako – the 'Cyprus issue'; politically sensitive and never forgotten by Greeks and Greek Cypriots

libations – in ancient Greece, wine or food which was offered to the gods

libation vessel – utensil from which the wine offered to the gods was poured; see *rhyton*

Linear A – Minoan script; so far undeciphered

Linear B – Mycenaean script; has been deciphered

lyra – small violin-like instrument, played on the knee; common in Cretan and Pontian music

malakas – literally 'wanker'; used as a familiar term of address, or as an insult, depending on context

mangas – 'wide boy' or 'dude'; originally a person of the underworld, now any streetwise person

mayiria – cook houses

megaron – central room of a Mycenaean palace

meltemi – north-easterly wind which blows throughout much of Greece during the summer

metope – sculpted section of a *Doric frieze*

meze (s), **mezedes** (pl) – appetiser

Middle Age – see *Archaic period*

Minoan civilisation (3000-1100 BC) – Bronze Age culture of Crete named after the mythical King Minos and characterised by pottery and metalwork of great beauty and artisanship

moni – monastery or convent

Mycenaean civilisation (1900-1100 BC) – first great civilisation of the Greek mainland, characterised by powerful independent city-states ruled by kings; also known as the Achaean civilisation

myzithra – soft sheep's milk cheese

narthex – porch of a church

nave – aisle of a church

Nea Dimokratia – New Democracy; conservative political party

necropolis – literally 'city of the dead'; ancient cemetery

nefos – cloud; usually used to refer to pollution in Athens

NEL – Naftiliaki Eteria Lesvou; Lesvos shipping company

neo kyma – 'new wave'; left-wing music of the boîtes and clubs of 1960s Athens

nomarhia – prefecture building

nomos – prefectures into which the regions and island groups of Greece are divided

nymphaeum – in ancient Greece, building containing a fountain and often dedicated to nymphs

OA – Olympiaki Aeroporia or Olympic Airways; Greece's national airline and major domestic air carrier

odeion – ancient Greek indoor theatre

odos – street

ohi – 'no'; what the Greeks said to Mussolini's ultimatum when he said surrender or be invaded; the Italians were subsequently repelled and the event is celebrated on October 28

omphalos – sacred stone at Delphi which the ancient Greeks believed marked the centre of the world

OSE – Organismos Sidirodromon Ellados; Greek railways organisation

OTE – Organismos Tilepikinonion Ellados; Greece's major telecommunications carrier

oud – a bulbous, stringed instrument with a sharply raked-back head

ouzeri (s), **ouzeria** (pl) – place which serves *ouzo* and light snacks

ouzo – a distilled spirit made from grapes and flavoured with aniseed

Panagia – Mother of God; name frequently used for churches

Pantokrator – painting or mosaic of Christ in the centre of the dome of a Byzantine church

pantopoleio – general store

PAO – official initials for Panathinaïkos football club

PAOK – main Thessaloniki football club

paralia – waterfront

PASOK – Panellinio Sosialistiko Komma; Greek socialist party

pediment – triangular section (often filled with sculpture) above the columns, found at the front and back of a classical Greek temple

periptero (s), **periptera** (pl) – streek kiosk

peristyle – columns surrounding a building (usually a temple) or courtyard

pinakotheke – picture gallery

pithos (s), **pithoi** (pl) – large Minoan storage jar

plateia – square

Politiki Anixi – Political Spring; centrist political party

Pomaks – minority, non-Turkic Muslim people from northern Greece

Pontians – Greeks whose ancestral home was on the Black Sea coast of Turkey

PRO-PO – Prognostiko Podosferou; Greek football pools

propylon (s), **propylaia** (pl) – elaborately built main entrance to an ancient city or sanctuary; a propylon had one gateway and a propylaia more than one

psistaria – restaurant serving grilled food

rembetika – blues songs commonly associated with the underworld of the 1920s

retsina – resinated white wine

rhyton – another name for a *libation vessel*

rizitika – traditional, patriotic songs of Crete

sacristy – room attached to a church where sacred vessels etc are kept

sandouri – hammered dulcimer from Asia Minor

Sarakatsani – Greek-speaking nomadic shepherd community from northern Greece

SEO – Syllogos Ellinon Orivaton; Greek mountaineers' association

skites (s), **skiti** (pl) – hermit's dwelling

Skopia – what the Greeks call the Former Yugoslav Republic of Macedonia (FYROM)

skyladika – literally 'dog songs'; popular, but not lyrically challenging, blues songs most often sung in *bouzoukia* nightclubs

spilia – cave

stele – grave stone which stands upright

stoa – long colonnaded building, usually in an *agora*; used as a meeting place and shelter in ancient Greece

taverna – traditional restaurant which serves food and wine

temblon – votive screen

tholos – Mycenaean tomb shaped like a beehive

toumberleki – small lap drum played with the fingers

triglyph – sections of a *Doric frieze* between the *metopes*

trireme – ancient Greek galley with three rows of oars on each side

tsikoudia – Cretan version of *tsipouro*

Tsingani – Gypsies or Romanies

tsipouro – distilled spirit made from grapes

vaulted – having an arched roof, normally of brick or stone

velenza – flokati rug

Vlach – traditional, seminomadic shepherds from northern Greece who speak a latin-based dialect

volta – promenade; evening stroll

volute – spiral decoration on *Ionic* capitals

xythomyzithra – soft sheep's milk cheese

zaharoplasteio (s), **zaharoplasteia** (pl) – pâtisserie; shop which sells cakes, chocolates, sweets and, sometimes, alcoholic drinks

Index

TEXT

LONELY PLANET TRAVEL ATLASES

Lonely Planet has long been famous for the number and quality of its guidebook maps. Now we've gone one step further and in conjunction with Steinhart Katzir Publishers produced a handy companion series: Lonely Planet travel atlases – maps of a country produced in book form.

Unlike other maps, which look good but lead travellers astray, our travel atlases have been researched on the road by Lonely Planet's experienced team of writers. All details are carefully checked to ensure the atlas corresponds with the equivalent Lonely Planet guidebook.

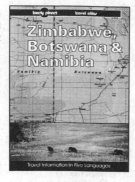

The handy atlas format means no holes, wrinkles, torn sections or constant folding and unfolding. These atlases can survive long periods on the road, unlike cumbersome fold-out maps. The comprehensive index ensures easy reference.

- full-colour throughout
- maps researched and checked by Lonely Planet authors
- place names correspond with Lonely Planet guidebooks
  – no confusing spelling differences
- legend and travelling information in English, French, German, Japanese and Spanish
- size: 230 x 160 mm

Available now:
Chile & Easter Island • Egypt • India & Bangladesh • Israel & the Palestinian Territories •Jordan, Syria & Lebanon • Kenya • Laos • Portugal • South Africa, Lesotho & Swaziland • Thailand • Turkey • Vietnam • Zimbabwe, Botswana & Namibia

---

LONELY PLANET TV SERIES & VIDEOS

Lonely Planet travel guides have been brought to life on television screens around the world. Like our guides, the programmes are based on the joy of independent travel, and look honestly at some of the most exciting, picturesque and frustrating places in the world. Each show is presented by one of three travellers from Australia, England or the USA and combines an innovative mixture of video, Super-8 film, atmospheric soundscapes and original music.

Videos of each episode – containing additional footage not shown on television – are available from good book and video shops, but the availability of individual videos varies with regional screening schedules.

Video destinations include: Alaska • American Rockies • Australia – The South-East • Baja California & the Copper Canyon • Brazil • Central Asia • Chile & Easter Island • Corsica, Sicily & Sardinia – The Mediterranean Islands • East Africa (Tanzania & Zanzibar) • Ecuador & the Galapagos Islands • Greenland & Iceland • Indonesia • Israel & the Sinai Desert • Jamaica • Japan • La Ruta Maya • Morocco • New York • North India • Pacific Islands (Fiji, Solomon Islands & Vanuatu) • South India • South West China • Turkey • Vietnam • West Africa • Zimbabwe, Botswana & Namibia

The Lonely Planet TV series is produced by:
Pilot Productions
The Old Studio
18 Middle Row
London W10 5AT UK

For video availability and ordering information contact your nearest Lonely Planet office.

Music from the TV series is available on CD & cassette.

PLANET TALK

Lonely Planet's FREE quarterly newsletter

We love hearing from you and think you'd like to hear from us.

*When...*is the right time to see reindeer in Finland?
*Where...*can you hear the best palm-wine music in Ghana?
*How...*do you get from Asunción to Areguá by steam train?
*What...*is the best way to see India?

For the answer to these and many other questions read PLANET TALK.

Every issue is packed with up-to-date travel news and advice including:

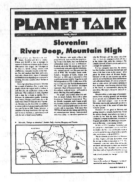

- a letter from Lonely Planet co-founders Tony and Maureen Wheeler
- go behind the scenes on the road with a Lonely Planet author
- feature article on an important and topical travel issue
- a selection of recent letters from travellers
- details on forthcoming Lonely Planet promotions
- complete list of Lonely Planet products

To join our mailing list contact any Lonely Planet office.

Also available: Lonely Planet T-shirts. 100% heavyweight cotton.

LONELY PLANET ONLINE

Get the latest travel information before you leave or while you're on the road

Whether you've just begun planning your next trip, or you're chasing down specific info on currency regulations or visa requirements, check out Lonely Planet Online for up-to-the-minute travel information.

As well as travel profiles of your favourite destinations (including maps and photos), you'll find current reports from our researchers and other travellers, updates on health and visas, travel advisories, and discussion of the ecological and political issues you need to be aware of as you travel.

There's also an online travellers' forum where you can share your experience of life on the road, meet travel companions and ask other travellers for their recommendations and advice. We also have plenty of links to other online sites useful to independent travellers.

And of course we have a complete and up-to-date list of all Lonely Planet travel products including guides, phrasebooks, atlases, Journeys and videos and a simple online ordering facility if you can't find the book you want elsewhere.

www.lonelyplanet.com
or
AOL keyword: lp

LONELY PLANET PRODUCTS

Lonely Planet is known worldwide for publishing practical, reliable and no-nonsense travel information in our guides and on our web site. The Lonely Planet list covers just about every accessible part of the world. Currently there are eight series: *travel guides*, *shoestring guides*, *walking guides*, *city guides*, *phrasebooks*, *audio packs*, *travel atlases* and *Journeys* – a unique collection of travel writing.

EUROPE

Amsterdam • Austria • Baltic States phrasebook • Britain • Central Europe on a shoestring • Central Europe phrasebook • Czech & Slovak Republics • Denmark • Dublin • Eastern Europe on a shoestring • Eastern Europe phrasebook • Estonia, Latvia & Lithuania • Finland • France • French phrasebook • German phrasebook • Greece • Greek phrasebook • Hungary • Iceland, Greenland & the Faroe Islands • Ireland • Italian phrasebook • Italy • Mediterranean Europe on a shoestring • Mediterranean Europe phrasebook • Paris • Poland • Portugal • Portugal travel atlas • Prague • Russia, Ukraine & Belarus • Russian phrasebook • Scandinavian & Baltic Europe on a shoestring • Scandinavian Europe phrasebook • Slovenia • Spain • Spanish phrasebook • St Petersburg • Switzerland • Trekking in Greece • Trekking in Spain • Ukrainian phrasebook • Vienna • Walking in Britain • Walking in Switzerland • Western Europe on a shoestring • Western Europe phrasebook

Travel Literature: The Olive Grove: Travels in Greece

NORTH AMERICA

Alaska • Backpacking in Alaska • Baja California • California & Nevada • Canada • Florida • Hawaii • Honolulu • Los Angeles • Mexico • Miami • New England • New Orleans • New York City • New York, New Jersey & Pennsylvania • Pacific Northwest USA • Rocky Mountain States • San Francisco • Southwest USA • USA phrasebook • Washington, DC & the Capital Region

CENTRAL AMERICA & THE CARIBBEAN

Bermuda • Central America on a shoestring • Costa Rica • Cuba • Eastern Caribbean • Guatemala, Belize & Yucatán: La Ruta Maya • Jamaica

SOUTH AMERICA

Argentina, Uruguay & Paraguay • Bolivia • Brazil • Brazilian phrasebook • Buenos Aires • Chile & Easter Island • Chile & Easter Island travel atlas • Colombia • Ecuador & the Galápagos Islands • Latin American Spanish phrasebook • Peru • Quechua phrasebook • Rio de Janeiro • South America on a shoestring • Trekking in the Patagonian Andes • Venezuela

Travel Literature: Full Circle: A South American Journey

ANTARCTICA

Antarctica

ISLANDS OF THE INDIAN OCEAN

Madagascar & Comoros • Maldives • Mauritius, Réunion & Seychelles

AFRICA

Africa - the South • Africa on a shoestring • Arabic (Moroccan) phrasebook • Cape Town • Central Africa • East Africa • Egypt • Egypt travel atlas • Ethiopian (Amharic) phrasebook • Kenya • Kenya travel atlas • Malawi, Mozambique & Zambia • Morocco • North Africa • South Africa, Lesotho & Swaziland • South Africa, Lesotho & Swaziland travel atlas • Swahili phrasebook • Trekking in East Africa • West Africa • Zimbabwe, Botswana & Namibia • Zimbabwe, Botswana & Namibia travel atlas

Travel Literature: The Rainbird: A Central African Journey • Songs to an African Sunset: A Zimbabwean Story

MAIL ORDER

Lonely Planet products are distributed worldwide. They are also available by mail order from Lonely Planet, so if you have difficulty finding a title please write to us. North American and South American residents should write to Embarcadero West, 155 Filbert St, Suite 251, Oakland CA 94607, USA; European and African residents should write to 10a Spring Place, London NW5 3BH; and residents of other countries to PO Box 617, Hawthorn, Victoria 3122, Australia.

NORTH-EAST ASIA

Beijing • Cantonese phrasebook • China • Hong Kong • Hong Kong, Macau & Guangzhou • Japan • Japanese phrasebook • Japanese audio pack • Korea • Korean phrasebook • Mandarin phrasebook • Mongolia • Mongolian phrasebook • North-East Asia on a shoestring • Seoul • Taiwan • Tibet • Tibet phrasebook • Tokyo

Travel Literature: Lost Japan

MIDDLE EAST & CENTRAL ASIA

Arab Gulf States • Arabic (Egyptian) phrasebook • Central Asia • Iran • Israel & the Palestinian Territories • Israel & the Palestinian Territories travel atlas • Istanbul • Jerusalem • Jordan & Syria • Jordan, Syria & Lebanon travel atlas • Lebanon • Middle East • Turkey • Turkish phrasebook • Turkey travel atlas • Yemen

Travel Literature: The Gates of Damascus • Kingdom of the Film Stars: Journey into Jordan

ALSO AVAILABLE:

Travel with Children • Traveller's Tales

INDIAN SUBCONTINENT

Bangladesh • Bengali phrasebook • Delhi • Hindi/Urdu phrasebook • India • India & Bangladesh travel atlas • Indian Himalaya • Karakoram Highway • Nepal • Nepali phrasebook • Pakistan • Rajasthan • Sri Lanka • Sri Lanka phrasebook • Trekking in the Indian Himalaya • Trekking in the Karakoram & Hindukush • Trekking in the Nepal Himalaya

Travel Literature: In Rajasthan • Shopping for Buddhas

SOUTH-EAST ASIA

Bali & Lombok • Bangkok • Burmese phrasebook • Cambodia • Ho Chi Minh City • Indonesia • Indonesian phrasebook • Indonesian audio pack • Jakarta • Java • Laos • Lao phrasebook • Laos travel atlas • Malay phrasebook • Malaysia, Singapore & Brunei • Myanmar (Burma) • Philippines • Pilipino phrasebook • Singapore • South-East Asia on a shoestring • South-East Asia phrasebook • Thailand • Thailand's Islands & Beaches • Thailand travel atlas • Thai phrasebook • Thai audio pack • Thai Hill Tribes phrasebook • Vietnam • Vietnamese phrasebook • Vietnam travel atlas

AUSTRALIA & THE PACIFIC

Australia • Australian phrasebook • Bushwalking in Australia • Bushwalking in Papua New Guinea • Fiji • Fijian phrasebook • Islands of Australia's Great Barrier Reef • Melbourne • Micronesia • New Caledonia • New South Wales & the ACT • New Zealand • Northern Territory • Outback Australia • Papua New Guinea • Papua New Guinea phrasebook • Queensland • Rarotonga & the Cook Islands • Samoa • Solomon Islands • South Australia • Sydney • Tahiti & French Polynesia • Tasmania • Tonga • Tramping in New Zealand • Vanuatu • Victoria • Western Australia

Travel Literature: Islands in the Clouds • Sean & David's Long Drive

THE LONELY PLANET STORY

Lonely Planet published its first book in 1973 in response to the numerous 'How did you do it?' questions Maureen and Tony Wheeler were asked after driving, bussing, hitching, sailing and railing their way from England to Australia.

Written at a kitchen table and hand collated, trimmed and stapled, *Across Asia on the Cheap* became an instant local bestseller, inspiring thoughts of another book.

Eighteen months in South-East Asia resulted in their second guide, *South-East Asia on a shoestring*, which they put together in a backstreet Chinese hotel in Singapore in 1975. The 'yellow bible', as it quickly became known to backpackers around the world, soon became *the* guide to the region. It has sold well over half a million copies and is now in its 9th edition, still retaining its familiar yellow cover.

Today there are over 240 titles, including travel guides, walking guides, language kits & phrasebooks, travel atlases and travel literature. The company is the largest independent travel publisher in the world. Although Lonely Planet initially specialised in guides to Asia, today there are few corners of the globe that have not been covered.

The emphasis continues to be on travel for independent travellers. Tony and Maureen still travel for several months of each year and play an active part in the writing, updating and quality control of Lonely Planet's guides.

They have been joined by over 70 authors and 170 staff at our offices in Melbourne (Australia), Oakland (USA), London (UK) and Paris (France). Travellers themselves also make a valuable contribution to the guides through the feedback we receive in thousands of letters each year and on our web site.

The people at Lonely Planet strongly believe that travellers can make a positive contribution to the countries they visit, both through their appreciation of the countries' culture, wildlife and natural features, and through the money they spend. In addition, the company makes a direct contribution to the countries and regions it covers. Since 1986 a percentage of the income from each book has been donated to ventures such as famine relief in Africa; aid projects in India; agricultural projects in Central America; Greenpeace's efforts to halt French nuclear testing in the Pacific; and Amnesty International.

'I hope we send people out with the right attitude about travel. You realise when you travel that there are so many different perspectives about the world, so we hope these books will make people more interested in what they see. Guidebooks can't really guide people. All you can do is point them in the right direction.'

– Tony Wheeler

LONELY PLANET PUBLICATIONS

Australia
PO Box 617, Hawthorn 3122, Victoria
tel: (03) 9819 1877 fax: (03) 9819 6459
e-mail: talk2us@lonelyplanet.com.au

USA
Embarcadero West, 155 Filbert St, Suite 251,
Oakland, CA 94607
tel: (510) 893 8555 TOLL FREE: 800 275-8555
fax: (510) 893 8563
e-mail: info@lonelyplanet.com

UK
10a Spring Place,
London NW5 3BH
tel: (0181) 742 3161 fax: (0181) 742 2772
e-mail: lonelyplanetuk@compuserve.com

France:
71 bis rue du Cardinal Lemoine, 75005 Paris
tel: 1 44 32 06 20 fax: 1 46 34 72 55
e-mail: 100560.415@compuserve.com

World Wide Web: http://www.lonelyplanet.com
or *AOL keyword: lp*